辰巳ヨシヒロ

ALSO BY YOSHIHIRO TATSUMI

The Push Man and Other Stories

Abandon the Old in Tokyo

Good-Bye

Edited, designed, and lettered by Adrian Tomine.

Translated by Taro Nettleton.

Special thanks to Mitsuhiro Asakawa, John Kuramoto, Alison Naturale, Taro Nettleton, and Andrew Wilmot.

Drawn & Quarterly

Post Office Box 48056

Montreal, Quebec

Canada H2V 4S8

www.drawnandquarterly.com

First edition: April 2009.

Printed in Canada.

10 9 8 7 6 5 4 3 2 1

This edition supported in part by The Japan Foundation.

Library and Archives Canada Cataloguing in Publication

Tatsumi, Yoshihiro, 1935–

   A Drifting Life: The epic autobiography of a manga master

author: Yoshihiro Tatsumi; editor: Adrian Tomine; translator: Taro Nettleton.

ISBN 978-1-897299-74-6

   I. Tomine, Adrian, 1974– II. Nettleton, Taro III. Tatsumi, Yoshihiro, 1935–

A Drifting Life. IV. Title.

PN6790.J33T38 2009   741.5'952   C2008-906621-9

Distributed in the USA and abroad by:

Farrar, Straus and Giroux

18 West 18th Street

New York, NY 10011

Orders: 888.330.8477

Distributed in Canada by:

Raincoast Books

9050 Shaughnessy Street

Vancouver, BC V6P 6E5

Orders: 800.663.5714

EDITOR'S NOTE

Although *A Drifting Life* is an autobiographical work, the author has chosen to alter some characters' names, most notably his own. In translating this book, we have made every effort to preserve the narrative flow without sacrificing crucial information. Due to the density of the text, ancillary information and more thorough explications have been placed in the book's appendix.

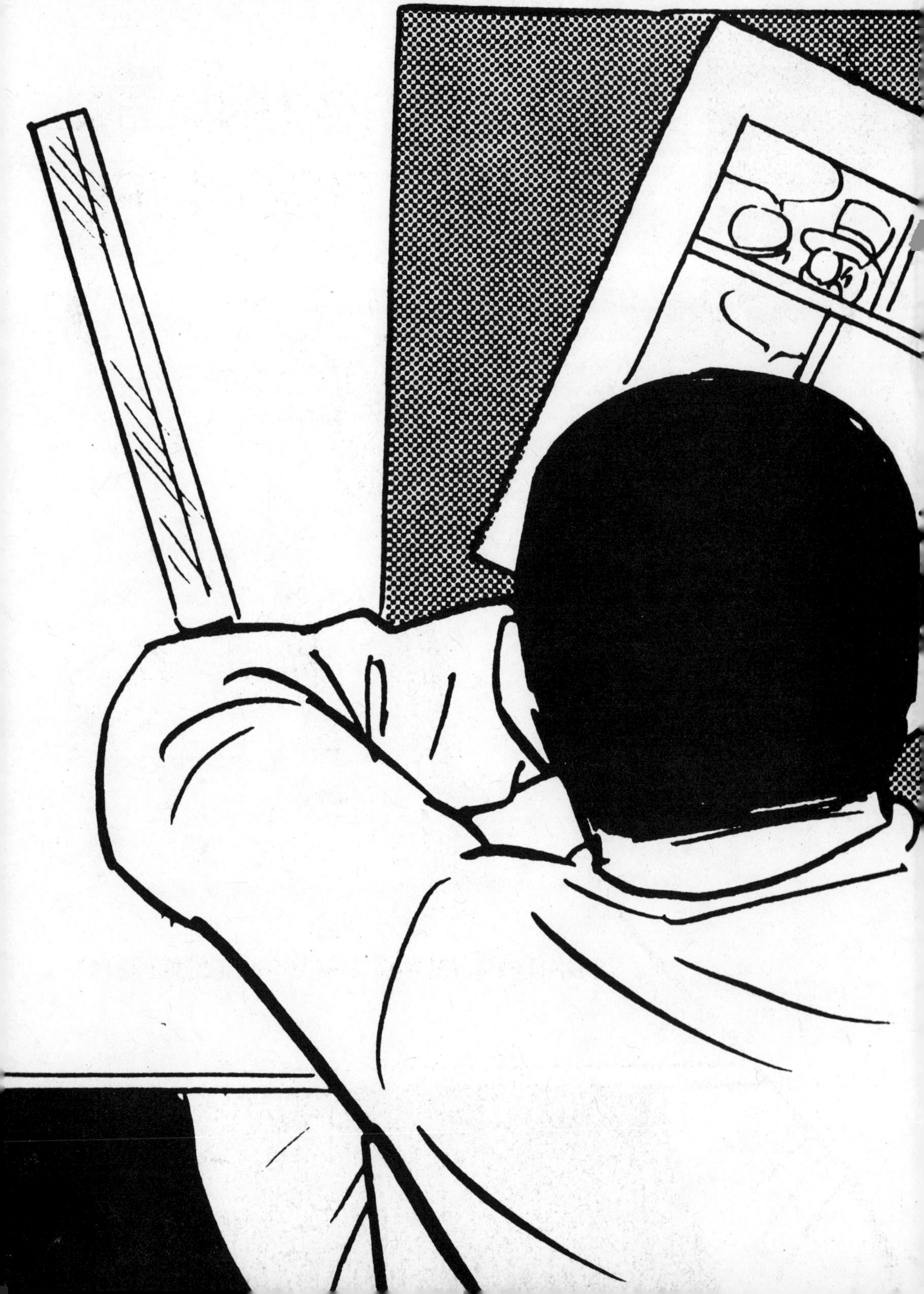

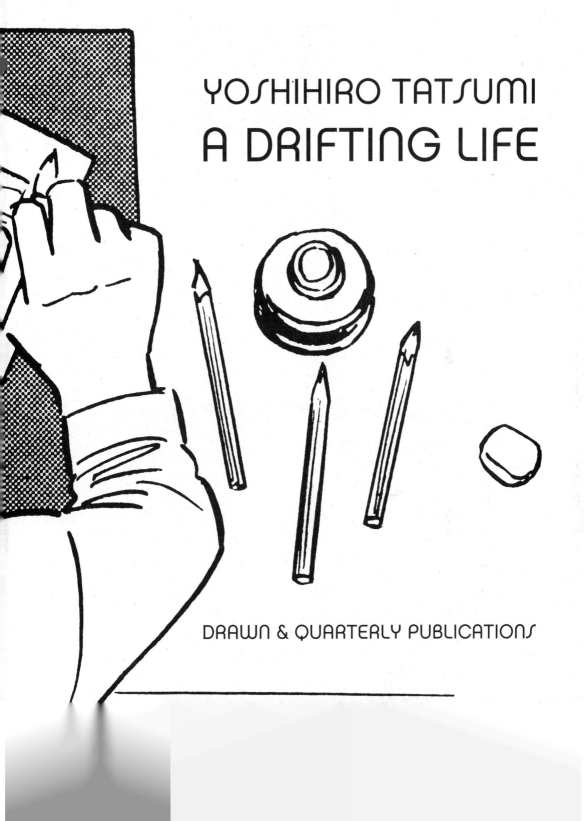

YOSHIHIRO TATSUMI

A DRIFTING LIFE

DRAWN & QUARTERLY PUBLICATIONS

A DRIFTING LIFE

THE BIRTH OF MANGA

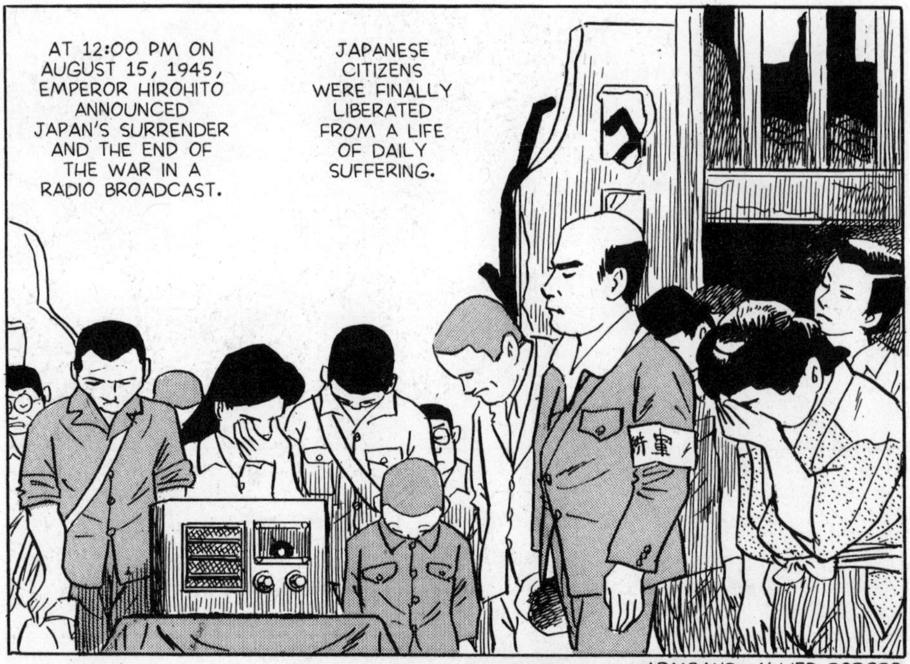
AT 12:00 PM ON AUGUST 15, 1945, EMPEROR HIROHITO ANNOUNCED JAPAN'S SURRENDER AND THE END OF THE WAR IN A RADIO BROADCAST.
JAPANESE CITIZENS WERE FINALLY LIBERATED FROM A LIFE OF DAILY SUFFERING.

ARMBAND: ALLIED FORCES

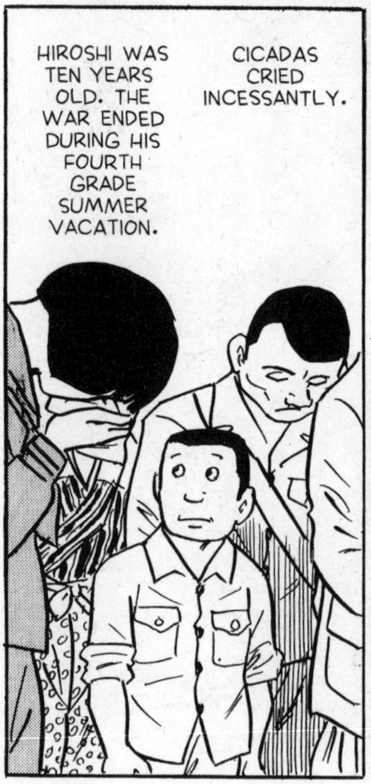
HIROSHI WAS TEN YEARS OLD. THE WAR ENDED DURING HIS FOURTH GRADE SUMMER VACATION.
CICADAS CRIED INCESSANTLY.

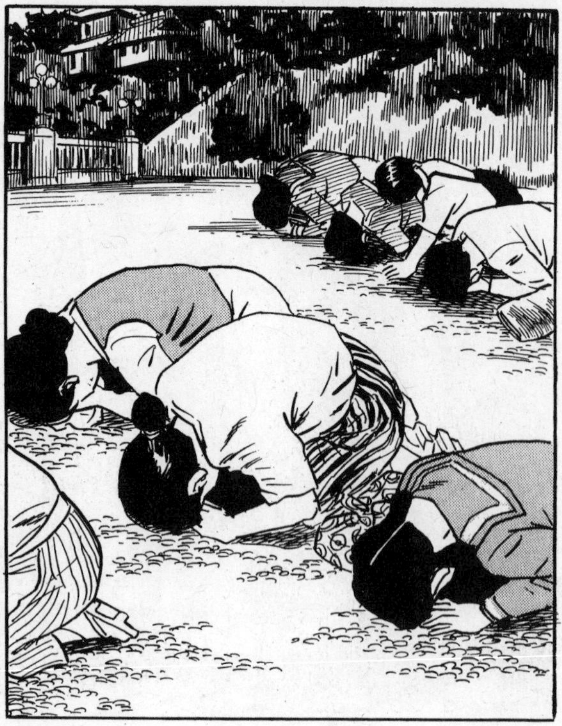

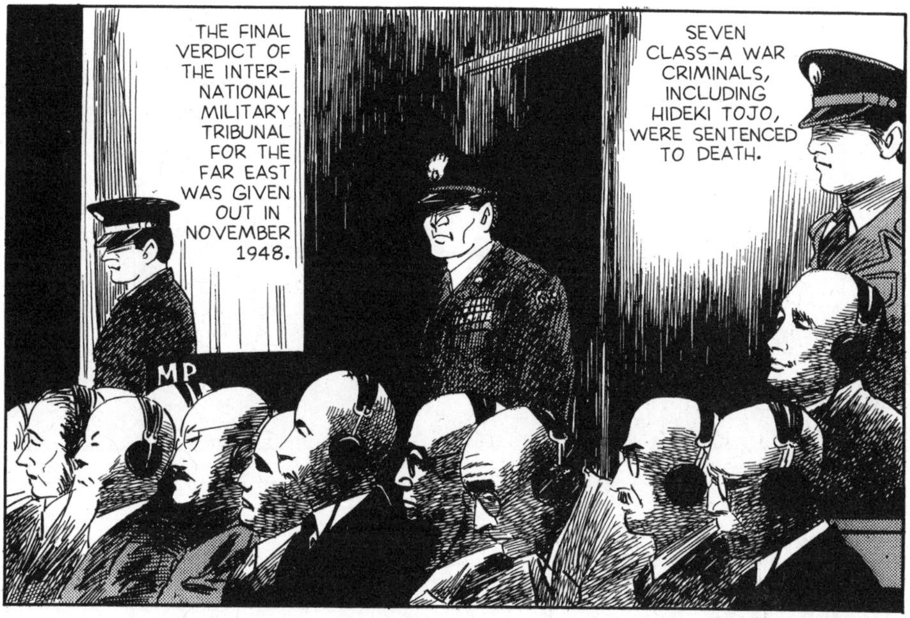
THE FINAL VERDICT OF THE INTER-NATIONAL MILITARY TRIBUNAL FOR THE FAR EAST WAS GIVEN OUT IN NOVEMBER 1948.
SEVEN CLASS-A WAR CRIMINALS, INCLUDING HIDEKI TOJO, WERE SENTENCED TO DEATH.
MP

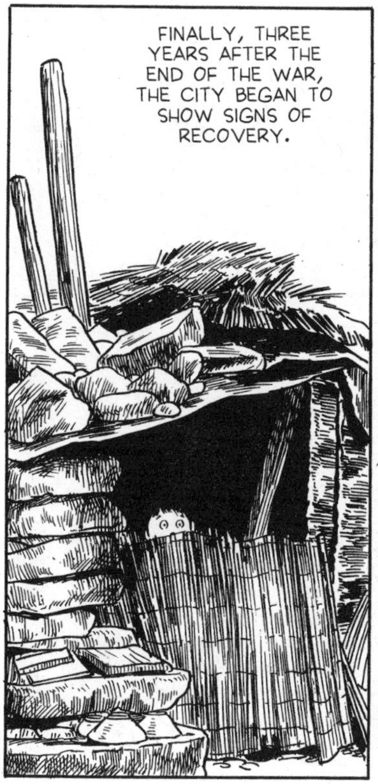
FINALLY, THREE YEARS AFTER THE END OF THE WAR, THE CITY BEGAN TO SHOW SIGNS OF RECOVERY.

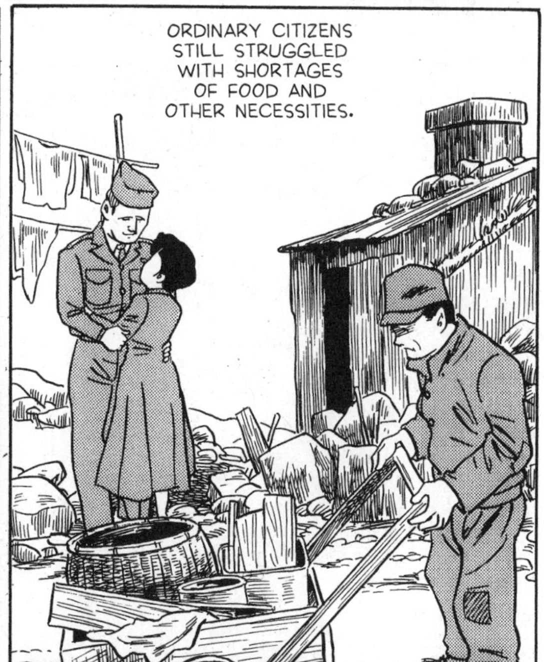
ORDINARY CITIZENS STILL STRUGGLED WITH SHORTAGES OF FOOD AND OTHER NECESSITIES.

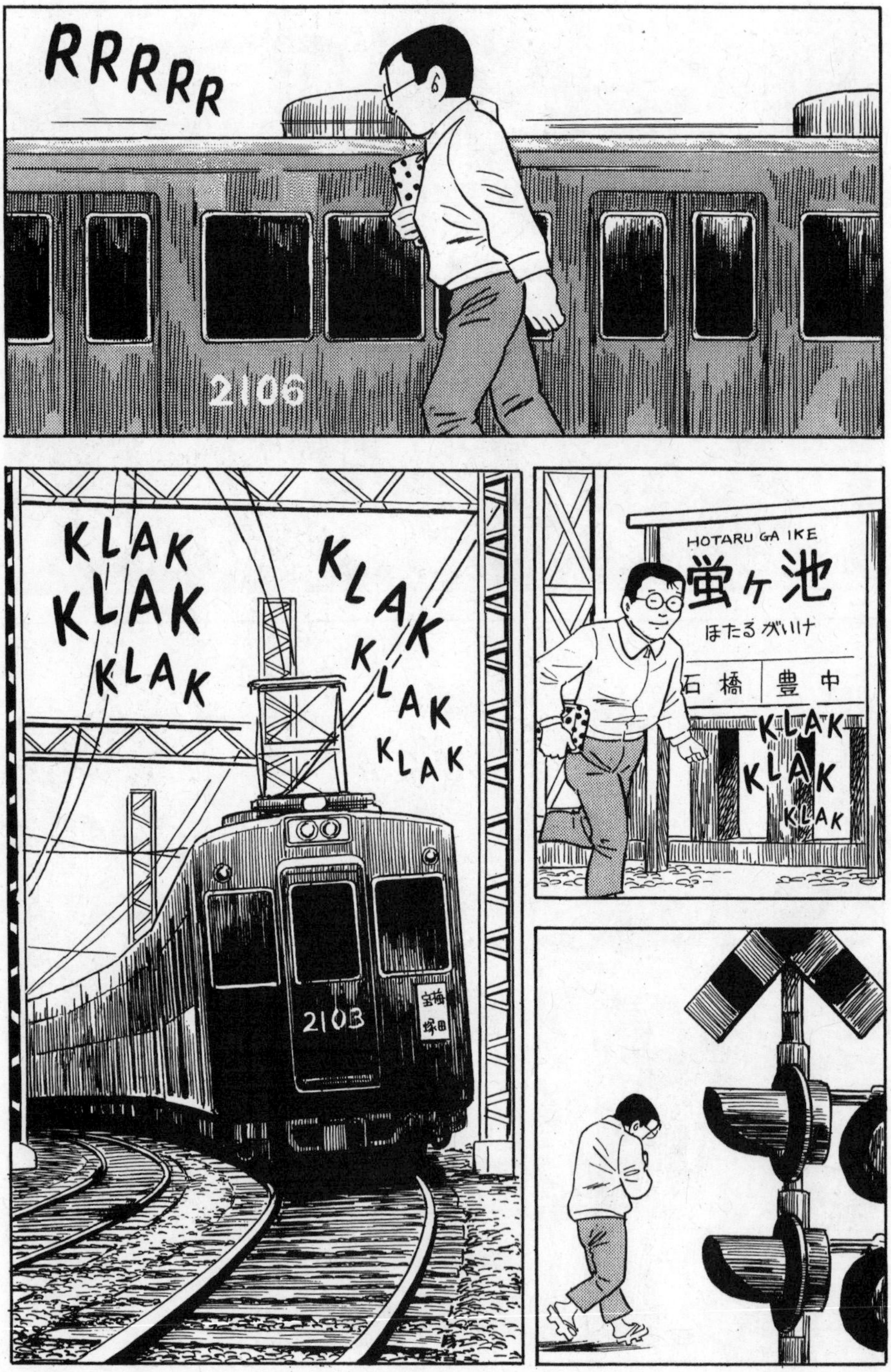
RRRRRR
2106
KLAK KLAK KLAK
KLAK KLAK KLAK KLAK
2103
HOTARU GA IKE
蛍ヶ池
ほたるがいけ
石橋 豊中
KLAK KLAK KLAK

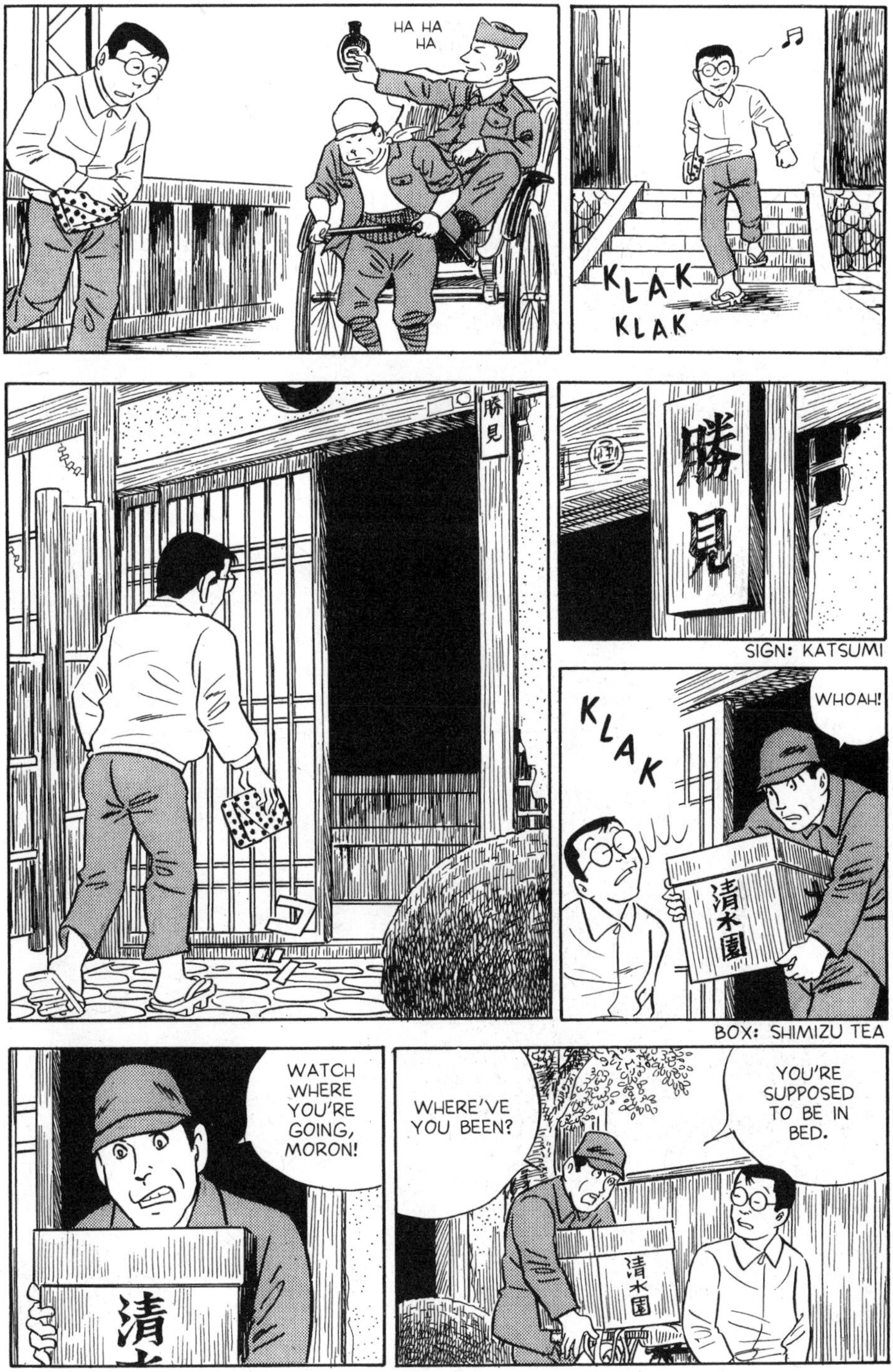
HA HA HA
KLAK KLAK
SIGN: KATSUMI
KLAK
WHOAH!
BOX: SHIMIZU TEA
WATCH WHERE YOU'RE GOING, MORON!
WHERE'VE YOU BEEN?
YOU'RE SUPPOSED TO BE IN BED.

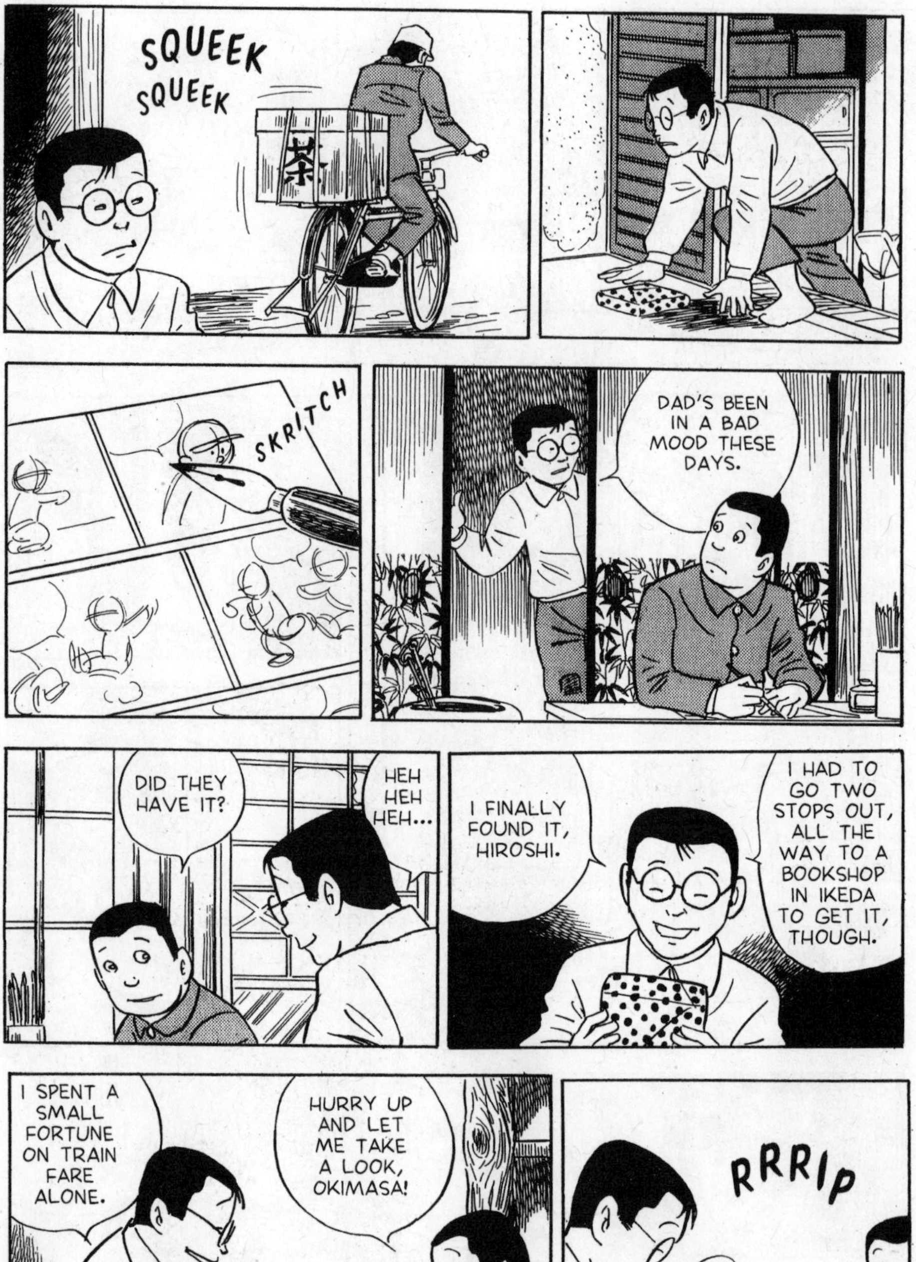
SQUEEK
SQUEEK
茶
SKRITCH
DAD'S BEEN IN A BAD MOOD THESE DAYS.
DID THEY HAVE IT?
HEH HEH HEH...
I FINALLY FOUND IT, HIROSHI.
I HAD TO GO TWO STOPS OUT, ALL THE WAY TO A BOOKSHOP IN IKEDA TO GET IT, THOUGH.
I SPENT A SMALL FORTUNE ON TRAIN FARE ALONE.
HURRY UP AND LET ME TAKE A LOOK, OKIMASA!
RRRIP

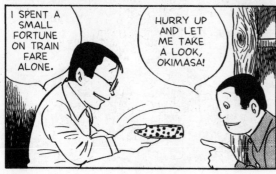

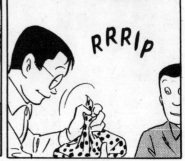

TITLES: ***LOST WORLD SPACE EDITION/***
LOST WORLD EARTH EDITION, BY OSAMU TEZUKA

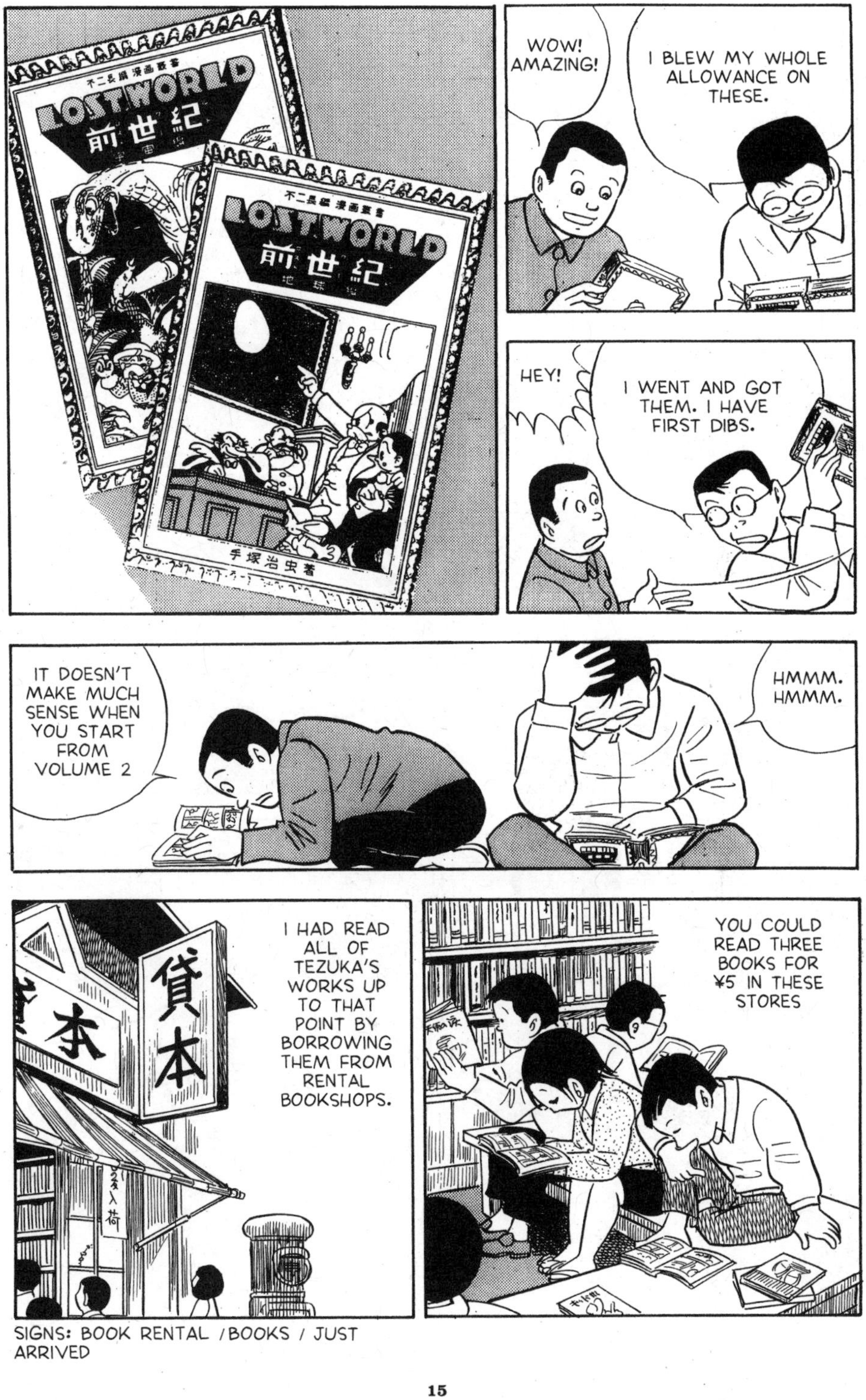
LOST WORLD
前世紀
LOST WORLD
前世紀
手塚治虫著
WOW! AMAZING!
I BLEW MY WHOLE ALLOWANCE ON THESE.
HEY!
I WENT AND GOT THEM. I HAVE FIRST DIBS.
IT DOESN'T MAKE MUCH SENSE WHEN YOU START FROM VOLUME 2
HMMM. HMMM.
I HAD READ ALL OF TEZUKA'S WORKS UP TO THAT POINT BY BORROWING THEM FROM RENTAL BOOKSHOPS.
貸本
YOU COULD READ THREE BOOKS FOR ¥5 IN THESE STORES

SIGNS: BOOK RENTAL / BOOKS / JUST ARRIVED

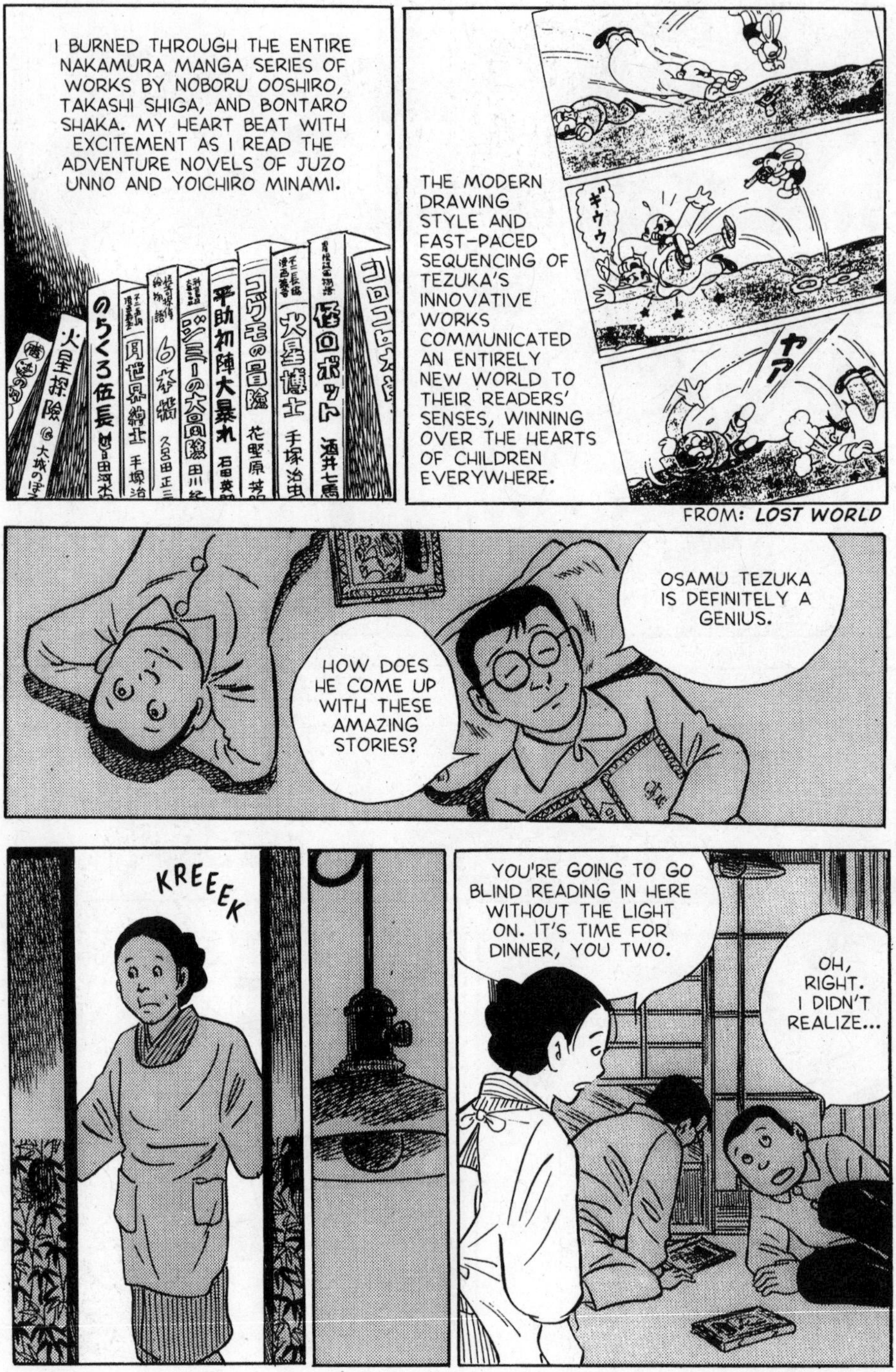
I BURNED THROUGH THE ENTIRE NAKAMURA MANGA SERIES OF WORKS BY NOBORU OOSHIRO, TAKASHI SHIGA, AND BONTARO SHAKA. MY HEART BEAT WITH EXCITEMENT AS I READ THE ADVENTURE NOVELS OF JUZO UNNO AND YOICHIRO MINAMI.
THE MODERN DRAWING STYLE AND FAST-PACED SEQUENCING OF TEZUKA'S INNOVATIVE WORKS COMMUNICATED AN ENTIRELY NEW WORLD TO THEIR READERS' SENSES, WINNING OVER THE HEARTS OF CHILDREN EVERYWHERE.
ギウウ
ヤア
FROM: *LOST WORLD*
HOW DOES HE COME UP WITH THESE AMAZING STORIES?
OSAMU TEZUKA IS DEFINITELY A GENIUS.
KREEEK
YOU'RE GOING TO GO BLIND READING IN HERE WITHOUT THE LIGHT ON. IT'S TIME FOR DINNER, YOU TWO.
OH, RIGHT. I DIDN'T REALIZE...

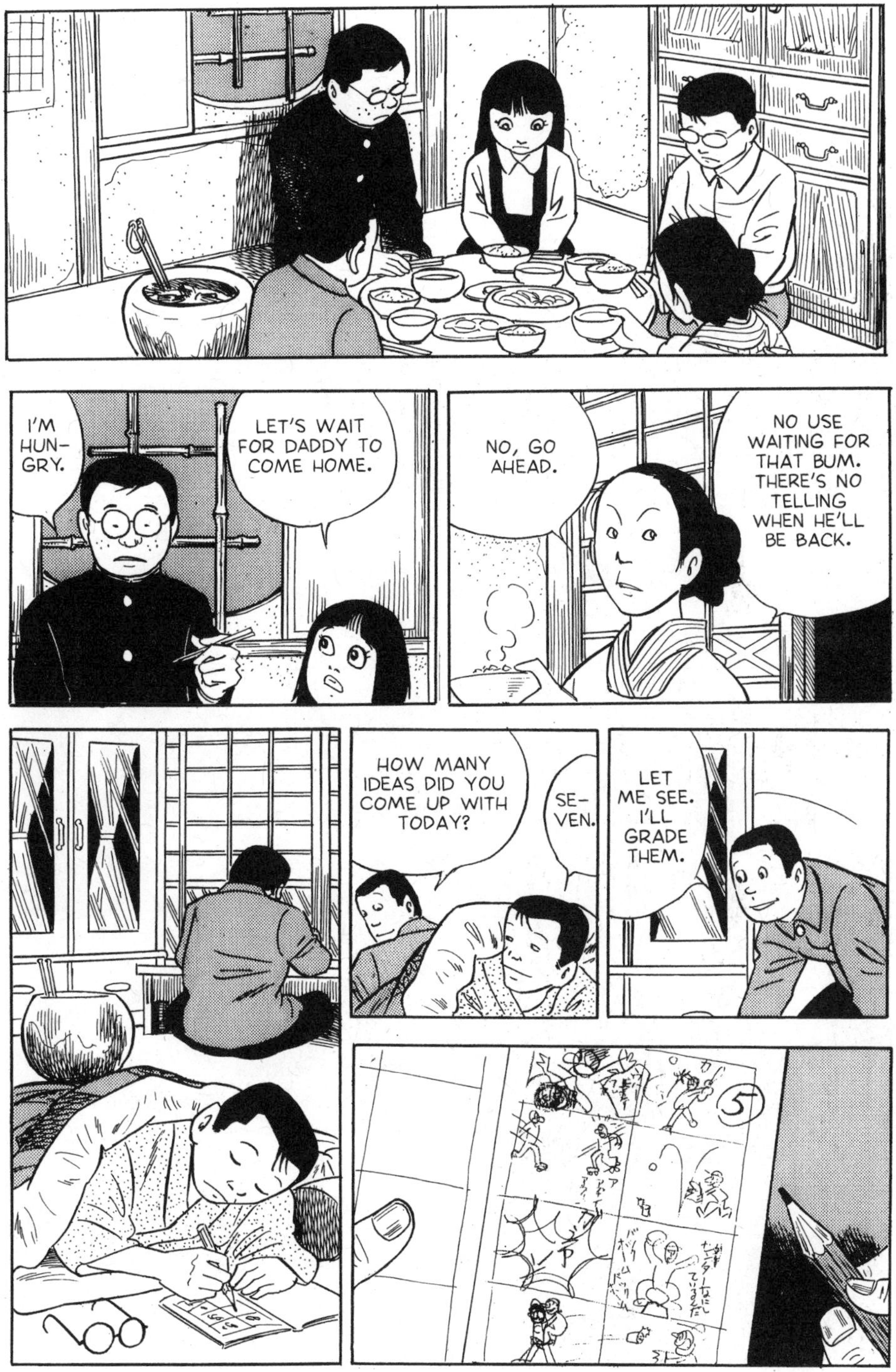
I'M HUN-GRY.
LET'S WAIT FOR DADDY TO COME HOME.
NO, GO AHEAD.
NO USE WAITING FOR THAT BUM. THERE'S NO TELLING WHEN HE'LL BE BACK.
HOW MANY IDEAS DID YOU COME UP WITH TODAY?
SE-VEN.
LET ME SEE. I'LL GRADE THEM.
5

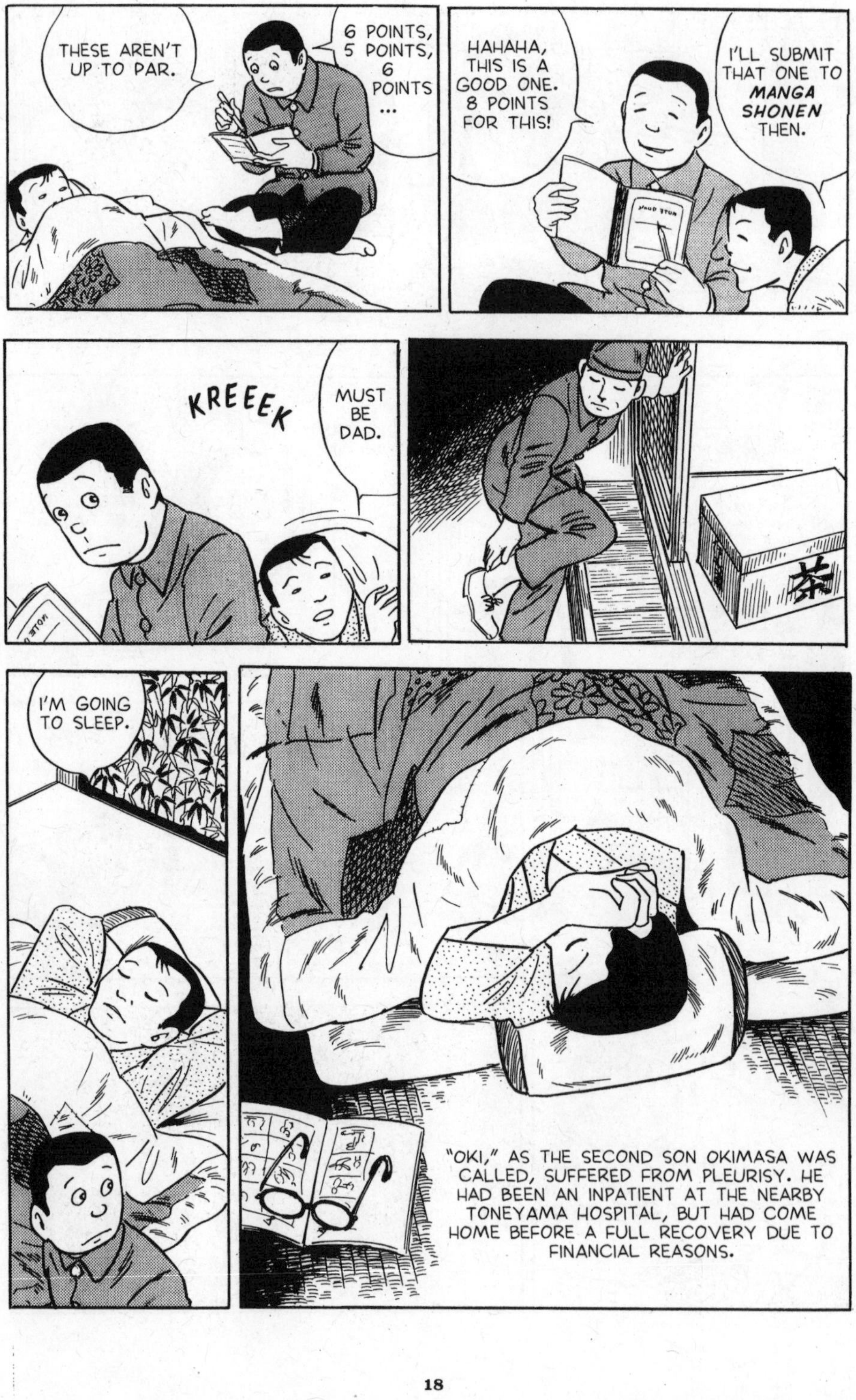
THESE AREN'T UP TO PAR.
6 POINTS, 5 POINTS, 6 POINTS ...
HAHAHA, THIS IS A GOOD ONE. 8 POINTS FOR THIS!
I'LL SUBMIT THAT ONE TO ***MANGA SHONEN*** THEN.
KREEEK
MUST BE DAD.
茶
I'M GOING TO SLEEP.
"OKI," AS THE SECOND SON OKIMASA WAS CALLED, SUFFERED FROM PLEURISY. HE HAD BEEN AN INPATIENT AT THE NEARBY TONEYAMA HOSPITAL, BUT HAD COME HOME BEFORE A FULL RECOVERY DUE TO FINANCIAL REASONS.

HIROSHI, WHO WAS IN SEVENTH GRADE, BEGAN DRAWING COMICS UNDER OKIMASA'S INFLUENCE...

...BUT HE PREFERRED STORY-BASED COMICS TO THEIR FOUR-PANEL COUNTERPARTS AND WORKED DAILY ON A GRAPHIC NOVEL.

TEZUKA'S WORKS, WHICH DEALT WITH THE ABSURD AND THE EMOTIONS OF MEN AND WOMEN, WERE ATTRACTIVE, BUT HIROSHI FELT CERTAIN THAT HE LACKED THE SKILLS TO EMULATE THEIR ACTION-FILLED DRAWINGS AND GRAND SCALE...

THEREFORE, HE USED THE QUIETER WORKS OF AUTHORS SUCH AS NOBORO OOSHIRO AS EXAMPLES.

SLURP

SLURP

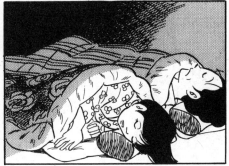

19

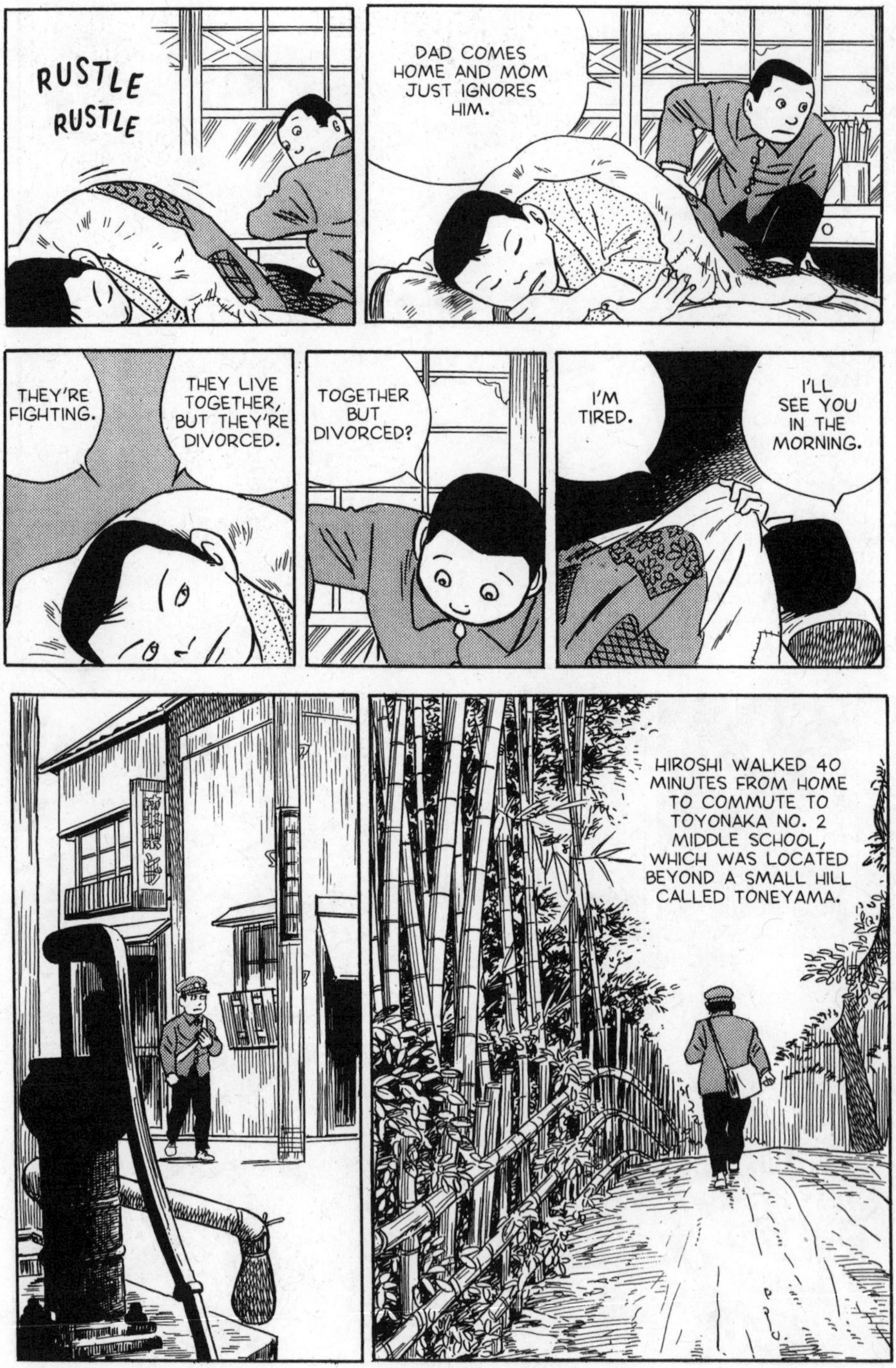
RUSTLE
RUSTLE
DAD COMES HOME AND MOM JUST IGNORES HIM.
THEY'RE FIGHTING.
THEY LIVE TOGETHER, BUT THEY'RE DIVORCED.
TOGETHER BUT DIVORCED?
I'M TIRED.
I'LL SEE YOU IN THE MORNING.
HIROSHI WALKED 40 MINUTES FROM HOME TO COMMUTE TO TOYONAKA NO. 2 MIDDLE SCHOOL, WHICH WAS LOCATED BEYOND A SMALL HILL CALLED TONEYAMA.

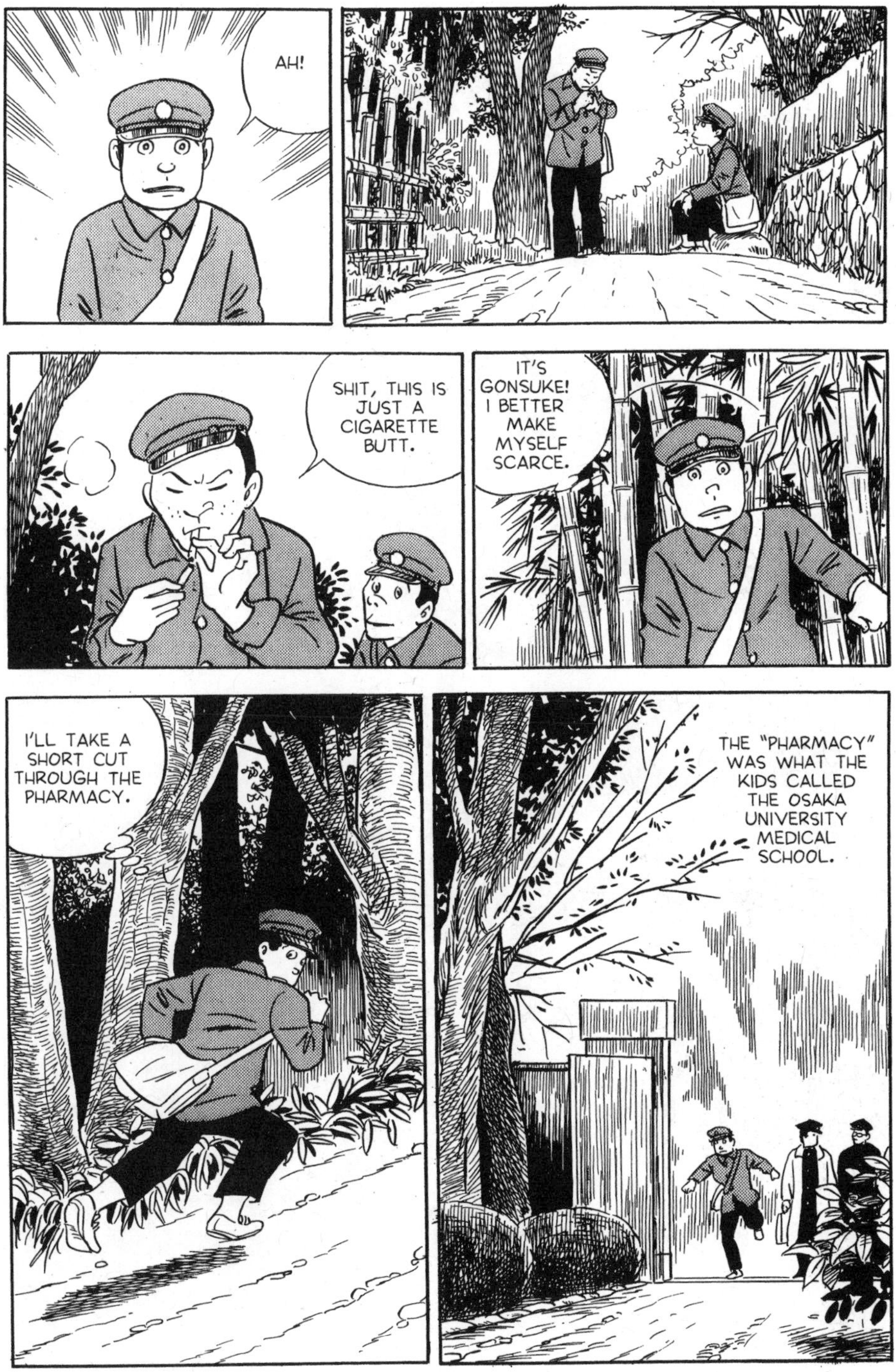
AH!
SHIT, THIS IS JUST A CIGARETTE BUTT.
IT'S GONSUKE! I BETTER MAKE MYSELF SCARCE.
I'LL TAKE A SHORT CUT THROUGH THE PHARMACY.
THE "PHARMACY" WAS WHAT THE KIDS CALLED THE OSAKA UNIVERSITY MEDICAL SCHOOL.

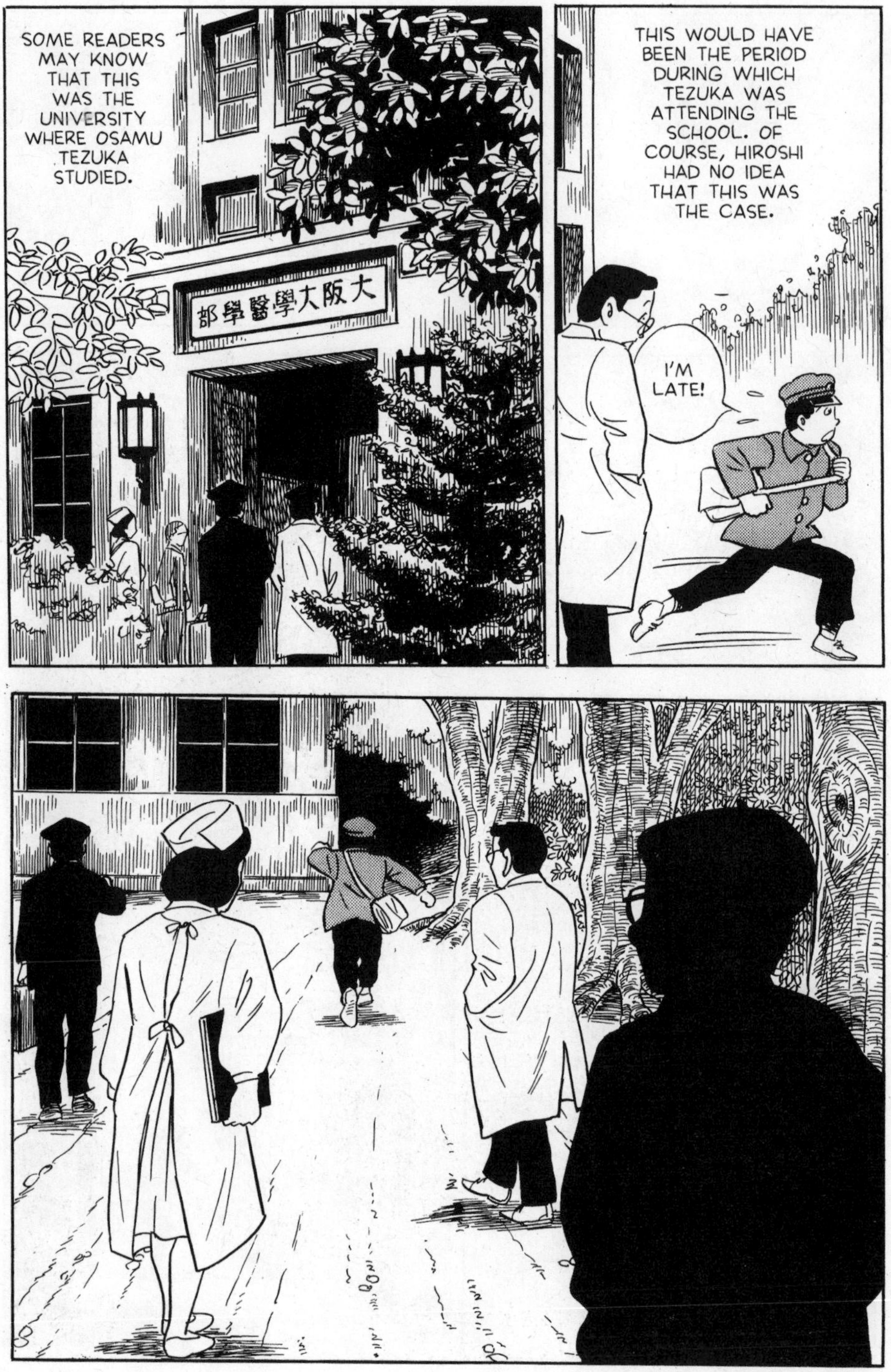
SOME READERS MAY KNOW THAT THIS WAS THE UNIVERSITY WHERE OSAMU TEZUKA STUDIED.
大阪大學醫學部
THIS WOULD HAVE BEEN THE PERIOD DURING WHICH TEZUKA WAS ATTENDING THE SCHOOL. OF COURSE, HIROSHI HAD NO IDEA THAT THIS WAS THE CASE.
I'M LATE!

MANGA OBSESSION

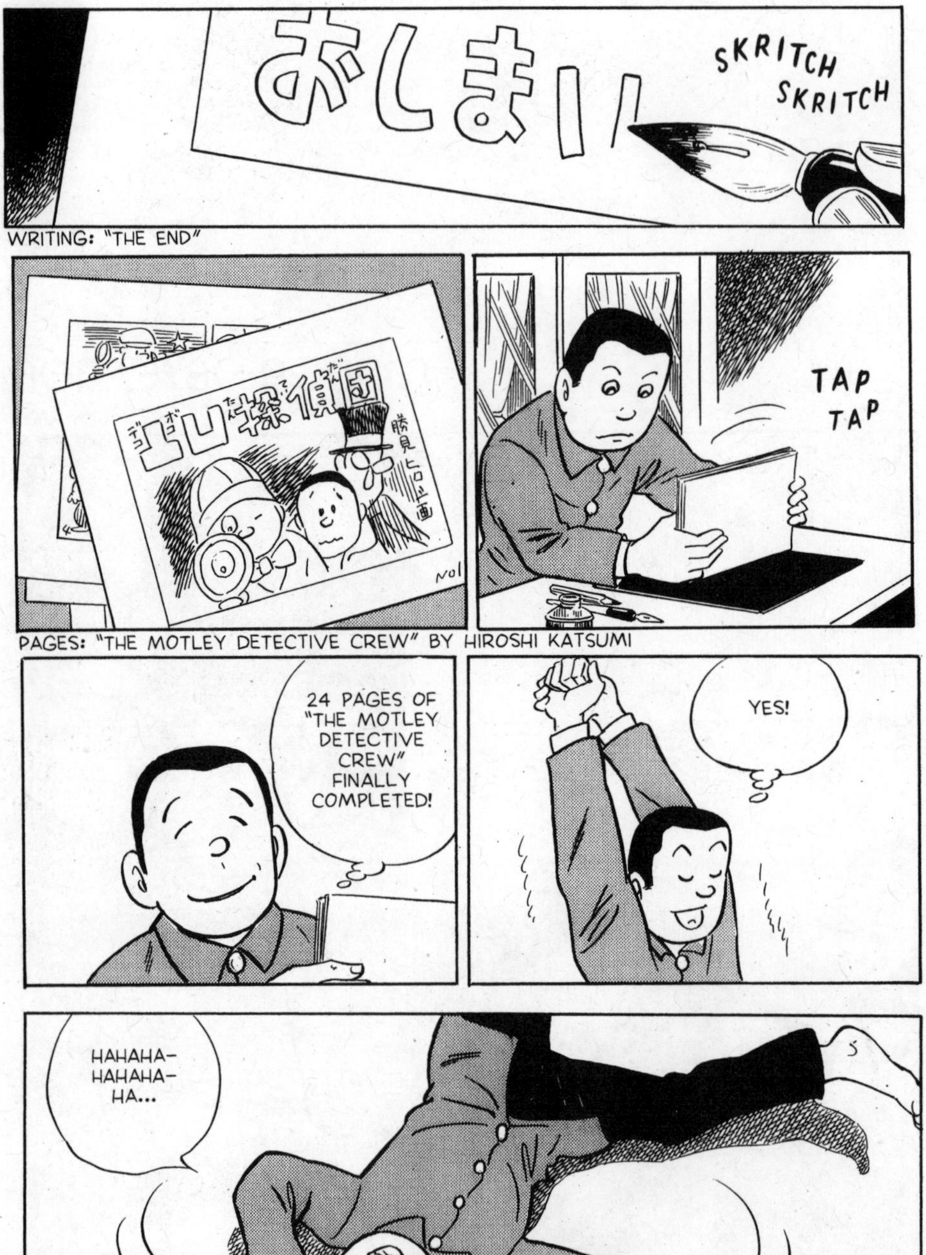
SKRITCH SKRITCH
WRITING: "THE END"
PAGES: "THE MOTLEY DETECTIVE CREW" BY HIROSHI KATSUMI
TAP TAP
24 PAGES OF "THE MOTLEY DETECTIVE CREW" FINALLY COMPLETED!
YES!
HAHAHA-HAHAHA-HA...

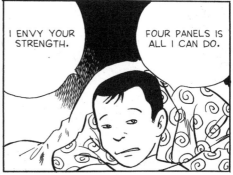

I ENVY YOUR STRENGTH.

FOUR PANELS IS ALL I CAN DO.

YOU DONE?

UH-HUH.

HEY... I KNOW YOU MUST BE TIRED, BUT I HAVE A FAVOR TO ASK.

MANGA SHONEN HITS THE STANDS TODAY.

COULD YOU GO CHECK ON THE RESULTS OF THE READER SUBMISSION CONTEST?

YOU SUB- MITTED SOME- THING...

TO SHONEN MANGA?

THAT'S RIGHT. THREE MONTHS AGO. THREE WHOLE PAGES.

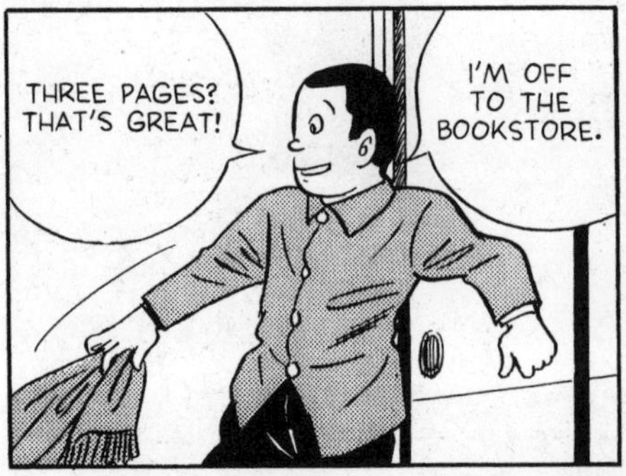
THREE PAGES? THAT'S GREAT!
I'M OFF TO THE BOOKSTORE.

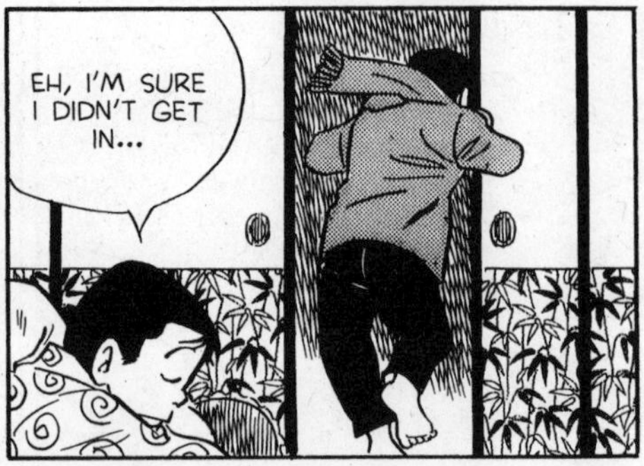
EH, I'M SURE I DIDN'T GET IN...

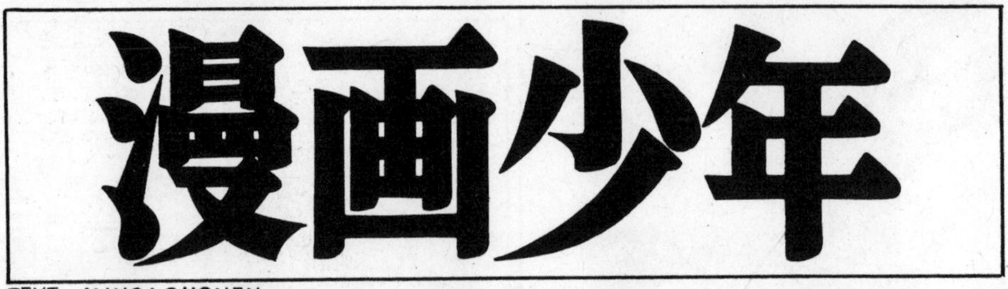
漫画少年

TEXT: *MANGA SHONEN*

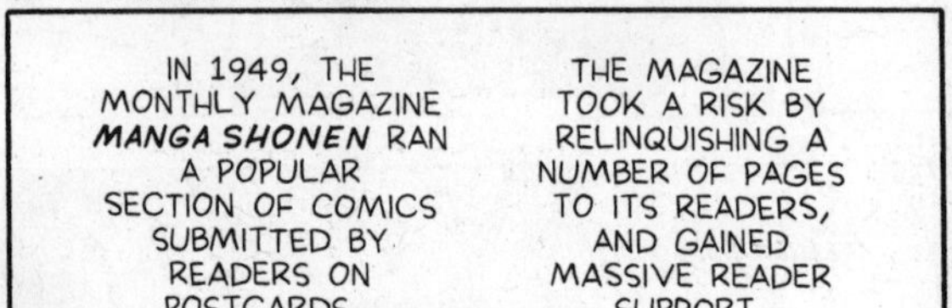
IN 1949, THE MONTHLY MAGAZINE *MANGA SHONEN* RAN A POPULAR SECTION OF COMICS SUBMITTED BY READERS ON POSTCARDS.
THE MAGAZINE TOOK A RISK BY RELINQUISHING A NUMBER OF PAGES TO ITS READERS, AND GAINED MASSIVE READER SUPPORT.
漫画少年
1

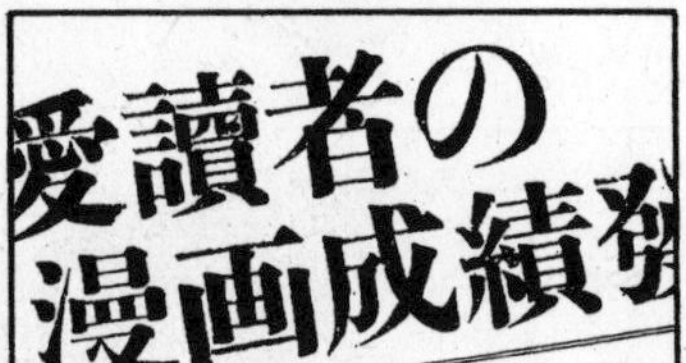
讀者の
漫画成績
福島縣
ハガキ漫画
入選漫画（特製メダル贈呈）
大阪府吹田市 桑田
東京都目黒区
岐阜縣恵那郡 小原
THE COMPETITION WAS FIERCE. THE CONTESTANTS WERE RANKED BY NAME LIKE SUMO WRESTLERS.
長尾和子 岩本
保坂良雄 芹沢
斎藤壽 古森
中沢勝喜 伊藤
武田政美 小笠原

DETAIL: RANKING OF READER-SUBMITTED WORKS / POSTCARD COMICS / WINNING COMICS (SPECIAL MEDAL AWARDED) / KUWATA (FUKIDA CITY, OSAKA)

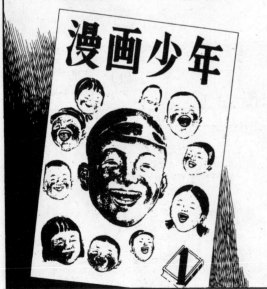

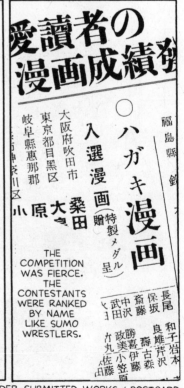

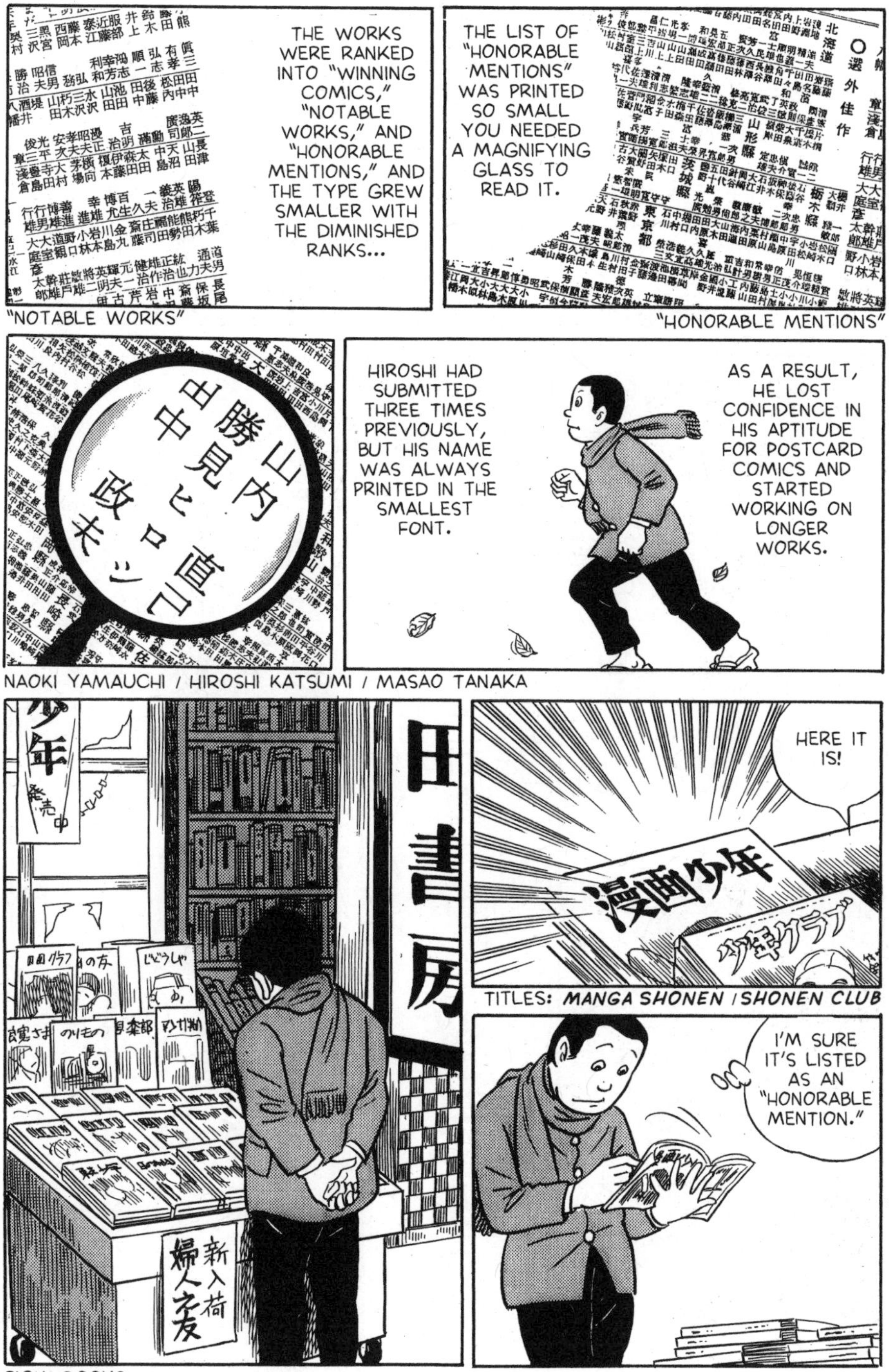
THE WORKS WERE RANKED INTO "WINNING COMICS," "NOTABLE WORKS," AND "HONORABLE MENTIONS," AND THE TYPE GREW SMALLER WITH THE DIMINISHED RANKS...
"NOTABLE WORKS"
THE LIST OF "HONORABLE MENTIONS" WAS PRINTED SO SMALL YOU NEEDED A MAGNIFYING GLASS TO READ IT.
"HONORABLE MENTIONS"
山内直己
勝見ヒロシ
田中政夫
NAOKI YAMAUCHI / HIROSHI KATSUMI / MASAO TANAKA
HIROSHI HAD SUBMITTED THREE TIMES PREVIOUSLY, BUT HIS NAME WAS ALWAYS PRINTED IN THE SMALLEST FONT.
AS A RESULT, HE LOST CONFIDENCE IN HIS APTITUDE FOR POSTCARD COMICS AND STARTED WORKING ON LONGER WORKS.
田書房
新入荷
婦人之友
SIGN: BOOKS
HERE IT IS!
漫画少年
少年クラブ
TITLES: *MANGA SHONEN* / *SHONEN CLUB*
I'M SURE IT'S LISTED AS AN "HONORABLE MENTION."

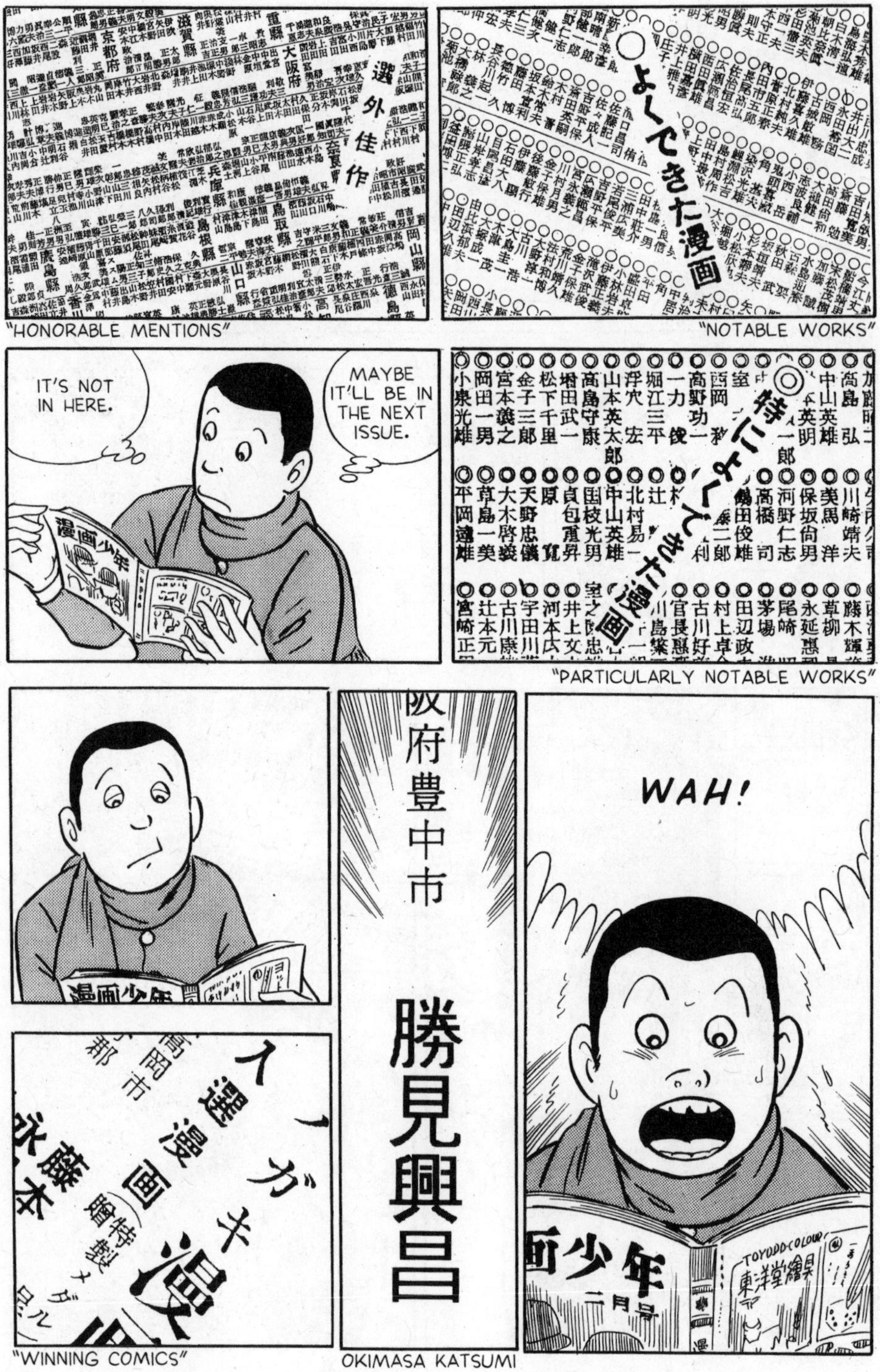
選外佳作
"HONORABLE MENTIONS"
よしできた漫画
"NOTABLE WORKS"
IT'S NOT IN HERE.
MAYBE IT'LL BE IN THE NEXT ISSUE.
漫画少年
特によしできた漫画
"PARTICULARLY NOTABLE WORKS"
漫画少年
入選漫画
"WINNING COMICS"
阪府豊中市
勝見興昌
OKIMASA KATSUMI
WAH!
画少年
二月号
TOYODO-COLOUR
東洋堂繪具

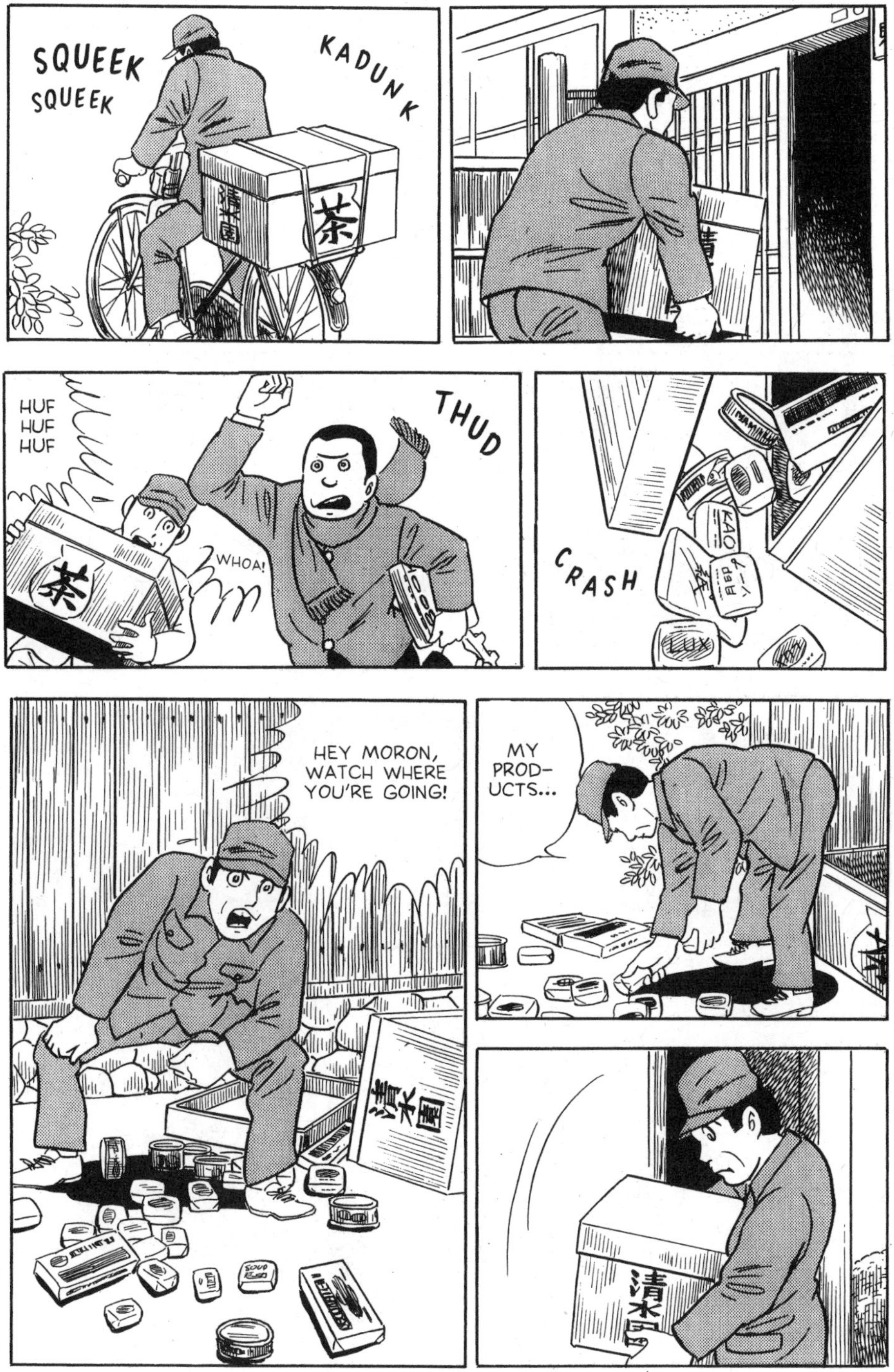
SQUEEK
SQUEEK
KADUNK
清水園
茶
HUF
HUF
HUF
THUD
WHOA!
茶
CRASH
KAO
LUX
HEY MORON, WATCH WHERE YOU'RE GOING!
MY PROD- UCTS...
清水園

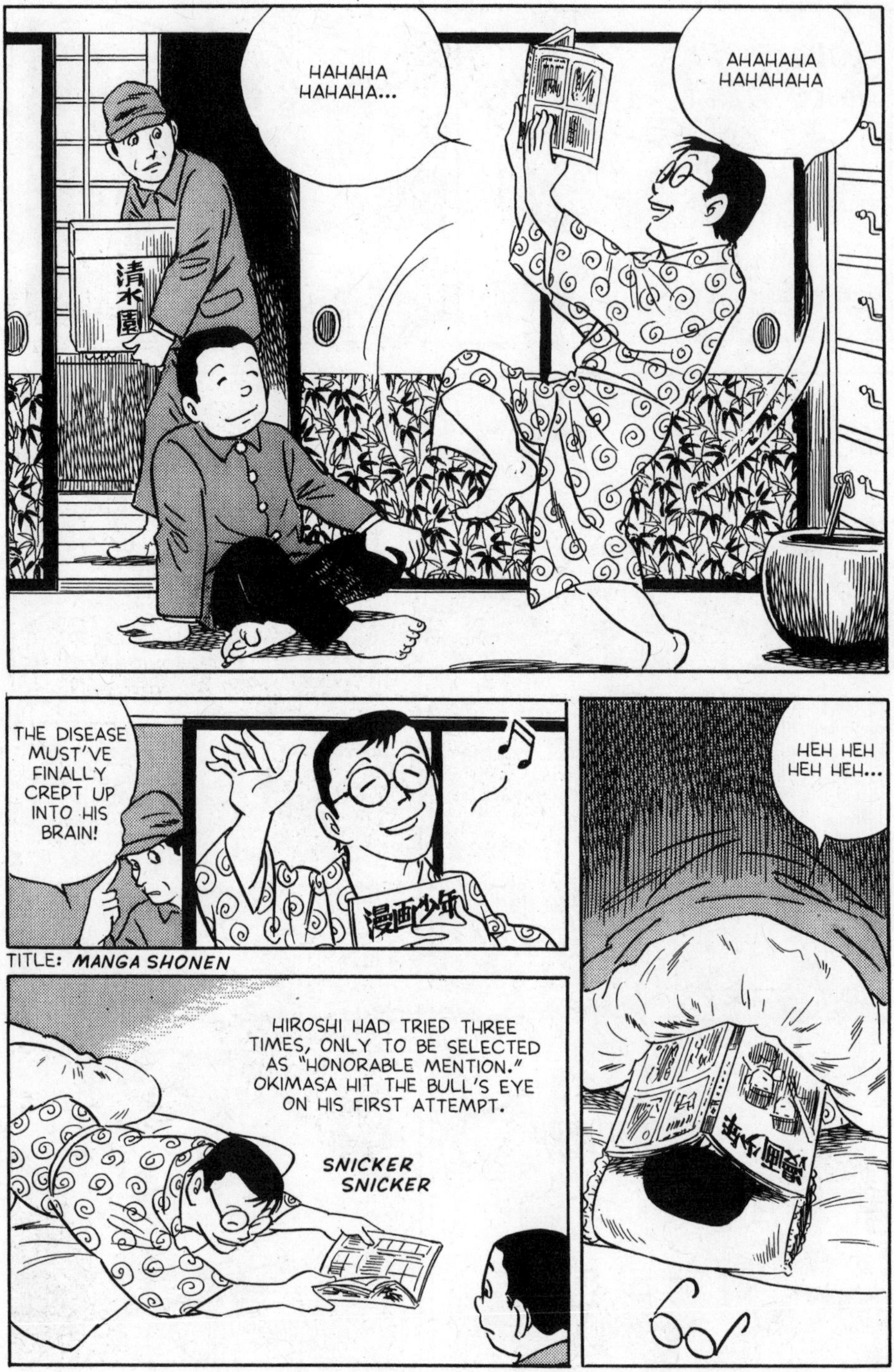
HAHAHA
HAHAHA...
AHAHAHA
HAHAHAHA
THE DISEASE MUST'VE FINALLY CREPT UP INTO HIS BRAIN!
漫画少年
TITLE: *MANGA SHONEN*
HEH HEH HEH HEH...
HIROSHI HAD TRIED THREE TIMES, ONLY TO BE SELECTED AS "HONORABLE MENTION." OKIMASA HIT THE BULL'S EYE ON HIS FIRST ATTEMPT.
SNICKER SNICKER

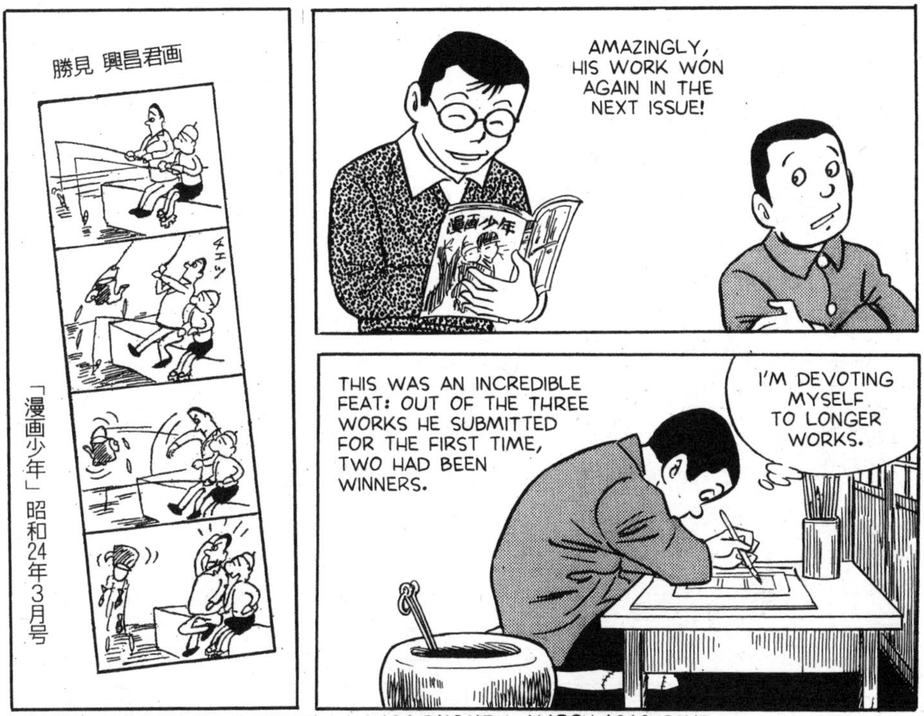
勝見 興昌君画
「漫画少年」昭和24年3月号
AMAZINGLY, HIS WORK WON AGAIN IN THE NEXT ISSUE!
漫画少年
THIS WAS AN INCREDIBLE FEAT: OUT OF THE THREE WORKS HE SUBMITTED FOR THE FIRST TIME, TWO HAD BEEN WINNERS.
I'M DEVOTING MYSELF TO LONGER WORKS.

HEADER: BY OKIMASA KATSUMI/ ***MANGA SHONEN***, MARCH 1949 ISSUE

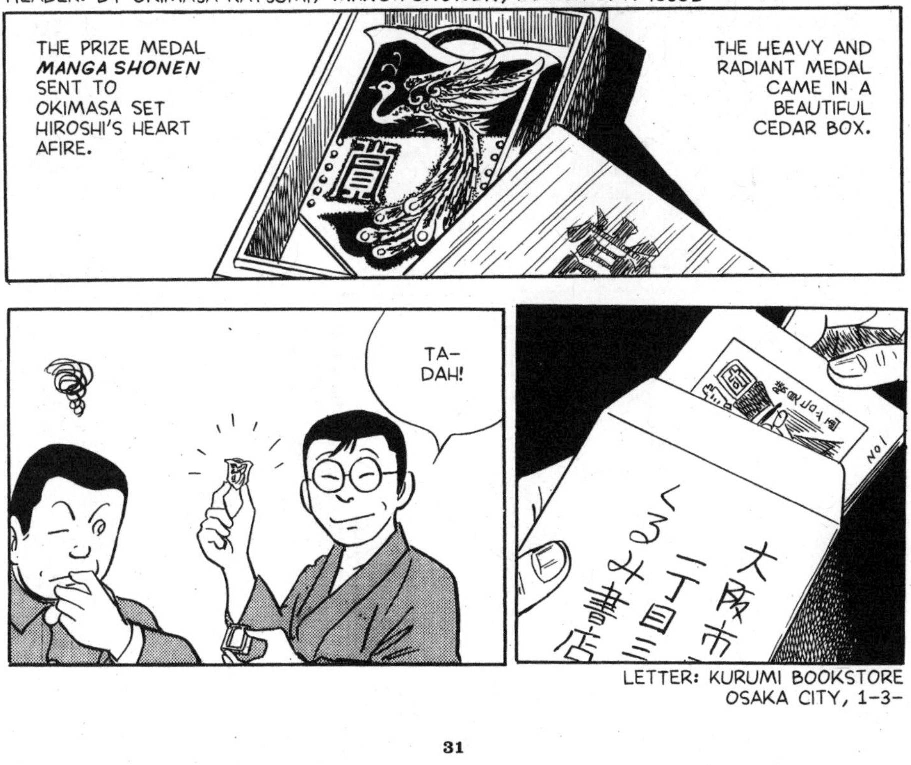
THE PRIZE MEDAL ***MANGA SHONEN*** SENT TO OKIMASA SET HIROSHI'S HEART AFIRE.
THE HEAVY AND RADIANT MEDAL CAME IN A BEAUTIFUL CEDAR BOX.
TA-DAH!
NO1
大阪市
二丁目三
くるみ書店

LETTER: KURUMI BOOKSTORE
OSAKA CITY, 1-3-

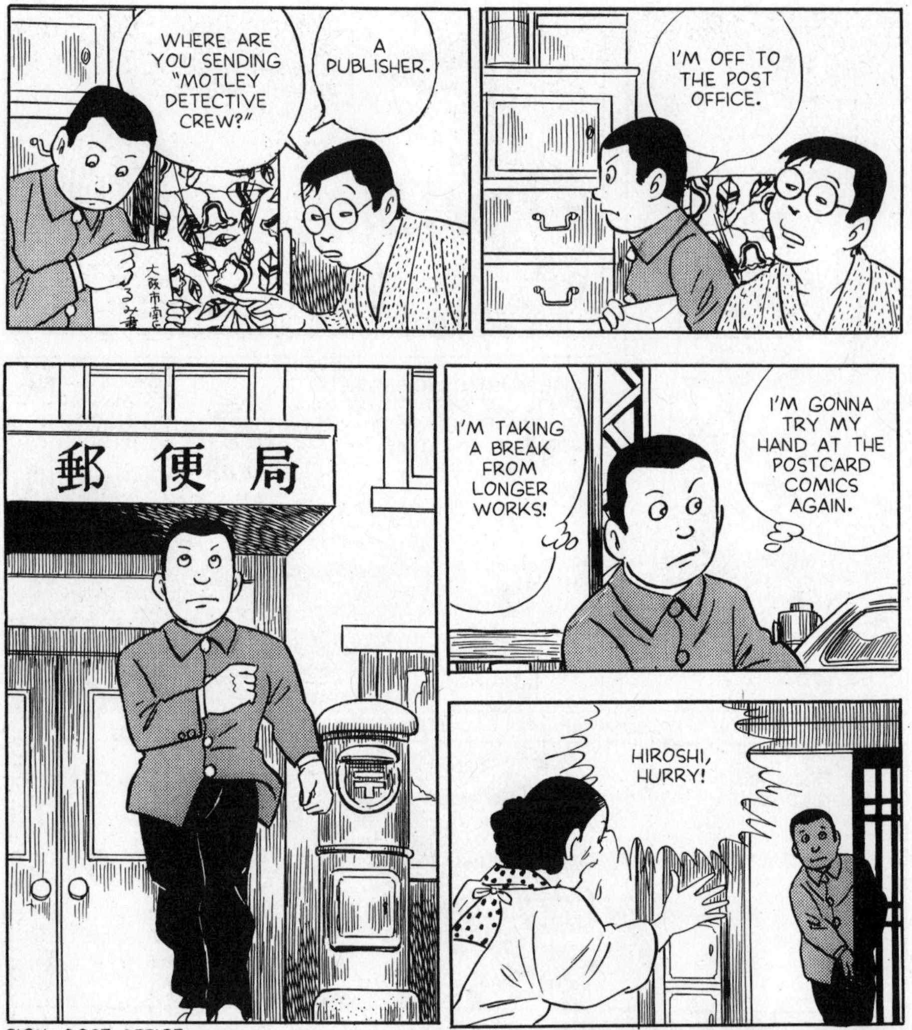
WHERE ARE YOU SENDING "MOTLEY DETECTIVE CREW?"
A PUBLISHER.
I'M OFF TO THE POST OFFICE.
郵便局
I'M TAKING A BREAK FROM LONGER WORKS!
I'M GONNA TRY MY HAND AT THE POSTCARD COMICS AGAIN.
HIROSHI, HURRY!

SIGN: POST OFFICE

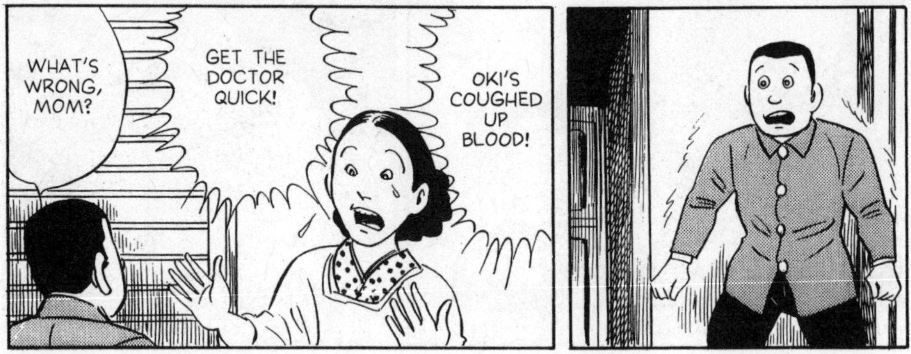
WHAT'S WRONG, MOM?
GET THE DOCTOR QUICK!
OKI'S COUGHED UP BLOOD!

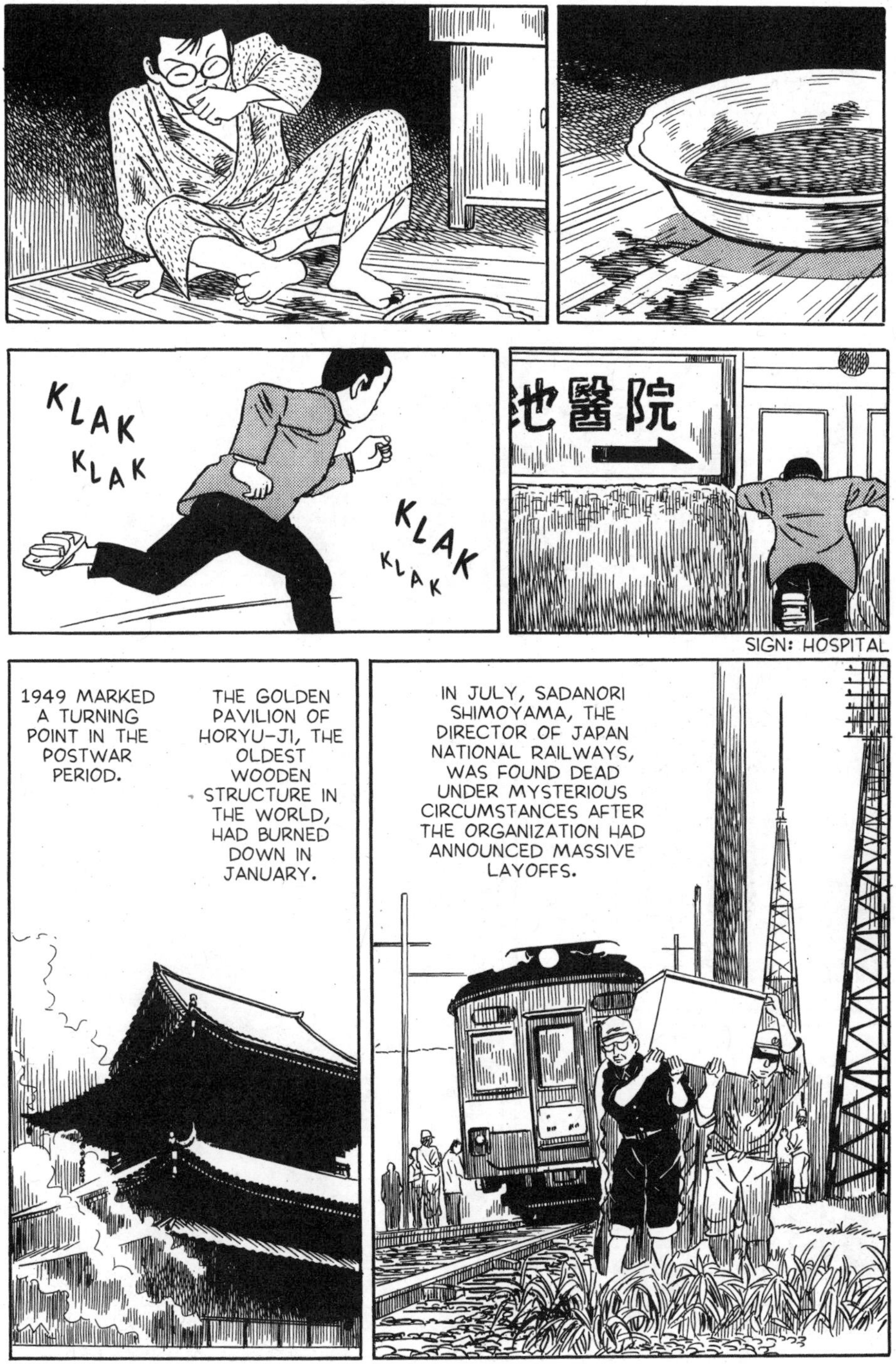
KLAK
KLAK
KLAK
KLAK
池醫院
SIGN: HOSPITAL
1949 MARKED A TURNING POINT IN THE POSTWAR PERIOD.
THE GOLDEN PAVILION OF HORYU-JI, THE OLDEST WOODEN STRUCTURE IN THE WORLD, HAD BURNED DOWN IN JANUARY.
IN JULY, SADANORI SHIMOYAMA, THE DIRECTOR OF JAPAN NATIONAL RAILWAYS, WAS FOUND DEAD UNDER MYSTERIOUS CIRCUMSTANCES AFTER THE ORGANIZATION HAD ANNOUNCED MASSIVE LAYOFFS.

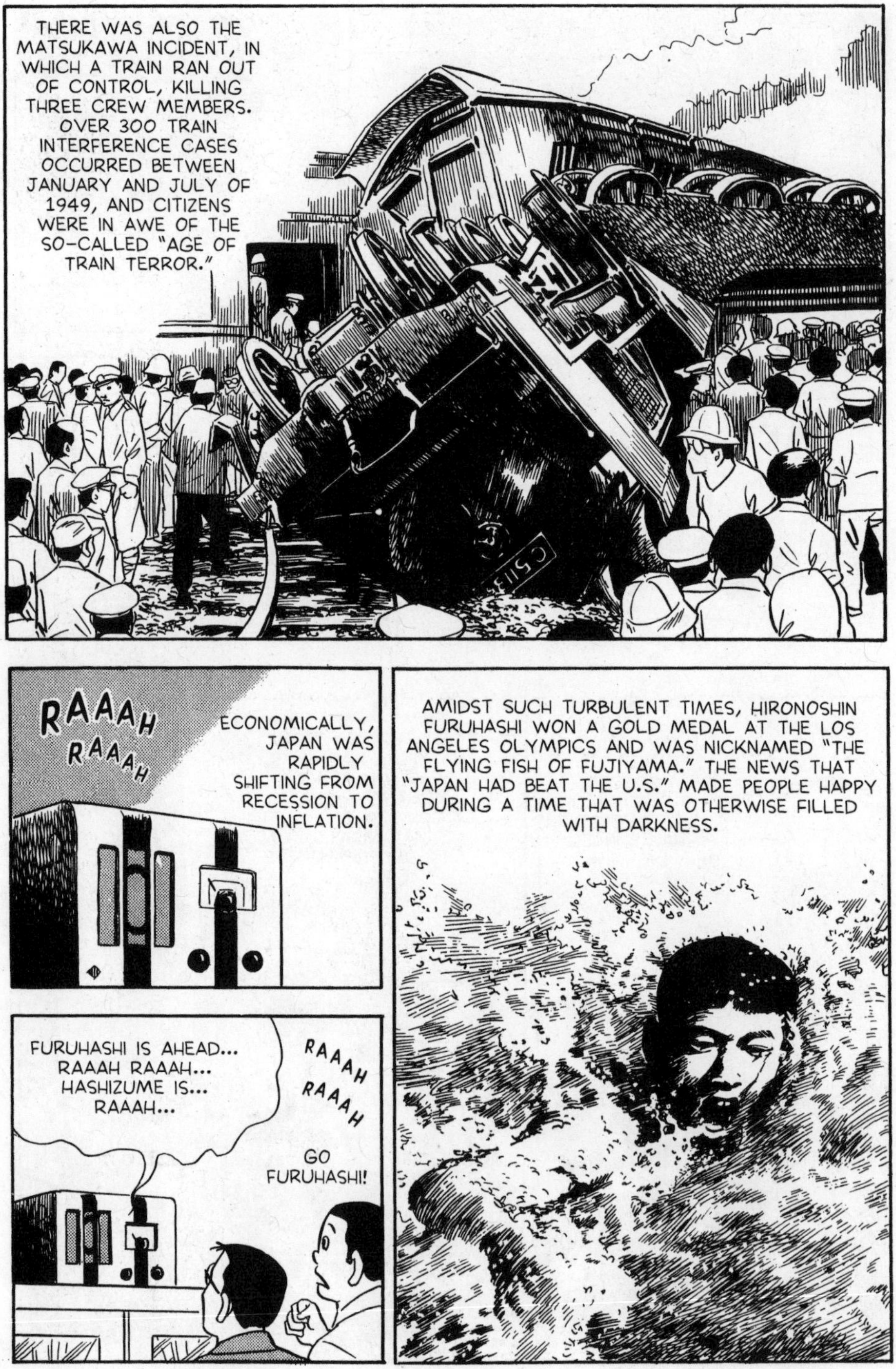
THERE WAS ALSO THE MATSUKAWA INCIDENT, IN WHICH A TRAIN RAN OUT OF CONTROL, KILLING THREE CREW MEMBERS. OVER 300 TRAIN INTERFERENCE CASES OCCURRED BETWEEN JANUARY AND JULY OF 1949, AND CITIZENS WERE IN AWE OF THE SO-CALLED "AGE OF TRAIN TERROR."
RAAAH RAAAH
ECONOMICALLY, JAPAN WAS RAPIDLY SHIFTING FROM RECESSION TO INFLATION.
FURUHASHI IS AHEAD... RAAAH RAAAH... HASHIZUME IS... RAAAH...
RAAAH RAAAH
GO FURUHASHI!
AMIDST SUCH TURBULENT TIMES, HIRONOSHIN FURUHASHI WON A GOLD MEDAL AT THE LOS ANGELES OLYMPICS AND WAS NICKNAMED "THE FLYING FISH OF FUJIYAMA." THE NEWS THAT "JAPAN HAD BEAT THE U.S." MADE PEOPLE HAPPY DURING A TIME THAT WAS OTHERWISE FILLED WITH DARKNESS.

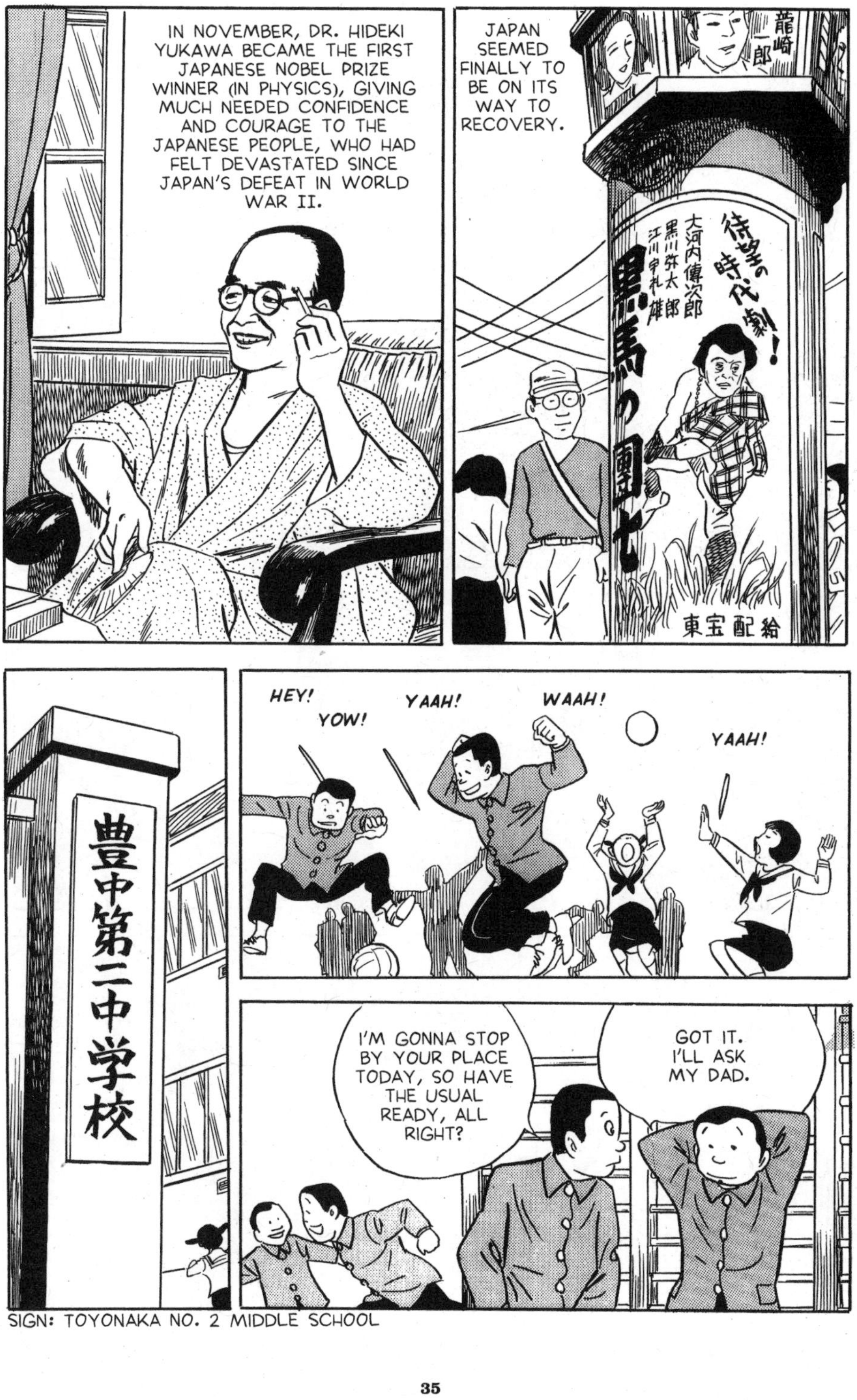
IN NOVEMBER, DR. HIDEKI YUKAWA BECAME THE FIRST JAPANESE NOBEL PRIZE WINNER (IN PHYSICS), GIVING MUCH NEEDED CONFIDENCE AND COURAGE TO THE JAPANESE PEOPLE, WHO HAD FELT DEVASTATED SINCE JAPAN'S DEFEAT IN WORLD WAR II.
JAPAN SEEMED FINALLY TO BE ON ITS WAY TO RECOVERY.
龍崎一郎
待望の時代劇！
大河内傳次郎
黒川弥太郎
江川宇礼雄
黒馬の團七
東宝配給
豊中第二中学校
HEY!
YOW!
YAAH!
WAAH!
YAAH!
I'M GONNA STOP BY YOUR PLACE TODAY, SO HAVE THE USUAL READY, ALL RIGHT?
GOT IT. I'LL ASK MY DAD.

SIGN: TOYONAKA NO. 2 MIDDLE SCHOOL

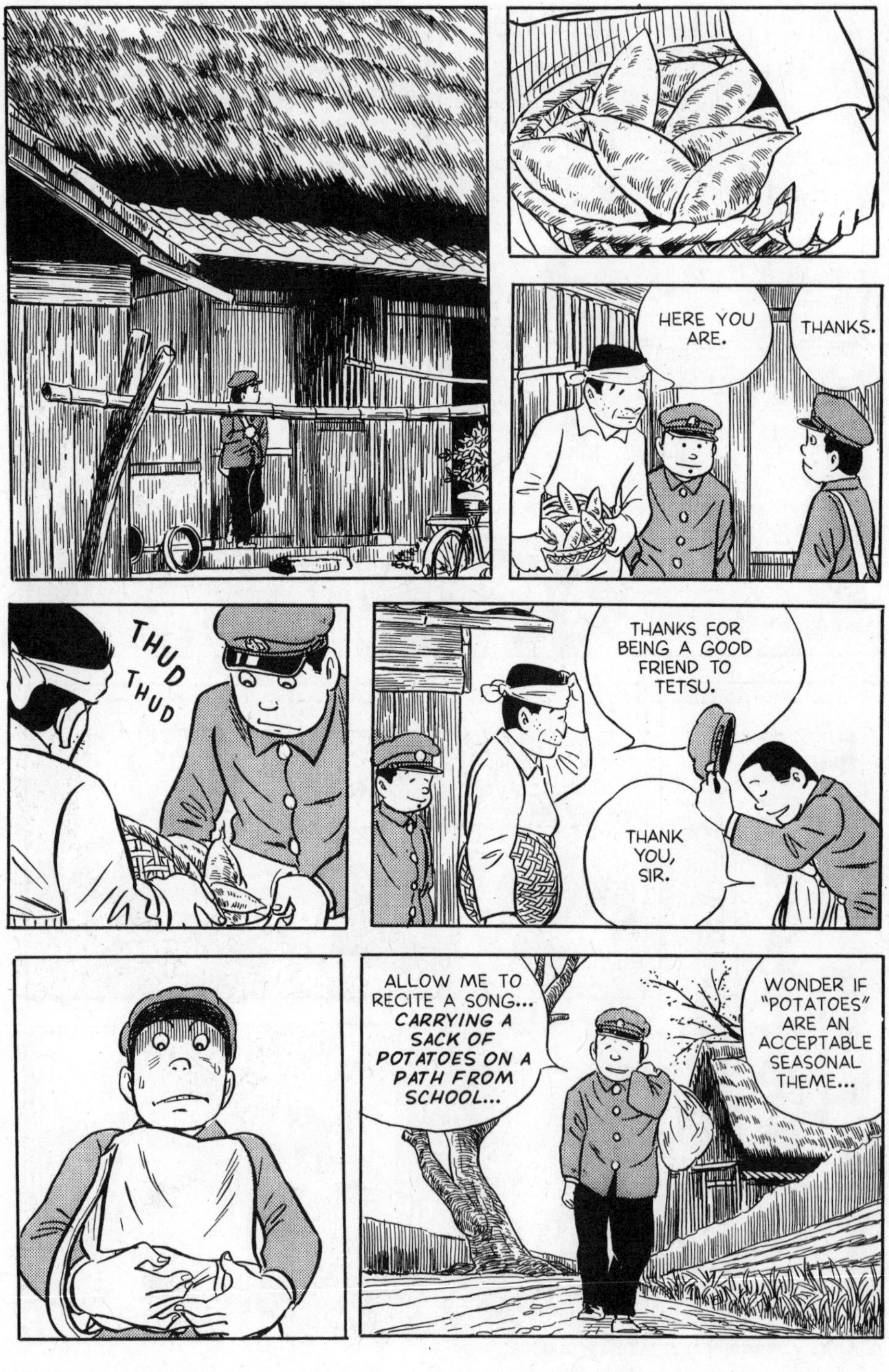
HERE YOU ARE.
THANKS.
THUD THUD
THANKS FOR BEING A GOOD FRIEND TO TETSU.
THANK YOU, SIR.
ALLOW ME TO RECITE A SONG... *CARRYING A SACK OF POTATOES ON A PATH FROM SCHOOL...*
WONDER IF "POTATOES" ARE AN ACCEPTABLE SEASONAL THEME...

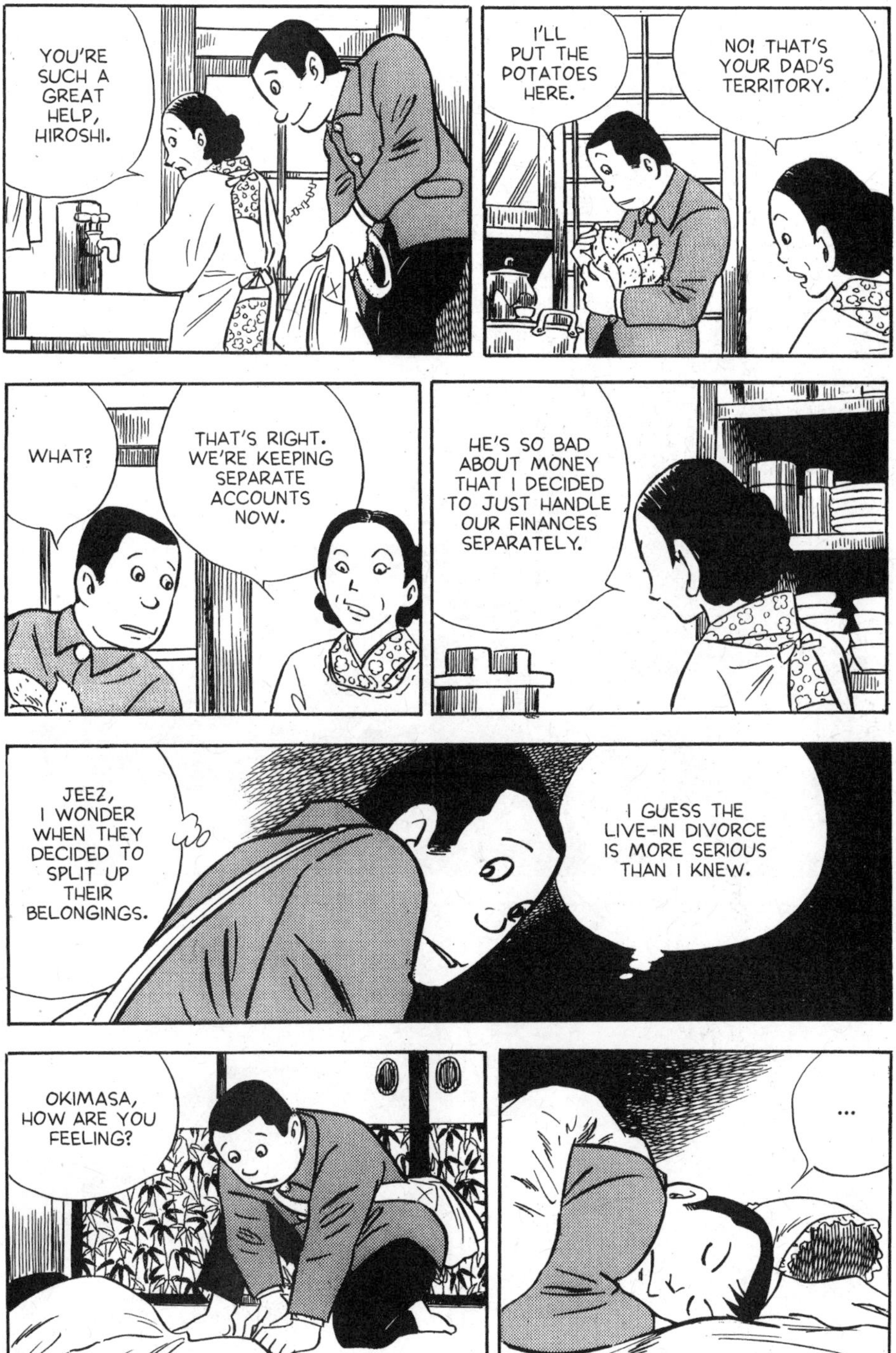
YOU'RE SUCH A GREAT HELP, HIROSHI.
I'LL PUT THE POTATOES HERE.
NO! THAT'S YOUR DAD'S TERRITORY.
WHAT?
THAT'S RIGHT. WE'RE KEEPING SEPARATE ACCOUNTS NOW.
HE'S SO BAD ABOUT MONEY THAT I DECIDED TO JUST HANDLE OUR FINANCES SEPARATELY.
JEEZ, I WONDER WHEN THEY DECIDED TO SPLIT UP THEIR BELONGINGS.
I GUESS THE LIVE-IN DIVORCE IS MORE SERIOUS THAN I KNEW.
OKIMASA, HOW ARE YOU FEELING?
...

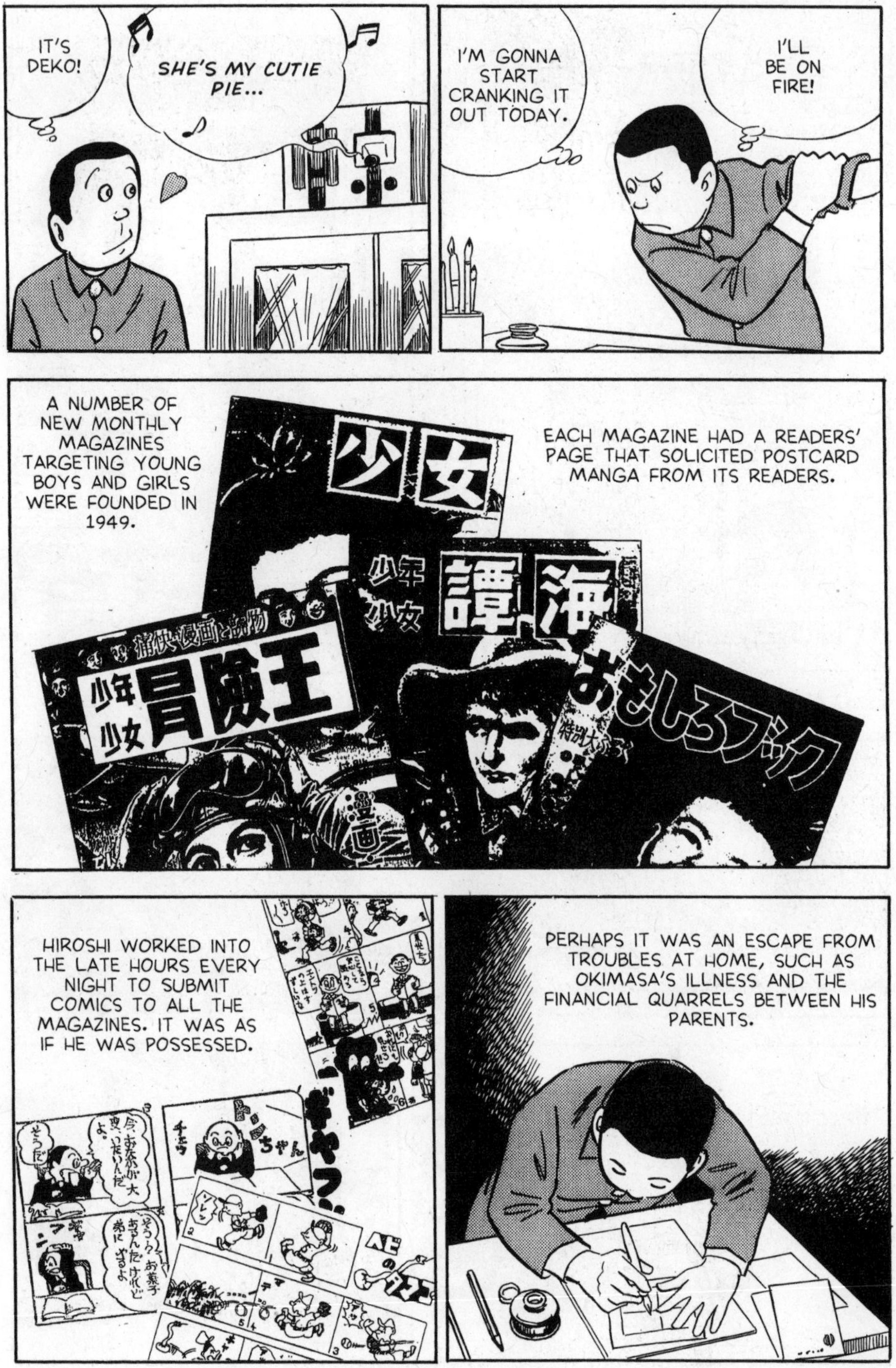
IT'S DEKO!
SHE'S MY CUTIE PIE...
I'M GONNA START CRANKING IT OUT TODAY.
I'LL BE ON FIRE!
A NUMBER OF NEW MONTHLY MAGAZINES TARGETING YOUNG BOYS AND GIRLS WERE FOUNDED IN 1949.
少女
少年少女
譚海
少年少女冒険王
おもしろブック
EACH MAGAZINE HAD A READERS' PAGE THAT SOLICITED POSTCARD MANGA FROM ITS READERS.
HIROSHI WORKED INTO THE LATE HOURS EVERY NIGHT TO SUBMIT COMICS TO ALL THE MAGAZINES. IT WAS AS IF HE WAS POSSESSED.
PERHAPS IT WAS AN ESCAPE FROM TROUBLES AT HOME, SUCH AS OKIMASA'S ILLNESS AND THE FINANCIAL QUARRELS BETWEEN HIS PARENTS.

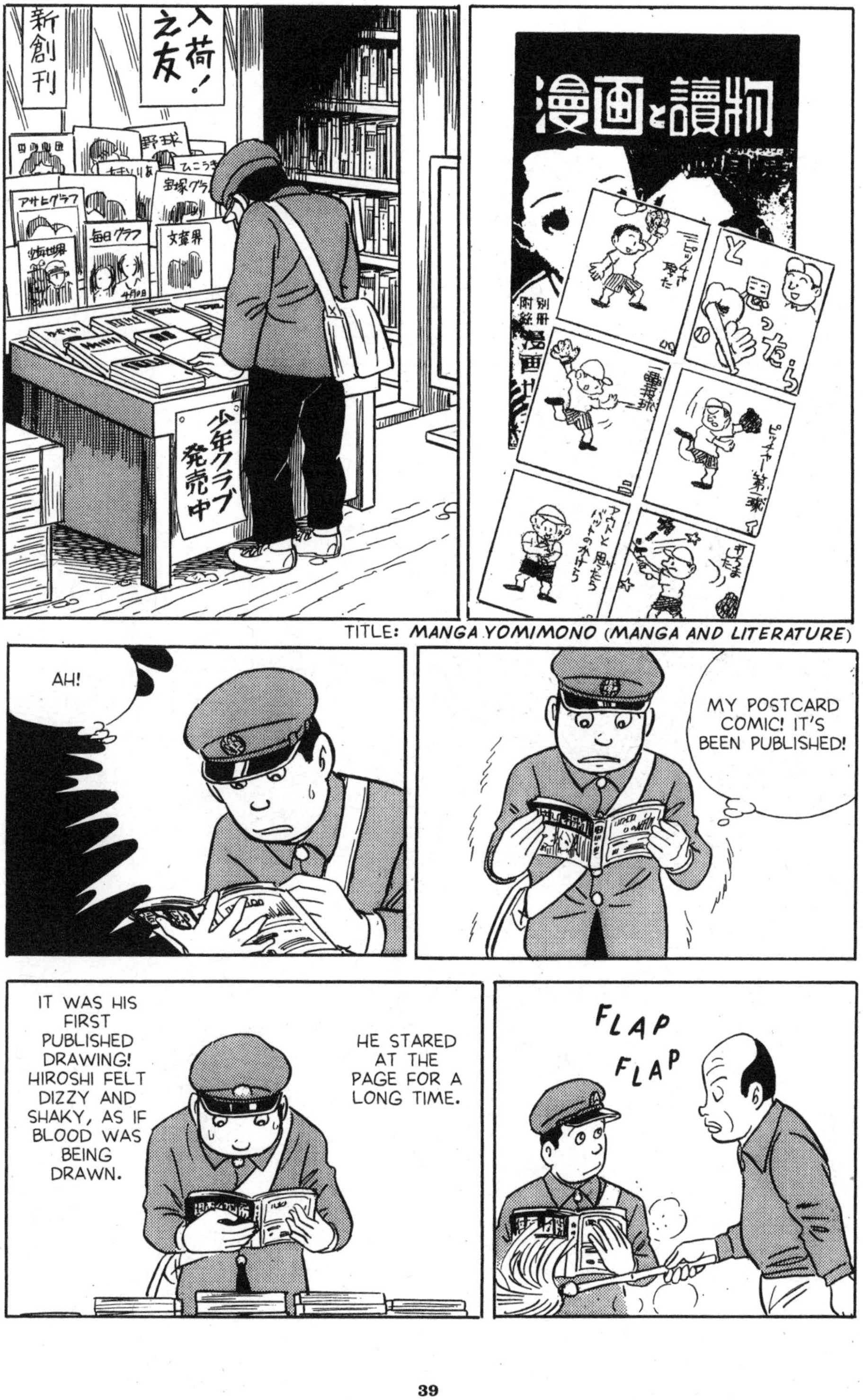
新創刊
入荷！
之友
野球
アサヒグラフ
毎日グラフ
少年クラブ発売中
漫画と讀物
TITLE: MANGA YOMIMONO (MANGA AND LITERATURE)
AH!
MY POSTCARD COMIC! IT'S BEEN PUBLISHED!
IT WAS HIS FIRST PUBLISHED DRAWING! HIROSHI FELT DIZZY AND SHAKY, AS IF BLOOD WAS BEING DRAWN.
HE STARED AT THE PAGE FOR A LONG TIME.
FLAP
FLAP

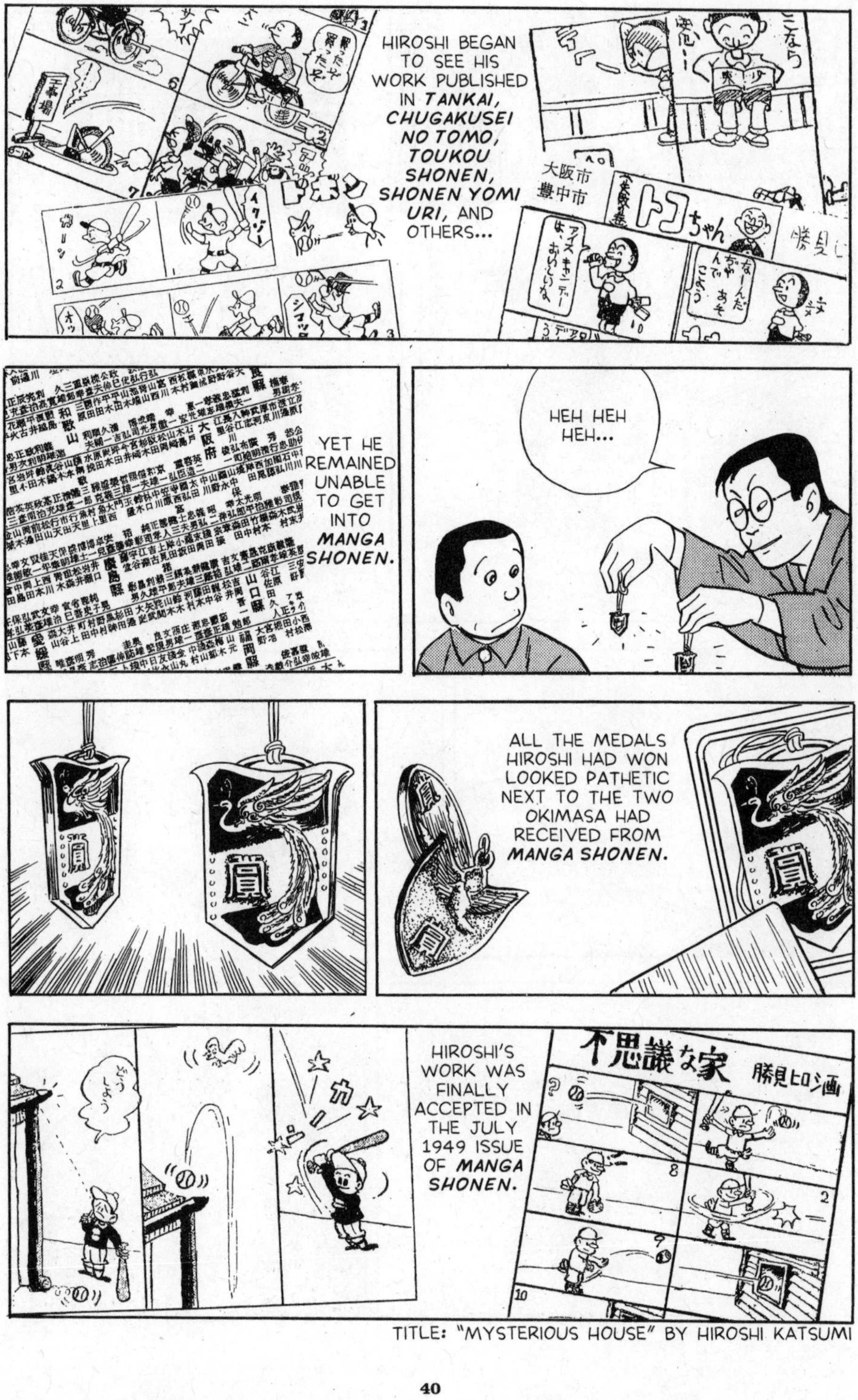
HIROSHI BEGAN TO SEE HIS WORK PUBLISHED IN TANKAI, CHUGAKUSEI NO TOMO, TOUKOU SHONEN, SHONEN YOMI URI, AND OTHERS...
大阪市
豊中市
YET HE REMAINED UNABLE TO GET INTO MANGA SHONEN.
HEH HEH HEH...
ALL THE MEDALS HIROSHI HAD WON LOOKED PATHETIC NEXT TO THE TWO OKIMASA HAD RECEIVED FROM MANGA SHONEN.
HIROSHI'S WORK WAS FINALLY ACCEPTED IN THE JULY 1949 ISSUE OF MANGA SHONEN.
不思議な家
勝見ヒロシ画

TITLE: "MYSTERIOUS HOUSE" BY HIROSHI KATSUMI

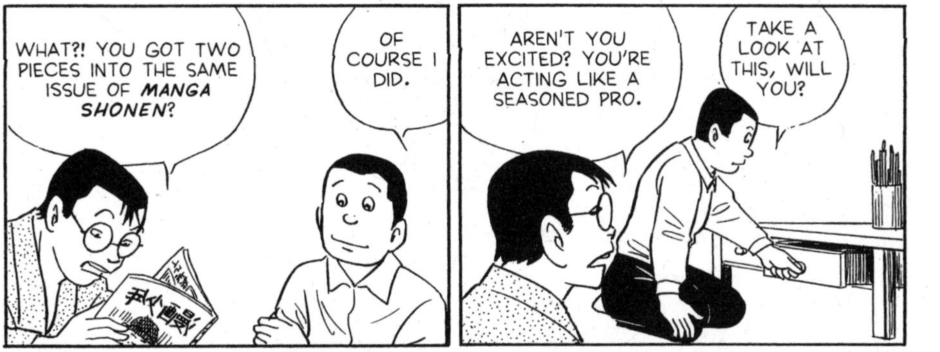
WHAT?! YOU GOT TWO PIECES INTO THE SAME ISSUE OF *MANGA SHONEN*?
OF COURSE I DID.
AREN'T YOU EXCITED? YOU'RE ACTING LIKE A SEASONED PRO.
TAKE A LOOK AT THIS, WILL YOU?

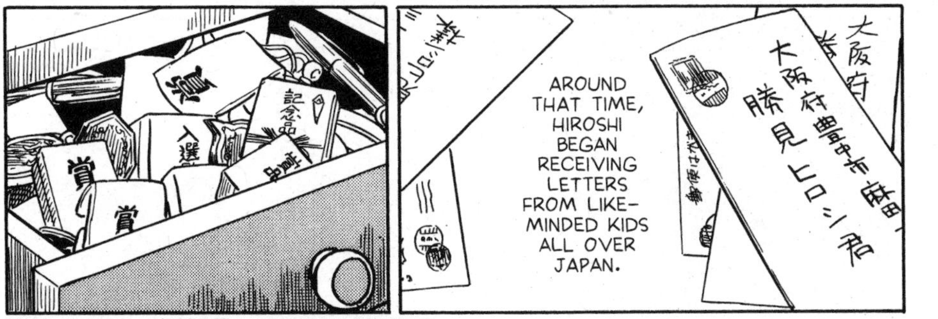
賞
入選
記念品
AROUND THAT TIME, HIROSHI BEGAN RECEIVING LETTERS FROM LIKE-MINDED KIDS ALL OVER JAPAN.
大阪府豊中市麻田
勝見ヒロシ君

TEXT: AWARD / ACCEPTED / COMMEMORATIVE

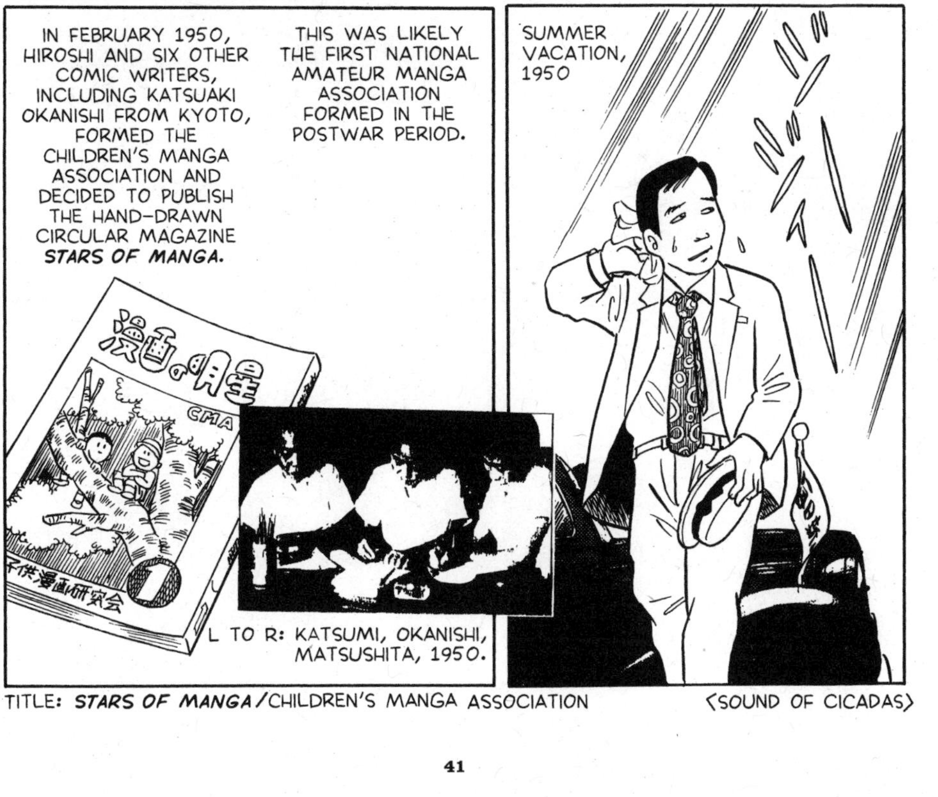
IN FEBRUARY 1950, HIROSHI AND SIX OTHER COMIC WRITERS, INCLUDING KATSUAKI OKANISHI FROM KYOTO, FORMED THE CHILDREN'S MANGA ASSOCIATION AND DECIDED TO PUBLISH THE HAND-DRAWN CIRCULAR MAGAZINE ***STARS OF MANGA***.
THIS WAS LIKELY THE FIRST NATIONAL AMATEUR MANGA ASSOCIATION FORMED IN THE POSTWAR PERIOD.
漫画の明星
CMA
子供漫画研究会
L TO R: KATSUMI, OKANISHI, MATSUSHITA, 1950.
SUMMER VACATION, 1950

TITLE: ***STARS OF MANGA*** / CHILDREN'S MANGA ASSOCIATION 〈SOUND OF CICADAS〉

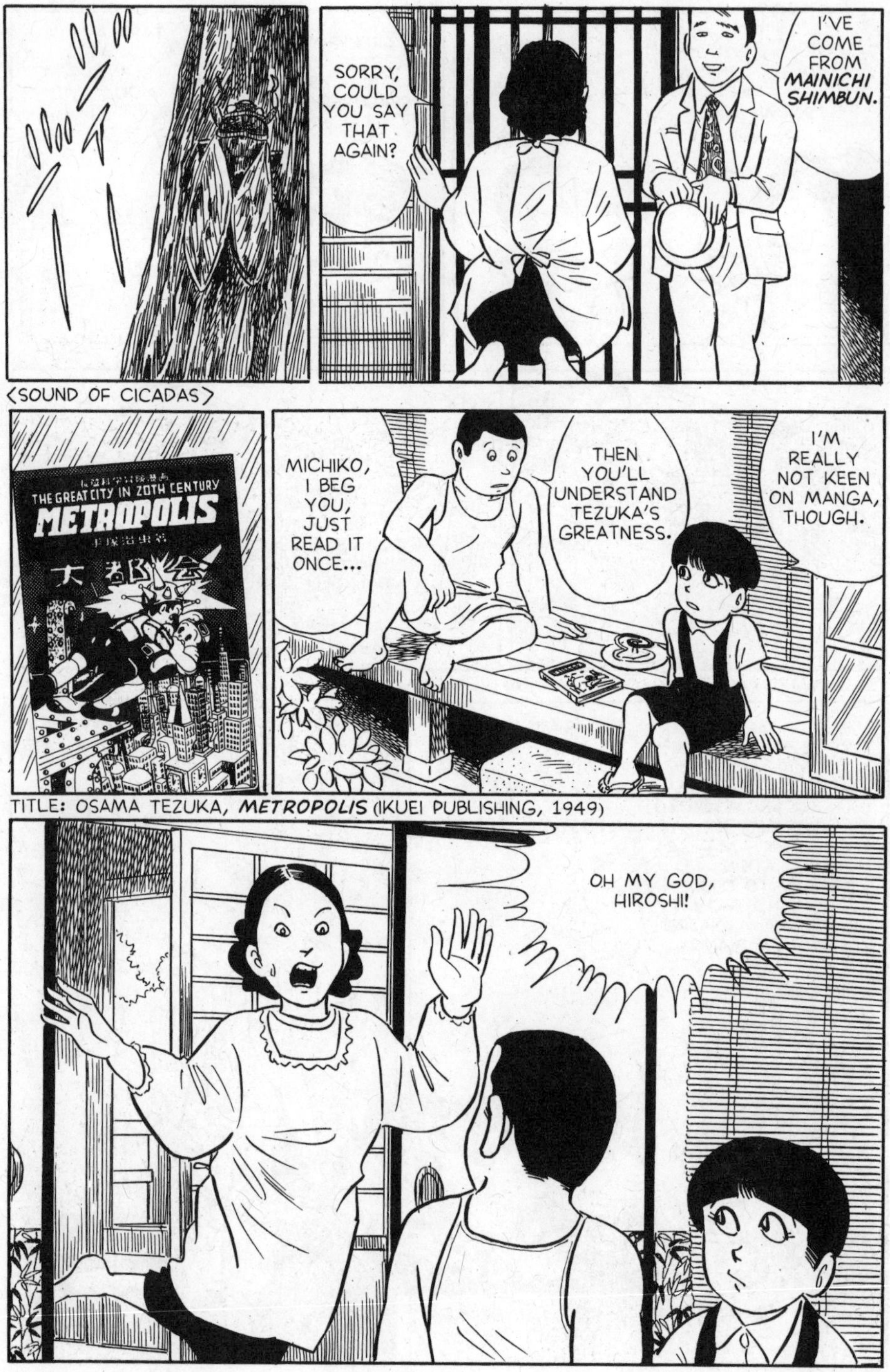
SORRY, COULD YOU SAY THAT AGAIN?
I'VE COME FROM *MAINICHI SHIMBUN*.
〈SOUND OF CICADAS〉
THE GREAT CITY IN 20TH CENTURY
METROPOLIS
大都会
MICHIKO, I BEG YOU, JUST READ IT ONCE...
THEN YOU'LL UNDERSTAND TEZUKA'S GREATNESS.
I'M REALLY NOT KEEN ON MANGA, THOUGH.
TITLE: OSAMA TEZUKA, *METROPOLIS* (IKUEI PUBLISHING, 1949)
OH MY GOD, HIROSHI!

THE JOURNALIST FROM MAINICHI SHIMBUN

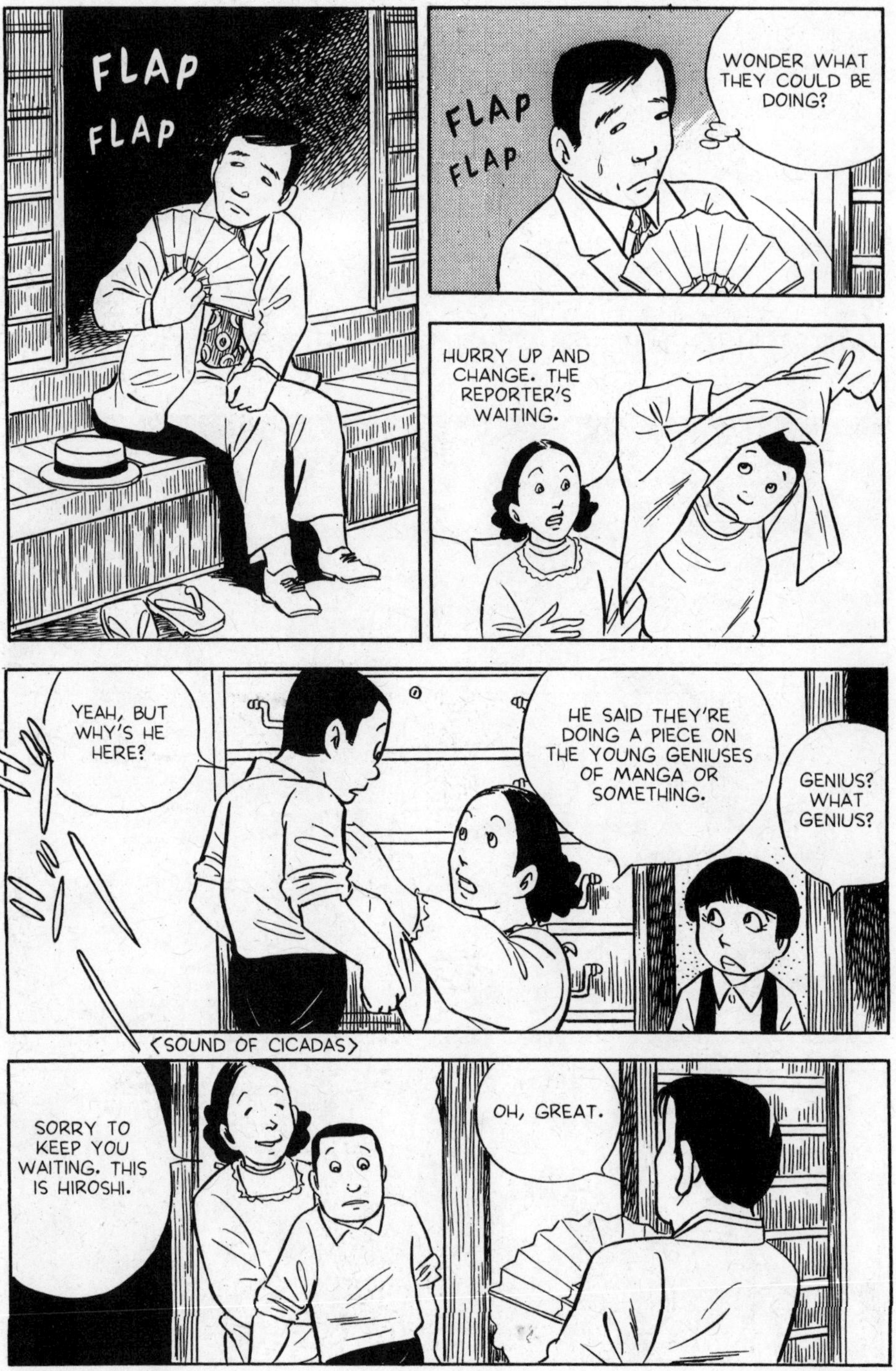
FLAP
FLAP
FLAP
FLAP
WONDER WHAT THEY COULD BE DOING?
HURRY UP AND CHANGE. THE REPORTER'S WAITING.
YEAH, BUT WHY'S HE HERE?
HE SAID THEY'RE DOING A PIECE ON THE YOUNG GENIUSES OF MANGA OR SOMETHING.
GENIUS? WHAT GENIUS?
〈SOUND OF CICADAS〉
SORRY TO KEEP YOU WAITING. THIS IS HIROSHI.
OH, GREAT.

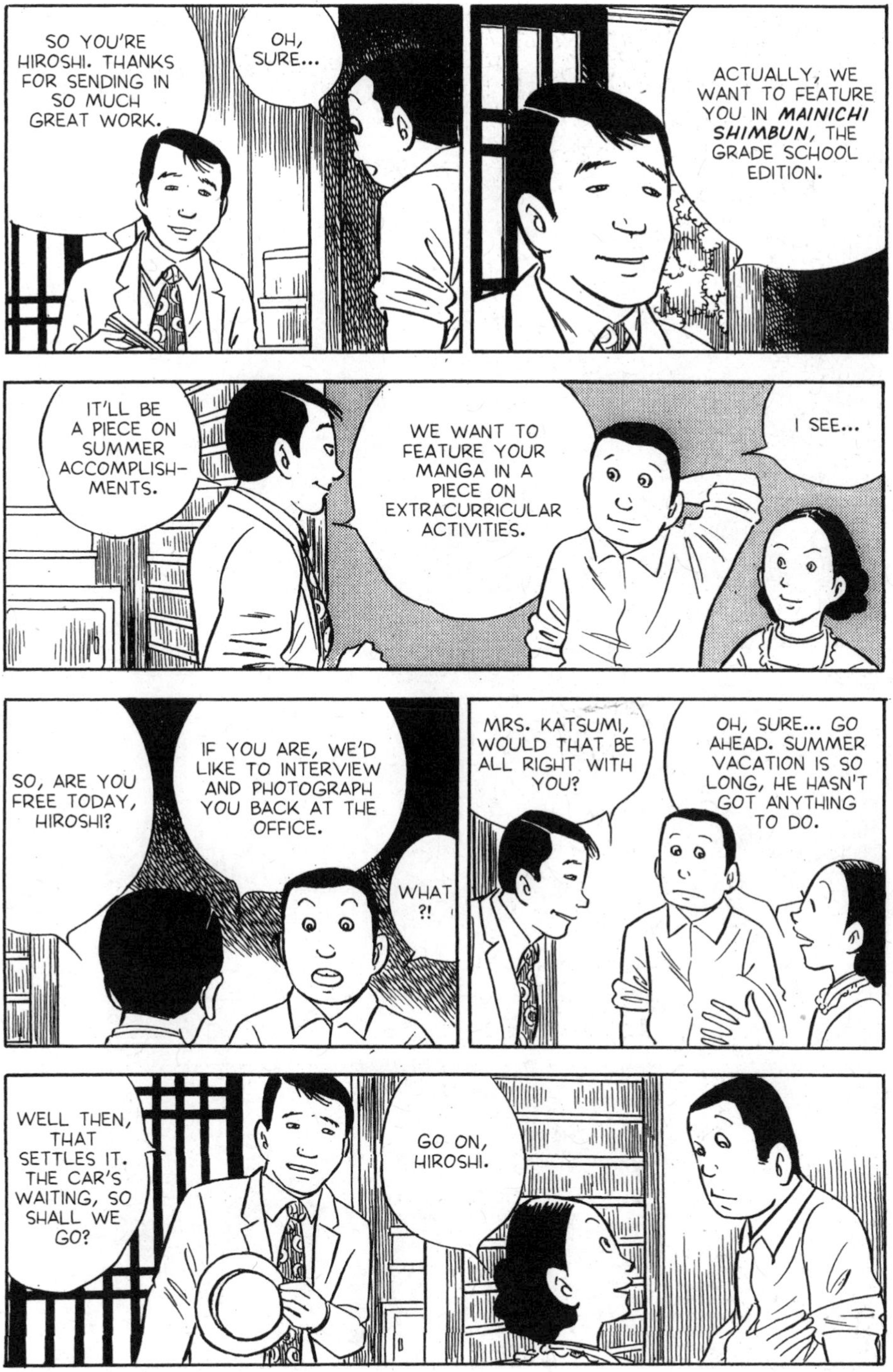
SO YOU'RE HIROSHI. THANKS FOR SENDING IN SO MUCH GREAT WORK.
OH, SURE...
ACTUALLY, WE WANT TO FEATURE YOU IN *MAINICHI SHIMBUN*, THE GRADE SCHOOL EDITION.
IT'LL BE A PIECE ON SUMMER ACCOMPLISH-MENTS.
WE WANT TO FEATURE YOUR MANGA IN A PIECE ON EXTRACURRICULAR ACTIVITIES.
I SEE...
SO, ARE YOU FREE TODAY, HIROSHI?
IF YOU ARE, WE'D LIKE TO INTERVIEW AND PHOTOGRAPH YOU BACK AT THE OFFICE.
WHAT ?!
MRS. KATSUMI, WOULD THAT BE ALL RIGHT WITH YOU?
OH, SURE... GO AHEAD. SUMMER VACATION IS SO LONG, HE HASN'T GOT ANYTHING TO DO.
WELL THEN, THAT SETTLES IT. THE CAR'S WAITING, SO SHALL WE GO?
GO ON, HIROSHI.

〈SOUND OF CICADAS〉

SURE IS HOT INSIDE THE CAR, HUH? MAKE YOURSELF COMFORTABLE.

FLAP
FLAP

THE CORPORATE FLAG FLUTTERED IN THE WIND AS THE CAR TOOK OFF.

IN 1950, GASOLINE USE WAS STILL REGULATED, AND MANY CARS WERE POWERED BY CHARCOAL GAS.

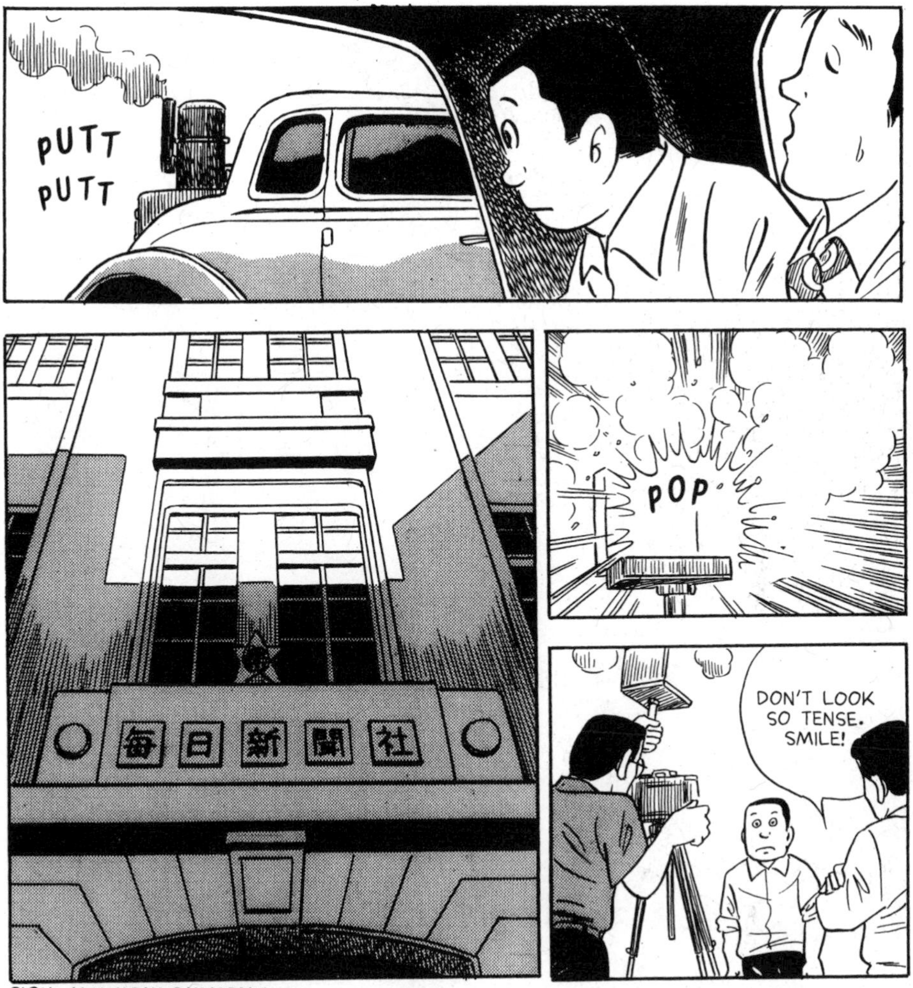
PUTT PUTT
毎日新聞社
POP
DON'T LOOK SO TENSE. SMILE!
SIGN: *MAINICHI SHIMBUN*

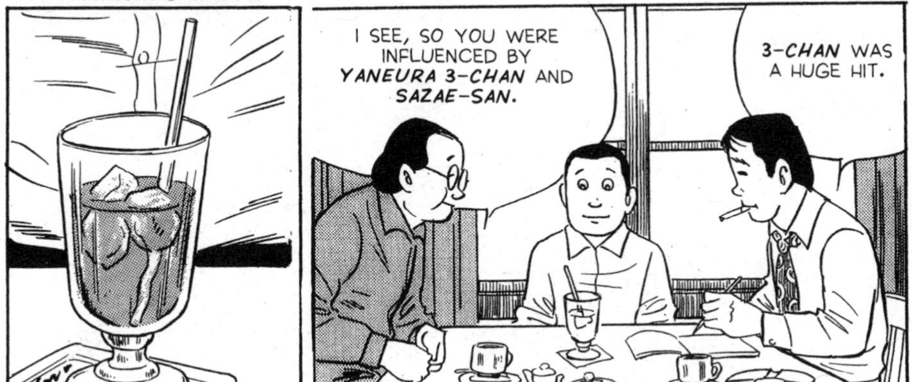
I SEE, SO YOU WERE INFLUENCED BY *YANEURA 3-CHAN* AND *SAZAE-SAN*.
3-CHAN WAS A HUGE HIT.

YES, BUT THERE IS A NEW MANGA ARTIST THAT I'M VERY EXCITED ABOUT RIGHT NOW!

REALLY? AND WHO'S THAT?

OSAMU TEZUKA.

I'VE READ ALL OF HIS WORKS.

OF COURSE, YOU'RE A TEZUKA FAN AS WELL.

"TEZUKA, TEZUKA," THAT'S WHAT ALL YOUNG MANGA ARTISTS SAY THESE DAYS.

THESE ARE THE SEVEN FOUR-PANEL STRIPS YOU'VE SENT US.

WE'LL PUBLISH THE THREE YOU CHOOSE.

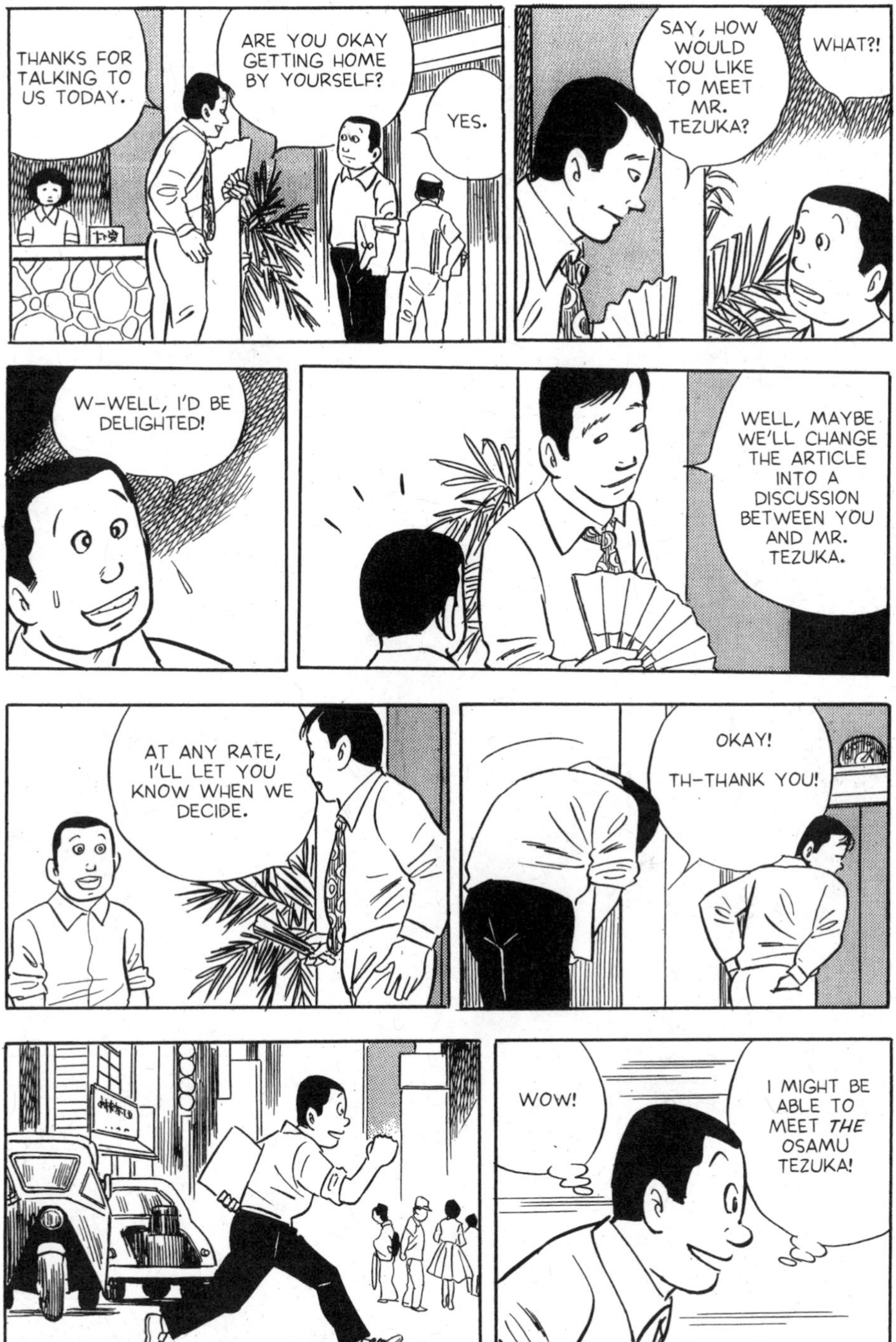
THANKS FOR TALKING TO US TODAY.
ARE YOU OKAY GETTING HOME BY YOURSELF?
YES.
SAY, HOW WOULD YOU LIKE TO MEET MR. TEZUKA?
WHAT?!
W-WELL, I'D BE DELIGHTED!
WELL, MAYBE WE'LL CHANGE THE ARTICLE INTO A DISCUSSION BETWEEN YOU AND MR. TEZUKA.
AT ANY RATE, I'LL LET YOU KNOW WHEN WE DECIDE.
OKAY!
TH-THANK YOU!
WOW!
I MIGHT BE ABLE TO MEET *THE* OSAMU TEZUKA!

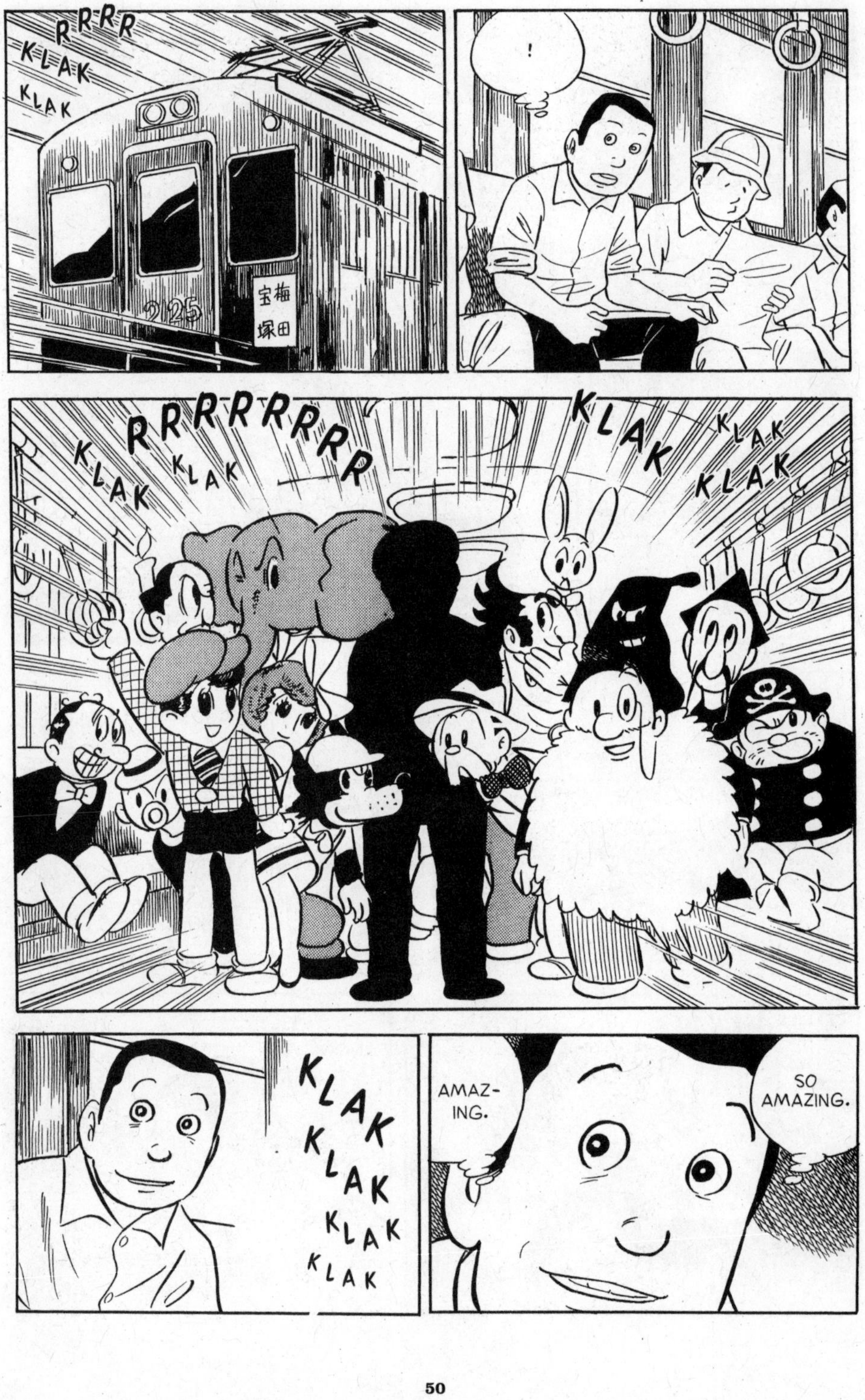
RRRR
KLAK
KLAK
梅田
宝塚
!
RRRRRRRRRR
KLAK
KLAK
KLAK
KLAK
KLAK
KLAK
KLAK
KLAK
KLAK
KLAK
AMAZ-
ING.
SO
AMAZING.

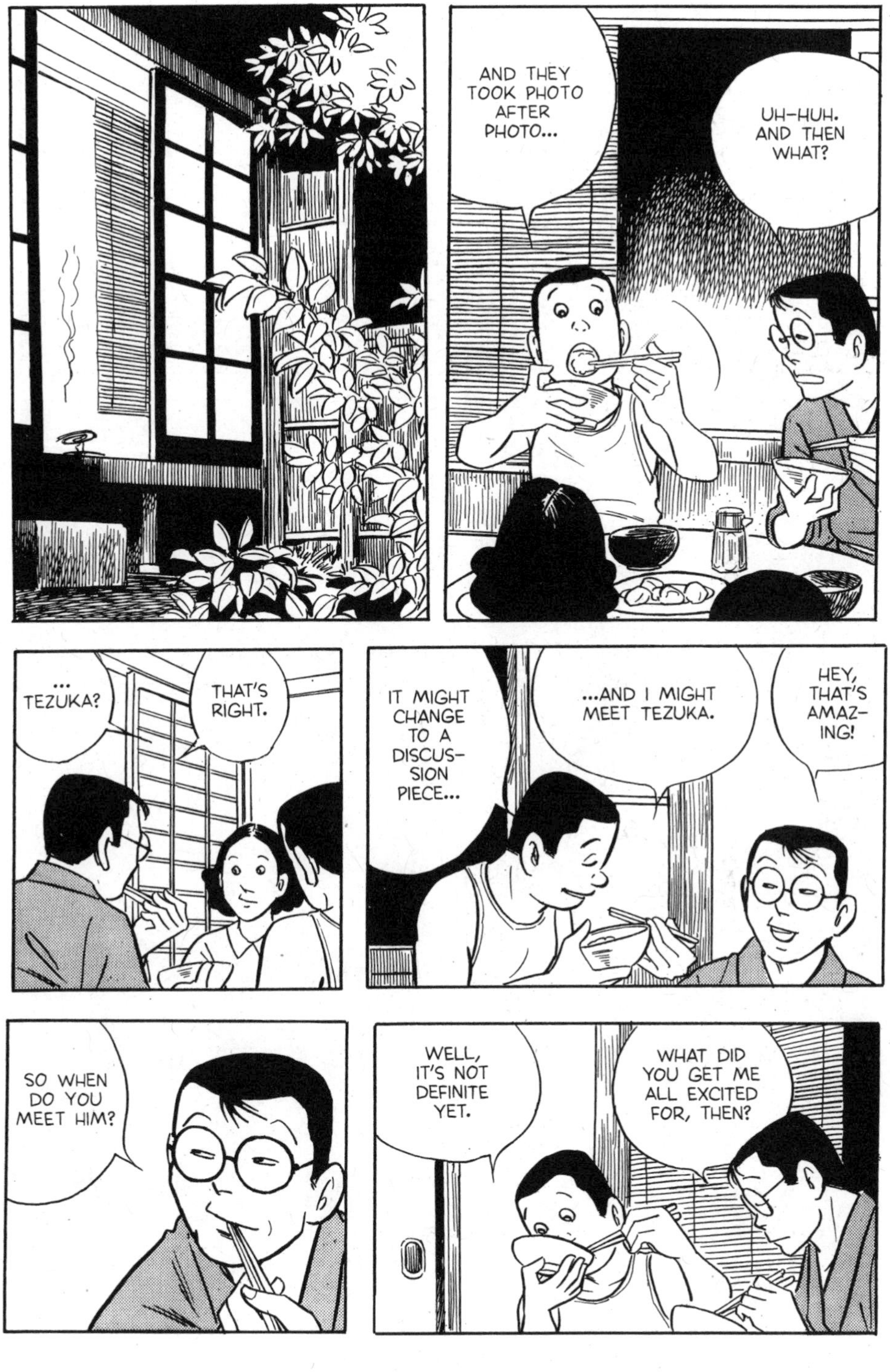
AND THEY TOOK PHOTO AFTER PHOTO...
UH-HUH. AND THEN WHAT?
... TEZUKA?
THAT'S RIGHT.
IT MIGHT CHANGE TO A DISCUSSION PIECE...
...AND I MIGHT MEET TEZUKA.
HEY, THAT'S AMAZING!
SO WHEN DO YOU MEET HIM?
WELL, IT'S NOT DEFINITE YET.
WHAT DID YOU GET ME ALL EXCITED FOR, THEN?

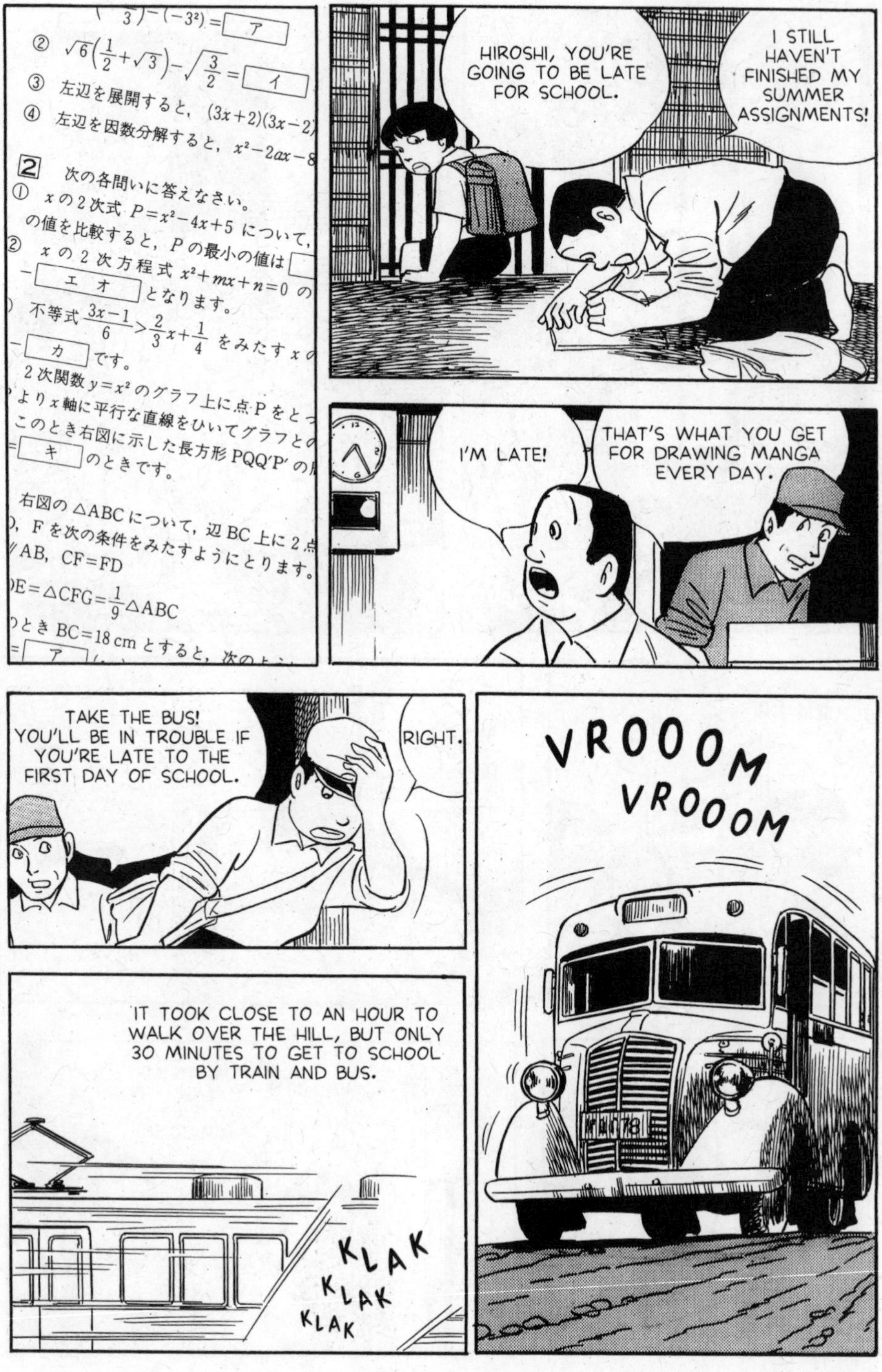

次の各問いに答えなさい。
となります。
です。
のときです。
HIROSHI, YOU'RE GOING TO BE LATE FOR SCHOOL.
I STILL HAVEN'T FINISHED MY SUMMER ASSIGNMENTS!
I'M LATE!
THAT'S WHAT YOU GET FOR DRAWING MANGA EVERY DAY.
TAKE THE BUS! YOU'LL BE IN TROUBLE IF YOU'RE LATE TO THE FIRST DAY OF SCHOOL.
RIGHT.
IT TOOK CLOSE TO AN HOUR TO WALK OVER THE HILL, BUT ONLY 30 MINUTES TO GET TO SCHOOL BY TRAIN AND BUS.
KLAK
KLAK
KLAK
VROOOM
VROOOM

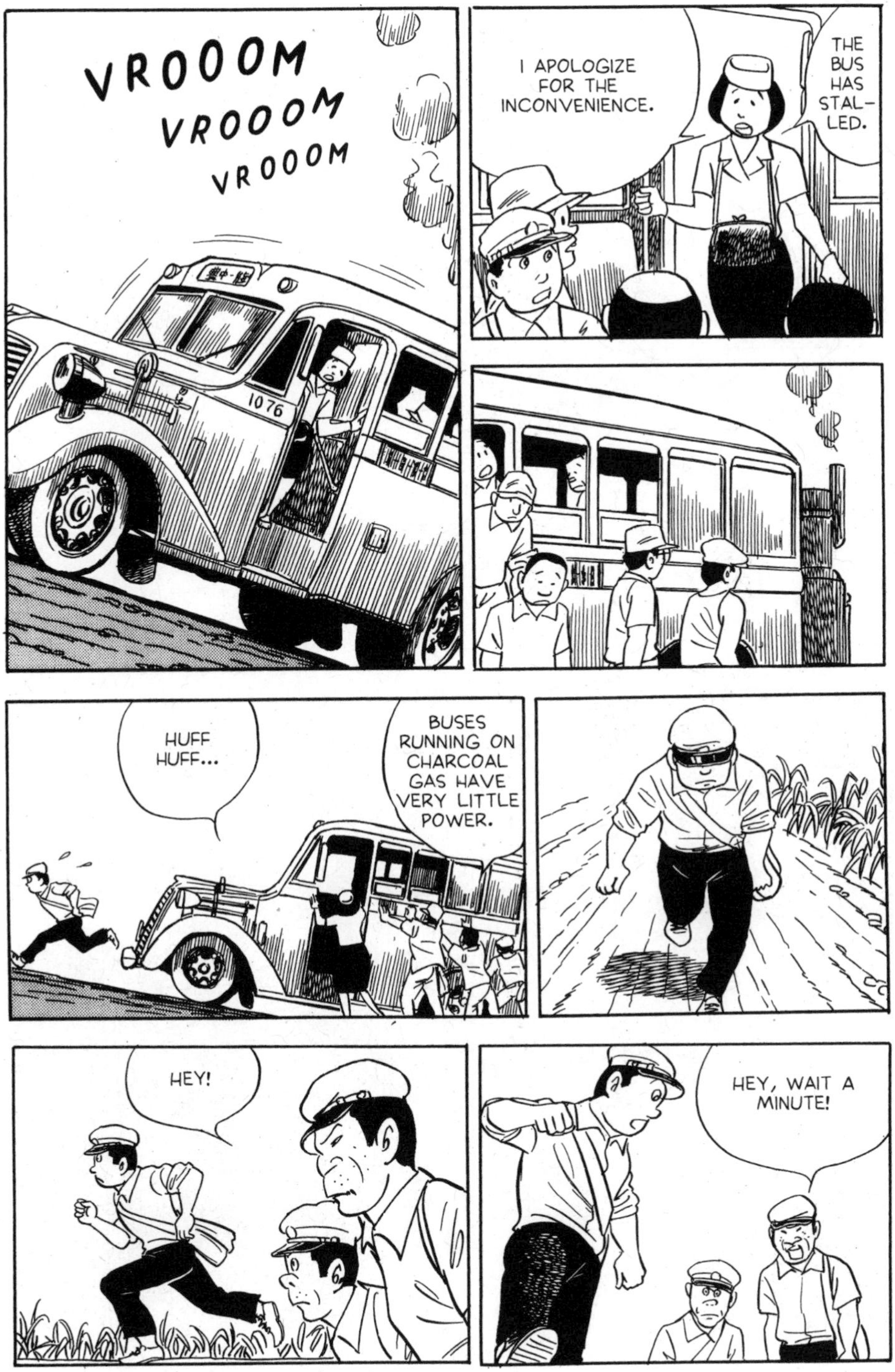
VROOOM
VROOOM
VROOOM
I APOLOGIZE FOR THE INCONVENIENCE.
THE BUS HAS STAL-LED.
1076
HUFF HUFF...
BUSES RUNNING ON CHARCOAL GAS HAVE VERY LITTLE POWER.
HEY!
HEY, WAIT A MINUTE!

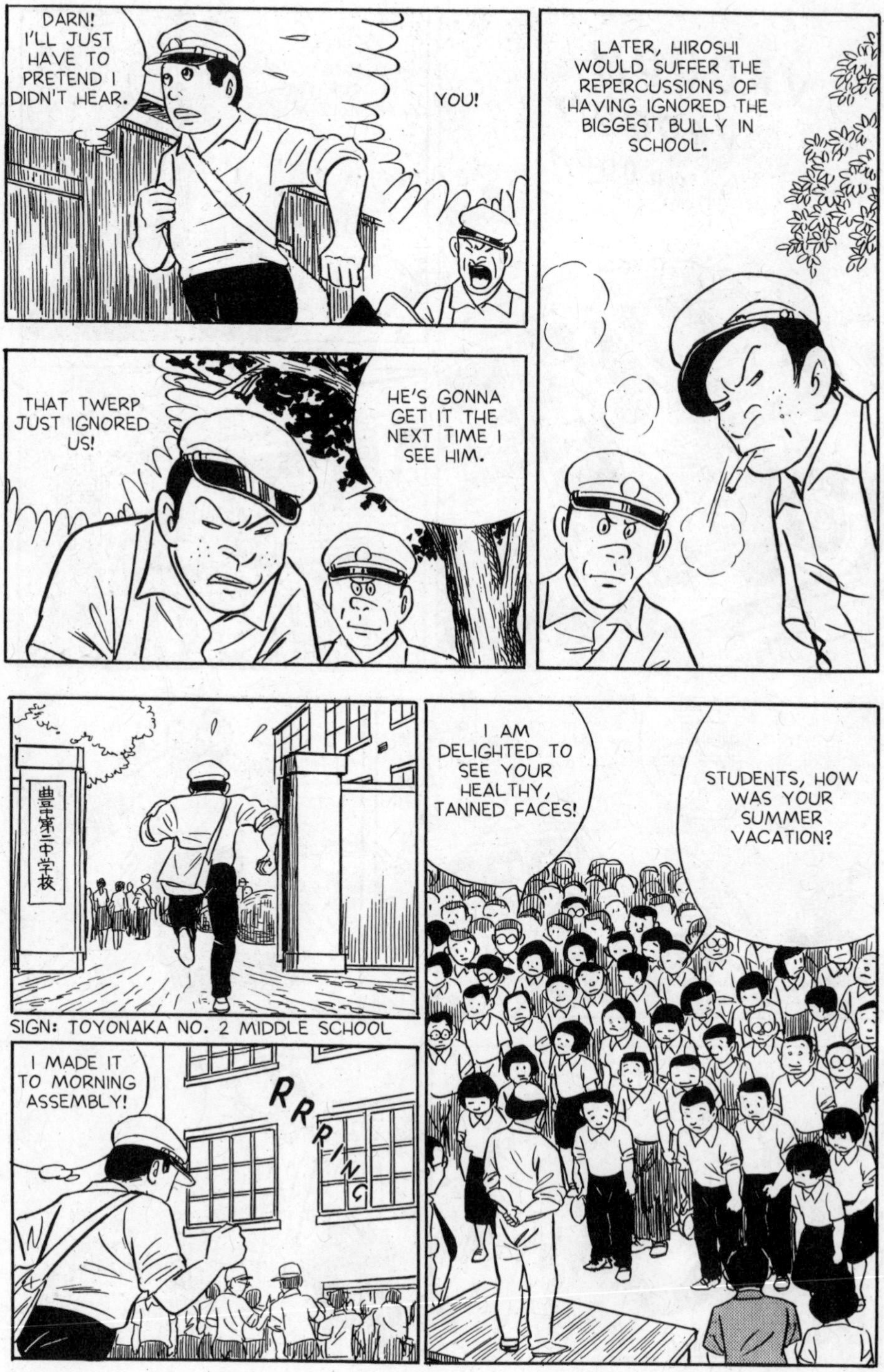
DARN! I'LL JUST HAVE TO PRETEND I DIDN'T HEAR.
YOU!
THAT TWERP JUST IGNORED US!
HE'S GONNA GET IT THE NEXT TIME I SEE HIM.
LATER, HIROSHI WOULD SUFFER THE REPERCUSSIONS OF HAVING IGNORED THE BIGGEST BULLY IN SCHOOL.
豊中第二中学校
SIGN: TOYONAKA NO. 2 MIDDLE SCHOOL
I MADE IT TO MORNING ASSEMBLY!
RRRING
I AM DELIGHTED TO SEE YOUR HEALTHY, TANNED FACES!
STUDENTS, HOW WAS YOUR SUMMER VACATION?

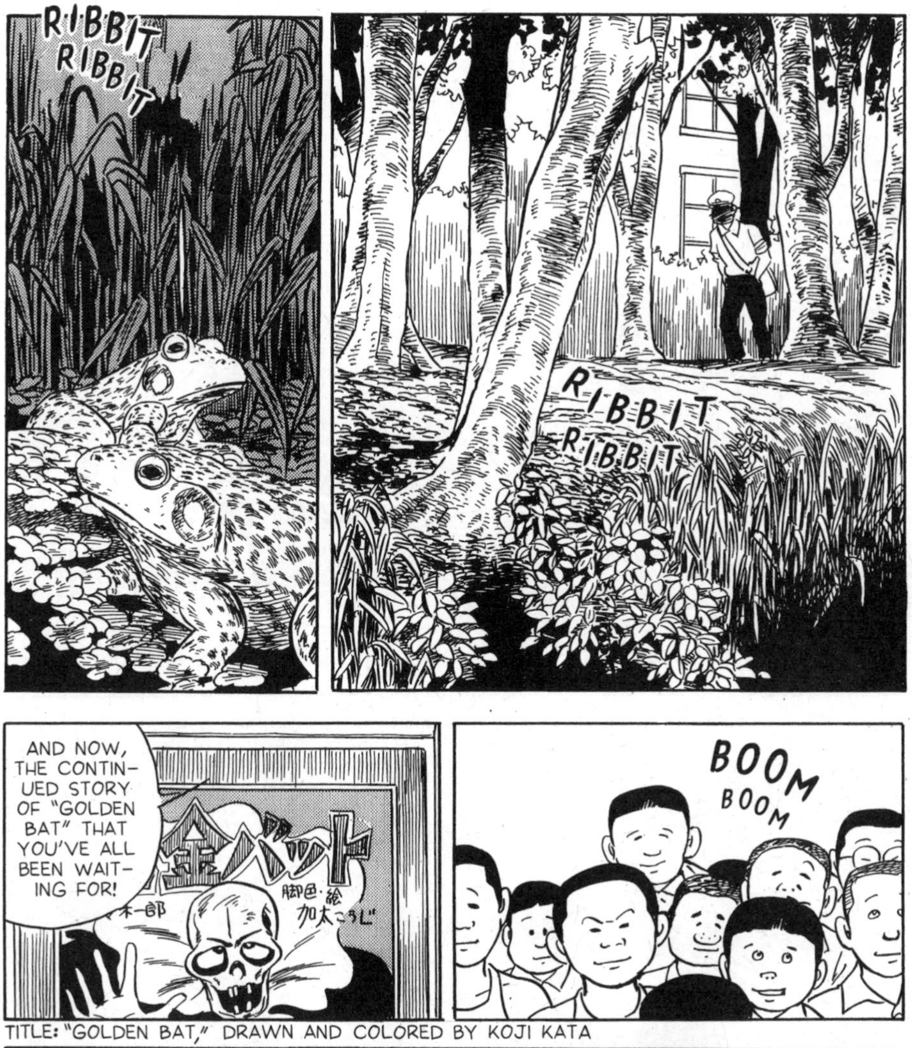
RIBBIT RIBBIT
RIBBIT RIBBIT
AND NOW, THE CONTINUED STORY OF "GOLDEN BAT" THAT YOU'VE ALL BEEN WAITING FOR!
脚色・絵
加太こうじ
BOOM BOOM

TITLE: "GOLDEN BAT," DRAWN AND COLORED BY KOJI KATA

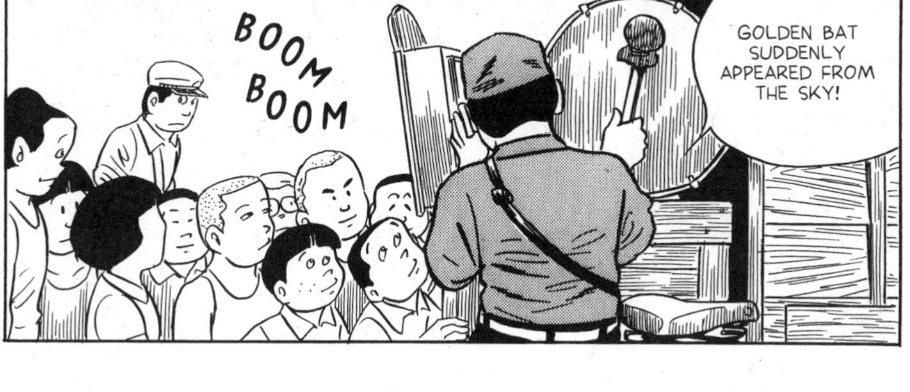
BOOM BOOM
GOLDEN BAT SUDDENLY APPEARED FROM THE SKY!

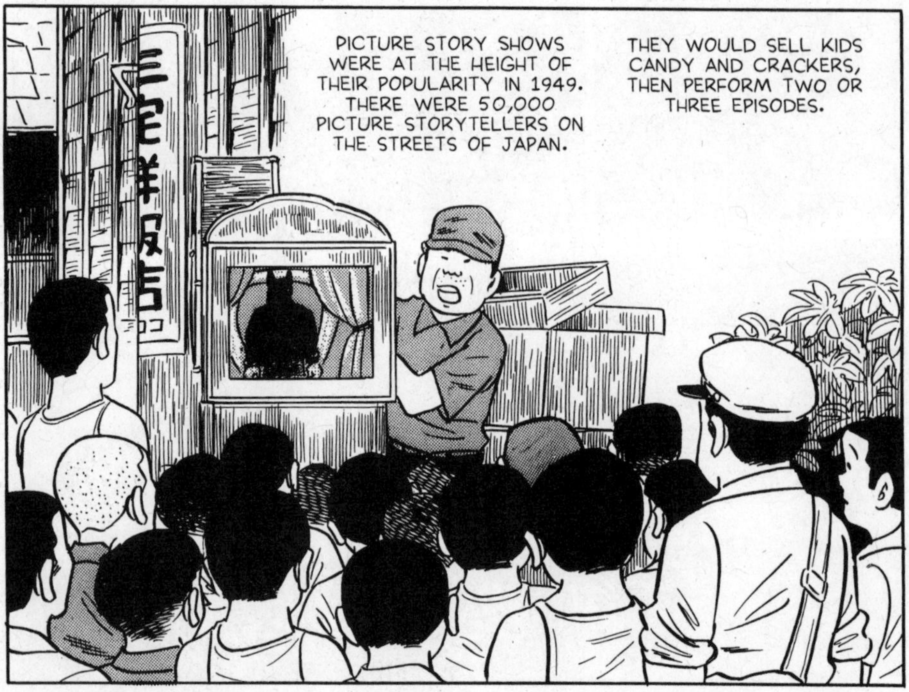
PICTURE STORY SHOWS WERE AT THE HEIGHT OF THEIR POPULARITY IN 1949. THERE WERE 50,000 PICTURE STORYTELLERS ON THE STREETS OF JAPAN.
THEY WOULD SELL KIDS CANDY AND CRACKERS, THEN PERFORM TWO OR THREE EPISODES.

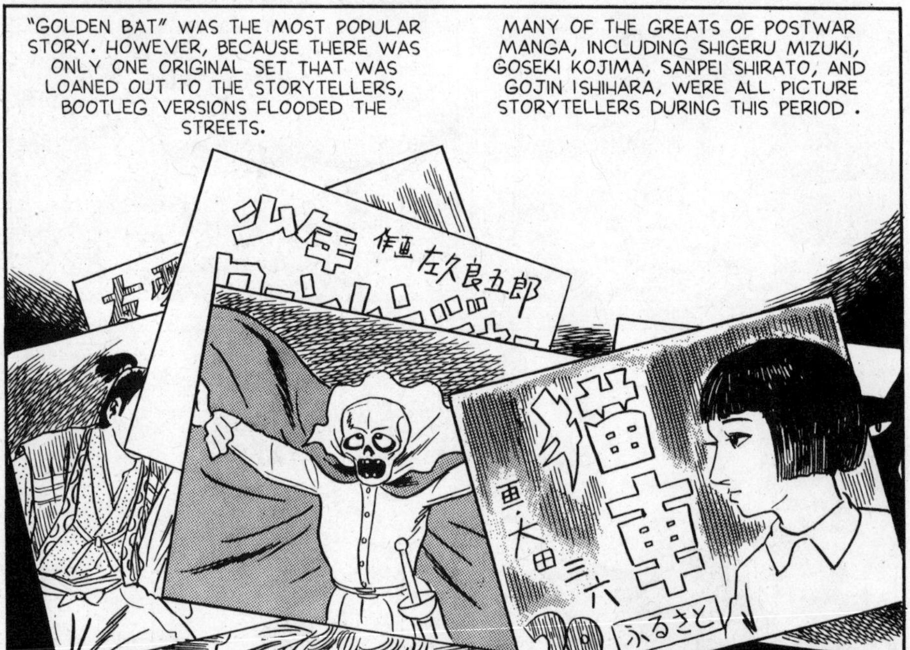
"GOLDEN BAT" WAS THE MOST POPULAR STORY. HOWEVER, BECAUSE THERE WAS ONLY ONE ORIGINAL SET THAT WAS LOANED OUT TO THE STORYTELLERS, BOOTLEG VERSIONS FLOODED THE STREETS.
MANY OF THE GREATS OF POSTWAR MANGA, INCLUDING SHIGERU MIZUKI, GOSEKI KOJIMA, SANPEI SHIRATO, AND GOJIN ISHIHARA, WERE ALL PICTURE STORYTELLERS DURING THIS PERIOD .
少年
作画 左久良五郎
猫車
画・大田三六
20
ふるさと

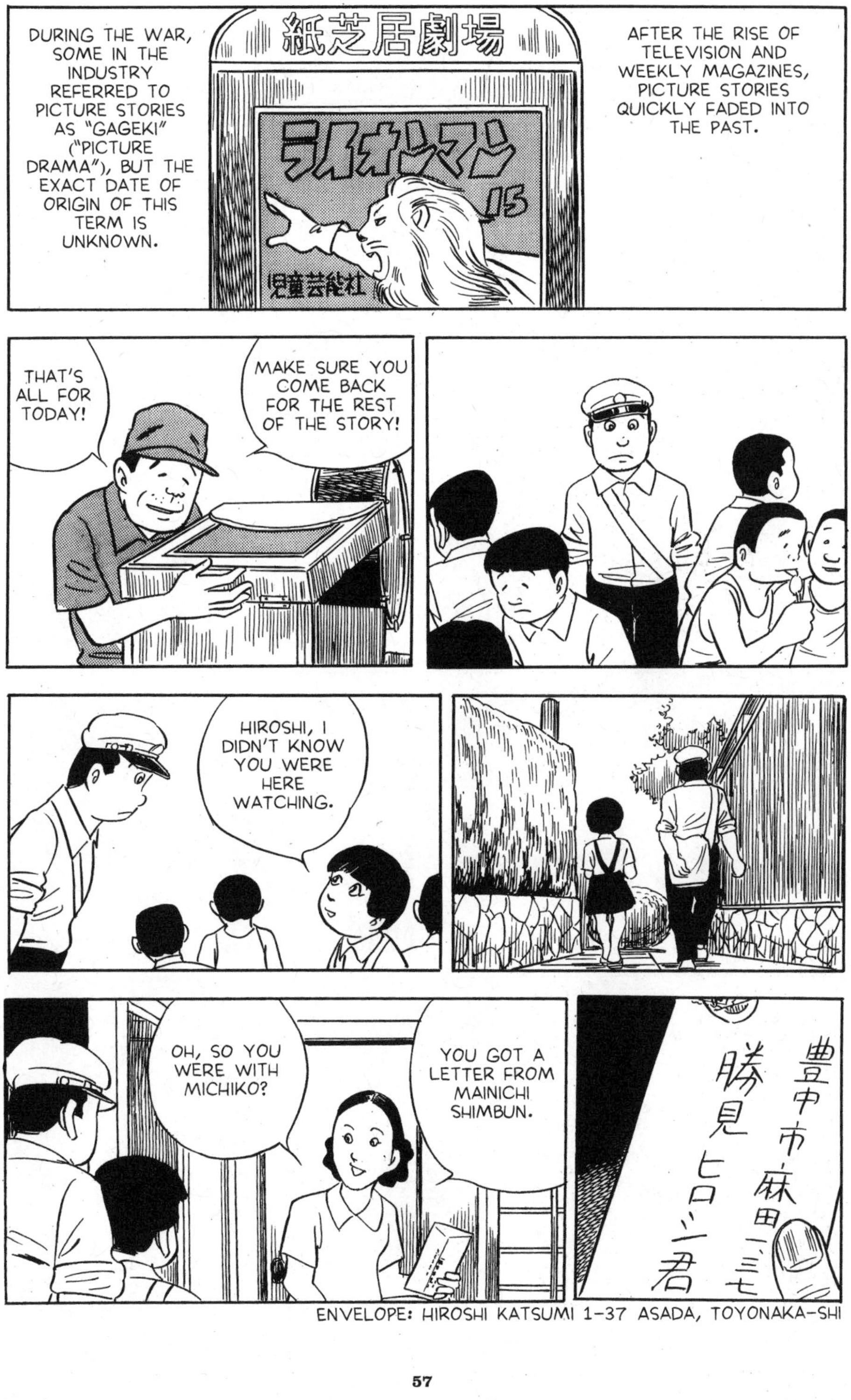

DURING THE WAR, SOME IN THE INDUSTRY REFERRED TO PICTURE STORIES AS "GAGEKI" ("PICTURE DRAMA"), BUT THE EXACT DATE OF ORIGIN OF THIS TERM IS UNKNOWN.
紙芝居劇場
ライオンマン
15
児童芸能社
AFTER THE RISE OF TELEVISION AND WEEKLY MAGAZINES, PICTURE STORIES QUICKLY FADED INTO THE PAST.
THAT'S ALL FOR TODAY!
MAKE SURE YOU COME BACK FOR THE REST OF THE STORY!
HIROSHI, I DIDN'T KNOW YOU WERE HERE WATCHING.
OH, SO YOU WERE WITH MICHIKO?
YOU GOT A LETTER FROM MAINICHI SHIMBUN.
豊中市麻田一ノ三七
勝見ヒロシ君

ENVELOPE: HIROSHI KATSUMI 1-37 ASADA, TOYONAKA-SHI

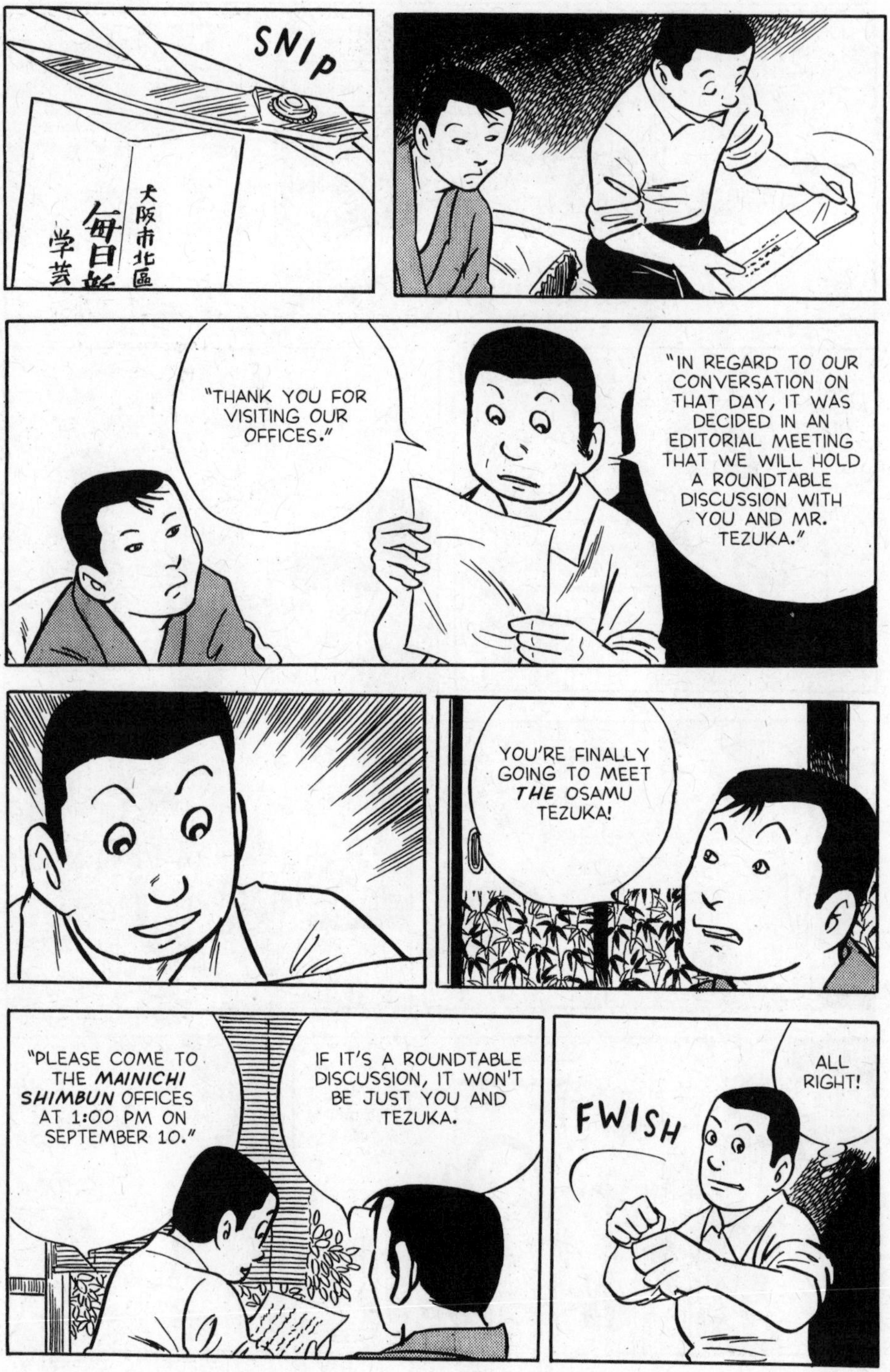
SNIP
大阪市北區
毎日新
学芸
"THANK YOU FOR VISITING OUR OFFICES."
"IN REGARD TO OUR CONVERSATION ON THAT DAY, IT WAS DECIDED IN AN EDITORIAL MEETING THAT WE WILL HOLD A ROUNDTABLE DISCUSSION WITH YOU AND MR. TEZUKA."
YOU'RE FINALLY GOING TO MEET *THE* OSAMU TEZUKA!
"PLEASE COME TO THE *MAINICHI SHIMBUN* OFFICES AT 1:00 PM ON SEPTEMBER 10."
IF IT'S A ROUNDTABLE DISCUSSION, IT WON'T BE JUST YOU AND TEZUKA.
ALL RIGHT!
FWISH

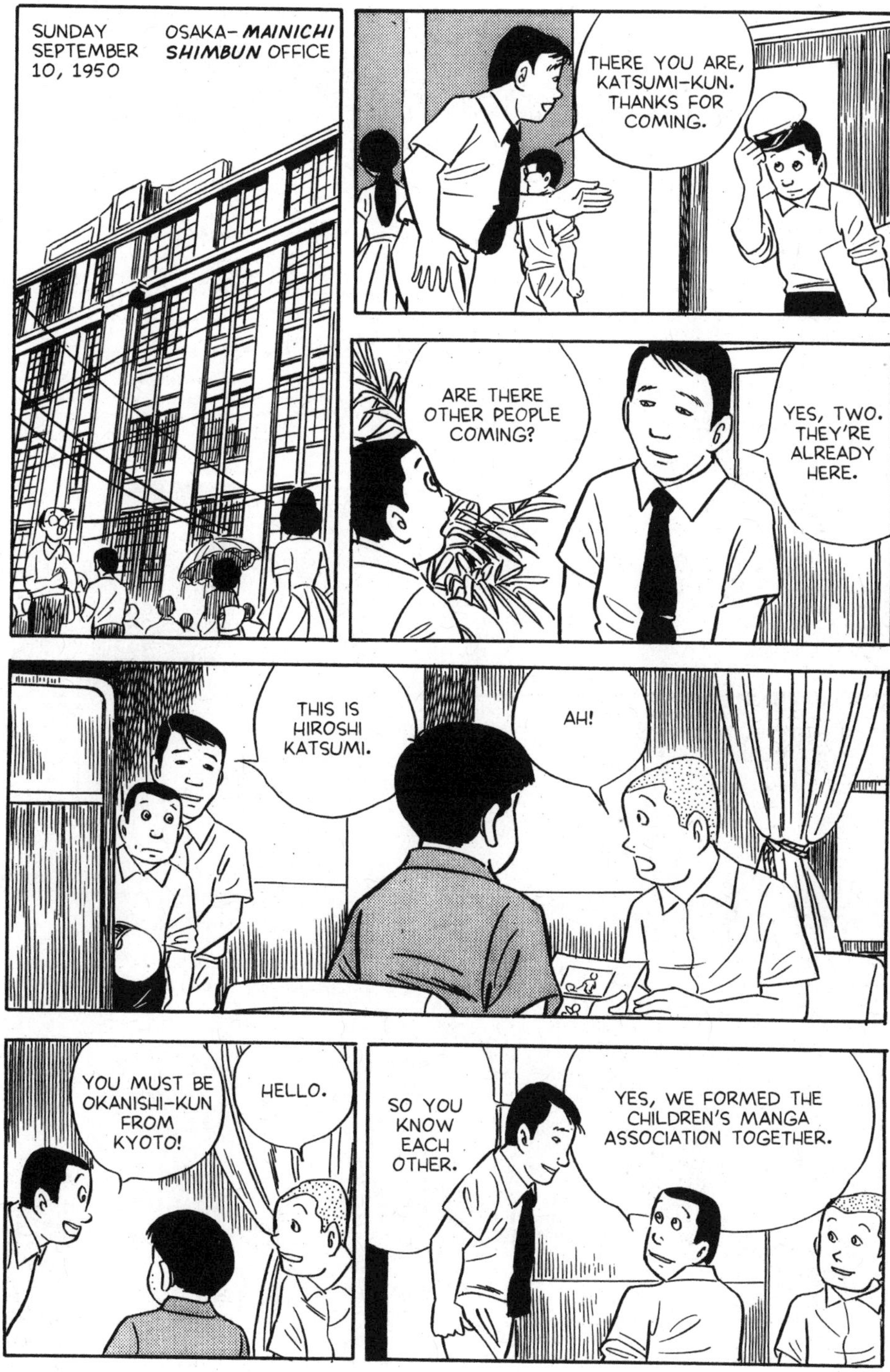
SUNDAY SEPTEMBER 10, 1950
OSAKA-*MAINICHI SHIMBUN* OFFICE
THERE YOU ARE, KATSUMI-KUN. THANKS FOR COMING.
ARE THERE OTHER PEOPLE COMING?
YES, TWO. THEY'RE ALREADY HERE.
THIS IS HIROSHI KATSUMI.
AH!
YOU MUST BE OKANISHI-KUN FROM KYOTO!
HELLO.
SO YOU KNOW EACH OTHER.
YES, WE FORMED THE CHILDREN'S MANGA ASSOCIATION TOGETHER.

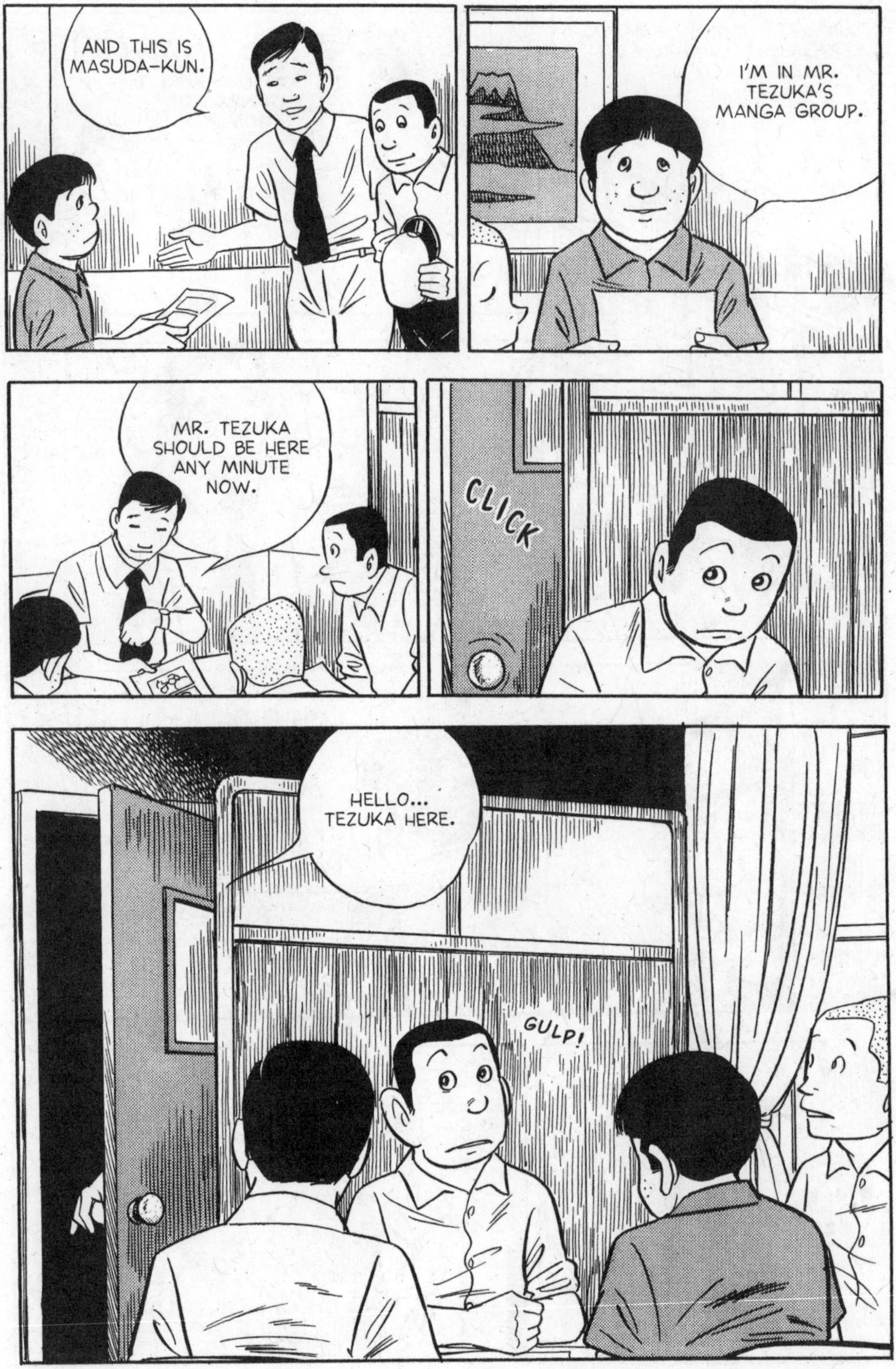
AND THIS IS MASUDA-KUN.
I'M IN MR. TEZUKA'S MANGA GROUP.
MR. TEZUKA SHOULD BE HERE ANY MINUTE NOW.
CLICK
HELLO... TEZUKA HERE.
GULP!

ENTER TEZUKA

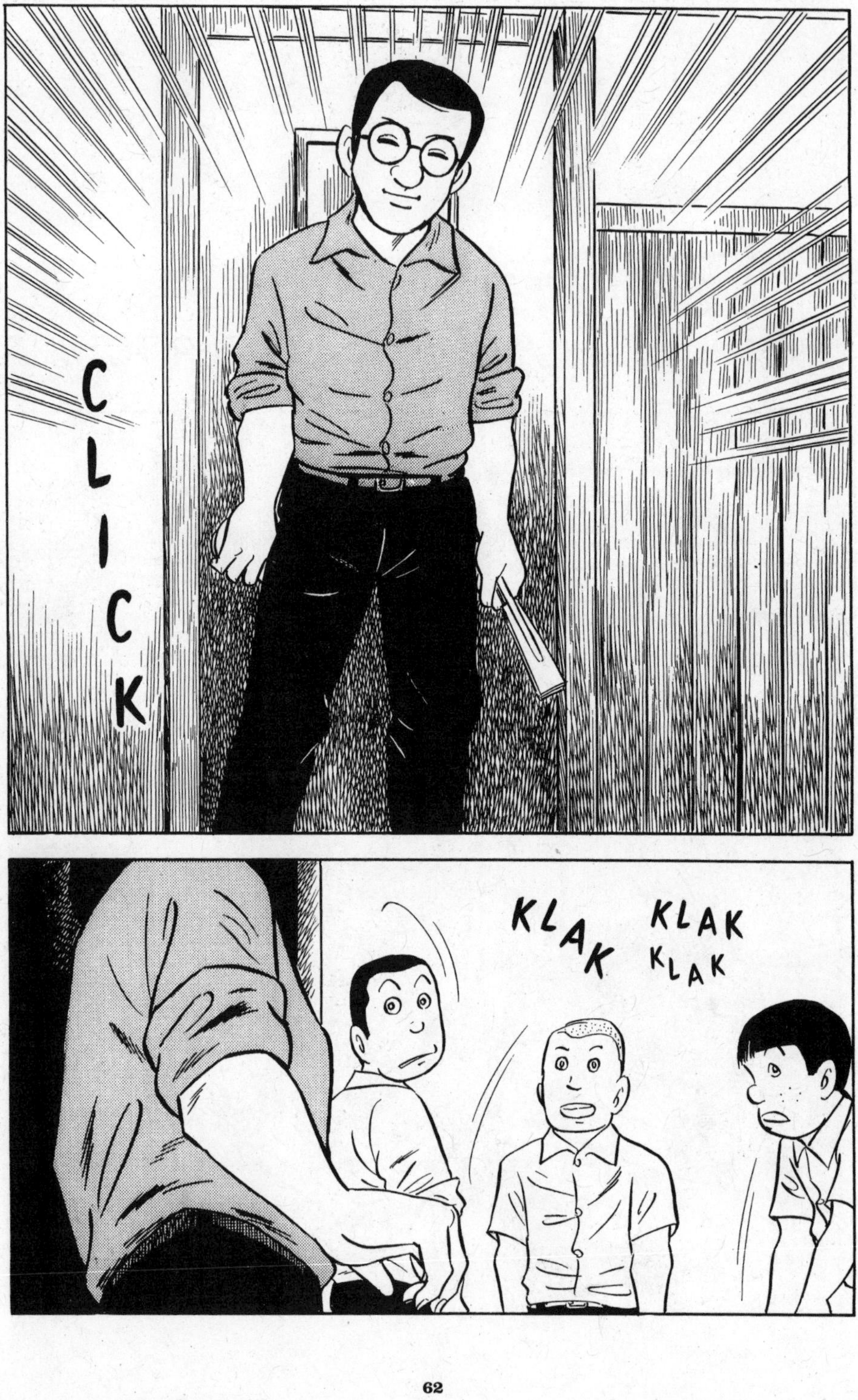
CLICK
KLAK
KLAK
KLAK
KLAK

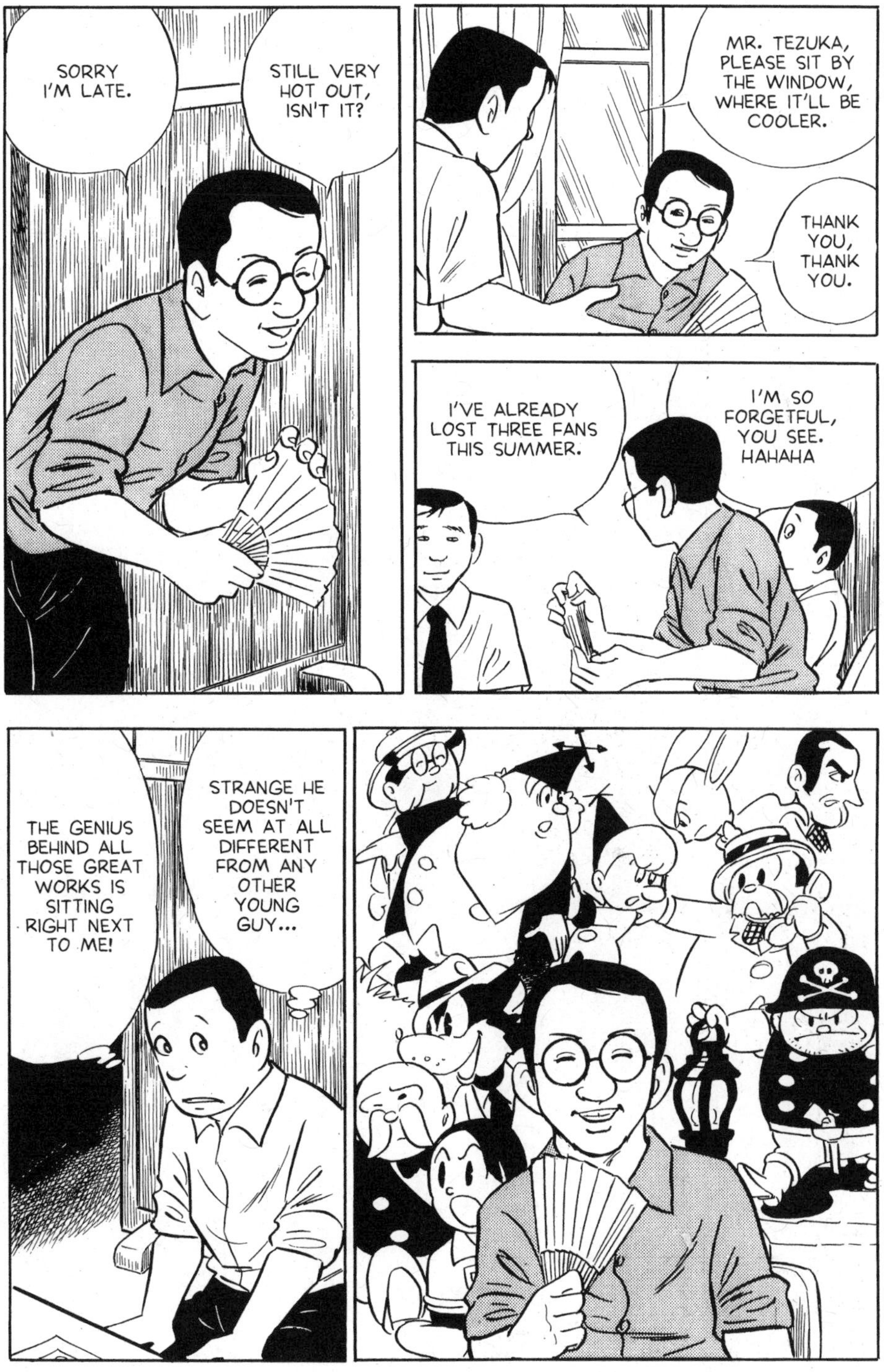
SORRY I'M LATE.
STILL VERY HOT OUT, ISN'T IT?
MR. TEZUKA, PLEASE SIT BY THE WINDOW, WHERE IT'LL BE COOLER.
THANK YOU, THANK YOU.
I'VE ALREADY LOST THREE FANS THIS SUMMER.
I'M SO FORGETFUL, YOU SEE. HAHAHA
THE GENIUS BEHIND ALL THOSE GREAT WORKS IS SITTING RIGHT NEXT TO ME!
STRANGE HE DOESN'T SEEM AT ALL DIFFERENT FROM ANY OTHER YOUNG GUY...

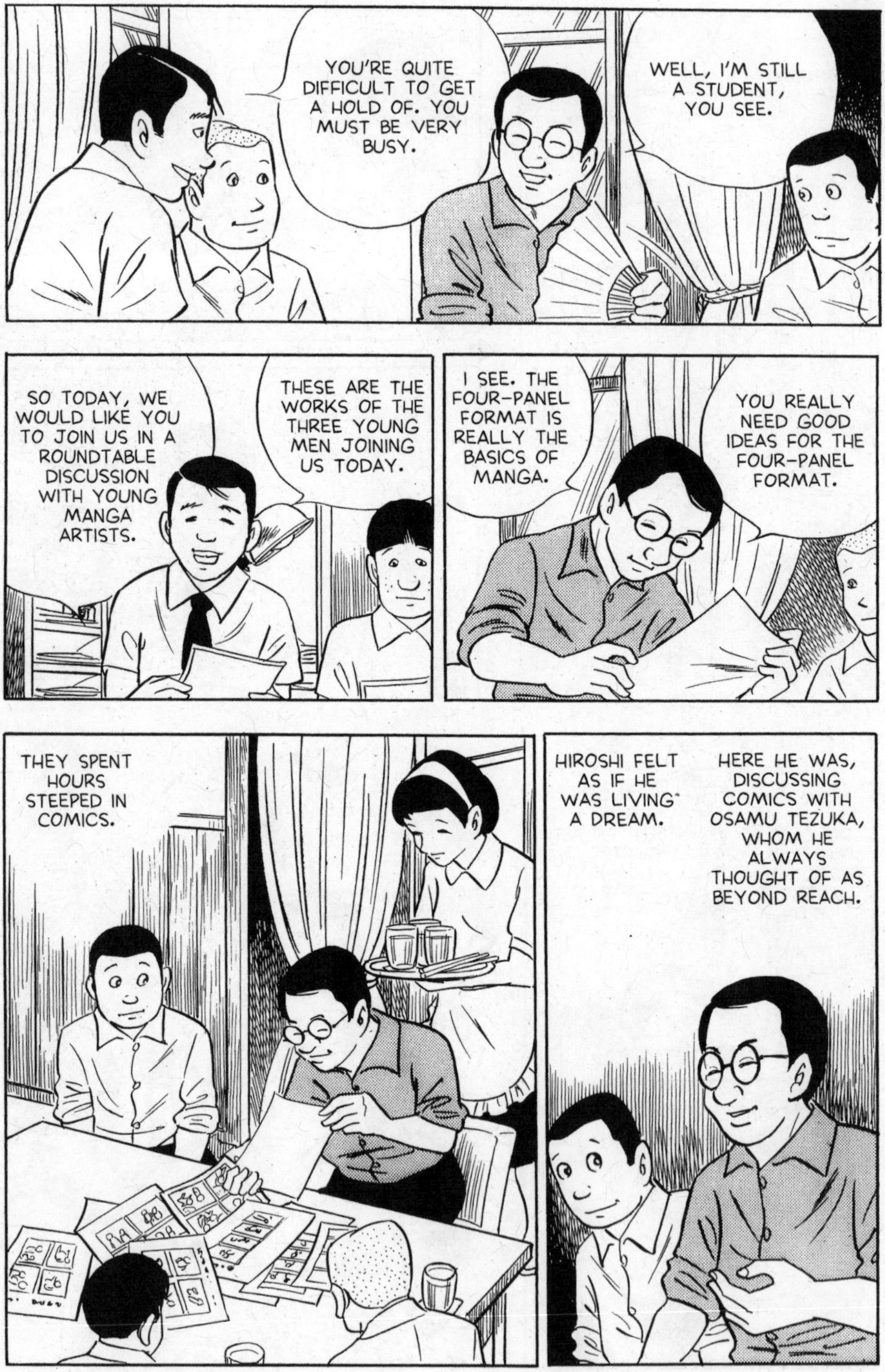
YOU'RE QUITE DIFFICULT TO GET A HOLD OF. YOU MUST BE VERY BUSY.
WELL, I'M STILL A STUDENT, YOU SEE.
SO TODAY, WE WOULD LIKE YOU TO JOIN US IN A ROUNDTABLE DISCUSSION WITH YOUNG MANGA ARTISTS.
THESE ARE THE WORKS OF THE THREE YOUNG MEN JOINING US TODAY.
I SEE. THE FOUR-PANEL FORMAT IS REALLY THE BASICS OF MANGA.
YOU REALLY NEED GOOD IDEAS FOR THE FOUR-PANEL FORMAT.
THEY SPENT HOURS STEEPED IN COMICS.
HIROSHI FELT AS IF HE WAS LIVING A DREAM.
HERE HE WAS, DISCUSSING COMICS WITH OSAMU TEZUKA, WHOM HE ALWAYS THOUGHT OF AS BEYOND REACH.

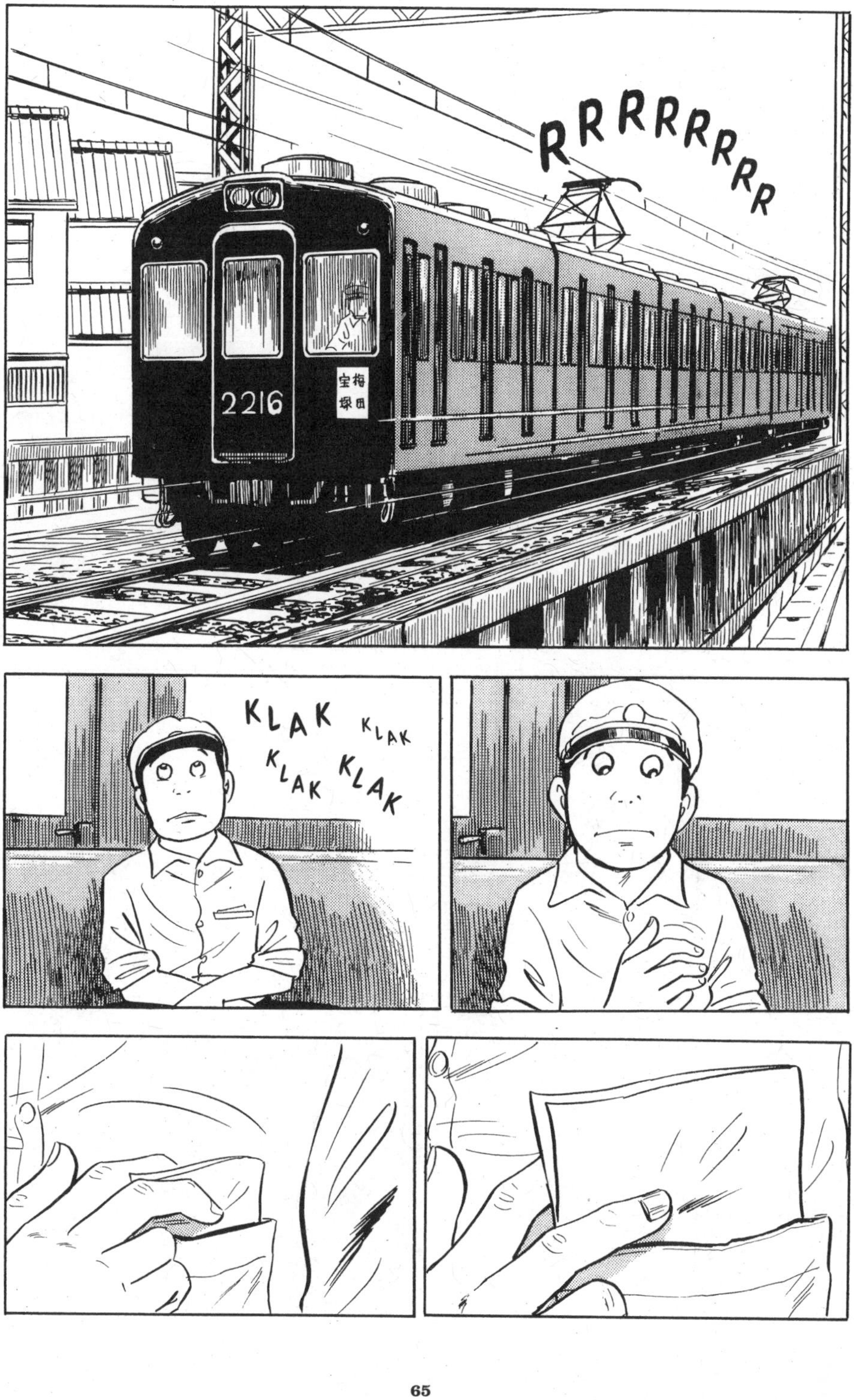
2216
梅田
宝塚
RRRRRRRR
KLAK
KLAK
KLAK
KLAK

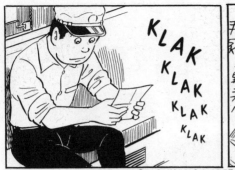

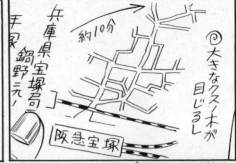

KLAK KLAK KLAK KLAK
◎大きなクスノ木が目じるし
約10分
兵庫県宝塚局
鍋野二九ノ
手塚
阪急宝塚
PAPER: LOOK FOR THE LARGE CINNAMON TREE; APPROX. 10 MINUTES (TEZUKA ADDRESS)
WE BOTH LIVE OFF THE HANKYU LINE.
WE'RE PRACTICALLY NEIGHBORS. COME VISIT ME SOMETIME.
SO MR. TEZUKA'S HOUSE IS IN TAKARAZUKA.
ON THE HANKYU LINE, TAKARAZUKA WAS APPROXIMATELY 20 MINUTES AWAY FROM HOTARUGAIKE, WHERE HIROSHI LIVED.
TAKARAZUKA
OSAMU TEZUKA RESIDENCE
HIROSHI'S HOUSE
ISHIBASHI
HOTARUG-AIKE
TOYONAKA
HANKYU TAKARAZUKA LINE
TO KYOTO
TO KOBE
JUSO
2132
UMEDA
(OSAKA STATION)

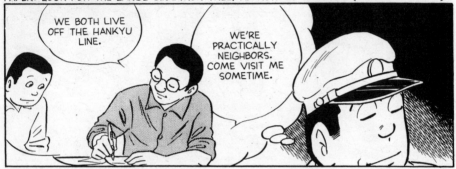

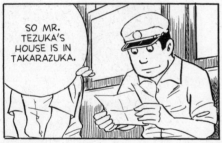

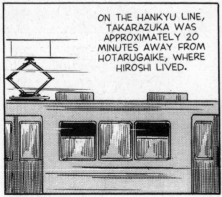

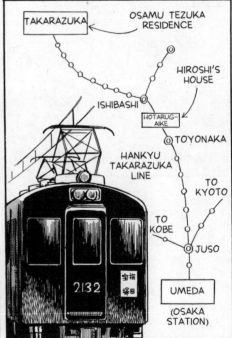

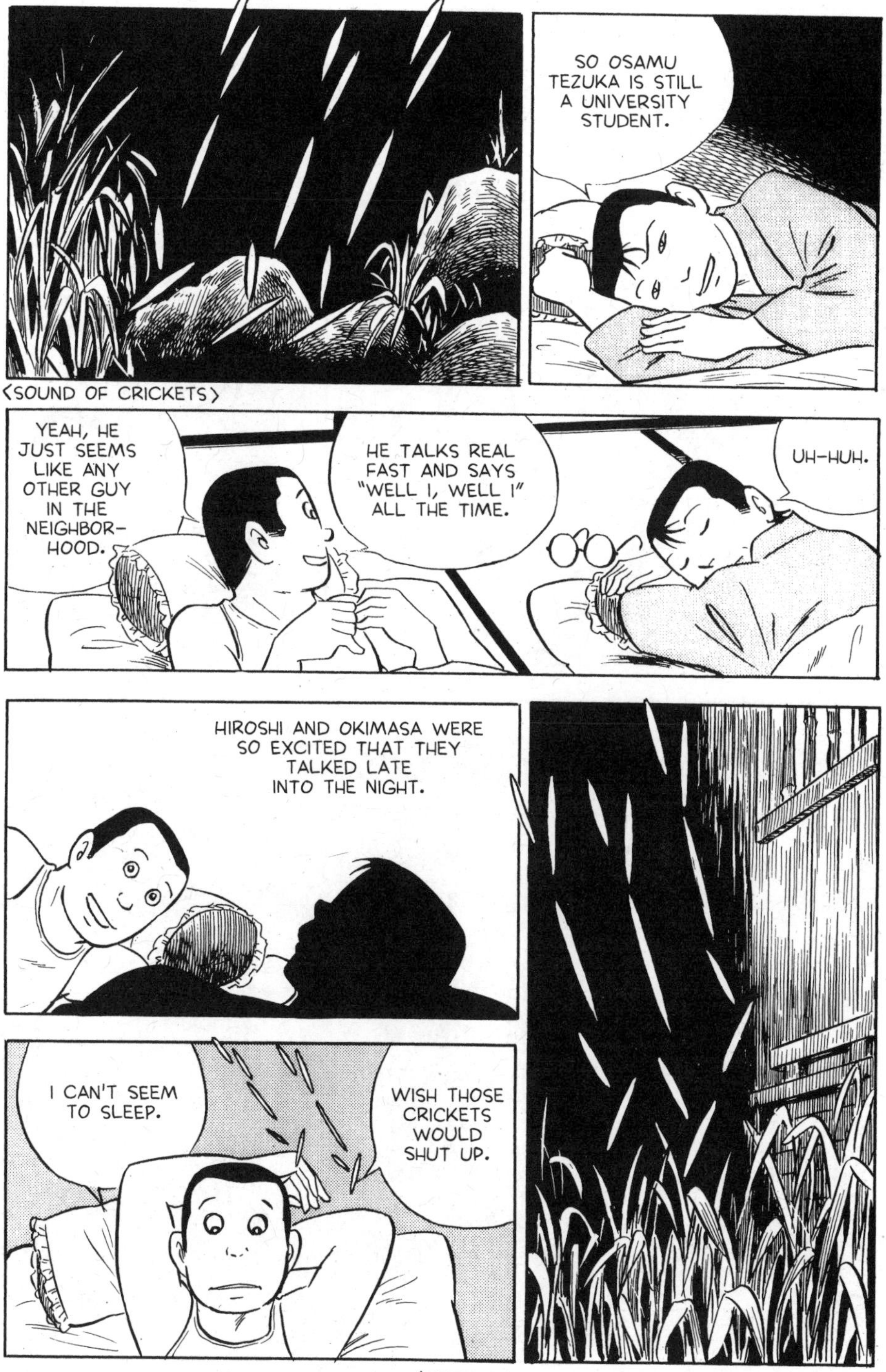
SO OSAMU TEZUKA IS STILL A UNIVERSITY STUDENT.
YEAH, HE JUST SEEMS LIKE ANY OTHER GUY IN THE NEIGHBOR-HOOD.
HE TALKS REAL FAST AND SAYS "WELL I, WELL I" ALL THE TIME.
UH-HUH.
HIROSHI AND OKIMASA WERE SO EXCITED THAT THEY TALKED LATE INTO THE NIGHT.
I CAN'T SEEM TO SLEEP.
WISH THOSE CRICKETS WOULD SHUT UP.

〈SOUND OF CRICKETS〉

〈FIFTH AND SIXTH PANELS: SOUND OF CRICKETS〉

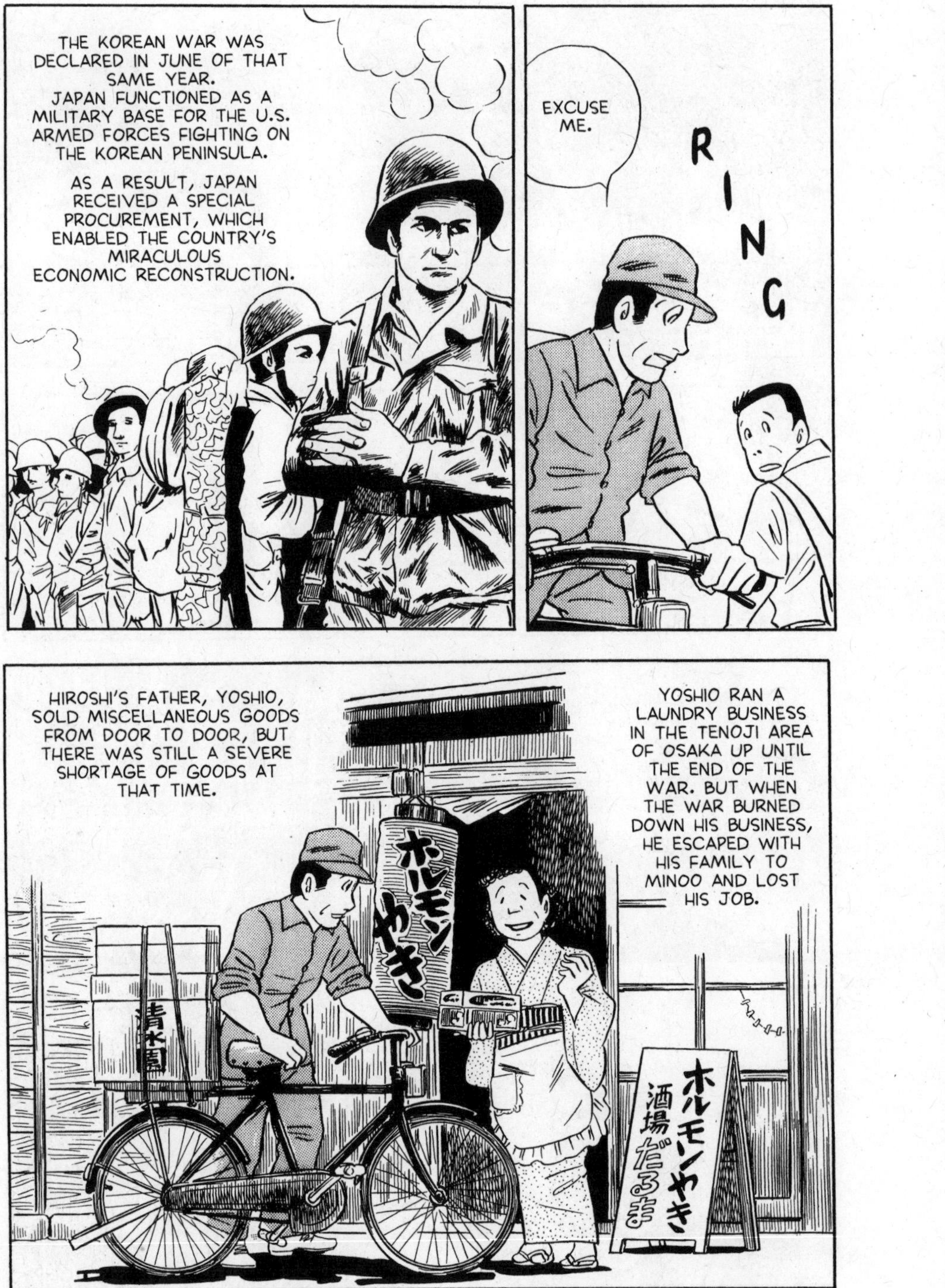
THE KOREAN WAR WAS DECLARED IN JUNE OF THAT SAME YEAR.
JAPAN FUNCTIONED AS A MILITARY BASE FOR THE U.S. ARMED FORCES FIGHTING ON THE KOREAN PENINSULA.
AS A RESULT, JAPAN RECEIVED A SPECIAL PROCUREMENT, WHICH ENABLED THE COUNTRY'S MIRACULOUS ECONOMIC RECONSTRUCTION.
EXCUSE ME.
RING
HIROSHI'S FATHER, YOSHIO, SOLD MISCELLANEOUS GOODS FROM DOOR TO DOOR, BUT THERE WAS STILL A SEVERE SHORTAGE OF GOODS AT THAT TIME.
YOSHIO RAN A LAUNDRY BUSINESS IN THE TENOJI AREA OF OSAKA UP UNTIL THE END OF THE WAR. BUT WHEN THE WAR BURNED DOWN HIS BUSINESS, HE ESCAPED WITH HIS FAMILY TO MINOO AND LOST HIS JOB.
ホルモンやき
清水園
ホルモンやき
酒場だるま

SIGN: BAR DARUMA / GRILLED OFFAL

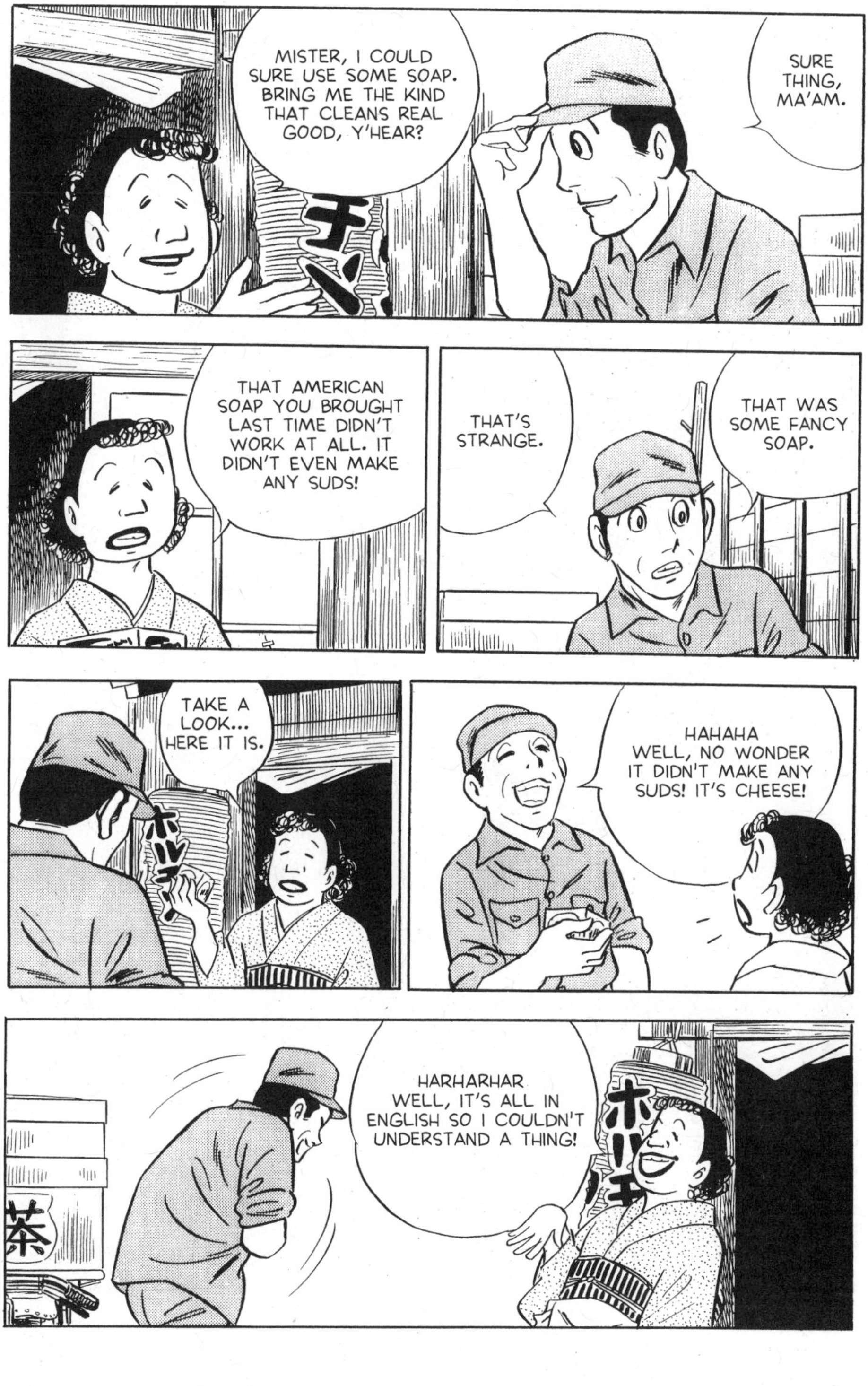

MISTER, I COULD SURE USE SOME SOAP. BRING ME THE KIND THAT CLEANS REAL GOOD, Y'HEAR?
SURE THING, MA'AM.
THAT AMERICAN SOAP YOU BROUGHT LAST TIME DIDN'T WORK AT ALL. IT DIDN'T EVEN MAKE ANY SUDS!
THAT'S STRANGE.
THAT WAS SOME FANCY SOAP.
TAKE A LOOK... HERE IT IS.
HAHAHA WELL, NO WONDER IT DIDN'T MAKE ANY SUDS! IT'S CHEESE!
HARHARHAR WELL, IT'S ALL IN ENGLISH SO I COULDN'T UNDERSTAND A THING!
茶

SURPLUS EVERYDAY GOODS FROM THE OCCUPATION ARMY WERE VERY POPULAR.

HIROSHI WATCHED HIS FATHER USE "MAGIC" TO INCREASE THE AMOUNT OF SCRAP PAPER HE COLLECTED.

FROM EACH STACK OF 500 SHEETS OF PAPER, HE WOULD SKIM OFF 20-30 SHEETS...

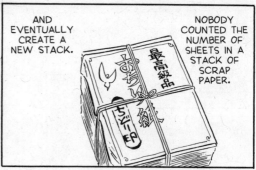

AND EVENTUALLY CREATE A NEW STACK.

NOBODY COUNTED THE NUMBER OF SHEETS IN A STACK OF SCRAP PAPER.

ADULTS ARE VILE.

I MEAN, I KNOW IT MUST BE ROUGH SUPPORTING A FAMILY OF SIX, BUT...

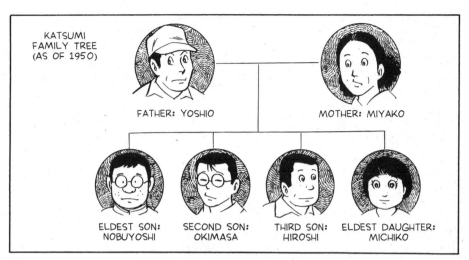

KATSUMI FAMILY TREE (AS OF 1950)

FATHER: YOSHIO

MOTHER: MIYAKO

ELDEST SON: NOBUYOSHI

SECOND SON: OKIMASA

THIRD SON: HIROSHI

ELDEST DAUGHTER: MICHIKO

ZZZZ

SUNDAY, SEPTEMBER 17, 1950

THUMP

BAM

WHAT TH--?

DO YOU KNOW WHAT TIME IT IS?

TODAY'S SUNDAY...

I GOT YOU A COPY OF *MAINICHI SHIMBUN,* THE GRADE SCHOOL EDITION.

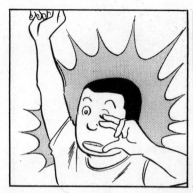

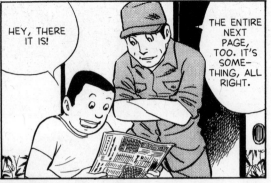

HEY, THERE IT IS!
THE ENTIRE NEXT PAGE, TOO. IT'S SOME-THING, ALL RIGHT.
少年マン画家座談会
機智で人をくすぐるマンガ……笑いで世の中を和やかにするマンガ……マンガの
社会的な意味は案外深くて広い。戦後マンガが流行しているが、明日のマンガを
健全ないいものにするのは、僕らの仕事だ。中学生マンガ家三人に寄ってもら
って、少年少女に圧倒的な人気のある手塚治虫先生をかこんで、
た。——
HEADLINE: "YOUNG MANGA ARTISTS' ROUNDTABLE DISCUSSION"
升田くん
絵より文
ヒロシ
勝見ヒロシ君
作品見せあって批判しあう
寝床や歩行中ひょいと思いつく
四コマ

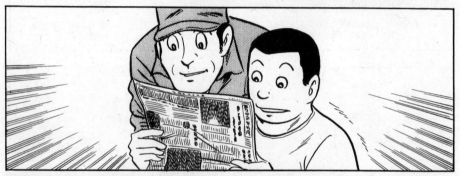

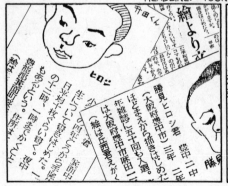

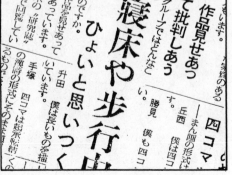

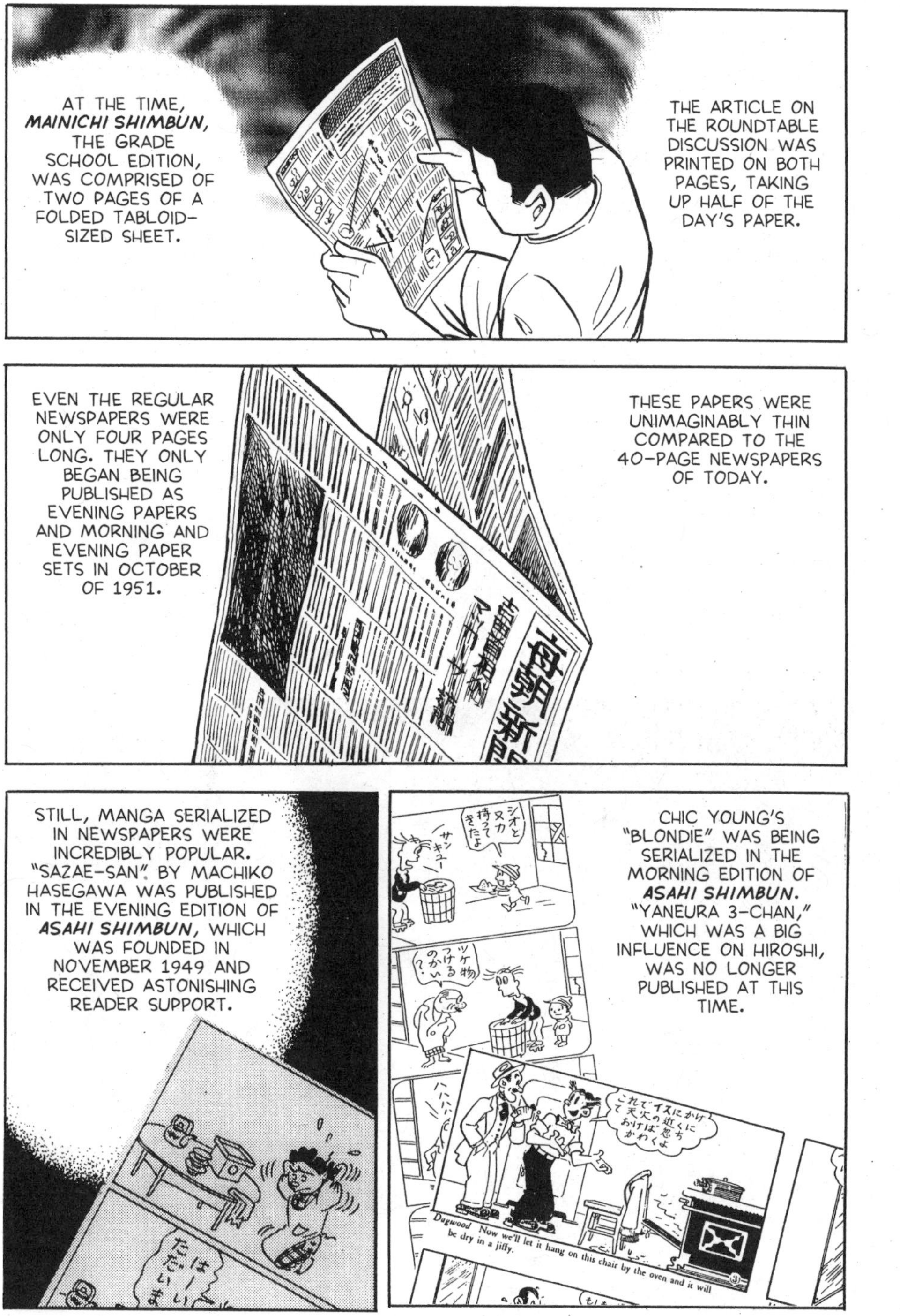
AT THE TIME, ***MAINICHI SHIMBUN,*** THE GRADE SCHOOL EDITION, WAS COMPRISED OF TWO PAGES OF A FOLDED TABLOID-SIZED SHEET.
THE ARTICLE ON THE ROUNDTABLE DISCUSSION WAS PRINTED ON BOTH PAGES, TAKING UP HALF OF THE DAY'S PAPER.
EVEN THE REGULAR NEWSPAPERS WERE ONLY FOUR PAGES LONG. THEY ONLY BEGAN BEING PUBLISHED AS EVENING PAPERS AND MORNING AND EVENING PAPER SETS IN OCTOBER OF 1951.
THESE PAPERS WERE UNIMAGINABLY THIN COMPARED TO THE 40-PAGE NEWSPAPERS OF TODAY.
STILL, MANGA SERIALIZED IN NEWSPAPERS WERE INCREDIBLY POPULAR. "SAZAE-SAN" BY MACHIKO HASEGAWA WAS PUBLISHED IN THE EVENING EDITION OF ***ASAHI SHIMBUN,*** WHICH WAS FOUNDED IN NOVEMBER 1949 AND RECEIVED ASTONISHING READER SUPPORT.
はーい
ただいま
CHIC YOUNG'S "BLONDIE" WAS BEING SERIALIZED IN THE MORNING EDITION OF ***ASAHI SHIMBUN.*** "YANEURA 3-CHAN," WHICH WAS A BIG INFLUENCE ON HIROSHI, WAS NO LONGER PUBLISHED AT THIS TIME.
シオとヌカ持ってきたよ
サンキュー
ツケ物つけるのかい？
ハハハハ
これでイスにかけて天火の近くにおけば忽ちかわくよ
Dagwood Now we'll let it hang on this chair by the oven and it will be dry in a jiffy.

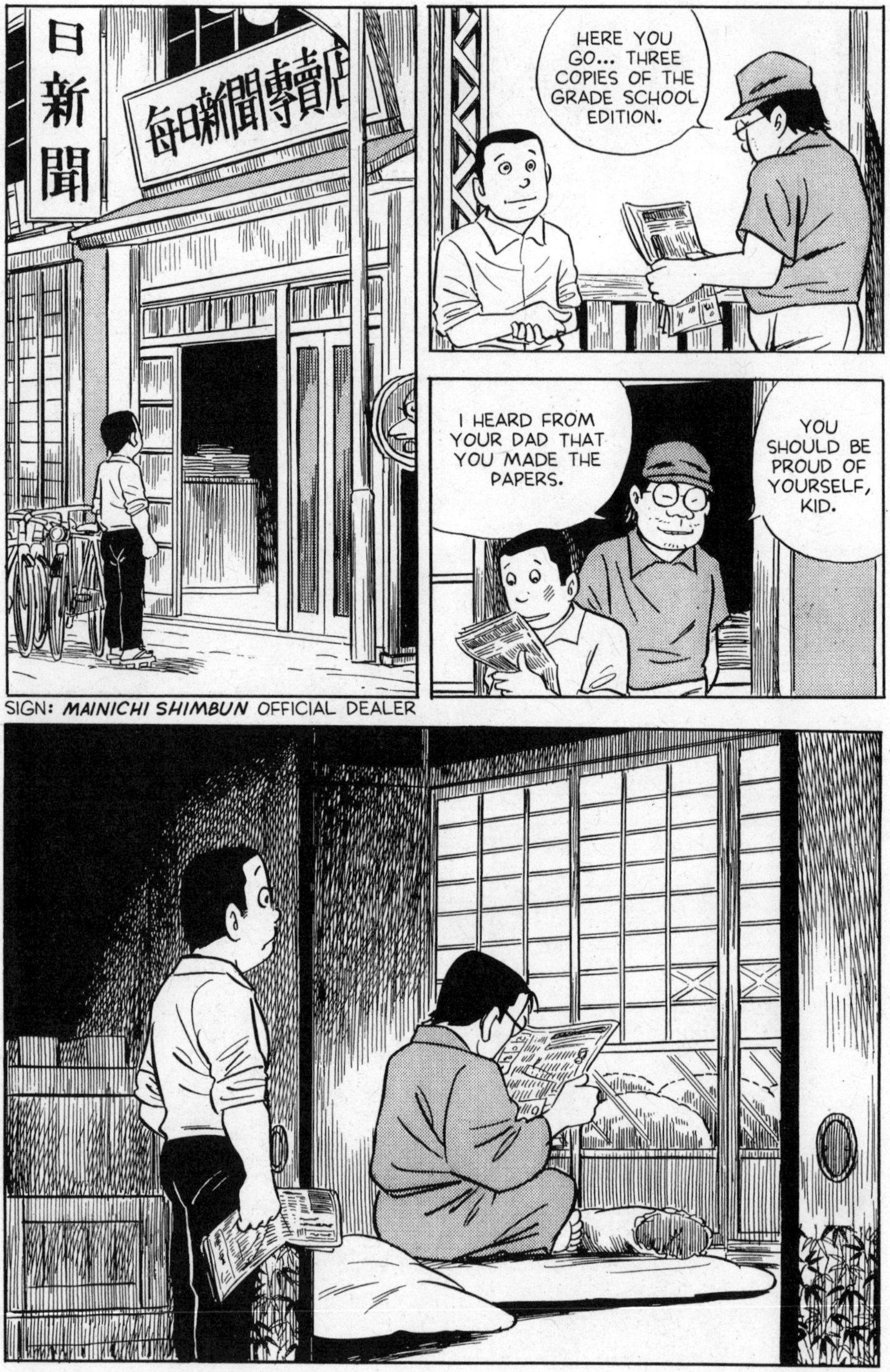
日新聞
毎日新聞專賣店
SIGN: *MAINICHI SHIMBUN* OFFICIAL DEALER
HERE YOU GO... THREE COPIES OF THE GRADE SCHOOL EDITION.
I HEARD FROM YOUR DAD THAT YOU MADE THE PAPERS.
YOU SHOULD BE PROUD OF YOURSELF, KID.

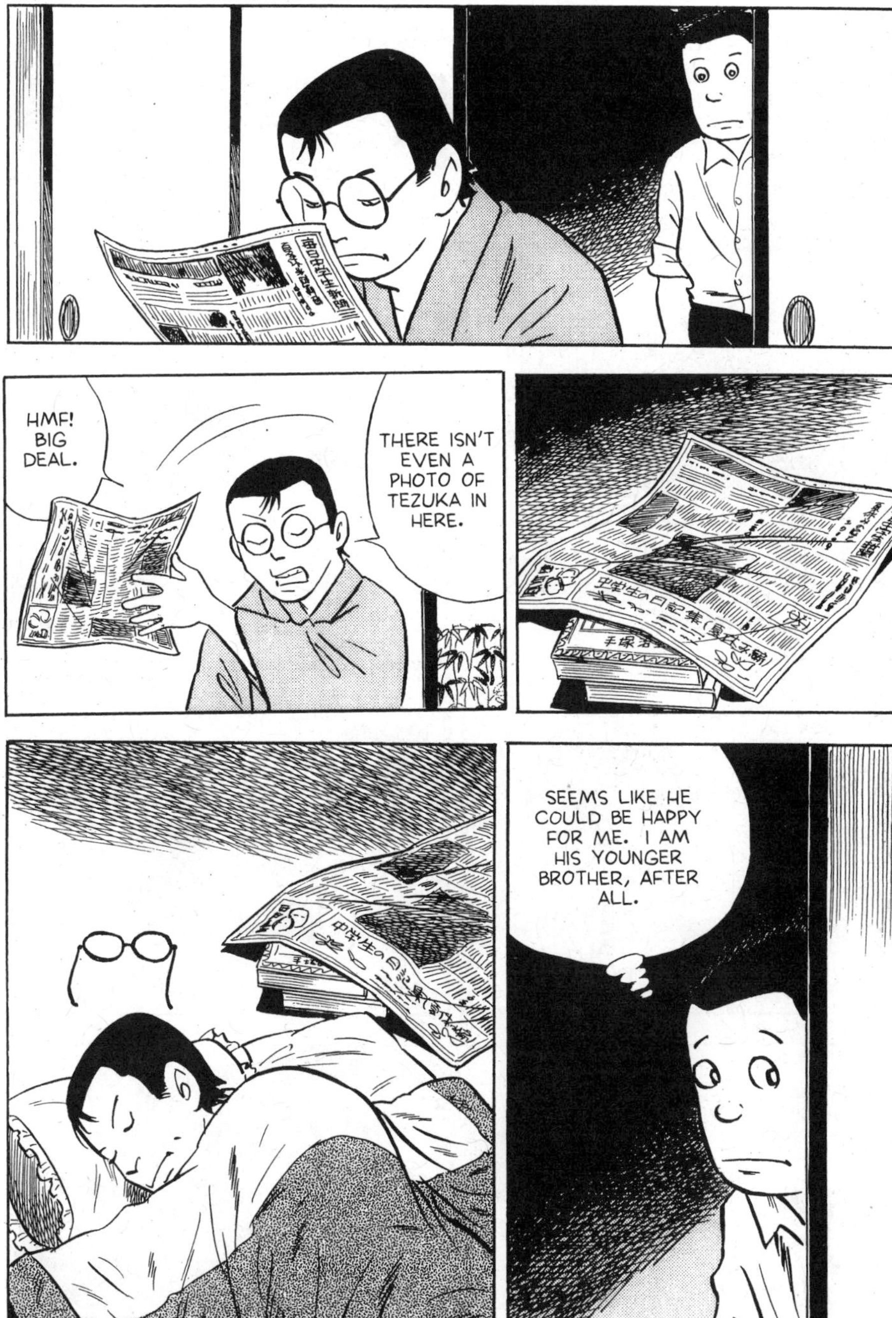
HMF! BIG DEAL.
THERE ISN'T EVEN A PHOTO OF TEZUKA IN HERE.
SEEMS LIKE HE COULD BE HAPPY FOR ME. I AM HIS YOUNGER BROTHER, AFTER ALL.

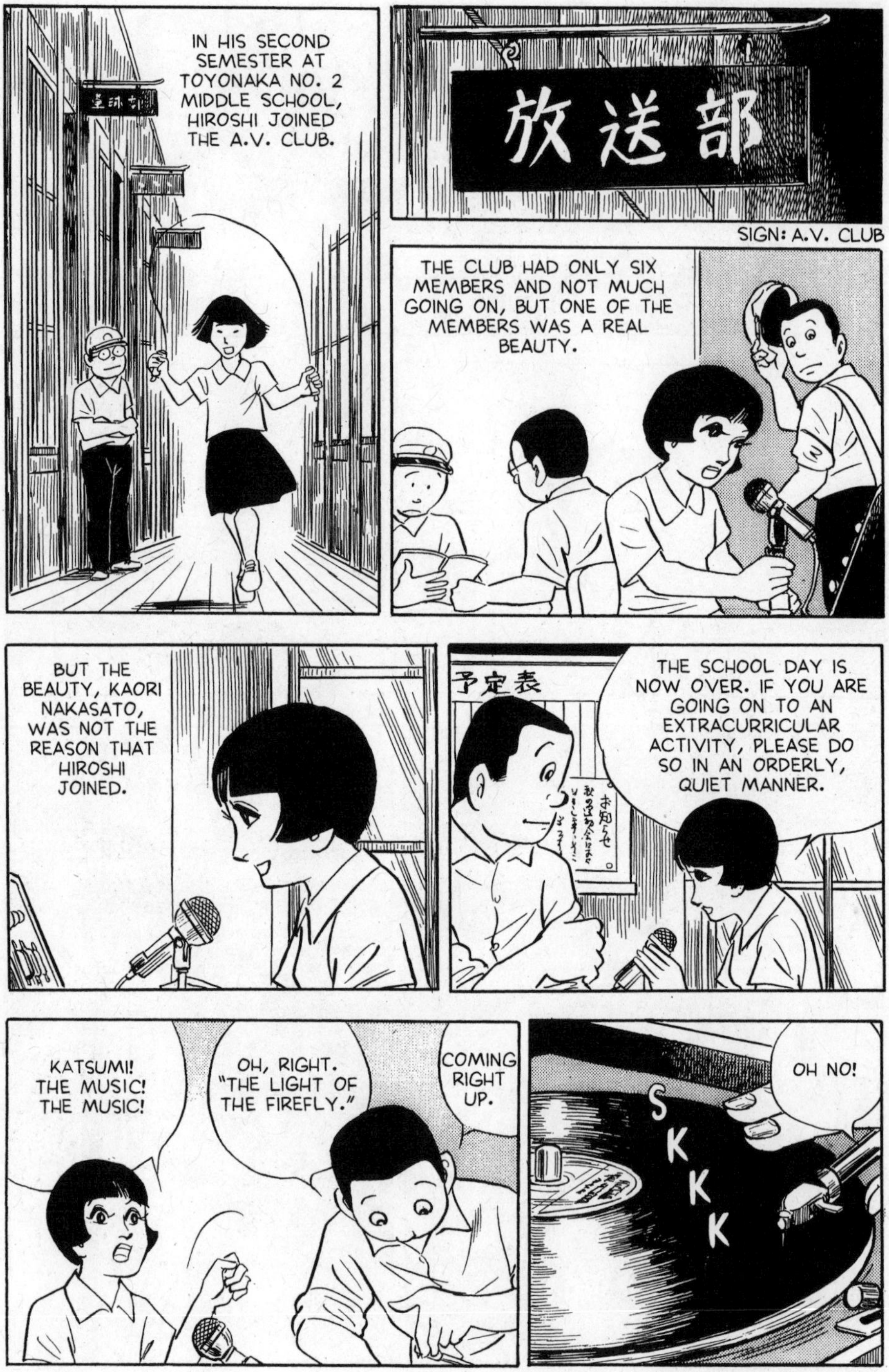
IN HIS SECOND SEMESTER AT TOYONAKA NO. 2 MIDDLE SCHOOL, HIROSHI JOINED THE A.V. CLUB.
放送部
SIGN: A.V. CLUB
THE CLUB HAD ONLY SIX MEMBERS AND NOT MUCH GOING ON, BUT ONE OF THE MEMBERS WAS A REAL BEAUTY.
BUT THE BEAUTY, KAORI NAKASATO, WAS NOT THE REASON THAT HIROSHI JOINED.
予定表
お知らせ
THE SCHOOL DAY IS NOW OVER. IF YOU ARE GOING ON TO AN EXTRACURRICULAR ACTIVITY, PLEASE DO SO IN AN ORDERLY, QUIET MANNER.
KATSUMI! THE MUSIC! THE MUSIC!
OH, RIGHT. "THE LIGHT OF THE FIREFLY."
COMING RIGHT UP.
OH NO!
SKKK

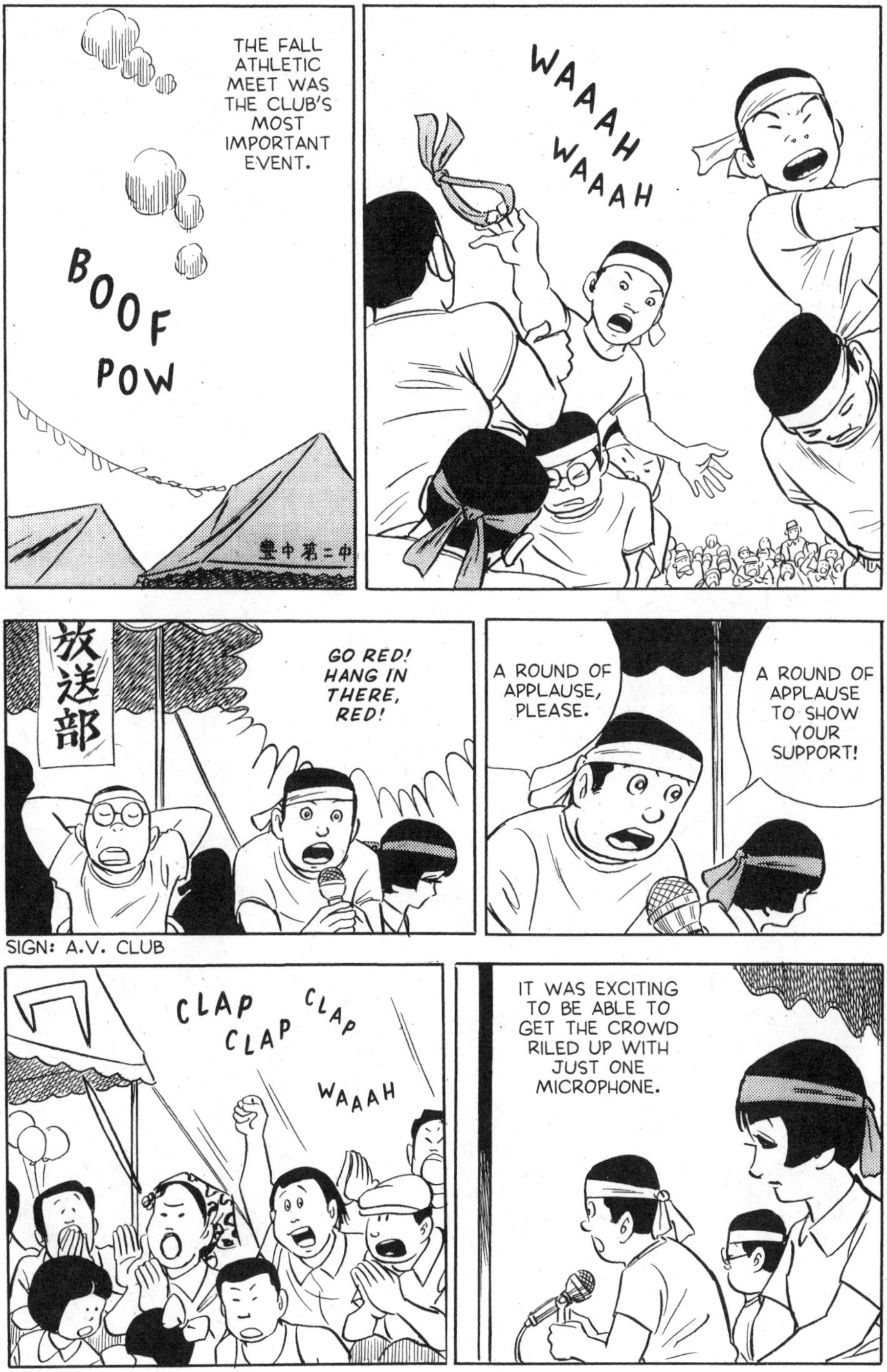
THE FALL ATHLETIC MEET WAS THE CLUB'S MOST IMPORTANT EVENT.
BOOF
POW
豊中第二中
WAAAH
WAAAH
放送部
GO RED! HANG IN THERE, RED!
SIGN: A.V. CLUB
A ROUND OF APPLAUSE, PLEASE.
A ROUND OF APPLAUSE TO SHOW YOUR SUPPORT!
CLAP
CLAP
CLAP
WAAAH
IT WAS EXCITING TO BE ABLE TO GET THE CROWD RILED UP WITH JUST ONE MICROPHONE.

KATSUMI-KUN, I HEARD YOU WERE MENTIONED IN THE NEWSPAPER...

I HAD NO IDEA THAT YOU WRITE MANGA.

YOU'RE PRETTY GOOD, AREN'T YOU, KATSUMI-KUN?

THAT NAKASATO-SAN HAD KNOWN ABOUT THE ARTICLE IN THE PAPER MADE HIROSHI FEEL AS IF HE HAD A MILLION SUPPORTERS. HE WAS ELATED.

WAAAH
WAAAH

WAAAH
WAAAH

THE CHILDREN'S MANGA ASSOCIATION (CMA), WHICH HAD SIX MEMBERS, REMAINED ACTIVE.

IT HAD PUBLISHED FOUR ISSUES OF *MANGA MEISEI* ("MANGA STAR").

TITLE: *MANGA MEISEI*

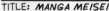

LET'S DO THIS!

A COLLABORATION?

THAT'S RIGHT. THE SIX CMA MEMBERS ARE GOING TO SUBMIT FOUR-PANEL MANGAS UNDER ONE TITLE.

78

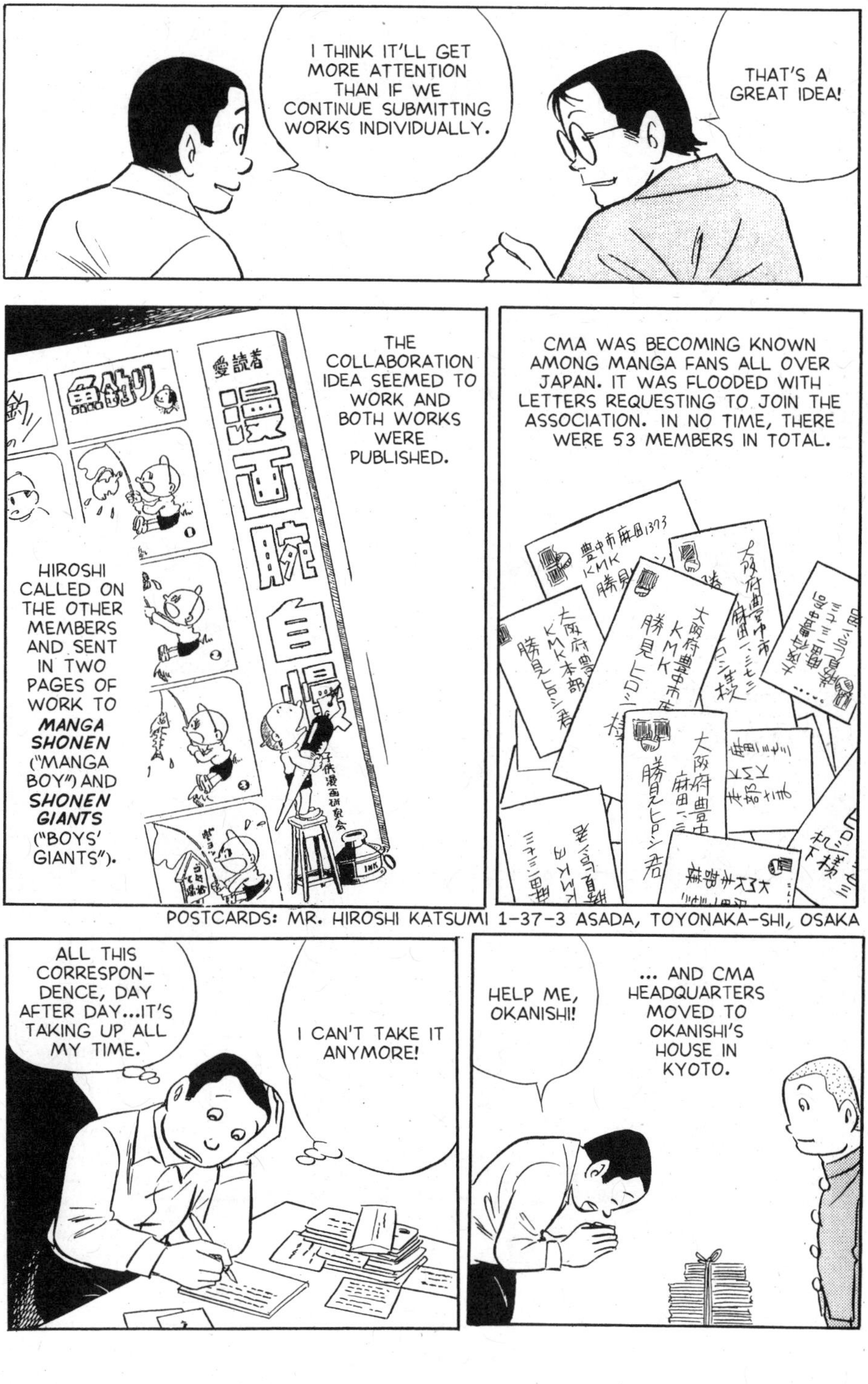
I THINK IT'LL GET MORE ATTENTION THAN IF WE CONTINUE SUBMITTING WORKS INDIVIDUALLY.
THAT'S A GREAT IDEA!
HIROSHI CALLED ON THE OTHER MEMBERS AND SENT IN TWO PAGES OF WORK TO ***MANGA SHONEN*** ("MANGA BOY") AND ***SHONEN GIANTS*** ("BOYS' GIANTS").
THE COLLABORATION IDEA SEEMED TO WORK AND BOTH WORKS WERE PUBLISHED.
愛読者
漫画腕自慢
CMA WAS BECOMING KNOWN AMONG MANGA FANS ALL OVER JAPAN. IT WAS FLOODED WITH LETTERS REQUESTING TO JOIN THE ASSOCIATION. IN NO TIME, THERE WERE 53 MEMBERS IN TOTAL.
POSTCARDS: MR. HIROSHI KATSUMI 1-37-3 ASADA, TOYONAKA-SHI, OSAKA
ALL THIS CORRESPON-DENCE, DAY AFTER DAY...IT'S TAKING UP ALL MY TIME.
I CAN'T TAKE IT ANYMORE!
HELP ME, OKANISHI!
... AND CMA HEADQUARTERS MOVED TO OKANISHI'S HOUSE IN KYOTO.

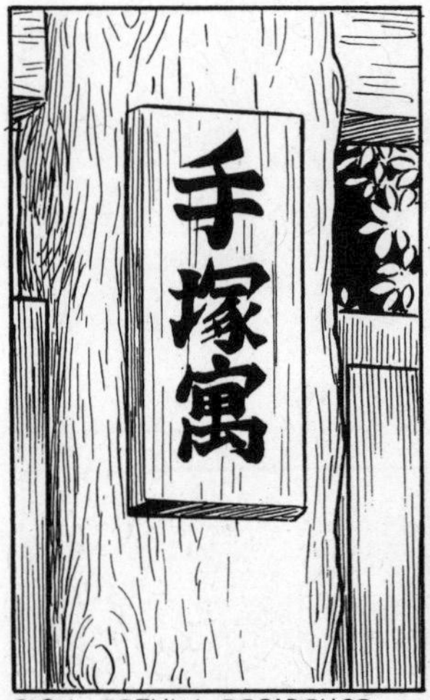
手塚寓

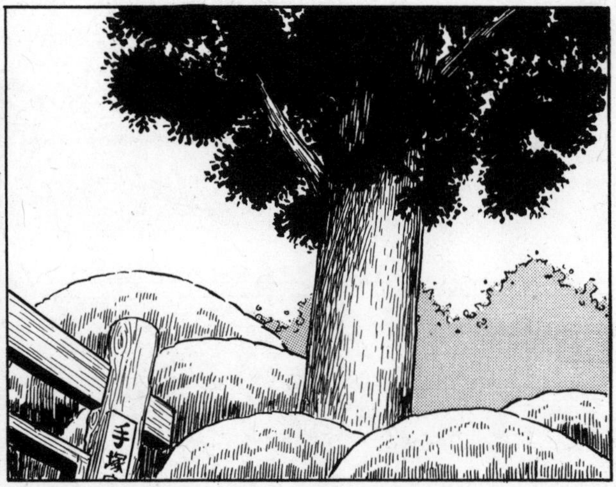

SIGN: TEZUKA RESIDENCE

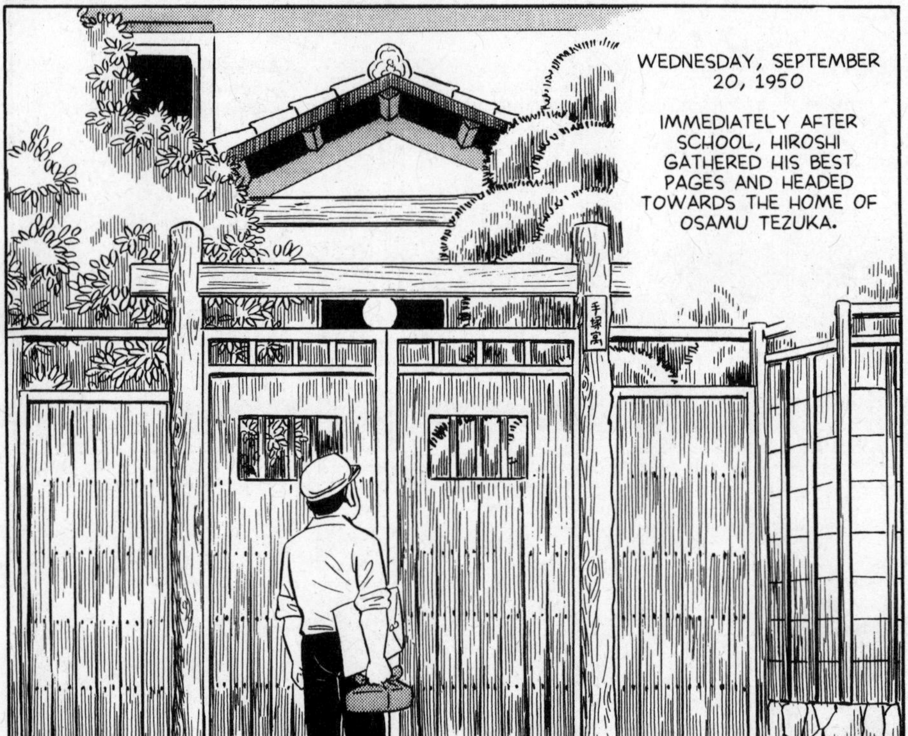
WEDNESDAY, SEPTEMBER 20, 1950
IMMEDIATELY AFTER SCHOOL, HIROSHI GATHERED HIS BEST PAGES AND HEADED TOWARDS THE HOME OF OSAMU TEZUKA.
手塚寓

SIBLING RIVALRY

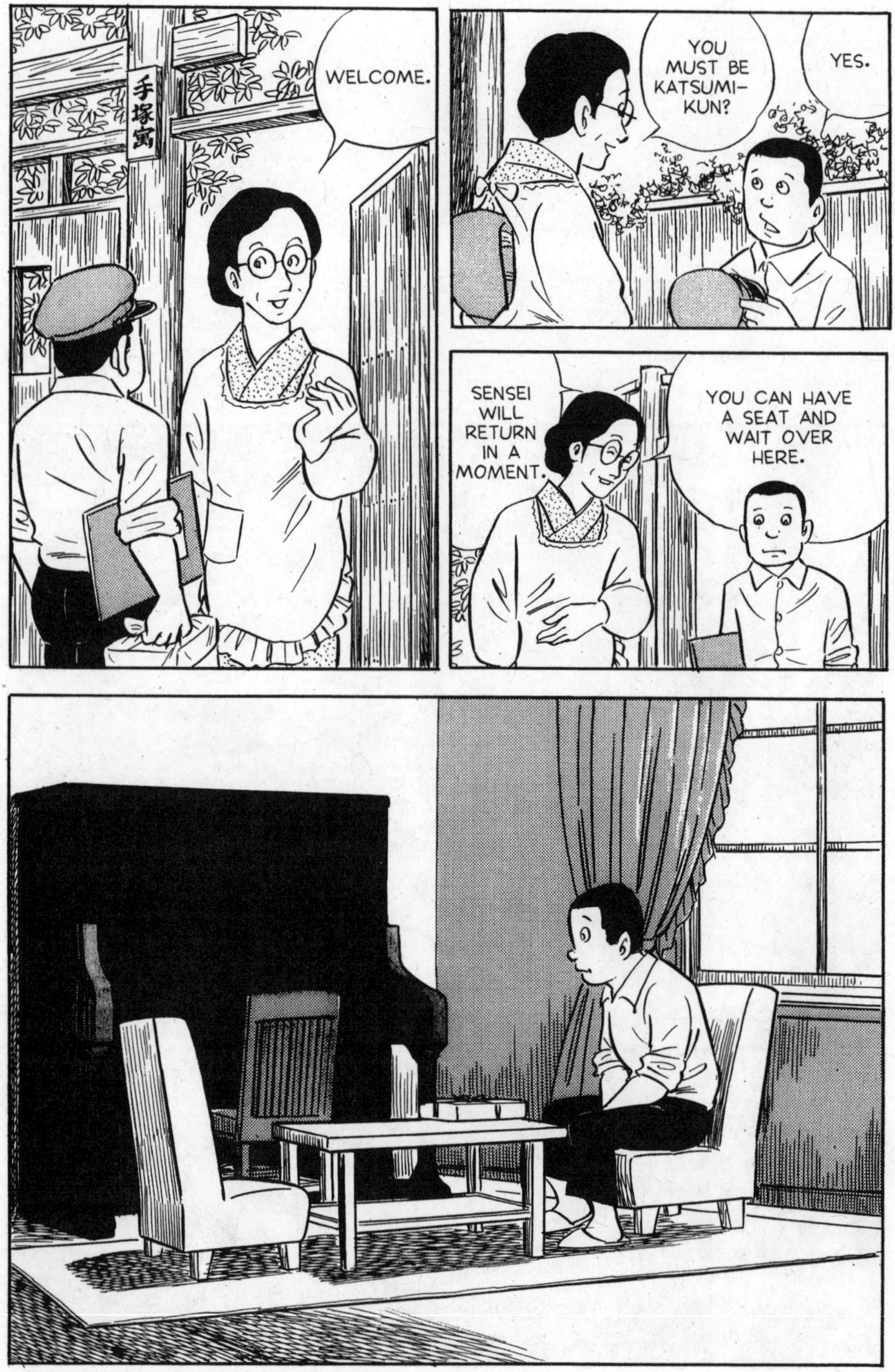

手塚寓
WELCOME.
YOU MUST BE KATSUMI-KUN?
YES.
SENSEI WILL RETURN IN A MOMENT.
YOU CAN HAVE A SEAT AND WAIT OVER HERE.

SHE CALLED OSAMU TEZUKA "SENSEI"...

COULD SHE BE A MAID?

HIROSHI MISTOOK TEZUKA'S MOTHER, WHO REFERRED TO HER SON AS "SENSEI," FOR A MAID.

HE'D NEVER HEARD ANYONE OTHER THAN THE TEACHERS AT SCHOOL CALLED SENSEI BEFORE.

HELLO, KATSUMI-KUN.

AH.

THIS IS A SOUVENIR FROM MY MOTHER.

THANK YOU SO MUCH.

BOW

IT WAS A BOX OF CINNAMON-FLAVORED SWEET POTATOES FROM A LOCAL CONFECTIONER.

LET'S GO OVER HERE.

WE CAN TALK IN MY STUDY.

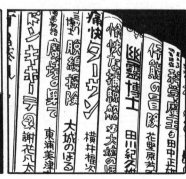

SUIHO TAGAWA, BONTARO SHAKA, NOBORU OOSHIRO... I'VE READ ALL OF THESE.

YOU LIKE THEM, TOO?

YES! I ESPECIALLY LIKE NOBORU OOSHIRO.

OH NO!

FLAP FLAP FLAP

QUICK, HOLD THAT END!

FLAP

I-I'M SORRY!

PHEW! FINALLY BACK IN PLACE.

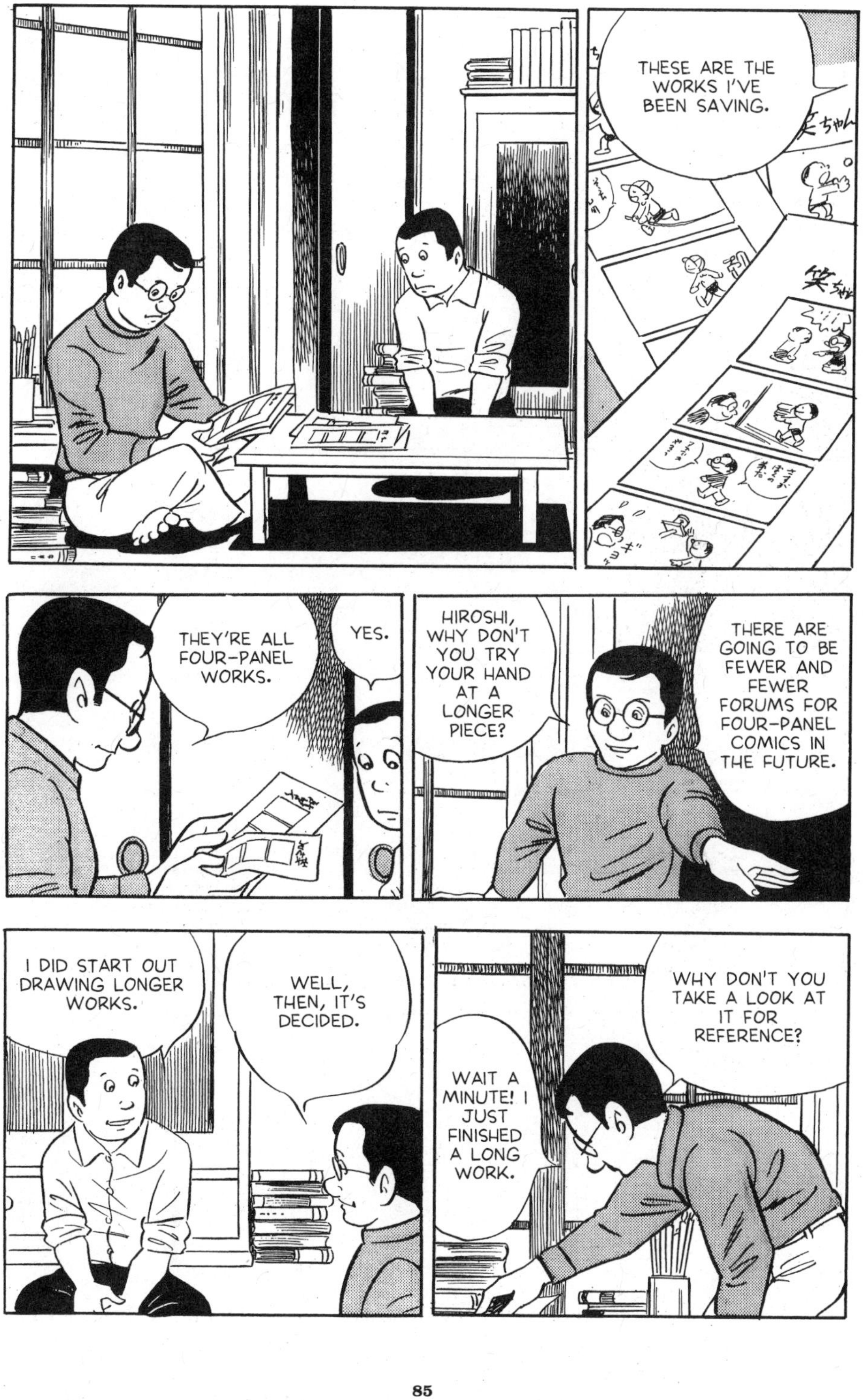
THESE ARE THE WORKS I'VE BEEN SAVING.
THEY'RE ALL FOUR-PANEL WORKS.
YES.
HIROSHI, WHY DON'T YOU TRY YOUR HAND AT A LONGER PIECE?
THERE ARE GOING TO BE FEWER AND FEWER FORUMS FOR FOUR-PANEL COMICS IN THE FUTURE.
I DID START OUT DRAWING LONGER WORKS.
WELL, THEN, IT'S DECIDED.
WAIT A MINUTE! I JUST FINISHED A LONG WORK.
WHY DON'T YOU TAKE A LOOK AT IT FOR REFERENCE?

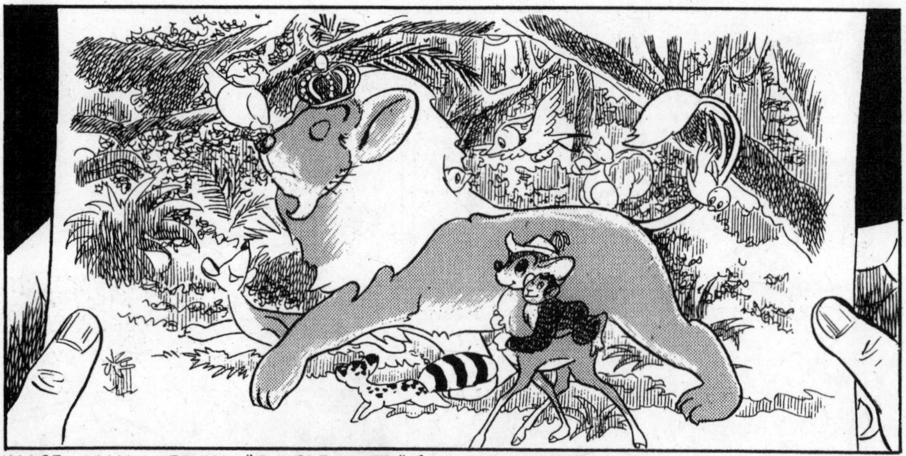

IMAGE: OSAMU TEZUKA, "JUNGLE TAITEI" (JUNGLE EMPEROR LEO)

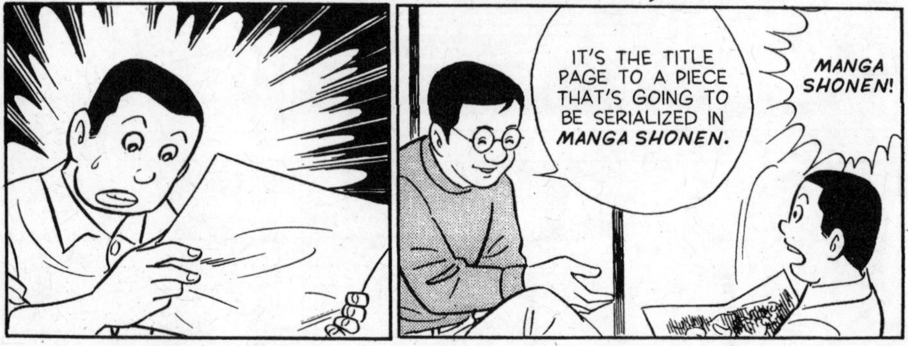
IT'S THE TITLE PAGE TO A PIECE THAT'S GOING TO BE SERIALIZED IN MANGA SHONEN.
MANGA SHONEN!

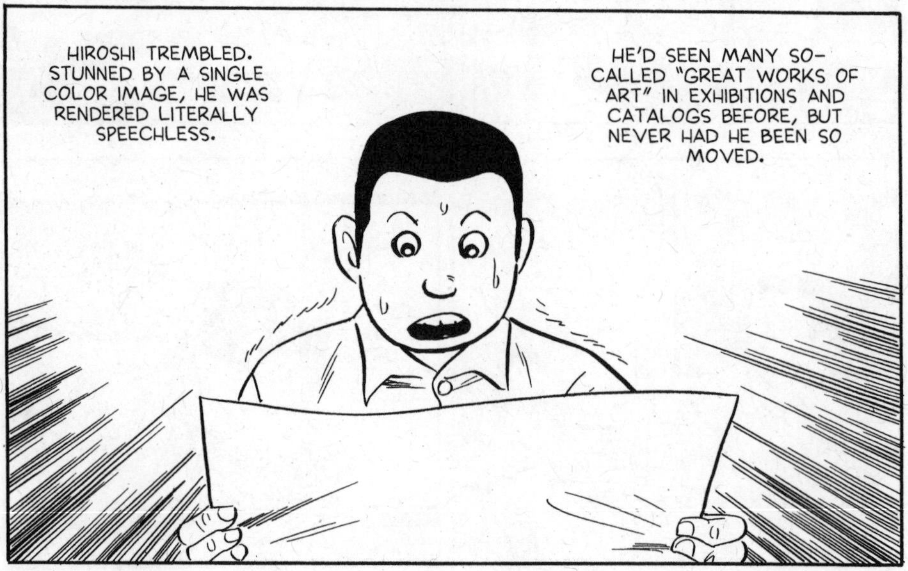
HIROSHI TREMBLED. STUNNED BY A SINGLE COLOR IMAGE, HE WAS RENDERED LITERALLY SPEECHLESS.
HE'D SEEN MANY SO-CALLED "GREAT WORKS OF ART" IN EXHIBITIONS AND CATALOGS BEFORE, BUT NEVER HAD HE BEEN SO MOVED.

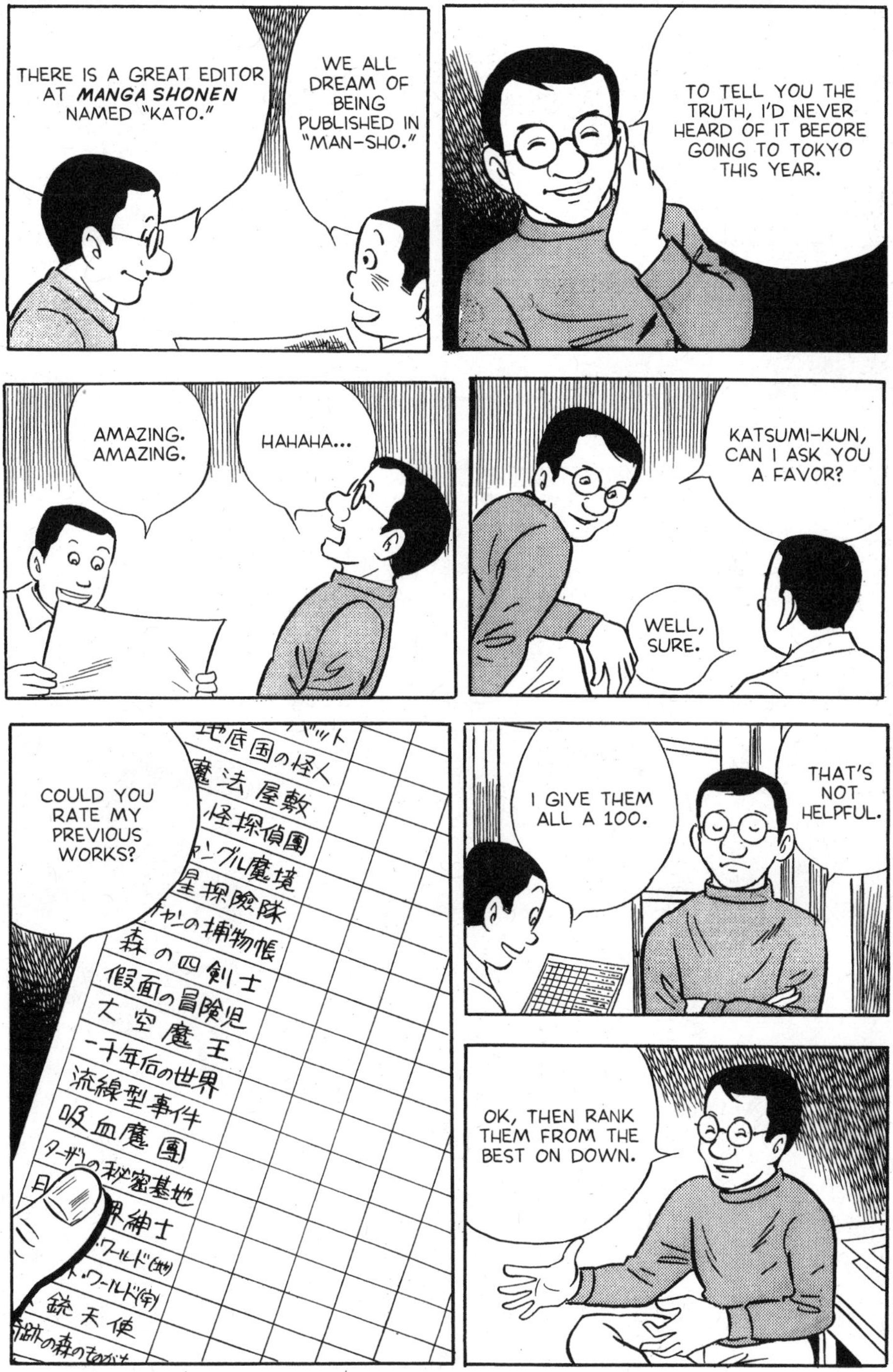
THERE IS A GREAT EDITOR AT **MANGA SHONEN** NAMED "KATO."
WE ALL DREAM OF BEING PUBLISHED IN "MAN-SHO."
TO TELL YOU THE TRUTH, I'D NEVER HEARD OF IT BEFORE GOING TO TOKYO THIS YEAR.
AMAZING. AMAZING.
HAHAHA...
KATSUMI-KUN, CAN I ASK YOU A FAVOR?
WELL, SURE.
COULD YOU RATE MY PREVIOUS WORKS?
地底国の怪人
魔法屋敷
森の四剣士
假面の冒険児
大空魔王
一千年后の世界
流線型事件
吸血魔團
ターザンの秘密基地
I GIVE THEM ALL A 100.
THAT'S NOT HELPFUL.
OK, THEN RANK THEM FROM THE BEST ON DOWN.

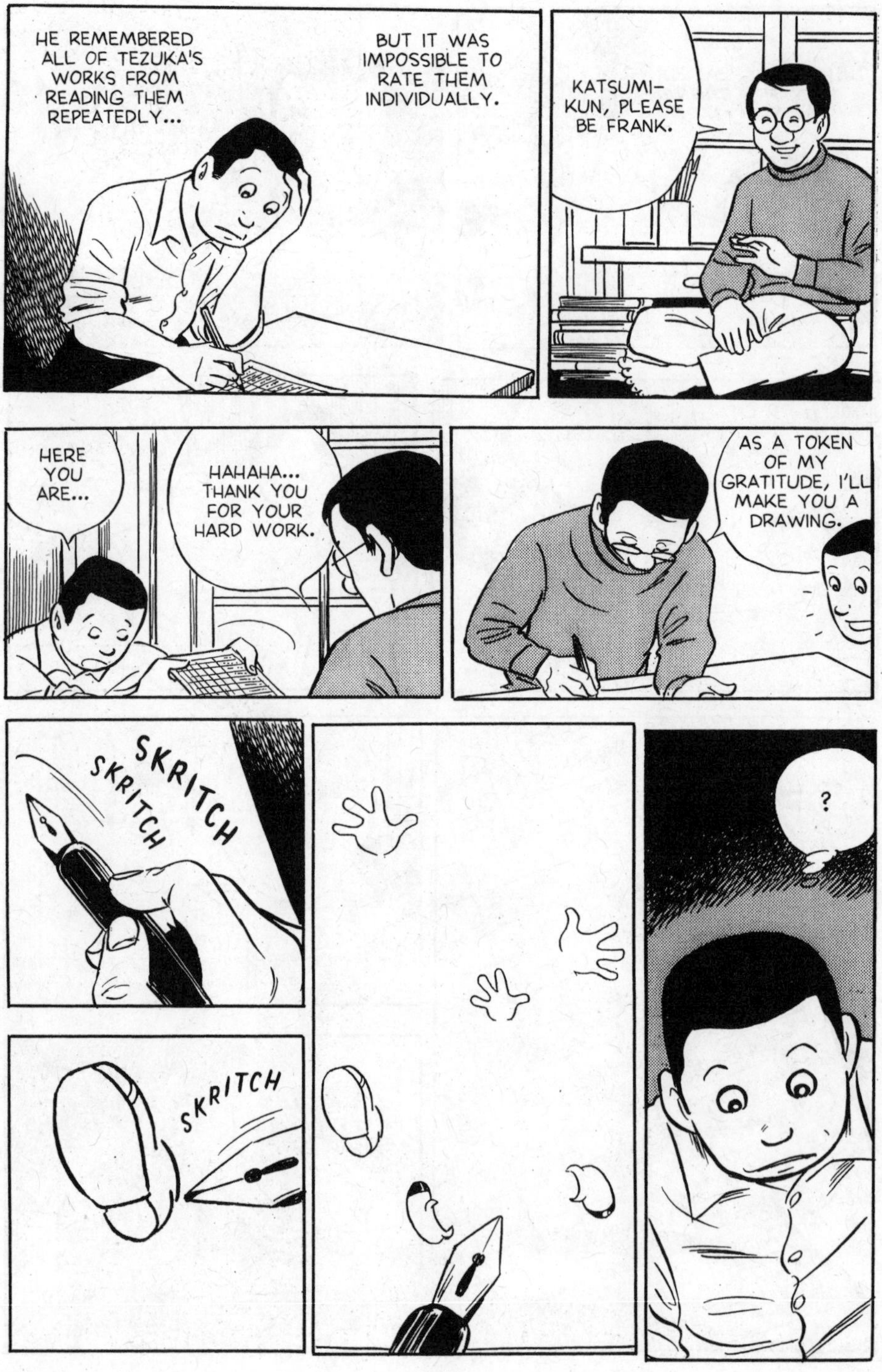
HE REMEMBERED ALL OF TEZUKA'S WORKS FROM READING THEM REPEATEDLY...
BUT IT WAS IMPOSSIBLE TO RATE THEM INDIVIDUALLY.
KATSUMI-KUN, PLEASE BE FRANK.
HERE YOU ARE...
HAHAHA... THANK YOU FOR YOUR HARD WORK.
AS A TOKEN OF MY GRATITUDE, I'LL MAKE YOU A DRAWING.
SKRITCH
SKRITCH
SKRITCH
?

SHHH

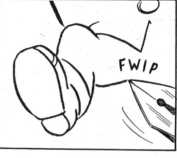

FWIP

TEZUKA FIRST DREW THE HANDS AND FEET, THEN THE FACES, AND THEN FINISHED THE REST IN A FLASH.

IT WAS TRULY MAGICAL.

THANK YOU FOR EVERYTHING.

I'M LOOKING FORWARD TO SEEING A LONGER PIECE FROM YOU.

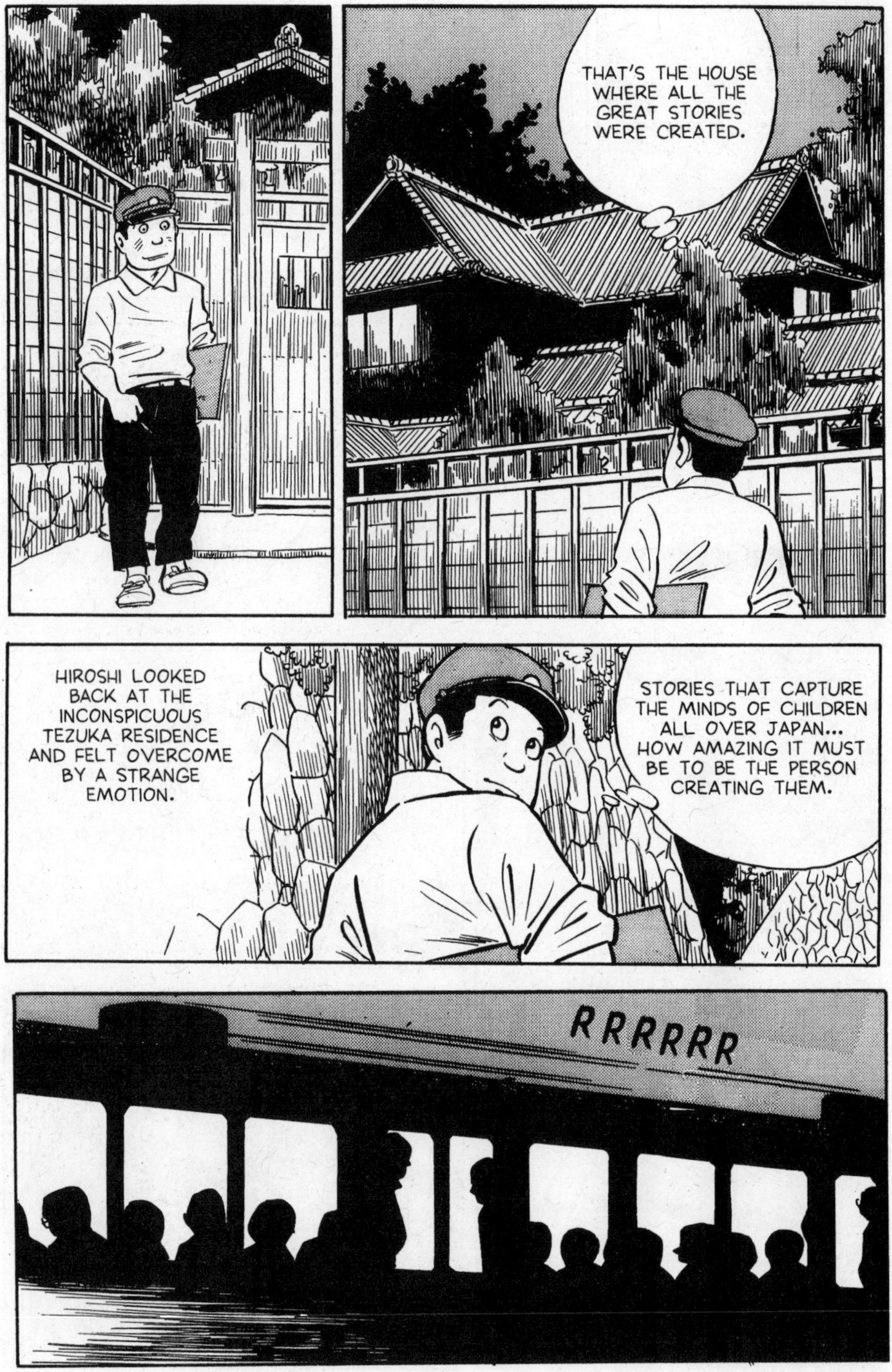
THAT'S THE HOUSE WHERE ALL THE GREAT STORIES WERE CREATED.
HIROSHI LOOKED BACK AT THE INCONSPICUOUS TEZUKA RESIDENCE AND FELT OVERCOME BY A STRANGE EMOTION.
STORIES THAT CAPTURE THE MINDS OF CHILDREN ALL OVER JAPAN... HOW AMAZING IT MUST BE TO BE THE PERSON CREATING THEM.
RRRRRR

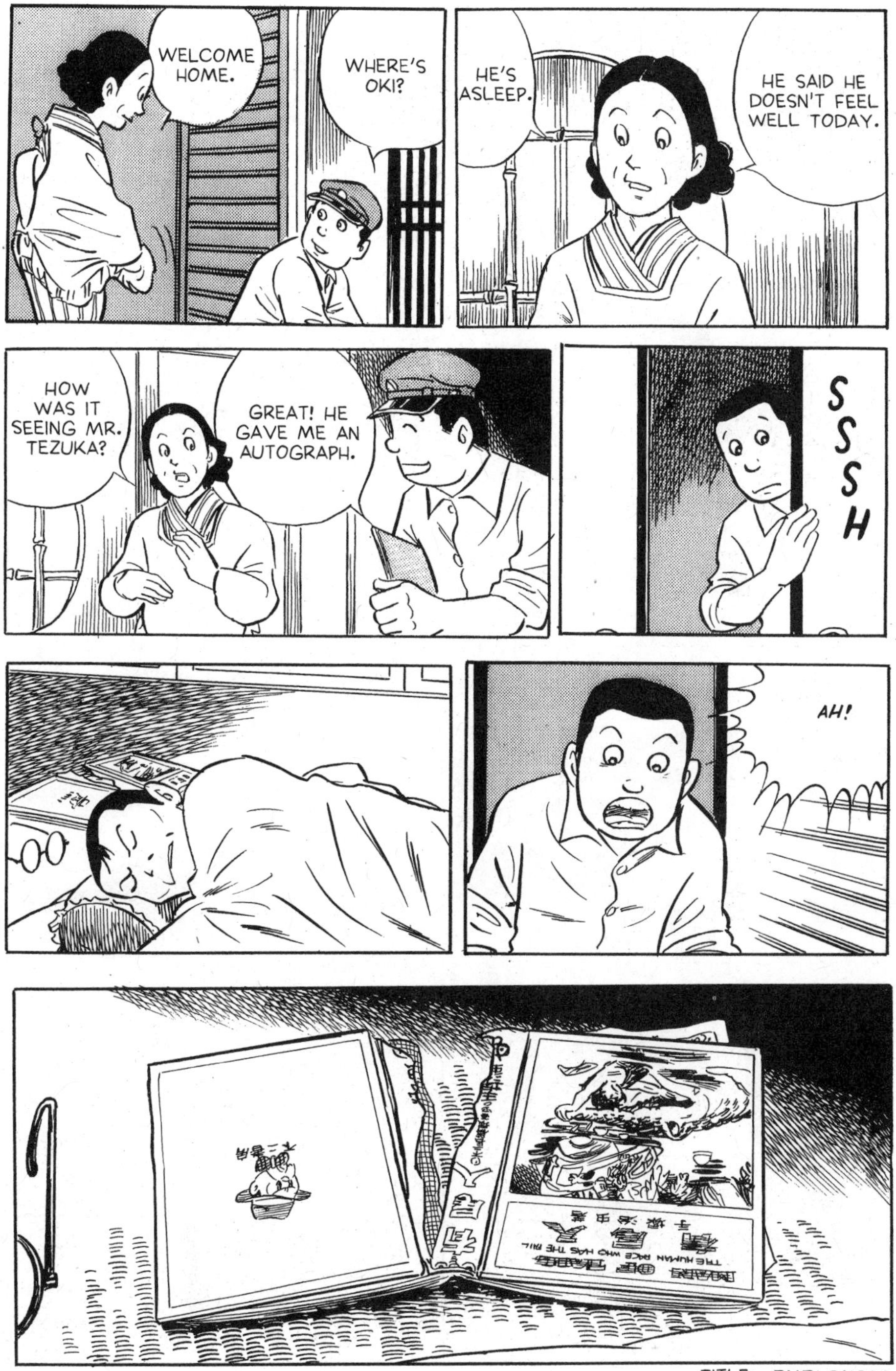
WELCOME HOME.
WHERE'S OKI?
HE'S ASLEEP.
HE SAID HE DOESN'T FEEL WELL TODAY.
HOW WAS IT SEEING MR. TEZUKA?
GREAT! HE GAVE ME AN AUTOGRAPH.
SSSH
AH!

TITLE: *FUJI SHOBO*

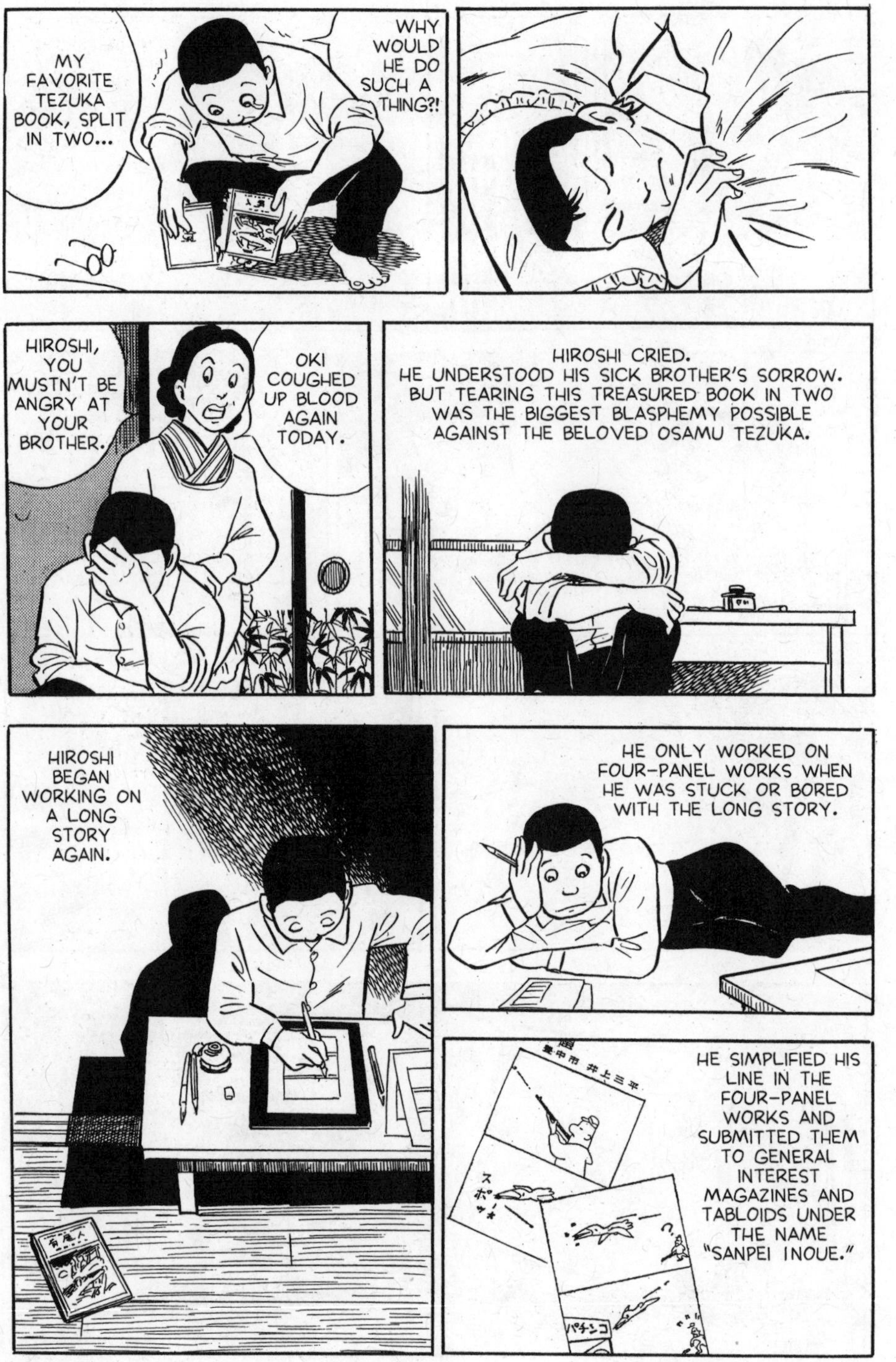
MY FAVORITE TEZUKA BOOK, SPLIT IN TWO...
WHY WOULD HE DO SUCH A THING?!
HIROSHI, YOU MUSTN'T BE ANGRY AT YOUR BROTHER.
OKI COUGHED UP BLOOD AGAIN TODAY.
HIROSHI CRIED. HE UNDERSTOOD HIS SICK BROTHER'S SORROW. BUT TEARING THIS TREASURED BOOK IN TWO WAS THE BIGGEST BLASPHEMY POSSIBLE AGAINST THE BELOVED OSAMU TEZUKA.
HIROSHI BEGAN WORKING ON A LONG STORY AGAIN.
HE ONLY WORKED ON FOUR-PANEL WORKS WHEN HE WAS STUCK OR BORED WITH THE LONG STORY.
HE SIMPLIFIED HIS LINE IN THE FOUR-PANEL WORKS AND SUBMITTED THEM TO GENERAL INTEREST MAGAZINES AND TABLOIDS UNDER THE NAME "SANPEI INOUE."

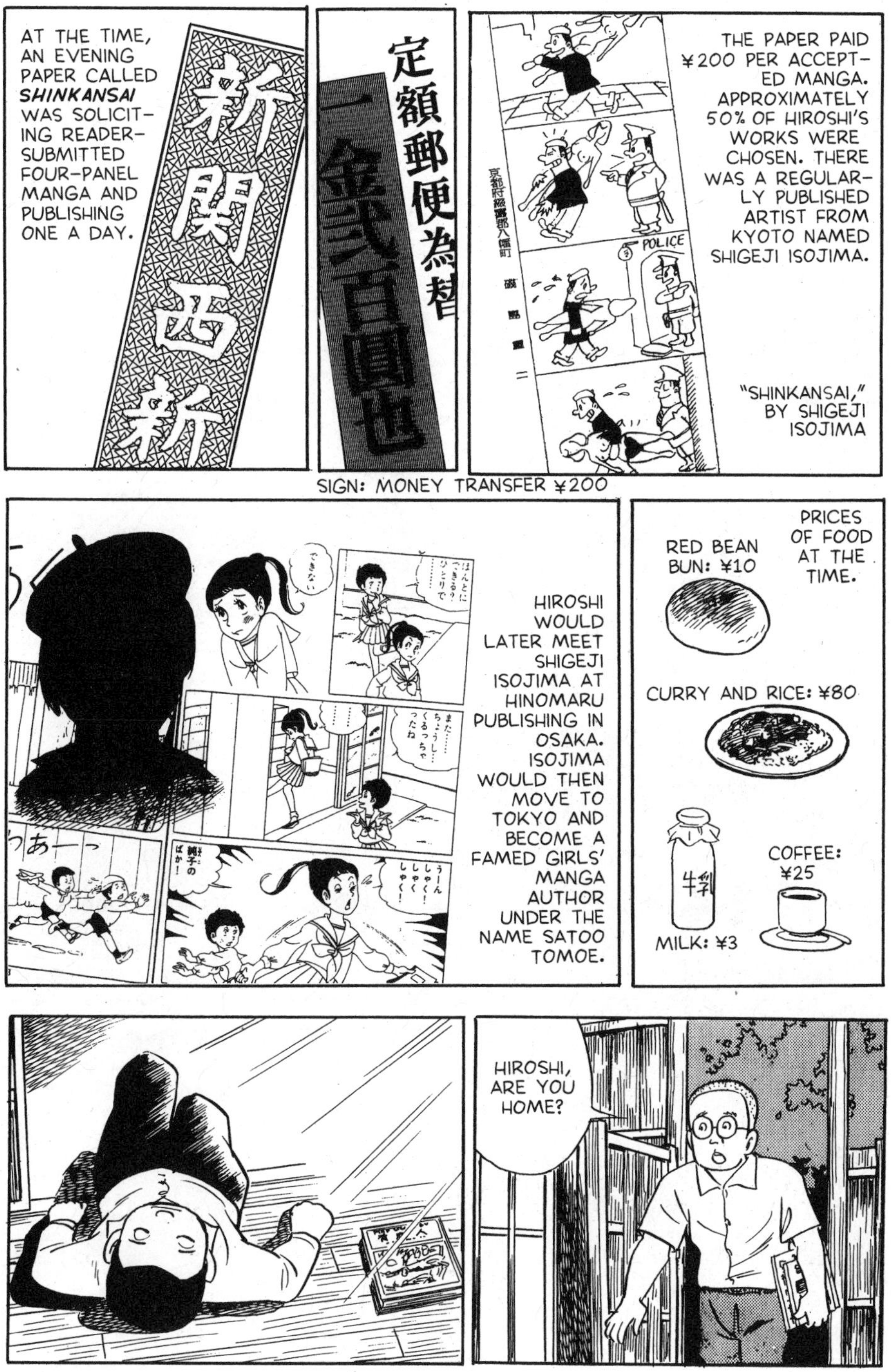
AT THE TIME, AN EVENING PAPER CALLED ***SHINKANSAI*** WAS SOLICITING READER-SUBMITTED FOUR-PANEL MANGA AND PUBLISHING ONE A DAY.
新関西新
定額郵便為替
一金弐百圓也
POLICE
THE PAPER PAID ¥200 PER ACCEPTED MANGA. APPROXIMATELY 50% OF HIROSHI'S WORKS WERE CHOSEN. THERE WAS A REGULARLY PUBLISHED ARTIST FROM KYOTO NAMED SHIGEJI ISOJIMA.
"SHINKANSAI," BY SHIGEJI ISOJIMA
SIGN: MONEY TRANSFER ¥200
できない
ほんとにできる?ひとりで……
HIROSHI WOULD LATER MEET SHIGEJI ISOJIMA AT HINOMARU PUBLISHING IN OSAKA. ISOJIMA WOULD THEN MOVE TO TOKYO AND BECOME A FAMED GIRLS' MANGA AUTHOR UNDER THE NAME SATOO TOMOE.
PRICES OF FOOD AT THE TIME.
RED BEAN BUN: ¥10
CURRY AND RICE: ¥80
牛乳
MILK: ¥3
COFFEE: ¥25
HIROSHI, ARE YOU HOME?

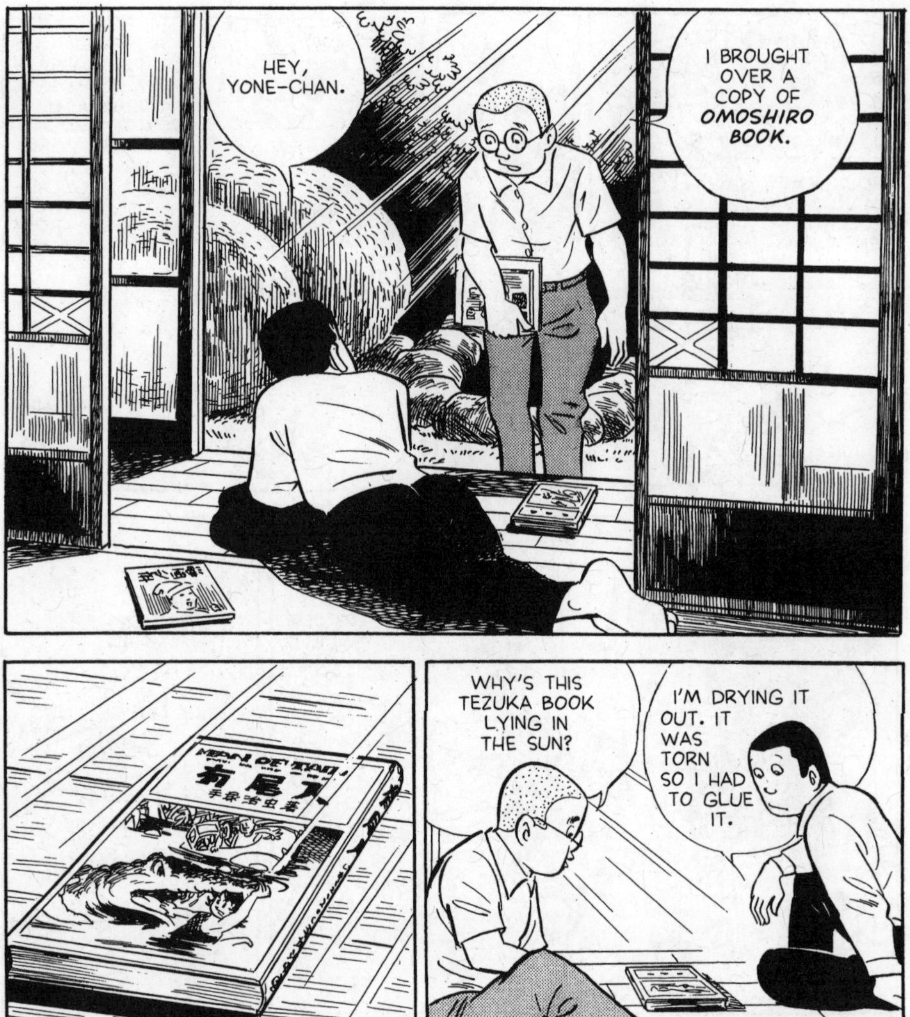
HEY, YONE-CHAN.
I BROUGHT OVER A COPY OF *OMOSHIRO BOOK*.
WHY'S THIS TEZUKA BOOK LYING IN THE SUN?
I'M DRYING IT OUT. IT WAS TORN SO I HAD TO GLUE IT.
BOOK: ***MANGA SHONEN*** BY OSAMU TEZUKA

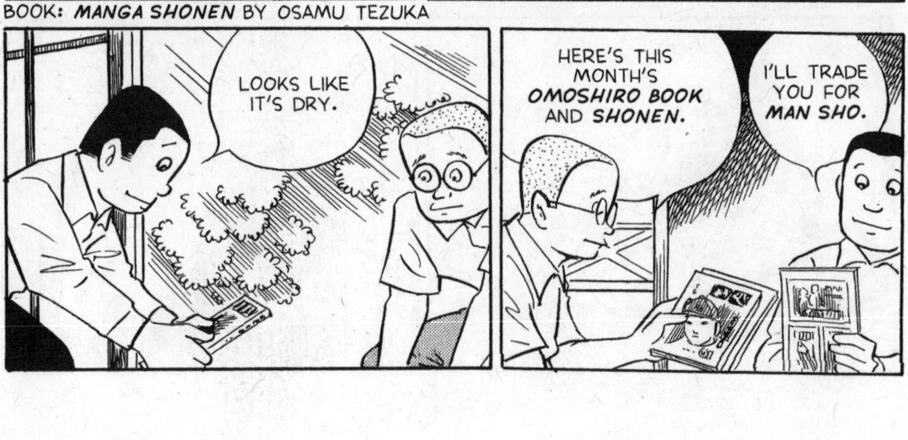
LOOKS LIKE IT'S DRY.
HERE'S THIS MONTH'S *OMOSHIRO BOOK* AND *SHONEN*.
I'LL TRADE YOU FOR *MAN SHO*.

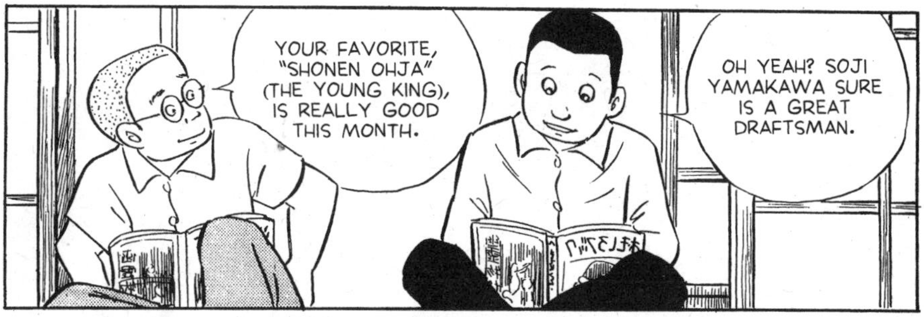
YOUR FAVORITE, "SHONEN OHJA" (THE YOUNG KING), IS REALLY GOOD THIS MONTH.
OH YEAH? SOJI YAMAKAWA SURE IS A GREAT DRAFTSMAN.

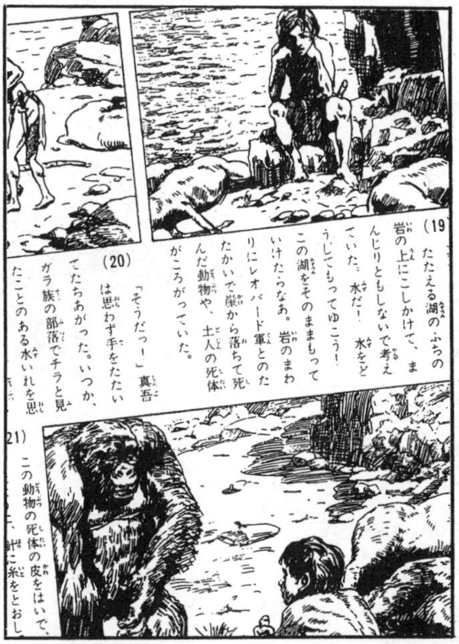
(19) たたえる湖のふちの岩の上にこしかけて、まんじりともしないで考えていた。水だ！水をどうしてもってゆこう！この湖をそのままもっていけたらなあ。岩のまわりにレオパード軍とのたたかいで崖から落ちて死んだ動物や、土人の死体がころがっていた。
(20) 「そうだっ！」真吾は思わず手をたたいてたちあがった。いつか、ガラ族の部落でチラと見たことのある水いれを思

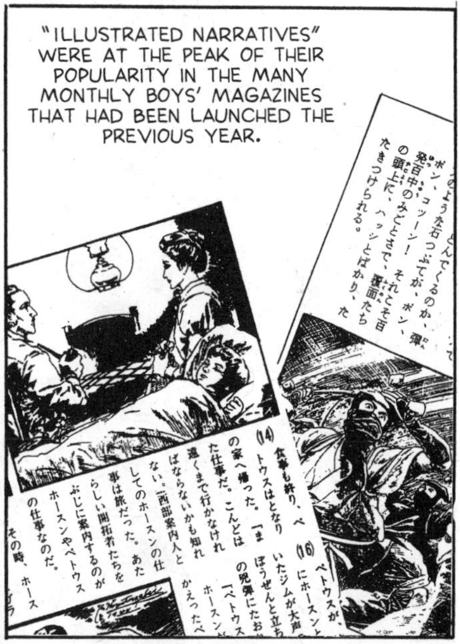
"ILLUSTRATED NARRATIVES" WERE AT THE PEAK OF THEIR POPULARITY IN THE MANY MONTHLY BOYS' MAGAZINES THAT HAD BEEN LAUNCHED THE PREVIOUS YEAR.

IMAGES: SHIGERU KOMATSUZAKI, "DAIHEI GENZI"; KOJIRO KOMIYA, "ADVENTURES OF BLACK HOOD."

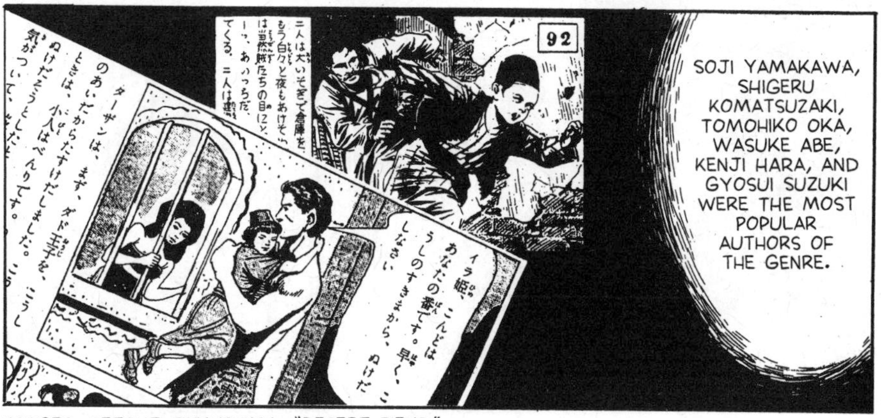
92
イラ姫、こんどはあなたの番です。早く、こうしのすきまから、ぬけだしなさい
SOJI YAMAKAWA, SHIGERU KOMATSUZAKI, TOMOHIKO OKA, WASUKE ABE, KENJI HARA, AND GYOSUI SUZUKI WERE THE MOST POPULAR AUTHORS OF THE GENRE.

IMAGES: TETZUJI FUKUSHIMA, "DESERT FIEND"; WASUKE ABE, "TARZAN AND THE MIDGET QUEEN."

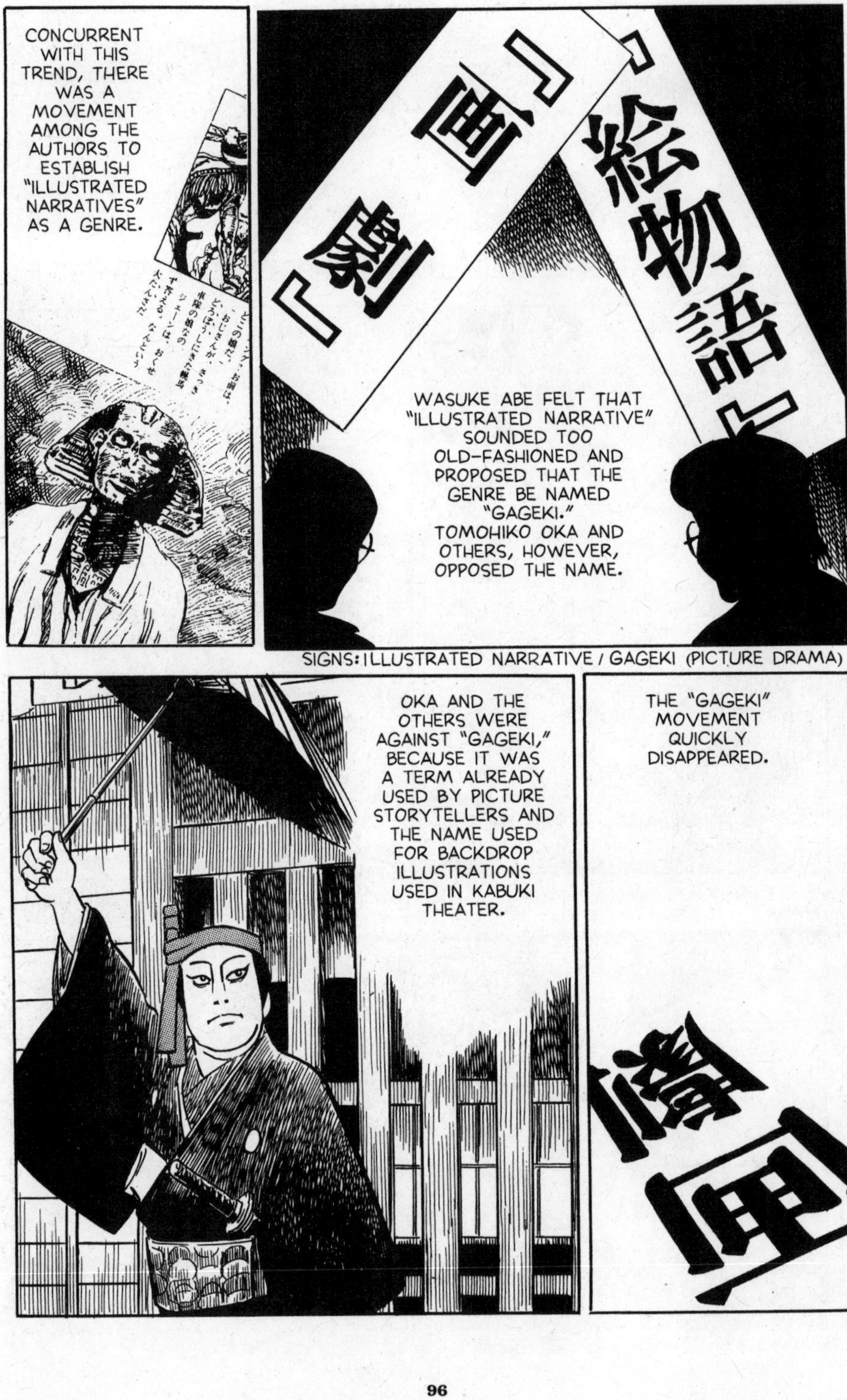
CONCURRENT WITH THIS TREND, THERE WAS A MOVEMENT AMONG THE AUTHORS TO ESTABLISH "ILLUSTRATED NARRATIVES" AS A GENRE.
『絵物語』
『画劇』
WASUKE ABE FELT THAT "ILLUSTRATED NARRATIVE" SOUNDED TOO OLD-FASHIONED AND PROPOSED THAT THE GENRE BE NAMED "GAGEKI." TOMOHIKO OKA AND OTHERS, HOWEVER, OPPOSED THE NAME.
SIGNS: ILLUSTRATED NARRATIVE / GAGEKI (PICTURE DRAMA)
OKA AND THE OTHERS WERE AGAINST "GAGEKI," BECAUSE IT WAS A TERM ALREADY USED BY PICTURE STORYTELLERS AND THE NAME USED FOR BACKDROP ILLUSTRATIONS USED IN KABUKI THEATER.
THE "GAGEKI" MOVEMENT QUICKLY DISAPPEARED.

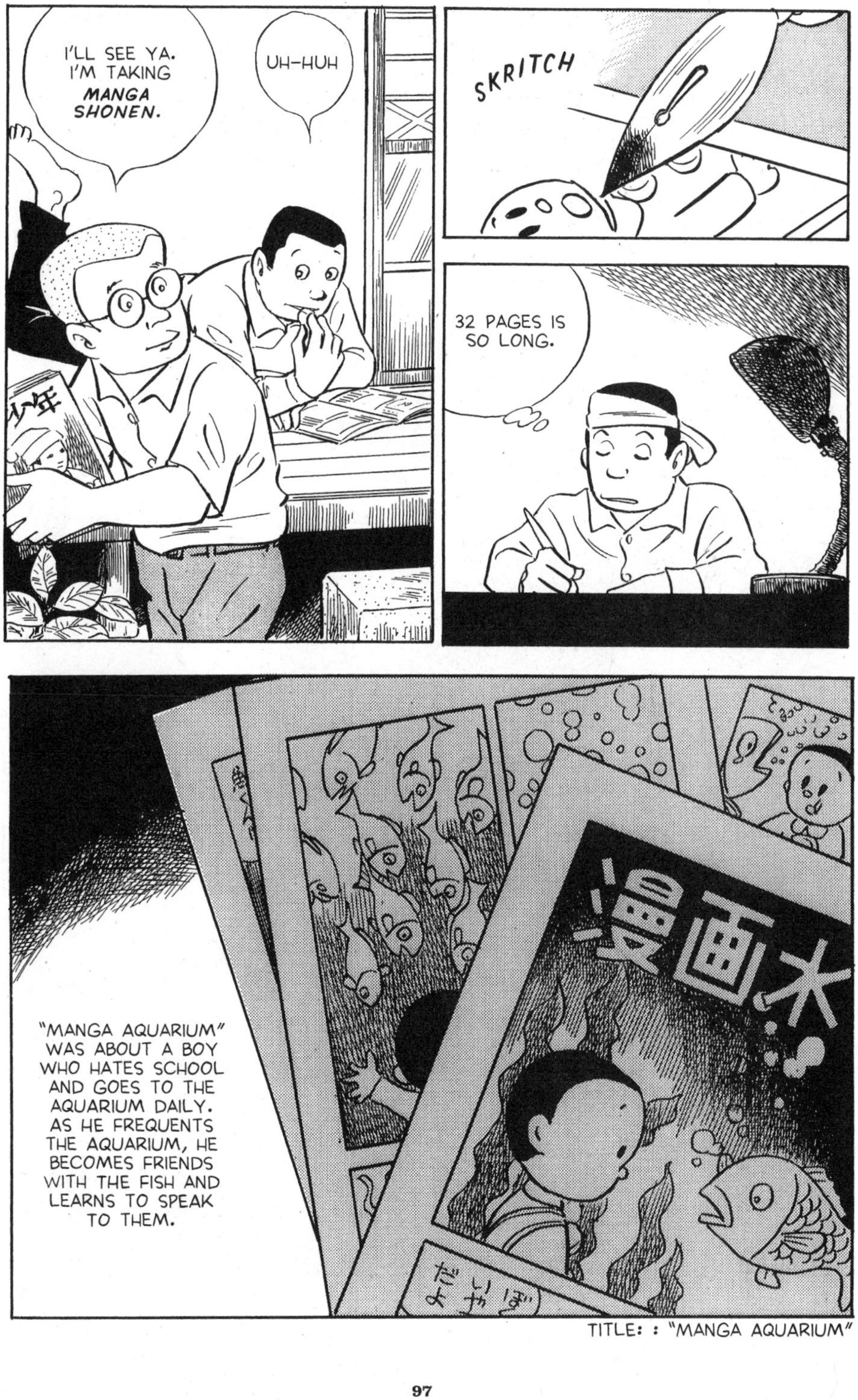
I'LL SEE YA. I'M TAKING *MANGA SHONEN.*
UH-HUH
少年
SKRITCH
32 PAGES IS SO LONG.
"MANGA AQUARIUM" WAS ABOUT A BOY WHO HATES SCHOOL AND GOES TO THE AQUARIUM DAILY. AS HE FREQUENTS THE AQUARIUM, HE BECOMES FRIENDS WITH THE FISH AND LEARNS TO SPEAK TO THEM.
漫画水
TITLE: : "MANGA AQUARIUM"

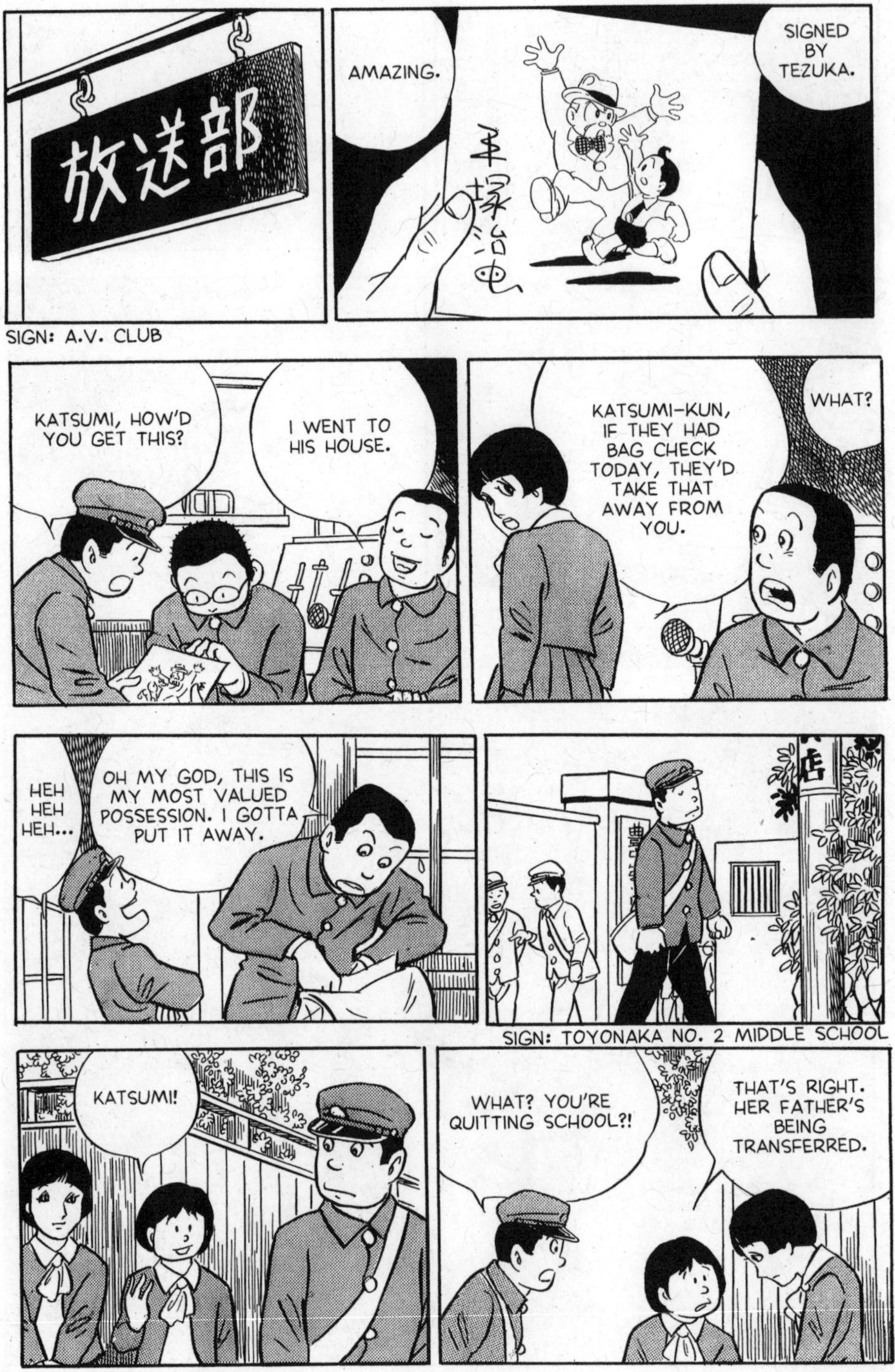
放送部
AMAZING.
手塚治虫
SIGNED BY TEZUKA.
SIGN: A.V. CLUB
KATSUMI, HOW'D YOU GET THIS?
I WENT TO HIS HOUSE.
KATSUMI-KUN, IF THEY HAD BAG CHECK TODAY, THEY'D TAKE THAT AWAY FROM YOU.
WHAT?
HEH HEH HEH...
OH MY GOD, THIS IS MY MOST VALUED POSSESSION. I GOTTA PUT IT AWAY.
SIGN: TOYONAKA NO. 2 MIDDLE SCHOOL
KATSUMI!
WHAT? YOU'RE QUITTING SCHOOL?!
THAT'S RIGHT. HER FATHER'S BEING TRANSFERRED.

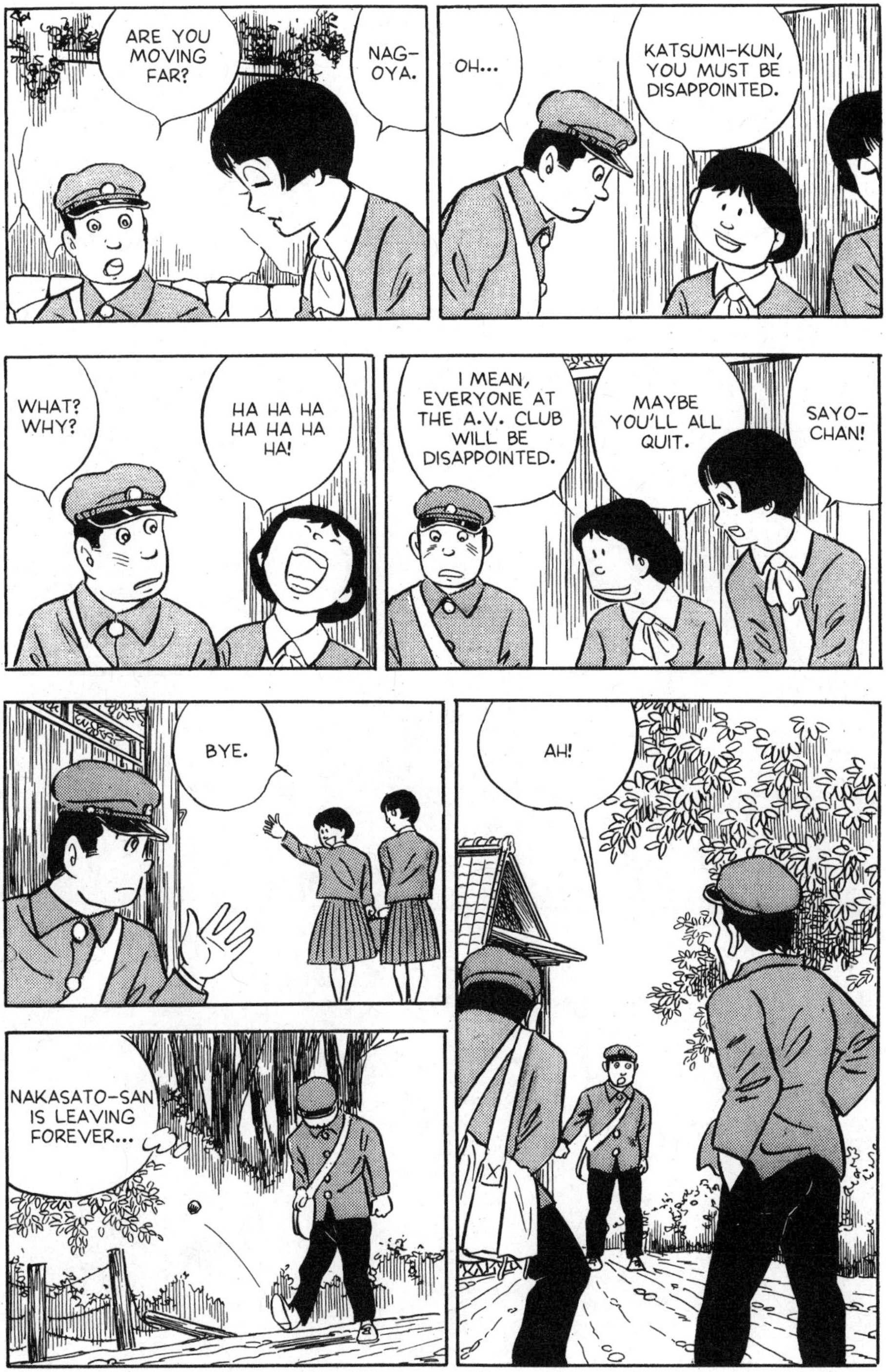
ARE YOU MOVING FAR?
NAG-OYA.
OH...
KATSUMI-KUN, YOU MUST BE DISAPPOINTED.
WHAT? WHY?
HA HA HA HA HA HA HA!
I MEAN, EVERYONE AT THE A.V. CLUB WILL BE DISAPPOINTED.
MAYBE YOU'LL ALL QUIT.
SAYO-CHAN!
BYE.
NAKASATO-SAN IS LEAVING FOREVER...
AH!

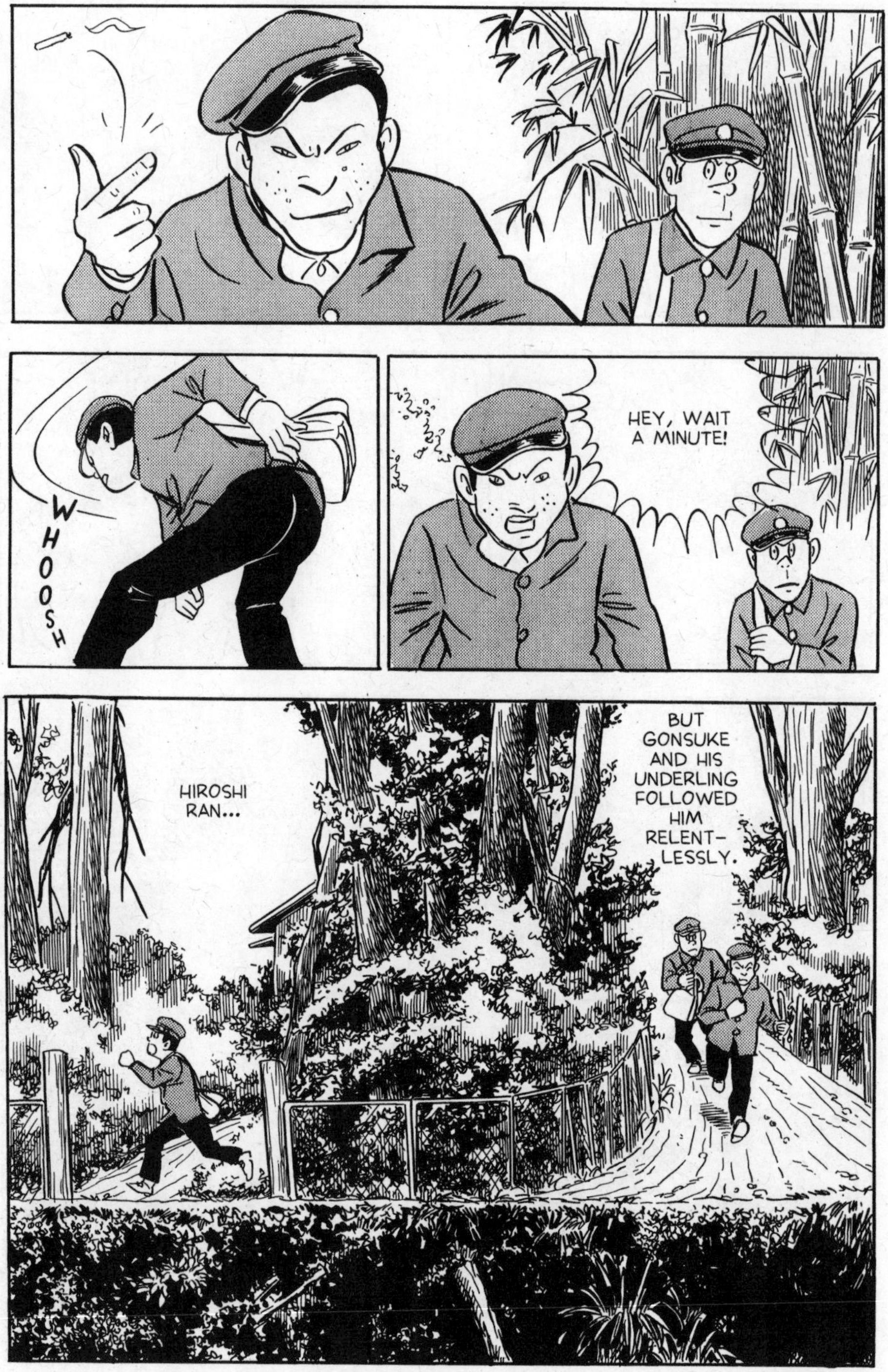
WHOOSH
HEY, WAIT A MINUTE!
HIROSHI RAN...
BUT GONSUKE AND HIS UNDERLING FOLLOWED HIM RELENTLESSLY.

TEZUKA VANISHES

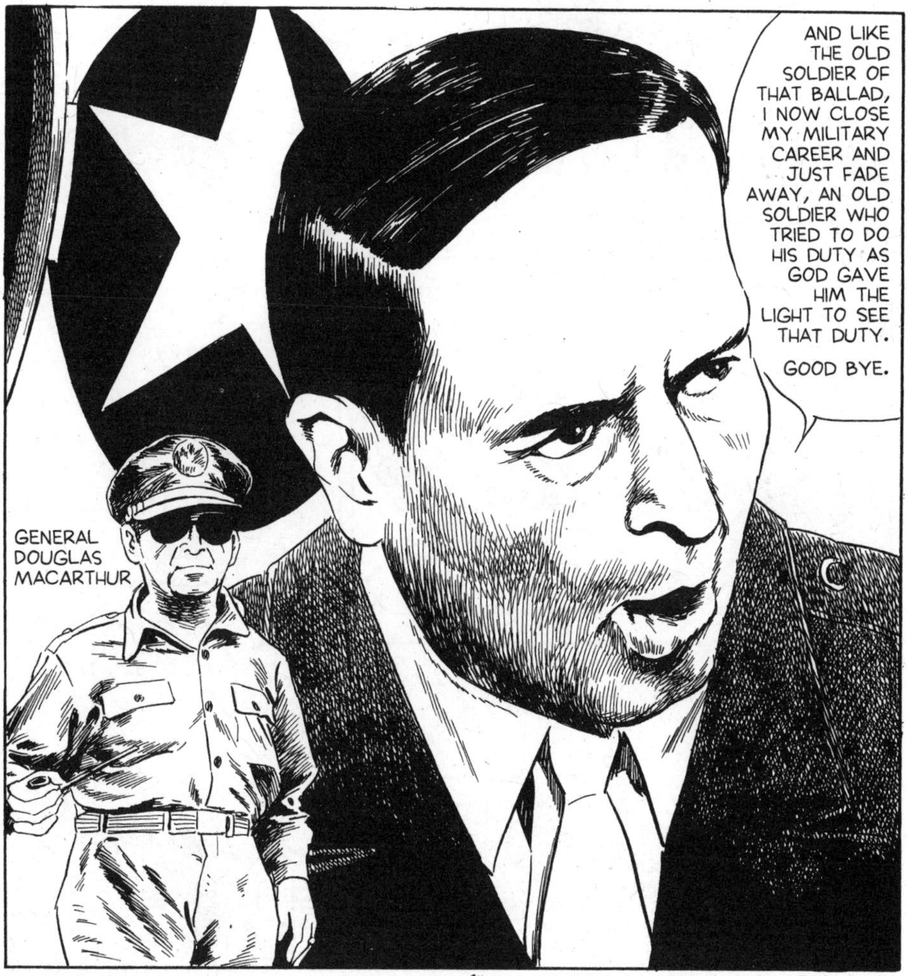
AND LIKE THE OLD SOLDIER OF THAT BALLAD, I NOW CLOSE MY MILITARY CAREER AND JUST FADE AWAY, AN OLD SOLDIER WHO TRIED TO DO HIS DUTY AS GOD GAVE HIM THE LIGHT TO SEE THAT DUTY.
GOOD BYE.
GENERAL DOUGLAS MACARTHUR

IMAGE SOURCE: ***ICHIOKUNIN NO SHOWA-SHI*** ("THE HISTORY OF 100 MILLION PEOPLE IN SHOWA"), MAINICHI SHIMBUN

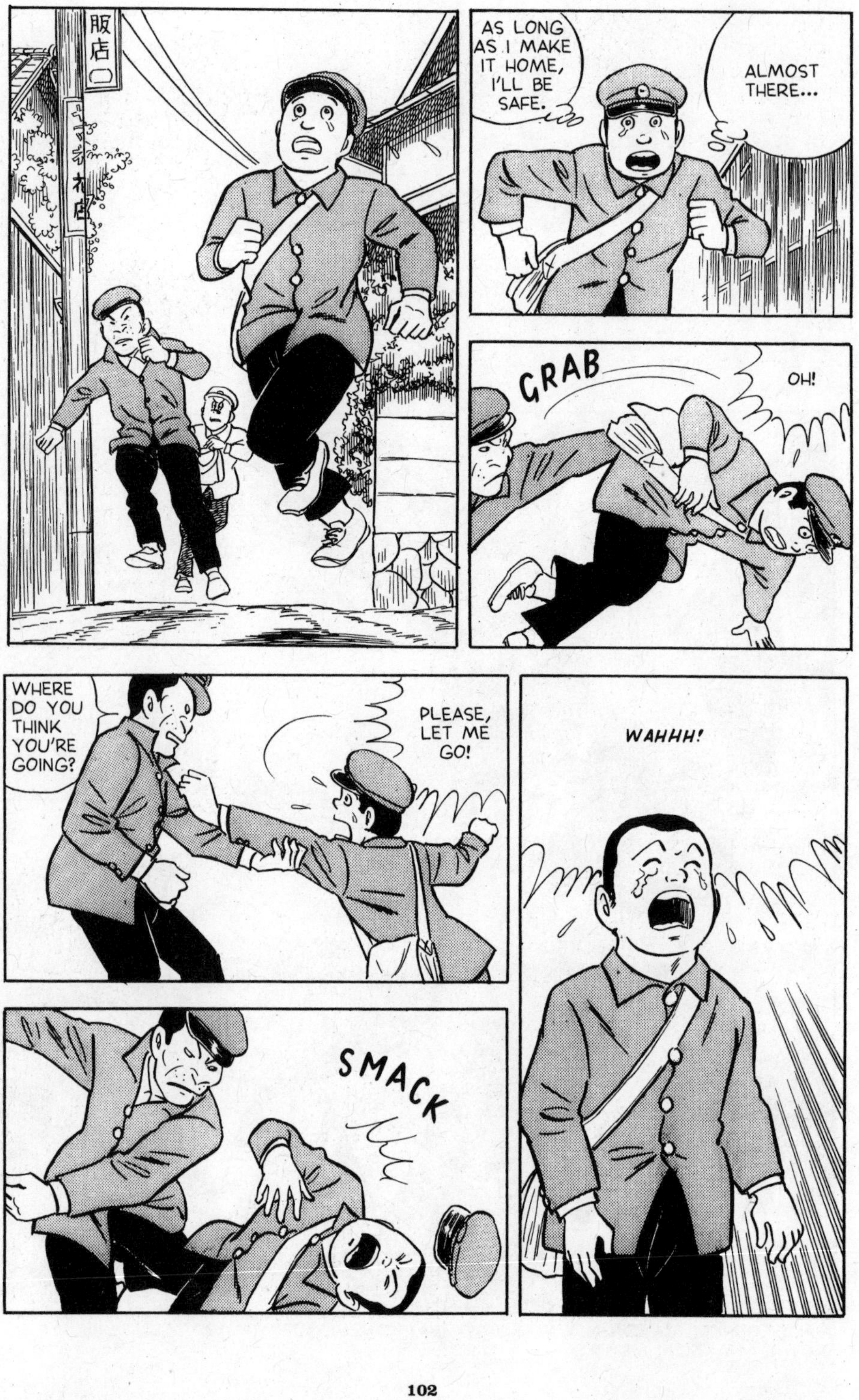
販店
AS LONG AS I MAKE IT HOME, I'LL BE SAFE.
ALMOST THERE...
GRAB
OH!
WHERE DO YOU THINK YOU'RE GOING?
PLEASE, LET ME GO!
SMACK
WAHHH!

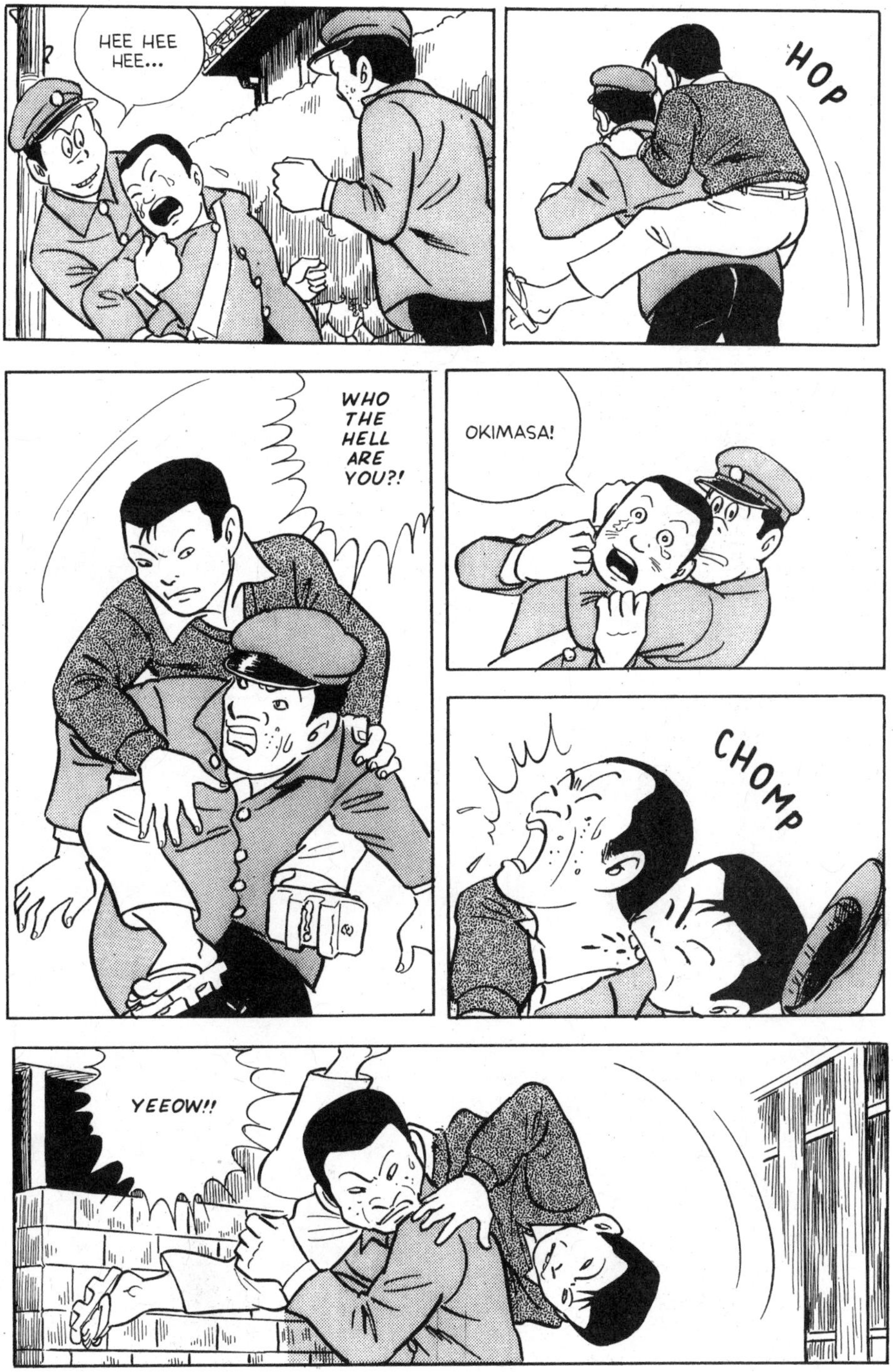
HEE HEE HEE...
HOP
WHO THE HELL ARE YOU?!
OKIMASA!
CHOMP
YEEOW!!

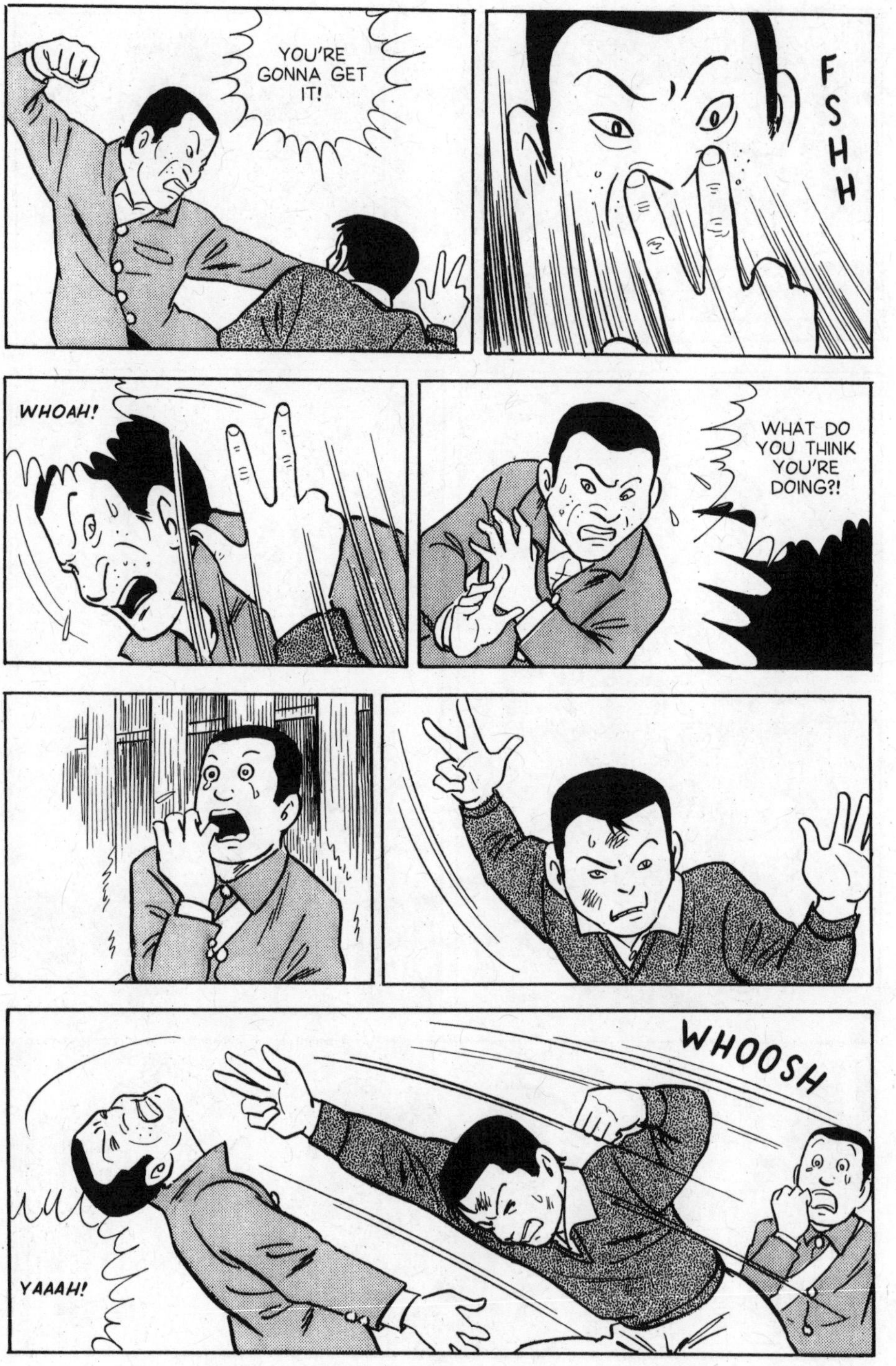
YOU'RE GONNA GET IT!
FSHH
WHOAH!
WHAT DO YOU THINK YOU'RE DOING?!
WHOOSH
YAAAH!

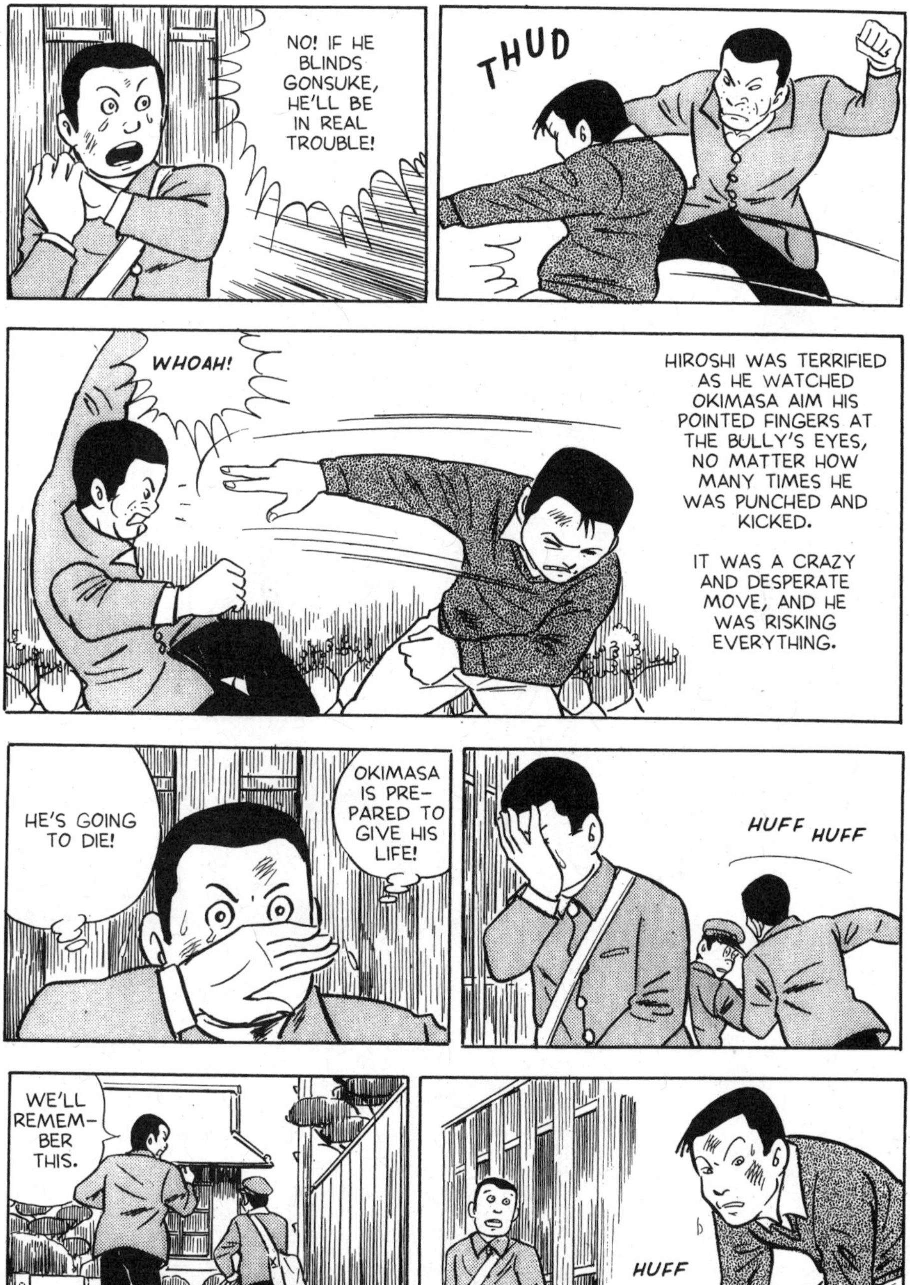
NO! IF HE BLINDS GONSUKE, HE'LL BE IN REAL TROUBLE!
THUD
WHOAH!
HIROSHI WAS TERRIFIED AS HE WATCHED OKIMASA AIM HIS POINTED FINGERS AT THE BULLY'S EYES, NO MATTER HOW MANY TIMES HE WAS PUNCHED AND KICKED.
IT WAS A CRAZY AND DESPERATE MOVE, AND HE WAS RISKING EVERYTHING.
HE'S GOING TO DIE!
OKIMASA IS PRE-PARED TO GIVE HIS LIFE!
HUFF HUFF
WE'LL REMEM-BER THIS.
HUFF HUFF

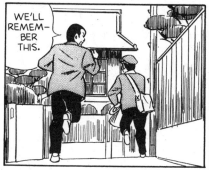

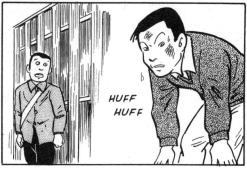

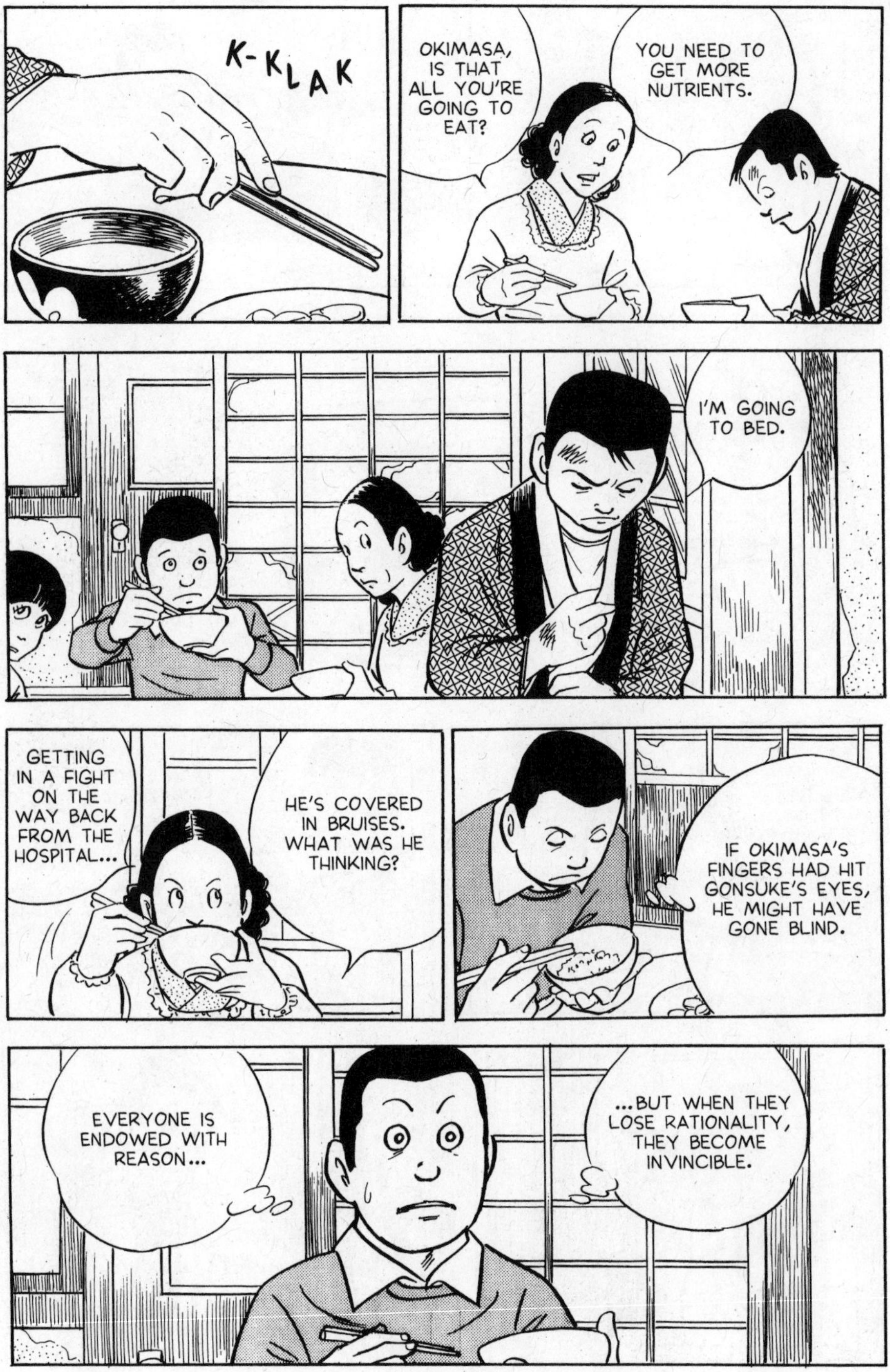
K-KLAK
OKIMASA, IS THAT ALL YOU'RE GOING TO EAT?
YOU NEED TO GET MORE NUTRIENTS.
I'M GOING TO BED.
GETTING IN A FIGHT ON THE WAY BACK FROM THE HOSPITAL...
HE'S COVERED IN BRUISES. WHAT WAS HE THINKING?
IF OKIMASA'S FINGERS HAD HIT GONSUKE'S EYES, HE MIGHT HAVE GONE BLIND.
EVERYONE IS ENDOWED WITH REASON...
...BUT WHEN THEY LOSE RATIONALITY, THEY BECOME INVINCIBLE.

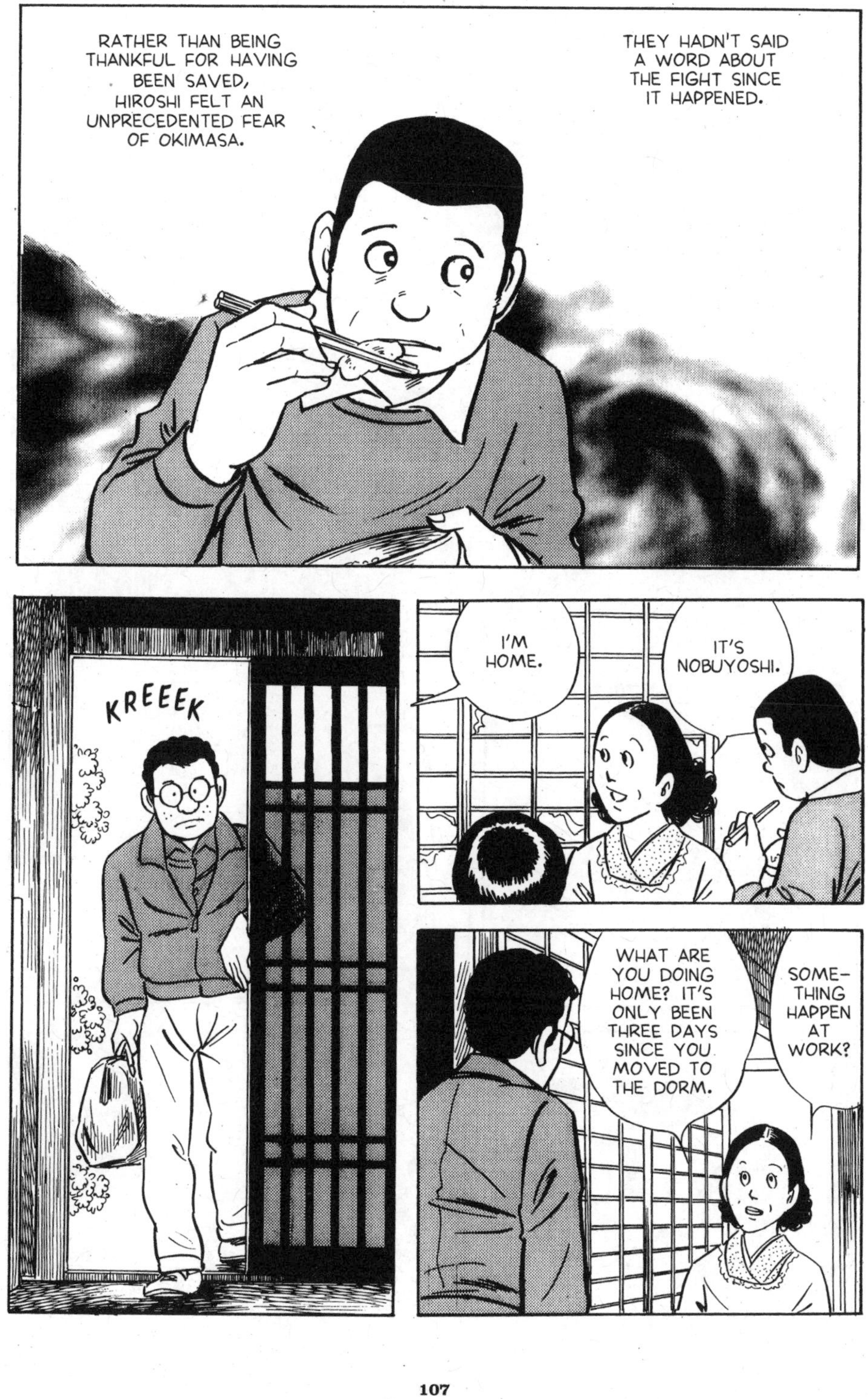
RATHER THAN BEING THANKFUL FOR HAVING BEEN SAVED, HIROSHI FELT AN UNPRECEDENTED FEAR OF OKIMASA.
THEY HADN'T SAID A WORD ABOUT THE FIGHT SINCE IT HAPPENED.
KREEEK
I'M HOME.
IT'S NOBUYOSHI.
WHAT ARE YOU DOING HOME? IT'S ONLY BEEN THREE DAYS SINCE YOU MOVED TO THE DORM.
SOME-THING HAPPEN AT WORK?

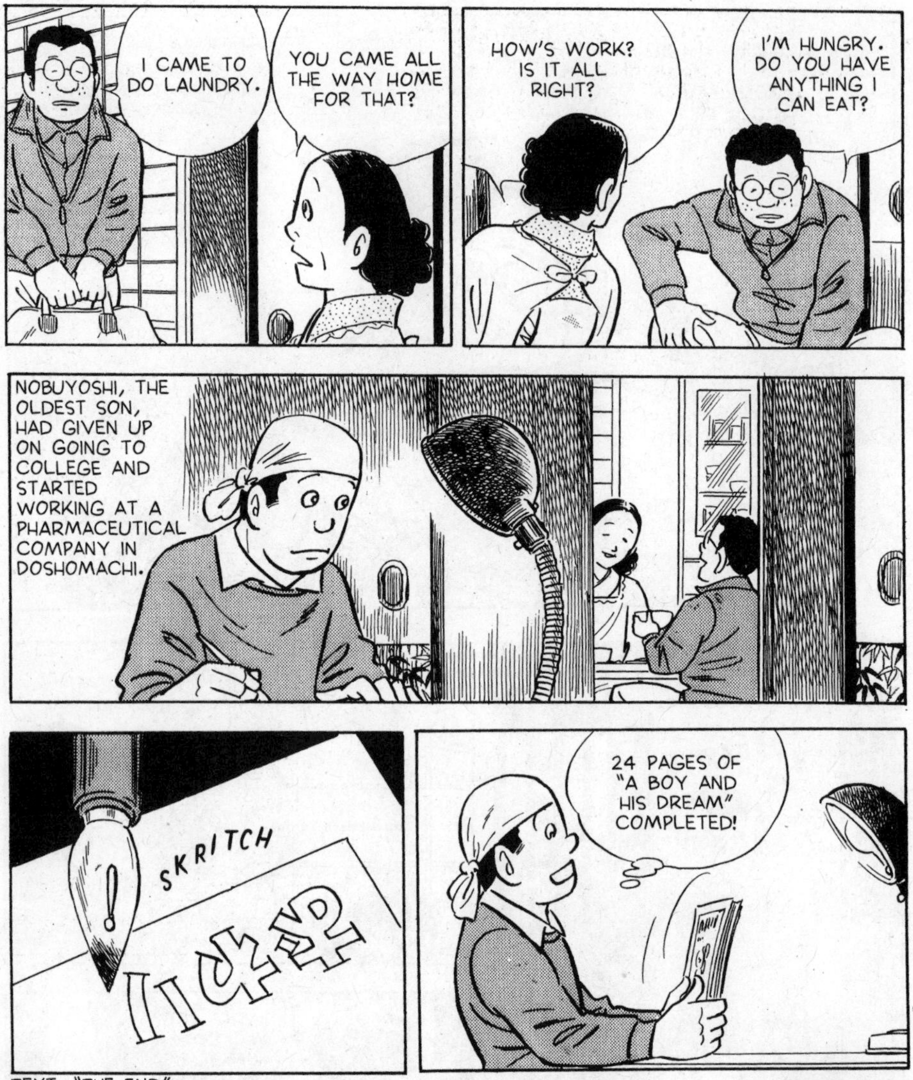
I CAME TO DO LAUNDRY.
YOU CAME ALL THE WAY HOME FOR THAT?
HOW'S WORK? IS IT ALL RIGHT?
I'M HUNGRY. DO YOU HAVE ANYTHING I CAN EAT?
NOBUYOSHI, THE OLDEST SON, HAD GIVEN UP ON GOING TO COLLEGE AND STARTED WORKING AT A PHARMACEUTICAL COMPANY IN DOSHOMACHI.
SKRITCH
24 PAGES OF "A BOY AND HIS DREAM" COMPLETED!

TEXT: "THE END"

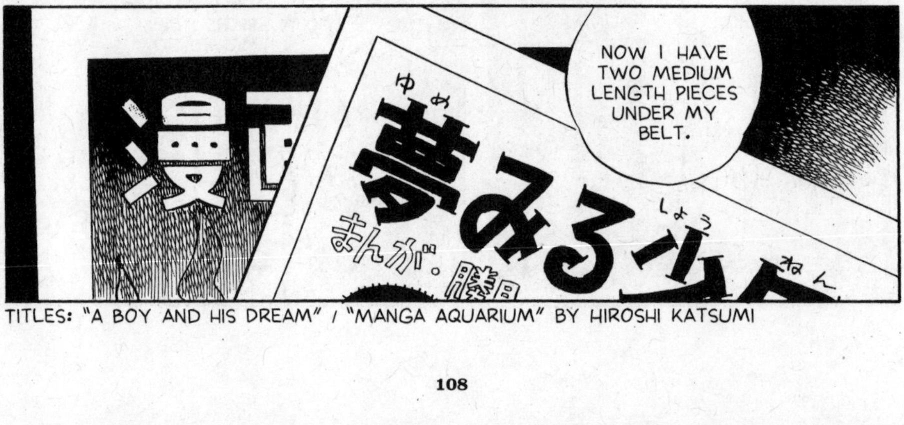
NOW I HAVE TWO MEDIUM LENGTH PIECES UNDER MY BELT.
夢みる
まんが。

TITLES: "A BOY AND HIS DREAM" / "MANGA AQUARIUM" BY HIROSHI KATSUMI

JANUARY 15, 1951 – HOLIDAY

HIROSHI MET UP WITH OKANISHI AND MATSUSHITA FROM KYOTO TO VISIT OSAMU TEZUKA AGAIN.

RRRRRRR

KLAK KLAK KLAK
KLAK KLAK

SIGN: TEZUKA

SO OKANISHI-KUN, WE MET LAST SUMMER AT *MAINICHI SHIMBUN*, RIGHT?

YES, WITH KATSUMI-KUN.

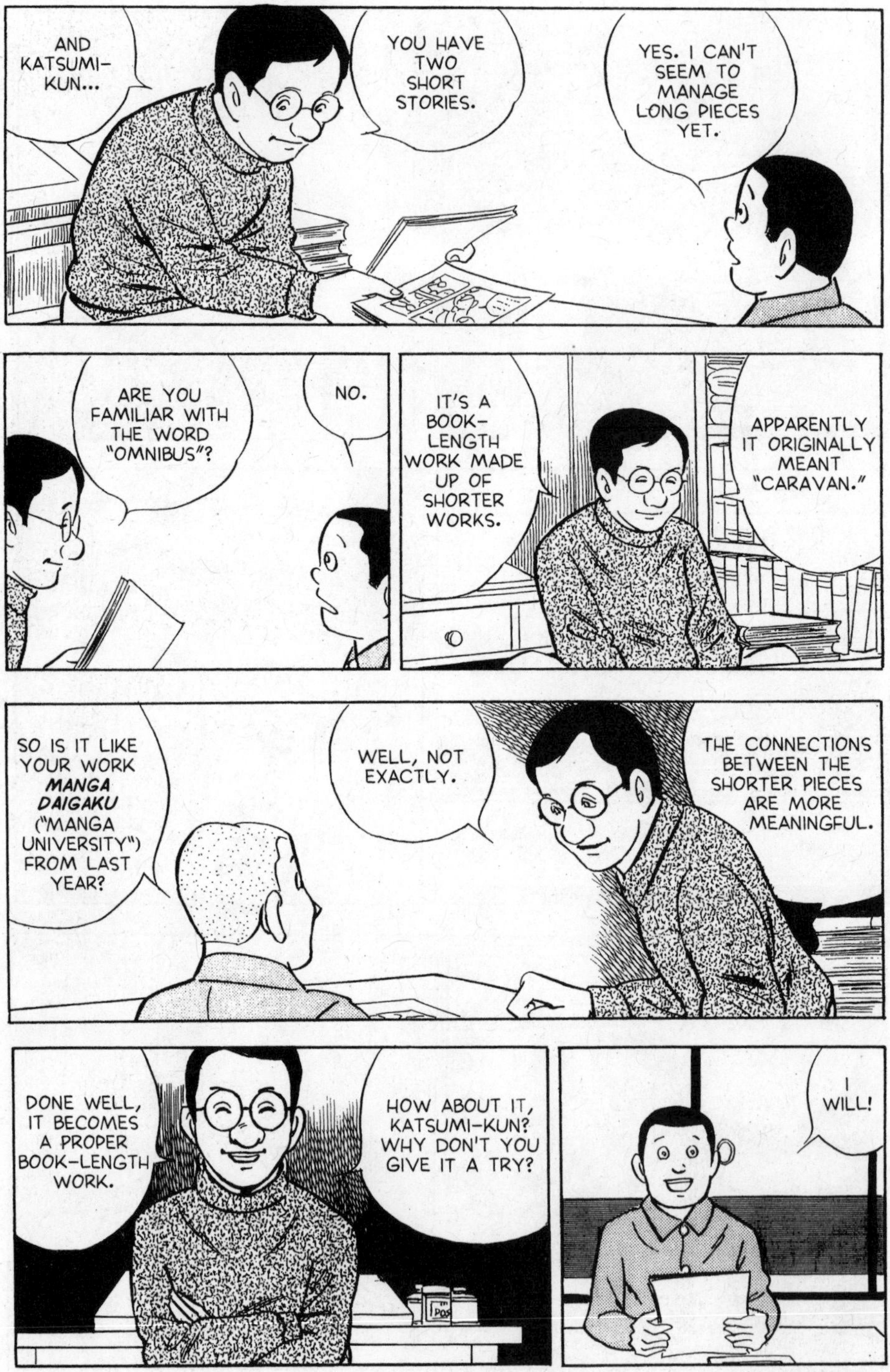
AND KATSUMI-KUN...
YOU HAVE TWO SHORT STORIES.
YES. I CAN'T SEEM TO MANAGE LONG PIECES YET.
ARE YOU FAMILIAR WITH THE WORD "OMNIBUS"?
NO.
IT'S A BOOK-LENGTH WORK MADE UP OF SHORTER WORKS.
APPARENTLY IT ORIGINALLY MEANT "CARAVAN."
SO IS IT LIKE YOUR WORK ***MANGA DAIGAKU*** ("MANGA UNIVERSITY") FROM LAST YEAR?
WELL, NOT EXACTLY.
THE CONNECTIONS BETWEEN THE SHORTER PIECES ARE MORE MEANINGFUL.
DONE WELL, IT BECOMES A PROPER BOOK-LENGTH WORK.
HOW ABOUT IT, KATSUMI-KUN? WHY DON'T YOU GIVE IT A TRY?
I WILL!

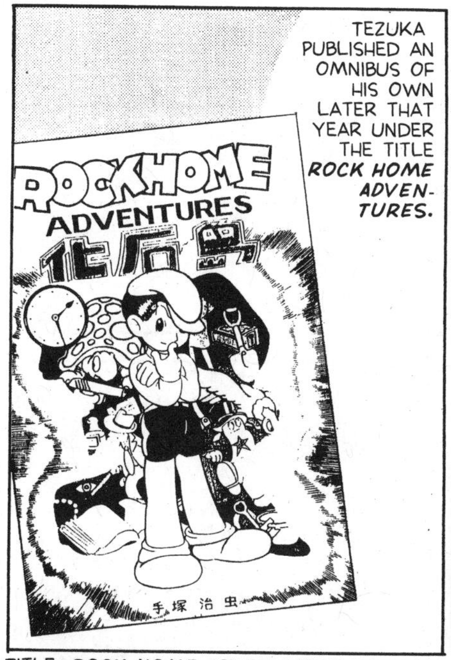
TEZUKA PUBLISHED AN OMNIBUS OF HIS OWN LATER THAT YEAR UNDER THE TITLE *ROCK HOME ADVENTURES*.
ROCKHOME ADVENTURES
手塚治虫

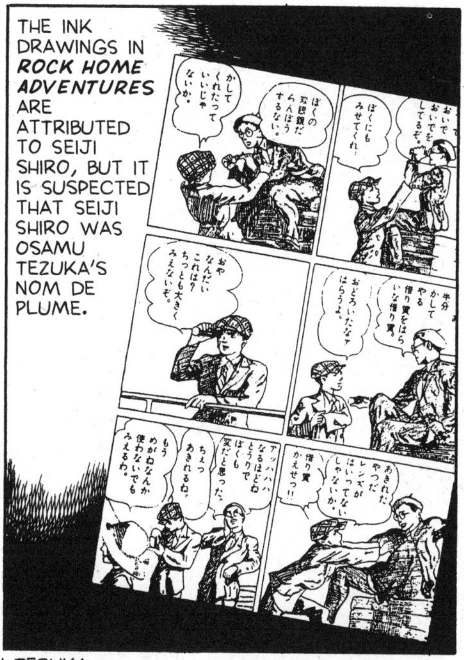
THE INK DRAWINGS IN *ROCK HOME ADVENTURES* ARE ATTRIBUTED TO SEIJI SHIRO, BUT IT IS SUSPECTED THAT SEIJI SHIRO WAS OSAMU TEZUKA'S NOM DE PLUME.

TITLE: *ROCK HOME ADVENTURES* BY OSAMU TEZUKA

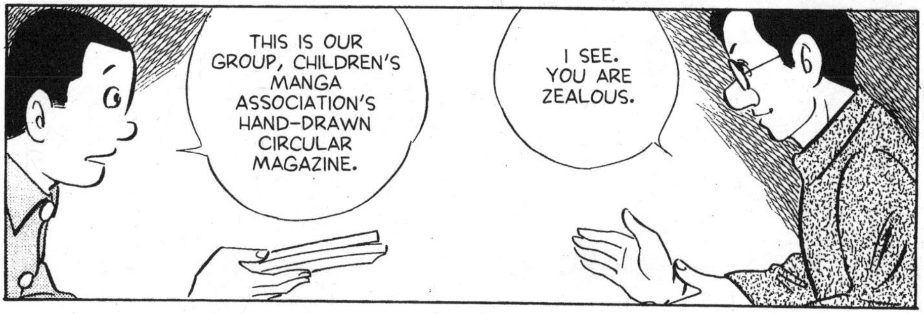
THIS IS OUR GROUP, CHILDREN'S MANGA ASSOCIATION'S HAND-DRAWN CIRCULAR MAGAZINE.
I SEE. YOU ARE ZEALOUS.

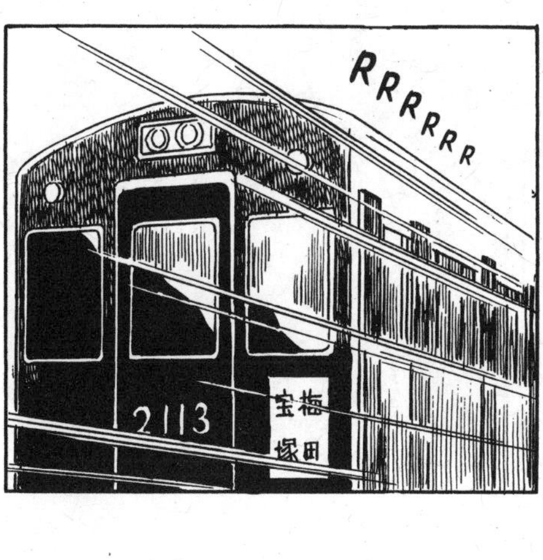
RRRRRRR
2113

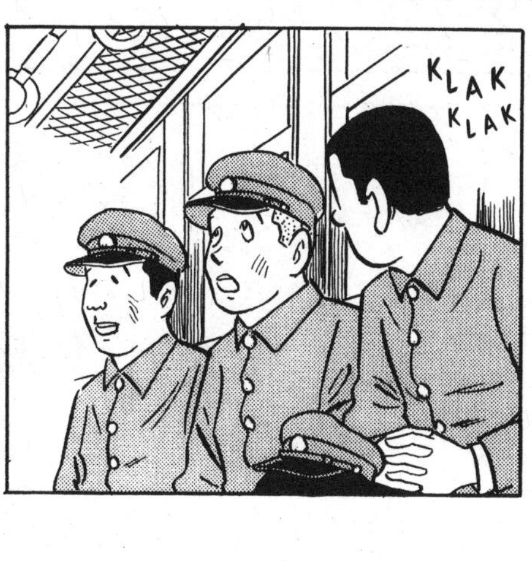
KLAK KLAK

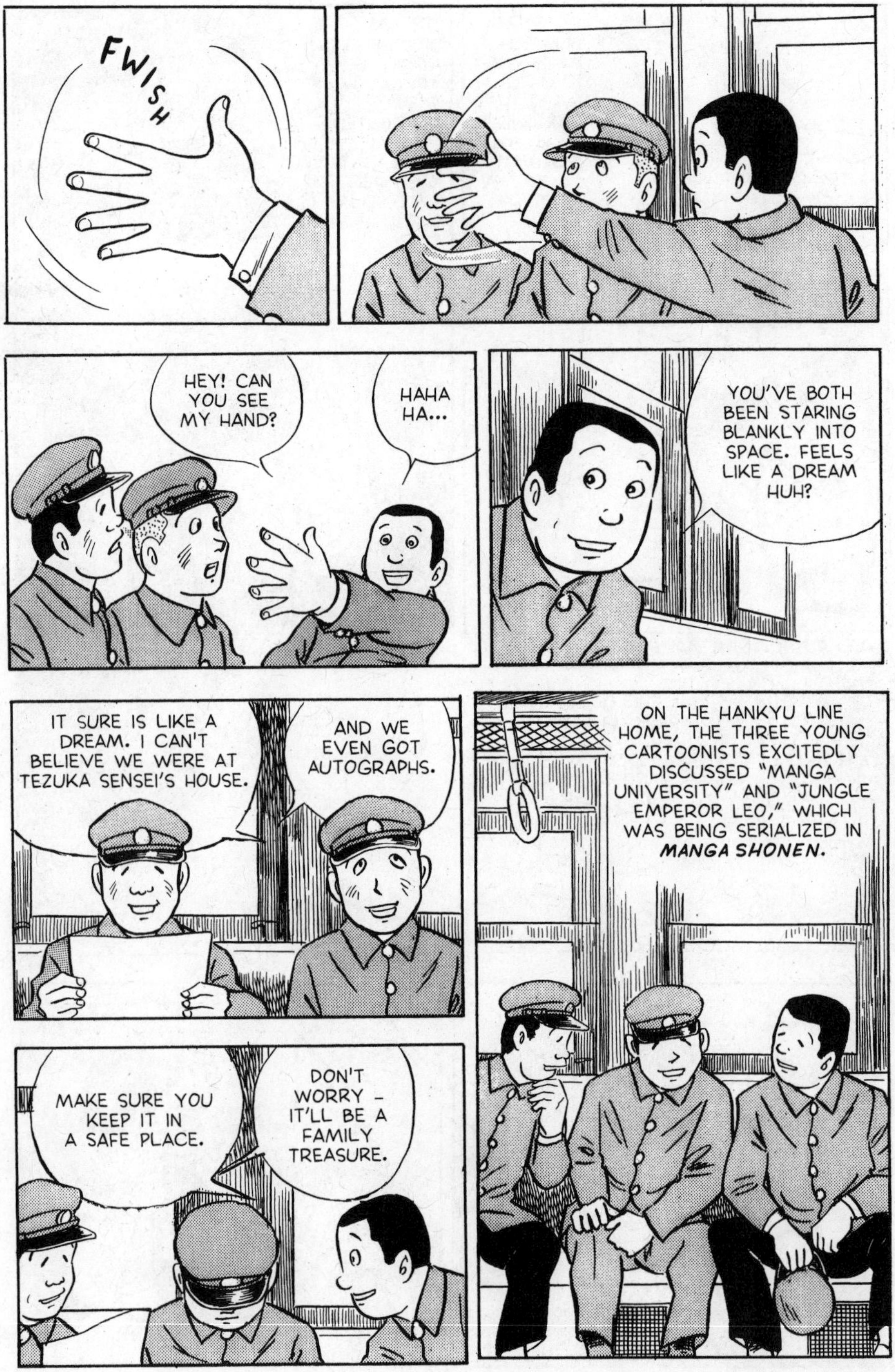
FWISH
HEY! CAN YOU SEE MY HAND?
HAHA HA...
YOU'VE BOTH BEEN STARING BLANKLY INTO SPACE. FEELS LIKE A DREAM HUH?
IT SURE IS LIKE A DREAM. I CAN'T BELIEVE WE WERE AT TEZUKA SENSEI'S HOUSE.
AND WE EVEN GOT AUTOGRAPHS.
MAKE SURE YOU KEEP IT IN A SAFE PLACE.
DON'T WORRY – IT'LL BE A FAMILY TREASURE.
ON THE HANKYU LINE HOME, THE THREE YOUNG CARTOONISTS EXCITEDLY DISCUSSED "MANGA UNIVERSITY" AND "JUNGLE EMPEROR LEO," WHICH WAS BEING SERIALIZED IN MANGA SHONEN.

TITLE: "FRIENDLY NEWSPAPER COMPANY"

YES! 23 PAGES OF "FRIENDLY NEWSPAPER COMPANY" ARE DONE!

COMBINED WITH "MANGA AQUARIUM" AND "A BOY AND HIS DREAM," I HAVE 79 PAGES.

ONE MORE AND I'LL HAVE 96 PAGES... ENOUGH FOR ONE BOOK.

DONE WELL, IT BECOMES A PROPER BOOK-LENGTH WORK.

HOW ABOUT IT, HIROSHI? WHY DON'T YOU GIVE IT A TRY?

AN "OMNIBUS"...

THE QUESTION IS, HOW TO CONNECT THE SHORTER PIECES...

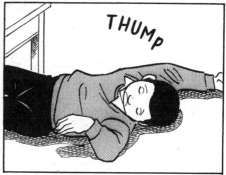

THUMP

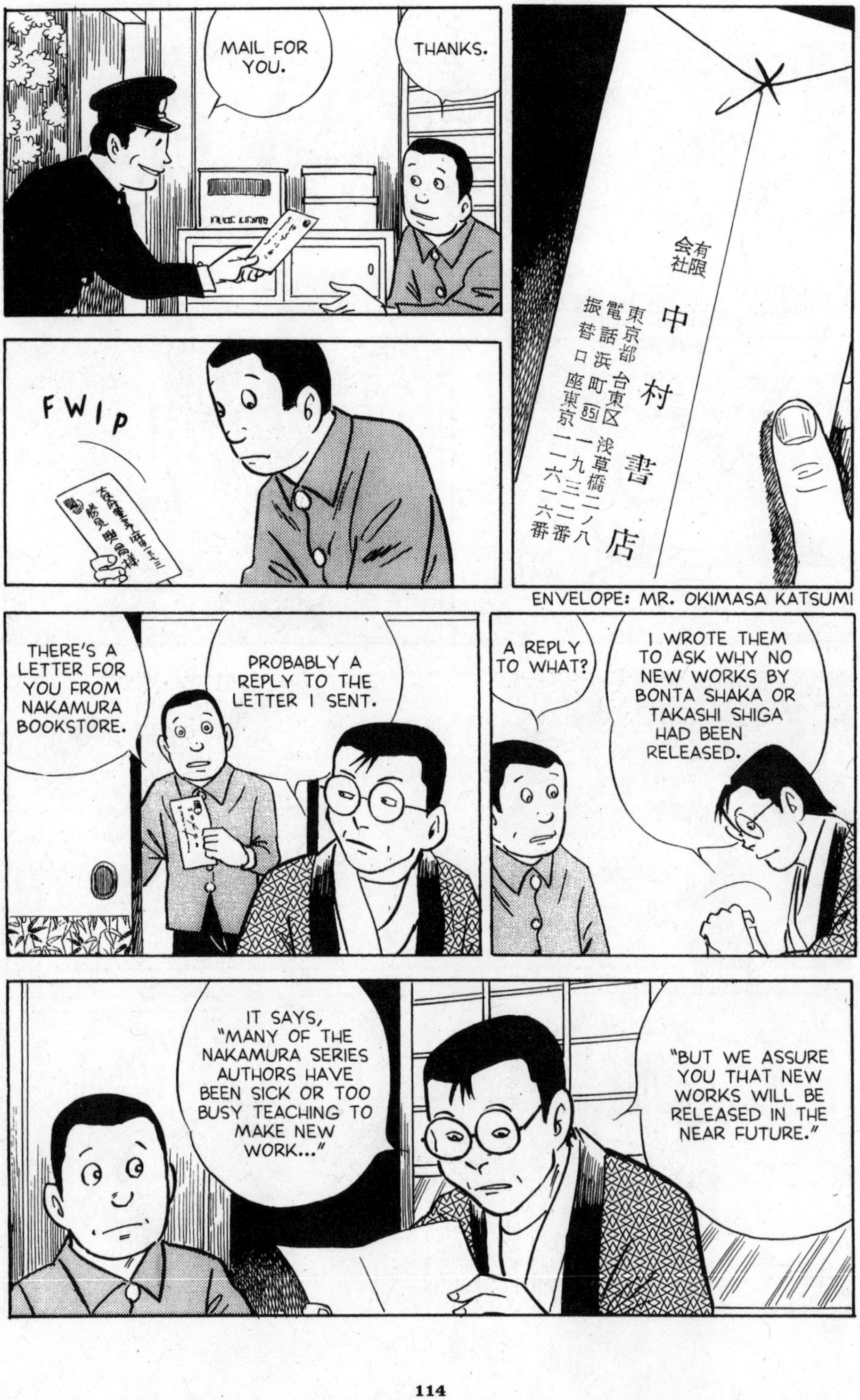
MAIL FOR YOU.
THANKS.
FWIP
ENVELOPE: MR. OKIMASA KATSUMI
有限会社
中村書店
東京都台東区浅草橋二ノ八
電話浜町(85)一九三二番
振替口座東京一一六一六番
THERE'S A LETTER FOR YOU FROM NAKAMURA BOOKSTORE.
PROBABLY A REPLY TO THE LETTER I SENT.
A REPLY TO WHAT?
I WROTE THEM TO ASK WHY NO NEW WORKS BY BONTA SHAKA OR TAKASHI SHIGA HAD BEEN RELEASED.
IT SAYS, "MANY OF THE NAKAMURA SERIES AUTHORS HAVE BEEN SICK OR TOO BUSY TEACHING TO MAKE NEW WORK..."
"BUT WE ASSURE YOU THAT NEW WORKS WILL BE RELEASED IN THE NEAR FUTURE."

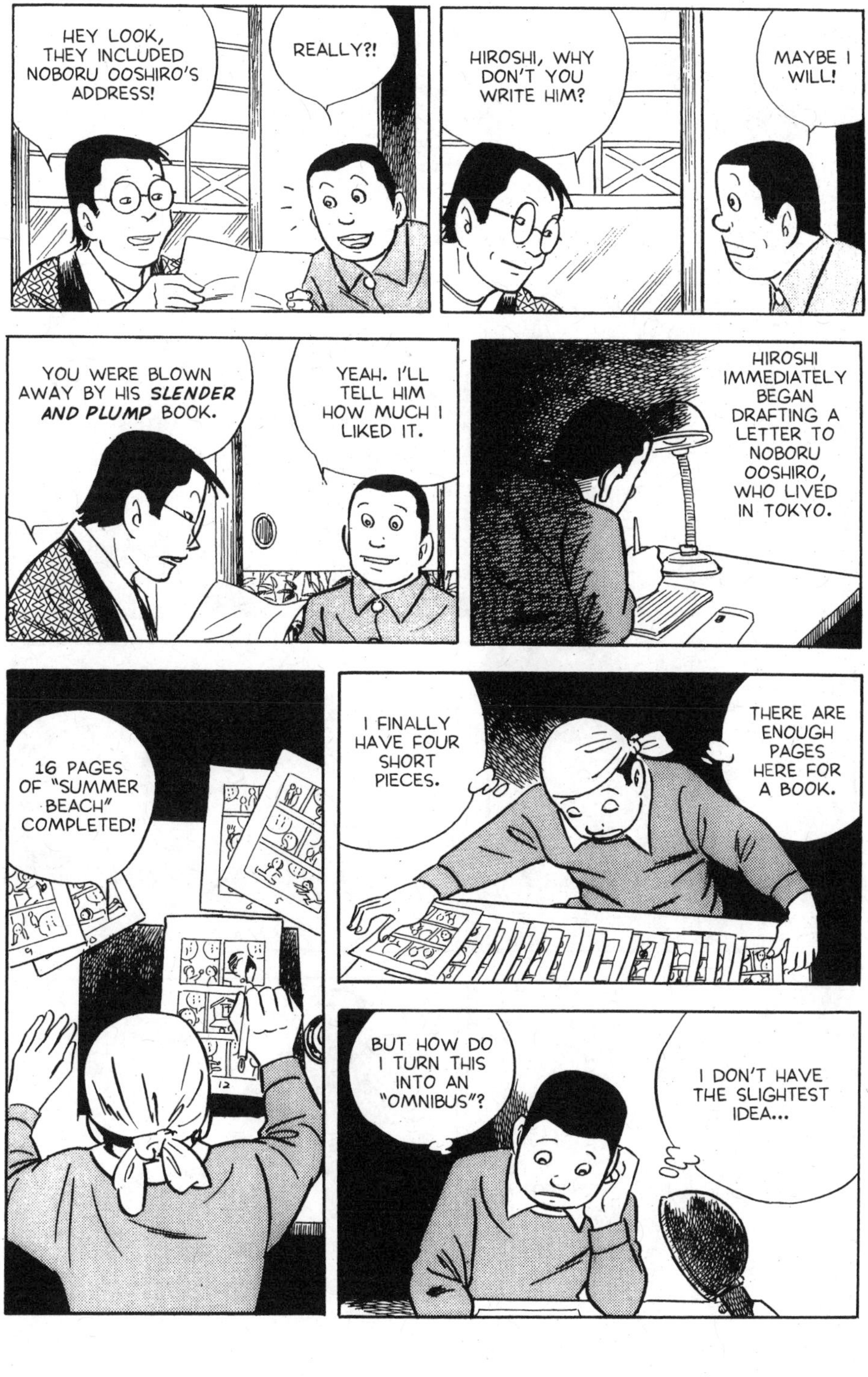
HEY LOOK, THEY INCLUDED NOBORU OOSHIRO'S ADDRESS!
REALLY?!
HIROSHI, WHY DON'T YOU WRITE HIM?
MAYBE I WILL!
YOU WERE BLOWN AWAY BY HIS **SLENDER AND PLUMP** BOOK.
YEAH. I'LL TELL HIM HOW MUCH I LIKED IT.
HIROSHI IMMEDIATELY BEGAN DRAFTING A LETTER TO NOBORU OOSHIRO, WHO LIVED IN TOKYO.
16 PAGES OF "SUMMER BEACH" COMPLETED!
I FINALLY HAVE FOUR SHORT PIECES.
THERE ARE ENOUGH PAGES HERE FOR A BOOK.
BUT HOW DO I TURN THIS INTO AN "OMNIBUS"?
I DON'T HAVE THE SLIGHTEST IDEA...

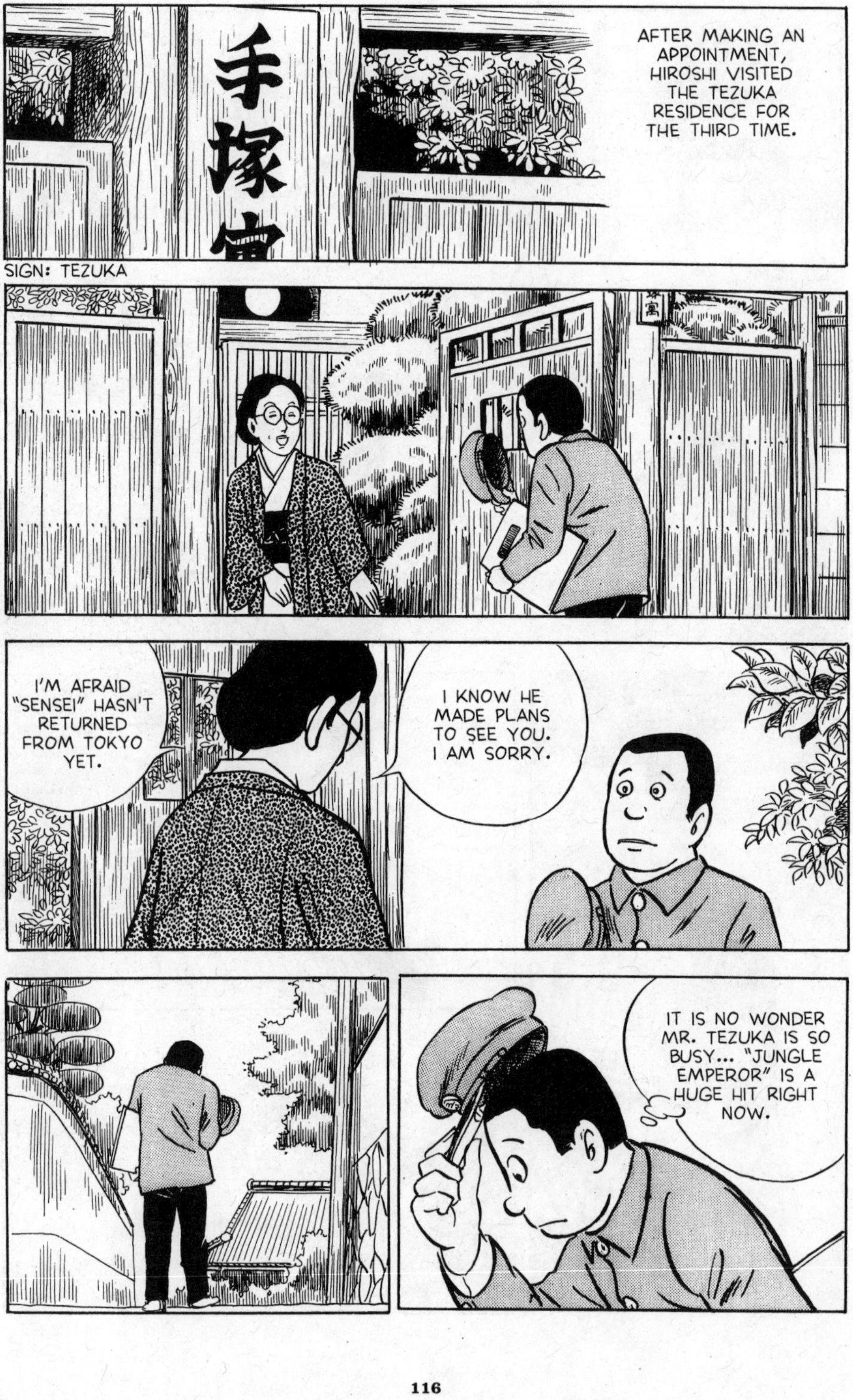

手塚
AFTER MAKING AN APPOINTMENT, HIROSHI VISITED THE TEZUKA RESIDENCE FOR THE THIRD TIME.
SIGN: TEZUKA
I'M AFRAID "SENSEI" HASN'T RETURNED FROM TOKYO YET.
I KNOW HE MADE PLANS TO SEE YOU. I AM SORRY.
IT IS NO WONDER MR. TEZUKA IS SO BUSY... "JUNGLE EMPEROR" IS A HUGE HIT RIGHT NOW.

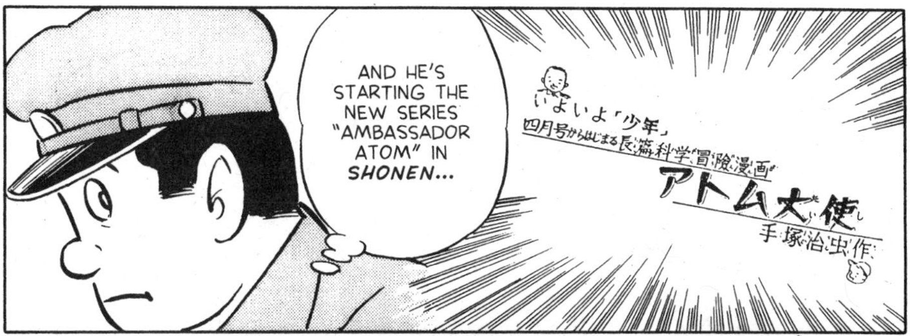
AND HE'S STARTING THE NEW SERIES "AMBASSADOR ATOM" IN **SHONEN...**
いよいよ「少年」
四月号からはじまる長篇科学冒険漫画
アトム大使
手塚治虫作

MAGAZINE TITLE: ***SHONEN,*** MARCH 1951 (KOBUNSHA)

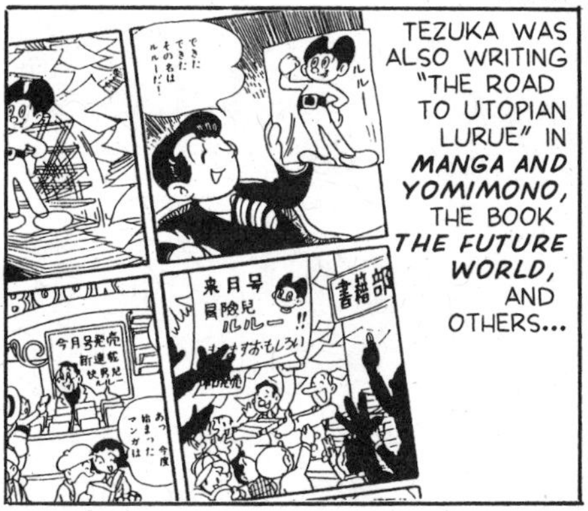
TEZUKA WAS ALSO WRITING "THE ROAD TO UTOPIAN LURUE" IN ***MANGA AND YOMIMONO,*** THE BOOK ***THE FUTURE WORLD,*** AND OTHERS...

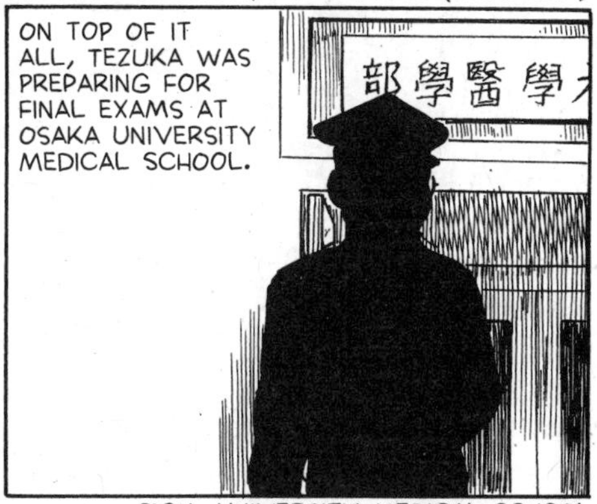
ON TOP OF IT ALL, TEZUKA WAS PREPARING FOR FINAL EXAMS AT OSAKA UNIVERSITY MEDICAL SCHOOL.

SIGN: UNIVERSITY MEDICAL SCHOOL

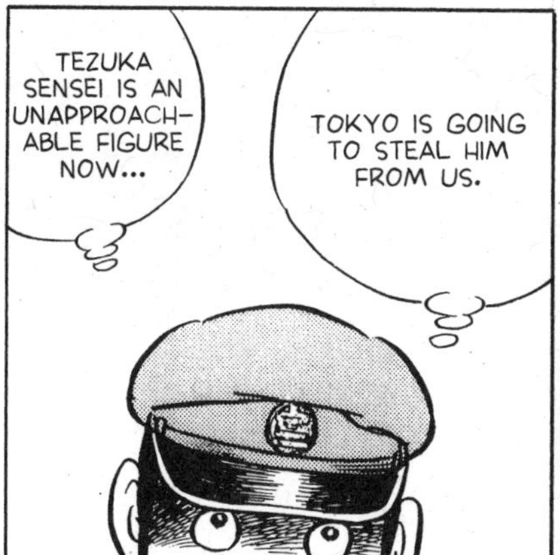
TEZUKA SENSEI IS AN UNAPPROACH-ABLE FIGURE NOW...
TOKYO IS GOING TO STEAL HIM FROM US.

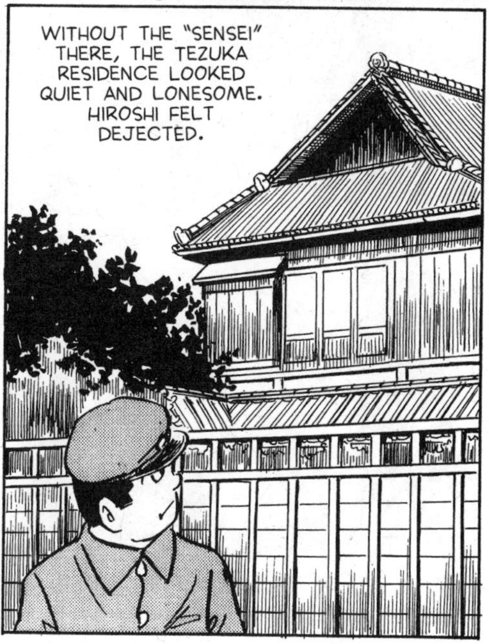
WITHOUT THE "SENSEI" THERE, THE TEZUKA RESIDENCE LOOKED QUIET AND LONESOME. HIROSHI FELT DEJECTED.

IN APRIL 1951,
HIROSHI WAS
ENROLLED
AT OSAKA
PREFECTURE
TOYONAKA
HIGH SCHOOL.

THERE WERE TWO
MAJOR EVENTS FOR THE
RECENTLY DEFEATED
JAPAN: ON APRIL 16,
GENERAL MACARTHUR
WAS REMOVED FROM
COMMAND AND LEFT
JAPAN. SOME 200,000
JAPANESE CITIZENS
FILLED THE ROAD TO
HANEDA AIRPORT TO SEE
THE FORMER GENERAL
OFF.

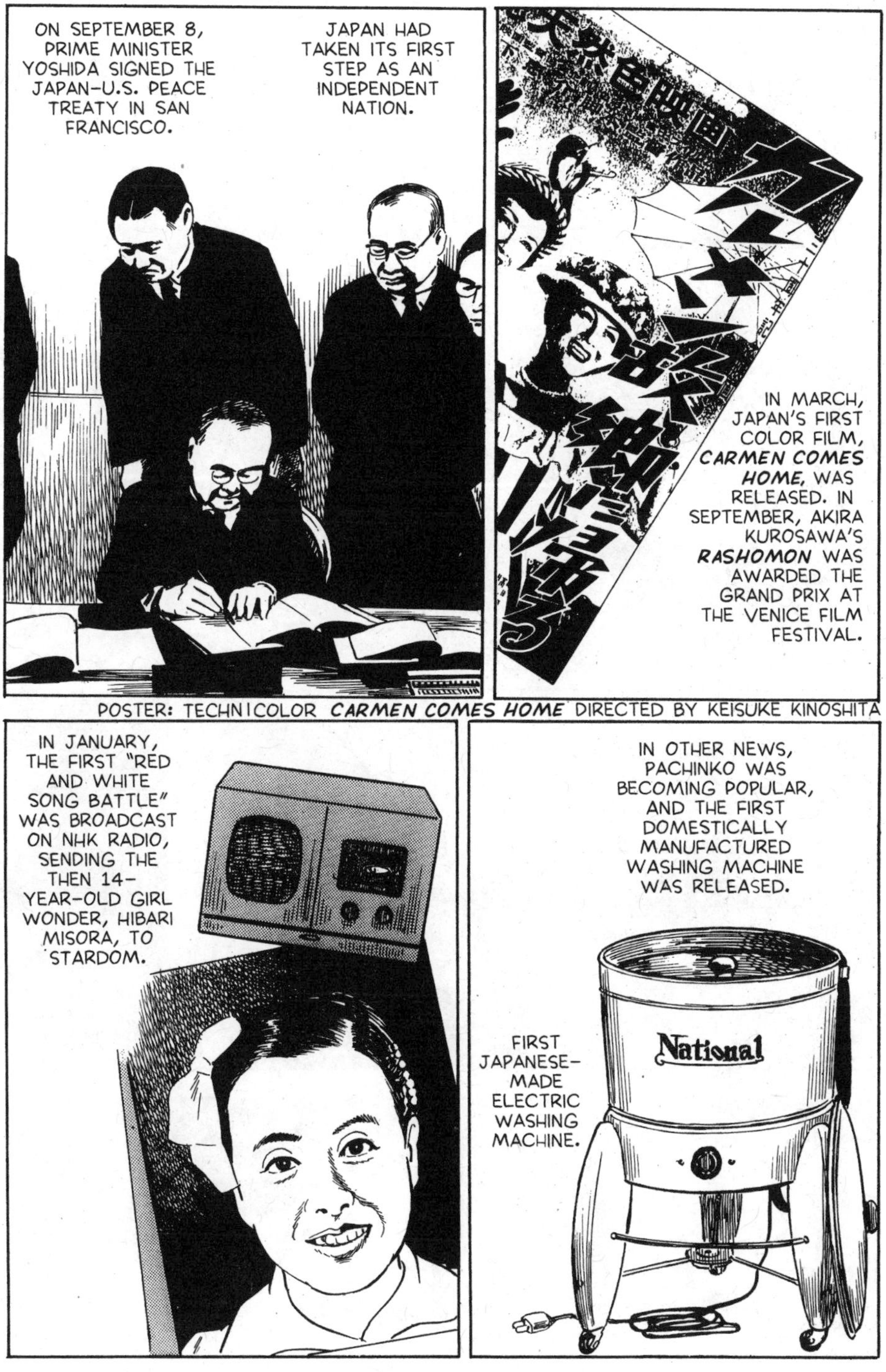
ON SEPTEMBER 8, PRIME MINISTER YOSHIDA SIGNED THE JAPAN-U.S. PEACE TREATY IN SAN FRANCISCO.
JAPAN HAD TAKEN ITS FIRST STEP AS AN INDEPENDENT NATION.
IN MARCH, JAPAN'S FIRST COLOR FILM, ***CARMEN COMES HOME,*** WAS RELEASED. IN SEPTEMBER, AKIRA KUROSAWA'S ***RASHOMON*** WAS AWARDED THE GRAND PRIX AT THE VENICE FILM FESTIVAL.
POSTER: TECHNICOLOR ***CARMEN COMES HOME*** DIRECTED BY KEISUKE KINOSHITA
IN JANUARY, THE FIRST "RED AND WHITE SONG BATTLE" WAS BROADCAST ON NHK RADIO, SENDING THE THEN 14-YEAR-OLD GIRL WONDER, HIBARI MISORA, TO STARDOM.
IN OTHER NEWS, PACHINKO WAS BECOMING POPULAR, AND THE FIRST DOMESTICALLY MANUFACTURED WASHING MACHINE WAS RELEASED.
FIRST JAPANESE-MADE ELECTRIC WASHING MACHINE.
National

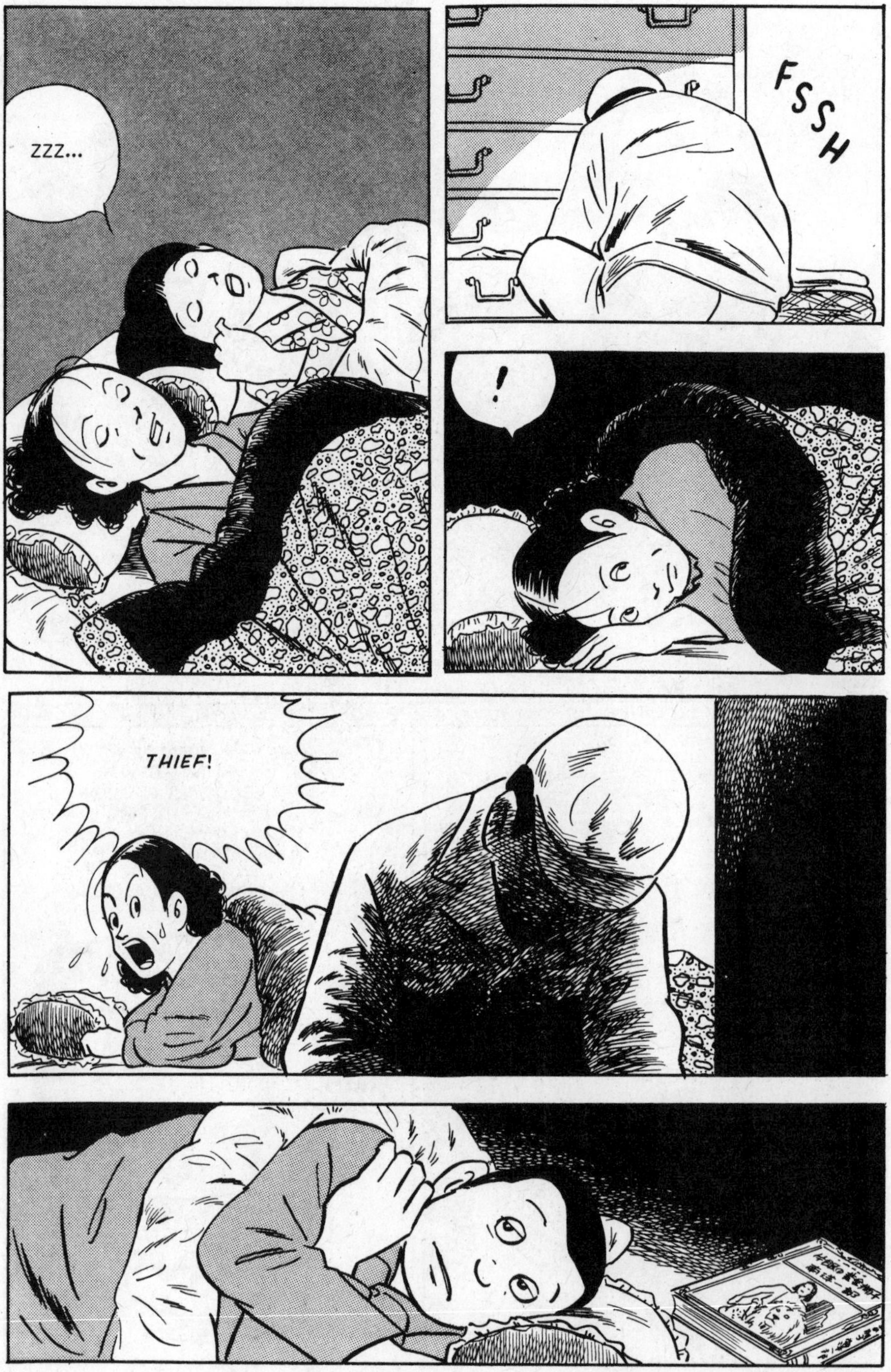
ZZZ...
FSSH
!
THIEF!

BOOK TITLE: ***THE ONE-EYED GOLDEN LION***, YOICHIRO MINAMI"

BELOVED MANGA

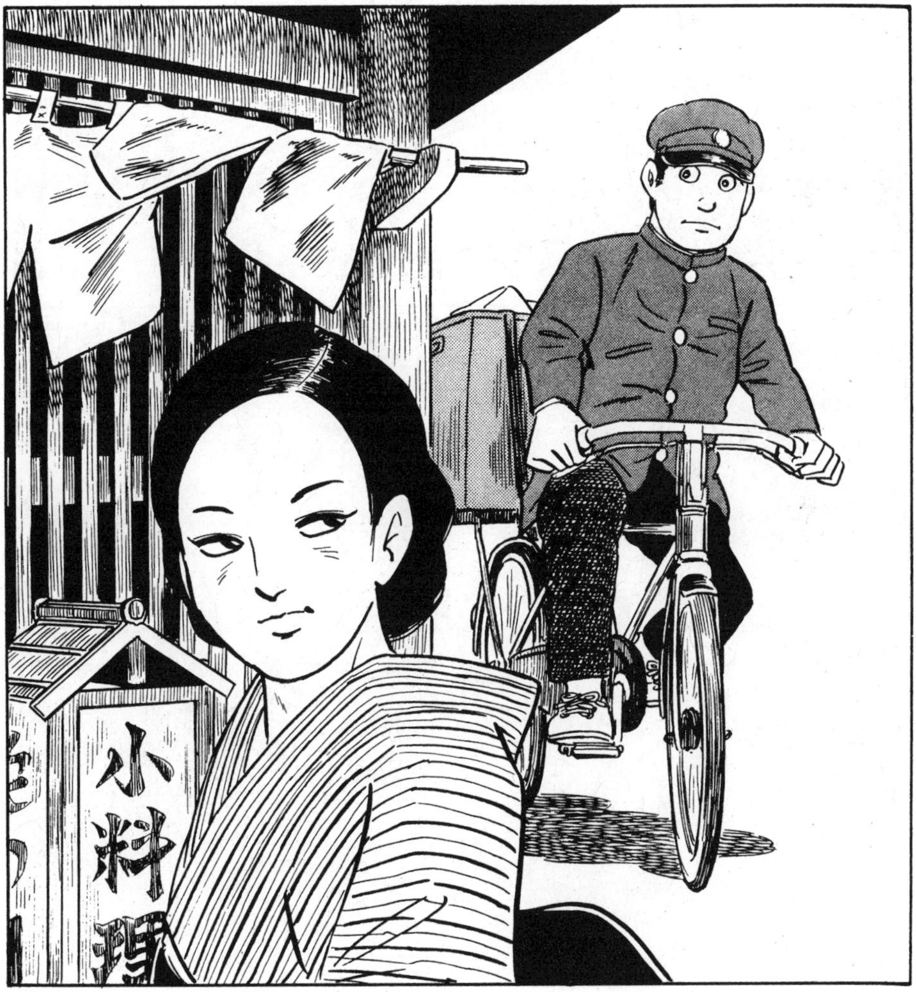
小料理

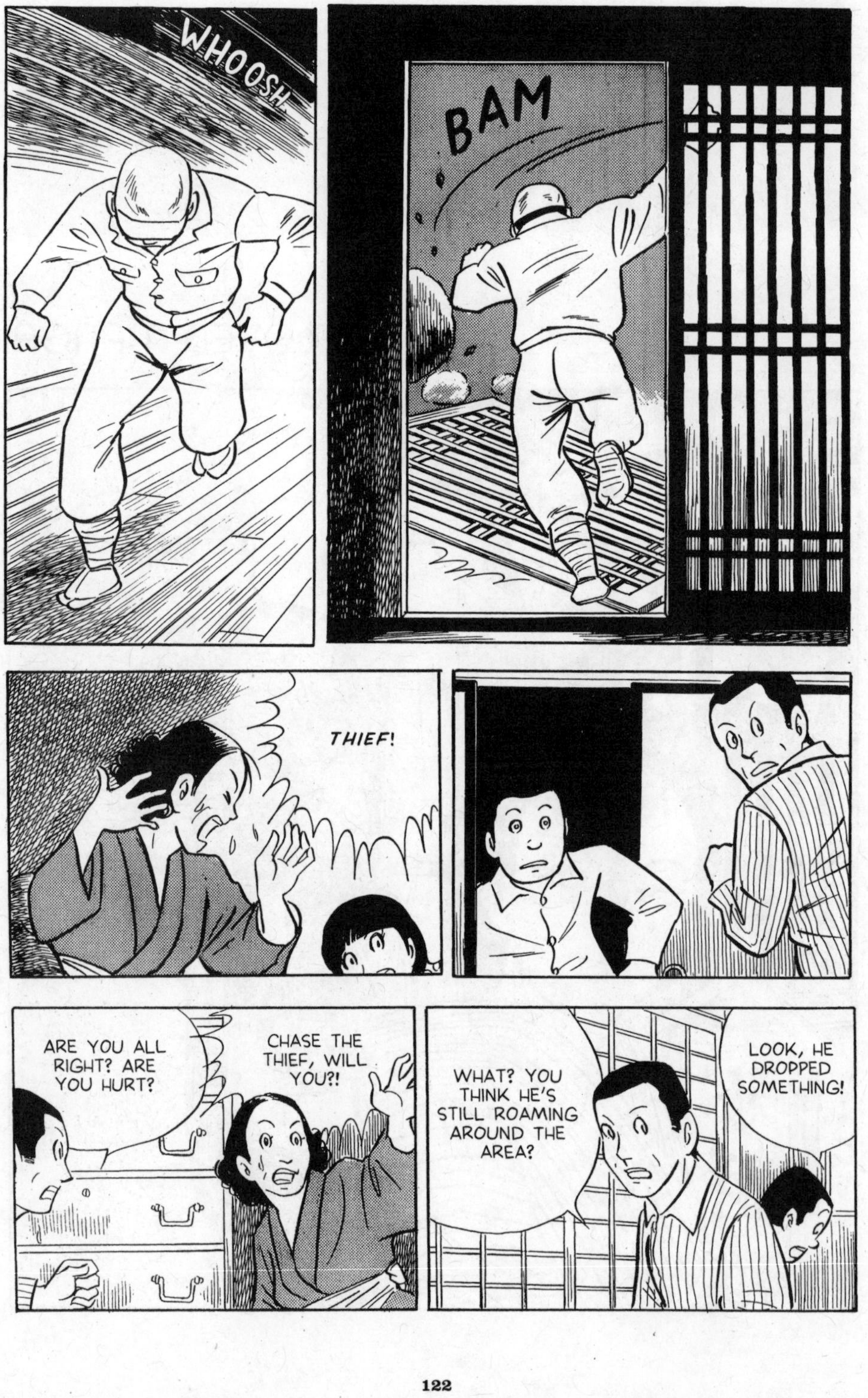
WHOOSH
BAM
THIEF!
ARE YOU ALL RIGHT? ARE YOU HURT?
CHASE THE THIEF, WILL YOU?!
WHAT? YOU THINK HE'S STILL ROAMING AROUND THE AREA?
LOOK, HE DROPPED SOMETHING!

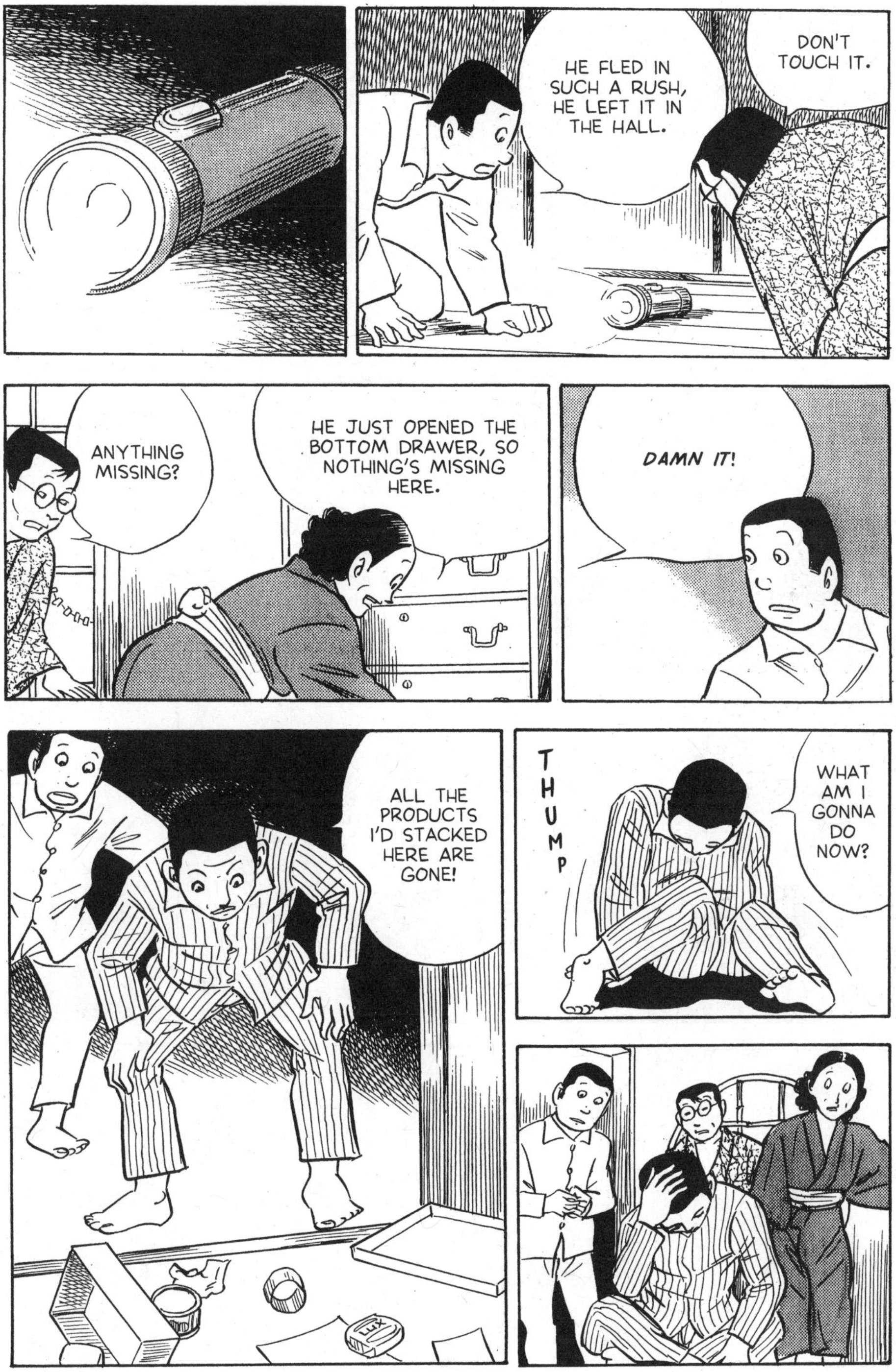
HE FLED IN SUCH A RUSH, HE LEFT IT IN THE HALL.
DON'T TOUCH IT.
ANYTHING MISSING?
HE JUST OPENED THE BOTTOM DRAWER, SO NOTHING'S MISSING HERE.
DAMN IT!
ALL THE PRODUCTS I'D STACKED HERE ARE GONE!
THUMP
WHAT AM I GONNA DO NOW?
LUX

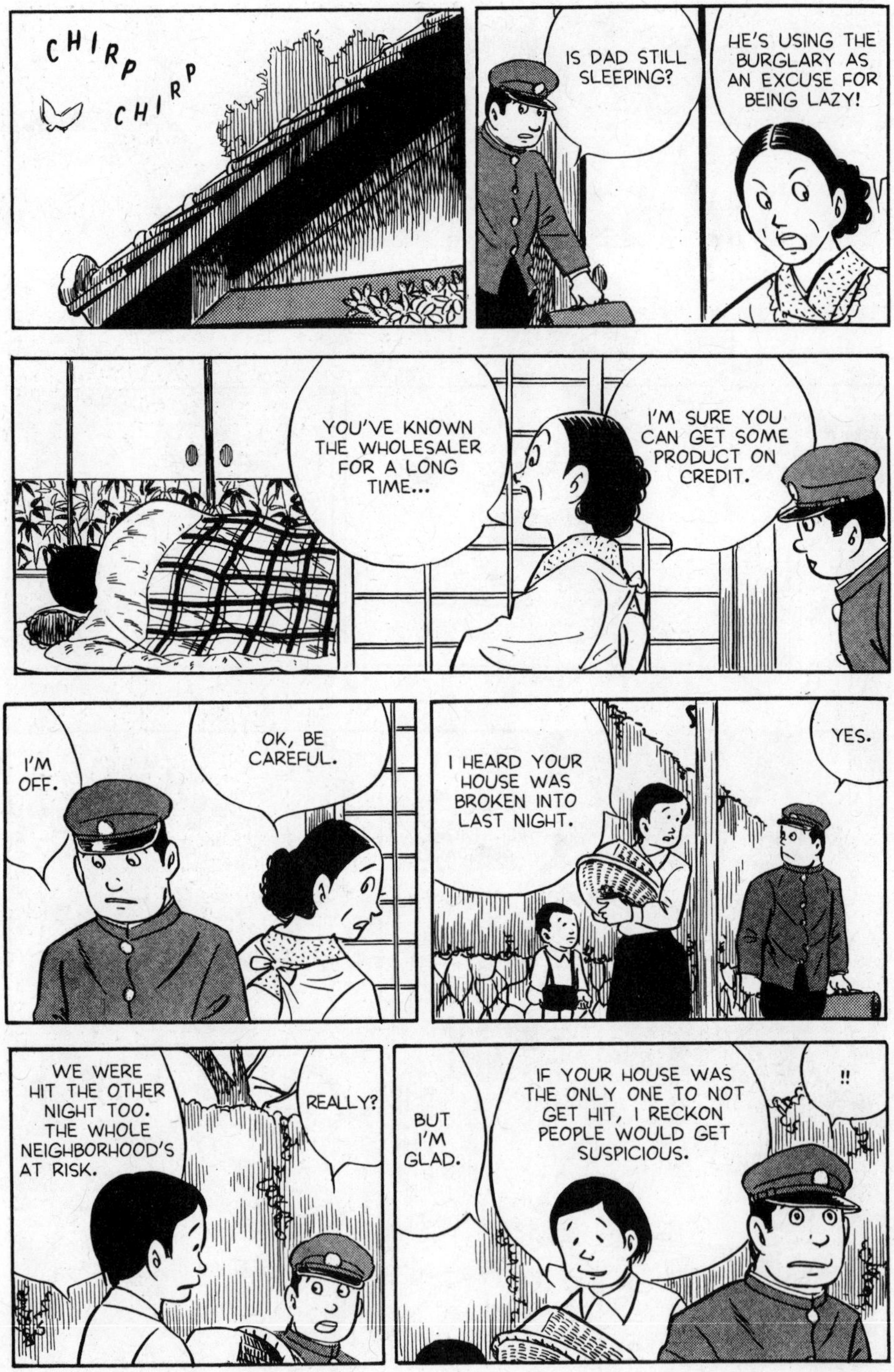
CHIRP
CHIRP
IS DAD STILL SLEEPING?
HE'S USING THE BURGLARY AS AN EXCUSE FOR BEING LAZY!
YOU'VE KNOWN THE WHOLESALER FOR A LONG TIME...
I'M SURE YOU CAN GET SOME PRODUCT ON CREDIT.
I'M OFF.
OK, BE CAREFUL.
I HEARD YOUR HOUSE WAS BROKEN INTO LAST NIGHT.
YES.
WE WERE HIT THE OTHER NIGHT TOO. THE WHOLE NEIGHBORHOOD'S AT RISK.
REALLY?
BUT I'M GLAD.
IF YOUR HOUSE WAS THE ONLY ONE TO NOT GET HIT, I RECKON PEOPLE WOULD GET SUSPICIOUS.
!!

HIROSHI'S FATHER CHANGED AFTER THE BURGLARY.

IT TOOK SOME TIME BEFORE HE RECOVERED AND STARTED WORKING AGAIN.

RING

ANYONE HOME?

I HAVE REGIS- TERED MAIL!

REGISTERED MAIL FOR YOU!

HERE YOU ARE... A LETTER AND TWO CASH ENVELOPES.

勝見様方
豊中市麻田一、三七三
勝見
上三平殿
現金書留
井上三平様

ENVELOPES: TO SANPEI INOUE C/O MR. KATSUMI 1-37-3 ASADA, TOYONAKA-SHI

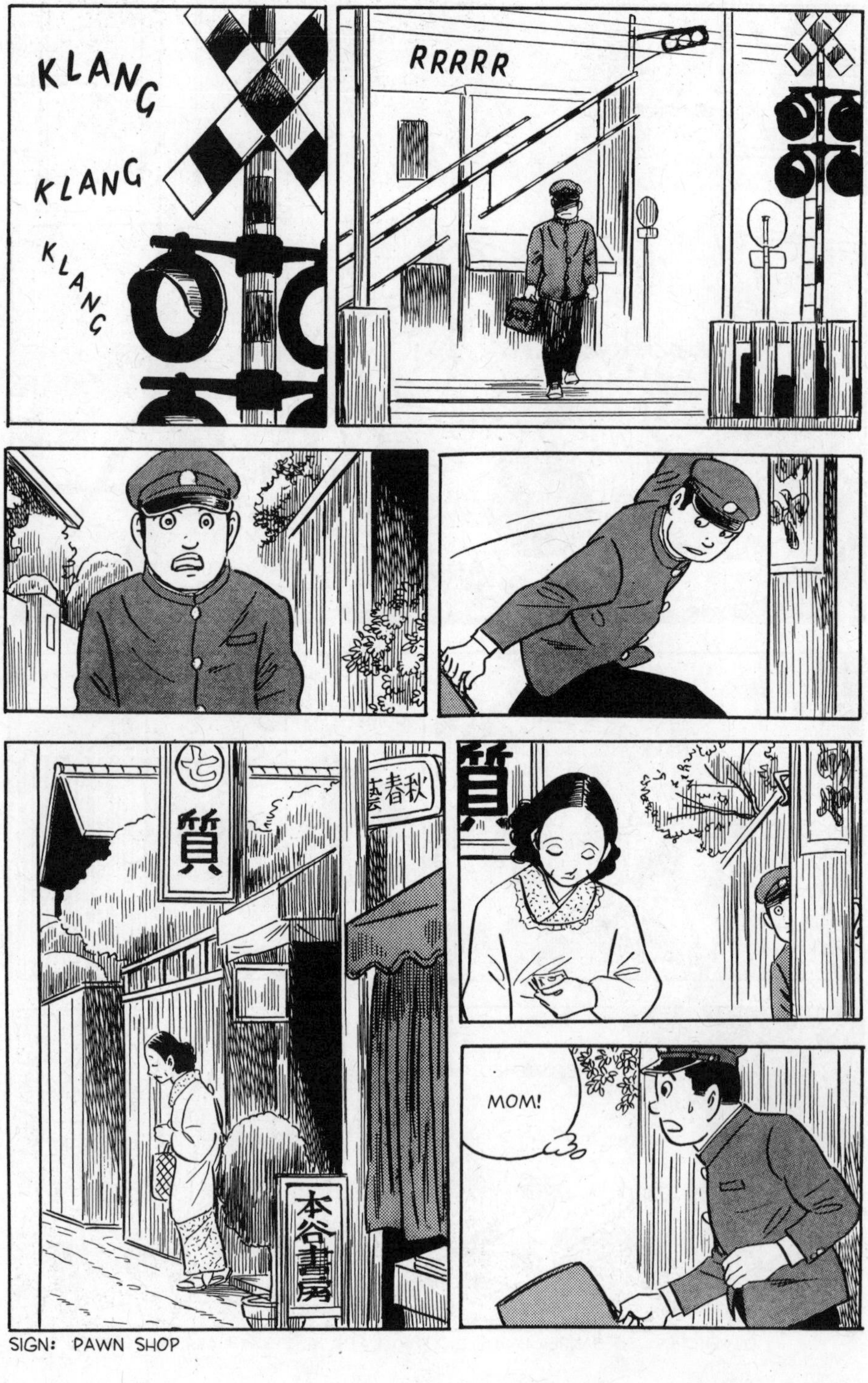
KLANG
KLANG
KLANG
RRRRR
質
本谷書房
質
MOM!
SIGN: PAWN SHOP

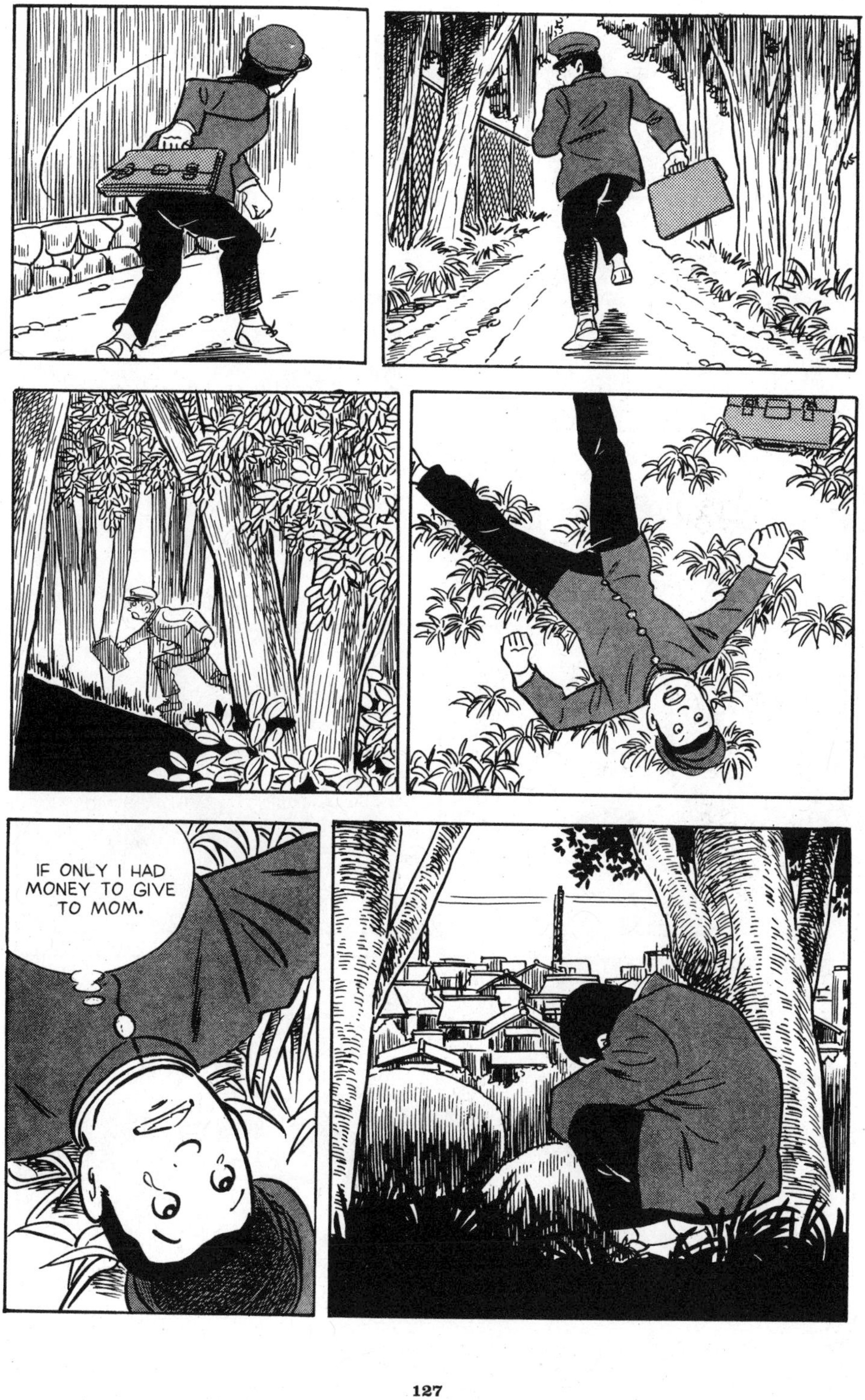
IF ONLY I HAD MONEY TO GIVE TO MOM.

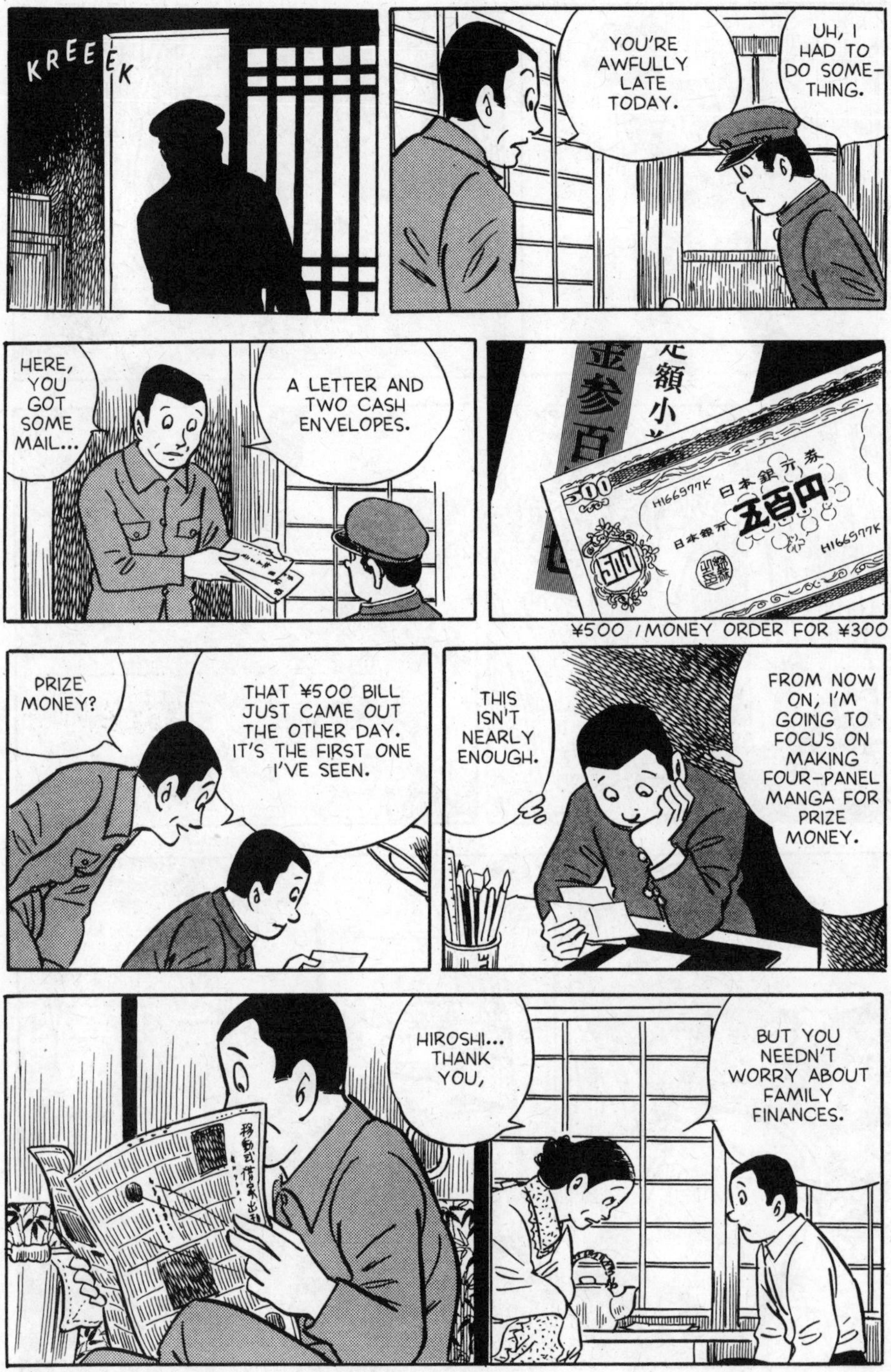
KREEEK
YOU'RE AWFULLY LATE TODAY.
UH, I HAD TO DO SOME-THING.
HERE, YOU GOT SOME MAIL...
A LETTER AND TWO CASH ENVELOPES.
五百円
¥500 / MONEY ORDER FOR ¥300
PRIZE MONEY?
THAT ¥500 BILL JUST CAME OUT THE OTHER DAY. IT'S THE FIRST ONE I'VE SEEN.
THIS ISN'T NEARLY ENOUGH.
FROM NOW ON, I'M GOING TO FOCUS ON MAKING FOUR-PANEL MANGA FOR PRIZE MONEY.
HIROSHI... THANK YOU,
BUT YOU NEEDN'T WORRY ABOUT FAMILY FINANCES.

HIROSHI SET HIMSELF A QUOTA OF TWO POSTCARD MANGA PER DAY AND SUBMITTED THEM TO MAGAZINES TARGETING ADULTS.

THE OMNIBUS WORK SUGGESTED BY OSAMU TEZUKA HAD BEEN PUT ON HOLD AFTER FOUR SHORT PIECES WERE COMPLETED.

HIROSHI WOULD SEND IN A POSTCARD, AND IT WOULD COME BACK AS CASH.

LITTLE BY LITTLE, HIROSHI WAS LOSING HIS DRIVE TO CREATE A FULL-LENGTH WORK.

I GOT A RESPONSE FROM NOBORU OOSHIRO!

WOW, REALLY?

LOOK AT THE PENMANSHIP: WRITTEN WITH A BRUSH ON ROLLED PAPER.

ENVELOPE: NOBORU OOSHIRO / HIGASHINAKANO

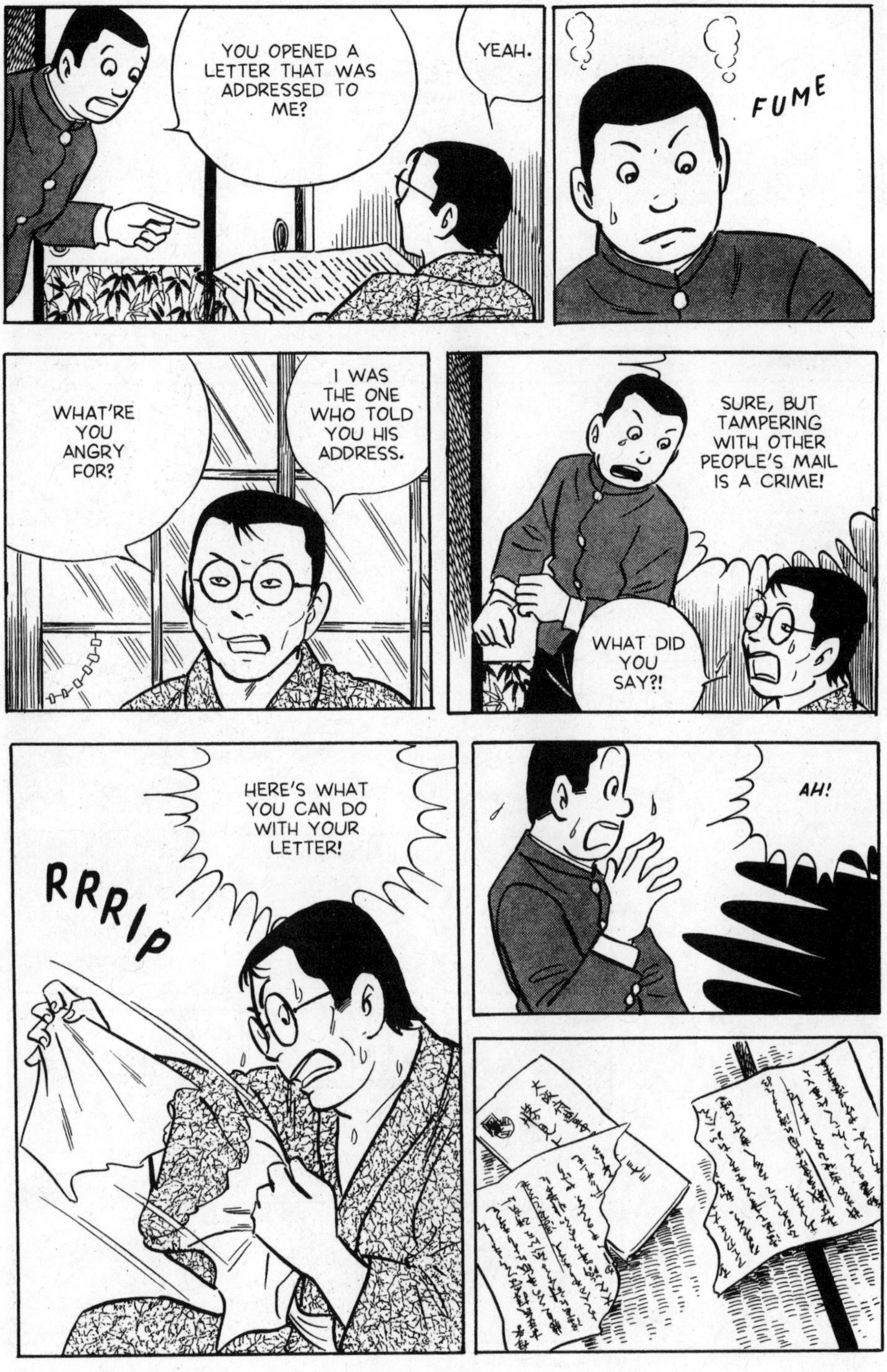
YOU OPENED A LETTER THAT WAS ADDRESSED TO ME?
YEAH.
FUME
WHAT'RE YOU ANGRY FOR?
I WAS THE ONE WHO TOLD YOU HIS ADDRESS.
SURE, BUT TAMPERING WITH OTHER PEOPLE'S MAIL IS A CRIME!
WHAT DID YOU SAY?!
HERE'S WHAT YOU CAN DO WITH YOUR LETTER!
RRRIP
AH!

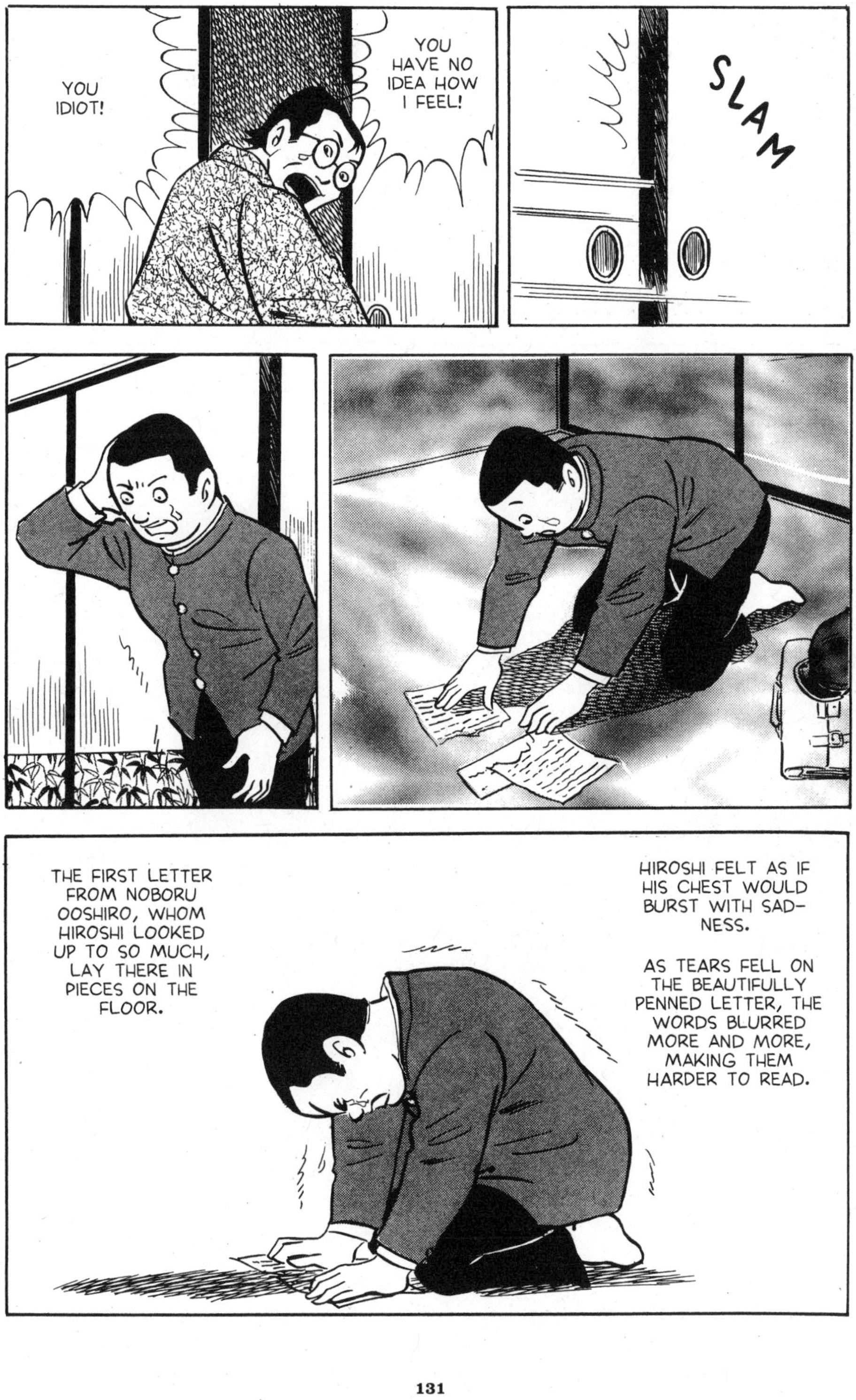
YOU IDIOT!
YOU HAVE NO IDEA HOW I FEEL!
SLAM
THE FIRST LETTER FROM NOBORU OOSHIRO, WHOM HIROSHI LOOKED UP TO SO MUCH, LAY THERE IN PIECES ON THE FLOOR.
HIROSHI FELT AS IF HIS CHEST WOULD BURST WITH SAD-NESS.
AS TEARS FELL ON THE BEAUTIFULLY PENNED LETTER, THE WORDS BLURRED MORE AND MORE, MAKING THEM HARDER TO READ.

IN THE LETTER, OOSHIRO HAD FRANKLY EXPRESSED HIS GENUINE VIEWS REGARDING MANGA.

THAT NIGHT, HIROSHI COULD NOT MOTIVATE HIMSELF TO FILL HIS QUOTA OF COMICS...

INSTEAD HE REREAD THE OOSHIRO WORKS IN HIS COLLECTION.

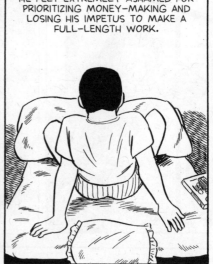

HE FELT EXTREMELY ASHAMED FOR PRIORITIZING MONEY-MAKING AND LOSING HIS IMPETUS TO MAKE A FULL-LENGTH WORK.

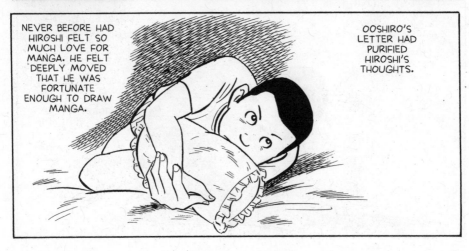

NEVER BEFORE HAD HIROSHI FELT SO MUCH LOVE FOR MANGA. HE FELT DEEPLY MOVED THAT HE WAS FORTUNATE ENOUGH TO DRAW MANGA.

OOSHIRO'S LETTER HAD PURIFIED HIROSHI'S THOUGHTS.

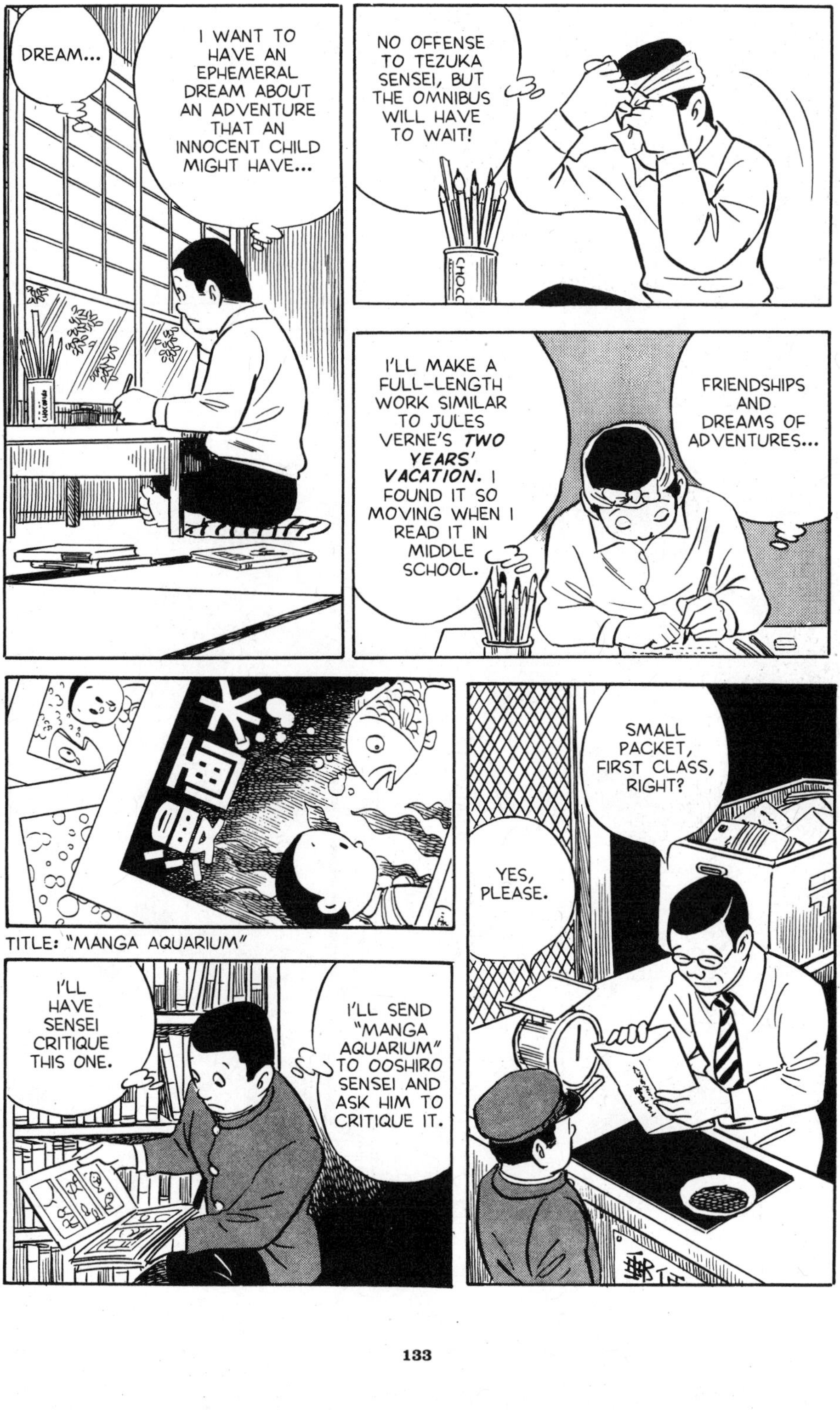
DREAM...
I WANT TO HAVE AN EPHEMERAL DREAM ABOUT AN ADVENTURE THAT AN INNOCENT CHILD MIGHT HAVE...
NO OFFENSE TO TEZUKA SENSEI, BUT THE OMNIBUS WILL HAVE TO WAIT!
I'LL MAKE A FULL-LENGTH WORK SIMILAR TO JULES VERNE'S ***TWO YEARS' VACATION.*** I FOUND IT SO MOVING WHEN I READ IT IN MIDDLE SCHOOL.
FRIENDSHIPS AND DREAMS OF ADVENTURES...
TITLE: "MANGA AQUARIUM"
I'LL HAVE SENSEI CRITIQUE THIS ONE.
I'LL SEND "MANGA AQUARIUM" TO OOSHIRO SENSEI AND ASK HIM TO CRITIQUE IT.
SMALL PACKET, FIRST CLASS, RIGHT?
YES, PLEASE.

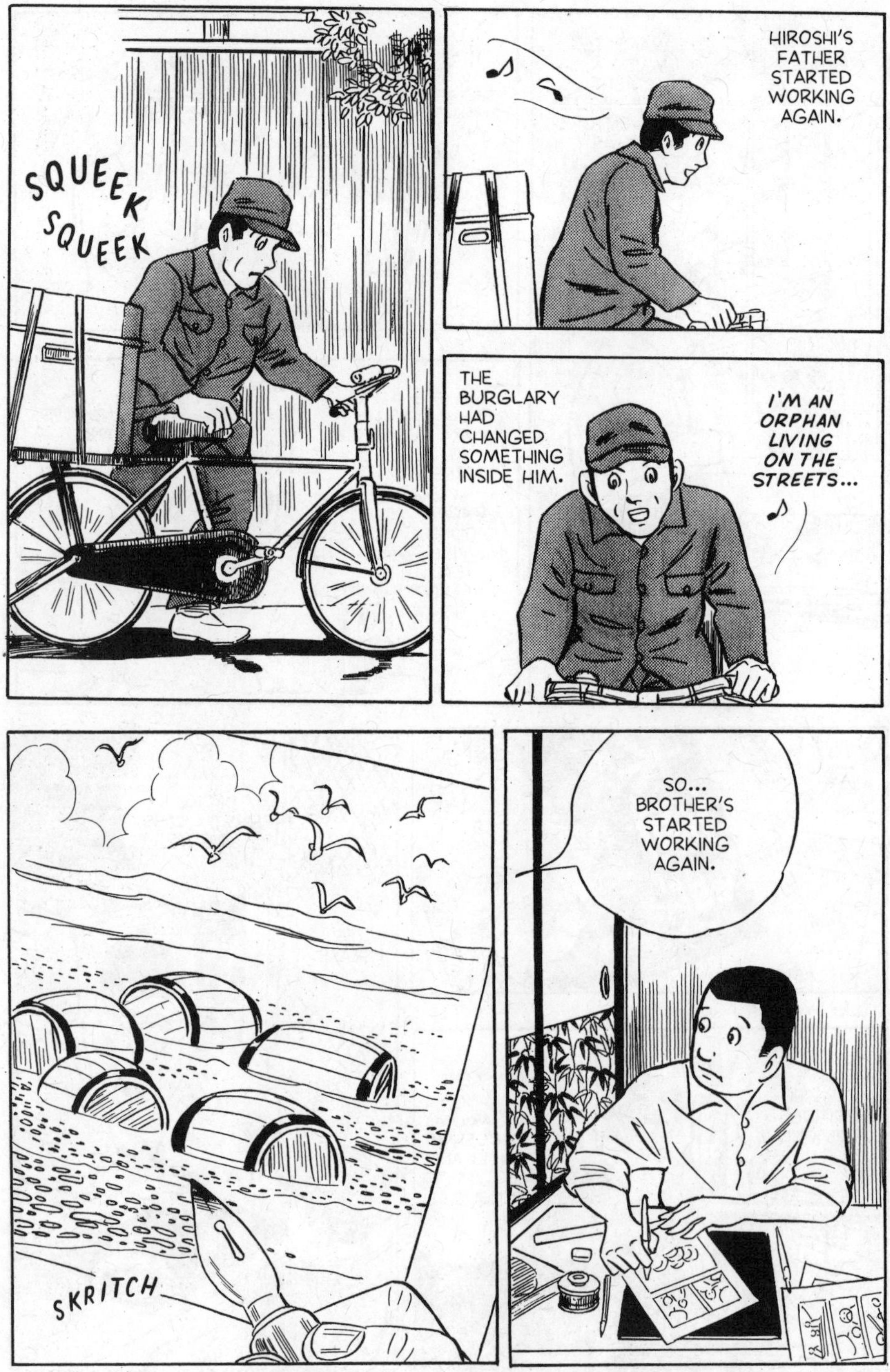
SQUEEK
SQUEEK
HIROSHI'S FATHER STARTED WORKING AGAIN.
THE BURGLARY HAD CHANGED SOMETHING INSIDE HIM.
I'M AN ORPHAN LIVING ON THE STREETS...
SKRITCH
SO... BROTHER'S STARTED WORKING AGAIN.

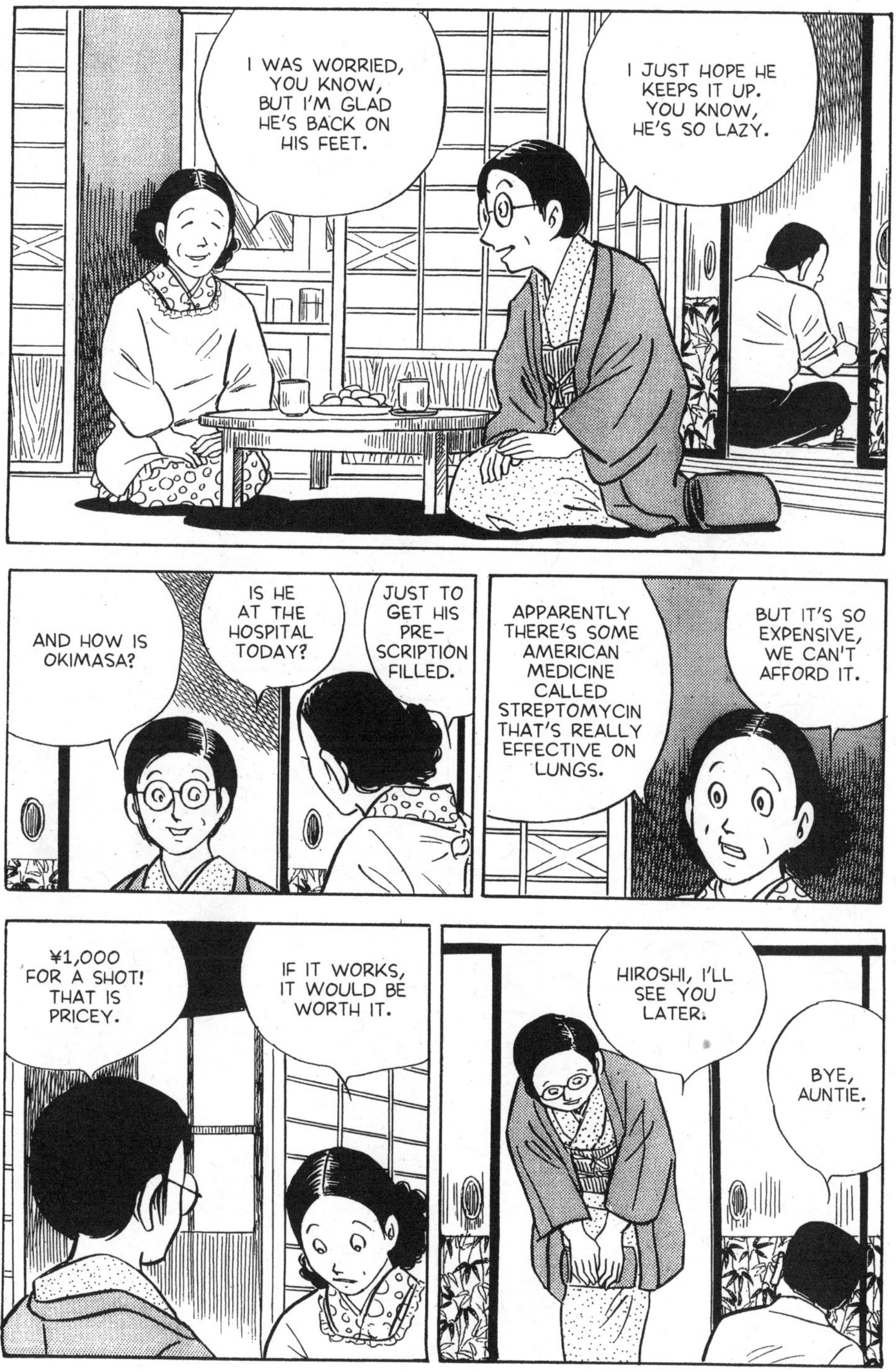
I WAS WORRIED, YOU KNOW, BUT I'M GLAD HE'S BACK ON HIS FEET.
I JUST HOPE HE KEEPS IT UP. YOU KNOW, HE'S SO LAZY.
AND HOW IS OKIMASA?
IS HE AT THE HOSPITAL TODAY?
JUST TO GET HIS PRE-SCRIPTION FILLED.
APPARENTLY THERE'S SOME AMERICAN MEDICINE CALLED STREPTOMYCIN THAT'S REALLY EFFECTIVE ON LUNGS.
BUT IT'S SO EXPENSIVE, WE CAN'T AFFORD IT.
¥1,000 FOR A SHOT! THAT IS PRICEY.
IF IT WORKS, IT WOULD BE WORTH IT.
HIROSHI, I'LL SEE YOU LATER.
BYE, AUNTIE.

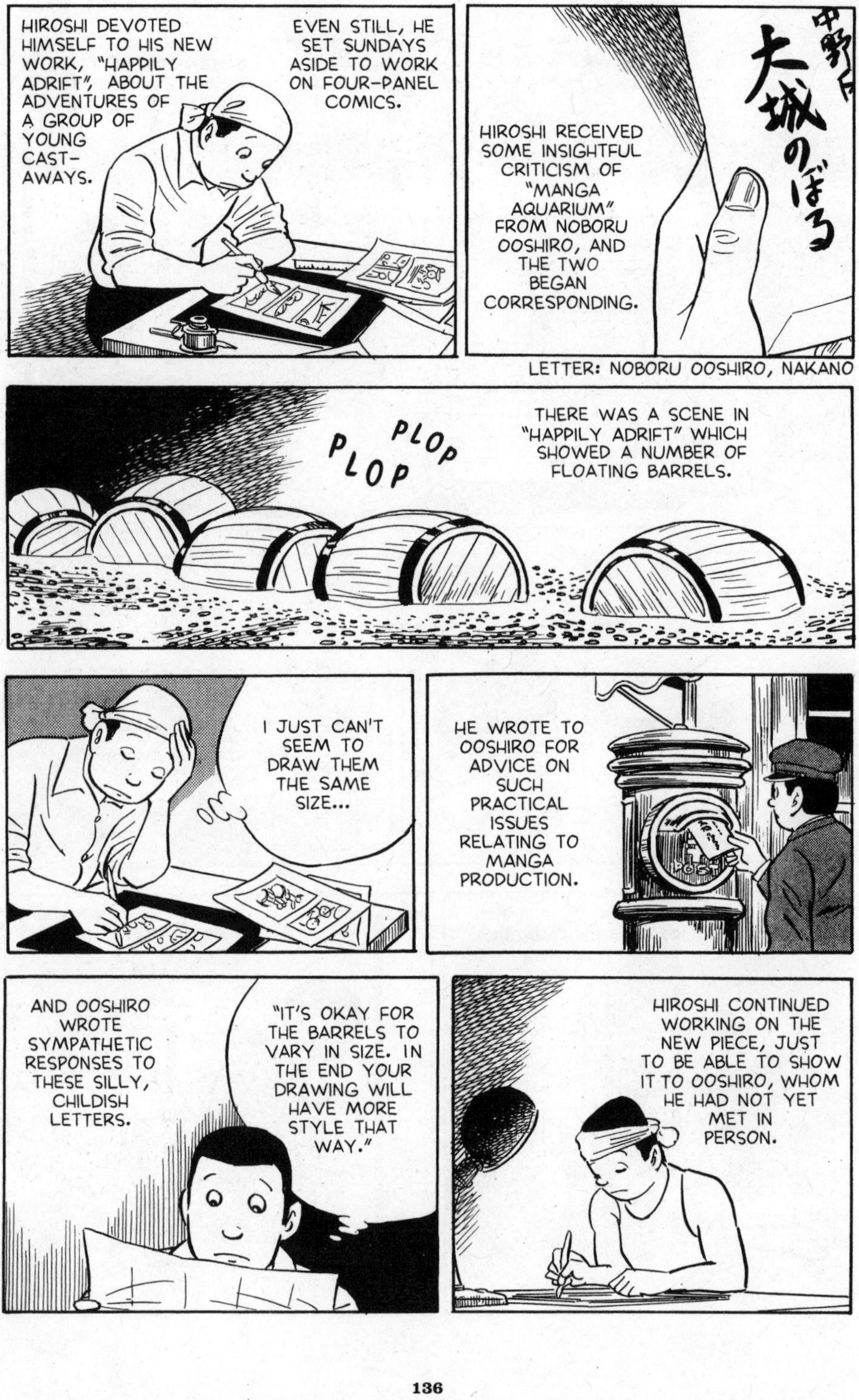
HIROSHI DEVOTED HIMSELF TO HIS NEW WORK, "HAPPILY ADRIFT", ABOUT THE ADVENTURES OF A GROUP OF YOUNG CAST-AWAYS.
EVEN STILL, HE SET SUNDAYS ASIDE TO WORK ON FOUR-PANEL COMICS.
大城のぼる
HIROSHI RECEIVED SOME INSIGHTFUL CRITICISM OF "MANGA AQUARIUM" FROM NOBORU OOSHIRO, AND THE TWO BEGAN CORRESPONDING.
LETTER: NOBORU OOSHIRO, NAKANO
PLOP PLOP
THERE WAS A SCENE IN "HAPPILY ADRIFT" WHICH SHOWED A NUMBER OF FLOATING BARRELS.
I JUST CAN'T SEEM TO DRAW THEM THE SAME SIZE...
HE WROTE TO OOSHIRO FOR ADVICE ON SUCH PRACTICAL ISSUES RELATING TO MANGA PRODUCTION.
AND OOSHIRO WROTE SYMPATHETIC RESPONSES TO THESE SILLY, CHILDISH LETTERS.
"IT'S OKAY FOR THE BARRELS TO VARY IN SIZE. IN THE END YOUR DRAWING WILL HAVE MORE STYLE THAT WAY."
HIROSHI CONTINUED WORKING ON THE NEW PIECE, JUST TO BE ABLE TO SHOW IT TO OOSHIRO, WHOM HE HAD NOT YET MET IN PERSON.

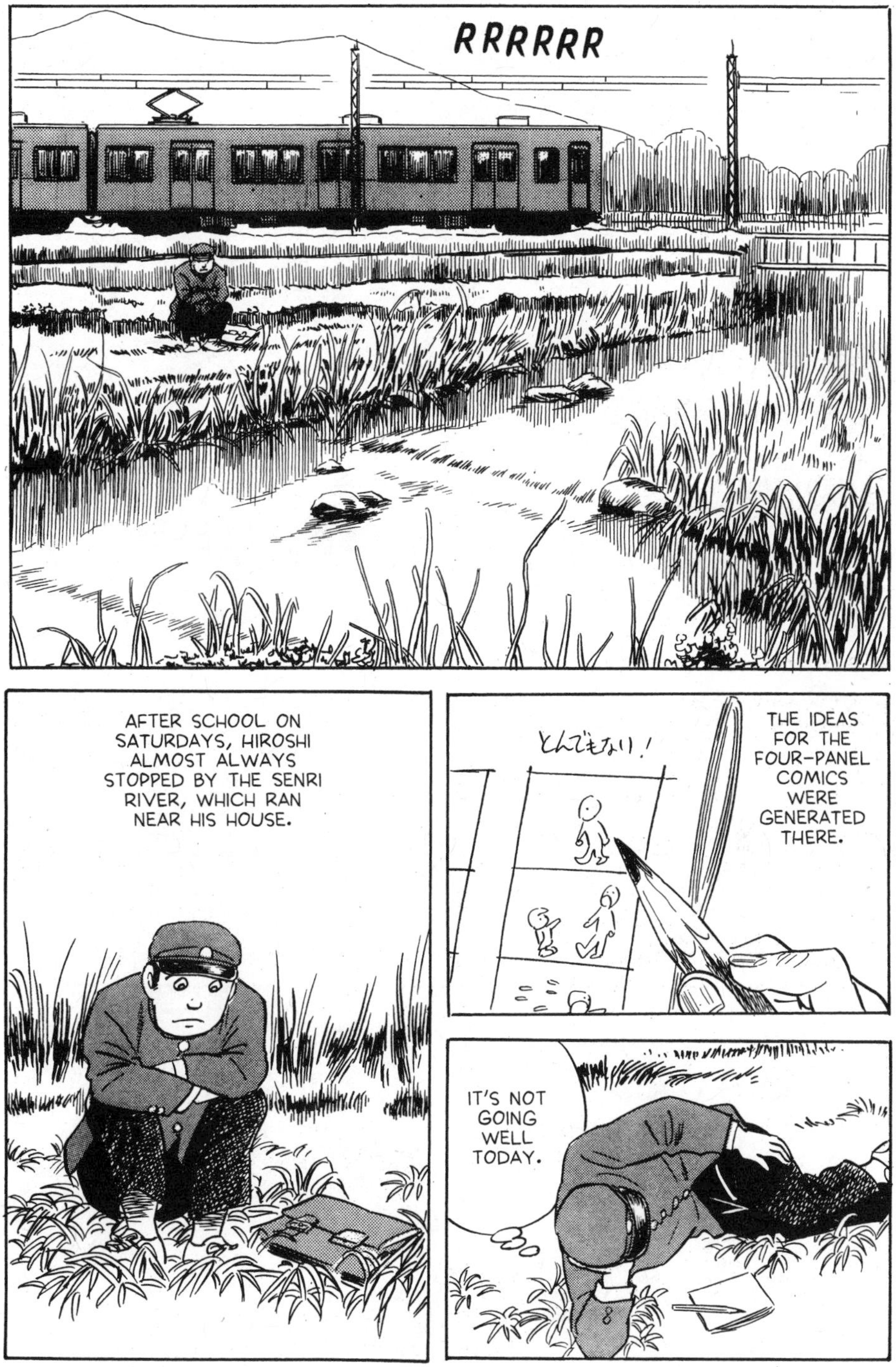
RRRRRR
AFTER SCHOOL ON SATURDAYS, HIROSHI ALMOST ALWAYS STOPPED BY THE SENRI RIVER, WHICH RAN NEAR HIS HOUSE.
とんでもなり！
THE IDEAS FOR THE FOUR-PANEL COMICS WERE GENERATED THERE.
IT'S NOT GOING WELL TODAY.

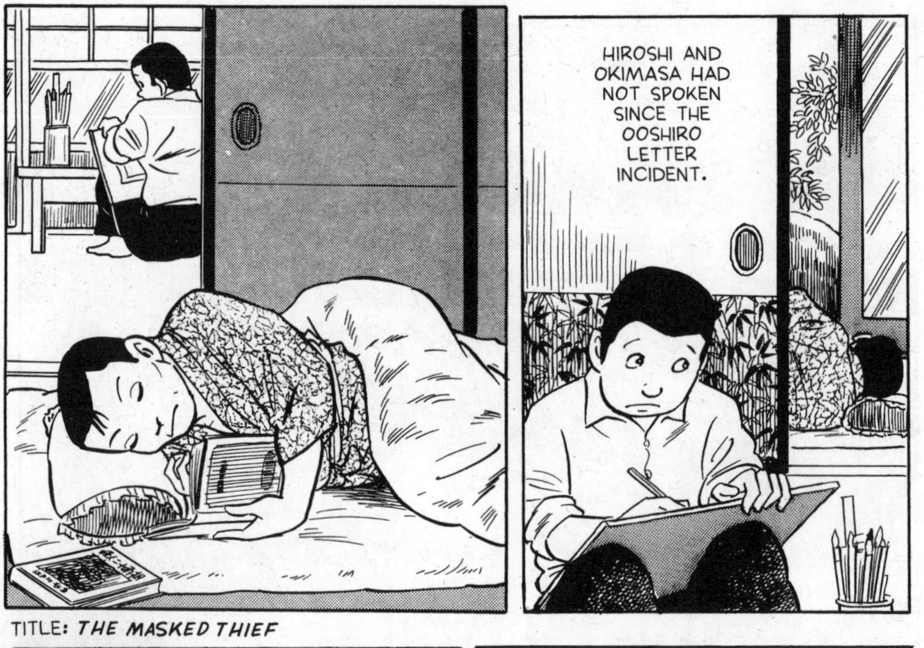
HIROSHI AND OKIMASA HAD NOT SPOKEN SINCE THE OOSHIRO LETTER INCIDENT.

TITLE: *THE MASKED THIEF*

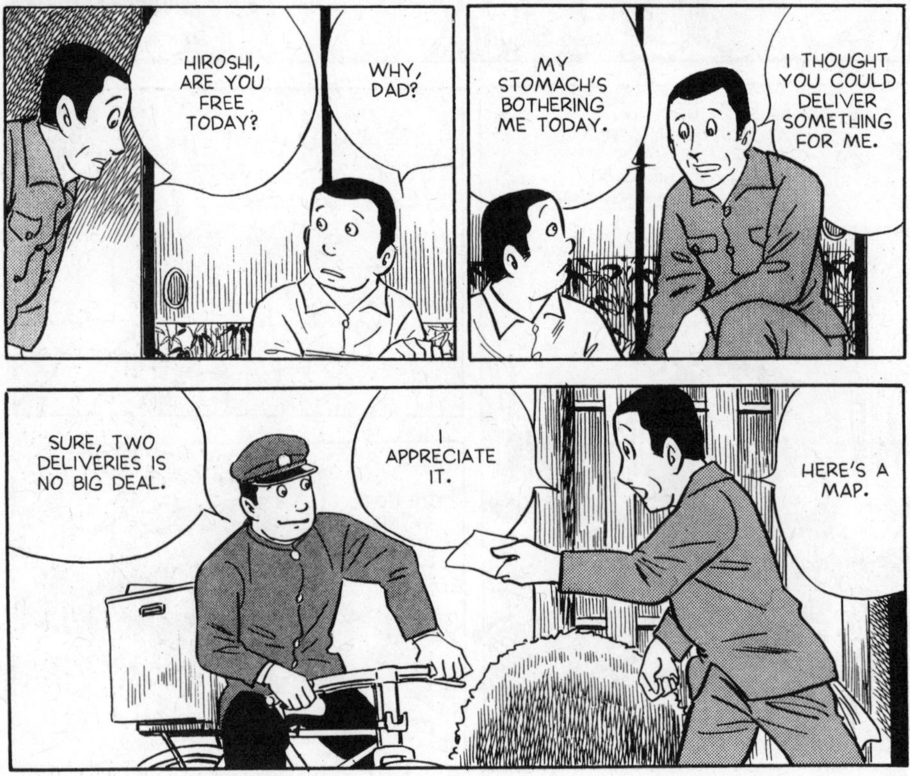
HIROSHI, ARE YOU FREE TODAY?
WHY, DAD?
MY STOMACH'S BOTHERING ME TODAY.
I THOUGHT YOU COULD DELIVER SOMETHING FOR ME.
SURE, TWO DELIVERIES IS NO BIG DEAL.
I APPRECIATE IT.
HERE'S A MAP.

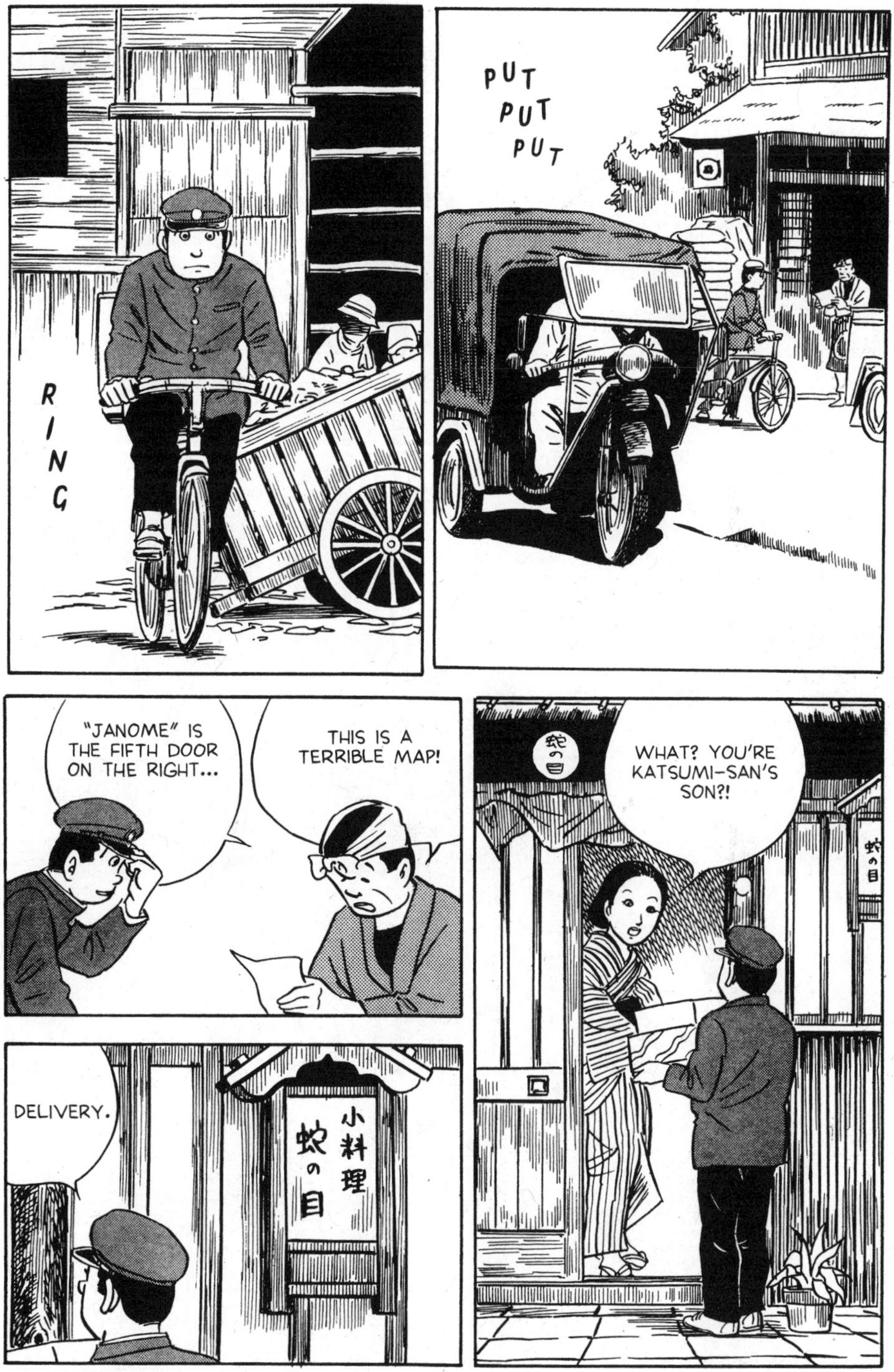
RING
PUT PUT PUT
"JANOME" IS THE FIFTH DOOR ON THE RIGHT...
THIS IS A TERRIBLE MAP!
DELIVERY.
小料理
蛇の目
WHAT? YOU'RE KATSUMI-SAN'S SON?!

SIGN: JANOME RESTAURANT

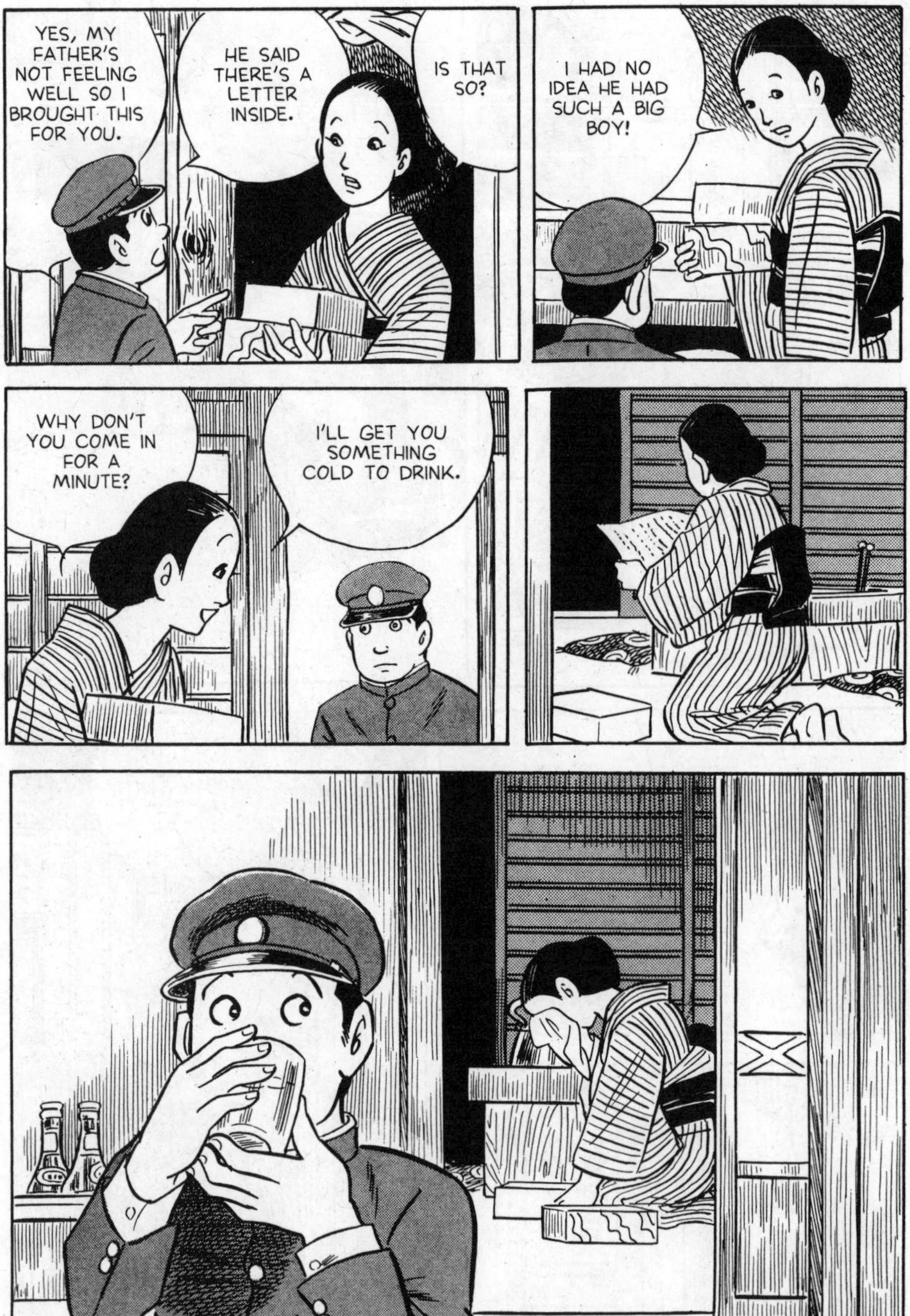
YES, MY FATHER'S NOT FEELING WELL SO I BROUGHT THIS FOR YOU.
HE SAID THERE'S A LETTER INSIDE.
IS THAT SO?
I HAD NO IDEA HE HAD SUCH A BIG BOY!
WHY DON'T YOU COME IN FOR A MINUTE?
I'LL GET YOU SOMETHING COLD TO DRINK.

TORN APART

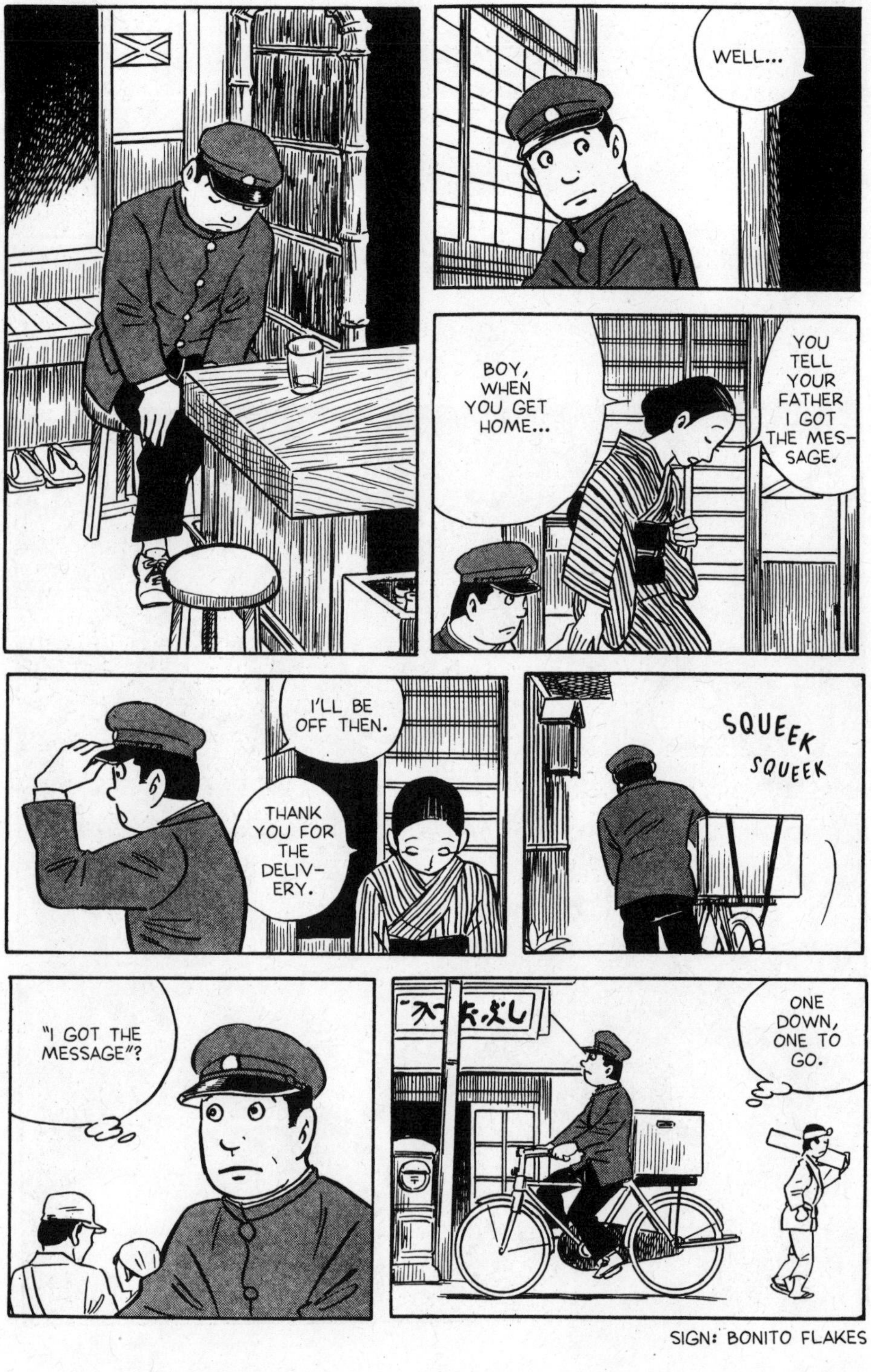
WELL...
BOY, WHEN YOU GET HOME...
YOU TELL YOUR FATHER I GOT THE MES-SAGE.
I'LL BE OFF THEN.
THANK YOU FOR THE DELIV-ERY.
SQUEEK
SQUEEK
"I GOT THE MESSAGE"?
ONE DOWN, ONE TO GO.
SIGN: BONITO FLAKES

SQEEK SQEEK

SIGN: IKEDA CLINIC

SKREECH

OH, YOU'RE MAKING DELIVERIES FOR YOUR FATHER?

THIS IS FOR YOU...

THIS IS THE SOAP I ORDERED.

AND I HAVE A LETTER...

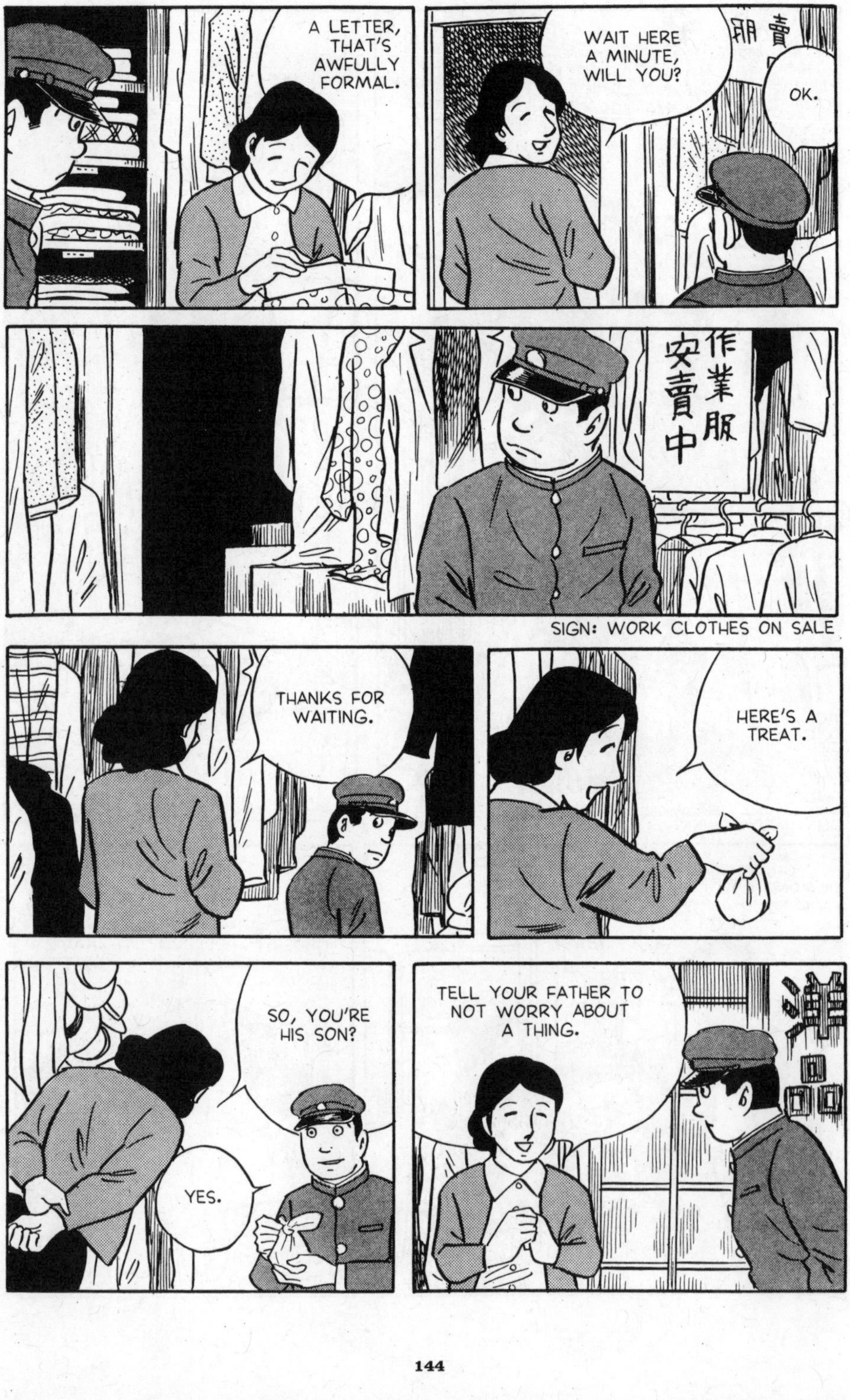
A LETTER, THAT'S AWFULLY FORMAL.
WAIT HERE A MINUTE, WILL YOU?
OK.
作業服安賣中
SIGN: WORK CLOTHES ON SALE
THANKS FOR WAITING.
HERE'S A TREAT.
SO, YOU'RE HIS SON?
YES.
TELL YOUR FATHER TO NOT WORRY ABOUT A THING.

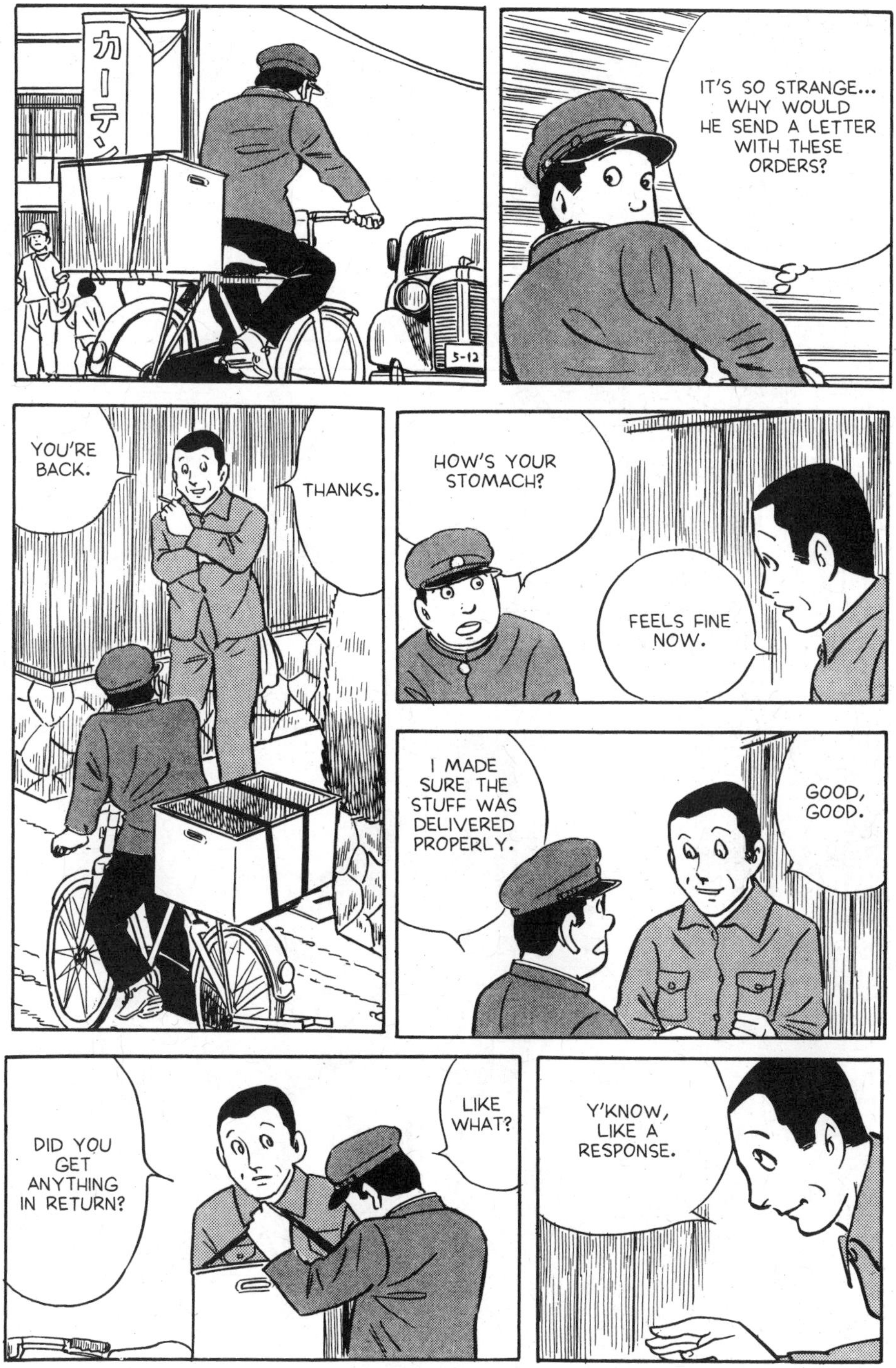
5-12
IT'S SO STRANGE... WHY WOULD HE SEND A LETTER WITH THESE ORDERS?
YOU'RE BACK.
THANKS.
HOW'S YOUR STOMACH?
FEELS FINE NOW.
I MADE SURE THE STUFF WAS DELIVERED PROPERLY.
GOOD, GOOD.
DID YOU GET ANYTHING IN RETURN?
LIKE WHAT?
Y'KNOW, LIKE A RESPONSE.

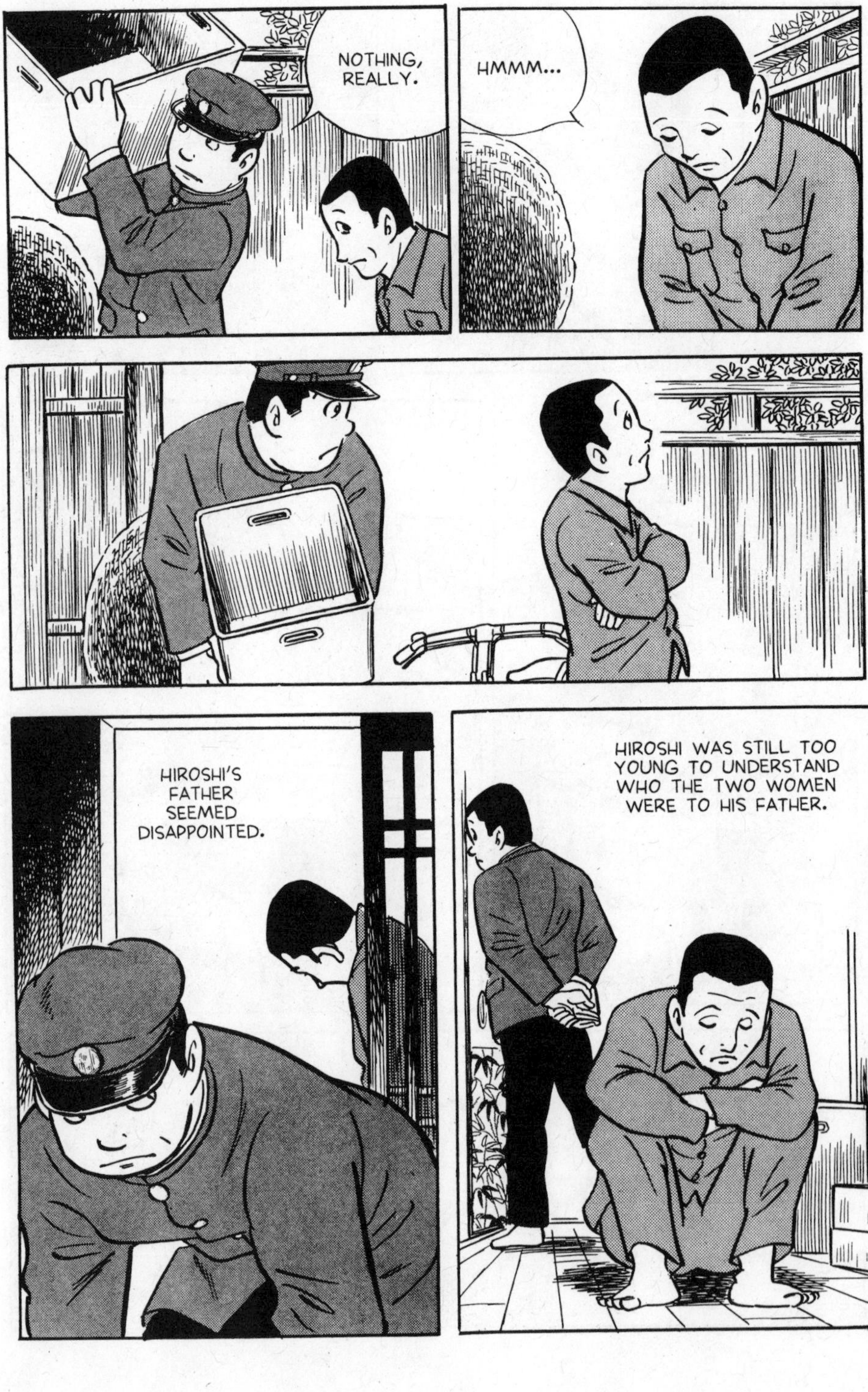
NOTHING, REALLY.
HMMM...
HIROSHI'S FATHER SEEMED DISAPPOINTED.
HIROSHI WAS STILL TOO YOUNG TO UNDERSTAND WHO THE TWO WOMEN WERE TO HIS FATHER.

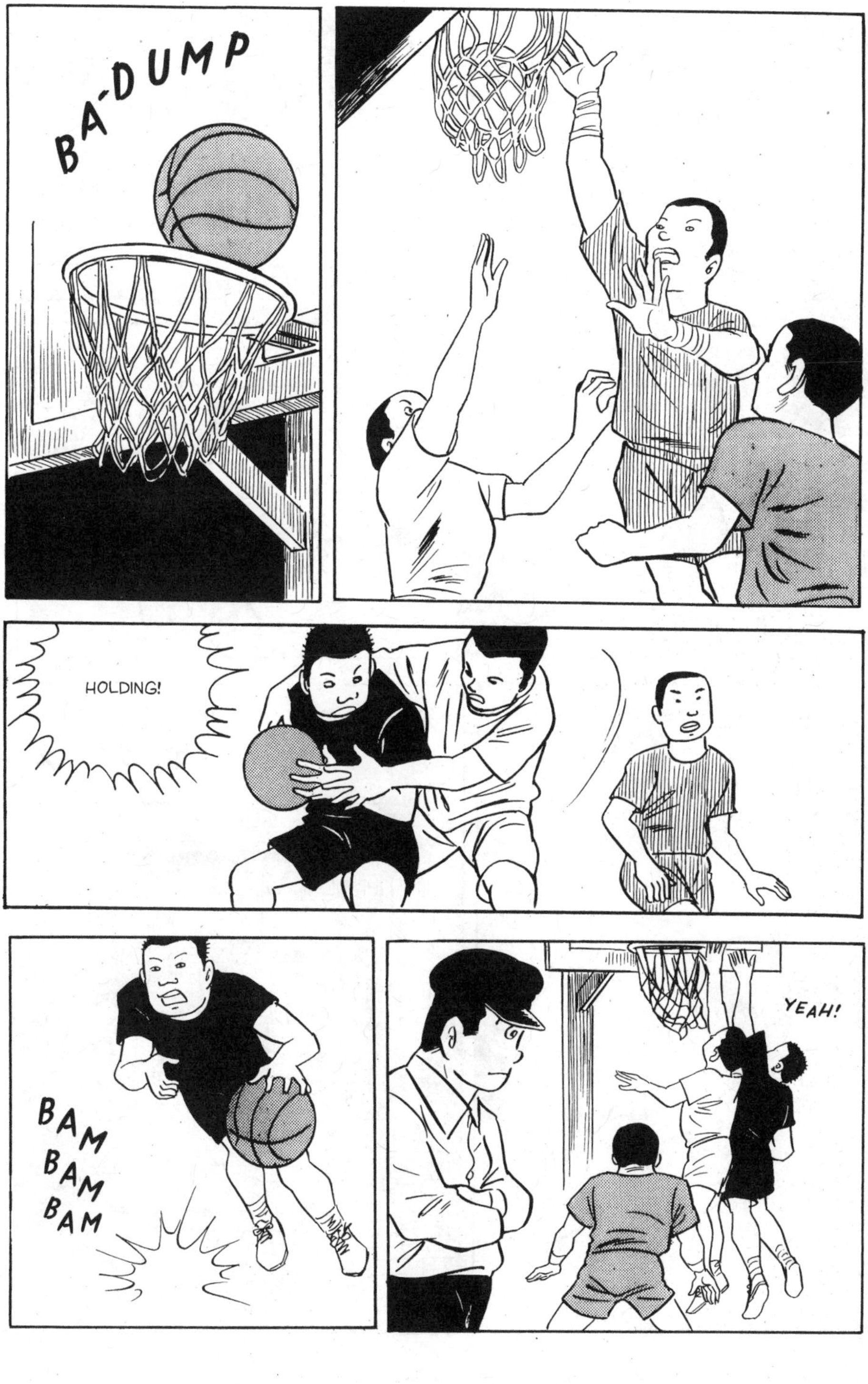
BA-DUMP
HOLDING!
BAM
BAM
BAM
YEAH!

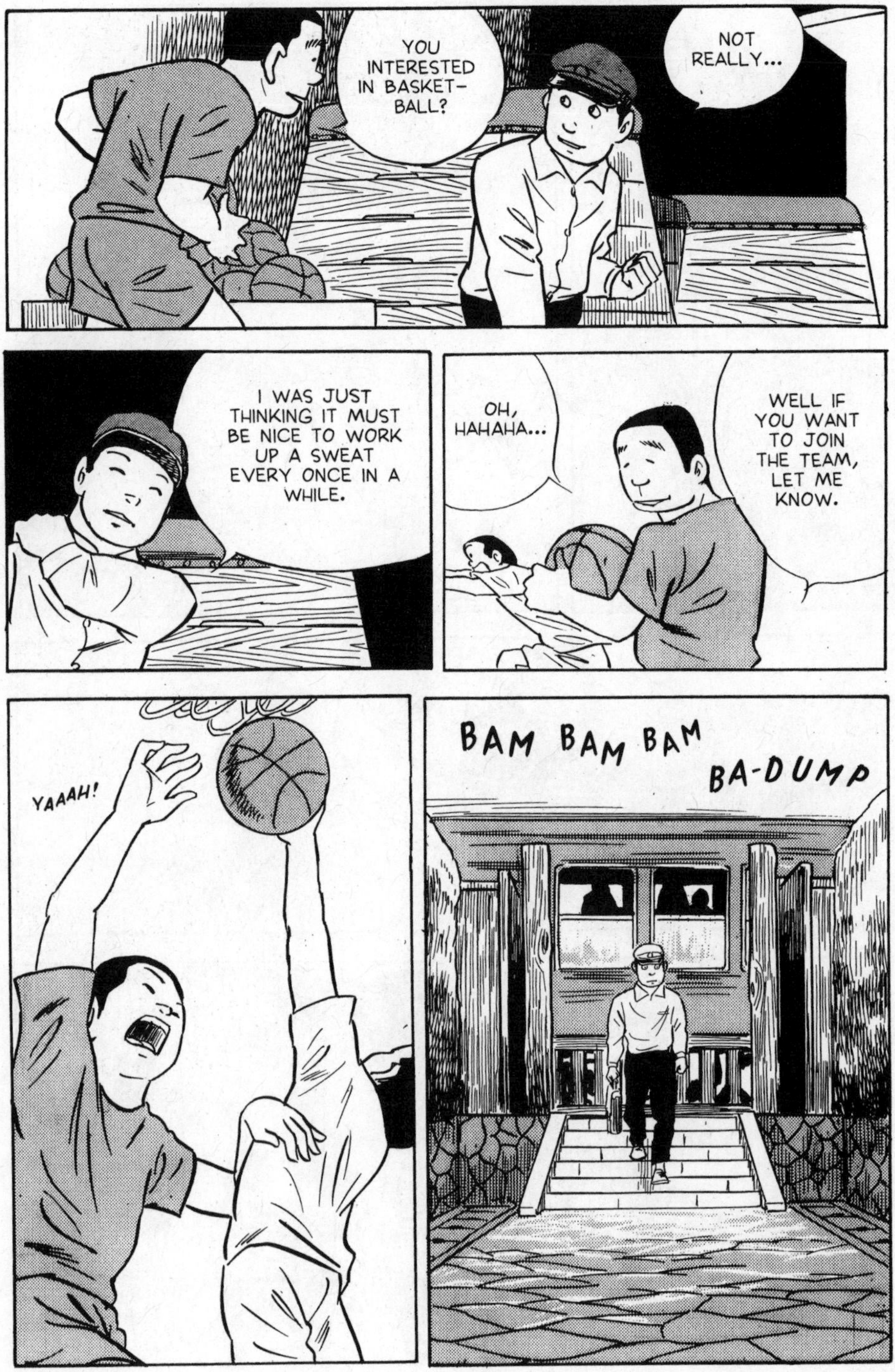

YOU INTERESTED IN BASKET-BALL?
NOT REALLY...
I WAS JUST THINKING IT MUST BE NICE TO WORK UP A SWEAT EVERY ONCE IN A WHILE.
OH, HAHAHA...
WELL IF YOU WANT TO JOIN THE TEAM, LET ME KNOW.
YAAAH!
BAM BAM BAM
BA-DUMP

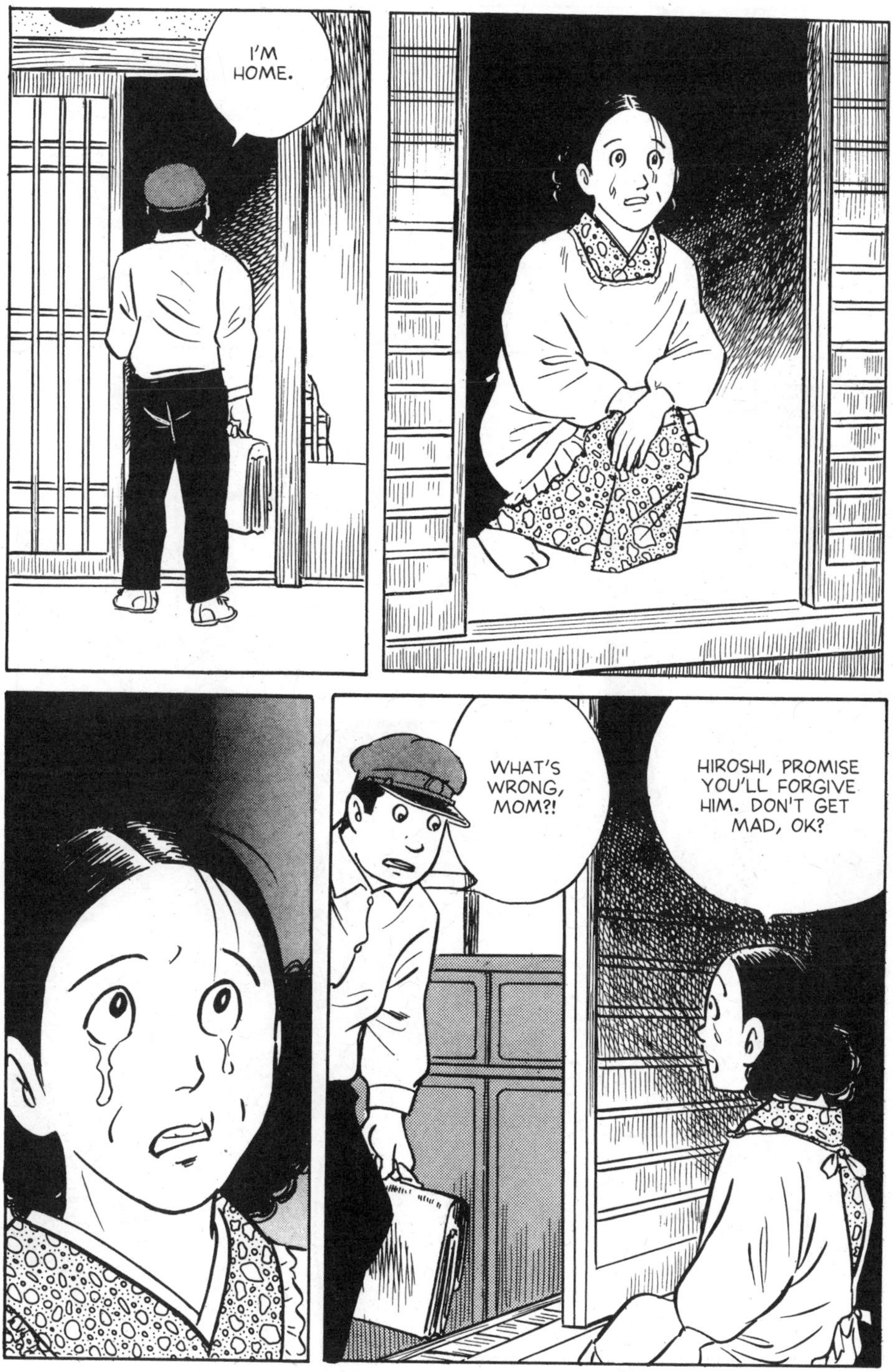
I'M HOME.
WHAT'S WRONG, MOM?!
HIROSHI, PROMISE YOU'LL FORGIVE HIM. DON'T GET MAD, OK?

WHAT'S THE MATTER?
OKIMASA'S HAD A HARD LIFE... YOU HAVE TO UNDERSTAND THAT.
FSSH

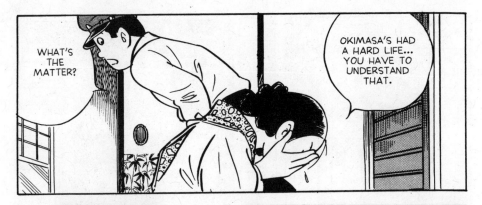

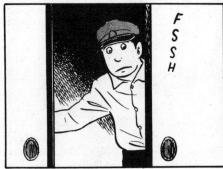

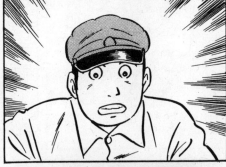

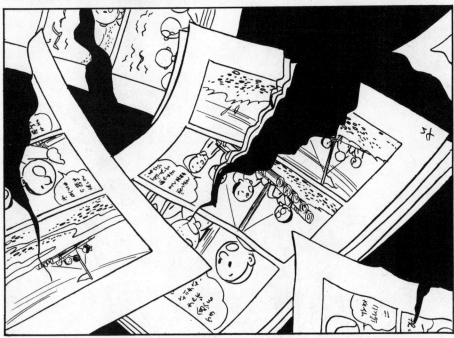

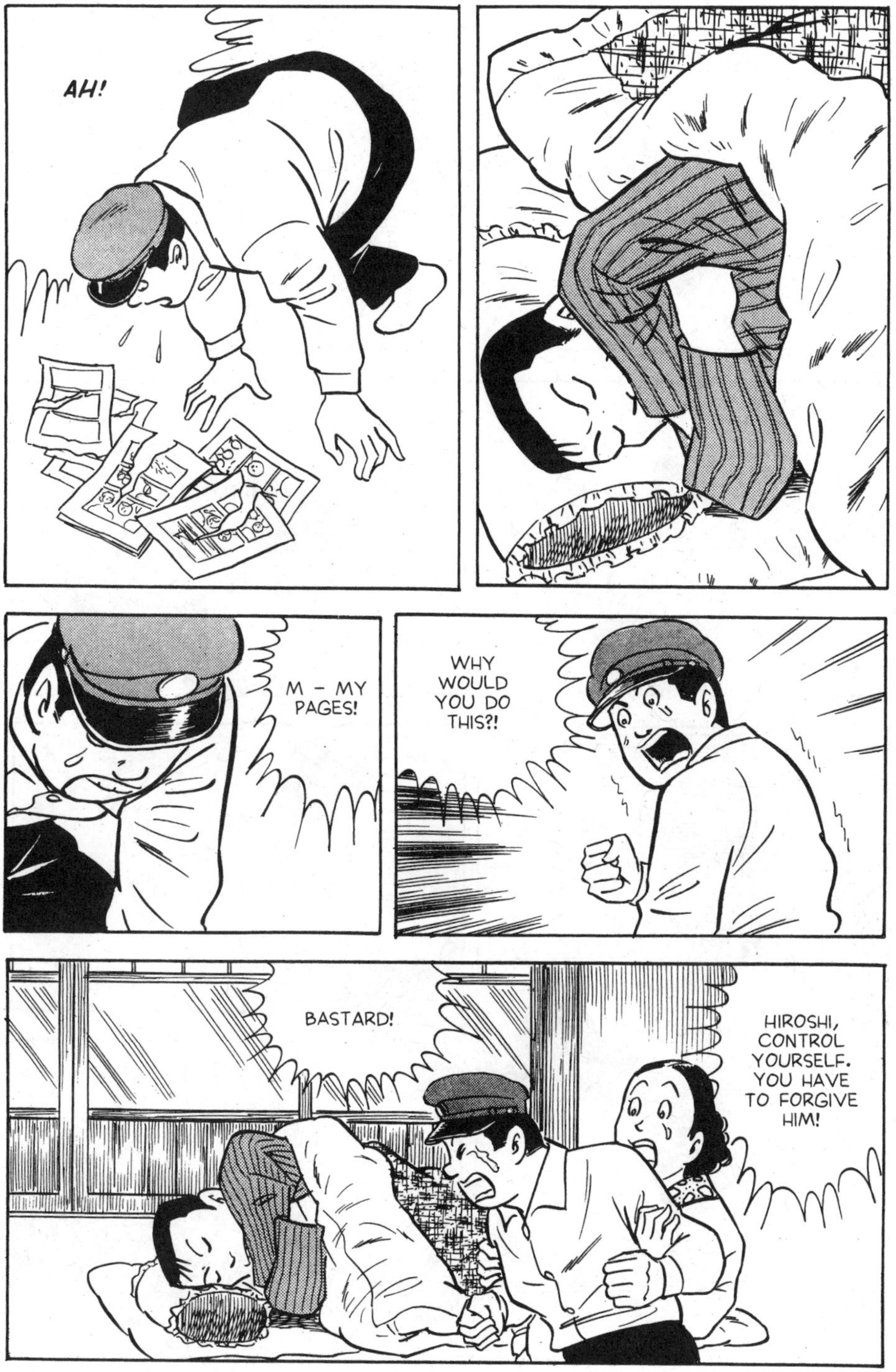
AH!
M - MY PAGES!
WHY WOULD YOU DO THIS?!
BASTARD!
HIROSHI, CONTROL YOURSELF. YOU HAVE TO FORGIVE HIM!

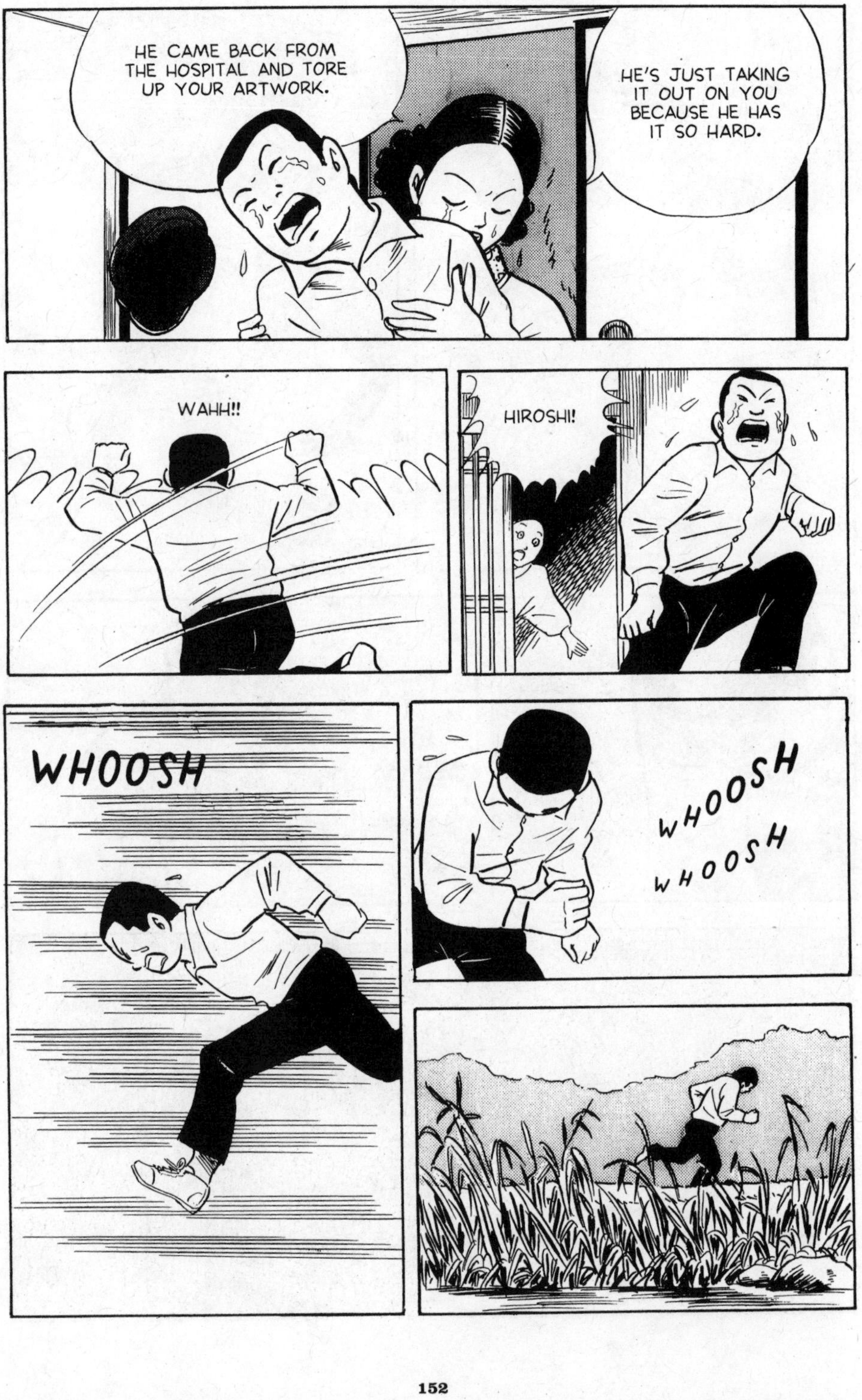
HE CAME BACK FROM THE HOSPITAL AND TORE UP YOUR ARTWORK.
HE'S JUST TAKING IT OUT ON YOU BECAUSE HE HAS IT SO HARD.
WAHH!!
HIROSHI!
WHOOSH
WHOOSH
WHOOSH

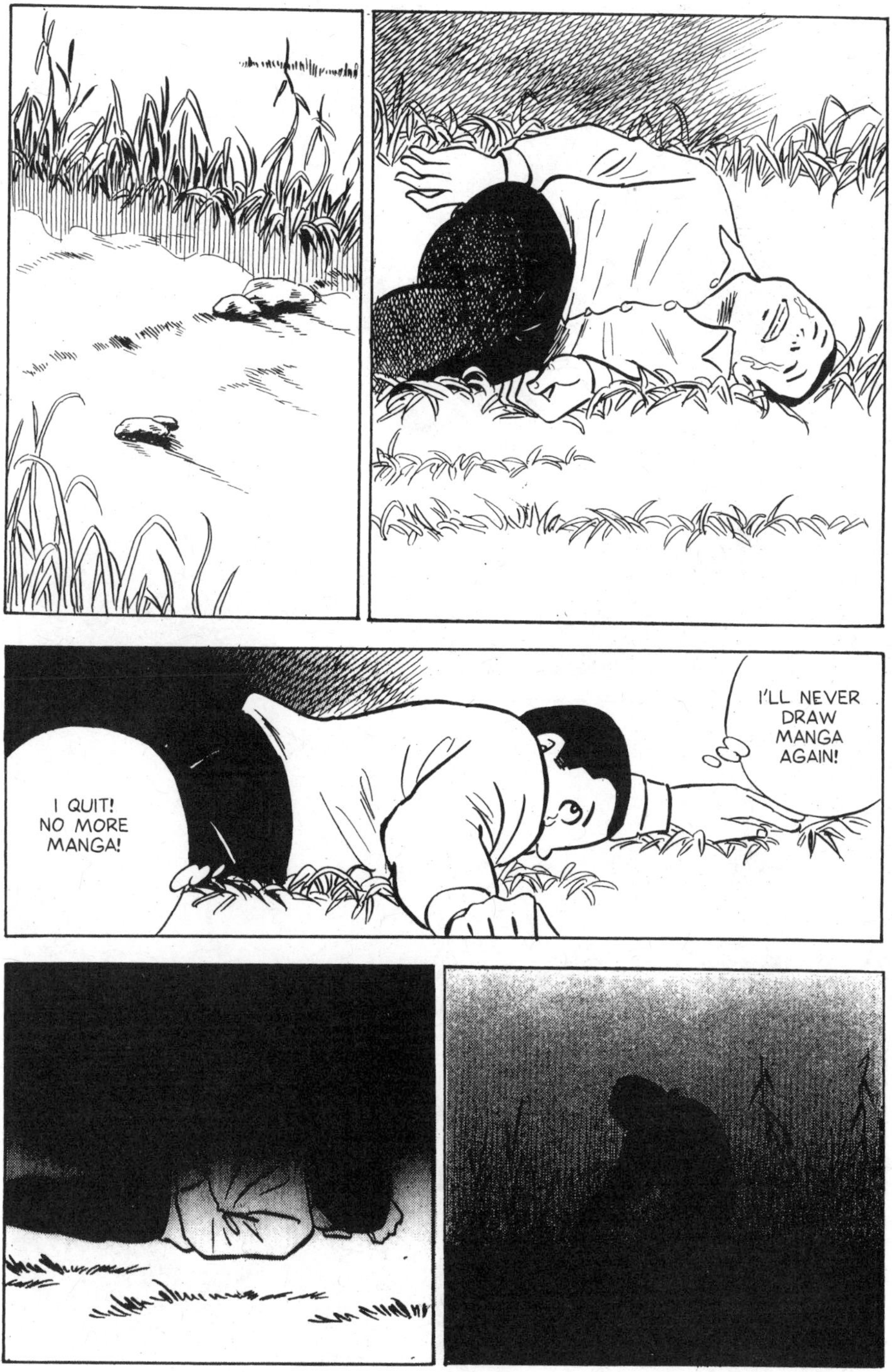
I QUIT! NO MORE MANGA!
I'LL NEVER DRAW MANGA AGAIN!

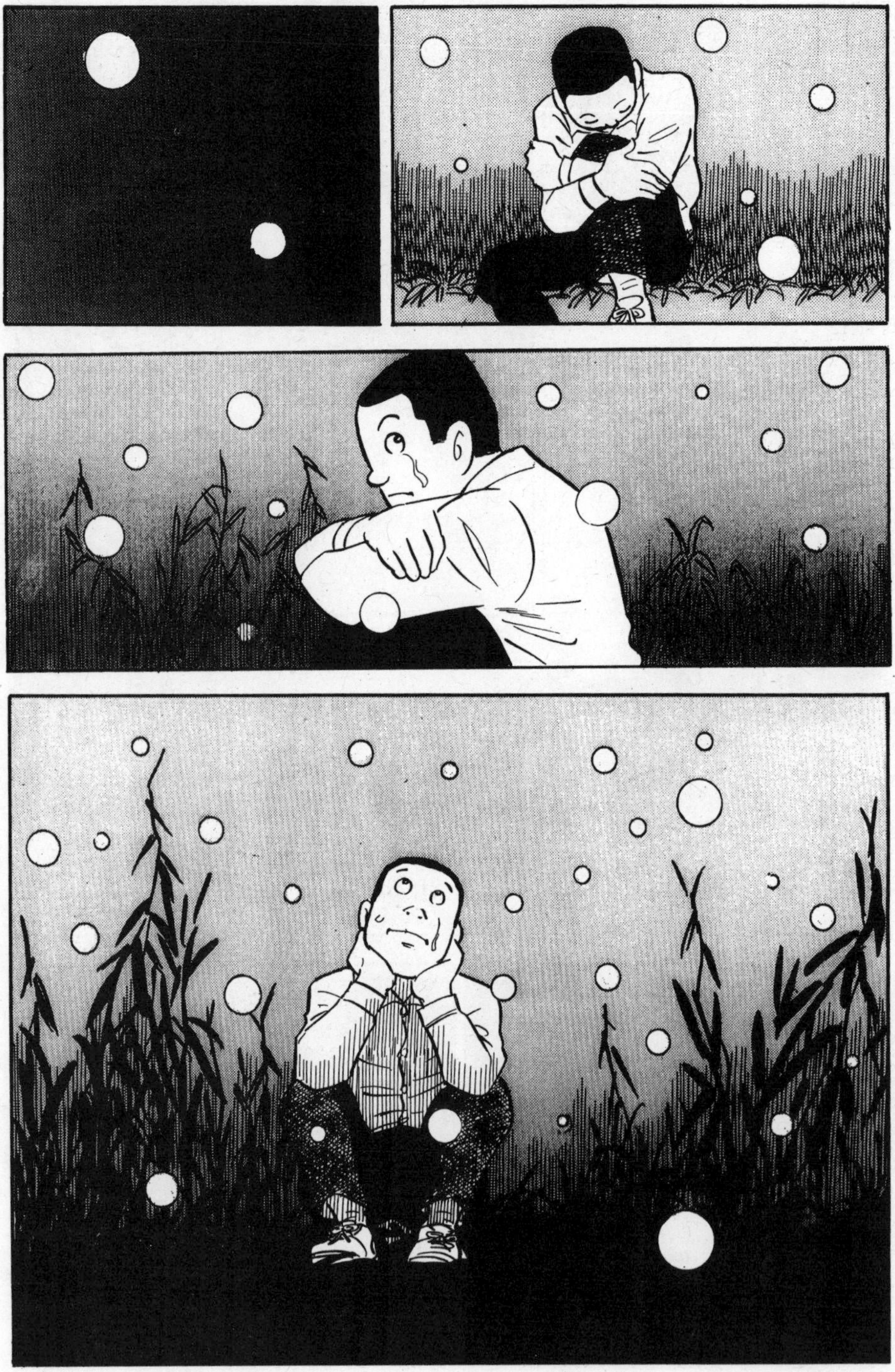

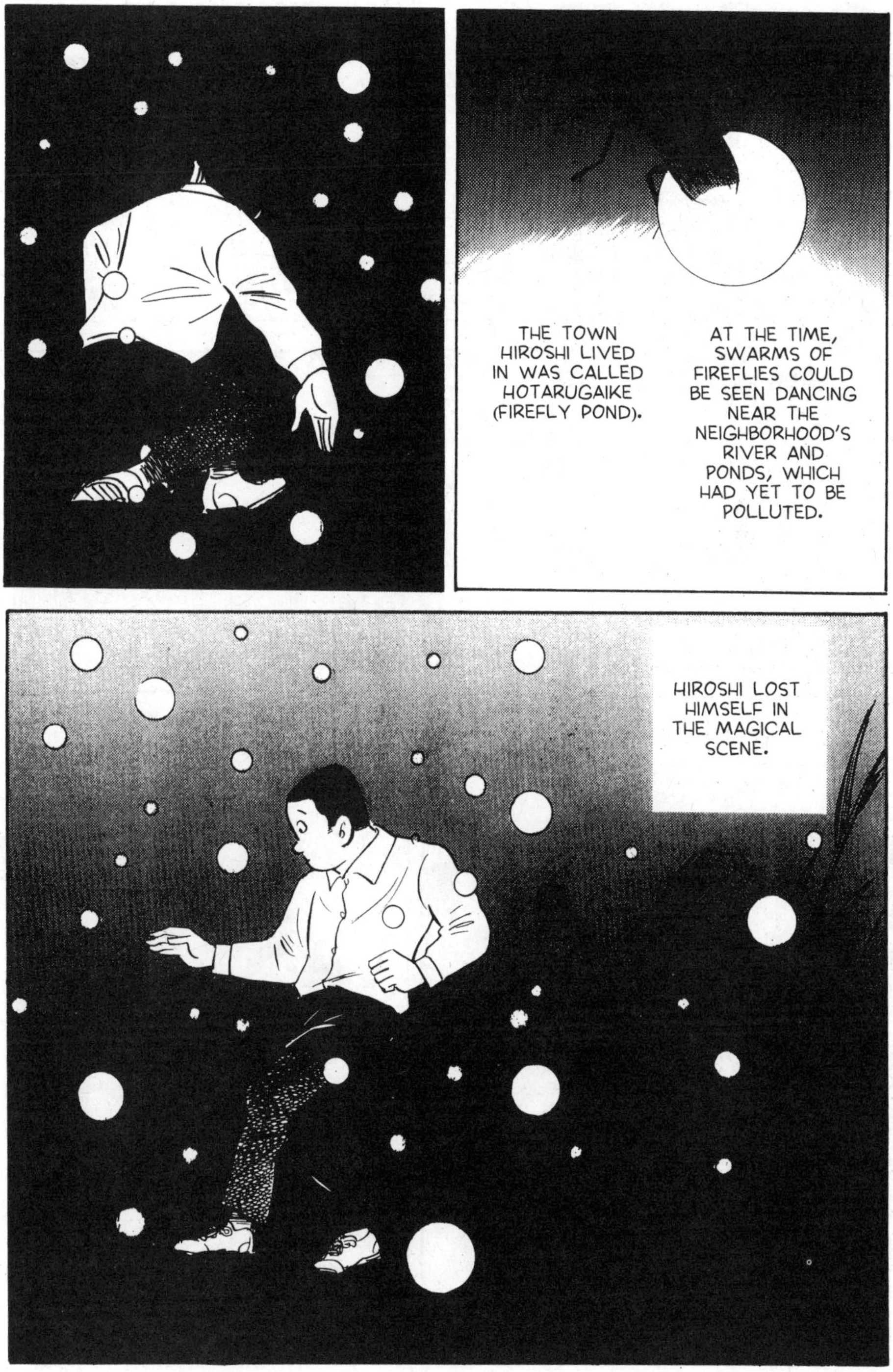
THE TOWN HIROSHI LIVED IN WAS CALLED HOTARUGAIKE (FIREFLY POND).
AT THE TIME, SWARMS OF FIREFLIES COULD BE SEEN DANCING NEAR THE NEIGHBORHOOD'S RIVER AND PONDS, WHICH HAD YET TO BE POLLUTED.
HIROSHI LOST HIMSELF IN THE MAGICAL SCENE.

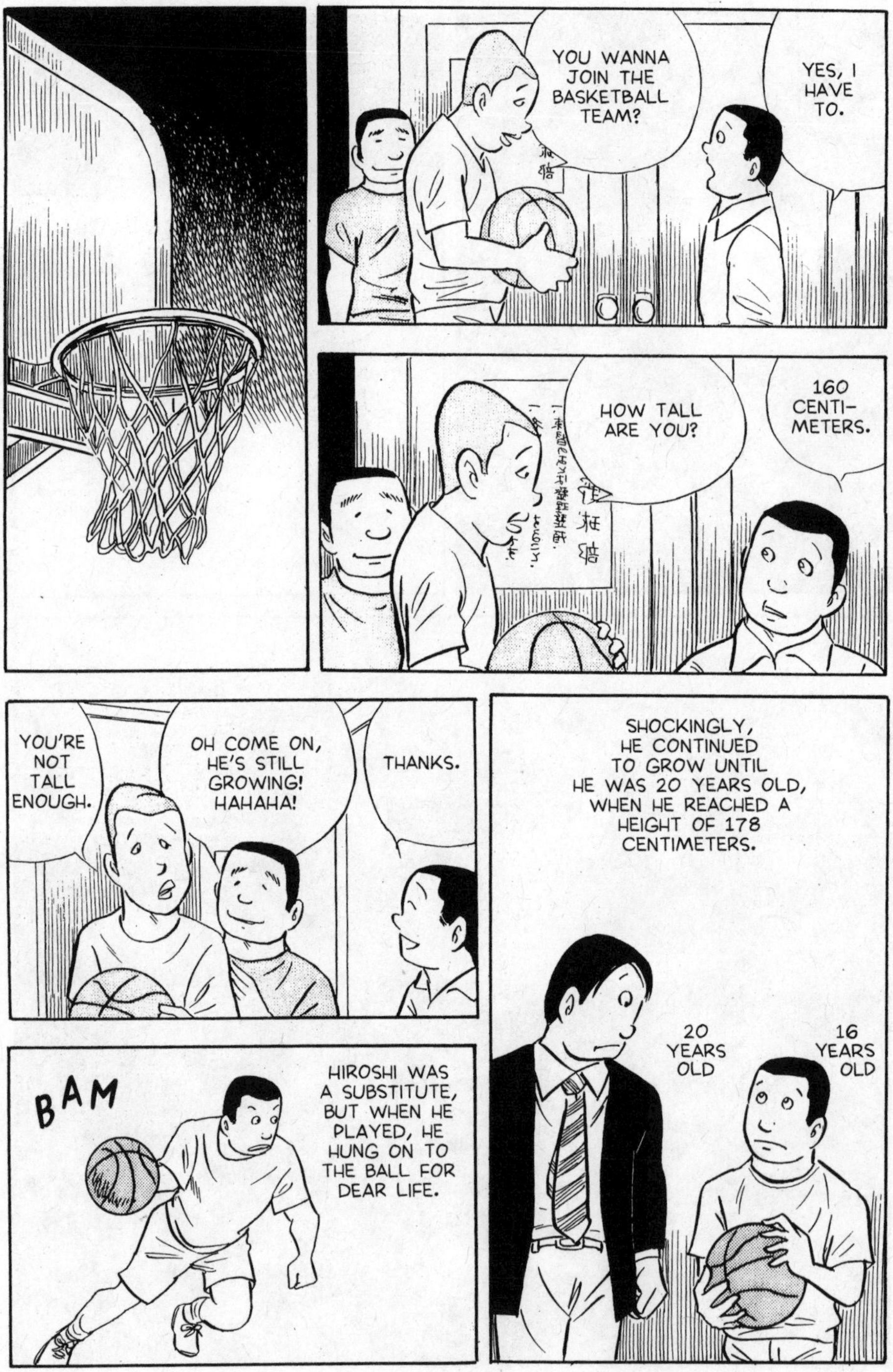
YOU WANNA JOIN THE BASKETBALL TEAM?
YES, I HAVE TO.
HOW TALL ARE YOU?
160 CENTI-METERS.
YOU'RE NOT TALL ENOUGH.
OH COME ON, HE'S STILL GROWING! HAHAHA!
THANKS.
BAM
HIROSHI WAS A SUBSTITUTE, BUT WHEN HE PLAYED, HE HUNG ON TO THE BALL FOR DEAR LIFE.
SHOCKINGLY, HE CONTINUED TO GROW UNTIL HE WAS 20 YEARS OLD, WHEN HE REACHED A HEIGHT OF 178 CENTIMETERS.
20 YEARS OLD
16 YEARS OLD

UNGH!

THUD

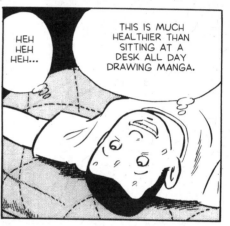

HEH HEH HEH...

THIS IS MUCH HEALTHIER THAN SITTING AT A DESK ALL DAY DRAWING MANGA.

HERE'S YOUR MAIL.

大城のぼる

東中野一丁目

拝

IT'S FROM OOSHIRO SENSEI.

LETTER: NOBORU OOSHIRO, 1 HIGASHI NAKANO

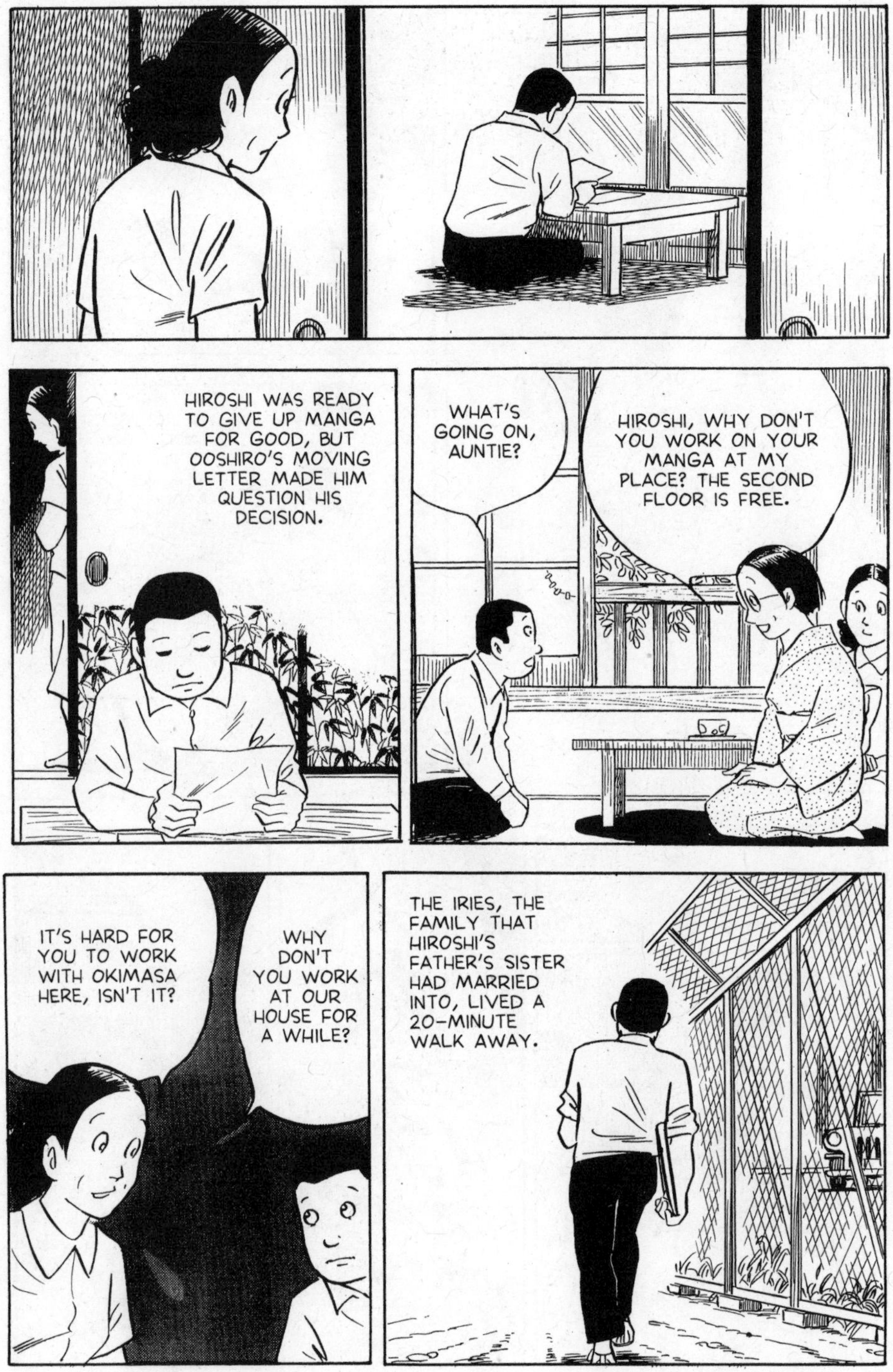
HIROSHI WAS READY TO GIVE UP MANGA FOR GOOD, BUT OOSHIRO'S MOVING LETTER MADE HIM QUESTION HIS DECISION.
WHAT'S GOING ON, AUNTIE?
HIROSHI, WHY DON'T YOU WORK ON YOUR MANGA AT MY PLACE? THE SECOND FLOOR IS FREE.
IT'S HARD FOR YOU TO WORK WITH OKIMASA HERE, ISN'T IT?
WHY DON'T YOU WORK AT OUR HOUSE FOR A WHILE?
THE IRIES, THE FAMILY THAT HIROSHI'S FATHER'S SISTER HAD MARRIED INTO, LIVED A 20-MINUTE WALK AWAY.

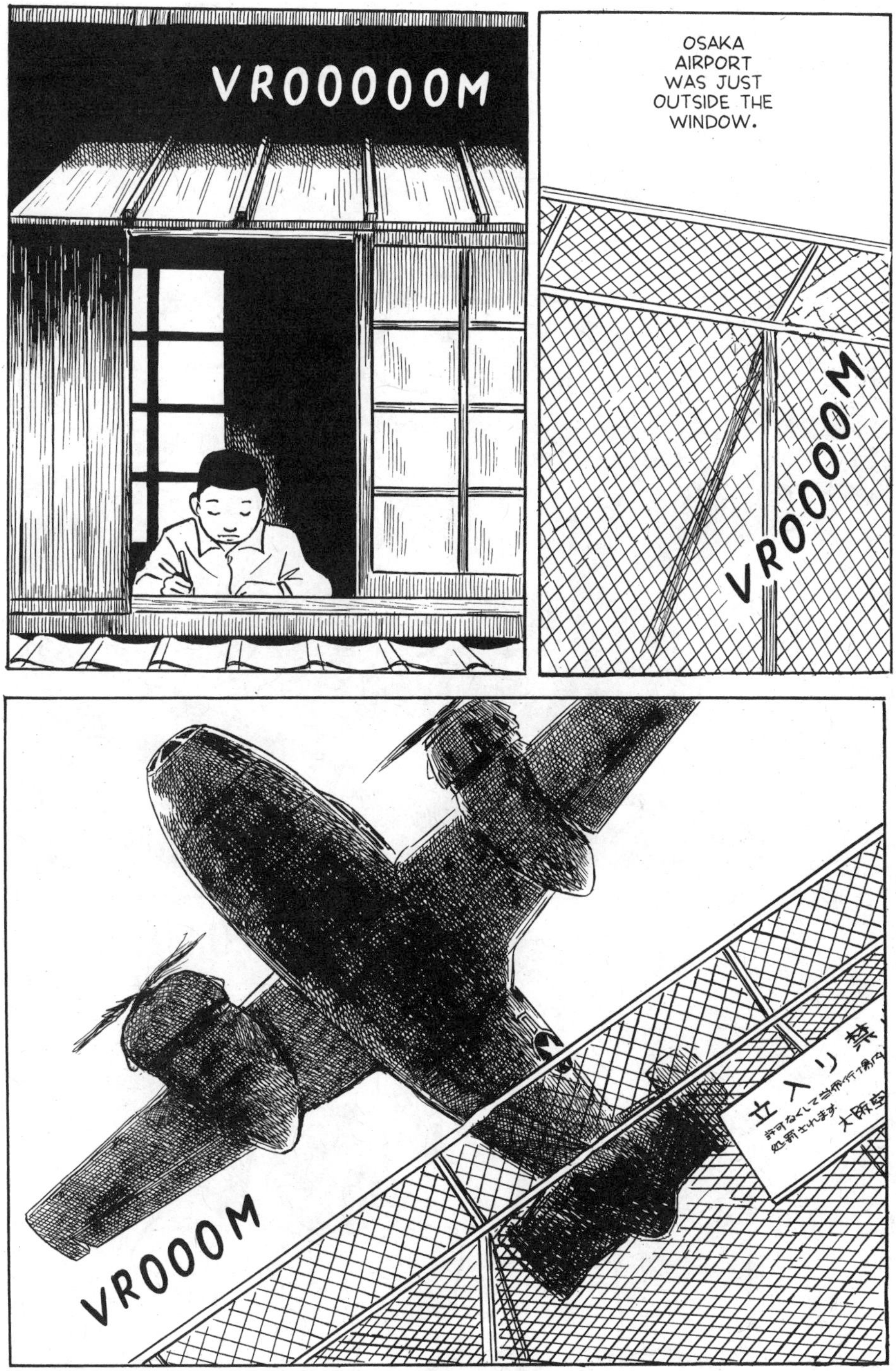
VROOOOOM
OSAKA AIRPORT WAS JUST OUTSIDE THE WINDOW.
VROOOOM
立入り禁
許可なくして当飛行場内
処罰されます
大阪空
VROOOM

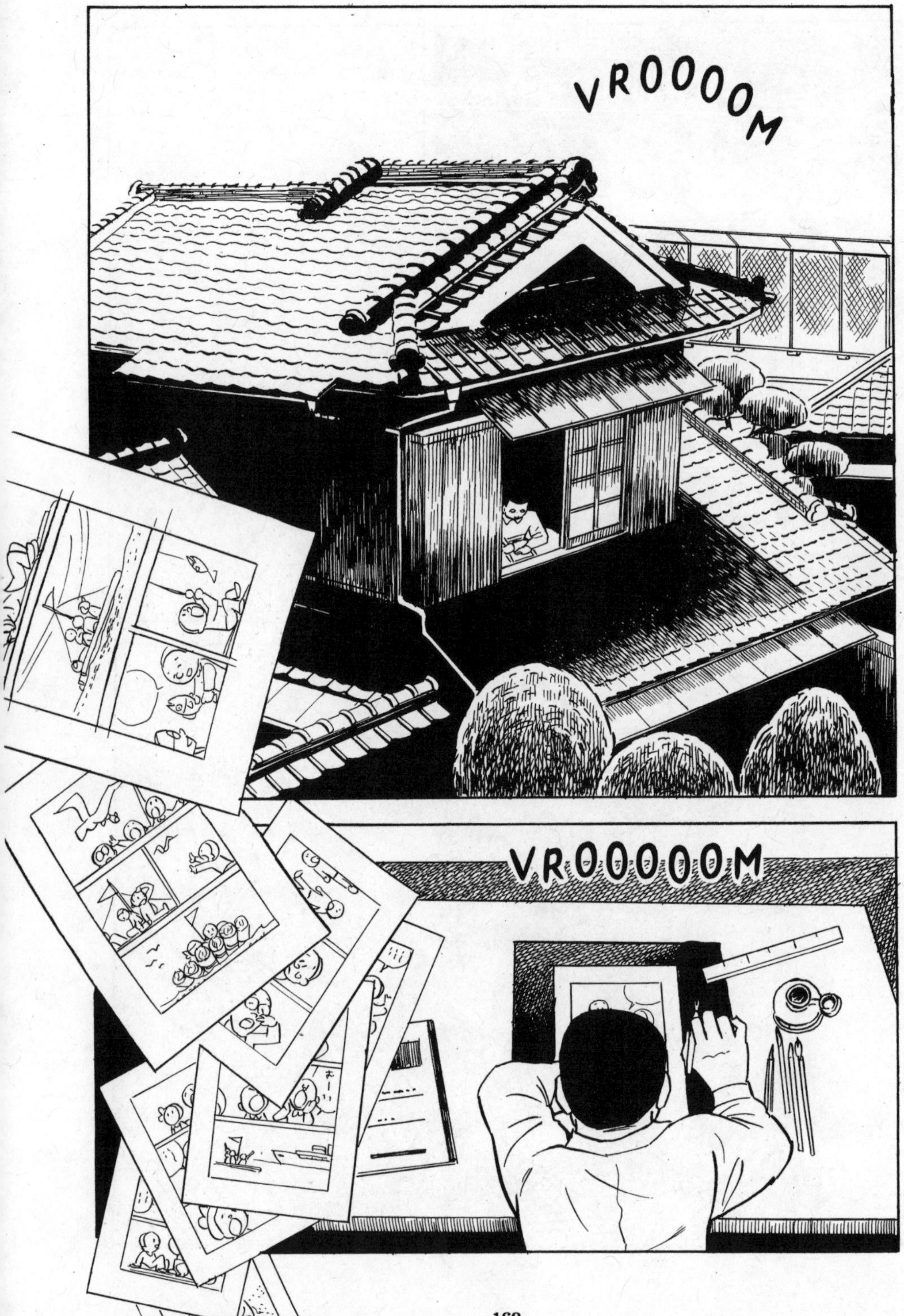
VROOOOM
VROOOOOM

SUMMERTIME DREAMS

AUGUST 1951

CIVIL AVIATION BEGINS
DEBUT OF "AIR GIRLS"
(FLIGHT ATTENDANTS)

日 本 航

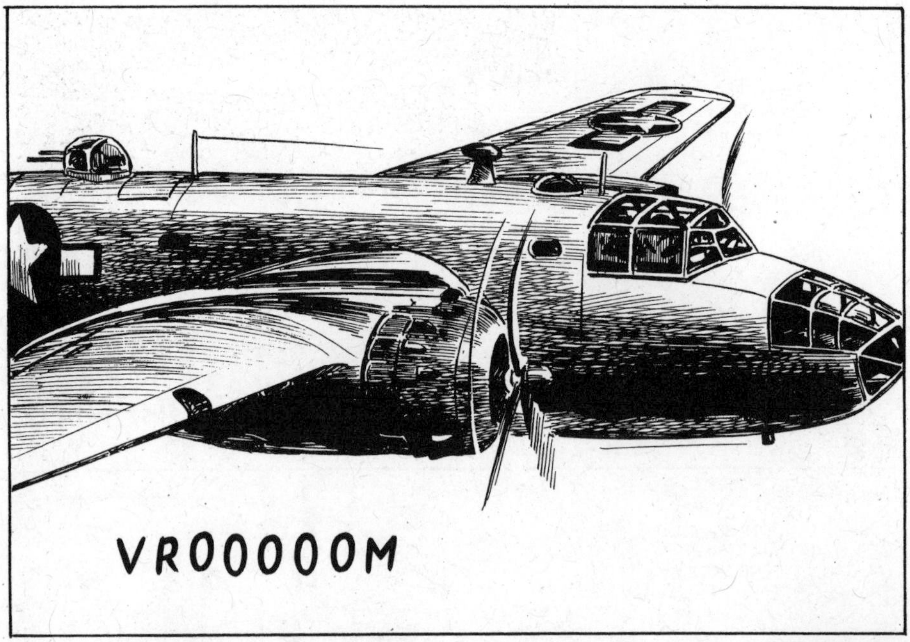
VROOOOOM

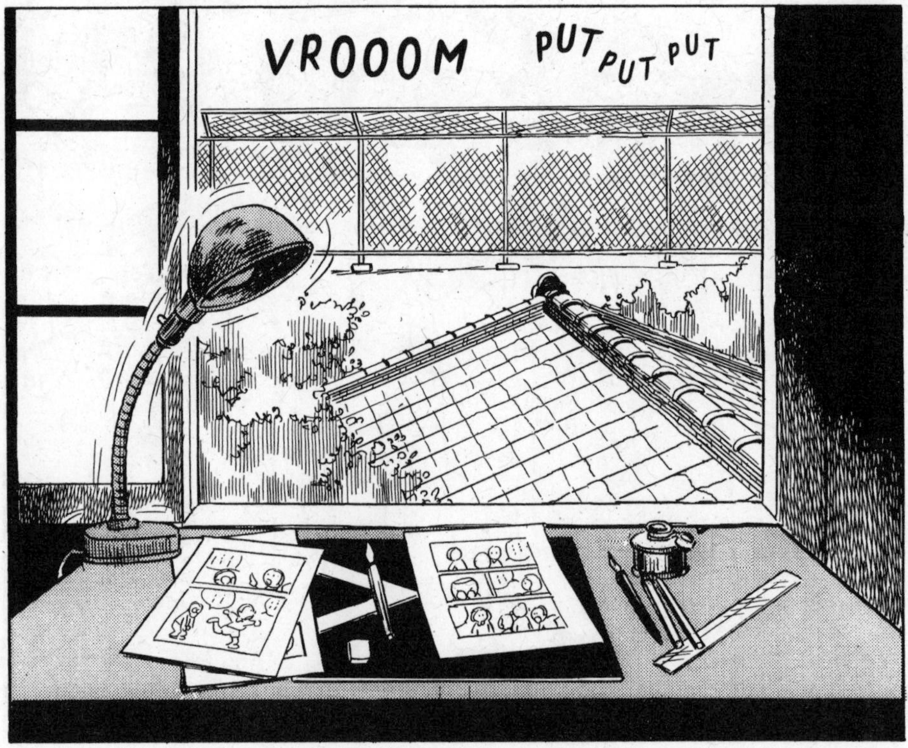
VROOOM
PUT PUT PUT

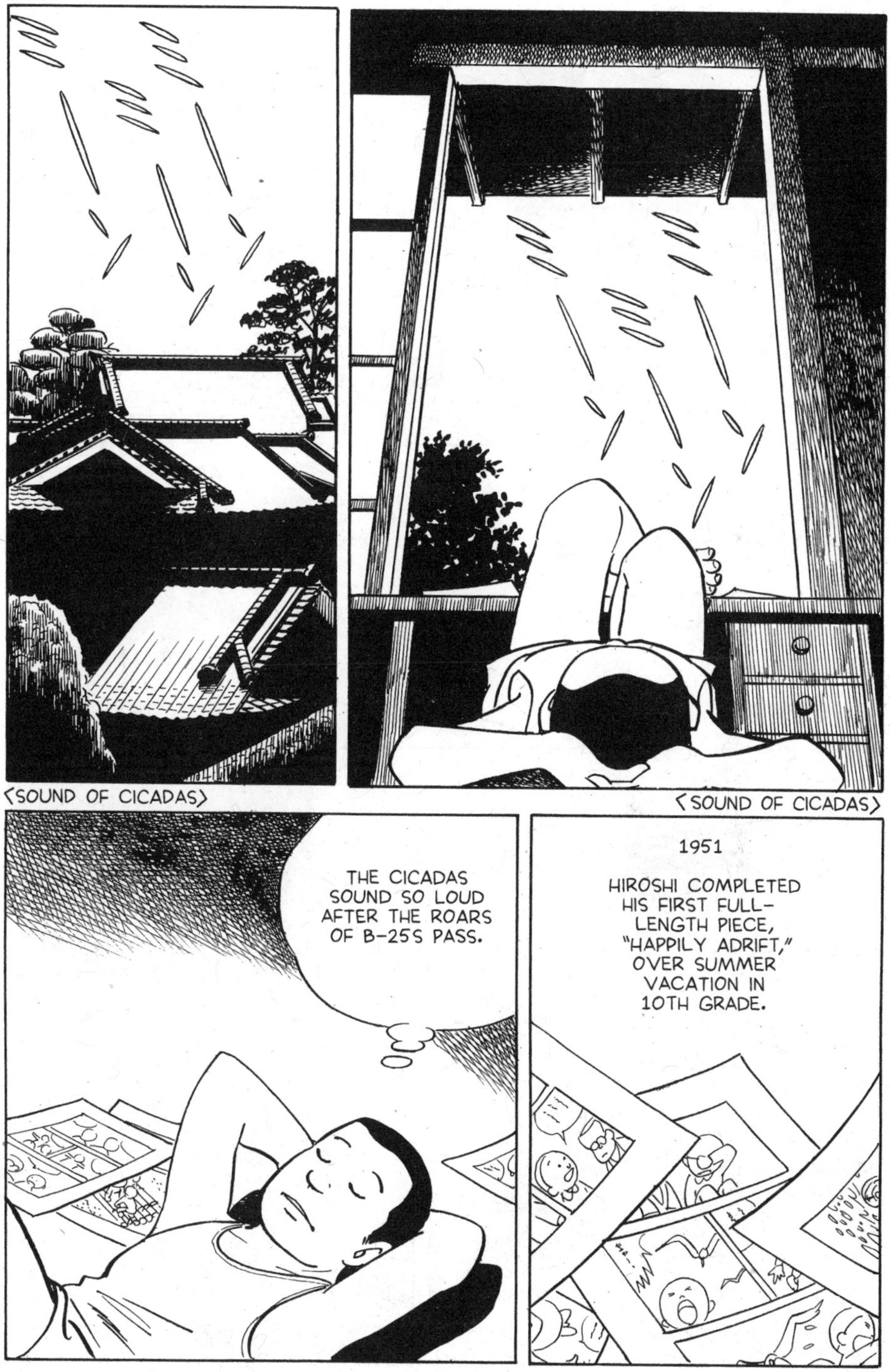
〈SOUND OF CICADAS〉
〈SOUND OF CICADAS〉
THE CICADAS SOUND SO LOUD AFTER THE ROARS OF B-25'S PASS.
1951
HIROSHI COMPLETED HIS FIRST FULL-LENGTH PIECE, "HAPPILY ADRIFT," OVER SUMMER VACATION IN 10TH GRADE.

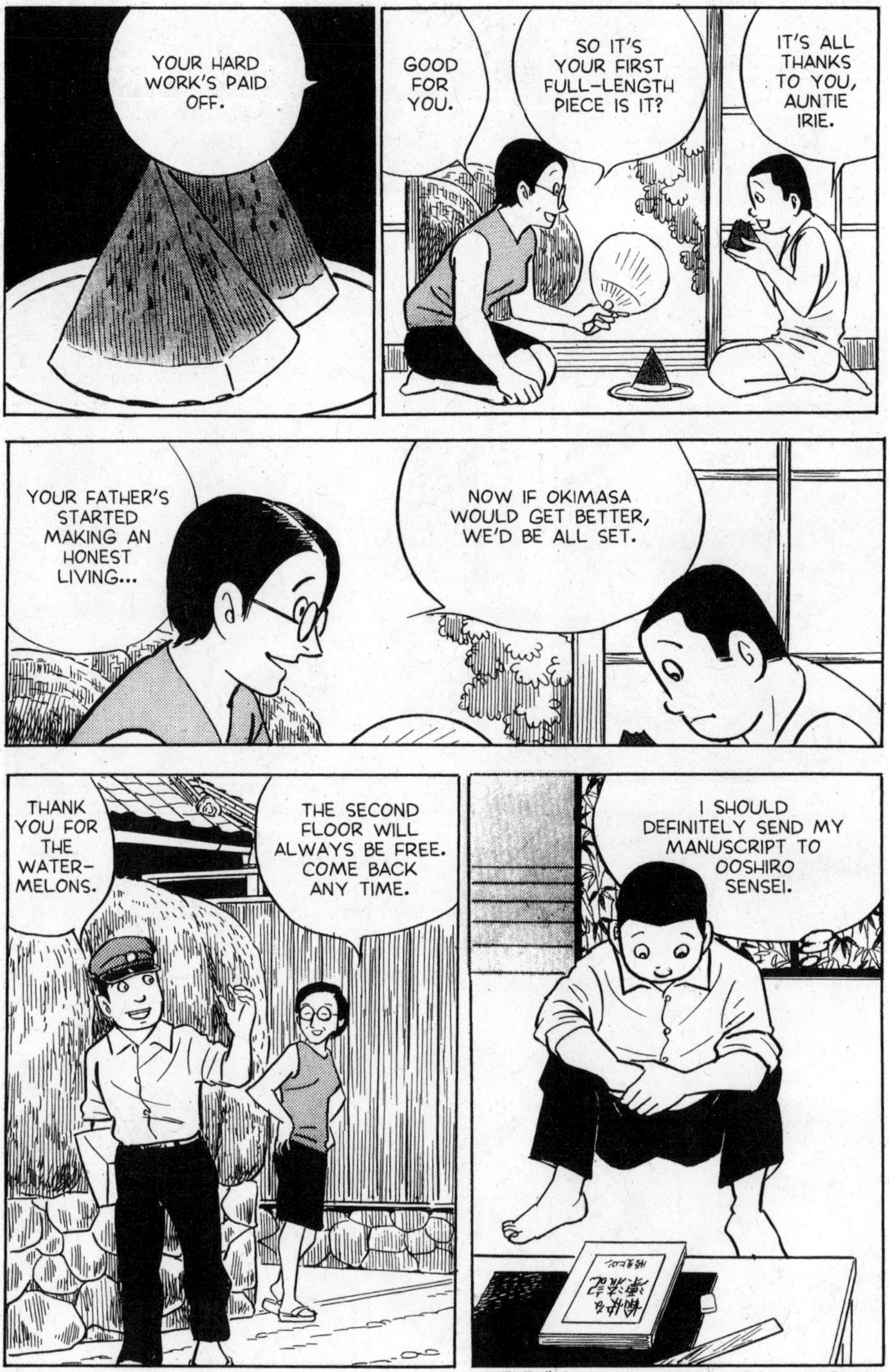
YOUR HARD WORK'S PAID OFF.
GOOD FOR YOU.
SO IT'S YOUR FIRST FULL-LENGTH PIECE IS IT?
IT'S ALL THANKS TO YOU, AUNTIE IRIE.
YOUR FATHER'S STARTED MAKING AN HONEST LIVING...
NOW IF OKIMASA WOULD GET BETTER, WE'D BE ALL SET.
THANK YOU FOR THE WATER-MELONS.
THE SECOND FLOOR WILL ALWAYS BE FREE. COME BACK ANY TIME.
I SHOULD DEFINITELY SEND MY MANUSCRIPT TO OOSHIRO SENSEI.
TITLE: "HAPPILY ADRIFT," HIROSHI KATSUMI

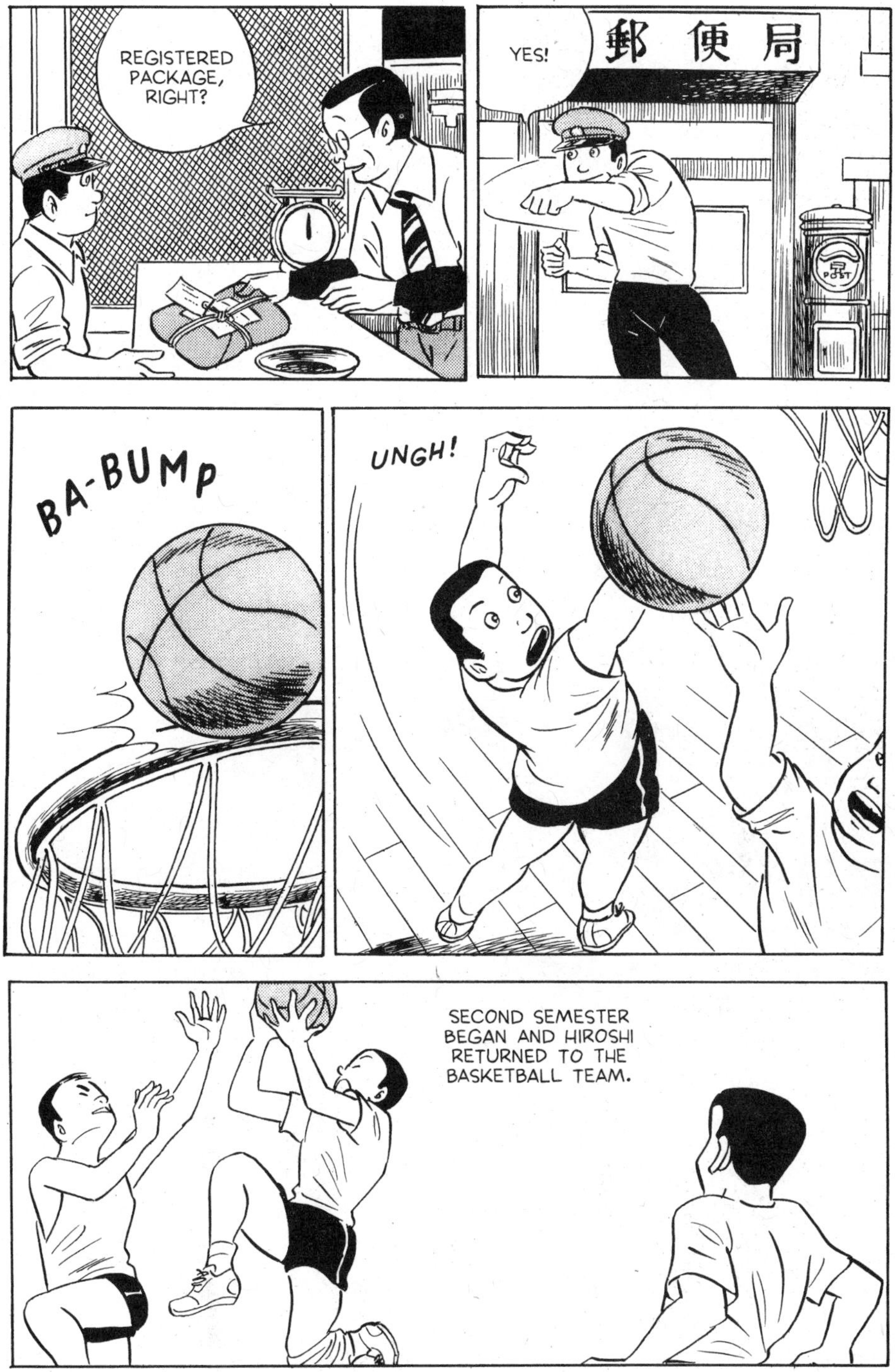
REGISTERED PACKAGE, RIGHT?
YES!
郵便局
POST
BA-BUMP
UNGH!
SECOND SEMESTER BEGAN AND HIROSHI RETURNED TO THE BASKETBALL TEAM.

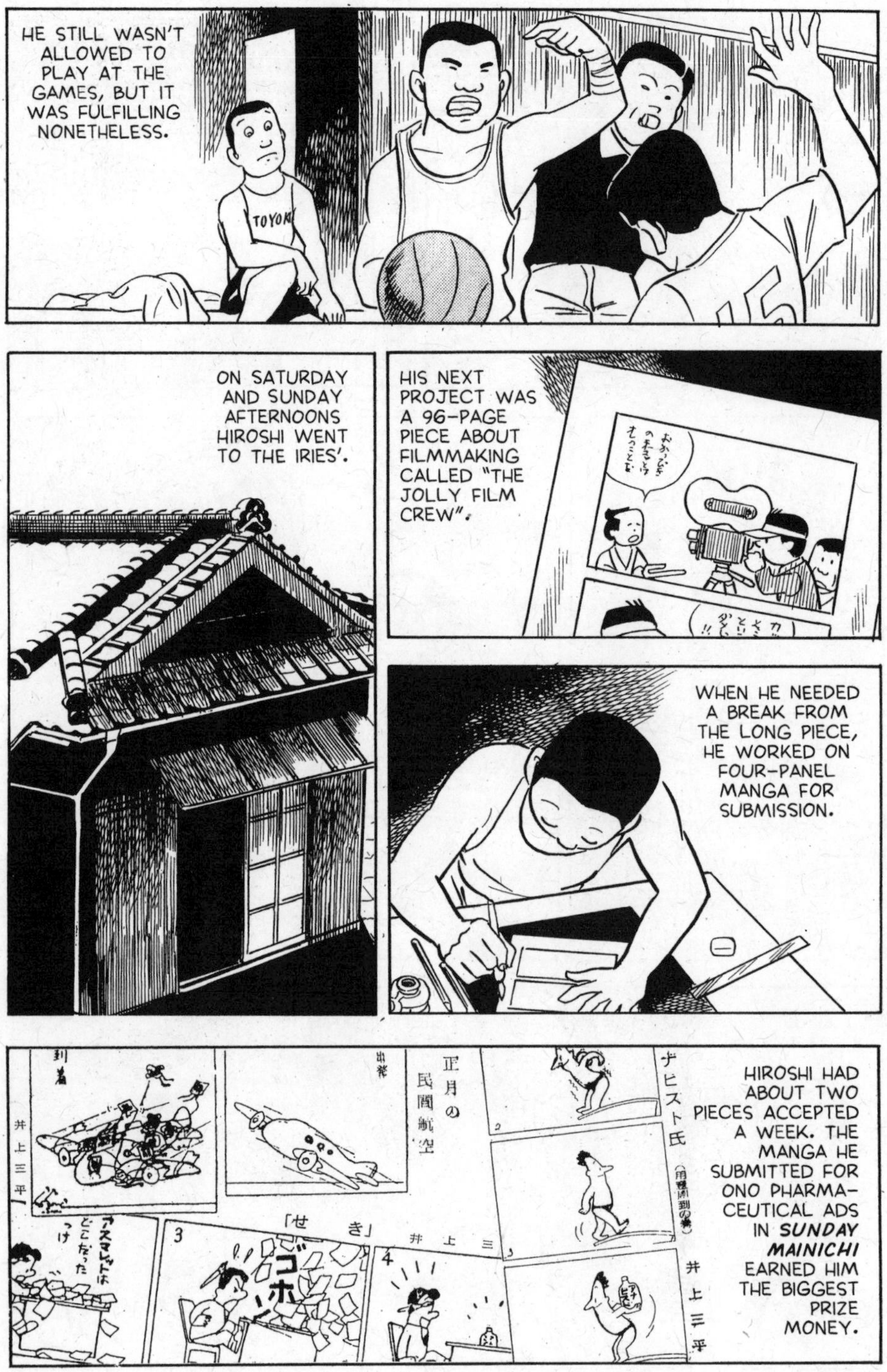
HE STILL WASN'T ALLOWED TO PLAY AT THE GAMES, BUT IT WAS FULFILLING NONETHELESS.
ON SATURDAY AND SUNDAY AFTERNOONS HIROSHI WENT TO THE IRIES'.
HIS NEXT PROJECT WAS A 96-PAGE PIECE ABOUT FILMMAKING CALLED "THE JOLLY FILM CREW".
WHEN HE NEEDED A BREAK FROM THE LONG PIECE, HE WORKED ON FOUR-PANEL MANGA FOR SUBMISSION.
HIROSHI HAD ABOUT TWO PIECES ACCEPTED A WEEK. THE MANGA HE SUBMITTED FOR ONO PHARMACEUTICAL ADS IN ***SUNDAY MAINICHI*** EARNED HIM THE BIGGEST PRIZE MONEY.
正月の民間航空
井上三平
「せき」

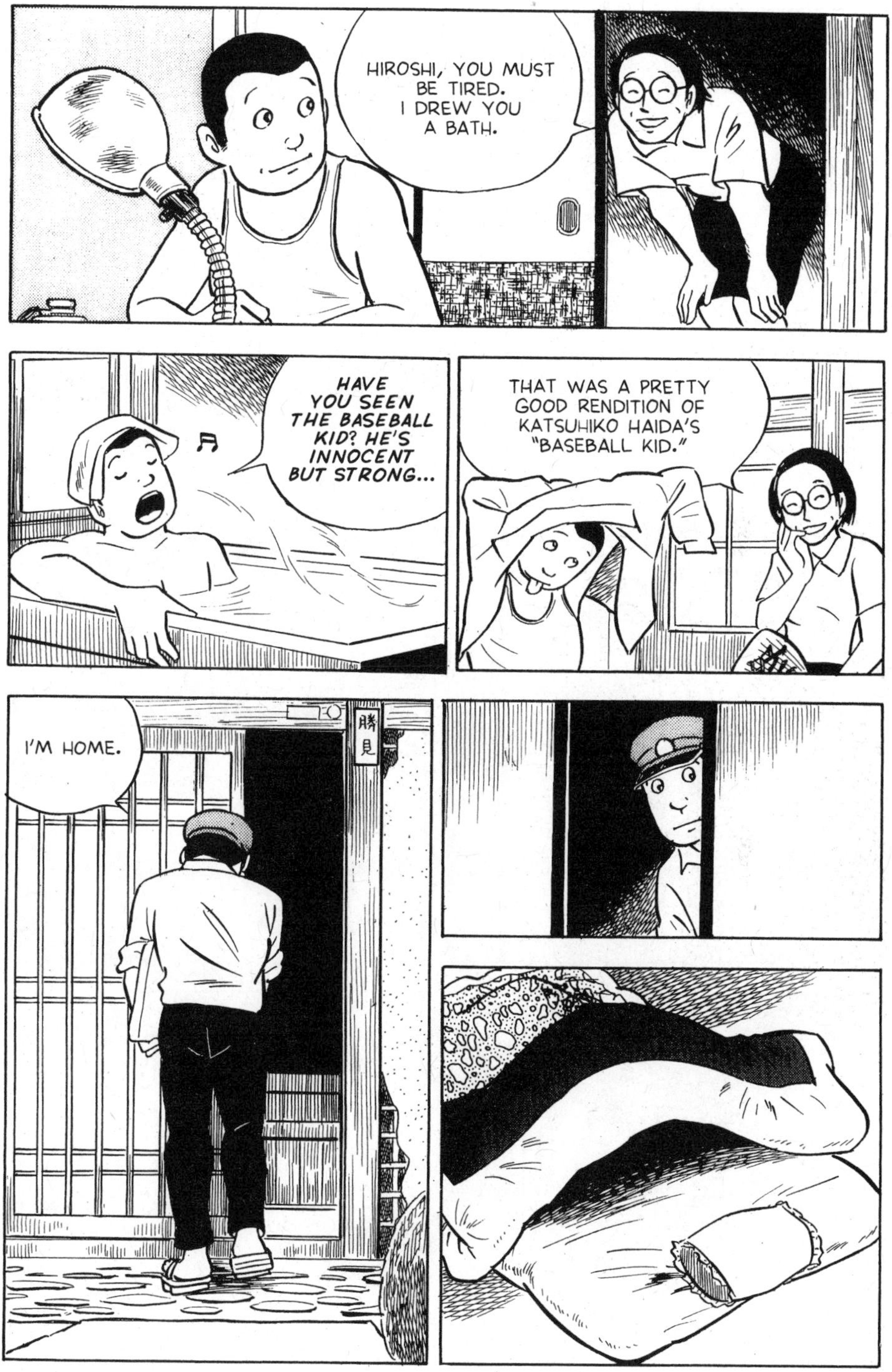
HIROSHI, YOU MUST BE TIRED. I DREW YOU A BATH.
HAVE YOU SEEN THE BASEBALL KID? HE'S INNOCENT BUT STRONG...
THAT WAS A PRETTY GOOD RENDITION OF KATSUHIKO HAIDA'S "BASEBALL KID."
I'M HOME.
勝見

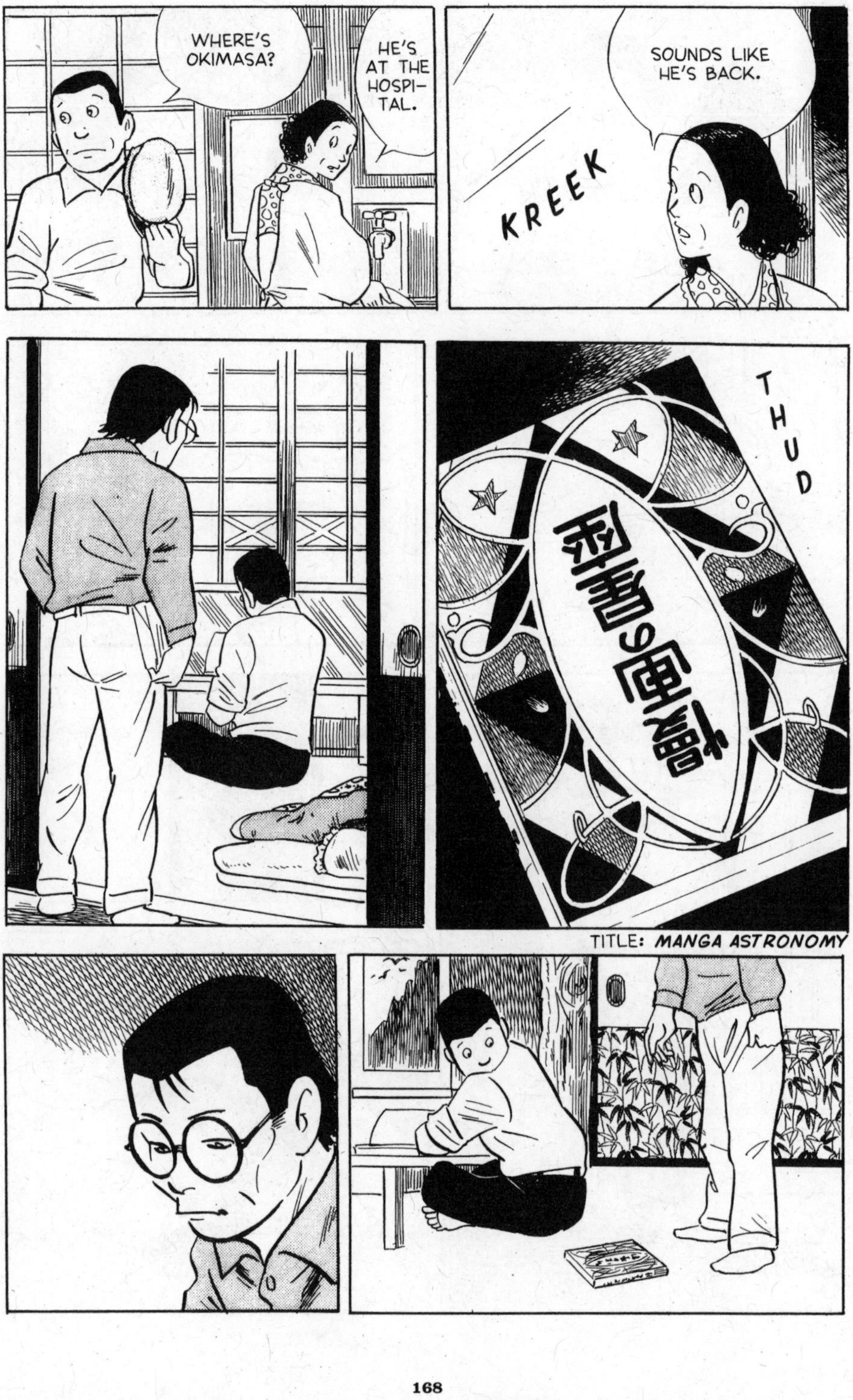
WHERE'S OKIMASA?
HE'S AT THE HOSPITAL.
KREEK
SOUNDS LIKE HE'S BACK.
THUD
TITLE: MANGA ASTRONOMY

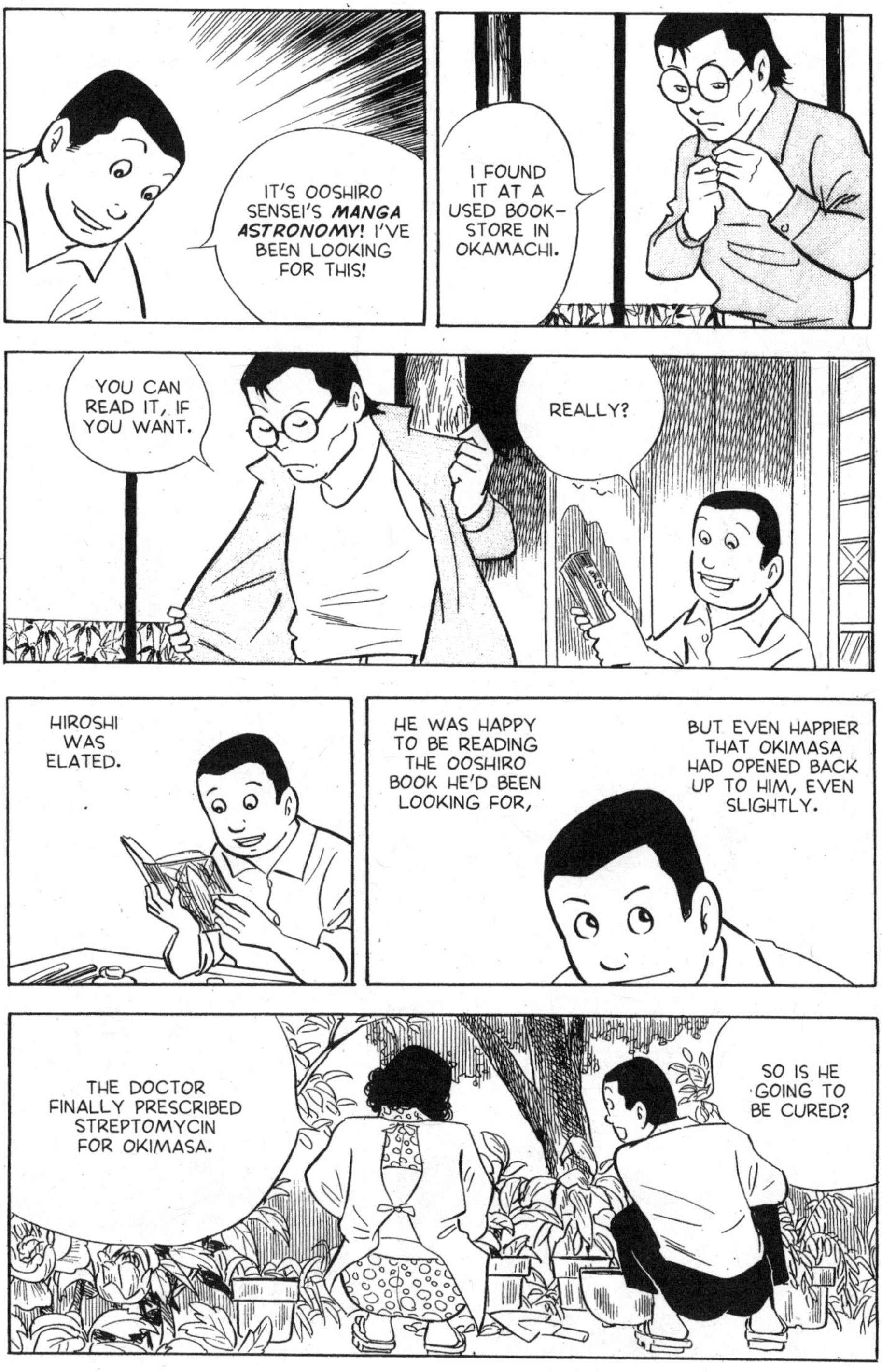
IT'S OOSHIRO SENSEI'S **MANGA ASTRONOMY**! I'VE BEEN LOOKING FOR THIS!
I FOUND IT AT A USED BOOK-STORE IN OKAMACHI.
YOU CAN READ IT, IF YOU WANT.
REALLY?
HIROSHI WAS ELATED.
HE WAS HAPPY TO BE READING THE OOSHIRO BOOK HE'D BEEN LOOKING FOR,
BUT EVEN HAPPIER THAT OKIMASA HAD OPENED BACK UP TO HIM, EVEN SLIGHTLY.
THE DOCTOR FINALLY PRESCRIBED STREPTOMYCIN FOR OKIMASA.
SO IS HE GOING TO BE CURED?

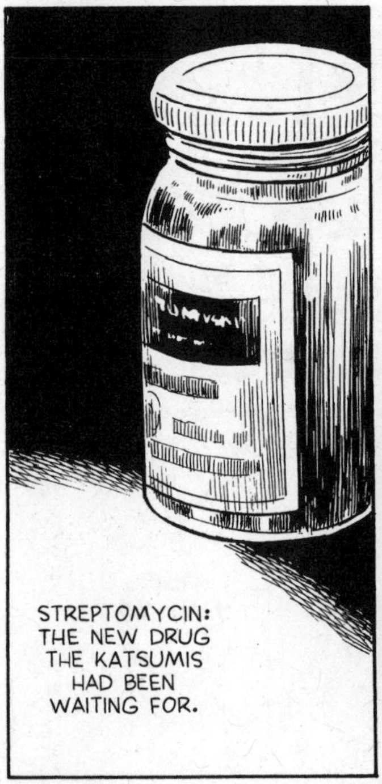
STREPTOMYCIN: THE NEW DRUG THE KATSUMIS HAD BEEN WAITING FOR.

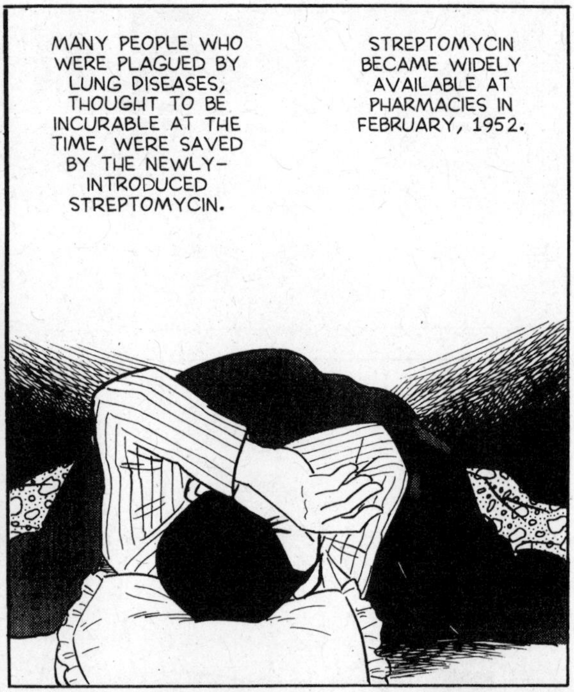
MANY PEOPLE WHO WERE PLAGUED BY LUNG DISEASES, THOUGHT TO BE INCURABLE AT THE TIME, WERE SAVED BY THE NEWLY-INTRODUCED STREPTOMYCIN.
STREPTOMYCIN BECAME WIDELY AVAILABLE AT PHARMACIES IN FEBRUARY, 1952.

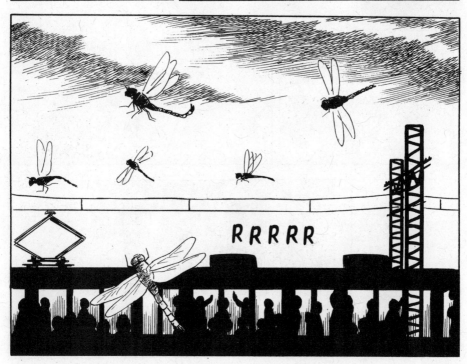

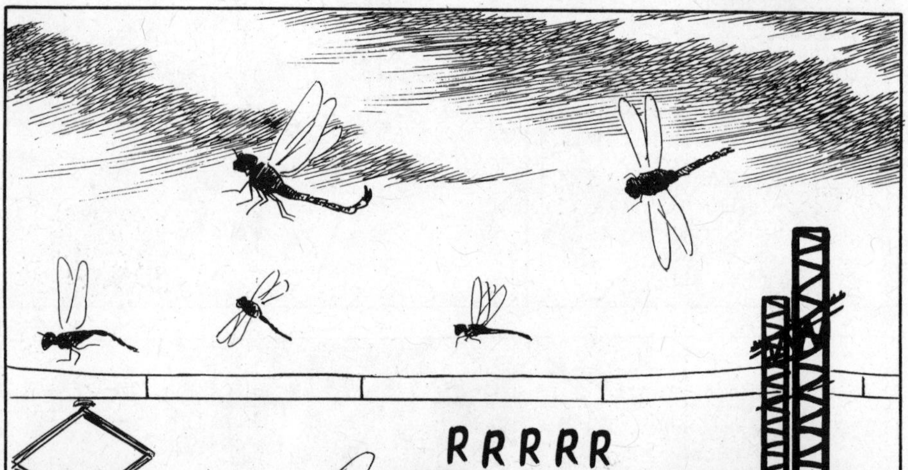
RRRRR

YOU'RE BACK... THERE'S A LETTER FOR YOU FROM OOSHIRO SENSEI.

WHOOSH

WHAT?!

貴君の作品「愉快な漂流記」を拝見いたしました。大へん面白いとくにストーリィが良いと思います

大城のぼる 拝

TEXT: DEAR HIROSHI...

TEXT: I HAVE AT LAST HAD THE CHANCE TO READ YOUR NEW WORK, "HAPPILY ADRIFT." IT IS A FINE WORK. THE STORY IS ESPECIALLY GOOD...

171

TEXT: I WAS MOVED BY THE PIECE AND I WOULD LIKE TO PUBLISH IT, WITH MY DRAWINGS. PLEASE LET ME KNOW...

TEXT: IT WOULD GIVE YOU SOME POCKET MONEY. I LOOK FORWARD...

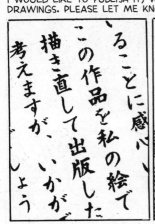

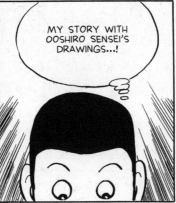

ることに感心
この作品を私の絵で
描き直して出版した
いかが
考えますが、
しょう
MY STORY WITH OOSHIRO SENSEI'S DRAWINGS...!
しょうか？
お小遣いくらいに
なりますよ。
って返事
"DRAWN BY NOBORU OOSHIRO (ORIGINAL CONCEPT BY HIROSHI KATSUMI)".
INCRED-IBLE!
HAHAHA HAHA...
THUMP
THUMP

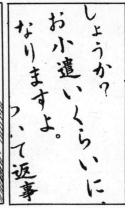

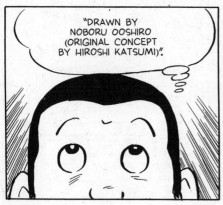

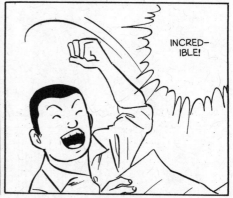

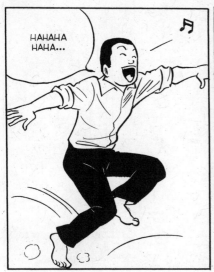

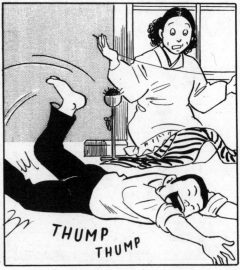

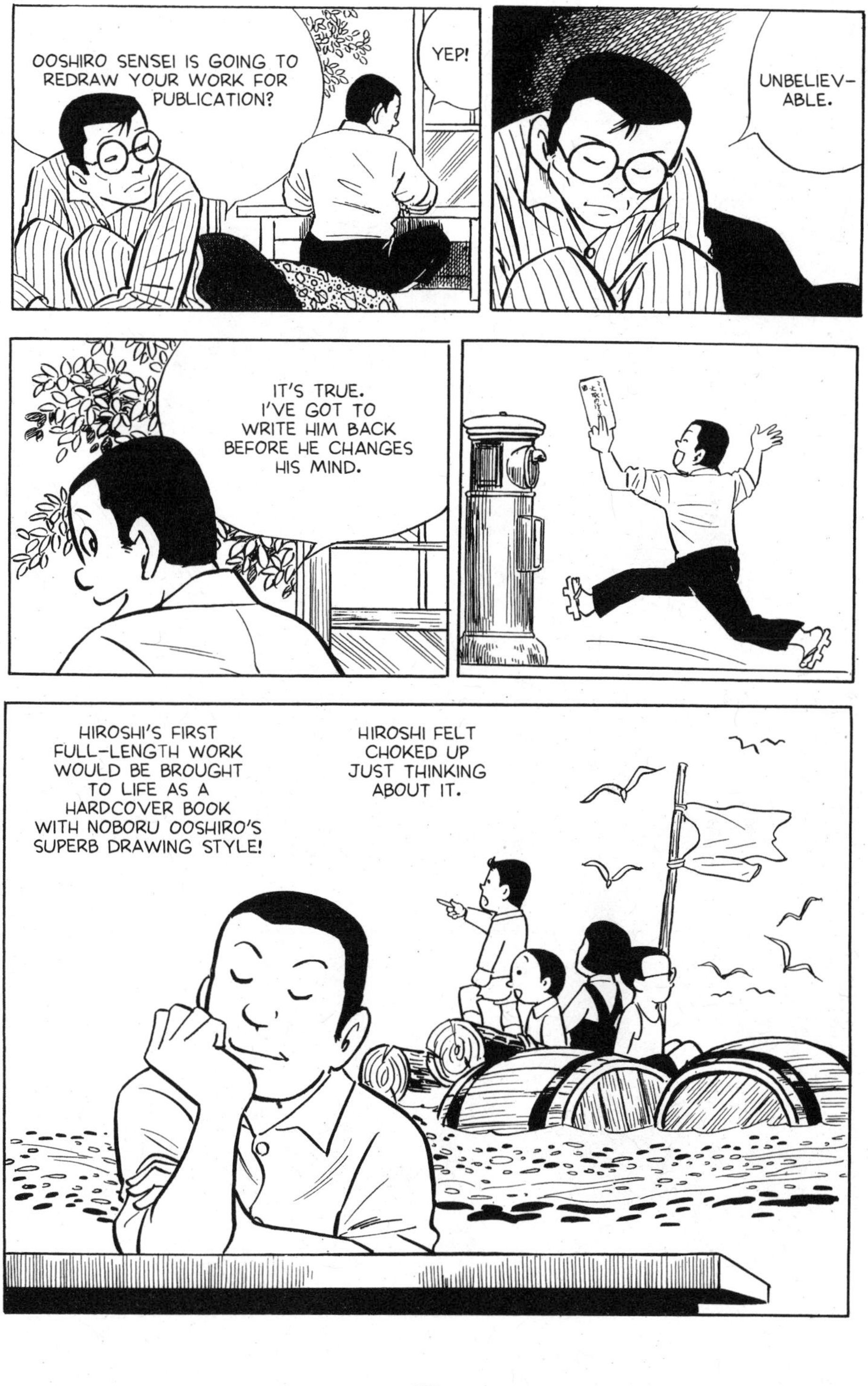
OOSHIRO SENSEI IS GOING TO REDRAW YOUR WORK FOR PUBLICATION?
YEP!
UNBELIEV-ABLE.
IT'S TRUE. I'VE GOT TO WRITE HIM BACK BEFORE HE CHANGES HIS MIND.
HIROSHI'S FIRST FULL-LENGTH WORK WOULD BE BROUGHT TO LIFE AS A HARDCOVER BOOK WITH NOBORU OOSHIRO'S SUPERB DRAWING STYLE!
HIROSHI FELT CHOKED UP JUST THINKING ABOUT IT.

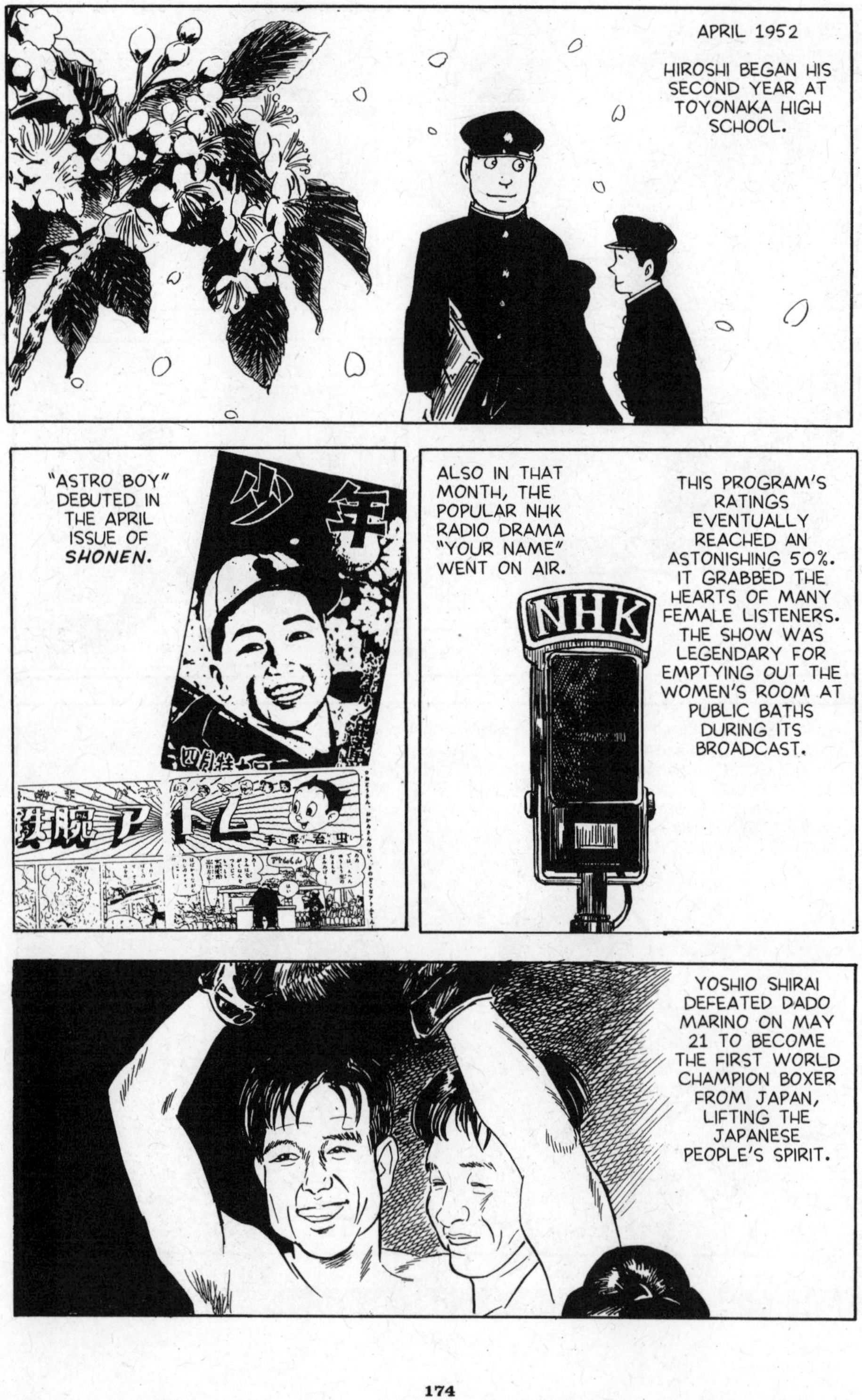
APRIL 1952
HIROSHI BEGAN HIS SECOND YEAR AT TOYONAKA HIGH SCHOOL.
"ASTRO BOY" DEBUTED IN THE APRIL ISSUE OF ***SHONEN***.
少年
鉄腕アトム
手塚治虫
ALSO IN THAT MONTH, THE POPULAR NHK RADIO DRAMA "YOUR NAME" WENT ON AIR.
THIS PROGRAM'S RATINGS EVENTUALLY REACHED AN ASTONISHING 50%. IT GRABBED THE HEARTS OF MANY FEMALE LISTENERS. THE SHOW WAS LEGENDARY FOR EMPTYING OUT THE WOMEN'S ROOM AT PUBLIC BATHS DURING ITS BROADCAST.
NHK
YOSHIO SHIRAI DEFEATED DADO MARINO ON MAY 21 TO BECOME THE FIRST WORLD CHAMPION BOXER FROM JAPAN, LIFTING THE JAPANESE PEOPLE'S SPIRIT.

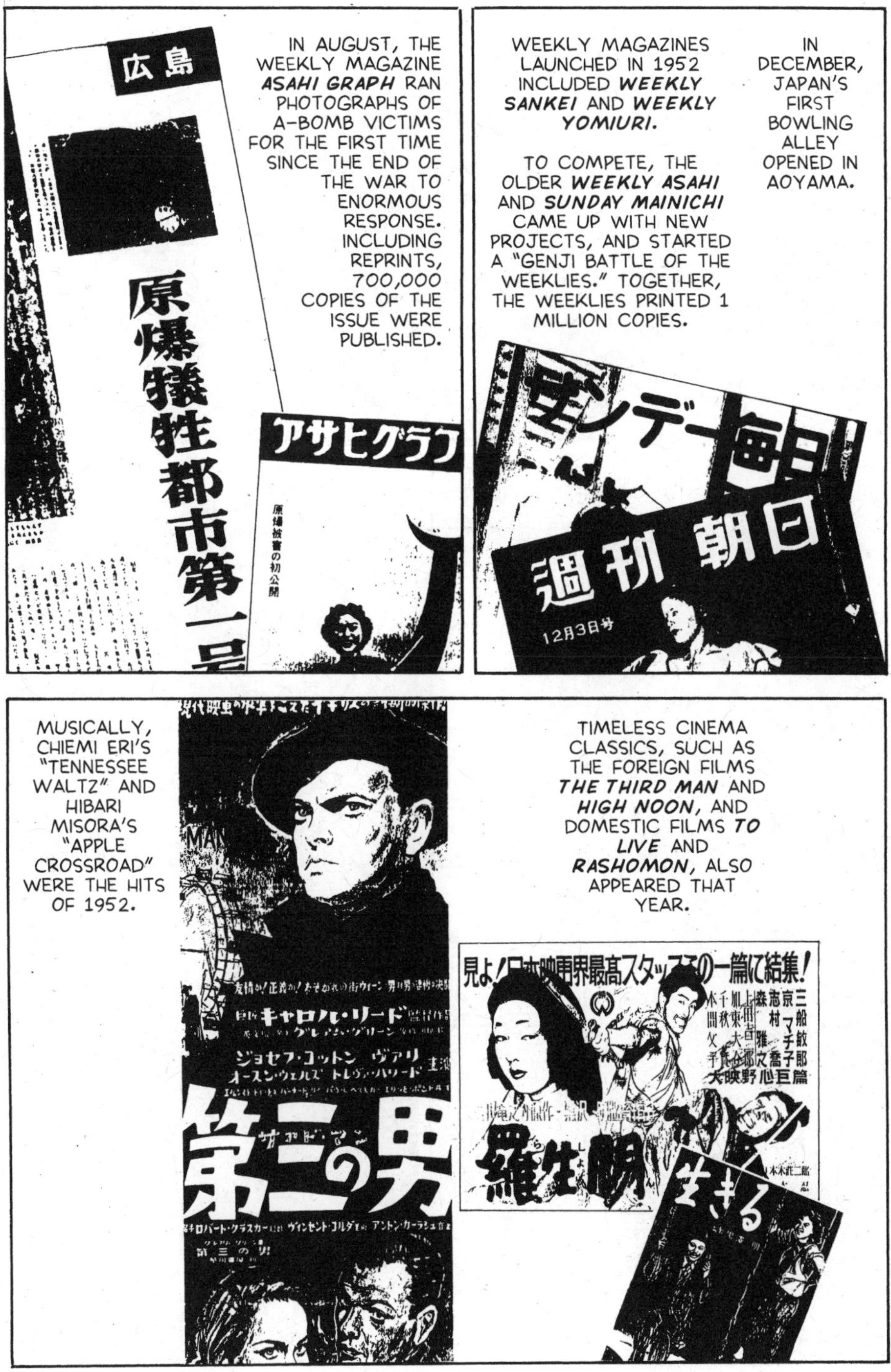

IN AUGUST, THE WEEKLY MAGAZINE ***ASAHI GRAPH*** RAN PHOTOGRAPHS OF A-BOMB VICTIMS FOR THE FIRST TIME SINCE THE END OF THE WAR TO ENORMOUS RESPONSE. INCLUDING REPRINTS, 700,000 COPIES OF THE ISSUE WERE PUBLISHED.
広島
原爆犠牲都市第一
アサヒグラフ
原爆被害の初公開
WEEKLY MAGAZINES LAUNCHED IN 1952 INCLUDED ***WEEKLY SANKEI*** AND ***WEEKLY YOMIURI.***
TO COMPETE, THE OLDER ***WEEKLY ASAHI*** AND ***SUNDAY MAINICHI*** CAME UP WITH NEW PROJECTS, AND STARTED A "GENJI BATTLE OF THE WEEKLIES." TOGETHER, THE WEEKLIES PRINTED 1 MILLION COPIES.
IN DECEMBER, JAPAN'S FIRST BOWLING ALLEY OPENED IN AOYAMA.
サンデー毎日
週刊朝日
12月3日号
MUSICALLY, CHIEMI ERI'S "TENNESSEE WALTZ" AND HIBARI MISORA'S "APPLE CROSSROAD" WERE THE HITS OF 1952.
キャロル・リード
ジョセフ・コットン　ヴァリ
オースン・ウェルズ　トレヴァ・ハワード
第三の男
TIMELESS CINEMA CLASSICS, SUCH AS THE FOREIGN FILMS ***THE THIRD MAN*** AND ***HIGH NOON,*** AND DOMESTIC FILMS ***TO LIVE*** AND ***RASHOMON,*** ALSO APPEARED THAT YEAR.
見よ！日本映画界最高スタッフその一篇に結集！
羅生門
生きる

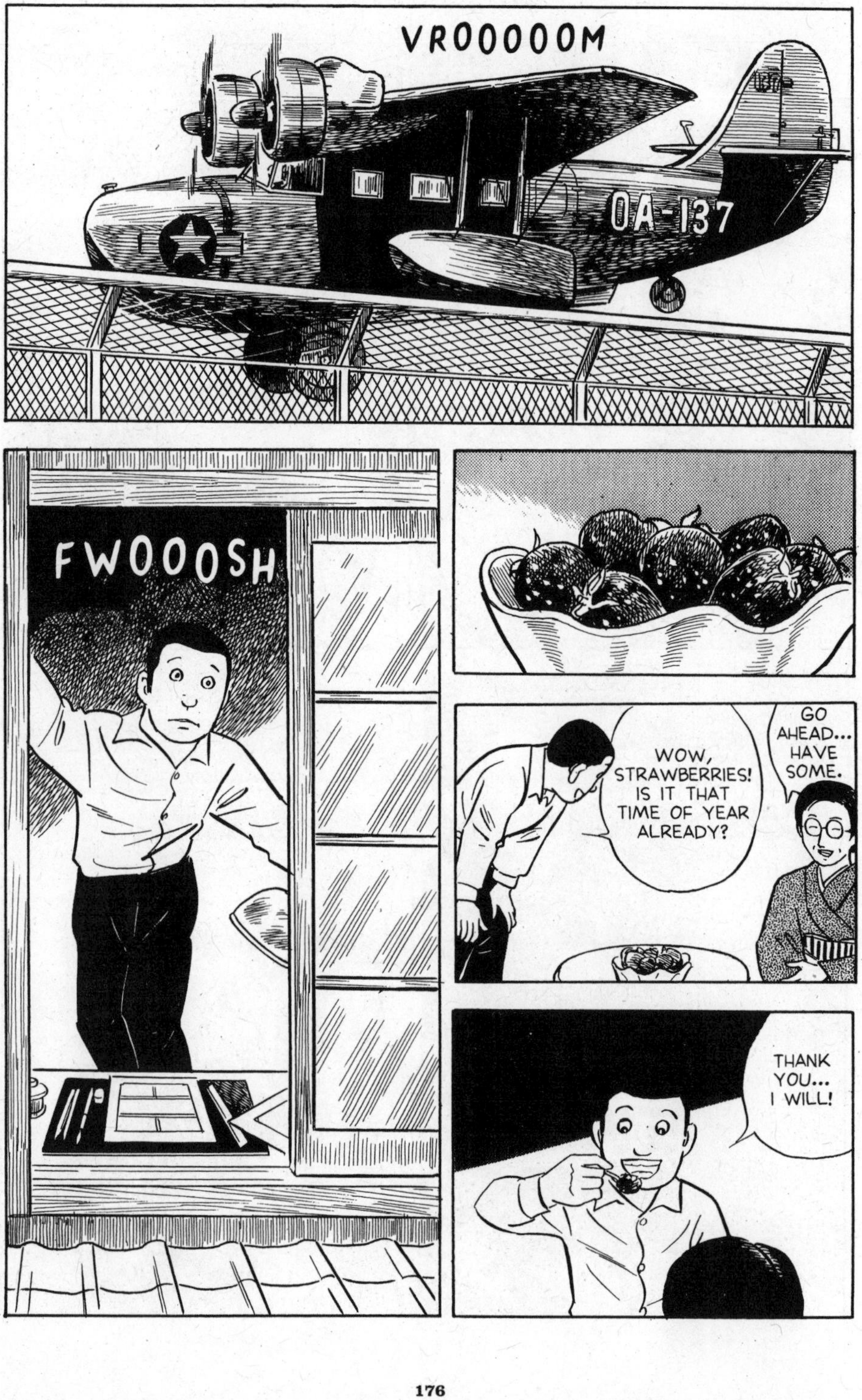
VROOOOOM
OA-137
FWOOOSH
WOW, STRAWBERRIES! IS IT THAT TIME OF YEAR ALREADY?
GO AHEAD... HAVE SOME.
THANK YOU... I WILL!

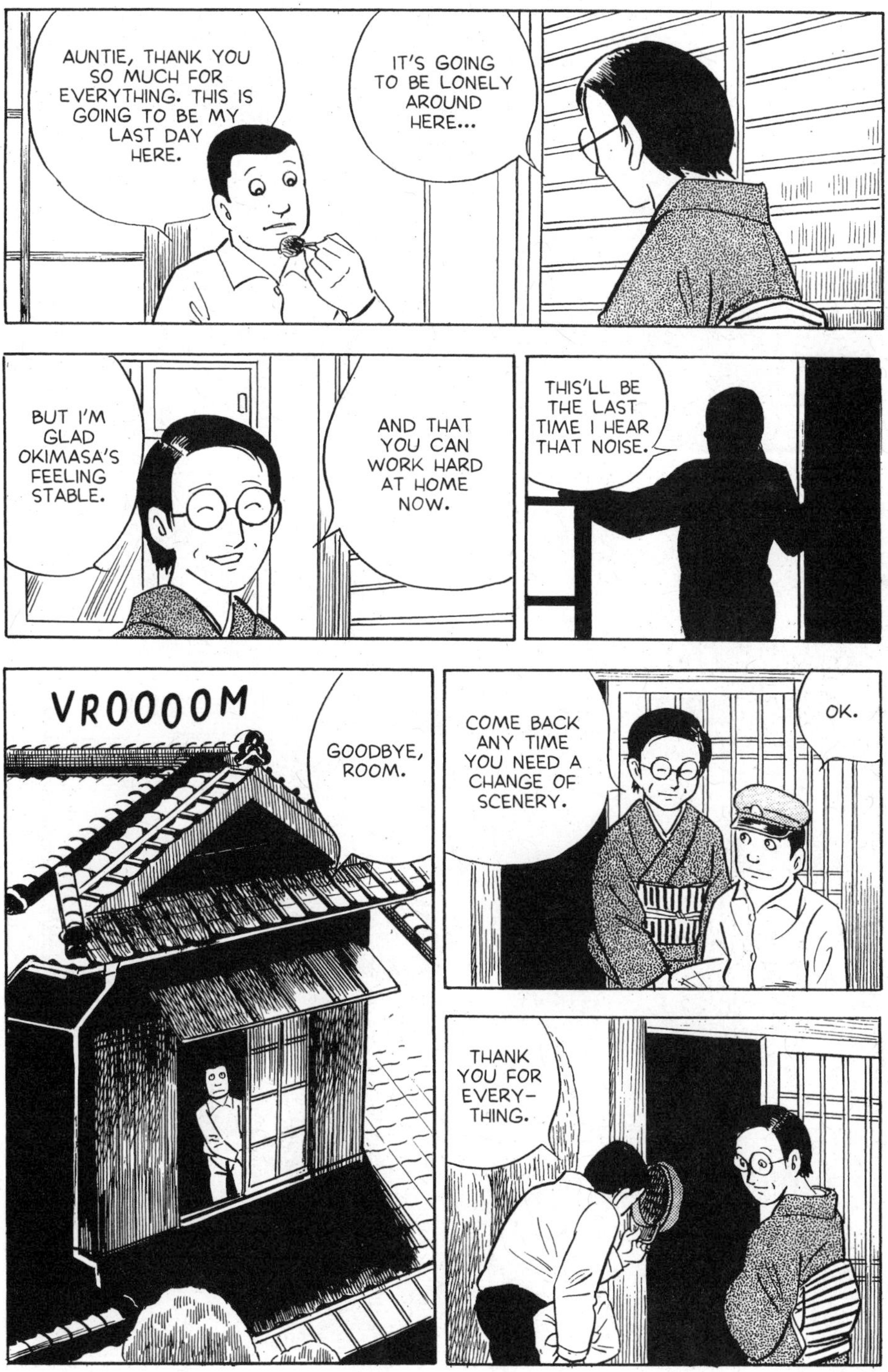
AUNTIE, THANK YOU SO MUCH FOR EVERYTHING. THIS IS GOING TO BE MY LAST DAY HERE.
IT'S GOING TO BE LONELY AROUND HERE...
BUT I'M GLAD OKIMASA'S FEELING STABLE.
AND THAT YOU CAN WORK HARD AT HOME NOW.
THIS'LL BE THE LAST TIME I HEAR THAT NOISE.
VROOOOM
GOODBYE, ROOM.
COME BACK ANY TIME YOU NEED A CHANGE OF SCENERY.
OK.
THANK YOU FOR EVERY-THING.

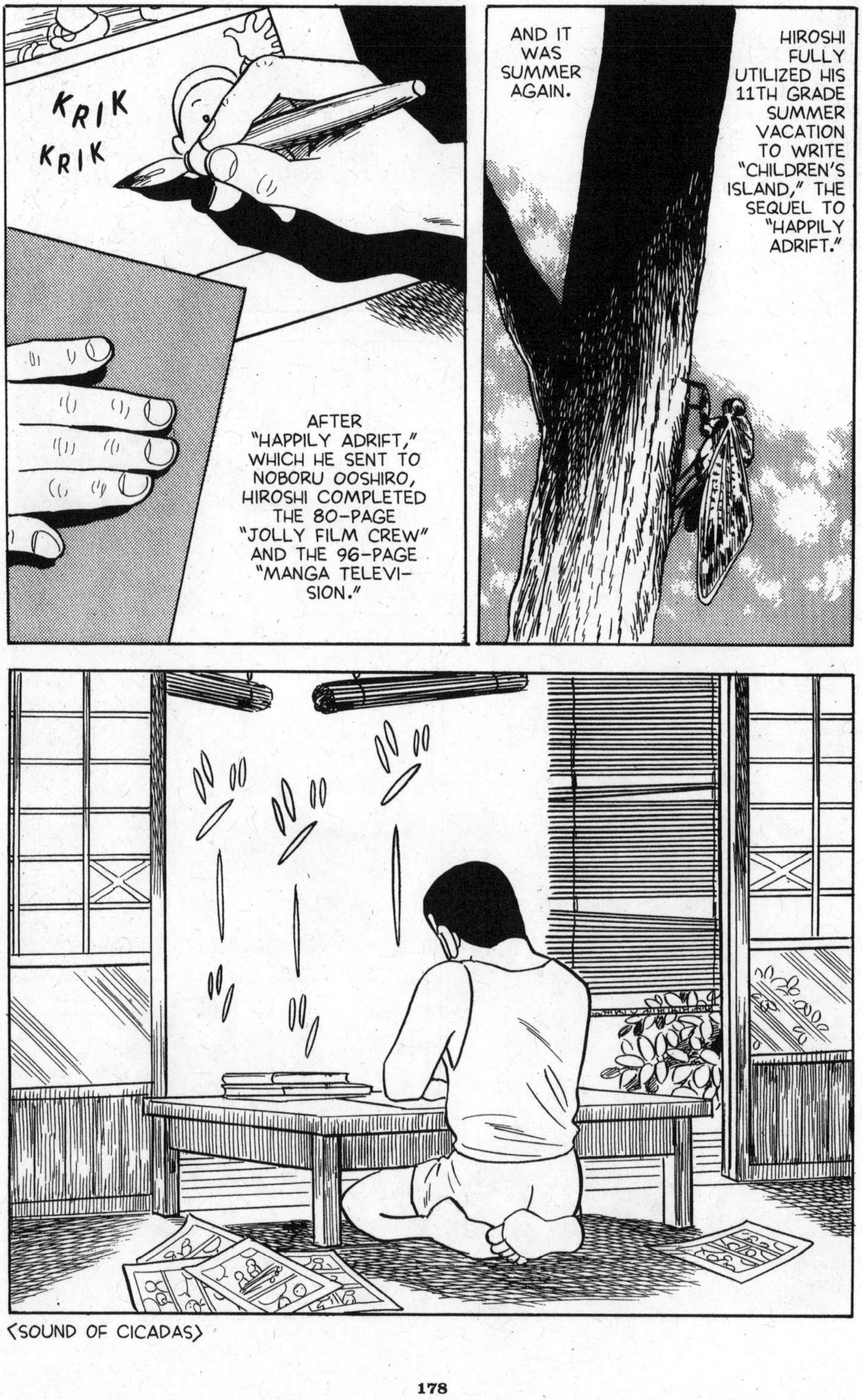
KRIK
KRIK
AFTER "HAPPILY ADRIFT," WHICH HE SENT TO NOBORU OOSHIRO, HIROSHI COMPLETED THE 80-PAGE "JOLLY FILM CREW" AND THE 96-PAGE "MANGA TELEVISION."
AND IT WAS SUMMER AGAIN.
HIROSHI FULLY UTILIZED HIS 11TH GRADE SUMMER VACATION TO WRITE "CHILDREN'S ISLAND," THE SEQUEL TO "HAPPILY ADRIFT."

<SOUND OF CICADAS>

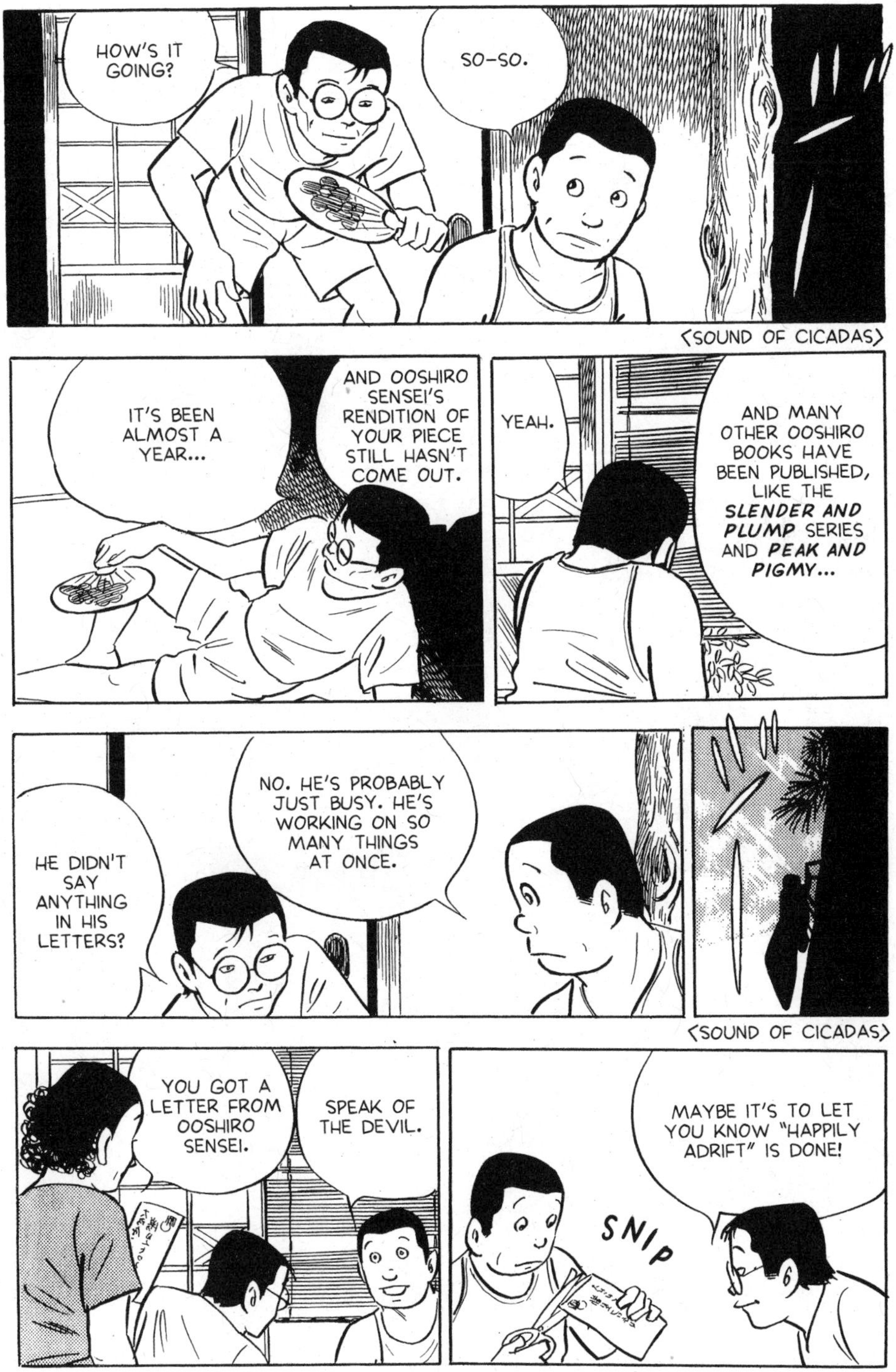
HOW'S IT GOING?
SO-SO.
⟨SOUND OF CICADAS⟩
IT'S BEEN ALMOST A YEAR...
AND OOSHIRO SENSEI'S RENDITION OF YOUR PIECE STILL HASN'T COME OUT.
YEAH.
AND MANY OTHER OOSHIRO BOOKS HAVE BEEN PUBLISHED, LIKE THE ***SLENDER AND PLUMP*** SERIES AND ***PEAK AND PIGMY...***
HE DIDN'T SAY ANYTHING IN HIS LETTERS?
NO. HE'S PROBABLY JUST BUSY. HE'S WORKING ON SO MANY THINGS AT ONCE.
⟨SOUND OF CICADAS⟩
YOU GOT A LETTER FROM OOSHIRO SENSEI.
SPEAK OF THE DEVIL.
SNIP
MAYBE IT'S TO LET YOU KNOW "HAPPILY ADRIFT" IS DONE!

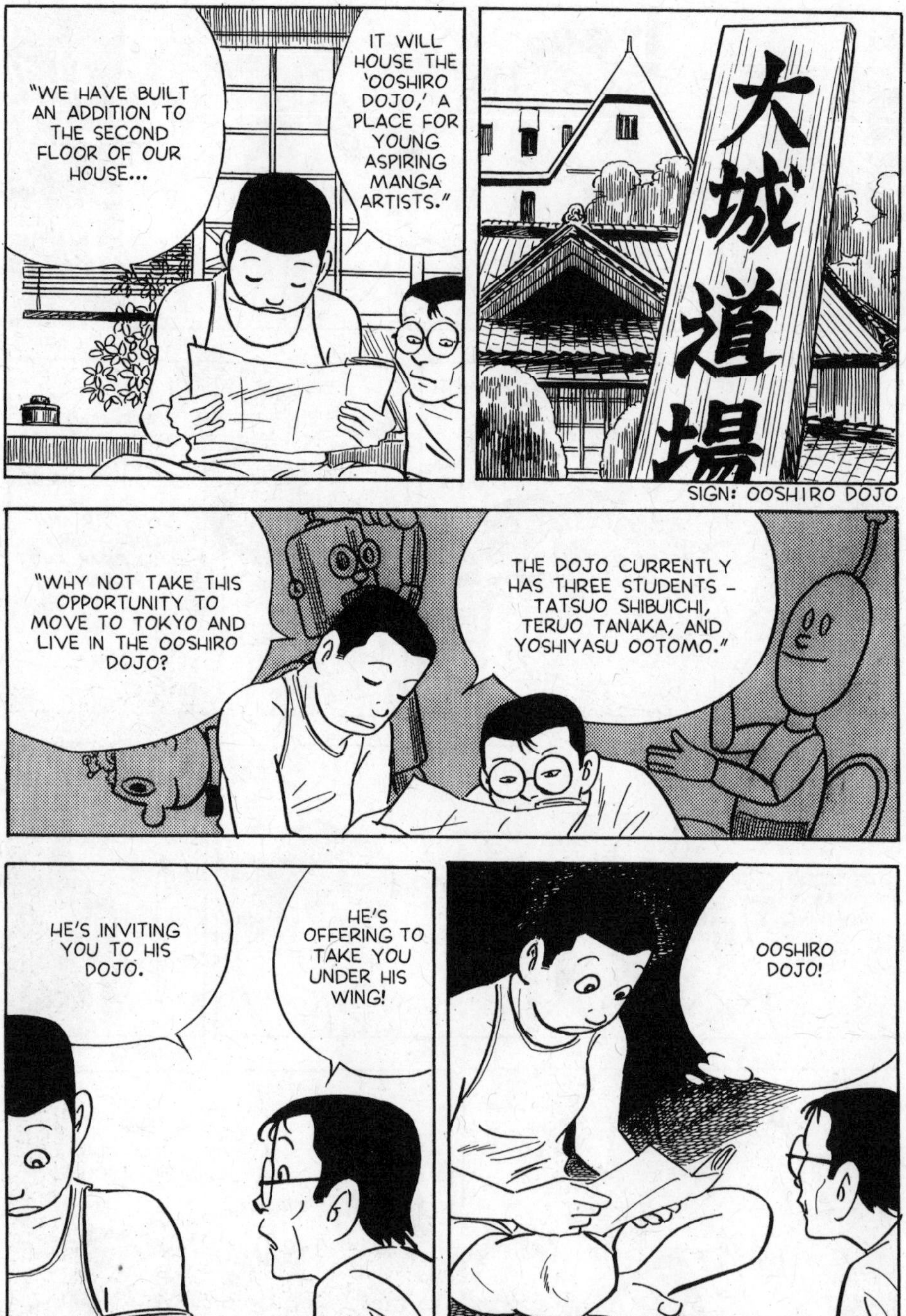
"WE HAVE BUILT AN ADDITION TO THE SECOND FLOOR OF OUR HOUSE...
IT WILL HOUSE THE 'OOSHIRO DOJO,' A PLACE FOR YOUNG ASPIRING MANGA ARTISTS."
大城道場
SIGN: OOSHIRO DOJO
"WHY NOT TAKE THIS OPPORTUNITY TO MOVE TO TOKYO AND LIVE IN THE OOSHIRO DOJO?
THE DOJO CURRENTLY HAS THREE STUDENTS – TATSUO SHIBUICHI, TERUO TANAKA, AND YOSHIYASU OOTOMO."
HE'S INVITING YOU TO HIS DOJO.
HE'S OFFERING TO TAKE YOU UNDER HIS WING!
OOSHIRO DOJO!

THE CON ARTIST

TEXT BELOW:
NAKAMURA MANGA SERIES
PINBO THE AUTOMATON
NOBORU OOSHIRO

ナカムラマンガシリーズ
人造人間のピン坊

大城のぼる

昭和27年の長谷川町子

TEXT ABOVE: MACHIKO
HASEGAWA IN 1952

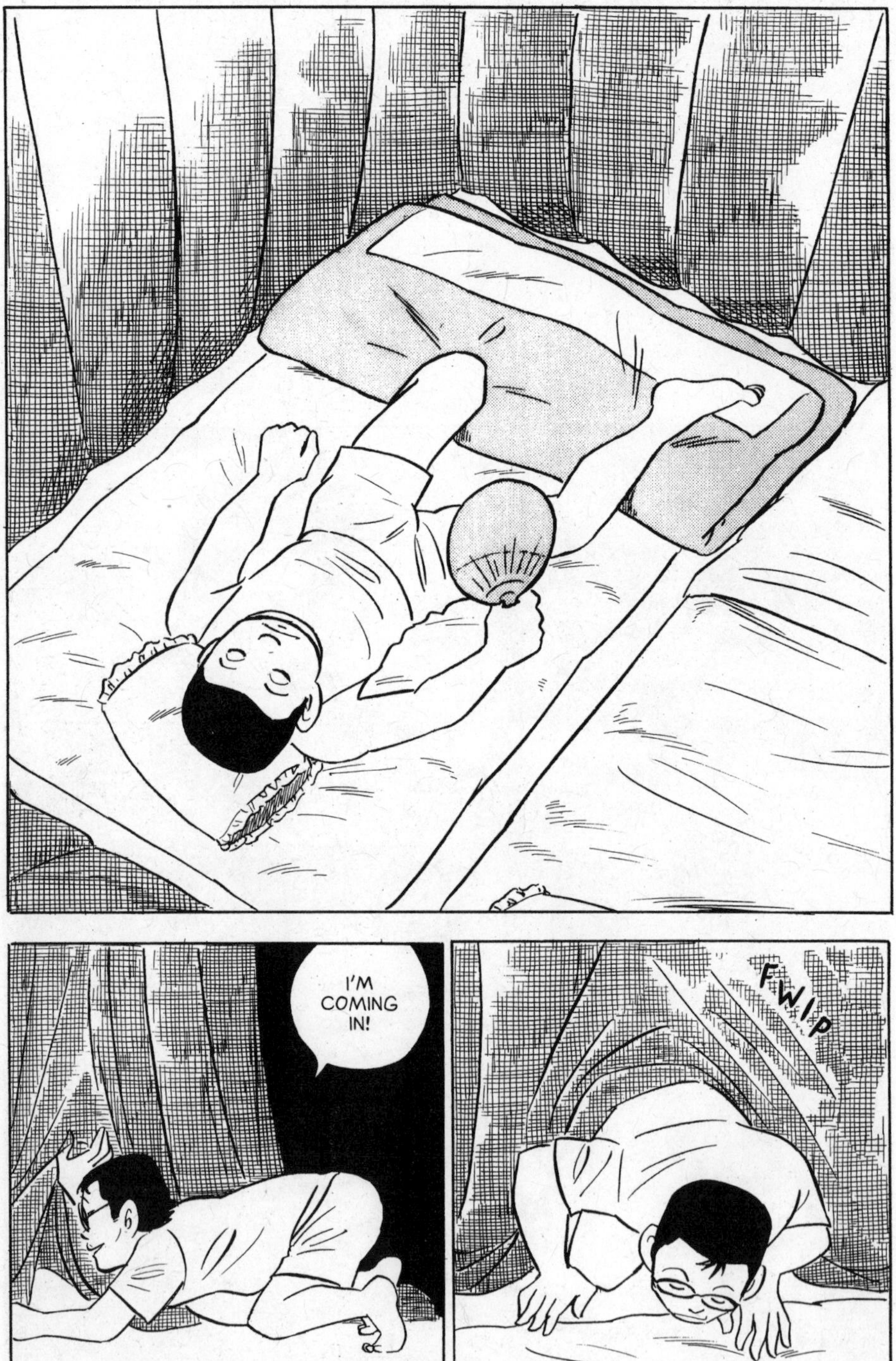
I'M COMING IN!
FWIP

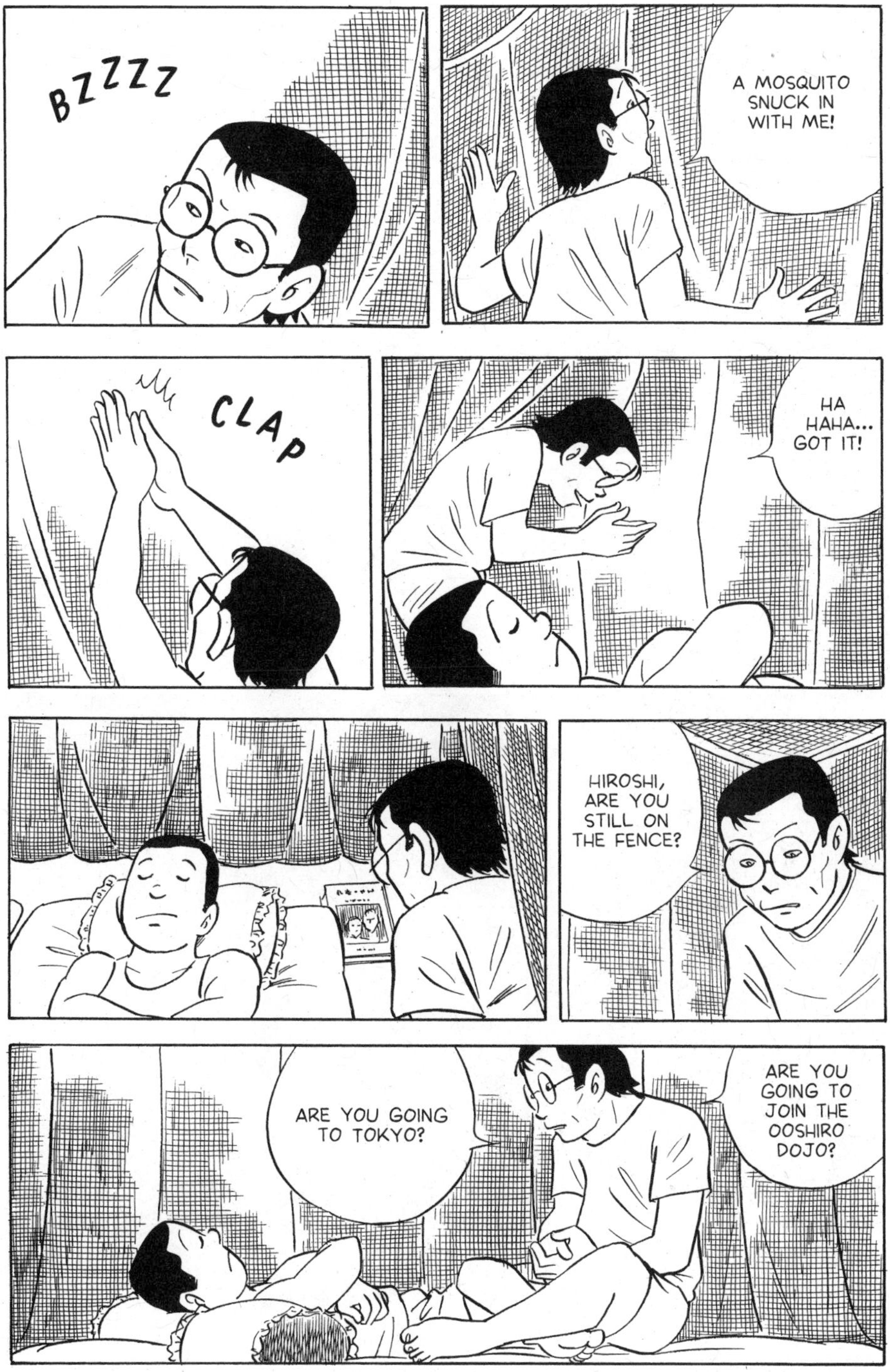
BZZZZ
A MOSQUITO SNUCK IN WITH ME!
CLAP
HA HAHA... GOT IT!
HIROSHI, ARE YOU STILL ON THE FENCE?
ARE YOU GOING TO TOKYO?
ARE YOU GOING TO JOIN THE OOSHIRO DOJO?

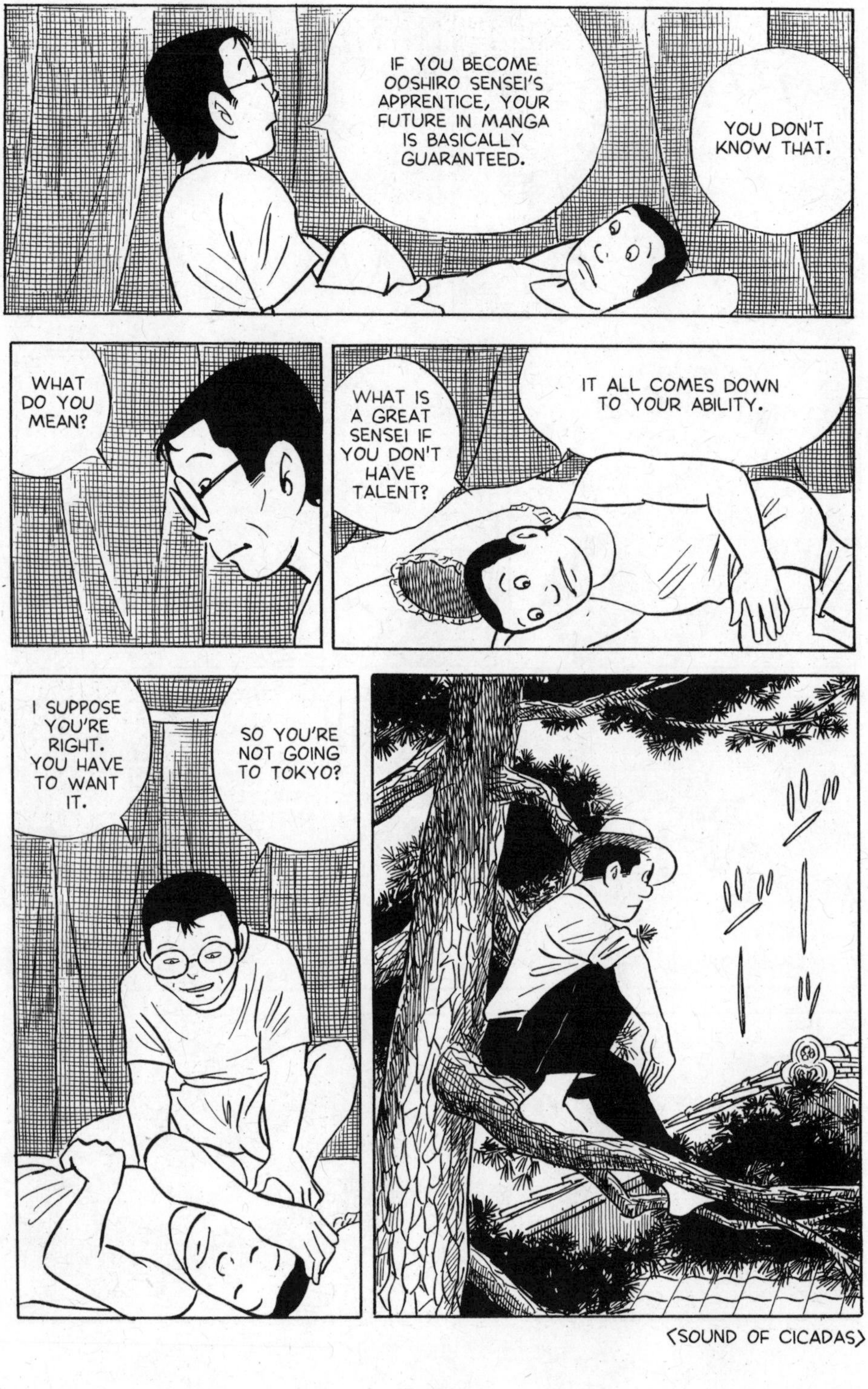
IF YOU BECOME OOSHIRO SENSEI'S APPRENTICE, YOUR FUTURE IN MANGA IS BASICALLY GUARANTEED.
YOU DON'T KNOW THAT.
WHAT DO YOU MEAN?
WHAT IS A GREAT SENSEI IF YOU DON'T HAVE TALENT?
IT ALL COMES DOWN TO YOUR ABILITY.
I SUPPOSE YOU'RE RIGHT. YOU HAVE TO WANT IT.
SO YOU'RE NOT GOING TO TOKYO?

〈SOUND OF CICADAS〉

HIROSHI FELT UNSURE.

THIS DECISION WOULD ALTER THE COURSE OF HIS LIFE.

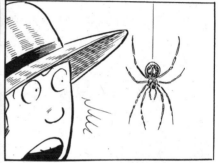

KRIK
KRIK

185

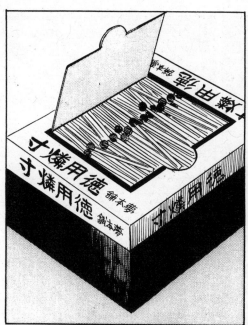

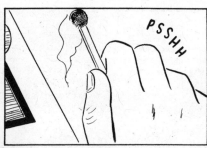

PSSHH

BOX: DREAM BRAND SAFETY MATCHES

SORRY YOU HAD TO HELP ME WITH THE BATH. I KNOW IT'S DELAYING YOUR WORK.

IT'S ALL RIGHT. I DON'T FEEL LIKE WORKING RIGHT NOW ANYWAY.

OKIMASA'S CONDITION'S IMPROVED THANKS TO THE STREPTO- MYCIN...

AND DAD'S BACK ON HIS FEET.

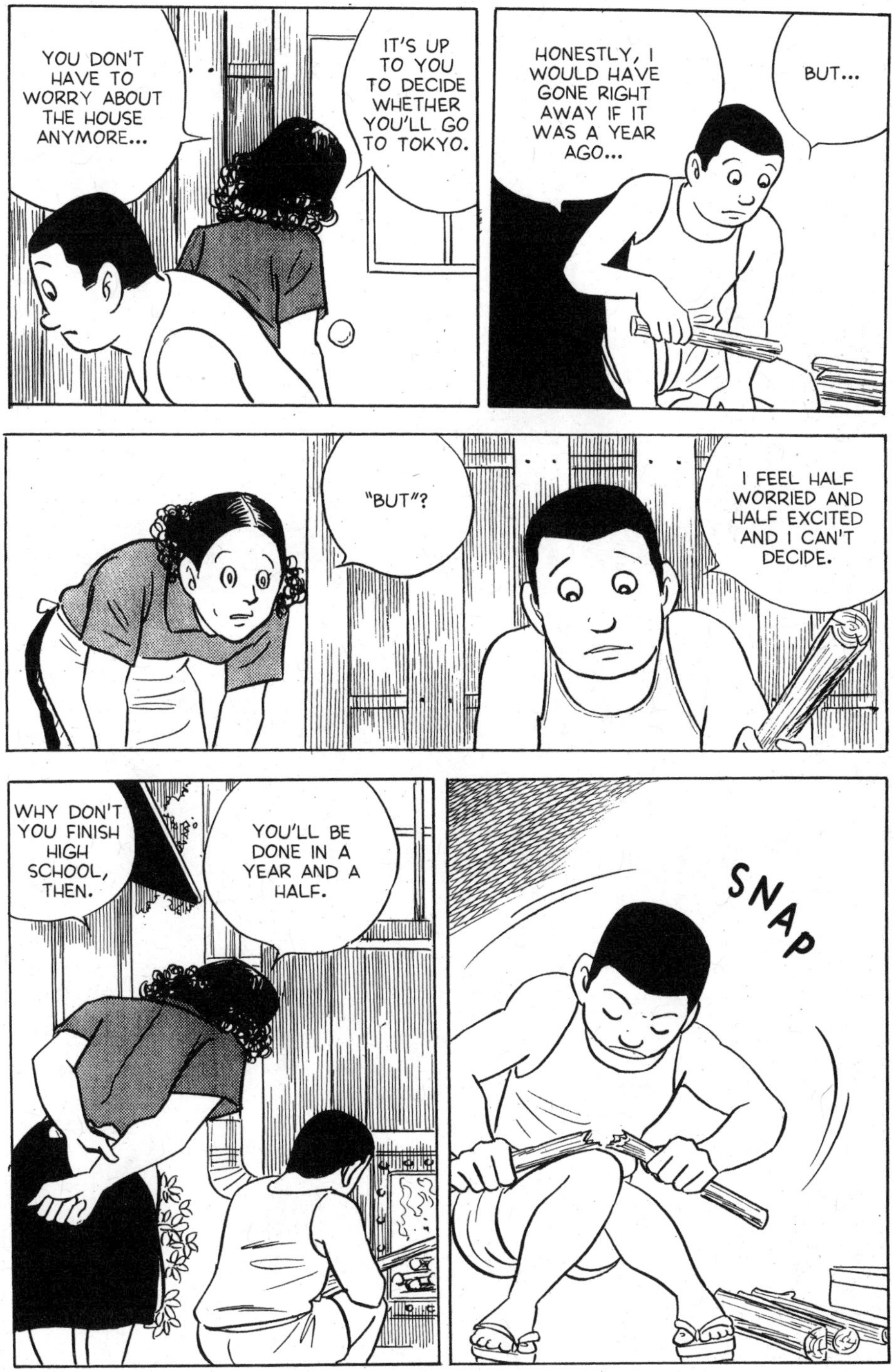
YOU DON'T HAVE TO WORRY ABOUT THE HOUSE ANYMORE...
IT'S UP TO YOU TO DECIDE WHETHER YOU'LL GO TO TOKYO.
HONESTLY, I WOULD HAVE GONE RIGHT AWAY IF IT WAS A YEAR AGO...
BUT...
"BUT"?
I FEEL HALF WORRIED AND HALF EXCITED AND I CAN'T DECIDE.
WHY DON'T YOU FINISH HIGH SCHOOL, THEN.
YOU'LL BE DONE IN A YEAR AND A HALF.
SNAP

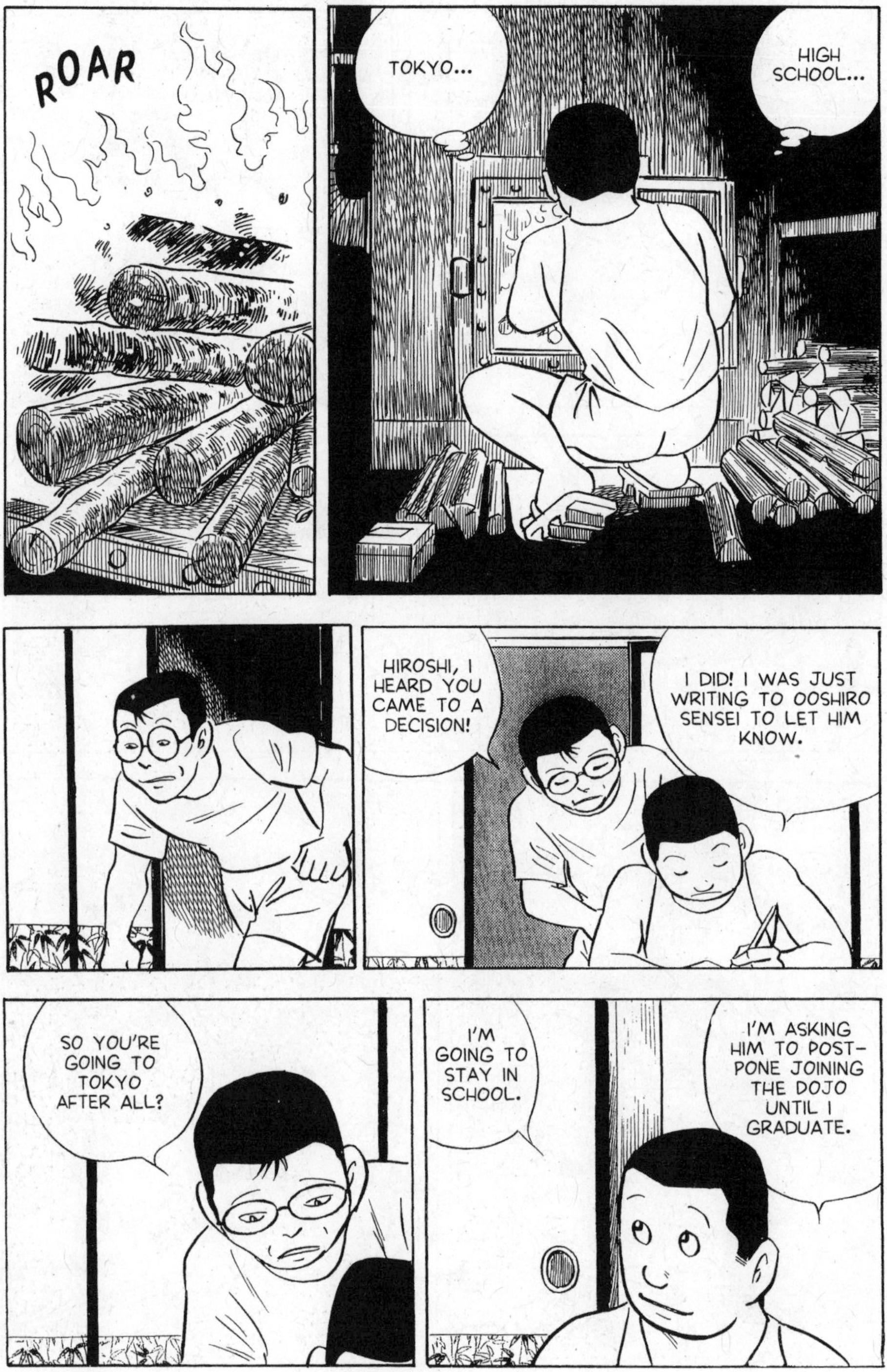
ROAR
TOKYO...
HIGH SCHOOL...
HIROSHI, I HEARD YOU CAME TO A DECISION!
I DID! I WAS JUST WRITING TO OOSHIRO SENSEI TO LET HIM KNOW.
SO YOU'RE GOING TO TOKYO AFTER ALL?
I'M GOING TO STAY IN SCHOOL.
I'M ASKING HIM TO POST-PONE JOINING THE DOJO UNTIL I GRADUATE.

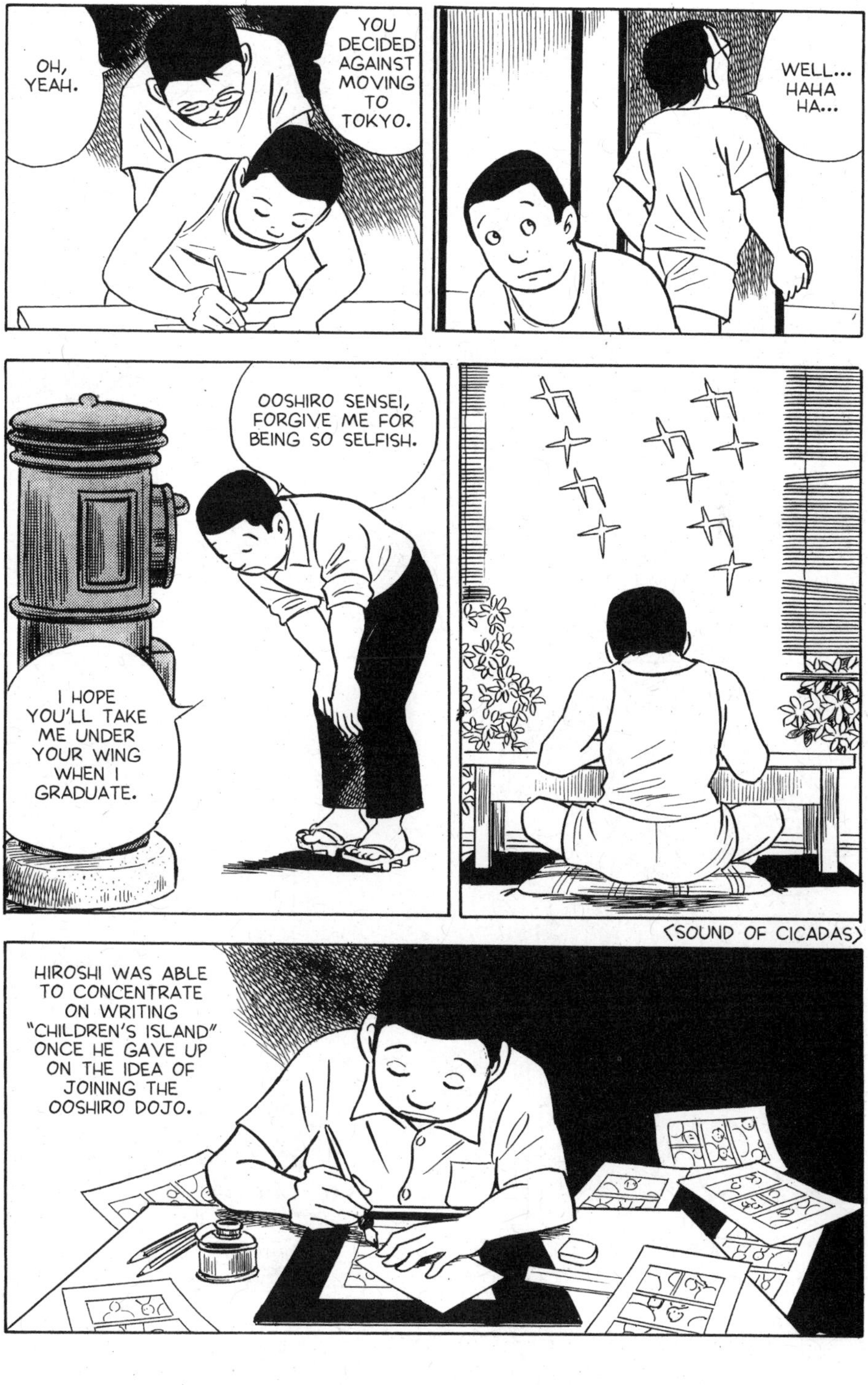
OH, YEAH.
YOU DECIDED AGAINST MOVING TO TOKYO.
WELL... HAHA HA...
OOSHIRO SENSEI, FORGIVE ME FOR BEING SO SELFISH.
I HOPE YOU'LL TAKE ME UNDER YOUR WING WHEN I GRADUATE.
〈SOUND OF CICADAS〉
HIROSHI WAS ABLE TO CONCENTRATE ON WRITING "CHILDREN'S ISLAND" ONCE HE GAVE UP ON THE IDEA OF JOINING THE OOSHIRO DOJO.

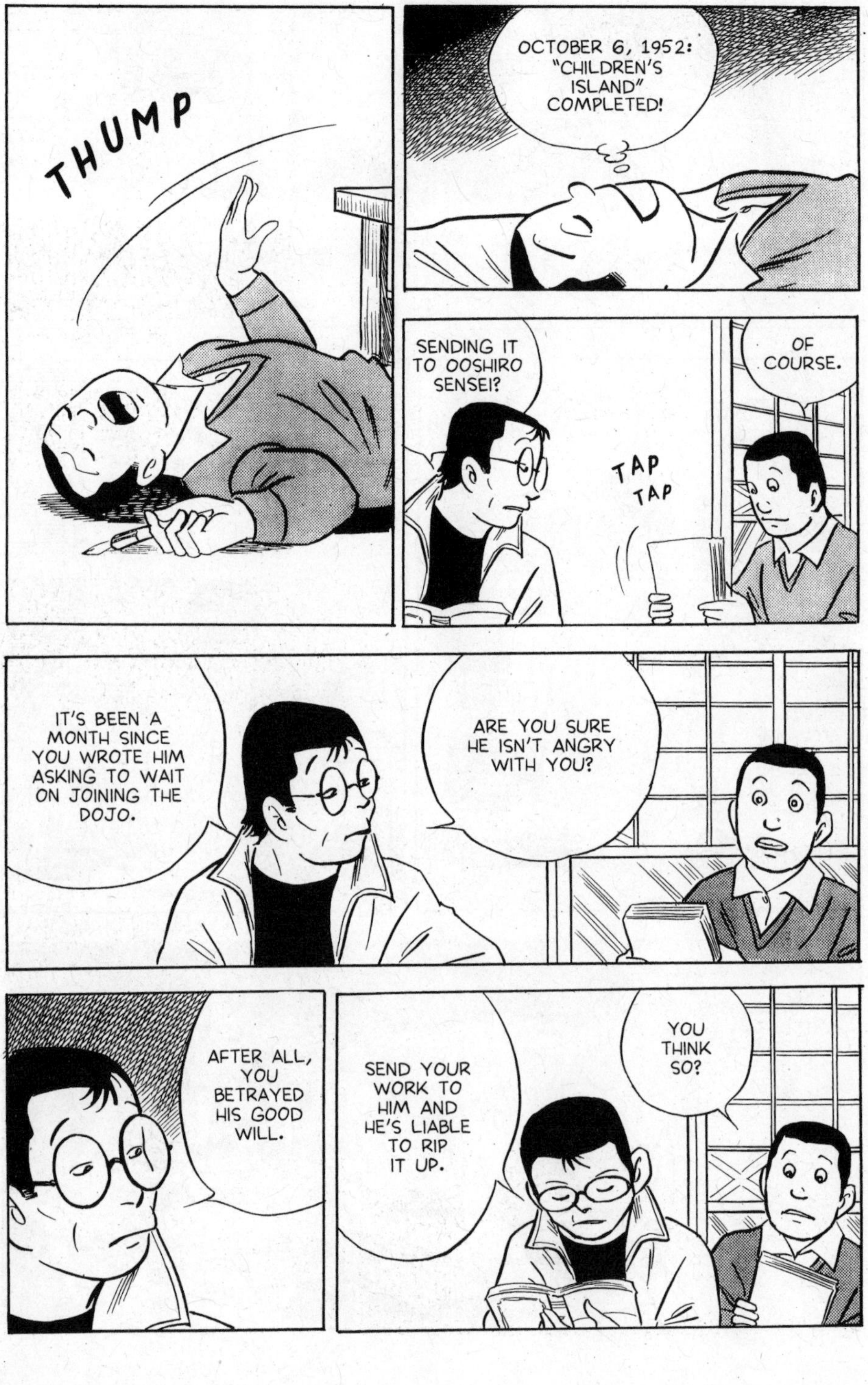
THUMP
OCTOBER 6, 1952: "CHILDREN'S ISLAND" COMPLETED!
SENDING IT TO OOSHIRO SENSEI?
OF COURSE.
TAP TAP
IT'S BEEN A MONTH SINCE YOU WROTE HIM ASKING TO WAIT ON JOINING THE DOJO.
ARE YOU SURE HE ISN'T ANGRY WITH YOU?
AFTER ALL, YOU BETRAYED HIS GOOD WILL.
SEND YOUR WORK TO HIM AND HE'S LIABLE TO RIP IT UP.
YOU THINK SO?

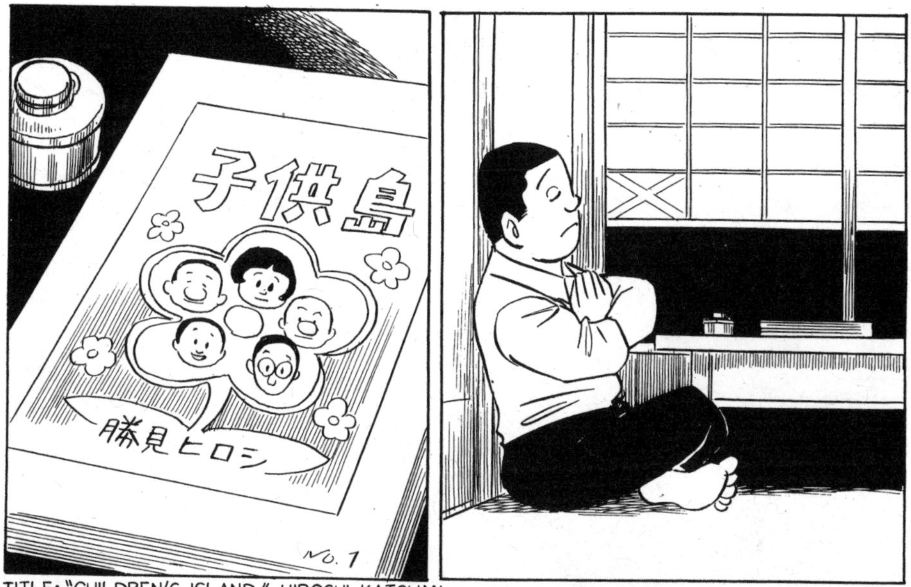
子供島
勝見ヒロシ
NO. 1

TITLE: "CHILDREN'S ISLAND," HIROSHI KATSUMI

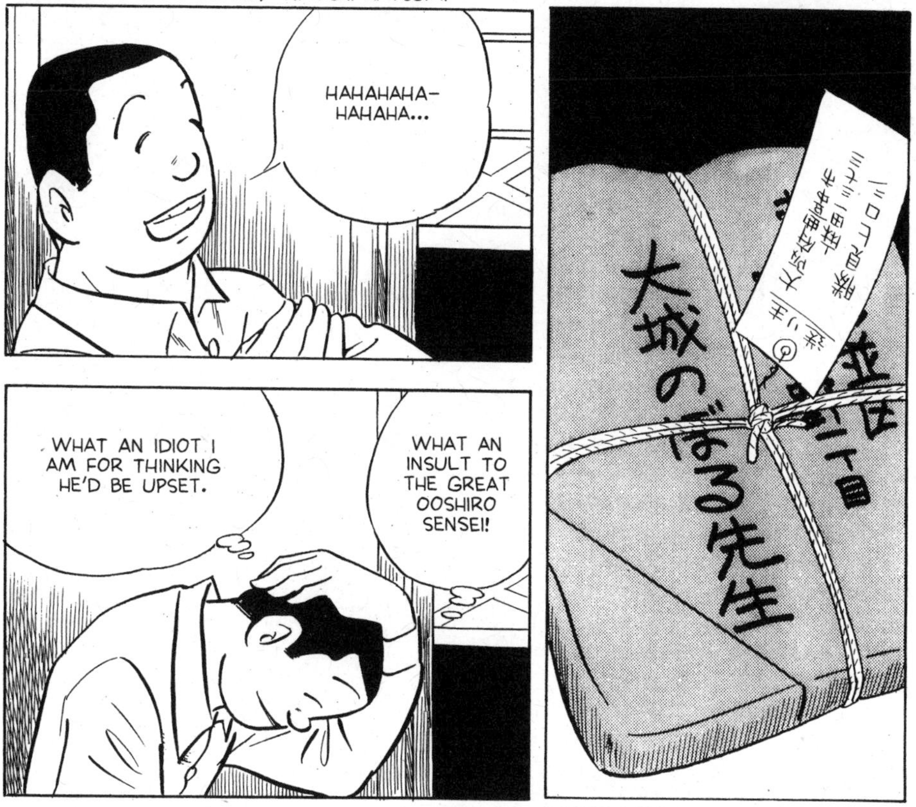
HAHAHAHA-
HAHAHA...
WHAT AN IDIOT I AM FOR THINKING HE'D BE UPSET.
WHAT AN INSULT TO THE GREAT OOSHIRO SENSEI!
大城のぼる先生

PARCEL TEXT:
TO: NOBORU OOSHIRO SENSEI
FROM: HIROSHI KATSUMI

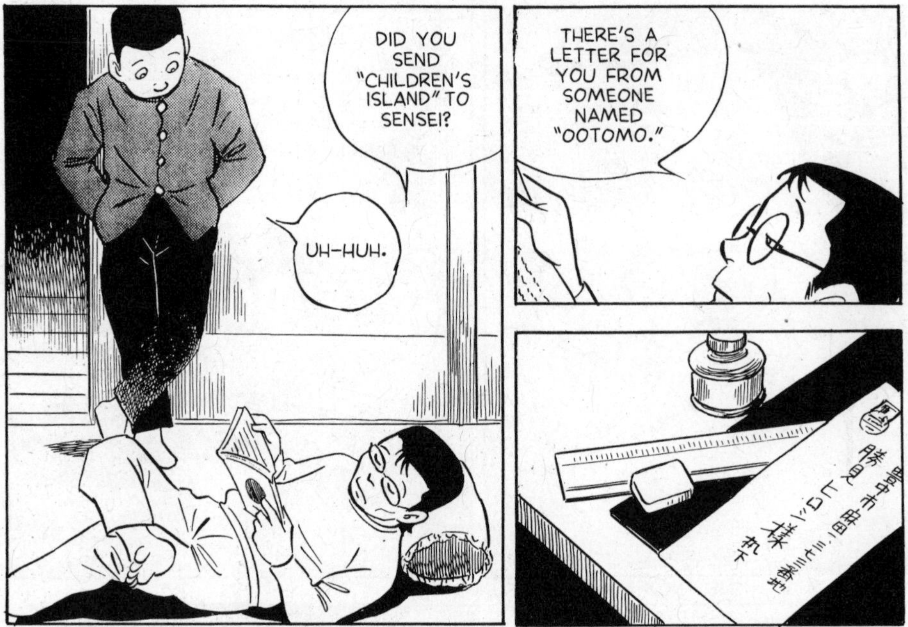
DID YOU SEND "CHILDREN'S ISLAND" TO SENSEI?
UH-HUH.
THERE'S A LETTER FOR YOU FROM SOMEONE NAMED "OOTOMO."

LETTER: HIROSHI KATSUMI 1-37-3 ASADA, TOYONAKA-SHI, OSAKA

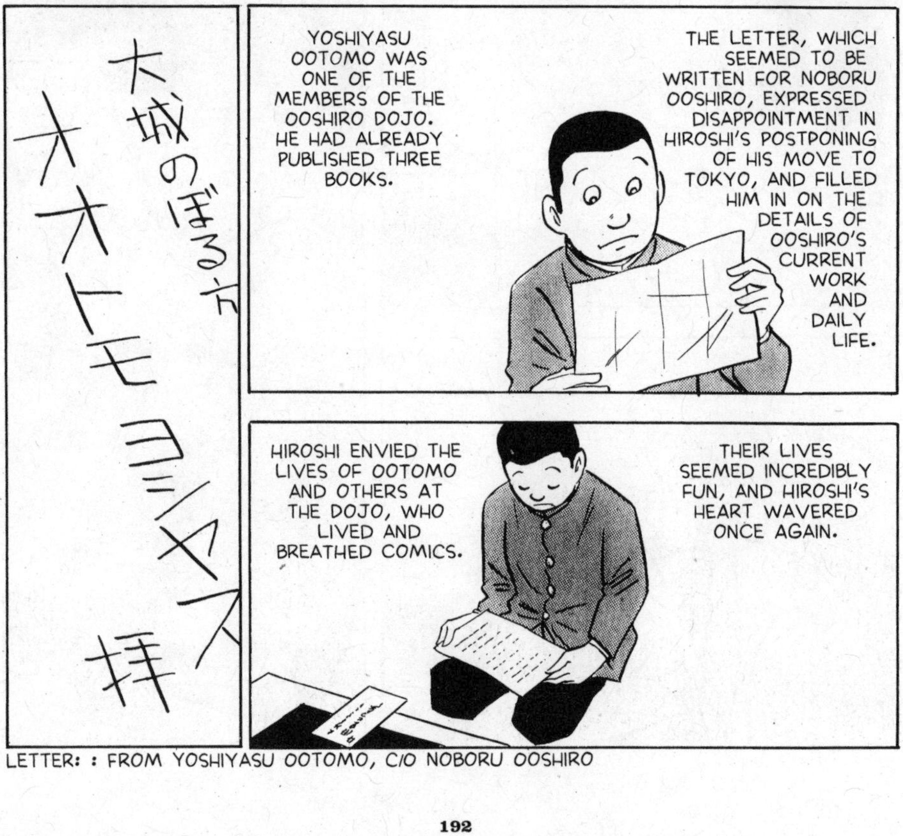
大城のぼる方
オオトモヨシヤス拝
YOSHIYASU OOTOMO WAS ONE OF THE MEMBERS OF THE OOSHIRO DOJO. HE HAD ALREADY PUBLISHED THREE BOOKS.
THE LETTER, WHICH SEEMED TO BE WRITTEN FOR NOBORU OOSHIRO, EXPRESSED DISAPPOINTMENT IN HIROSHI'S POSTPONING OF HIS MOVE TO TOKYO, AND FILLED HIM IN ON THE DETAILS OF OOSHIRO'S CURRENT WORK AND DAILY LIFE.
HIROSHI ENVIED THE LIVES OF OOTOMO AND OTHERS AT THE DOJO, WHO LIVED AND BREATHED COMICS.
THEIR LIVES SEEMED INCREDIBLY FUN, AND HIROSHI'S HEART WAVERED ONCE AGAIN.

LETTER: : FROM YOSHIYASU OOTOMO, C/O NOBORU OOSHIRO

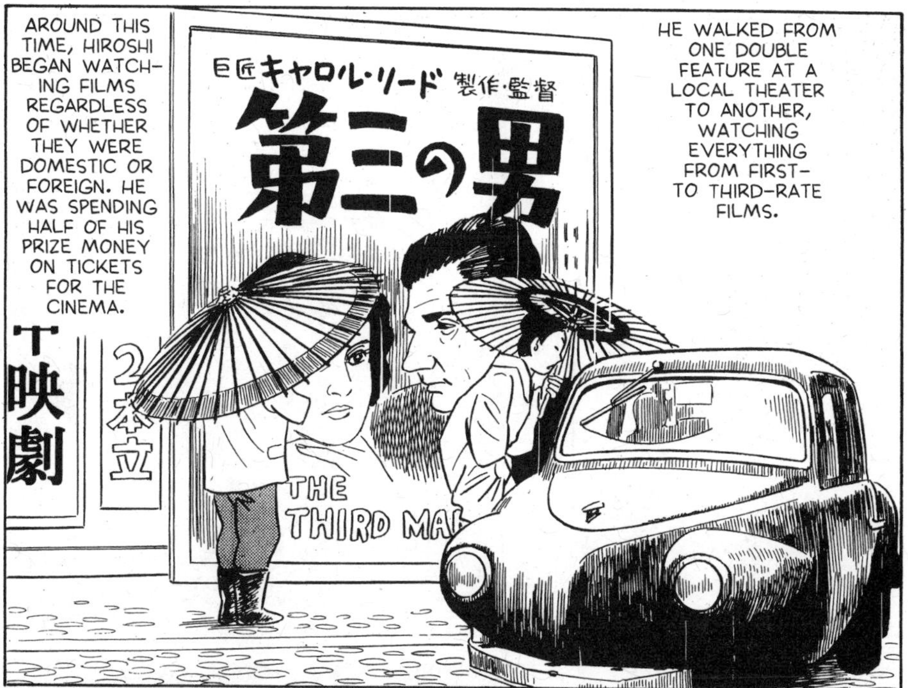
AROUND THIS TIME, HIROSHI BEGAN WATCHING FILMS REGARDLESS OF WHETHER THEY WERE DOMESTIC OR FOREIGN. HE WAS SPENDING HALF OF HIS PRIZE MONEY ON TICKETS FOR THE CINEMA.
巨匠キャロル・リード 製作・監督
第三の男
THE THIRD MA
映劇
2本立
HE WALKED FROM ONE DOUBLE FEATURE AT A LOCAL THEATER TO ANOTHER, WATCHING EVERYTHING FROM FIRST- TO THIRD-RATE FILMS.

POSTER: DIRECTED AND PRODUCED BY THE GREAT CAROL REED / ***THE THIRD MAN***

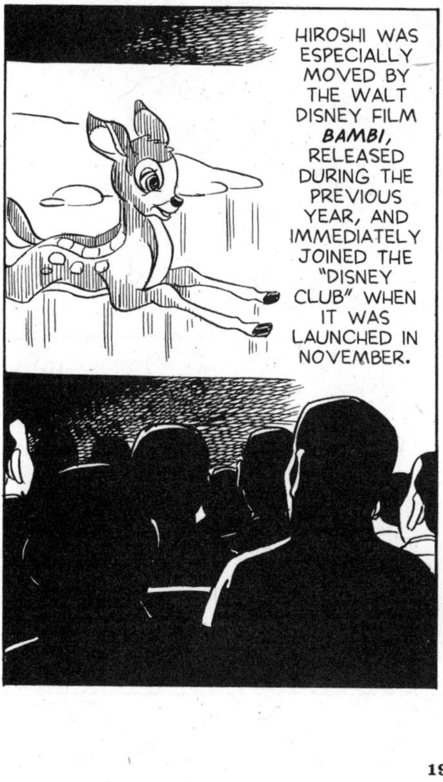
HIROSHI WAS ESPECIALLY MOVED BY THE WALT DISNEY FILM ***BAMBI***, RELEASED DURING THE PREVIOUS YEAR, AND IMMEDIATELY JOINED THE "DISNEY CLUB" WHEN IT WAS LAUNCHED IN NOVEMBER.

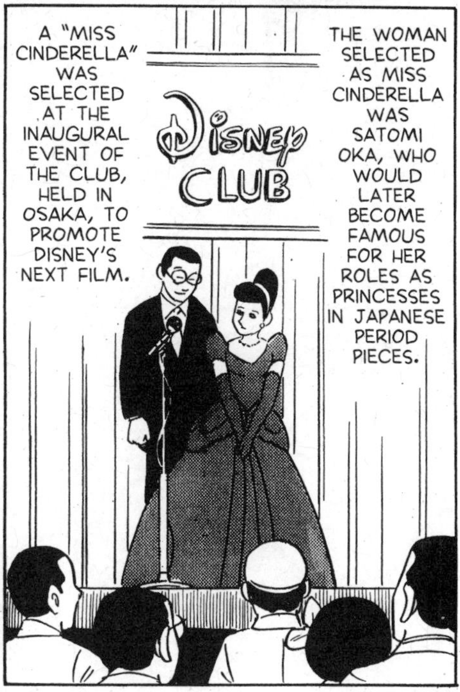
A "MISS CINDERELLA" WAS SELECTED AT THE INAUGURAL EVENT OF THE CLUB, HELD IN OSAKA, TO PROMOTE DISNEY'S NEXT FILM.
DISNEY CLUB
THE WOMAN SELECTED AS MISS CINDERELLA WAS SATOMI OKA, WHO WOULD LATER BECOME FAMOUS FOR HER ROLES AS PRINCESSES IN JAPANESE PERIOD PIECES.

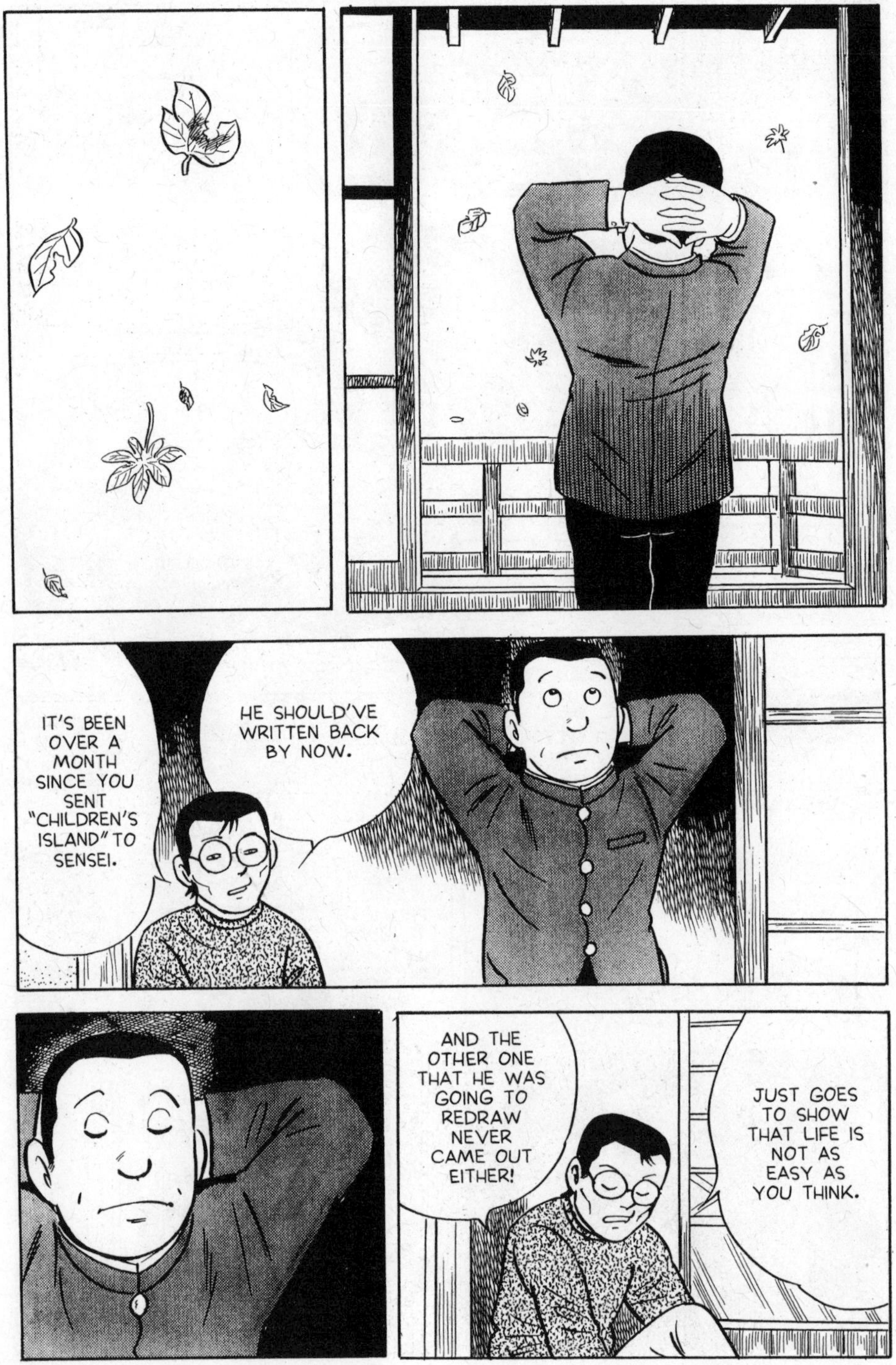
IT'S BEEN OVER A MONTH SINCE YOU SENT "CHILDREN'S ISLAND" TO SENSEI.
HE SHOULD'VE WRITTEN BACK BY NOW.
AND THE OTHER ONE THAT HE WAS GOING TO REDRAW NEVER CAME OUT EITHER!
JUST GOES TO SHOW THAT LIFE IS NOT AS EASY AS YOU THINK.

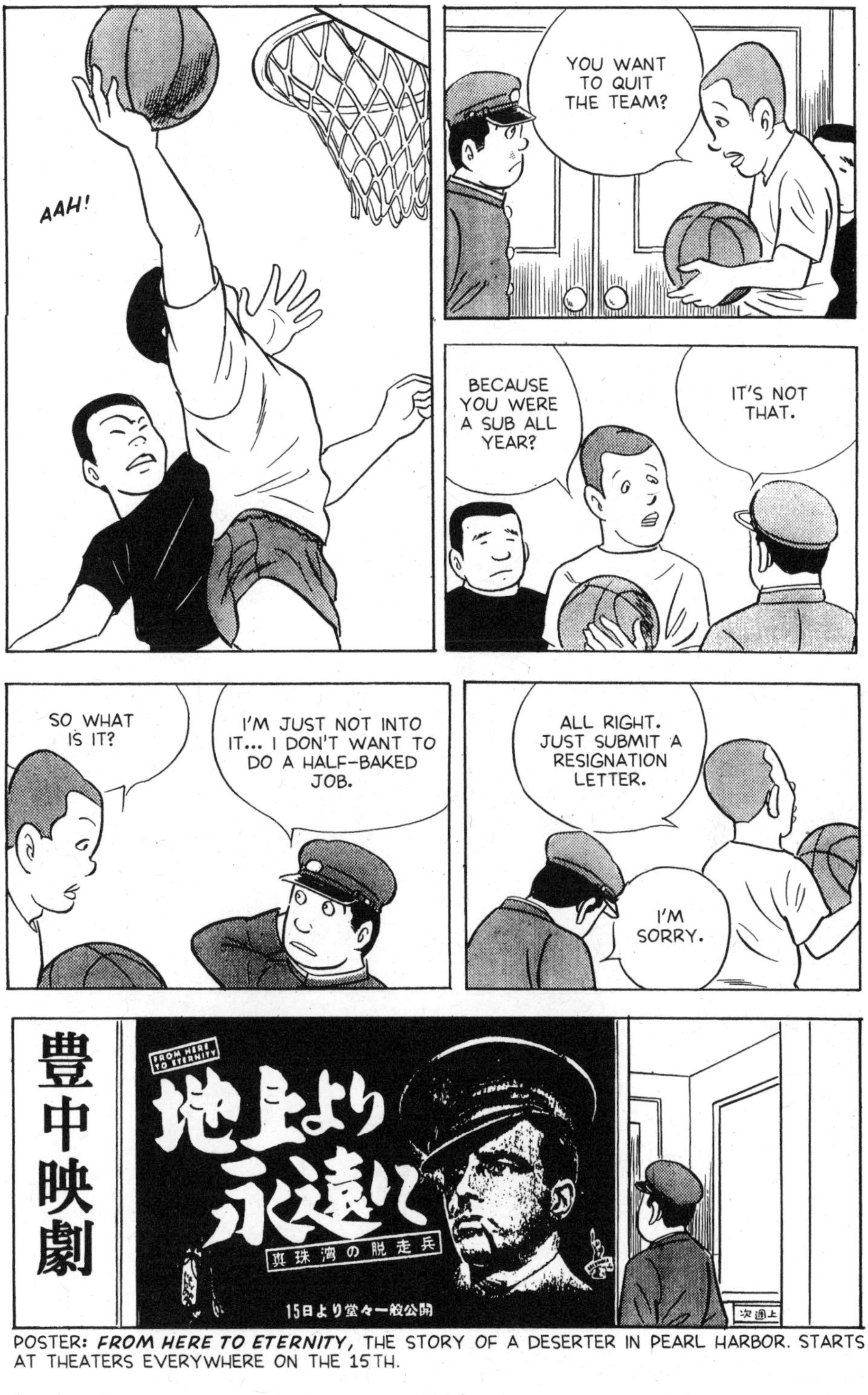
AAH!
YOU WANT TO QUIT THE TEAM?
BECAUSE YOU WERE A SUB ALL YEAR?
IT'S NOT THAT.
SO WHAT IS IT?
I'M JUST NOT INTO IT... I DON'T WANT TO DO A HALF-BAKED JOB.
ALL RIGHT. JUST SUBMIT A RESIGNATION LETTER.
I'M SORRY.
豊中映劇
FROM HERE TO ETERNITY
地上より永遠に
真珠湾の脱走兵
15日より堂々一般公開
次週上
POSTER: ***FROM HERE TO ETERNITY***, THE STORY OF A DESERTER IN PEARL HARBOR. STARTS AT THEATERS EVERYWHERE ON THE 15TH.

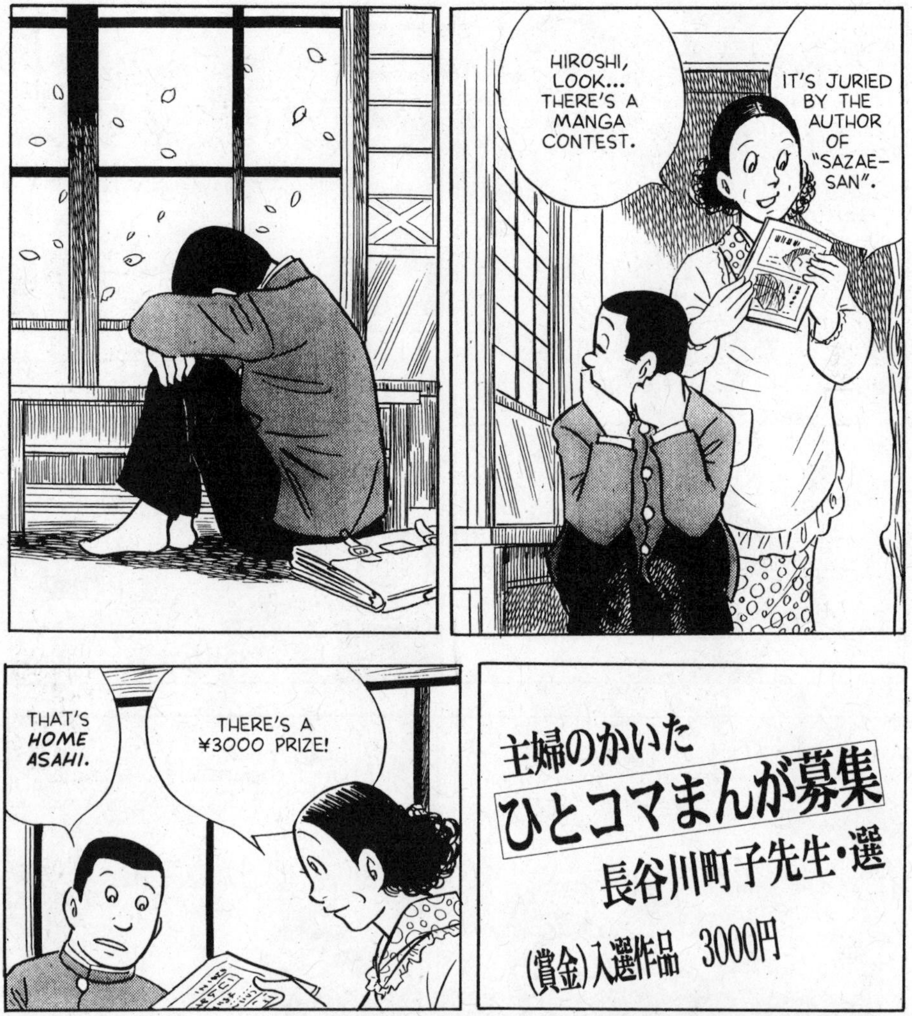
HIROSHI, LOOK... THERE'S A MANGA CONTEST.
IT'S JURIED BY THE AUTHOR OF "SAZAE-SAN".
THAT'S *HOME ASAHI.*
THERE'S A ¥3000 PRIZE!
主婦のかいた
ひとコマまんが募集
長谷川町子先生・選
(賞金)入選作品 3000円

PANEL 4: WANTED FOR SUBMISSION: 1-PANEL MANGA DRAWN BY HOUSEWIVES...

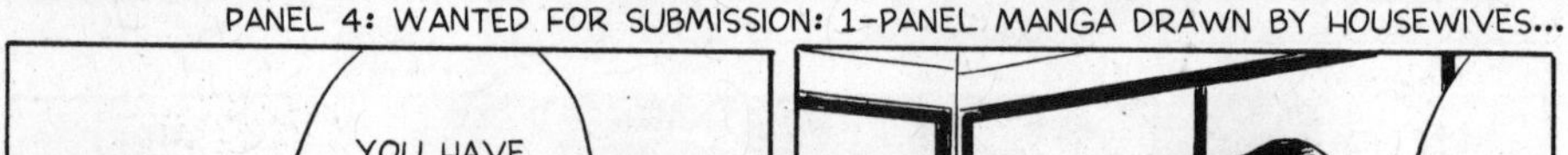
YOU HAVE TO BE A HOUSEWIFE TO ENTER.
OH, THAT'S NO GOOD.
TOO BAD...

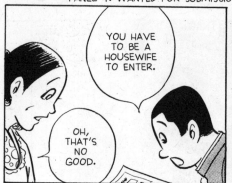

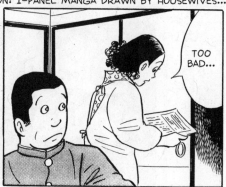

MACHIKO HASEGAWA, THE AUTHOR OF THE POPULAR "SAZAE-SAN", IS THE JUROR.

"SAZAE-SAN" BEGAN BEING PUBLISHED IN *ASAHI SHIMBUN* IN APRIL. ITS PROTAGONIST, SAZAE-SAN, RECEIVED OVERWHELMING SUPPORT FROM READERS FOR BEING AN ACTIVE HOUSEWIFE.

サザエさん
長谷川町子作

おねえ
ボクら
いく

HIROSHI BORROWED HIS SISTER'S NAME AND APPLIED AS A 23 YEAR-OLD WOMAN.

MY CONSCIENCE IS BOTHERING ME SLIGHTLY, BUT...

I PROBABLY WON'T BE ACCEPTED ANYWAY.

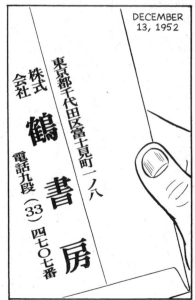

DECEMBER 13, 1952

東京都千代田区富士見町一八

株式
会社

鶴　書　房

電話九段（33）四七〇七番

TSURU SHOBO? WHAT COULD THIS BE ABOUT?

THERE'S ONLY ONE WAY TO KNOW. GO AHEAD AND OPEN IT. THE SUSPENSE IS KILLING ME.

LETTER: TSURU SHOBO CO., LTD. 1-8 FUJIMI-CHO, CHIYODA-KU, TOKYO TEL: (33) 4707

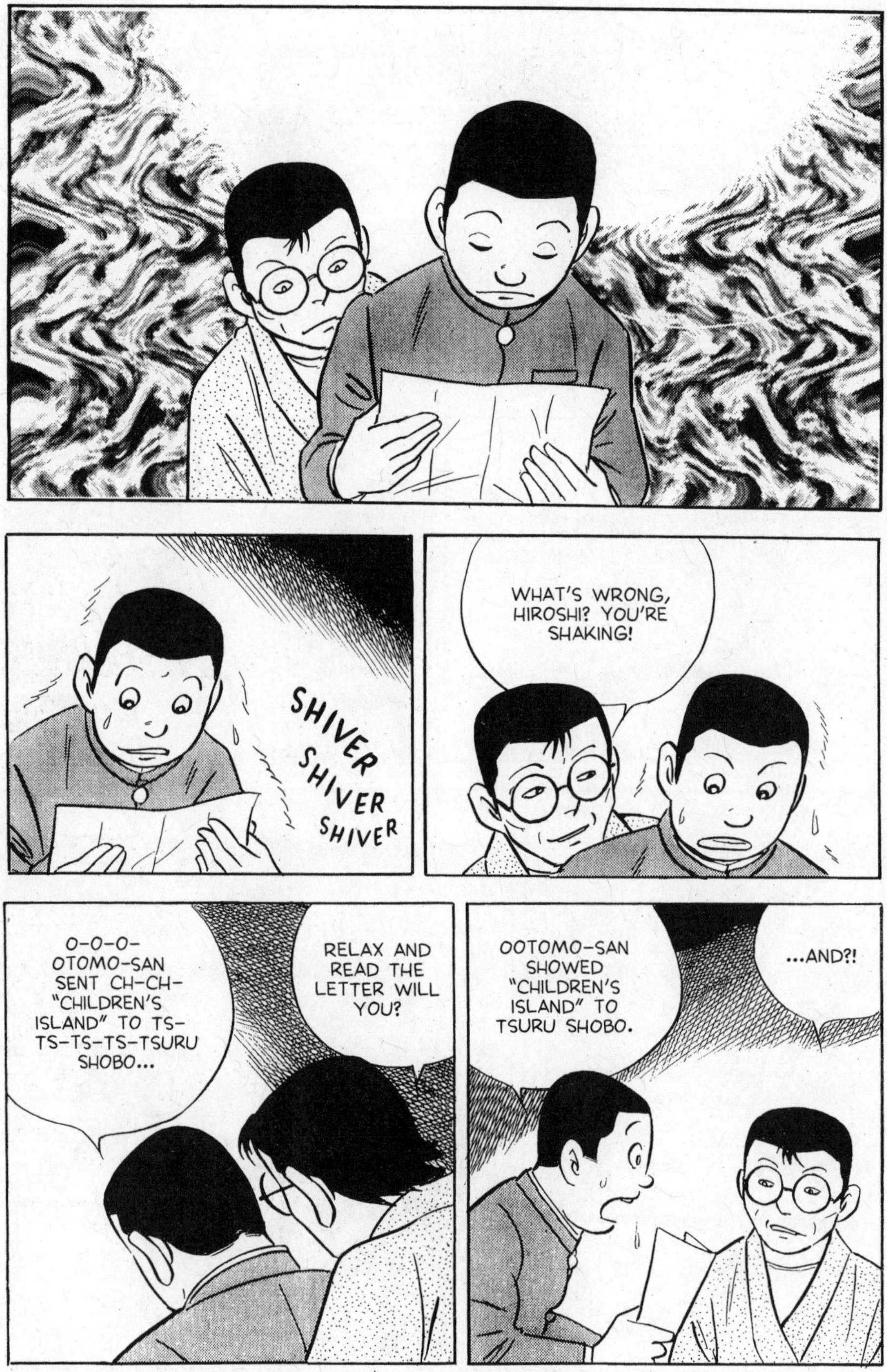
SHIVER SHIVER SHIVER
WHAT'S WRONG, HIROSHI? YOU'RE SHAKING!
O-O-O-OTOMO-SAN SENT CH-CH-"CHILDREN'S ISLAND" TO TS-TS-TS-TS-TSURU SHOBO...
RELAX AND READ THE LETTER WILL YOU?
OOTOMO-SAN SHOWED "CHILDREN'S ISLAND" TO TSURU SHOBO.
...AND?!

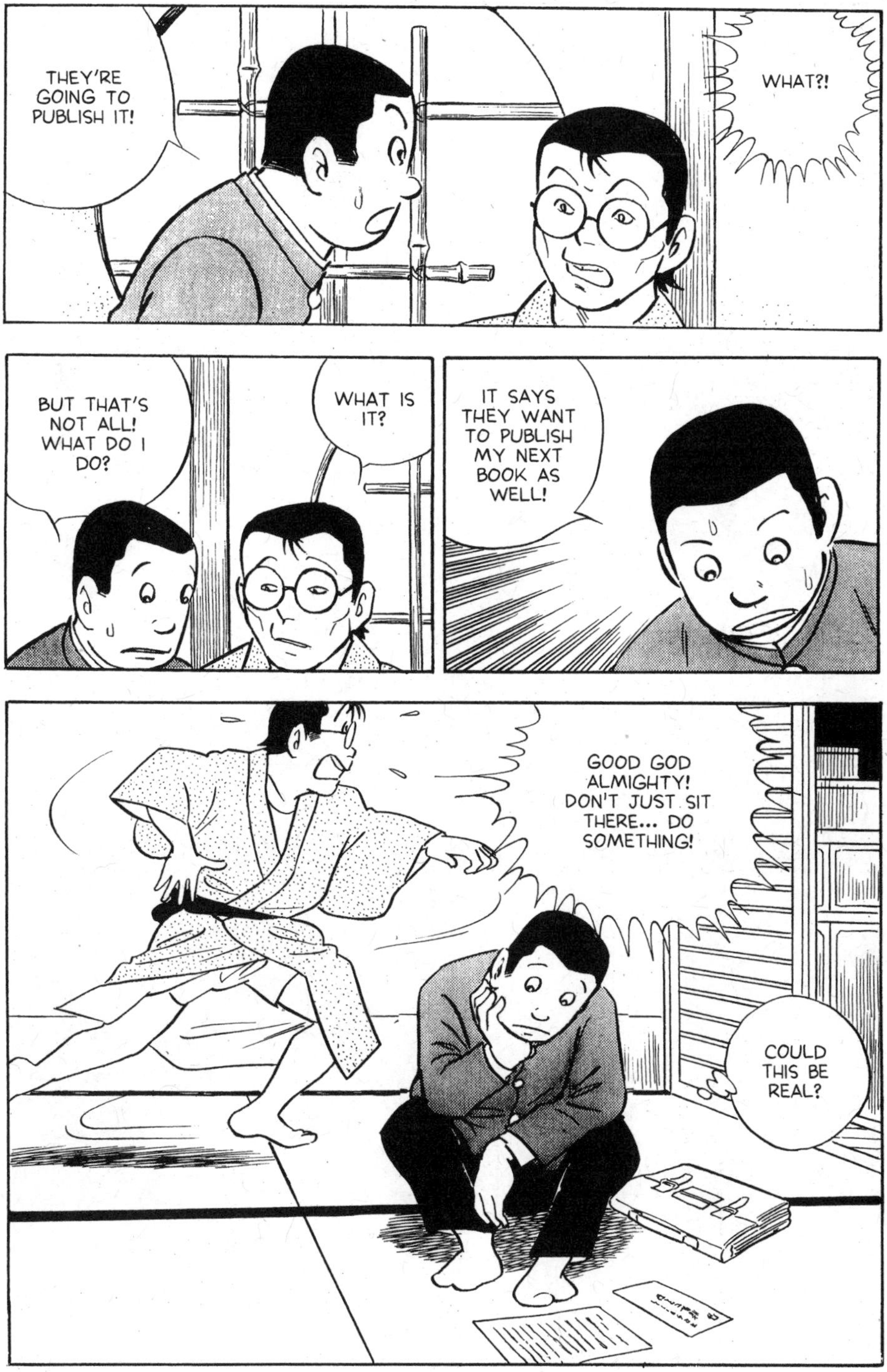
THEY'RE GOING TO PUBLISH IT!
WHAT?!
BUT THAT'S NOT ALL! WHAT DO I DO?
WHAT IS IT?
IT SAYS THEY WANT TO PUBLISH MY NEXT BOOK AS WELL!
GOOD GOD ALMIGHTY! DON'T JUST SIT THERE... DO SOMETHING!
COULD THIS BE REAL?

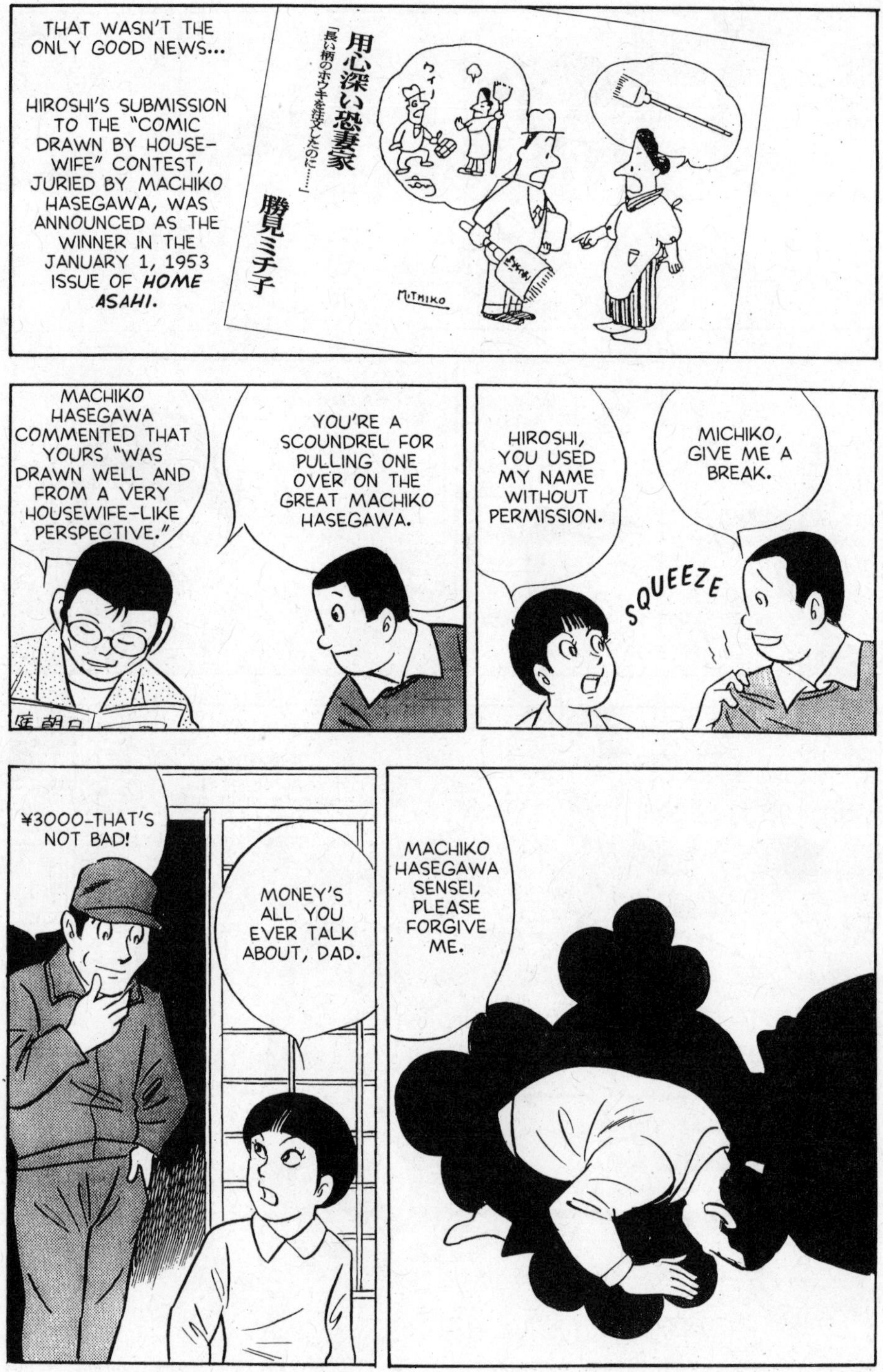
THAT WASN'T THE ONLY GOOD NEWS...
HIROSHI'S SUBMISSION TO THE "COMIC DRAWN BY HOUSE-WIFE" CONTEST, JURIED BY MACHIKO HASEGAWA, WAS ANNOUNCED AS THE WINNER IN THE JANUARY 1, 1953 ISSUE OF ***HOME ASAHI***.
用心深い恐妻家
「長い柄のホウキを注文したのに……」
勝見ミチ子
MITIKO
MACHIKO HASEGAWA COMMENTED THAT YOURS "WAS DRAWN WELL AND FROM A VERY HOUSEWIFE-LIKE PERSPECTIVE."
YOU'RE A SCOUNDREL FOR PULLING ONE OVER ON THE GREAT MACHIKO HASEGAWA.
HIROSHI, YOU USED MY NAME WITHOUT PERMISSION.
MICHIKO, GIVE ME A BREAK.
SQUEEZE
¥3000–THAT'S NOT BAD!
MONEY'S ALL YOU EVER TALK ABOUT, DAD.
MACHIKO HASEGAWA SENSEI, PLEASE FORGIVE ME.

THE ROAD TO SUCCESS

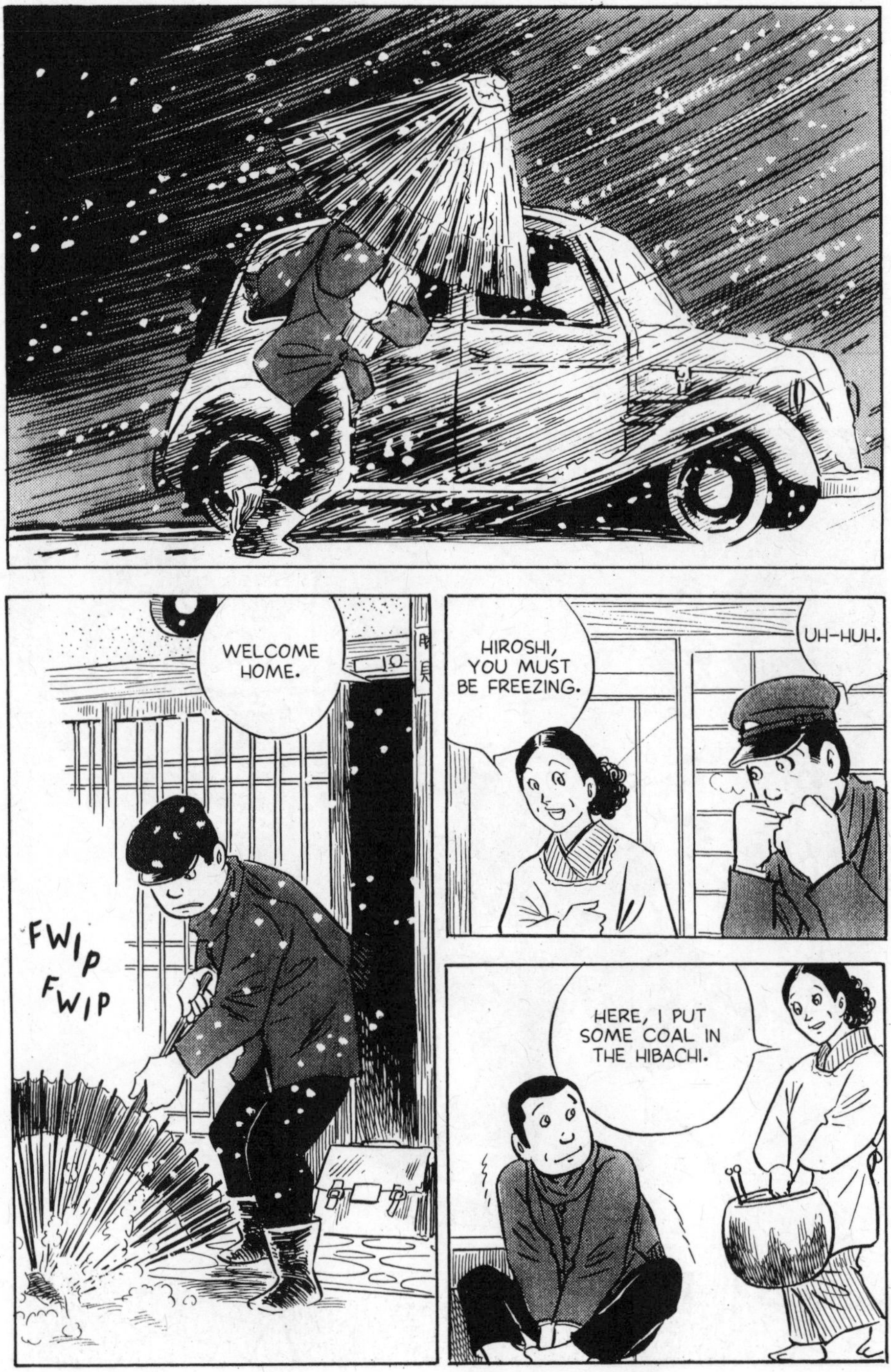

WELCOME HOME.
FWIP FWIP
HIROSHI, YOU MUST BE FREEZING.
UH-HUH.
HERE, I PUT SOME COAL IN THE HIBACHI.

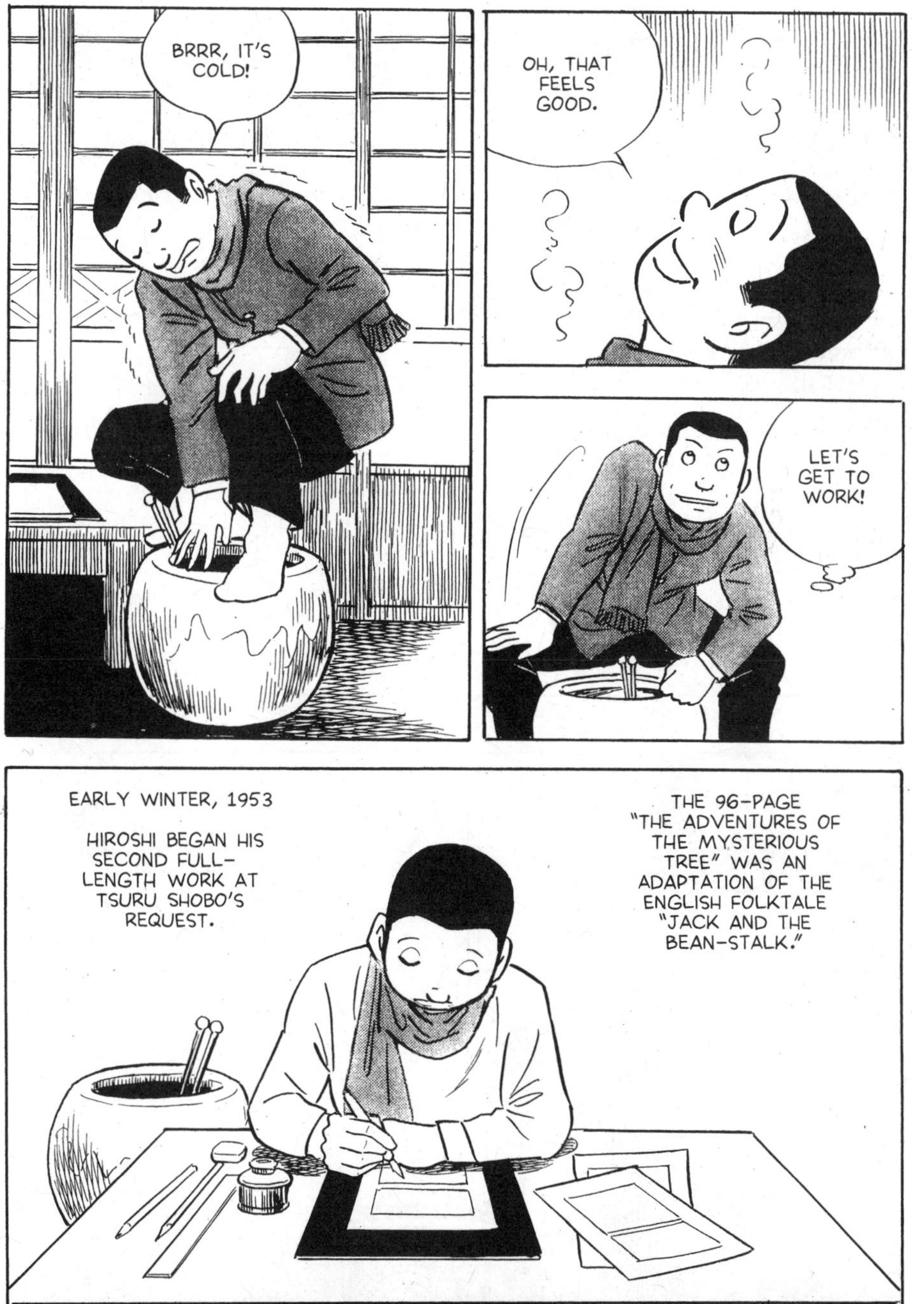
BRRR, IT'S COLD!
OH, THAT FEELS GOOD.
LET'S GET TO WORK!
EARLY WINTER, 1953
HIROSHI BEGAN HIS SECOND FULL-LENGTH WORK AT TSURU SHOBO'S REQUEST.
THE 96-PAGE "THE ADVENTURES OF THE MYSTERIOUS TREE" WAS AN ADAPTATION OF THE ENGLISH FOLKTALE "JACK AND THE BEAN-STALK."

HE SENT THE PIECE IN THREE INSTALLMENTS, SENDING THE FIRST 45 PAGES TO TSURU SHOBO ON FEBRUARY 23.

A POSTCARD FROM TSURU SHOBO. THEY GOT THE FIRST INSTALLMENT.

というこ とになっ
あくまで學業に差しさわり
のないように、作品を描き
続けて下さい。

次作を期待しています

鶴書房 太田

LETTER: PLEASE MAKE SURE THAT YOUR WORK ON "THE ADVENTURES..." DOES NOT INTERFERE WITH YOUR SCHOOL. WE SINCERELY LOOK FORWARD TO THE NEXT INSTALLMENT, TSURU SHOBO

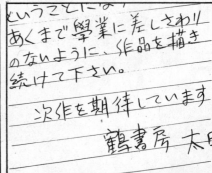

OKAY. LET ME RETIE MY HEADBAND, AND WE'RE READY TO GO.

ENVELOPE: HIROSHI KATSUMI, 1-37-3 ASADA, TOYONAKA-SHI, OSAKA

SECOND INSTALLMENT OF 21 PAGES SENT ON MARCH 24.

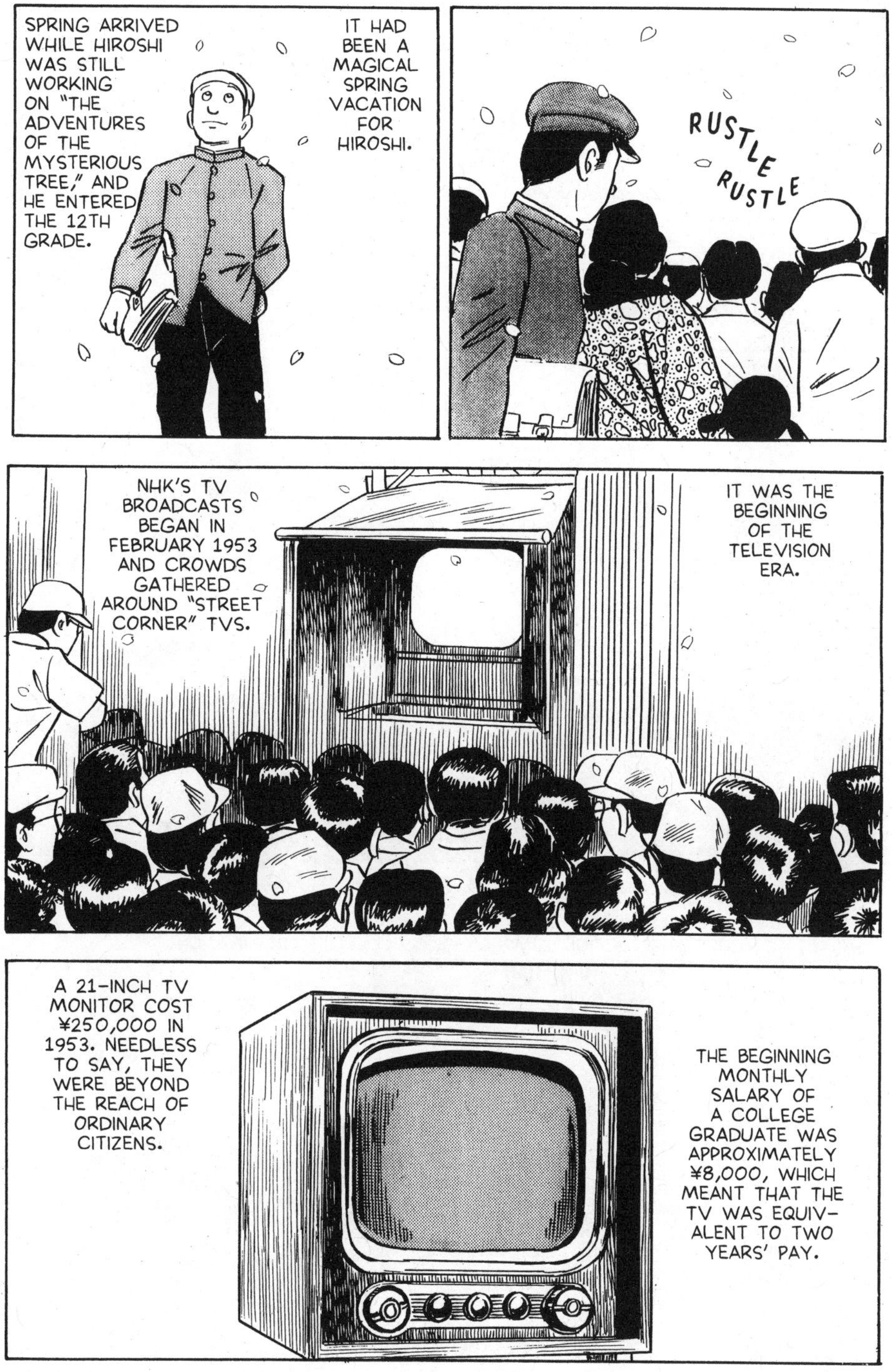
SPRING ARRIVED WHILE HIROSHI WAS STILL WORKING ON "THE ADVENTURES OF THE MYSTERIOUS TREE," AND HE ENTERED THE 12TH GRADE.
IT HAD BEEN A MAGICAL SPRING VACATION FOR HIROSHI.
RUSTLE RUSTLE
NHK'S TV BROADCASTS BEGAN IN FEBRUARY 1953 AND CROWDS GATHERED AROUND "STREET CORNER" TVS.
IT WAS THE BEGINNING OF THE TELEVISION ERA.
A 21-INCH TV MONITOR COST ¥250,000 IN 1953. NEEDLESS TO SAY, THEY WERE BEYOND THE REACH OF ORDINARY CITIZENS.
THE BEGINNING MONTHLY SALARY OF A COLLEGE GRADUATE WAS APPROXIMATELY ¥8,000, WHICH MEANT THAT THE TV WAS EQUIV-ALENT TO TWO YEARS' PAY.

WOW, A TV...

SOON WE'LL BE ABLE TO WATCH FILMS AT HOME.

WHEN THAT HAPPENS, MANGA MAY BE DOOMED.

FOR NOW, I NEED TO MOVE FORWARD ON THIS PIECE.

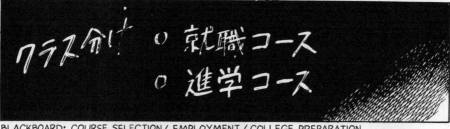

クラス分け ○ 就職コース ○ 進学コース

BLACKBOARD: COURSE SELECTION / EMPLOYMENT / COLLEGE PREPARATION

YOU CAN'T GO ON TO COLLEGE UNLESS YOU'RE REALLY SERIOUS.

就職コース
進学コース

THEREFORE, 12TH GRADERS WILL BE SPLIT INTO TWO DISTINCT PATHS...

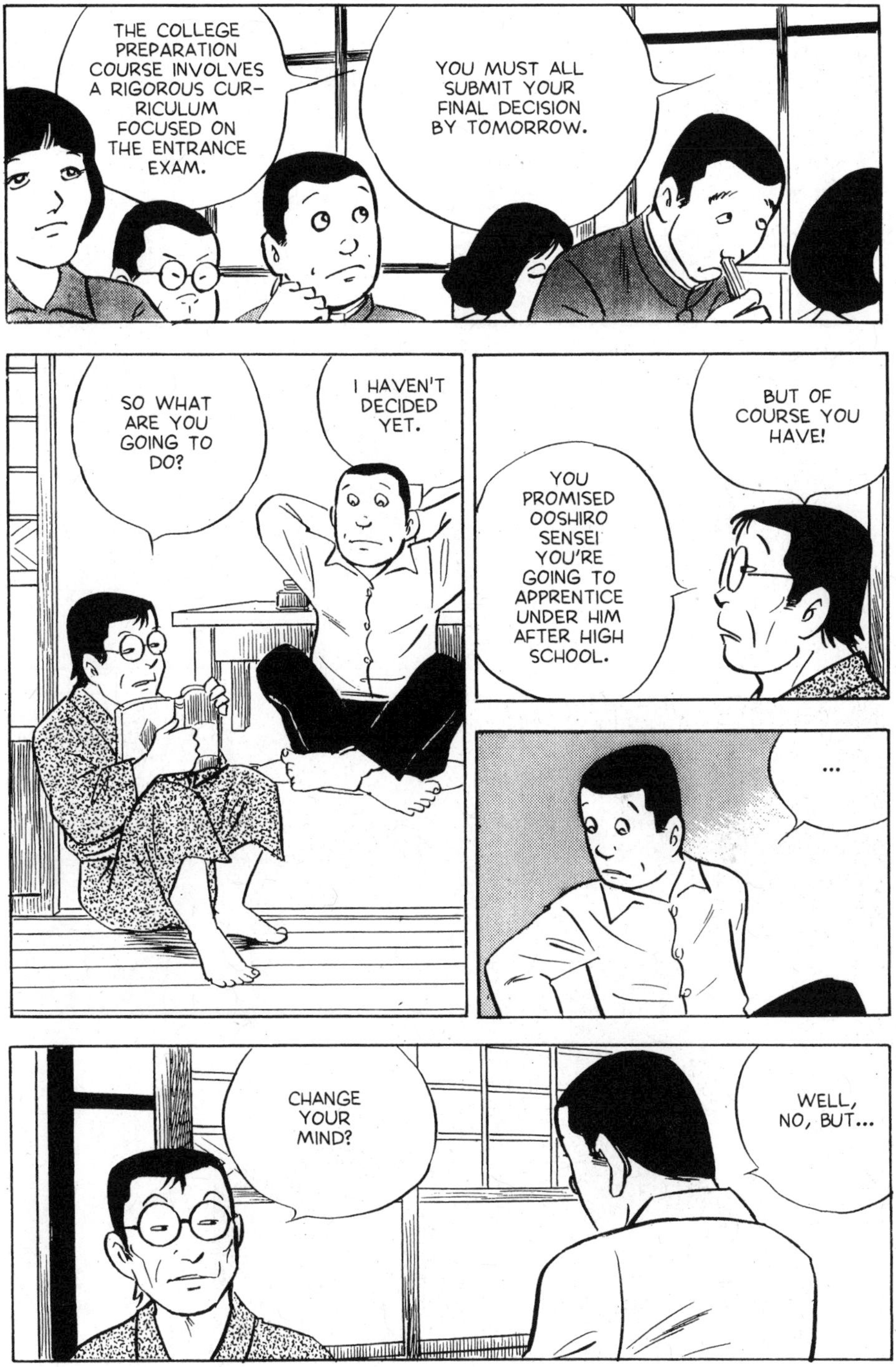
THE COLLEGE PREPARATION COURSE INVOLVES A RIGOROUS CURRICULUM FOCUSED ON THE ENTRANCE EXAM.
YOU MUST ALL SUBMIT YOUR FINAL DECISION BY TOMORROW.
SO WHAT ARE YOU GOING TO DO?
I HAVEN'T DECIDED YET.
BUT OF COURSE YOU HAVE!
YOU PROMISED OOSHIRO SENSEI YOU'RE GOING TO APPRENTICE UNDER HIM AFTER HIGH SCHOOL.
...
CHANGE YOUR MIND?
WELL, NO, BUT...

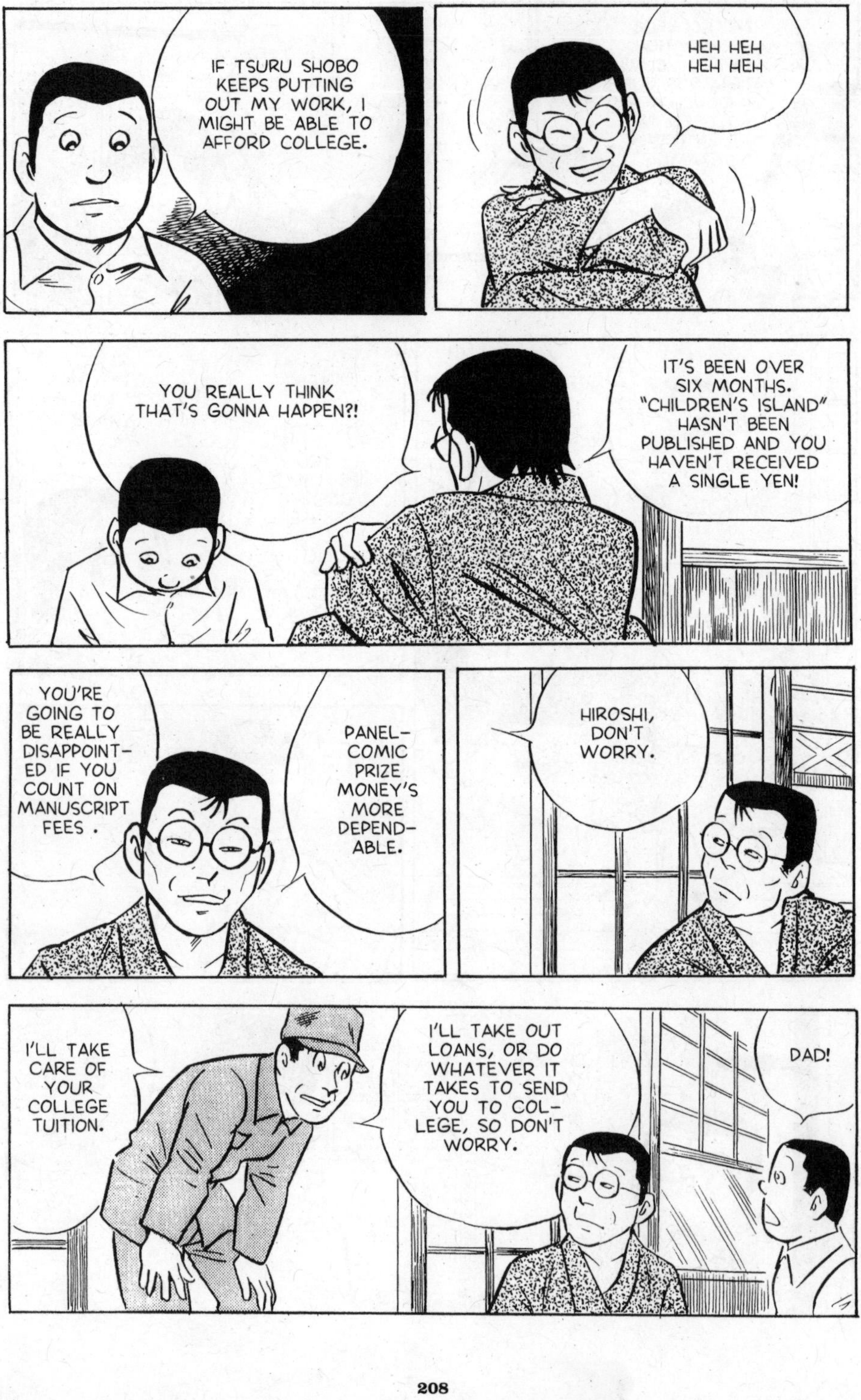

IF TSURU SHOBO KEEPS PUTTING OUT MY WORK, I MIGHT BE ABLE TO AFFORD COLLEGE.
HEH HEH HEH HEH
YOU REALLY THINK THAT'S GONNA HAPPEN?!
IT'S BEEN OVER SIX MONTHS. "CHILDREN'S ISLAND" HASN'T BEEN PUBLISHED AND YOU HAVEN'T RECEIVED A SINGLE YEN!
YOU'RE GOING TO BE REALLY DISAPPOINT-ED IF YOU COUNT ON MANUSCRIPT FEES .
PANEL-COMIC PRIZE MONEY'S MORE DEPEND-ABLE.
HIROSHI, DON'T WORRY.
I'LL TAKE CARE OF YOUR COLLEGE TUITION.
I'LL TAKE OUT LOANS, OR DO WHATEVER IT TAKES TO SEND YOU TO COL-LEGE, SO DON'T WORRY.
DAD!

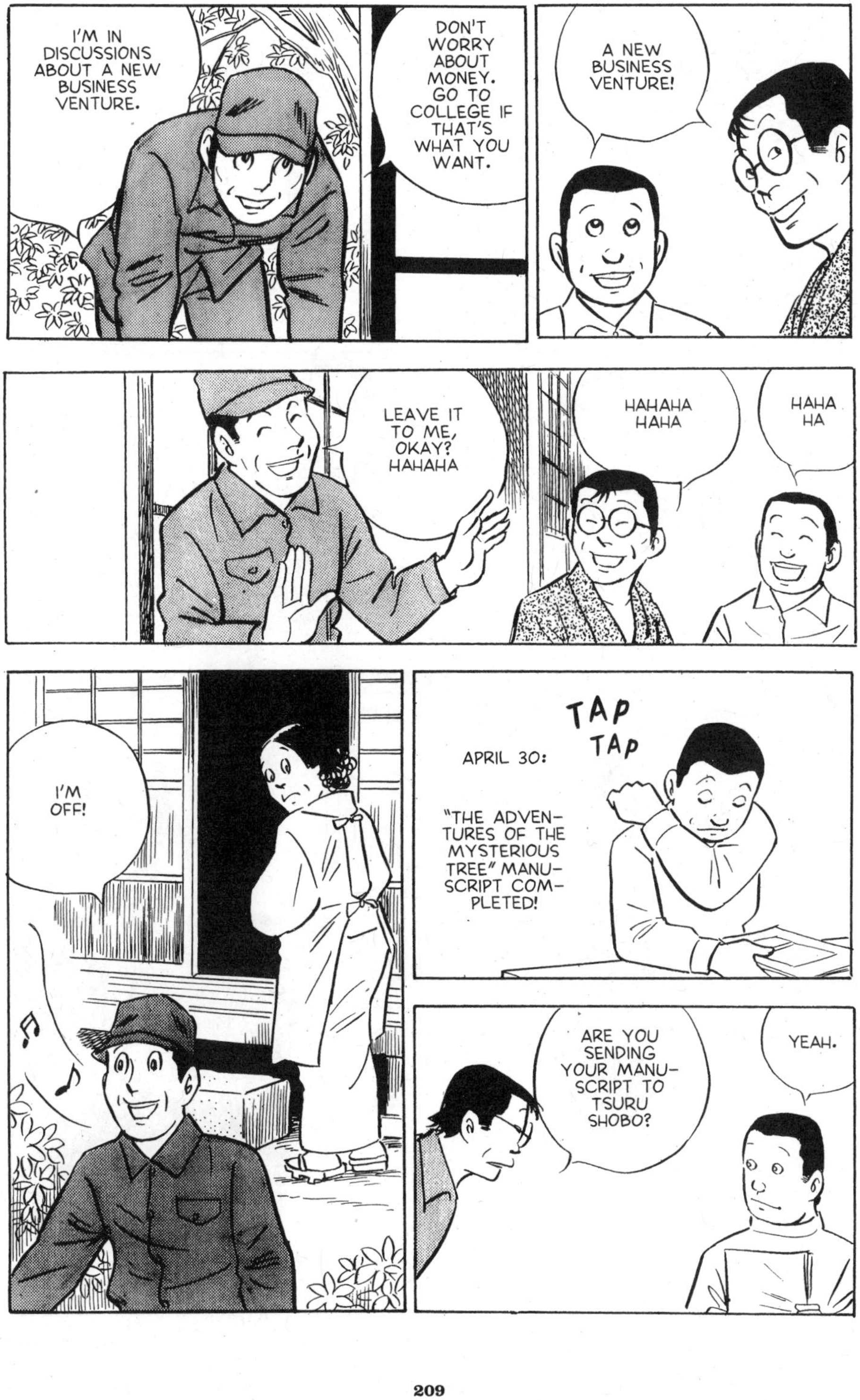
I'M IN DISCUSSIONS ABOUT A NEW BUSINESS VENTURE.
DON'T WORRY ABOUT MONEY. GO TO COLLEGE IF THAT'S WHAT YOU WANT.
A NEW BUSINESS VENTURE!
LEAVE IT TO ME, OKAY? HAHAHA
HAHAHA HAHA
HAHA HA
I'M OFF!
APRIL 30:
"THE ADVENTURES OF THE MYSTERIOUS TREE" MANUSCRIPT COMPLETED!
TAP TAP
ARE YOU SENDING YOUR MANUSCRIPT TO TSURU SHOBO?
YEAH.

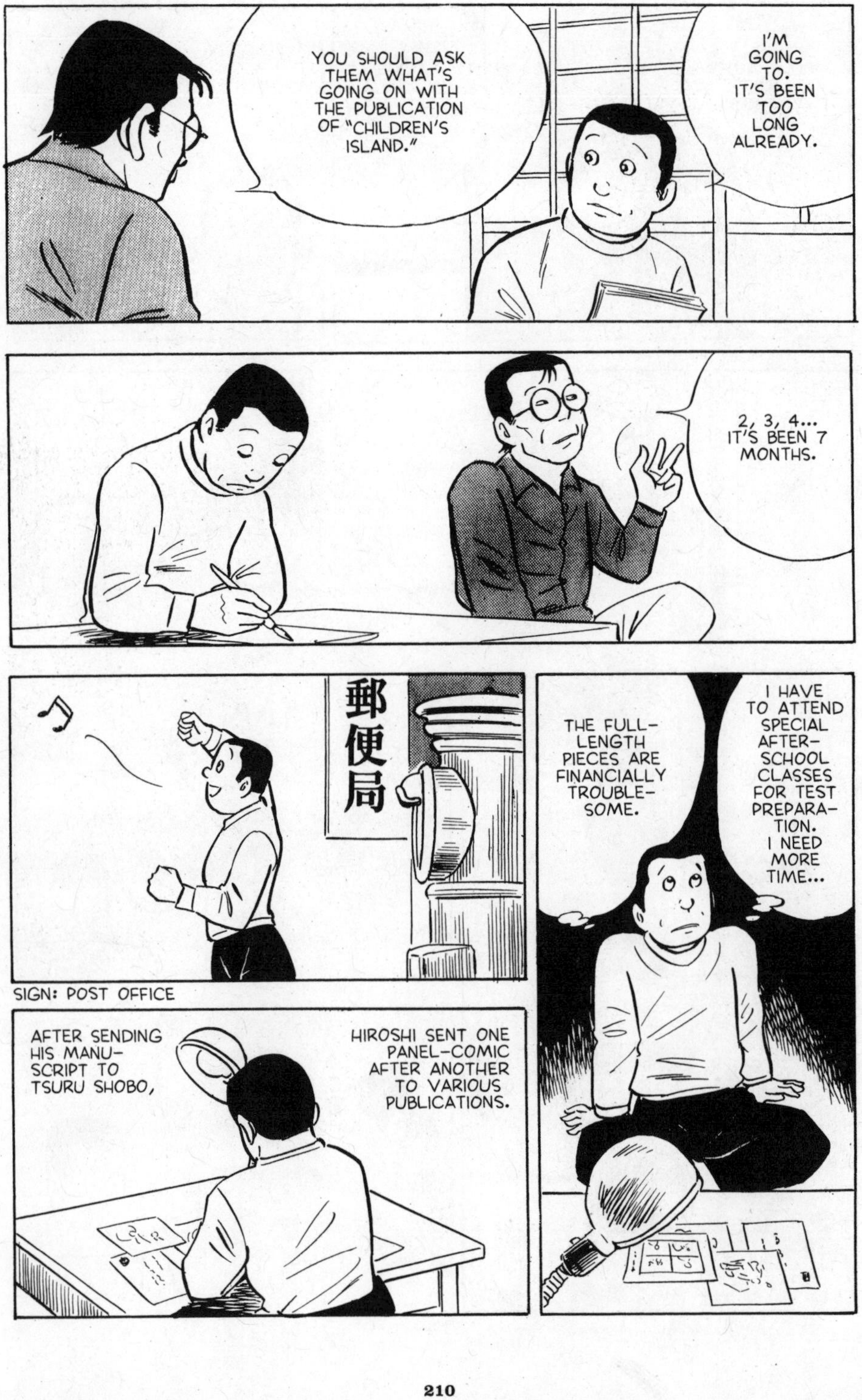
YOU SHOULD ASK THEM WHAT'S GOING ON WITH THE PUBLICATION OF "CHILDREN'S ISLAND."
I'M GOING TO. IT'S BEEN TOO LONG ALREADY.
2, 3, 4... IT'S BEEN 7 MONTHS.
郵便局
SIGN: POST OFFICE
AFTER SENDING HIS MANU-SCRIPT TO TSURU SHOBO,
HIROSHI SENT ONE PANEL-COMIC AFTER ANOTHER TO VARIOUS PUBLICATIONS.
THE FULL-LENGTH PIECES ARE FINANCIALLY TROUBLE-SOME.
I HAVE TO ATTEND SPECIAL AFTER-SCHOOL CLASSES FOR TEST PREPARA-TION. I NEED MORE TIME...

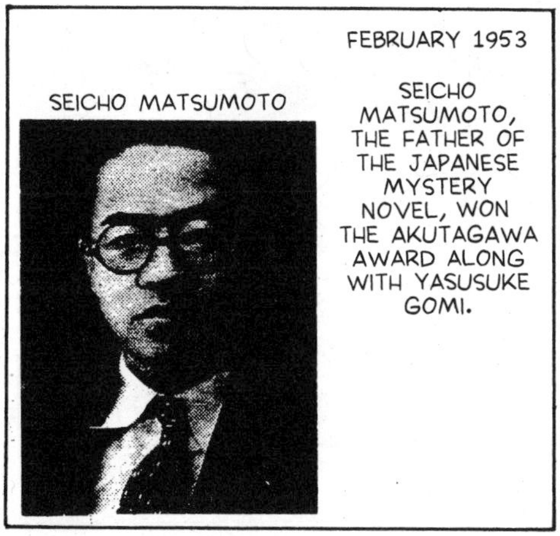
FEBRUARY 1953
SEICHO MATSUMOTO
SEICHO MATSUMOTO, THE FATHER OF THE JAPANESE MYSTERY NOVEL, WON THE AKUTAGAWA AWARD ALONG WITH YASUSUKE GOMI.
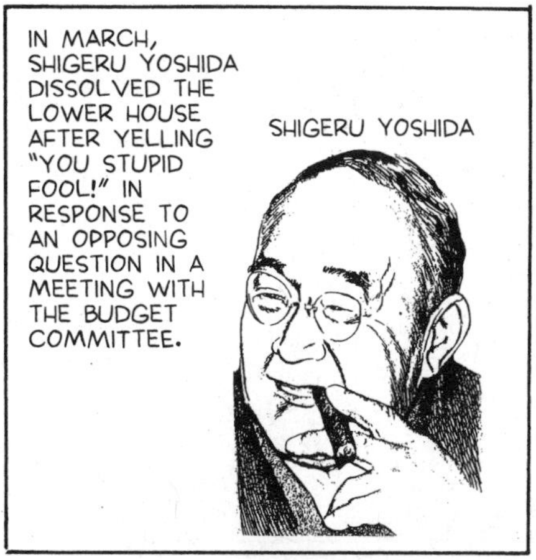
IN MARCH, SHIGERU YOSHIDA DISSOLVED THE LOWER HOUSE AFTER YELLING "YOU STUPID FOOL!" IN RESPONSE TO AN OPPOSING QUESTION IN A MEETING WITH THE BUDGET COMMITTEE.
SHIGERU YOSHIDA
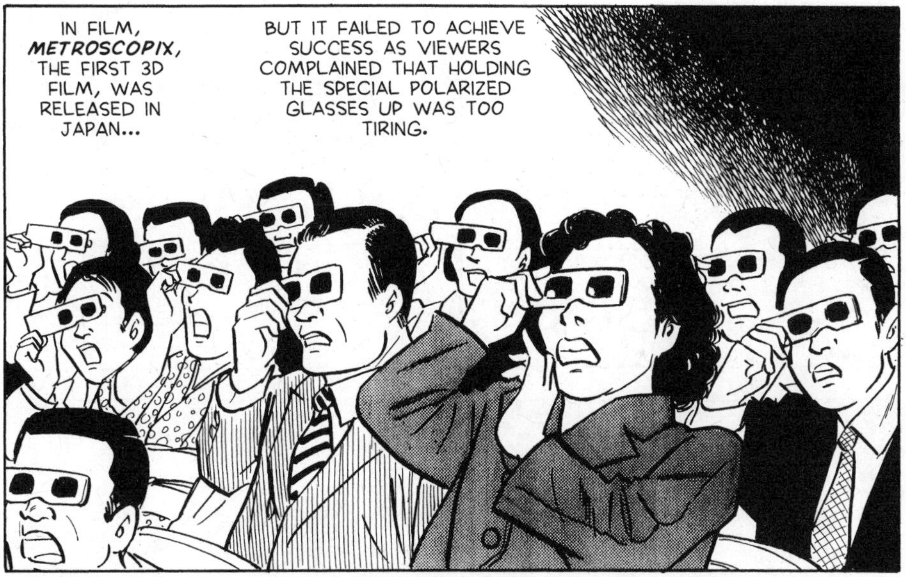
IN FILM, *METROSCOPIX,* THE FIRST 3D FILM, WAS RELEASED IN JAPAN...
BUT IT FAILED TO ACHIEVE SUCCESS AS VIEWERS COMPLAINED THAT HOLDING THE SPECIAL POLARIZED GLASSES UP WAS TOO TIRING.
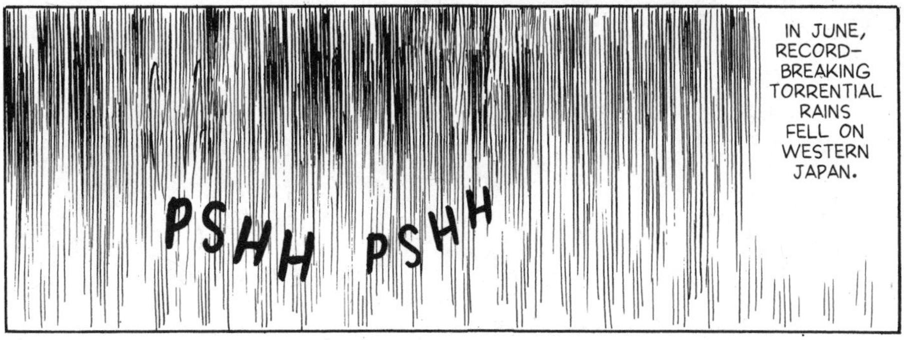
IN JUNE, RECORD-BREAKING TORRENTIAL RAINS FELL ON WESTERN JAPAN.
PSHH PSHH

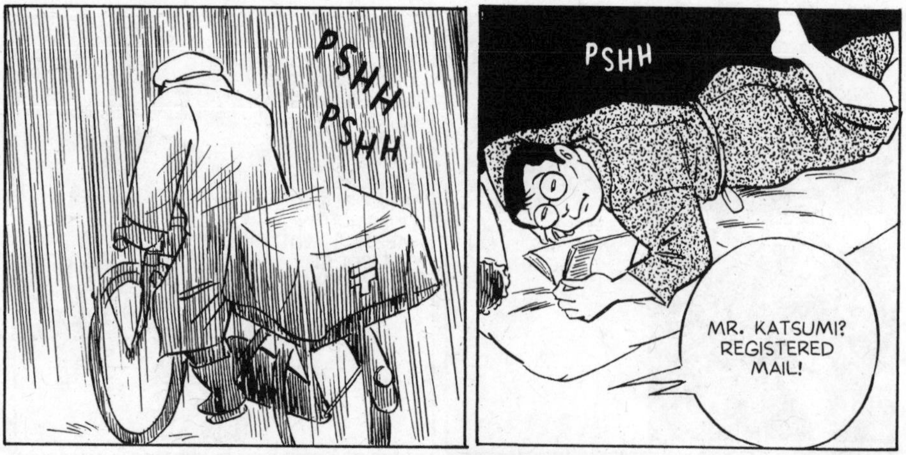
PSHH
PSHH
PSHH
PSHH
MR. KATSUMI? REGISTERED MAIL!

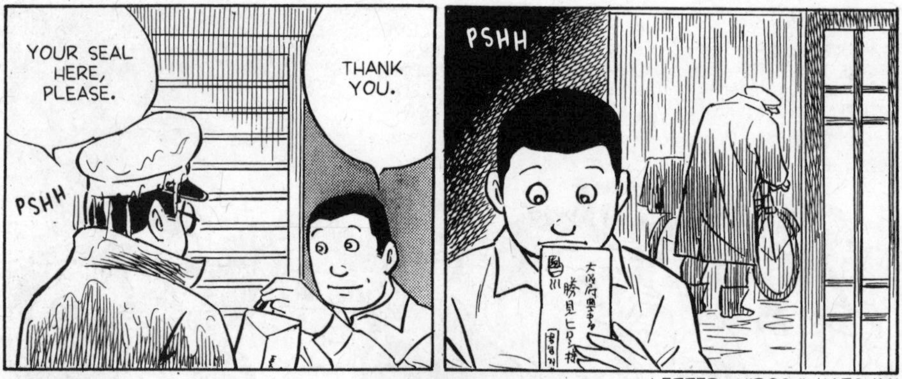
YOUR SEAL HERE, PLEASE.
PSHH
THANK YOU.
PSHH

LETTER: HIROSHI KATSUMI

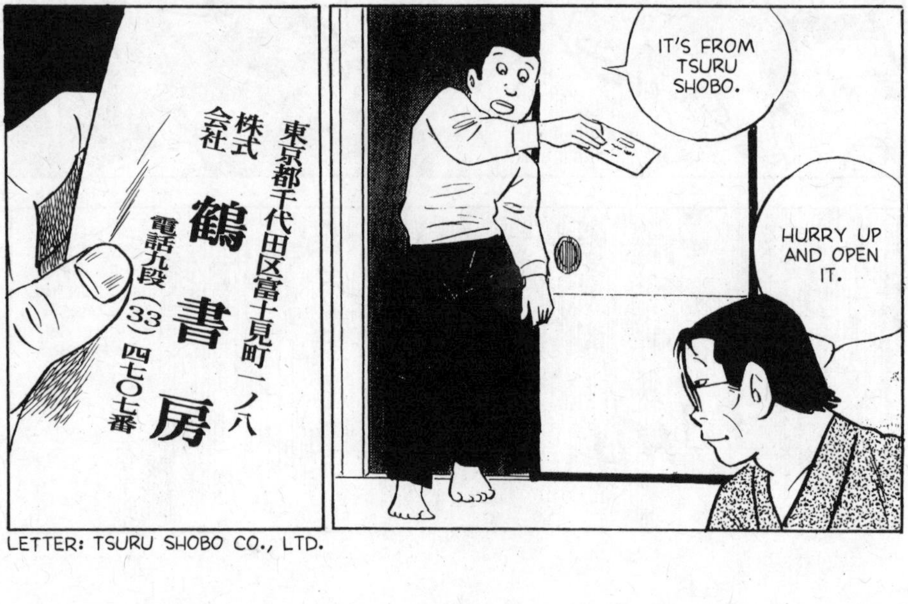
東京都千代田区富士見町一ノ八
株式会社
鶴書房
電話九段(33)四七〇七番
IT'S FROM TSURU SHOBO.
HURRY UP AND OPEN IT.

LETTER: TSURU SHOBO CO., LTD.

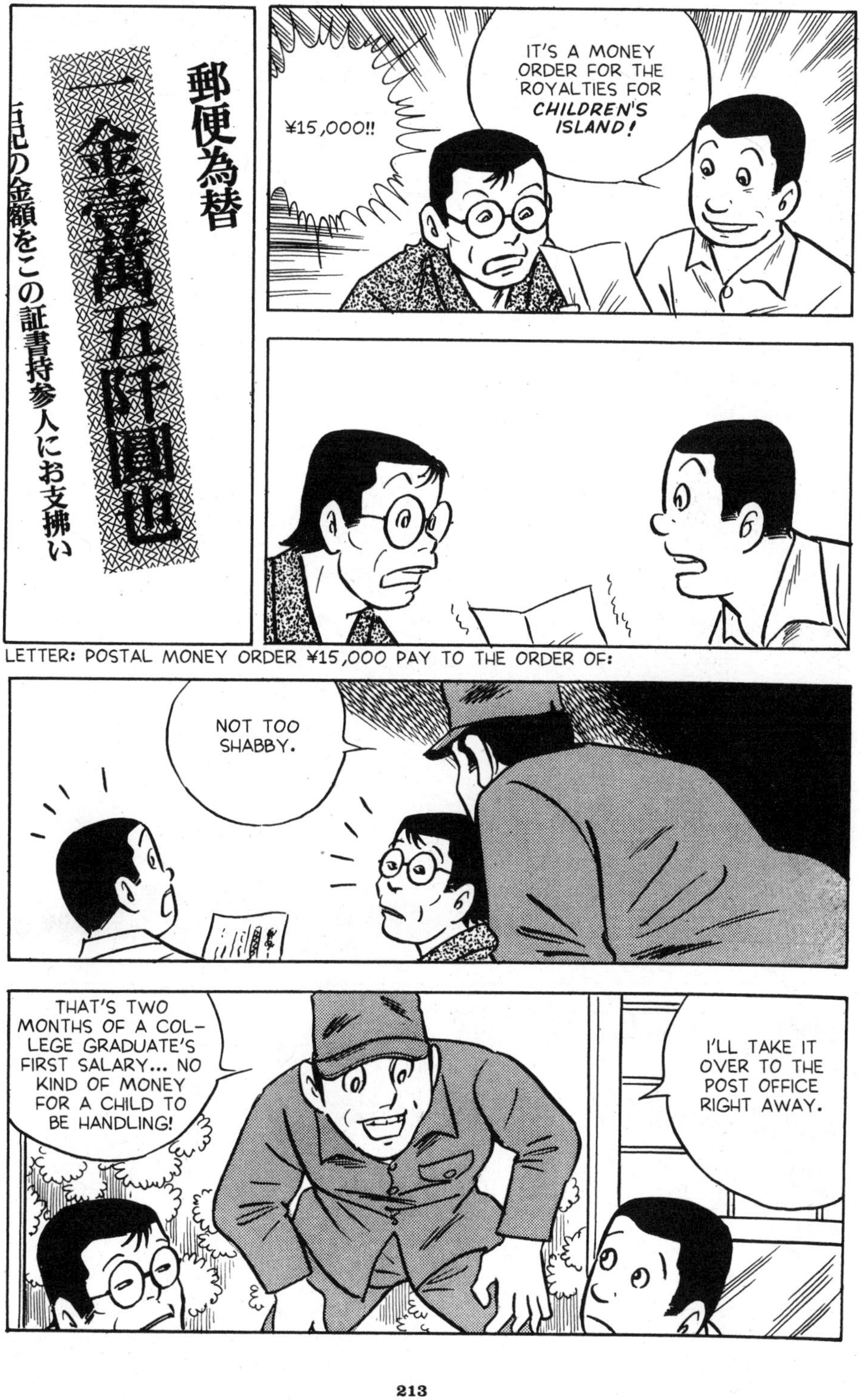
郵便為替
一金壹萬五阡圓也
右記の金額をこの証書持参人にお支拂い
¥15,000!!
IT'S A MONEY ORDER FOR THE ROYALTIES FOR CHILDREN'S ISLAND!
LETTER: POSTAL MONEY ORDER ¥15,000 PAY TO THE ORDER OF:
NOT TOO SHABBY.
THAT'S TWO MONTHS OF A COL-LEGE GRADUATE'S FIRST SALARY... NO KIND OF MONEY FOR A CHILD TO BE HANDLING!
I'LL TAKE IT OVER TO THE POST OFFICE RIGHT AWAY.

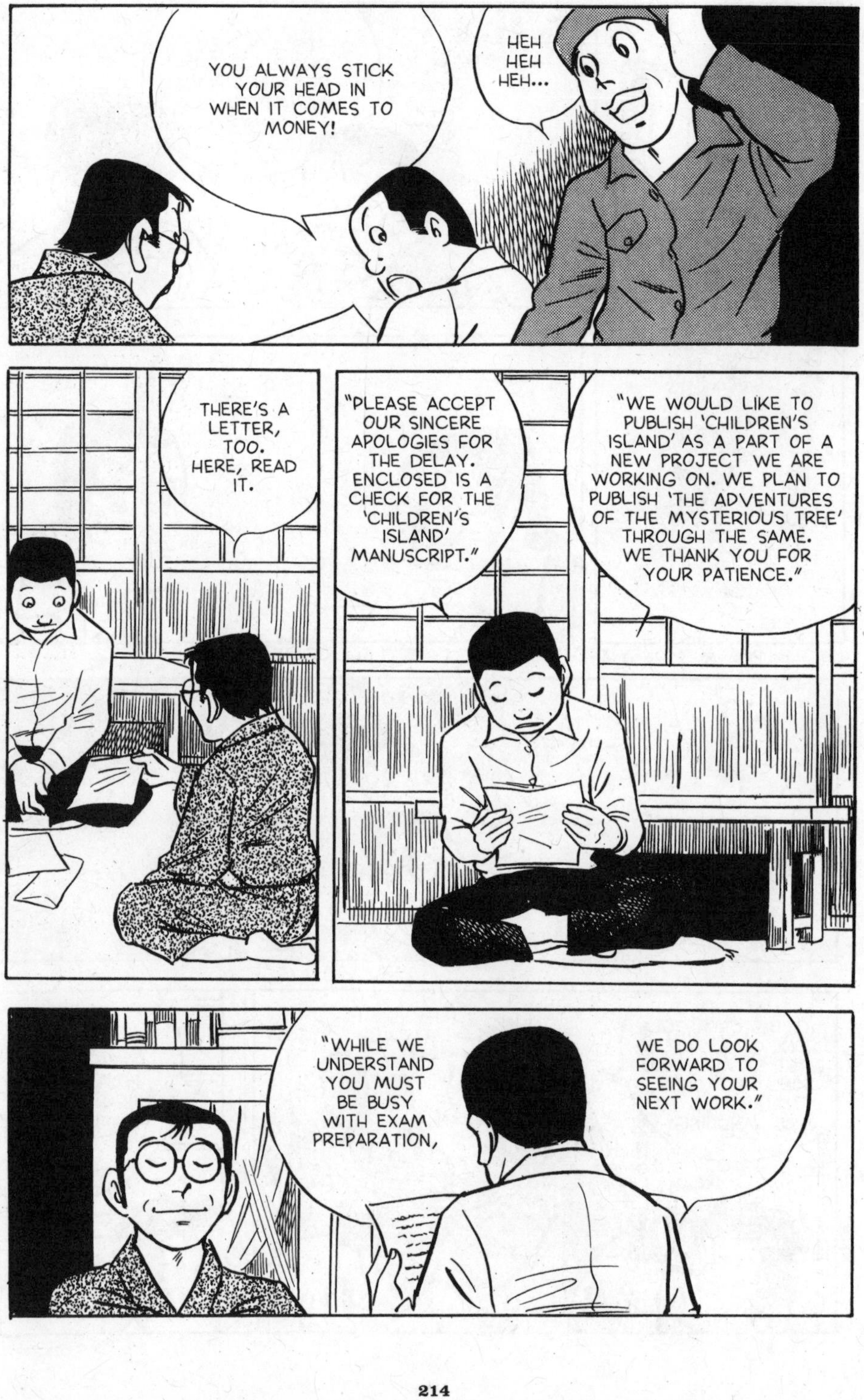
YOU ALWAYS STICK YOUR HEAD IN WHEN IT COMES TO MONEY!
HEH HEH HEH...
THERE'S A LETTER, TOO. HERE, READ IT.
"PLEASE ACCEPT OUR SINCERE APOLOGIES FOR THE DELAY. ENCLOSED IS A CHECK FOR THE 'CHILDREN'S ISLAND' MANUSCRIPT."
"WE WOULD LIKE TO PUBLISH 'CHILDREN'S ISLAND' AS A PART OF A NEW PROJECT WE ARE WORKING ON. WE PLAN TO PUBLISH 'THE ADVENTURES OF THE MYSTERIOUS TREE' THROUGH THE SAME. WE THANK YOU FOR YOUR PATIENCE."
"WHILE WE UNDERSTAND YOU MUST BE BUSY WITH EXAM PREPARATION,
WE DO LOOK FORWARD TO SEEING YOUR NEXT WORK."

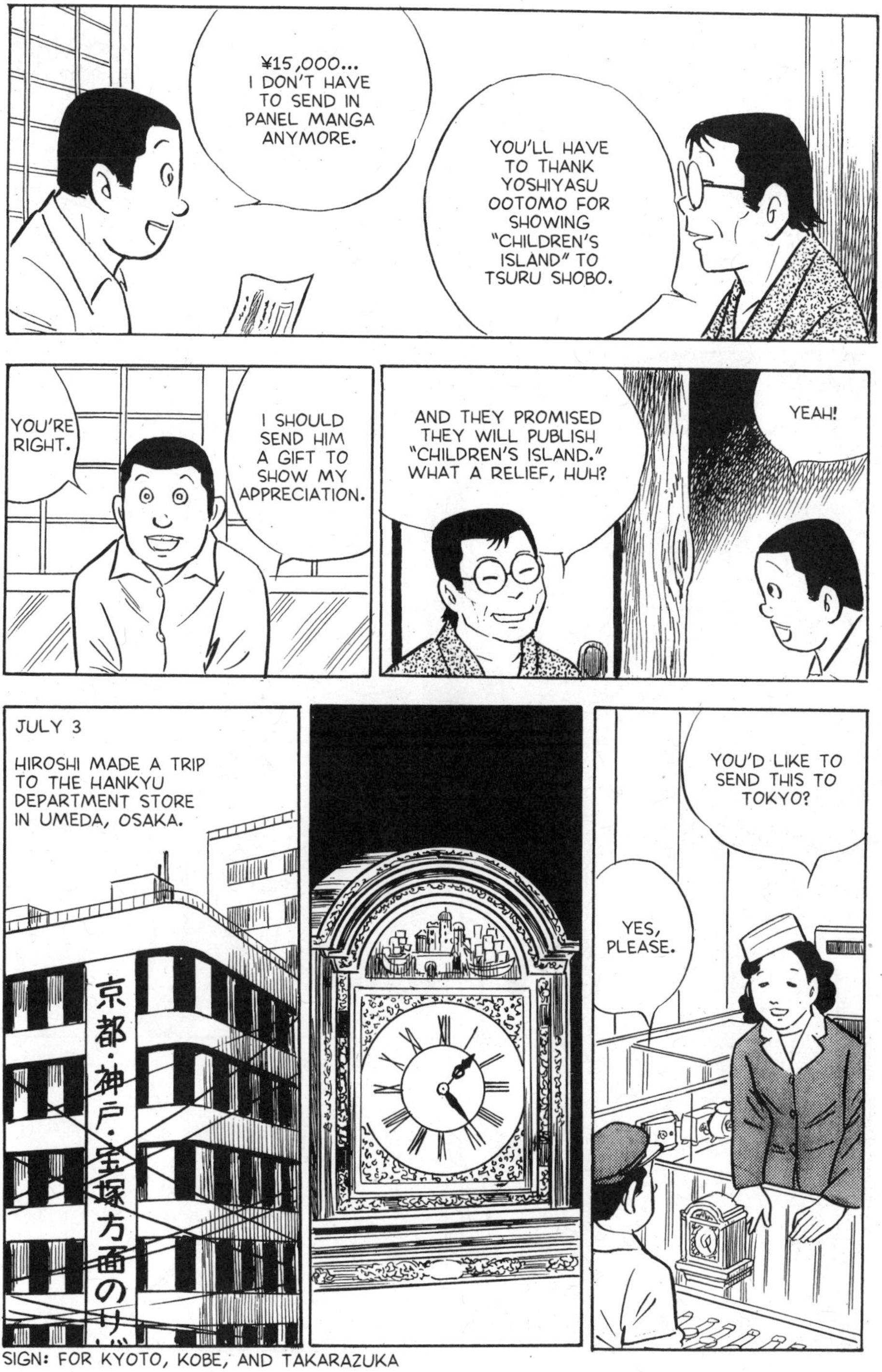
¥15,000... I DON'T HAVE TO SEND IN PANEL MANGA ANYMORE.
YOU'LL HAVE TO THANK YOSHIYASU OOTOMO FOR SHOWING "CHILDREN'S ISLAND" TO TSURU SHOBO.
YOU'RE RIGHT.
I SHOULD SEND HIM A GIFT TO SHOW MY APPRECIATION.
AND THEY PROMISED THEY WILL PUBLISH "CHILDREN'S ISLAND." WHAT A RELIEF, HUH?
YEAH!
JULY 3
HIROSHI MADE A TRIP TO THE HANKYU DEPARTMENT STORE IN UMEDA, OSAKA.
京都・神戸・宝塚方面のり
YOU'D LIKE TO SEND THIS TO TOKYO?
YES, PLEASE.

SIGN: FOR KYOTO, KOBE, AND TAKARAZUKA

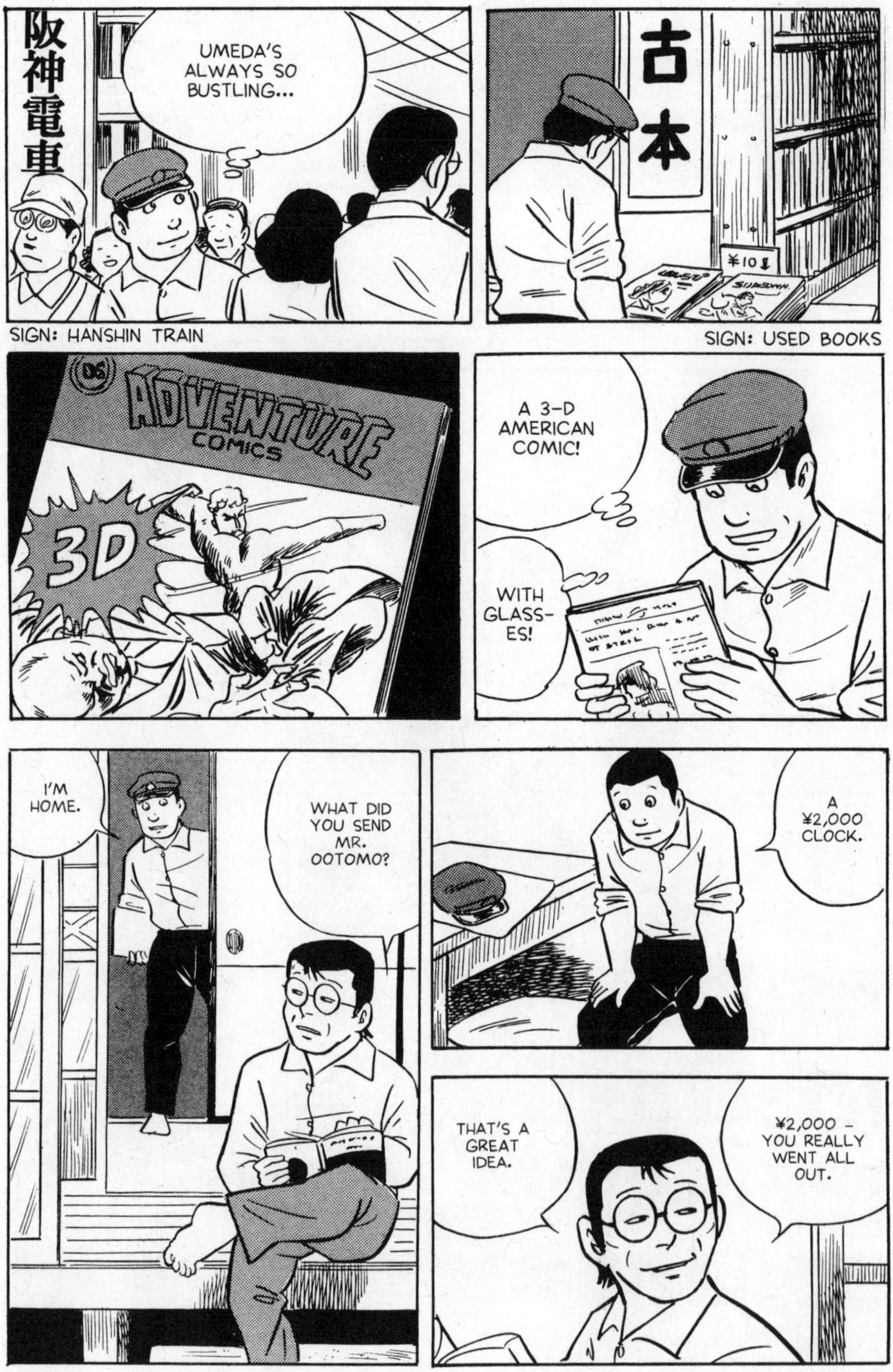
阪神電車
UMEDA'S ALWAYS SO BUSTLING...
SIGN: HANSHIN TRAIN
古本
¥10
SIGN: USED BOOKS
DC
ADVENTURE COMICS
3D
A 3-D AMERICAN COMIC!
WITH GLASS-ES!
I'M HOME.
WHAT DID YOU SEND MR. OOTOMO?
A ¥2,000 CLOCK.
THAT'S A GREAT IDEA.
¥2,000 - YOU REALLY WENT ALL OUT.

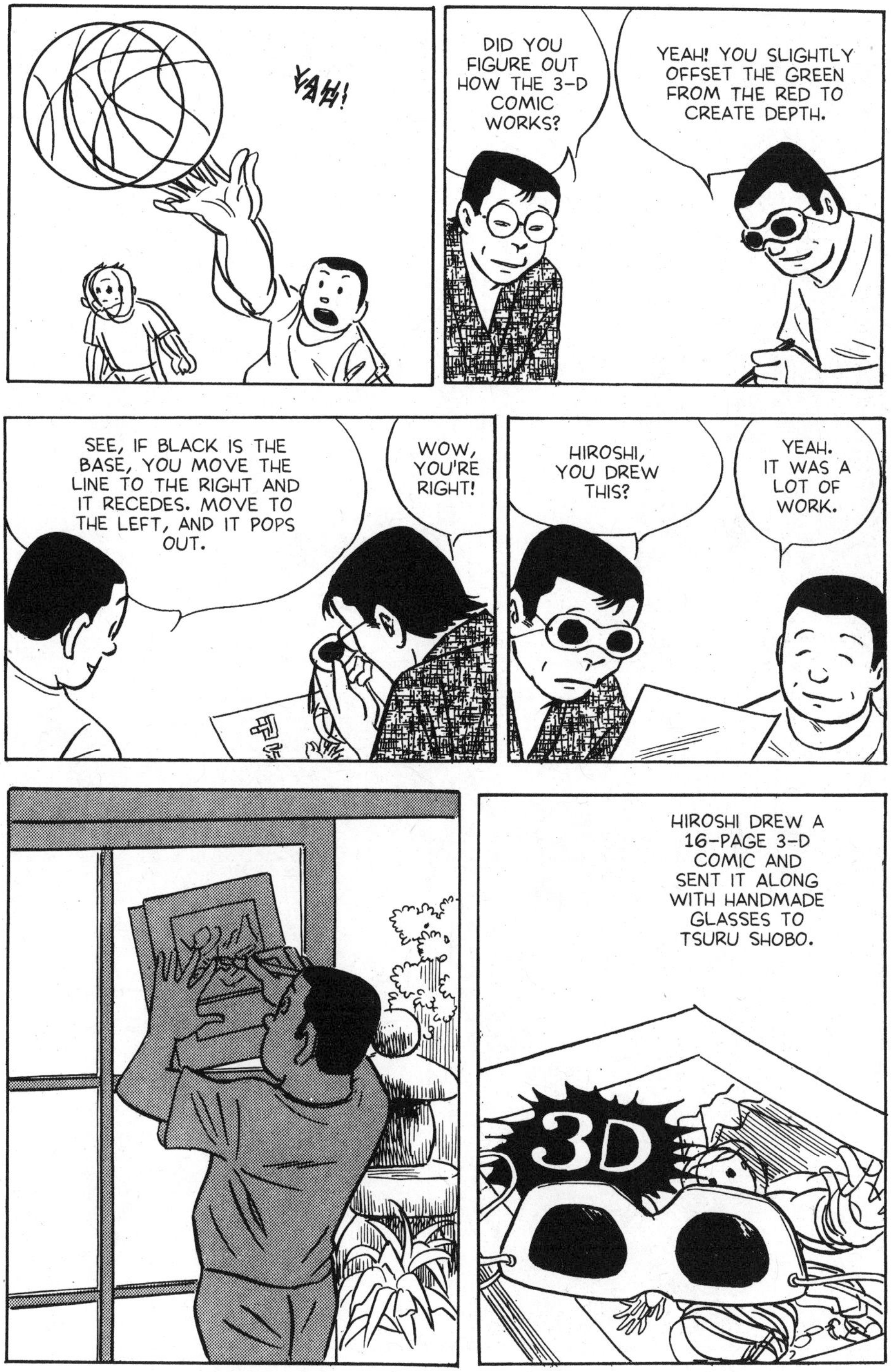
YAH!
DID YOU FIGURE OUT HOW THE 3-D COMIC WORKS?
YEAH! YOU SLIGHTLY OFFSET THE GREEN FROM THE RED TO CREATE DEPTH.
SEE, IF BLACK IS THE BASE, YOU MOVE THE LINE TO THE RIGHT AND IT RECEDES. MOVE TO THE LEFT, AND IT POPS OUT.
WOW, YOU'RE RIGHT!
HIROSHI, YOU DREW THIS?
YEAH. IT WAS A LOT OF WORK.
HIROSHI DREW A 16-PAGE 3-D COMIC AND SENT IT ALONG WITH HANDMADE GLASSES TO TSURU SHOBO.
3D

IN JULY, KINUKO ITO PLACED THIRD IN THE MISS UNIVERSE CONTEST, POPULARIZING THE PHRASE "8-HEADS-TALL BEAUTY."

I GOT A RESPONSE FROM TSURU SHOBO: "3-D COMICS MAY BE TOO ADVANCED FOR THE JAPANESE MARKET. WE LOOK FORWARD TO YOUR NEXT WORK."

THOUGHT SO.

IT WAS HIROSHI'S LAST SUMMER BREAK AS A HIGH SCHOOL STUDENT.

⟨SOUND OF CICADAS⟩

HIROSHI UTILIZED THE BREAK TO THE FULLEST TO CREATE "JUNGLE GIANT," HIS LAST PIECE AS A HIGH SCHOOL STUDENT.

⟨SOUND OF CICADAS⟩

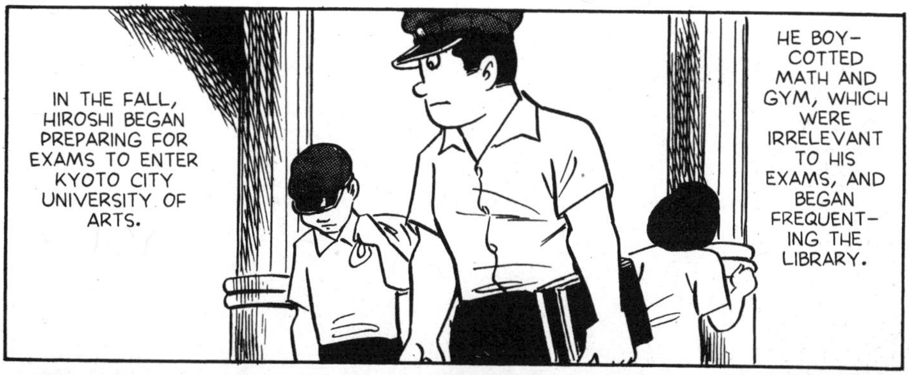
IN THE FALL, HIROSHI BEGAN PREPARING FOR EXAMS TO ENTER KYOTO CITY UNIVERSITY OF ARTS.
HE BOY-COTTED MATH AND GYM, WHICH WERE IRRELEVANT TO HIS EXAMS, AND BEGAN FREQUENT-ING THE LIBRARY.

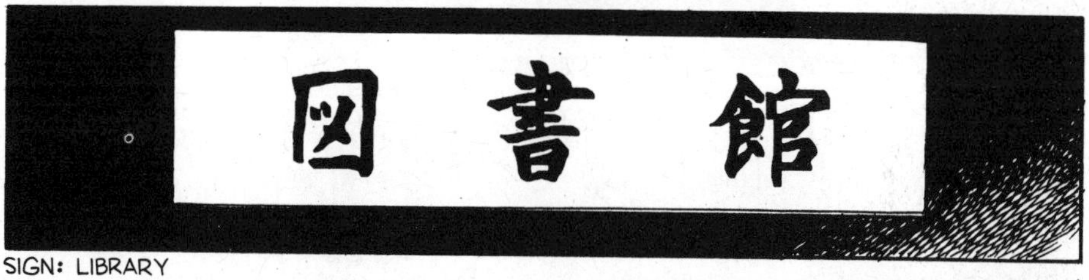
図書館

SIGN: LIBRARY

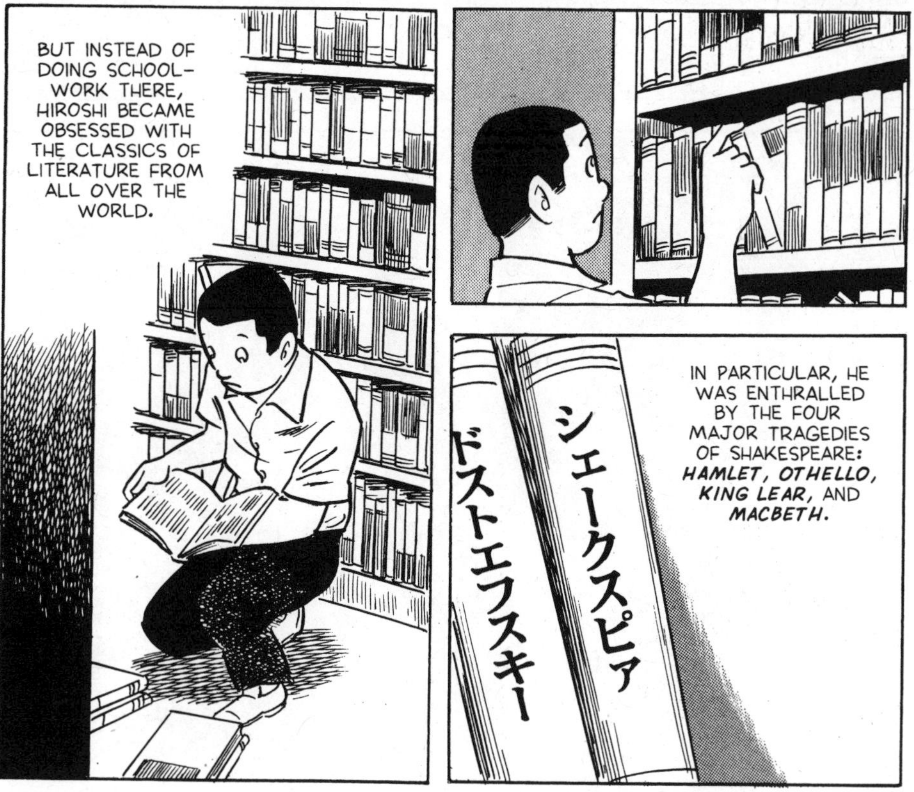
BUT INSTEAD OF DOING SCHOOL-WORK THERE, HIROSHI BECAME OBSESSED WITH THE CLASSICS OF LITERATURE FROM ALL OVER THE WORLD.
IN PARTICULAR, HE WAS ENTHRALLED BY THE FOUR MAJOR TRAGEDIES OF SHAKESPEARE: ***HAMLET***, ***OTHELLO***, ***KING LEAR***, AND ***MACBETH***.
シェークスピア
ドストエフスキー

BOOKS: SHAKESPEARE, DOSTOEVSKY

MACBETH, WHO KILLED KING DUNCAN TO USURP HIS THRONE, BELIEVED THE WITCH'S PREDICTION, THAT HE NEED FEAR NO DEFEAT "TILL BIRNAM FOREST COME TO DUNSINANE."

ゴォォ

BUT IT MOVED!

⟨SOUND OF FOREST MOVING⟩

A MOVING FOREST! SUCH DYNAMIC SCALE...

I WANT TO MAKE A MANGA VERSION OF MACBETH...

HIROSHI QUICKLY FORGOT ABOUT EXAM PREPARATION AND SPIRALED BACK INTO THE WORLD OF MANGA.

(HIROSHI WORE GLASSES TO EMULATE TEZUKA)

220

DEBUT

THE AMERICAN FILM *SHANE* (1953), DIRECTED BY GEORGE STEVENS
AND STARRING ALAN LADD

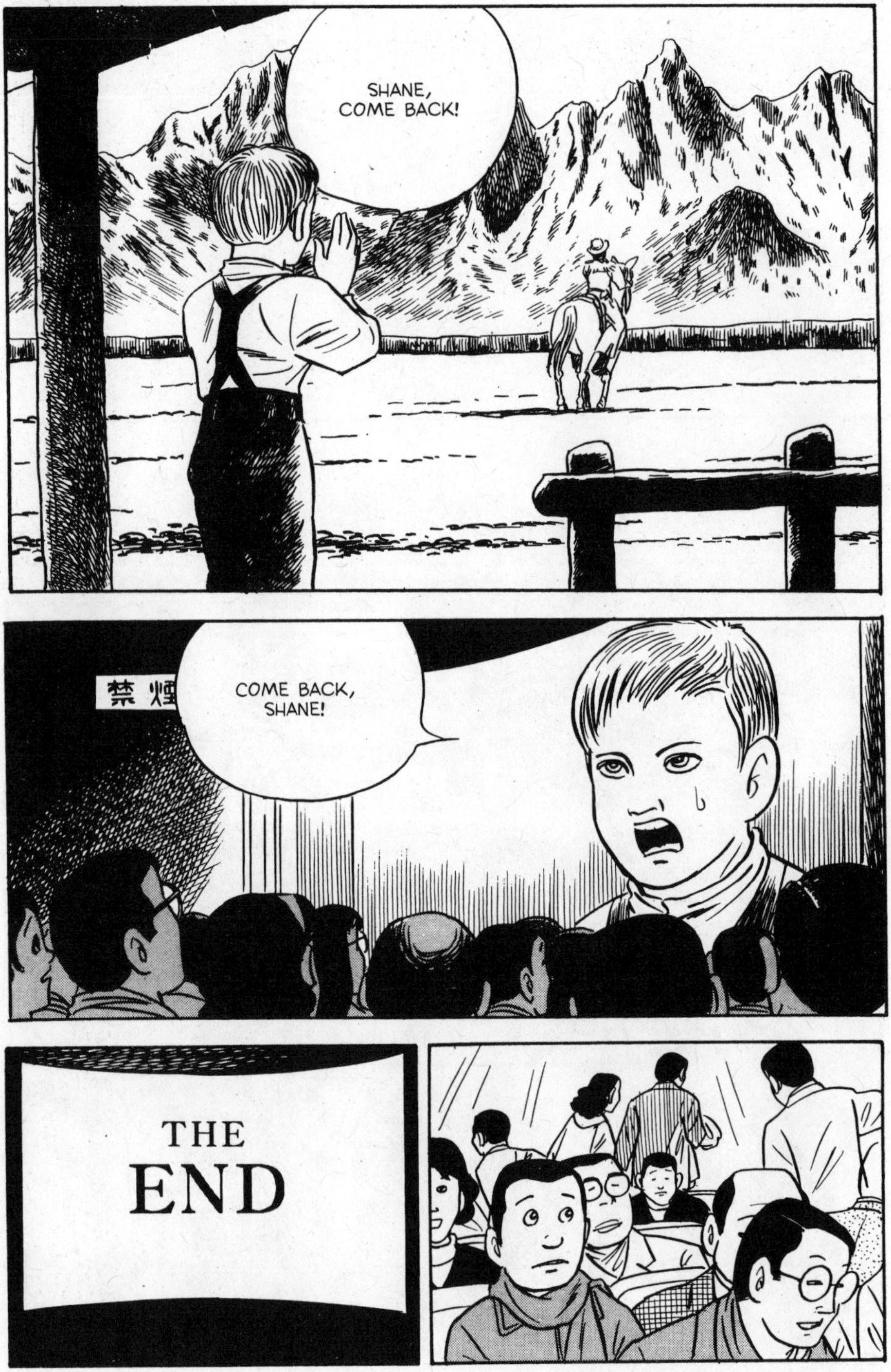
SHANE,
COME BACK!
禁煙
COME BACK,
SHANE!
THE
END

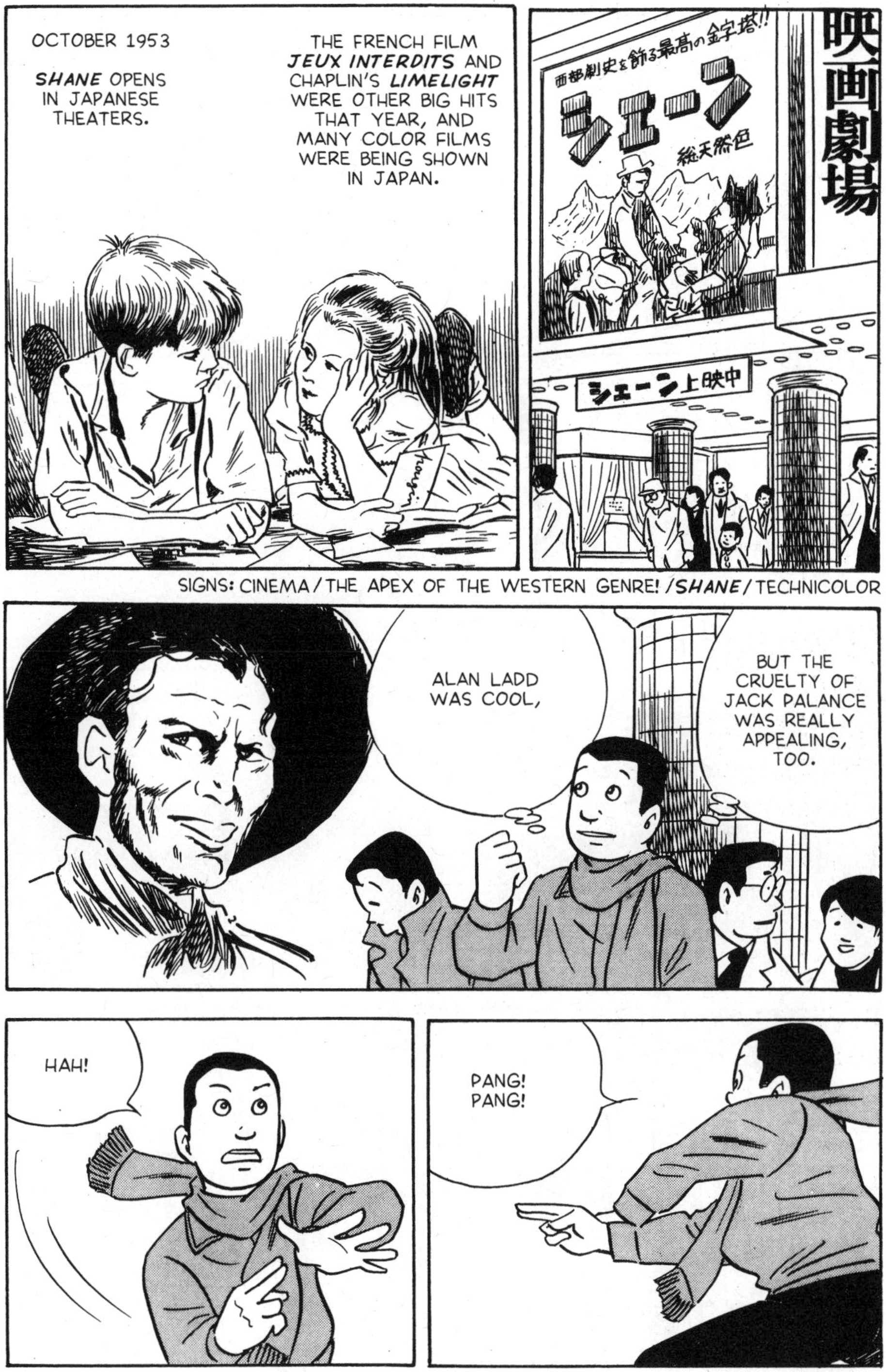
OCTOBER 1953
SHANE OPENS IN JAPANESE THEATERS.
THE FRENCH FILM ***JEUX INTERDITS*** AND CHAPLIN'S ***LIMELIGHT*** WERE OTHER BIG HITS THAT YEAR, AND MANY COLOR FILMS WERE BEING SHOWN IN JAPAN.
映画劇場
西部劇史を飾る最高の金字塔!!
シェーン
総天然色
シェーン上映中
SIGNS: CINEMA / THE APEX OF THE WESTERN GENRE! / ***SHANE*** / TECHNICOLOR
ALAN LADD WAS COOL,
BUT THE CRUELTY OF JACK PALANCE WAS REALLY APPEALING, TOO.
HAH!
PANG! PANG!

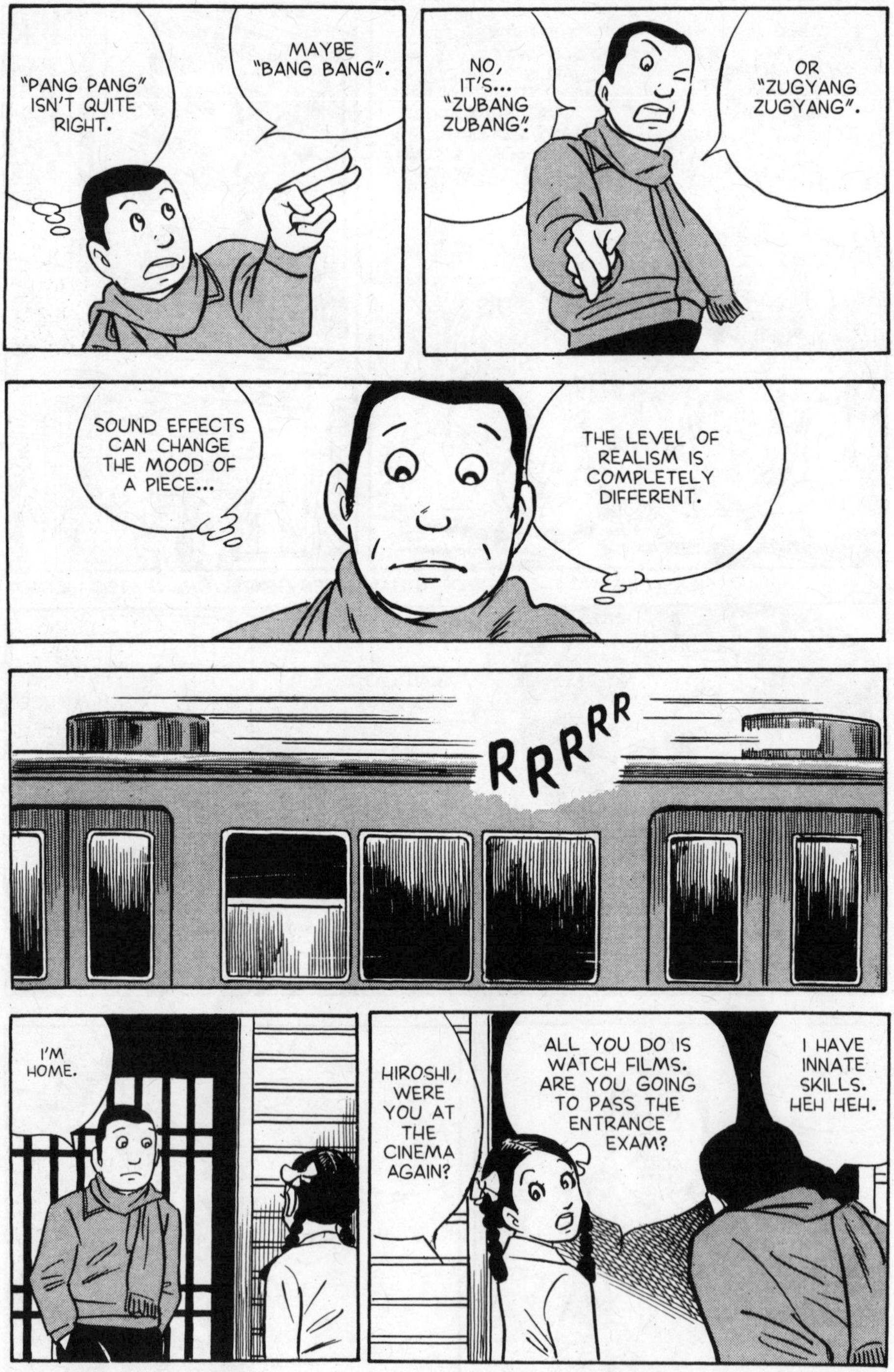
"PANG PANG" ISN'T QUITE RIGHT.
MAYBE "BANG BANG".
NO, IT'S... "ZUBANG ZUBANG".
OR "ZUGYANG ZUGYANG".
SOUND EFFECTS CAN CHANGE THE MOOD OF A PIECE...
THE LEVEL OF REALISM IS COMPLETELY DIFFERENT.
RRRRR
I'M HOME.
HIROSHI, WERE YOU AT THE CINEMA AGAIN?
ALL YOU DO IS WATCH FILMS. ARE YOU GOING TO PASS THE ENTRANCE EXAM?
I HAVE INNATE SKILLS. HEH HEH.

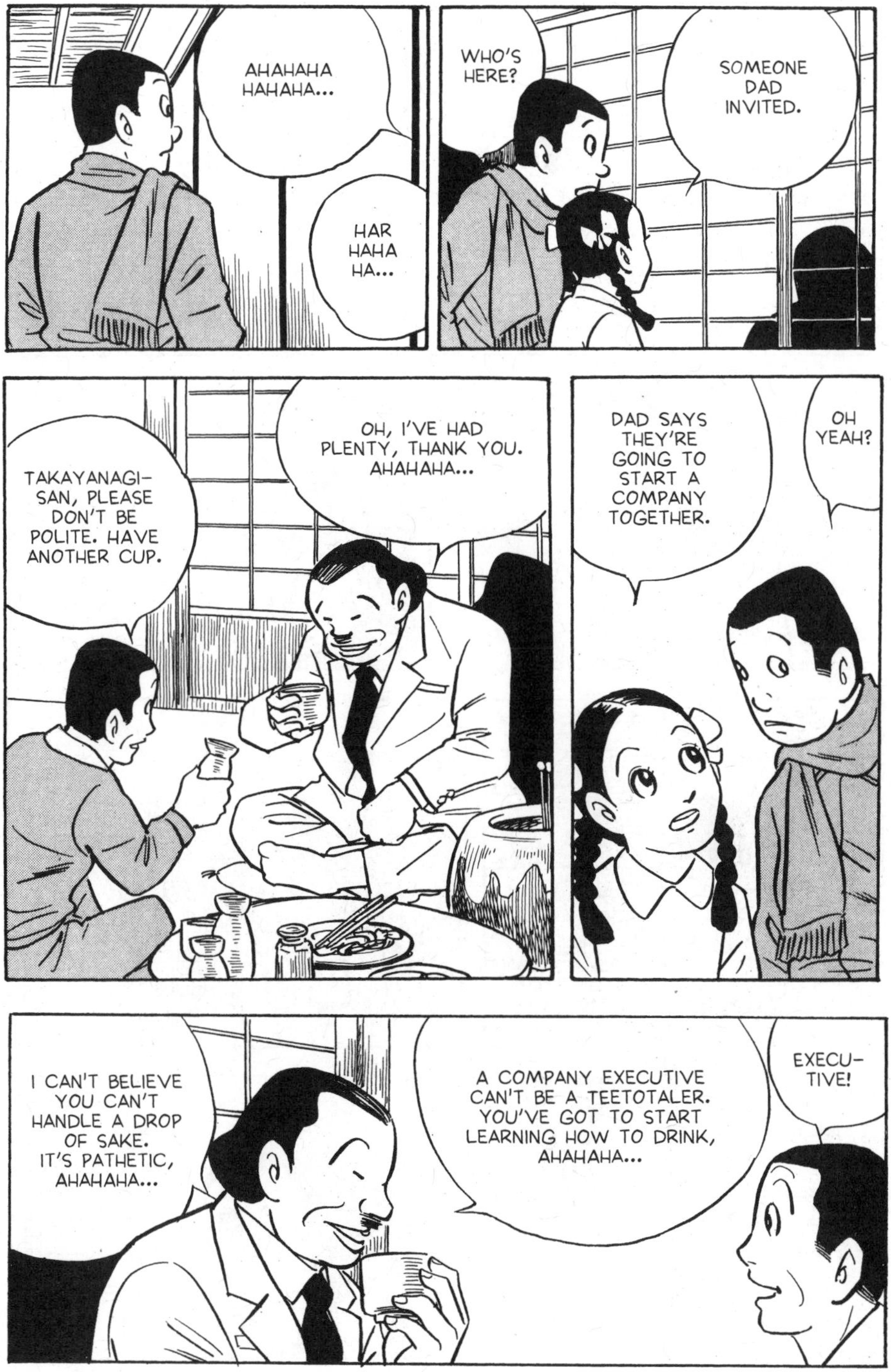
AHAHAHA HAHAHA...
HAR HAHA HA...
WHO'S HERE?
SOMEONE DAD INVITED.
TAKAYANAGI-SAN, PLEASE DON'T BE POLITE. HAVE ANOTHER CUP.
OH, I'VE HAD PLENTY, THANK YOU. AHAHAHA...
DAD SAYS THEY'RE GOING TO START A COMPANY TOGETHER.
OH YEAH?
I CAN'T BELIEVE YOU CAN'T HANDLE A DROP OF SAKE. IT'S PATHETIC, AHAHAHA...
A COMPANY EXECUTIVE CAN'T BE A TEETOTALER. YOU'VE GOT TO START LEARNING HOW TO DRINK, AHAHAHA...
EXECU-TIVE!

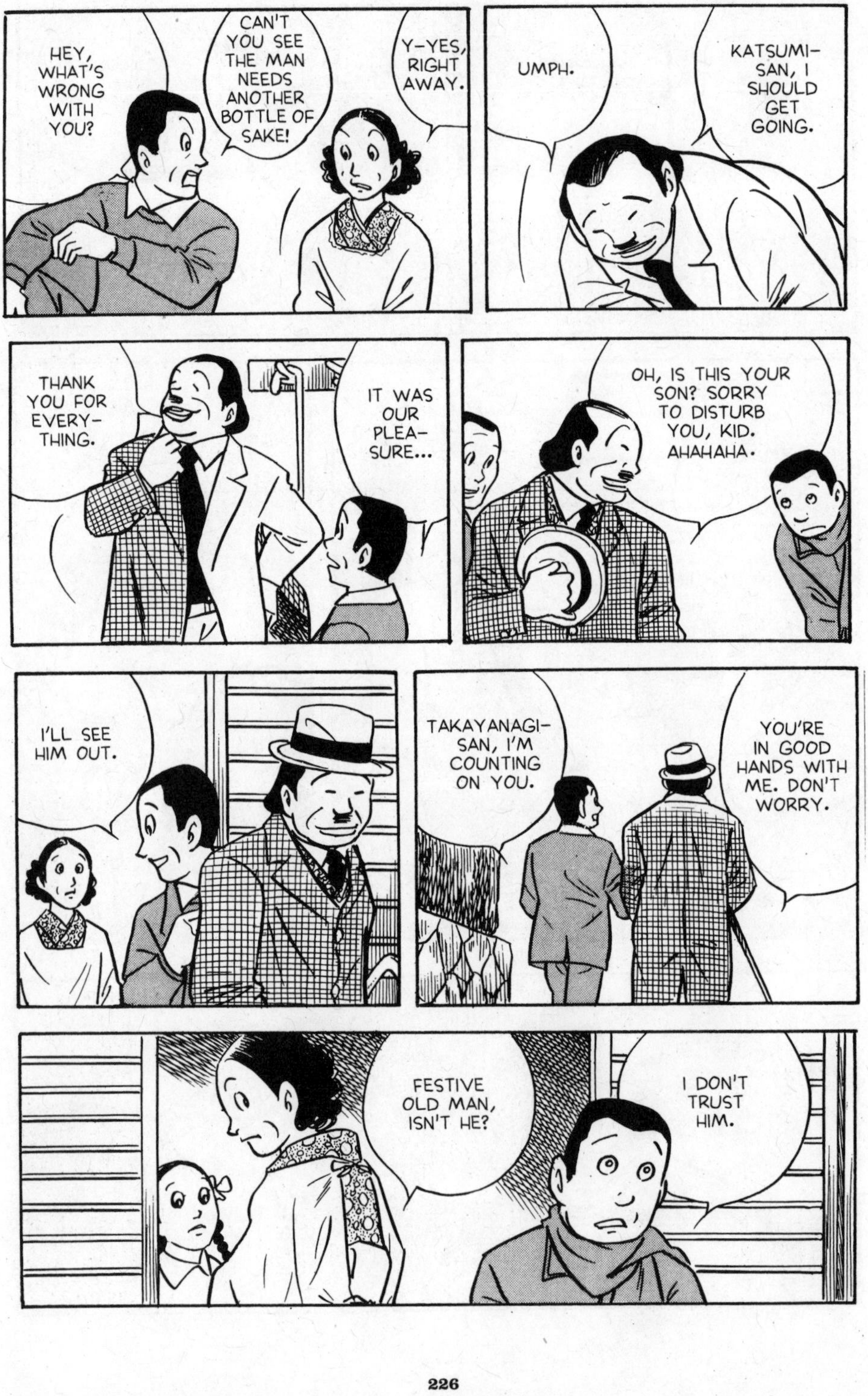
HEY, WHAT'S WRONG WITH YOU?
CAN'T YOU SEE THE MAN NEEDS ANOTHER BOTTLE OF SAKE!
Y-YES, RIGHT AWAY.
UMPH.
KATSUMI-SAN, I SHOULD GET GOING.
THANK YOU FOR EVERY-THING.
IT WAS OUR PLEA-SURE...
OH, IS THIS YOUR SON? SORRY TO DISTURB YOU, KID. AHAHAHA.
I'LL SEE HIM OUT.
TAKAYANAGI-SAN, I'M COUNTING ON YOU.
YOU'RE IN GOOD HANDS WITH ME. DON'T WORRY.
FESTIVE OLD MAN, ISN'T HE?
I DON'T TRUST HIM.

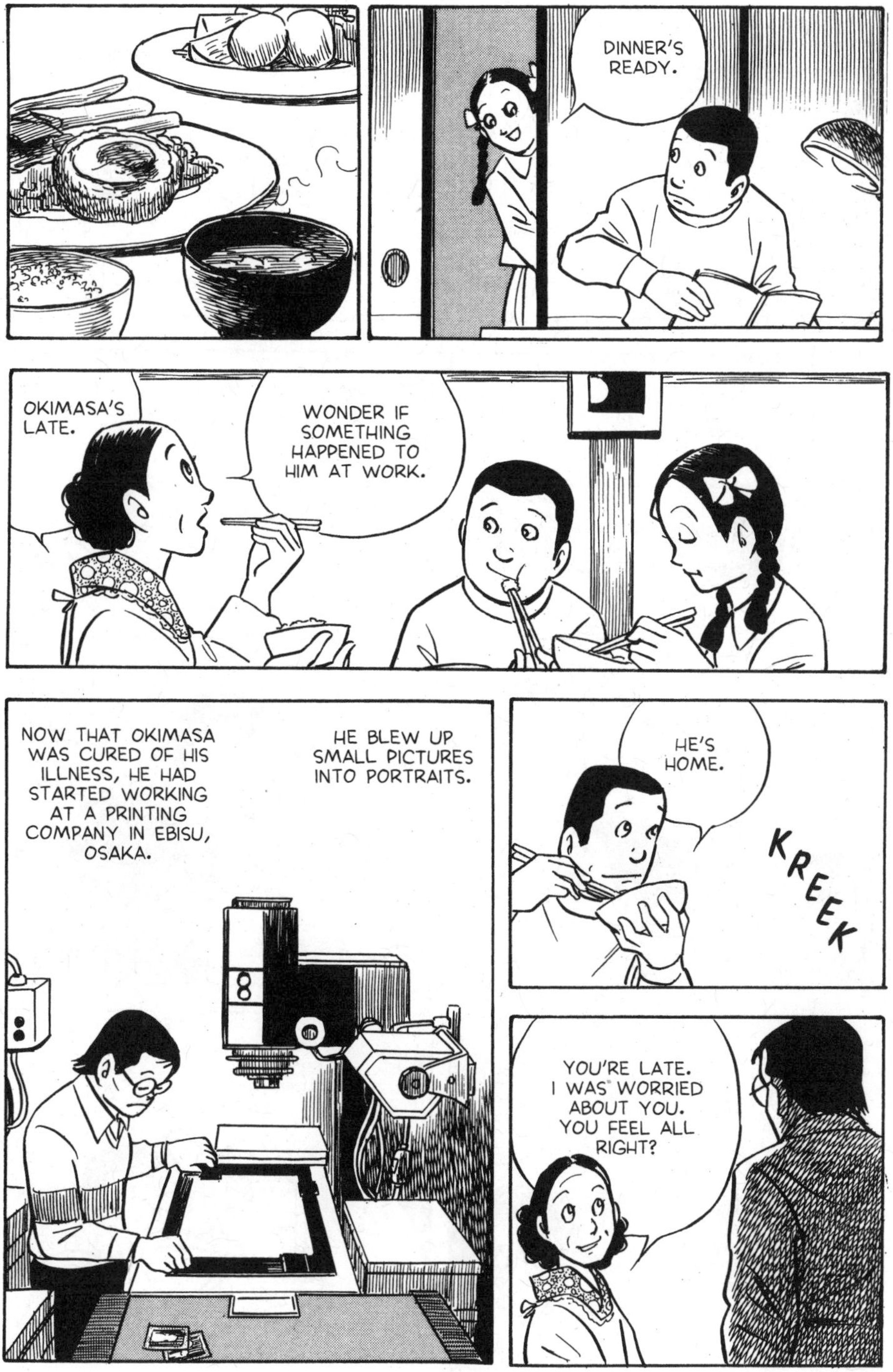
DINNER'S READY.
OKIMASA'S LATE.
WONDER IF SOMETHING HAPPENED TO HIM AT WORK.
NOW THAT OKIMASA WAS CURED OF HIS ILLNESS, HE HAD STARTED WORKING AT A PRINTING COMPANY IN EBISU, OSAKA.
HE BLEW UP SMALL PICTURES INTO PORTRAITS.
HE'S HOME.
KREEK
YOU'RE LATE. I WAS WORRIED ABOUT YOU. YOU FEEL ALL RIGHT?

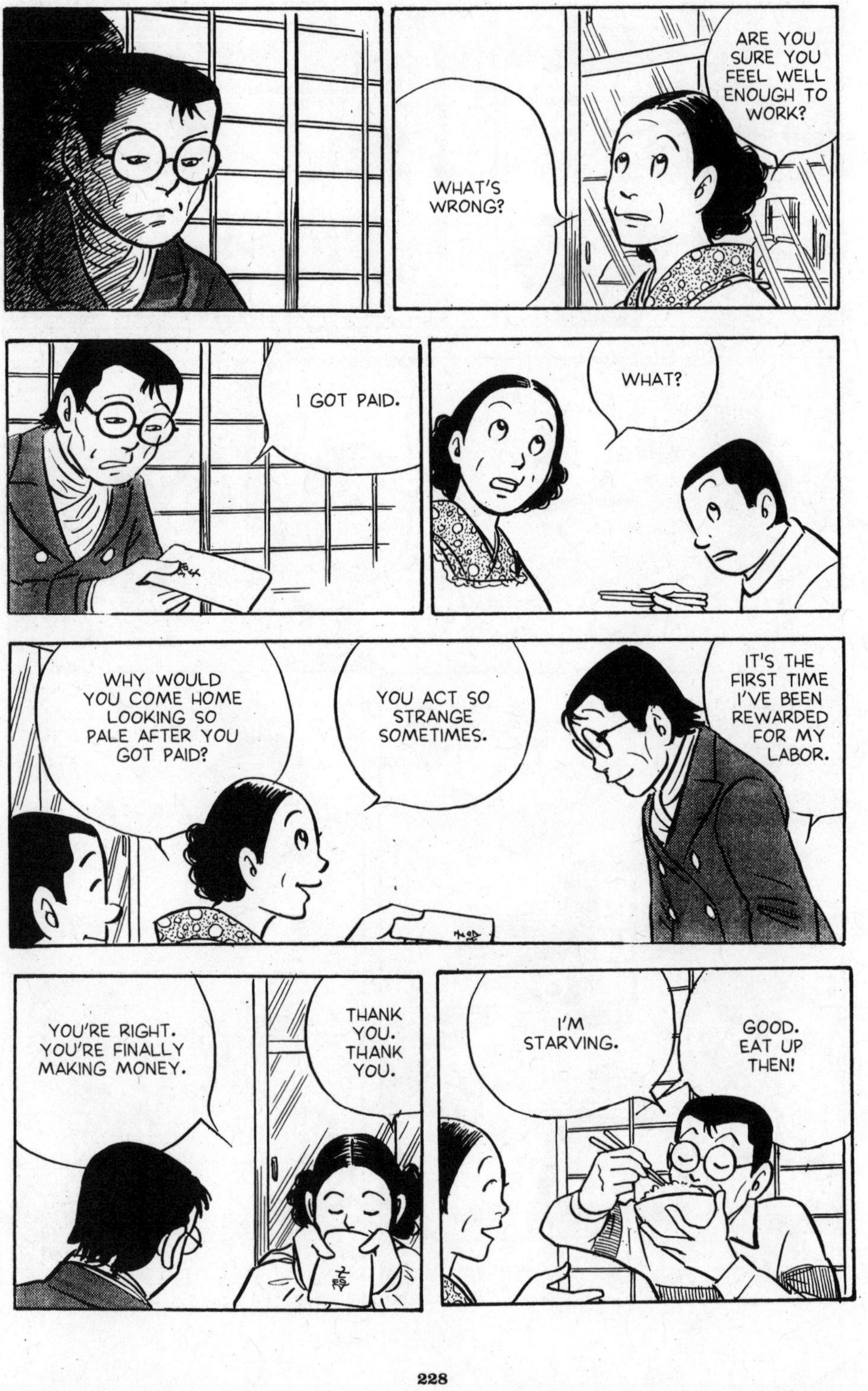
WHAT'S WRONG?
ARE YOU SURE YOU FEEL WELL ENOUGH TO WORK?
I GOT PAID.
WHAT?
WHY WOULD YOU COME HOME LOOKING SO PALE AFTER YOU GOT PAID?
YOU ACT SO STRANGE SOMETIMES.
IT'S THE FIRST TIME I'VE BEEN REWARDED FOR MY LABOR.
YOU'RE RIGHT. YOU'RE FINALLY MAKING MONEY.
THANK YOU. THANK YOU.
I'M STARVING.
GOOD. EAT UP THEN!

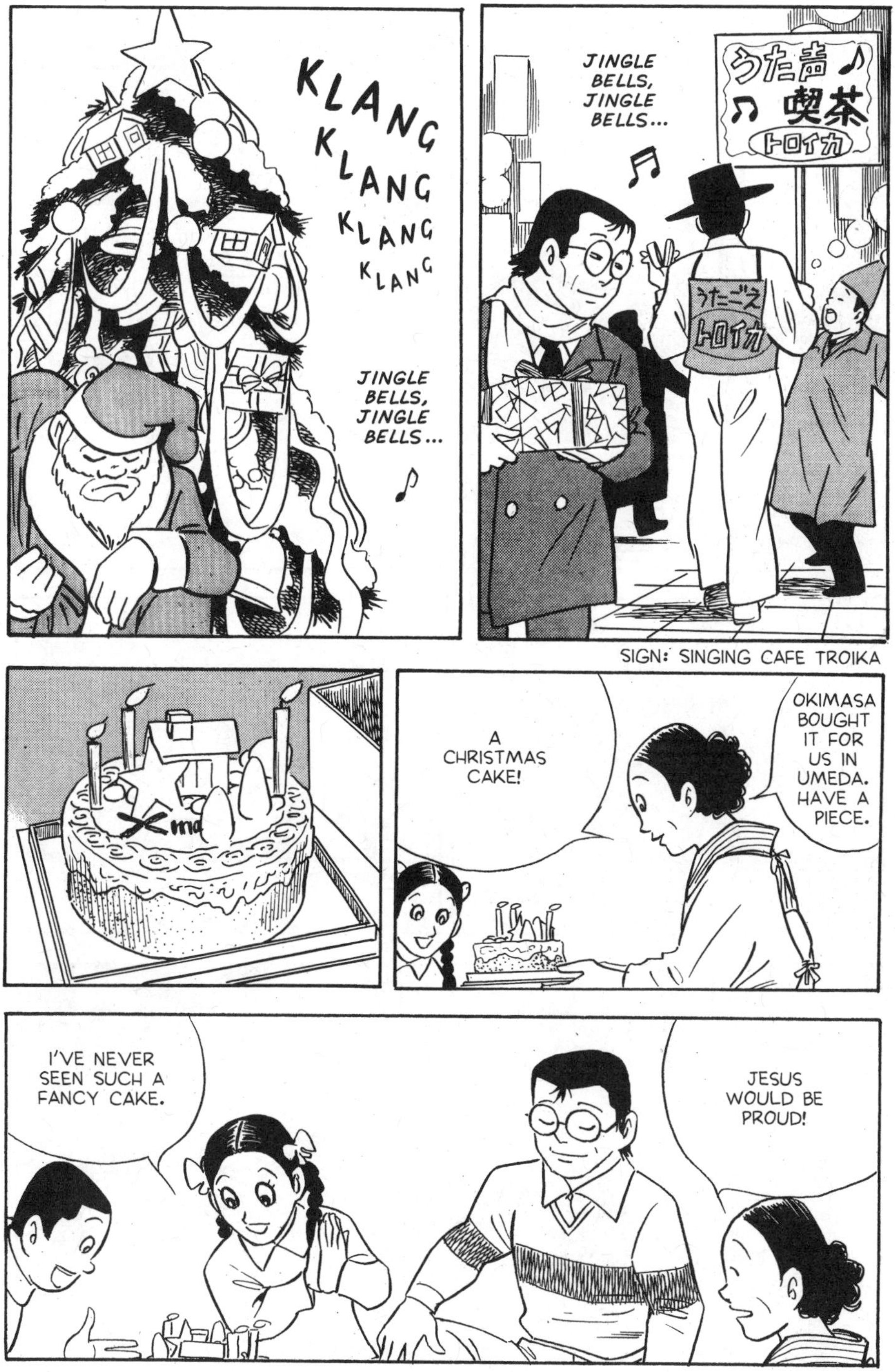
KLANG
KLANG
KLANG
KLANG
JINGLE BELLS, JINGLE BELLS...
JINGLE BELLS, JINGLE BELLS...
うた声♪
♪ 喫茶
トロイカ
うたごえ
トロイカ
SIGN: SINGING CAFE TROIKA
A CHRISTMAS CAKE!
OKIMASA BOUGHT IT FOR US IN UMEDA. HAVE A PIECE.
I'VE NEVER SEEN SUCH A FANCY CAKE.
JESUS WOULD BE PROUD!

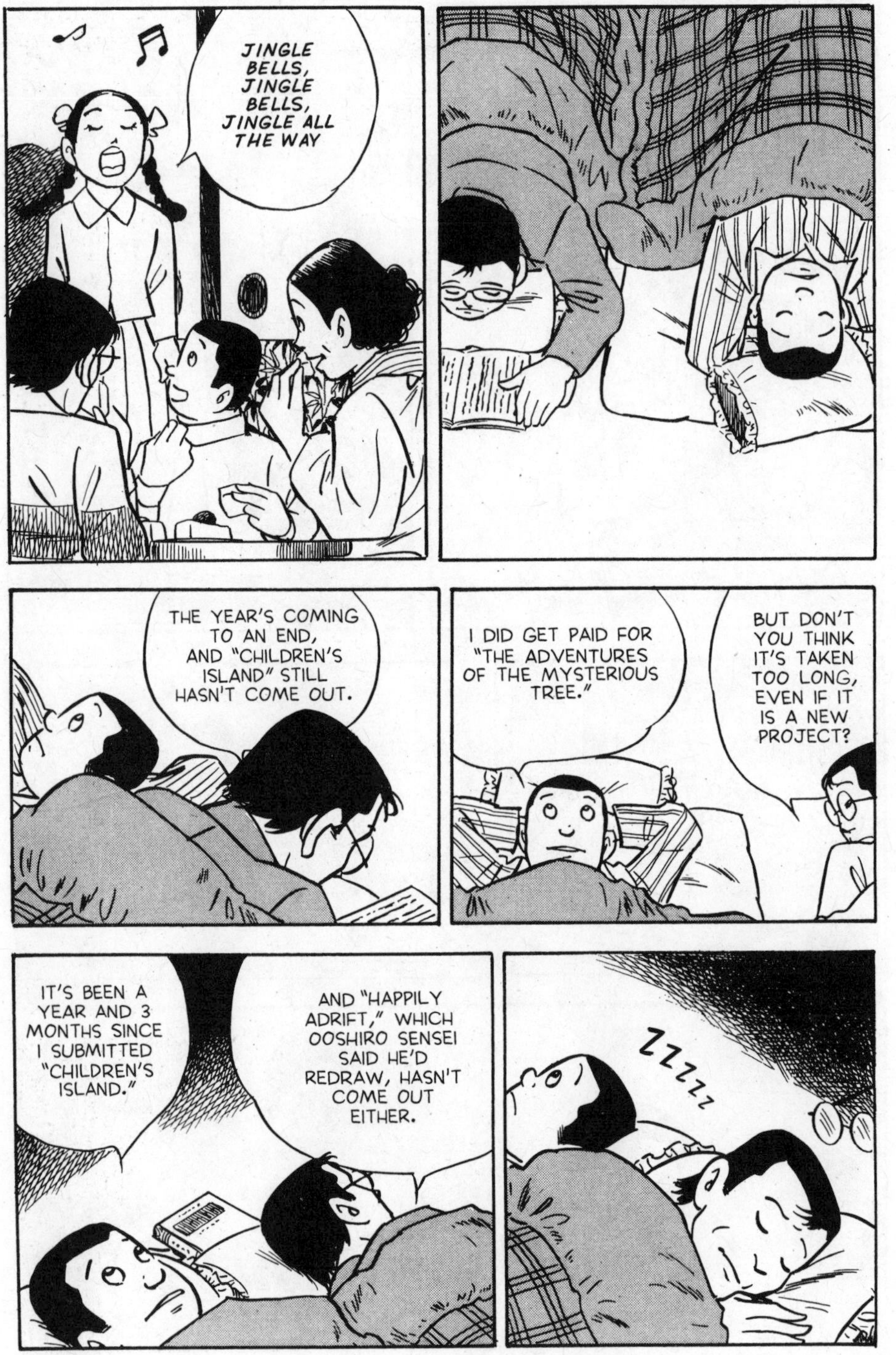
JINGLE BELLS, JINGLE BELLS, JINGLE ALL THE WAY
THE YEAR'S COMING TO AN END, AND "CHILDREN'S ISLAND" STILL HASN'T COME OUT.
I DID GET PAID FOR "THE ADVENTURES OF THE MYSTERIOUS TREE."
BUT DON'T YOU THINK IT'S TAKEN TOO LONG, EVEN IF IT IS A NEW PROJECT?
IT'S BEEN A YEAR AND 3 MONTHS SINCE I SUBMITTED "CHILDREN'S ISLAND."
AND "HAPPILY ADRIFT," WHICH OOSHIRO SENSEI SAID HE'D REDRAW, HASN'T COME OUT EITHER.
ZZZZZ

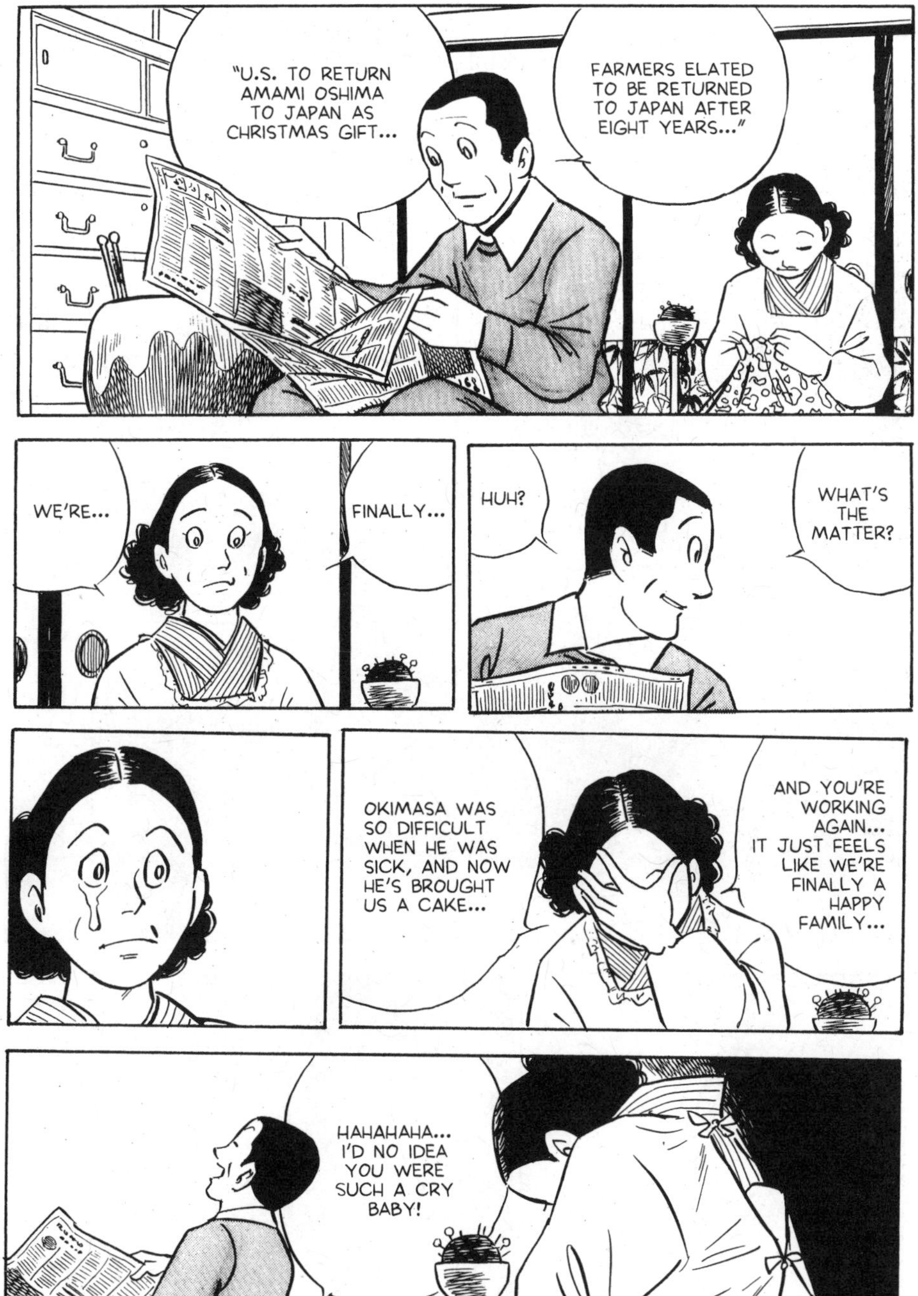
"U.S. TO RETURN AMAMI OSHIMA TO JAPAN AS CHRISTMAS GIFT...
FARMERS ELATED TO BE RETURNED TO JAPAN AFTER EIGHT YEARS..."
WE'RE...
FINALLY...
HUH?
WHAT'S THE MATTER?
OKIMASA WAS SO DIFFICULT WHEN HE WAS SICK, AND NOW HE'S BROUGHT US A CAKE...
AND YOU'RE WORKING AGAIN... IT JUST FEELS LIKE WE'RE FINALLY A HAPPY FAMILY...
HAHAHAHA... I'D NO IDEA YOU WERE SUCH A CRY BABY!

NEW YEAR'S DAY, 1954
380,000 PEOPLE VISITED THE IMPERIAL RESIDENCE TO CELEBRATE THE NEW YEAR.
IN THE CHAOTIC AFTERMATH, 16 PEOPLE WERE TRAMPLED TO DEATH NEAR NIJUBASHI.
都市立美術大學
入學試驗願書
受付
THUMP
立美術大学
受領

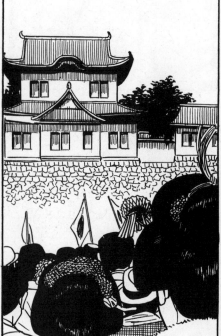

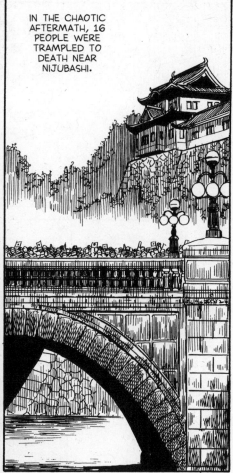

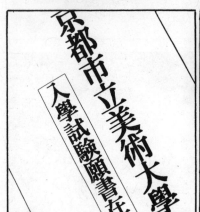

ENVELOPE: KYOTO CITY UNIVERSITY OF THE ARTS ENTRANCE EXAMINATION

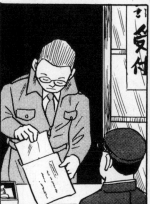

SIGN: RECEPTION

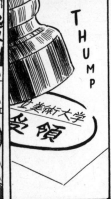

STAMP: RECEIVED–KYOTO CITY UNIVERSITY OF THE ARTS

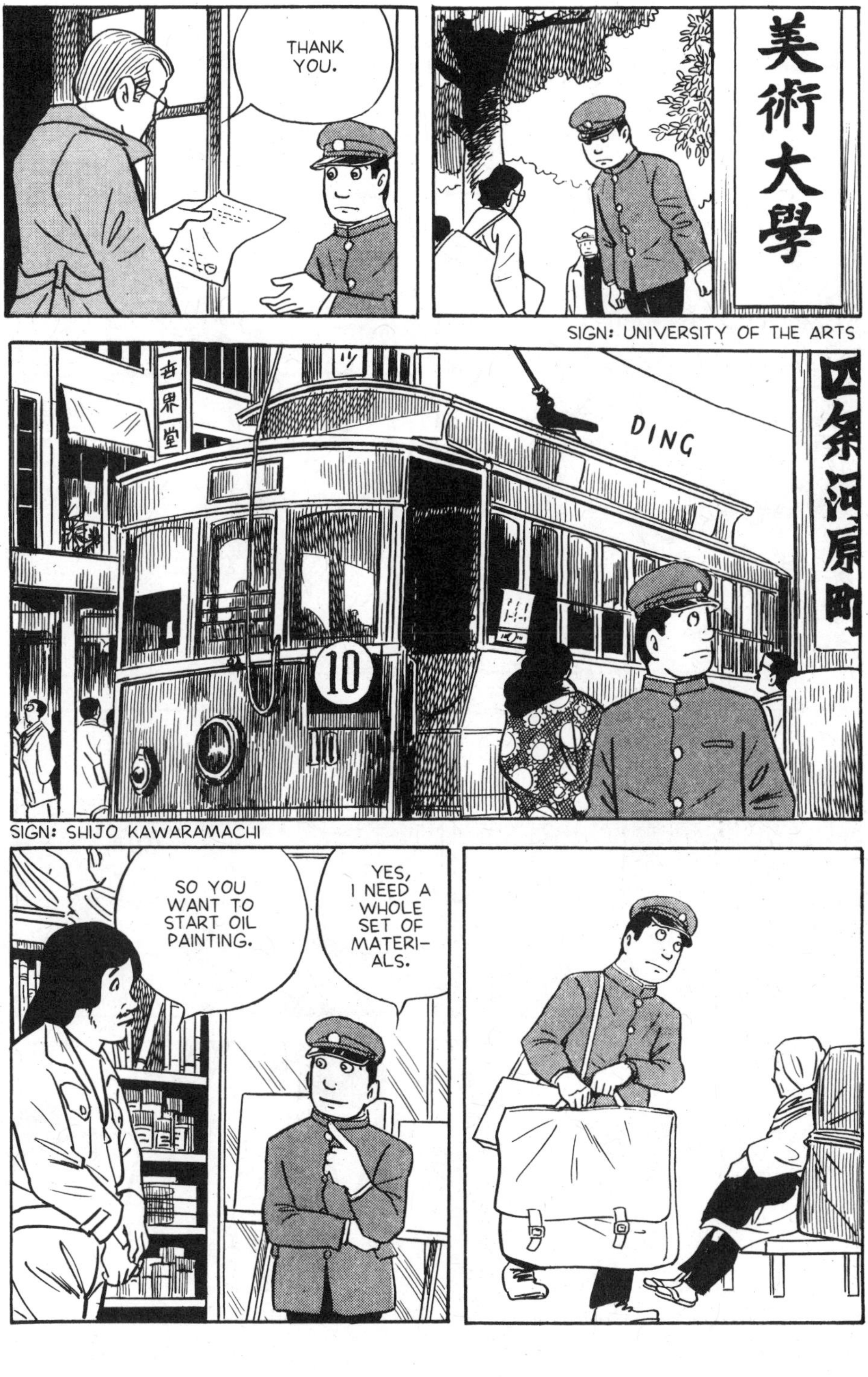
THANK YOU.
美術大學
SIGN: UNIVERSITY OF THE ARTS
DING
四条河原町
10
SIGN: SHIJO KAWARAMACHI
SO YOU WANT TO START OIL PAINTING.
YES, I NEED A WHOLE SET OF MATERI-ALS.

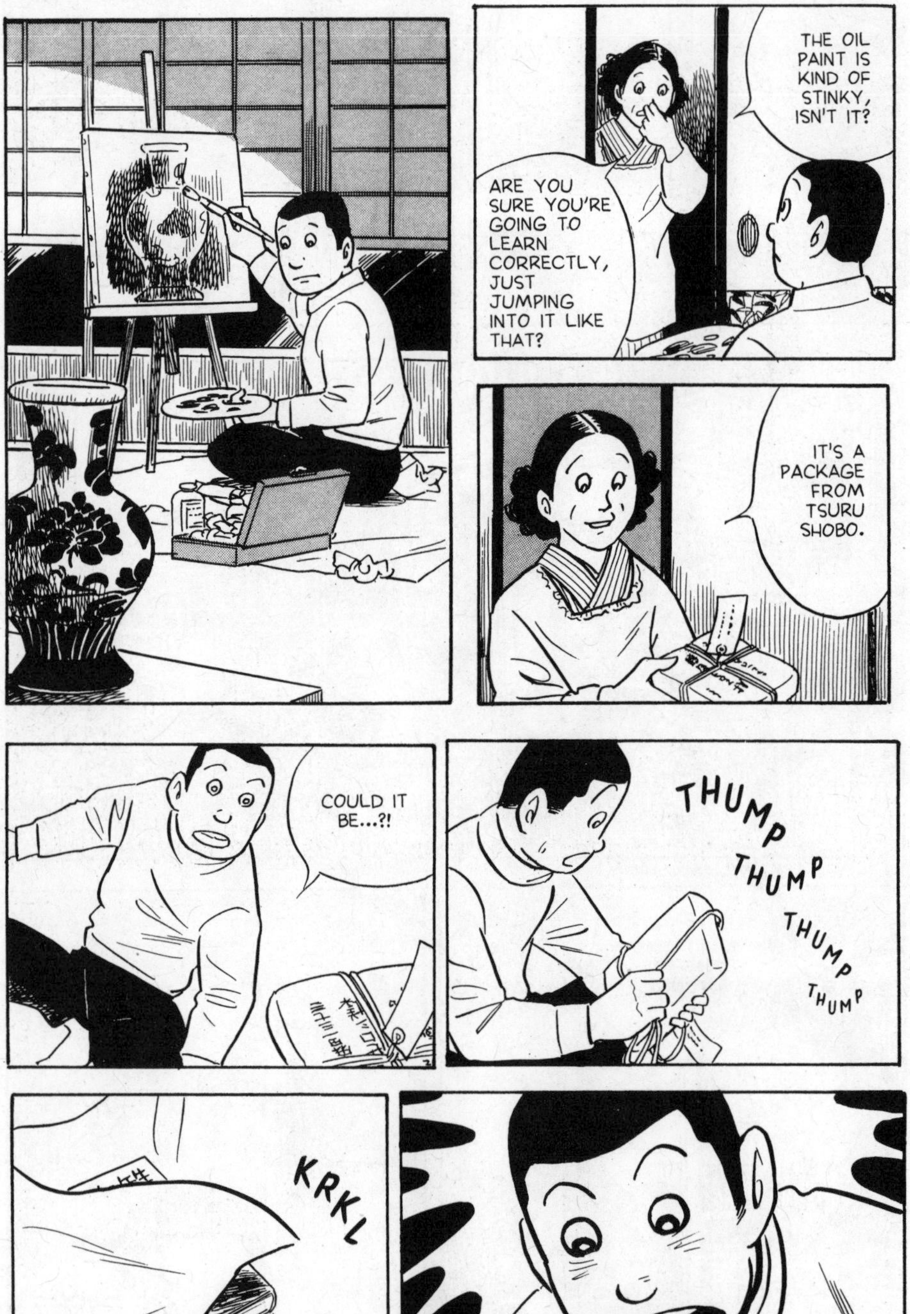
THE OIL PAINT IS KIND OF STINKY, ISN'T IT?
ARE YOU SURE YOU'RE GOING TO LEARN CORRECTLY, JUST JUMPING INTO IT LIKE THAT?
IT'S A PACKAGE FROM TSURU SHOBO.
COULD IT BE...?!
THUMP THUMP THUMP THUMP
KRKL

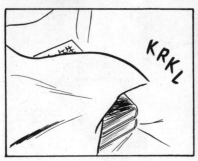

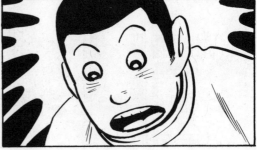

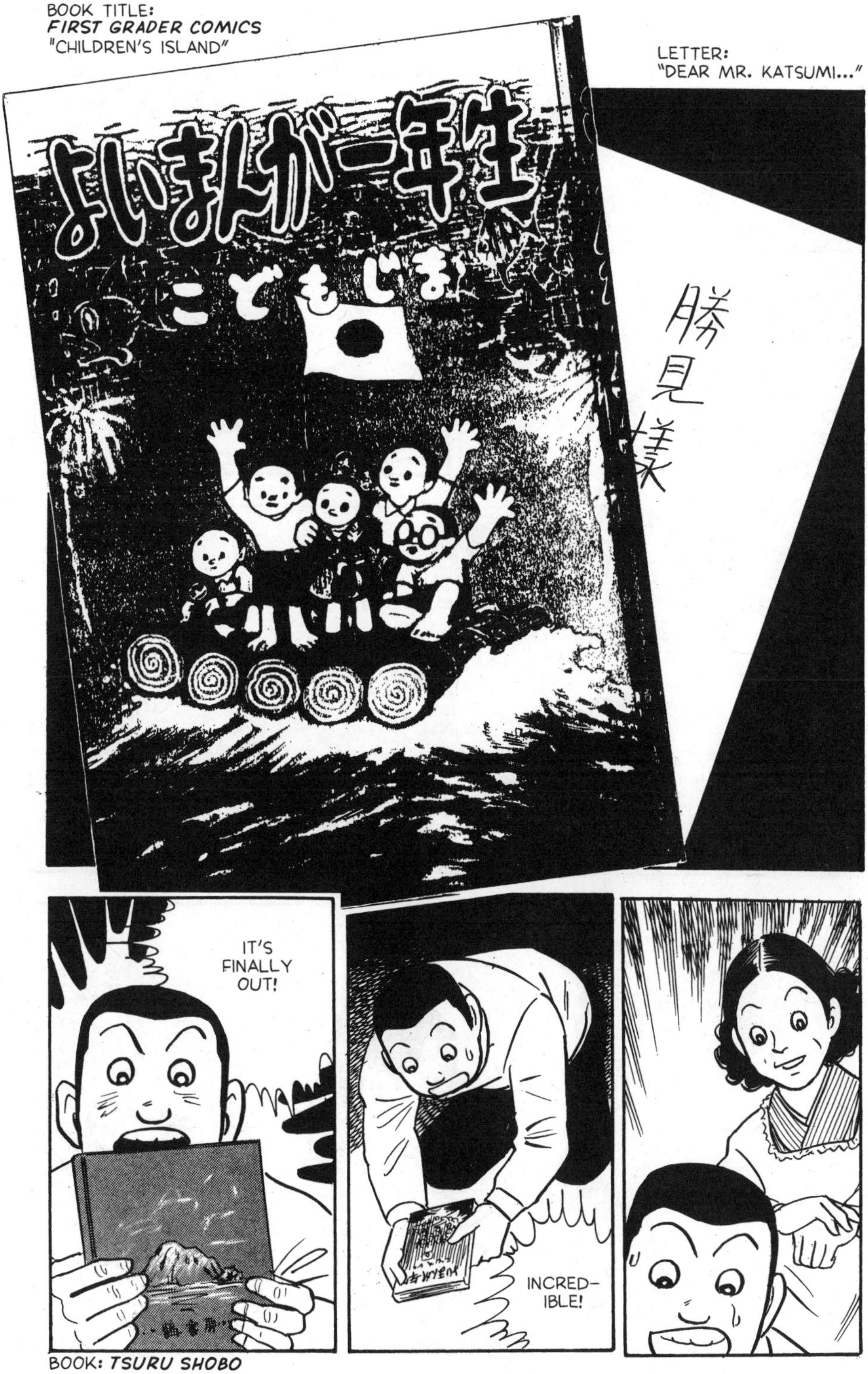
BOOK TITLE:
FIRST GRADER COMICS
"CHILDREN'S ISLAND"
よいまんが一年生
こどもじま
LETTER:
"DEAR MR. KATSUMI..."
勝見様
IT'S FINALLY OUT!
BOOK: TSURU SHOBO
INCRED-IBLE!

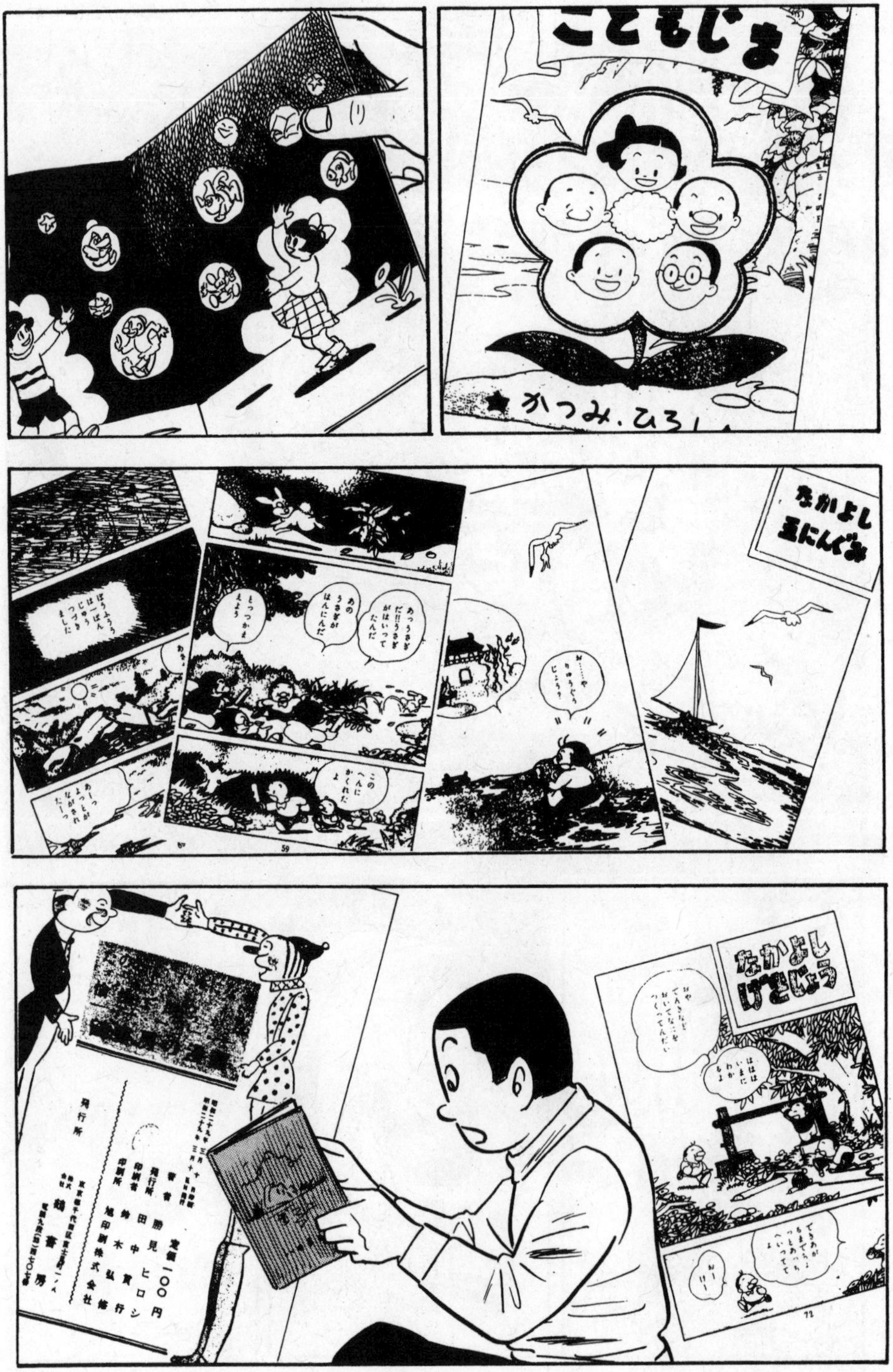
こどもじま
かつみ.ひろ
ぼうふうう は一ばん じゅう つづきました
あーっ よっとが ながされ たーっ
あっうさぎだ!!うさぎがはいってたんだ
あのうさぎがはんにんだ
とっつかまえよう
このへんにかくれたよ
59
お……や りゅうぐう じょう?
なかよし 五にんぐみ
定価一〇〇円
著者 勝見ヒロシ
発行所 田中貫行
印刷者 鈴木弘行
印刷所 旭印刷株式会社
発行所
株式会社 鶴書房
なかよし げきじょう
おや てんきなど おいてなにを つくってんだい
ははは いまに わかるよ
てきおがきまでちょっとおかへいってて よ
おーりー
72

I'M HOME.

I HEAR "CHILDREN'S ISLAND" CAME OUT?

YEAH!

WITH A COVER BY OOSHIRO SENSEI, HUH?

WHAT A GREAT IMAGE!

IT'S A NICE BOOK. IT WAS WORTH WAITING A YEAR AND 4 MONTHS FOR.

YEAH, BUT I'M NOT CRAZY ABOUT THIS "FIRST GRADER" BIT.

I GUESS THE SUCCESSFUL ONES WILL CONTINUE TO SECOND AND THIRD GRADERS' COMICS.

DON'T YOU THINK IT MAKES THE WORK SEEM JUVENILE?

SURE, THEY'RE SAYING YOUR WORK IS CHILDISH!

HMPH.

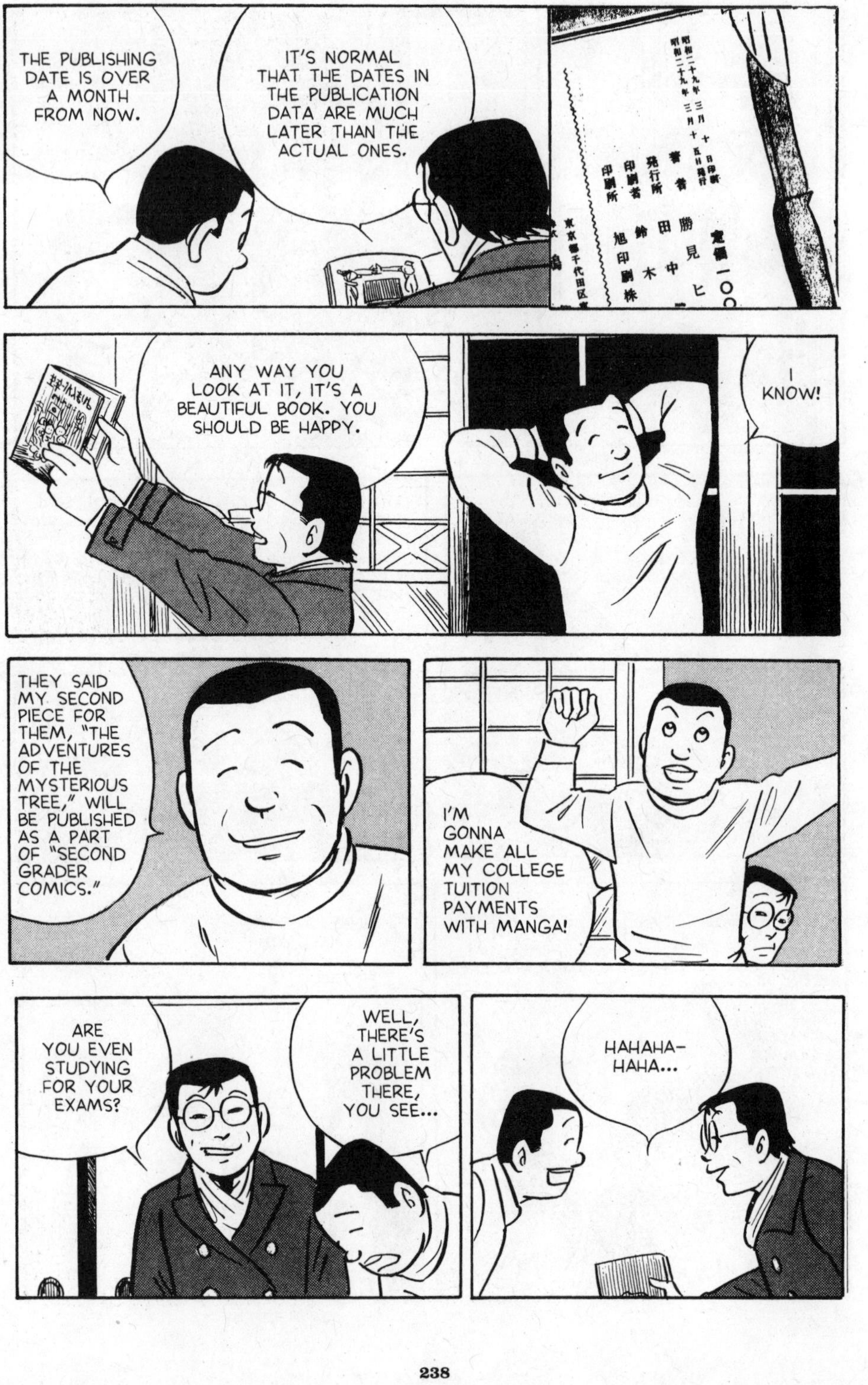

THE PUBLISHING DATE IS OVER A MONTH FROM NOW.
IT'S NORMAL THAT THE DATES IN THE PUBLICATION DATA ARE MUCH LATER THAN THE ACTUAL ONES.
ANY WAY YOU LOOK AT IT, IT'S A BEAUTIFUL BOOK. YOU SHOULD BE HAPPY.
I KNOW!
THEY SAID MY SECOND PIECE FOR THEM, "THE ADVENTURES OF THE MYSTERIOUS TREE," WILL BE PUBLISHED AS A PART OF "SECOND GRADER COMICS."
I'M GONNA MAKE ALL MY COLLEGE TUITION PAYMENTS WITH MANGA!
ARE YOU EVEN STUDYING FOR YOUR EXAMS?
WELL, THERE'S A LITTLE PROBLEM THERE, YOU SEE...
HAHAHA-HAHA...

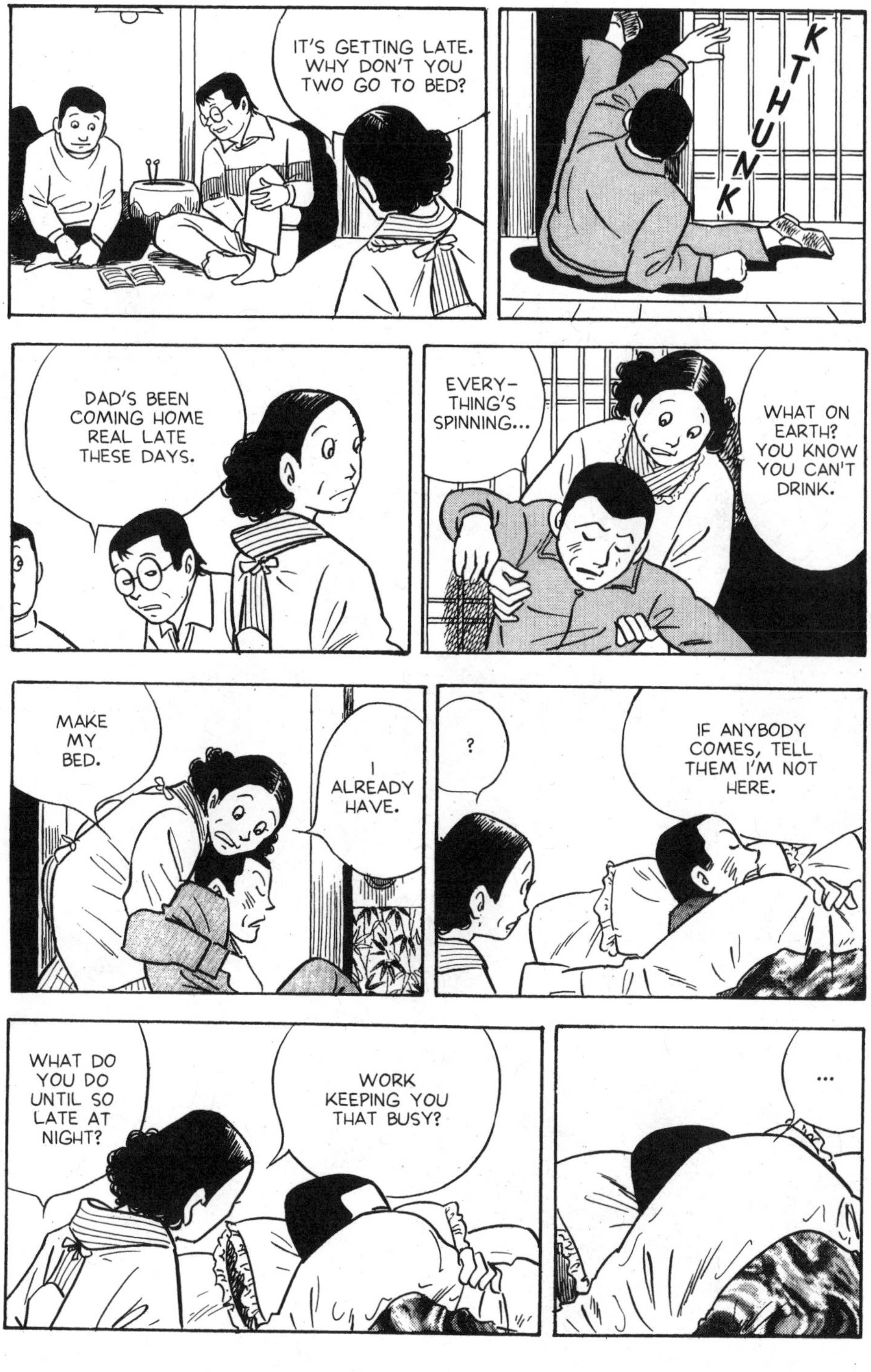
IT'S GETTING LATE. WHY DON'T YOU TWO GO TO BED?
KTHUNK
DAD'S BEEN COMING HOME REAL LATE THESE DAYS.
EVERY-THING'S SPINNING...
WHAT ON EARTH? YOU KNOW YOU CAN'T DRINK.
MAKE MY BED.
I ALREADY HAVE.
?
IF ANYBODY COMES, TELL THEM I'M NOT HERE.
WHAT DO YOU DO UNTIL SO LATE AT NIGHT?
WORK KEEPING YOU THAT BUSY?
...

HIROSHI NEVER LET HIS COPY OF "CHILDREN'S ISLAND" OUT OF HIS SIGHT THAT DAY.

THE TEXTURE, THE SMELL OF PRINTING INK.... IT'S AMAZING.

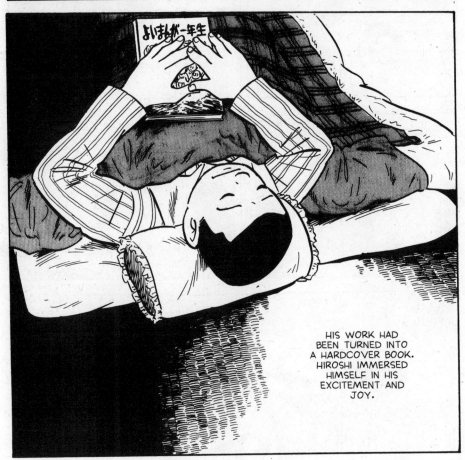

HIS WORK HAD BEEN TURNED INTO A HARDCOVER BOOK. HIROSHI IMMERSED HIMSELF IN HIS EXCITEMENT AND JOY.

THE SUN SETS ON HIGH SCHOOL DAYS

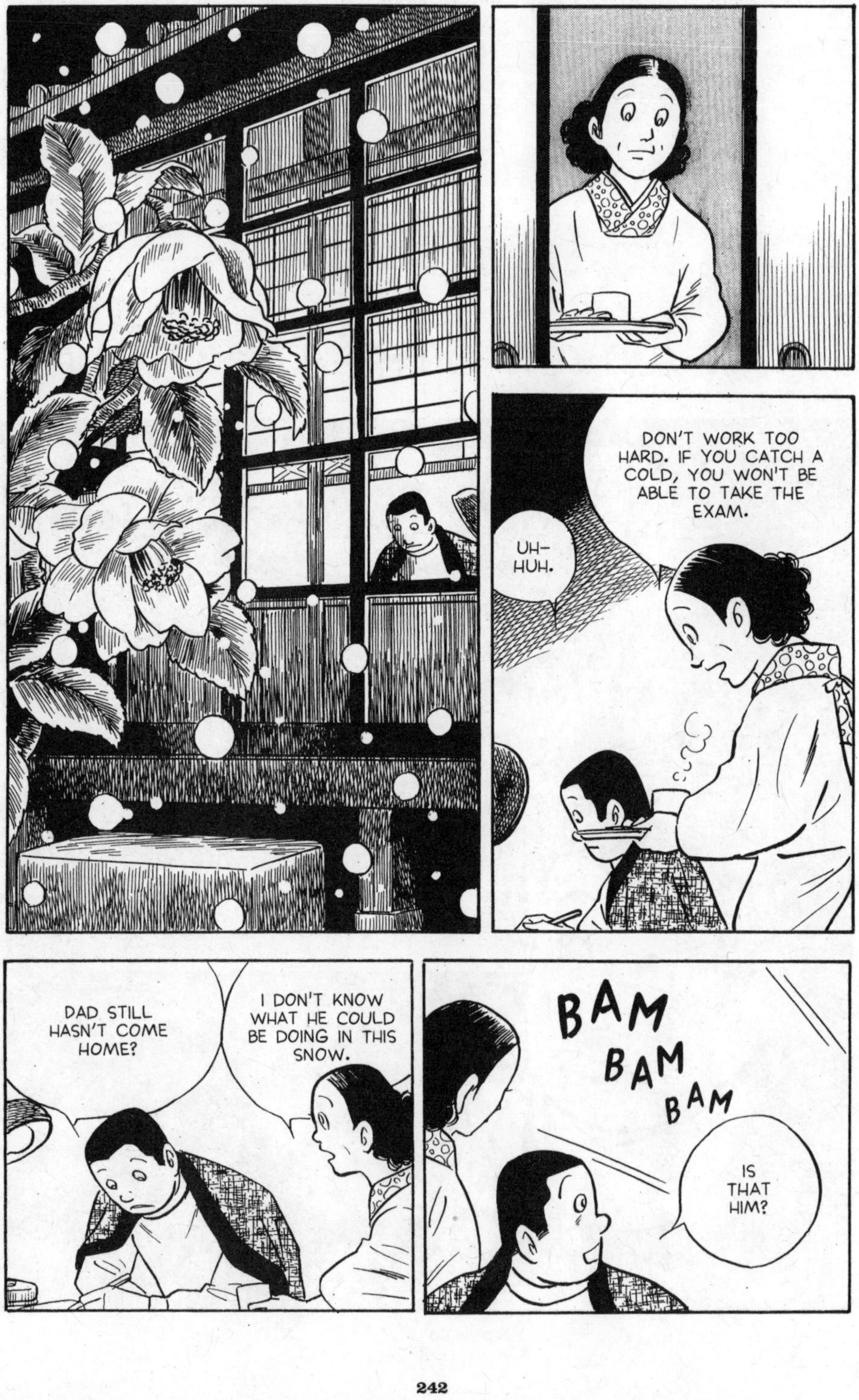
DON'T WORK TOO HARD. IF YOU CATCH A COLD, YOU WON'T BE ABLE TO TAKE THE EXAM.
UH-HUH.
DAD STILL HASN'T COME HOME?
I DON'T KNOW WHAT HE COULD BE DOING IN THIS SNOW.
BAM BAM BAM
IS THAT HIM?

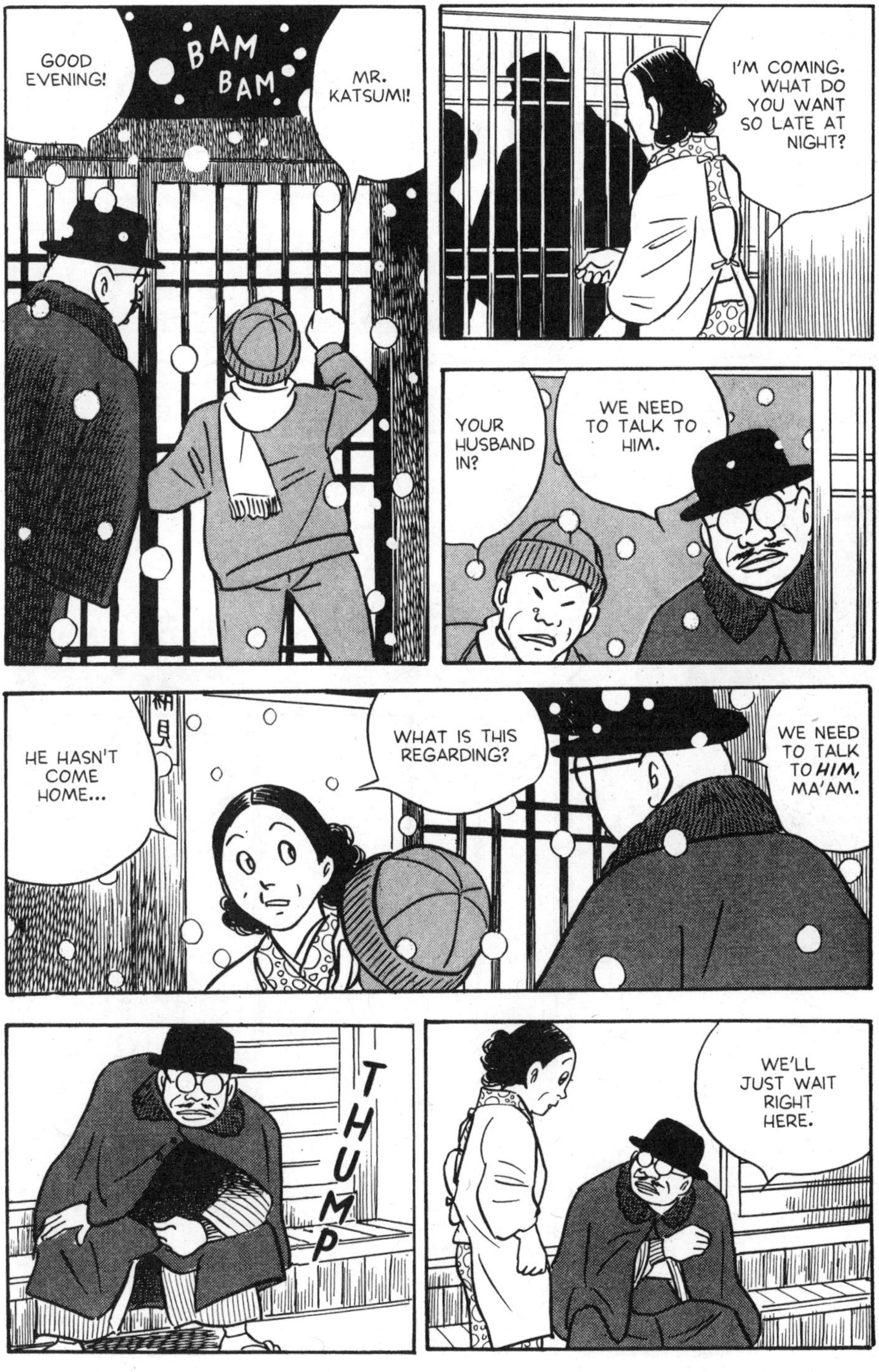
GOOD EVENING!
BAM BAM
MR. KATSUMI!
I'M COMING. WHAT DO YOU WANT SO LATE AT NIGHT?
YOUR HUSBAND IN?
WE NEED TO TALK TO HIM.
HE HASN'T COME HOME...
WHAT IS THIS REGARDING?
WE NEED TO TALK TO *HIM*, MA'AM.
THUMP
WE'LL JUST WAIT RIGHT HERE.

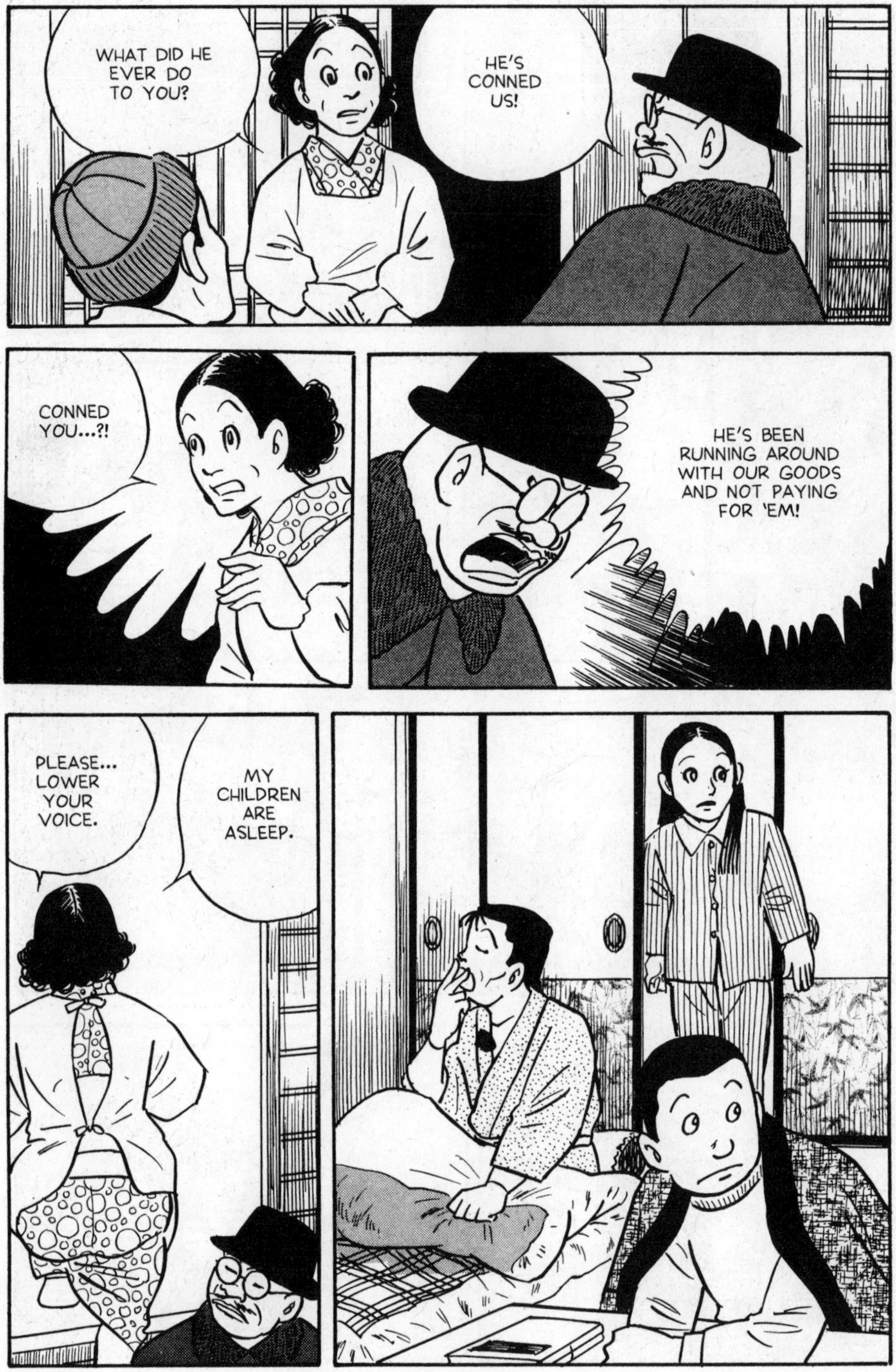
WHAT DID HE EVER DO TO YOU?
HE'S CONNED US!
CONNED YOU...?!
HE'S BEEN RUNNING AROUND WITH OUR GOODS AND NOT PAYING FOR 'EM!
PLEASE... LOWER YOUR VOICE.
MY CHILDREN ARE ASLEEP.

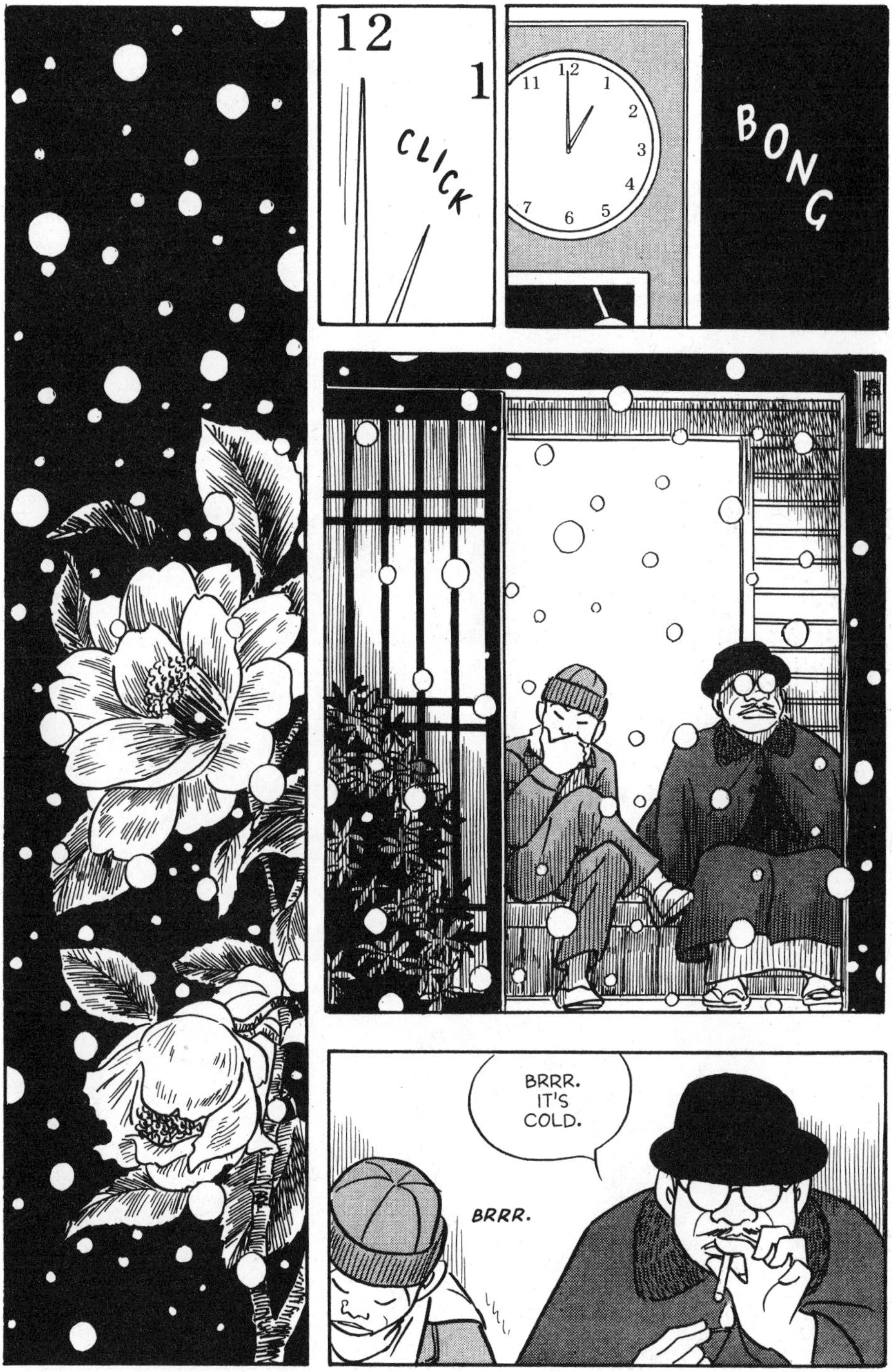
12
1
CLICK
BONG
BRRR. IT'S COLD.
BRRR.

HERE, I BROUGHT YOU SOME HOT TEA.

THANK YOU.

SSSLURRRP

WELL, MAKE YOURSELF AT HOME.

MA'AM...

WE'LL COME BACK.

WE'RE LEAVING FOR NOW, BUT DON'T THINK THAT THIS IS THE END OF IT.

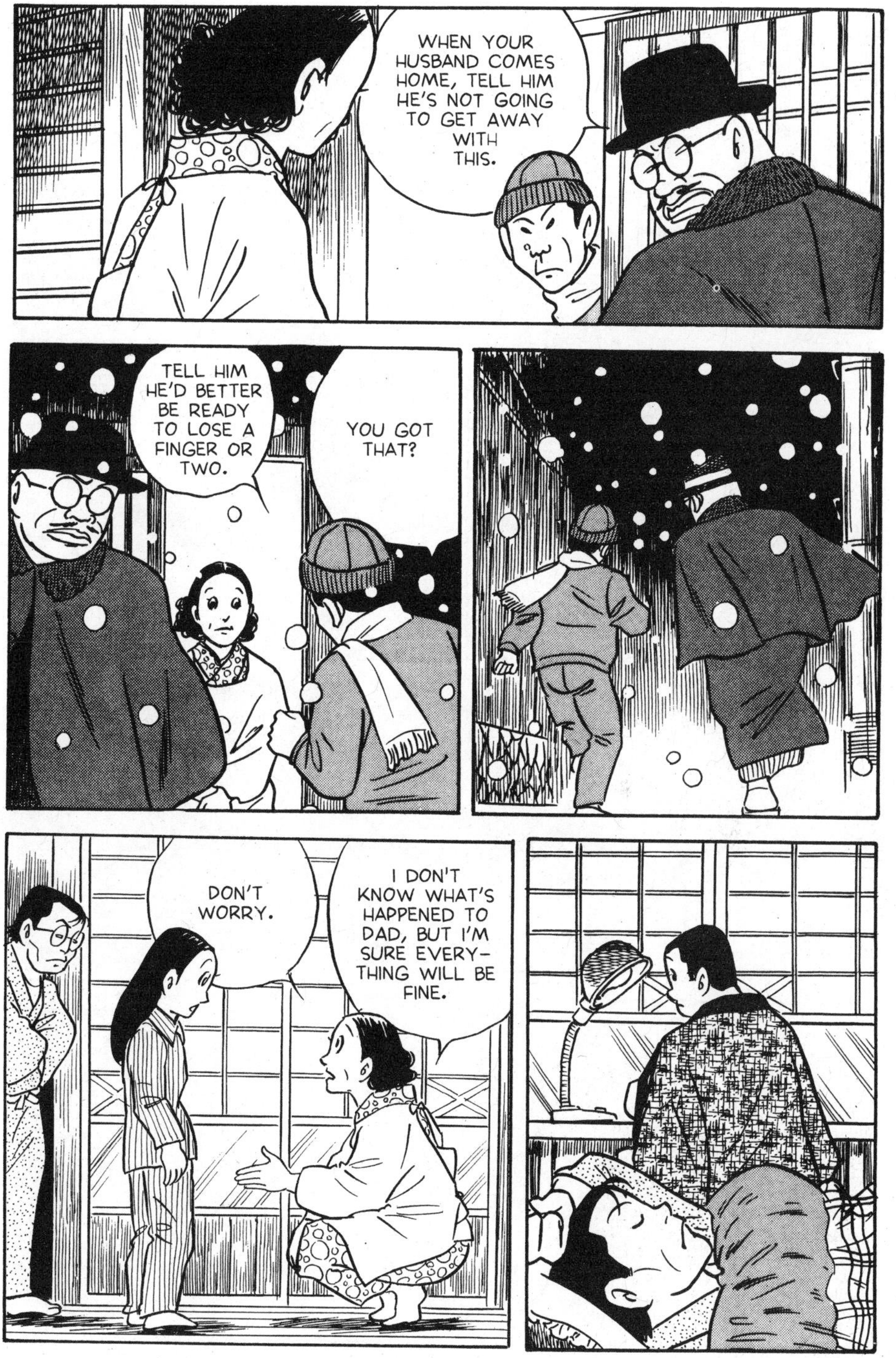
WHEN YOUR HUSBAND COMES HOME, TELL HIM HE'S NOT GOING TO GET AWAY WITH THIS.
TELL HIM HE'D BETTER BE READY TO LOSE A FINGER OR TWO.
YOU GOT THAT?
DON'T WORRY.
I DON'T KNOW WHAT'S HAPPENED TO DAD, BUT I'M SURE EVERY-THING WILL BE FINE.

SQUEEK
SQUEEK
よつば牛乳
SIGN: YOTSUBA MILK
KREEK
CHOP
CHOP
CHOP
CHOP
MORN-
ING.
WHY ARE YOU COMING IN FROM THE BACK?
WHERE ON EARTH WERE YOU LAST NIGHT?!
THERE WERE PEOPLE HERE MAKING A RUCKUS LATE INTO THE NIGHT.
I KNOW. PUT THAT DOWN, IT'S DAN-GEROUS.
I'VE GOT MYSELF INTO SOME REAL TROUBLE JUST FOR PUTTING MY SIGNATURE SEAL AS THE GUARANTOR ON THE COMPANY FORMATION CONTRACT.
I'M THE VICTIM HERE.

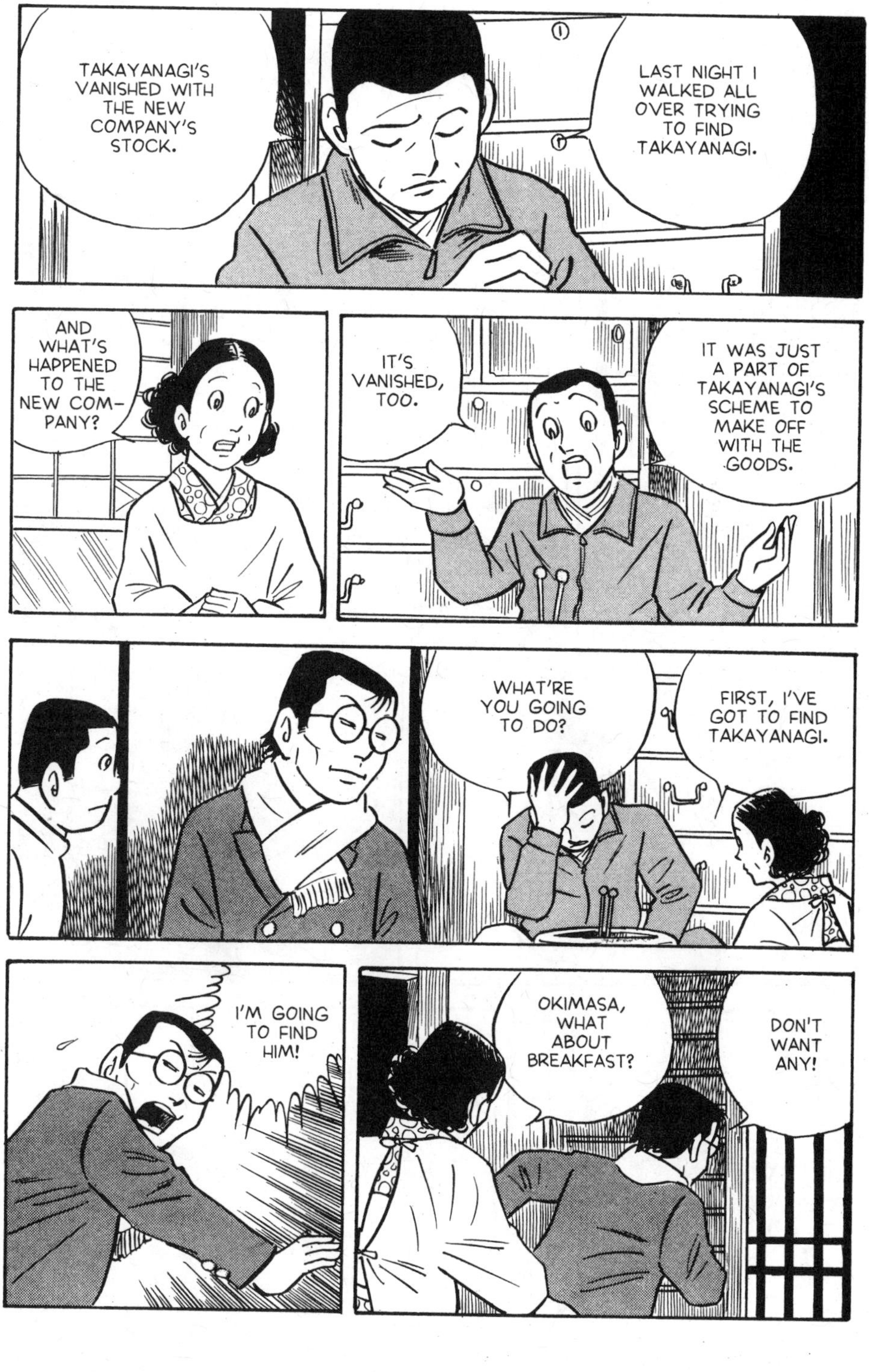
TAKAYANAGI'S VANISHED WITH THE NEW COMPANY'S STOCK.
LAST NIGHT I WALKED ALL OVER TRYING TO FIND TAKAYANAGI.
AND WHAT'S HAPPENED TO THE NEW COMPANY?
IT'S VANISHED, TOO.
IT WAS JUST A PART OF TAKAYANAGI'S SCHEME TO MAKE OFF WITH THE GOODS.
WHAT'RE YOU GOING TO DO?
FIRST, I'VE GOT TO FIND TAKAYANAGI.
I'M GOING TO FIND HIM!
OKIMASA, WHAT ABOUT BREAKFAST?
DON'T WANT ANY!

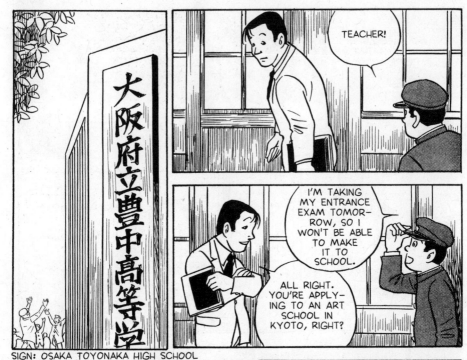

TEACHER!

I'M TAKING MY ENTRANCE EXAM TOMORROW, SO I WON'T BE ABLE TO MAKE IT TO SCHOOL.

ALL RIGHT. YOU'RE APPLYING TO AN ART SCHOOL IN KYOTO, RIGHT?

SIGN: OSAKA TOYONAKA HIGH SCHOOL

LISTEN, JUST RELAX AND DO YOUR BEST. YOU'LL DO FINE.

THANK YOU.

YOU'RE BACK EARLY.

DON'T RUSH. TAKE YOUR TIME AND PREPARE CAREFULLY FOR TOMORROW.

UH-HUH.

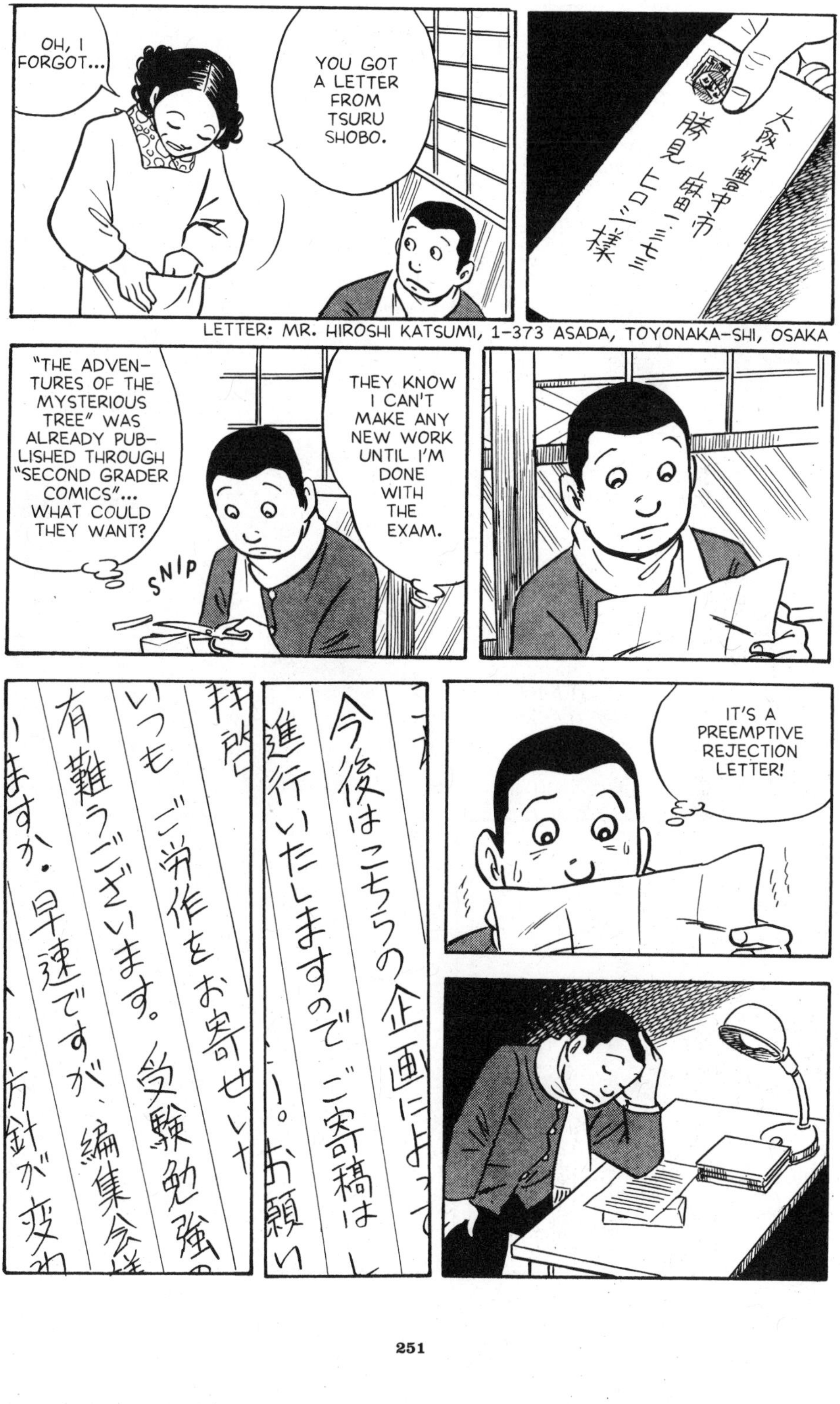
OH, I FORGOT...
YOU GOT A LETTER FROM TSURU SHOBO.
勝見
LETTER: MR. HIROSHI KATSUMI, 1-373 ASADA, TOYONAKA-SHI, OSAKA
"THE ADVENTURES OF THE MYSTERIOUS TREE" WAS ALREADY PUBLISHED THROUGH "SECOND GRADER COMICS"... WHAT COULD THEY WANT?
SNIP
THEY KNOW I CAN'T MAKE ANY NEW WORK UNTIL I'M DONE WITH THE EXAM.
拝啓
いつも ご労作をお寄せい
有難うございます。受験勉強
早速ですが、編集会
今後はこちらの企画によっ
進行いたしますので ご寄稿は
お願い
IT'S A PREEMPTIVE REJECTION LETTER!

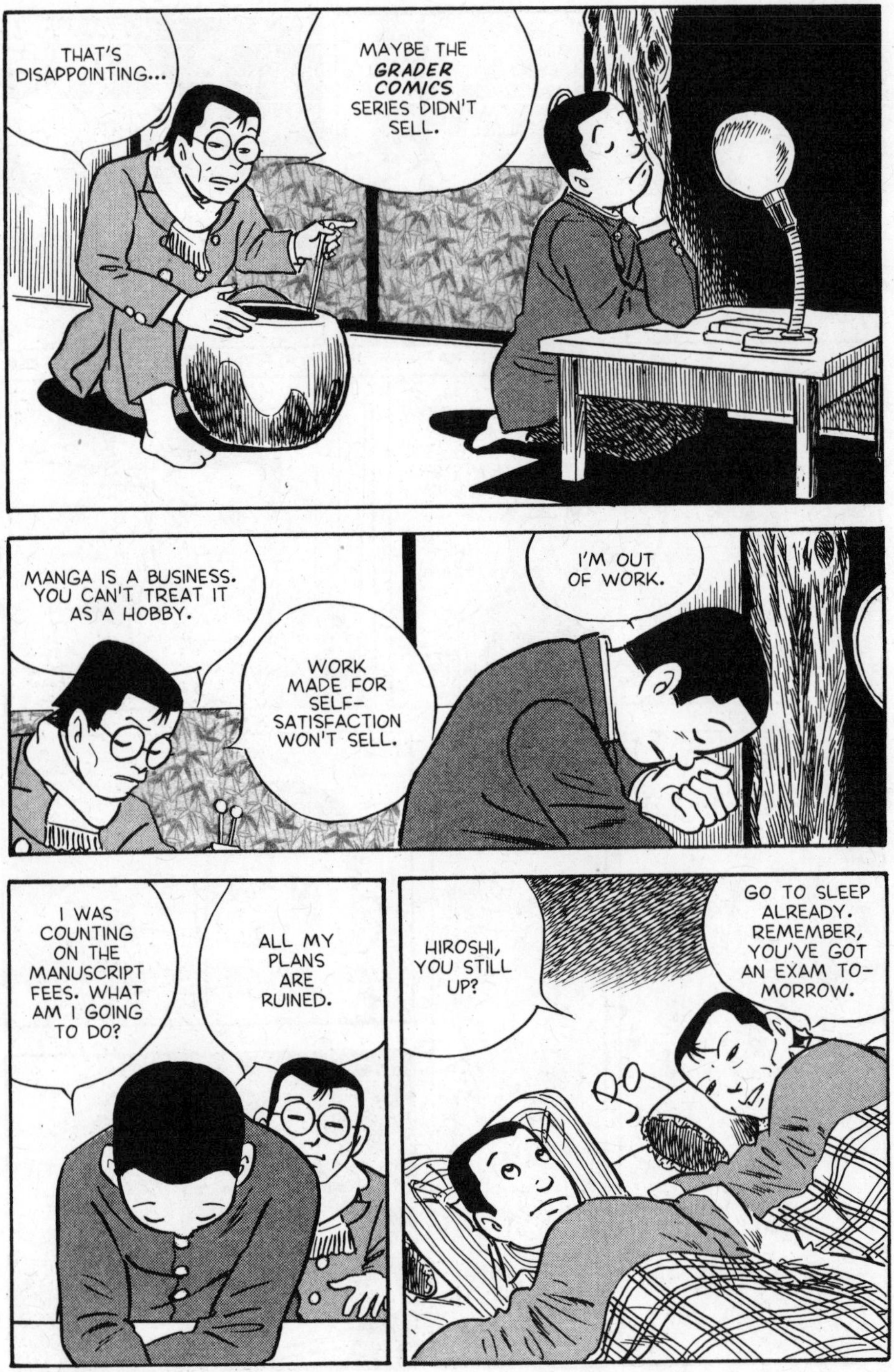
THAT'S DISAPPOINTING...
MAYBE THE GRADER COMICS SERIES DIDN'T SELL.
MANGA IS A BUSINESS. YOU CAN'T TREAT IT AS A HOBBY.
WORK MADE FOR SELF-SATISFACTION WON'T SELL.
I'M OUT OF WORK.
I WAS COUNTING ON THE MANUSCRIPT FEES. WHAT AM I GOING TO DO?
ALL MY PLANS ARE RUINED.
HIROSHI, YOU STILL UP?
GO TO SLEEP ALREADY. REMEMBER, YOU'VE GOT AN EXAM TO-MORROW.

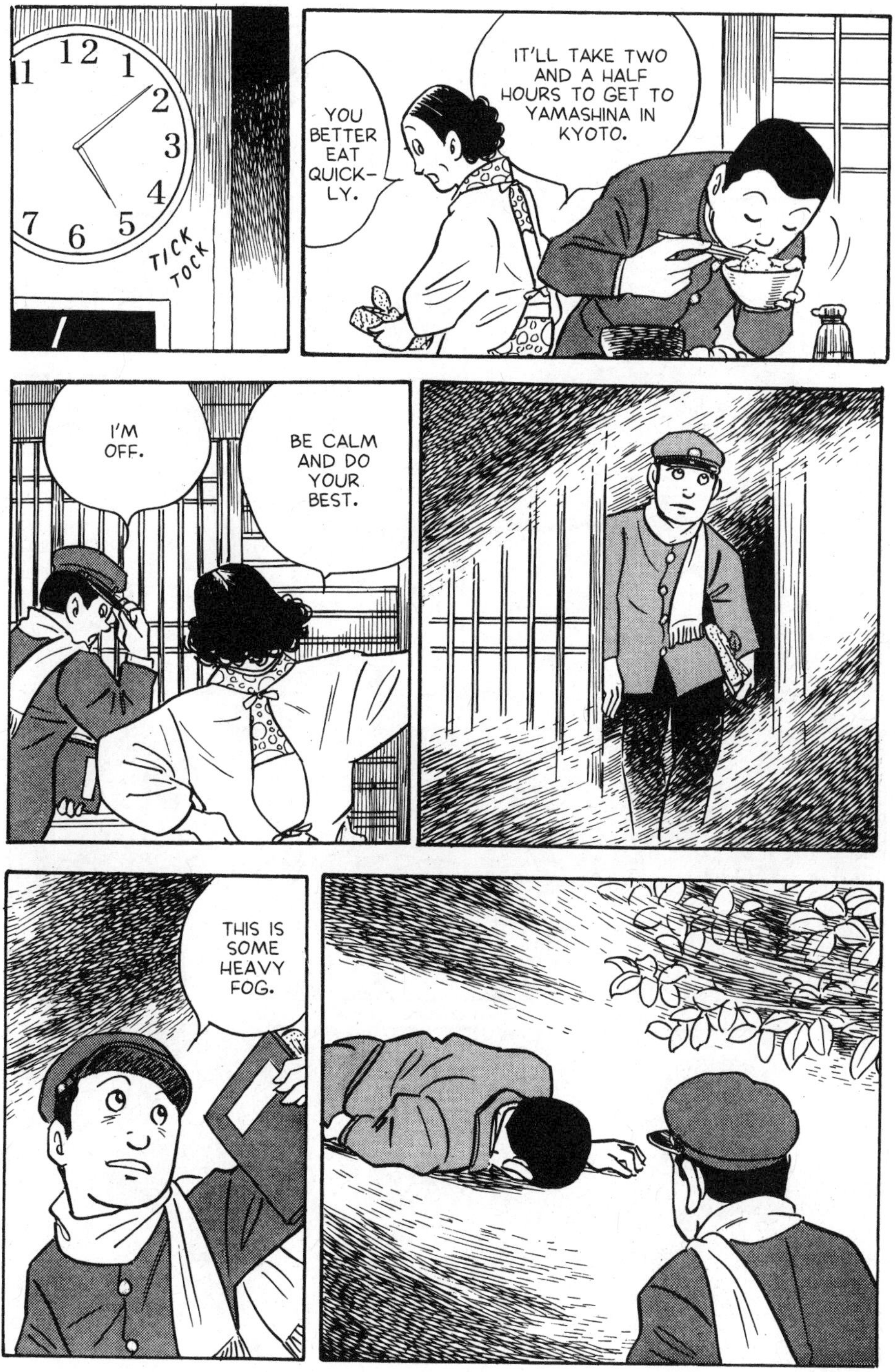
TICK TOCK
IT'LL TAKE TWO AND A HALF HOURS TO GET TO YAMASHINA IN KYOTO.
YOU BETTER EAT QUICK-LY.
I'M OFF.
BE CALM AND DO YOUR BEST.
THIS IS SOME HEAVY FOG.

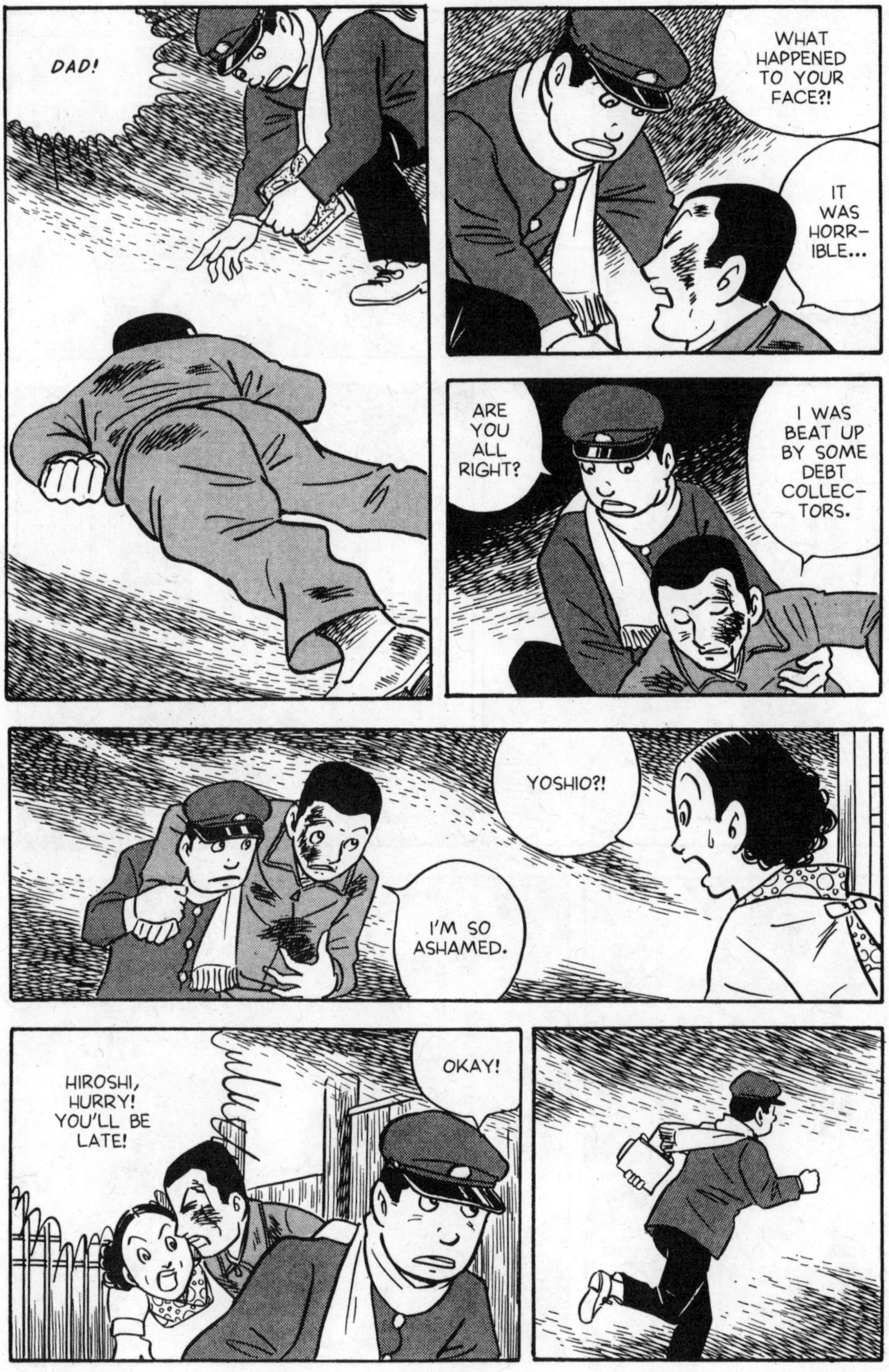
DAD!
WHAT HAPPENED TO YOUR FACE?!
IT WAS HORRIBLE...
ARE YOU ALL RIGHT?
I WAS BEAT UP BY SOME DEBT COLLECTORS.
YOSHIO?!
I'M SO ASHAMED.
HIROSHI, HURRY! YOU'LL BE LATE!
OKAY!

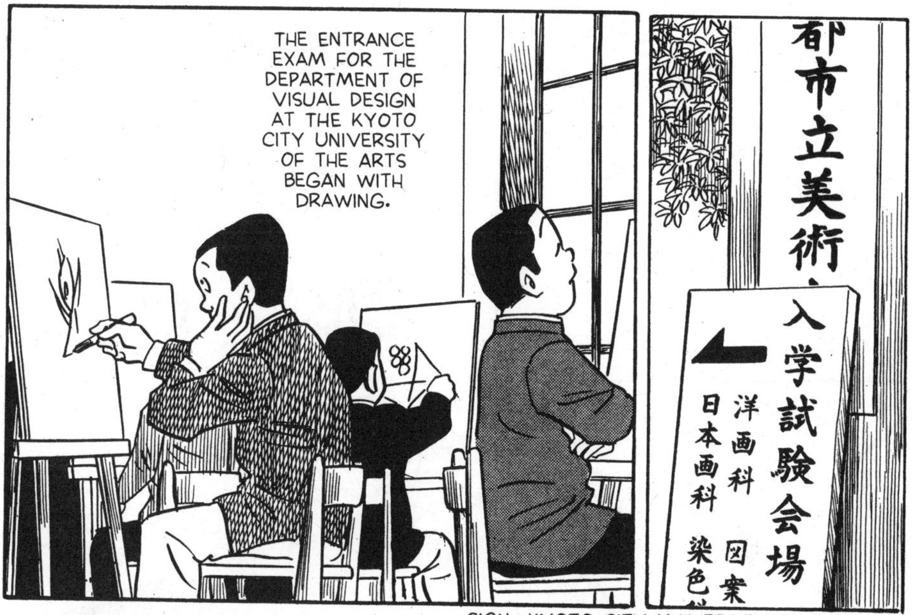
THE ENTRANCE EXAM FOR THE DEPARTMENT OF VISUAL DESIGN AT THE KYOTO CITY UNIVERSITY OF THE ARTS BEGAN WITH DRAWING.
都市立美術
入学試験会場
洋画科
日本画科
図案
染色

SIGN: KYOTO CITY UNIVERSITY OF THE ARTS

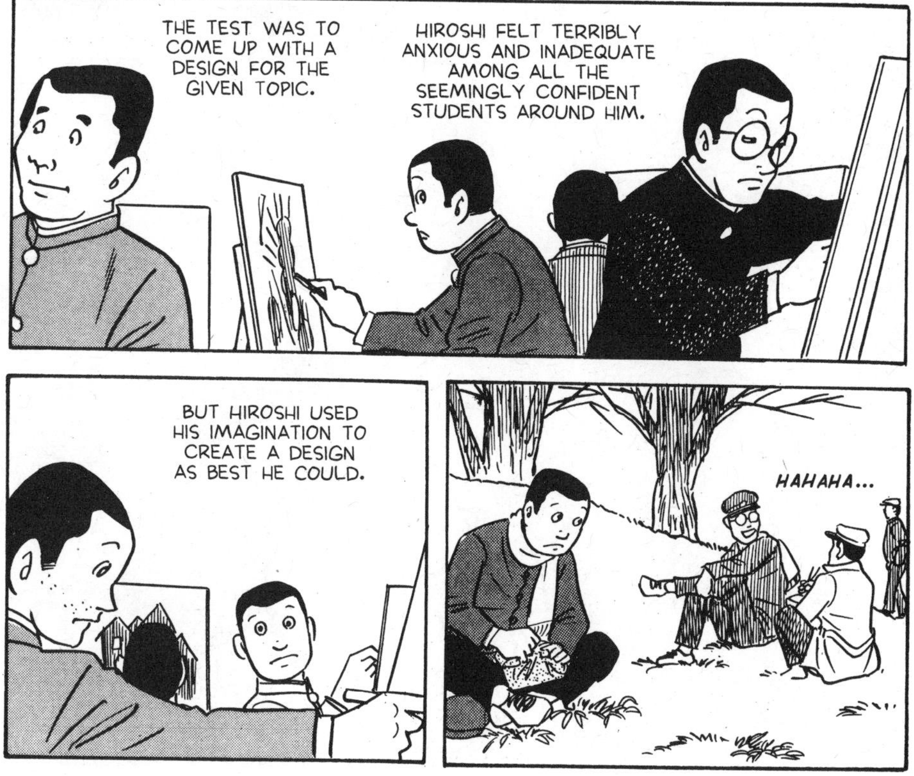
THE TEST WAS TO COME UP WITH A DESIGN FOR THE GIVEN TOPIC.
HIROSHI FELT TERRIBLY ANXIOUS AND INADEQUATE AMONG ALL THE SEEMINGLY CONFIDENT STUDENTS AROUND HIM.
BUT HIROSHI USED HIS IMAGINATION TO CREATE A DESIGN AS BEST HE COULD.
HAHAHA...

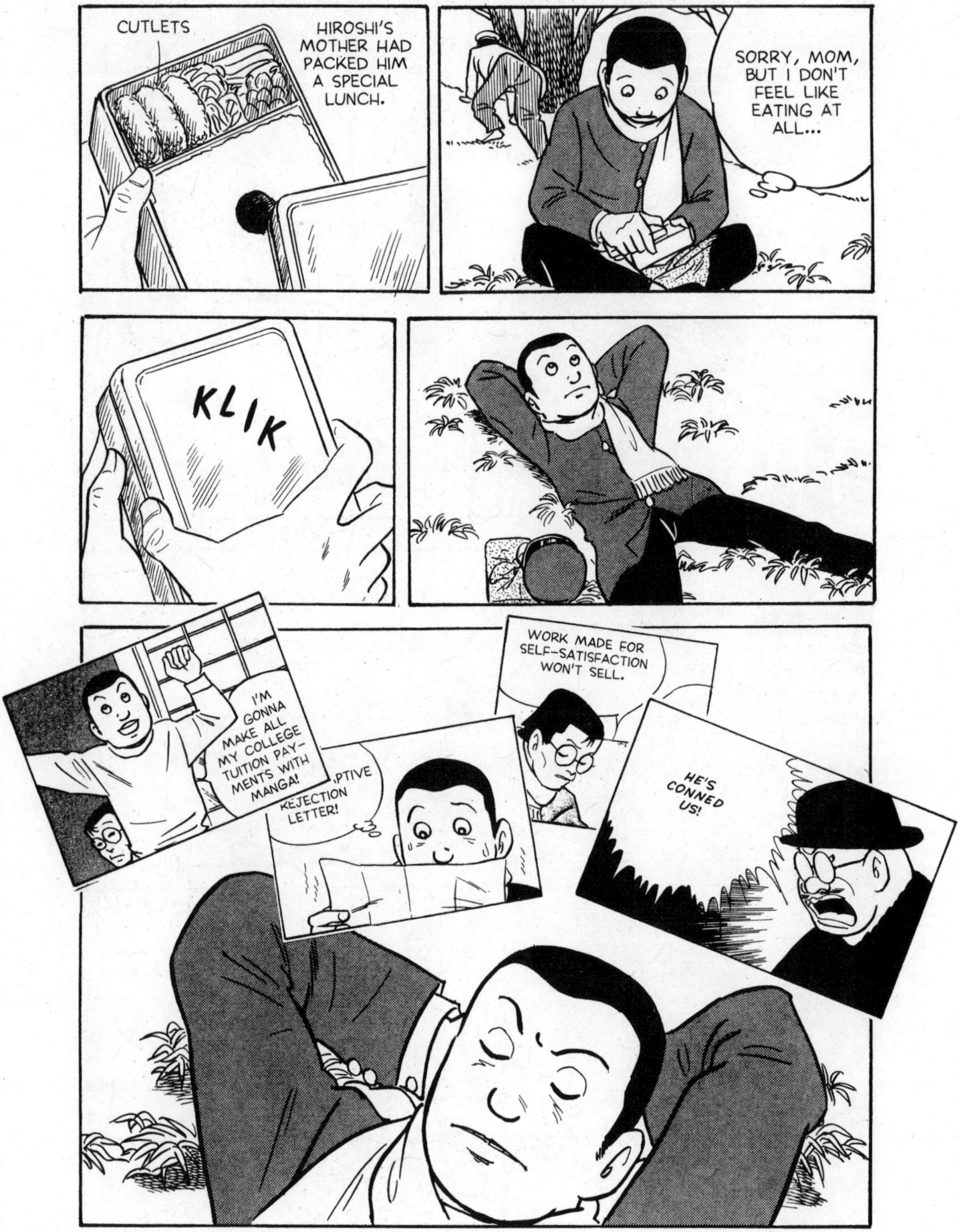
CUTLETS
HIROSHI'S MOTHER HAD PACKED HIM A SPECIAL LUNCH.
SORRY, MOM, BUT I DON'T FEEL LIKE EATING AT ALL...
KLIK
I'M GONNA MAKE ALL MY COLLEGE TUITION PAYMENTS WITH MANGA!
PTIVE REJECTION LETTER!
WORK MADE FOR SELF-SATISFACTION WON'T SELL.
HE'S CONNED US!

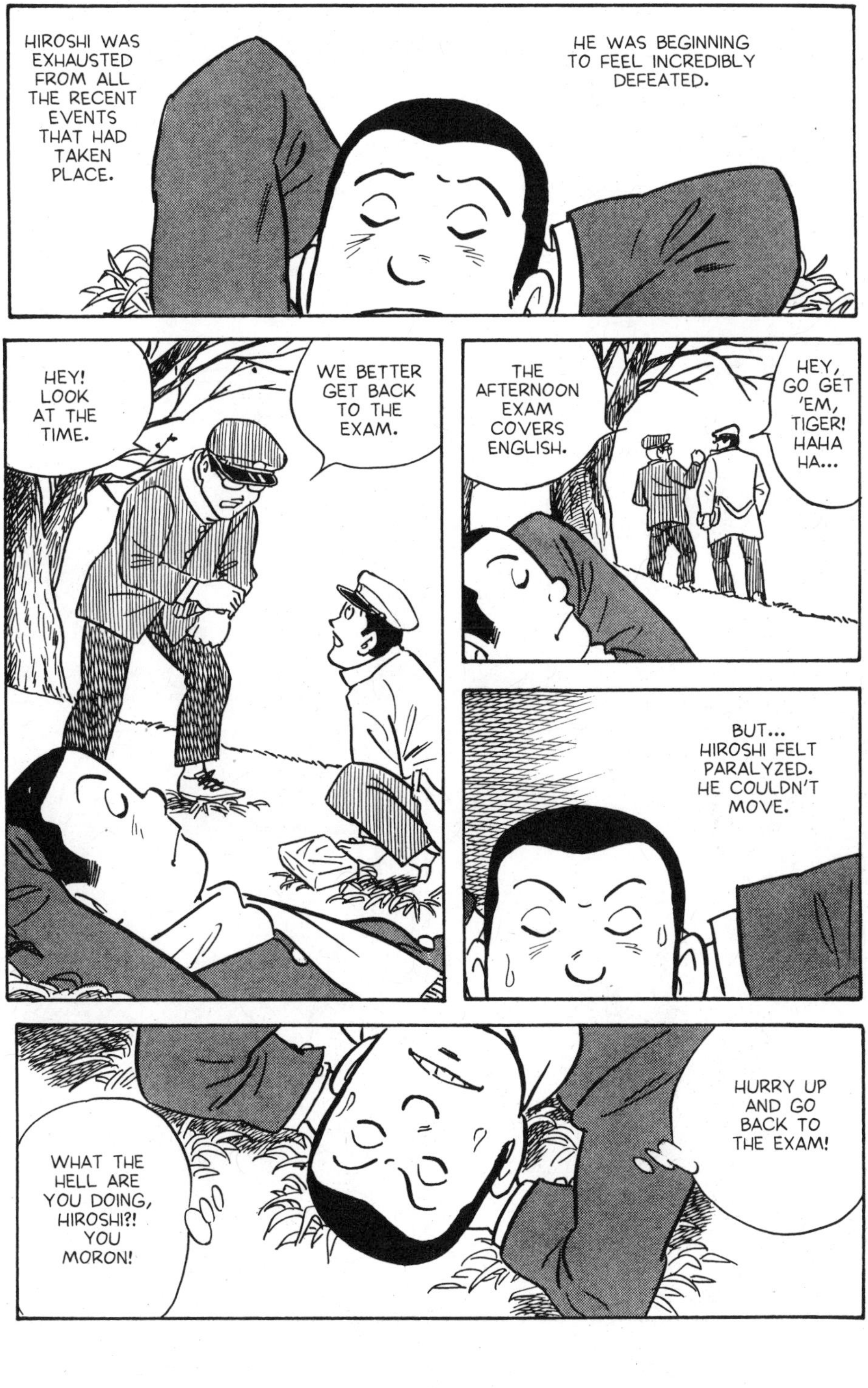
HIROSHI WAS EXHAUSTED FROM ALL THE RECENT EVENTS THAT HAD TAKEN PLACE.
HE WAS BEGINNING TO FEEL INCREDIBLY DEFEATED.
HEY! LOOK AT THE TIME.
WE BETTER GET BACK TO THE EXAM.
THE AFTERNOON EXAM COVERS ENGLISH.
HEY, GO GET 'EM, TIGER! HAHA HA...
BUT... HIROSHI FELT PARALYZED. HE COULDN'T MOVE.
WHAT THE HELL ARE YOU DOING, HIROSHI?! YOU MORON!
HURRY UP AND GO BACK TO THE EXAM!

RING
RING
RING
RING
RING

THERE SHOULD BE AN EXAM ANSWER FORM IN FRONT OF YOU.

WE'LL NOW BEGIN THE ENGLISH LANGUAGE EXAM.

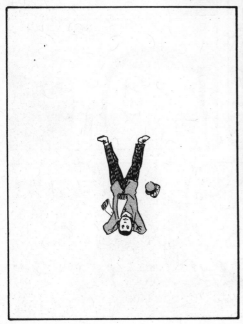

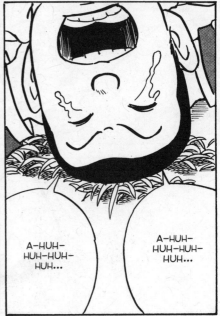

A-HUH-HUH-HUH-HUH...

A-HUH-HUH-HUH-HUH...

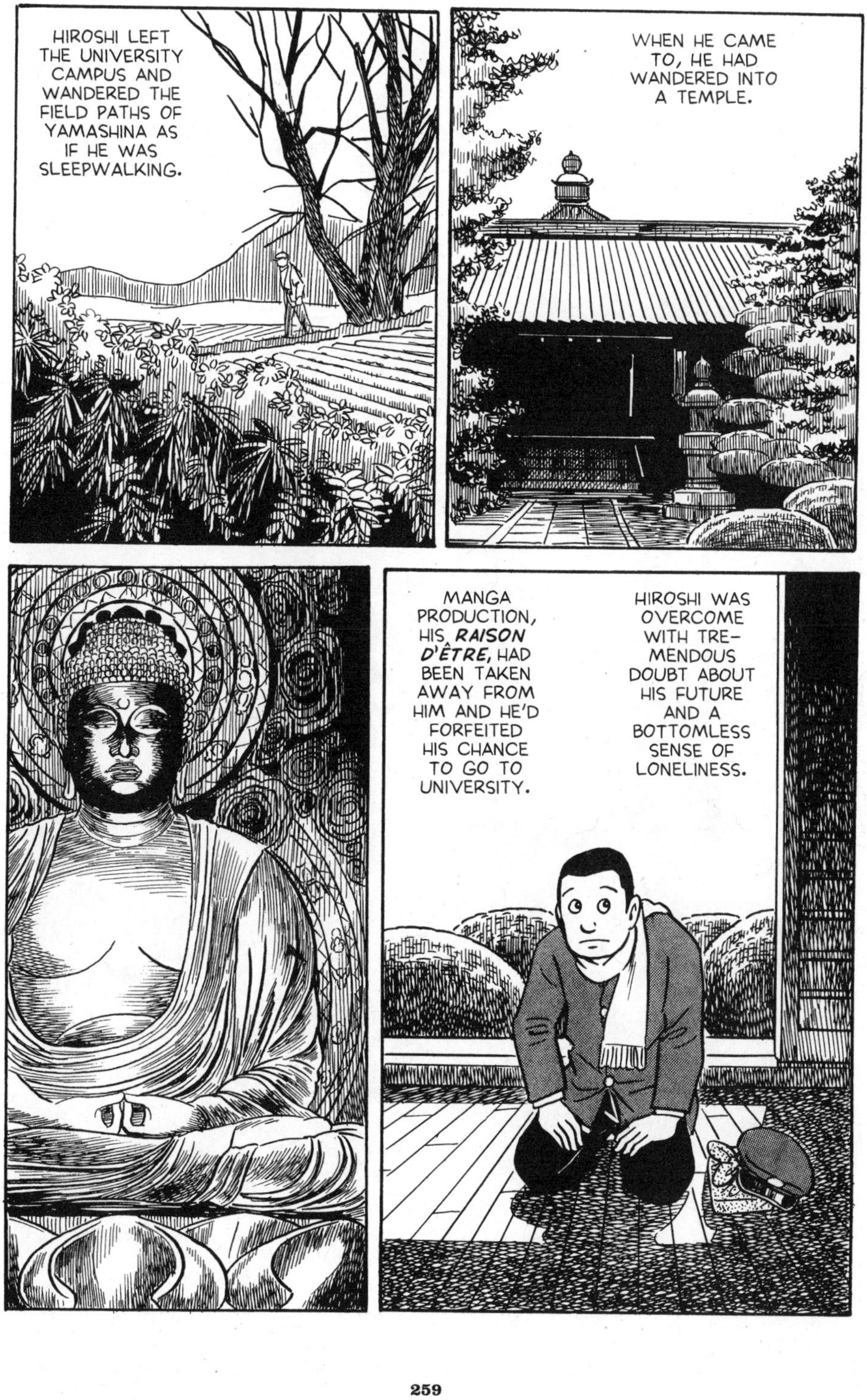
HIROSHI LEFT THE UNIVERSITY CAMPUS AND WANDERED THE FIELD PATHS OF YAMASHINA AS IF HE WAS SLEEPWALKING.
WHEN HE CAME TO, HE HAD WANDERED INTO A TEMPLE.
MANGA PRODUCTION, HIS ***RAISON D'ÊTRE***, HAD BEEN TAKEN AWAY FROM HIM AND HE'D FORFEITED HIS CHANCE TO GO TO UNIVERSITY.
HIROSHI WAS OVERCOME WITH TRE-MENDOUS DOUBT ABOUT HIS FUTURE AND A BOTTOMLESS SENSE OF LONELINESS.

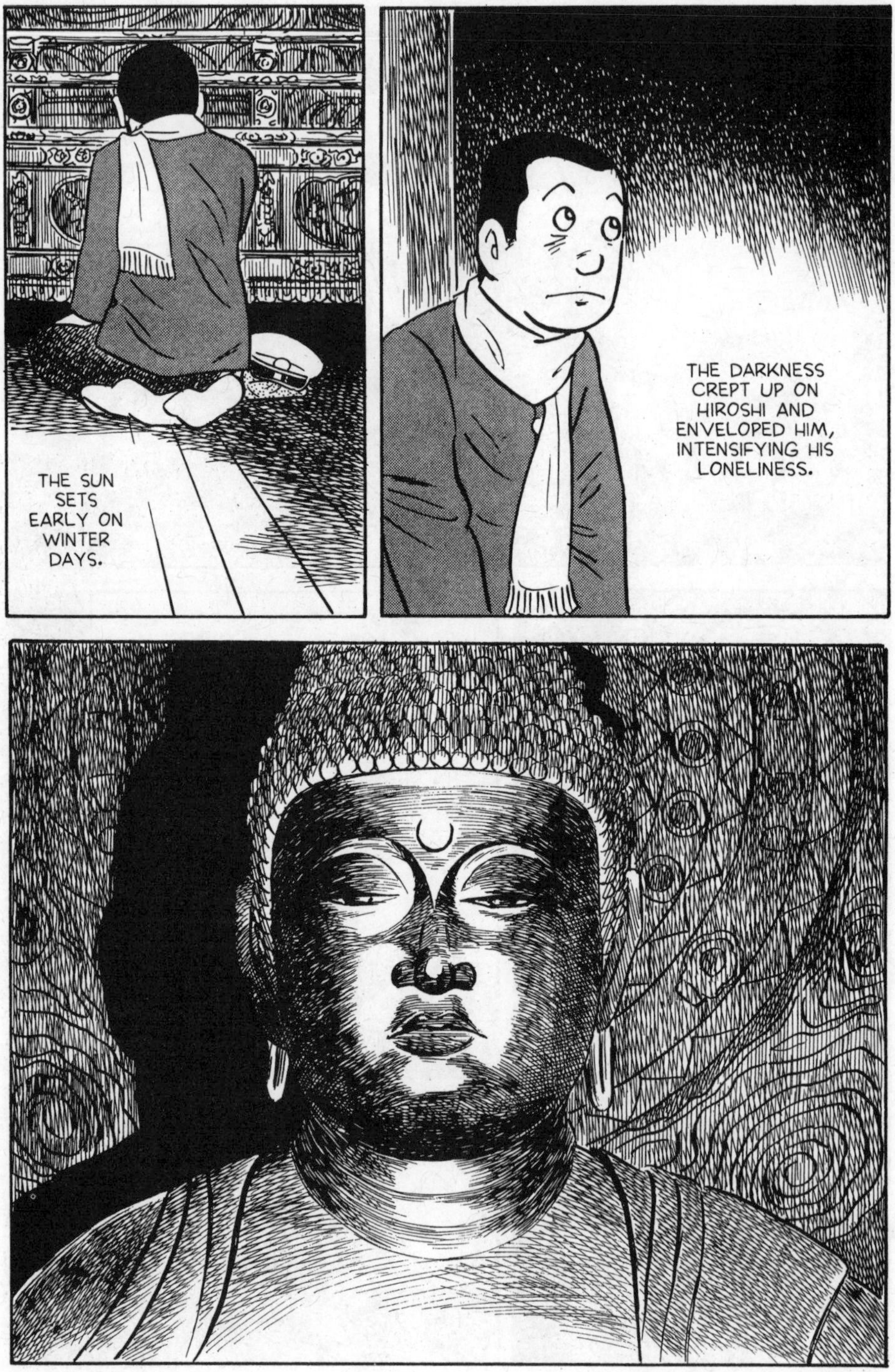
THE SUN SETS EARLY ON WINTER DAYS.
THE DARKNESS CREPT UP ON HIROSHI AND ENVELOPED HIM, INTENSIFYING HIS LONELINESS.

DESERT TRAVELER

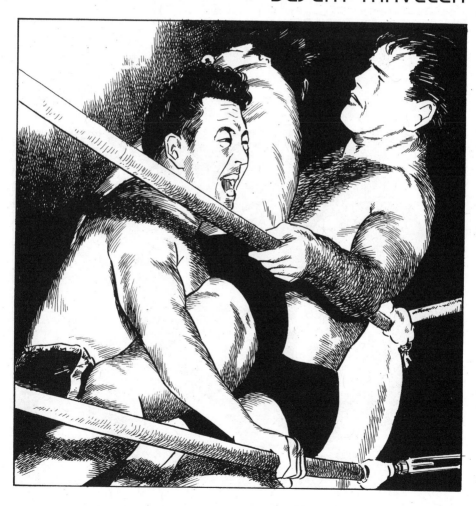

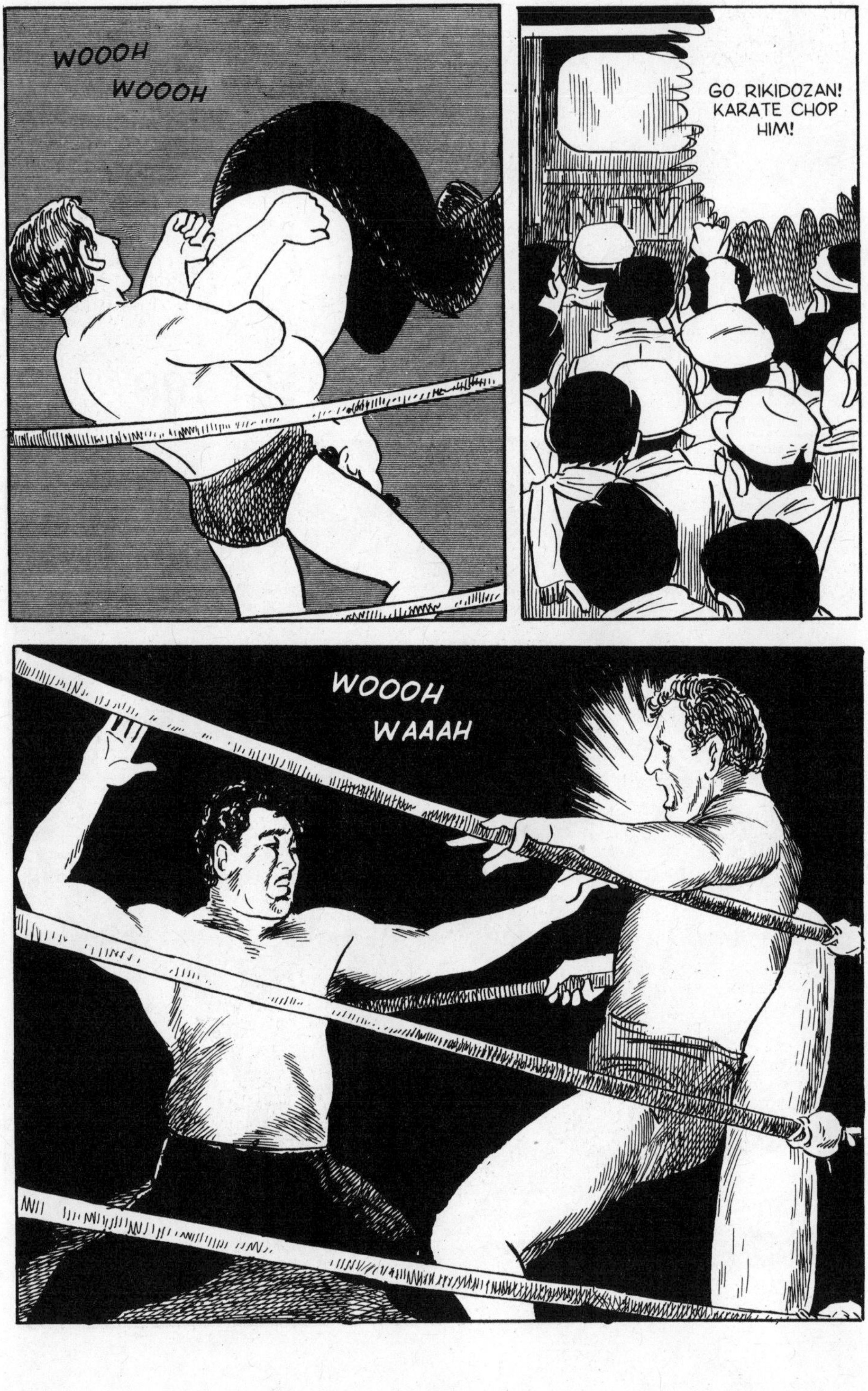
WOOOH
WOOOH
GO RIKIDOZAN! KARATE CHOP HIM!
WOOOH
WAAAH

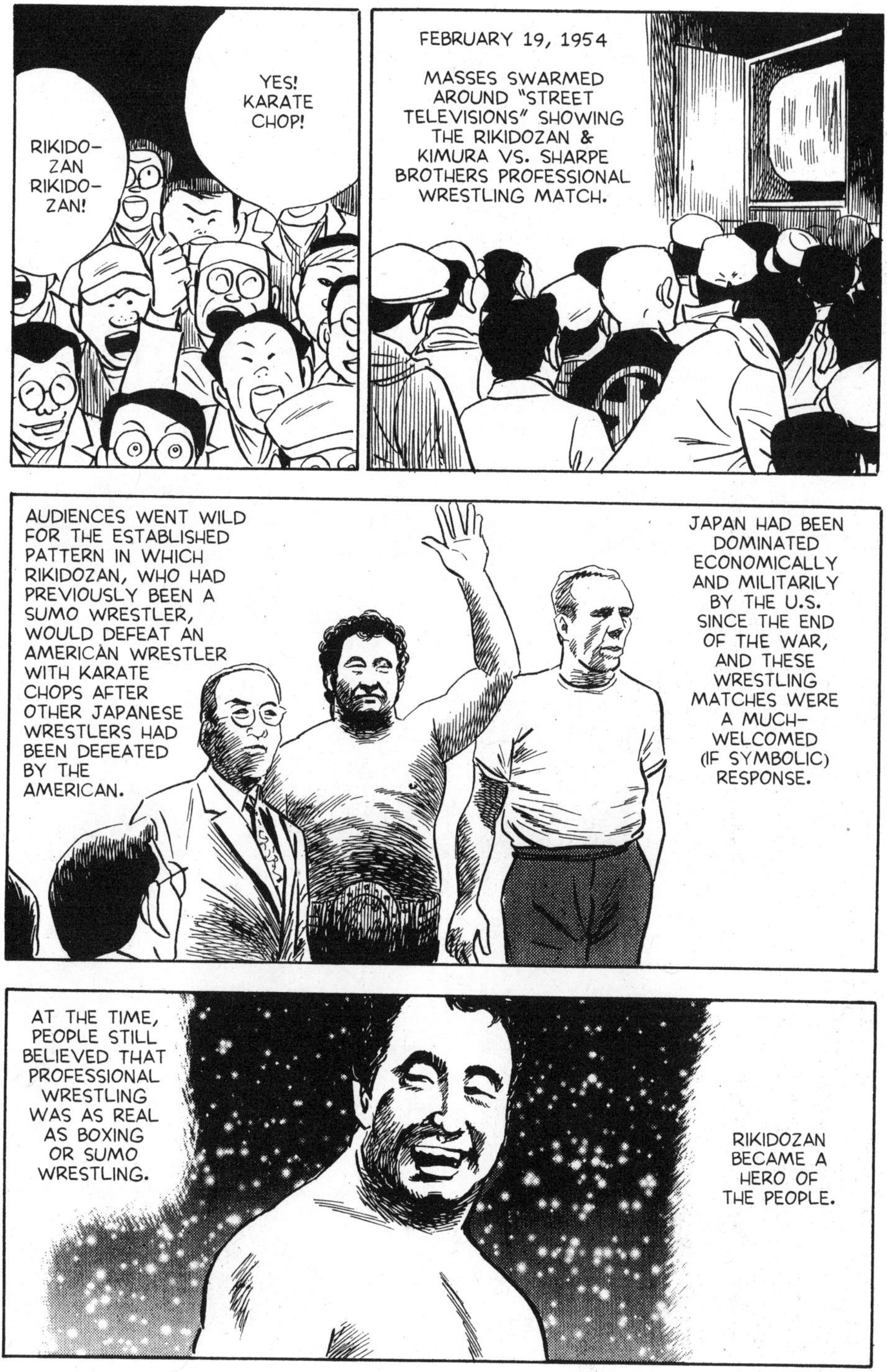
RIKIDO-ZAN RIKIDO-ZAN!
YES! KARATE CHOP!
FEBRUARY 19, 1954
MASSES SWARMED AROUND "STREET TELEVISIONS" SHOWING THE RIKIDOZAN & KIMURA VS. SHARPE BROTHERS PROFESSIONAL WRESTLING MATCH.
AUDIENCES WENT WILD FOR THE ESTABLISHED PATTERN IN WHICH RIKIDOZAN, WHO HAD PREVIOUSLY BEEN A SUMO WRESTLER, WOULD DEFEAT AN AMERICAN WRESTLER WITH KARATE CHOPS AFTER OTHER JAPANESE WRESTLERS HAD BEEN DEFEATED BY THE AMERICAN.
JAPAN HAD BEEN DOMINATED ECONOMICALLY AND MILITARILY BY THE U.S. SINCE THE END OF THE WAR, AND THESE WRESTLING MATCHES WERE A MUCH-WELCOMED (IF SYMBOLIC) RESPONSE.
AT THE TIME, PEOPLE STILL BELIEVED THAT PROFESSIONAL WRESTLING WAS AS REAL AS BOXING OR SUMO WRESTLING.
RIKIDOZAN BECAME A HERO OF THE PEOPLE.

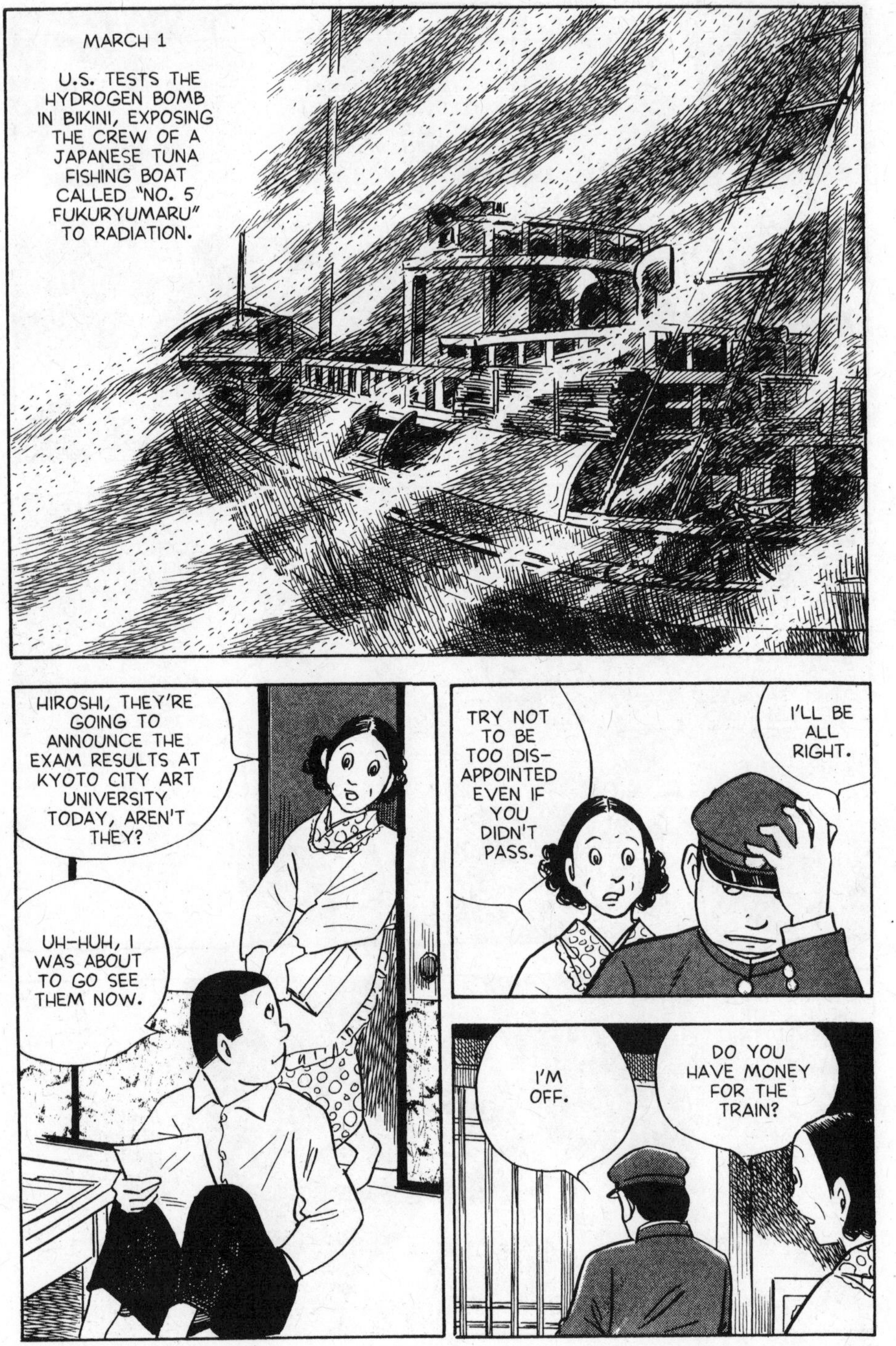
MARCH 1
U.S. TESTS THE HYDROGEN BOMB IN BIKINI, EXPOSING THE CREW OF A JAPANESE TUNA FISHING BOAT CALLED "NO. 5 FUKURYUMARU" TO RADIATION.
HIROSHI, THEY'RE GOING TO ANNOUNCE THE EXAM RESULTS AT KYOTO CITY ART UNIVERSITY TODAY, AREN'T THEY?
UH-HUH, I WAS ABOUT TO GO SEE THEM NOW.
TRY NOT TO BE TOO DIS-APPOINTED EVEN IF YOU DIDN'T PASS.
I'LL BE ALL RIGHT.
I'M OFF.
DO YOU HAVE MONEY FOR THE TRAIN?

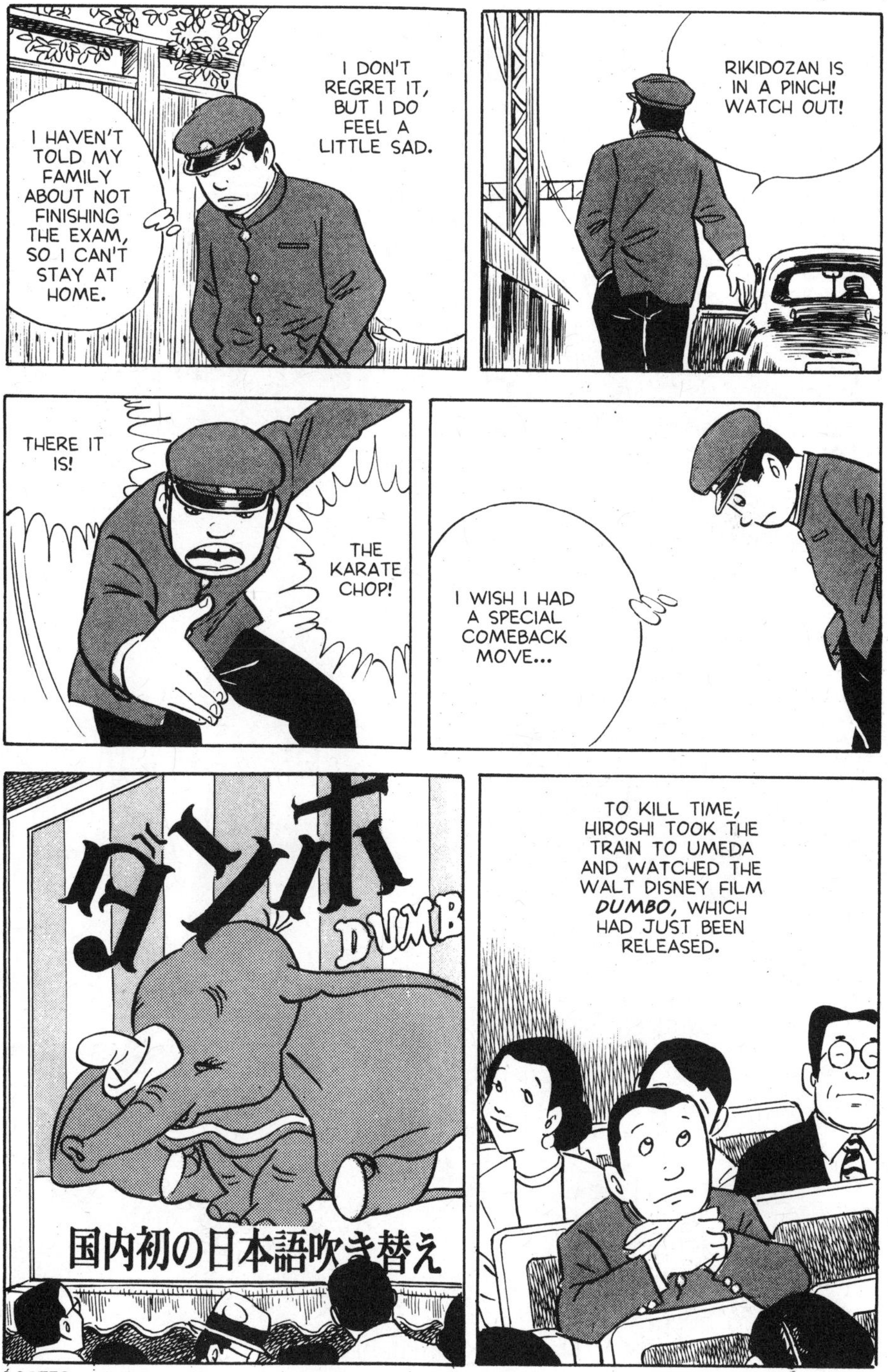
I HAVEN'T TOLD MY FAMILY ABOUT NOT FINISHING THE EXAM, SO I CAN'T STAY AT HOME.
I DON'T REGRET IT, BUT I DO FEEL A LITTLE SAD.
RIKIDOZAN IS IN A PINCH! WATCH OUT!
THERE IT IS!
THE KARATE CHOP!
I WISH I HAD A SPECIAL COMEBACK MOVE...
ダンボ
DUMB
国内初の日本語吹き替え
TO KILL TIME, HIROSHI TOOK THE TRAIN TO UMEDA AND WATCHED THE WALT DISNEY FILM *DUMBO*, WHICH HAD JUST BEEN RELEASED.
POSTER: ***DUMBO*** / FIRST FOREIGN FILM DUBBED IN JAPANESE

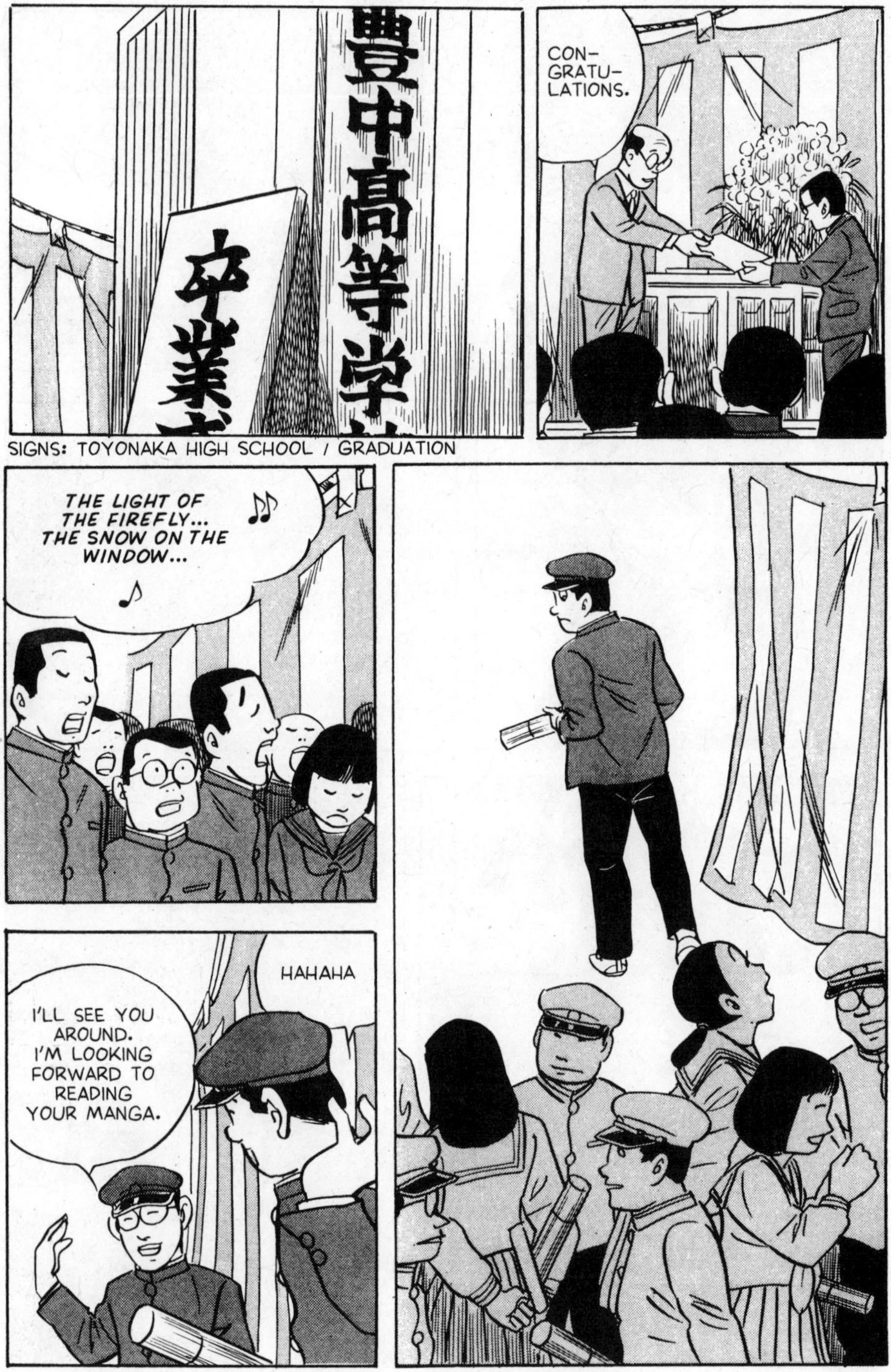
豐中高等学
卒業
CON-GRATU-LATIONS.
SIGNS: TOYONAKA HIGH SCHOOL / GRADUATION
THE LIGHT OF THE FIREFLY... THE SNOW ON THE WINDOW...
HAHAHA
I'LL SEE YOU AROUND. I'M LOOKING FORWARD TO READING YOUR MANGA.

WHAT'S THIS MONEY?!

IT'S THE MONEY I SAVED FOR COLLEGE. THERE'S A LITTLE OVER ¥10,000. COULDN'T YOU USE IT?

YOU HAVE A LONG LIFE AHEAD OF YOU. ONE OR TWO YEARS OFF WON'T DO ANY HARM.

IT'S TOO BAD ABOUT KYOTO ART UNIVERSITY, BUT...

DON'T WORRY. I FEEL LIKE EVERYTHING I DID IN HIGH SCHOOL WAS HALF-BAKED.

THIS YEAR, I'M GOING TO THINK SERIOUSLY ABOUT WHAT I'M GOING TO DO WITH MY LIFE.

IS THAT RIGHT? WELL, YOU CAN ALWAYS TAKE THE EXAM AGAIN IN A YEAR IF YOU DECIDE YOU WANT TO STUDY.

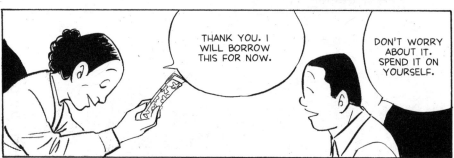

THANK YOU. I WILL BORROW THIS FOR NOW.

DON'T WORRY ABOUT IT. SPEND IT ON YOURSELF.

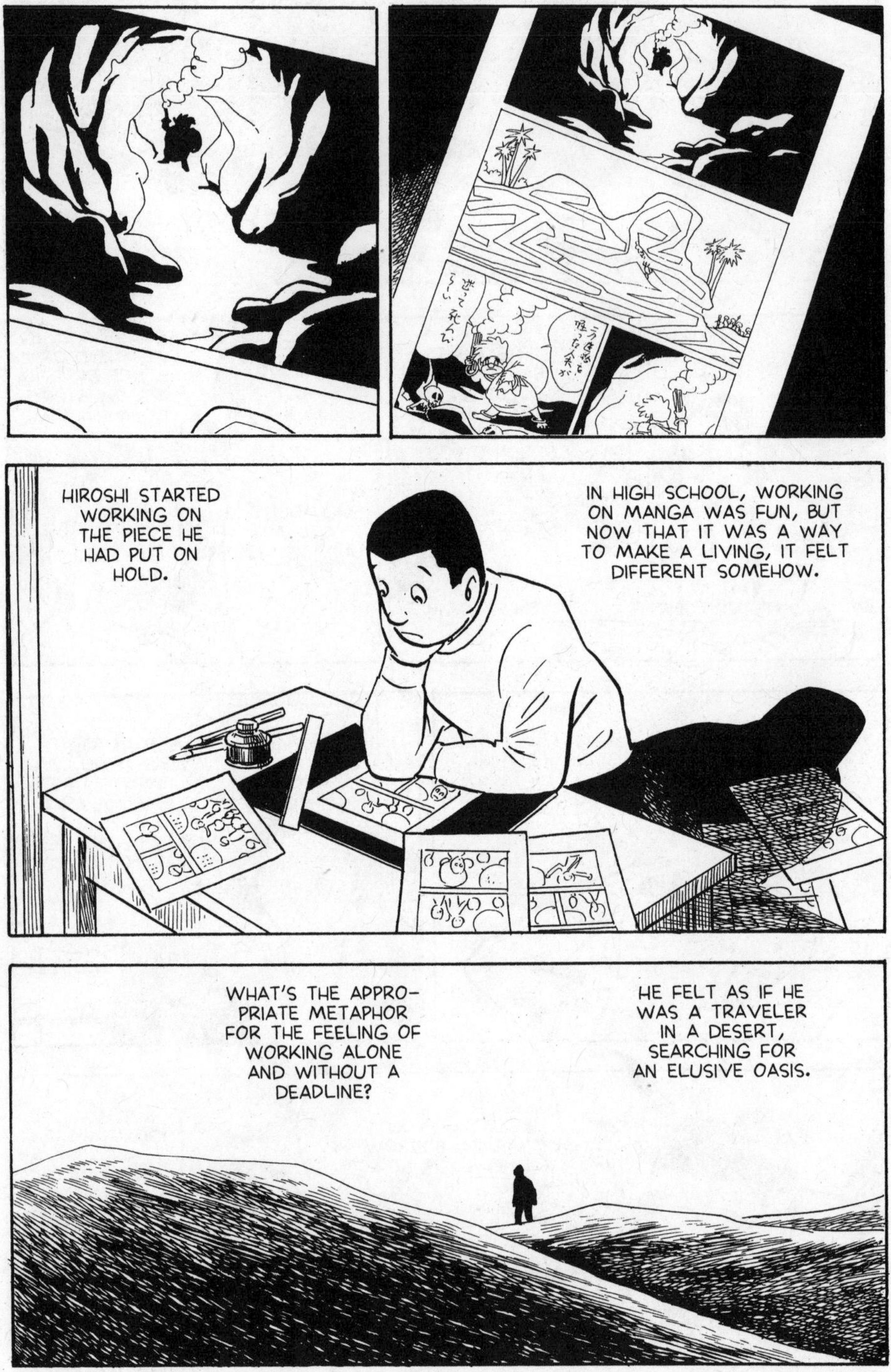
HIROSHI STARTED WORKING ON THE PIECE HE HAD PUT ON HOLD.
IN HIGH SCHOOL, WORKING ON MANGA WAS FUN, BUT NOW THAT IT WAS A WAY TO MAKE A LIVING, IT FELT DIFFERENT SOMEHOW.
WHAT'S THE APPROPRIATE METAPHOR FOR THE FEELING OF WORKING ALONE AND WITHOUT A DEADLINE?
HE FELT AS IF HE WAS A TRAVELER IN A DESERT, SEARCHING FOR AN ELUSIVE OASIS.

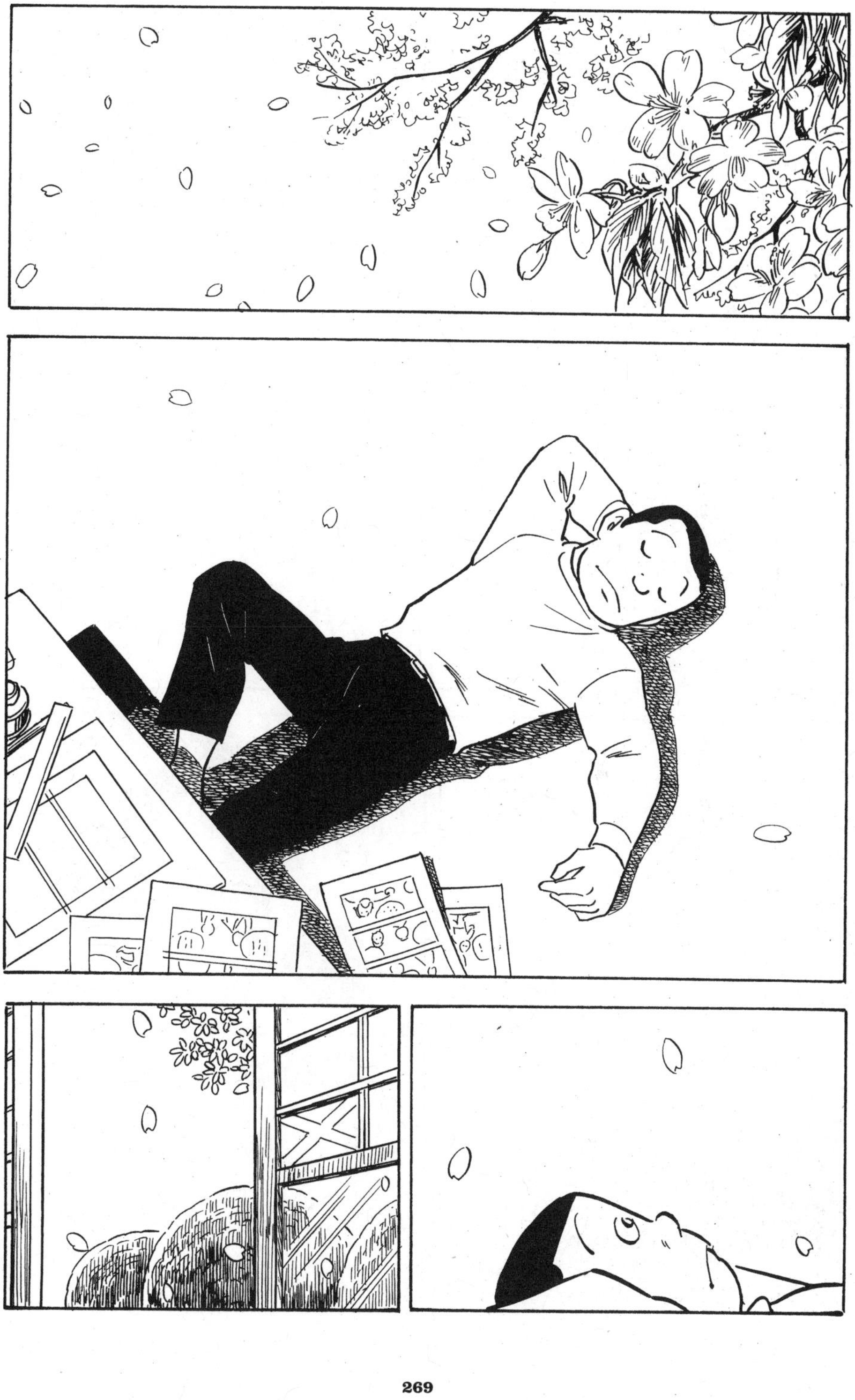

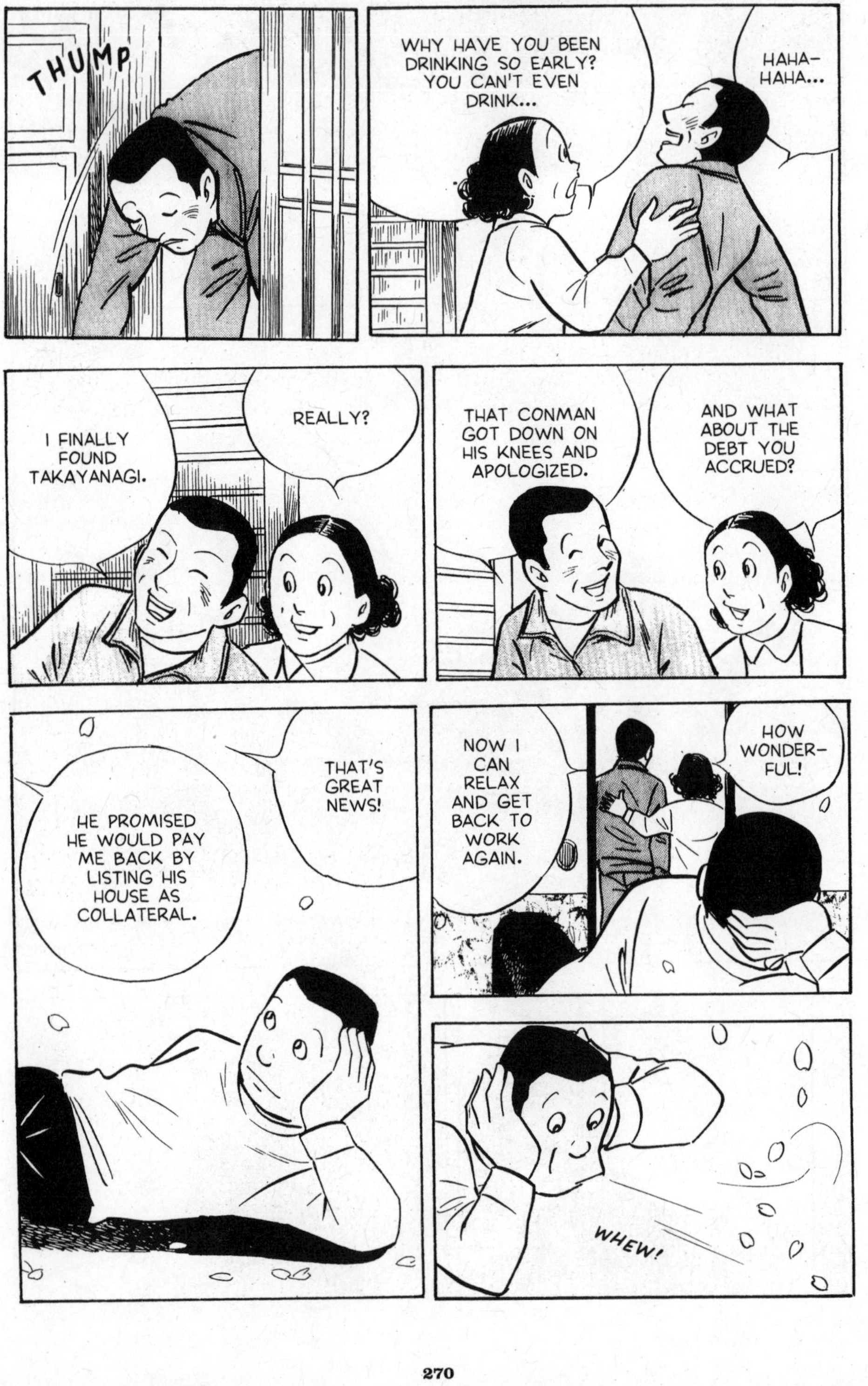
THUMP
WHY HAVE YOU BEEN DRINKING SO EARLY? YOU CAN'T EVEN DRINK...
HAHA-HAHA...
I FINALLY FOUND TAKAYANAGI.
REALLY?
THAT CONMAN GOT DOWN ON HIS KNEES AND APOLOGIZED.
AND WHAT ABOUT THE DEBT YOU ACCRUED?
HE PROMISED HE WOULD PAY ME BACK BY LISTING HIS HOUSE AS COLLATERAL.
THAT'S GREAT NEWS!
NOW I CAN RELAX AND GET BACK TO WORK AGAIN.
HOW WONDER-FUL!
WHEW!

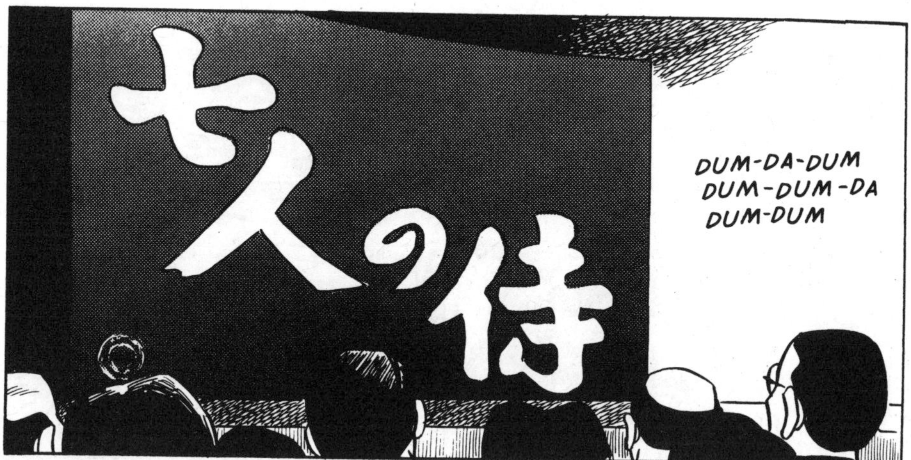
七人の侍
DUM-DA-DUM
DUM-DUM-DA
DUM-DUM
TITLE: *SEVEN SAMURAI*

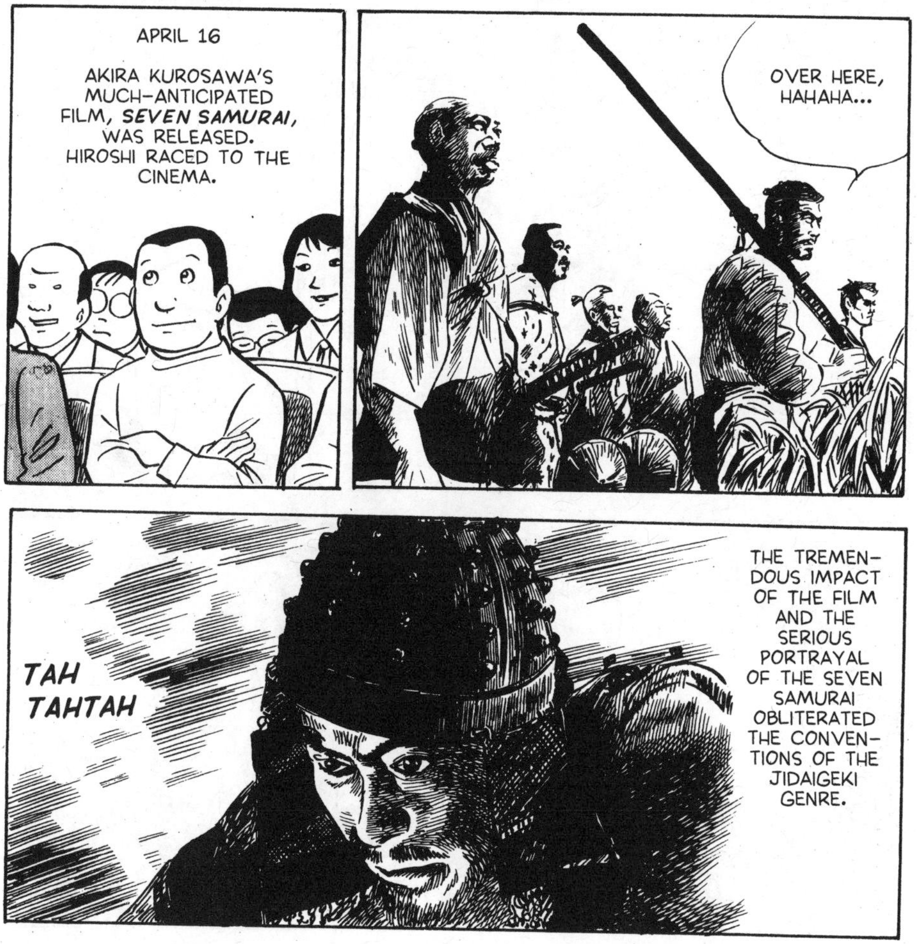
APRIL 16
AKIRA KUROSAWA'S MUCH-ANTICIPATED FILM, SEVEN SAMURAI, WAS RELEASED. HIROSHI RACED TO THE CINEMA.
OVER HERE, HAHAHA...
TAH
TAHTAH
THE TREMEN-DOUS IMPACT OF THE FILM AND THE SERIOUS PORTRAYAL OF THE SEVEN SAMURAI OBLITERATED THE CONVEN-TIONS OF THE JIDAIGEKI GENRE.

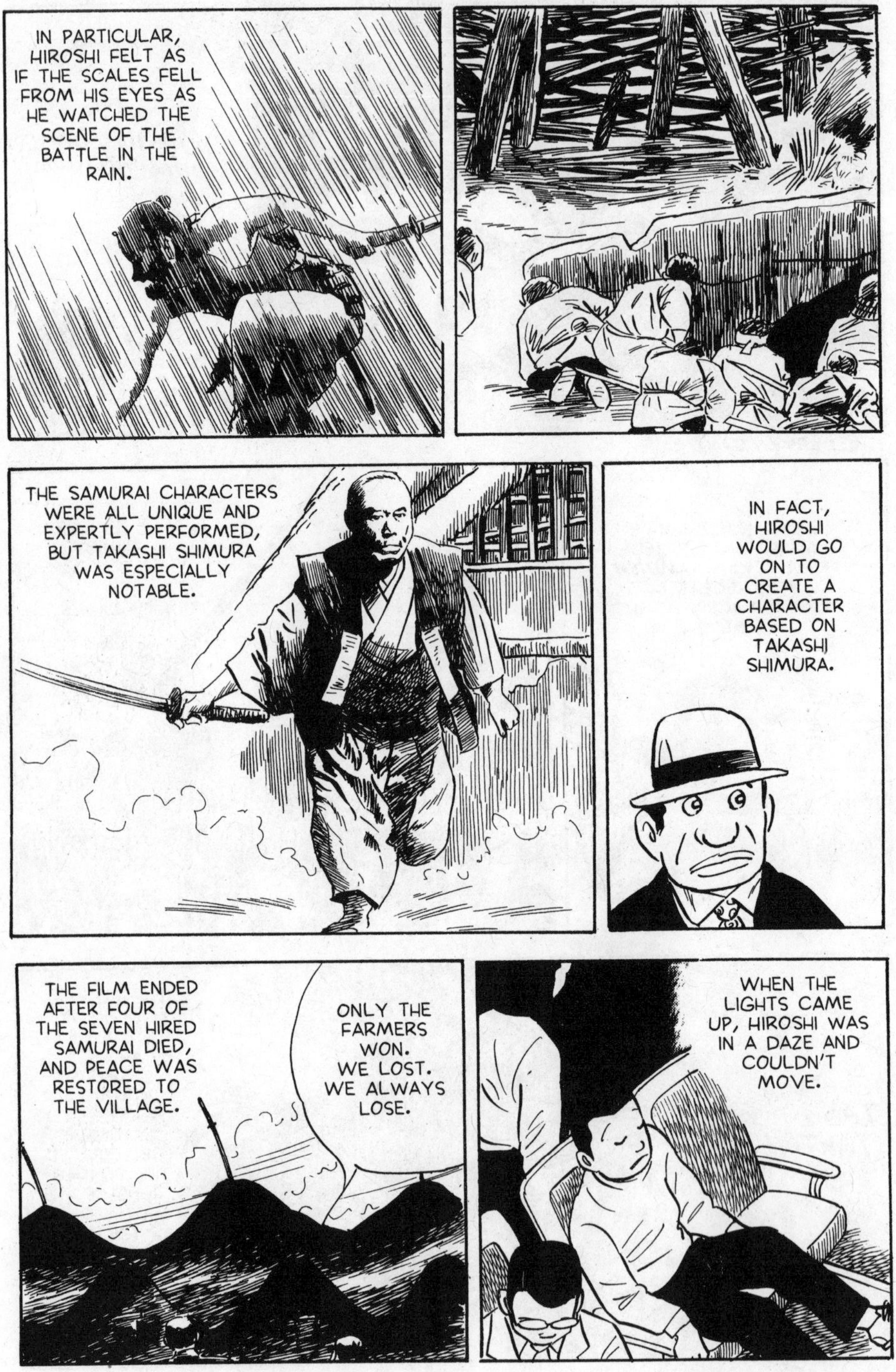
IN PARTICULAR, HIROSHI FELT AS IF THE SCALES FELL FROM HIS EYES AS HE WATCHED THE SCENE OF THE BATTLE IN THE RAIN.
THE SAMURAI CHARACTERS WERE ALL UNIQUE AND EXPERTLY PERFORMED, BUT TAKASHI SHIMURA WAS ESPECIALLY NOTABLE.
IN FACT, HIROSHI WOULD GO ON TO CREATE A CHARACTER BASED ON TAKASHI SHIMURA.
THE FILM ENDED AFTER FOUR OF THE SEVEN HIRED SAMURAI DIED, AND PEACE WAS RESTORED TO THE VILLAGE.
ONLY THE FARMERS WON. WE LOST. WE ALWAYS LOSE.
WHEN THE LIGHTS CAME UP, HIROSHI WAS IN A DAZE AND COULDN'T MOVE.

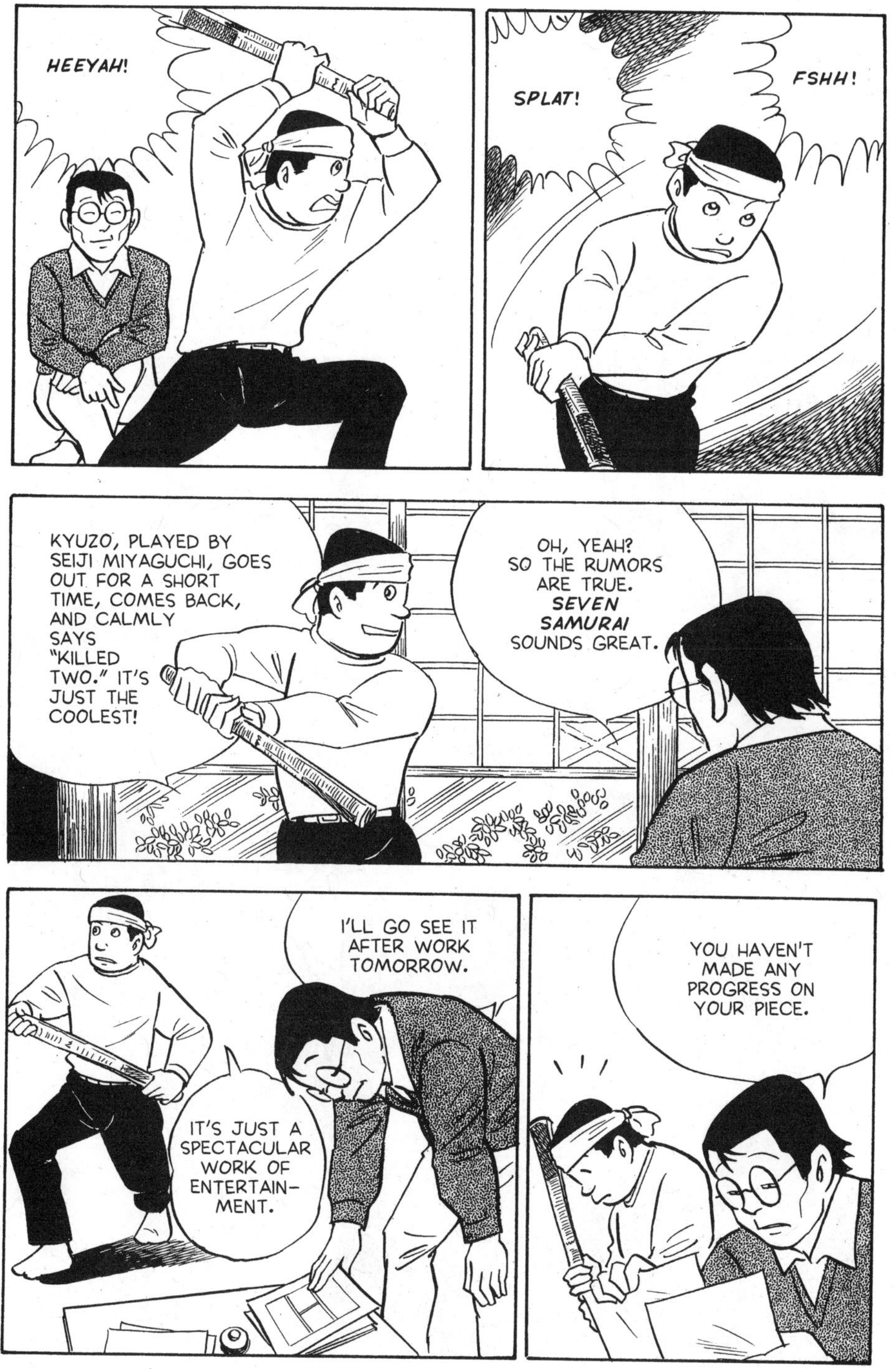
HEEYAH!
SPLAT!
FSHH!
KYUZO, PLAYED BY SEIJI MIYAGUCHI, GOES OUT FOR A SHORT TIME, COMES BACK, AND CALMLY SAYS "KILLED TWO." IT'S JUST THE COOLEST!
OH, YEAH? SO THE RUMORS ARE TRUE. ***SEVEN SAMURAI*** SOUNDS GREAT.
I'LL GO SEE IT AFTER WORK TOMORROW.
IT'S JUST A SPECTACULAR WORK OF ENTERTAIN-MENT.
YOU HAVEN'T MADE ANY PROGRESS ON YOUR PIECE.

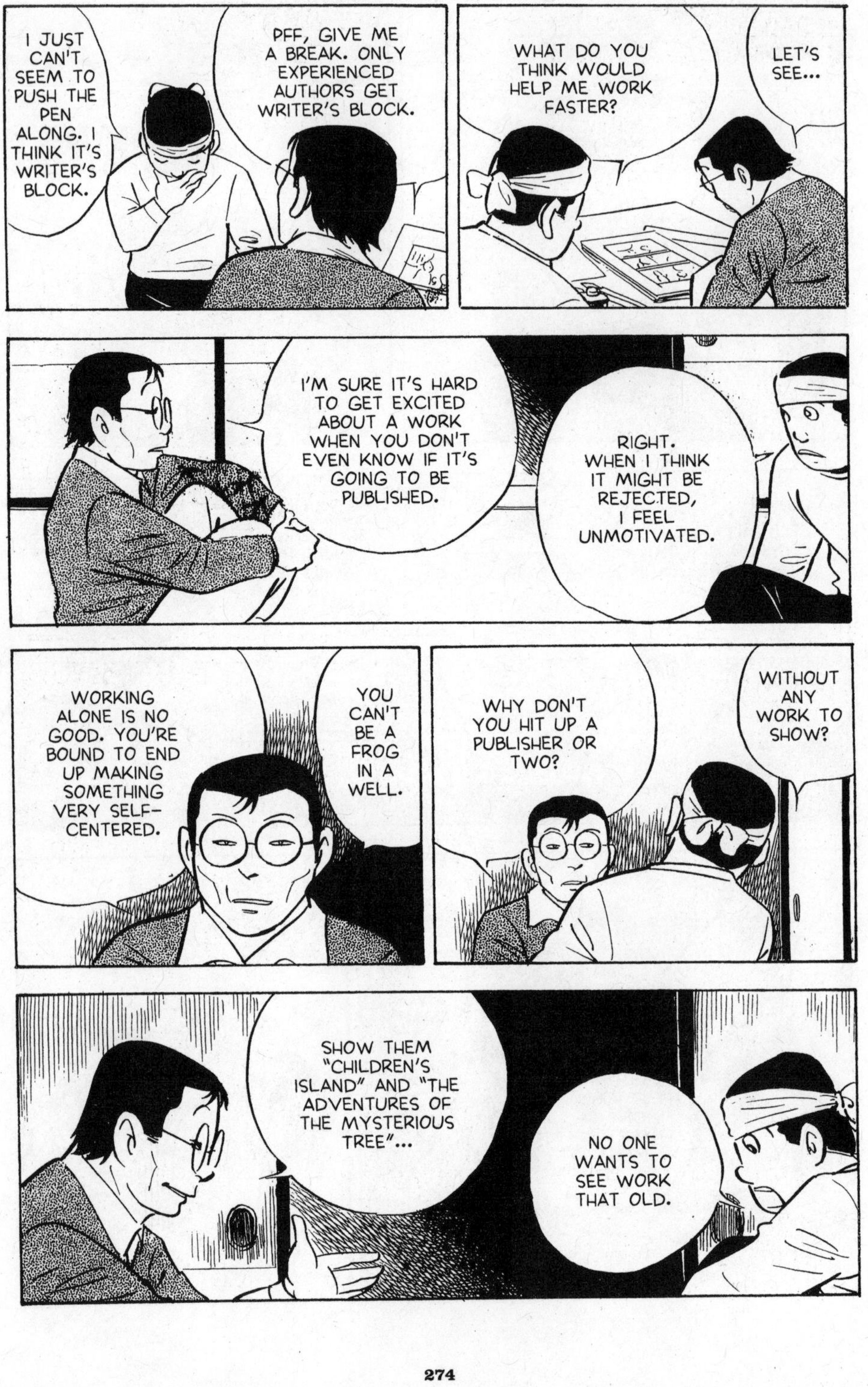
I JUST CAN'T SEEM TO PUSH THE PEN ALONG. I THINK IT'S WRITER'S BLOCK.
PFF, GIVE ME A BREAK. ONLY EXPERIENCED AUTHORS GET WRITER'S BLOCK.
WHAT DO YOU THINK WOULD HELP ME WORK FASTER?
LET'S SEE...
I'M SURE IT'S HARD TO GET EXCITED ABOUT A WORK WHEN YOU DON'T EVEN KNOW IF IT'S GOING TO BE PUBLISHED.
RIGHT. WHEN I THINK IT MIGHT BE REJECTED, I FEEL UNMOTIVATED.
WORKING ALONE IS NO GOOD. YOU'RE BOUND TO END UP MAKING SOMETHING VERY SELF-CENTERED.
YOU CAN'T BE A FROG IN A WELL.
WHY DON'T YOU HIT UP A PUBLISHER OR TWO?
WITHOUT ANY WORK TO SHOW?
SHOW THEM "CHILDREN'S ISLAND" AND "THE ADVENTURES OF THE MYSTERIOUS TREE"...
NO ONE WANTS TO SEE WORK THAT OLD.

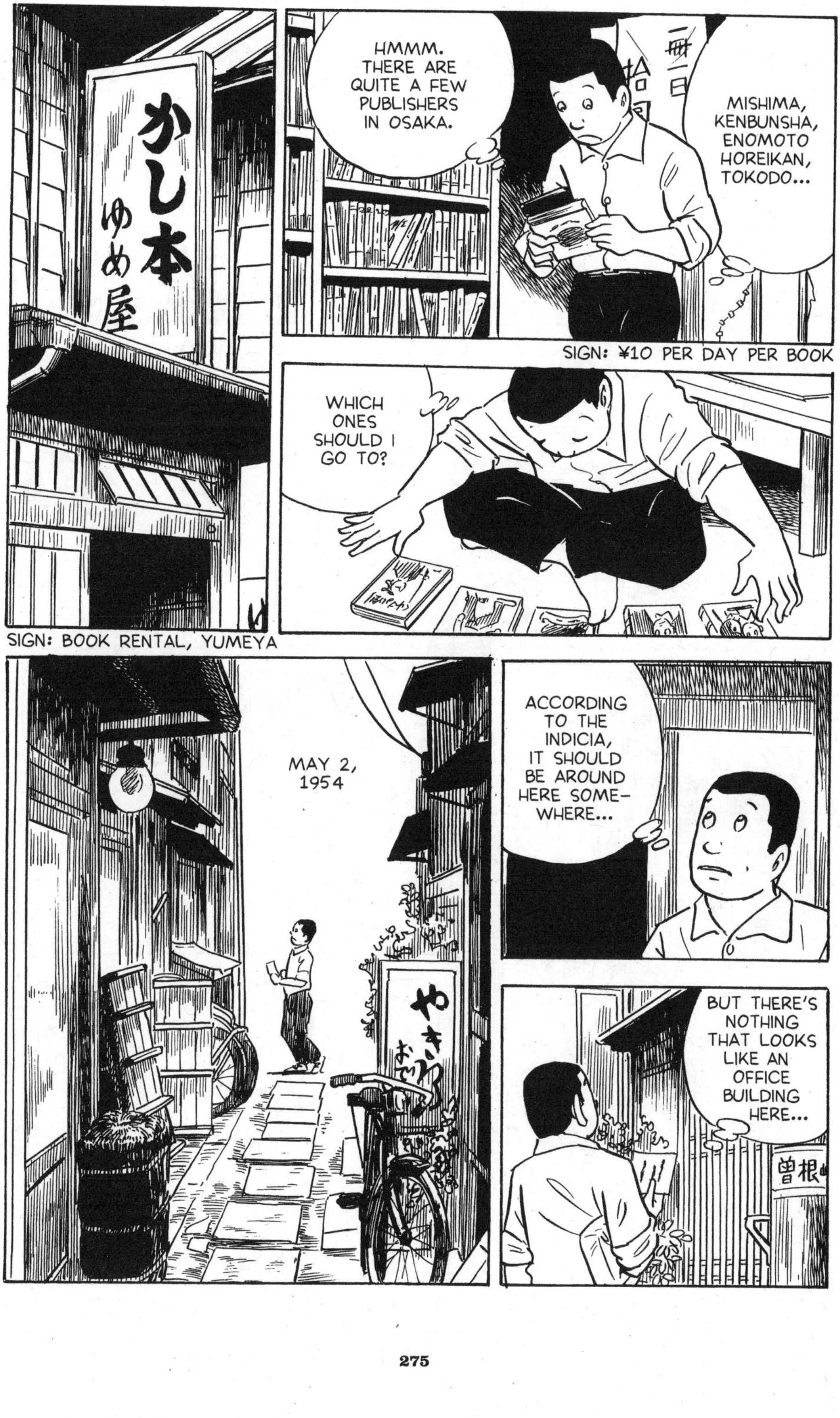

かし本
ゆめ屋
SIGN: BOOK RENTAL, YUMEYA
HMMM. THERE ARE QUITE A FEW PUBLISHERS IN OSAKA.
MISHIMA, KENBUNSHA, ENOMOTO HOREIKAN, TOKODO...
SIGN: ¥10 PER DAY PER BOOK
WHICH ONES SHOULD I GO TO?
MAY 2, 1954
ACCORDING TO THE INDICIA, IT SHOULD BE AROUND HERE SOME-WHERE...
BUT THERE'S NOTHING THAT LOOKS LIKE AN OFFICE BUILDING HERE...

KENBUN-SHA?

YES, I'M LOOKING FOR A PUBLISHER BY THAT NAME THAT PUTS OUT SAMURAI MANGA.

NEVER HEARD OF IT.

BESIDES, THERE AIN'T NO PUBLISHERS AROUND THESE PARTS.

MAYBE IT'S THAT, YOU KNOW...

HUH?

OH YEAH, THERE IS A PLACE WITH A PILE OF BOOKS OUT FRONT.

MUST BE THE ONE.

KENBUNSHA'S IN HERE IN THE BACK.

SIGN: KENBUNSHA

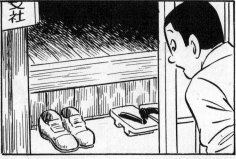

HELLO...?

ANYONE HOME?

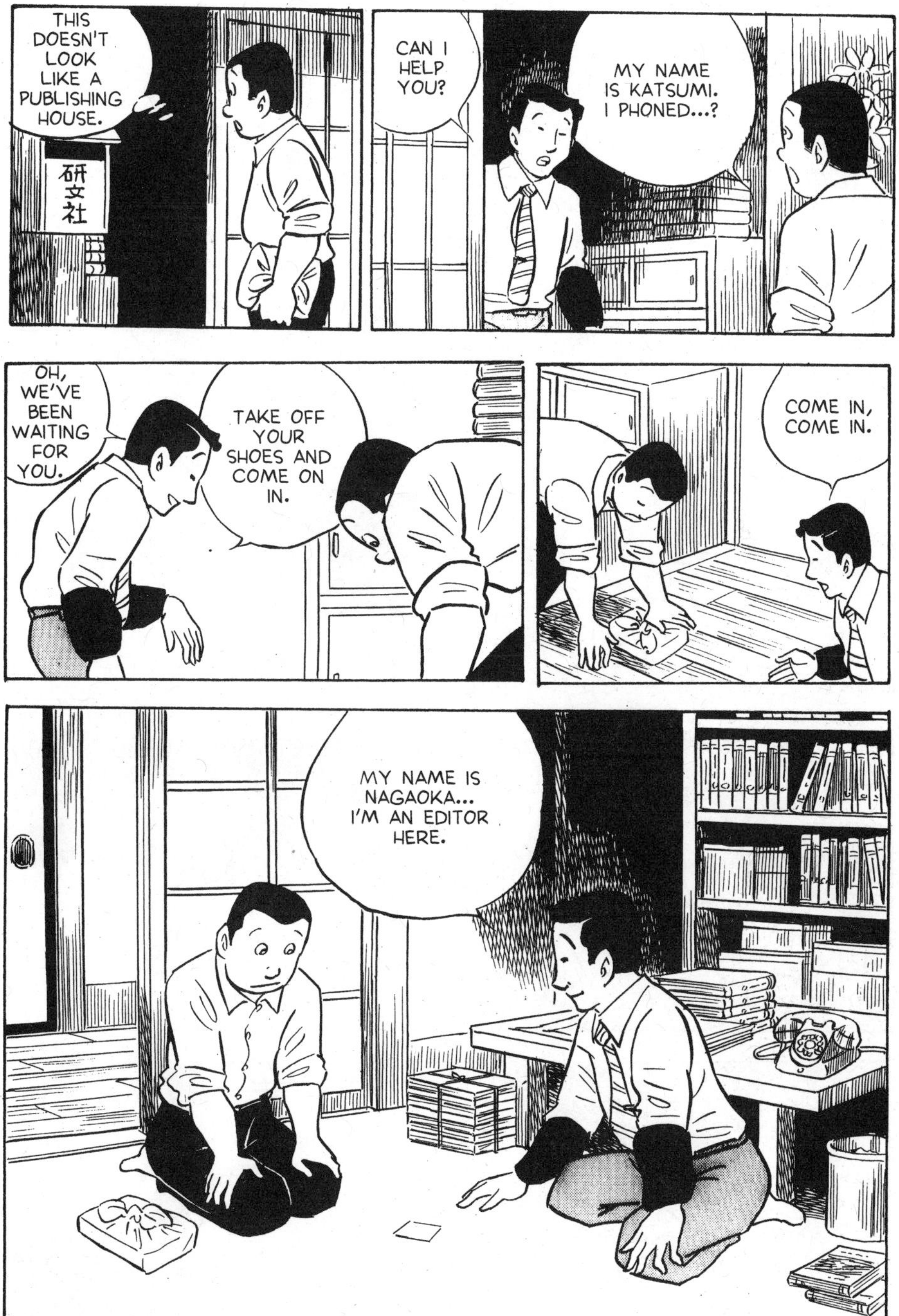
THIS DOESN'T LOOK LIKE A PUBLISHING HOUSE.
研文社
CAN I HELP YOU?
MY NAME IS KATSUMI. I PHONED...?
OH, WE'VE BEEN WAITING FOR YOU.
TAKE OFF YOUR SHOES AND COME ON IN.
COME IN, COME IN.
MY NAME IS NAGAOKA... I'M AN EDITOR HERE.

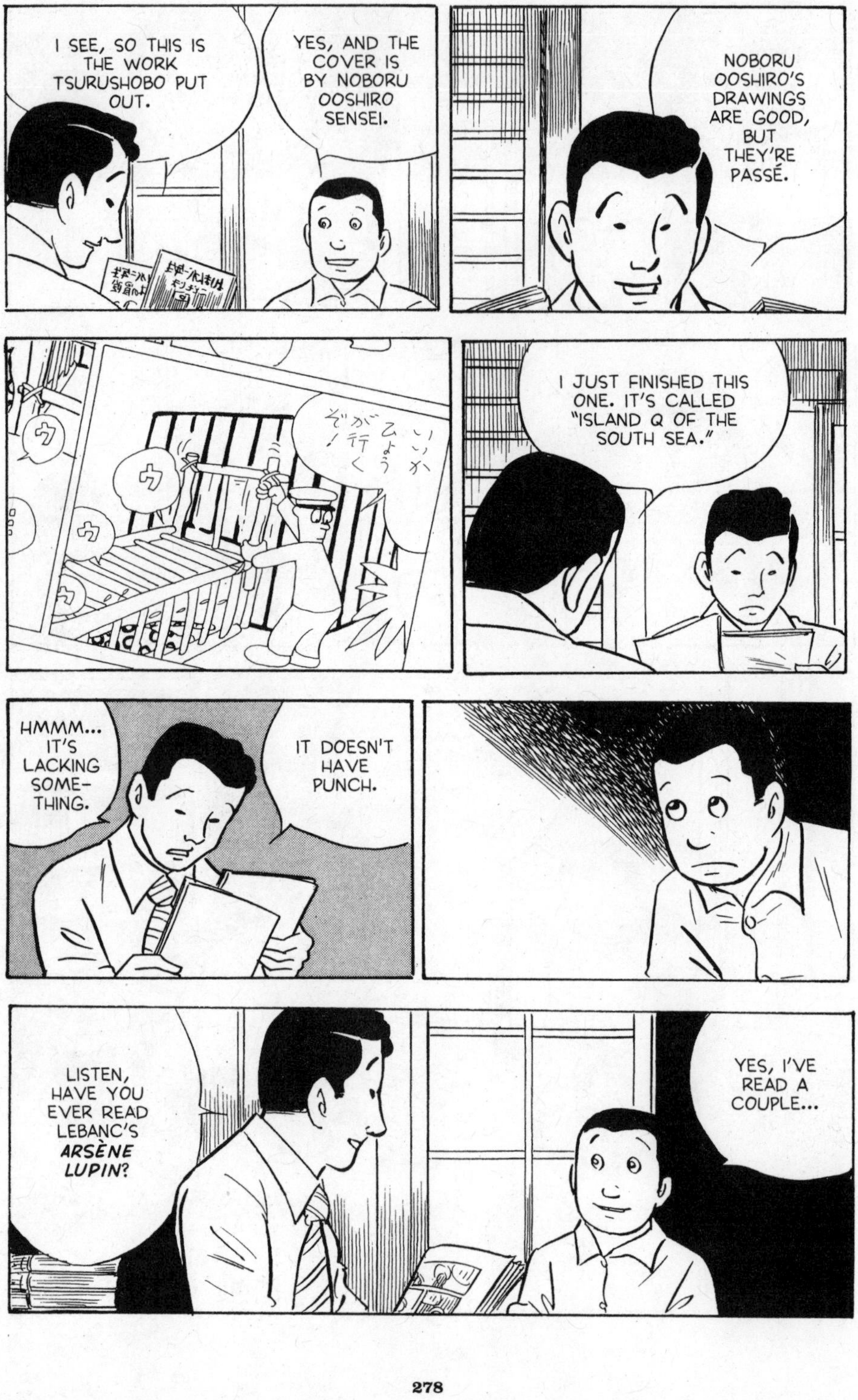
I SEE, SO THIS IS THE WORK TSURUSHOBO PUT OUT.
YES, AND THE COVER IS BY NOBORU OOSHIRO SENSEI.
NOBORU OOSHIRO'S DRAWINGS ARE GOOD, BUT THEY'RE PASSÉ.
ウ
ウ
ウ
ウ
いいか乙ようが行くぞ！
I JUST FINISHED THIS ONE. IT'S CALLED "ISLAND Q OF THE SOUTH SEA."
HMMM... IT'S LACKING SOME-THING.
IT DOESN'T HAVE PUNCH.
LISTEN, HAVE YOU EVER READ LEBANC'S ***ARSÈNE LUPIN***?
YES, I'VE READ A COUPLE...

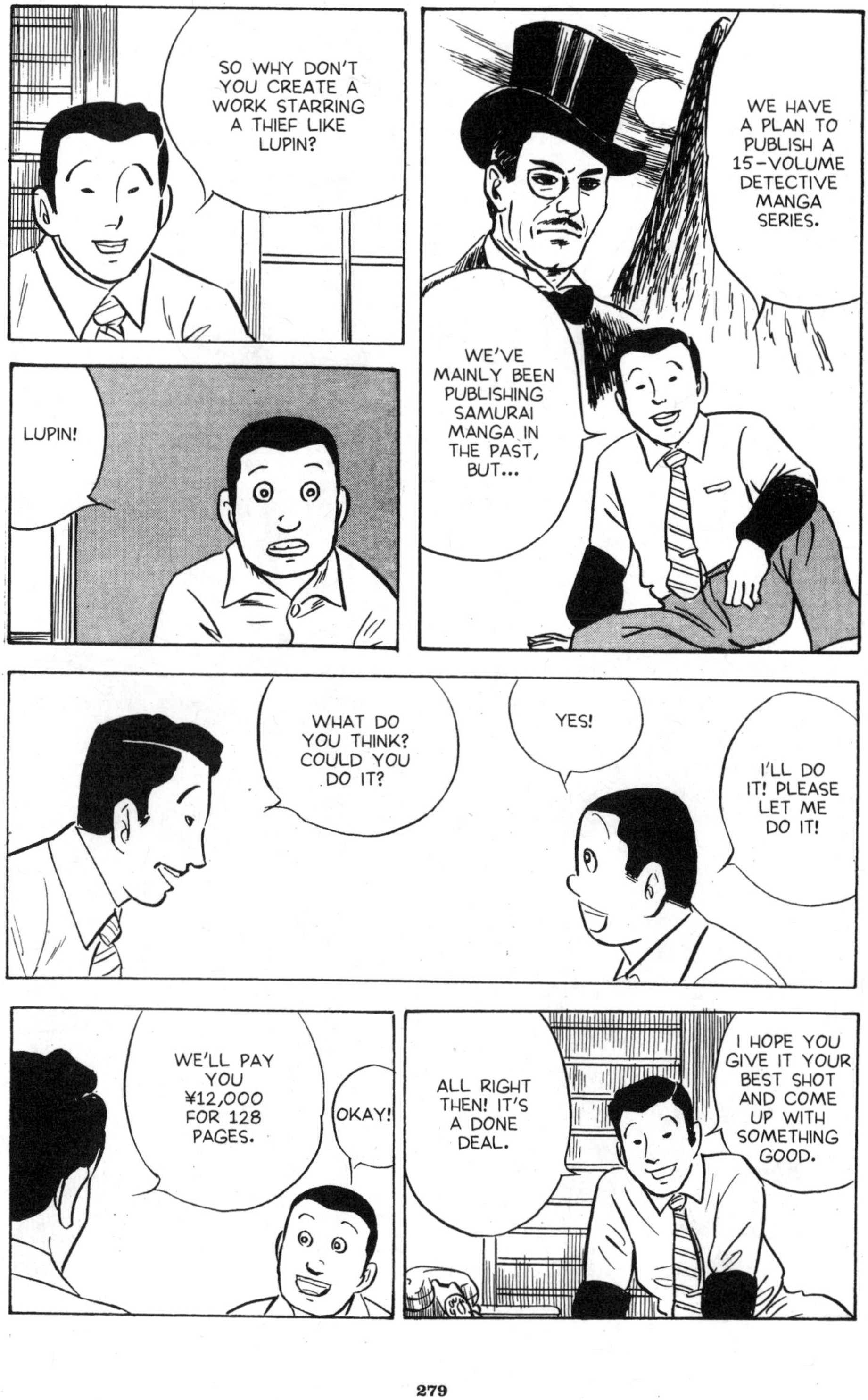

SO WHY DON'T YOU CREATE A WORK STARRING A THIEF LIKE LUPIN?
LUPIN!
WE HAVE A PLAN TO PUBLISH A 15-VOLUME DETECTIVE MANGA SERIES.
WE'VE MAINLY BEEN PUBLISHING SAMURAI MANGA IN THE PAST, BUT...
WHAT DO YOU THINK? COULD YOU DO IT?
YES!
I'LL DO IT! PLEASE LET ME DO IT!
WE'LL PAY YOU ¥12,000 FOR 128 PAGES.
OKAY!
ALL RIGHT THEN! IT'S A DONE DEAL.
I HOPE YOU GIVE IT YOUR BEST SHOT AND COME UP WITH SOMETHING GOOD.

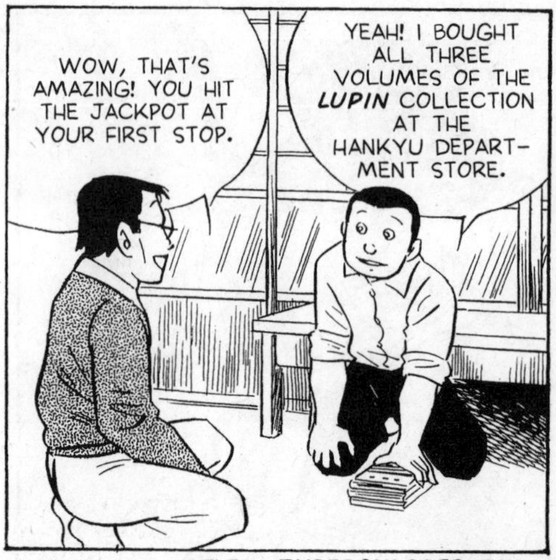
WOW, THAT'S AMAZING! YOU HIT THE JACKPOT AT YOUR FIRST STOP.
YEAH! I BOUGHT ALL THREE VOLUMES OF THE ***LUPIN*** COLLECTION AT THE HANKYU DEPARTMENT STORE.

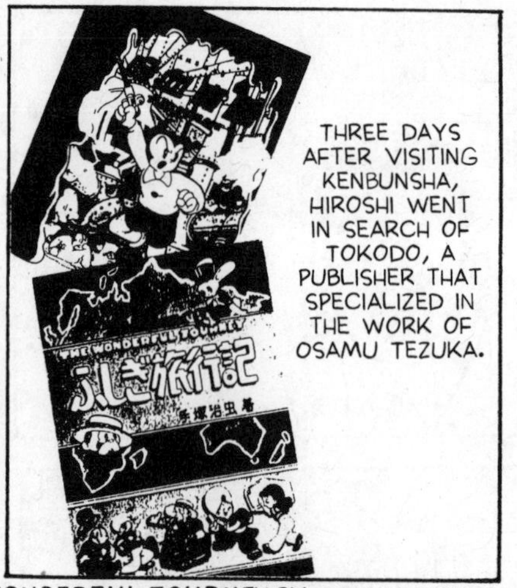
THREE DAYS AFTER VISITING KENBUNSHA, HIROSHI WENT IN SEARCH OF TOKODO, A PUBLISHER THAT SPECIALIZED IN THE WORK OF OSAMU TEZUKA.

TITLES: *TUBERCULOSES* / *THE WONDERFUL JOURNEY* BY OSAMU TEZUKA

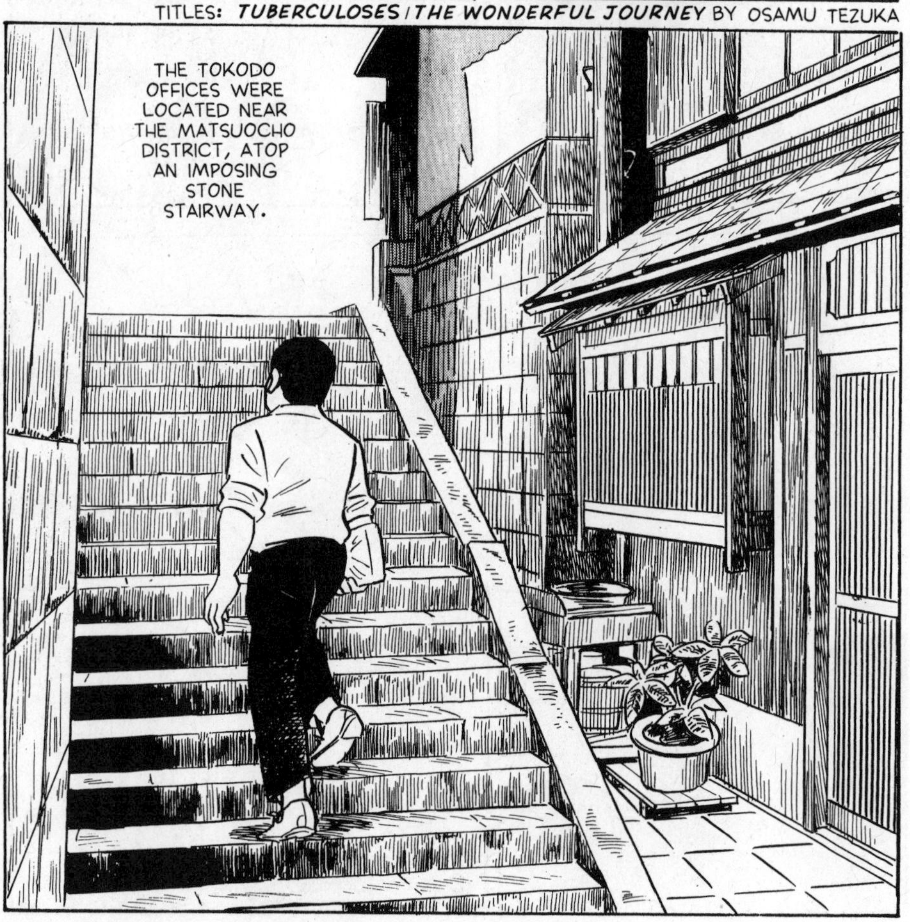
THE TOKODO OFFICES WERE LOCATED NEAR THE MATSUOCHO DISTRICT, ATOP AN IMPOSING STONE STAIRWAY.

A DREAM FULFILLED

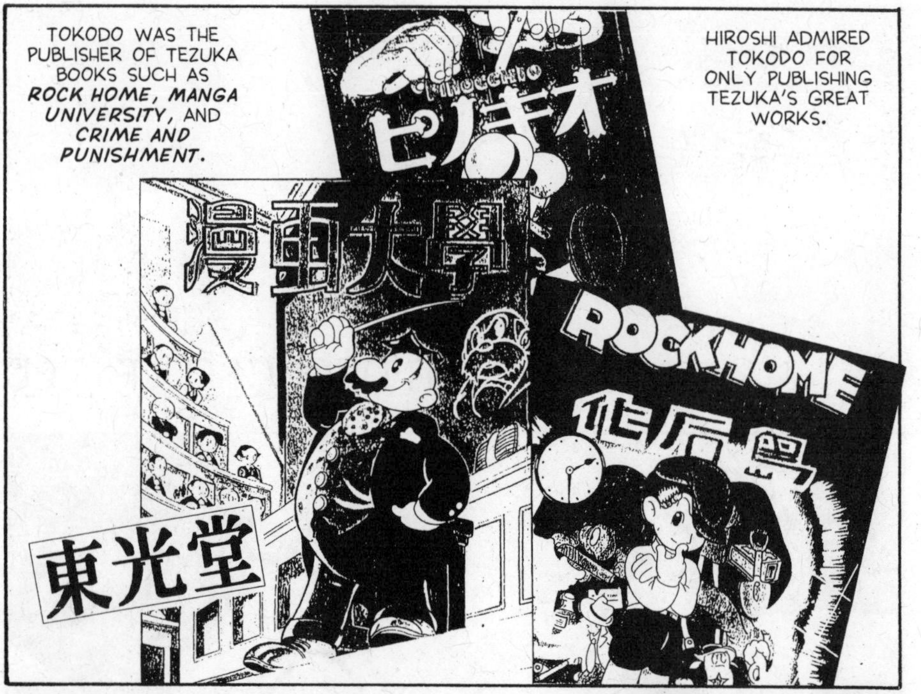
TOKODO WAS THE PUBLISHER OF TEZUKA BOOKS SUCH AS ***ROCK HOME, MANGA UNIVERSITY,*** AND ***CRIME AND PUNISHMENT***.
ピノキオ
漫画大學
ROCKHOME
化石島
東光堂
HIROSHI ADMIRED TOKODO FOR ONLY PUBLISHING TEZUKA'S GREAT WORKS.

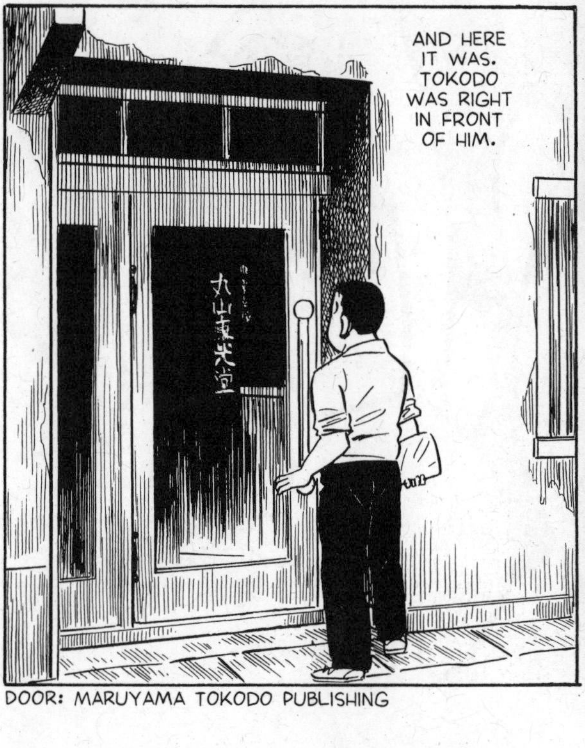
AND HERE IT WAS. TOKODO WAS RIGHT IN FRONT OF HIM.
丸山東光堂

DOOR: MARUYAMA TOKODO PUBLISHING

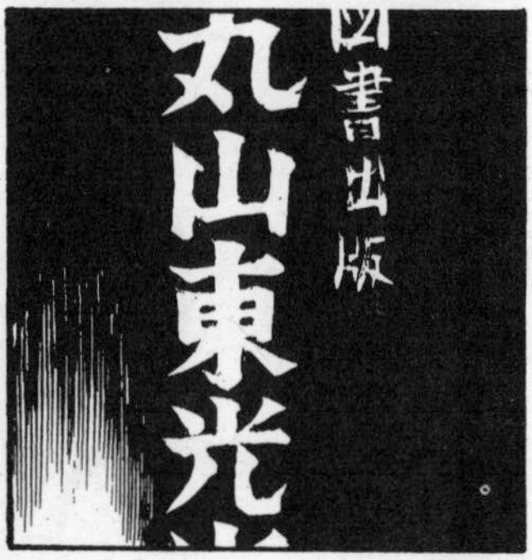
図書出版
丸山東光

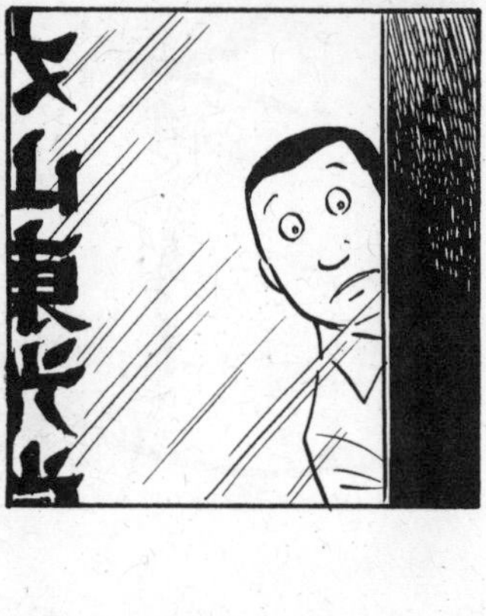

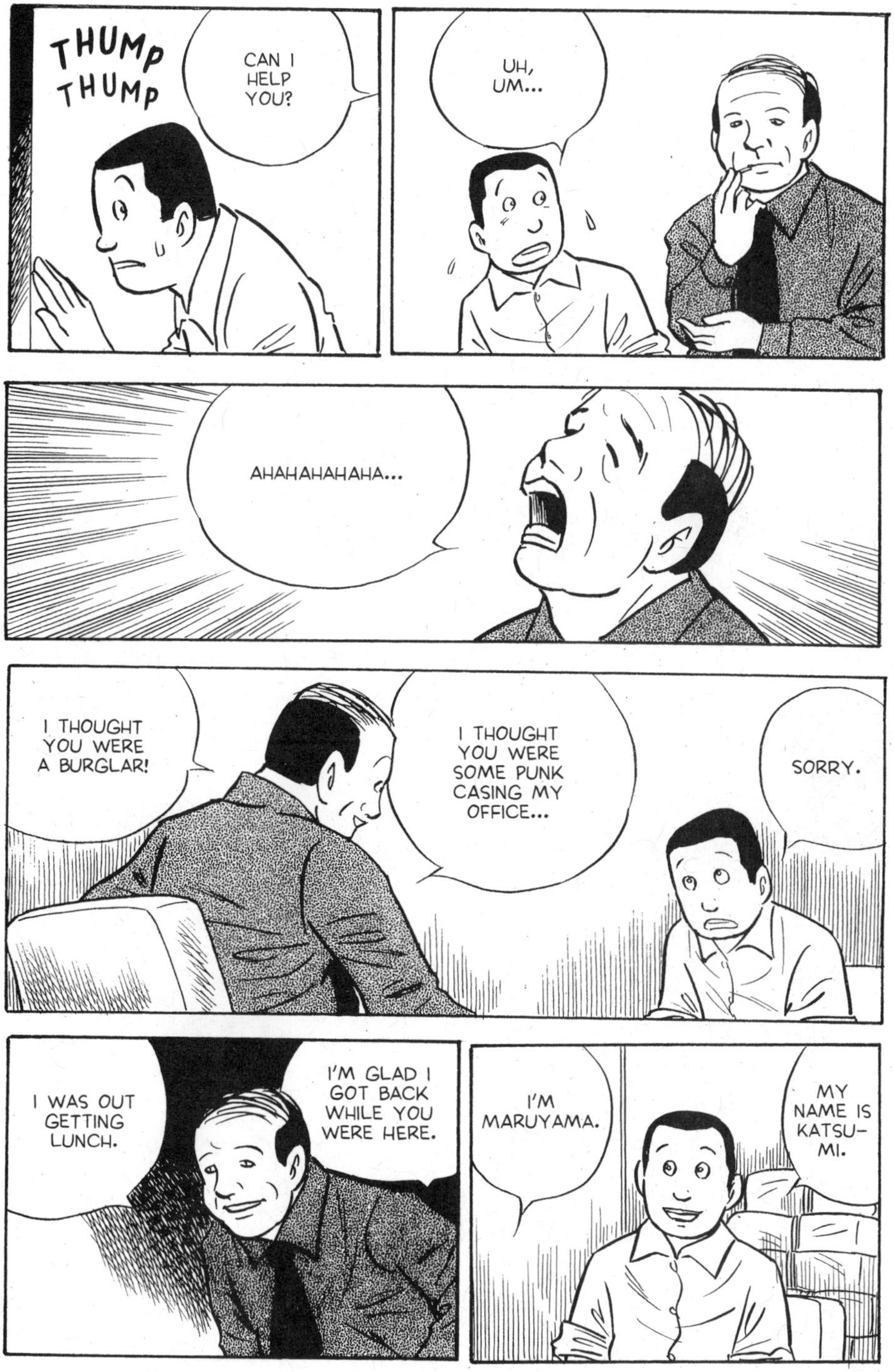
THUMP THUMP
CAN I HELP YOU?
UH, UM...
AHAHAHAHAHA...
I THOUGHT YOU WERE A BURGLAR!
I THOUGHT YOU WERE SOME PUNK CASING MY OFFICE...
SORRY.
I WAS OUT GETTING LUNCH.
I'M GLAD I GOT BACK WHILE YOU WERE HERE.
I'M MARUYAMA.
MY NAME IS KATSU-MI.

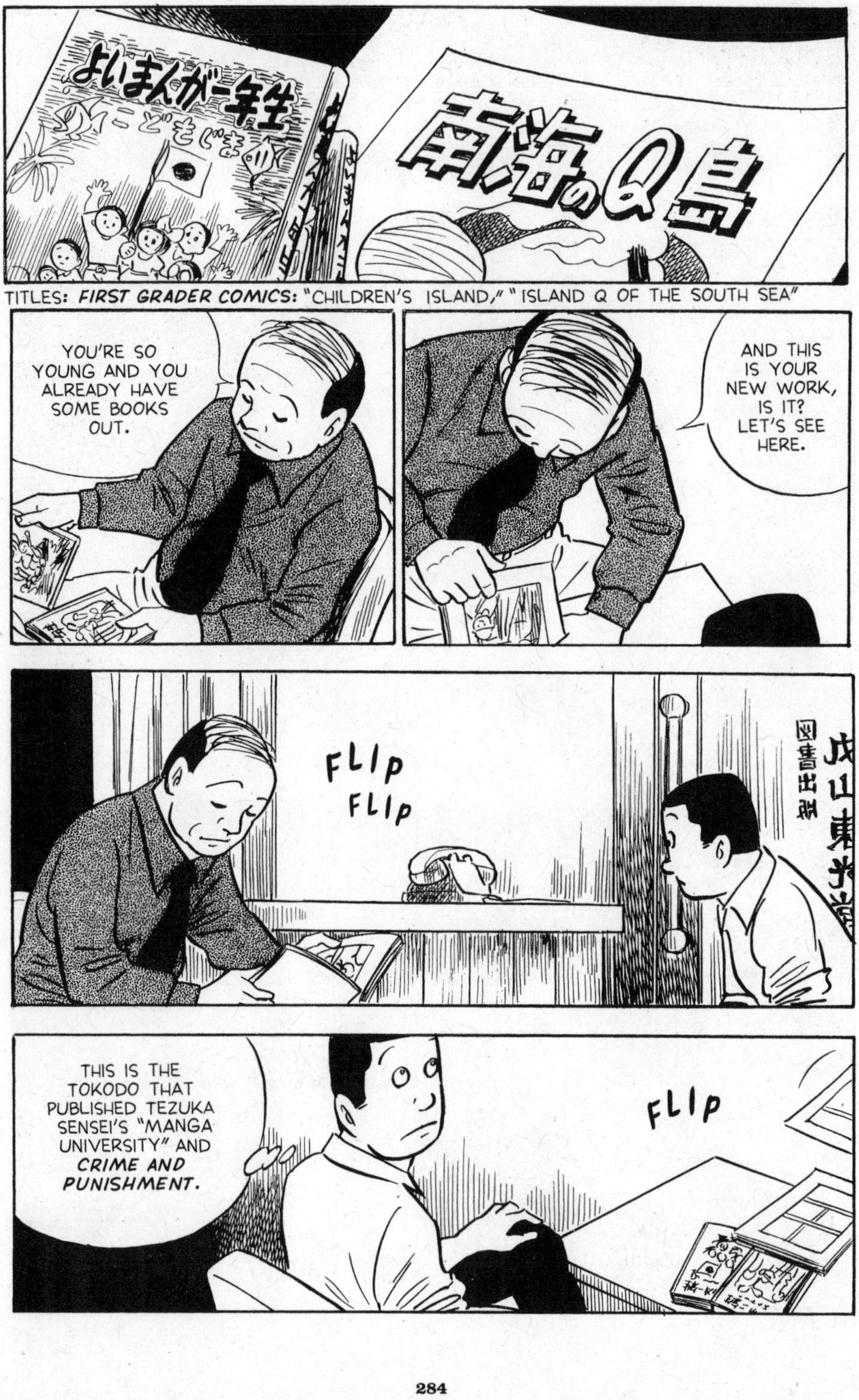
よいまんが一年生
南海のQ島
TITLES: FIRST GRADER COMICS: "CHILDREN'S ISLAND," "ISLAND Q OF THE SOUTH SEA"
YOU'RE SO YOUNG AND YOU ALREADY HAVE SOME BOOKS OUT.
AND THIS IS YOUR NEW WORK, IS IT? LET'S SEE HERE.
FLIP FLIP
図書出版
THIS IS THE TOKODO THAT PUBLISHED TEZUKA SENSEI'S "MANGA UNIVERSITY" AND CRIME AND PUNISHMENT.
FLIP

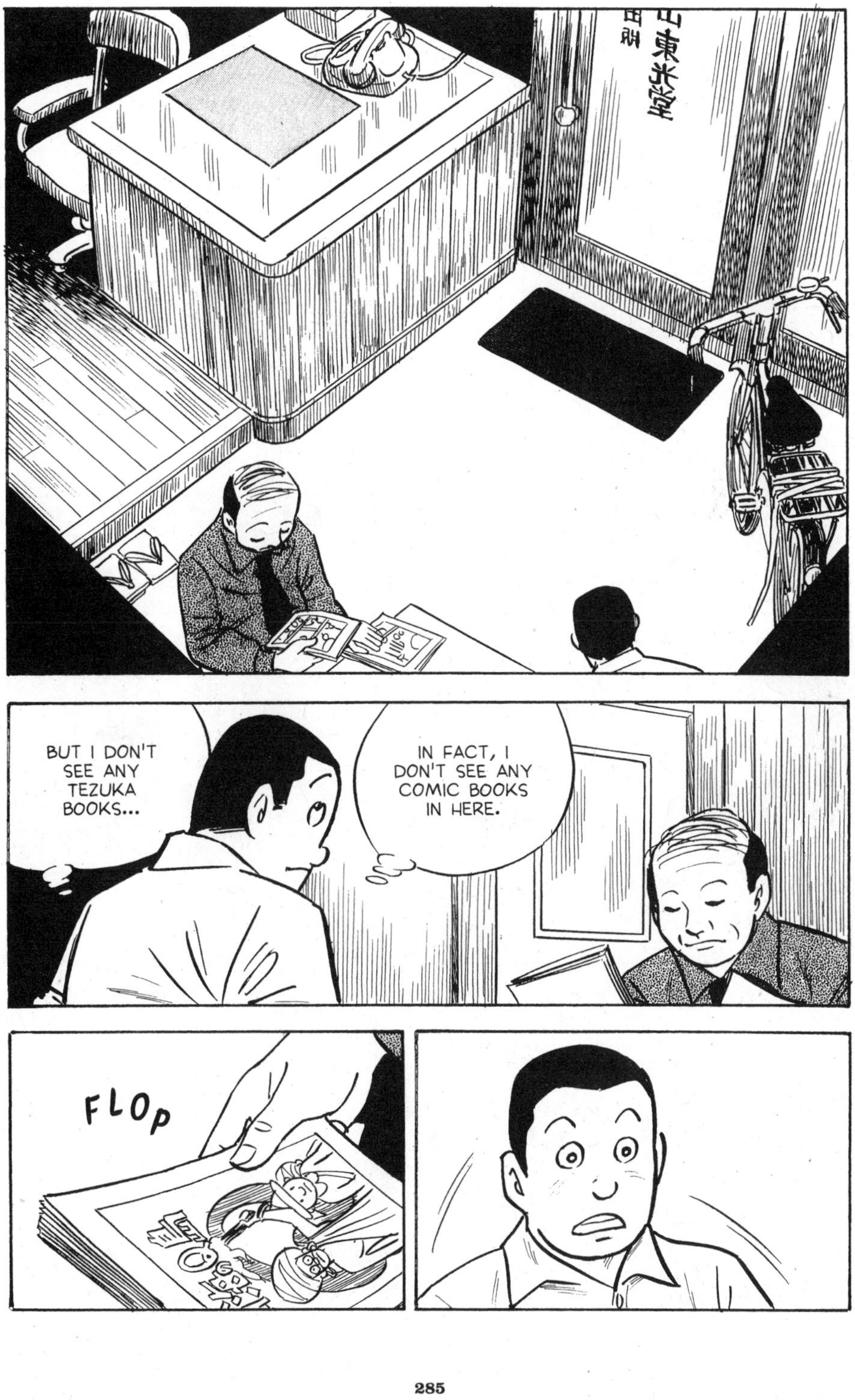
BUT I DON'T SEE ANY TEZUKA BOOKS...
IN FACT, I DON'T SEE ANY COMIC BOOKS IN HERE.
FLOP

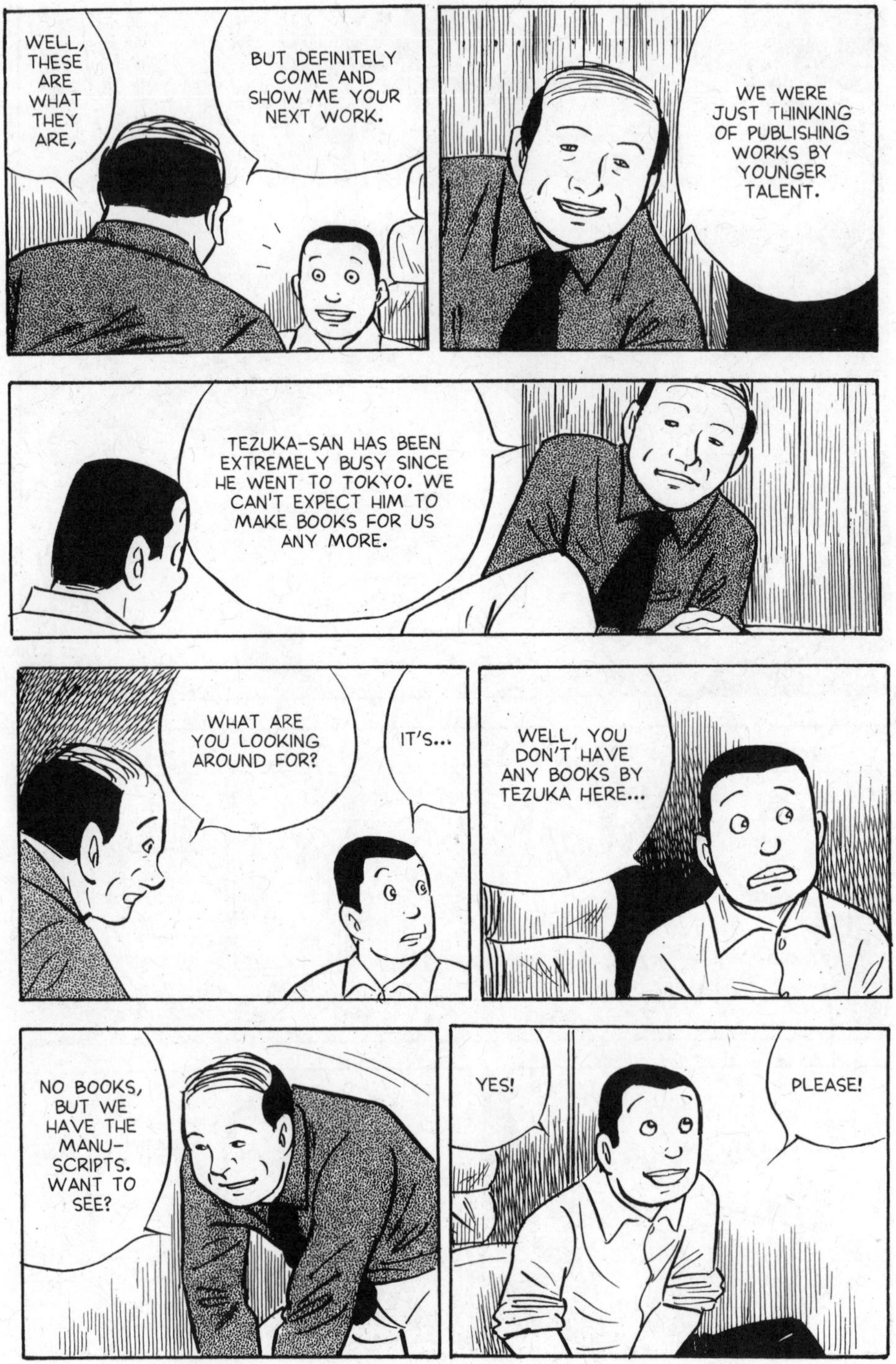
WELL, THESE ARE WHAT THEY ARE,
BUT DEFINITELY COME AND SHOW ME YOUR NEXT WORK.
WE WERE JUST THINKING OF PUBLISHING WORKS BY YOUNGER TALENT.
TEZUKA-SAN HAS BEEN EXTREMELY BUSY SINCE HE WENT TO TOKYO. WE CAN'T EXPECT HIM TO MAKE BOOKS FOR US ANY MORE.
WHAT ARE YOU LOOKING AROUND FOR?
IT'S...
WELL, YOU DON'T HAVE ANY BOOKS BY TEZUKA HERE...
NO BOOKS, BUT WE HAVE THE MANU-SCRIPTS. WANT TO SEE?
YES!
PLEASE!

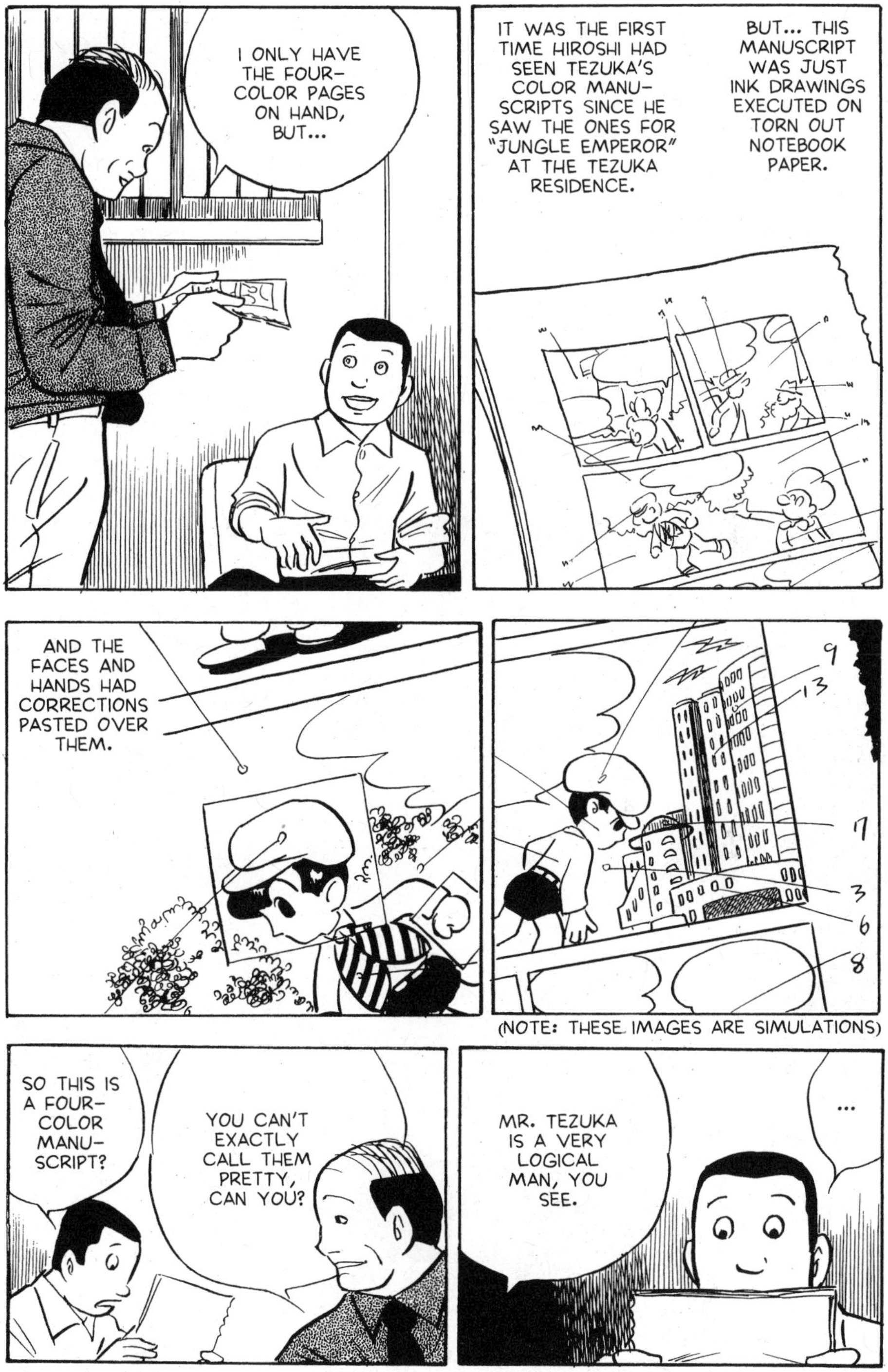
I ONLY HAVE THE FOUR-COLOR PAGES ON HAND, BUT...
IT WAS THE FIRST TIME HIROSHI HAD SEEN TEZUKA'S COLOR MANU-SCRIPTS SINCE HE SAW THE ONES FOR "JUNGLE EMPEROR" AT THE TEZUKA RESIDENCE.
BUT... THIS MANUSCRIPT WAS JUST INK DRAWINGS EXECUTED ON TORN OUT NOTEBOOK PAPER.
AND THE FACES AND HANDS HAD CORRECTIONS PASTED OVER THEM.
(NOTE: THESE IMAGES ARE SIMULATIONS)
SO THIS IS A FOUR-COLOR MANU-SCRIPT?
YOU CAN'T EXACTLY CALL THEM PRETTY, CAN YOU?
MR. TEZUKA IS A VERY LOGICAL MAN, YOU SEE.
...

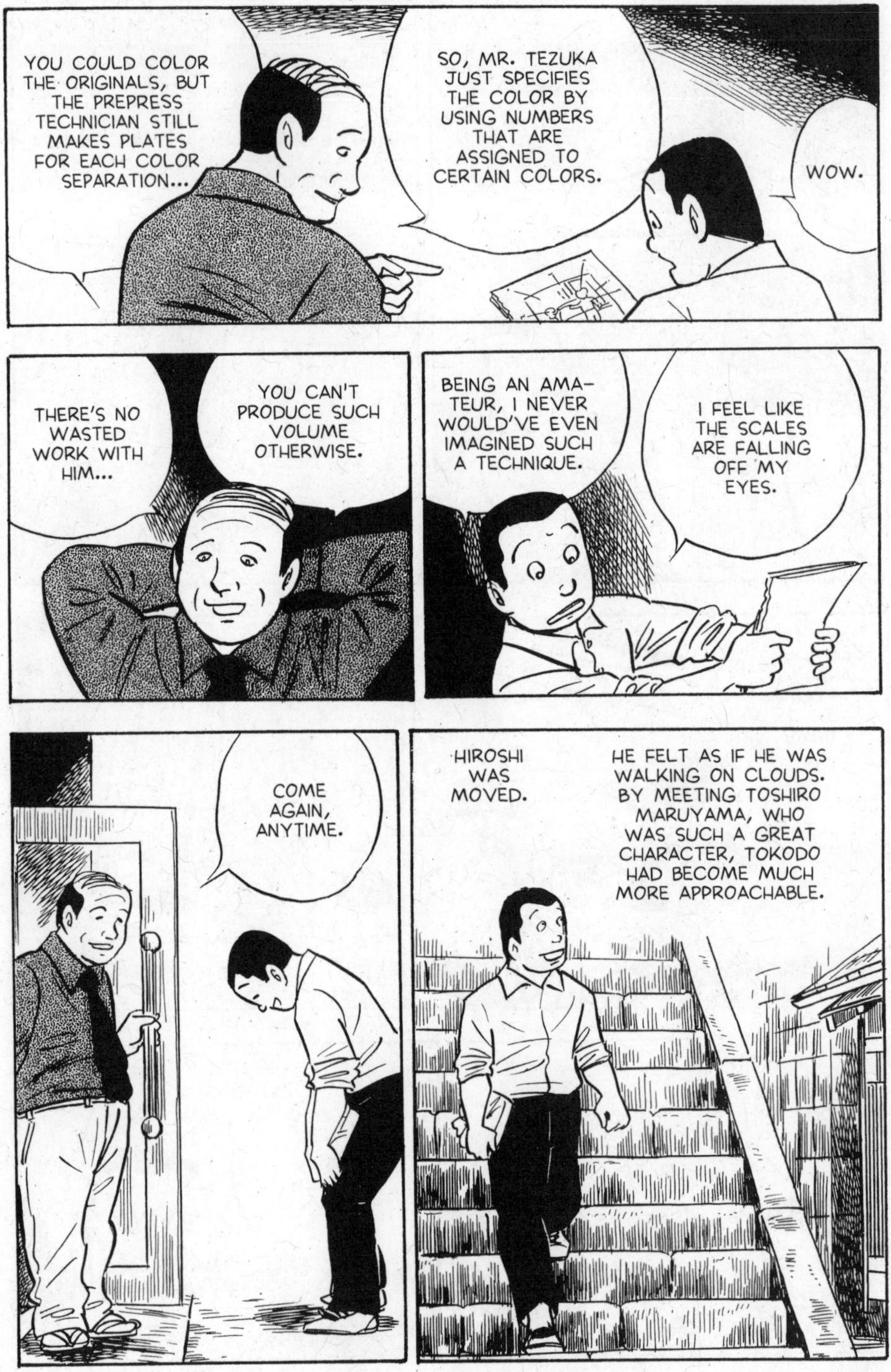
YOU COULD COLOR THE ORIGINALS, BUT THE PREPRESS TECHNICIAN STILL MAKES PLATES FOR EACH COLOR SEPARATION...
SO, MR. TEZUKA JUST SPECIFIES THE COLOR BY USING NUMBERS THAT ARE ASSIGNED TO CERTAIN COLORS.
WOW.
THERE'S NO WASTED WORK WITH HIM...
YOU CAN'T PRODUCE SUCH VOLUME OTHERWISE.
BEING AN AMATEUR, I NEVER WOULD'VE EVEN IMAGINED SUCH A TECHNIQUE.
I FEEL LIKE THE SCALES ARE FALLING OFF MY EYES.
COME AGAIN, ANYTIME.
HIROSHI WAS MOVED.
HE FELT AS IF HE WAS WALKING ON CLOUDS. BY MEETING TOSHIRO MARUYAMA, WHO WAS SUCH A GREAT CHARACTER, TOKODO HAD BECOME MUCH MORE APPROACHABLE.

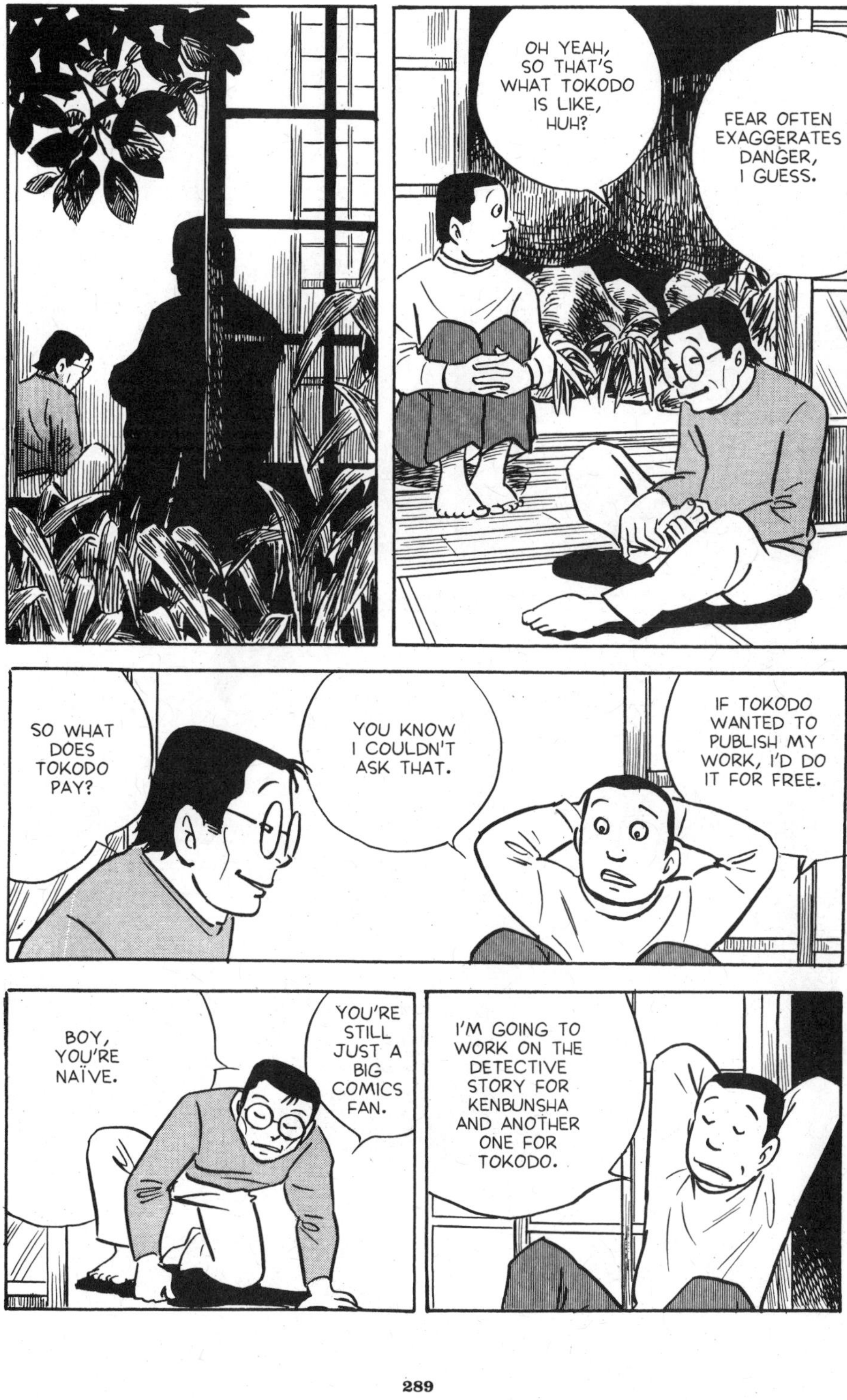
OH YEAH, SO THAT'S WHAT TOKODO IS LIKE, HUH?
FEAR OFTEN EXAGGERATES DANGER, I GUESS.
SO WHAT DOES TOKODO PAY?
YOU KNOW I COULDN'T ASK THAT.
IF TOKODO WANTED TO PUBLISH MY WORK, I'D DO IT FOR FREE.
BOY, YOU'RE NAÏVE.
YOU'RE STILL JUST A BIG COMICS FAN.
I'M GOING TO WORK ON THE DETECTIVE STORY FOR KENBUNSHA AND ANOTHER ONE FOR TOKODO.

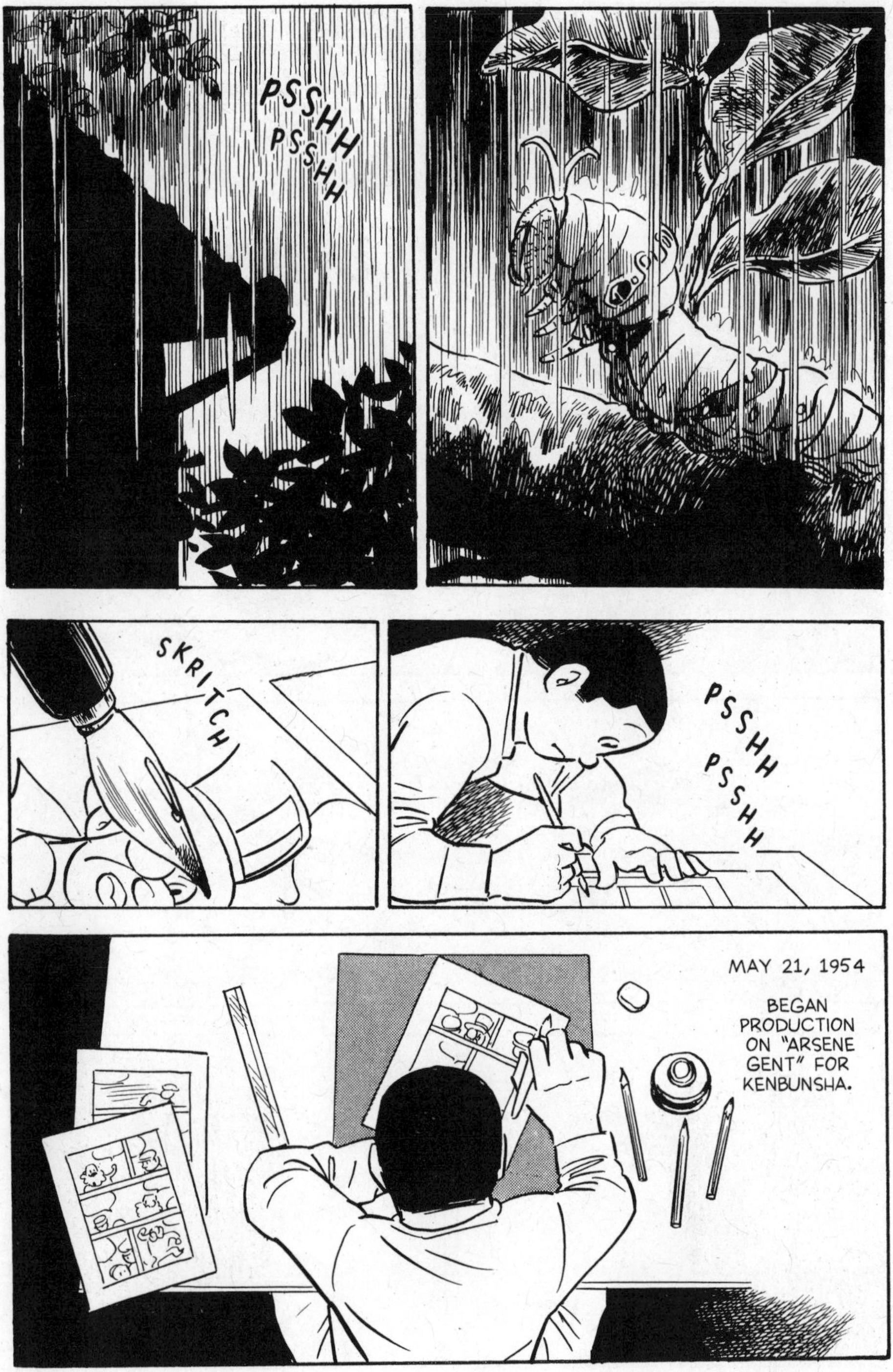
PSSHH
PSSHH
SKRITCH
PSSHH
PSSHH
MAY 21, 1954
BEGAN PRODUCTION ON "ARSENE GENT" FOR KENBUNSHA.

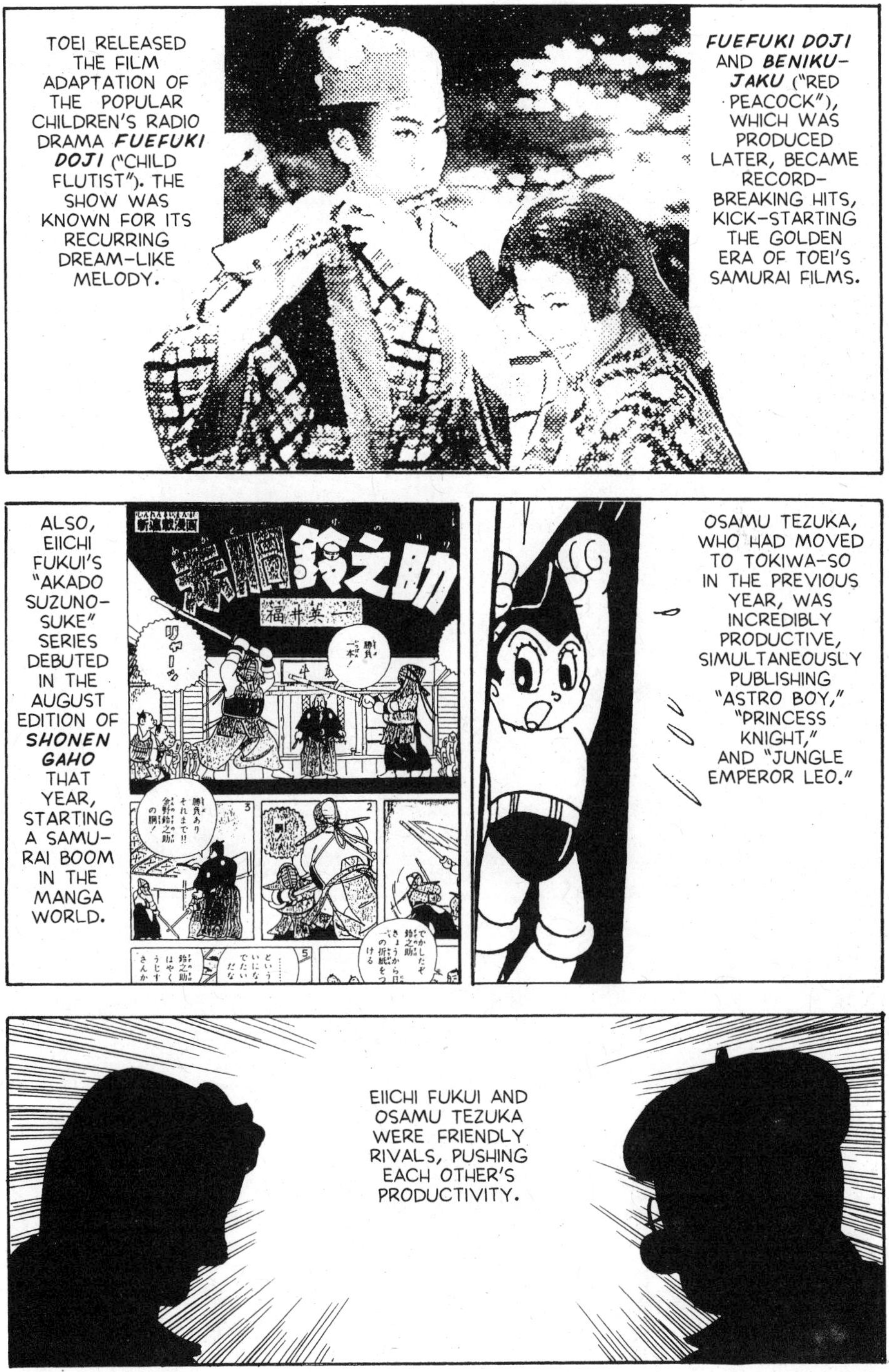
TOEI RELEASED THE FILM ADAPTATION OF THE POPULAR CHILDREN'S RADIO DRAMA ***FUEFUKI DOJI*** ("CHILD FLUTIST"). THE SHOW WAS KNOWN FOR ITS RECURRING DREAM-LIKE MELODY.
FUEFUKI DOJI AND ***BENIKU-JAKU*** ("RED PEACOCK"), WHICH WAS PRODUCED LATER, BECAME RECORD-BREAKING HITS, KICK-STARTING THE GOLDEN ERA OF TOEI'S SAMURAI FILMS.
ALSO, EIICHI FUKUI'S "AKADO SUZUNO-SUKE" SERIES DEBUTED IN THE AUGUST EDITION OF ***SHONEN GAHO*** THAT YEAR, STARTING A SAMU-RAI BOOM IN THE MANGA WORLD.
鈴之助
福井英一
OSAMU TEZUKA, WHO HAD MOVED TO TOKIWA-SO IN THE PREVIOUS YEAR, WAS INCREDIBLY PRODUCTIVE, SIMULTANEOUSLY PUBLISHING "ASTRO BOY," "PRINCESS KNIGHT," AND "JUNGLE EMPEROR LEO."
EIICHI FUKUI AND OSAMU TEZUKA WERE FRIENDLY RIVALS, PUSHING EACH OTHER'S PRODUCTIVITY.

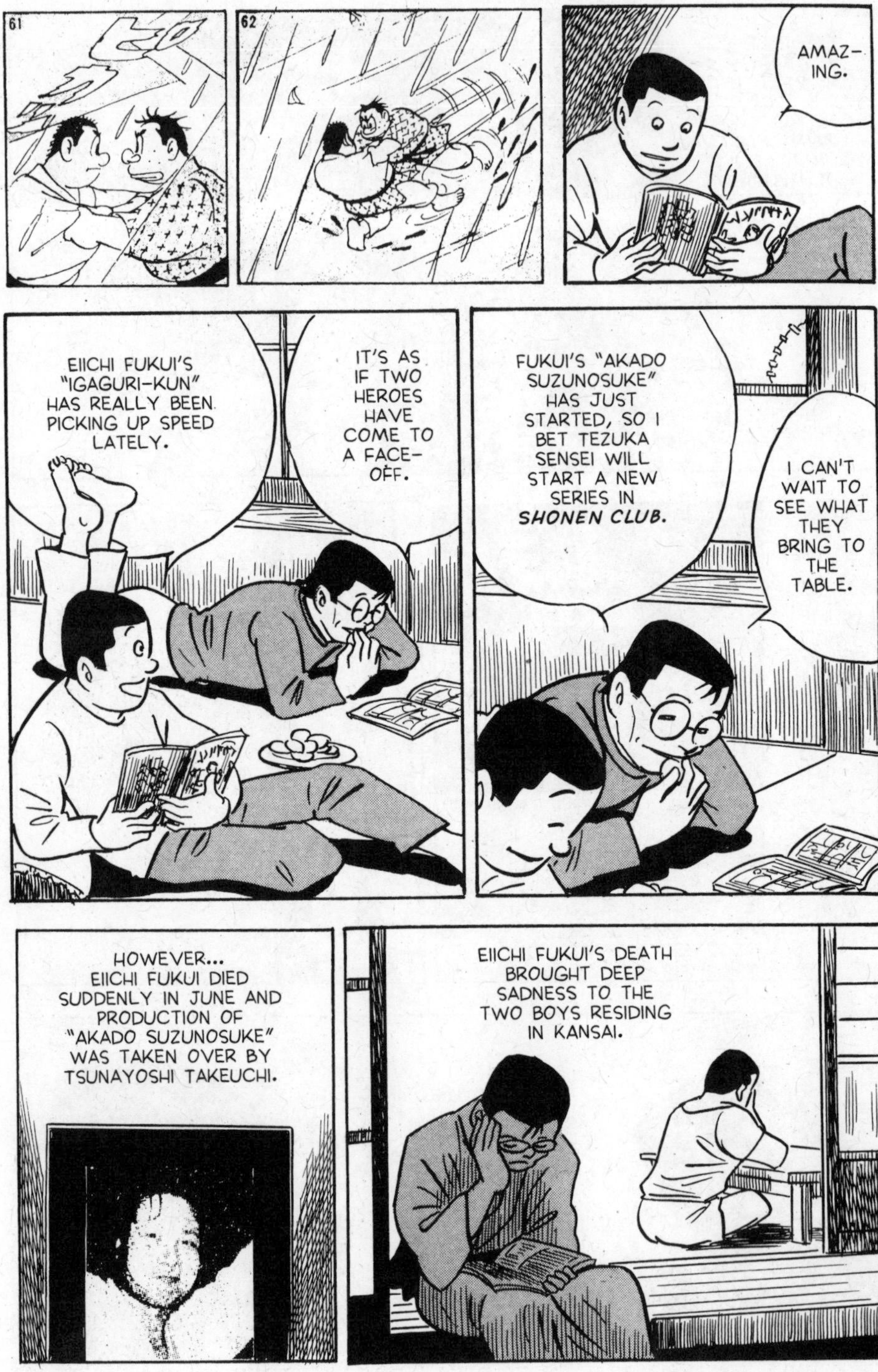
61
62
AMAZ-ING.
EIICHI FUKUI'S "IGAGURI-KUN" HAS REALLY BEEN PICKING UP SPEED LATELY.
IT'S AS IF TWO HEROES HAVE COME TO A FACE-OFF.
FUKUI'S "AKADO SUZUNOSUKE" HAS JUST STARTED, SO I BET TEZUKA SENSEI WILL START A NEW SERIES IN SHONEN CLUB.
I CAN'T WAIT TO SEE WHAT THEY BRING TO THE TABLE.
HOWEVER... EIICHI FUKUI DIED SUDDENLY IN JUNE AND PRODUCTION OF "AKADO SUZUNOSUKE" WAS TAKEN OVER BY TSUNAYOSHI TAKEUCHI.
EIICHI FUKUI'S DEATH BROUGHT DEEP SADNESS TO THE TWO BOYS RESIDING IN KANSAI.

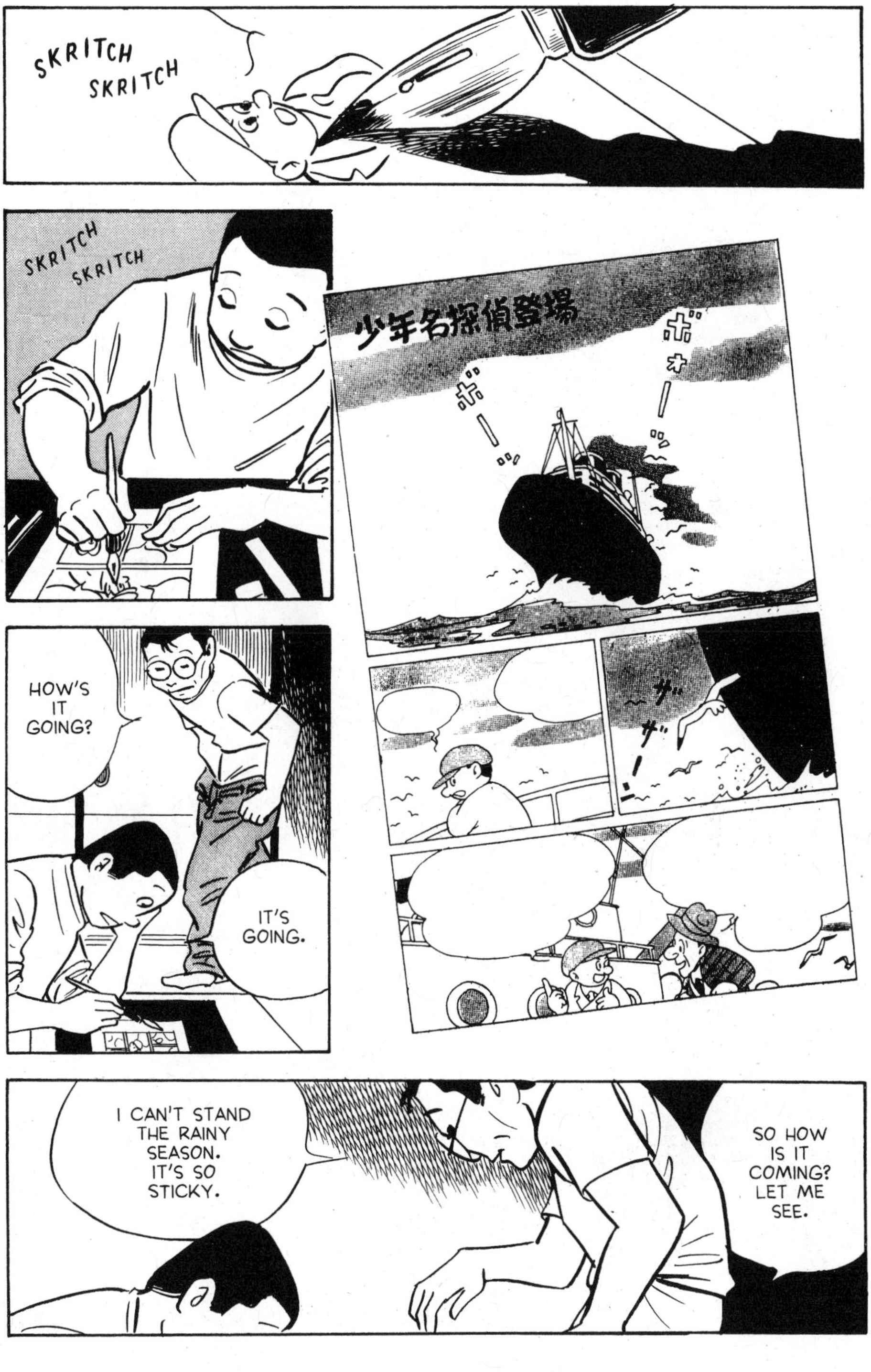
SKRITCH SKRITCH
SKRITCH SKRITCH
HOW'S IT GOING?
IT'S GOING.
少年名探偵登場
ボーッ
ボォーッ
ザザーッ
I CAN'T STAND THE RAINY SEASON. IT'S SO STICKY.
SO HOW IS IT COMING? LET ME SEE.

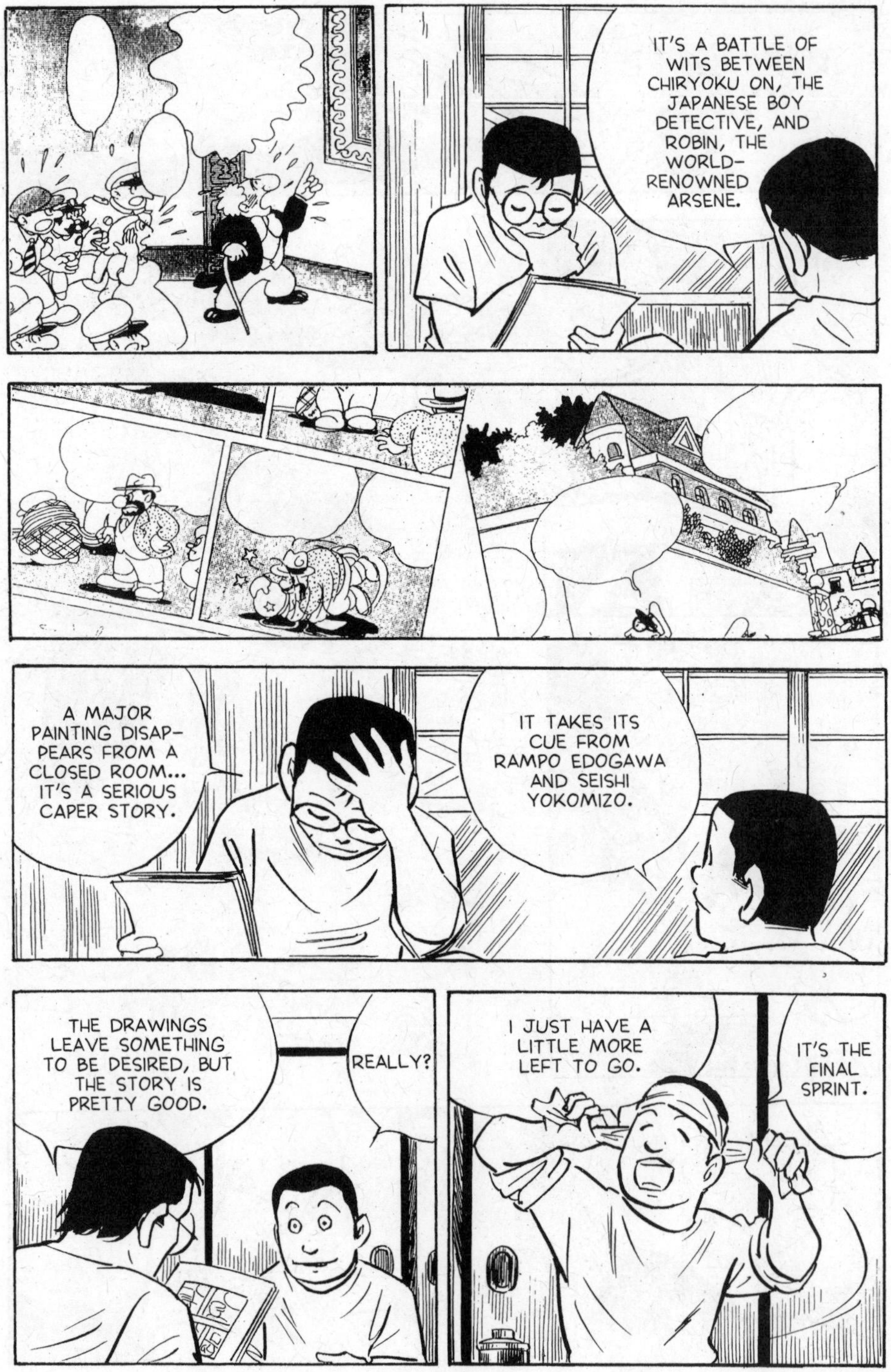
IT'S A BATTLE OF WITS BETWEEN CHIRYOKU ON, THE JAPANESE BOY DETECTIVE, AND ROBIN, THE WORLD-RENOWNED ARSENE.
A MAJOR PAINTING DISAPPEARS FROM A CLOSED ROOM... IT'S A SERIOUS CAPER STORY.
IT TAKES ITS CUE FROM RAMPO EDOGAWA AND SEISHI YOKOMIZO.
THE DRAWINGS LEAVE SOMETHING TO BE DESIRED, BUT THE STORY IS PRETTY GOOD.
REALLY?
I JUST HAVE A LITTLE MORE LEFT TO GO.
IT'S THE FINAL SPRINT.

AND THE BOAT SAILED QUIETLY AWAY.

SKRIT

TEXT: "END"

TAP

YEAH!

"ARSENE GENT" FINALLY COMPLETED!

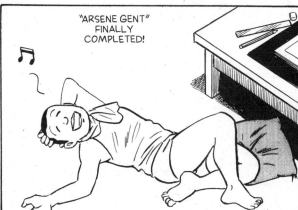

I'M HOME.

YOU FINISHED?

IT'S THE FIRST WORK OF MY PRO-FESSIONAL CAREER.

PROFESSIONAL MY ASS.

HEH HEH HEH HEH...

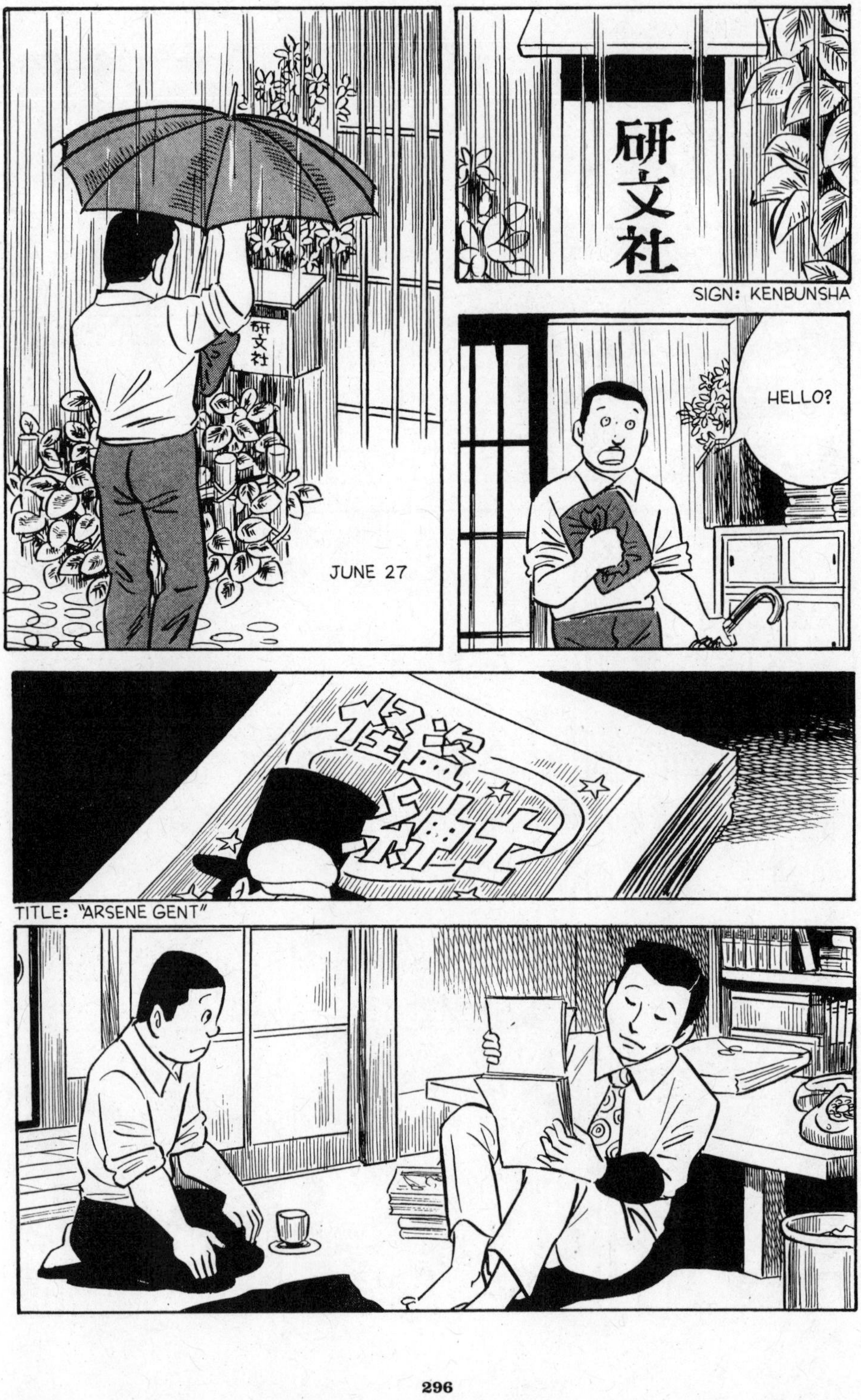
研文社
JUNE 27
研文社
SIGN: KENBUNSHA
HELLO?
怪盗紳士
TITLE: "ARSENE GENT"

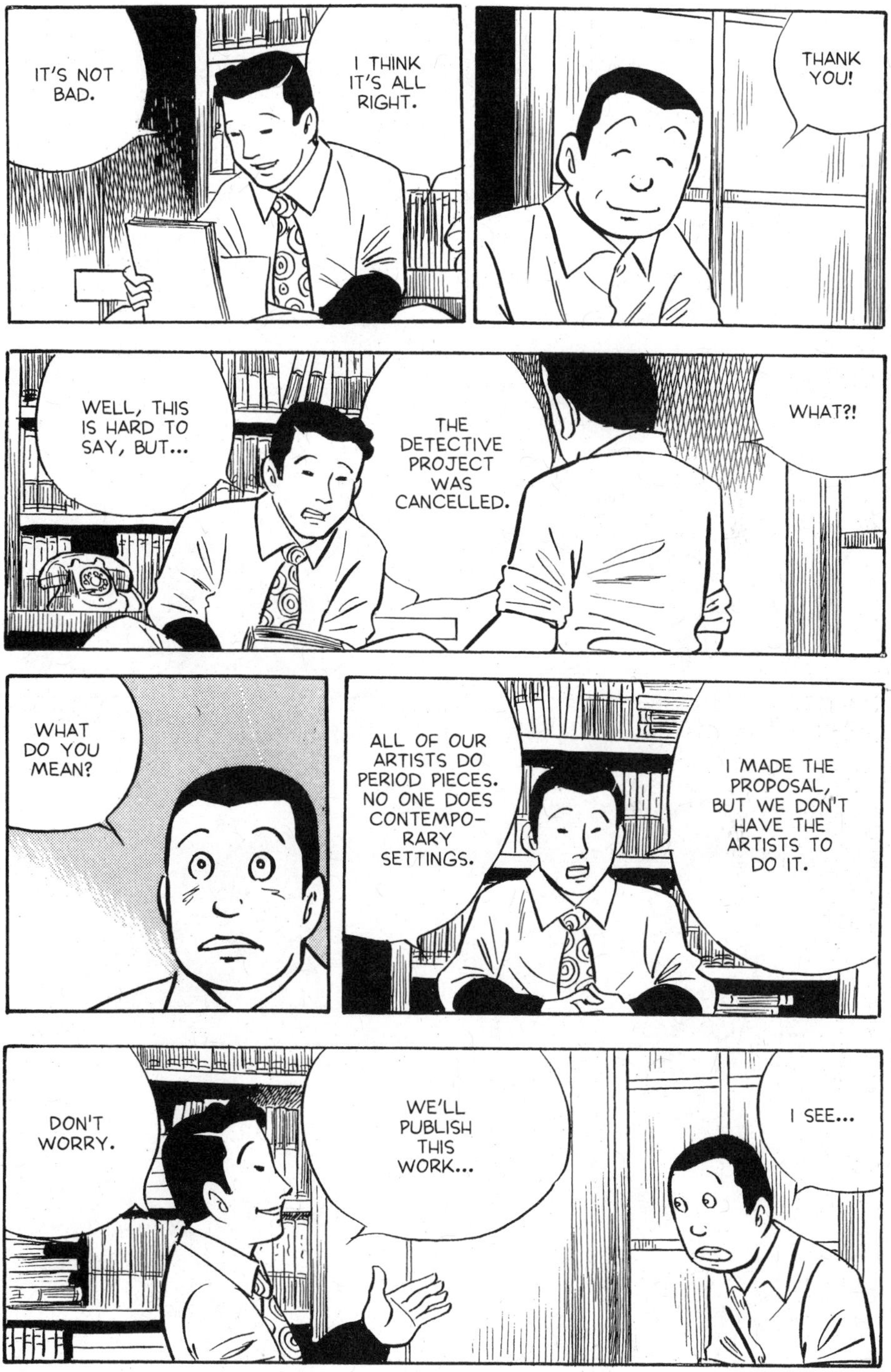
IT'S NOT BAD.
I THINK IT'S ALL RIGHT.
THANK YOU!
WELL, THIS IS HARD TO SAY, BUT...
THE DETECTIVE PROJECT WAS CANCELLED.
WHAT?!
WHAT DO YOU MEAN?
ALL OF OUR ARTISTS DO PERIOD PIECES. NO ONE DOES CONTEMPO-RARY SETTINGS.
I MADE THE PROPOSAL, BUT WE DON'T HAVE THE ARTISTS TO DO IT.
DON'T WORRY.
WE'LL PUBLISH THIS WORK...
I SEE...

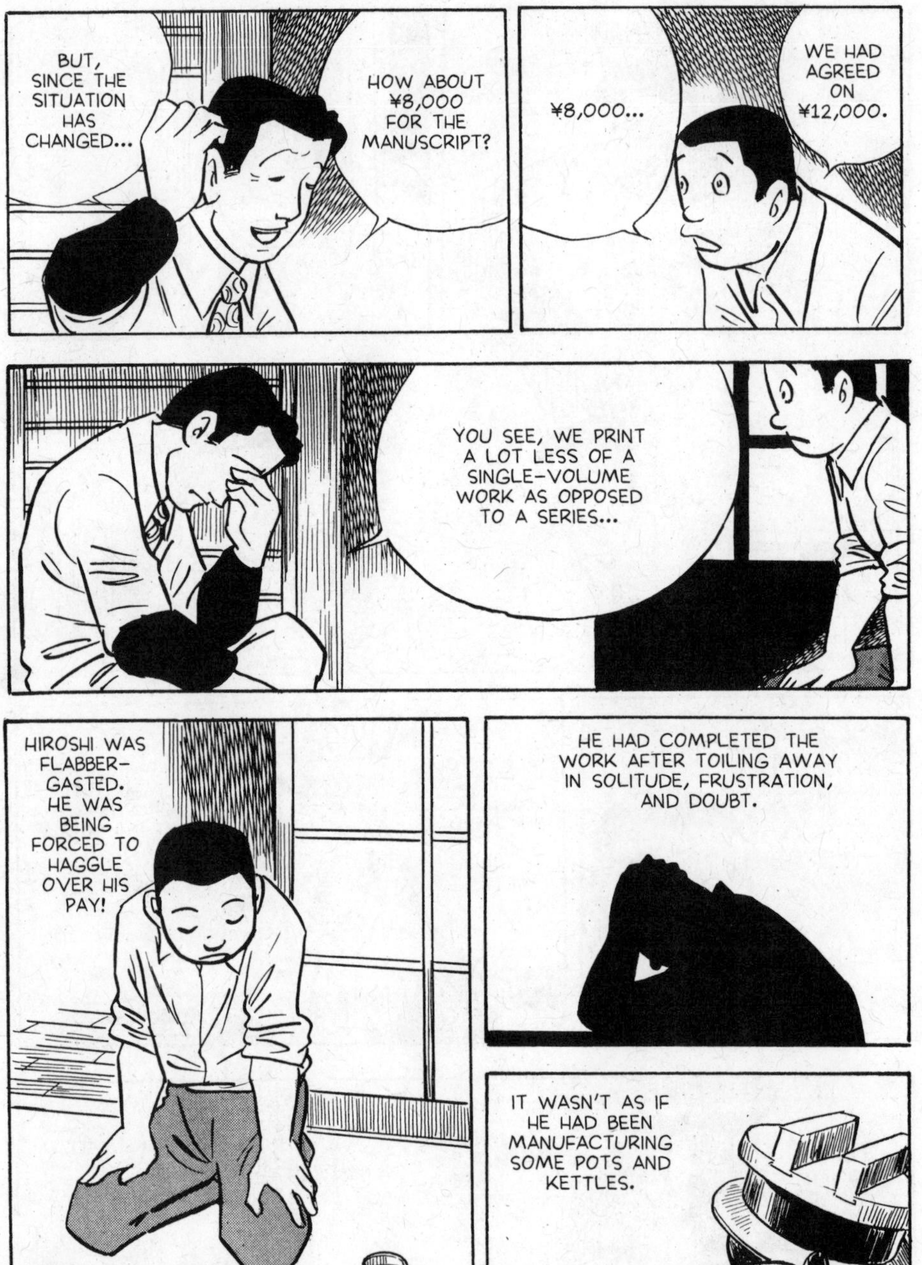
BUT, SINCE THE SITUATION HAS CHANGED...
HOW ABOUT ¥8,000 FOR THE MANUSCRIPT?
¥8,000...
WE HAD AGREED ON ¥12,000.
YOU SEE, WE PRINT A LOT LESS OF A SINGLE-VOLUME WORK AS OPPOSED TO A SERIES...
HIROSHI WAS FLABBER-GASTED. HE WAS BEING FORCED TO HAGGLE OVER HIS PAY!
HE HAD COMPLETED THE WORK AFTER TOILING AWAY IN SOLITUDE, FRUSTRATION, AND DOUBT.
IT WASN'T AS IF HE HAD BEEN MANUFACTURING SOME POTS AND KETTLES.

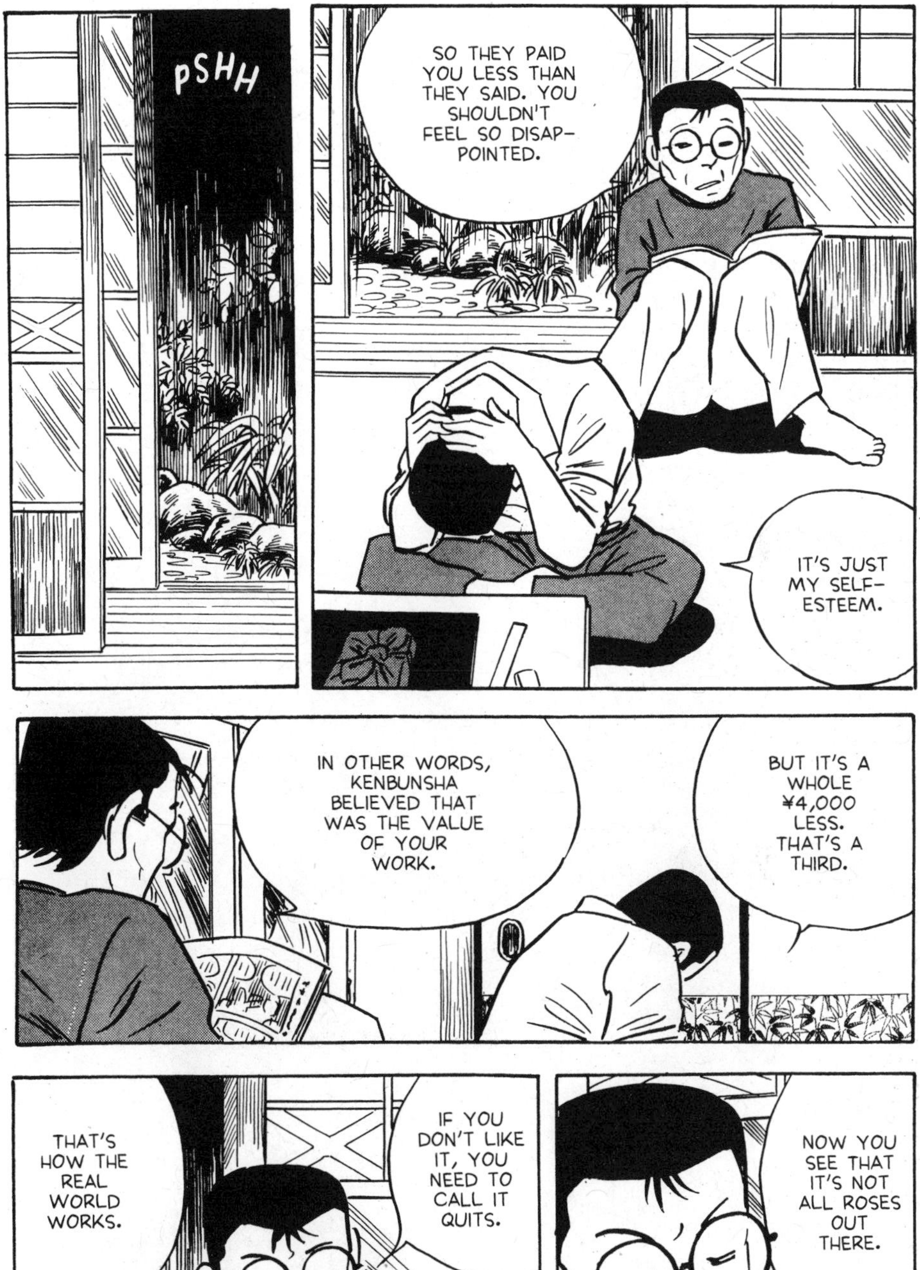
PSHH
SO THEY PAID YOU LESS THAN THEY SAID. YOU SHOULDN'T FEEL SO DISAP-POINTED.
IT'S JUST MY SELF-ESTEEM.
IN OTHER WORDS, KENBUNSHA BELIEVED THAT WAS THE VALUE OF YOUR WORK.
BUT IT'S A WHOLE ¥4,000 LESS. THAT'S A THIRD.
THAT'S HOW THE REAL WORLD WORKS.
IF YOU DON'T LIKE IT, YOU NEED TO CALL IT QUITS.
NOW YOU SEE THAT IT'S NOT ALL ROSES OUT THERE.

IS THIS THE SAME OKIMASA THAT TURNED PALE WHEN HE GOT HIS FIRST PAYCHECK?
I GUESS THE REAL WORLD HARDENS YOU QUICKLY.
WELL, I COMMEND YOU FOR NOT TAKING THE MONEY.
"ARSENE GENT" MARKS YOUR FIRST WORK AS A PRO. YOU SHOULD TREAT IT WELL.
THERE'S NO RUSH. JUST FIND ANOTHER PUBLISHER.
IF YOU WANT, I'LL GO WITH YOU. WE'LL HIT EVERY PUBLISHER IN OSAKA.

COLD CALLING

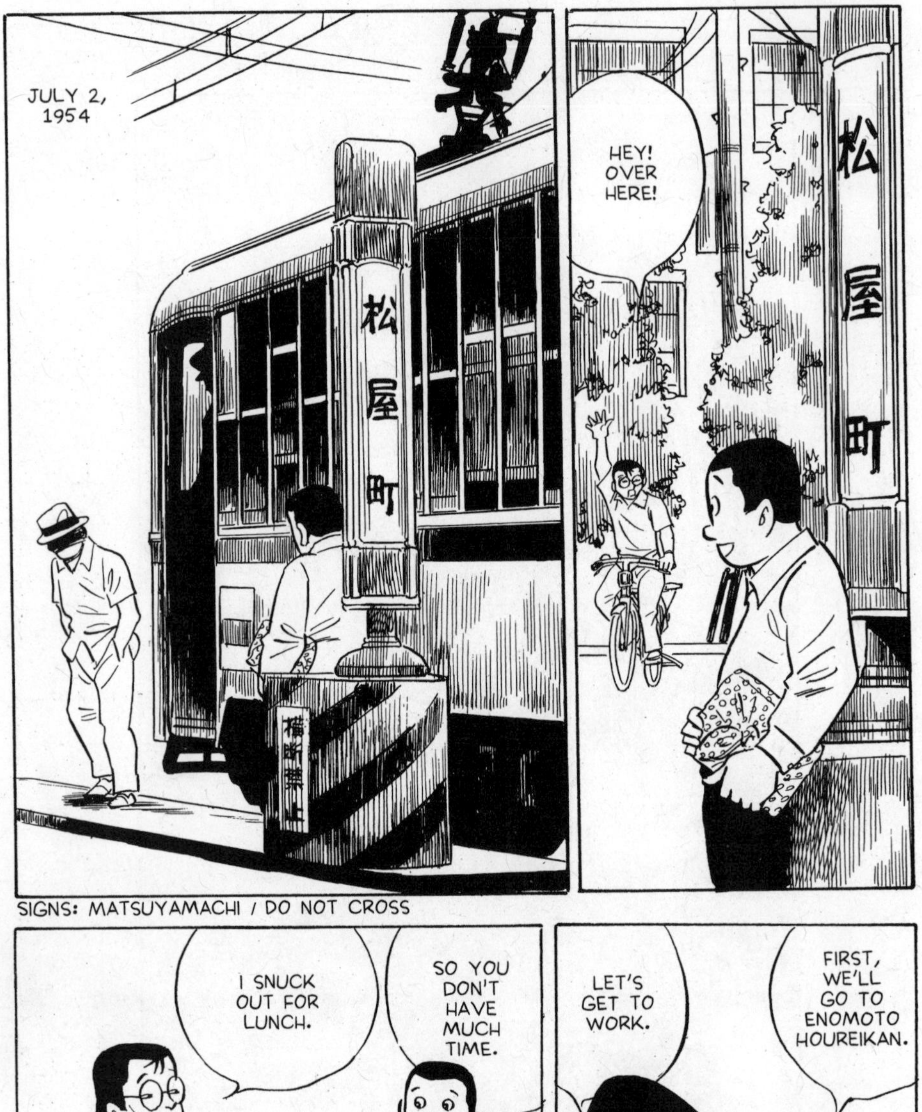

JULY 2, 1954
松屋町
横断禁止
HEY! OVER HERE!
松屋町

SIGNS: MATSUYAMACHI / DO NOT CROSS

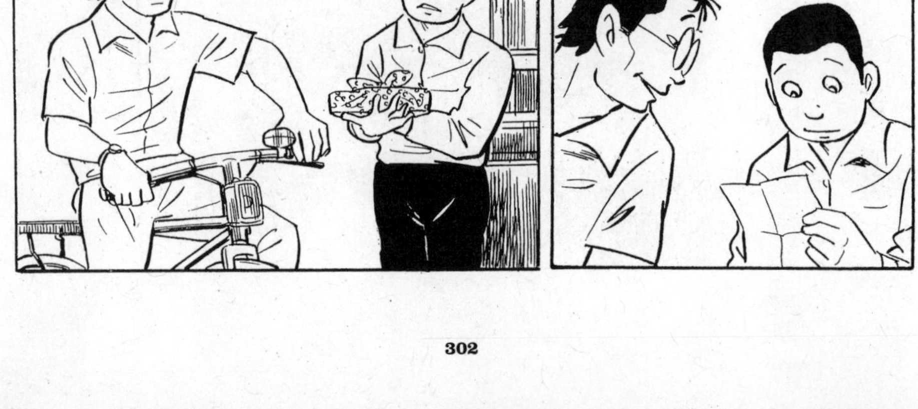

I SNUCK OUT FOR LUNCH.
SO YOU DON'T HAVE MUCH TIME.
LET'S GET TO WORK.
FIRST, WE'LL GO TO ENOMOTO HOUREIKAN.

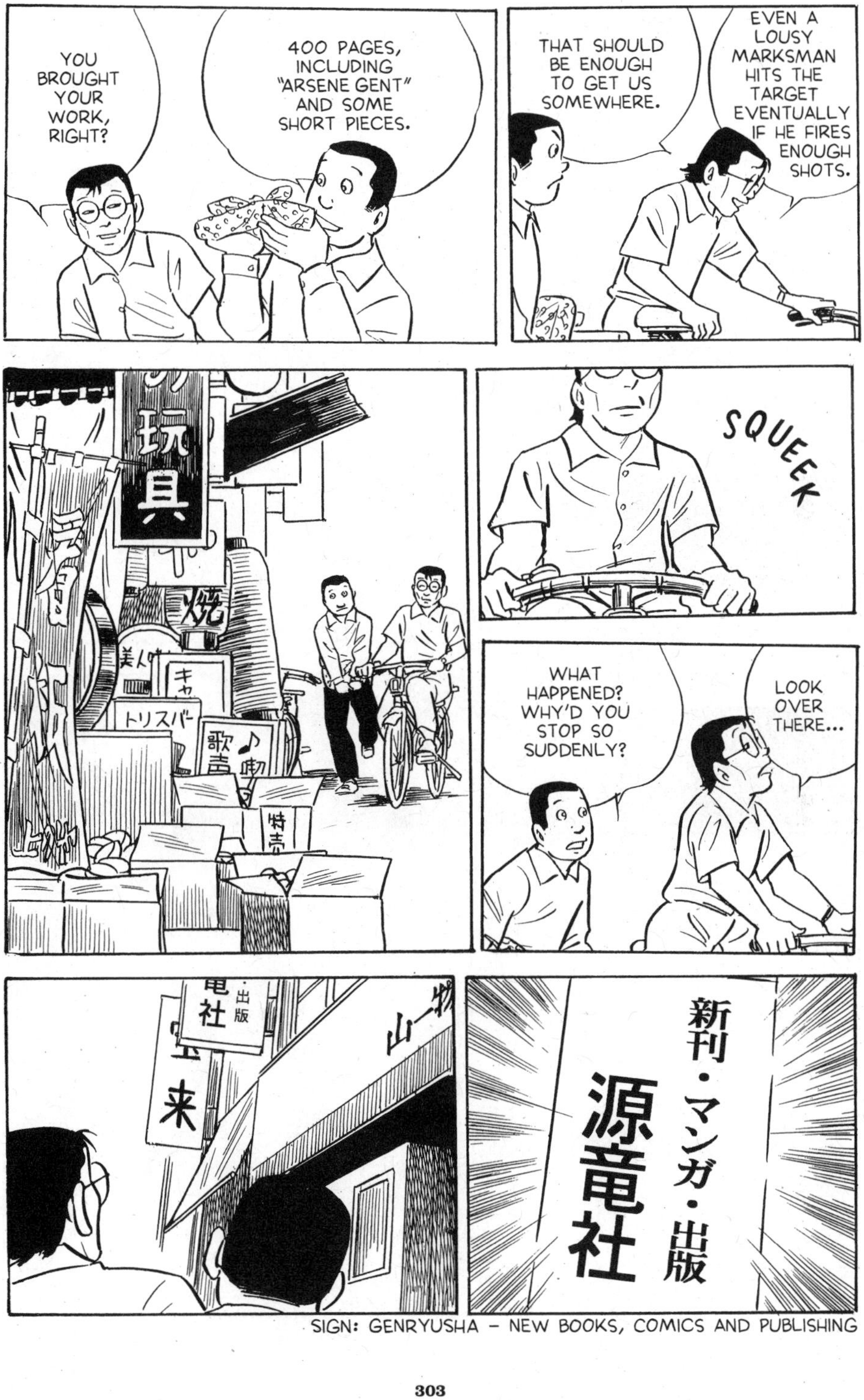

YOU BROUGHT YOUR WORK, RIGHT?
400 PAGES, INCLUDING "ARSENE GENT" AND SOME SHORT PIECES.
THAT SHOULD BE ENOUGH TO GET US SOMEWHERE.
EVEN A LOUSY MARKSMAN HITS THE TARGET EVENTUALLY IF HE FIRES ENOUGH SHOTS.
玩具
焼
トリスバー
SQUEEK
WHAT HAPPENED? WHY'D YOU STOP SO SUDDENLY?
LOOK OVER THERE...
新刊・マンガ・出版
源竜社

SIGN: GENRYUSHA – NEW BOOKS, COMICS AND PUBLISHING

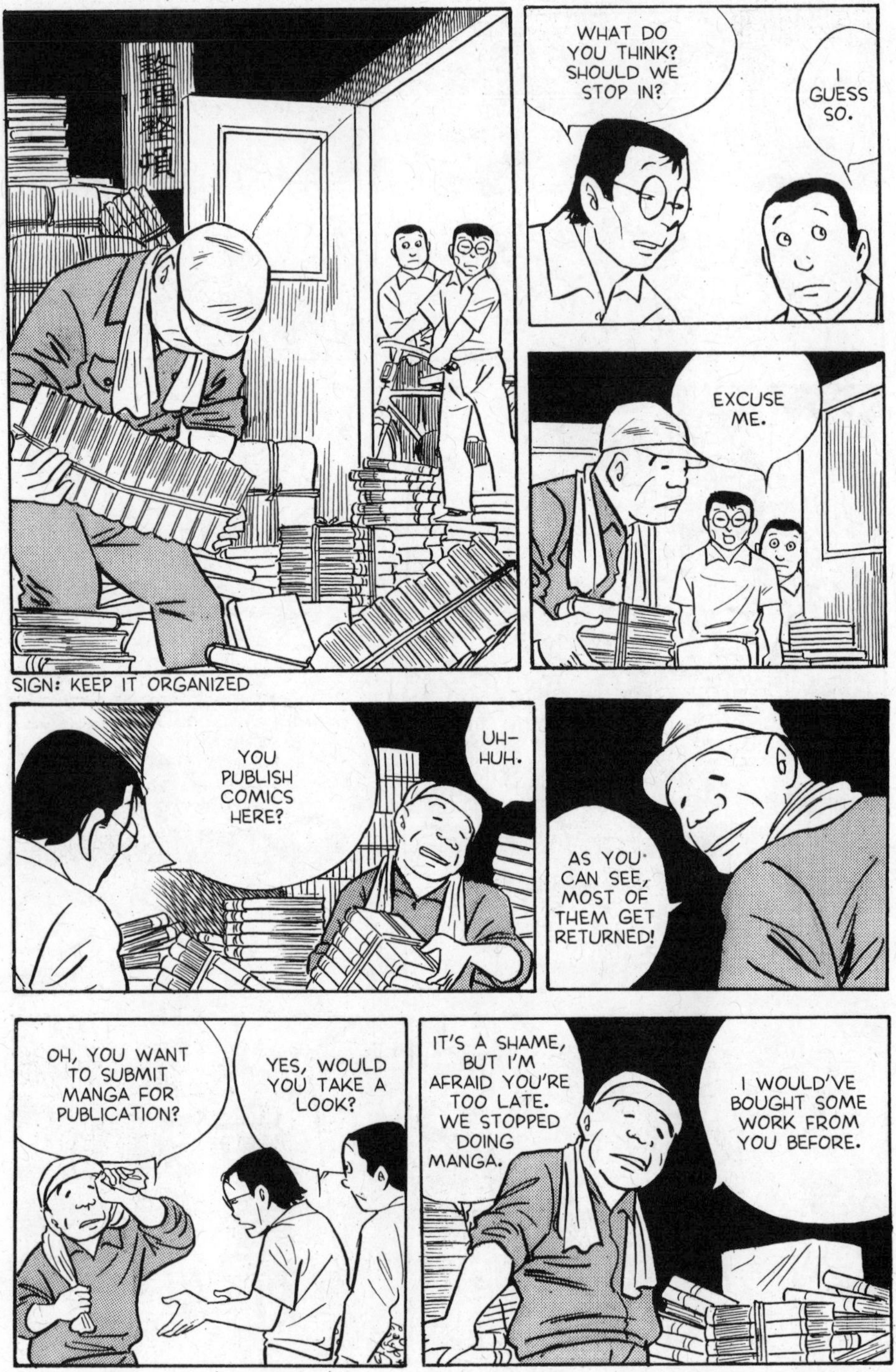
整理整頓
WHAT DO YOU THINK? SHOULD WE STOP IN?
I GUESS SO.
EXCUSE ME.
SIGN: KEEP IT ORGANIZED
YOU PUBLISH COMICS HERE?
UH-HUH.
AS YOU CAN SEE, MOST OF THEM GET RETURNED!
OH, YOU WANT TO SUBMIT MANGA FOR PUBLICATION?
YES, WOULD YOU TAKE A LOOK?
IT'S A SHAME, BUT I'M AFRAID YOU'RE TOO LATE. WE STOPPED DOING MANGA.
I WOULD'VE BOUGHT SOME WORK FROM YOU BEFORE.

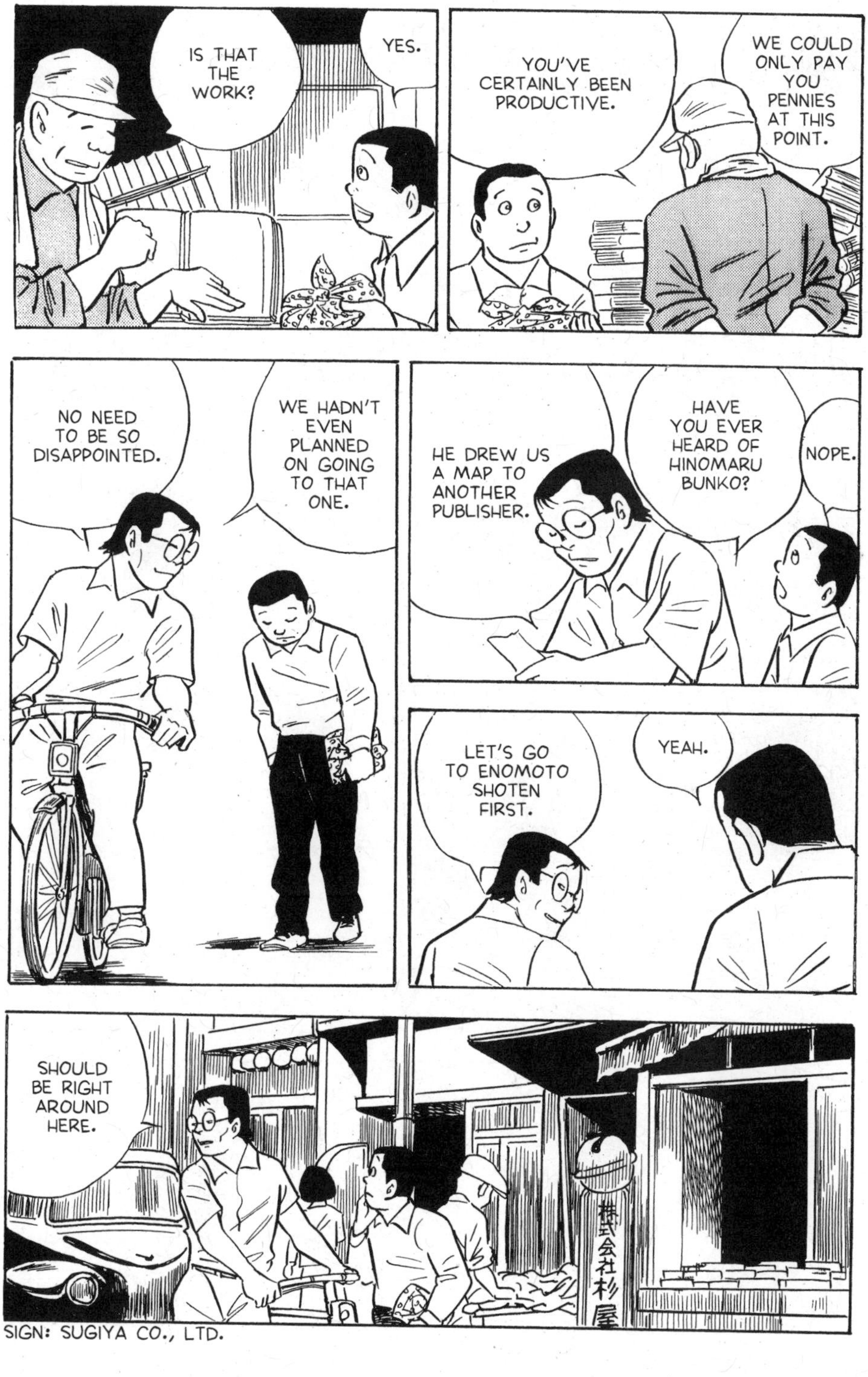
IS THAT THE WORK?
YES.
YOU'VE CERTAINLY BEEN PRODUCTIVE.
WE COULD ONLY PAY YOU PENNIES AT THIS POINT.
NO NEED TO BE SO DISAPPOINTED.
WE HADN'T EVEN PLANNED ON GOING TO THAT ONE.
HE DREW US A MAP TO ANOTHER PUBLISHER.
HAVE YOU EVER HEARD OF HINOMARU BUNKO?
NOPE.
LET'S GO TO ENOMOTO SHOTEN FIRST.
YEAH.
SHOULD BE RIGHT AROUND HERE.
株式会社杉屋
SIGN: SUGIYA CO., LTD.

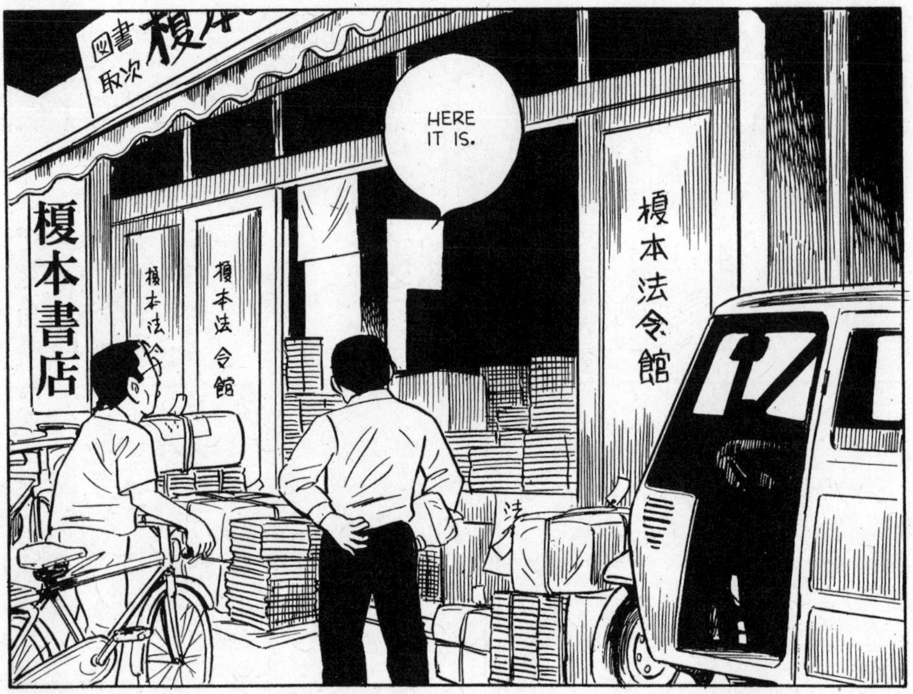
榎本書店
榎本法令館
HERE IT IS.

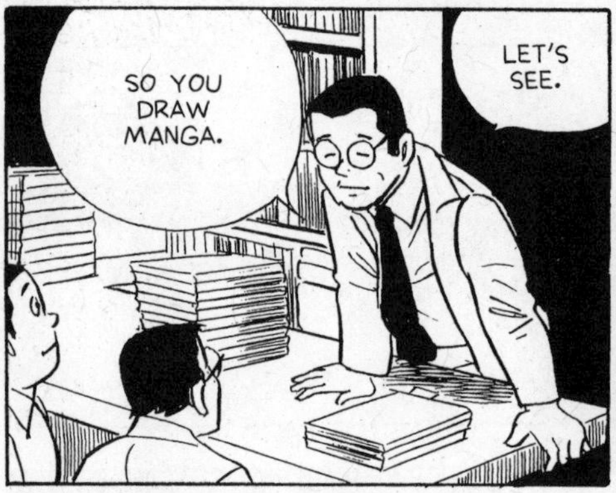
SO YOU DRAW MANGA.
LET'S SEE.

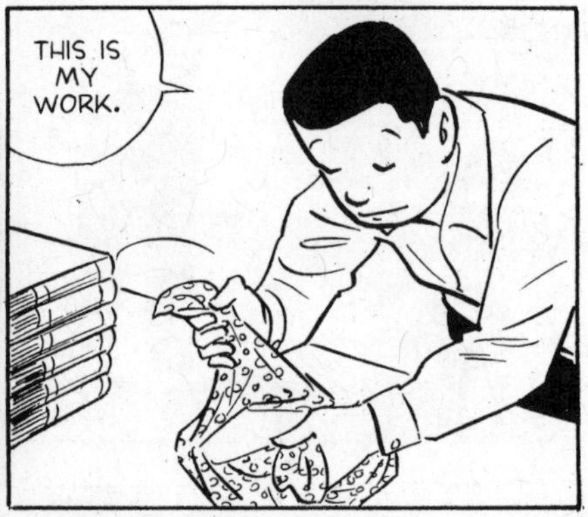
THIS IS MY WORK.

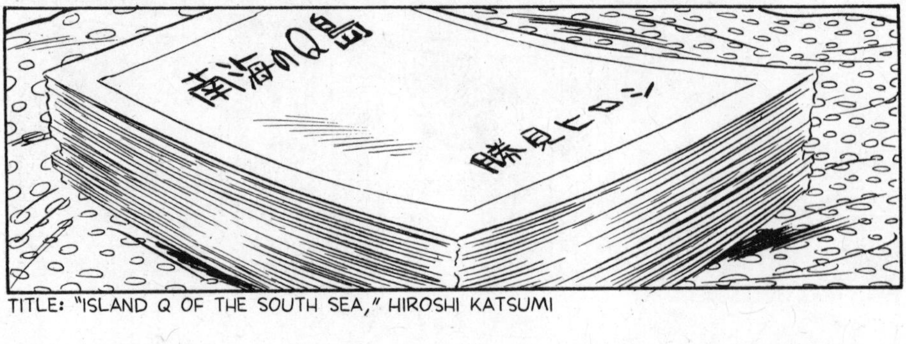
南海のQ島
勝見ヒロシ

TITLE: "ISLAND Q OF THE SOUTH SEA," HIROSHI KATSUMI

HAVE A SEAT OVER THERE WHILE I TAKE A LOOK.

SIGN: BOOKS NOW IN STOCK!

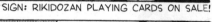

SIGN: RIKIDOZAN PLAYING CARDS ON SALE!

TITLE: "ARSENE GENT"

THANKS FOR WAITING.

I THINK WE MAY BE ABLE TO PUBLISH "ARSENE GENT."

REALLY?!

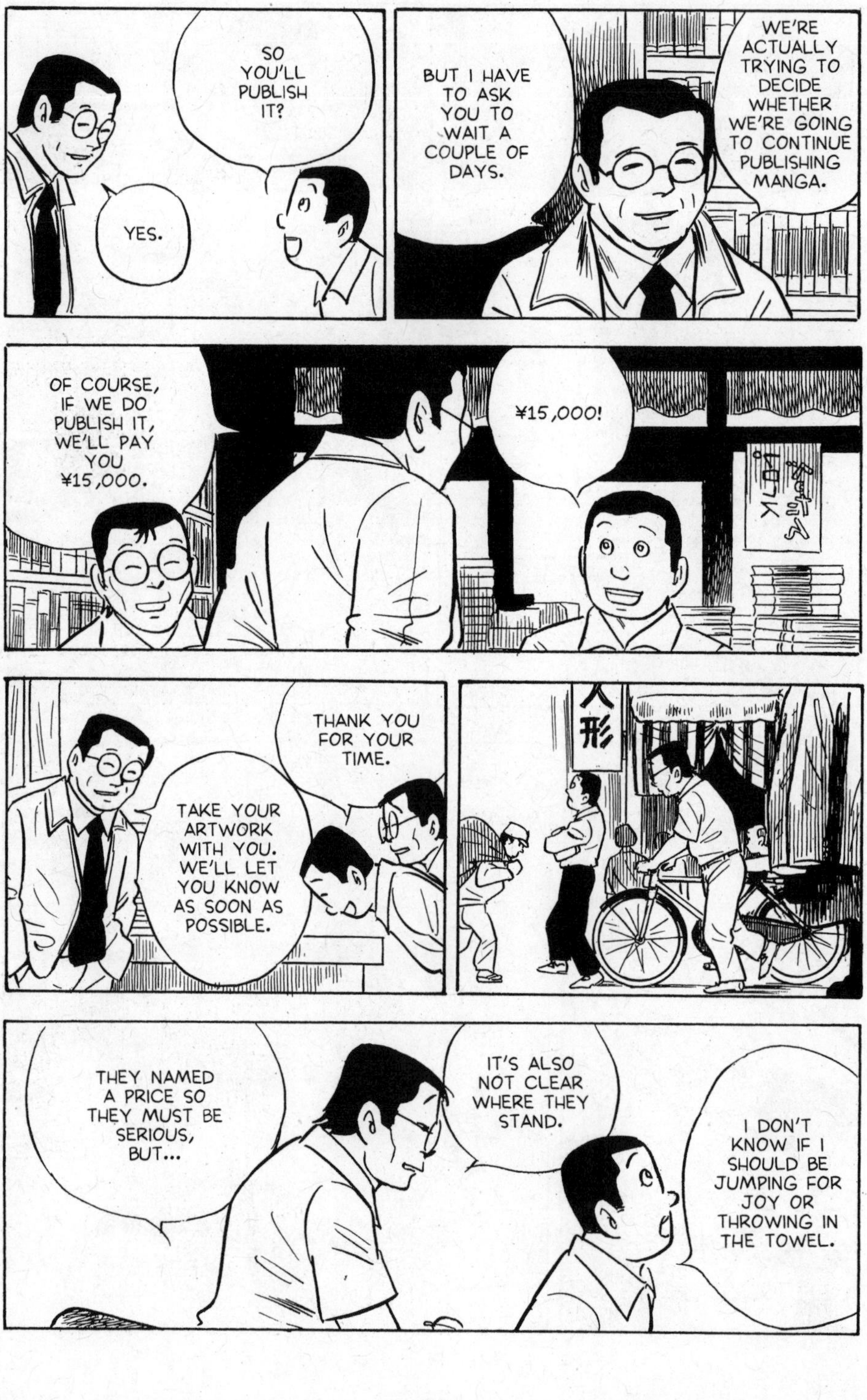
SO YOU'LL PUBLISH IT?
YES.
BUT I HAVE TO ASK YOU TO WAIT A COUPLE OF DAYS.
WE'RE ACTUALLY TRYING TO DECIDE WHETHER WE'RE GOING TO CONTINUE PUBLISHING MANGA.
OF COURSE, IF WE DO PUBLISH IT, WE'LL PAY YOU ¥15,000.
¥15,000!
THANK YOU FOR YOUR TIME.
TAKE YOUR ARTWORK WITH YOU. WE'LL LET YOU KNOW AS SOON AS POSSIBLE.
人形
THEY NAMED A PRICE SO THEY MUST BE SERIOUS, BUT...
IT'S ALSO NOT CLEAR WHERE THEY STAND.
I DON'T KNOW IF I SHOULD BE JUMPING FOR JOY OR THROWING IN THE TOWEL.

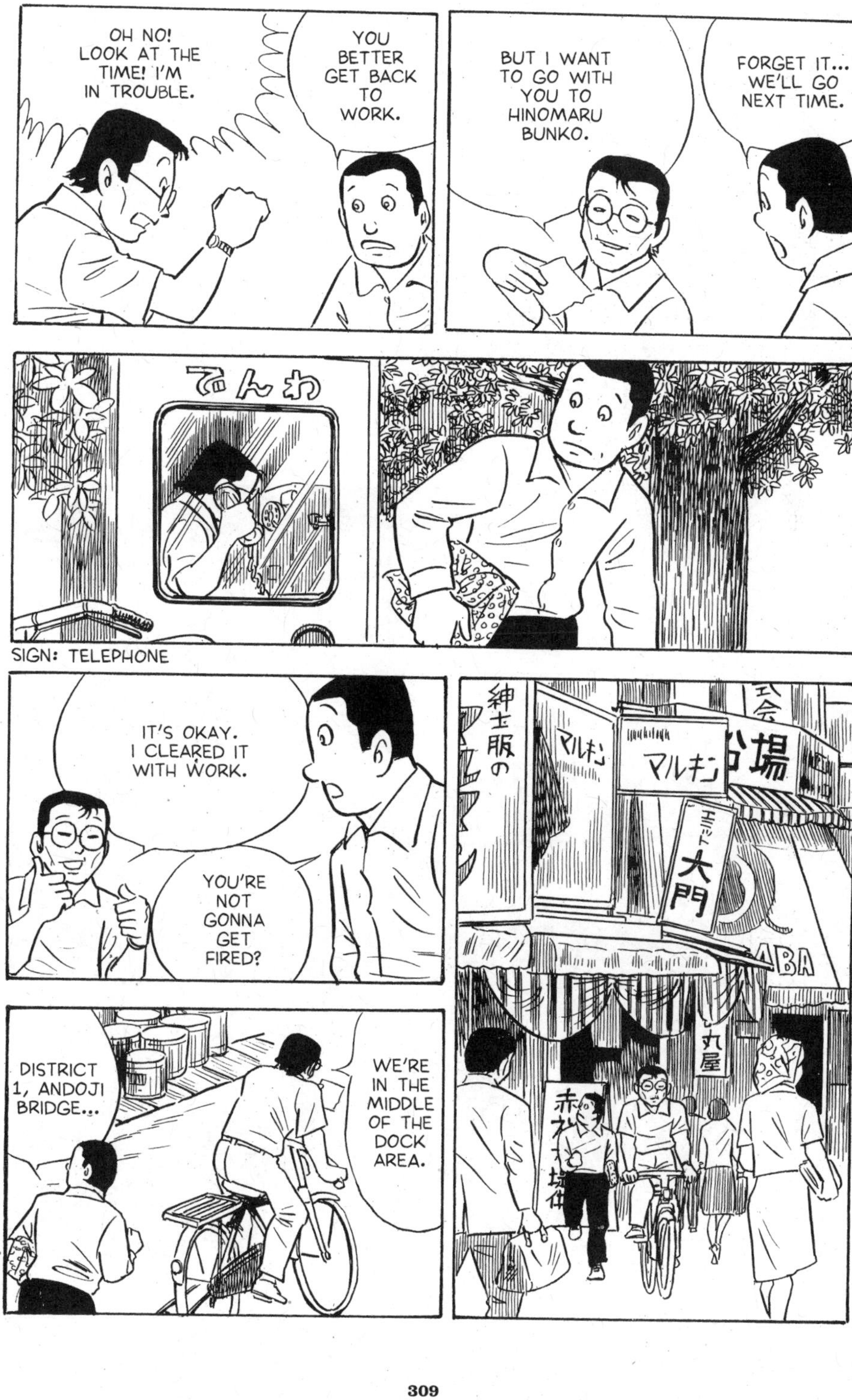
OH NO! LOOK AT THE TIME! I'M IN TROUBLE.
YOU BETTER GET BACK TO WORK.
BUT I WANT TO GO WITH YOU TO HINOMARU BUNKO.
FORGET IT... WE'LL GO NEXT TIME.
でんわ
SIGN: TELEPHONE
IT'S OKAY. I CLEARED IT WITH WORK.
YOU'RE NOT GONNA GET FIRED?
DISTRICT 1, ANDOJI BRIDGE...
WE'RE IN THE MIDDLE OF THE DOCK AREA.
紳士服の
マルキン
マルキン
大門

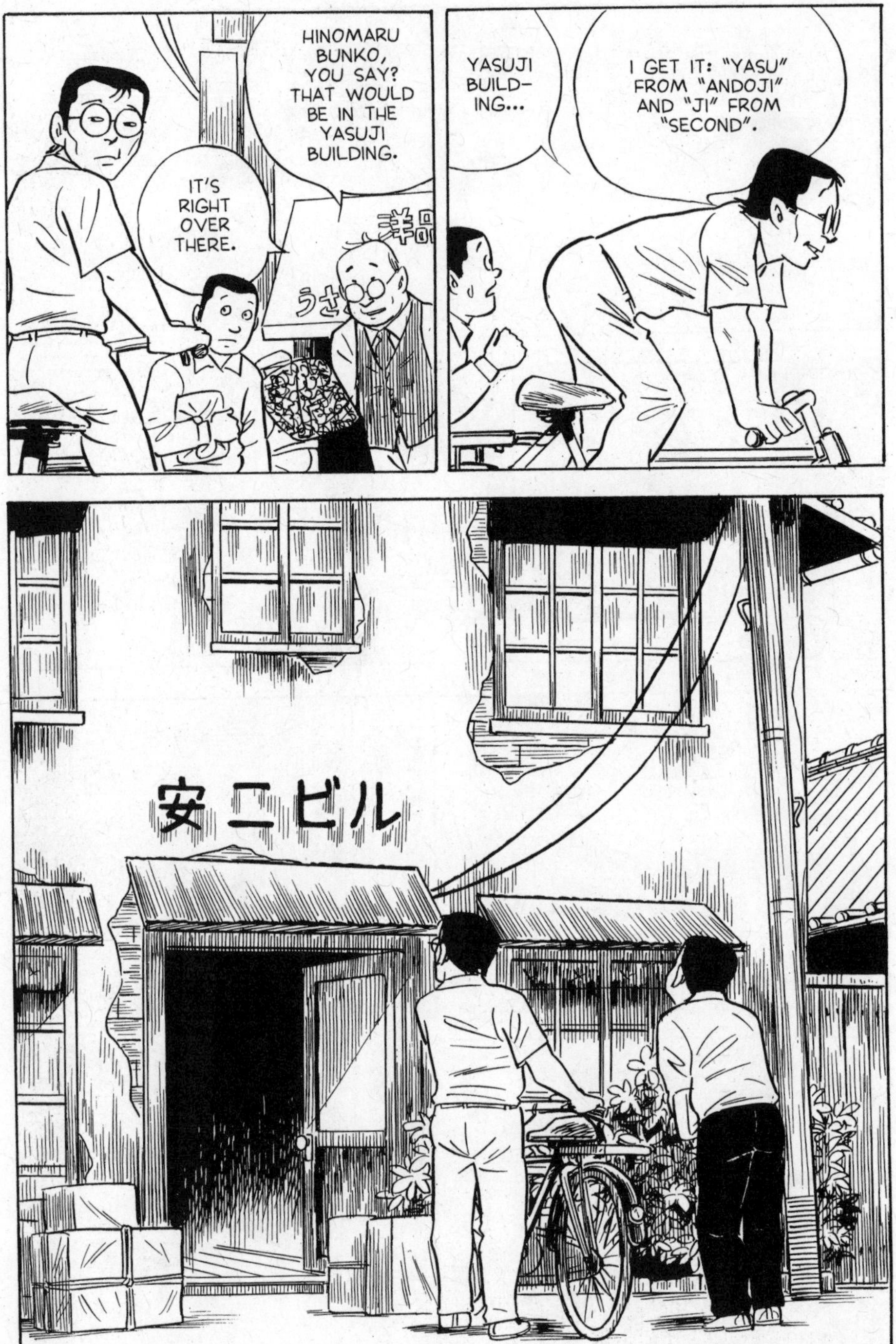
HINOMARU BUNKO, YOU SAY? THAT WOULD BE IN THE YASUJI BUILDING.
IT'S RIGHT OVER THERE.
YASUJI BUILDING...
I GET IT: "YASU" FROM "ANDOJI" AND "JI" FROM "SECOND".
安二ビル
SIGN: YASUJI BUILDING

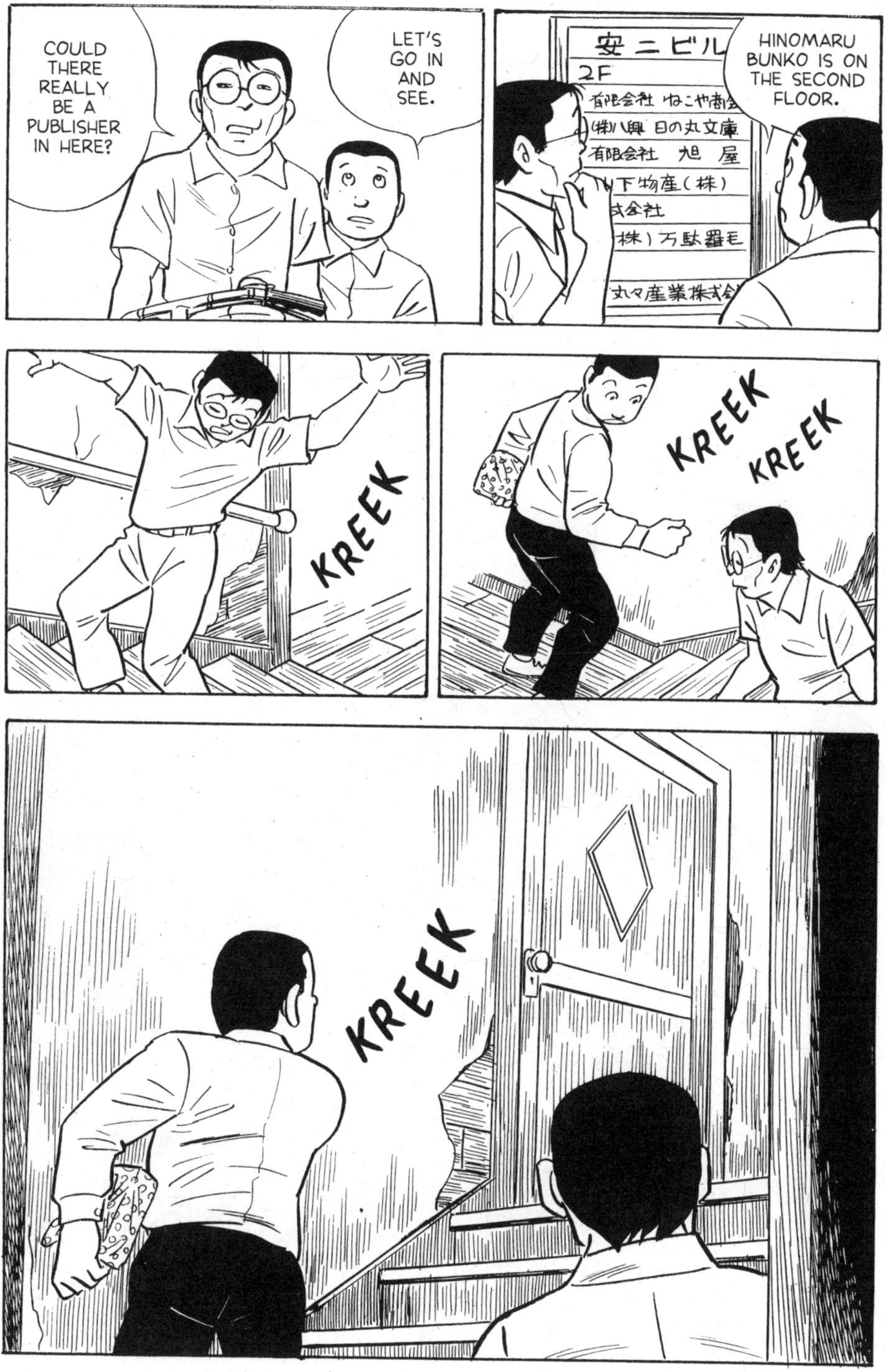
COULD THERE REALLY BE A PUBLISHER IN HERE?
LET'S GO IN AND SEE.
安ニビル
2F
(株)八興 日の丸文庫
有限会社 旭屋
HINOMARU BUNKO IS ON THE SECOND FLOOR.
KREEK
KREEK
KREEK
KREEK

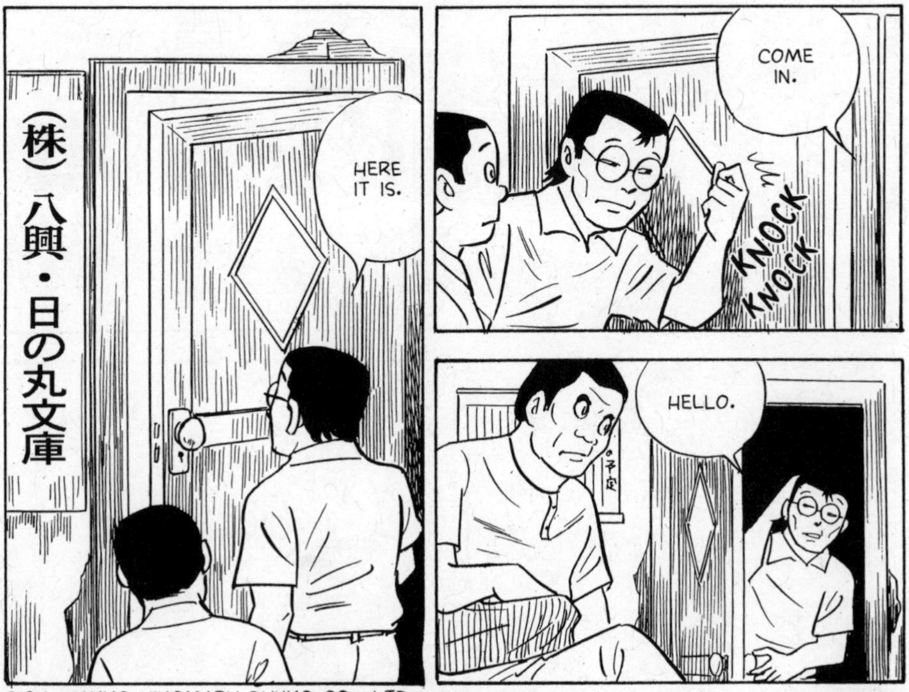
(株) 八興・日の丸文庫
HERE IT IS.
COME IN.
KNOCK KNOCK
HELLO.

SIGN: HAKKO HINOMARU BUNKO CO., LTD.

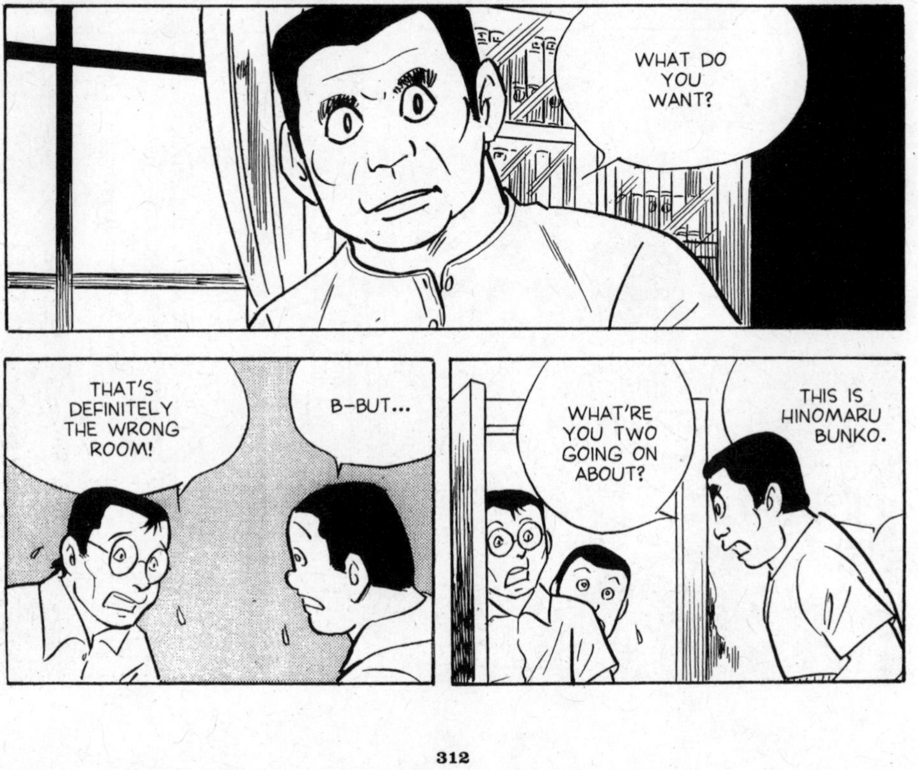
WHAT DO YOU WANT?
THAT'S DEFINITELY THE WRONG ROOM!
B-BUT...
WHAT'RE YOU TWO GOING ON ABOUT?
THIS IS HINOMARU BUNKO.

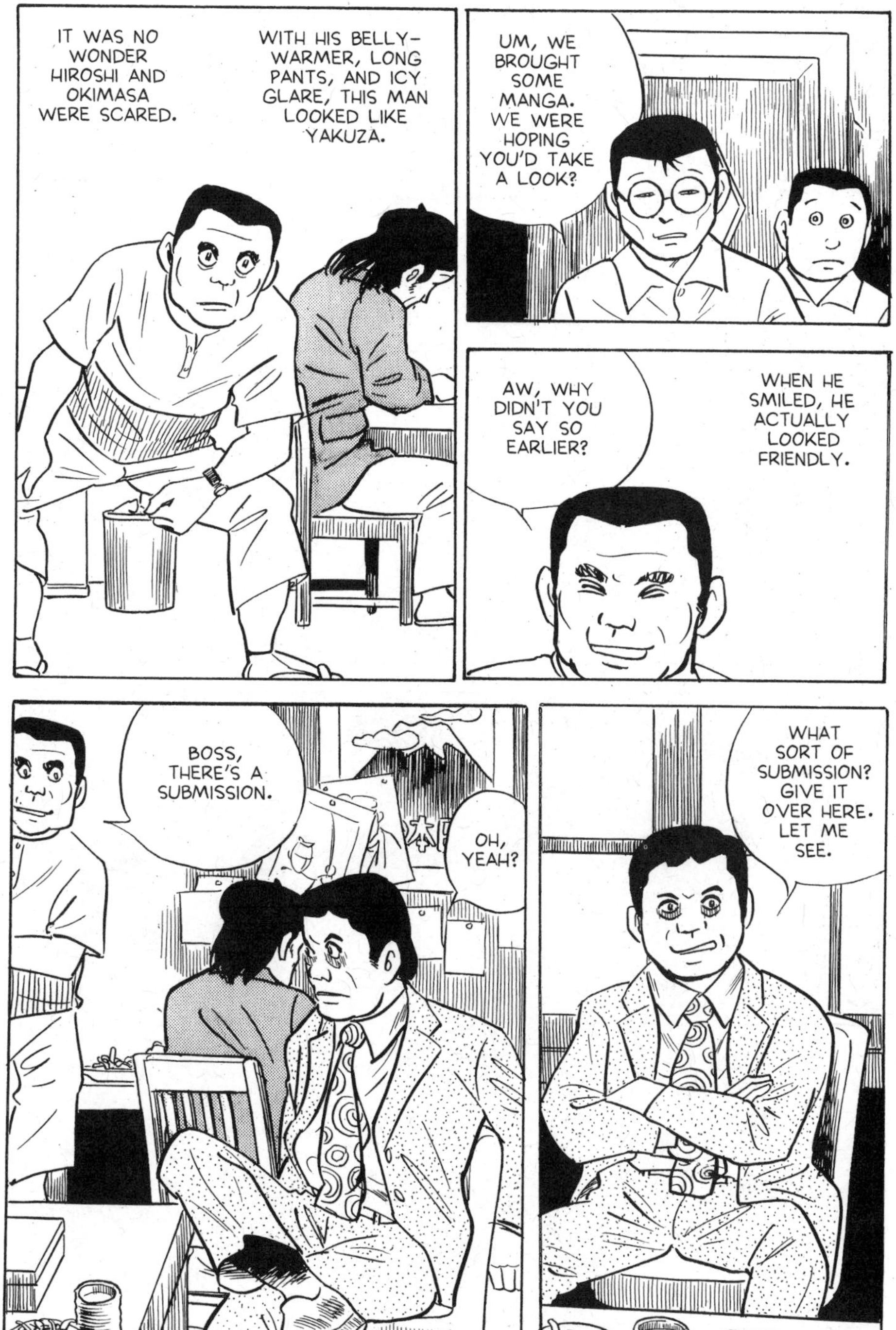
IT WAS NO WONDER HIROSHI AND OKIMASA WERE SCARED.
WITH HIS BELLY-WARMER, LONG PANTS, AND ICY GLARE, THIS MAN LOOKED LIKE YAKUZA.
UM, WE BROUGHT SOME MANGA. WE WERE HOPING YOU'D TAKE A LOOK?
AW, WHY DIDN'T YOU SAY SO EARLIER?
WHEN HE SMILED, HE ACTUALLY LOOKED FRIENDLY.
BOSS, THERE'S A SUBMISSION.
OH, YEAH?
WHAT SORT OF SUBMISSION? GIVE IT OVER HERE. LET ME SEE.

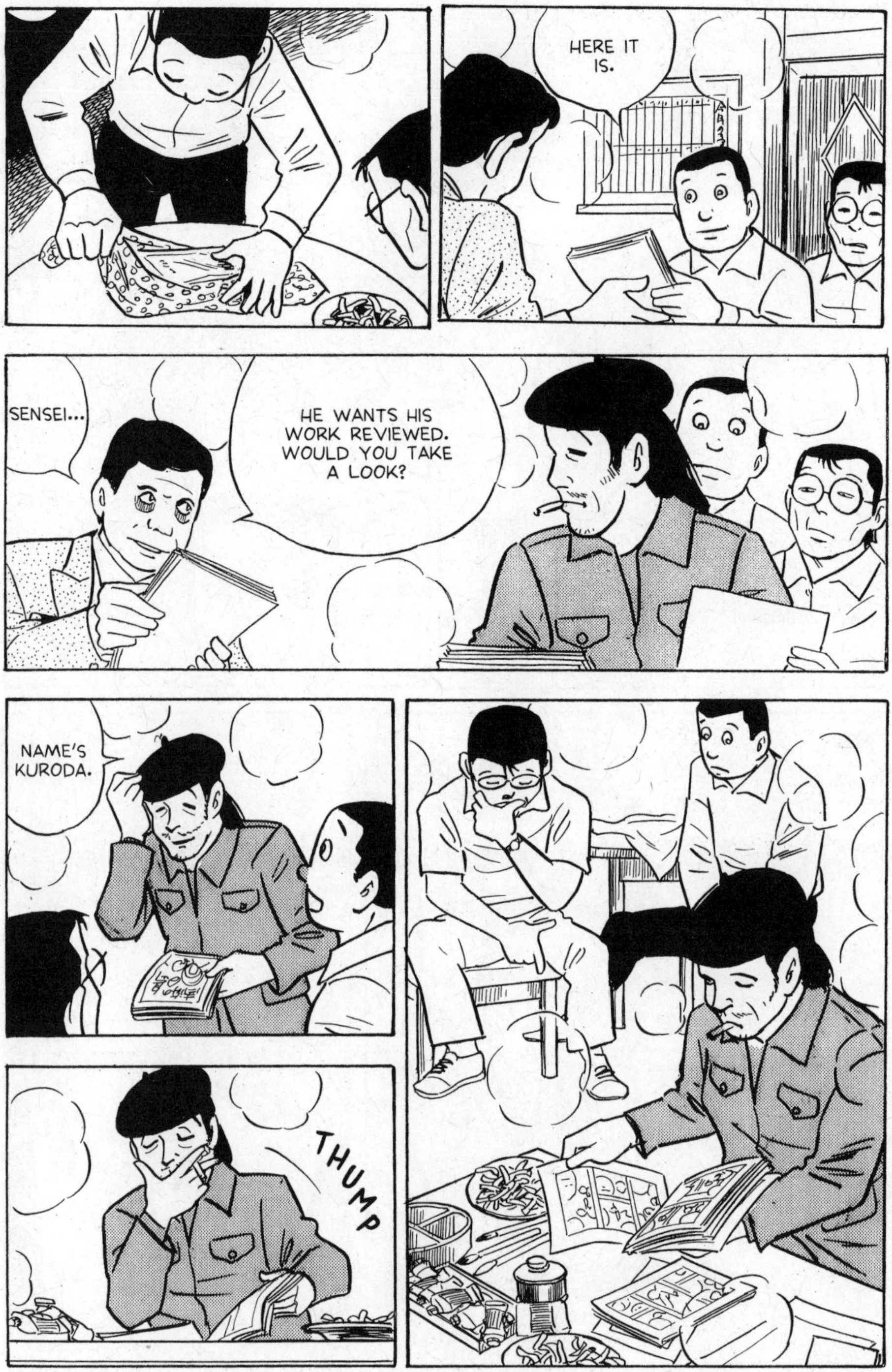
HERE IT IS.
SENSEI...
HE WANTS HIS WORK REVIEWED. WOULD YOU TAKE A LOOK?
NAME'S KURODA.
THUMP

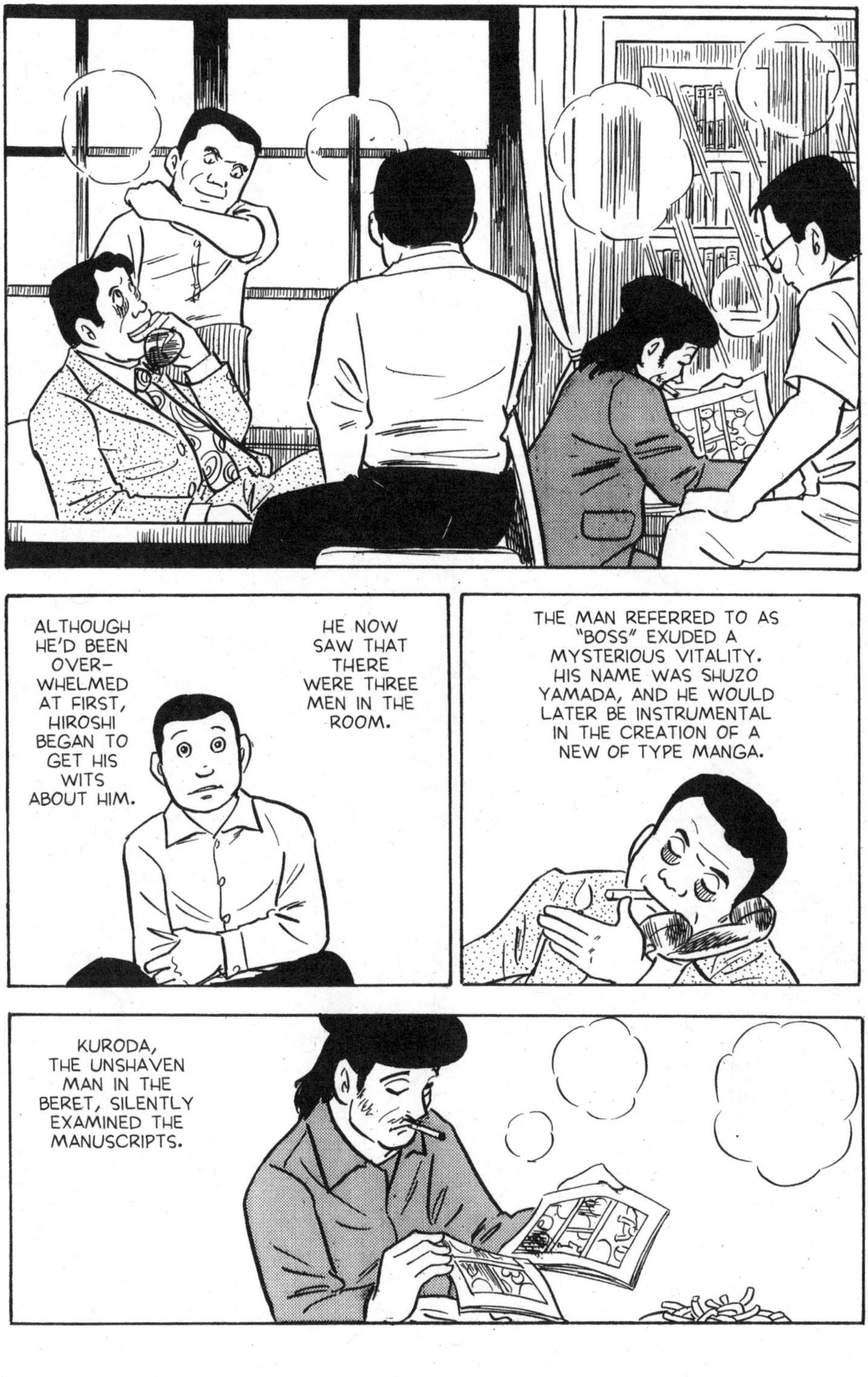
ALTHOUGH HE'D BEEN OVER-WHELMED AT FIRST, HIROSHI BEGAN TO GET HIS WITS ABOUT HIM.
HE NOW SAW THAT THERE WERE THREE MEN IN THE ROOM.
THE MAN REFERRED TO AS "BOSS" EXUDED A MYSTERIOUS VITALITY. HIS NAME WAS SHUZO YAMADA, AND HE WOULD LATER BE INSTRUMENTAL IN THE CREATION OF A NEW OF TYPE MANGA.
KURODA, THE UNSHAVEN MAN IN THE BERET, SILENTLY EXAMINED THE MANUSCRIPTS.

BOSS...

THUMP

THIS SHIT IS PASSÉ!

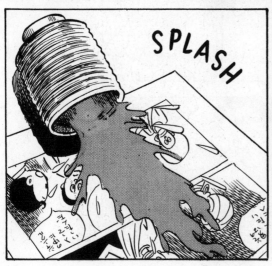

SPLASH

HINOMARU BUNKO, RENTAL MANGA PUBLISHER

THE TEA!
FWIP
SPLAT
IT'S NOT QUITE THERE.
GRRRRR...
I HAVE MORE WORK.

TITLE: "ISLAND Q OF THE SOUTH SEA", HIROSHI KATSUMI TITLE: "ARSENE GENT"

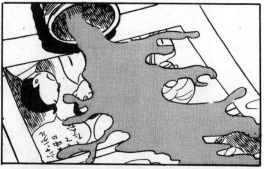

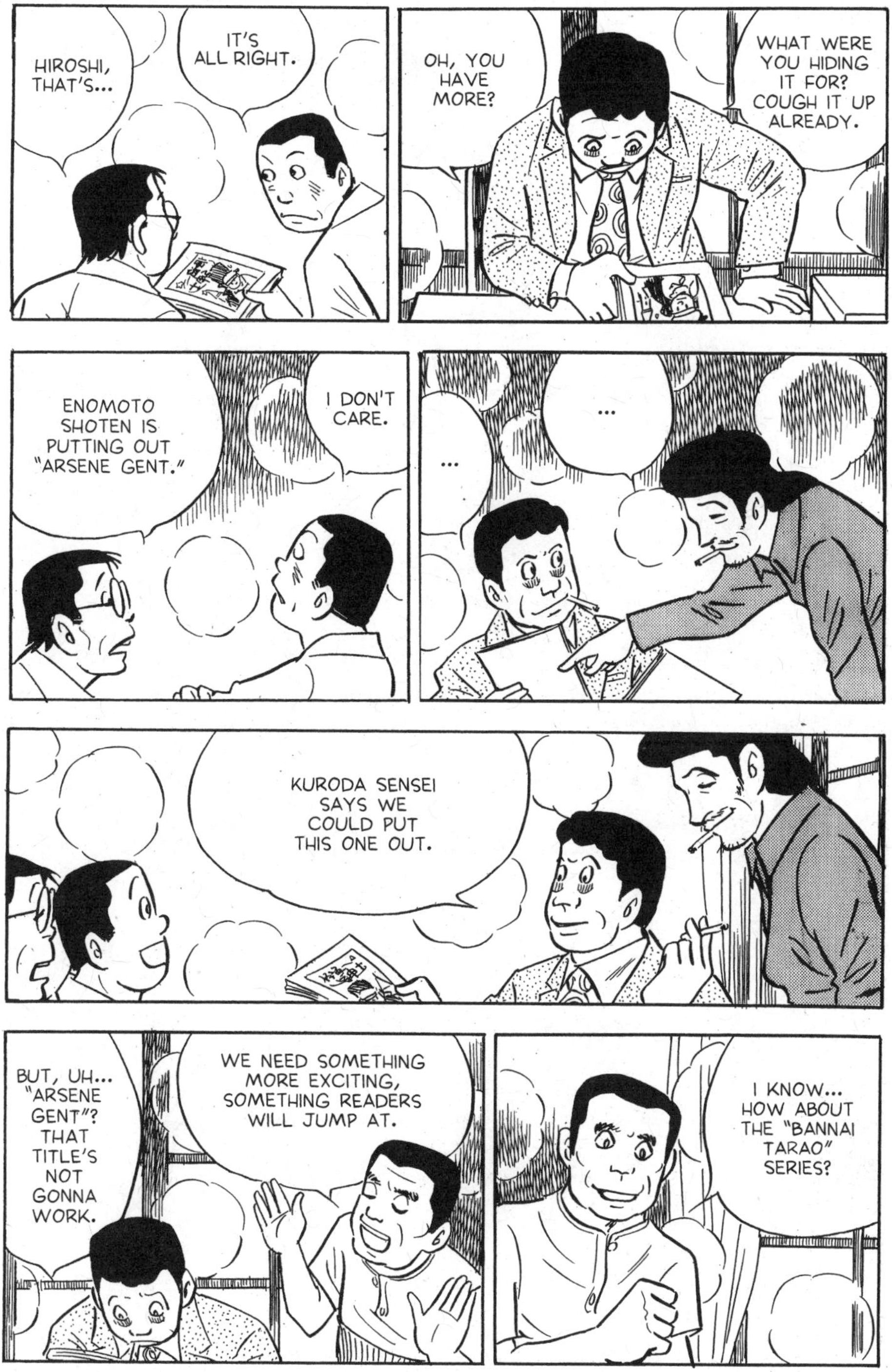
HIROSHI, THAT'S...
IT'S ALL RIGHT.
OH, YOU HAVE MORE?
WHAT WERE YOU HIDING IT FOR? COUGH IT UP ALREADY.
ENOMOTO SHOTEN IS PUTTING OUT "ARSENE GENT."
I DON'T CARE.
...
...
KURODA SENSEI SAYS WE COULD PUT THIS ONE OUT.
BUT, UH... "ARSENE GENT"? THAT TITLE'S NOT GONNA WORK.
WE NEED SOMETHING MORE EXCITING, SOMETHING READERS WILL JUMP AT.
I KNOW... HOW ABOUT THE "BANNAI TARAO" SERIES?

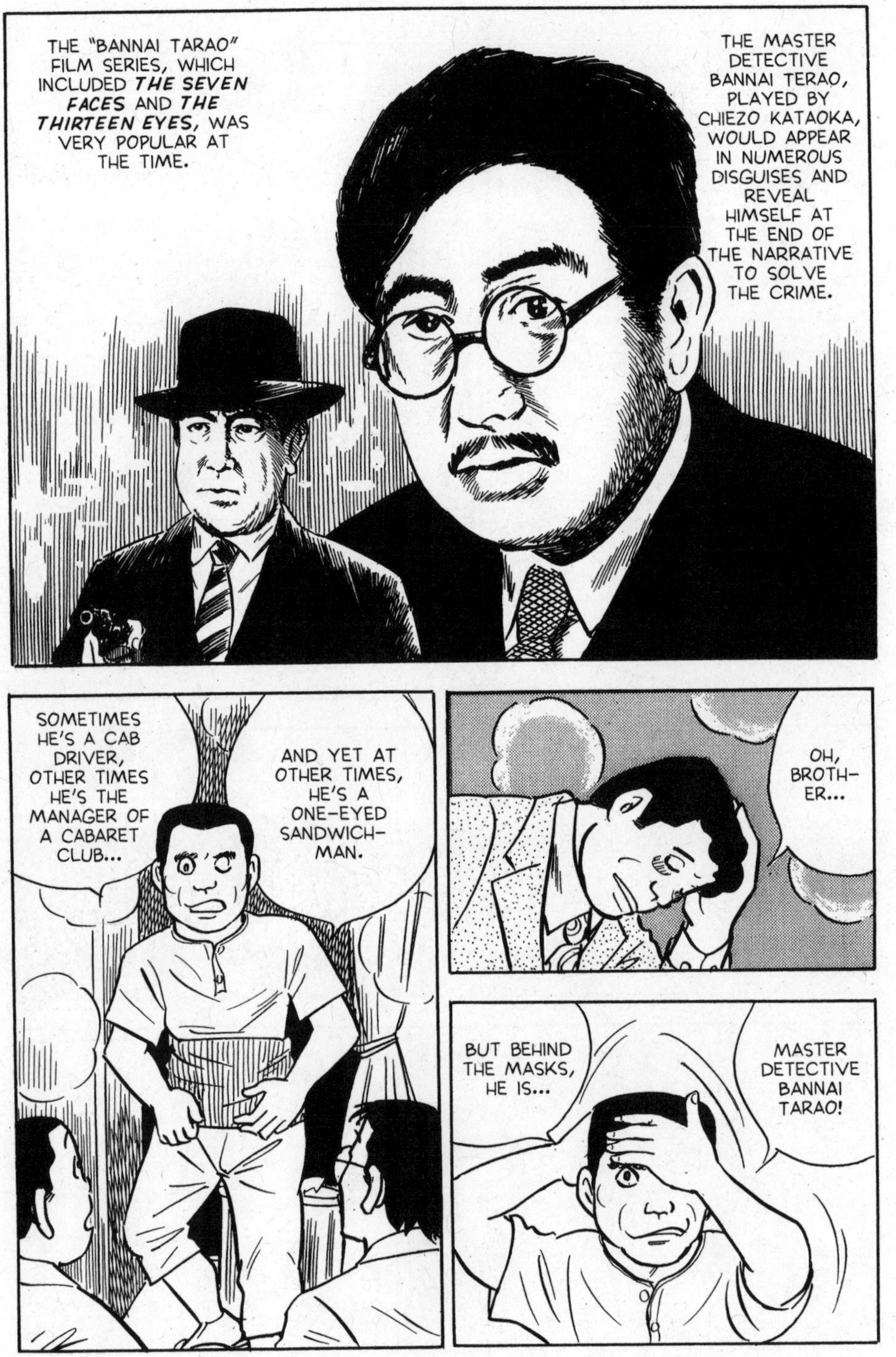

THE "BANNAI TARAO" FILM SERIES, WHICH INCLUDED ***THE SEVEN FACES*** AND ***THE THIRTEEN EYES,*** WAS VERY POPULAR AT THE TIME.
THE MASTER DETECTIVE BANNAI TERAO, PLAYED BY CHIEZO KATAOKA, WOULD APPEAR IN NUMEROUS DISGUISES AND REVEAL HIMSELF AT THE END OF THE NARRATIVE TO SOLVE THE CRIME.
SOMETIMES HE'S A CAB DRIVER, OTHER TIMES HE'S THE MANAGER OF A CABARET CLUB...
AND YET AT OTHER TIMES, HE'S A ONE-EYED SANDWICH-MAN.
OH, BROTH-ER...
BUT BEHIND THE MASKS, HE IS...
MASTER DETECTIVE BANNAI TARAO!

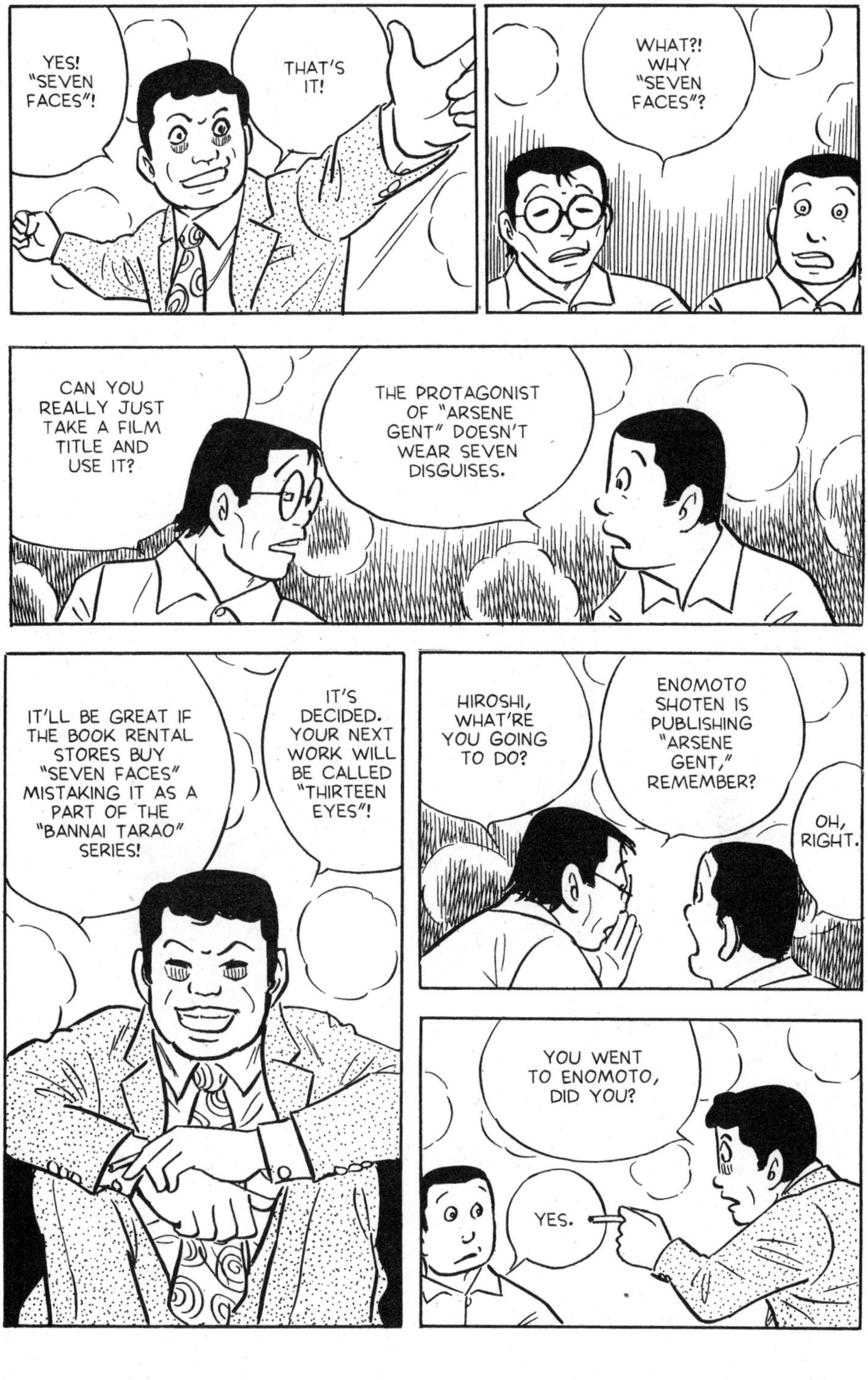
YES! "SEVEN FACES"!
THAT'S IT!
WHAT?! WHY "SEVEN FACES"?
CAN YOU REALLY JUST TAKE A FILM TITLE AND USE IT?
THE PROTAGONIST OF "ARSENE GENT" DOESN'T WEAR SEVEN DISGUISES.
IT'LL BE GREAT IF THE BOOK RENTAL STORES BUY "SEVEN FACES" MISTAKING IT AS A PART OF THE "BANNAI TARAO" SERIES!
IT'S DECIDED. YOUR NEXT WORK WILL BE CALLED "THIRTEEN EYES"!
HIROSHI, WHAT'RE YOU GOING TO DO?
ENOMOTO SHOTEN IS PUBLISHING "ARSENE GENT," REMEMBER?
OH, RIGHT.
YOU WENT TO ENOMOTO, DID YOU?
YES.

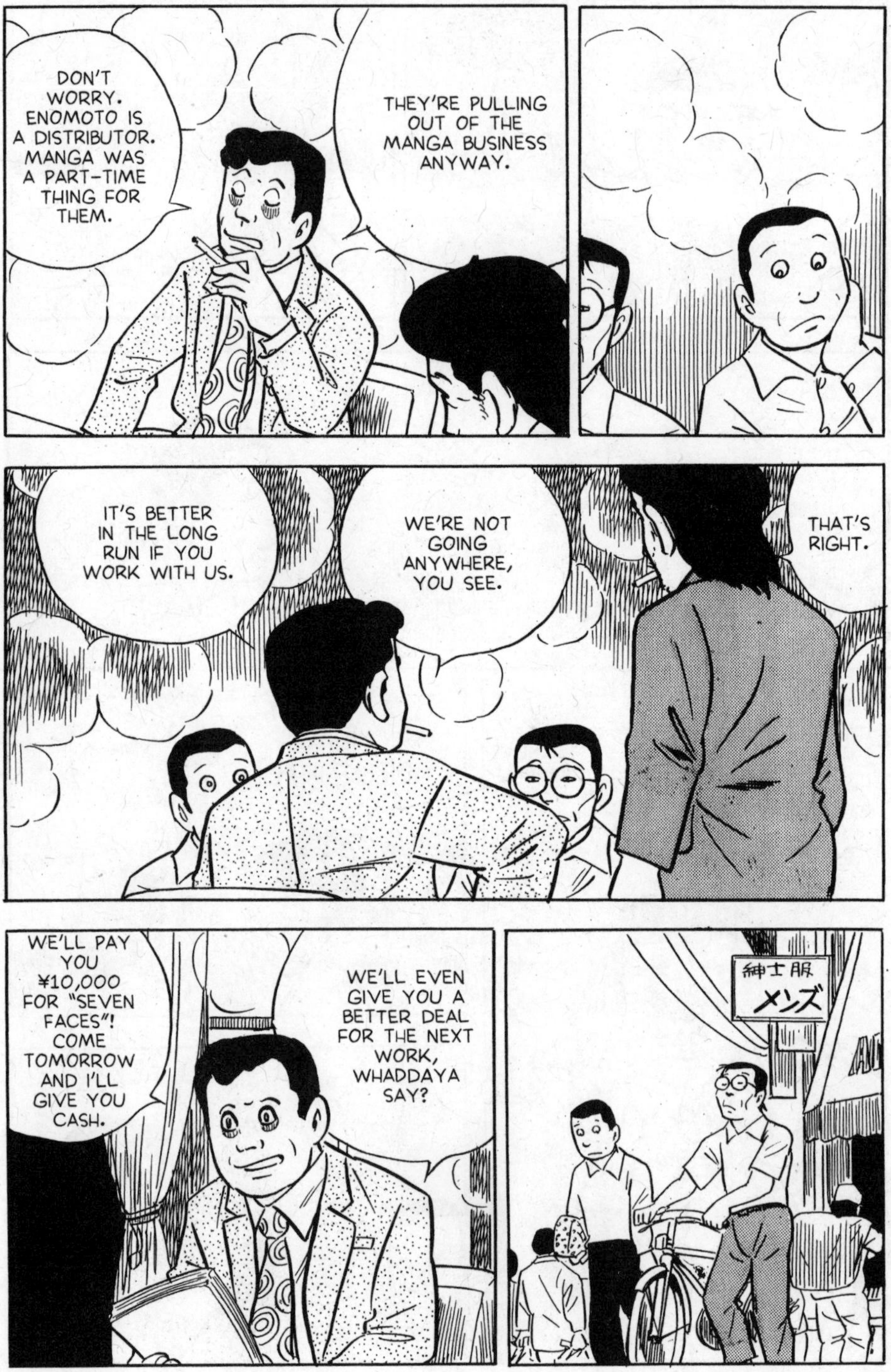
DON'T WORRY. ENOMOTO IS A DISTRIBUTOR. MANGA WAS A PART-TIME THING FOR THEM.
THEY'RE PULLING OUT OF THE MANGA BUSINESS ANYWAY.
IT'S BETTER IN THE LONG RUN IF YOU WORK WITH US.
WE'RE NOT GOING ANYWHERE, YOU SEE.
THAT'S RIGHT.
WE'LL PAY YOU ¥10,000 FOR "SEVEN FACES"! COME TOMORROW AND I'LL GIVE YOU CASH.
WE'LL EVEN GIVE YOU A BETTER DEAL FOR THE NEXT WORK, WHADDAYA SAY?
紳士服
メンズ

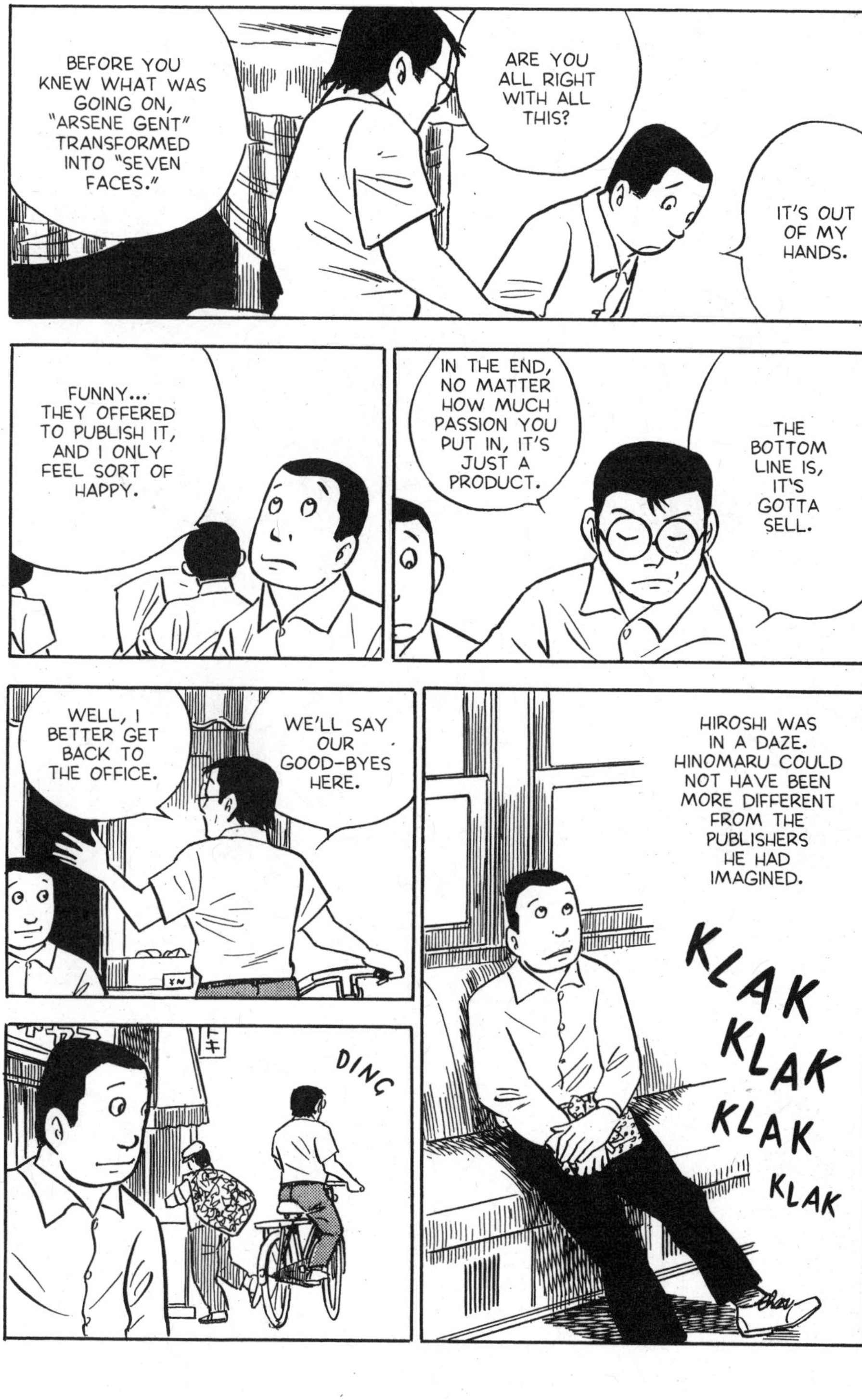
BEFORE YOU KNEW WHAT WAS GOING ON, "ARSENE GENT" TRANSFORMED INTO "SEVEN FACES."
ARE YOU ALL RIGHT WITH ALL THIS?
IT'S OUT OF MY HANDS.
FUNNY... THEY OFFERED TO PUBLISH IT, AND I ONLY FEEL SORT OF HAPPY.
IN THE END, NO MATTER HOW MUCH PASSION YOU PUT IN, IT'S JUST A PRODUCT.
THE BOTTOM LINE IS, IT'S GOTTA SELL.
WELL, I BETTER GET BACK TO THE OFFICE.
WE'LL SAY OUR GOOD-BYES HERE.
DING
HIROSHI WAS IN A DAZE. HINOMARU COULD NOT HAVE BEEN MORE DIFFERENT FROM THE PUBLISHERS HE HAD IMAGINED.
KLAK
KLAK
KLAK
KLAK

安ニビル
JULY 3

SIGN: YASUJI BUILDING

WE HAVE IT ALL READY FOR YOU. WE JUST NEED A RECEIPT.

YES, YES. OKAY.

RECEIPT: ¥10,000 RECEIVED BY ASADA, TOYONAKA-SHI OSAKA, HIROSHI KATSU

DID YOU MAKE SURE THERE'S TEN OF THOSE IN THERE?

NO.

WELL, IF YOU FIND THERE'S ONLY NINE OF THEM IN THERE LATER, IT'LL BE TOO LATE.

YES, I SEE.

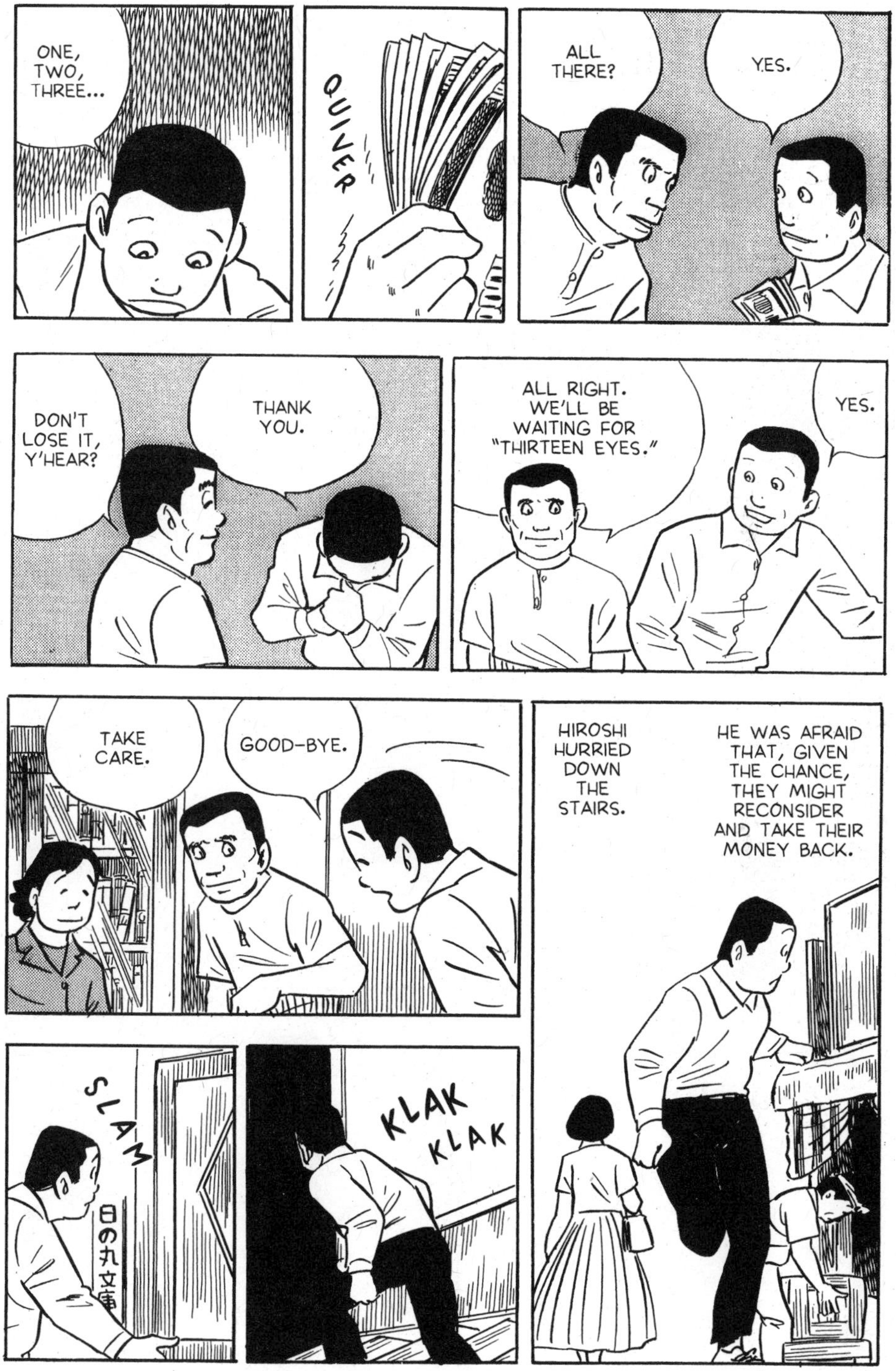
ONE, TWO, THREE...
QUIVER
ALL THERE?
YES.
DON'T LOSE IT, Y'HEAR?
THANK YOU.
ALL RIGHT. WE'LL BE WAITING FOR "THIRTEEN EYES."
YES.
TAKE CARE.
GOOD-BYE.
SLAM
日の丸文庫
KLAK KLAK
HIROSHI HURRIED DOWN THE STAIRS.
HE WAS AFRAID THAT, GIVEN THE CHANCE, THEY MIGHT RECONSIDER AND TAKE THEIR MONEY BACK.

YOU MORON, AHAHA...

YOU DIDN'T NEED TO RUN HOME.

I'VE NEVER EXCHANGED MY WORK FOR CASH BEFORE...

I FELT EMBARRASSED TO SELL MY WORK AS A PRODUCT.

AT ANY RATE, THE "ARSENE GENT" CASE IS NOW CLOSED.

ARE YOU MAKING ANY PROGRESS ON THE PIECE FOR TOKAIDO?

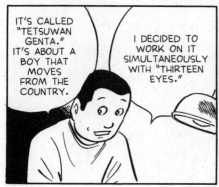

IT'S CALLED "TETSUWAN GENTA." IT'S ABOUT A BOY THAT MOVES FROM THE COUNTRY.

I DECIDED TO WORK ON IT SIMULTANEOUSLY WITH "THIRTEEN EYES."

THERE'S STILL THE ENOMOTO THING.

I HOPE THEY JUST FORGET TO CALL ME.

郵便はがき

大阪府豊中市
麻田二三七

勝見ヒロシ

BUT THREE DAYS LATER...

I HEARD YOU GOT A CARD FROM ENOMOTO SHOTEN?

I'M IN A BIND!

LETTER: HIROSHI KATSUMI, 1-37 ASADA, TOYONAKA-SHI, OSAKA

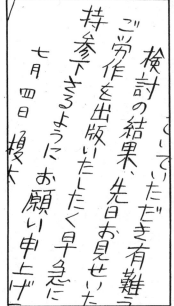

検討の結果有難う

ご労作を出版いたしたく早急に

持参下さるようにお願い申上げ

七月四日　榎本

OH NO! YOU DON'T EVEN HAVE THE MANUSCRIPT ANYMORE.

SHOULD I GO TO HINOMARU AND GIVE THEM THEIR MONEY BACK?

YOU FOOL! YOU REALLY THINK THEY'D GO FOR THAT?

WHAT DO I DO?

LETTER: "JULY 4, 1954 / AFTER MUCH CONSIDERATION, WE HAVE DECIDED THAT WE WOULD VERY MUCH LIKE TO PUBLISH YOUR PIECE. PLEASE BRING YOUR MANUSCRIPT IN AT YOUR EARLIEST CONVENIENCE. —ENOMOTO"

I COULD HAVE MADE ¥15,000 BY GOING WITH ENOMOTO SHOTEN.

I JUST LOST ¥5,000!

THAT'S NOT THE ISSUE HERE.

SLAP

OW!

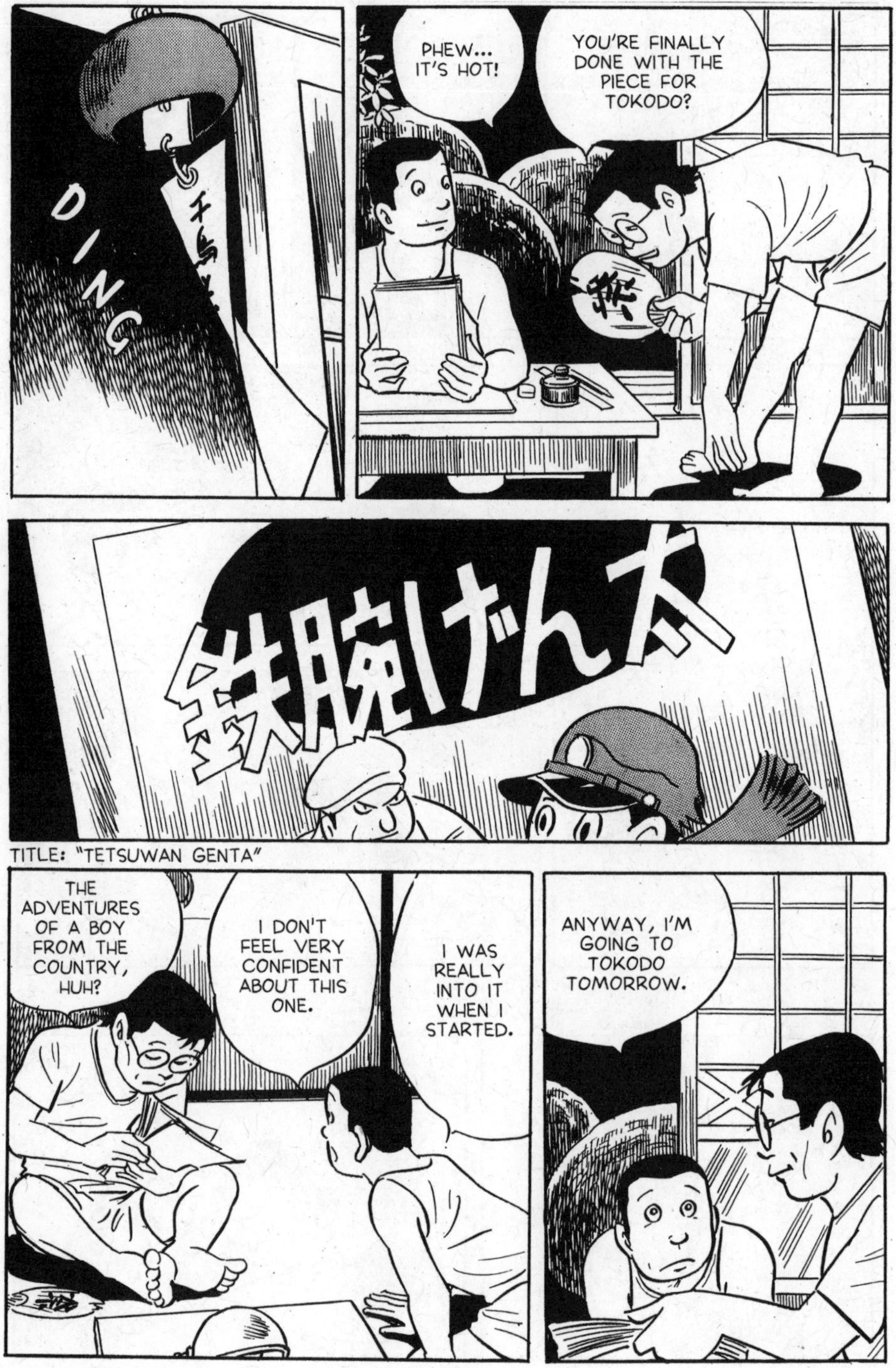
DING
PHEW... IT'S HOT!
YOU'RE FINALLY DONE WITH THE PIECE FOR TOKODO?
鉄腕げん太
TITLE: "TETSUWAN GENTA"
THE ADVENTURES OF A BOY FROM THE COUNTRY, HUH?
I DON'T FEEL VERY CONFIDENT ABOUT THIS ONE.
I WAS REALLY INTO IT WHEN I STARTED.
ANYWAY, I'M GOING TO TOKODO TOMORROW.

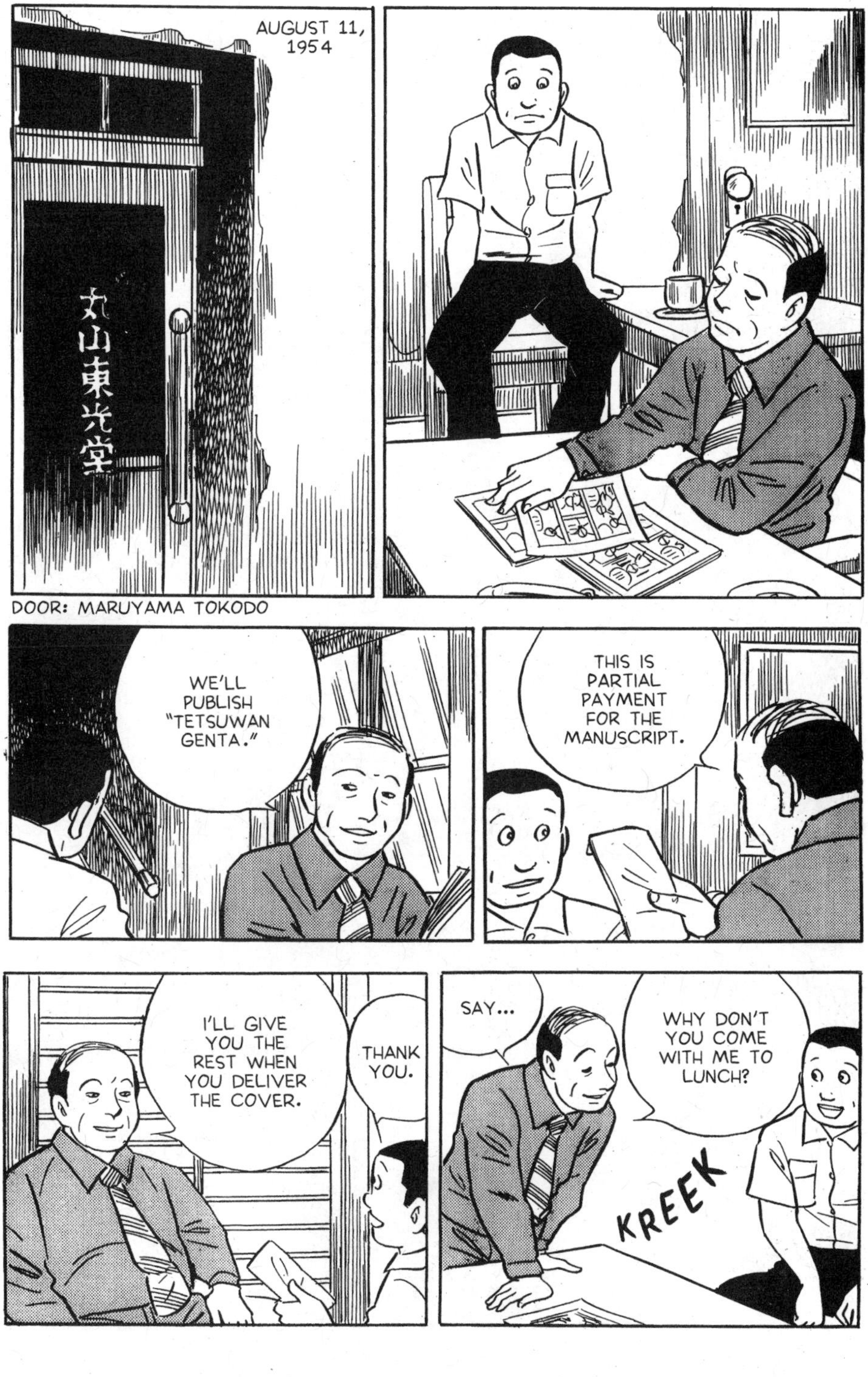
AUGUST 11, 1954
丸山東光堂
DOOR: MARUYAMA TOKODO
WE'LL PUBLISH "TETSUWAN GENTA."
THIS IS PARTIAL PAYMENT FOR THE MANUSCRIPT.
I'LL GIVE YOU THE REST WHEN YOU DELIVER THE COVER.
THANK YOU.
SAY...
WHY DON'T YOU COME WITH ME TO LUNCH?
KREEK

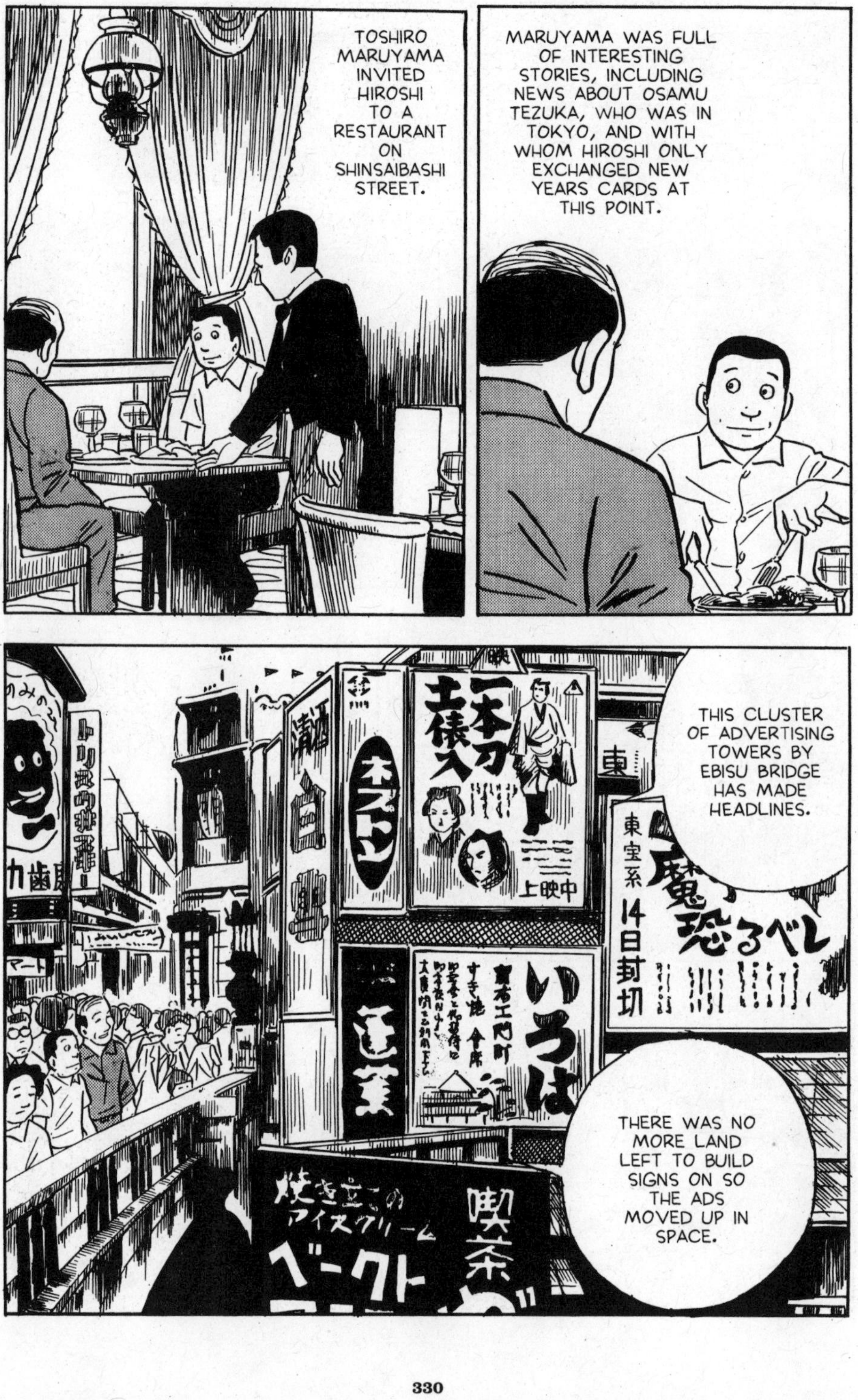
TOSHIRO MARUYAMA INVITED HIROSHI TO A RESTAURANT ON SHINSAIBASHI STREET.
MARUYAMA WAS FULL OF INTERESTING STORIES, INCLUDING NEWS ABOUT OSAMU TEZUKA, WHO WAS IN TOKYO, AND WITH WHOM HIROSHI ONLY EXCHANGED NEW YEARS CARDS AT THIS POINT.
上映中
東宝系
14日封切
THIS CLUSTER OF ADVERTISING TOWERS BY EBISU BRIDGE HAS MADE HEADLINES.
喫茶
THERE WAS NO MORE LAND LEFT TO BUILD SIGNS ON SO THE ADS MOVED UP IN SPACE.

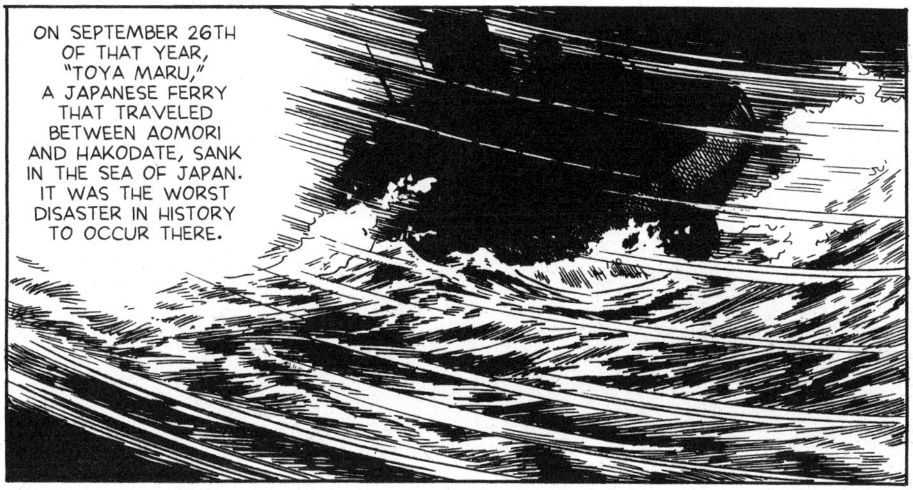
ON SEPTEMBER 26TH OF THAT YEAR, "TOYA MARU," A JAPANESE FERRY THAT TRAVELED BETWEEN AOMORI AND HAKODATE, SANK IN THE SEA OF JAPAN. IT WAS THE WORST DISASTER IN HISTORY TO OCCUR THERE.

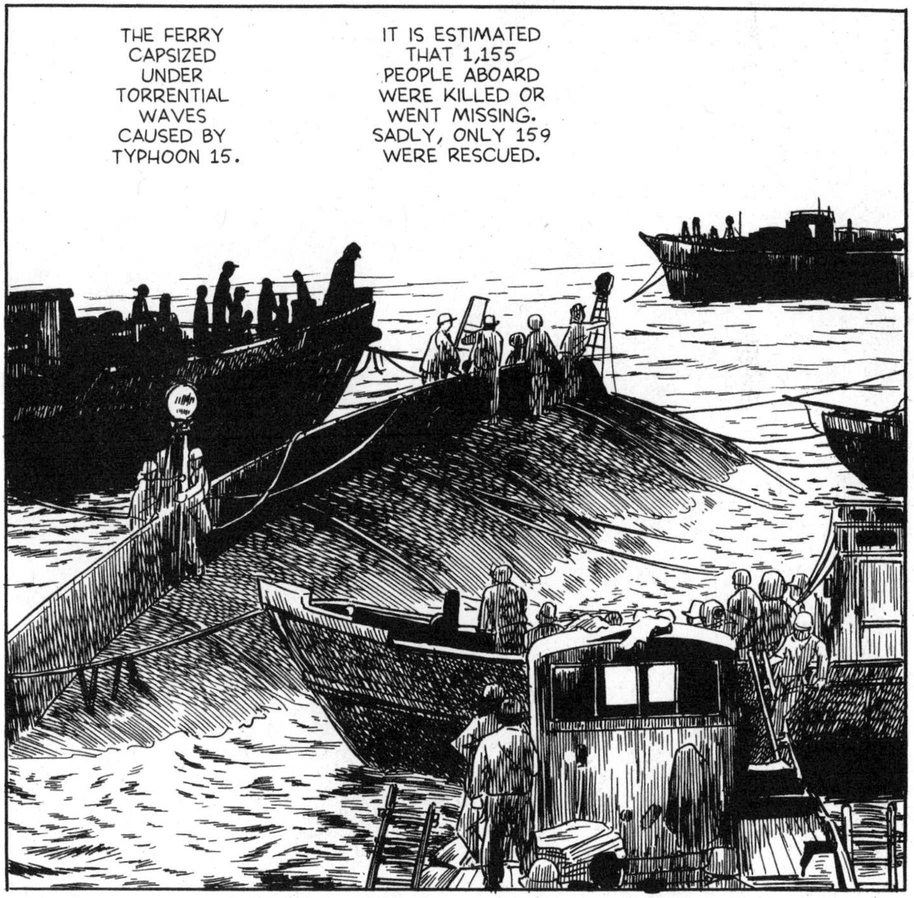
THE FERRY CAPSIZED UNDER TORRENTIAL WAVES CAUSED BY TYPHOON 15.
IT IS ESTIMATED THAT 1,155 PEOPLE ABOARD WERE KILLED OR WENT MISSING. SADLY, ONLY 159 WERE RESCUED.

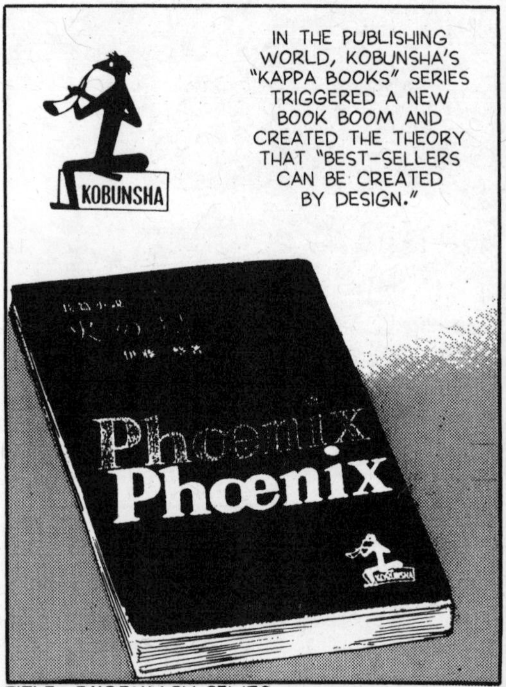
KOBUNSHA
IN THE PUBLISHING WORLD, KOBUNSHA'S "KAPPA BOOKS" SERIES TRIGGERED A NEW BOOK BOOM AND CREATED THE THEORY THAT "BEST-SELLERS CAN BE CREATED BY DESIGN."
Phœnix
Phœnix

TITLE: *PHOENIX* BY SEI ITO

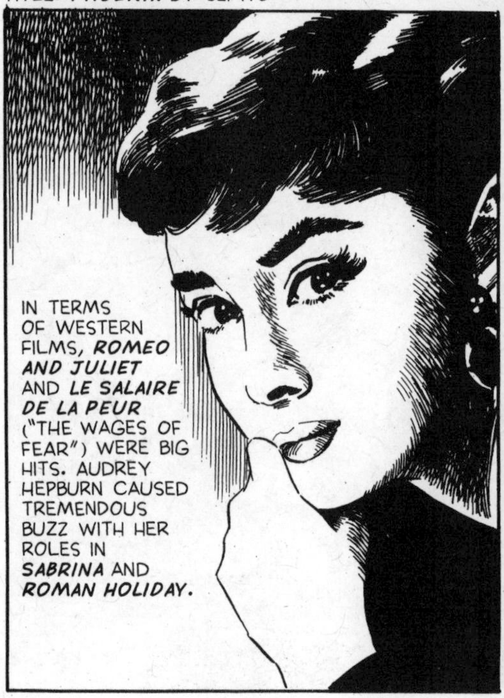
IN TERMS OF WESTERN FILMS, ***ROMEO AND JULIET*** AND ***LE SALAIRE DE LA PEUR*** ("THE WAGES OF FEAR") WERE BIG HITS. AUDREY HEPBURN CAUSED TREMENDOUS BUZZ WITH HER ROLES IN ***SABRINA*** AND ***ROMAN HOLIDAY***.

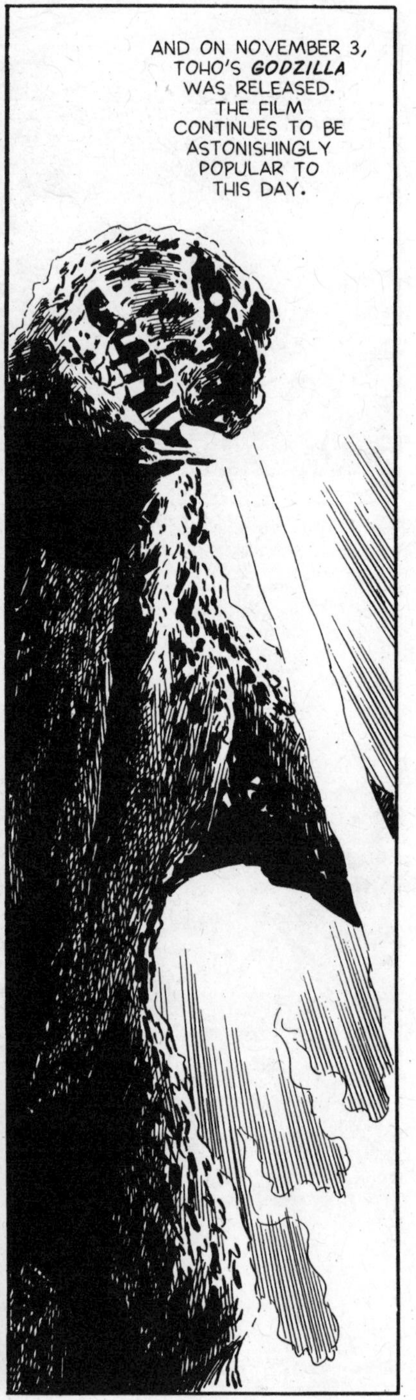
AND ON NOVEMBER 3, TOHO'S ***GODZILLA*** WAS RELEASED. THE FILM CONTINUES TO BE ASTONISHINGLY POPULAR TO THIS DAY.

NOM DE PLUME

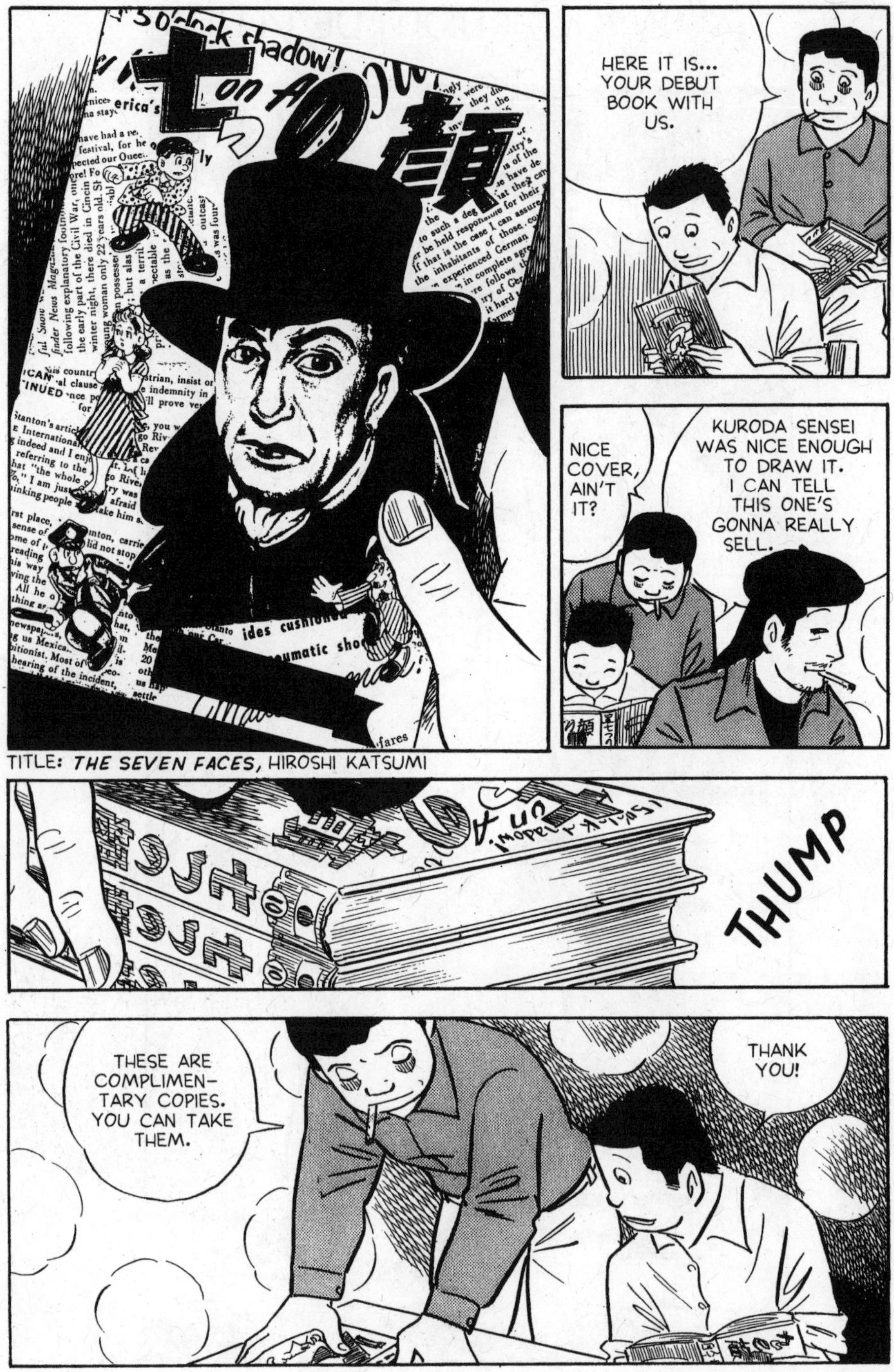

HERE IT IS... YOUR DEBUT BOOK WITH US.
NICE COVER, AIN'T IT?
KURODA SENSEI WAS NICE ENOUGH TO DRAW IT. I CAN TELL THIS ONE'S GONNA REALLY SELL.
TITLE: *THE SEVEN FACES*, HIROSHI KATSUMI
THUMP
THESE ARE COMPLIMEN-TARY COPIES. YOU CAN TAKE THEM.
THANK YOU!

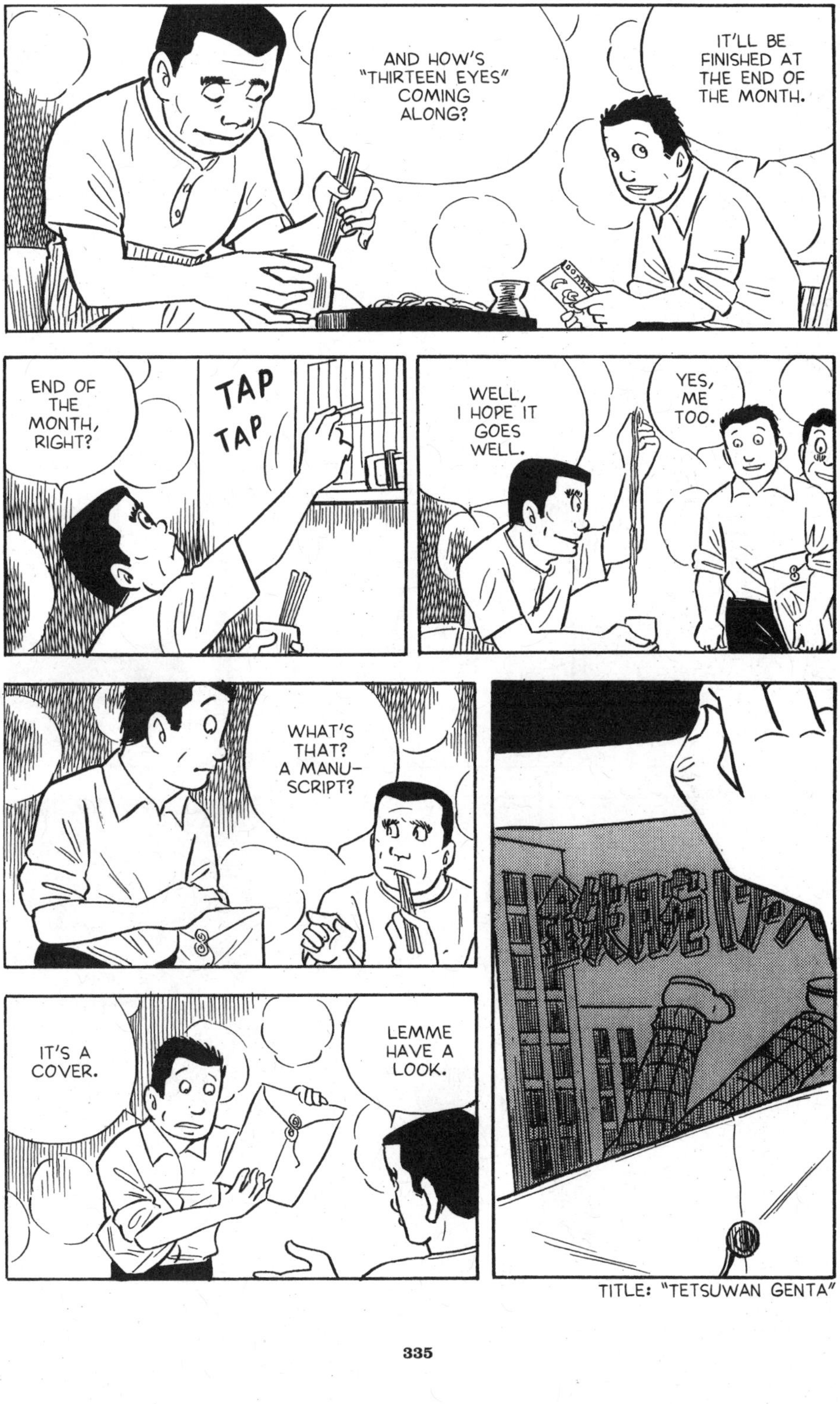
AND HOW'S "THIRTEEN EYES" COMING ALONG?
IT'LL BE FINISHED AT THE END OF THE MONTH.
END OF THE MONTH, RIGHT?
TAP TAP
WELL, I HOPE IT GOES WELL.
YES, ME TOO.
WHAT'S THAT? A MANU-SCRIPT?
IT'S A COVER.
LEMME HAVE A LOOK.
TITLE: "TETSUWAN GENTA"

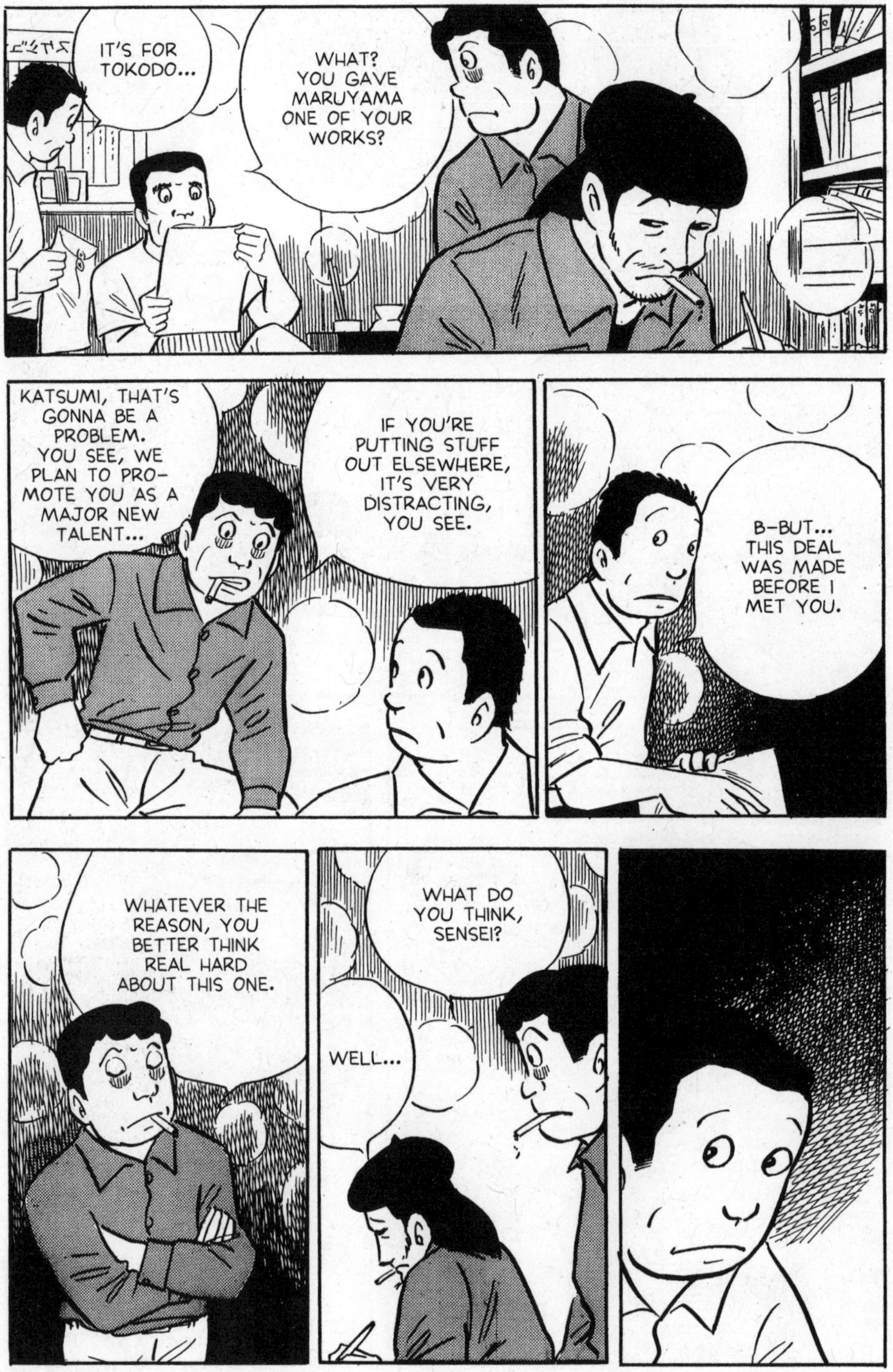
IT'S FOR TOKODO...
WHAT? YOU GAVE MARUYAMA ONE OF YOUR WORKS?
KATSUMI, THAT'S GONNA BE A PROBLEM. YOU SEE, WE PLAN TO PRO-MOTE YOU AS A MAJOR NEW TALENT...
IF YOU'RE PUTTING STUFF OUT ELSEWHERE, IT'S VERY DISTRACTING, YOU SEE.
B-BUT... THIS DEAL WAS MADE BEFORE I MET YOU.
WHATEVER THE REASON, YOU BETTER THINK REAL HARD ABOUT THIS ONE.
WHAT DO YOU THINK, SENSEI?
WELL...

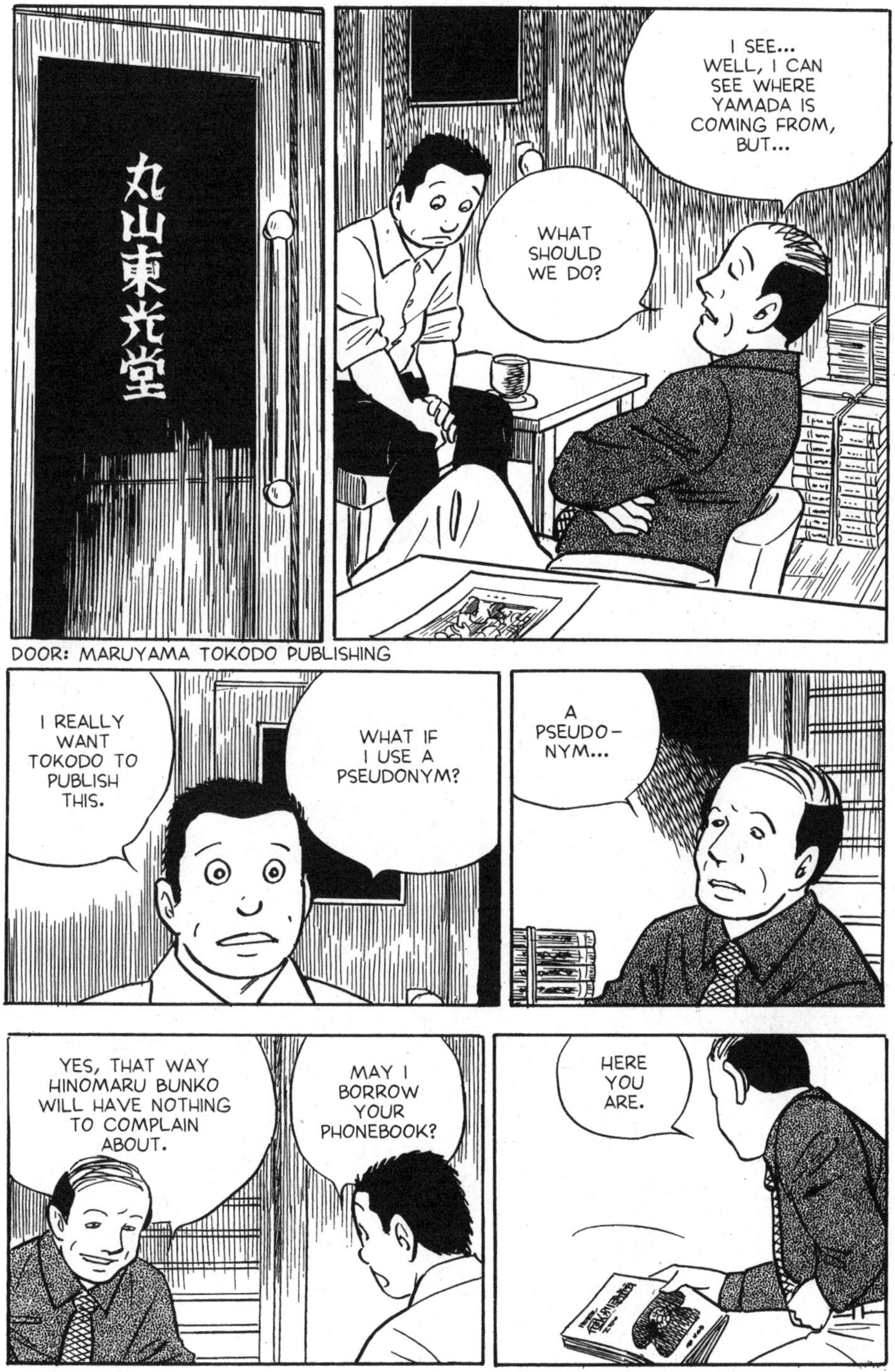
丸山東光堂
I SEE... WELL, I CAN SEE WHERE YAMADA IS COMING FROM, BUT...
WHAT SHOULD WE DO?
DOOR: MARUYAMA TOKODO PUBLISHING
I REALLY WANT TOKODO TO PUBLISH THIS.
WHAT IF I USE A PSEUDONYM?
A PSEUDO-NYM...
YES, THAT WAY HINOMARU BUNKO WILL HAVE NOTHING TO COMPLAIN ABOUT.
MAY I BORROW YOUR PHONEBOOK?
HERE YOU ARE.

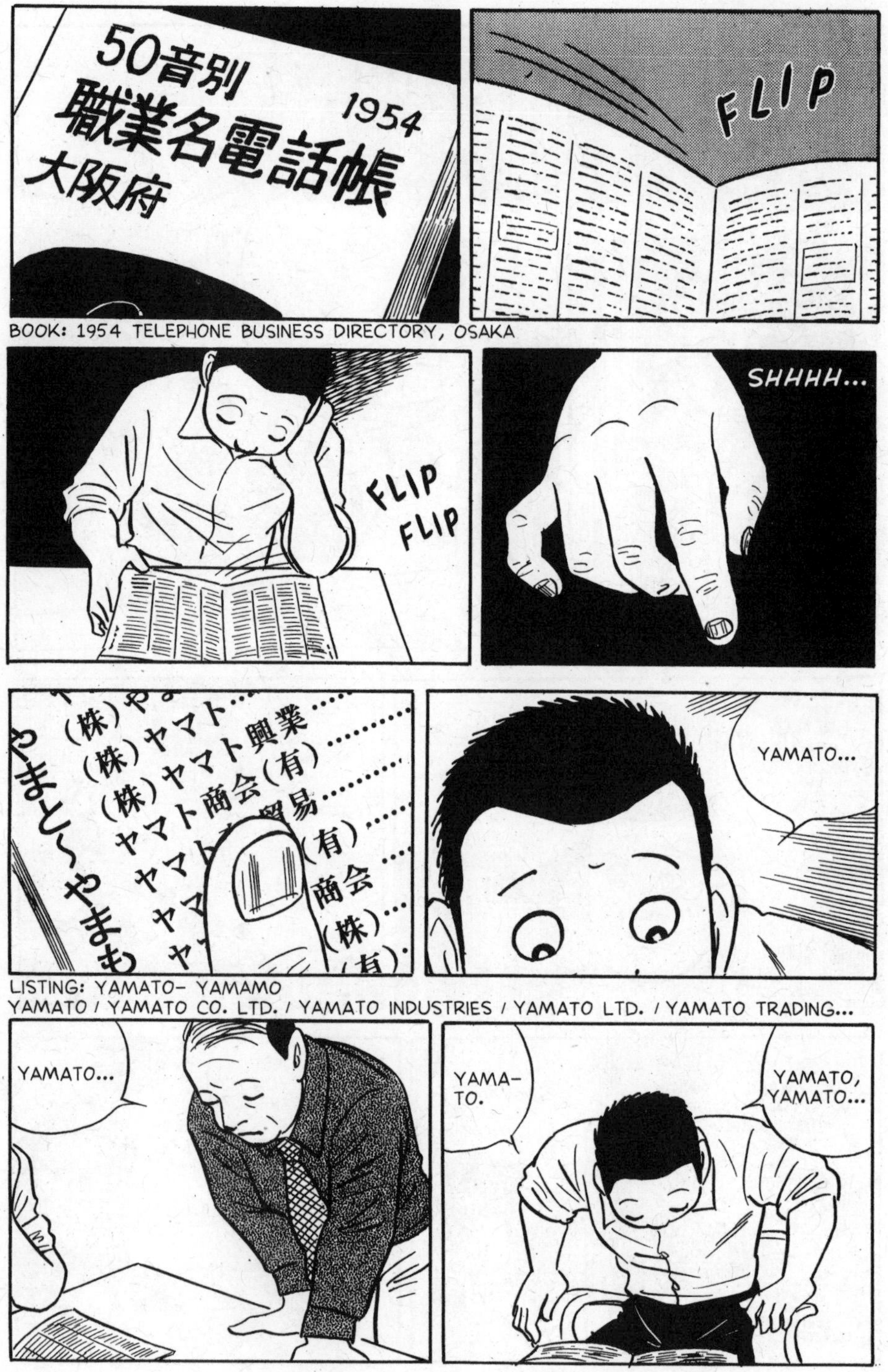
50音別
1954
職業名電話帳
大阪府
FLIP
BOOK: 1954 TELEPHONE BUSINESS DIRECTORY, OSAKA
FLIP
FLIP
SHHHH...
やまと～やまも
(株)ヤマト……
(株)ヤマト興業……
(株)ヤマト商会(有)……
YAMATO...
LISTING: YAMATO– YAMAMO
YAMATO / YAMATO CO. LTD. / YAMATO INDUSTRIES / YAMATO LTD. / YAMATO TRADING...
YAMATO...
YAMA-
TO.
YAMATO,
YAMATO...

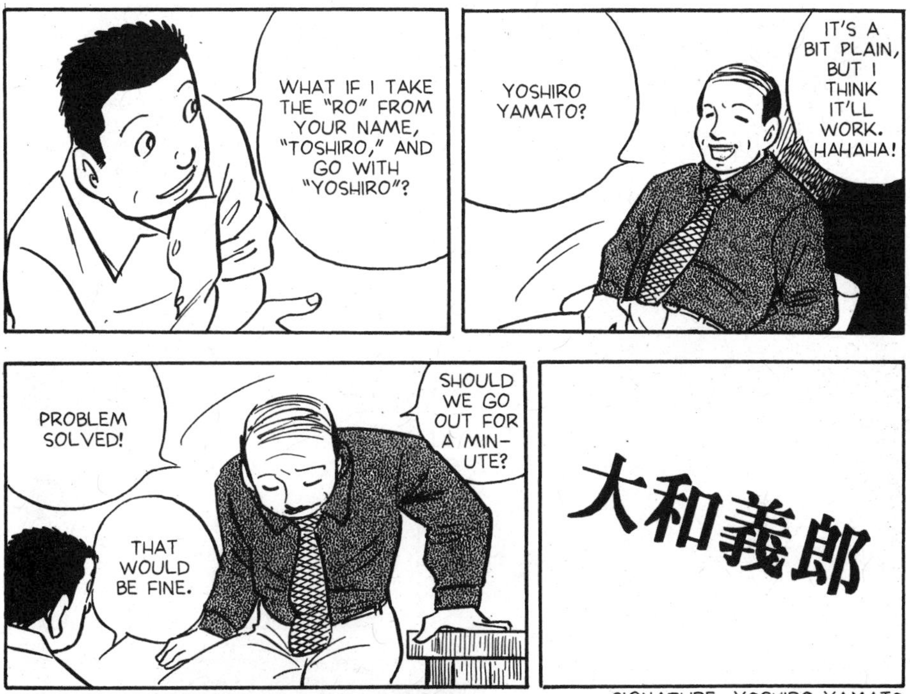
WHAT IF I TAKE THE "RO" FROM YOUR NAME, "TOSHIRO," AND GO WITH "YOSHIRO"?
YOSHIRO YAMATO?
IT'S A BIT PLAIN, BUT I THINK IT'LL WORK. HAHAHA!
PROBLEM SOLVED!
SHOULD WE GO OUT FOR A MIN-UTE?
THAT WOULD BE FINE.
大和義郎
SIGNATURE: YOSHIRO YAMATO

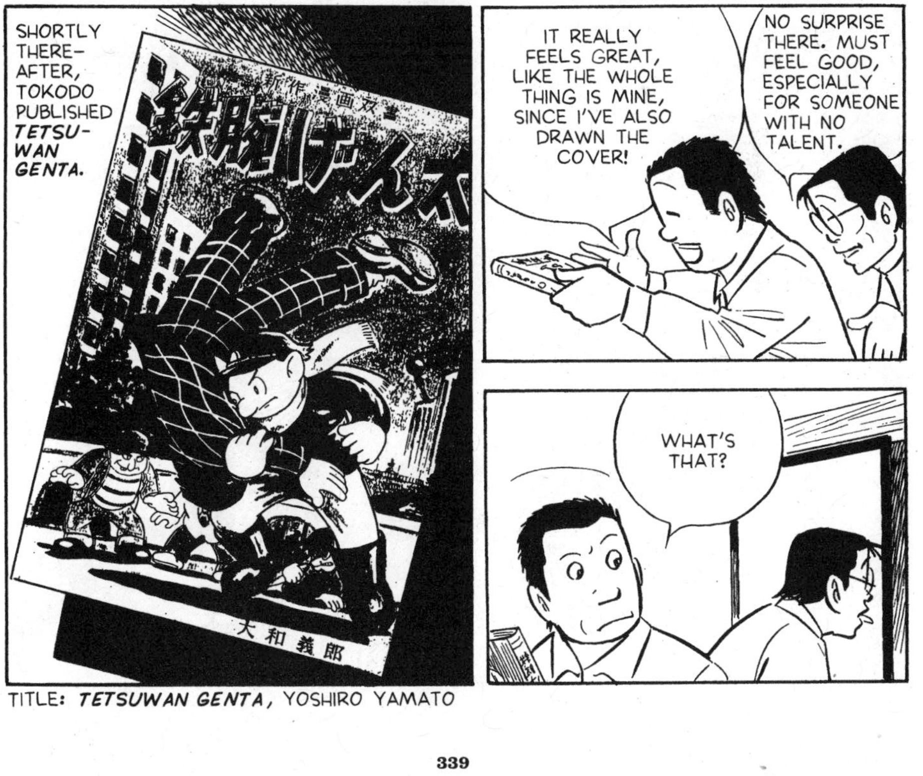
SHORTLY THERE-AFTER, TOKODO PUBLISHED *TETSU-WAN GENTA*.
大和義郎
IT REALLY FEELS GREAT, LIKE THE WHOLE THING IS MINE, SINCE I'VE ALSO DRAWN THE COVER!
NO SURPRISE THERE. MUST FEEL GOOD, ESPECIALLY FOR SOMEONE WITH NO TALENT.
WHAT'S THAT?
TITLE: ***TETSUWAN GENTA***, YOSHIRO YAMATO

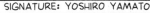

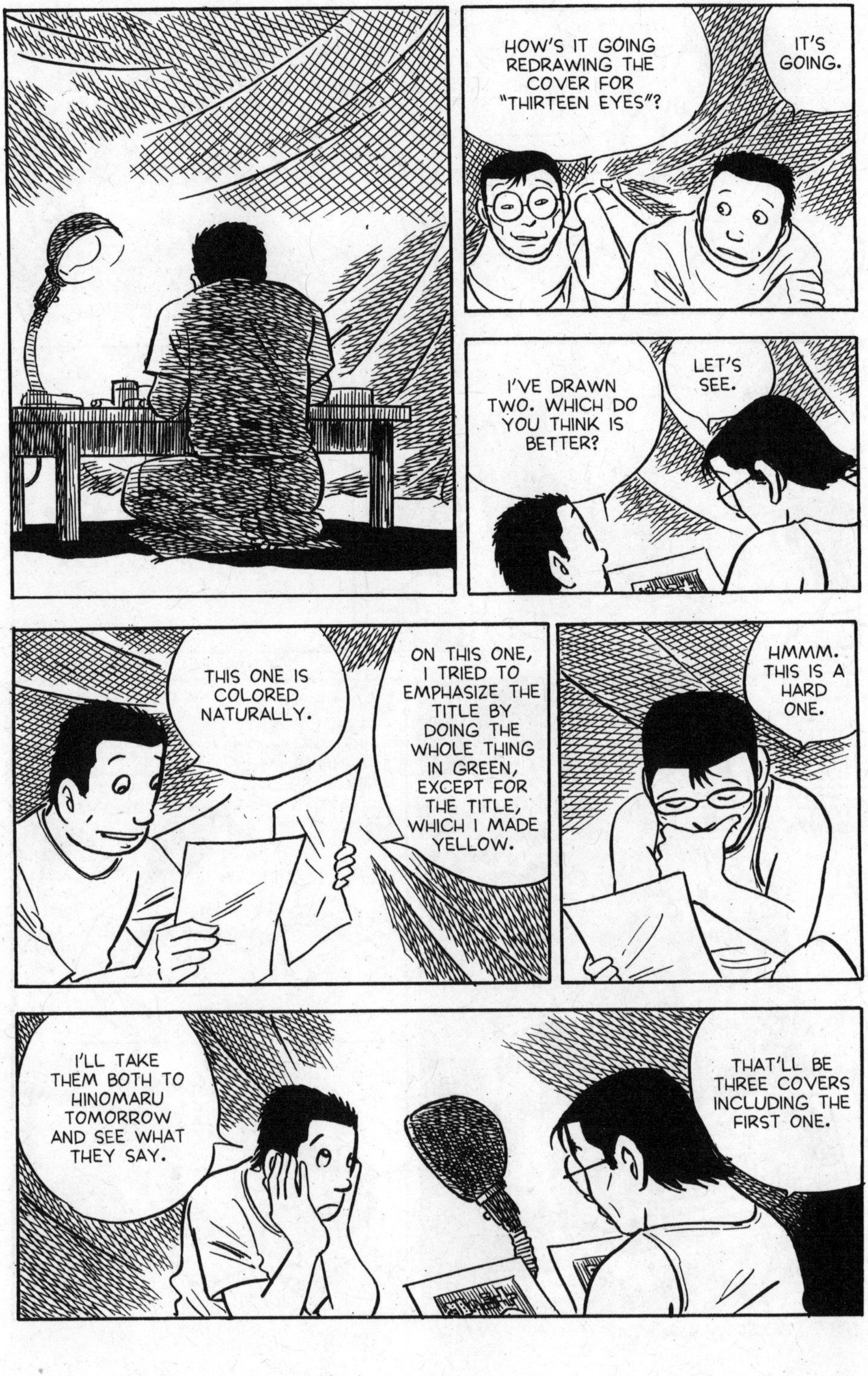
HOW'S IT GOING REDRAWING THE COVER FOR "THIRTEEN EYES"?
IT'S GOING.
I'VE DRAWN TWO. WHICH DO YOU THINK IS BETTER?
LET'S SEE.
THIS ONE IS COLORED NATURALLY.
ON THIS ONE, I TRIED TO EMPHASIZE THE TITLE BY DOING THE WHOLE THING IN GREEN, EXCEPT FOR THE TITLE, WHICH I MADE YELLOW.
HMMM. THIS IS A HARD ONE.
I'LL TAKE THEM BOTH TO HINOMARU TOMORROW AND SEE WHAT THEY SAY.
THAT'LL BE THREE COVERS INCLUDING THE FIRST ONE.

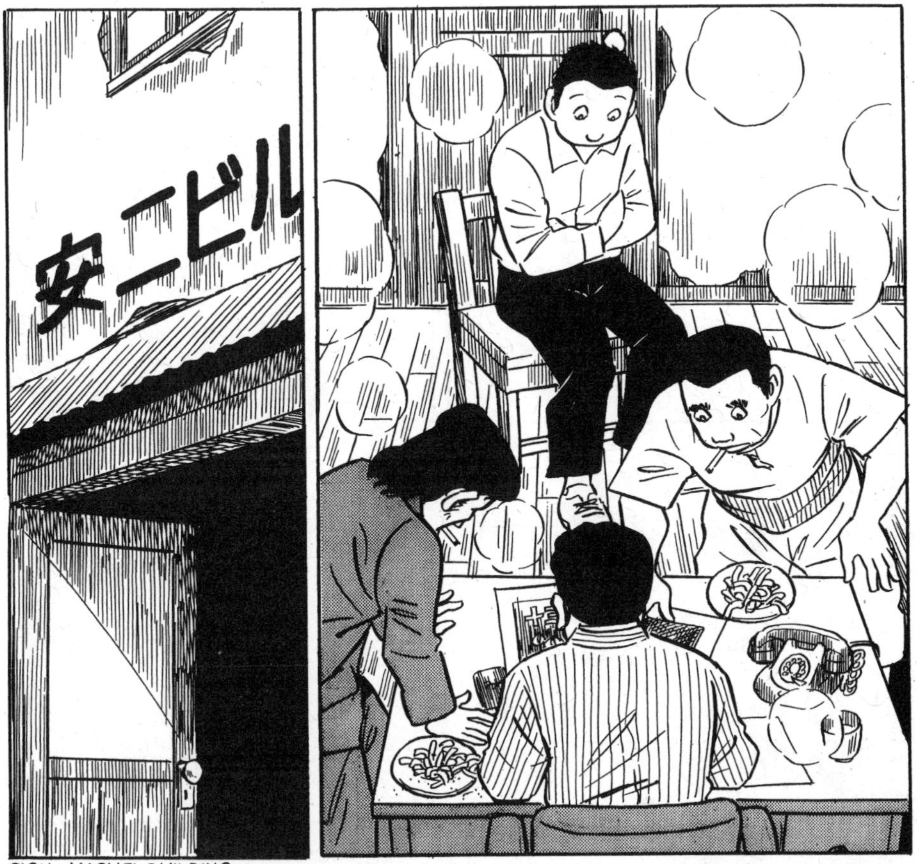
安二ビル

SIGN: YASUJI BUILDING

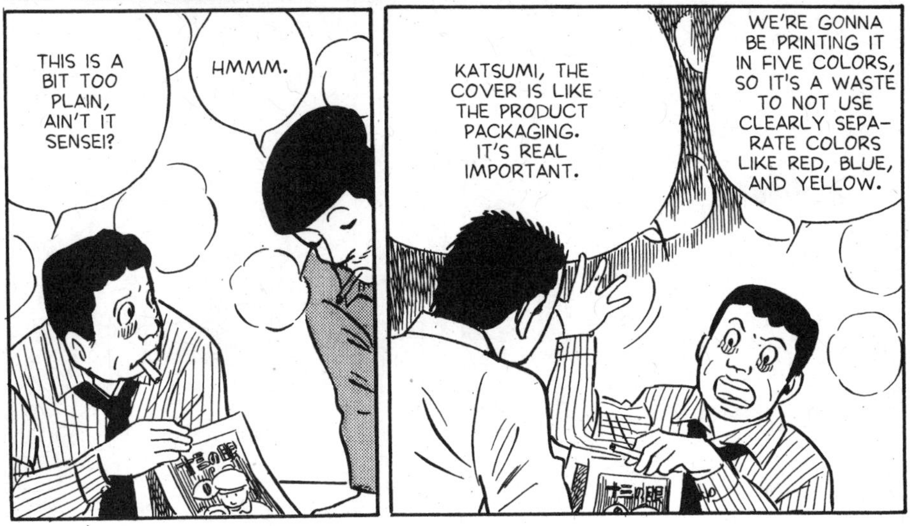
THIS IS A BIT TOO PLAIN, AIN'T IT SENSEI?
HMMM.
KATSUMI, THE COVER IS LIKE THE PRODUCT PACKAGING. IT'S REAL IMPORTANT.
WE'RE GONNA BE PRINTING IT IN FIVE COLORS, SO IT'S A WASTE TO NOT USE CLEARLY SEPARATE COLORS LIKE RED, BLUE, AND YELLOW.

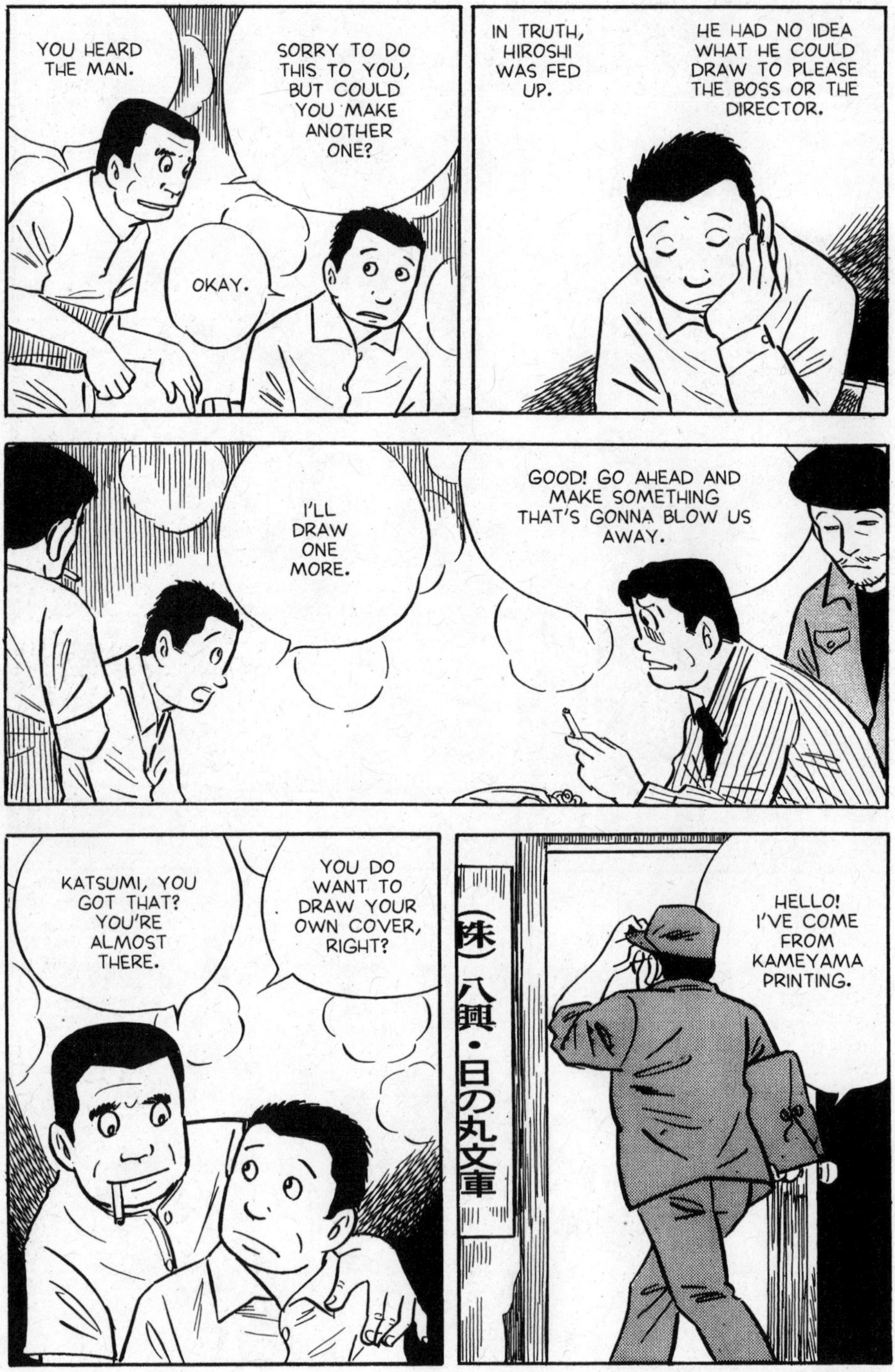
YOU HEARD THE MAN.
SORRY TO DO THIS TO YOU, BUT COULD YOU MAKE ANOTHER ONE?
OKAY.
IN TRUTH, HIROSHI WAS FED UP.
HE HAD NO IDEA WHAT HE COULD DRAW TO PLEASE THE BOSS OR THE DIRECTOR.
I'LL DRAW ONE MORE.
GOOD! GO AHEAD AND MAKE SOMETHING THAT'S GONNA BLOW US AWAY.
KATSUMI, YOU GOT THAT? YOU'RE ALMOST THERE.
YOU DO WANT TO DRAW YOUR OWN COVER, RIGHT?
(株)八興・日の丸文庫
HELLO! I'VE COME FROM KAMEYAMA PRINTING.

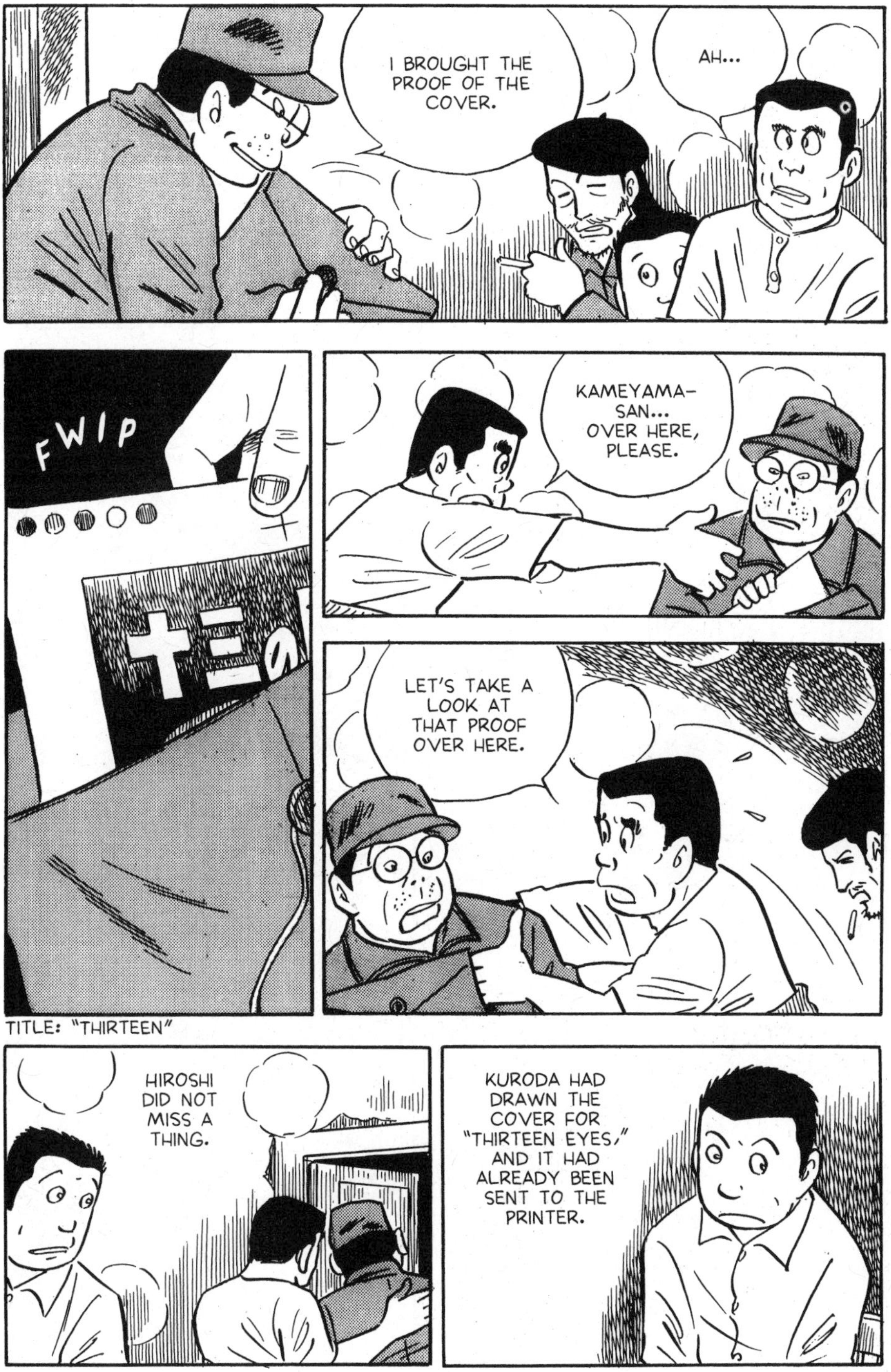
I BROUGHT THE PROOF OF THE COVER.
AH...
FWIP
十三の
KAMEYAMA-SAN... OVER HERE, PLEASE.
LET'S TAKE A LOOK AT THAT PROOF OVER HERE.
TITLE: "THIRTEEN"
HIROSHI DID NOT MISS A THING.
KURODA HAD DRAWN THE COVER FOR "THIRTEEN EYES," AND IT HAD ALREADY BEEN SENT TO THE PRINTER.

THERE WAS AN AWKWARD MOMENT IN THE OFFICE.

HEY!

GOOD TO SEE YOU, MATSU-MOTO!

WE WERE ALL WAITING FOR YA! COME ON IN!

HELLO.

A VACANT BUT WHOLESOME-LOOKING YOUNG MAN STOOD IN THE ENTRYWAY.

IT WAS MASAHIKO MATSUMOTO, WHO HAD BEEN AT HINOMARU A YEAR LONGER THAN HIROSHI.

MATSUMOTO HAD ALREADY RELEASED SEVERAL BOOKS THROUGH HINOMARU BUNKO, AND HIS SKILLS WERE PROVEN. HIS "SABOTEN-KUN" SERIES PLACED THIRD IN A POPULARITY SURVEY CONDUCTED BY *MAINICHI SHIMBUN.*

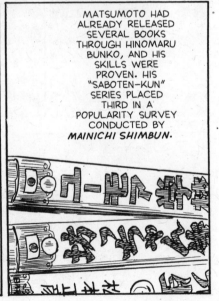

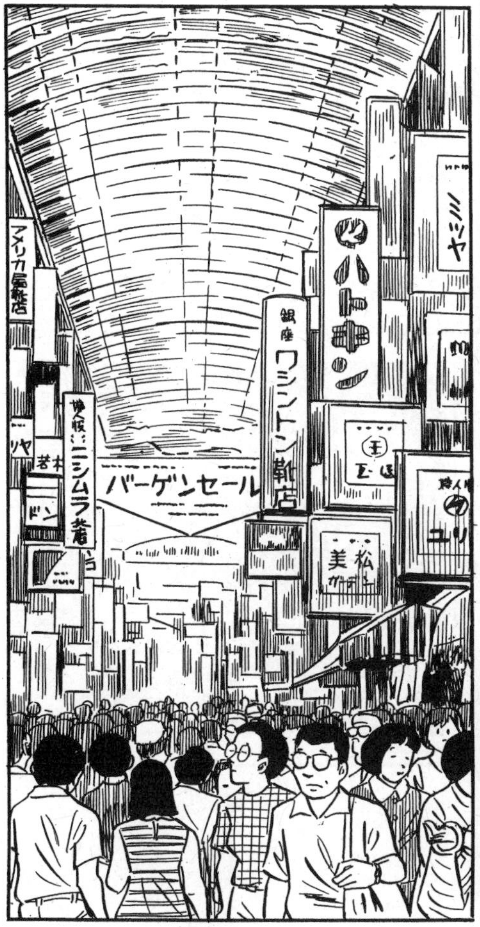
ミツヤ
バーゲンセール
銀座
ワシントン靴店
美松

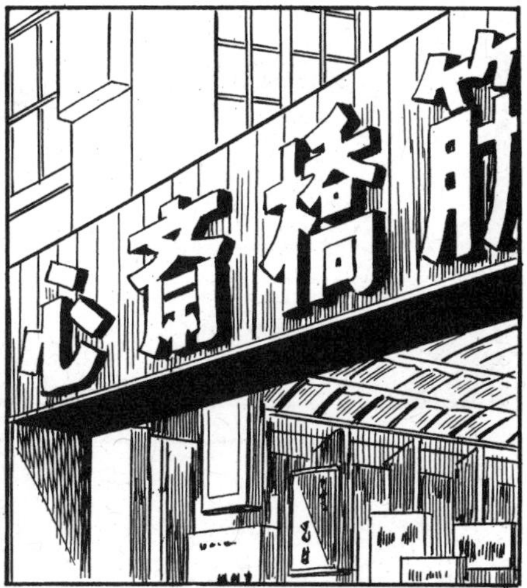
心斎橋

SIGN: SHINSAIBASHISUJI

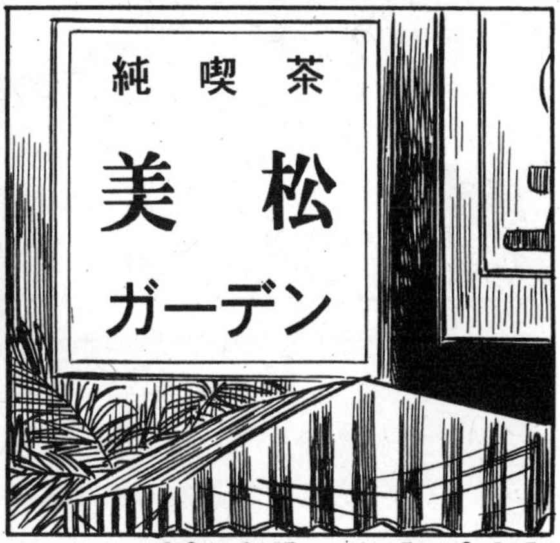
純喫茶
美松
ガーデン

SIGN: CAFE / MIMATSU GARDEN

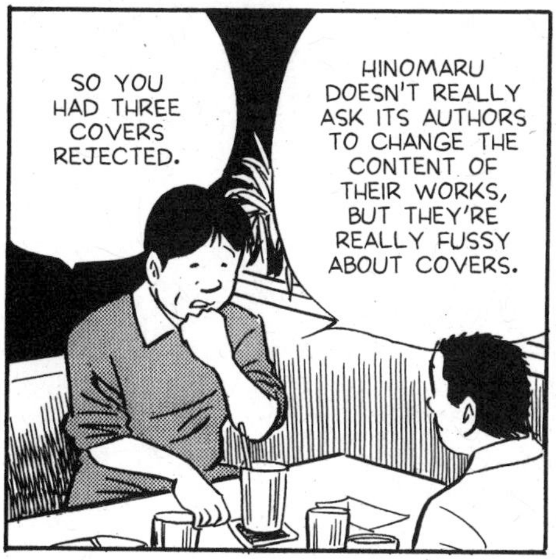
SO YOU HAD THREE COVERS REJECTED.
HINOMARU DOESN'T REALLY ASK ITS AUTHORS TO CHANGE THE CONTENT OF THEIR WORKS, BUT THEY'RE REALLY FUSSY ABOUT COVERS.

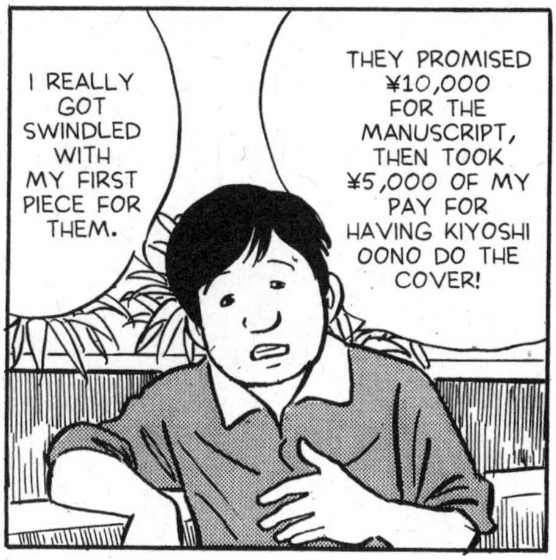
I REALLY GOT SWINDLED WITH MY FIRST PIECE FOR THEM.
THEY PROMISED ¥10,000 FOR THE MANUSCRIPT, THEN TOOK ¥5,000 OF MY PAY FOR HAVING KIYOSHI OONO DO THE COVER!

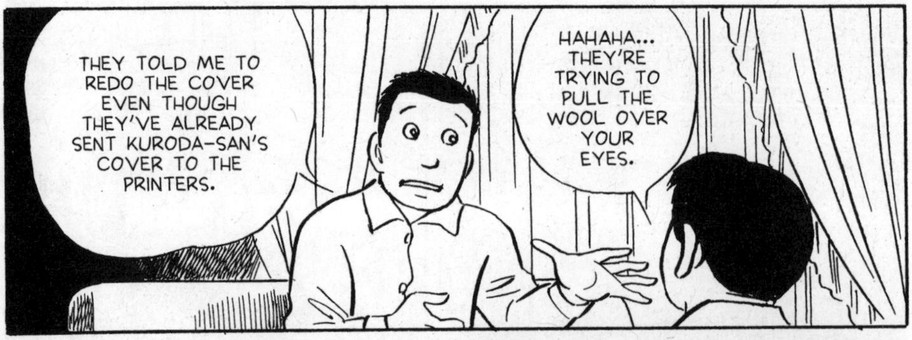
THEY TOLD ME TO REDO THE COVER EVEN THOUGH THEY'VE ALREADY SENT KURODA-SAN'S COVER TO THE PRINTERS.
HAHAHA... THEY'RE TRYING TO PULL THE WOOL OVER YOUR EYES.

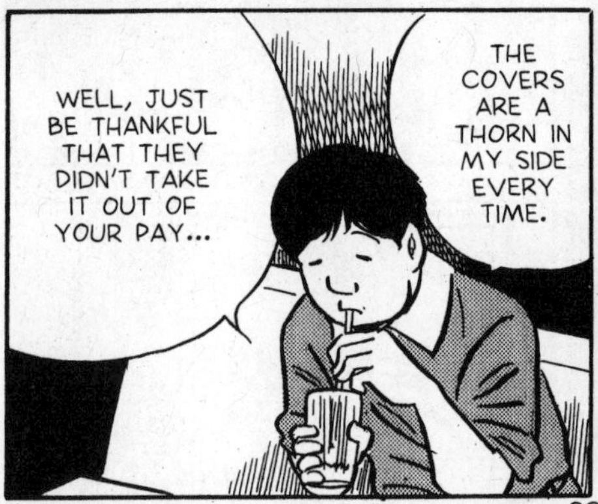
WELL, JUST BE THANKFUL THAT THEY DIDN'T TAKE IT OUT OF YOUR PAY...
THE COVERS ARE A THORN IN MY SIDE EVERY TIME.

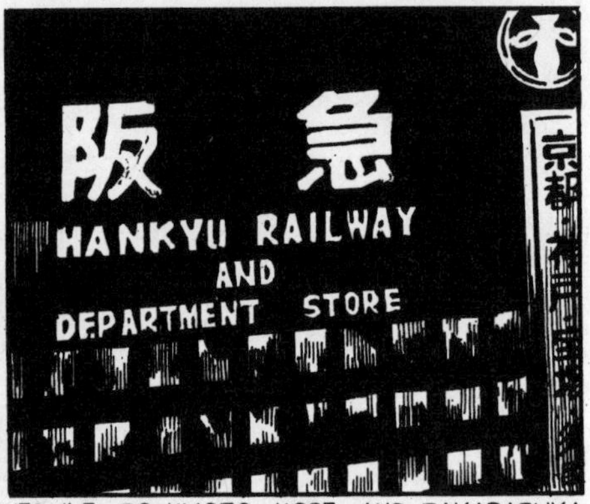
阪急
HANKYU RAILWAY
AND
DEPARTMENT STORE

SCHEDULE: TO KYOTO, KOBE, AND TAKARAZUKA

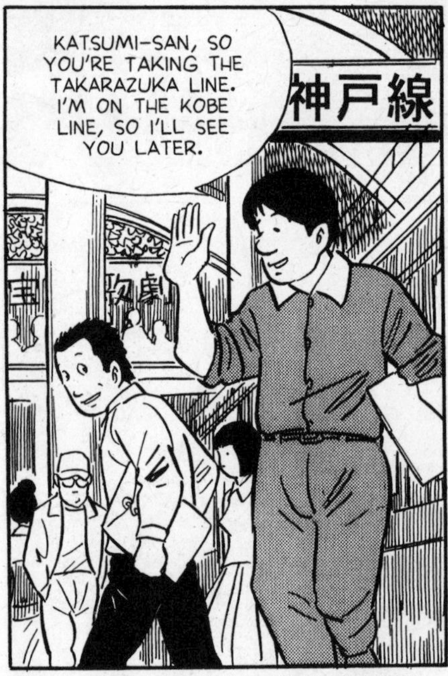
KATSUMI-SAN, SO YOU'RE TAKING THE TAKARAZUKA LINE. I'M ON THE KOBE LINE, SO I'LL SEE YOU LATER.
神戸線

SIGNS: KOBE LINE / TAKRAZUKA THEATER

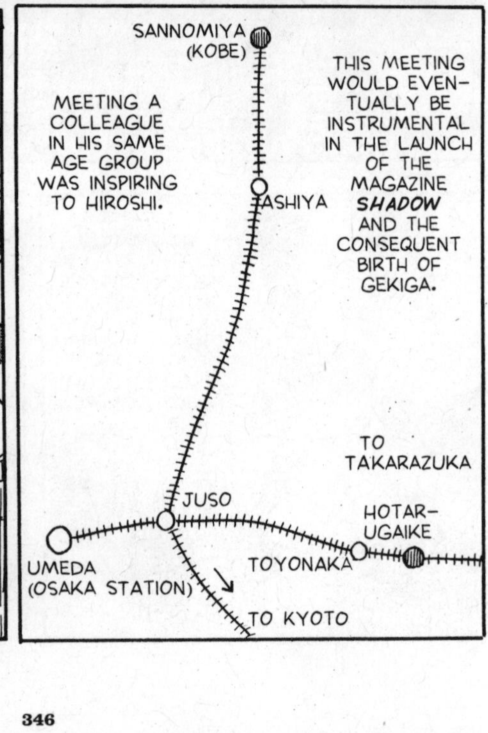
SANNOMIYA (KOBE)
MEETING A COLLEAGUE IN HIS SAME AGE GROUP WAS INSPIRING TO HIROSHI.
THIS MEETING WOULD EVENTUALLY BE INSTRUMENTAL IN THE LAUNCH OF THE MAGAZINE ***SHADOW*** AND THE CONSEQUENT BIRTH OF GEKIGA.
ASHIYA
TO TAKARAZUKA
JUSO
HOTARUGAIKE
UMEDA (OSAKA STATION)
TOYONAKA
TO KYOTO

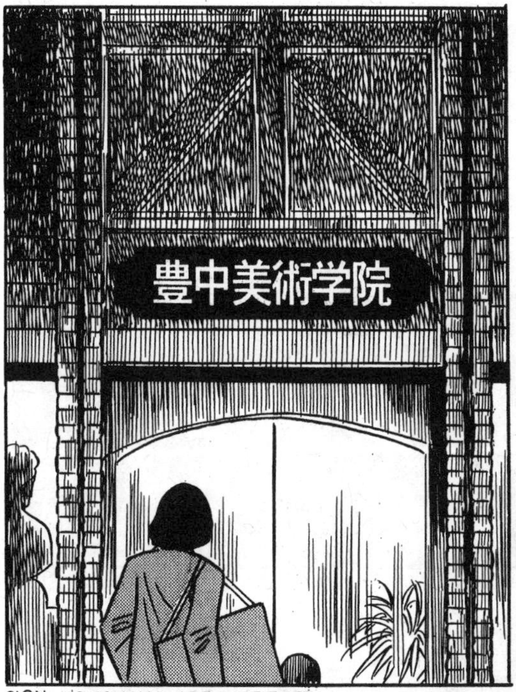
豊中美術学院

SIGN: TOYONAKA ART INSTITUTE

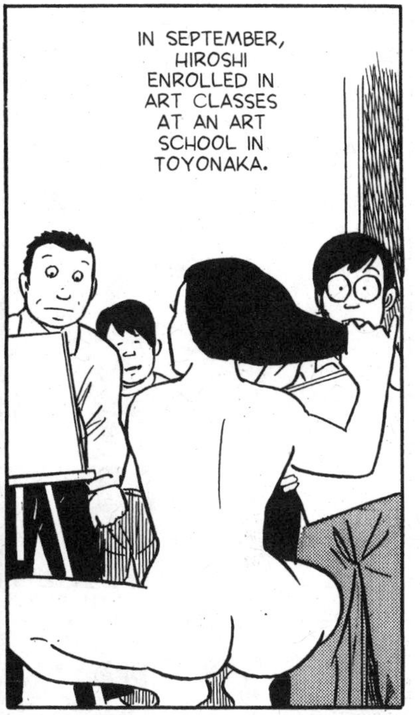
IN SEPTEMBER, HIROSHI ENROLLED IN ART CLASSES AT AN ART SCHOOL IN TOYONAKA.

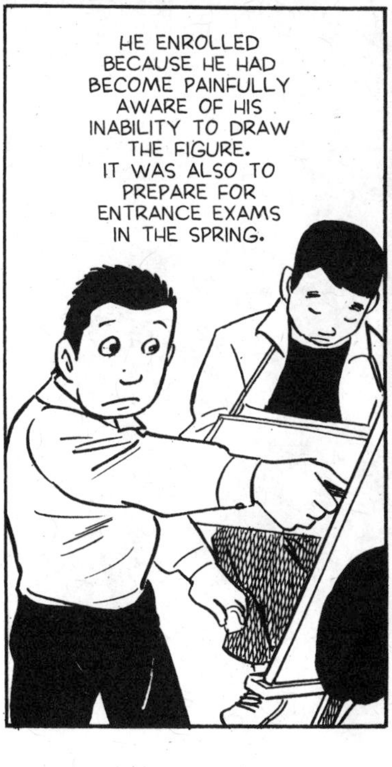
HE ENROLLED BECAUSE HE HAD BECOME PAINFULLY AWARE OF HIS INABILITY TO DRAW THE FIGURE.
IT WAS ALSO TO PREPARE FOR ENTRANCE EXAMS IN THE SPRING.

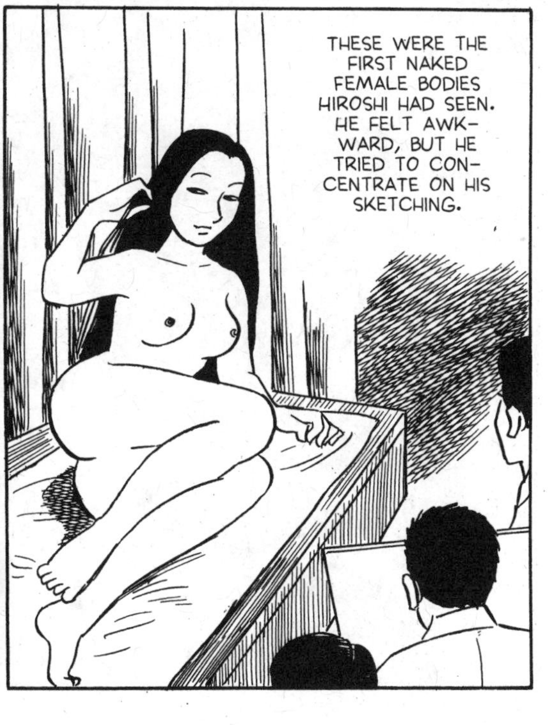
THESE WERE THE FIRST NAKED FEMALE BODIES HIROSHI HAD SEEN. HE FELT AWK-WARD, BUT HE TRIED TO CON-CENTRATE ON HIS SKETCHING.

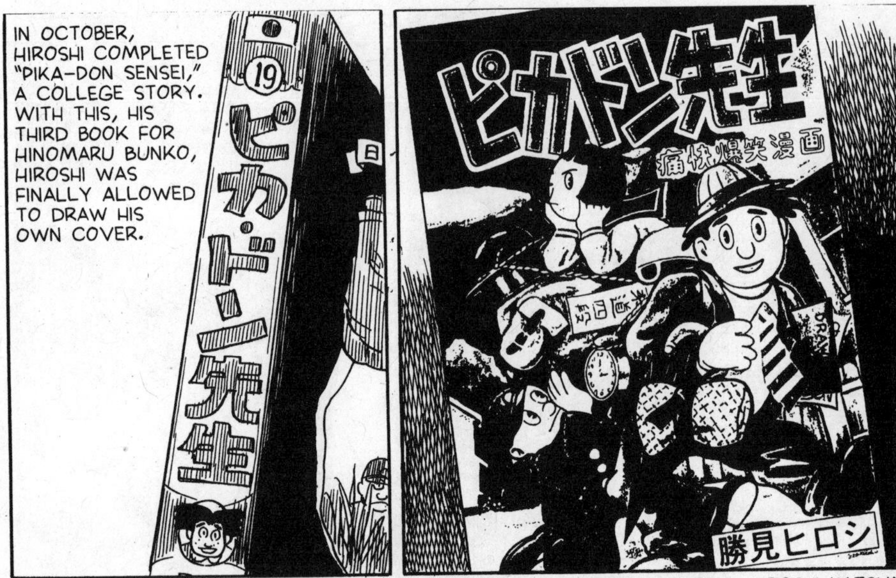
IN OCTOBER, HIROSHI COMPLETED "PIKA-DON SENSEI," A COLLEGE STORY. WITH THIS, HIS THIRD BOOK FOR HINOMARU BUNKO, HIROSHI WAS FINALLY ALLOWED TO DRAW HIS OWN COVER.
19
ピカドン先生
ピカドン先生
痛快爆笑漫画
勝見ヒロシ

TITLE: ***PIKA-DON SENSEI,*** MANGA COMEDY, HIROSHI KATSUMI

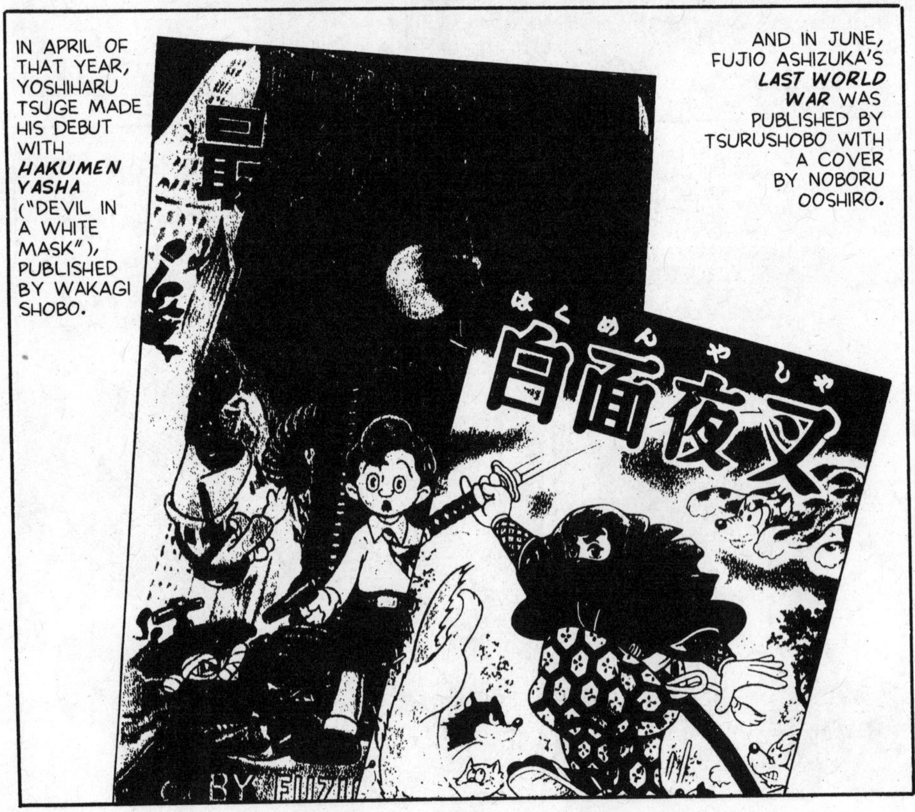
IN APRIL OF THAT YEAR, YOSHIHARU TSUGE MADE HIS DEBUT WITH ***HAKUMEN YASHA*** ("DEVIL IN A WHITE MASK"), PUBLISHED BY WAKAGI SHOBO.
AND IN JUNE, FUJIO ASHIZUKA'S ***LAST WORLD WAR*** WAS PUBLISHED BY TSURUSHOBO WITH A COVER BY NOBORU OOSHIRO.
はくめんやしゃ
白面夜叉

AN INFINITELY FREE WORLD

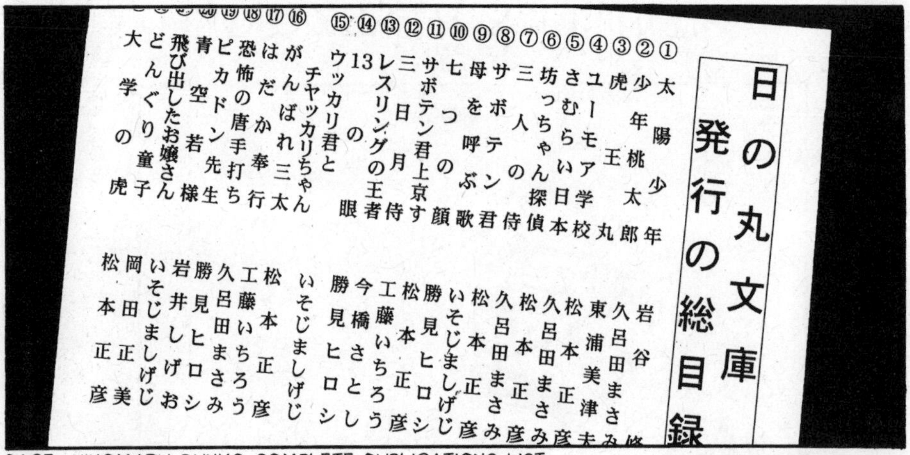
日の丸文庫
発行の総目録
① 太陽少年
岩谷
② 少年桃太郎
久呂田まさみ
③ 虎王丸
東浦美津
④ ユーモア学校
松本正彦
⑤ さむらい日本
久呂田まさみ
⑥ 坊っちゃん探偵
松本正彦
⑦ 三人の侍
久呂田まさみ
⑧ サボテン君
松本正彦
⑨ 母を呼ぶ歌
いそじましげじ
⑩ 七つの顔
勝見ヒロシ
⑪ サボテン君上京す
松本正彦
⑫ 三日月侍
工藤いちろう
⑬ レスリングの王者
今橋さとし
⑭ 13の眼
勝見ヒロシ
⑮ ウッカリ君とチャッカリちゃん
いそじましげじ
⑯ がんばれ三太
松本正彦
⑰ はだか奉行
工藤いちろう
⑱ 恐怖の唐手打ち
久呂田まさみ
⑲ ピカドン先生
勝見ヒロシ
⑳ 青空若様
岩井しげお
飛び出したお嬢さん
いそじましげじ
どんぐり童子
岡田正美
大学の虎
松本正彦
PAGE: HINOMARU BUNKO COMPLETE PUBLICATIONS LIST

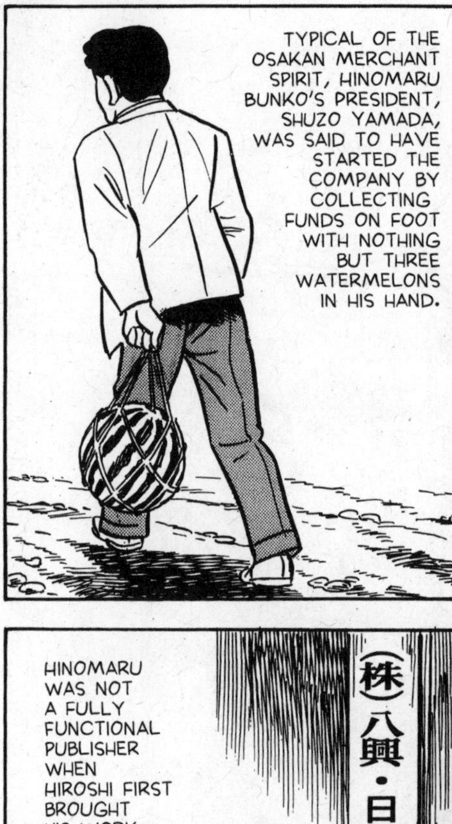
TYPICAL OF THE OSAKAN MERCHANT SPIRIT, HINOMARU BUNKO'S PRESIDENT, SHUZO YAMADA, WAS SAID TO HAVE STARTED THE COMPANY BY COLLECTING FUNDS ON FOOT WITH NOTHING BUT THREE WATERMELONS IN HIS HAND.

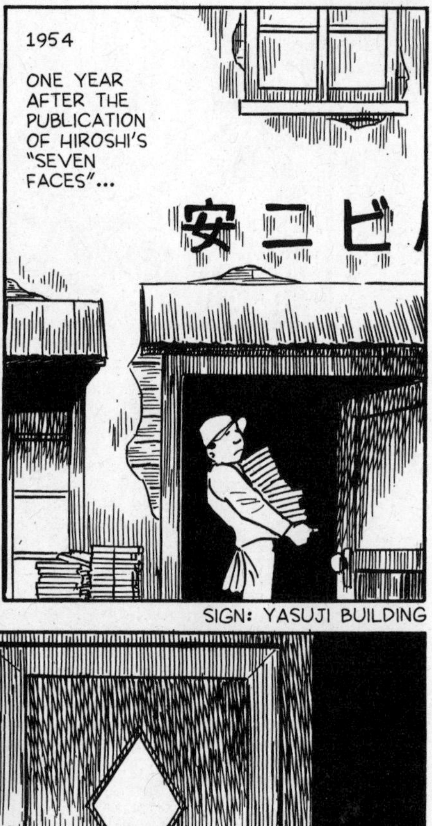
1954
ONE YEAR AFTER THE PUBLICATION OF HIROSHI'S "SEVEN FACES"...
安二ビ
SIGN: YASUJI BUILDING

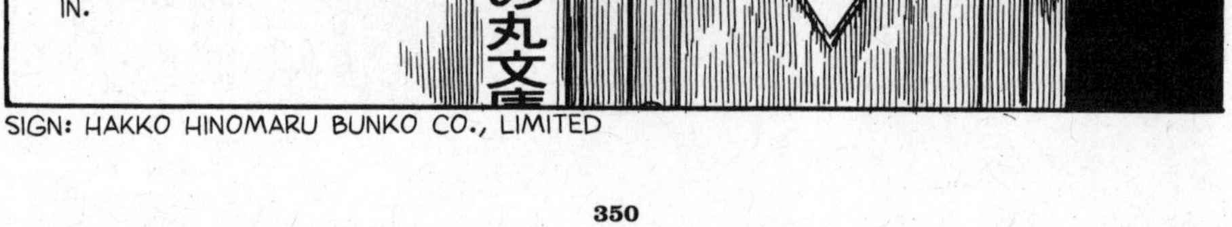
HINOMARU WAS NOT A FULLY FUNCTIONAL PUBLISHER WHEN HIROSHI FIRST BROUGHT HIS WORK IN.
㈱八興・日の丸文
SIGN: HAKKO HINOMARU BUNKO CO., LIMITED

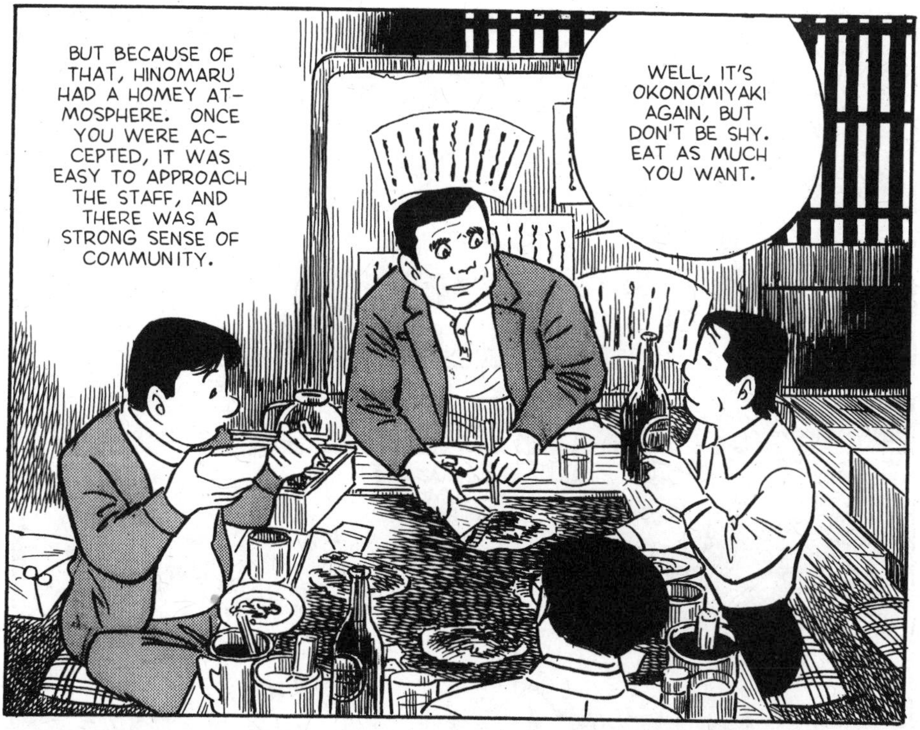
BUT BECAUSE OF THAT, HINOMARU HAD A HOMEY ATMOSPHERE. ONCE YOU WERE ACCEPTED, IT WAS EASY TO APPROACH THE STAFF, AND THERE WAS A STRONG SENSE OF COMMUNITY.
WELL, IT'S OKONOMIYAKI AGAIN, BUT DON'T BE SHY. EAT AS MUCH YOU WANT.

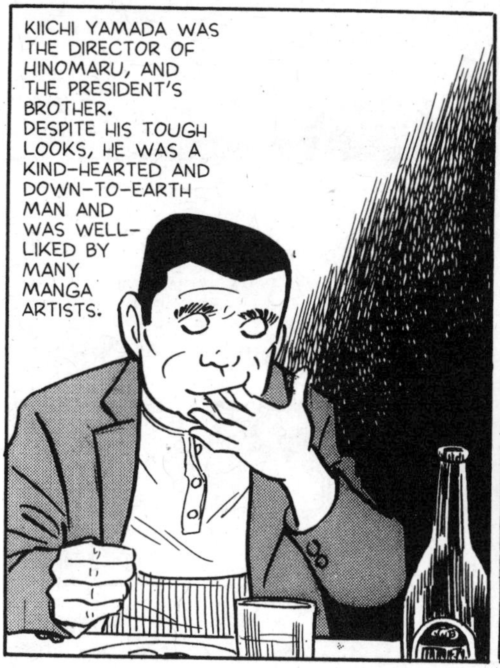
KIICHI YAMADA WAS THE DIRECTOR OF HINOMARU, AND THE PRESIDENT'S BROTHER.
DESPITE HIS TOUGH LOOKS, HE WAS A KIND-HEARTED AND DOWN-TO-EARTH MAN AND WAS WELL-LIKED BY MANY MANGA ARTISTS.

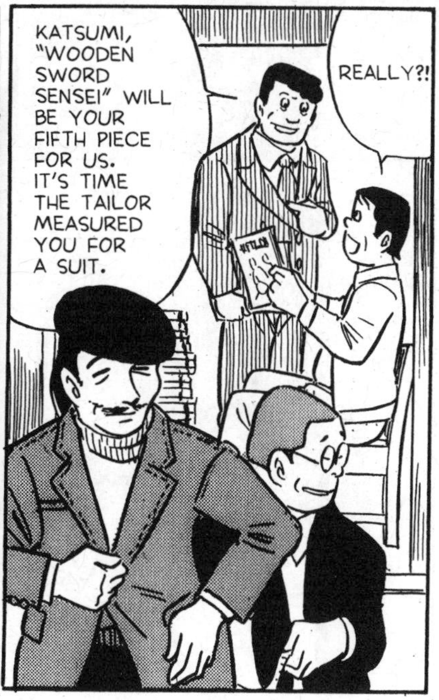
KATSUMI, "WOODEN SWORD SENSEI" WILL BE YOUR FIFTH PIECE FOR US. IT'S TIME THE TAILOR MEASURED YOU FOR A SUIT.
REALLY?!

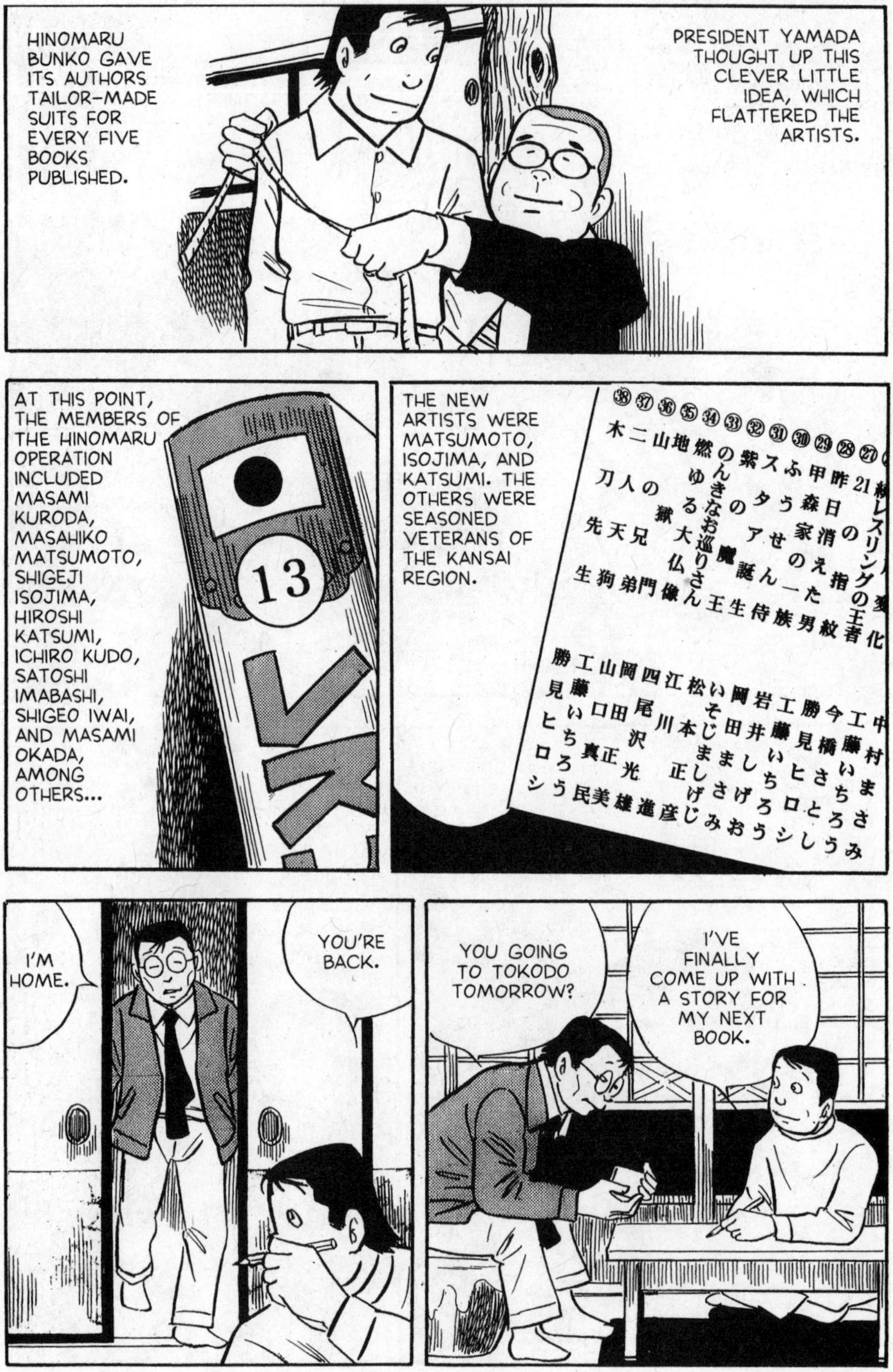
HINOMARU BUNKO GAVE ITS AUTHORS TAILOR-MADE SUITS FOR EVERY FIVE BOOKS PUBLISHED.
PRESIDENT YAMADA THOUGHT UP THIS CLEVER LITTLE IDEA, WHICH FLATTERED THE ARTISTS.
AT THIS POINT, THE MEMBERS OF THE HINOMARU OPERATION INCLUDED MASAMI KURODA, MASAHIKO MATSUMOTO, SHIGEJI ISOJIMA, HIROSHI KATSUMI, ICHIRO KUDO, SATOSHI IMABASHI, SHIGEO IWAI, AND MASAMI OKADA, AMONG OTHERS...
13
THE NEW ARTISTS WERE MATSUMOTO, ISOJIMA, AND KATSUMI. THE OTHERS WERE SEASONED VETERANS OF THE KANSAI REGION.
I'M HOME.
YOU'RE BACK.
YOU GOING TO TOKODO TOMORROW?
I'VE FINALLY COME UP WITH A STORY FOR MY NEXT BOOK.

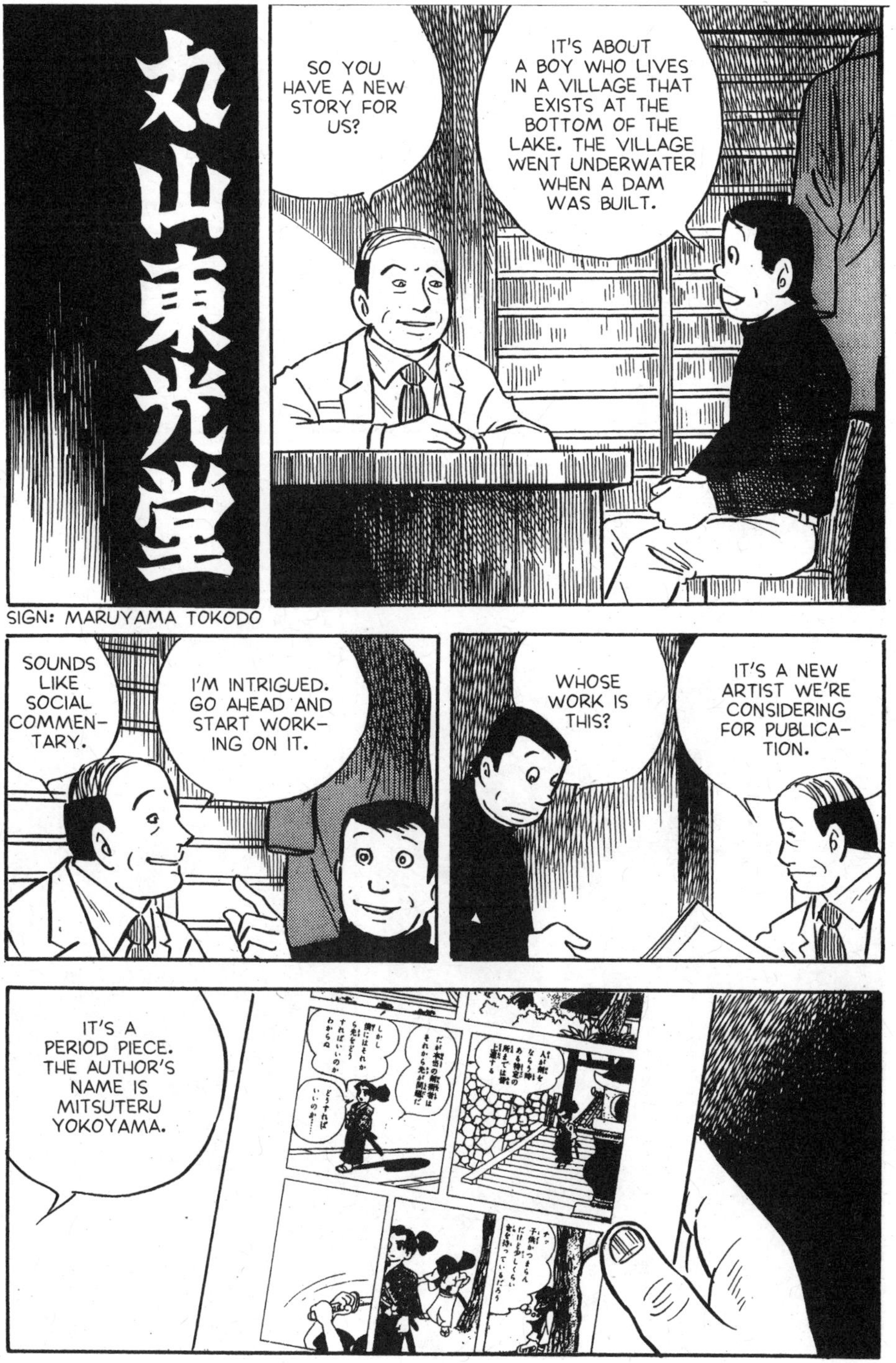
丸山東光堂
SO YOU HAVE A NEW STORY FOR US?
IT'S ABOUT A BOY WHO LIVES IN A VILLAGE THAT EXISTS AT THE BOTTOM OF THE LAKE. THE VILLAGE WENT UNDERWATER WHEN A DAM WAS BUILT.
SIGN: MARUYAMA TOKODO
SOUNDS LIKE SOCIAL COMMENTARY.
I'M INTRIGUED. GO AHEAD AND START WORKING ON IT.
WHOSE WORK IS THIS?
IT'S A NEW ARTIST WE'RE CONSIDERING FOR PUBLICATION.
IT'S A PERIOD PIECE. THE AUTHOR'S NAME IS MITSUTERU YOKOYAMA.
人が剣をならう時ある特定の所までは割に上達する
だが本当の剣術者はそれから先が問題だ
しかし僕にはそれから先をどうすればいいのかわからぬ
どうすればいいのか……
ナァ子供がつまらんだけど少しくらい金を持っているだろう

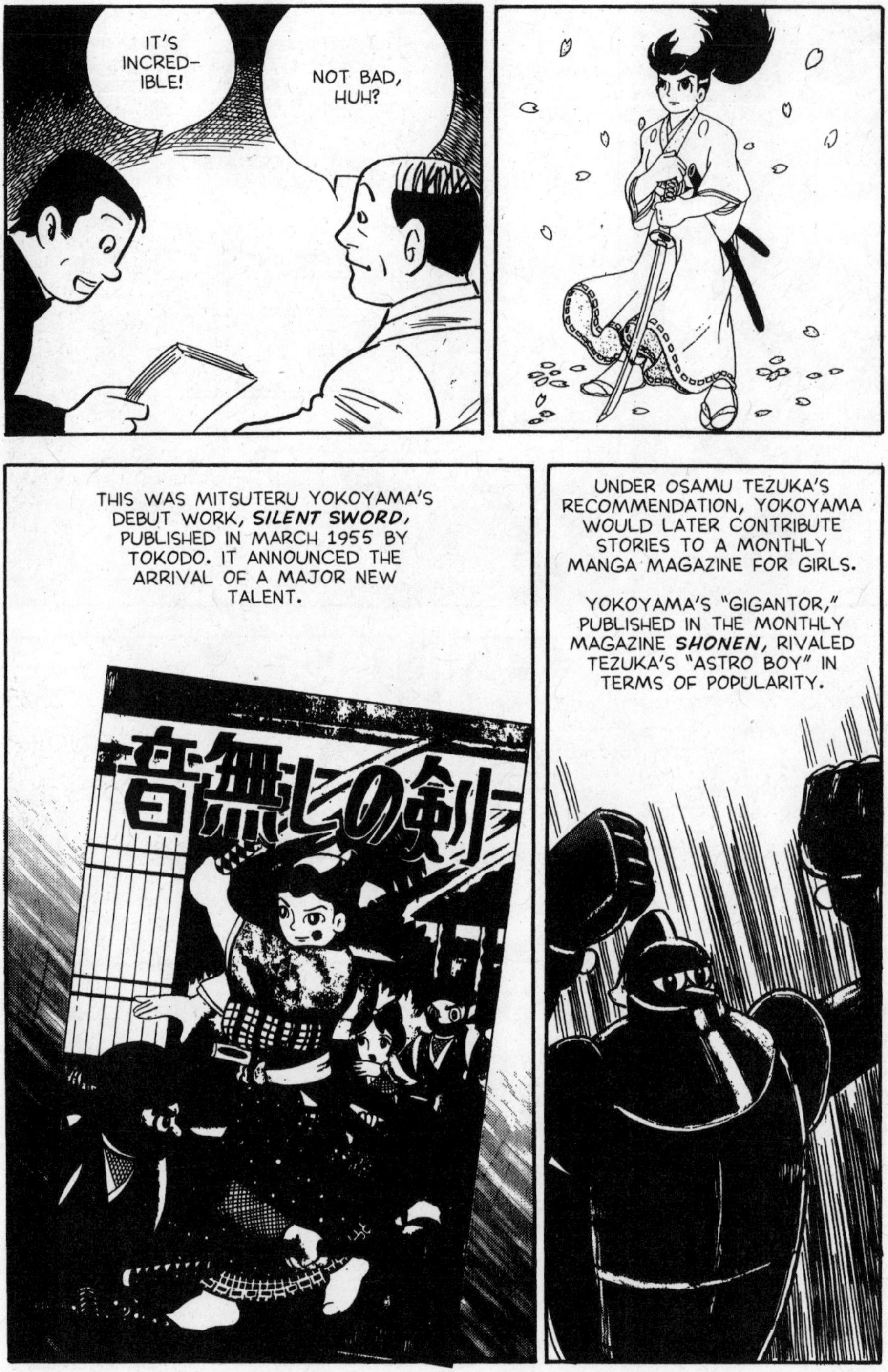
IT'S INCRED-IBLE!
NOT BAD, HUH?
THIS WAS MITSUTERU YOKOYAMA'S DEBUT WORK, ***SILENT SWORD,*** PUBLISHED IN MARCH 1955 BY TOKODO. IT ANNOUNCED THE ARRIVAL OF A MAJOR NEW TALENT.
音無しの剣
UNDER OSAMU TEZUKA'S RECOMMENDATION, YOKOYAMA WOULD LATER CONTRIBUTE STORIES TO A MONTHLY MANGA MAGAZINE FOR GIRLS.
YOKOYAMA'S "GIGANTOR," PUBLISHED IN THE MONTHLY MAGAZINE ***SHONEN,*** RIVALED TEZUKA'S "ASTRO BOY" IN TERMS OF POPULARITY.

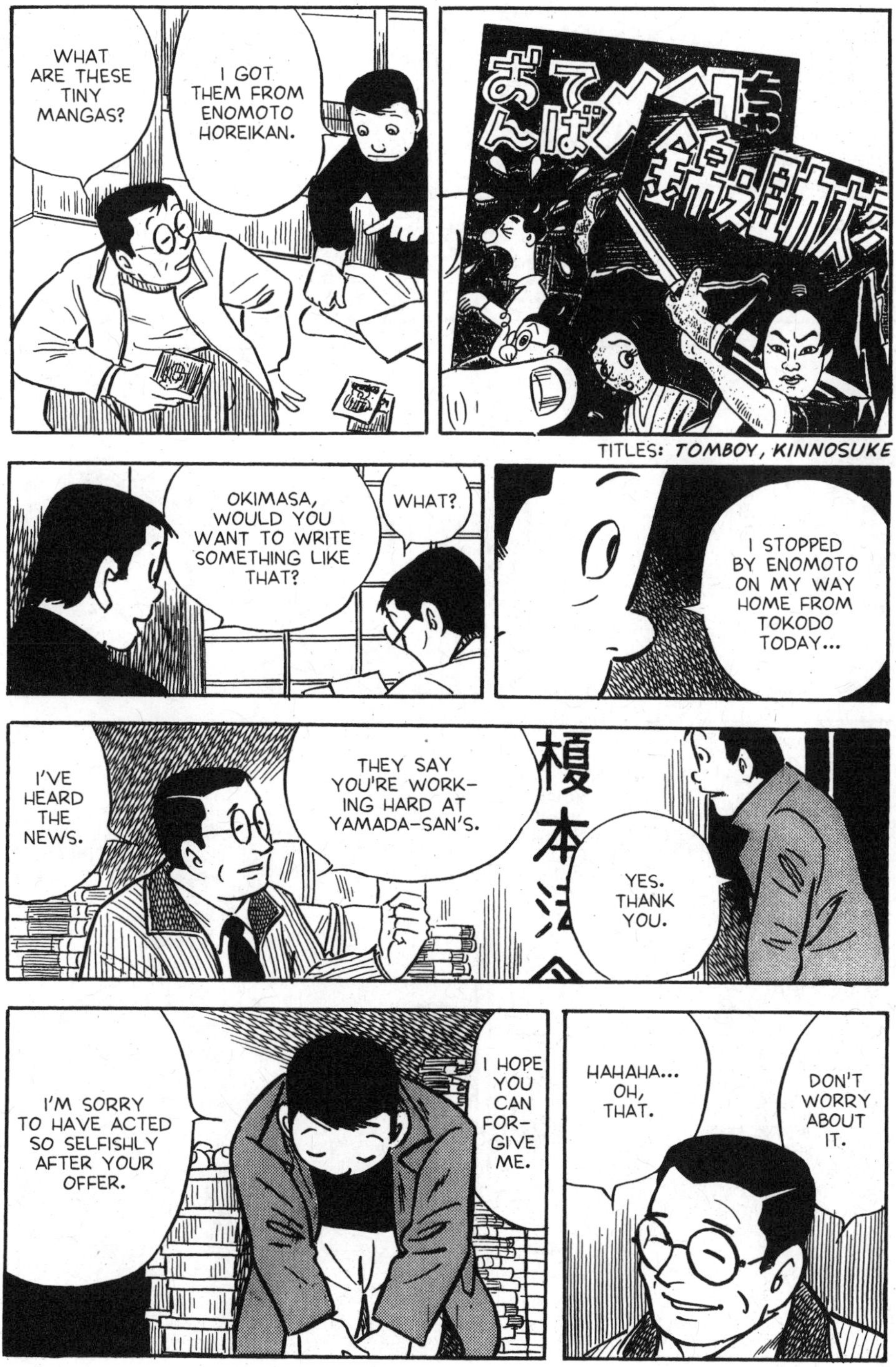
WHAT ARE THESE TINY MANGAS?
I GOT THEM FROM ENOMOTO HOREIKAN.
TITLES: TOMBOY, KINNOSUKE
OKIMASA, WOULD YOU WANT TO WRITE SOMETHING LIKE THAT?
WHAT?
I STOPPED BY ENOMOTO ON MY WAY HOME FROM TOKODO TODAY...
I'VE HEARD THE NEWS.
THEY SAY YOU'RE WORKING HARD AT YAMADA-SAN'S.
榎本法
YES. THANK YOU.
I'M SORRY TO HAVE ACTED SO SELFISHLY AFTER YOUR OFFER.
I HOPE YOU CAN FORGIVE ME.
HAHAHA... OH, THAT.
DON'T WORRY ABOUT IT.

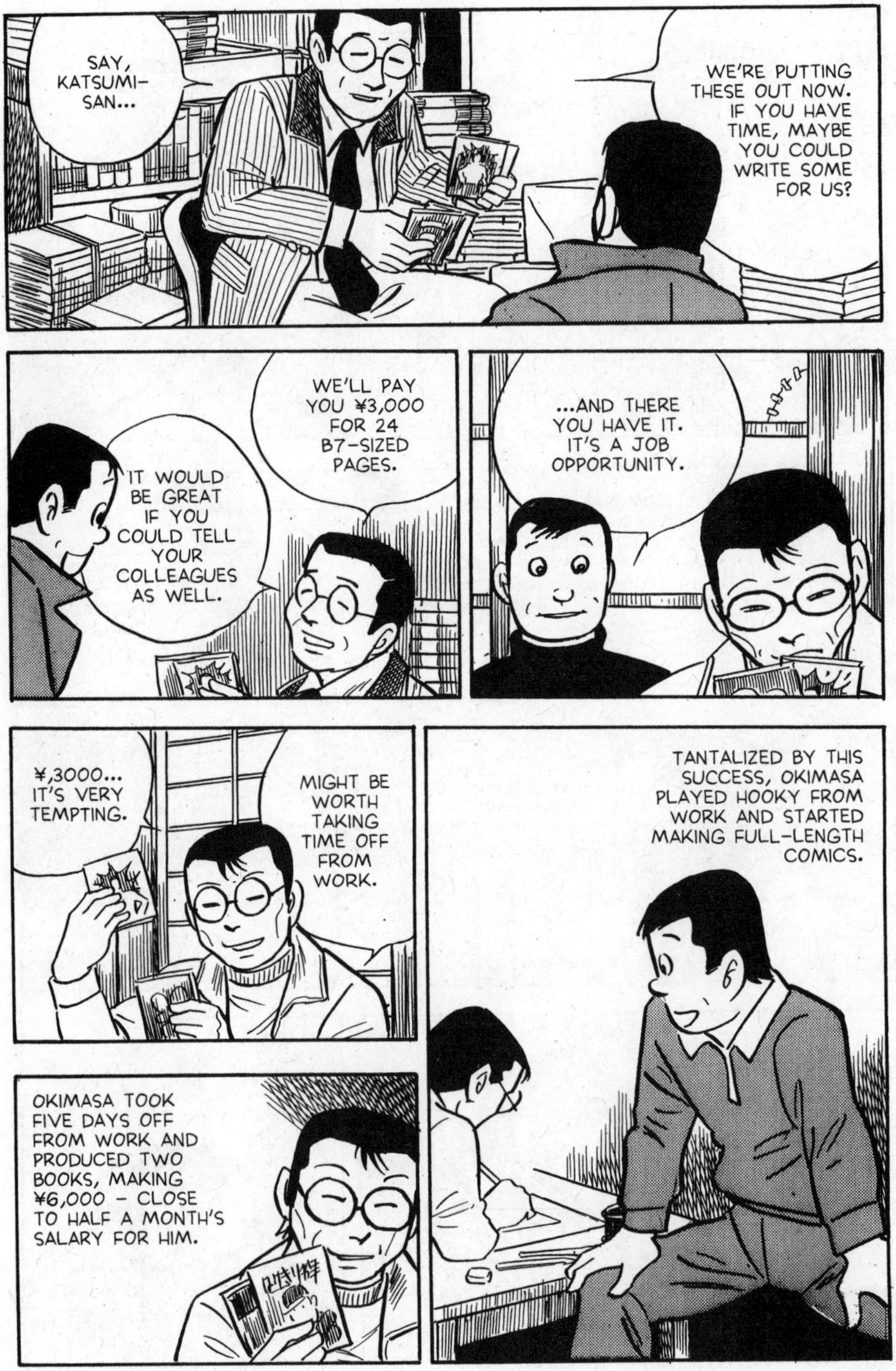

SAY, KATSUMI-SAN...
WE'RE PUTTING THESE OUT NOW. IF YOU HAVE TIME, MAYBE YOU COULD WRITE SOME FOR US?
WE'LL PAY YOU ¥3,000 FOR 24 B7-SIZED PAGES.
IT WOULD BE GREAT IF YOU COULD TELL YOUR COLLEAGUES AS WELL.
...AND THERE YOU HAVE IT. IT'S A JOB OPPORTUNITY.
¥3000... IT'S VERY TEMPTING.
MIGHT BE WORTH TAKING TIME OFF FROM WORK.
OKIMASA TOOK FIVE DAYS OFF FROM WORK AND PRODUCED TWO BOOKS, MAKING ¥6,000 – CLOSE TO HALF A MONTH'S SALARY FOR HIM.
TANTALIZED BY THIS SUCCESS, OKIMASA PLAYED HOOKY FROM WORK AND STARTED MAKING FULL-LENGTH COMICS.

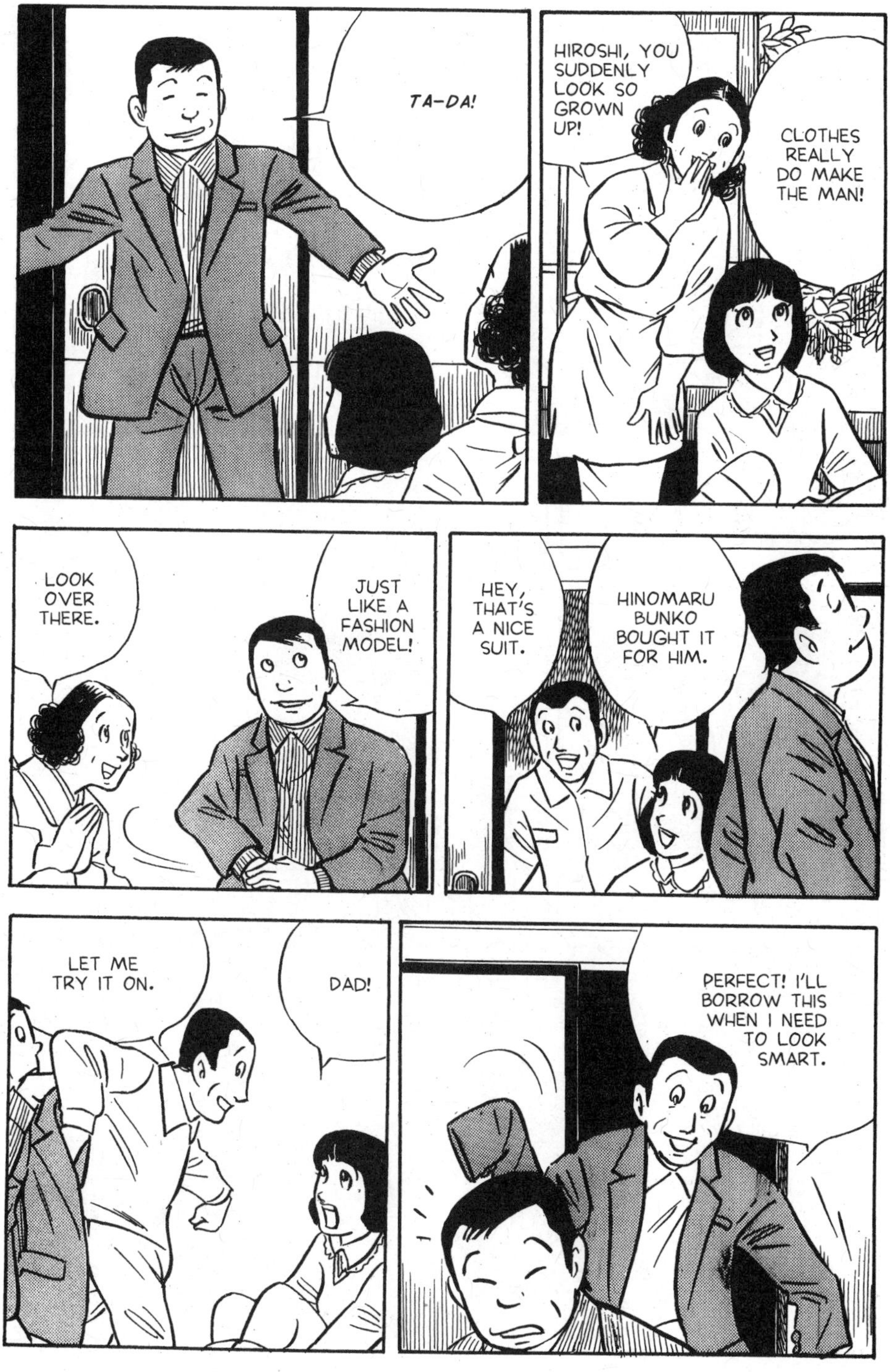
TA-DA!
HIROSHI, YOU SUDDENLY LOOK SO GROWN UP!
CLOTHES REALLY DO MAKE THE MAN!
LOOK OVER THERE.
JUST LIKE A FASHION MODEL!
HEY, THAT'S A NICE SUIT.
HINOMARU BUNKO BOUGHT IT FOR HIM.
LET ME TRY IT ON.
DAD!
PERFECT! I'LL BORROW THIS WHEN I NEED TO LOOK SMART.

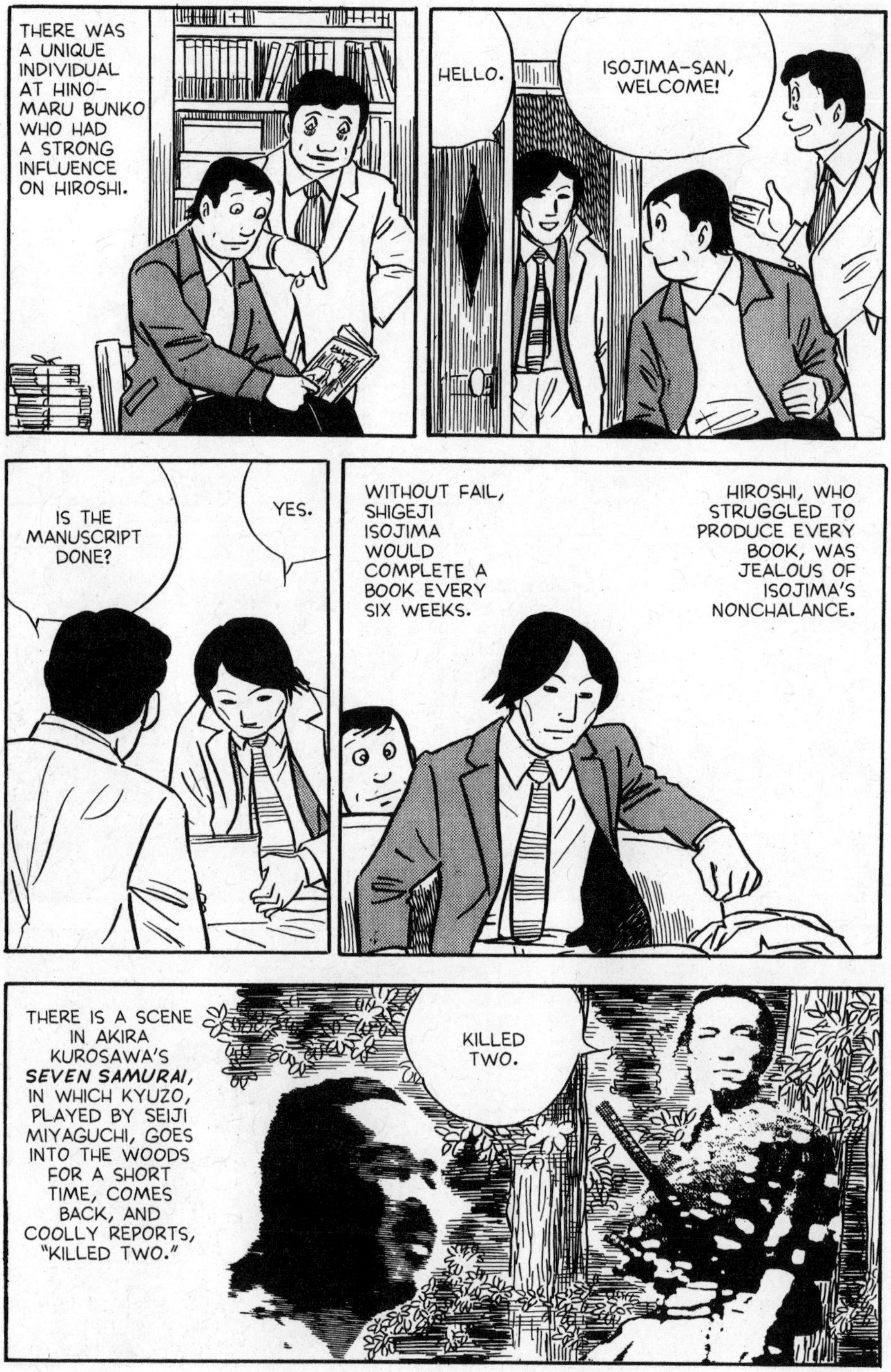
THERE WAS A UNIQUE INDIVIDUAL AT HINO-MARU BUNKO WHO HAD A STRONG INFLUENCE ON HIROSHI.
HELLO.
ISOJIMA-SAN, WELCOME!
IS THE MANUSCRIPT DONE?
YES.
WITHOUT FAIL, SHIGEJI ISOJIMA WOULD COMPLETE A BOOK EVERY SIX WEEKS.
HIROSHI, WHO STRUGGLED TO PRODUCE EVERY BOOK, WAS JEALOUS OF ISOJIMA'S NONCHALANCE.
THERE IS A SCENE IN AKIRA KUROSAWA'S ***SEVEN SAMURAI,*** IN WHICH KYUZO, PLAYED BY SEIJI MIYAGUCHI, GOES INTO THE WOODS FOR A SHORT TIME, COMES BACK, AND COOLLY REPORTS, "KILLED TWO."
KILLED TWO.

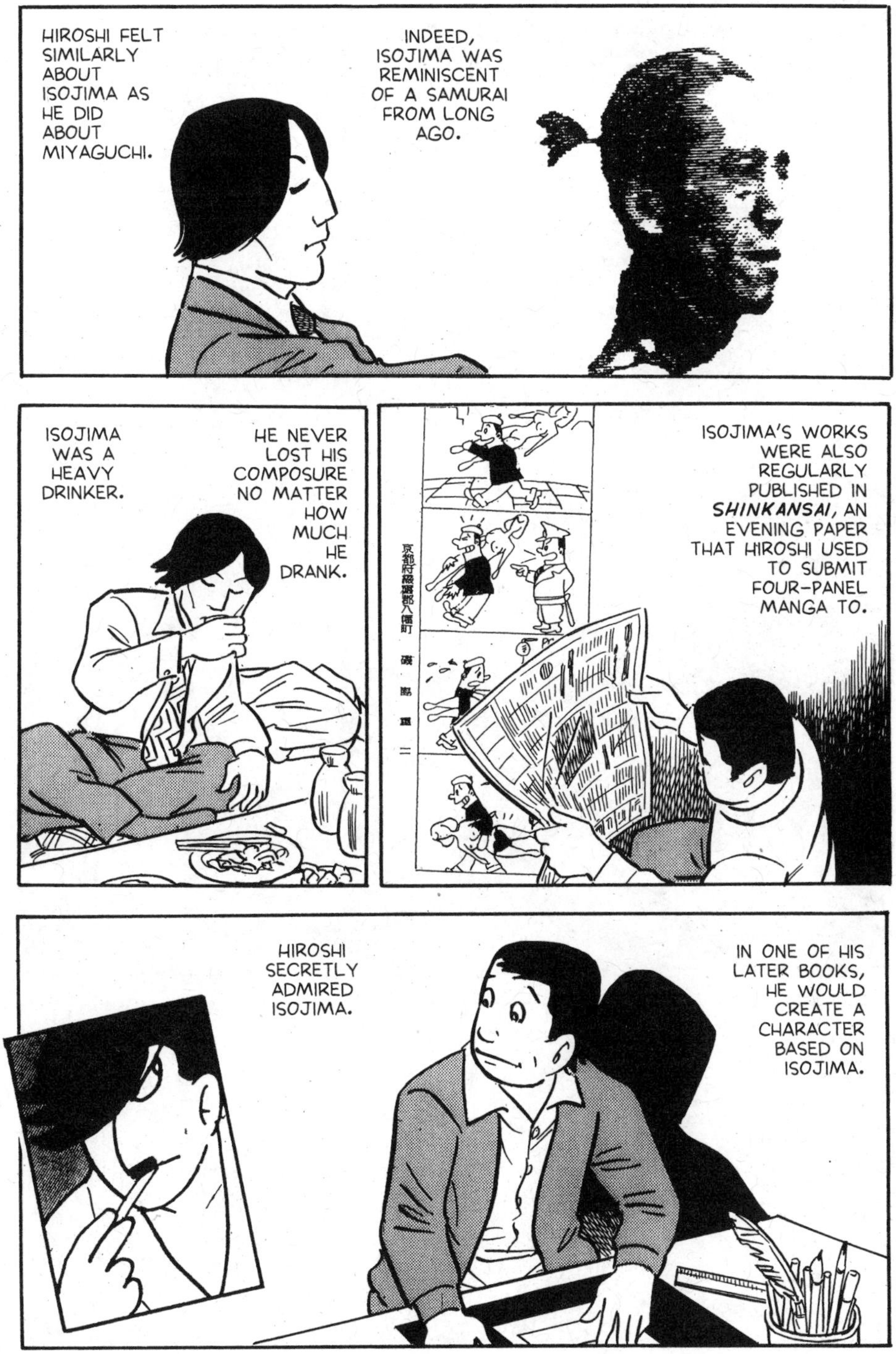
HIROSHI FELT SIMILARLY ABOUT ISOJIMA AS HE DID ABOUT MIYAGUCHI.
INDEED, ISOJIMA WAS REMINISCENT OF A SAMURAI FROM LONG AGO.
ISOJIMA WAS A HEAVY DRINKER.
HE NEVER LOST HIS COMPOSURE NO MATTER HOW MUCH HE DRANK.
ISOJIMA'S WORKS WERE ALSO REGULARLY PUBLISHED IN *SHINKANSAI*, AN EVENING PAPER THAT HIROSHI USED TO SUBMIT FOUR-PANEL MANGA TO.
HIROSHI SECRETLY ADMIRED ISOJIMA.
IN ONE OF HIS LATER BOOKS, HE WOULD CREATE A CHARACTER BASED ON ISOJIMA.

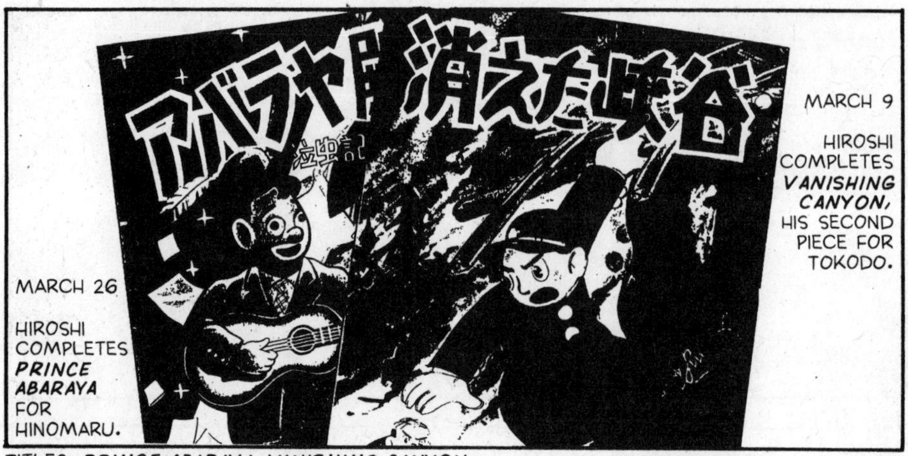

アバラヤ
消えた峡谷
MARCH 9
HIROSHI COMPLETES ***VANISHING CANYON,*** HIS SECOND PIECE FOR TOKODO.
MARCH 26
HIROSHI COMPLETES ***PRINCE ABARAYA*** FOR HINOMARU.

TITLES: ***PRINCE ABARAYA, VANISHING CANYON***

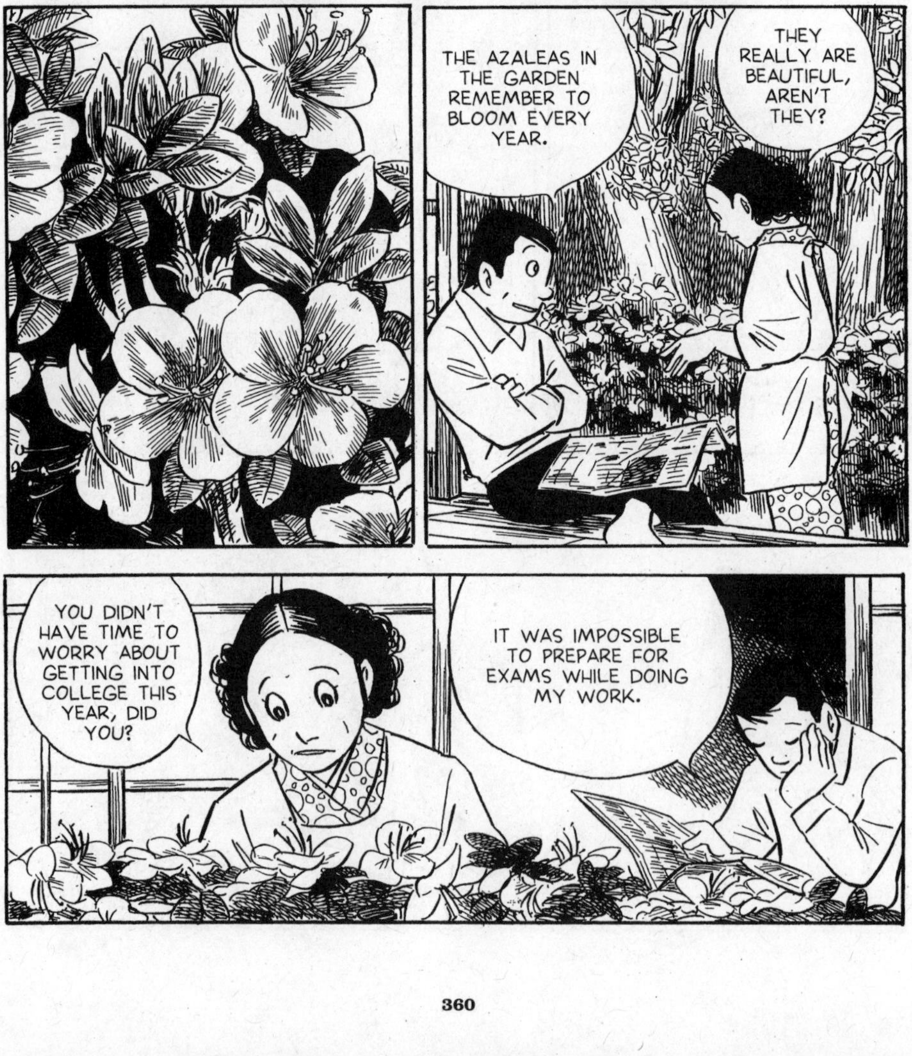

THE AZALEAS IN THE GARDEN REMEMBER TO BLOOM EVERY YEAR.
THEY REALLY ARE BEAUTIFUL, AREN'T THEY?
YOU DIDN'T HAVE TIME TO WORRY ABOUT GETTING INTO COLLEGE THIS YEAR, DID YOU?
IT WAS IMPOSSIBLE TO PREPARE FOR EXAMS WHILE DOING MY WORK.

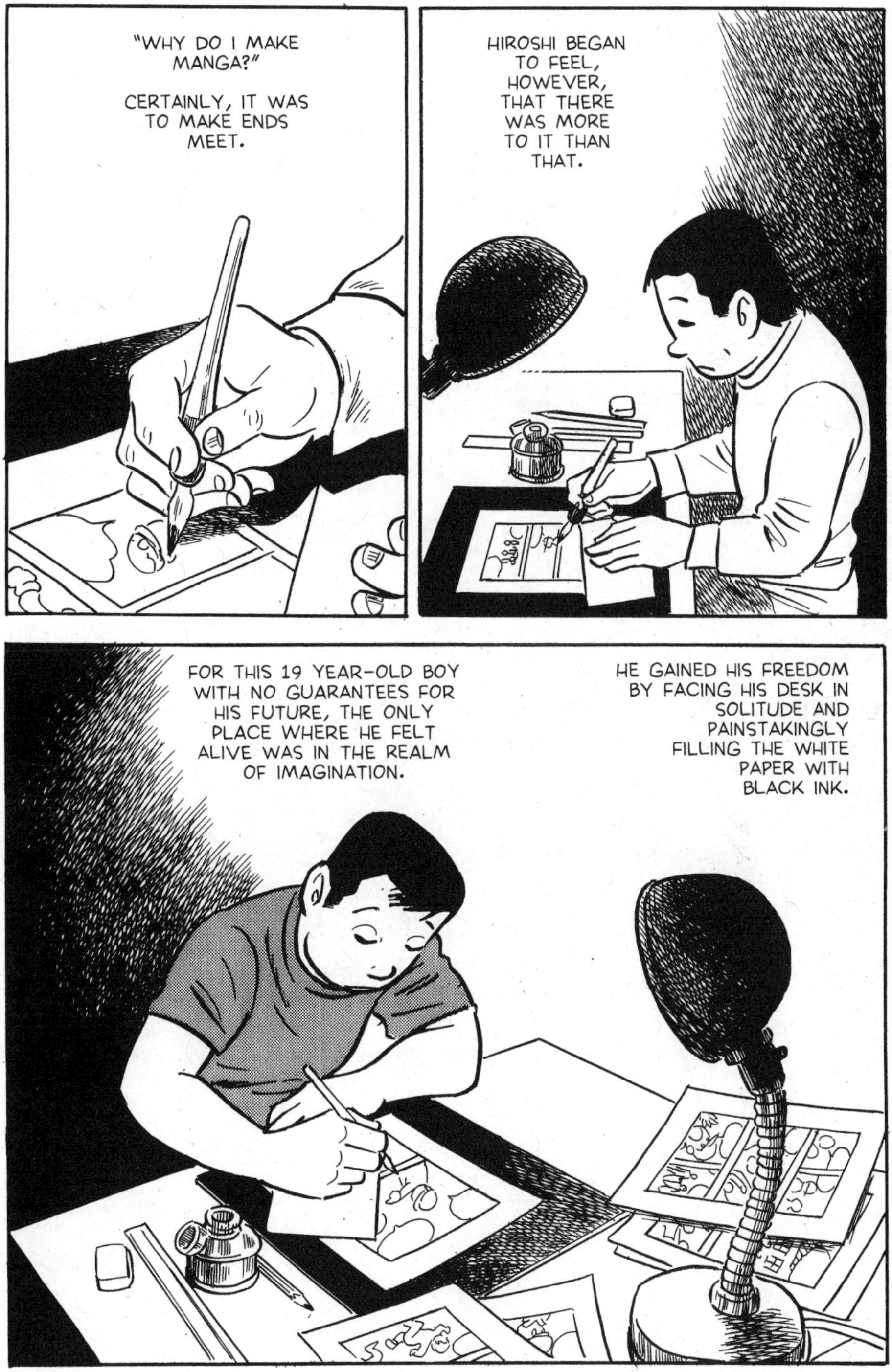
"WHY DO I MAKE MANGA?"
CERTAINLY, IT WAS TO MAKE ENDS MEET.
HIROSHI BEGAN TO FEEL, HOWEVER, THAT THERE WAS MORE TO IT THAN THAT.
FOR THIS 19 YEAR-OLD BOY WITH NO GUARANTEES FOR HIS FUTURE, THE ONLY PLACE WHERE HE FELT ALIVE WAS IN THE REALM OF IMAGINATION.
HE GAINED HIS FREEDOM BY FACING HIS DESK IN SOLITUDE AND PAINSTAKINGLY FILLING THE WHITE PAPER WITH BLACK INK.

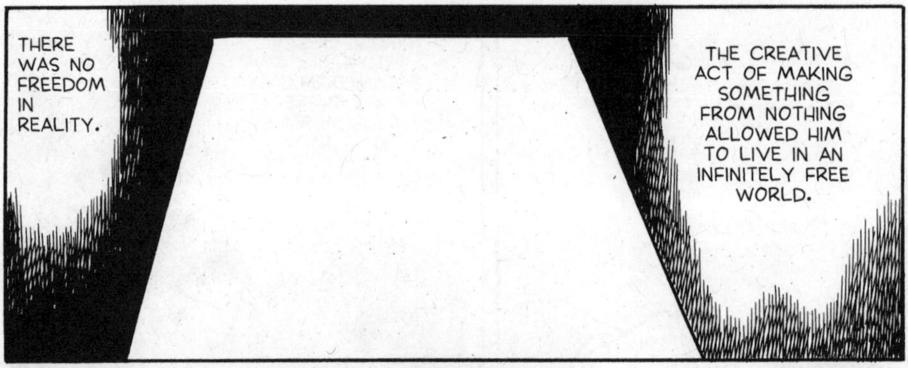
THERE WAS NO FREEDOM IN REALITY.
THE CREATIVE ACT OF MAKING SOMETHING FROM NOTHING ALLOWED HIM TO LIVE IN AN INFINITELY FREE WORLD.

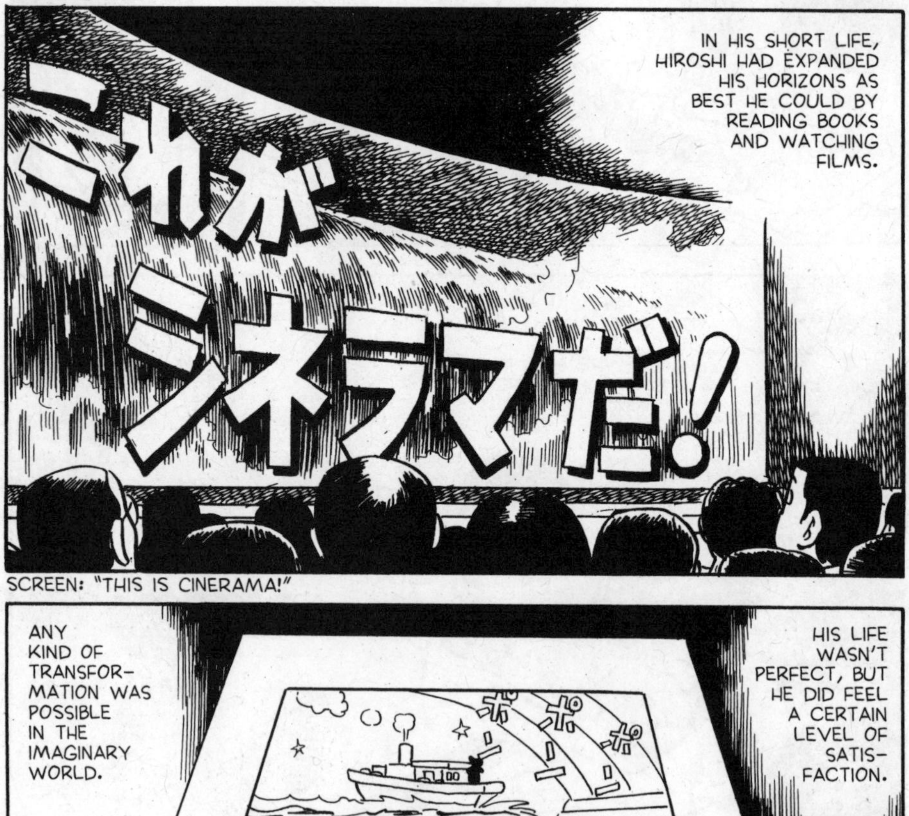
IN HIS SHORT LIFE, HIROSHI HAD EXPANDED HIS HORIZONS AS BEST HE COULD BY READING BOOKS AND WATCHING FILMS.
これが
シネラマだ!

SCREEN: "THIS IS CINERAMA!"

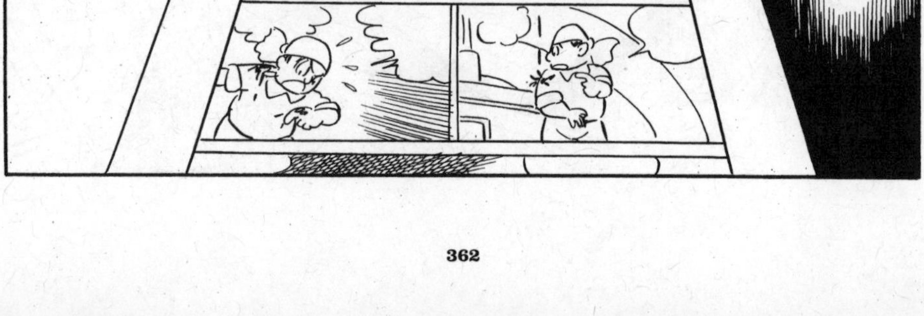
ANY KIND OF TRANSFORMATION WAS POSSIBLE IN THE IMAGINARY WORLD.
HIS LIFE WASN'T PERFECT, BUT HE DID FEEL A CERTAIN LEVEL OF SATISFACTION.

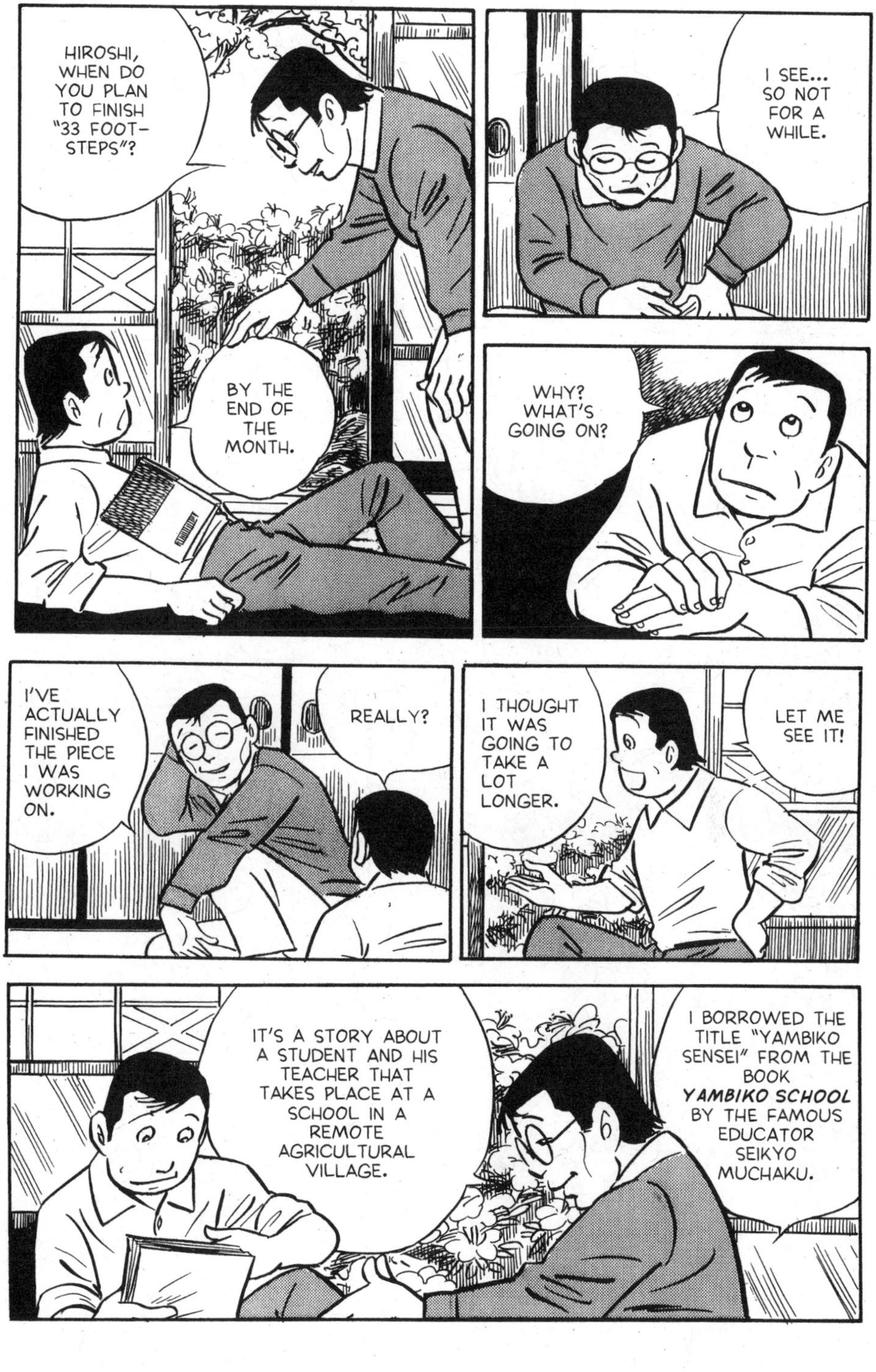
HIROSHI, WHEN DO YOU PLAN TO FINISH "33 FOOT-STEPS"?
BY THE END OF THE MONTH.
I SEE... SO NOT FOR A WHILE.
WHY? WHAT'S GOING ON?
I'VE ACTUALLY FINISHED THE PIECE I WAS WORKING ON.
REALLY?
I THOUGHT IT WAS GOING TO TAKE A LOT LONGER.
LET ME SEE IT!
IT'S A STORY ABOUT A STUDENT AND HIS TEACHER THAT TAKES PLACE AT A SCHOOL IN A REMOTE AGRICULTURAL VILLAGE.
I BORROWED THE TITLE "YAMBIKO SENSEI" FROM THE BOOK ***YAMBIKO SCHOOL*** BY THE FAMOUS EDUCATOR SEIKYO MUCHAKU.

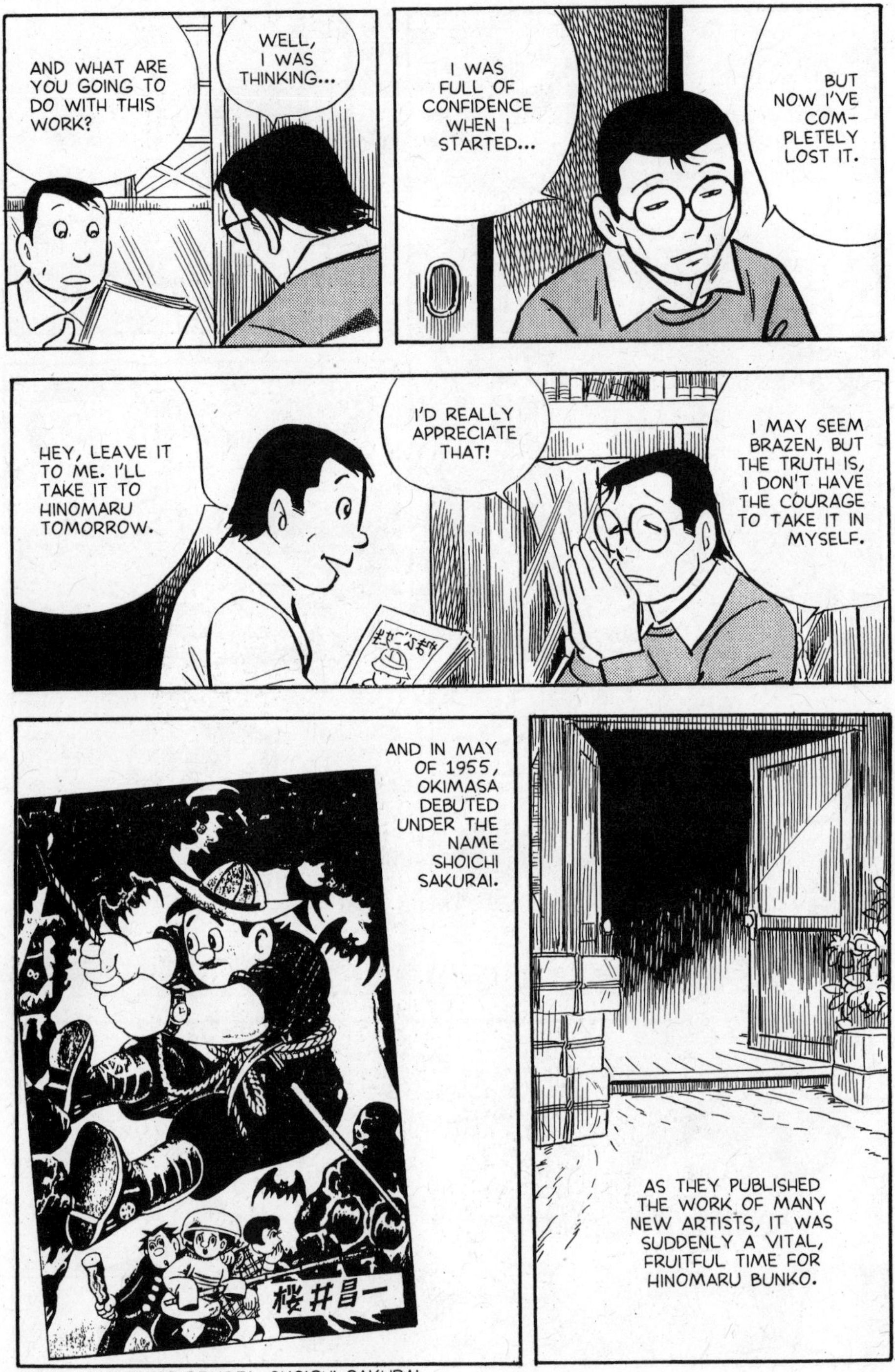
AND WHAT ARE YOU GOING TO DO WITH THIS WORK?
WELL, I WAS THINKING...
I WAS FULL OF CONFIDENCE WHEN I STARTED...
BUT NOW I'VE COM-PLETELY LOST IT.
HEY, LEAVE IT TO ME. I'LL TAKE IT TO HINOMARU TOMORROW.
I'D REALLY APPRECIATE THAT!
I MAY SEEM BRAZEN, BUT THE TRUTH IS, I DON'T HAVE THE COURAGE TO TAKE IT IN MYSELF.
AND IN MAY OF 1955, OKIMASA DEBUTED UNDER THE NAME SHOICHI SAKURAI.
桜井昌一
AS THEY PUBLISHED THE WORK OF MANY NEW ARTISTS, IT WAS SUDDENLY A VITAL, FRUITFUL TIME FOR HINOMARU BUNKO.

TITLE: *YAMABIKO SENSEI*, SHOICHI SAKURAI

THE MANGA MONSTER

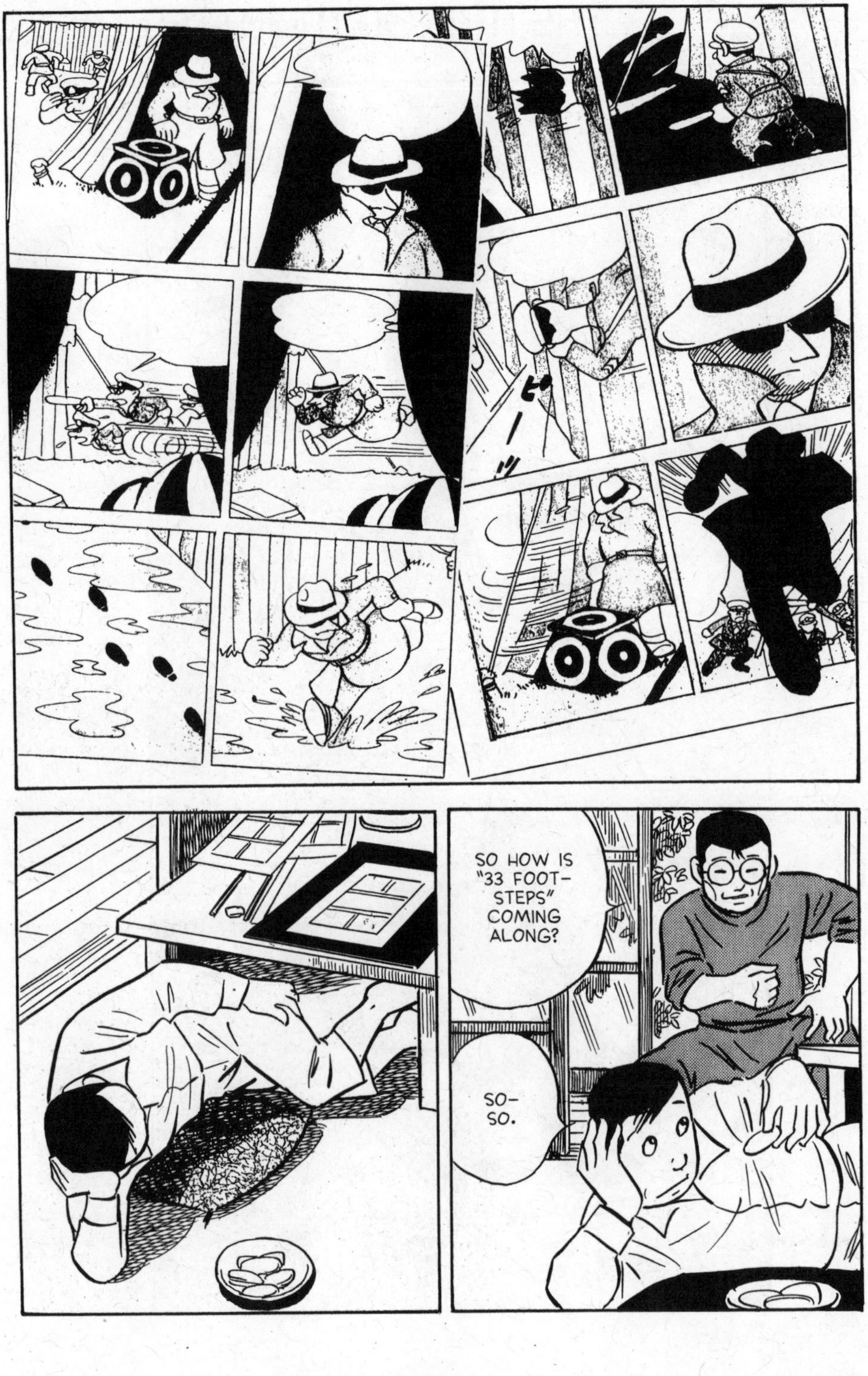
SO HOW IS "33 FOOT-STEPS" COMING ALONG?
SO-SO.

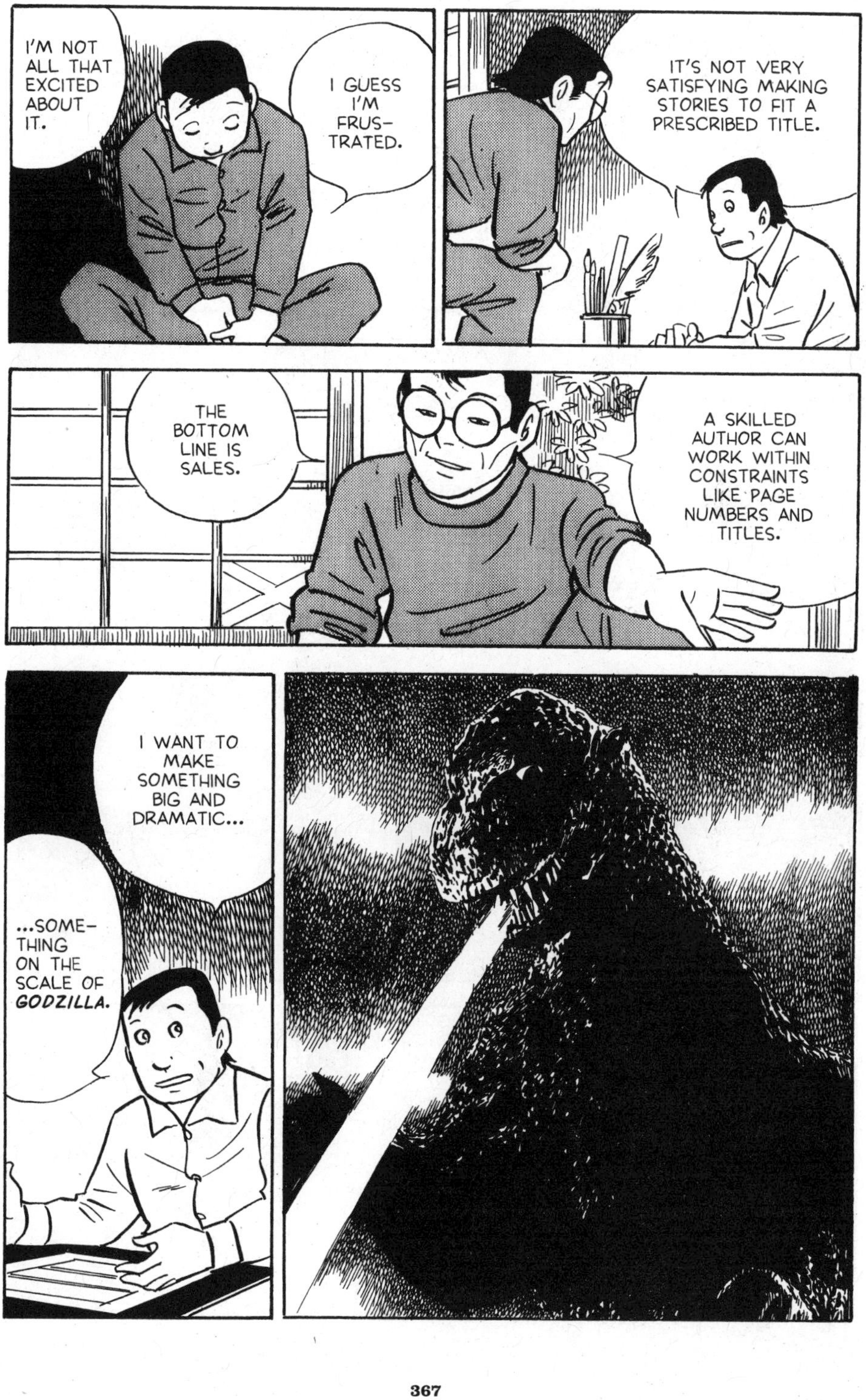
I'M NOT ALL THAT EXCITED ABOUT IT.
I GUESS I'M FRUS-TRATED.
IT'S NOT VERY SATISFYING MAKING STORIES TO FIT A PRESCRIBED TITLE.
THE BOTTOM LINE IS SALES.
A SKILLED AUTHOR CAN WORK WITHIN CONSTRAINTS LIKE PAGE NUMBERS AND TITLES.
I WANT TO MAKE SOMETHING BIG AND DRAMATIC...
...SOME-THING ON THE SCALE OF *GODZILLA*.

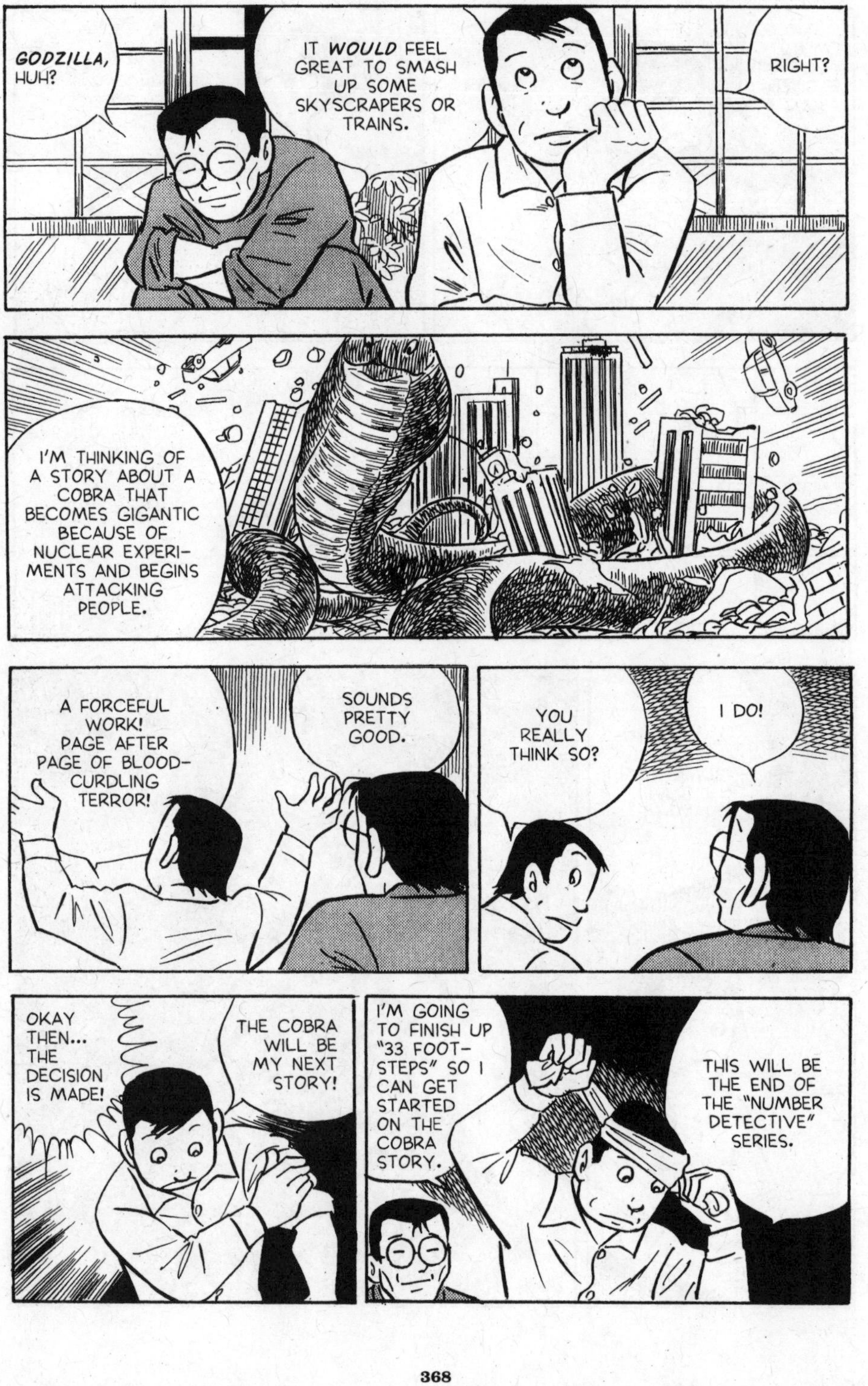
GODZILLA, HUH?
IT *WOULD* FEEL GREAT TO SMASH UP SOME SKYSCRAPERS OR TRAINS.
RIGHT?
I'M THINKING OF A STORY ABOUT A COBRA THAT BECOMES GIGANTIC BECAUSE OF NUCLEAR EXPERIMENTS AND BEGINS ATTACKING PEOPLE.
A FORCEFUL WORK! PAGE AFTER PAGE OF BLOOD-CURDLING TERROR!
SOUNDS PRETTY GOOD.
YOU REALLY THINK SO?
I DO!
OKAY THEN... THE DECISION IS MADE!
THE COBRA WILL BE MY NEXT STORY!
I'M GOING TO FINISH UP "33 FOOT-STEPS" SO I CAN GET STARTED ON THE COBRA STORY.
THIS WILL BE THE END OF THE "NUMBER DETECTIVE" SERIES.

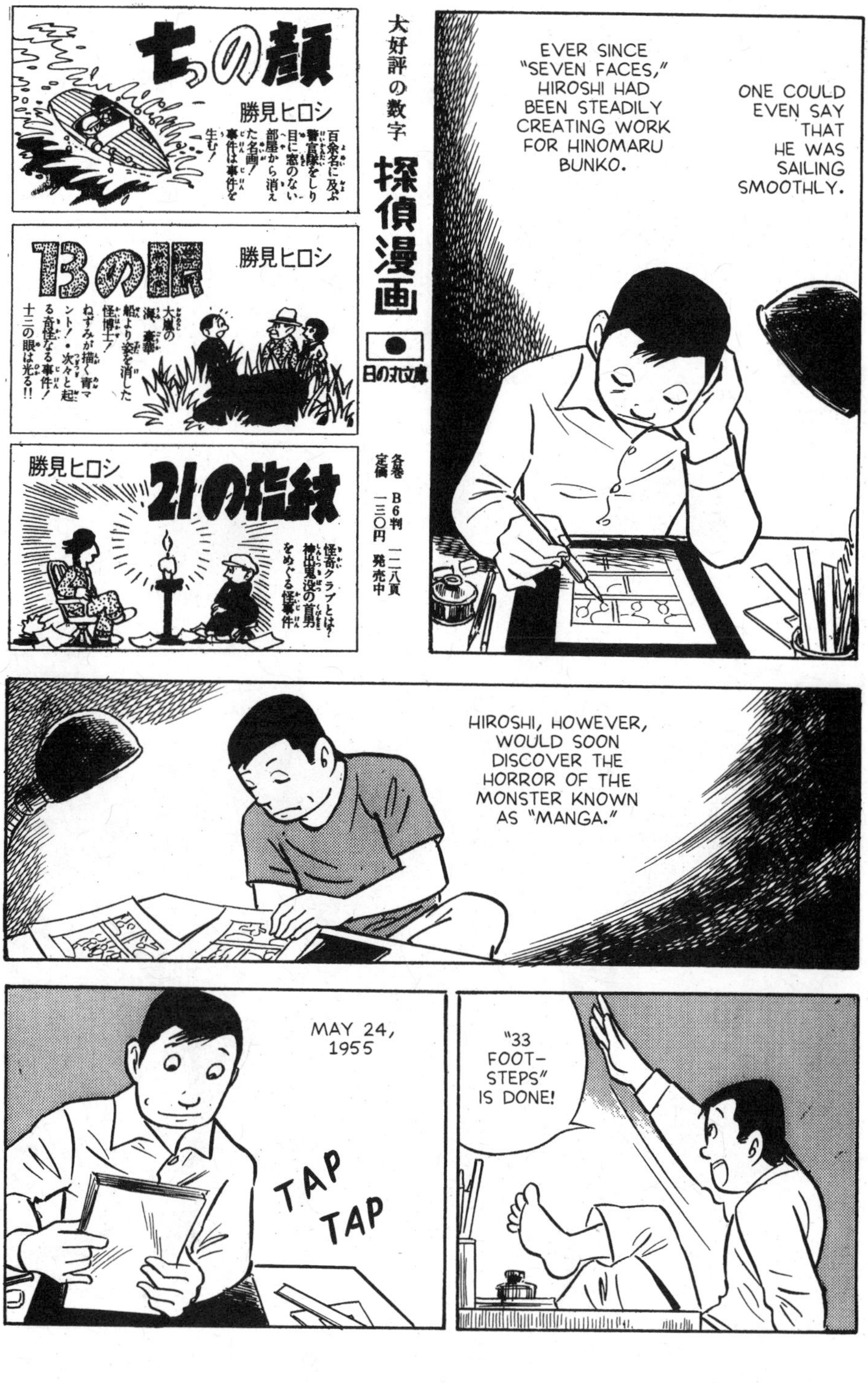
大好評の数字
探偵漫画
日の丸文庫
七つの顔
勝見ヒロシ
百余名に及ぶ警官隊をしり目に窓のない部屋から消えた名画！事件は事件を生む！
13の眼
勝見ヒロシ
大嵐の海、豪華船より姿を消した怪博士！ねずみが描く青マント！・次々と起る奇怪なる事件！十三の眼は光る!!
21の指紋
勝見ヒロシ
怪奇クラブとは？神出鬼没の首男をめぐる怪事件
各巻 B6判 一二八頁
定価 一三〇円 発売中
EVER SINCE "SEVEN FACES," HIROSHI HAD BEEN STEADILY CREATING WORK FOR HINOMARU BUNKO.
ONE COULD EVEN SAY THAT HE WAS SAILING SMOOTHLY.
HIROSHI, HOWEVER, WOULD SOON DISCOVER THE HORROR OF THE MONSTER KNOWN AS "MANGA."
MAY 24, 1955
TAP TAP
"33 FOOT-STEPS" IS DONE!

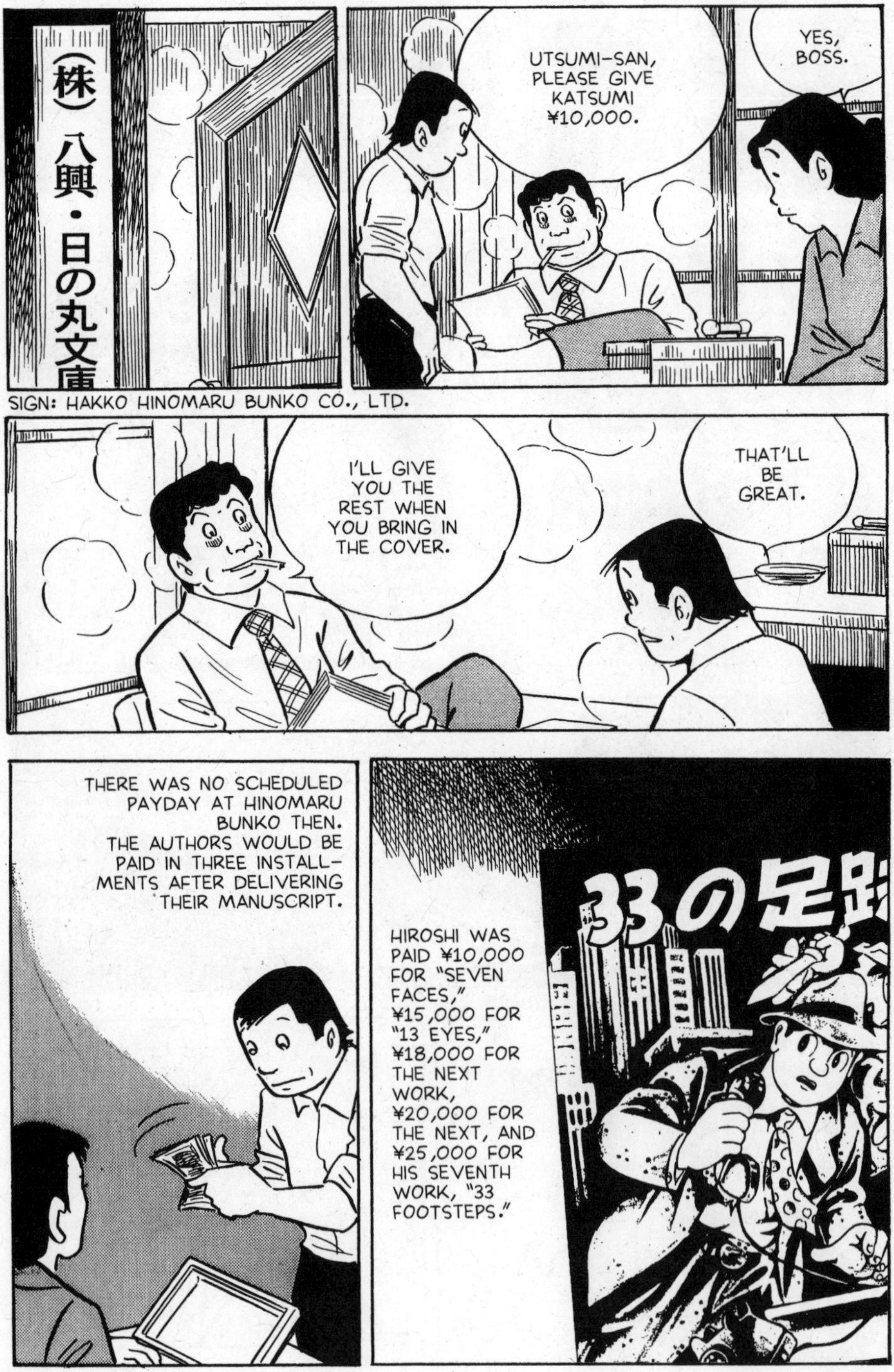
(株) 八興・日の丸文庫
UTSUMI-SAN, PLEASE GIVE KATSUMI ¥10,000.
YES, BOSS.
SIGN: HAKKO HINOMARU BUNKO CO., LTD.
I'LL GIVE YOU THE REST WHEN YOU BRING IN THE COVER.
THAT'LL BE GREAT.
THERE WAS NO SCHEDULED PAYDAY AT HINOMARU BUNKO THEN. THE AUTHORS WOULD BE PAID IN THREE INSTALL-MENTS AFTER DELIVERING THEIR MANUSCRIPT.
HIROSHI WAS PAID ¥10,000 FOR "SEVEN FACES," ¥15,000 FOR "13 EYES," ¥18,000 FOR THE NEXT WORK, ¥20,000 FOR THE NEXT, AND ¥25,000 FOR HIS SEVENTH WORK, "33 FOOTSTEPS."
33の足

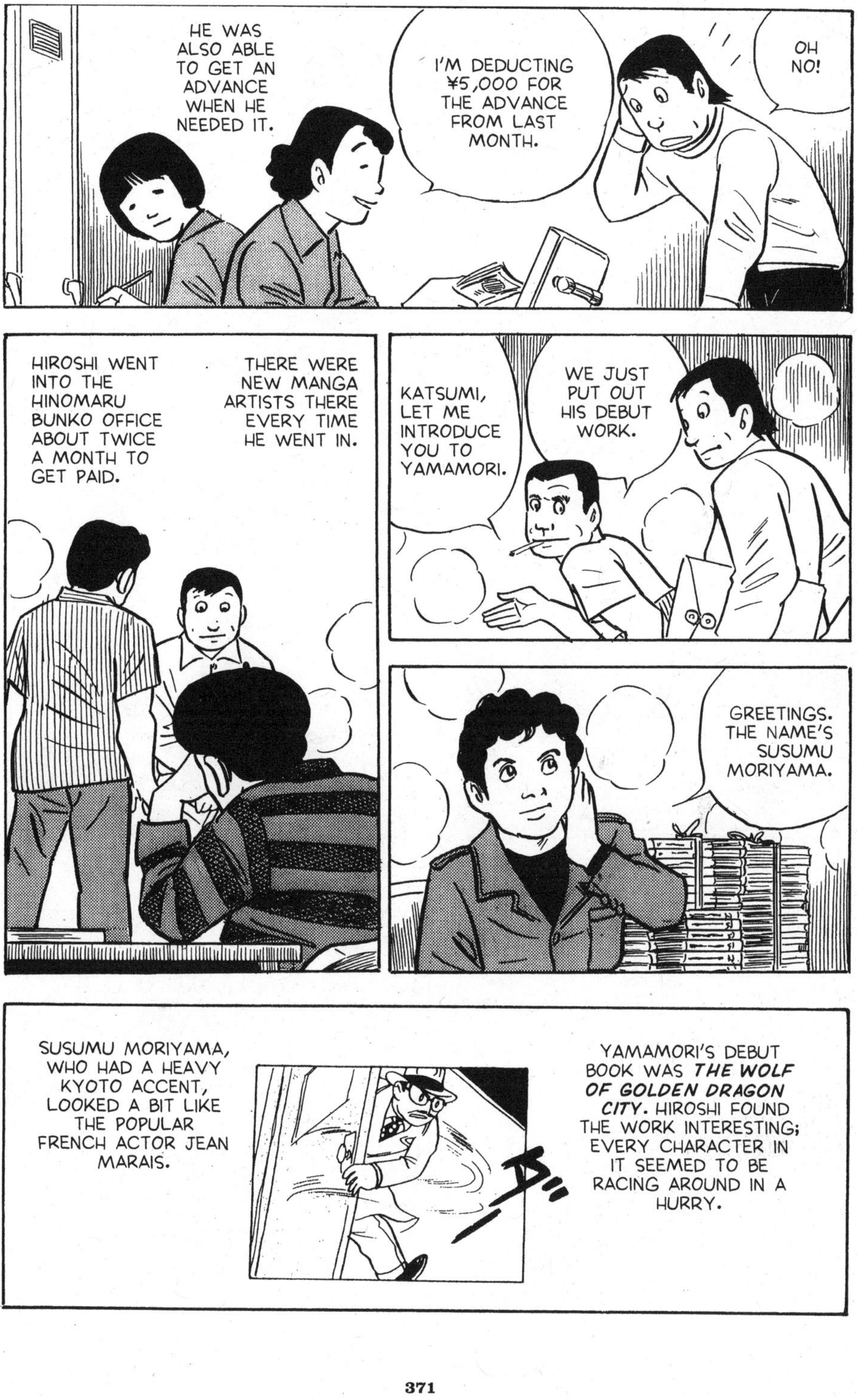
HE WAS ALSO ABLE TO GET AN ADVANCE WHEN HE NEEDED IT.
I'M DEDUCTING ¥5,000 FOR THE ADVANCE FROM LAST MONTH.
OH NO!
HIROSHI WENT INTO THE HINOMARU BUNKO OFFICE ABOUT TWICE A MONTH TO GET PAID.
THERE WERE NEW MANGA ARTISTS THERE EVERY TIME HE WENT IN.
KATSUMI, LET ME INTRODUCE YOU TO YAMAMORI.
WE JUST PUT OUT HIS DEBUT WORK.
GREETINGS. THE NAME'S SUSUMU MORIYAMA.
SUSUMU MORIYAMA, WHO HAD A HEAVY KYOTO ACCENT, LOOKED A BIT LIKE THE POPULAR FRENCH ACTOR JEAN MARAIS.
YAMAMORI'S DEBUT BOOK WAS **THE WOLF OF GOLDEN DRAGON CITY**. HIROSHI FOUND THE WORK INTERESTING; EVERY CHARACTER IN IT SEEMED TO BE RACING AROUND IN A HURRY.

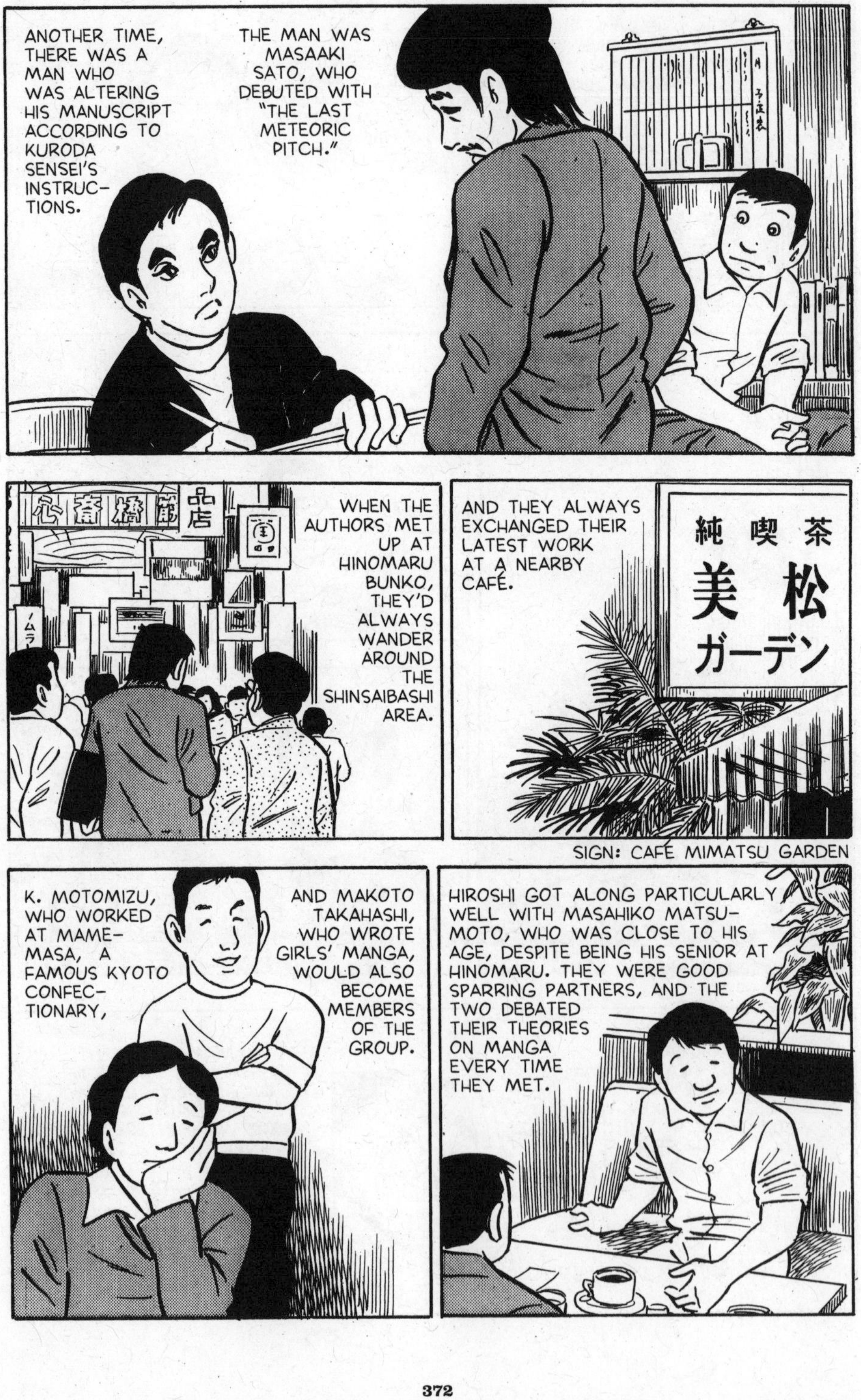
ANOTHER TIME, THERE WAS A MAN WHO WAS ALTERING HIS MANUSCRIPT ACCORDING TO KURODA SENSEI'S INSTRUCTIONS.
THE MAN WAS MASAAKI SATO, WHO DEBUTED WITH "THE LAST METEORIC PITCH."
WHEN THE AUTHORS MET UP AT HINOMARU BUNKO, THEY'D ALWAYS WANDER AROUND THE SHINSAIBASHI AREA.
AND THEY ALWAYS EXCHANGED THEIR LATEST WORK AT A NEARBY CAFÉ.
純喫茶
美松
ガーデン
SIGN: CAFÉ MIMATSU GARDEN
K. MOTOMIZU, WHO WORKED AT MAME-MASA, A FAMOUS KYOTO CONFECTIONARY,
AND MAKOTO TAKAHASHI, WHO WROTE GIRLS' MANGA, WOULD ALSO BECOME MEMBERS OF THE GROUP.
HIROSHI GOT ALONG PARTICULARLY WELL WITH MASAHIKO MATSUMOTO, WHO WAS CLOSE TO HIS AGE, DESPITE BEING HIS SENIOR AT HINOMARU. THEY WERE GOOD SPARRING PARTNERS, AND THE TWO DEBATED THEIR THEORIES ON MANGA EVERY TIME THEY MET.

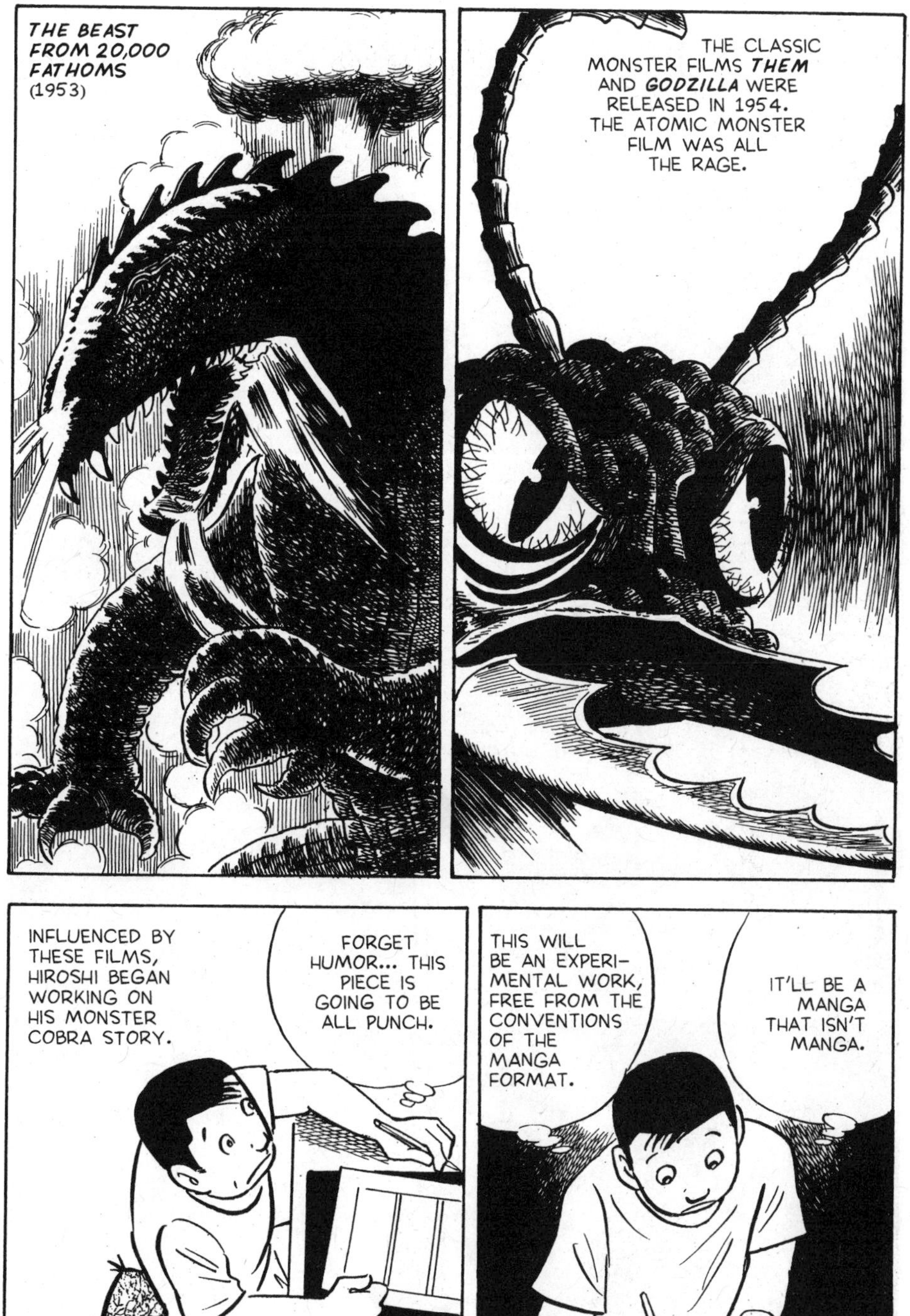
THE BEAST FROM 20,000 FATHOMS (1953)
THE CLASSIC MONSTER FILMS THEM AND GODZILLA WERE RELEASED IN 1954. THE ATOMIC MONSTER FILM WAS ALL THE RAGE.
INFLUENCED BY THESE FILMS, HIROSHI BEGAN WORKING ON HIS MONSTER COBRA STORY.
FORGET HUMOR... THIS PIECE IS GOING TO BE ALL PUNCH.
THIS WILL BE AN EXPERIMENTAL WORK, FREE FROM THE CONVENTIONS OF THE MANGA FORMAT.
IT'LL BE A MANGA THAT ISN'T MANGA.

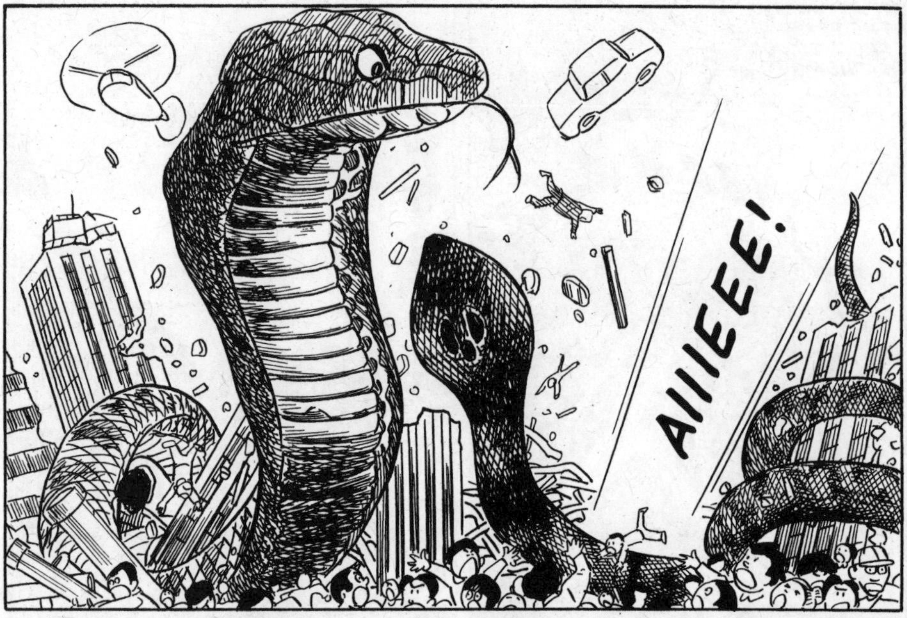
AIIIEEE!
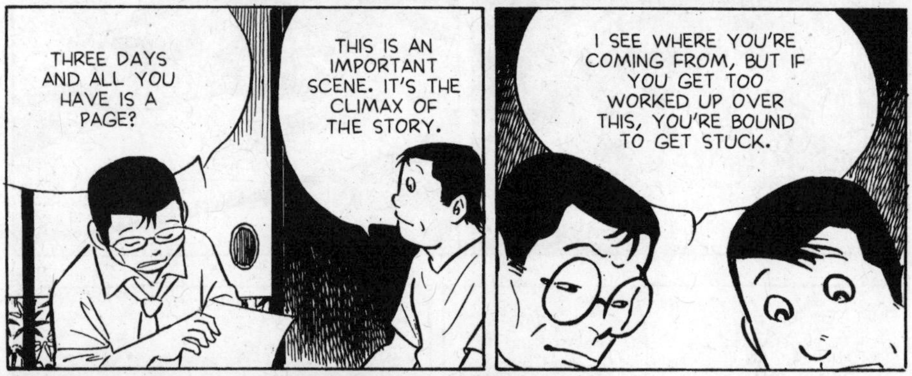
THREE DAYS AND ALL YOU HAVE IS A PAGE?
THIS IS AN IMPORTANT SCENE. IT'S THE CLIMAX OF THE STORY.
I SEE WHERE YOU'RE COMING FROM, BUT IF YOU GET TOO WORKED UP OVER THIS, YOU'RE BOUND TO GET STUCK.
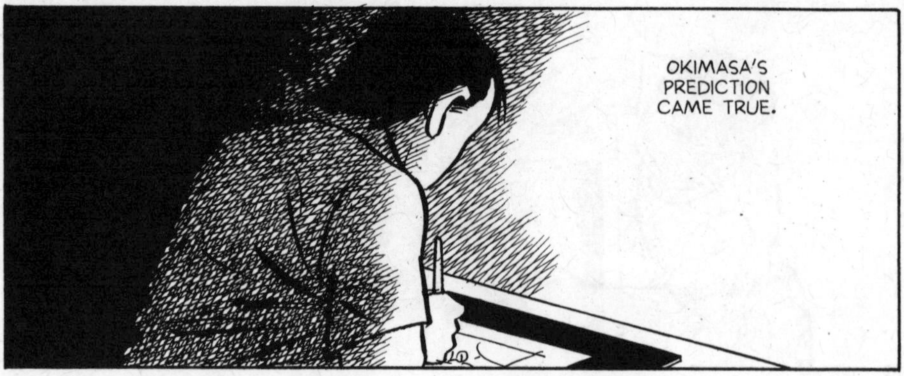
OKIMASA'S PREDICTION CAME TRUE.

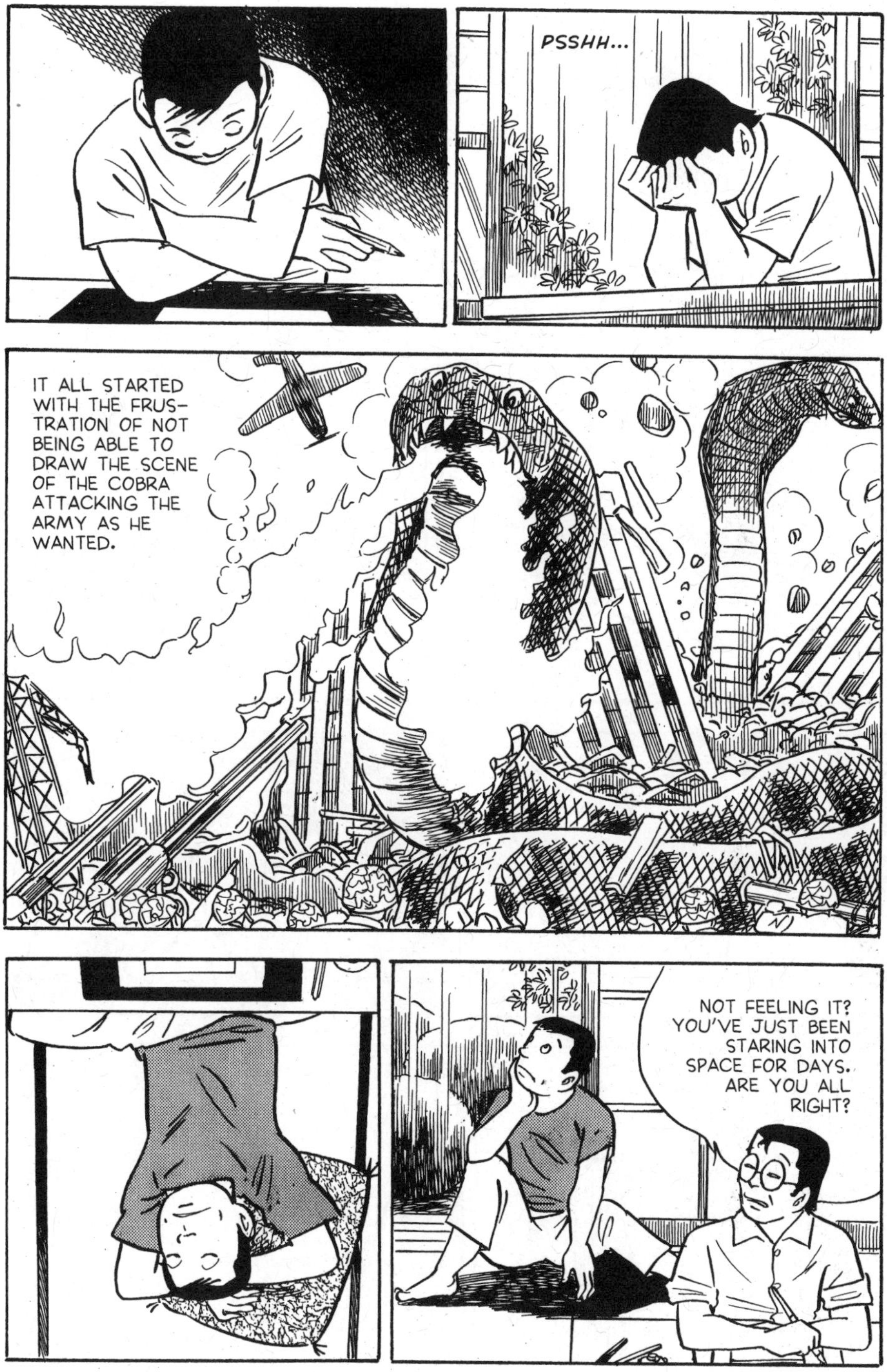
PSSHH...
IT ALL STARTED WITH THE FRUS-TRATION OF NOT BEING ABLE TO DRAW THE SCENE OF THE COBRA ATTACKING THE ARMY AS HE WANTED.
NOT FEELING IT? YOU'VE JUST BEEN STARING INTO SPACE FOR DAYS. ARE YOU ALL RIGHT?

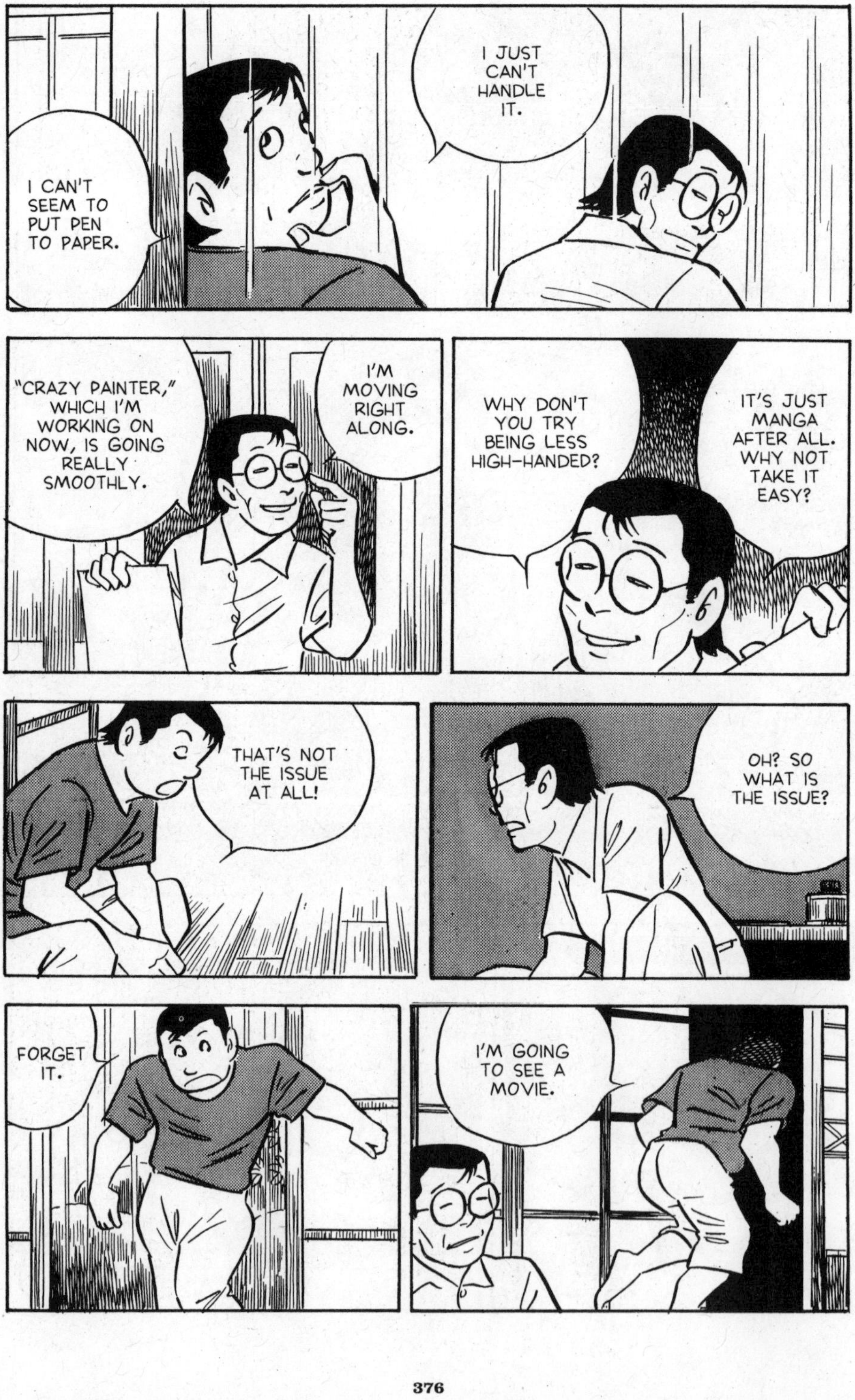
I CAN'T SEEM TO PUT PEN TO PAPER.
I JUST CAN'T HANDLE IT.
"CRAZY PAINTER," WHICH I'M WORKING ON NOW, IS GOING REALLY SMOOTHLY.
I'M MOVING RIGHT ALONG.
WHY DON'T YOU TRY BEING LESS HIGH-HANDED?
IT'S JUST MANGA AFTER ALL. WHY NOT TAKE IT EASY?
THAT'S NOT THE ISSUE AT ALL!
OH? SO WHAT IS THE ISSUE?
FORGET IT.
I'M GOING TO SEE A MOVIE.

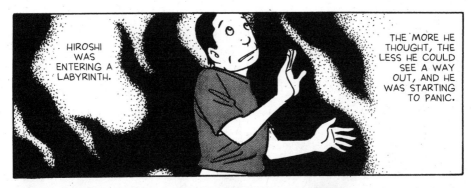

HIROSHI WAS ENTERING A LABYRINTH.
THE MORE HE THOUGHT, THE LESS HE COULD SEE A WAY OUT, AND HE WAS STARTING TO PANIC.
IF YOU HAVE TOO MANY PUNCHY SCENES, THEY LOSE THEIR PUNCH. AND YOU CAN'T CONSTRUCT A NARRATIVE BY SIMPLY STRINGING TOGETHER ONE ACTION SCENE AFTER ANOTHER.
HIROSHI HAD FORGOTTEN THE MOST BASIC ELEMENTS OF STORYTELLING.
まんが
THE IDEA OF A NON-COMEDIC MANGA HAD GROWN GIANT AND OUT OF CONTROL IN HIS MIND.
パラマウント映画
グレイス・ケリー
喝采
かっさい
THE COUNTRY GIRL
上映中

TEXT: MANGA POSTER: NOW SHOWING / PARAMOUNT PICTURES / GRACE KELLY IN *THE COUNTRY GIRL* / BING CROSBY / WILLIAM HOLDEN

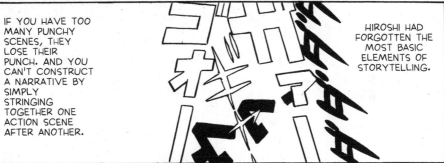

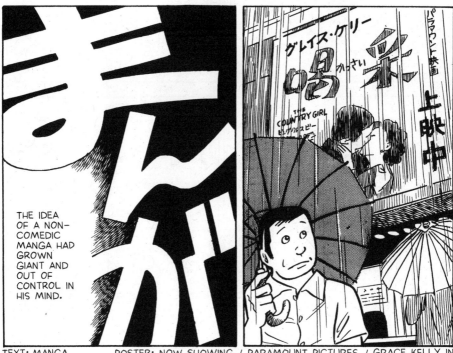

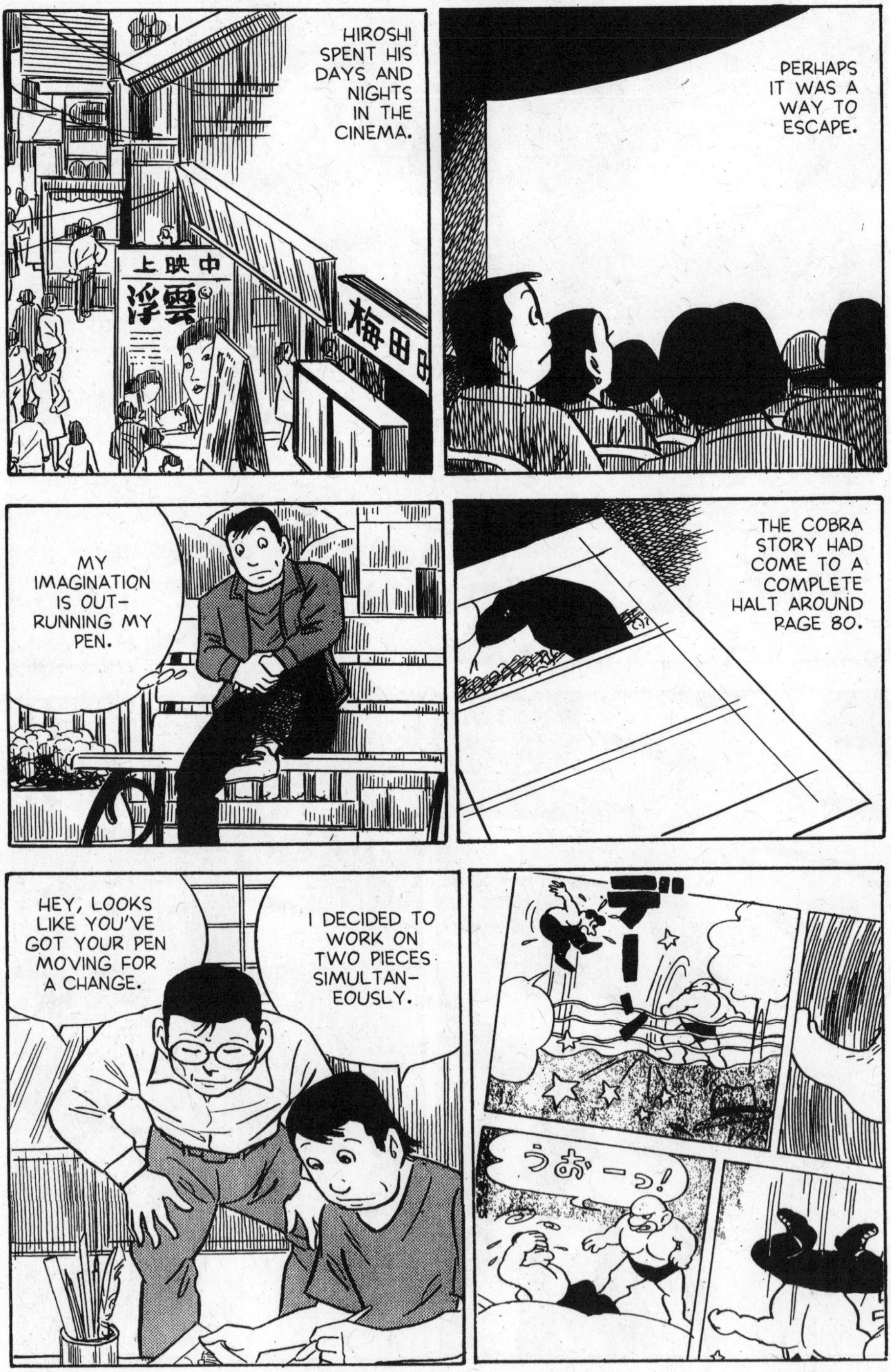
HIROSHI SPENT HIS DAYS AND NIGHTS IN THE CINEMA.
上映中
浮雲
梅田
PERHAPS IT WAS A WAY TO ESCAPE.
MY IMAGINATION IS OUT-RUNNING MY PEN.
THE COBRA STORY HAD COME TO A COMPLETE HALT AROUND PAGE 80.
HEY, LOOKS LIKE YOU'VE GOT YOUR PEN MOVING FOR A CHANGE.
I DECIDED TO WORK ON TWO PIECES SIMULTAN-EOUSLY.
デーン
うおーっ!

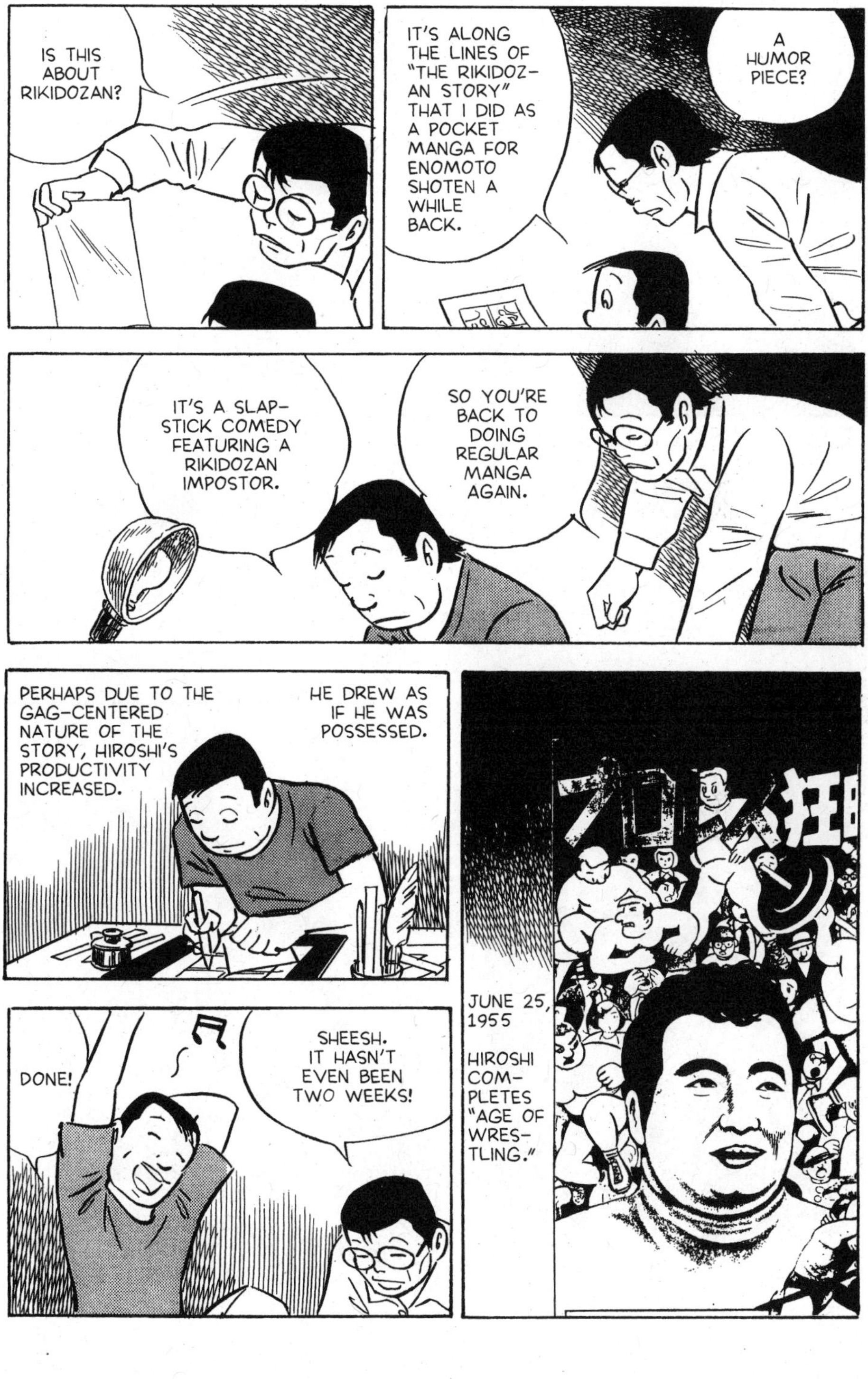
IS THIS ABOUT RIKIDOZAN?
IT'S ALONG THE LINES OF "THE RIKIDOZ-AN STORY" THAT I DID AS A POCKET MANGA FOR ENOMOTO SHOTEN A WHILE BACK.
A HUMOR PIECE?
IT'S A SLAP-STICK COMEDY FEATURING A RIKIDOZAN IMPOSTOR.
SO YOU'RE BACK TO DOING REGULAR MANGA AGAIN.
PERHAPS DUE TO THE GAG-CENTERED NATURE OF THE STORY, HIROSHI'S PRODUCTIVITY INCREASED.
HE DREW AS IF HE WAS POSSESSED.
DONE!
SHEESH. IT HASN'T EVEN BEEN TWO WEEKS!
JUNE 25, 1955
HIROSHI COM-PLETES "AGE OF WRES-TLING."

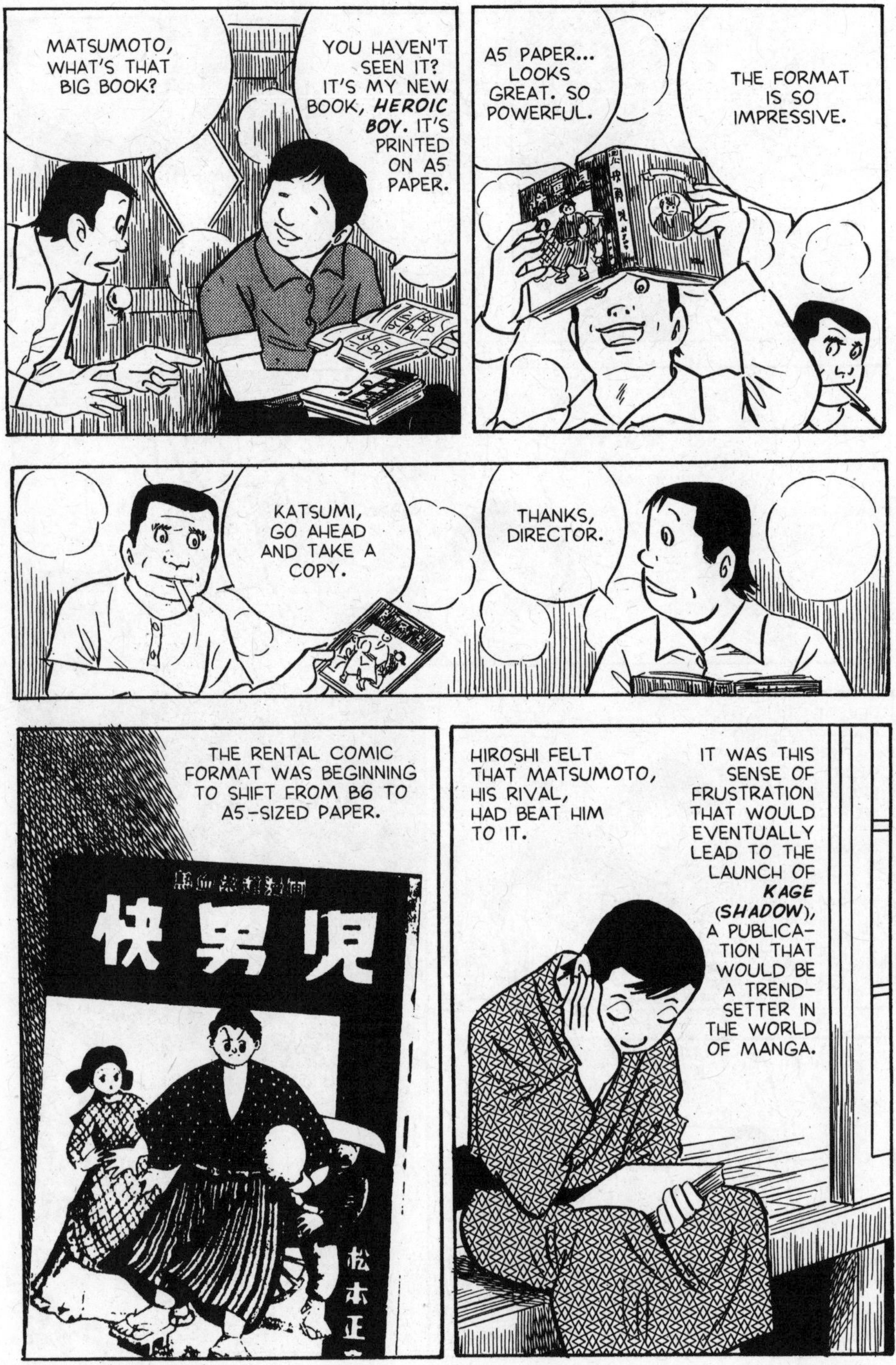
MATSUMOTO, WHAT'S THAT BIG BOOK?
YOU HAVEN'T SEEN IT? IT'S MY NEW BOOK, ***HEROIC BOY***. IT'S PRINTED ON A5 PAPER.
A5 PAPER... LOOKS GREAT. SO POWERFUL.
THE FORMAT IS SO IMPRESSIVE.
KATSUMI, GO AHEAD AND TAKE A COPY.
THANKS, DIRECTOR.
THE RENTAL COMIC FORMAT WAS BEGINNING TO SHIFT FROM B6 TO A5-SIZED PAPER.
快男児
HIROSHI FELT THAT MATSUMOTO, HIS RIVAL, HAD BEAT HIM TO IT.
IT WAS THIS SENSE OF FRUSTRATION THAT WOULD EVENTUALLY LEAD TO THE LAUNCH OF ***KAGE*** (***SHADOW***), A PUBLICATION THAT WOULD BE A TREND-SETTER IN THE WORLD OF MANGA.

TITLE: ***HEROIC BOY***

SEARCHING FOR A NEW METHOD

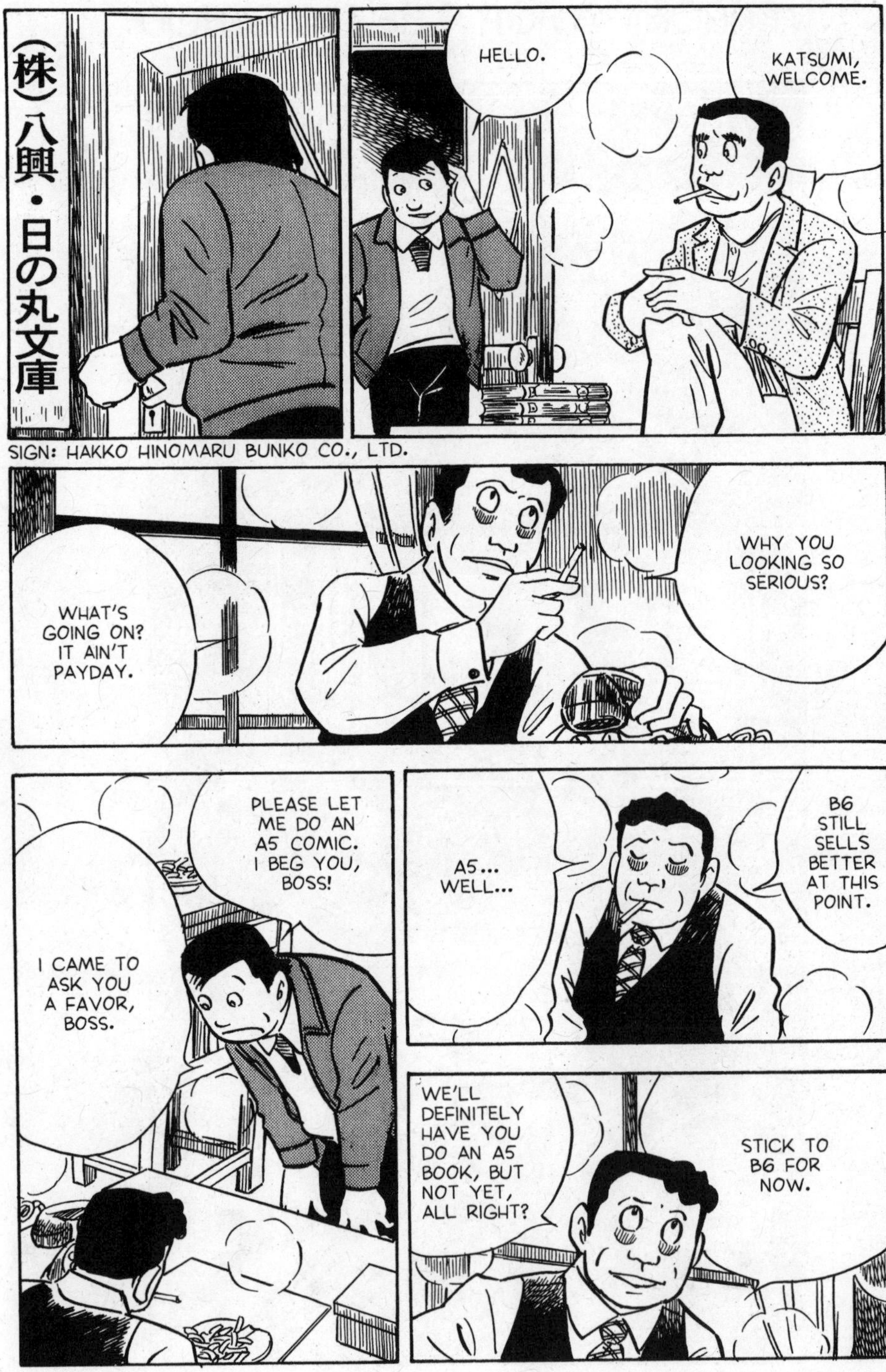
(株) 八興・日の丸文庫
HELLO.
KATSUMI, WELCOME.
SIGN: HAKKO HINOMARU BUNKO CO., LTD.
WHAT'S GOING ON? IT AIN'T PAYDAY.
WHY YOU LOOKING SO SERIOUS?
I CAME TO ASK YOU A FAVOR, BOSS.
PLEASE LET ME DO AN A5 COMIC. I BEG YOU, BOSS!
A5... WELL...
B6 STILL SELLS BETTER AT THIS POINT.
WE'LL DEFINITELY HAVE YOU DO AN A5 BOOK, BUT NOT YET, ALL RIGHT?
STICK TO B6 FOR NOW.

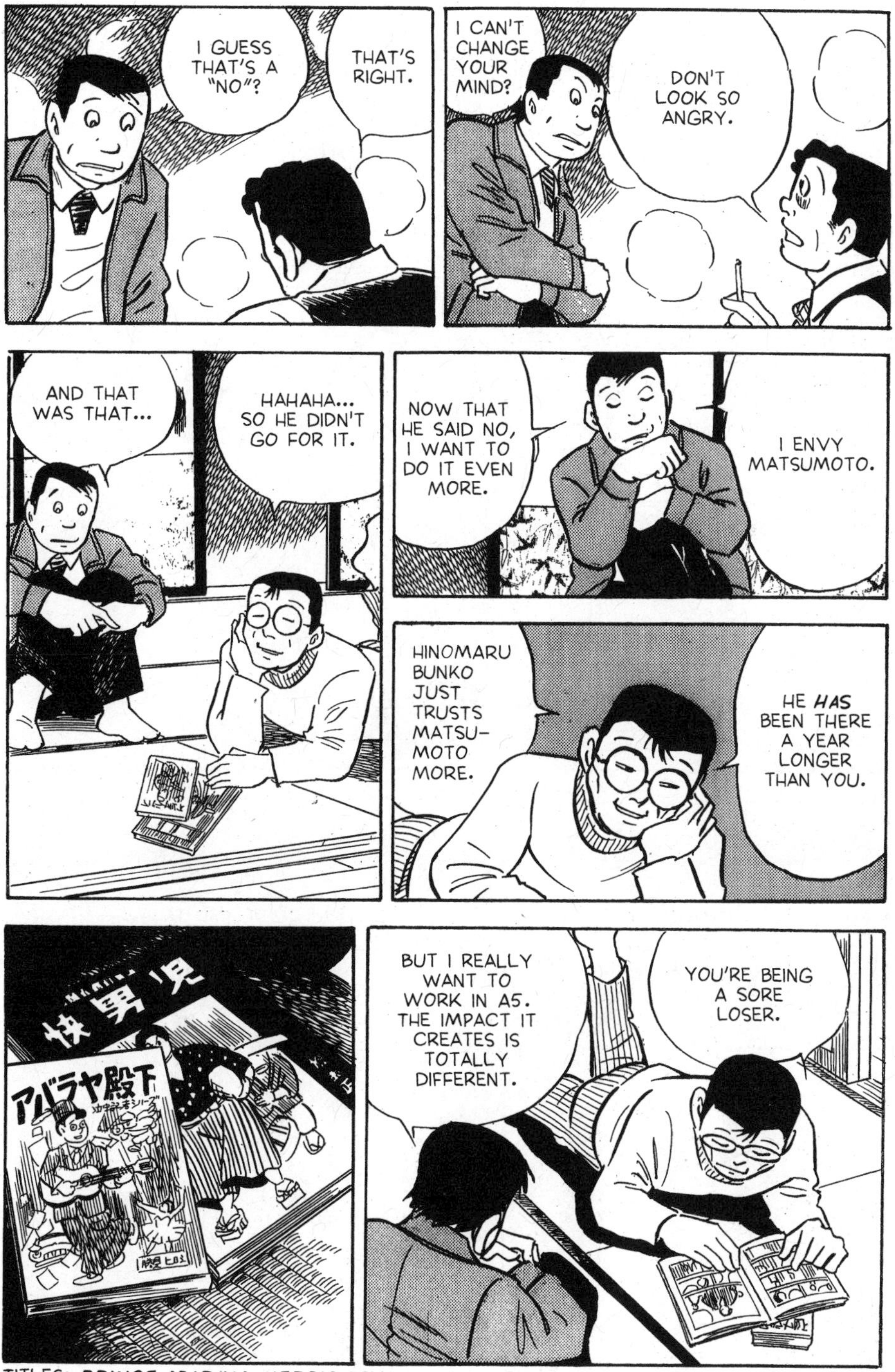
I GUESS THAT'S A "NO"?
THAT'S RIGHT.
I CAN'T CHANGE YOUR MIND?
DON'T LOOK SO ANGRY.
AND THAT WAS THAT...
HAHAHA... SO HE DIDN'T GO FOR IT.
NOW THAT HE SAID NO, I WANT TO DO IT EVEN MORE.
I ENVY MATSUMOTO.
HINOMARU BUNKO JUST TRUSTS MATSU-MOTO MORE.
HE *HAS* BEEN THERE A YEAR LONGER THAN YOU.
快男児
アバラヤ殿下
BUT I REALLY WANT TO WORK IN A5. THE IMPACT IT CREATES IS TOTALLY DIFFERENT.
YOU'RE BEING A SORE LOSER.

TITLES: ***PRINCE ABARAYA, HEROIC BOY***

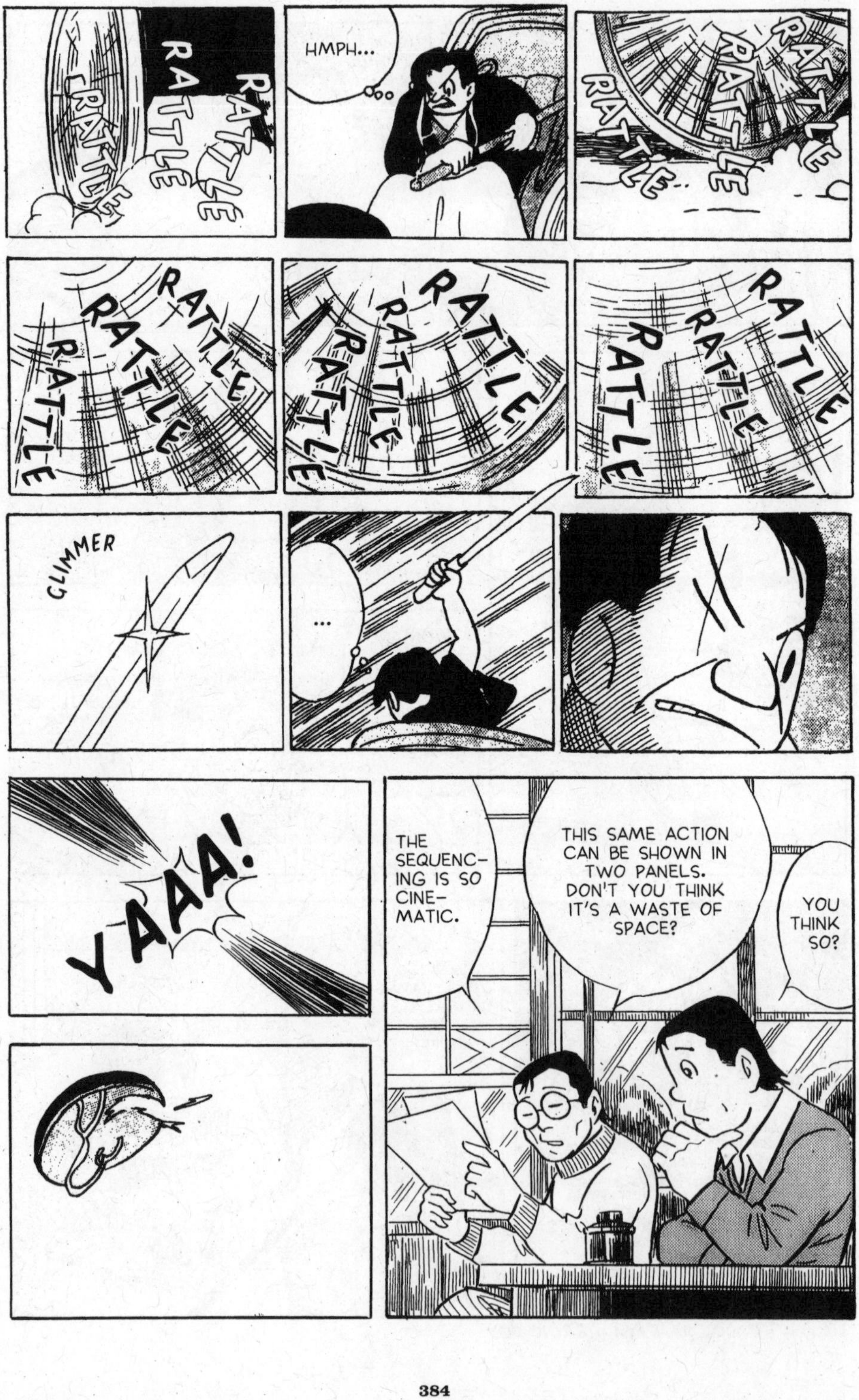
RATTLE
RATTLE
RATTLE
HMPH...
RATTLE
RATTLE
RATTLE
RATTLE
RATTLE
RATTLE
RATTLE
RATTLE
RATTLE
RATTLE
RATTLE
RATTLE
GLIMMER
...
YAAA!
THE SEQUENCING IS SO CINEMATIC.
THIS SAME ACTION CAN BE SHOWN IN TWO PANELS. DON'T YOU THINK IT'S A WASTE OF SPACE?
YOU THINK SO?

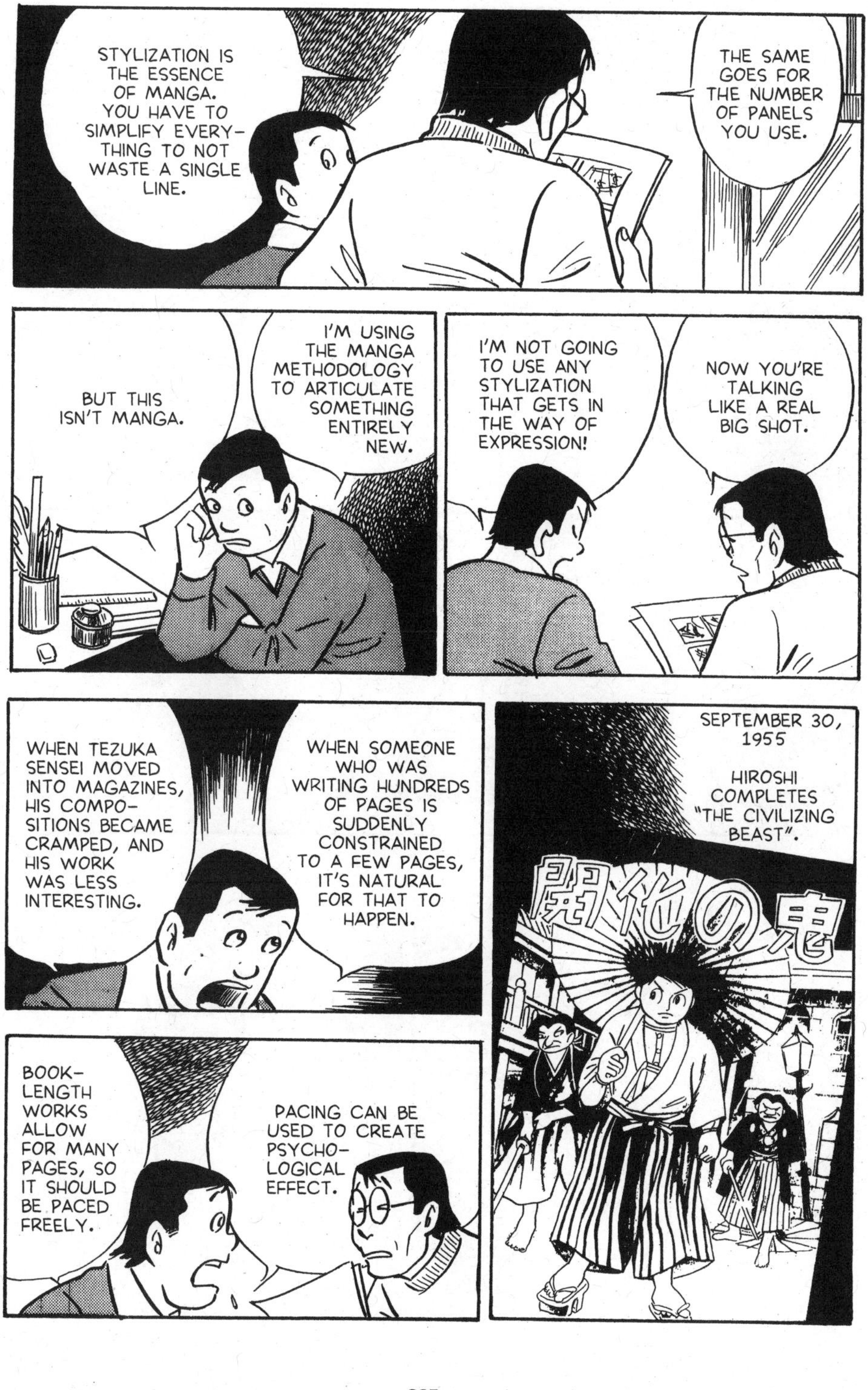
STYLIZATION IS THE ESSENCE OF MANGA. YOU HAVE TO SIMPLIFY EVERY-THING TO NOT WASTE A SINGLE LINE.
THE SAME GOES FOR THE NUMBER OF PANELS YOU USE.
BUT THIS ISN'T MANGA.
I'M USING THE MANGA METHODOLOGY TO ARTICULATE SOMETHING ENTIRELY NEW.
I'M NOT GOING TO USE ANY STYLIZATION THAT GETS IN THE WAY OF EXPRESSION!
NOW YOU'RE TALKING LIKE A REAL BIG SHOT.
WHEN TEZUKA SENSEI MOVED INTO MAGAZINES, HIS COMPO-SITIONS BECAME CRAMPED, AND HIS WORK WAS LESS INTERESTING.
WHEN SOMEONE WHO WAS WRITING HUNDREDS OF PAGES IS SUDDENLY CONSTRAINED TO A FEW PAGES, IT'S NATURAL FOR THAT TO HAPPEN.
BOOK-LENGTH WORKS ALLOW FOR MANY PAGES, SO IT SHOULD BE PACED FREELY.
PACING CAN BE USED TO CREATE PSYCHO-LOGICAL EFFECT.
SEPTEMBER 30, 1955
HIROSHI COMPLETES "THE CIVILIZING BEAST".
開化の鬼

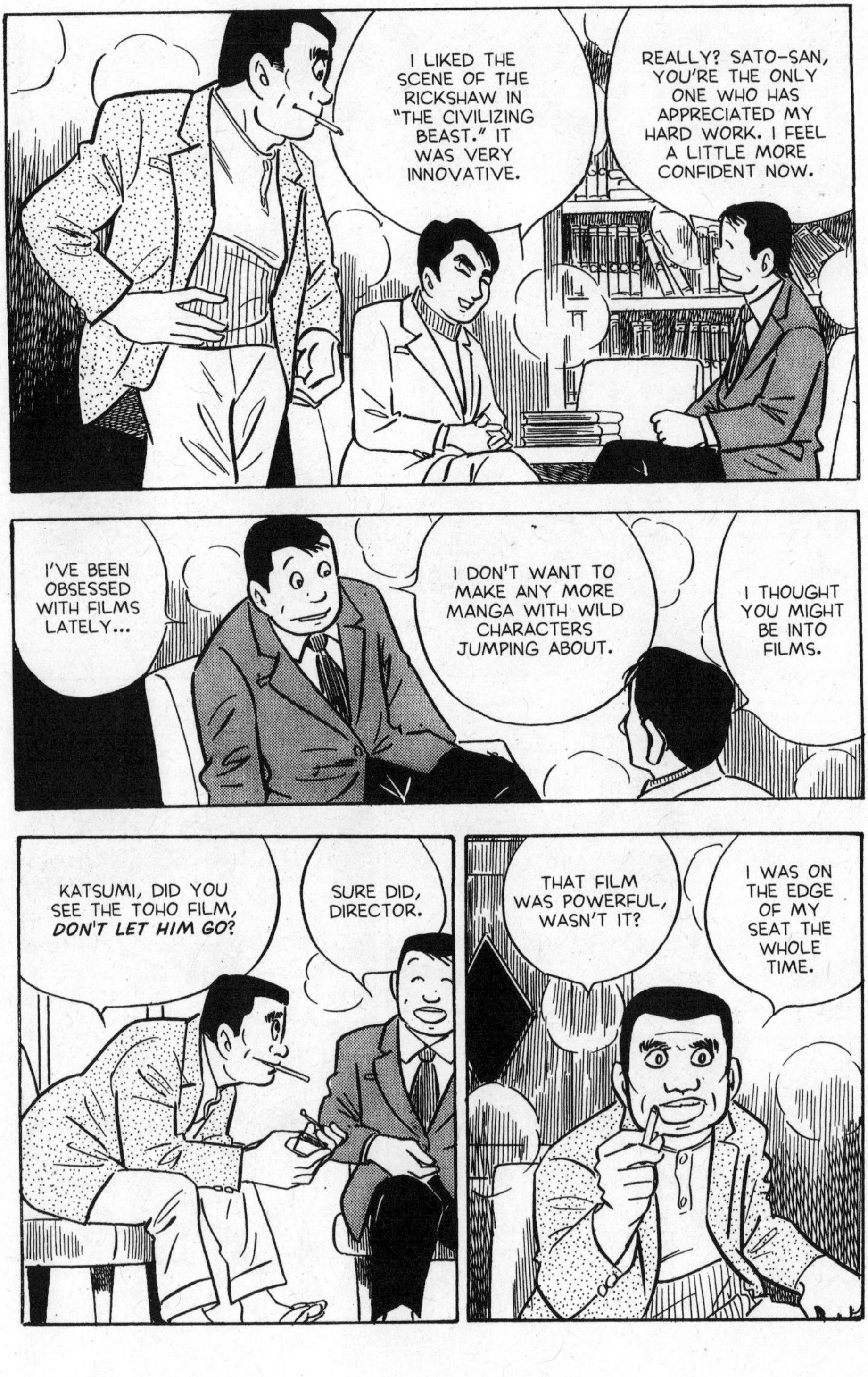
I LIKED THE SCENE OF THE RICKSHAW IN "THE CIVILIZING BEAST." IT WAS VERY INNOVATIVE.
REALLY? SATO-SAN, YOU'RE THE ONLY ONE WHO HAS APPRECIATED MY HARD WORK. I FEEL A LITTLE MORE CONFIDENT NOW.
I'VE BEEN OBSESSED WITH FILMS LATELY...
I DON'T WANT TO MAKE ANY MORE MANGA WITH WILD CHARACTERS JUMPING ABOUT.
I THOUGHT YOU MIGHT BE INTO FILMS.
KATSUMI, DID YOU SEE THE TOHO FILM, *DON'T LET HIM GO*?
SURE DID, DIRECTOR.
THAT FILM WAS POWERFUL, WASN'T IT?
I WAS ON THE EDGE OF MY SEAT THE WHOLE TIME.

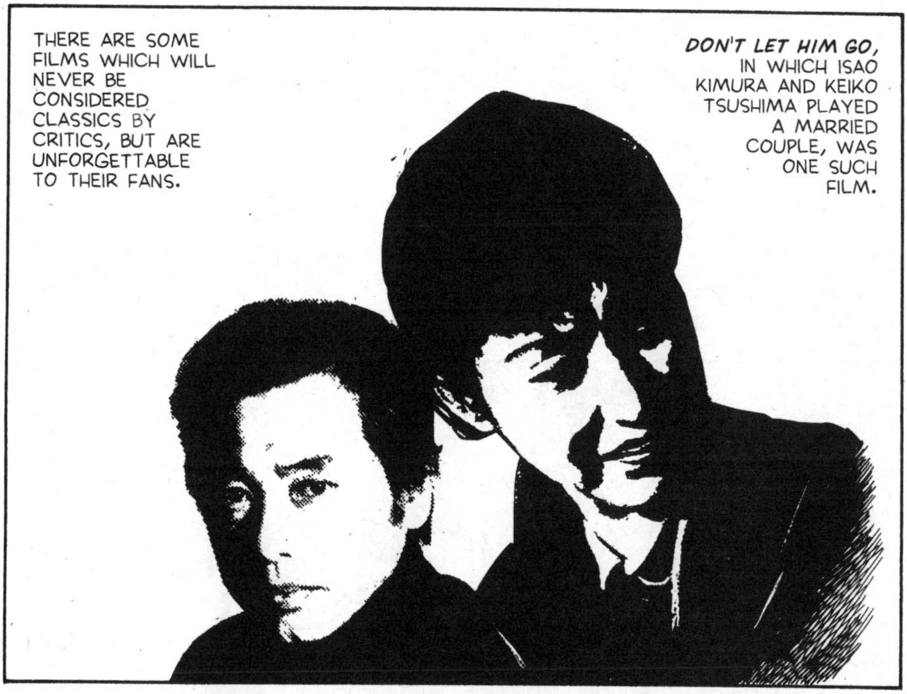
THERE ARE SOME FILMS WHICH WILL NEVER BE CONSIDERED CLASSICS BY CRITICS, BUT ARE UNFORGETTABLE TO THEIR FANS.
DON'T LET HIM GO, IN WHICH ISAO KIMURA AND KEIKO TSUSHIMA PLAYED A MARRIED COUPLE, WAS ONE SUCH FILM.

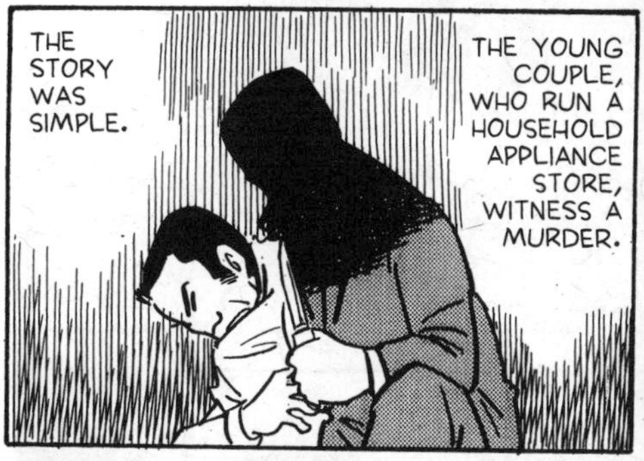
THE STORY WAS SIMPLE.
THE YOUNG COUPLE, WHO RUN A HOUSEHOLD APPLIANCE STORE, WITNESS A MURDER.

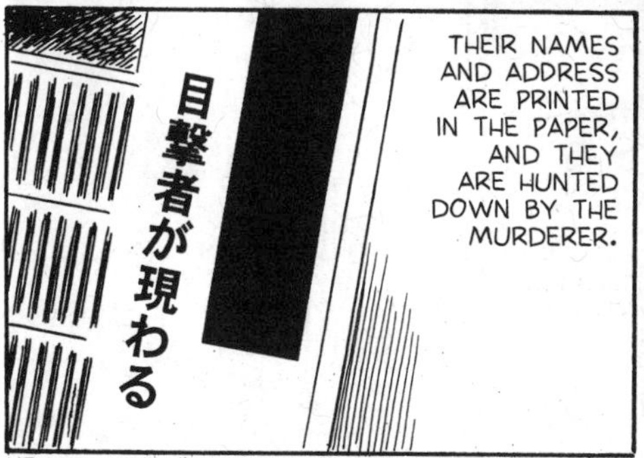
目撃者が現わる
THEIR NAMES AND ADDRESS ARE PRINTED IN THE PAPER, AND THEY ARE HUNTED DOWN BY THE MURDERER.

NEWSPAPER: "WITNESSES STEP FORTH"

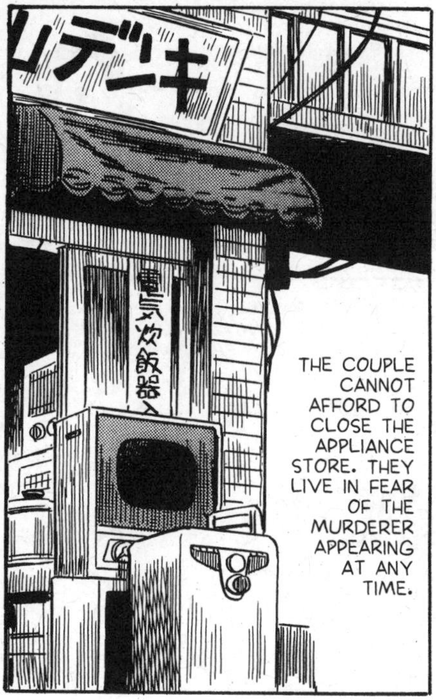
電気炊飯器入
THE COUPLE CANNOT AFFORD TO CLOSE THE APPLIANCE STORE. THEY LIVE IN FEAR OF THE MURDERER APPEARING AT ANY TIME.

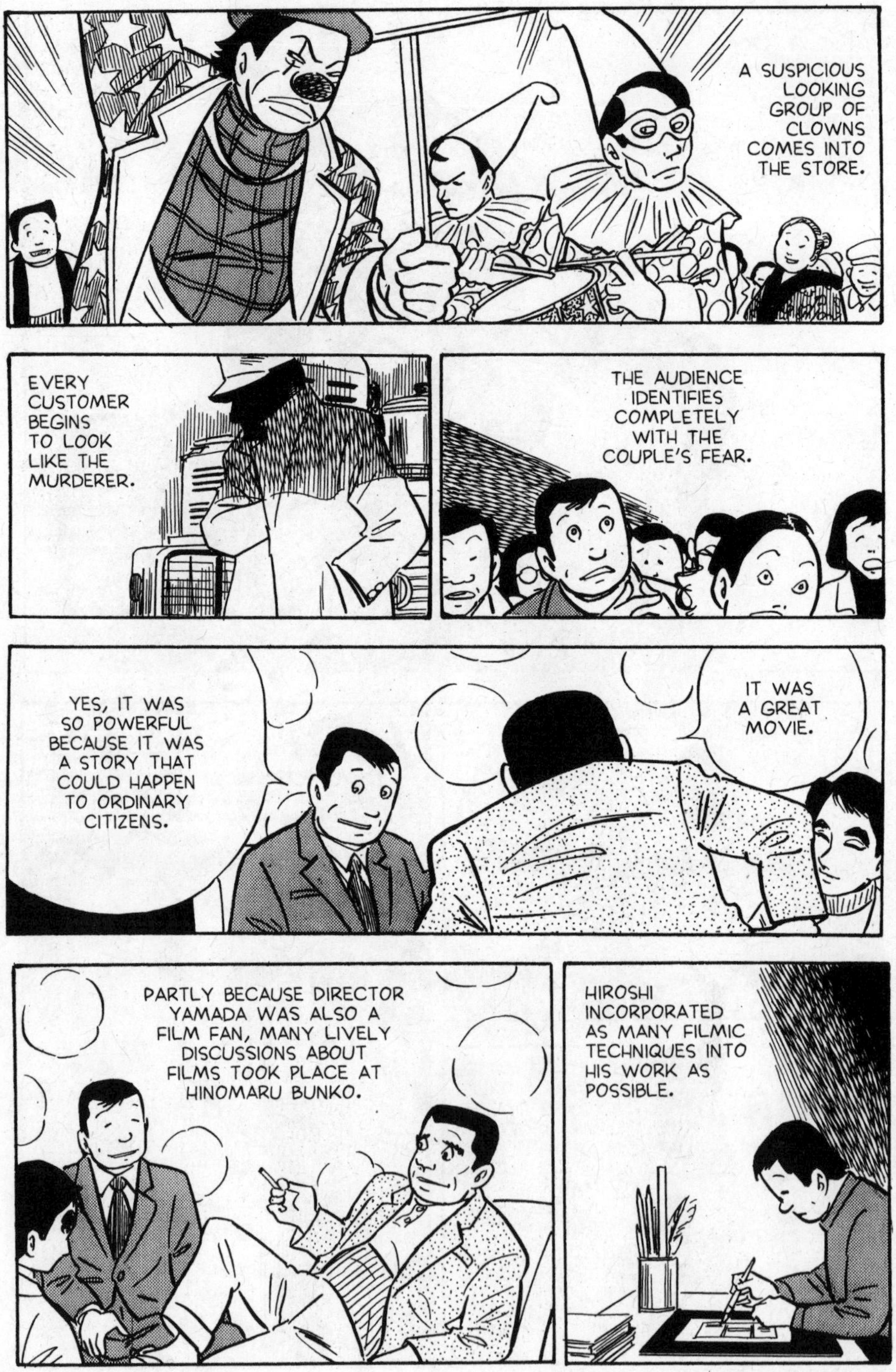
A SUSPICIOUS LOOKING GROUP OF CLOWNS COMES INTO THE STORE.
EVERY CUSTOMER BEGINS TO LOOK LIKE THE MURDERER.
THE AUDIENCE IDENTIFIES COMPLETELY WITH THE COUPLE'S FEAR.
YES, IT WAS SO POWERFUL BECAUSE IT WAS A STORY THAT COULD HAPPEN TO ORDINARY CITIZENS.
IT WAS A GREAT MOVIE.
PARTLY BECAUSE DIRECTOR YAMADA WAS ALSO A FILM FAN, MANY LIVELY DISCUSSIONS ABOUT FILMS TOOK PLACE AT HINOMARU BUNKO.
HIROSHI INCORPORATED AS MANY FILMIC TECHNIQUES INTO HIS WORK AS POSSIBLE.

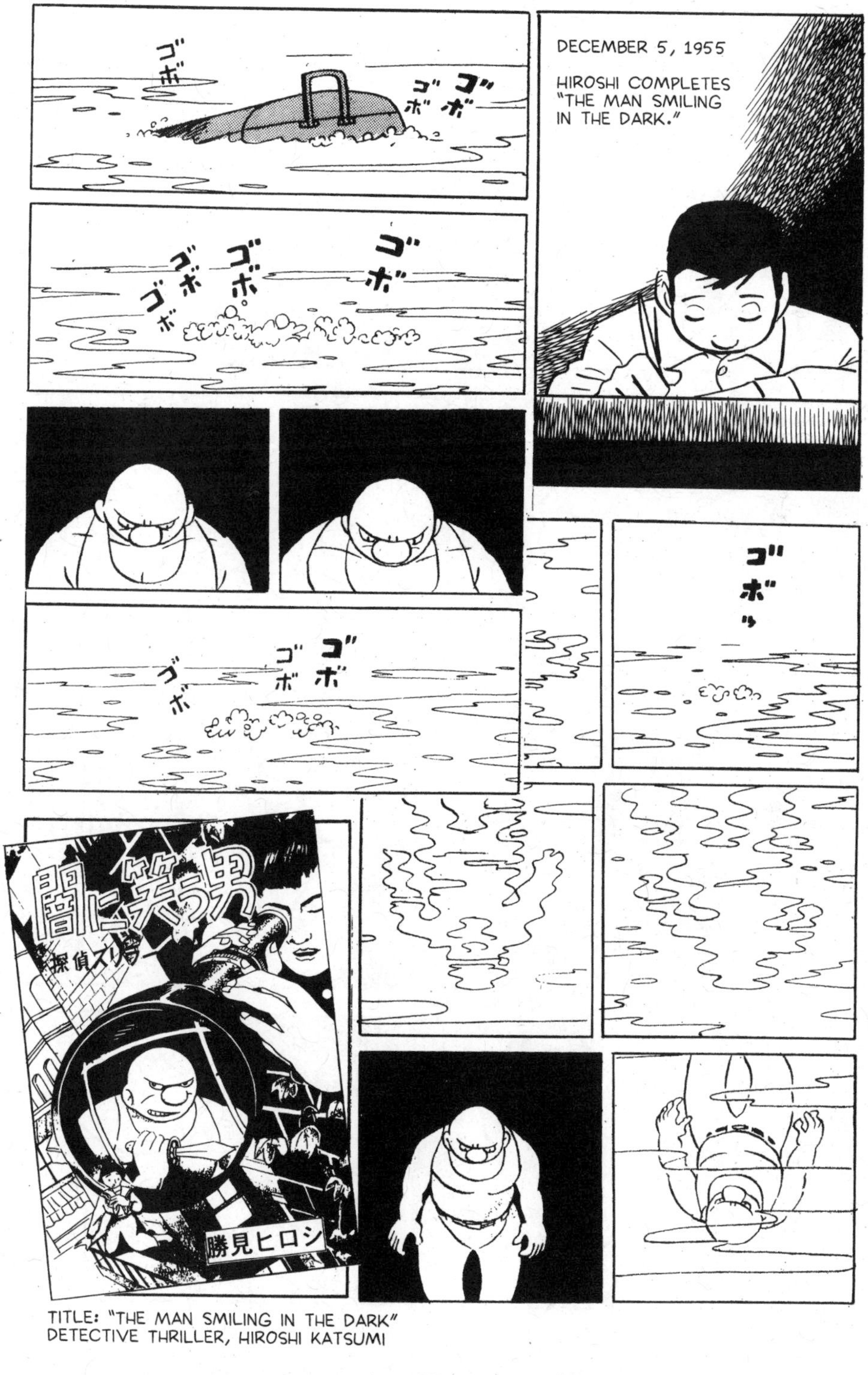
ゴボ
ゴボ
ゴボ
ゴボ
ゴボ
ゴボ
ゴボ
DECEMBER 5, 1955
HIROSHI COMPLETES "THE MAN SMILING IN THE DARK."
ゴボ
ゴボ
ゴボ
ゴボッ
闇に笑う男
探偵スリラー
勝見ヒロシ
TITLE: "THE MAN SMILING IN THE DARK"
DETECTIVE THRILLER, HIROSHI KATSUMI

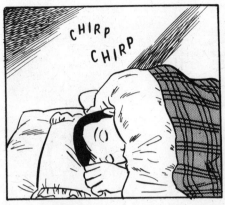

CHIRP CHIRP

HIROSHI, GET UP.

MOM'S GETTING MAD BECAUSE SHE CAN'T CLEAR THE TABLE.

LET ME SLEEP JUST A LITTLE LONGER. I WAS UP LATE LAST NIGHT.

NO!

HEY, WATCH IT!

JEEZ. CAN'T EVEN SLEEP IN THIS HOUSE.

HURRY UP AND WASH YOUR FACE. THE MISO SOUP'S GETTING COLD.

BRUSH BRUSH

GOOD MORNING, KATSUMI-SAN.

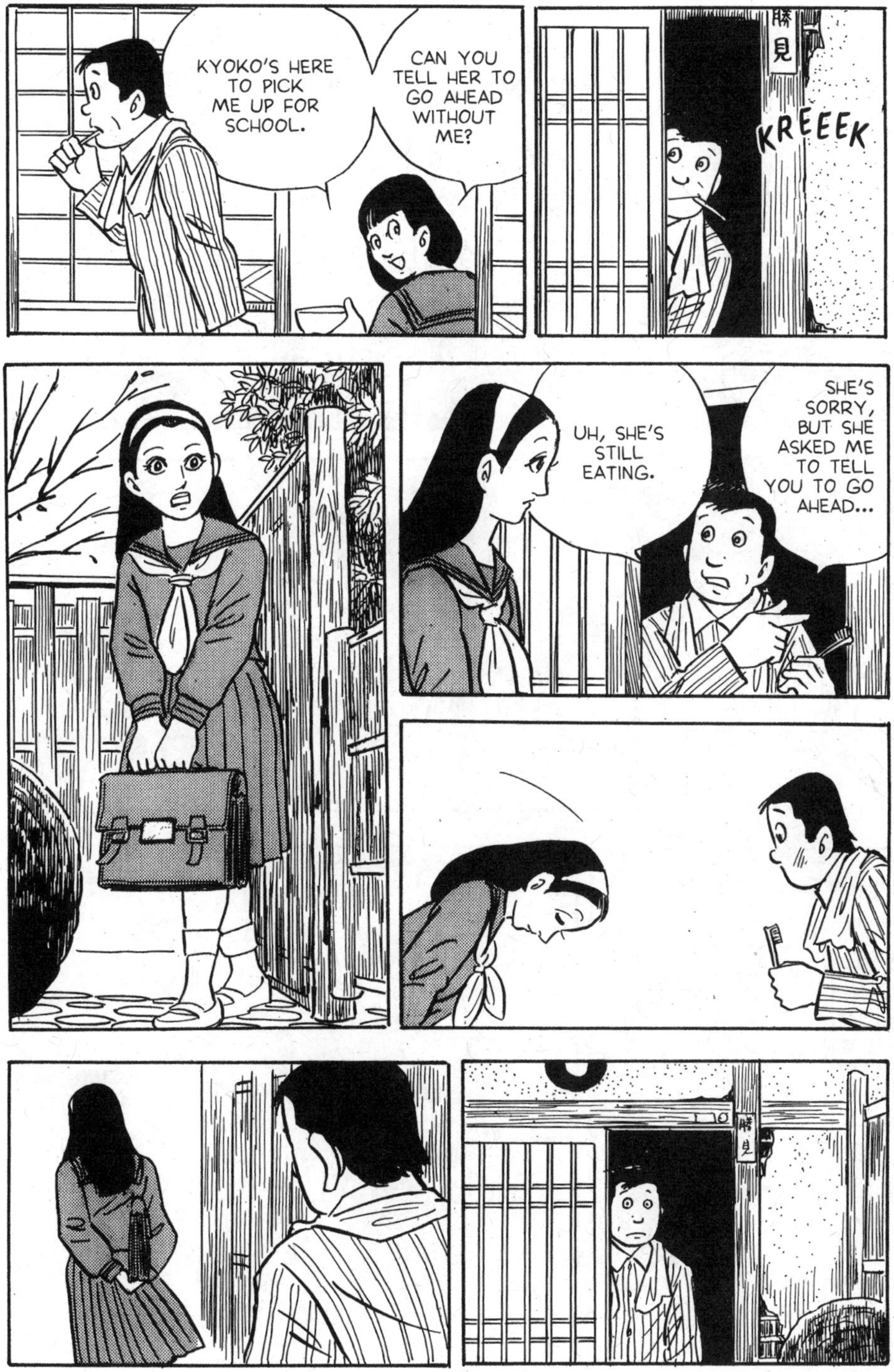
KYOKO'S HERE TO PICK ME UP FOR SCHOOL.
CAN YOU TELL HER TO GO AHEAD WITHOUT ME?
勝見
KREEEK
UH, SHE'S STILL EATING.
SHE'S SORRY, BUT SHE ASKED ME TO TELL YOU TO GO AHEAD...

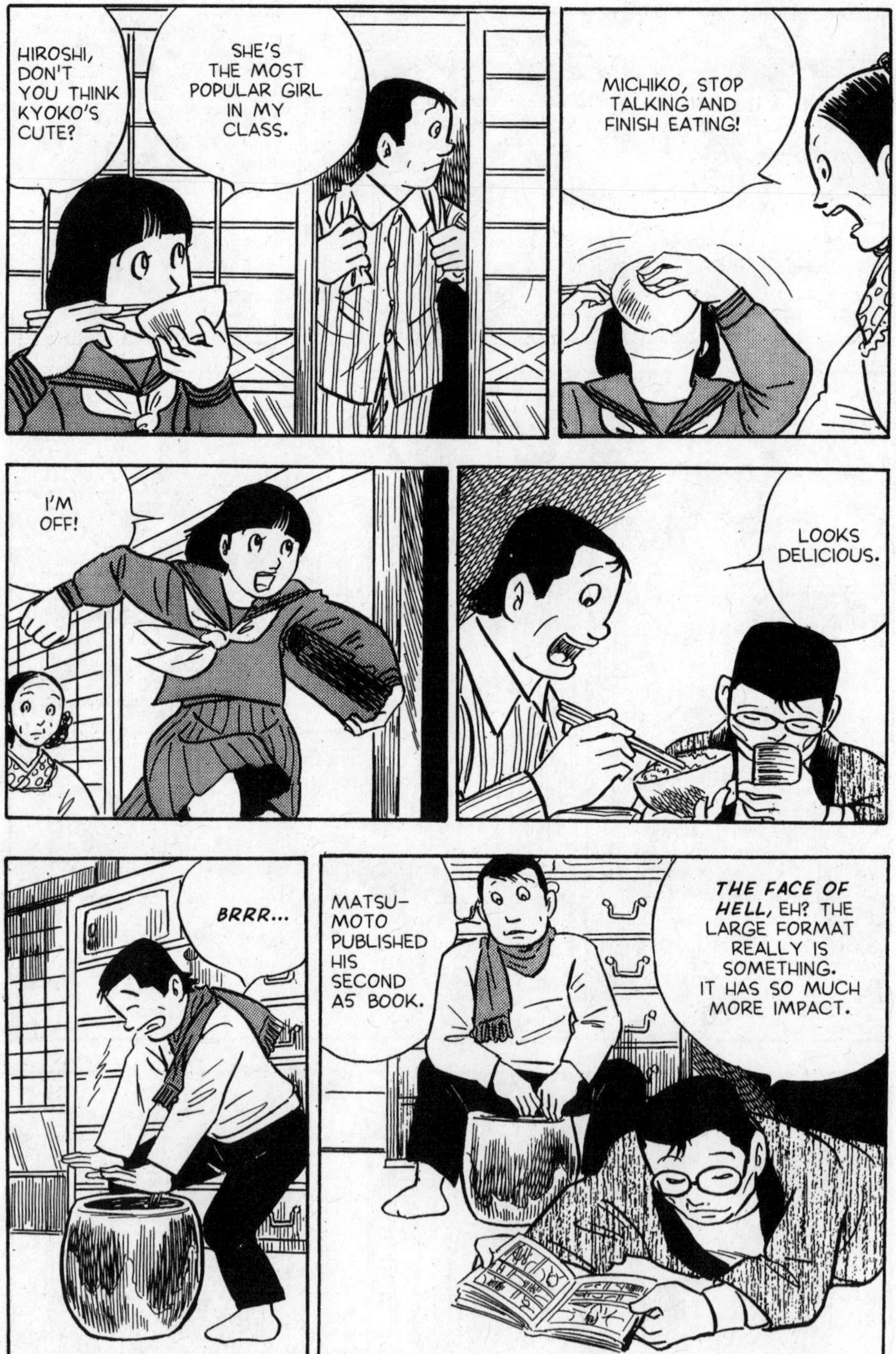
HIROSHI, DON'T YOU THINK KYOKO'S CUTE?
SHE'S THE MOST POPULAR GIRL IN MY CLASS.
MICHIKO, STOP TALKING AND FINISH EATING!
I'M OFF!
LOOKS DELICIOUS.
BRRR...
MATSUMOTO PUBLISHED HIS SECOND A5 BOOK.
THE FACE OF HELL, EH? THE LARGE FORMAT REALLY IS SOMETHING. IT HAS SO MUCH MORE IMPACT.

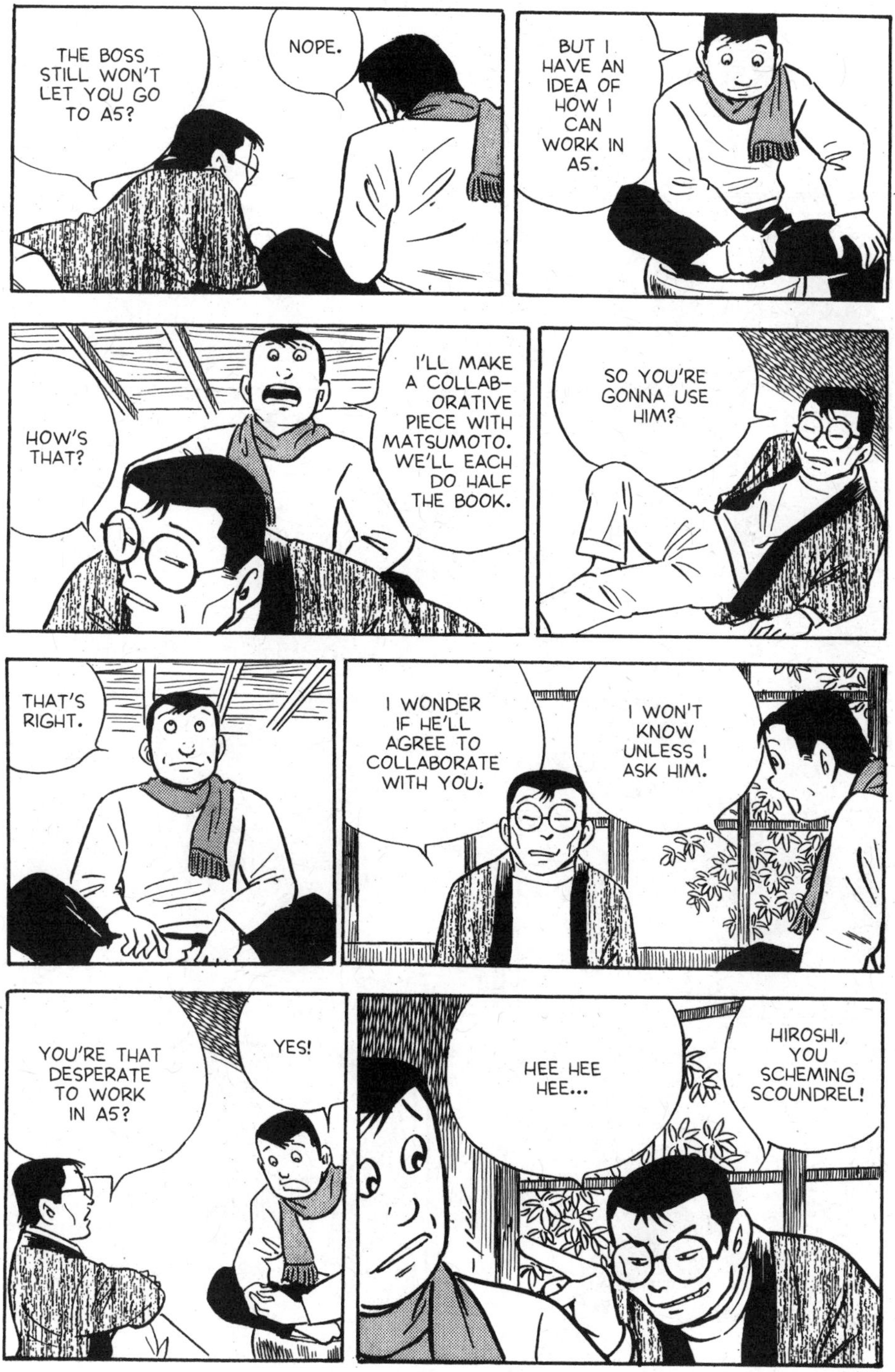
THE BOSS STILL WON'T LET YOU GO TO A5?
NOPE.
BUT I HAVE AN IDEA OF HOW I CAN WORK IN A5.
HOW'S THAT?
I'LL MAKE A COLLAB-ORATIVE PIECE WITH MATSUMOTO. WE'LL EACH DO HALF THE BOOK.
SO YOU'RE GONNA USE HIM?
THAT'S RIGHT.
I WONDER IF HE'LL AGREE TO COLLABORATE WITH YOU.
I WON'T KNOW UNLESS I ASK HIM.
YOU'RE THAT DESPERATE TO WORK IN A5?
YES!
HEE HEE HEE...
HIROSHI, YOU SCHEMING SCOUNDREL!

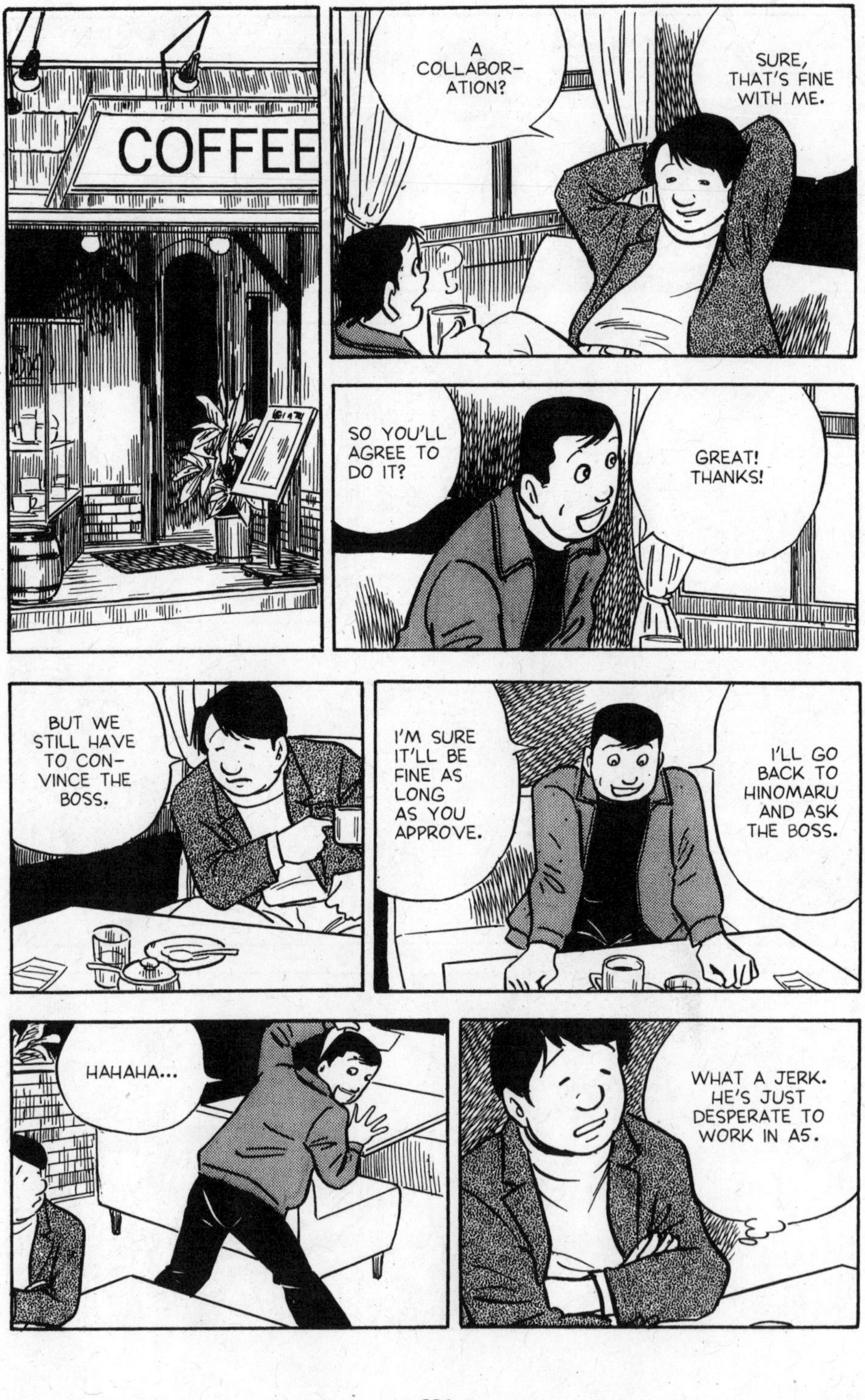
COFFEE
A COLLABOR-ATION?
SURE, THAT'S FINE WITH ME.
SO YOU'LL AGREE TO DO IT?
GREAT! THANKS!
BUT WE STILL HAVE TO CON-VINCE THE BOSS.
I'M SURE IT'LL BE FINE AS LONG AS YOU APPROVE.
I'LL GO BACK TO HINOMARU AND ASK THE BOSS.
HAHAHA...
WHAT A JERK. HE'S JUST DESPERATE TO WORK IN A5.

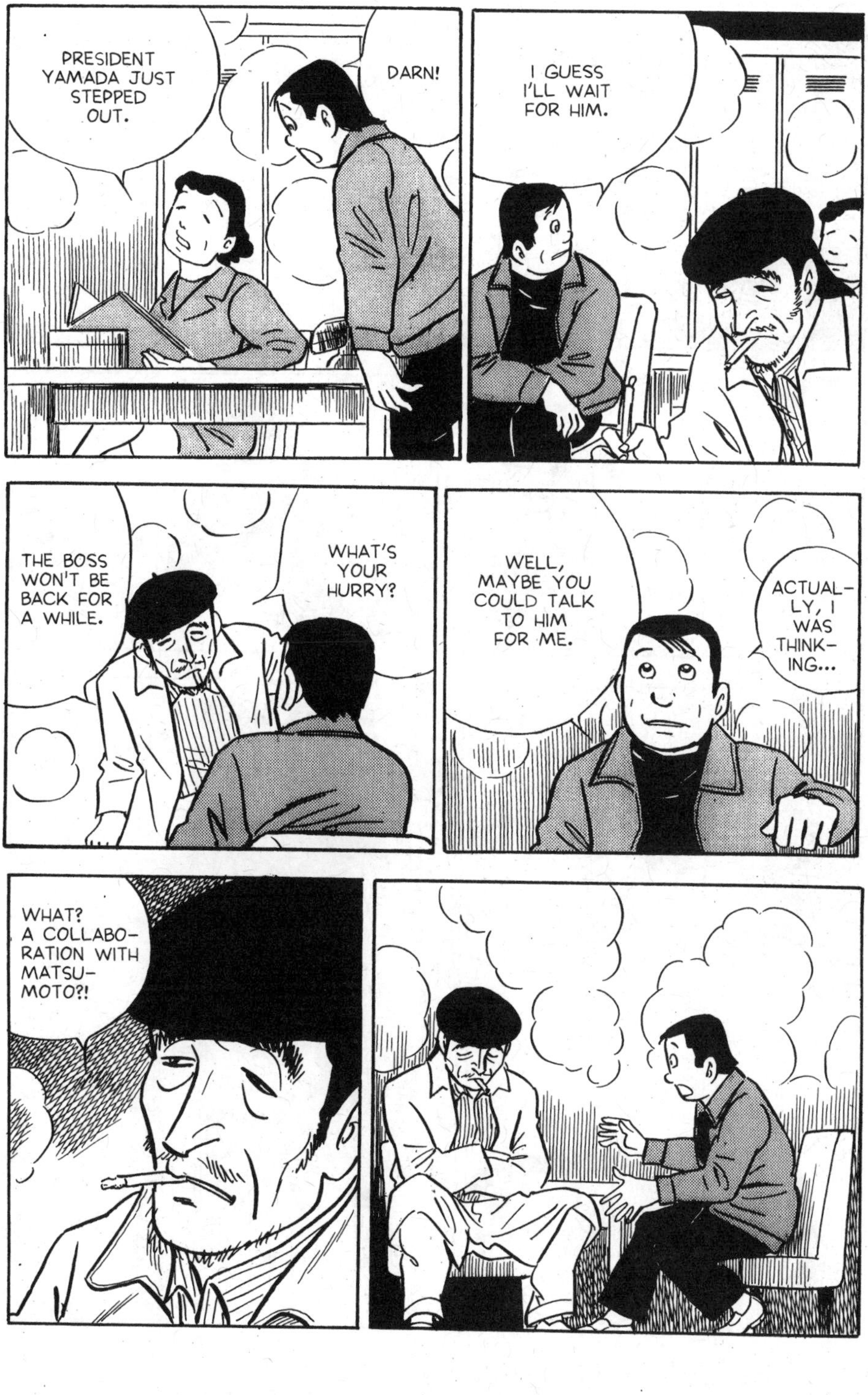
PRESIDENT YAMADA JUST STEPPED OUT.
DARN!
I GUESS I'LL WAIT FOR HIM.
THE BOSS WON'T BE BACK FOR A WHILE.
WHAT'S YOUR HURRY?
WELL, MAYBE YOU COULD TALK TO HIM FOR ME.
ACTUAL-LY, I WAS THINK-ING...
WHAT? A COLLABO-RATION WITH MATSU-MOTO?!

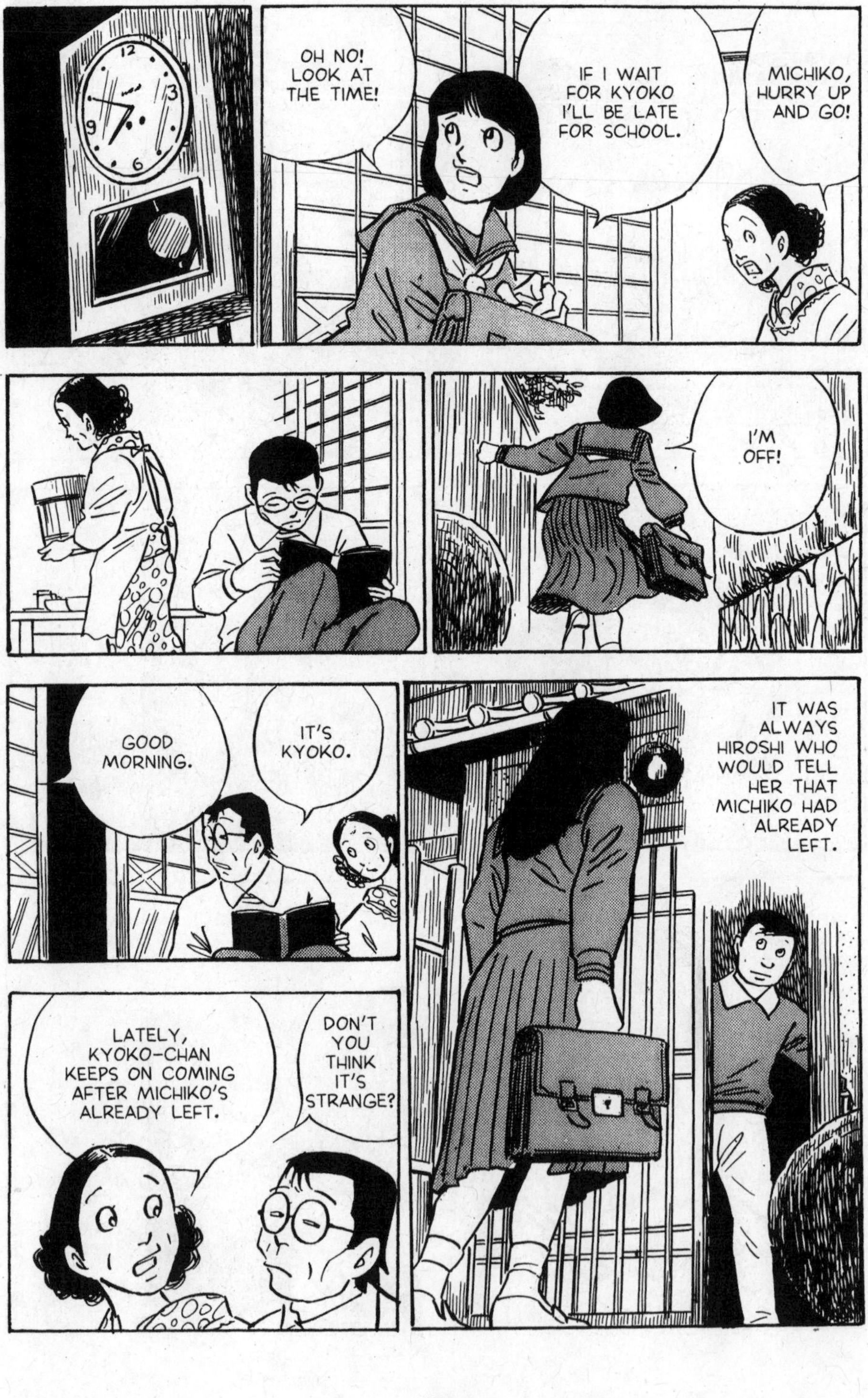
OH NO! LOOK AT THE TIME!
IF I WAIT FOR KYOKO I'LL BE LATE FOR SCHOOL.
MICHIKO, HURRY UP AND GO!
I'M OFF!
GOOD MORNING.
IT'S KYOKO.
LATELY, KYOKO-CHAN KEEPS ON COMING AFTER MICHIKO'S ALREADY LEFT.
DON'T YOU THINK IT'S STRANGE?
IT WAS ALWAYS HIROSHI WHO WOULD TELL HER THAT MICHIKO HAD ALREADY LEFT.

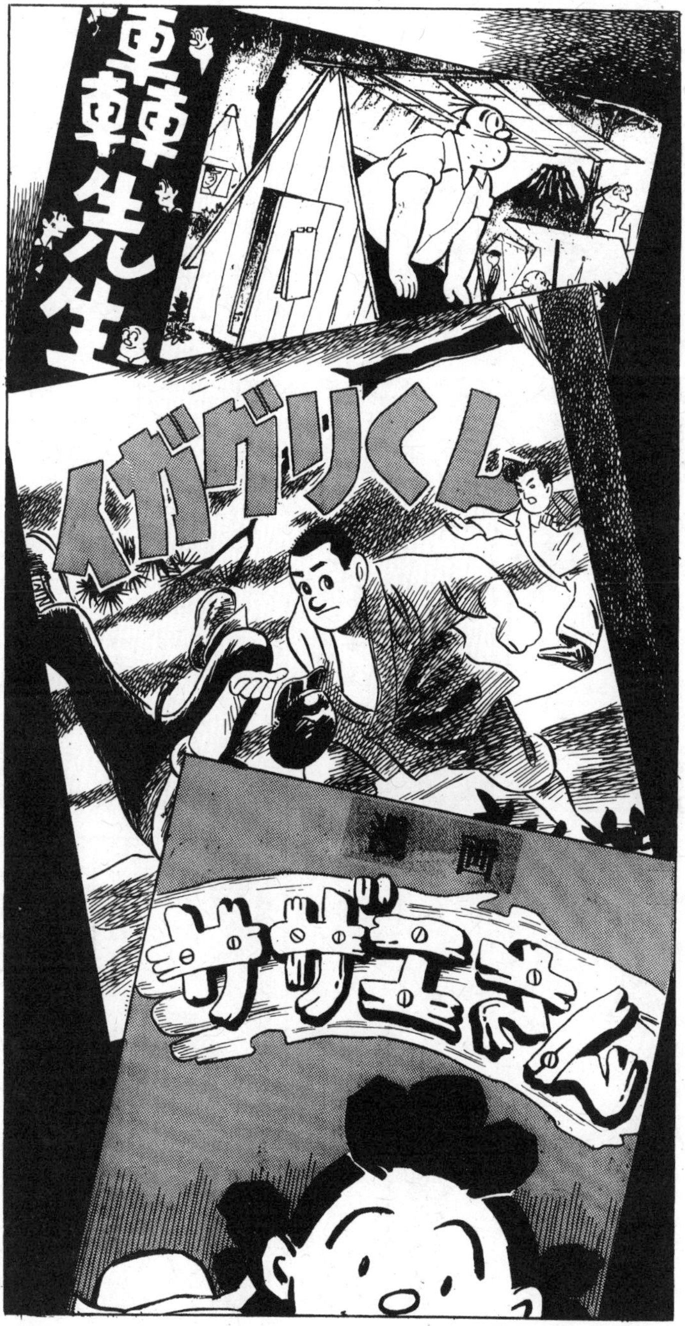
轟先生
イガグリくん
サザエさん

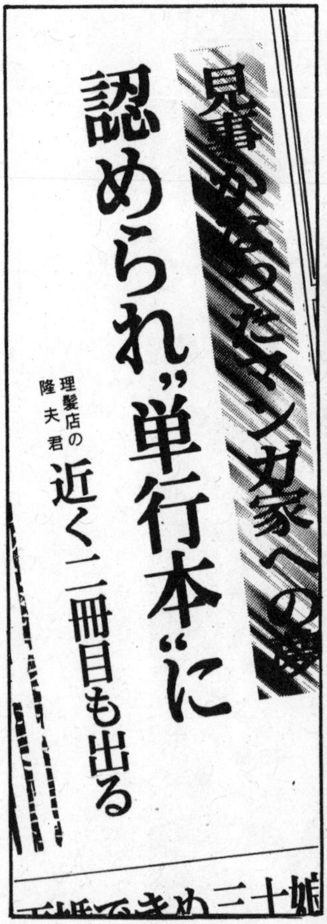
認められ"単行本"に
理髪店の隆夫君
近く二冊目も出る

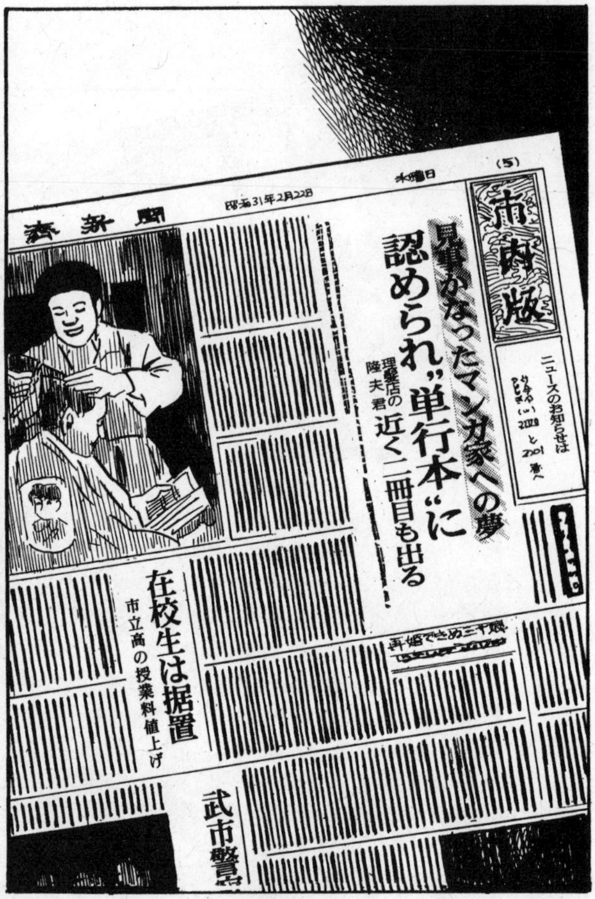
昭和31年2月22日
水曜日
(5)
市内版
ニュースのお知らせは
見事かなったマンガ家への夢
認められ"単行本"に
理髪店の隆夫君
近く二冊目も出る
在校生は据置
市立高の授業料値上げ
再婚できぬ三十娘

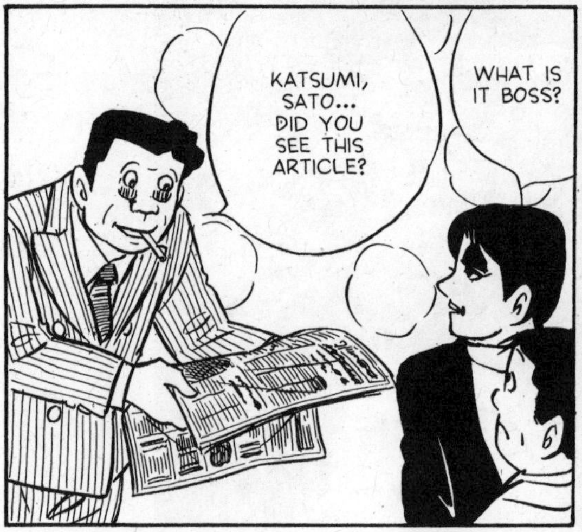
KATSUMI, SATO... DID YOU SEE THIS ARTICLE?
WHAT IS IT BOSS?

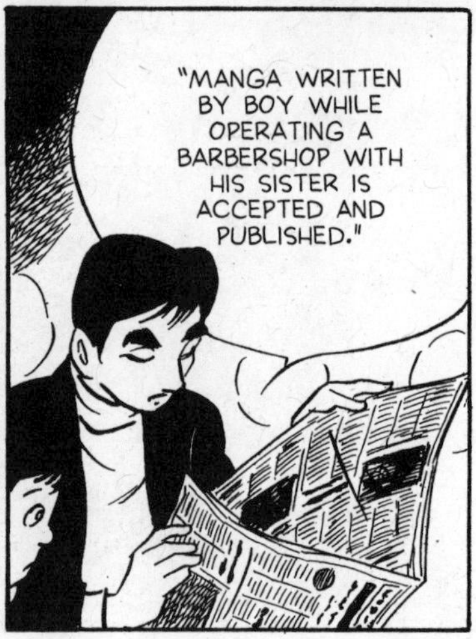
"MANGA WRITTEN BY BOY WHILE OPERATING A BARBERSHOP WITH HIS SISTER IS ACCEPTED AND PUBLISHED."

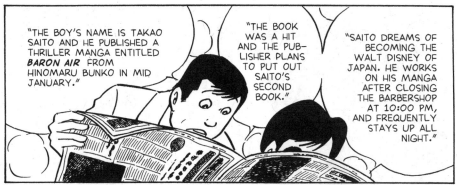

"THE BOY'S NAME IS TAKAO SAITO AND HE PUBLISHED A THRILLER MANGA ENTITLED *BARON AIR* FROM HINOMARU BUNKO IN MID JANUARY."

"THE BOOK WAS A HIT AND THE PUBLISHER PLANS TO PUT OUT SAITO'S SECOND BOOK."

"SAITO DREAMS OF BECOMING THE WALT DISNEY OF JAPAN. HE WORKS ON HIS MANGA AFTER CLOSING THE BARBERSHOP AT 10:00 PM, AND FREQUENTLY STAYS UP ALL NIGHT."

I'M QUOTED IN THERE, TOO.

READ THAT PART, WILL YA?

"SHUZO YAMADA, PRESIDENT OF HAKKO HINOMARU PUBLISHING, COMMENTED AS FOLLOWS: 'WE HAVE TWO TO THREE NEW AUTHORS COME IN WITH SUBMISSIONS EVERY DAY.'"

"'SAITO CAME IN LAST NOVEMBER AND HIS WORK WAS VERY INTERESTING, SO WE PUBLISHED IT. HE'S PRETTY GOOD FOR A NEW ARTIST. WE EXPECT GREAT THINGS FROM HIM.'"

BOSS, ISN'T "TWO TO THREE NEW ARTISTS" AN EXAGGERATION?

WELL, A LITTLE EMBELLISHMENT NEVER HURT. THE REPORTER WAS DELIGHTED WITH MY STORY.

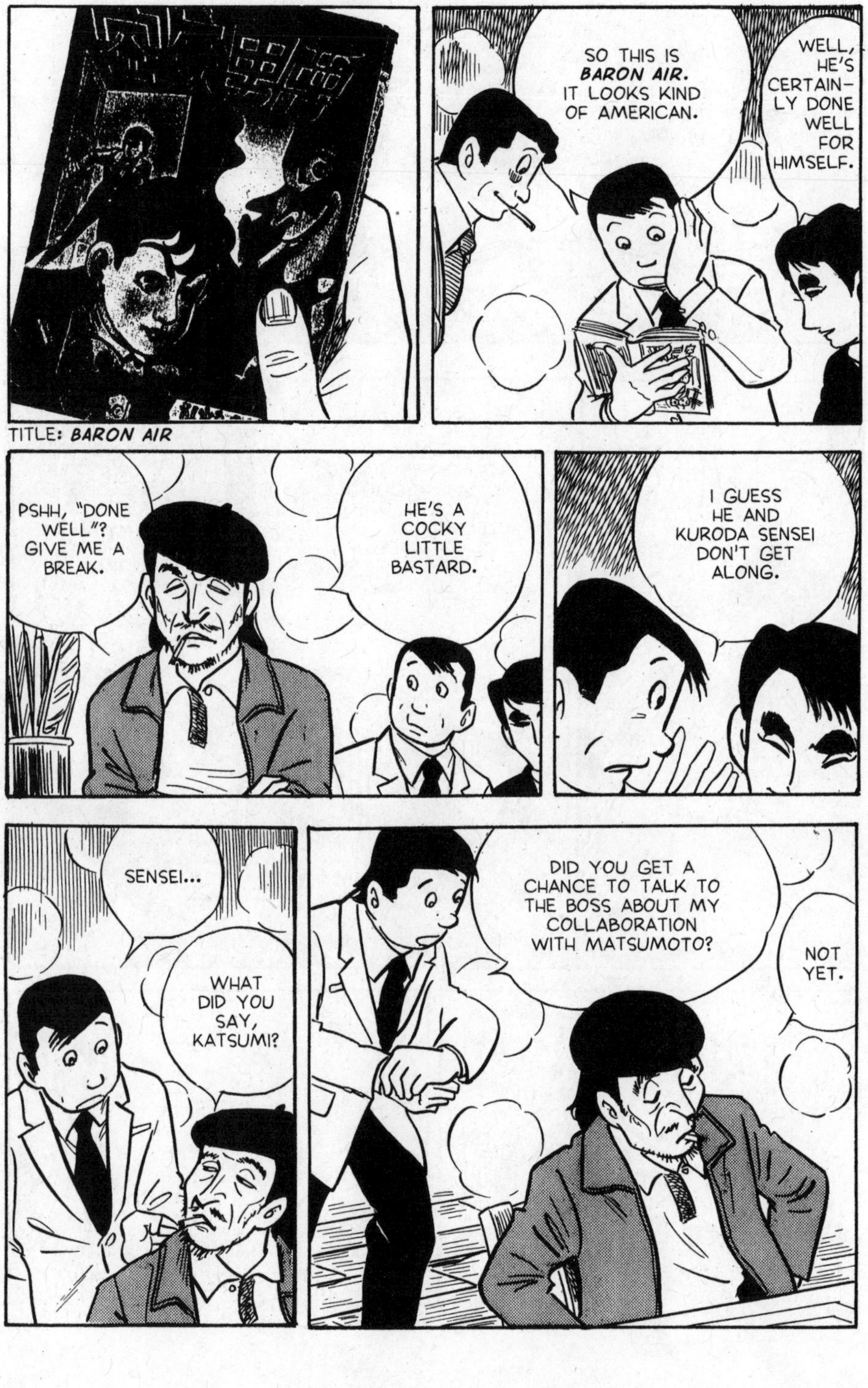
TITLE: BARON AIR
SO THIS IS BARON AIR. IT LOOKS KIND OF AMERICAN.
WELL, HE'S CERTAIN-LY DONE WELL FOR HIMSELF.
PSHH, "DONE WELL"? GIVE ME A BREAK.
HE'S A COCKY LITTLE BASTARD.
I GUESS HE AND KURODA SENSEI DON'T GET ALONG.
SENSEI...
WHAT DID YOU SAY, KATSUMI?
DID YOU GET A CHANCE TO TALK TO THE BOSS ABOUT MY COLLABORATION WITH MATSUMOTO?
NOT YET.

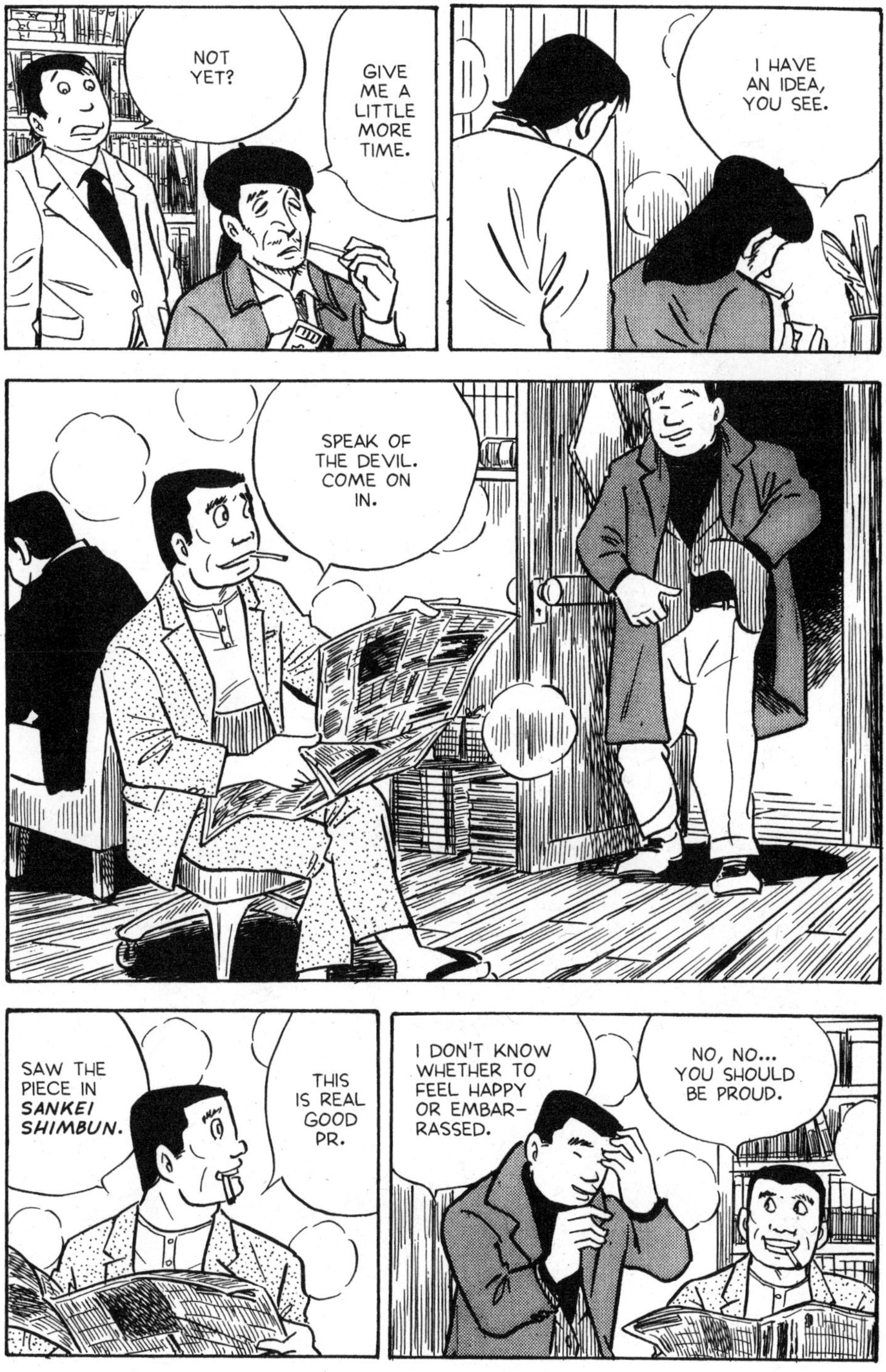
NOT YET?
GIVE ME A LITTLE MORE TIME.
I HAVE AN IDEA, YOU SEE.
SPEAK OF THE DEVIL. COME ON IN.
SAW THE PIECE IN SANKEI SHIMBUN.
THIS IS REAL GOOD PR.
I DON'T KNOW WHETHER TO FEEL HAPPY OR EMBARRASSED.
NO, NO... YOU SHOULD BE PROUD.

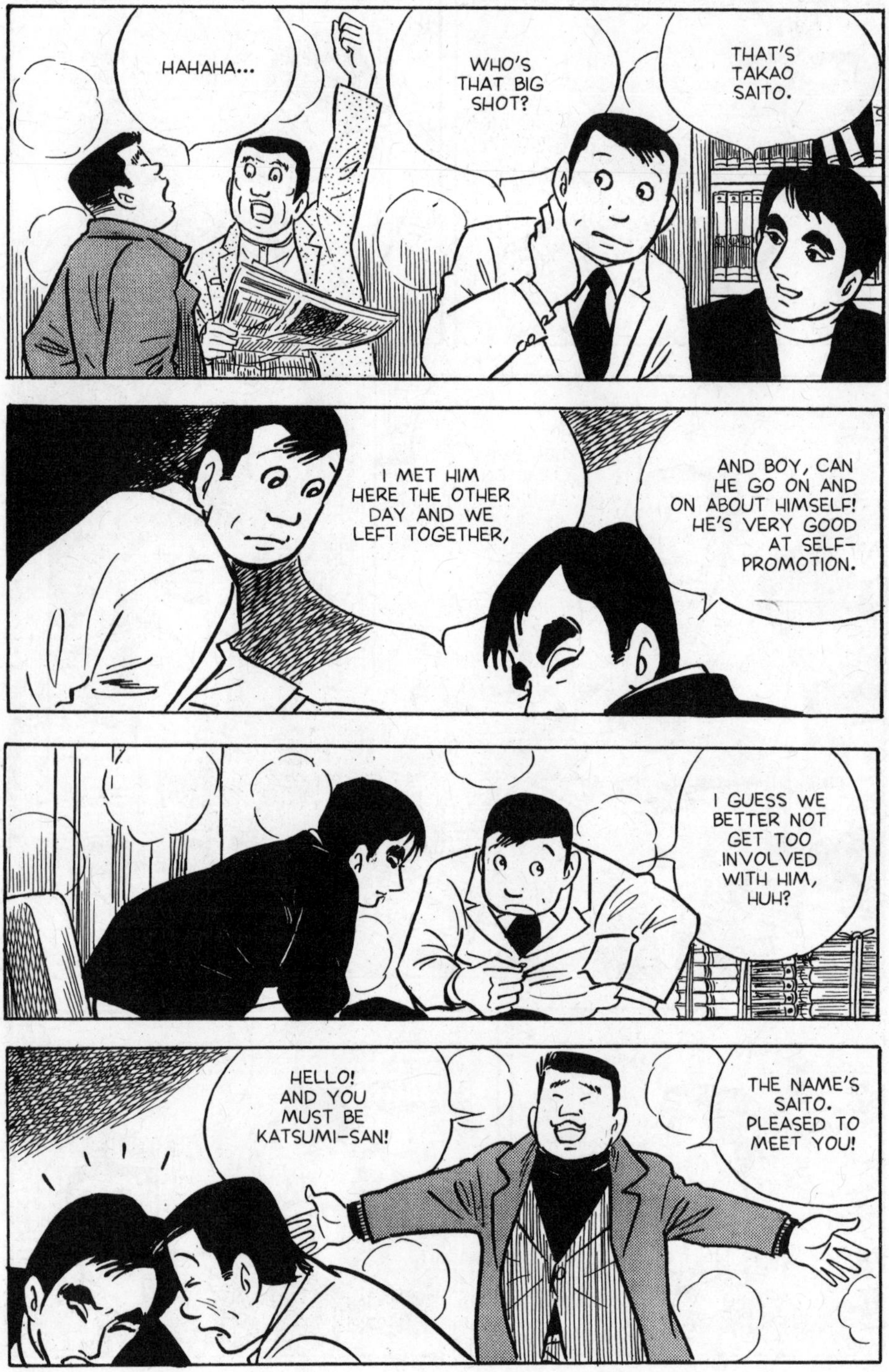
HAHAHA...
WHO'S THAT BIG SHOT?
THAT'S TAKAO SAITO.
I MET HIM HERE THE OTHER DAY AND WE LEFT TOGETHER,
AND BOY, CAN HE GO ON AND ON ABOUT HIMSELF! HE'S VERY GOOD AT SELF-PROMOTION.
I GUESS WE BETTER NOT GET TOO INVOLVED WITH HIM, HUH?
HELLO! AND YOU MUST BE KATSUMI-SAN!
THE NAME'S SAITO. PLEASED TO MEET YOU!

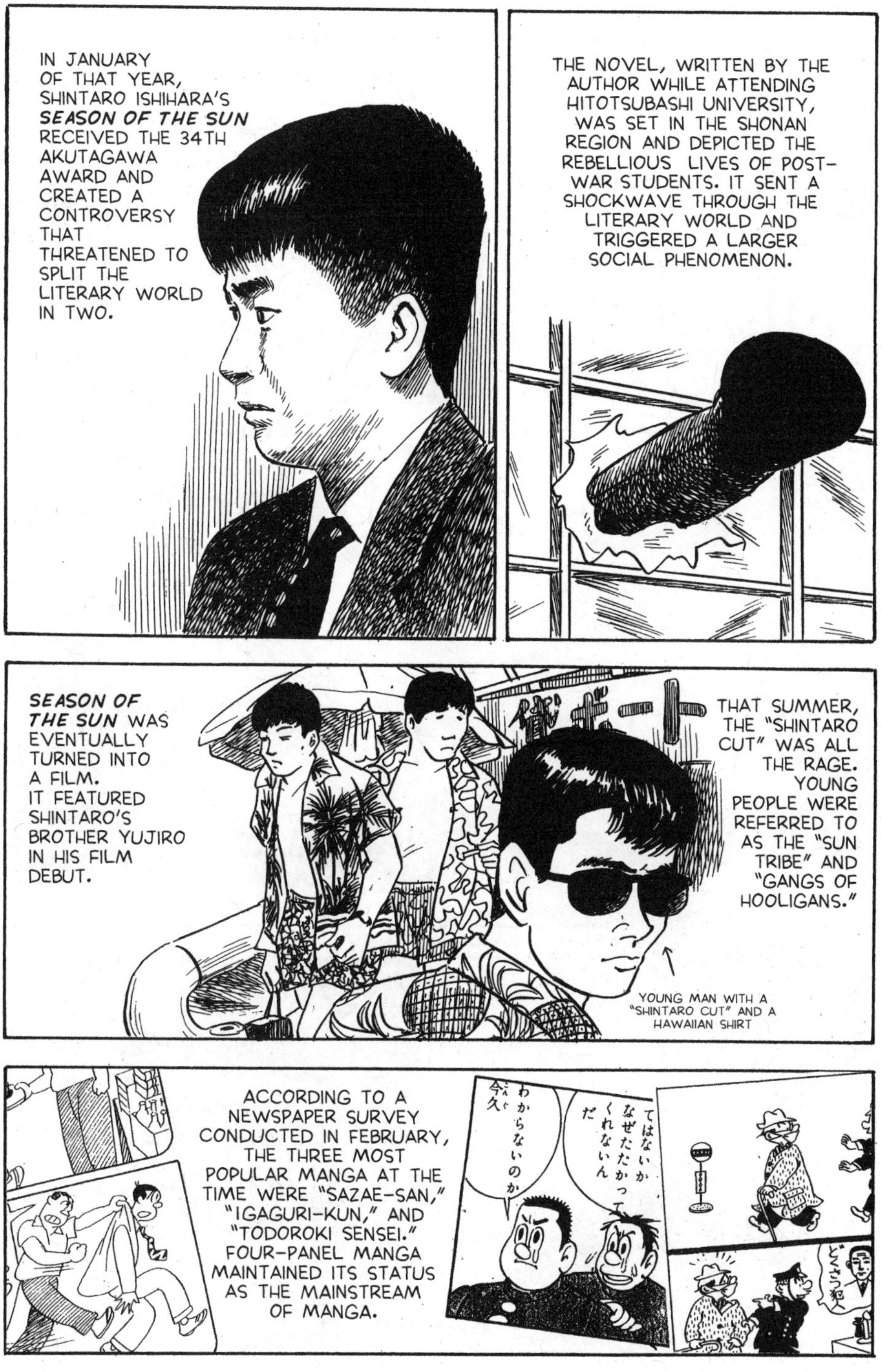
IN JANUARY OF THAT YEAR, SHINTARO ISHIHARA'S ***SEASON OF THE SUN*** RECEIVED THE 34TH AKUTAGAWA AWARD AND CREATED A CONTROVERSY THAT THREATENED TO SPLIT THE LITERARY WORLD IN TWO.
THE NOVEL, WRITTEN BY THE AUTHOR WHILE ATTENDING HITOTSUBASHI UNIVERSITY, WAS SET IN THE SHONAN REGION AND DEPICTED THE REBELLIOUS LIVES OF POST-WAR STUDENTS. IT SENT A SHOCKWAVE THROUGH THE LITERARY WORLD AND TRIGGERED A LARGER SOCIAL PHENOMENON.
SEASON OF THE SUN WAS EVENTUALLY TURNED INTO A FILM. IT FEATURED SHINTARO'S BROTHER YUJIRO IN HIS FILM DEBUT.
THAT SUMMER, THE "SHINTARO CUT" WAS ALL THE RAGE. YOUNG PEOPLE WERE REFERRED TO AS THE "SUN TRIBE" AND "GANGS OF HOOLIGANS."
YOUNG MAN WITH A "SHINTARO CUT" AND A HAWAIIAN SHIRT
ACCORDING TO A NEWSPAPER SURVEY CONDUCTED IN FEBRUARY, THE THREE MOST POPULAR MANGA AT THE TIME WERE "SAZAE-SAN," "IGAGURI-KUN," AND "TODOROKI SENSEI." FOUR-PANEL MANGA MAINTAINED ITS STATUS AS THE MAINSTREAM OF MANGA.
てはないか なぜたたかって くれないんだ
今久 わからないのか
どくさつ犯人

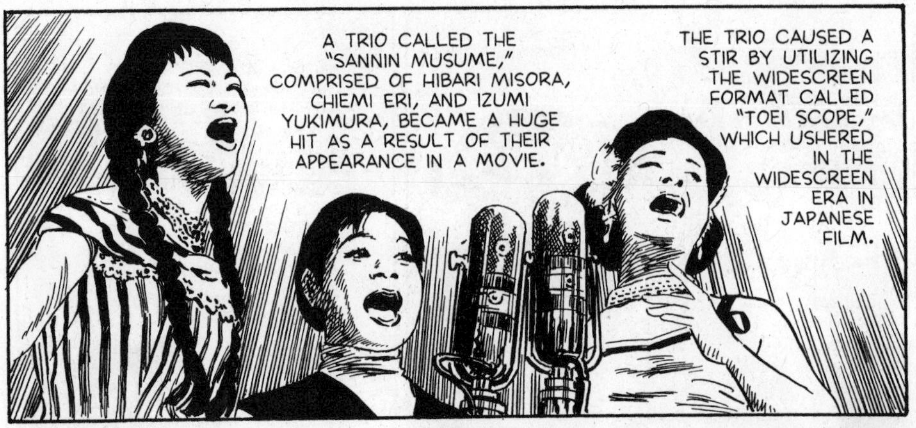
A TRIO CALLED THE "SANNIN MUSUME," COMPRISED OF HIBARI MISORA, CHIEMI ERI, AND IZUMI YUKIMURA, BECAME A HUGE HIT AS A RESULT OF THEIR APPEARANCE IN A MOVIE.
THE TRIO CAUSED A STIR BY UTILIZING THE WIDESCREEN FORMAT CALLED "TOEI SCOPE," WHICH USHERED IN THE WIDESCREEN ERA IN JAPANESE FILM.

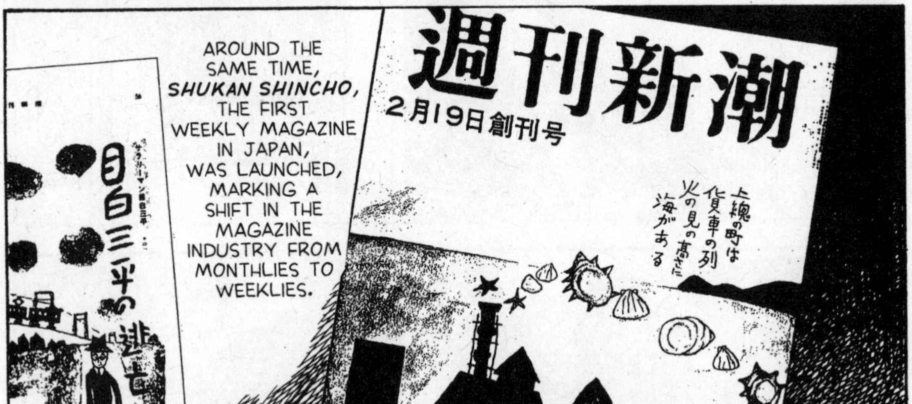
AROUND THE SAME TIME, ***SHUKAN SHINCHO,*** THE FIRST WEEKLY MAGAZINE IN JAPAN, WAS LAUNCHED, MARKING A SHIFT IN THE MAGAZINE INDUSTRY FROM MONTHLIES TO WEEKLIES.
目白三平の
週刊新潮
2月19日創刊号
貨車の列
火の見の高さに
海がある

TITLE: ***SHUKAN SHINCHO,*** FEB, 2/19 INAUGURAL ISSUE

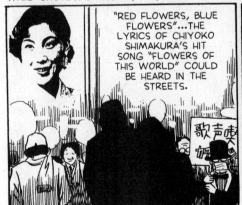

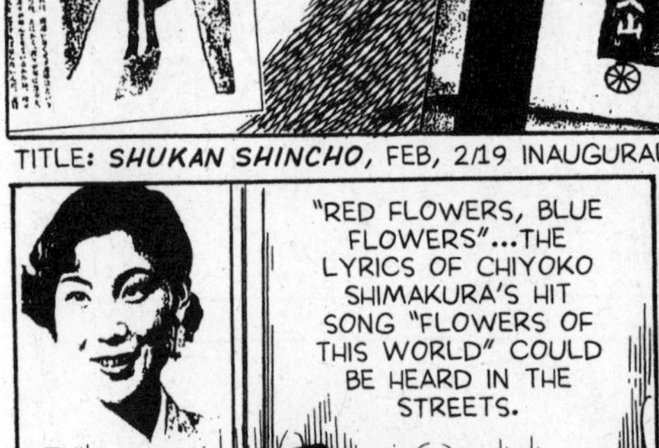
"RED FLOWERS, BLUE FLOWERS"...THE LYRICS OF CHIYOKO SHIMAKURA'S HIT SONG "FLOWERS OF THIS WORLD" COULD BE HEARD IN THE STREETS.

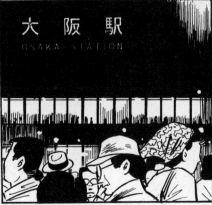

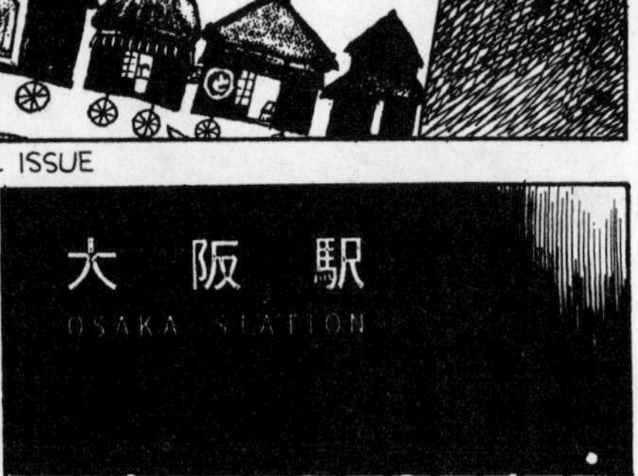
大阪駅
OSAKA STATION

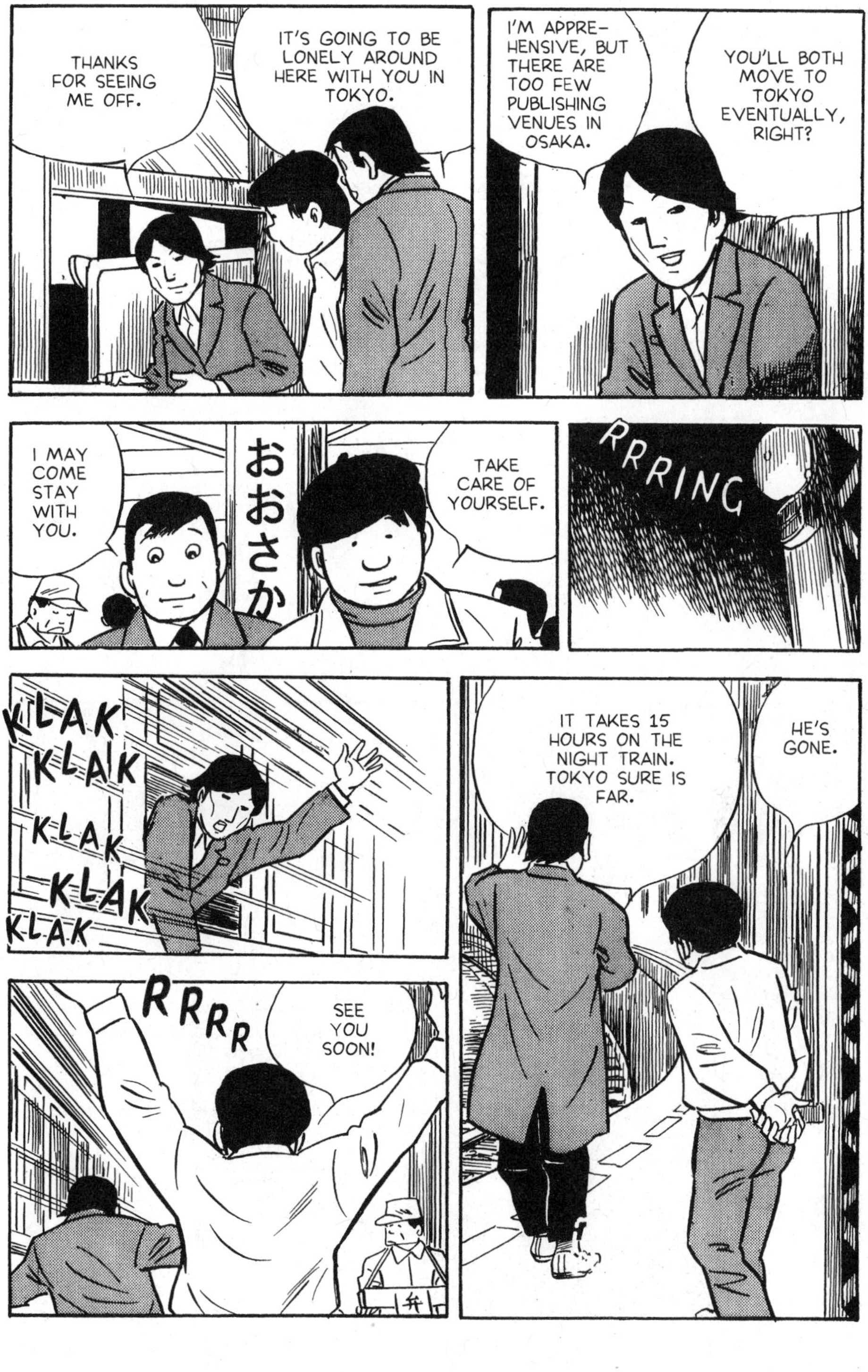
THANKS FOR SEEING ME OFF.
IT'S GOING TO BE LONELY AROUND HERE WITH YOU IN TOKYO.
I'M APPRE-HENSIVE, BUT THERE ARE TOO FEW PUBLISHING VENUES IN OSAKA.
YOU'LL BOTH MOVE TO TOKYO EVENTUALLY, RIGHT?
I MAY COME STAY WITH YOU.
おおさか
TAKE CARE OF YOURSELF.
RRRING
KLAK KLAK KLAK KLAK KLAK
IT TAKES 15 HOURS ON THE NIGHT TRAIN. TOKYO SURE IS FAR.
HE'S GONE.
RRRR
SEE YOU SOON!

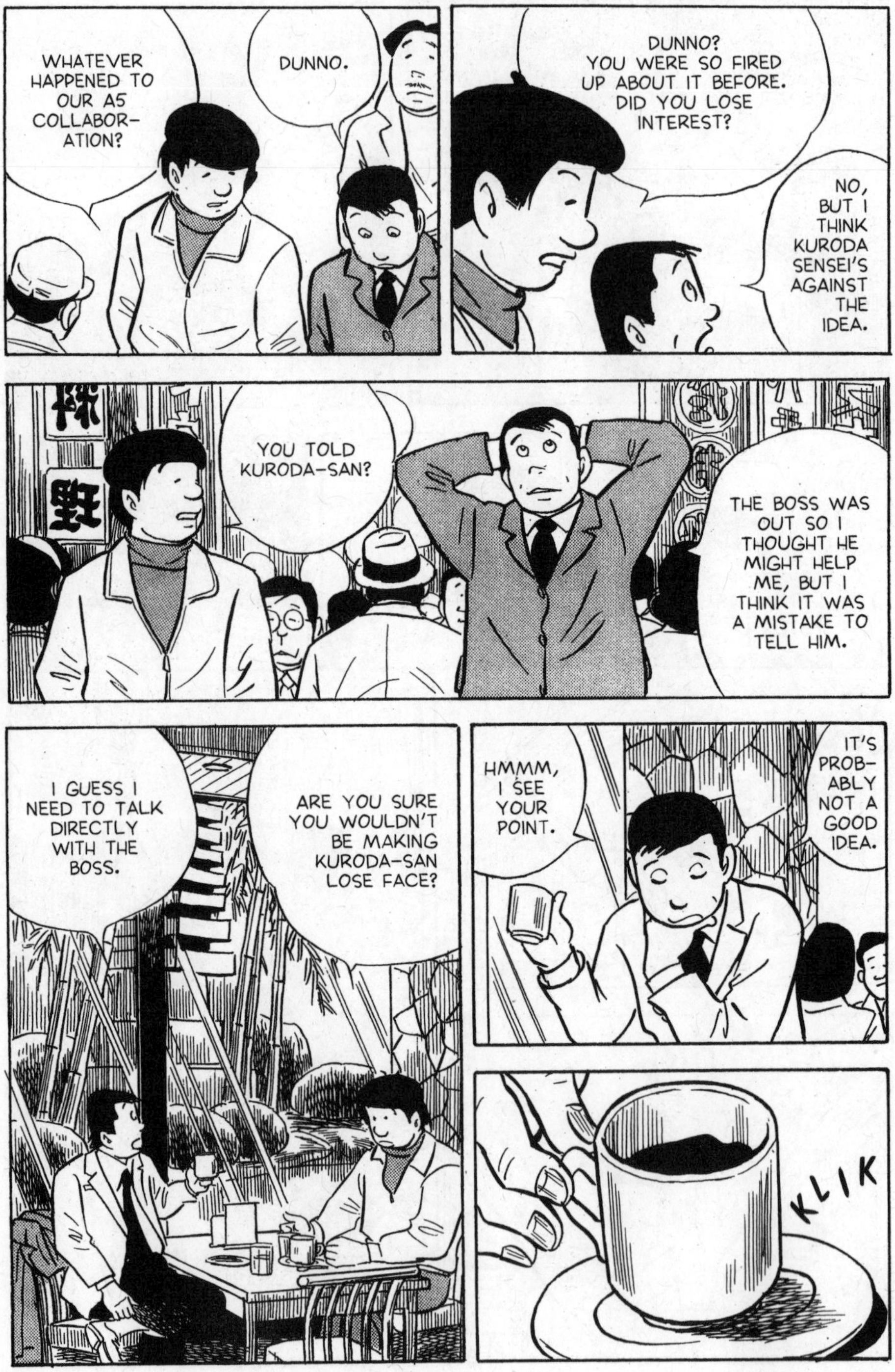
WHATEVER HAPPENED TO OUR A5 COLLABOR-ATION?
DUNNO.
DUNNO? YOU WERE SO FIRED UP ABOUT IT BEFORE. DID YOU LOSE INTEREST?
NO, BUT I THINK KURODA SENSEI'S AGAINST THE IDEA.
YOU TOLD KURODA-SAN?
THE BOSS WAS OUT SO I THOUGHT HE MIGHT HELP ME, BUT I THINK IT WAS A MISTAKE TO TELL HIM.
I GUESS I NEED TO TALK DIRECTLY WITH THE BOSS.
ARE YOU SURE YOU WOULDN'T BE MAKING KURODA-SAN LOSE FACE?
HMMM, I SEE YOUR POINT.
IT'S PROB-ABLY NOT A GOOD IDEA.
KLIK

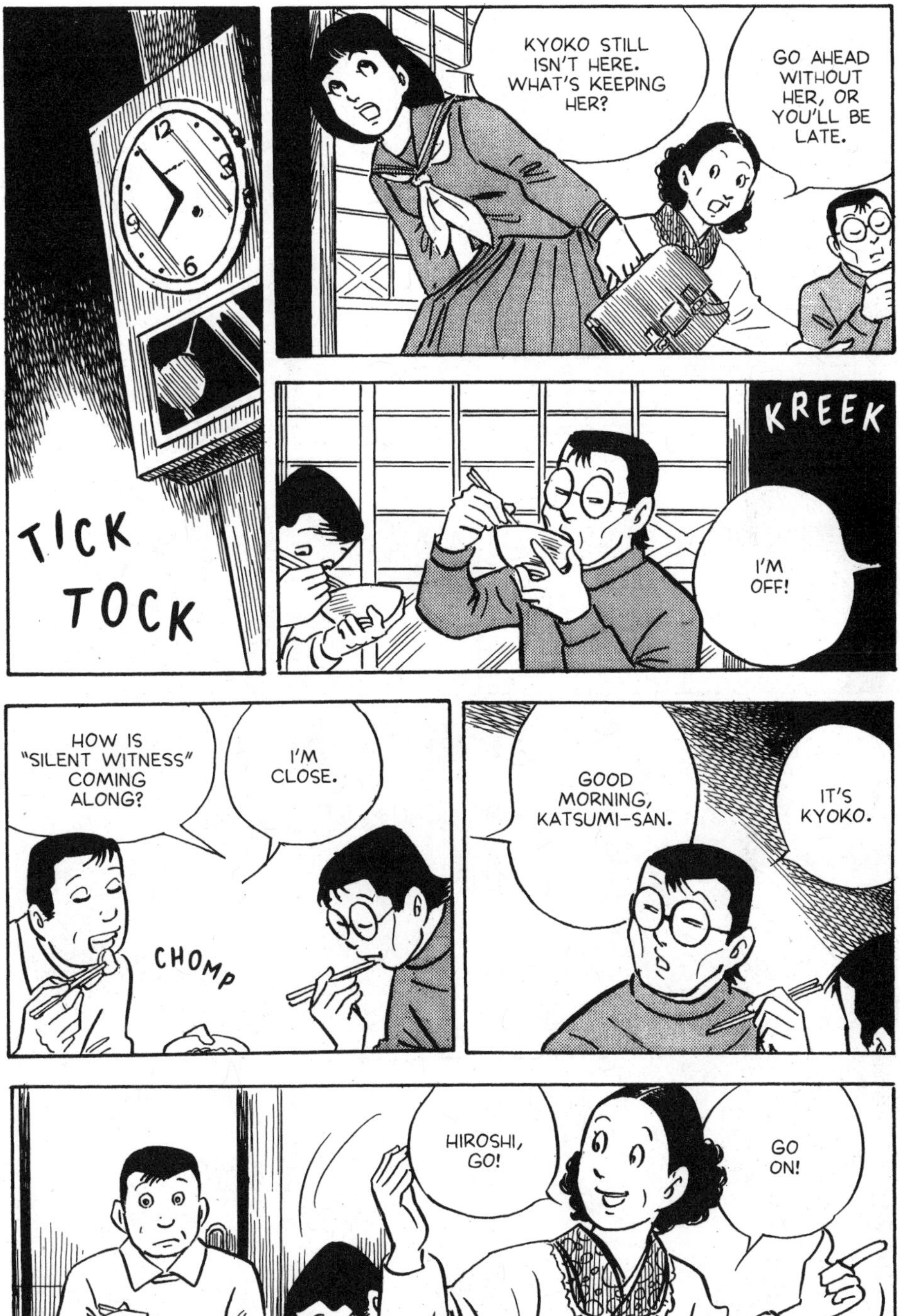
TICK
TOCK
KYOKO STILL ISN'T HERE. WHAT'S KEEPING HER?
GO AHEAD WITHOUT HER, OR YOU'LL BE LATE.
KREEK
I'M OFF!
HOW IS "SILENT WITNESS" COMING ALONG?
I'M CLOSE.
CHOMP
GOOD MORNING, KATSUMI-SAN.
IT'S KYOKO.
HIROSHI, GO!
GO ON!

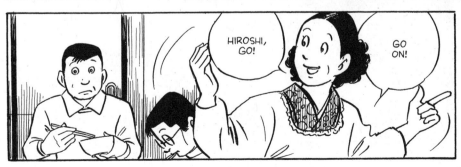

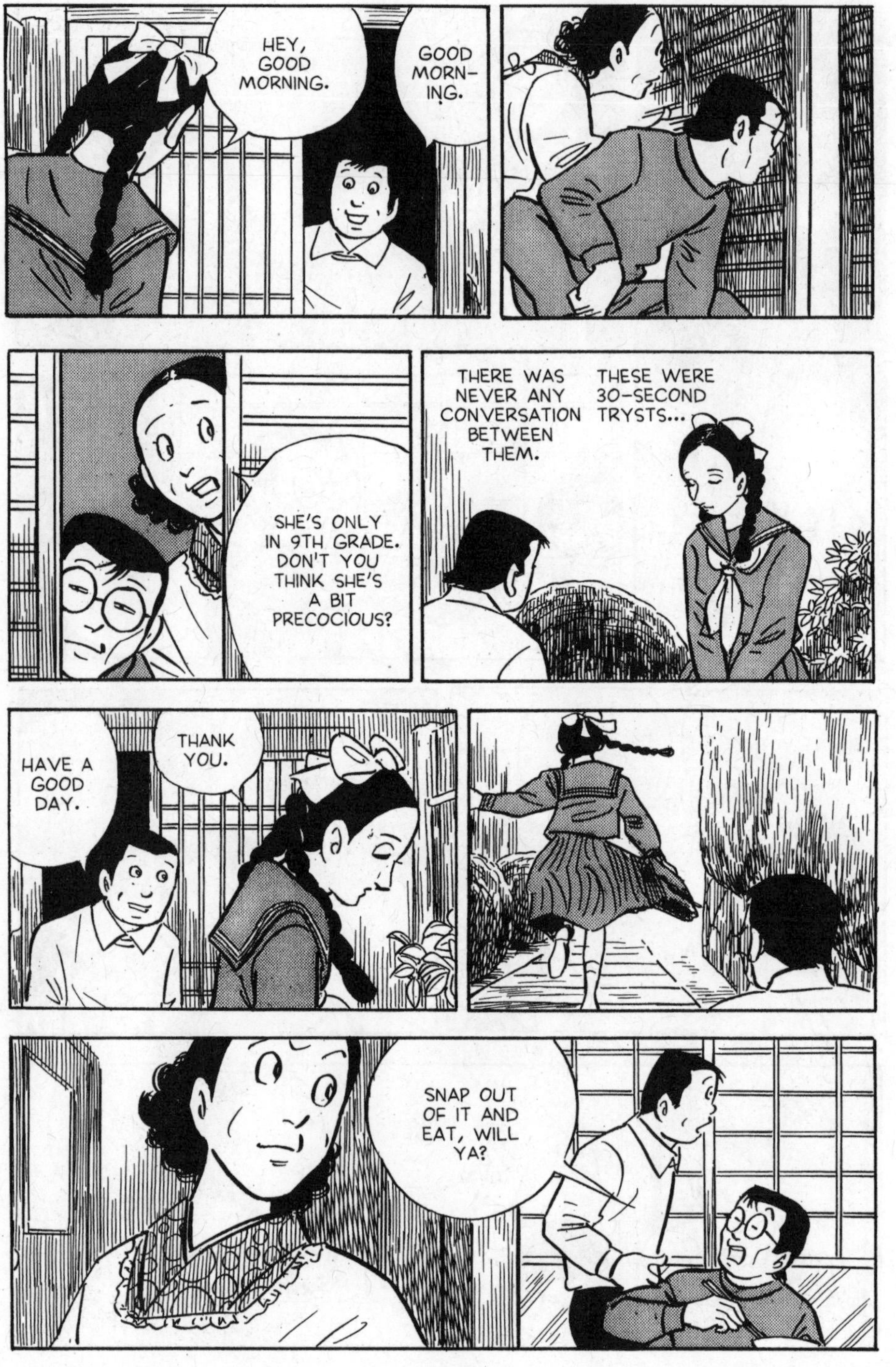
HEY, GOOD MORNING.
GOOD MORN-ING.
SHE'S ONLY IN 9TH GRADE. DON'T YOU THINK SHE'S A BIT PRECOCIOUS?
THERE WAS NEVER ANY CONVERSATION BETWEEN THEM.
THESE WERE 30-SECOND TRYSTS...
HAVE A GOOD DAY.
THANK YOU.
SNAP OUT OF IT AND EAT, WILL YA?

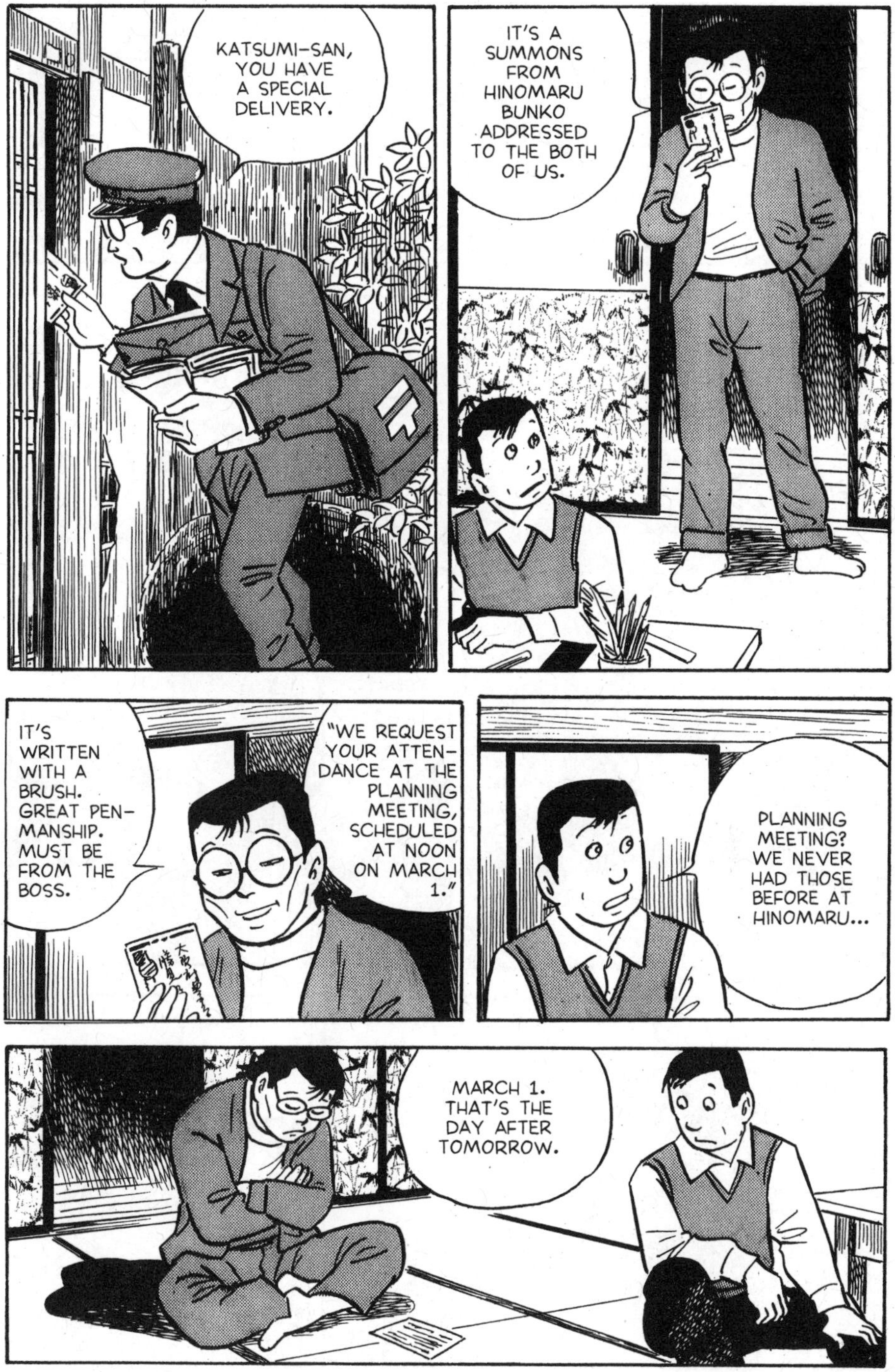
KATSUMI-SAN, YOU HAVE A SPECIAL DELIVERY.
IT'S A SUMMONS FROM HINOMARU BUNKO ADDRESSED TO THE BOTH OF US.
IT'S WRITTEN WITH A BRUSH. GREAT PEN-MANSHIP. MUST BE FROM THE BOSS.
"WE REQUEST YOUR ATTEN-DANCE AT THE PLANNING MEETING, SCHEDULED AT NOON ON MARCH 1."
PLANNING MEETING? WE NEVER HAD THOSE BEFORE AT HINOMARU...
MARCH 1. THAT'S THE DAY AFTER TOMORROW.

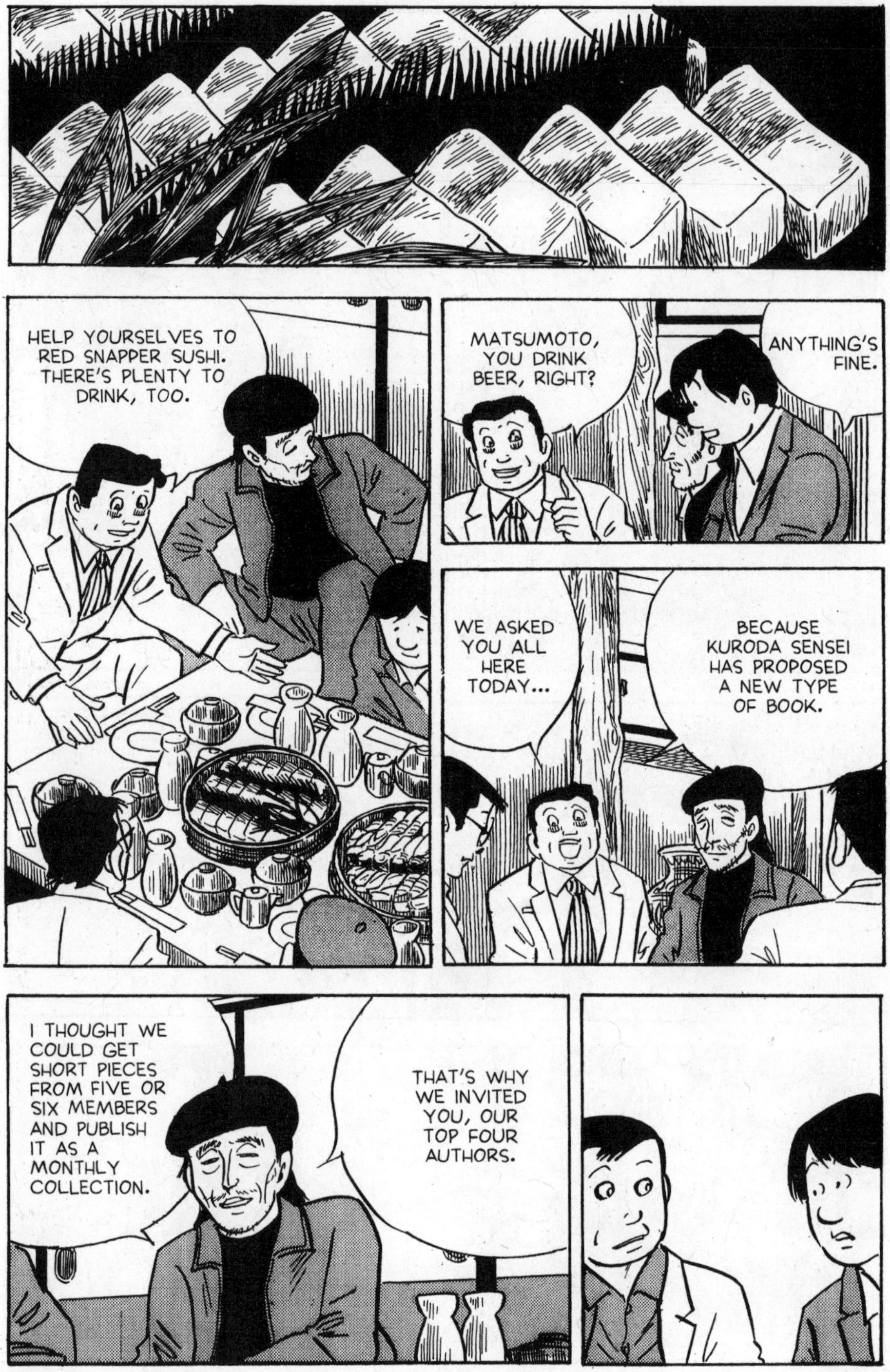
HELP YOURSELVES TO RED SNAPPER SUSHI. THERE'S PLENTY TO DRINK, TOO.
MATSUMOTO, YOU DRINK BEER, RIGHT?
ANYTHING'S FINE.
WE ASKED YOU ALL HERE TODAY...
BECAUSE KURODA SENSEI HAS PROPOSED A NEW TYPE OF BOOK.
I THOUGHT WE COULD GET SHORT PIECES FROM FIVE OR SIX MEMBERS AND PUBLISH IT AS A MONTHLY COLLECTION.
THAT'S WHY WE INVITED YOU, OUR TOP FOUR AUTHORS.

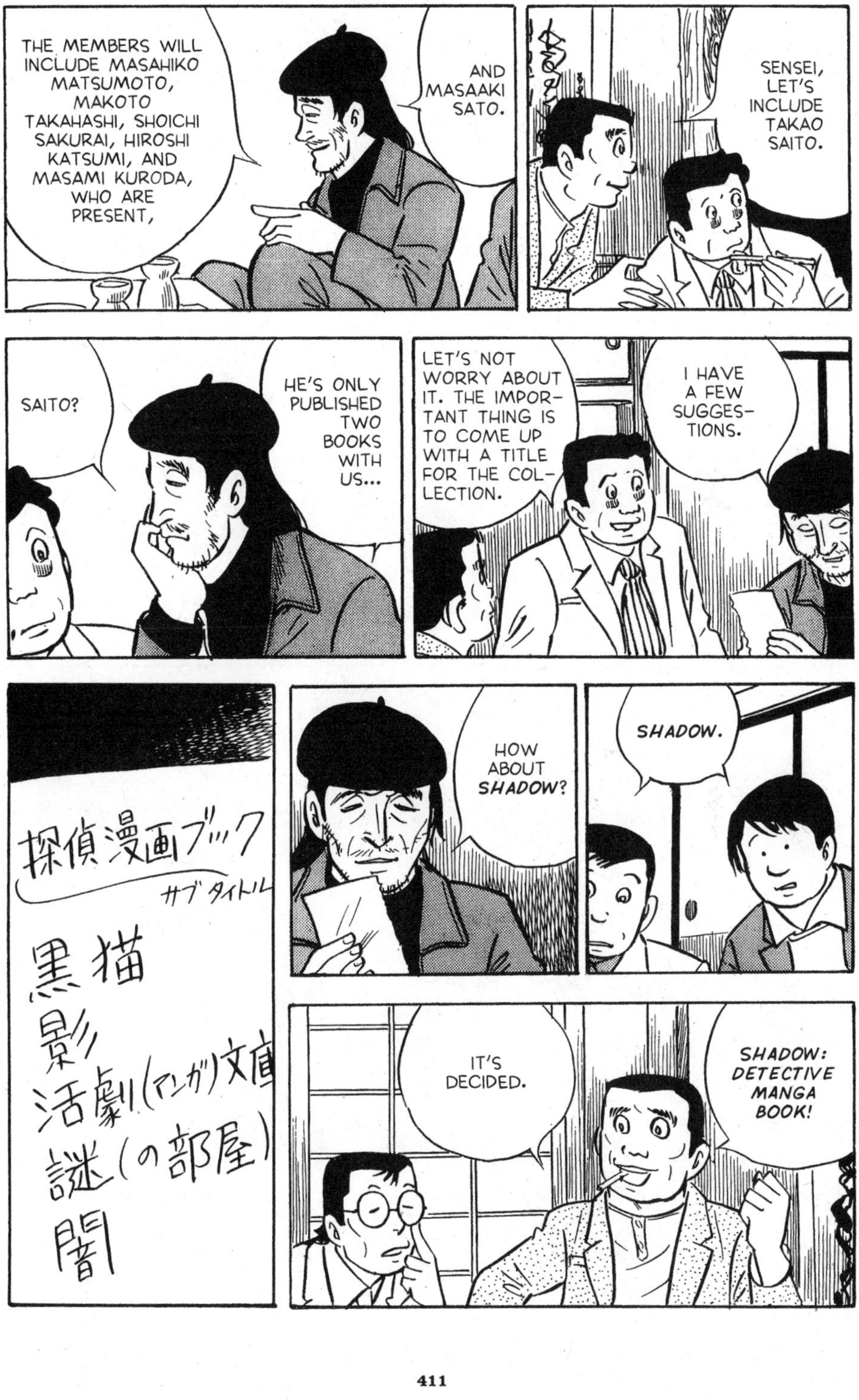
THE MEMBERS WILL INCLUDE MASAHIKO MATSUMOTO, MAKOTO TAKAHASHI, SHOICHI SAKURAI, HIROSHI KATSUMI, AND MASAMI KURODA, WHO ARE PRESENT,
AND MASAAKI SATO.
SENSEI, LET'S INCLUDE TAKAO SAITO.
SAITO?
HE'S ONLY PUBLISHED TWO BOOKS WITH US...
LET'S NOT WORRY ABOUT IT. THE IMPORTANT THING IS TO COME UP WITH A TITLE FOR THE COLLECTION.
I HAVE A FEW SUGGESTIONS.
探偵漫画ブック
サブタイトル
黒猫
影
活劇(アンガ)文
謎(の部屋)
闇
HOW ABOUT *SHADOW*?
SHADOW.
IT'S DECIDED.
SHADOW: DETECTIVE MANGA BOOK!

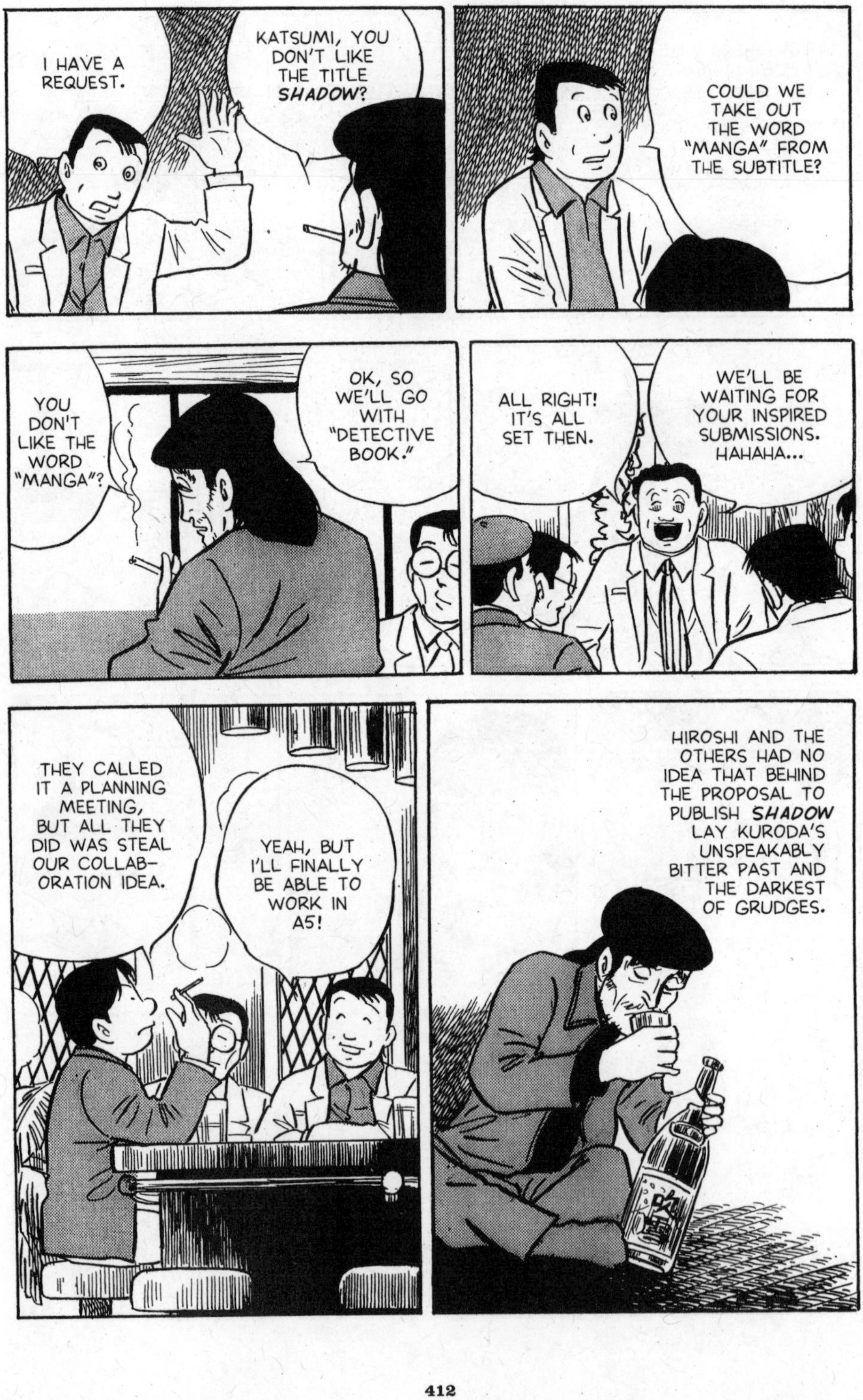
I HAVE A REQUEST.
KATSUMI, YOU DON'T LIKE THE TITLE SHADOW?
COULD WE TAKE OUT THE WORD "MANGA" FROM THE SUBTITLE?
YOU DON'T LIKE THE WORD "MANGA"?
OK, SO WE'LL GO WITH "DETECTIVE BOOK."
ALL RIGHT! IT'S ALL SET THEN.
WE'LL BE WAITING FOR YOUR INSPIRED SUBMISSIONS. HAHAHA...
THEY CALLED IT A PLANNING MEETING, BUT ALL THEY DID WAS STEAL OUR COLLAB-ORATION IDEA.
YEAH, BUT I'LL FINALLY BE ABLE TO WORK IN A5!
HIROSHI AND THE OTHERS HAD NO IDEA THAT BEHIND THE PROPOSAL TO PUBLISH SHADOW LAY KURODA'S UNSPEAKABLY BITTER PAST AND THE DARKEST OF GRUDGES.

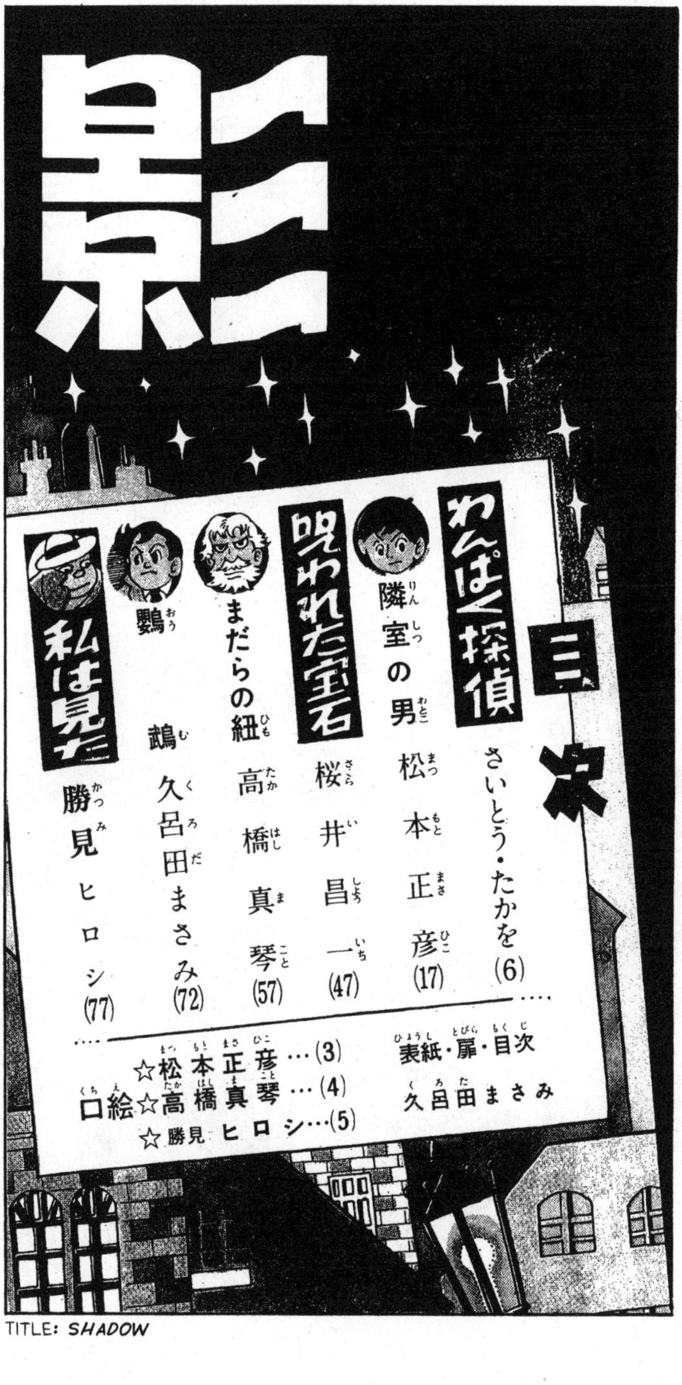
影
目次
わんぱく探偵 さいとう・たかを(6)
隣室の男 松本正彦(17)
呪われた宝石 桜井昌一(47)
まだらの紐 高橋真琴(57)
鸚鵡 久呂田まさみ(72)
私は見た 勝見ヒロシ(77)
表紙・扉・目次 久呂田まさみ
口絵☆松本正彦…(3)
☆高橋真琴…(4)
☆勝見ヒロシ…(5)

TITLE: *SHADOW*

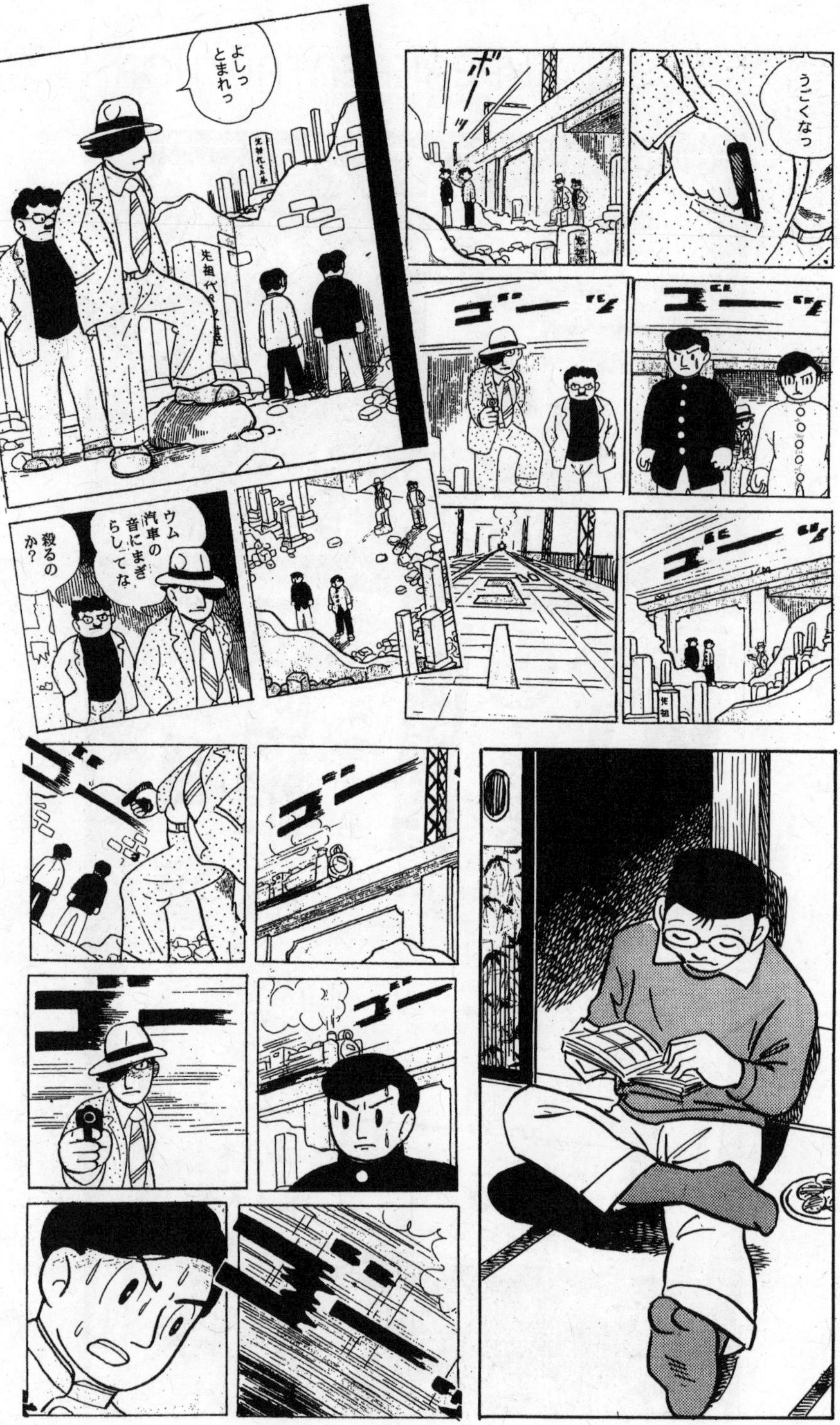
よしっ
とまれっ
ボーッ
うごくなっ
ゴーッ
ゴーッ
殺るのか?
ウム
汽車の音にまぎらしてな
ゴーーッ
ゴー
ゴー
ゴー
ゴー

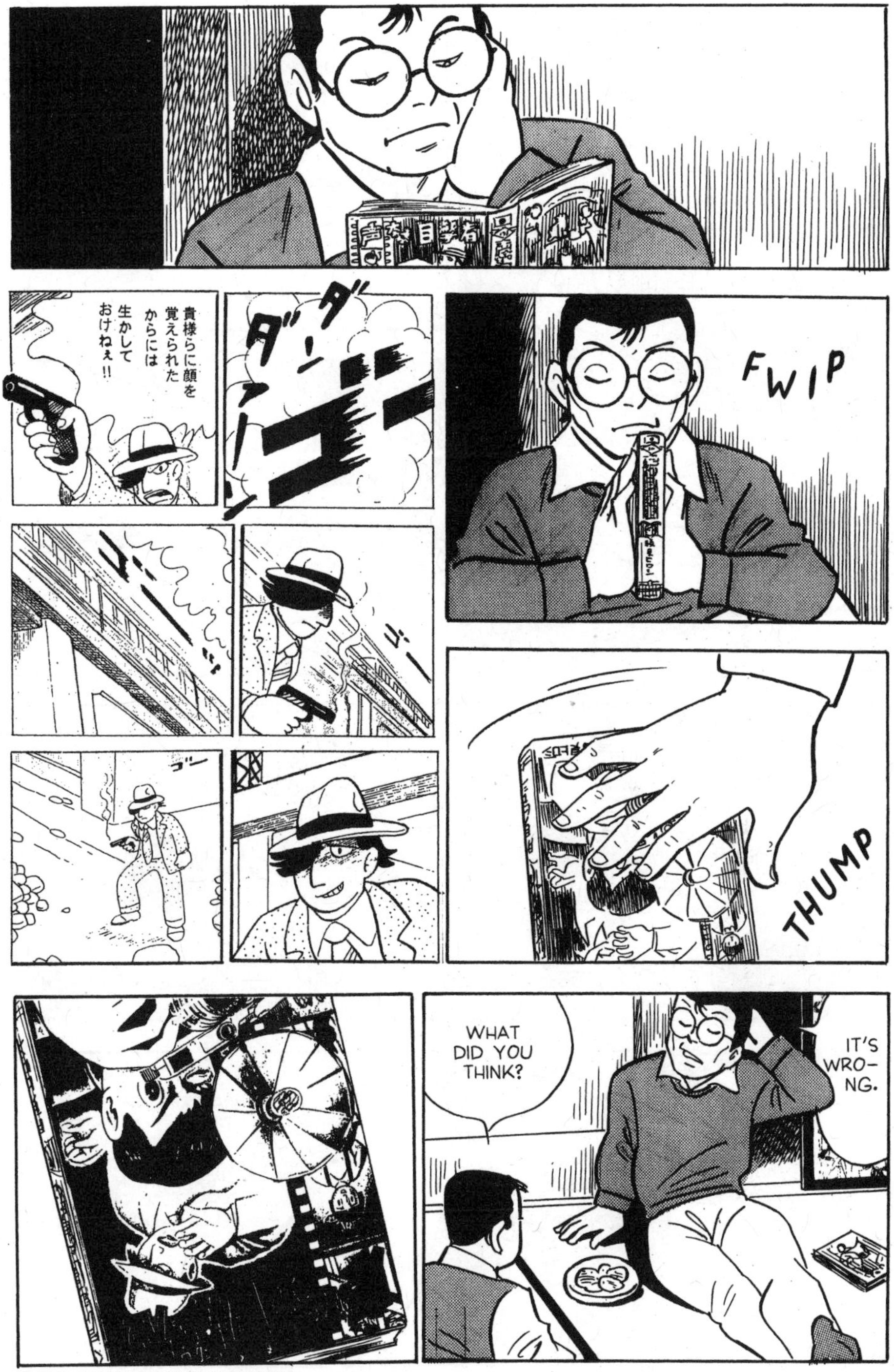

貴様らに顔を覚えられたからには生かしておけねぇ!!
FWIP
THUMP
WHAT DID YOU THINK?
IT'S WRO-NG.

TITLE: *THE SILENT WITNESS*

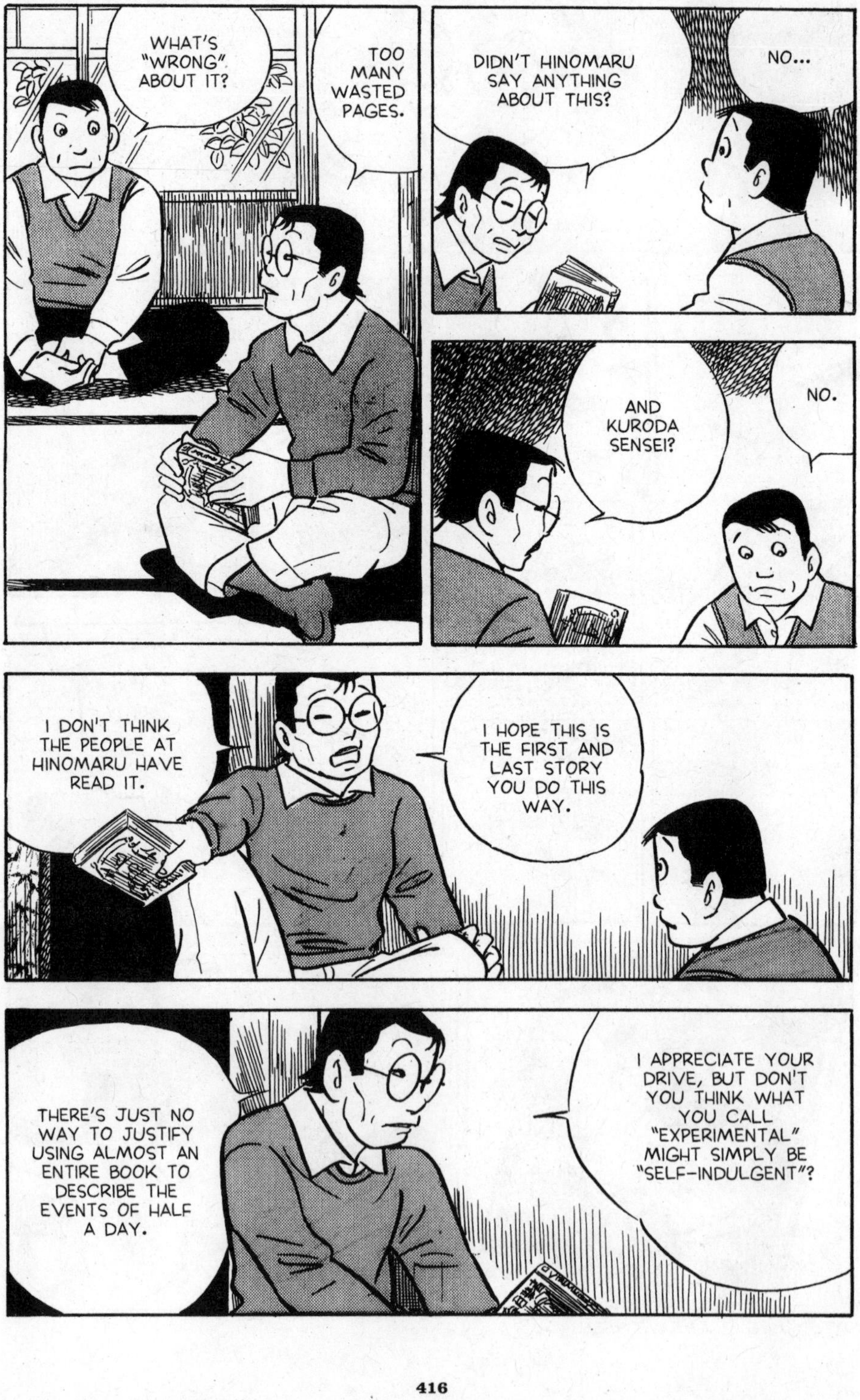
WHAT'S "WRONG" ABOUT IT?
TOO MANY WASTED PAGES.
DIDN'T HINOMARU SAY ANYTHING ABOUT THIS?
NO...
AND KURODA SENSEI?
NO.
I DON'T THINK THE PEOPLE AT HINOMARU HAVE READ IT.
I HOPE THIS IS THE FIRST AND LAST STORY YOU DO THIS WAY.
THERE'S JUST NO WAY TO JUSTIFY USING ALMOST AN ENTIRE BOOK TO DESCRIBE THE EVENTS OF HALF A DAY.
I APPRECIATE YOUR DRIVE, BUT DON'T YOU THINK WHAT YOU CALL "EXPERIMENTAL" MIGHT SIMPLY BE "SELF-INDULGENT"?

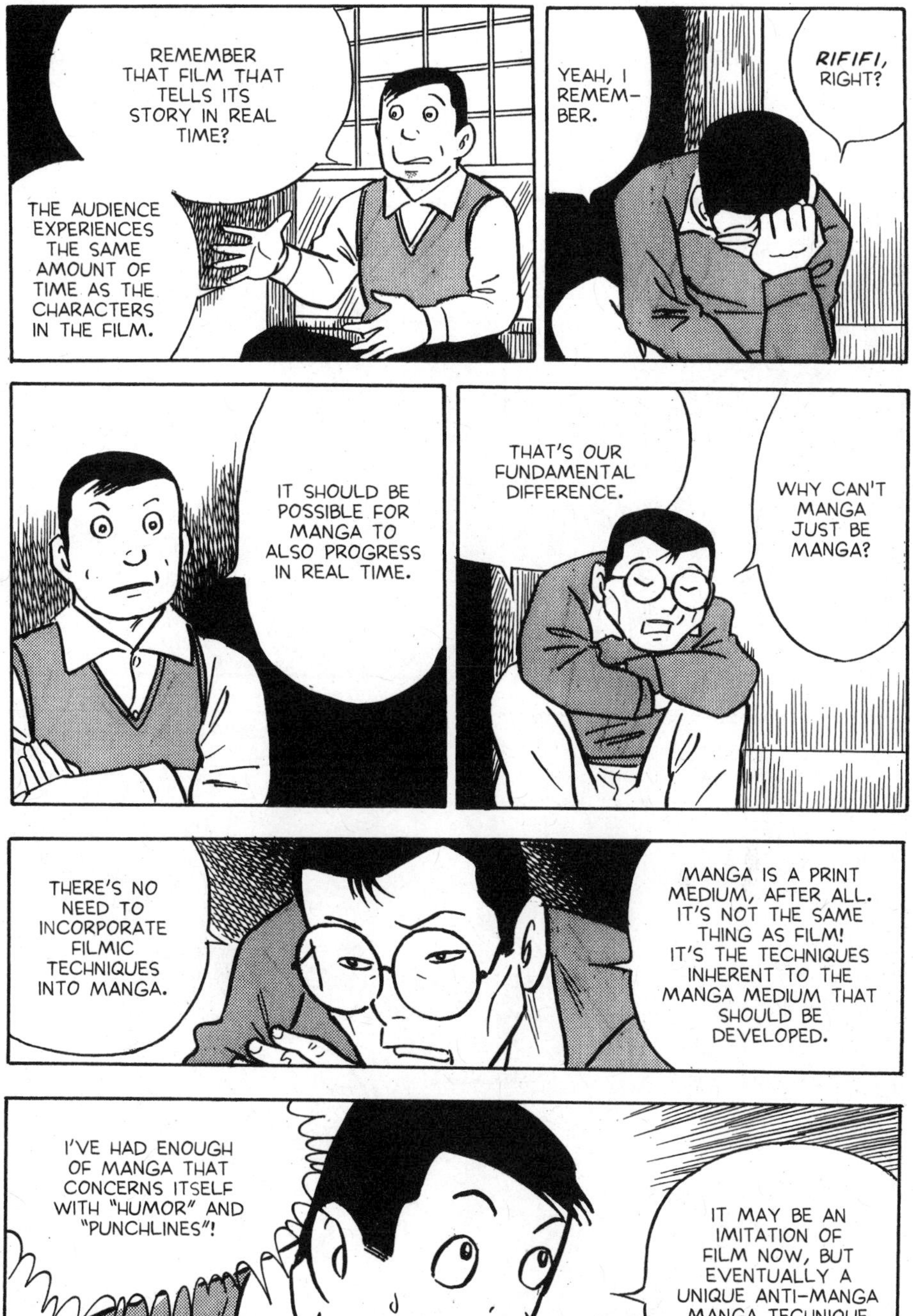

REMEMBER THAT FILM THAT TELLS ITS STORY IN REAL TIME?
THE AUDIENCE EXPERIENCES THE SAME AMOUNT OF TIME AS THE CHARACTERS IN THE FILM.
YEAH, I REMEMBER.
RIFIFI, RIGHT?
IT SHOULD BE POSSIBLE FOR MANGA TO ALSO PROGRESS IN REAL TIME.
THAT'S OUR FUNDAMENTAL DIFFERENCE.
WHY CAN'T MANGA JUST BE MANGA?
THERE'S NO NEED TO INCORPORATE FILMIC TECHNIQUES INTO MANGA.
MANGA IS A PRINT MEDIUM, AFTER ALL. IT'S NOT THE SAME THING AS FILM! IT'S THE TECHNIQUES INHERENT TO THE MANGA MEDIUM THAT SHOULD BE DEVELOPED.
I'VE HAD ENOUGH OF MANGA THAT CONCERNS ITSELF WITH "HUMOR" AND "PUNCHLINES"!
IT MAY BE AN IMITATION OF FILM NOW, BUT EVENTUALLY A UNIQUE ANTI-MANGA MANGA TECHNIQUE WILL BE DEVELOPED.

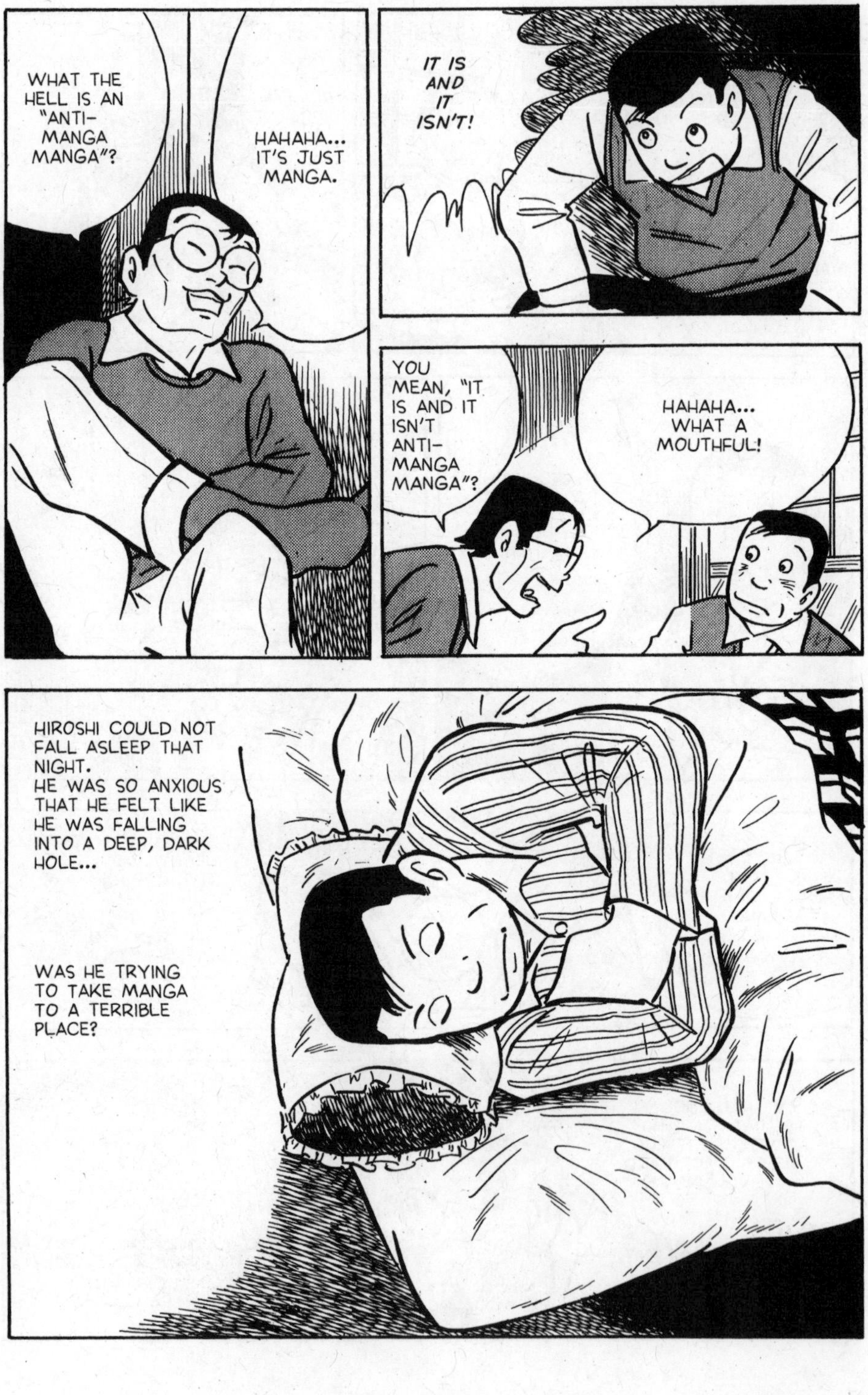
WHAT THE HELL IS AN "ANTI-MANGA MANGA"?
HAHAHA... IT'S JUST MANGA.
IT IS AND IT ISN'T!
YOU MEAN, "IT IS AND IT ISN'T ANTI-MANGA MANGA"?
HAHAHA... WHAT A MOUTHFUL!
HIROSHI COULD NOT FALL ASLEEP THAT NIGHT.
HE WAS SO ANXIOUS THAT HE FELT LIKE HE WAS FALLING INTO A DEEP, DARK HOLE...
WAS HE TRYING TO TAKE MANGA TO A TERRIBLE PLACE?

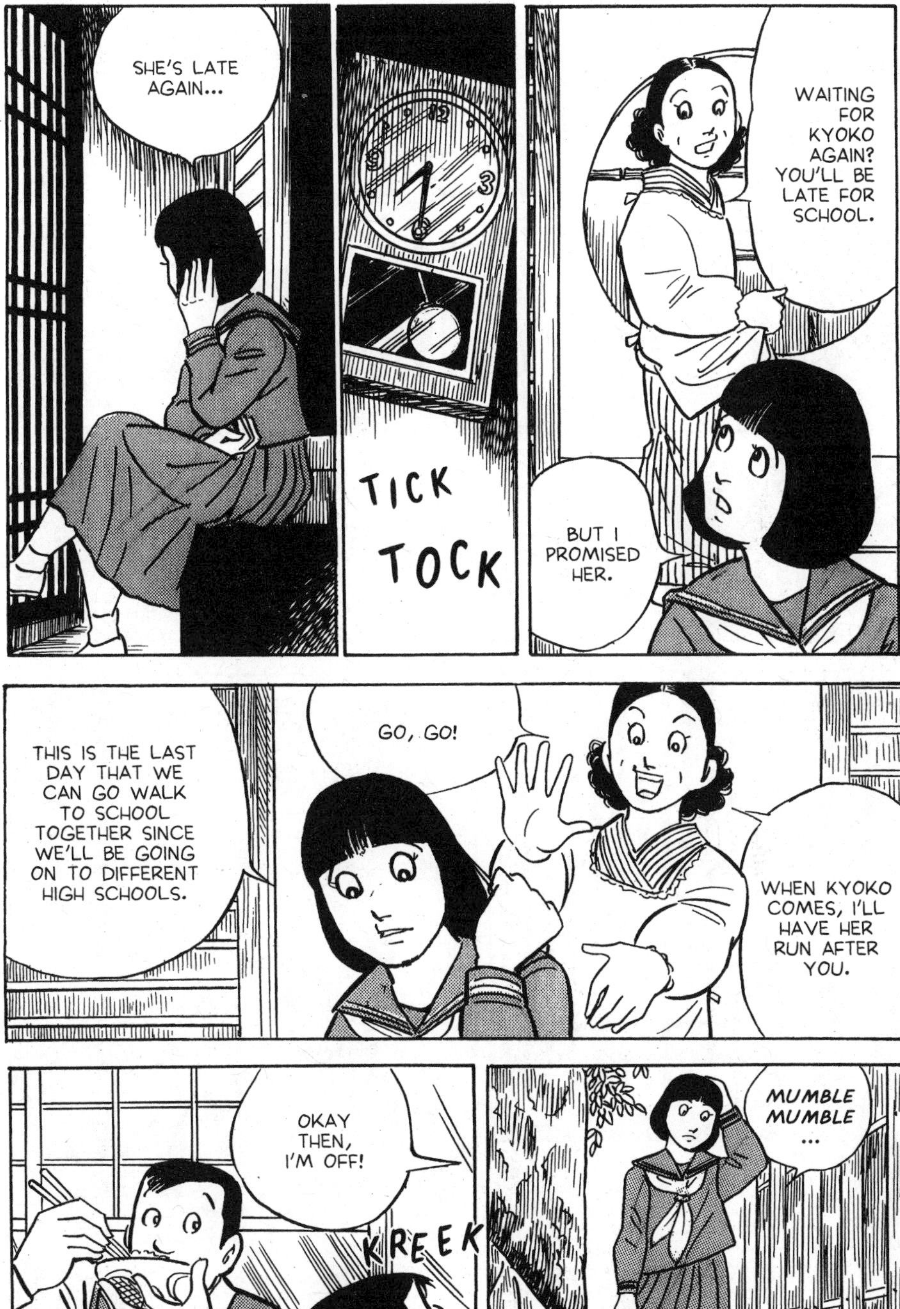
SHE'S LATE AGAIN...
TICK
TOCK
WAITING FOR KYOKO AGAIN? YOU'LL BE LATE FOR SCHOOL.
BUT I PROMISED HER.
THIS IS THE LAST DAY THAT WE CAN GO WALK TO SCHOOL TOGETHER SINCE WE'LL BE GOING ON TO DIFFERENT HIGH SCHOOLS.
GO, GO!
WHEN KYOKO COMES, I'LL HAVE HER RUN AFTER YOU.
OKAY THEN, I'M OFF!
KREEK
MUMBLE MUMBLE ...

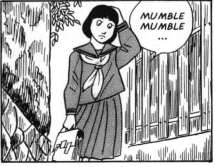

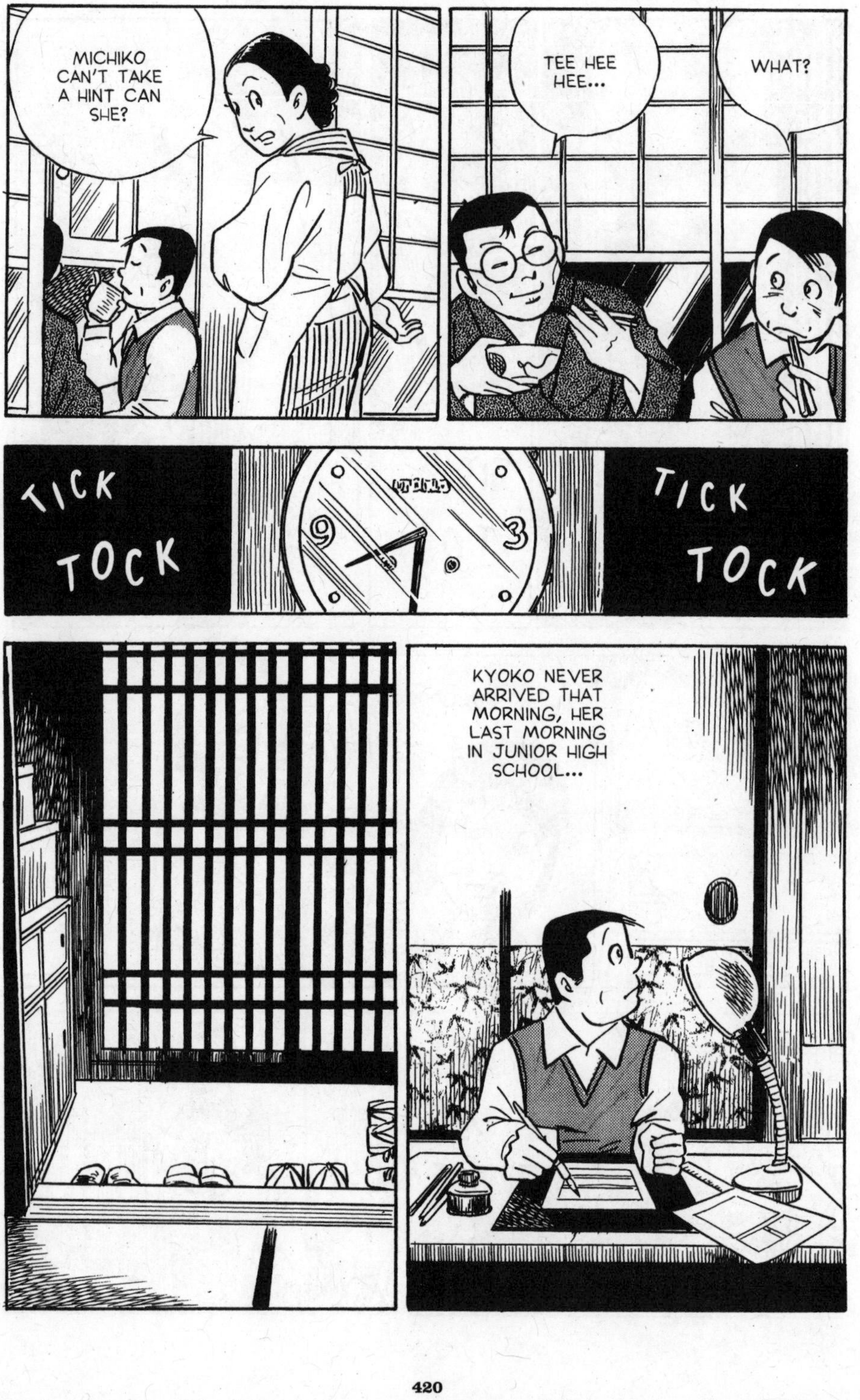

MICHIKO CAN'T TAKE A HINT CAN SHE?
TEE HEE HEE...
WHAT?
TICK TOCK
TICK TOCK
KYOKO NEVER ARRIVED THAT MORNING, HER LAST MORNING IN JUNIOR HIGH SCHOOL...

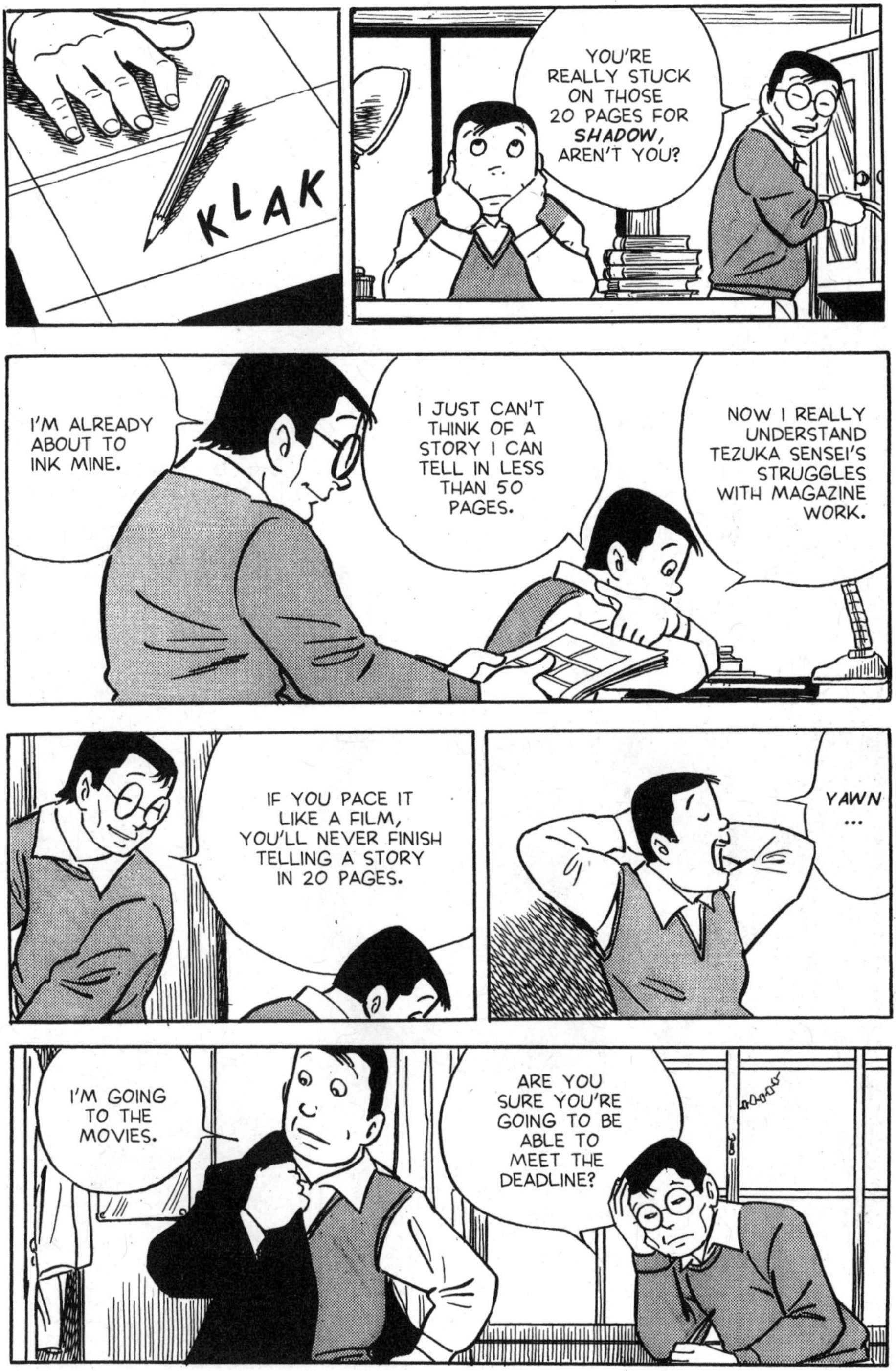
KLAK
YOU'RE REALLY STUCK ON THOSE 20 PAGES FOR SHADOW, AREN'T YOU?
I'M ALREADY ABOUT TO INK MINE.
I JUST CAN'T THINK OF A STORY I CAN TELL IN LESS THAN 50 PAGES.
NOW I REALLY UNDERSTAND TEZUKA SENSEI'S STRUGGLES WITH MAGAZINE WORK.
IF YOU PACE IT LIKE A FILM, YOU'LL NEVER FINISH TELLING A STORY IN 20 PAGES.
YAWN ...
I'M GOING TO THE MOVIES.
ARE YOU SURE YOU'RE GOING TO BE ABLE TO MEET THE DEADLINE?

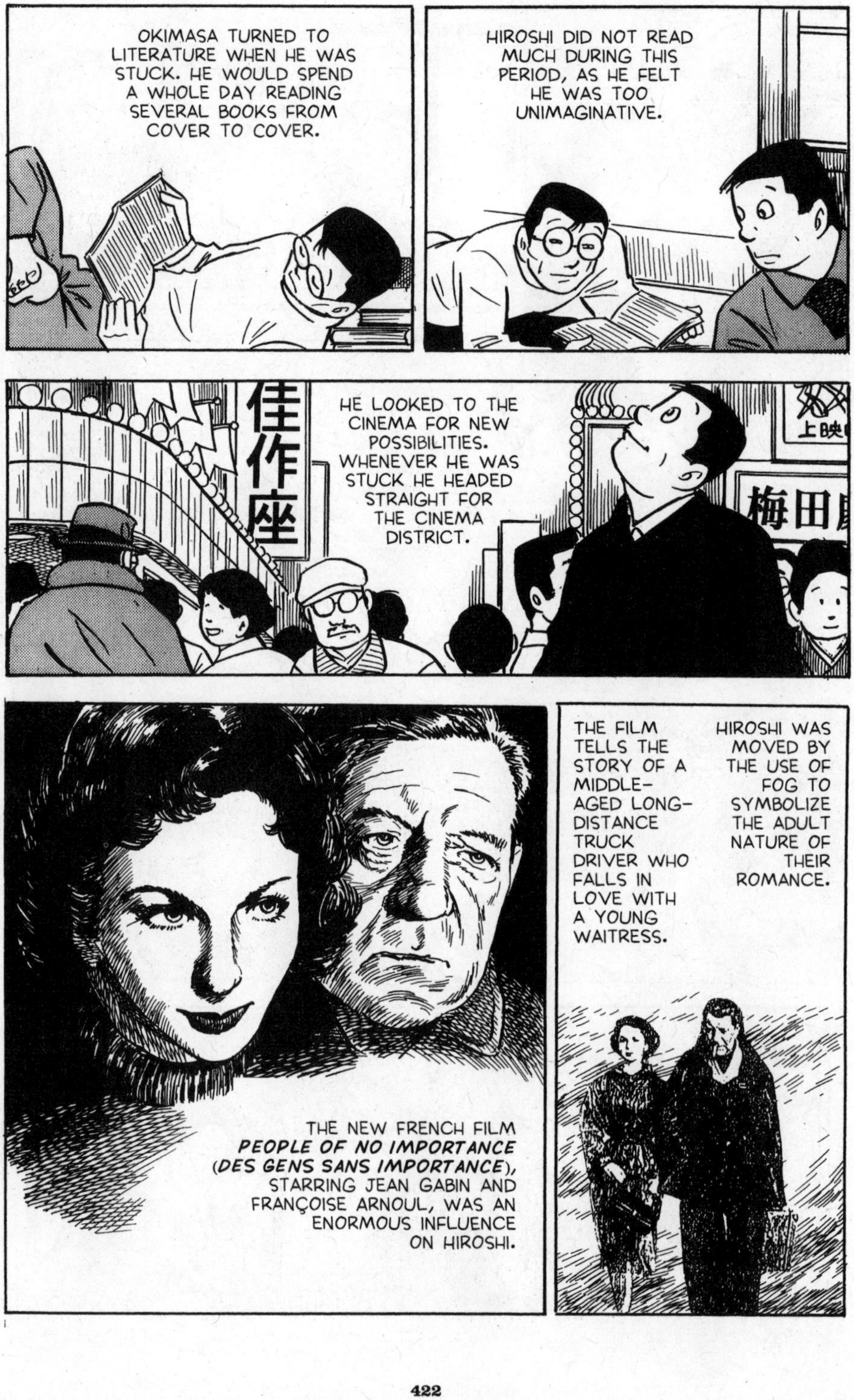
OKIMASA TURNED TO LITERATURE WHEN HE WAS STUCK. HE WOULD SPEND A WHOLE DAY READING SEVERAL BOOKS FROM COVER TO COVER.
HIROSHI DID NOT READ MUCH DURING THIS PERIOD, AS HE FELT HE WAS TOO UNIMAGINATIVE.
佳作座
HE LOOKED TO THE CINEMA FOR NEW POSSIBILITIES. WHENEVER HE WAS STUCK HE HEADED STRAIGHT FOR THE CINEMA DISTRICT.
上映
梅田
THE NEW FRENCH FILM ***PEOPLE OF NO IMPORTANCE*** (***DES GENS SANS IMPORTANCE***), STARRING JEAN GABIN AND FRANÇOISE ARNOUL, WAS AN ENORMOUS INFLUENCE ON HIROSHI.
THE FILM TELLS THE STORY OF A MIDDLE-AGED LONG-DISTANCE TRUCK DRIVER WHO FALLS IN LOVE WITH A YOUNG WAITRESS.
HIROSHI WAS MOVED BY THE USE OF FOG TO SYMBOLIZE THE ADULT NATURE OF THEIR ROMANCE.

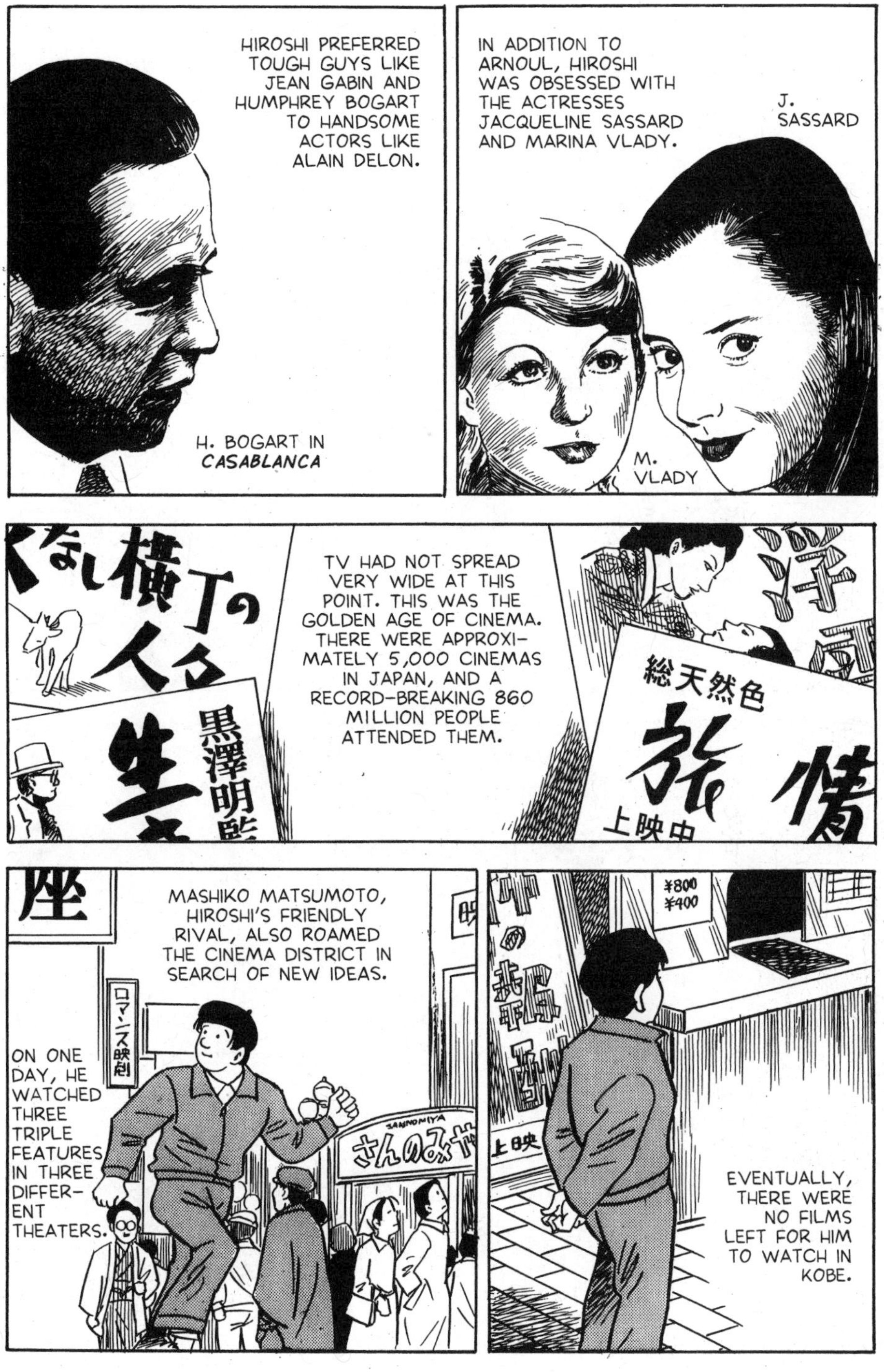

HIROSHI PREFERRED TOUGH GUYS LIKE JEAN GABIN AND HUMPHREY BOGART TO HANDSOME ACTORS LIKE ALAIN DELON.
H. BOGART IN *CASABLANCA*
IN ADDITION TO ARNOUL, HIROSHI WAS OBSESSED WITH THE ACTRESSES JACQUELINE SASSARD AND MARINA VLADY.
J. SASSARD
M. VLADY
なし横丁の人々
黒澤明監
TV HAD NOT SPREAD VERY WIDE AT THIS POINT. THIS WAS THE GOLDEN AGE OF CINEMA. THERE WERE APPROXI-MATELY 5,000 CINEMAS IN JAPAN, AND A RECORD-BREAKING 860 MILLION PEOPLE ATTENDED THEM.
総天然色
旅情
上映中
座
MASHIKO MATSUMOTO, HIROSHI'S FRIENDLY RIVAL, ALSO ROAMED THE CINEMA DISTRICT IN SEARCH OF NEW IDEAS.
ロマンス映劇
ON ONE DAY, HE WATCHED THREE TRIPLE FEATURES IN THREE DIFFER-ENT THEATERS.
SANNOMIYA
さんのみや
¥800
¥400
上映
EVENTUALLY, THERE WERE NO FILMS LEFT FOR HIM TO WATCH IN KOBE.

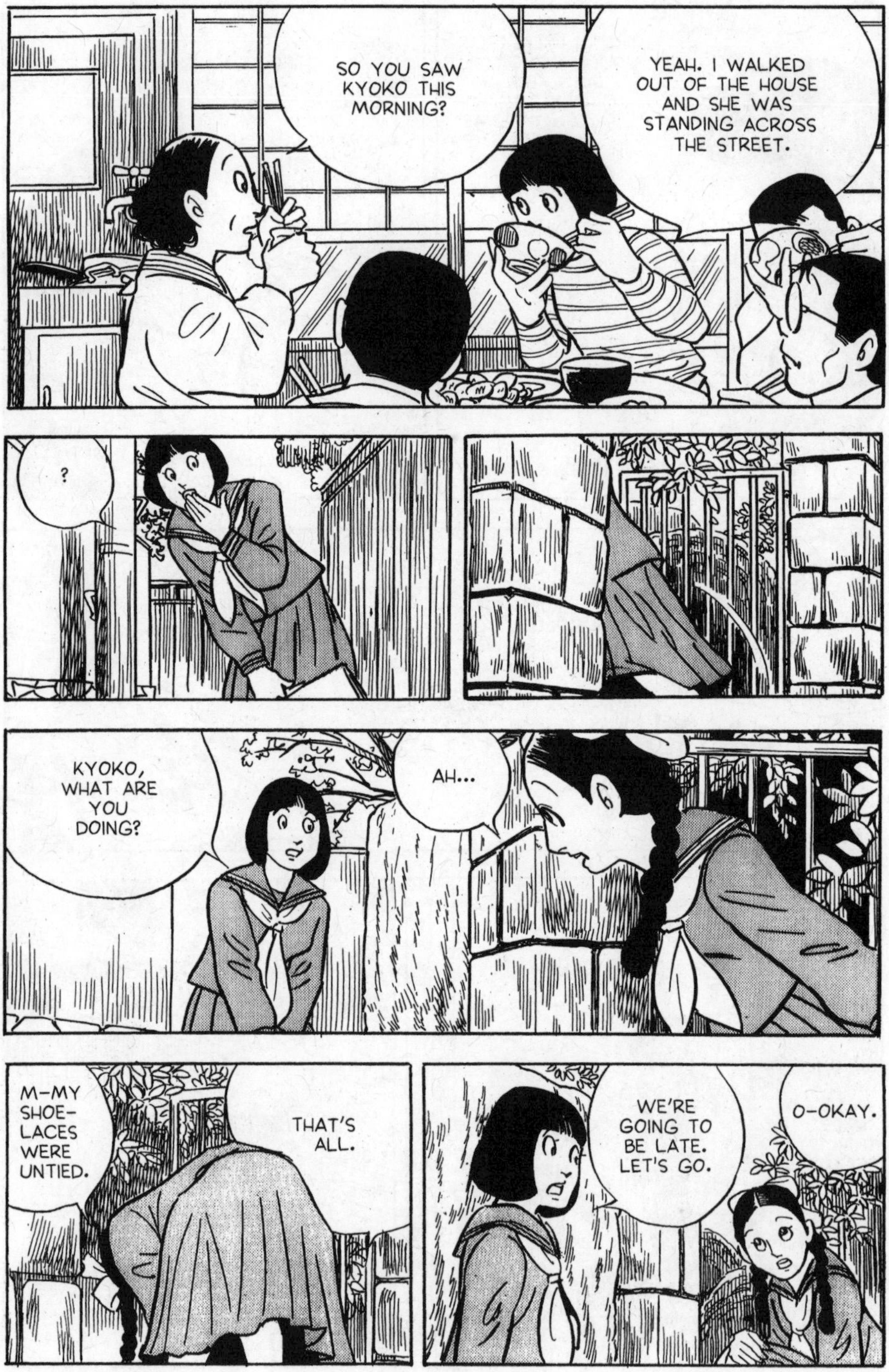
SO YOU SAW KYOKO THIS MORNING?
YEAH. I WALKED OUT OF THE HOUSE AND SHE WAS STANDING ACROSS THE STREET.
?
KYOKO, WHAT ARE YOU DOING?
AH...
M-MY SHOE-LACES WERE UNTIED.
THAT'S ALL.
WE'RE GOING TO BE LATE. LET'S GO.
O-OKAY.

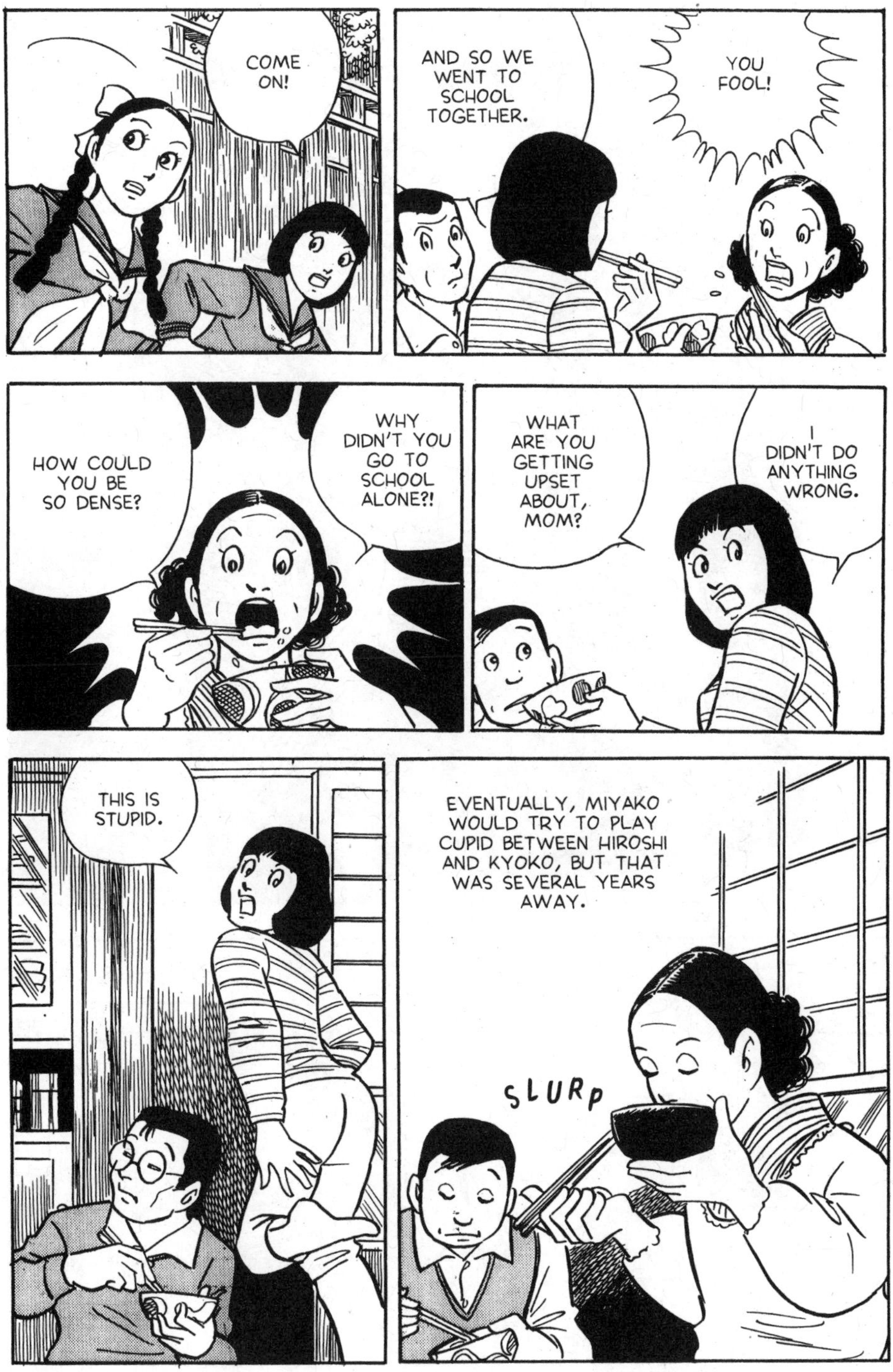
COME ON!
AND SO WE WENT TO SCHOOL TOGETHER.
YOU FOOL!
HOW COULD YOU BE SO DENSE?
WHY DIDN'T YOU GO TO SCHOOL ALONE?!
WHAT ARE YOU GETTING UPSET ABOUT, MOM?
I DIDN'T DO ANYTHING WRONG.
THIS IS STUPID.
EVENTUALLY, MIYAKO WOULD TRY TO PLAY CUPID BETWEEN HIROSHI AND KYOKO, BUT THAT WAS SEVERAL YEARS AWAY.
SLURP

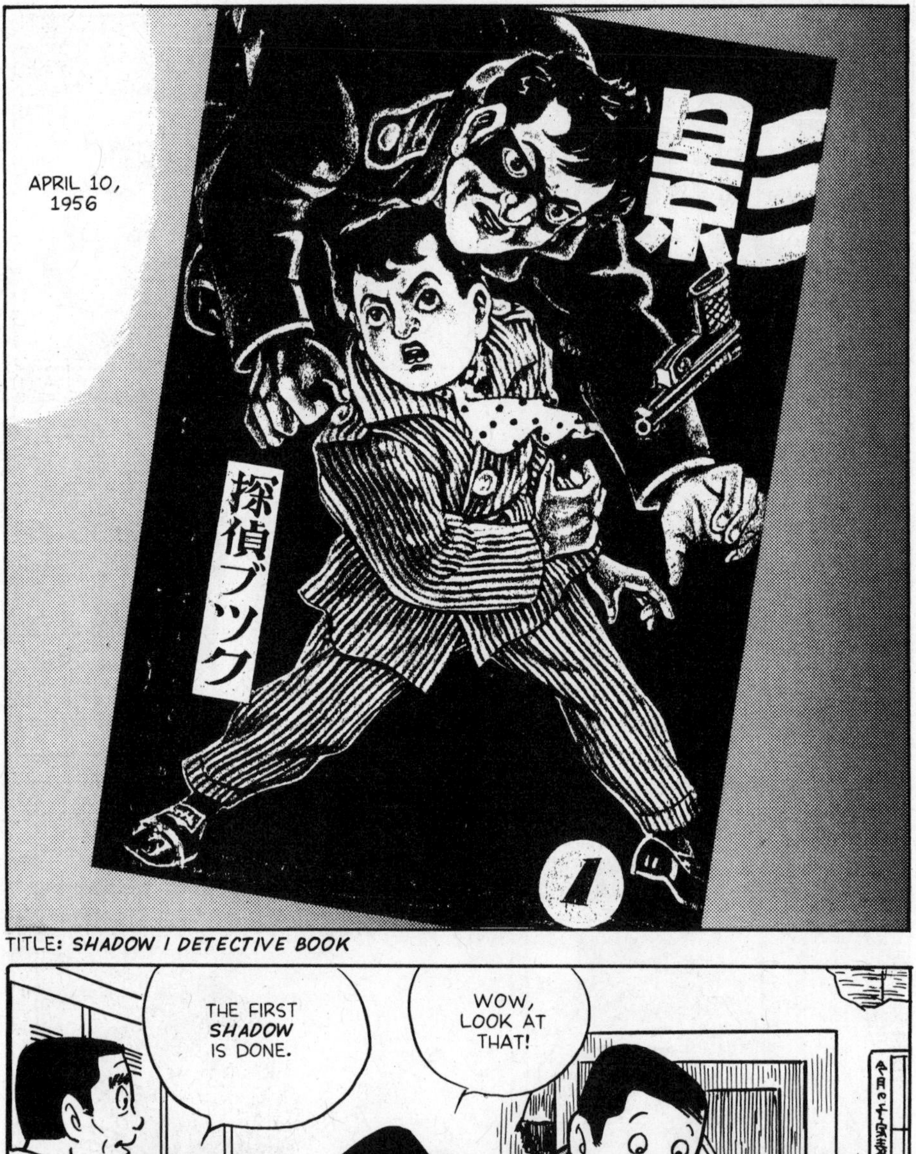
APRIL 10, 1956
影
探偵ブック
1
TITLE: *SHADOW I DETECTIVE BOOK*

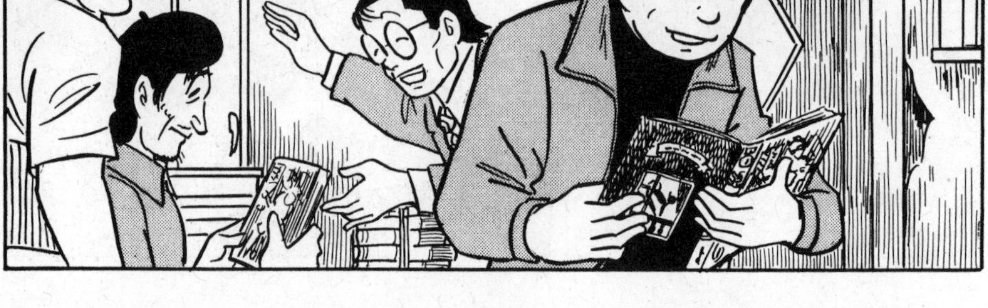
THE FIRST *SHADOW* IS DONE.
WOW, LOOK AT THAT!

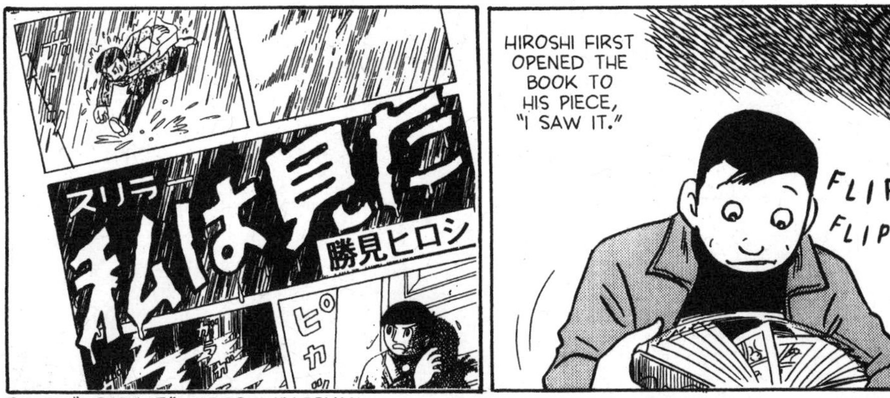

スリラー
私は見た
勝見ヒロシ
HIROSHI FIRST OPENED THE BOOK TO HIS PIECE, "I SAW IT."
FLIP FLIP

TITLE: "I SAW IT", HIROSHI KATSUMI

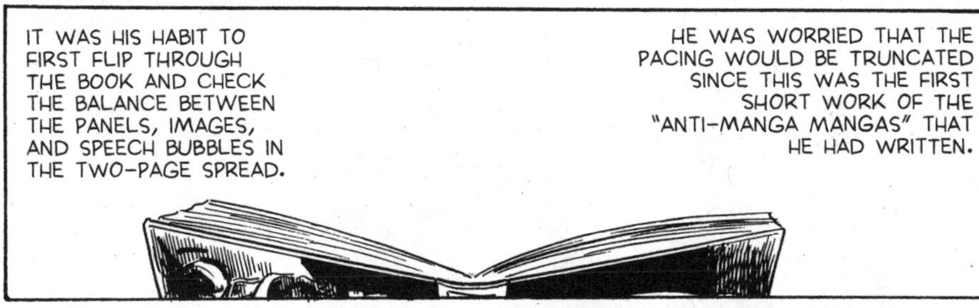

IT WAS HIS HABIT TO FIRST FLIP THROUGH THE BOOK AND CHECK THE BALANCE BETWEEN THE PANELS, IMAGES, AND SPEECH BUBBLES IN THE TWO-PAGE SPREAD.
HE WAS WORRIED THAT THE PACING WOULD BE TRUNCATED SINCE THIS WAS THE FIRST SHORT WORK OF THE "ANTI-MANGA MANGAS" THAT HE HAD WRITTEN.

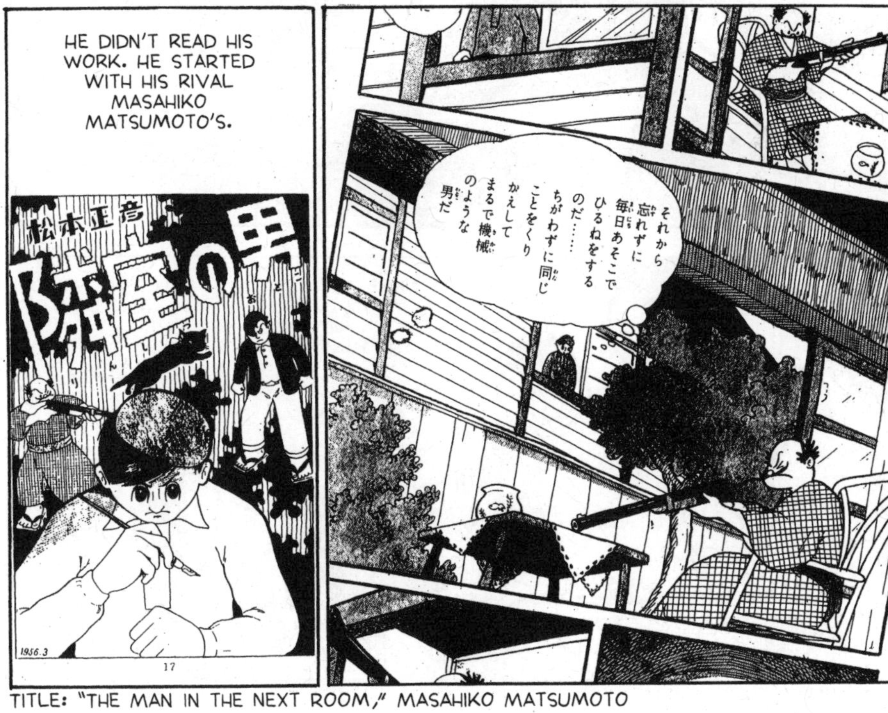

HE DIDN'T READ HIS WORK. HE STARTED WITH HIS RIVAL MASAHIKO MATSUMOTO'S.
松本正彦
隣室の男
1956.3
17
それから忘れずに毎日あそこでひるねをするのだ……ちがわずに同じことをくりかえしてまるで機械のような男だ

TITLE: "THE MAN IN THE NEXT ROOM," MASAHIKO MATSUMOTO

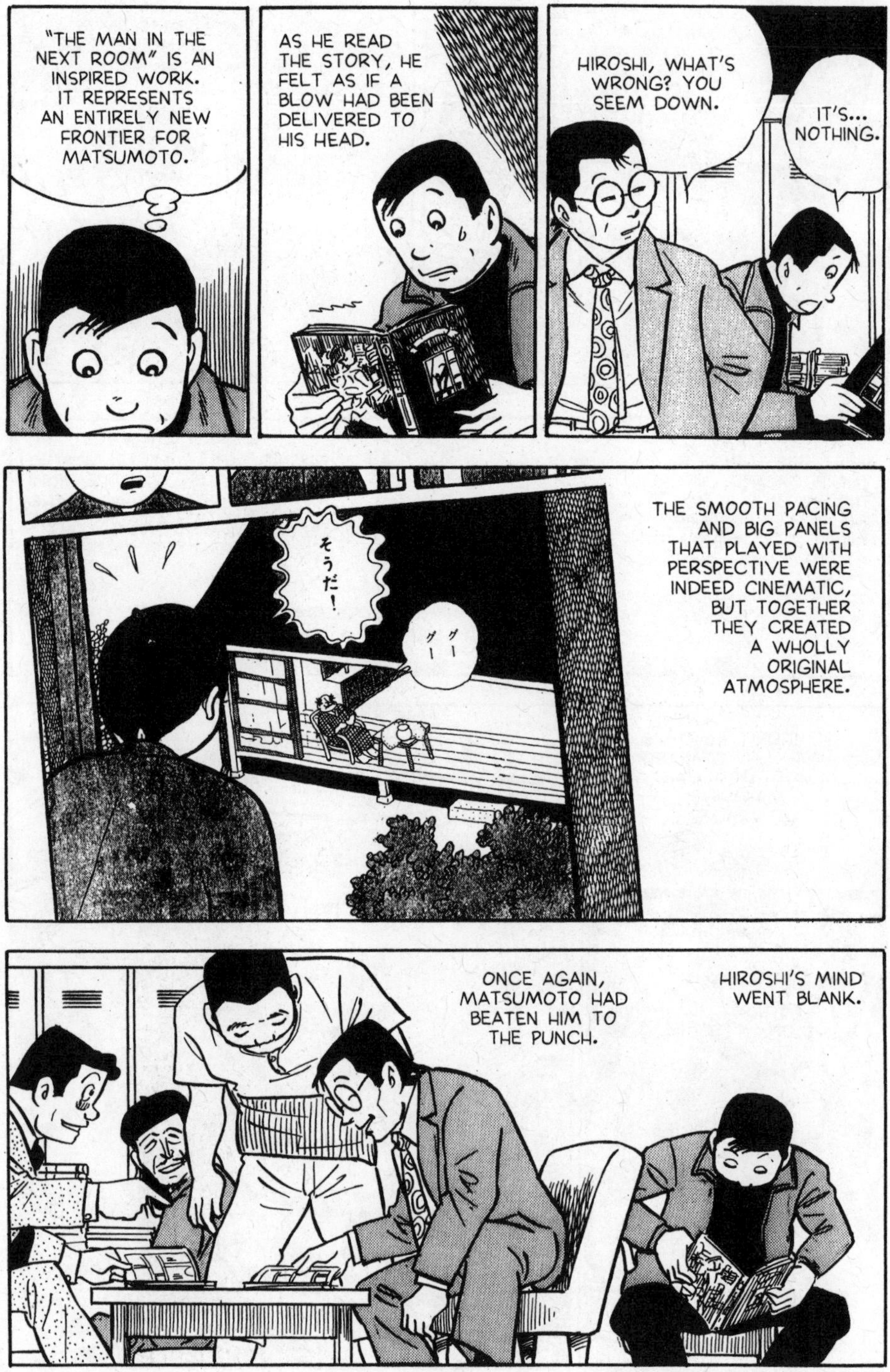
"THE MAN IN THE NEXT ROOM" IS AN INSPIRED WORK. IT REPRESENTS AN ENTIRELY NEW FRONTIER FOR MATSUMOTO.
AS HE READ THE STORY, HE FELT AS IF A BLOW HAD BEEN DELIVERED TO HIS HEAD.
HIROSHI, WHAT'S WRONG? YOU SEEM DOWN.
IT'S... NOTHING.
そうだ！
THE SMOOTH PACING AND BIG PANELS THAT PLAYED WITH PERSPECTIVE WERE INDEED CINEMATIC, BUT TOGETHER THEY CREATED A WHOLLY ORIGINAL ATMOSPHERE.
ONCE AGAIN, MATSUMOTO HAD BEATEN HIM TO THE PUNCH.
HIROSHI'S MIND WENT BLANK.

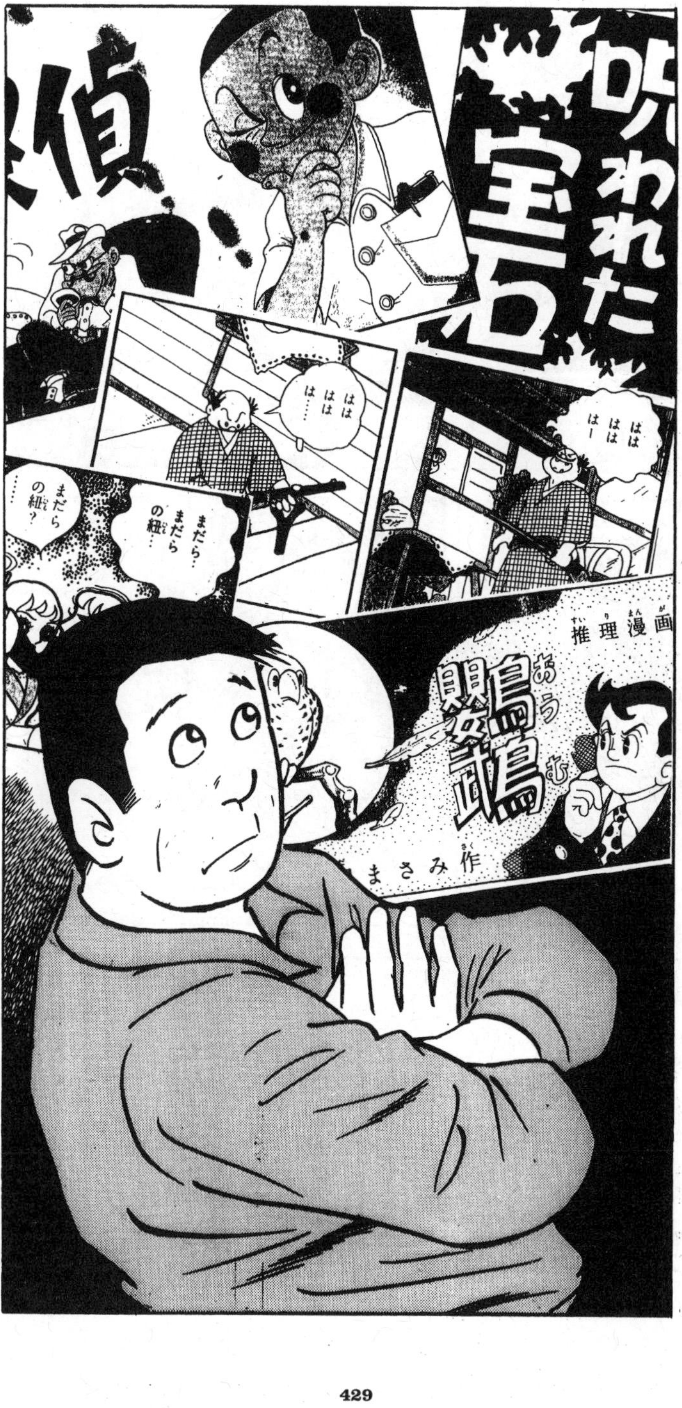
偵
呪われた宝石
ははははは……
ははははは ー
まだらの紐？……
まだら…まだらの紐…
推理漫画
鸚鵡
まさみ作

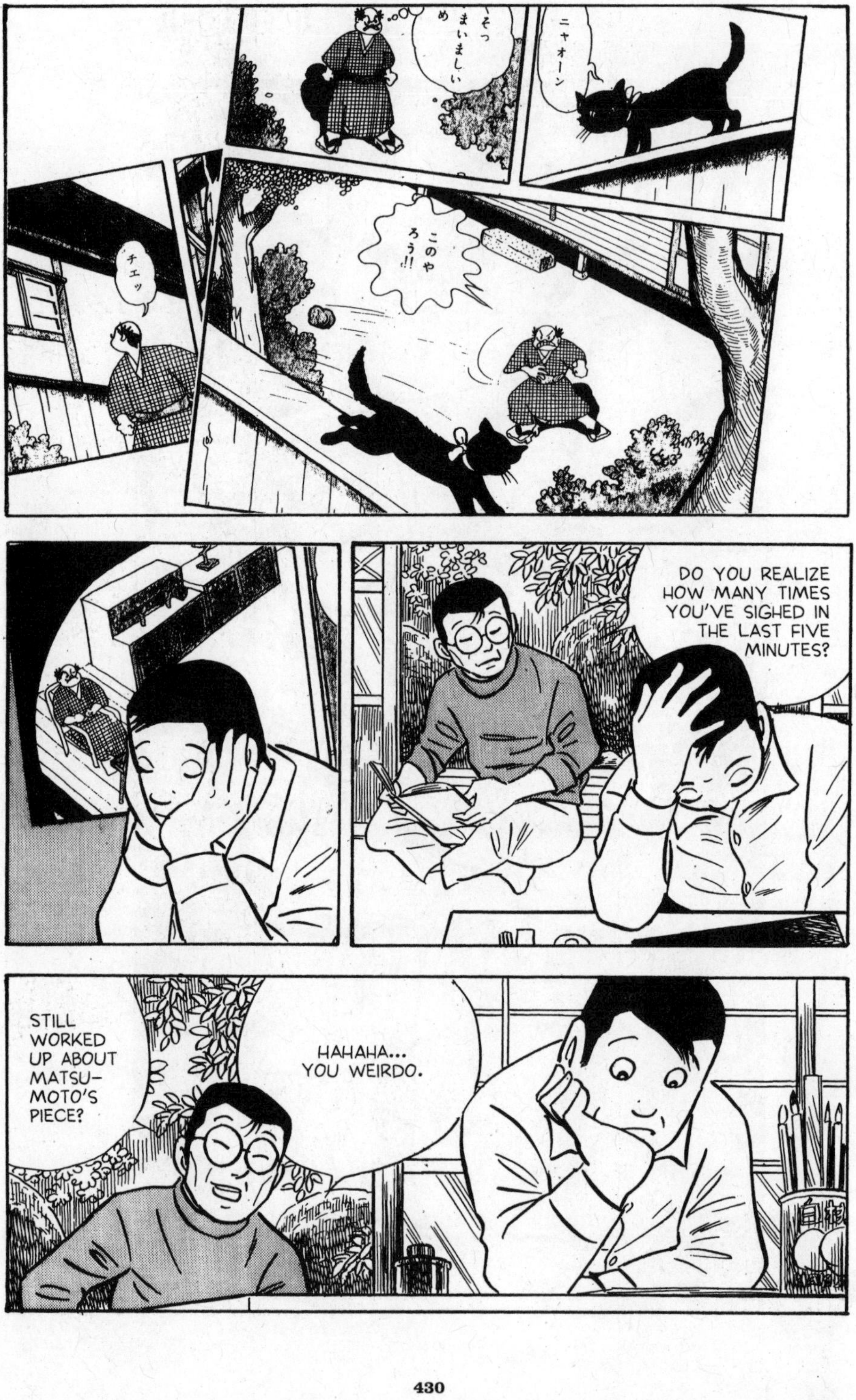
そっ まいましい め
ニャオーン
チェッ
このやろう!!
DO YOU REALIZE HOW MANY TIMES YOU'VE SIGHED IN THE LAST FIVE MINUTES?
STILL WORKED UP ABOUT MATSU-MOTO'S PIECE?
HAHAHA... YOU WEIRDO.

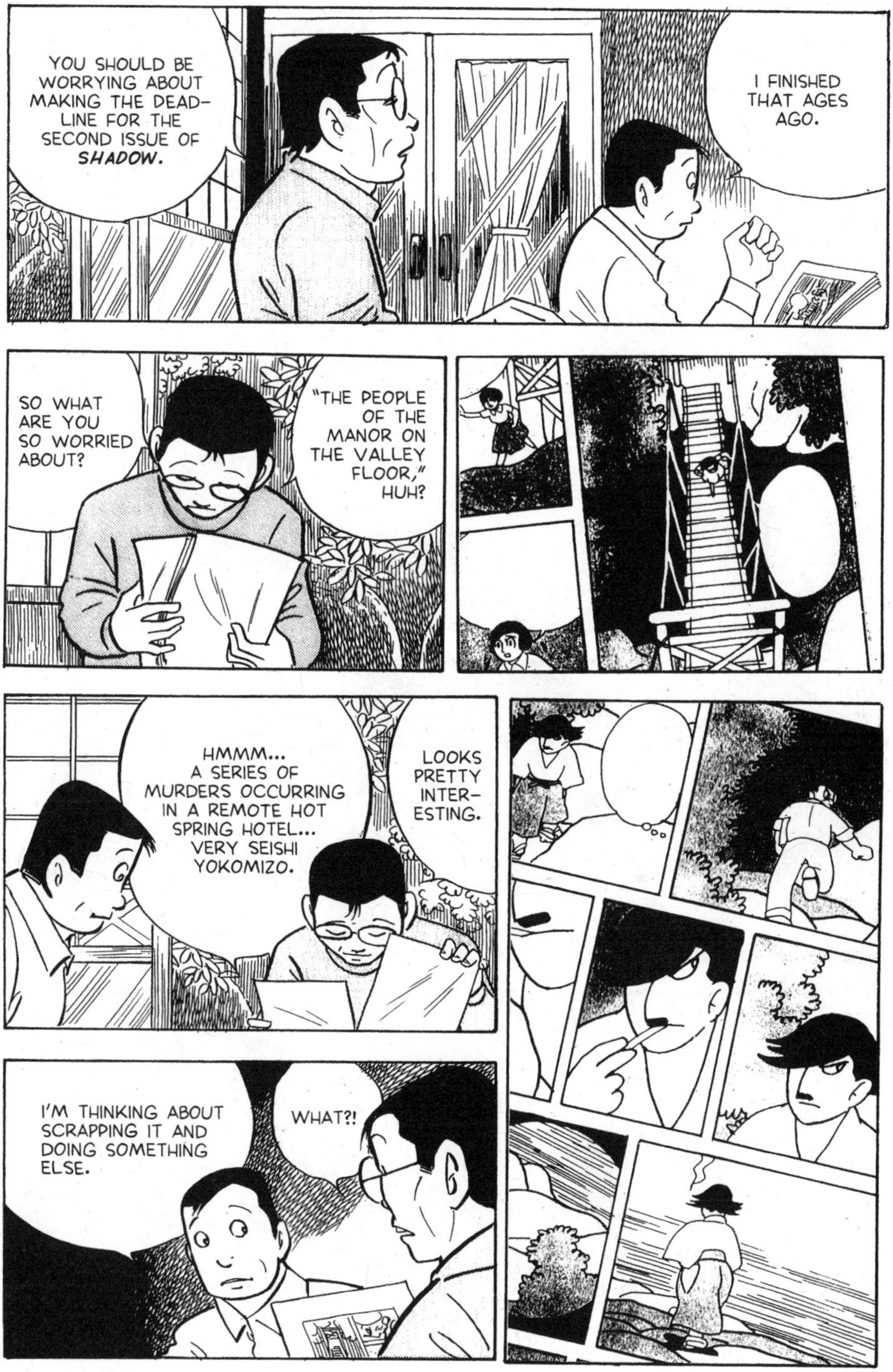
YOU SHOULD BE WORRYING ABOUT MAKING THE DEAD-LINE FOR THE SECOND ISSUE OF *SHADOW*.
I FINISHED THAT AGES AGO.
SO WHAT ARE YOU SO WORRIED ABOUT?
"THE PEOPLE OF THE MANOR ON THE VALLEY FLOOR," HUH?
HMMM... A SERIES OF MURDERS OCCURRING IN A REMOTE HOT SPRING HOTEL... VERY SEISHI YOKOMIZO.
LOOKS PRETTY INTER-ESTING.
I'M THINKING ABOUT SCRAPPING IT AND DOING SOMETHING ELSE.
WHAT?!

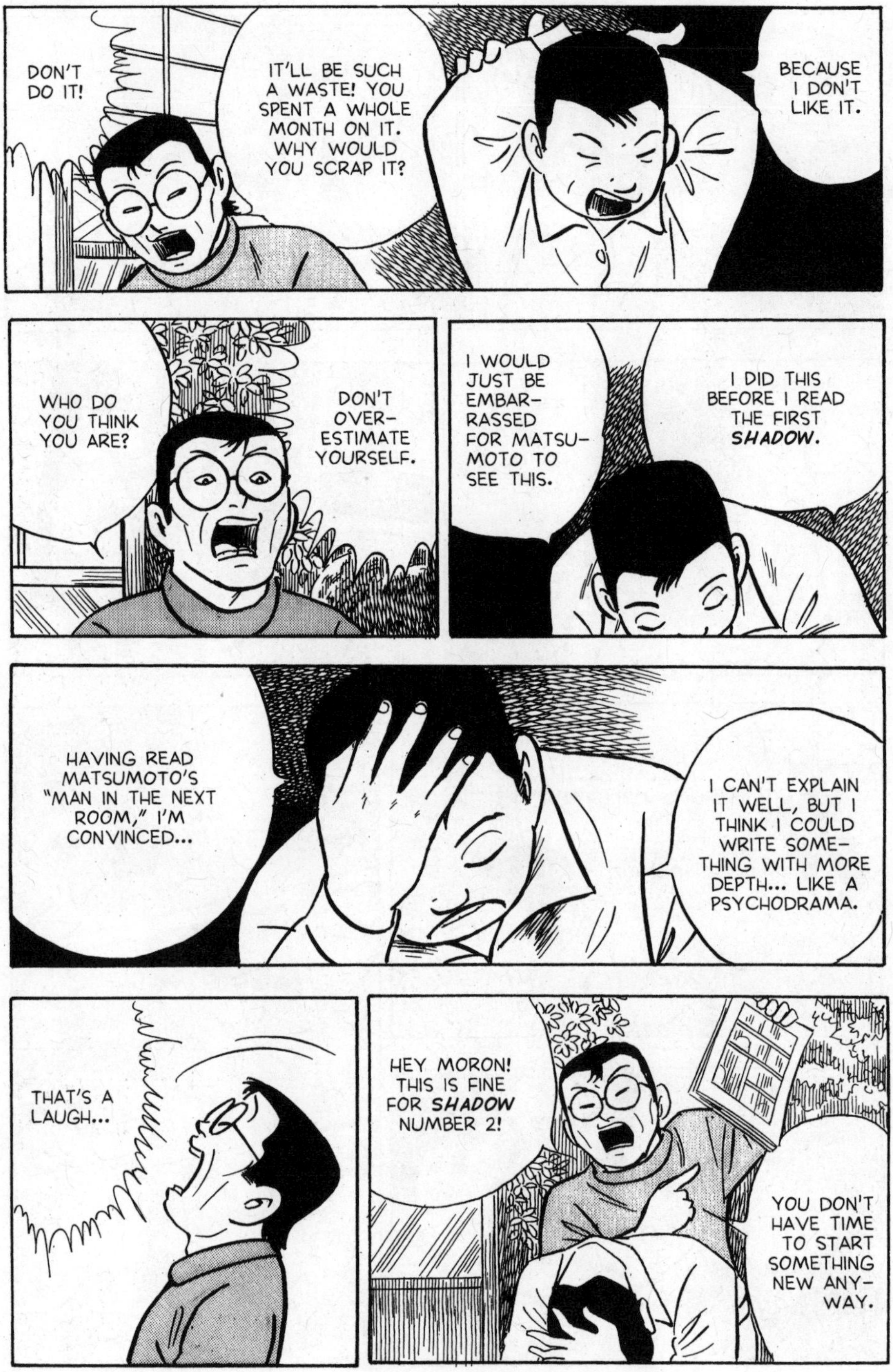
DON'T DO IT!
IT'LL BE SUCH A WASTE! YOU SPENT A WHOLE MONTH ON IT. WHY WOULD YOU SCRAP IT?
BECAUSE I DON'T LIKE IT.
WHO DO YOU THINK YOU ARE?
DON'T OVER-ESTIMATE YOURSELF.
I WOULD JUST BE EMBAR-RASSED FOR MATSU-MOTO TO SEE THIS.
I DID THIS BEFORE I READ THE FIRST SHADOW.
HAVING READ MATSUMOTO'S "MAN IN THE NEXT ROOM," I'M CONVINCED...
I CAN'T EXPLAIN IT WELL, BUT I THINK I COULD WRITE SOME-THING WITH MORE DEPTH... LIKE A PSYCHODRAMA.
THAT'S A LAUGH...
HEY MORON! THIS IS FINE FOR SHADOW NUMBER 2!
YOU DON'T HAVE TIME TO START SOMETHING NEW ANY-WAY.

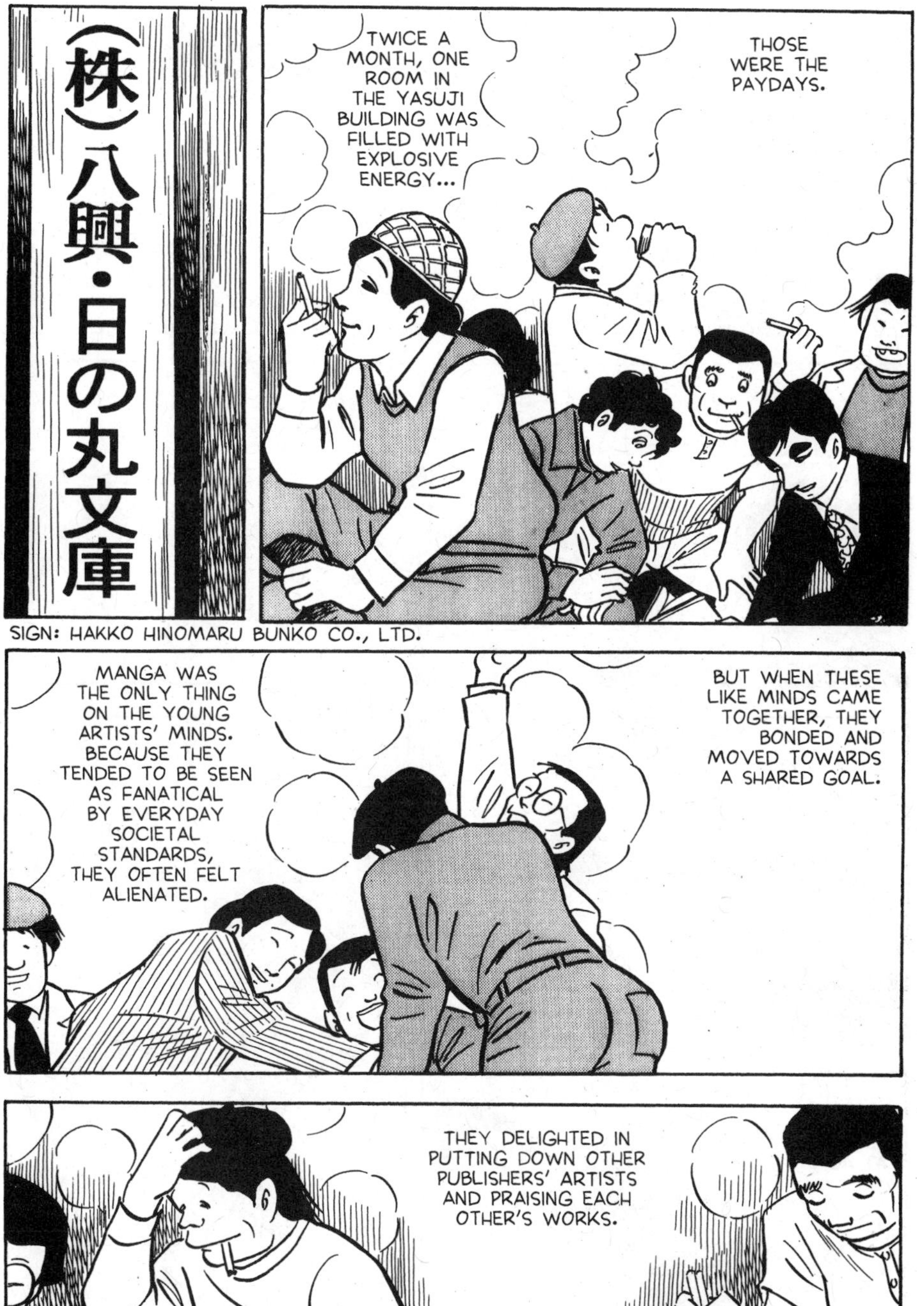
(株)八興・日の丸文庫
TWICE A MONTH, ONE ROOM IN THE YASUJI BUILDING WAS FILLED WITH EXPLOSIVE ENERGY...
THOSE WERE THE PAYDAYS.
SIGN: HAKKO HINOMARU BUNKO CO., LTD.
MANGA WAS THE ONLY THING ON THE YOUNG ARTISTS' MINDS. BECAUSE THEY TENDED TO BE SEEN AS FANATICAL BY EVERYDAY SOCIETAL STANDARDS, THEY OFTEN FELT ALIENATED.
BUT WHEN THESE LIKE MINDS CAME TOGETHER, THEY BONDED AND MOVED TOWARDS A SHARED GOAL.
THEY DELIGHTED IN PUTTING DOWN OTHER PUBLISHERS' ARTISTS AND PRAISING EACH OTHER'S WORKS.

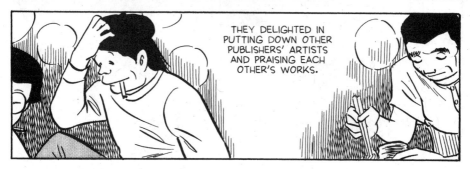

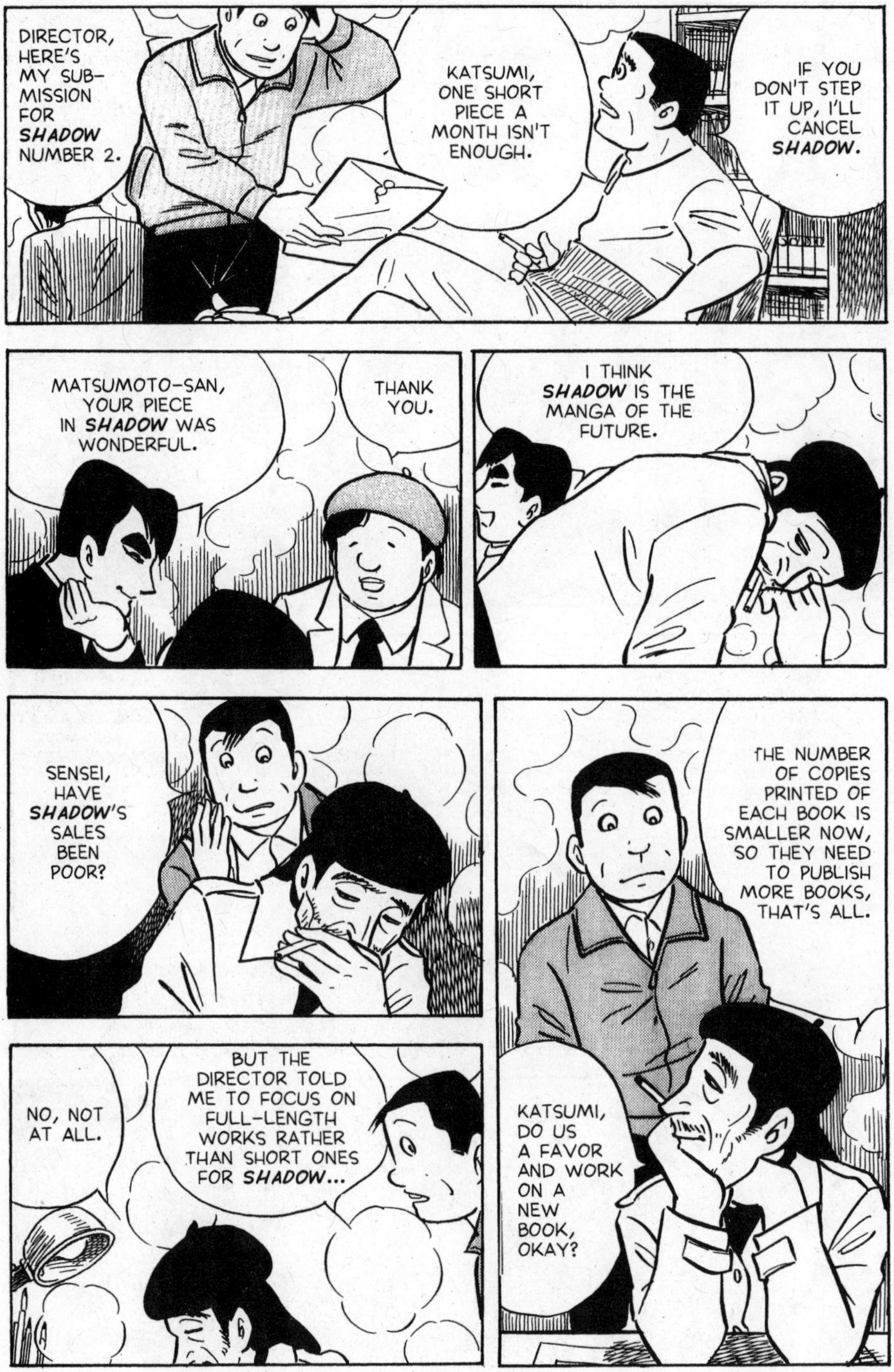
DIRECTOR, HERE'S MY SUB-MISSION FOR SHADOW NUMBER 2.
KATSUMI, ONE SHORT PIECE A MONTH ISN'T ENOUGH.
IF YOU DON'T STEP IT UP, I'LL CANCEL SHADOW.
MATSUMOTO-SAN, YOUR PIECE IN SHADOW WAS WONDERFUL.
THANK YOU.
I THINK SHADOW IS THE MANGA OF THE FUTURE.
SENSEI, HAVE SHADOW'S SALES BEEN POOR?
NO, NOT AT ALL.
BUT THE DIRECTOR TOLD ME TO FOCUS ON FULL-LENGTH WORKS RATHER THAN SHORT ONES FOR SHADOW...
THE NUMBER OF COPIES PRINTED OF EACH BOOK IS SMALLER NOW, SO THEY NEED TO PUBLISH MORE BOOKS, THAT'S ALL.
KATSUMI, DO US A FAVOR AND WORK ON A NEW BOOK, OKAY?

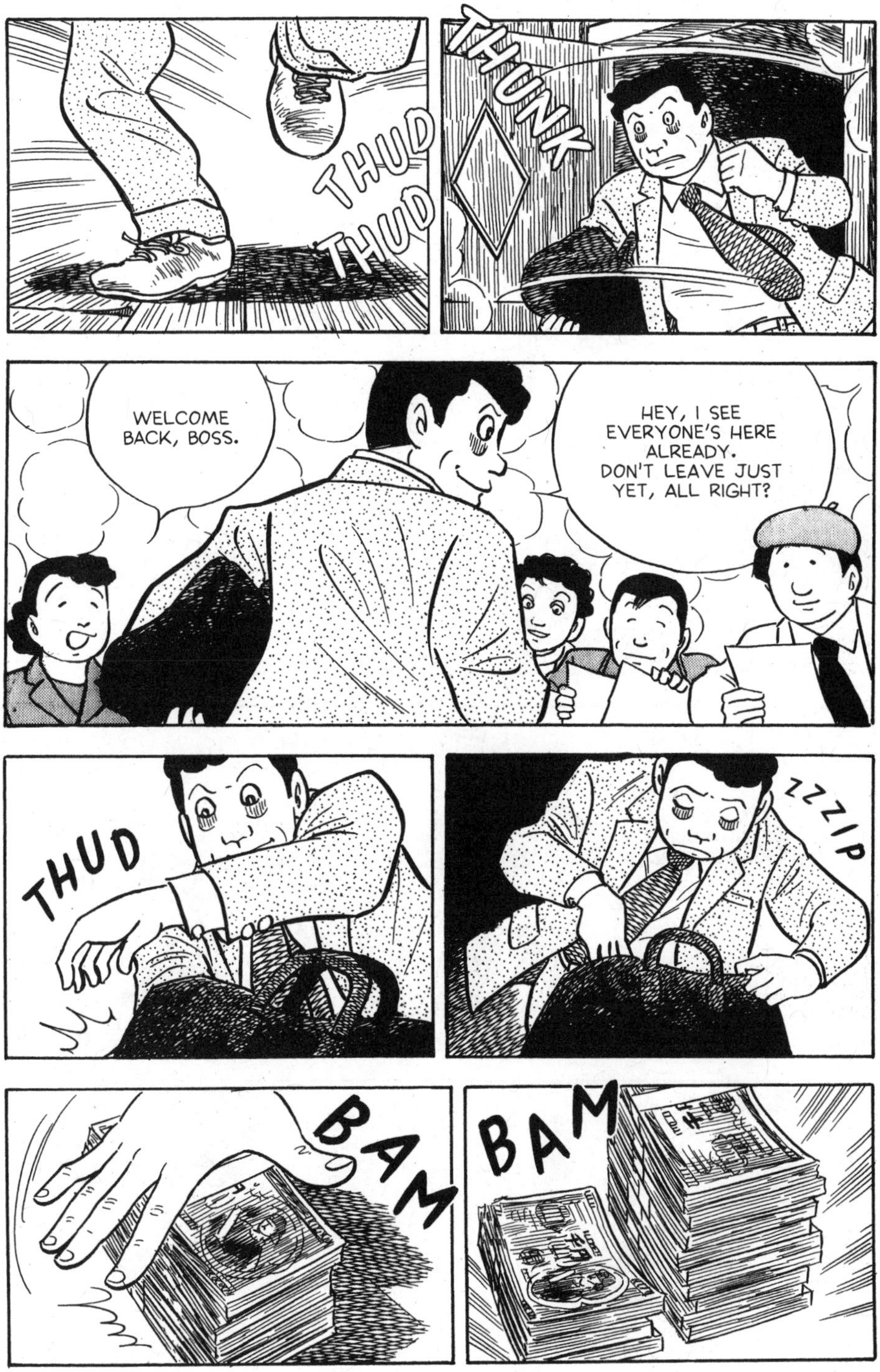
THUD
THUD
THUNK
WELCOME BACK, BOSS.
HEY, I SEE EVERYONE'S HERE ALREADY. DON'T LEAVE JUST YET, ALL RIGHT?
THUD
ZZZZIP
BAM
BAM

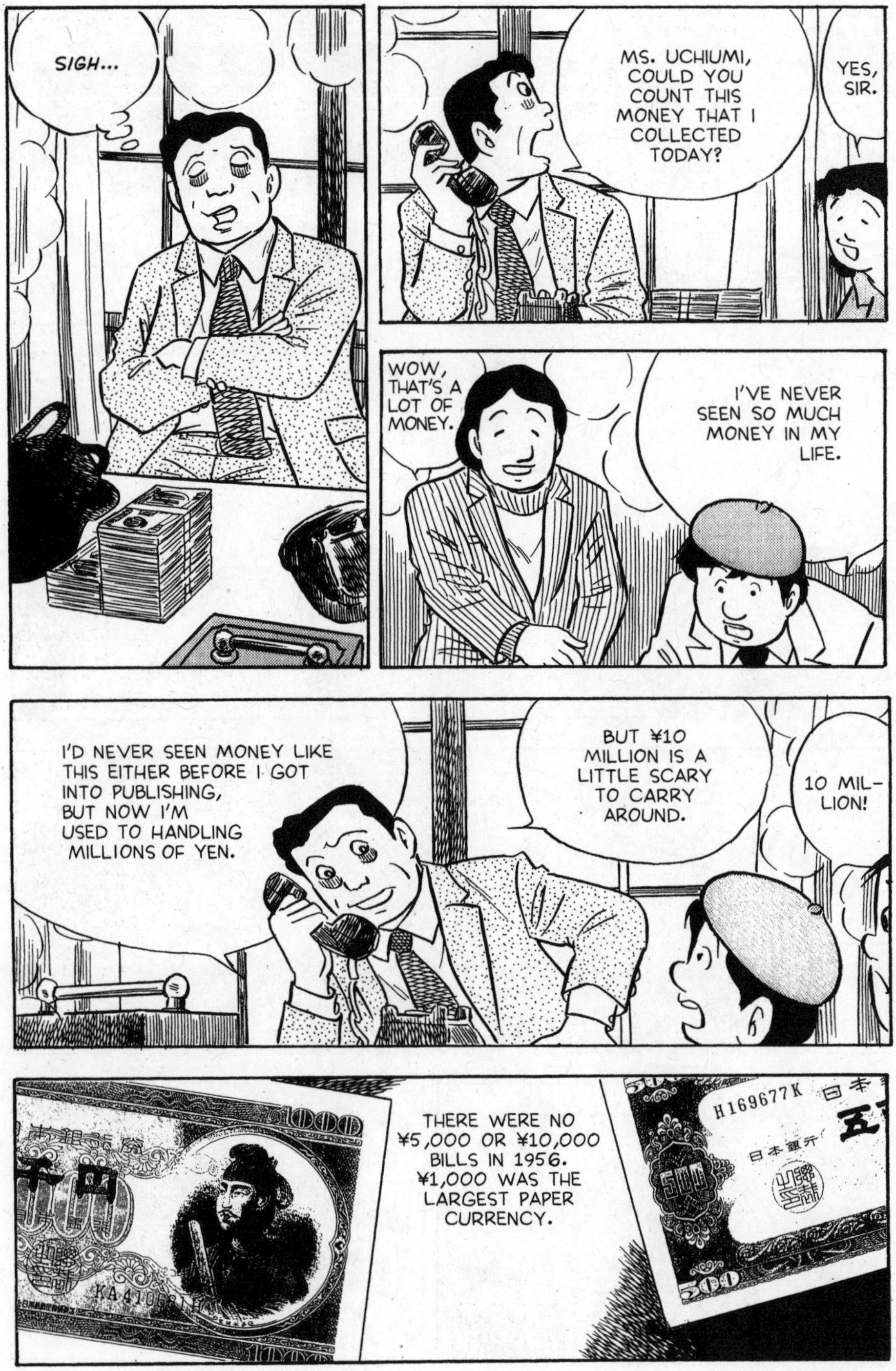
SIGH...
MS. UCHIUMI, COULD YOU COUNT THIS MONEY THAT I COLLECTED TODAY?
YES, SIR.
WOW, THAT'S A LOT OF MONEY.
I'VE NEVER SEEN SO MUCH MONEY IN MY LIFE.
I'D NEVER SEEN MONEY LIKE THIS EITHER BEFORE I GOT INTO PUBLISHING, BUT NOW I'M USED TO HANDLING MILLIONS OF YEN.
BUT ¥10 MILLION IS A LITTLE SCARY TO CARRY AROUND.
10 MIL-LION!
THERE WERE NO ¥5,000 OR ¥10,000 BILLS IN 1956. ¥1,000 WAS THE LARGEST PAPER CURRENCY.
H169677K

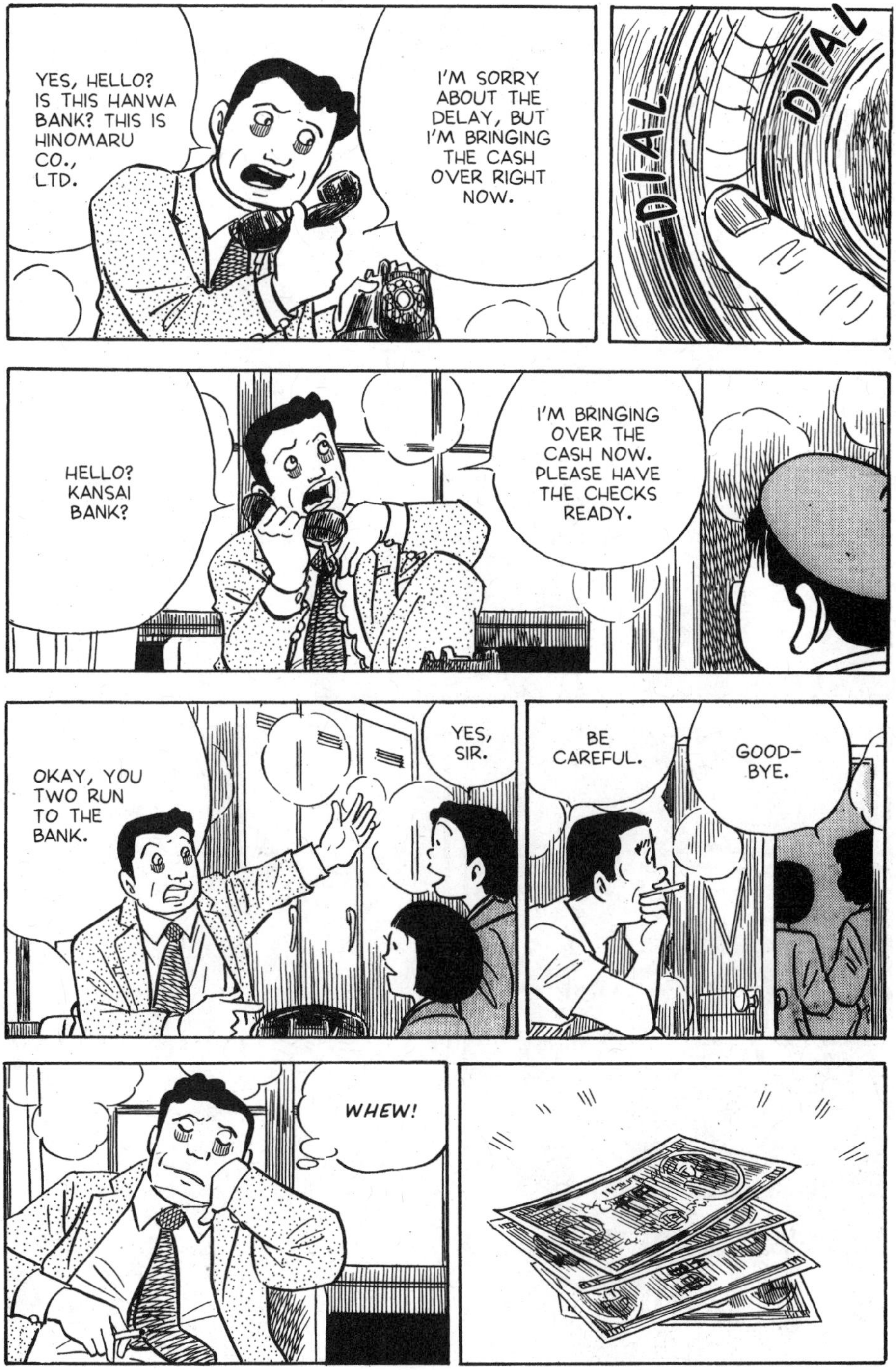
YES, HELLO? IS THIS HANWA BANK? THIS IS HINOMARU CO., LTD.
I'M SORRY ABOUT THE DELAY, BUT I'M BRINGING THE CASH OVER RIGHT NOW.
DIAL
DIAL
HELLO? KANSAI BANK?
I'M BRINGING OVER THE CASH NOW. PLEASE HAVE THE CHECKS READY.
OKAY, YOU TWO RUN TO THE BANK.
YES, SIR.
BE CAREFUL.
GOOD-BYE.
WHEW!

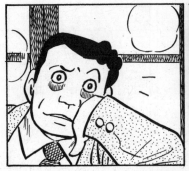

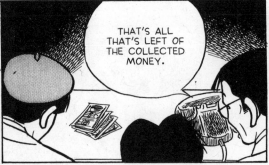

THAT'S ALL THAT'S LEFT OF THE COLLECTED MONEY.
DON'T WORRY, YOUR PAY IS RIGHT HERE IN THE SAFE.
PHEW!
お好み焼
DRAWING CLINICS?
I THINK OUR BIGGEST WEAKNESS IS DRAFTSMANSHIP.
PAT PAT
SIGN: OKONOMIYAKI

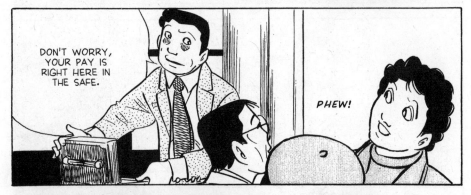

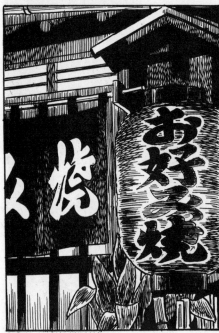

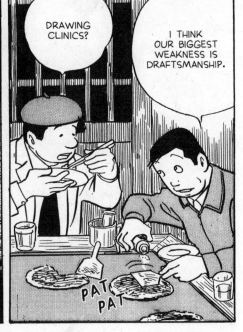

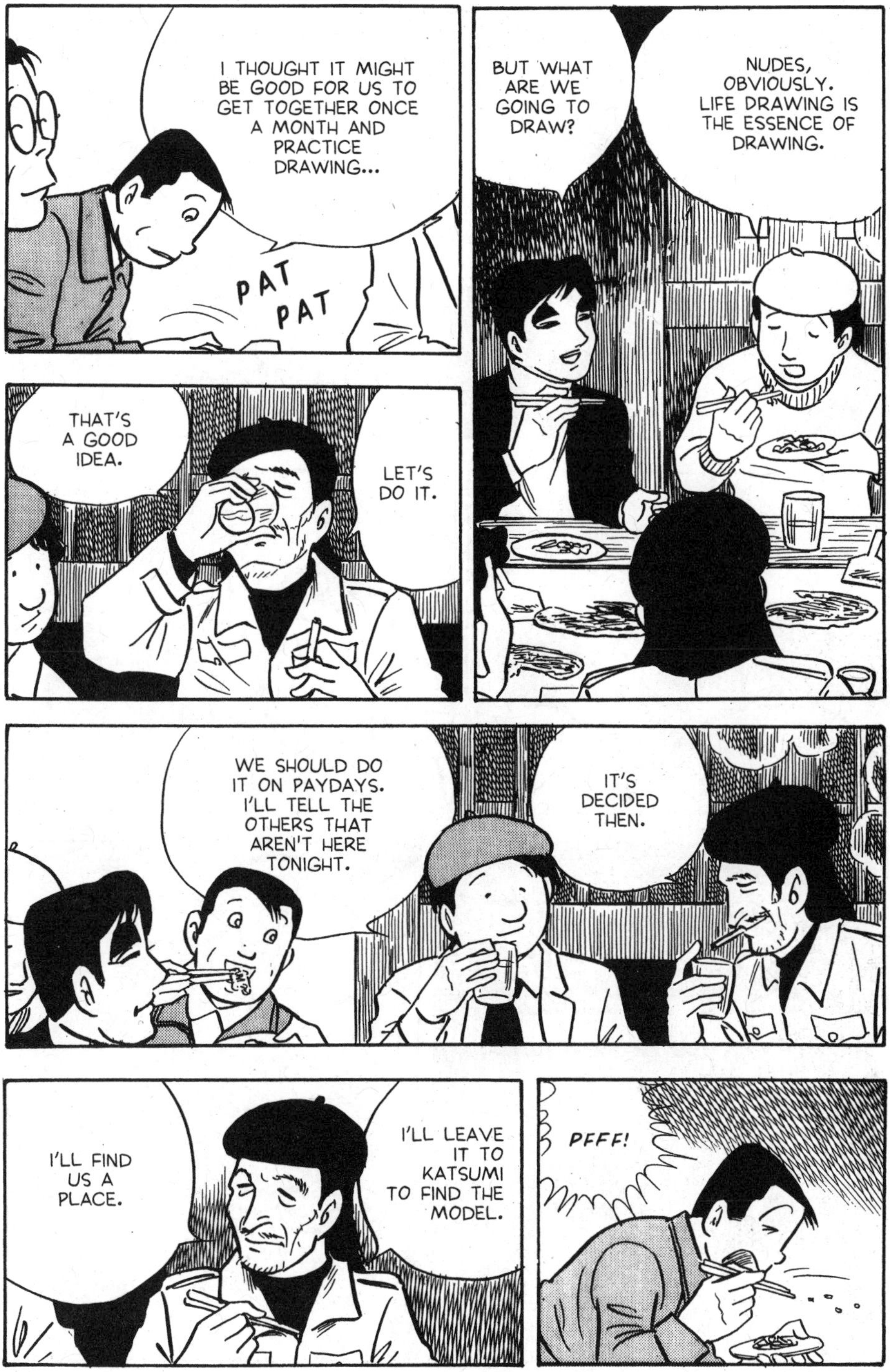
I THOUGHT IT MIGHT BE GOOD FOR US TO GET TOGETHER ONCE A MONTH AND PRACTICE DRAWING...
PAT PAT
BUT WHAT ARE WE GOING TO DRAW?
NUDES, OBVIOUSLY. LIFE DRAWING IS THE ESSENCE OF DRAWING.
THAT'S A GOOD IDEA.
LET'S DO IT.
WE SHOULD DO IT ON PAYDAYS. I'LL TELL THE OTHERS THAT AREN'T HERE TONIGHT.
IT'S DECIDED THEN.
I'LL FIND US A PLACE.
I'LL LEAVE IT TO KATSUMI TO FIND THE MODEL.
PFFF!

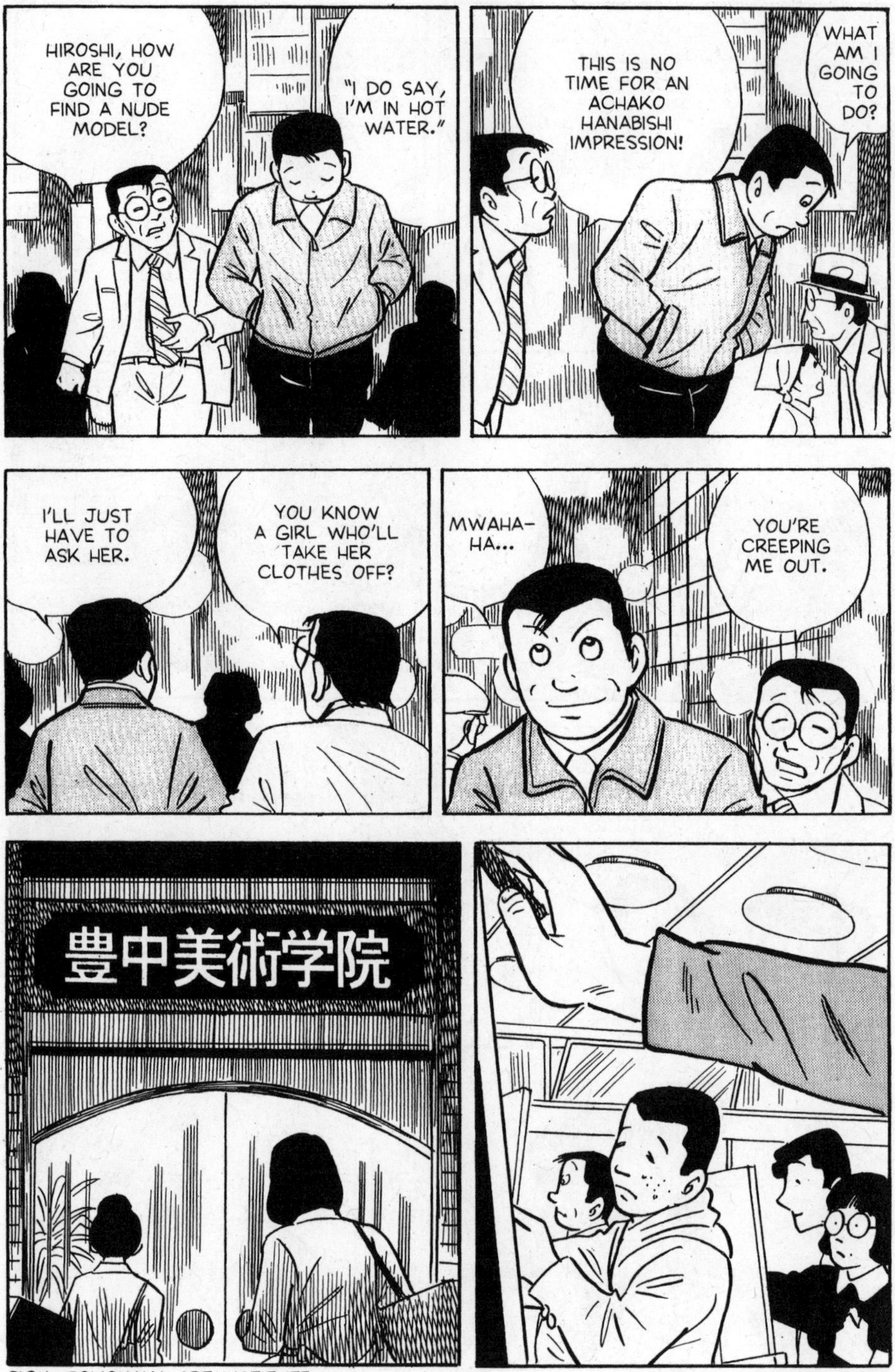
HIROSHI, HOW ARE YOU GOING TO FIND A NUDE MODEL?
"I DO SAY, I'M IN HOT WATER."
THIS IS NO TIME FOR AN ACHAKO HANABISHI IMPRESSION!
WHAT AM I GOING TO DO?
I'LL JUST HAVE TO ASK HER.
YOU KNOW A GIRL WHO'LL TAKE HER CLOTHES OFF?
MWAHA-HA...
YOU'RE CREEPING ME OUT.
豊中美術学院
SIGN: TOYONAKA ART INSTITUTE

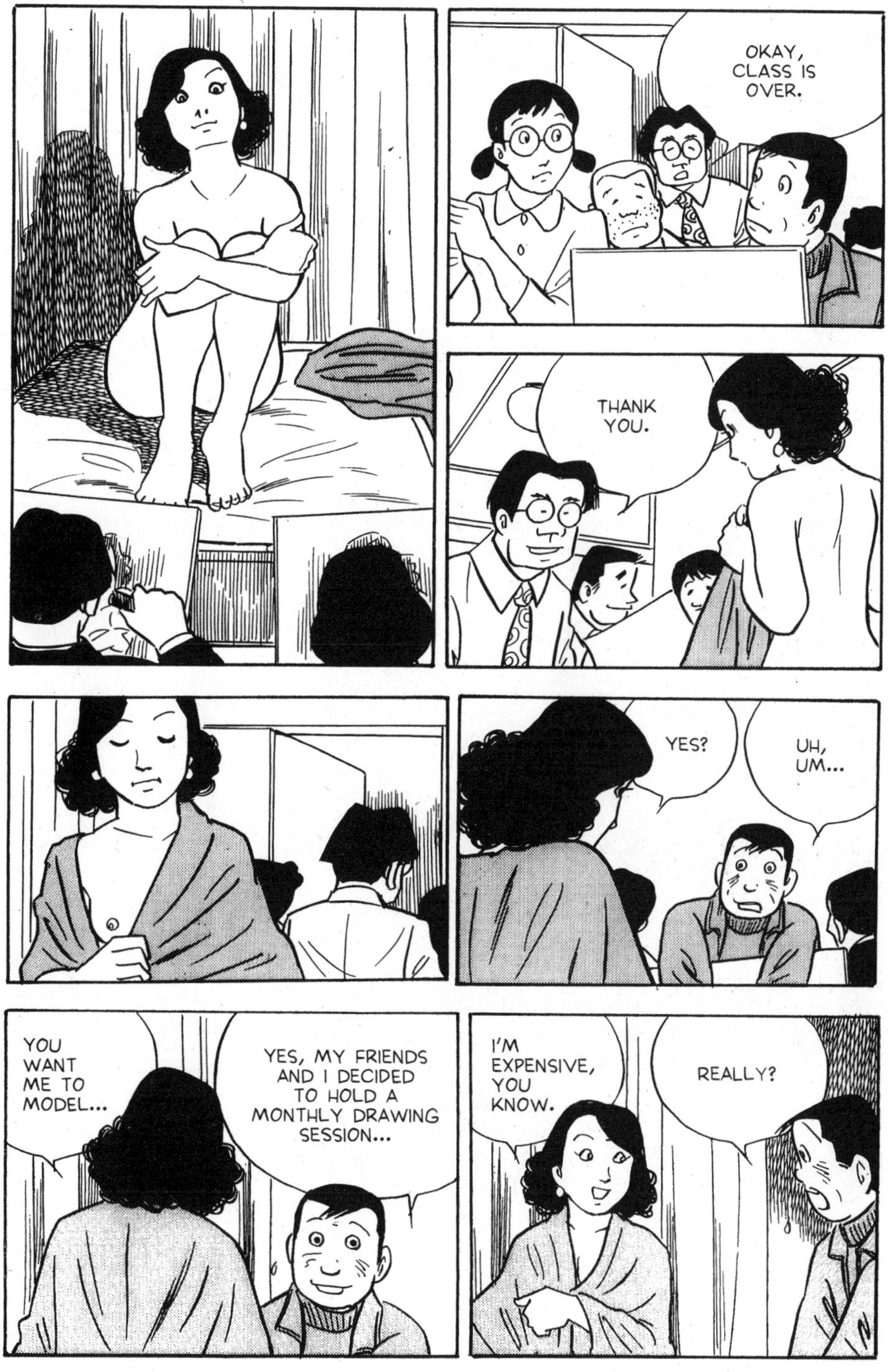
OKAY, CLASS IS OVER.
THANK YOU.
YES?
UH, UM...
YOU WANT ME TO MODEL...
YES, MY FRIENDS AND I DECIDED TO HOLD A MONTHLY DRAWING SESSION...
I'M EXPENSIVE, YOU KNOW.
REALLY?

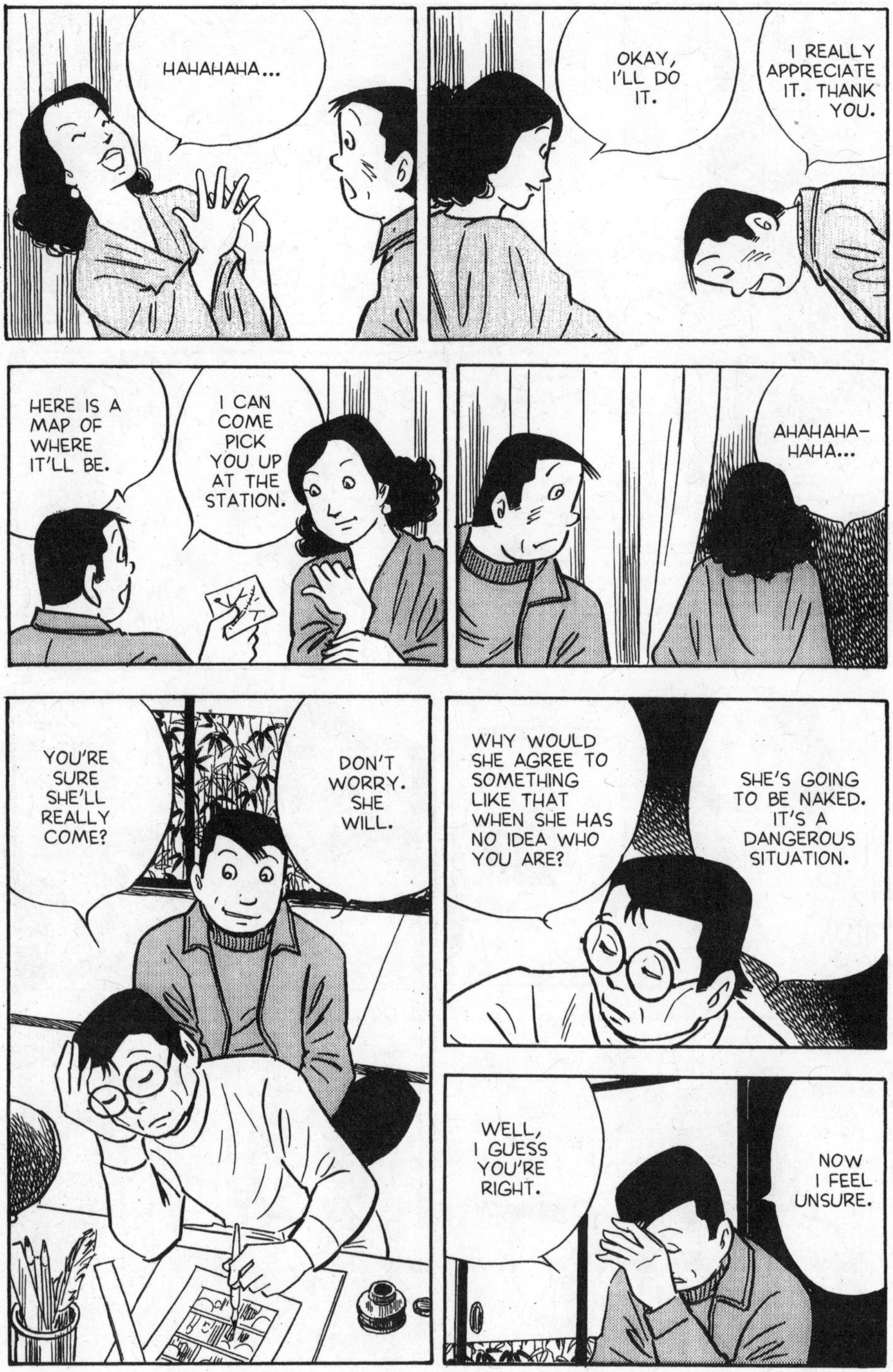
HAHAHAHA...
OKAY, I'LL DO IT.
I REALLY APPRECIATE IT. THANK YOU.
HERE IS A MAP OF WHERE IT'LL BE.
I CAN COME PICK YOU UP AT THE STATION.
AHAHAHA-HAHA...
YOU'RE SURE SHE'LL REALLY COME?
DON'T WORRY. SHE WILL.
WHY WOULD SHE AGREE TO SOMETHING LIKE THAT WHEN SHE HAS NO IDEA WHO YOU ARE?
SHE'S GOING TO BE NAKED. IT'S A DANGEROUS SITUATION.
WELL, I GUESS YOU'RE RIGHT.
NOW I FEEL UNSURE.

DING

RRRRR

IT'S TIME.

EVERY-ONE'S PROBABLY WAITING FOR US.

IF SHE DOESN'T COME, YOU'RE GONNA HAVE TO MODEL INSTEAD.

WHAT?!

HERE SHE COMES!

SKREEECH

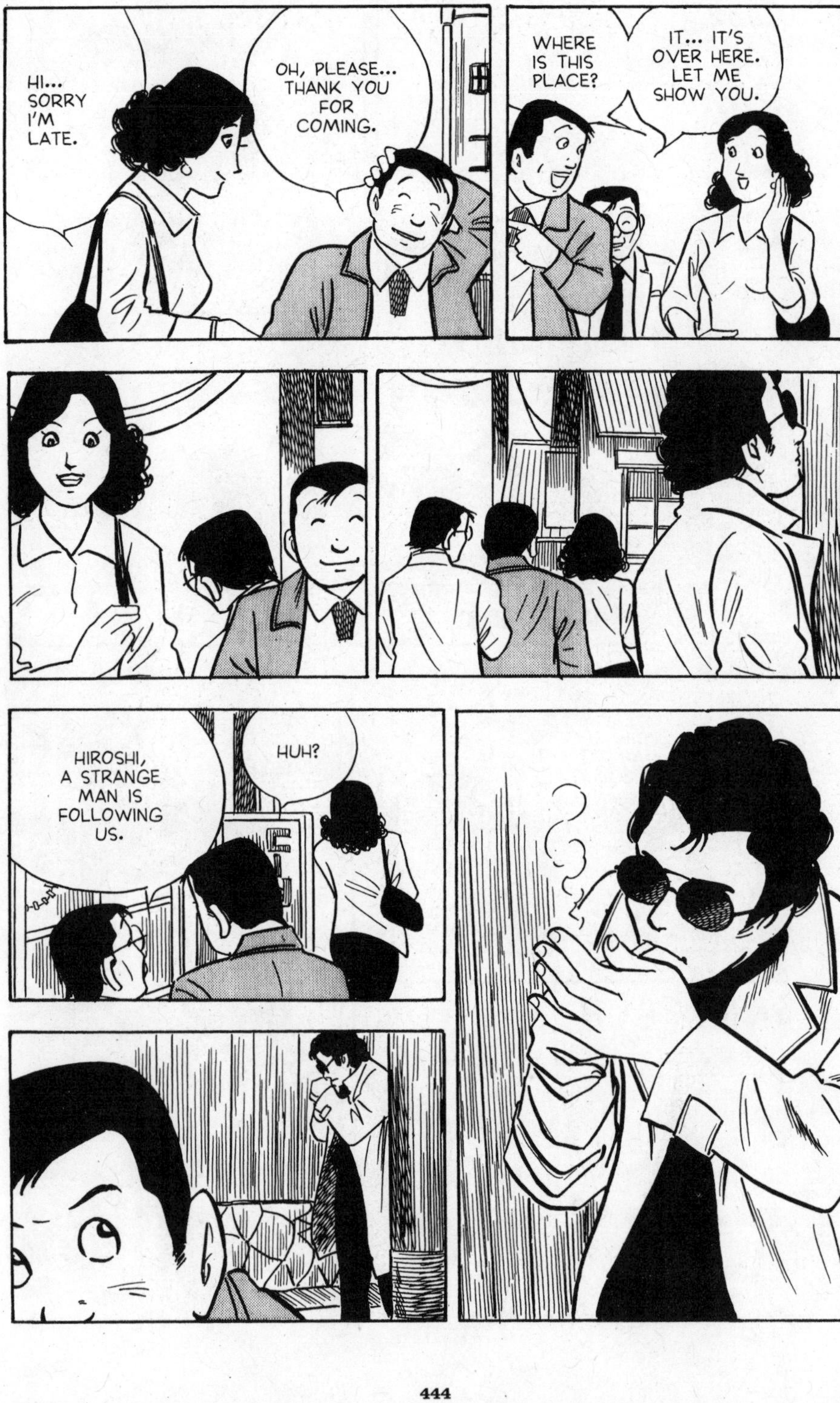
HI... SORRY I'M LATE.
OH, PLEASE... THANK YOU FOR COMING.
WHERE IS THIS PLACE?
IT... IT'S OVER HERE. LET ME SHOW YOU.
HIROSHI, A STRANGE MAN IS FOLLOWING US.
HUH?

MASAMI KURODA'S PAST

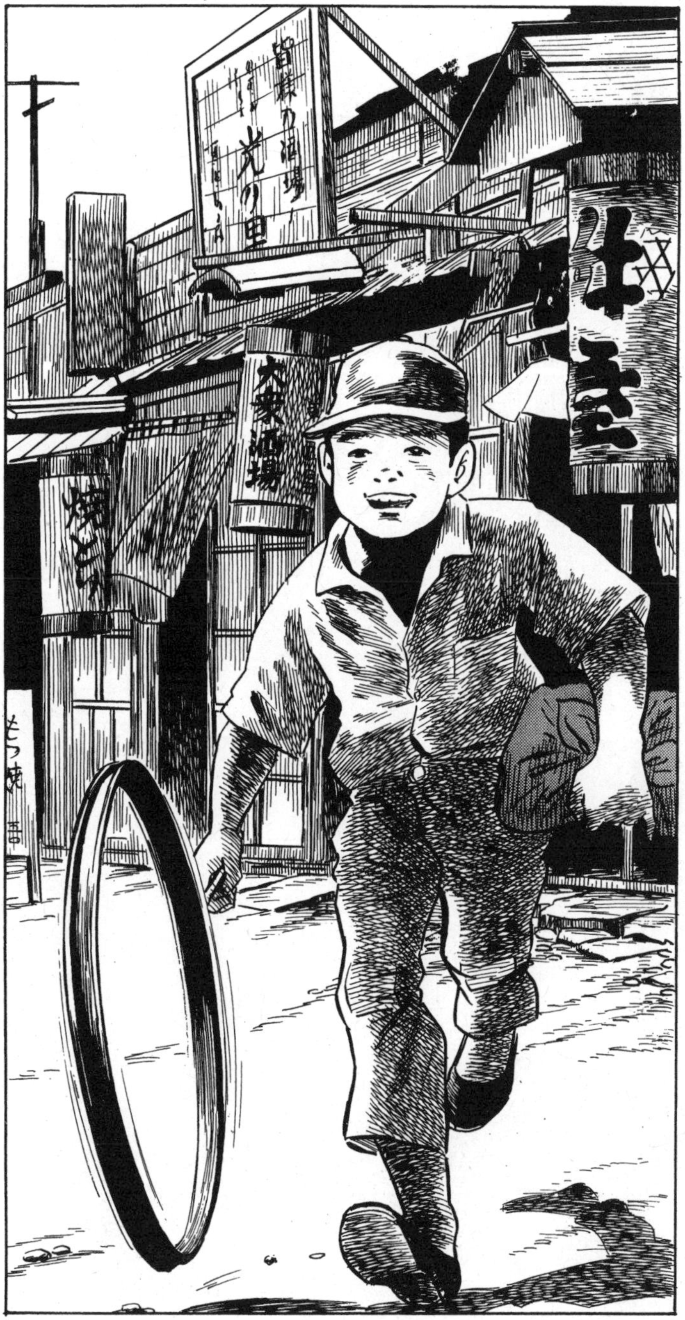
皆様の酒場
光の里
大衆酒場

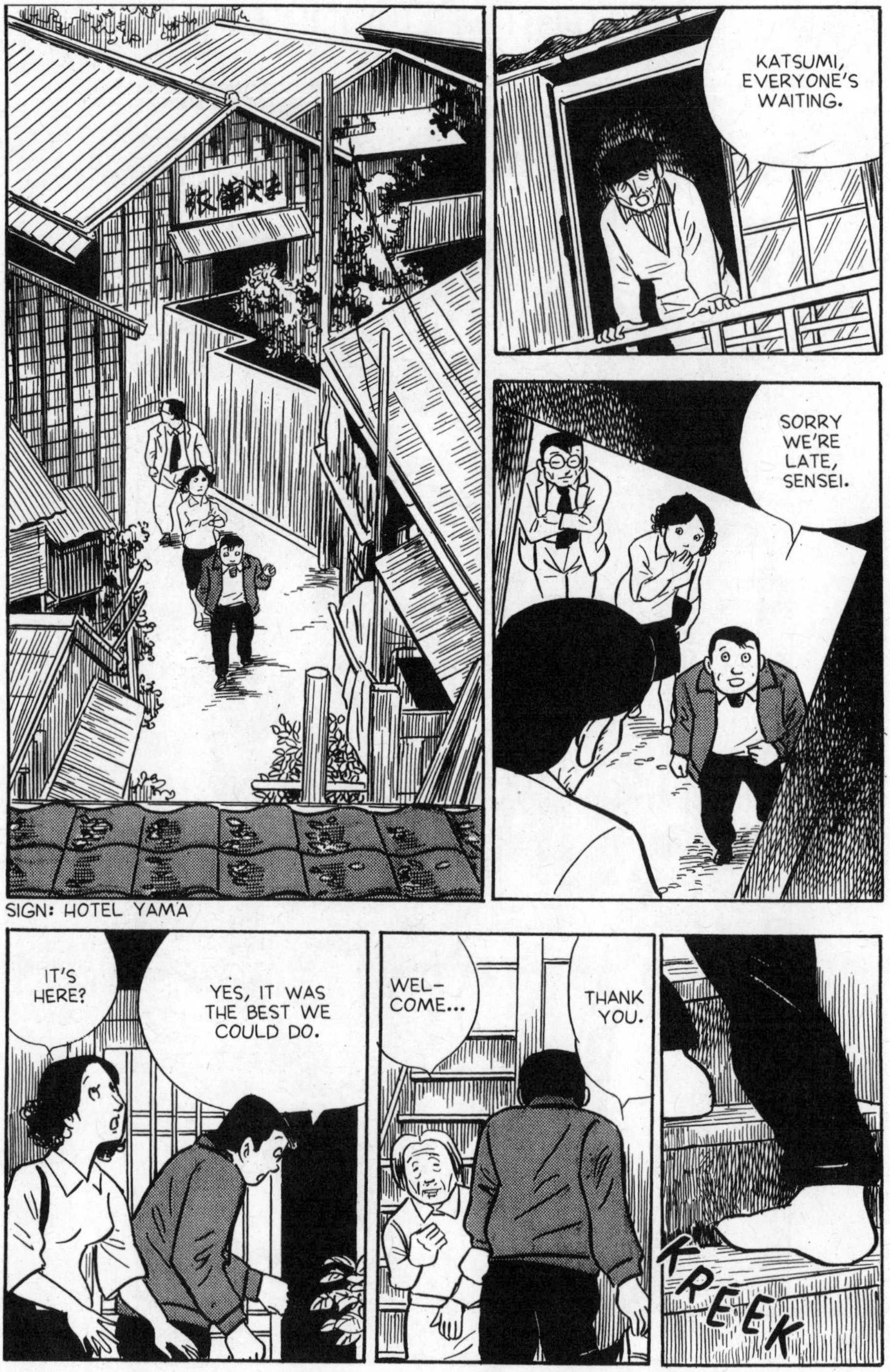

KATSUMI, EVERYONE'S WAITING.
SORRY WE'RE LATE, SENSEI.
IT'S HERE?
YES, IT WAS THE BEST WE COULD DO.
WEL-COME...
THANK YOU.
KREEK

SIGN: HOTEL YAMA

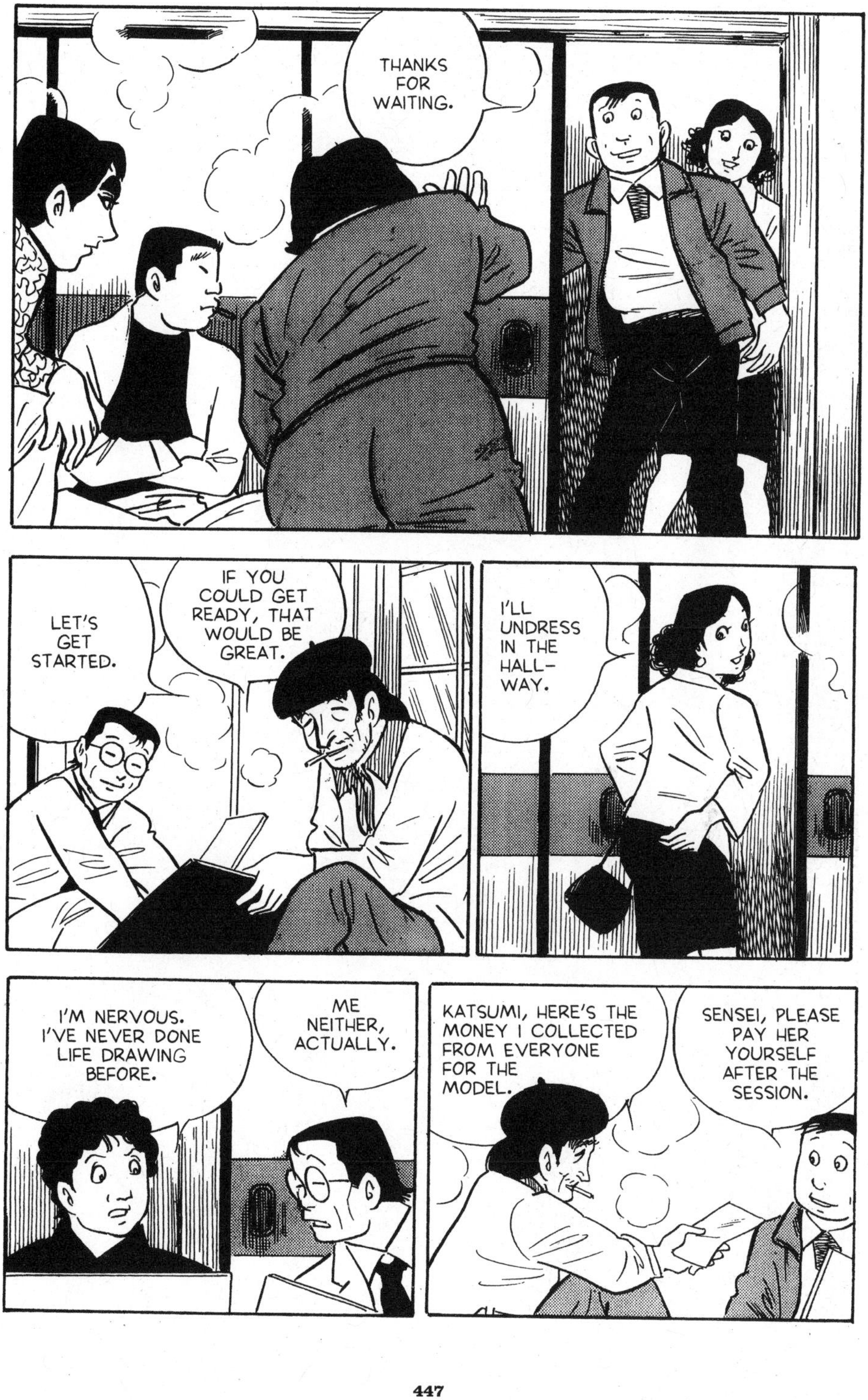
THANKS FOR WAITING.
LET'S GET STARTED.
IF YOU COULD GET READY, THAT WOULD BE GREAT.
I'LL UNDRESS IN THE HALL-WAY.
I'M NERVOUS. I'VE NEVER DONE LIFE DRAWING BEFORE.
ME NEITHER, ACTUALLY.
KATSUMI, HERE'S THE MONEY I COLLECTED FROM EVERYONE FOR THE MODEL.
SENSEI, PLEASE PAY HER YOURSELF AFTER THE SESSION.

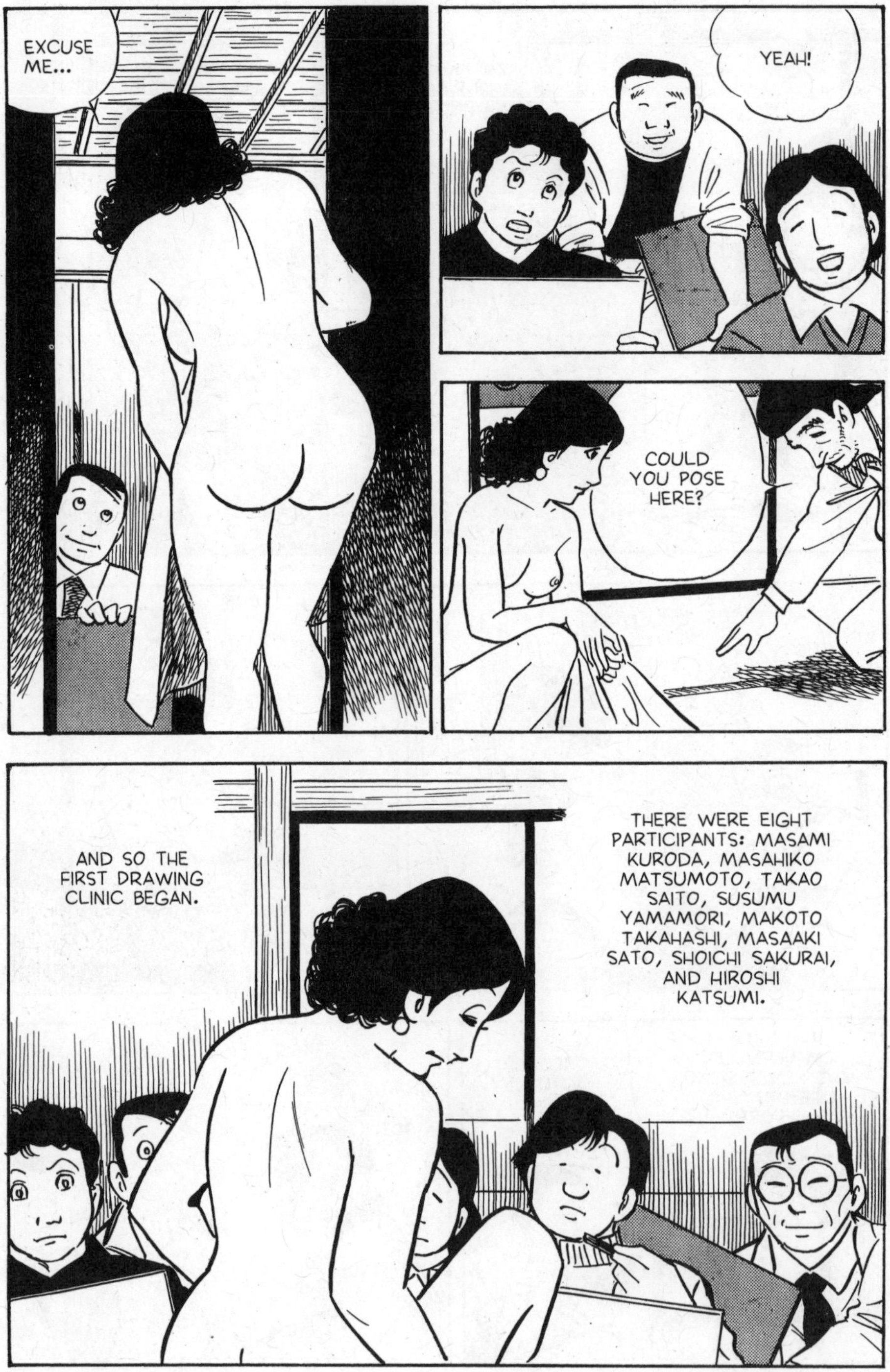
EXCUSE ME...
YEAH!
COULD YOU POSE HERE?
AND SO THE FIRST DRAWING CLINIC BEGAN.
THERE WERE EIGHT PARTICIPANTS: MASAMI KURODA, MASAHIKO MATSUMOTO, TAKAO SAITO, SUSUMU YAMAMORI, MAKOTO TAKAHASHI, MASAAKI SATO, SHOICHI SAKURAI, AND HIROSHI KATSUMI.

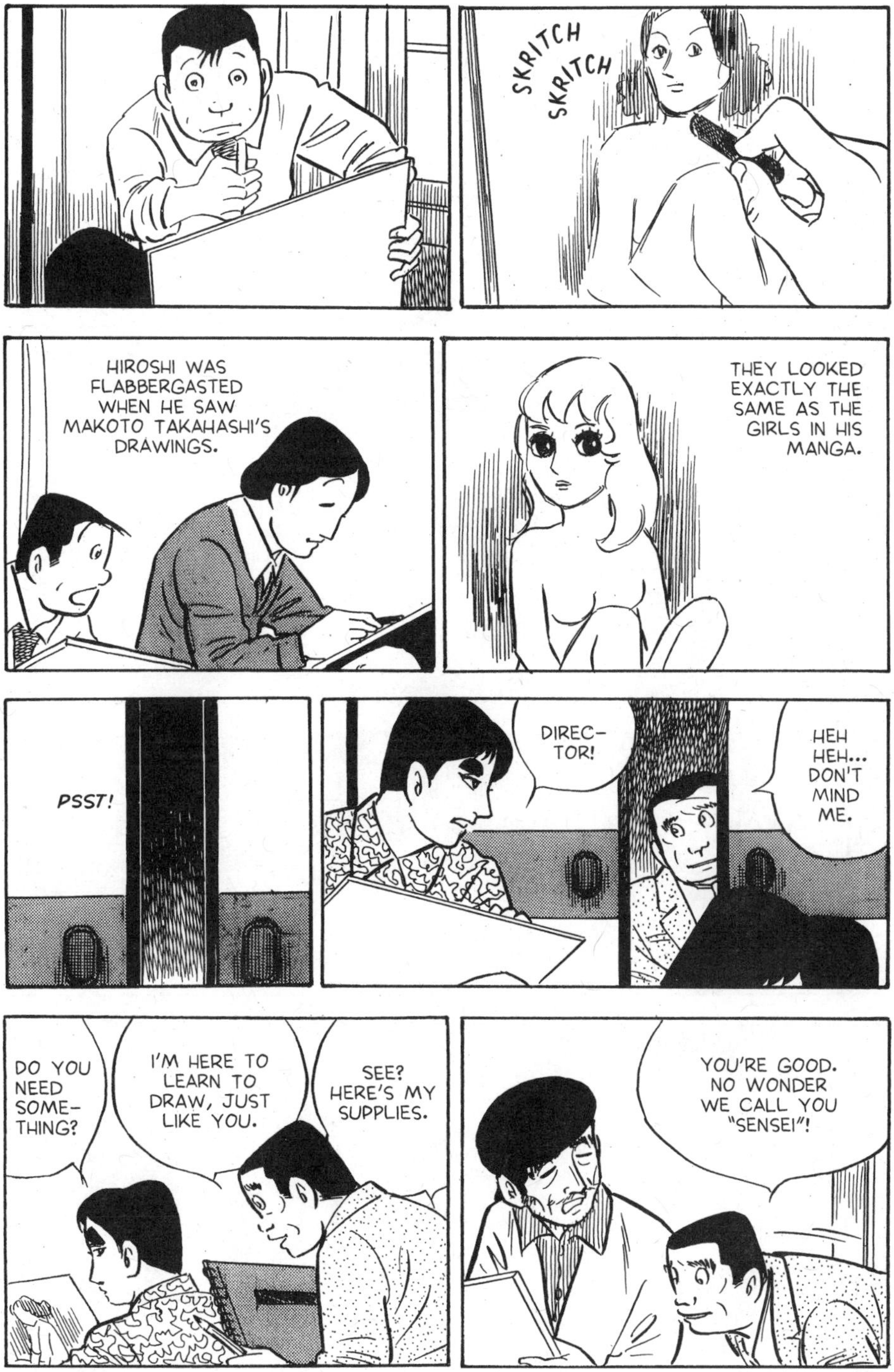
SKRITCH
SKRITCH
HIROSHI WAS FLABBERGASTED WHEN HE SAW MAKOTO TAKAHASHI'S DRAWINGS.
THEY LOOKED EXACTLY THE SAME AS THE GIRLS IN HIS MANGA.
PSST!
DIREC-TOR!
HEH HEH... DON'T MIND ME.
DO YOU NEED SOME-THING?
I'M HERE TO LEARN TO DRAW, JUST LIKE YOU.
SEE? HERE'S MY SUPPLIES.
YOU'RE GOOD. NO WONDER WE CALL YOU "SENSEI"!

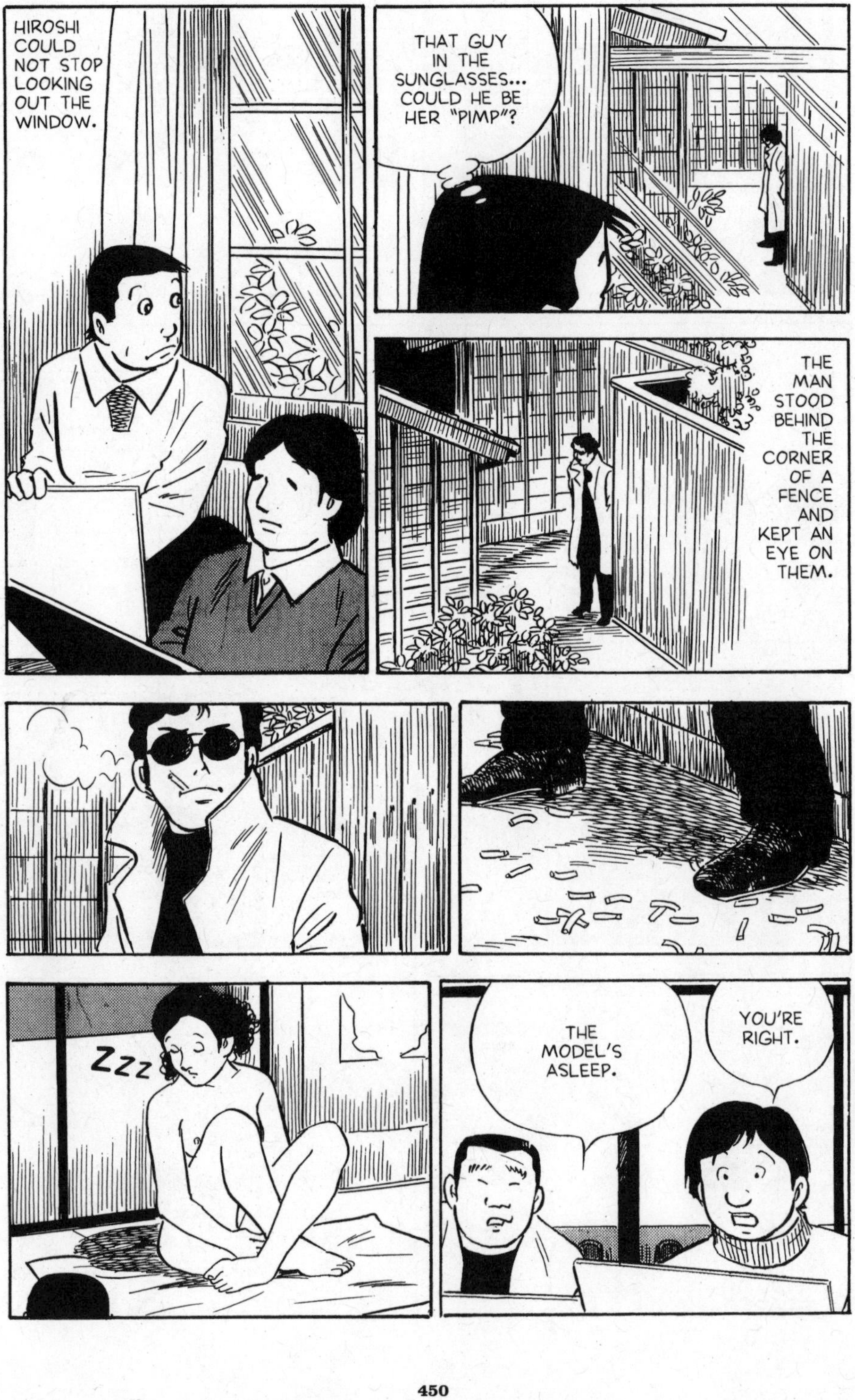
HIROSHI COULD NOT STOP LOOKING OUT THE WINDOW.
THAT GUY IN THE SUNGLASSES... COULD HE BE HER "PIMP"?
THE MAN STOOD BEHIND THE CORNER OF A FENCE AND KEPT AN EYE ON THEM.
ZZZ
THE MODEL'S ASLEEP.
YOU'RE RIGHT.

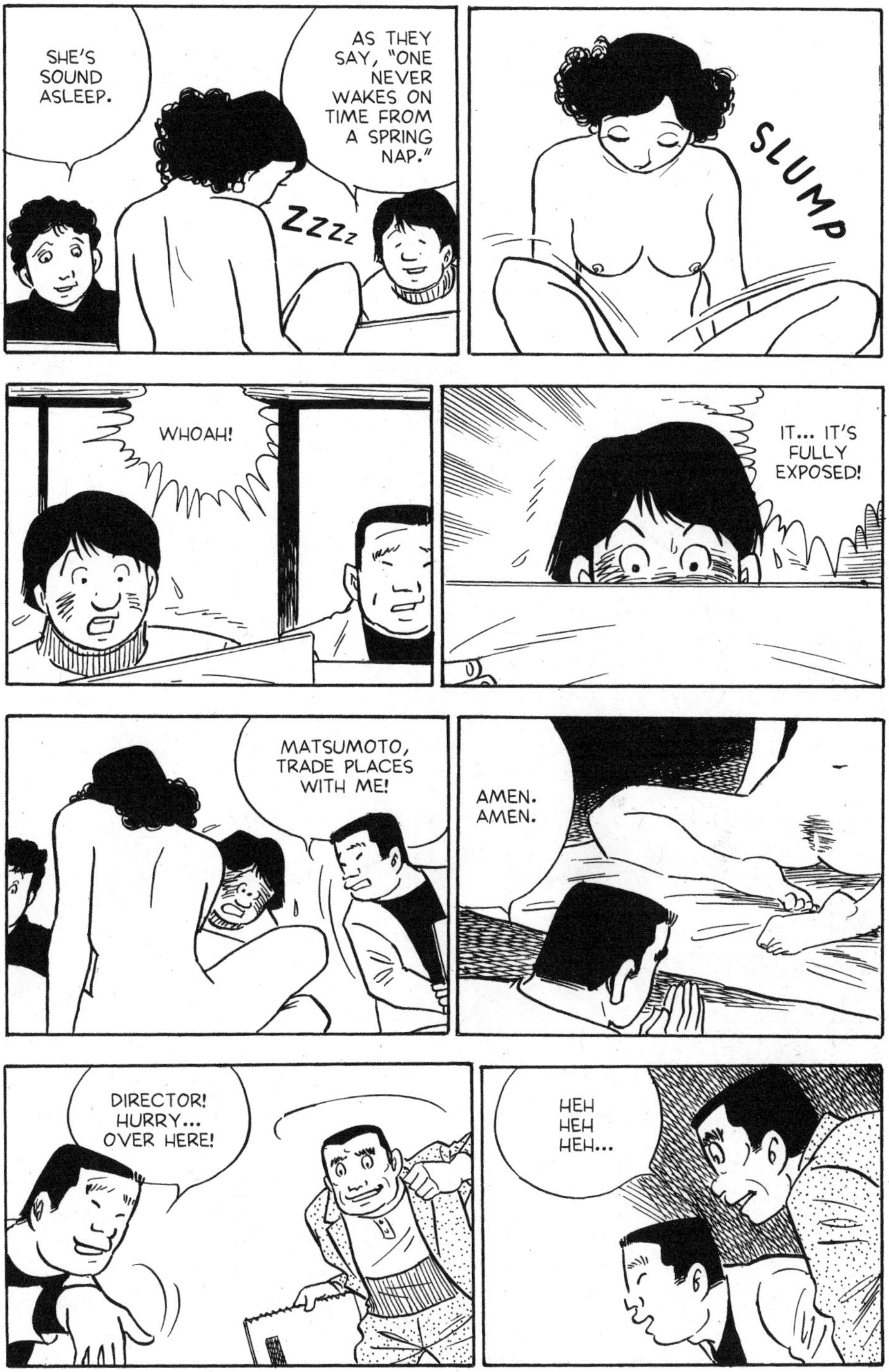
SHE'S SOUND ASLEEP.
AS THEY SAY, "ONE NEVER WAKES ON TIME FROM A SPRING NAP."
ZZZZ
SLUMP
WHOAH!
IT... IT'S FULLY EXPOSED!
MATSUMOTO, TRADE PLACES WITH ME!
AMEN. AMEN.
DIRECTOR! HURRY... OVER HERE!
HEH HEH HEH...

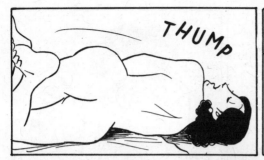

THUMP

AH!

I... I'M SORRY! I MUST'VE FALLEN ASLEEP.

IT'S VERY WARM AND SUNNY IN HERE. HAHAHA...

HIROSHI COULDN'T STOP THINKING ABOUT THE MAN OUTSIDE.

THE SOLITARY FIGURE STANDING AGAINST THE SETTING SUN LOOKED LIKE A SCENE FROM A FILM.

THE PIMPING BUSINESS CAN'T BE EASY.

I WONDER IF I COULD EXPRESS SOMETHING LIKE THAT IN MANGA?

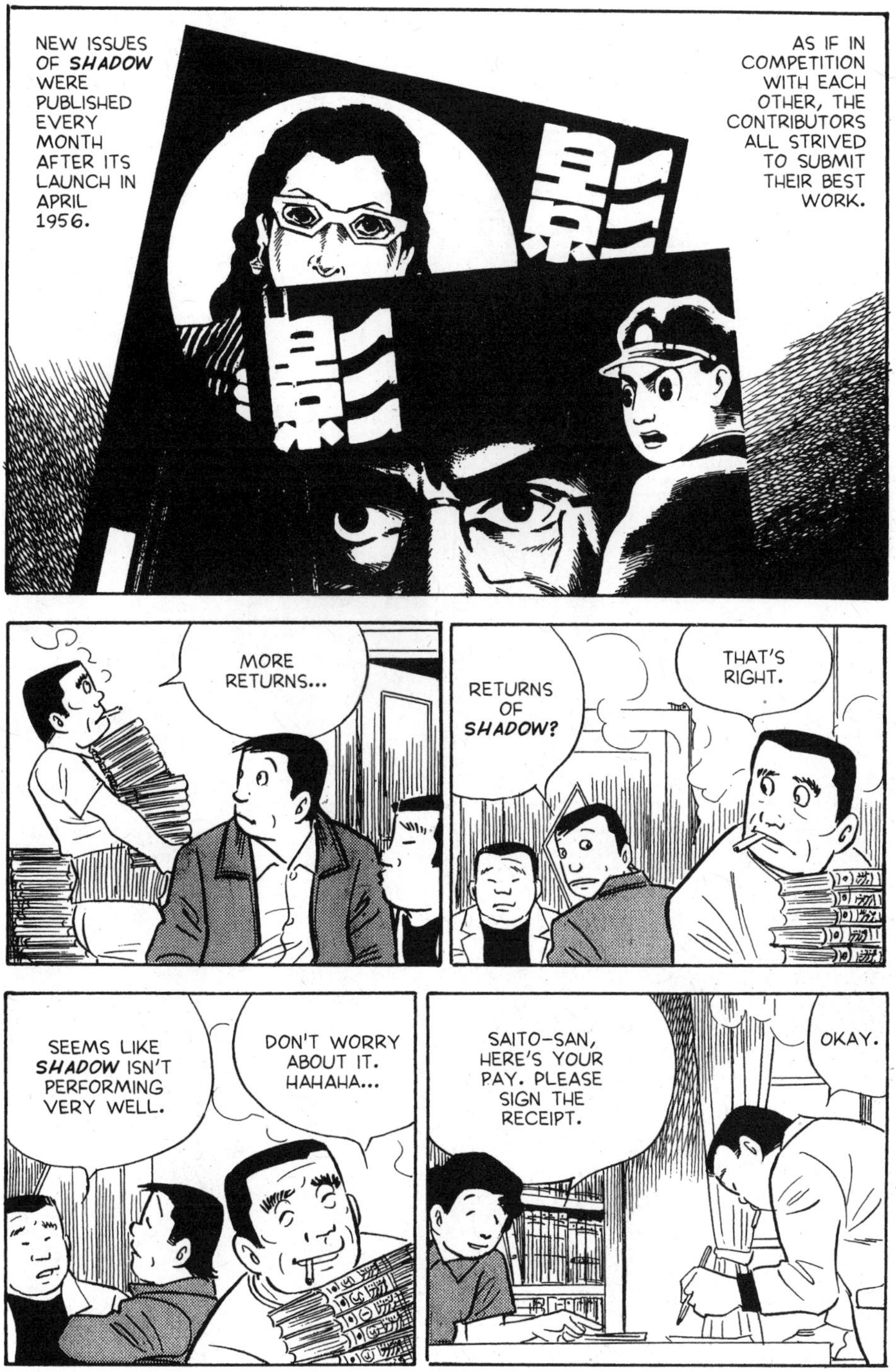

NEW ISSUES OF SHADOW WERE PUBLISHED EVERY MONTH AFTER ITS LAUNCH IN APRIL 1956.
AS IF IN COMPETITION WITH EACH OTHER, THE CONTRIBUTORS ALL STRIVED TO SUBMIT THEIR BEST WORK.
MORE RETURNS...
RETURNS OF SHADOW?
THAT'S RIGHT.
SEEMS LIKE SHADOW ISN'T PERFORMING VERY WELL.
DON'T WORRY ABOUT IT. HAHAHA...
SAITO-SAN, HERE'S YOUR PAY. PLEASE SIGN THE RECEIPT.
OKAY.

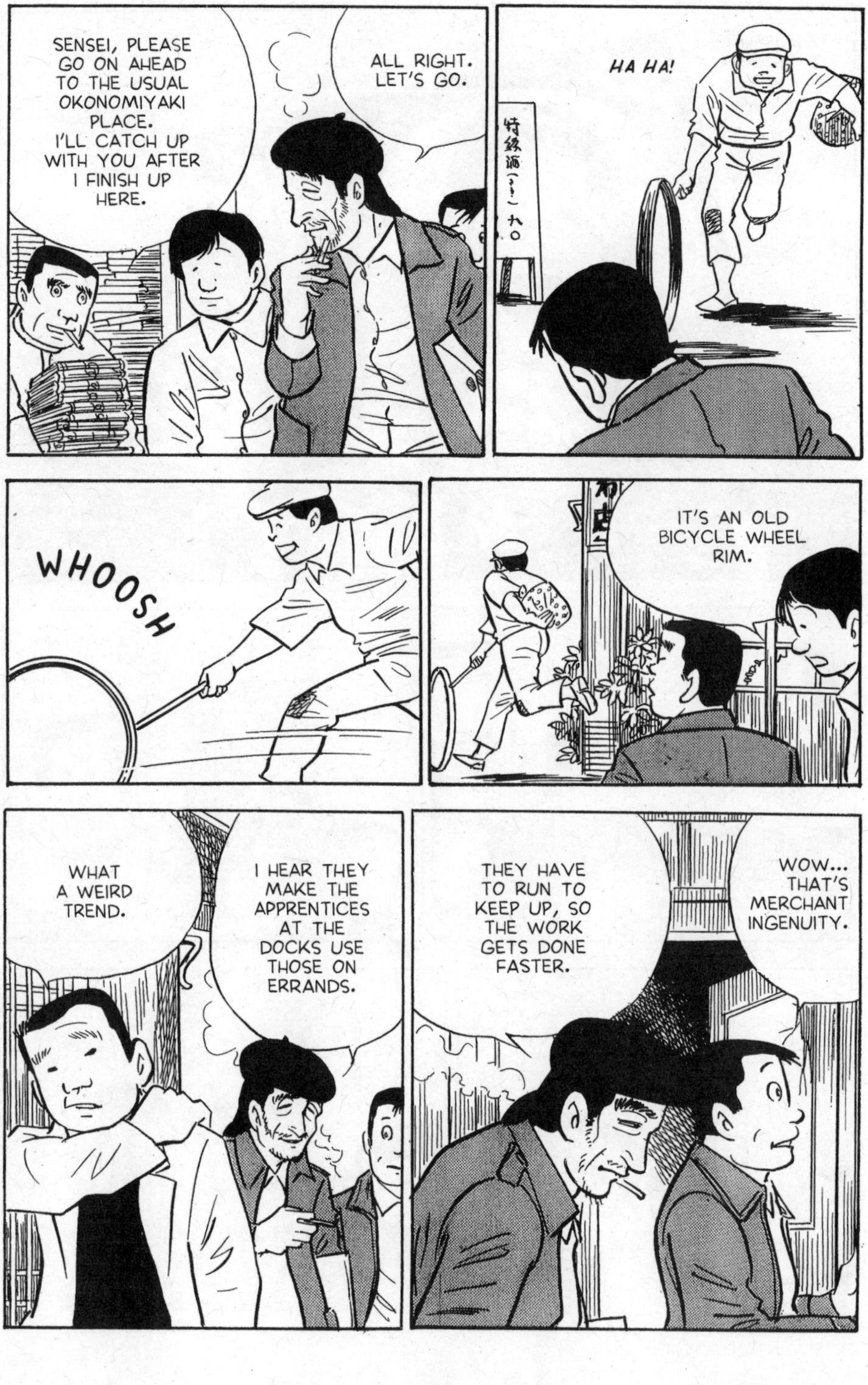
SENSEI, PLEASE GO ON AHEAD TO THE USUAL OKONOMIYAKI PLACE. I'LL CATCH UP WITH YOU AFTER I FINISH UP HERE.
ALL RIGHT. LET'S GO.
HA HA!
WHOOSH
IT'S AN OLD BICYCLE WHEEL RIM.
WHAT A WEIRD TREND.
I HEAR THEY MAKE THE APPRENTICES AT THE DOCKS USE THOSE ON ERRANDS.
THEY HAVE TO RUN TO KEEP UP, SO THE WORK GETS DONE FASTER.
WOW... THAT'S MERCHANT INGENUITY.

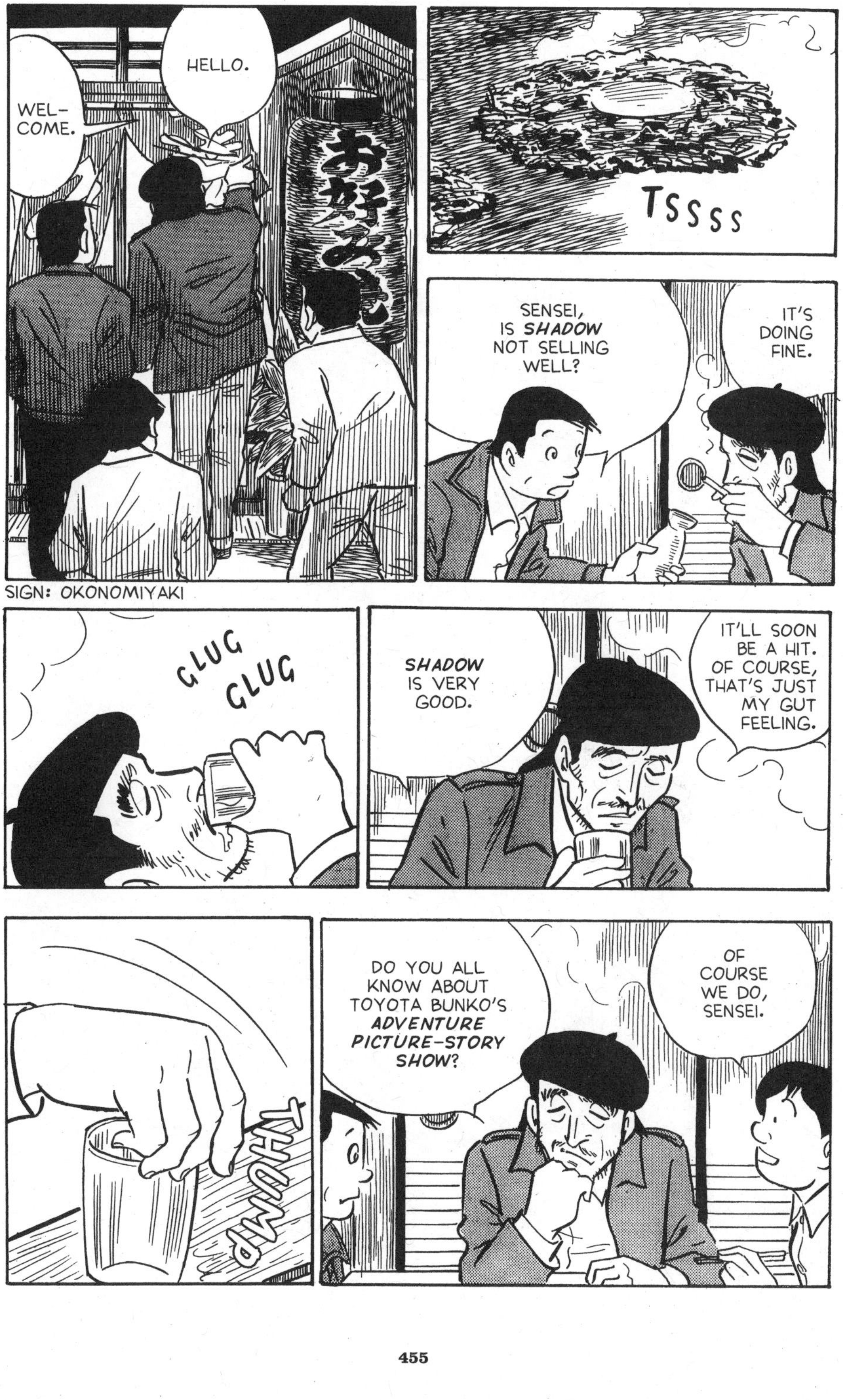
WEL-COME.
HELLO.
SIGN: OKONOMIYAKI
TSSSS
SENSEI, IS *SHADOW* NOT SELLING WELL?
IT'S DOING FINE.
GLUG GLUG
SHADOW IS VERY GOOD.
IT'LL SOON BE A HIT. OF COURSE, THAT'S JUST MY GUT FEELING.
THUMP
DO YOU ALL KNOW ABOUT TOYOTA BUNKO'S *ADVENTURE PICTURE-STORY SHOW*?
OF COURSE WE DO, SENSEI.

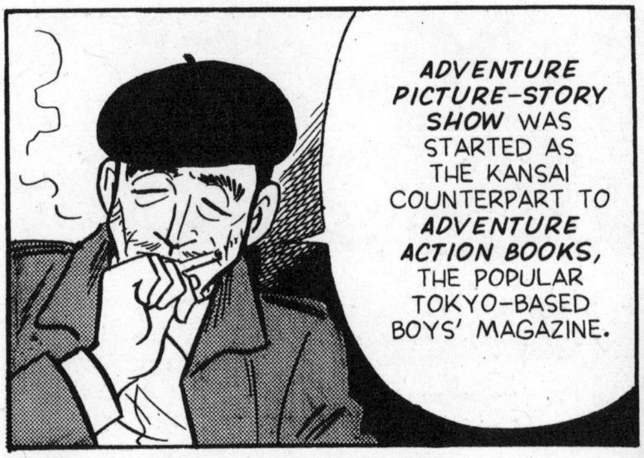
ADVENTURE PICTURE-STORY SHOW WAS STARTED AS THE KANSAI COUNTERPART TO *ADVENTURE ACTION BOOKS,* THE POPULAR TOKYO-BASED BOYS' MAGAZINE.

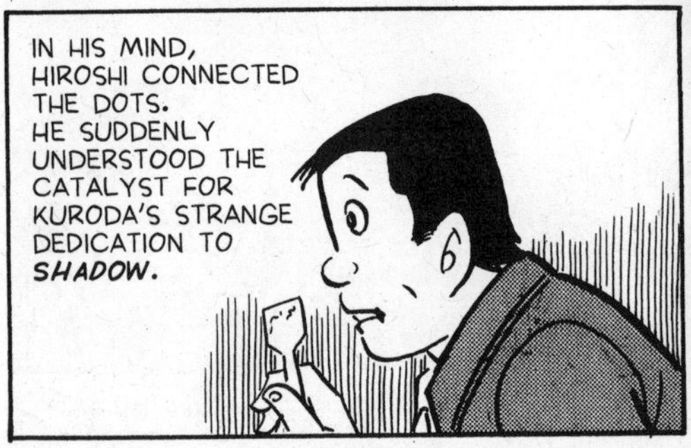
IN HIS MIND, HIROSHI CONNECTED THE DOTS.
HE SUDDENLY UNDERSTOOD THE CATALYST FOR KURODA'S STRANGE DEDICATION TO *SHADOW*.

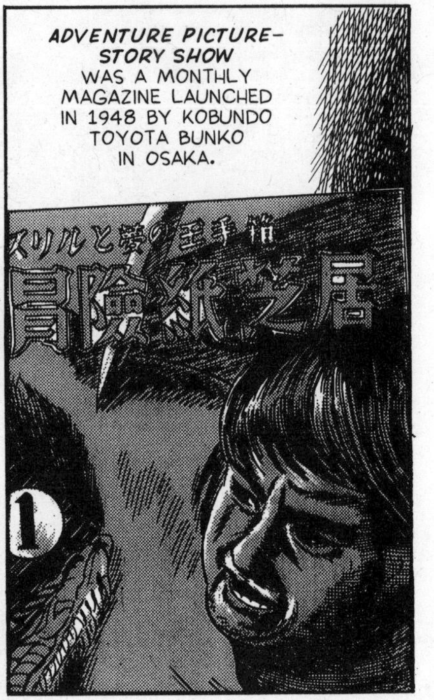
ADVENTURE PICTURE-STORY SHOW WAS A MONTHLY MAGAZINE LAUNCHED IN 1948 BY KOBUNDO TOYOTA BUNKO IN OSAKA.
冒険紙芝居
1

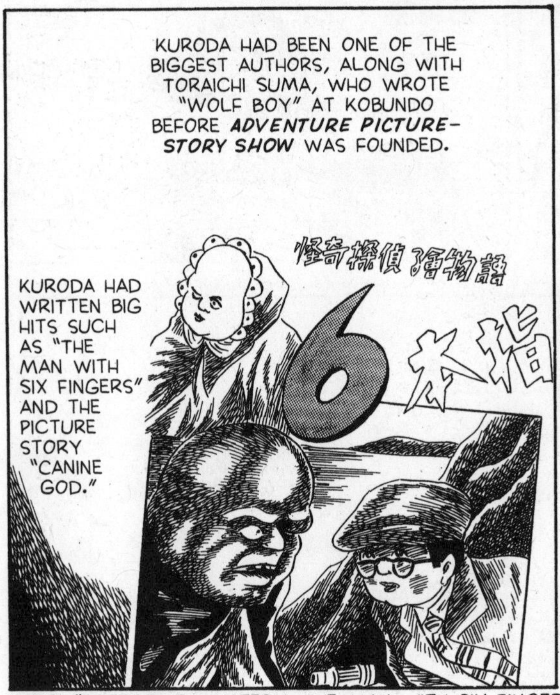
KURODA HAD BEEN ONE OF THE BIGGEST AUTHORS, ALONG WITH TORAICHI SUMA, WHO WROTE "WOLF BOY" AT KOBUNDO BEFORE *ADVENTURE PICTURE-STORY SHOW* WAS FOUNDED.
KURODA HAD WRITTEN BIG HITS SUCH AS "THE MAN WITH SIX FINGERS" AND THE PICTURE STORY "CANINE GOD."
6本指

TITLE: "DETECTIVE MYSTERY: THE MAN WITH SIX FINGERS"

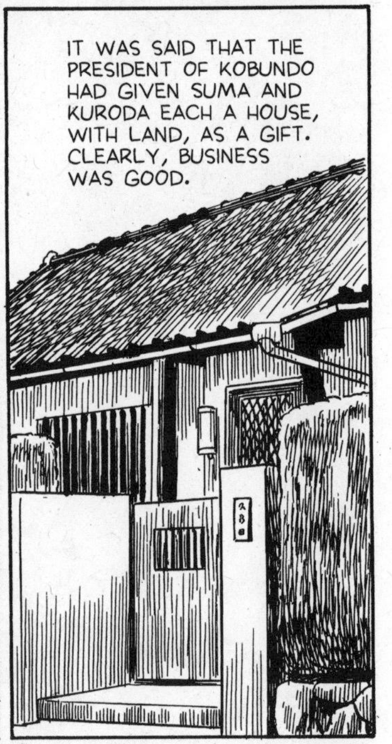
IT WAS SAID THAT THE PRESIDENT OF KOBUNDO HAD GIVEN SUMA AND KURODA EACH A HOUSE, WITH LAND, AS A GIFT. CLEARLY, BUSINESS WAS GOOD.

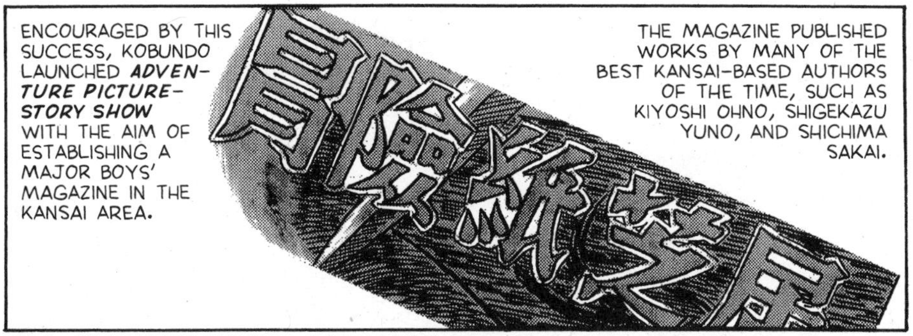
ENCOURAGED BY THIS SUCCESS, KOBUNDO LAUNCHED ***ADVENTURE PICTURE-STORY SHOW*** WITH THE AIM OF ESTABLISHING A MAJOR BOYS' MAGAZINE IN THE KANSAI AREA.
冒険紙芝居
THE MAGAZINE PUBLISHED WORKS BY MANY OF THE BEST KANSAI-BASED AUTHORS OF THE TIME, SUCH AS KIYOSHI OHNO, SHIGEKAZU YUNO, AND SHICHIMA SAKAI.
TITLE: ***ADVENTURE PICTURE-STORY SHOW***

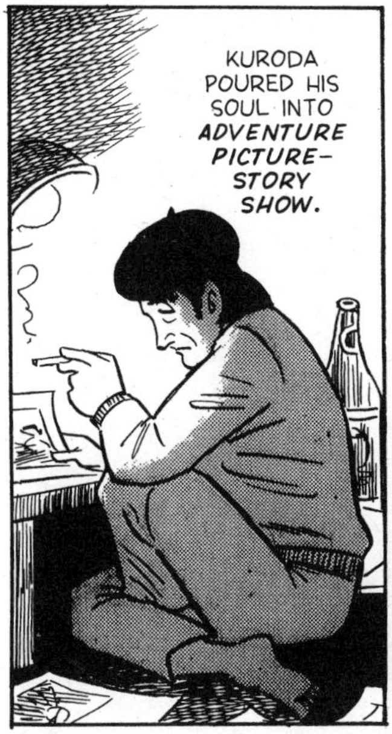
KURODA POURED HIS SOUL INTO ***ADVENTURE PICTURE-STORY SHOW.***

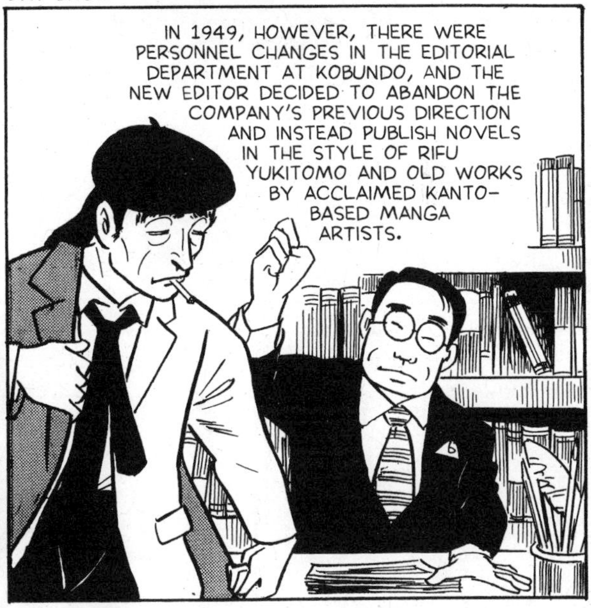
IN 1949, HOWEVER, THERE WERE PERSONNEL CHANGES IN THE EDITORIAL DEPARTMENT AT KOBUNDO, AND THE NEW EDITOR DECIDED TO ABANDON THE COMPANY'S PREVIOUS DIRECTION AND INSTEAD PUBLISH NOVELS IN THE STYLE OF RIFU YUKITOMO AND OLD WORKS BY ACCLAIMED KANTO-BASED MANGA ARTISTS.

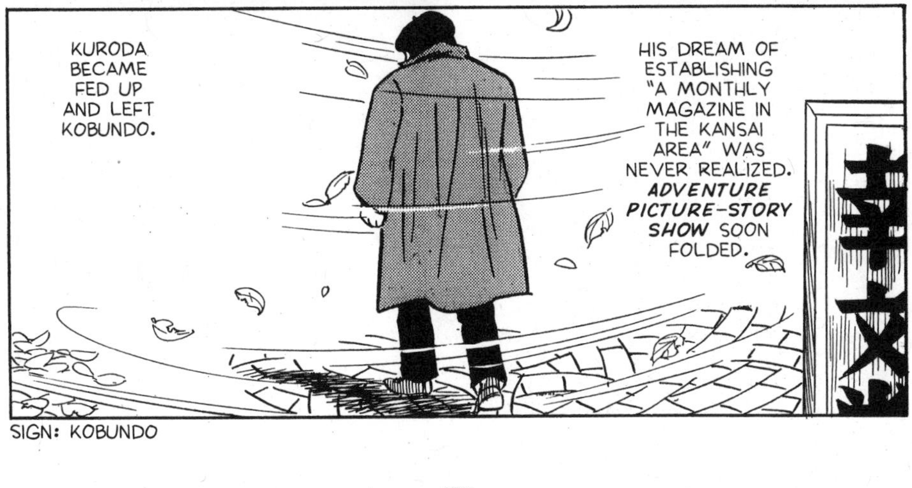
KURODA BECAME FED UP AND LEFT KOBUNDO.
HIS DREAM OF ESTABLISHING "A MONTHLY MAGAZINE IN THE KANSAI AREA" WAS NEVER REALIZED. ***ADVENTURE PICTURE-STORY SHOW*** SOON FOLDED.
SIGN: KOBUNDO

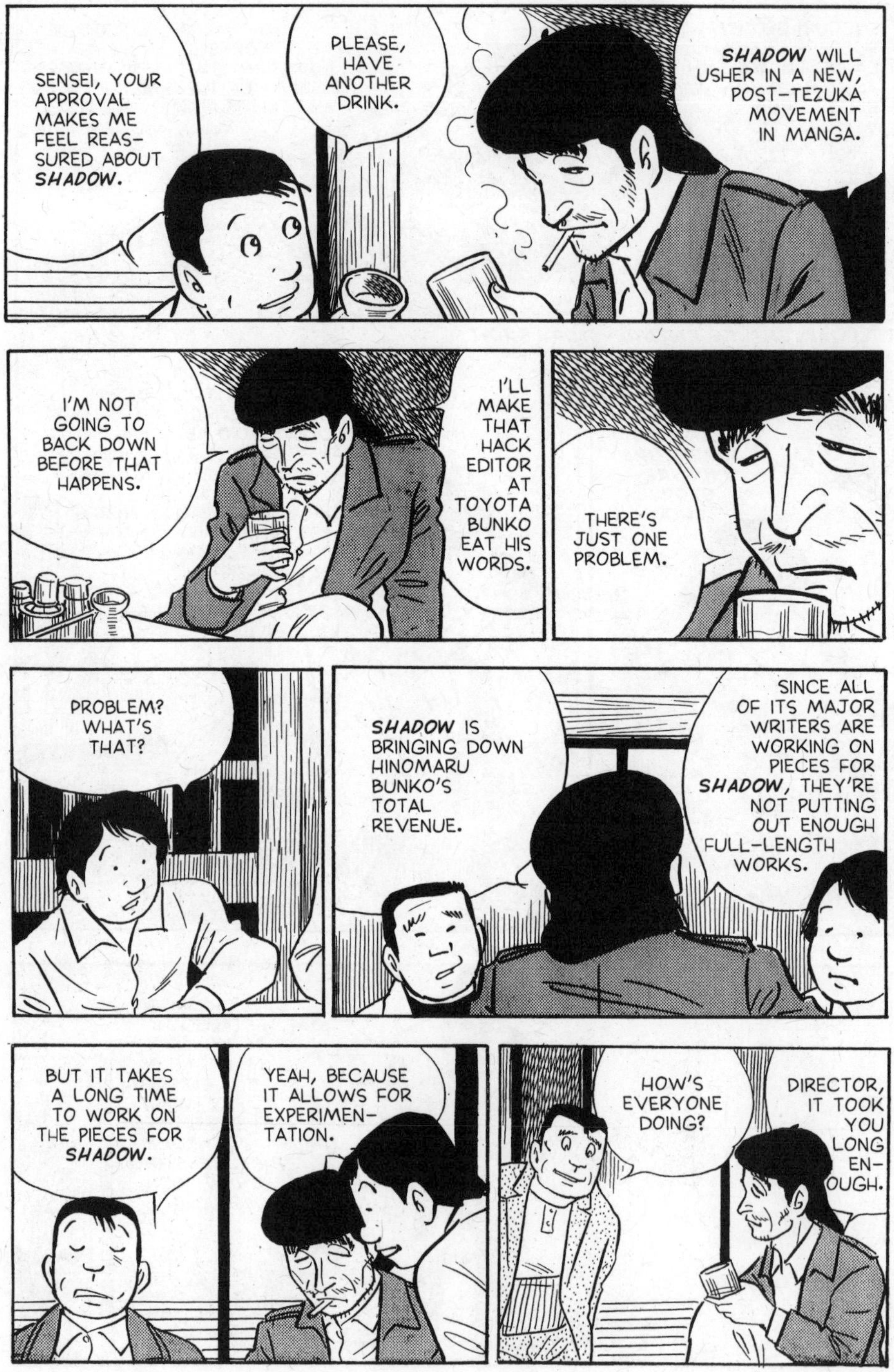

SENSEI, YOUR APPROVAL MAKES ME FEEL REAS-SURED ABOUT SHADOW.
PLEASE, HAVE ANOTHER DRINK.
SHADOW WILL USHER IN A NEW, POST-TEZUKA MOVEMENT IN MANGA.
I'M NOT GOING TO BACK DOWN BEFORE THAT HAPPENS.
I'LL MAKE THAT HACK EDITOR AT TOYOTA BUNKO EAT HIS WORDS.
THERE'S JUST ONE PROBLEM.
PROBLEM? WHAT'S THAT?
SHADOW IS BRINGING DOWN HINOMARU BUNKO'S TOTAL REVENUE.
SINCE ALL OF ITS MAJOR WRITERS ARE WORKING ON PIECES FOR SHADOW, THEY'RE NOT PUTTING OUT ENOUGH FULL-LENGTH WORKS.
BUT IT TAKES A LONG TIME TO WORK ON THE PIECES FOR SHADOW.
YEAH, BECAUSE IT ALLOWS FOR EXPERIMEN-TATION.
HOW'S EVERYONE DOING?
DIRECTOR, IT TOOK YOU LONG EN-OUGH.

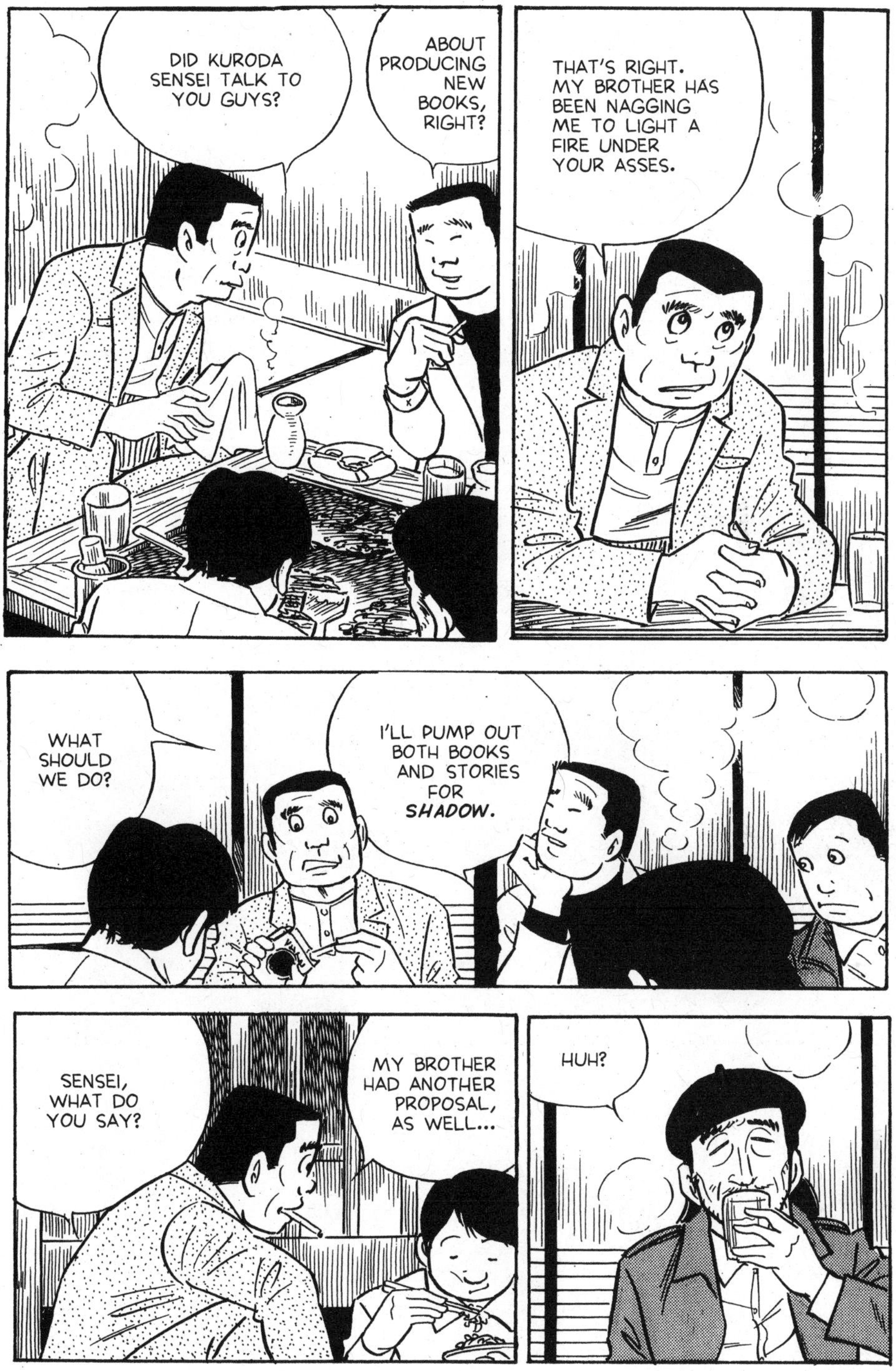
DID KURODA SENSEI TALK TO YOU GUYS?
ABOUT PRODUCING NEW BOOKS, RIGHT?
THAT'S RIGHT. MY BROTHER HAS BEEN NAGGING ME TO LIGHT A FIRE UNDER YOUR ASSES.
WHAT SHOULD WE DO?
I'LL PUMP OUT BOTH BOOKS AND STORIES FOR SHADOW.
SENSEI, WHAT DO YOU SAY?
MY BROTHER HAD ANOTHER PROPOSAL, AS WELL...
HUH?

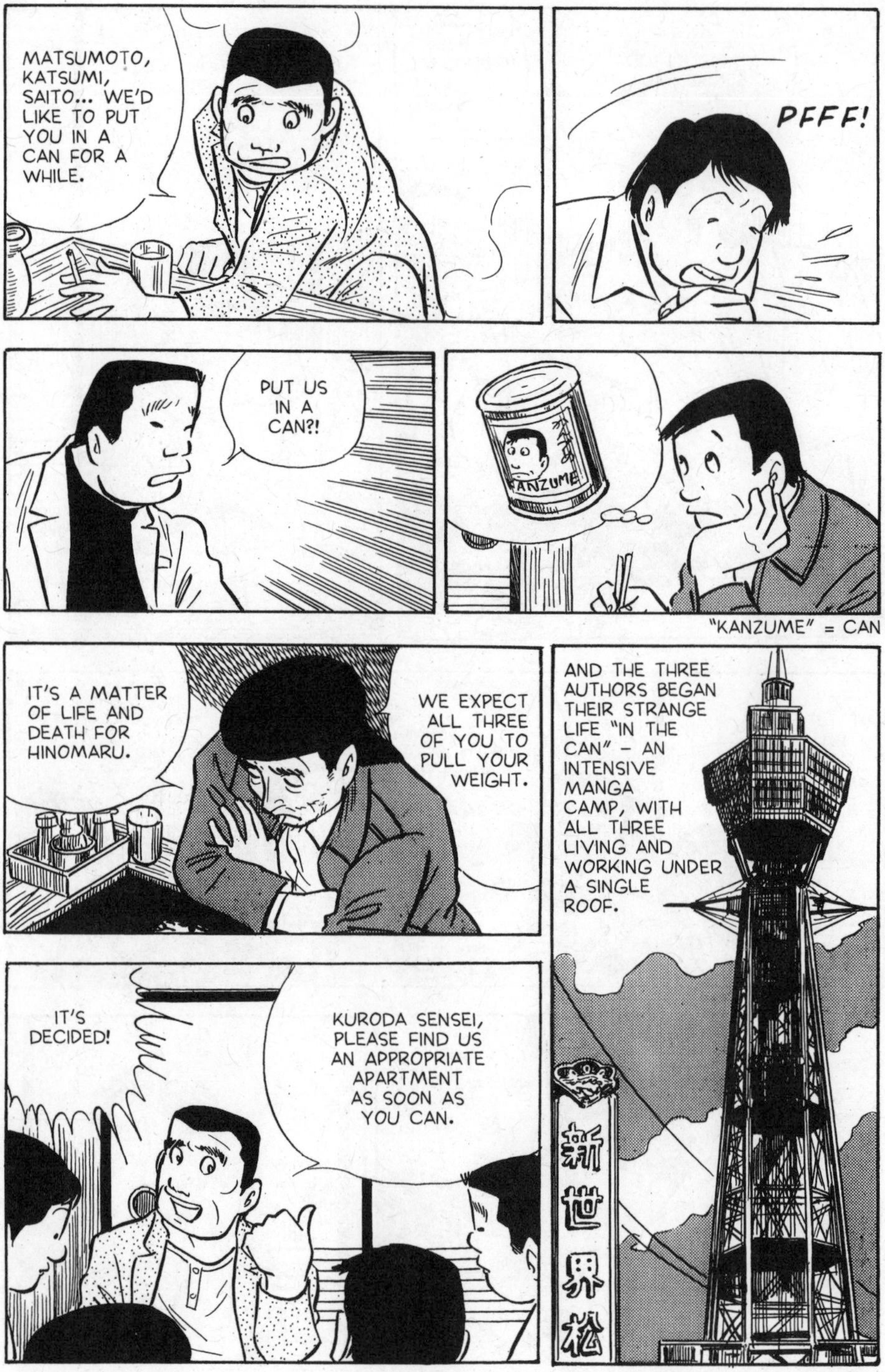
MATSUMOTO, KATSUMI, SAITO... WE'D LIKE TO PUT YOU IN A CAN FOR A WHILE.
PFFF!
PUT US IN A CAN?!
KANZUME
"KANZUME" = CAN
IT'S A MATTER OF LIFE AND DEATH FOR HINOMARU.
WE EXPECT ALL THREE OF YOU TO PULL YOUR WEIGHT.
IT'S DECIDED!
KURODA SENSEI, PLEASE FIND US AN APPROPRIATE APARTMENT AS SOON AS YOU CAN.
AND THE THREE AUTHORS BEGAN THEIR STRANGE LIFE "IN THE CAN" – AN INTENSIVE MANGA CAMP, WITH ALL THREE LIVING AND WORKING UNDER A SINGLE ROOF.
新世界松

SUMMER TRAINING CAMP

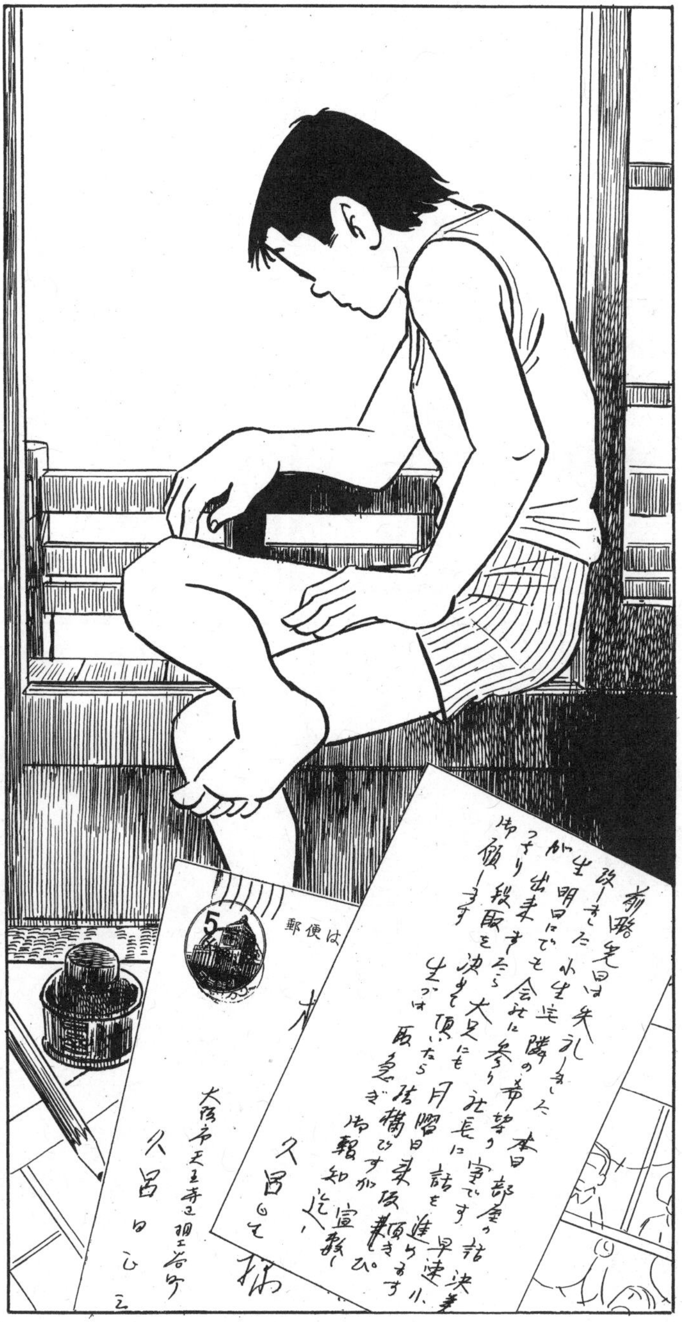
郵便は

(A POSTCARD SENT TO MASAHIKO MATSUMOTO FROM MASAMI KURODA IN AUGUST 1956)

PLEASE EXCUSE ME FOR MY BEHAVIOR THE OTHER DAY. I HAVE FOUND A ROOM IN A BUILDING NEXT TO MY HOME. I SHALL GO IN TO THE OFFICE AS SOON AS TOMORROW, AND TELL THE BOSS ABOUT THE PROCEEDINGS, BUT I SHALL BE VERY GRATEFUL IF YOU COULD COME ON MONDAY TO FINALIZE YOUR ARRANGEMENT.

MASAMI KURODA

JULY 1956

THE ECONOMIC PLANNING AGENCY PUBLISHED ITS ECONOMIC SURVEY, WHICH DECLARED THAT JAPAN WAS "NO LONGER IN THE POSTWAR PERIOD."

A DECADE HAD PASSED SINCE THE END OF WWII, AND JAPAN WAS ABOUT TO ENTER ITS PERIOD OF HIGH ECONOMIC GROWTH.

MEMBERS OF THE "SUN TRIBE," AND GIRLS IN UM-BRELLA SKIRTS FILLED THE BRIGHTLY-LIT CITY STREETS.

SHIINAMACHI, TOSHIMA-KU, TOKYO

⟨SOUND OF CICADAS⟩

462

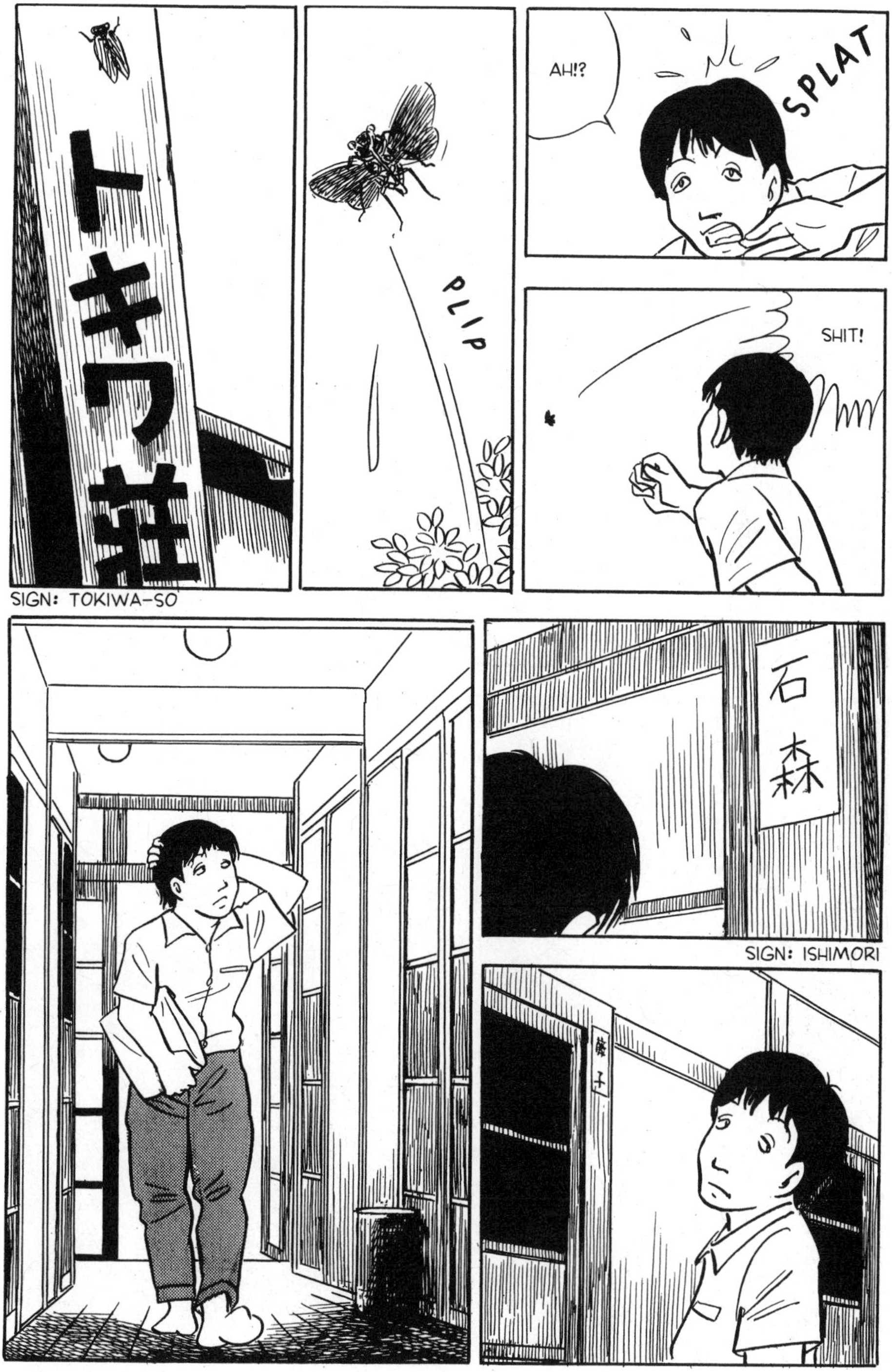
トキワ荘
SIGN: TOKIWA-SO
PLIP
AH!?
SPLAT
SHIT!
石森
SIGN: ISHIMORI

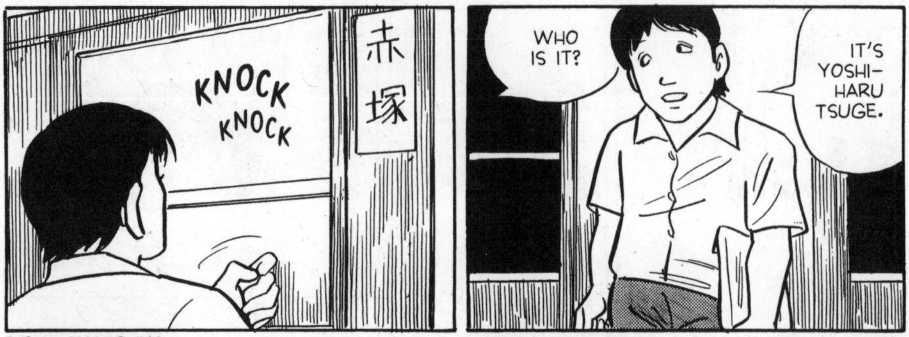
KNOCK
KNOCK
WHO IS IT?
IT'S YOSHI-HARU TSUGE.

SIGN: AKATSUKA

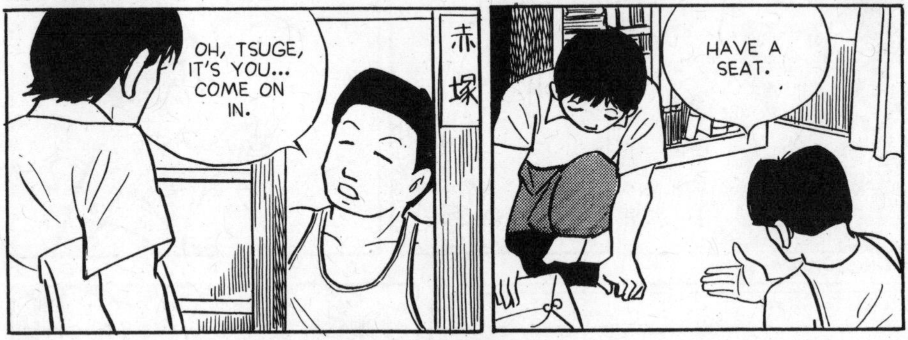
OH, TSUGE, IT'S YOU... COME ON IN.
HAVE A SEAT.

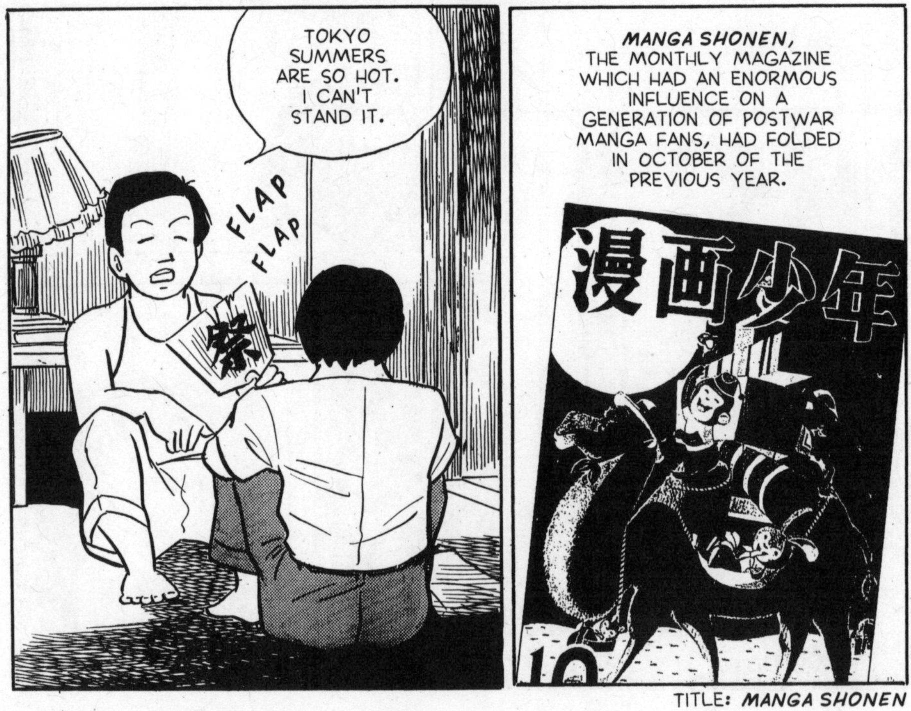
TOKYO SUMMERS ARE SO HOT. I CAN'T STAND IT.
FLAP
FLAP
MANGA SHONEN, THE MONTHLY MAGAZINE WHICH HAD AN ENORMOUS INFLUENCE ON A GENERATION OF POSTWAR MANGA FANS, HAD FOLDED IN OCTOBER OF THE PREVIOUS YEAR.
漫画少年
10

TITLE: *MANGA SHONEN*

HIROO TERADA AND SHOTARO ISHIMORI, WHO WERE PUBLISHING WORK IN *MANGA SHONEN*, HAD MOVED IN TO TOKIWA-SO AFTER OSAMU TEZUKA HAD MOVED OUT. LATER, FUJIKO FUJIO, FUJIO AKATSUKA, AND JIRO TSUNODA ALSO MOVED IN AND STARTED A NEW MANGA MOVEMENT.

TITLE: "MAKKURO-KUN: THE ADVENTURES OF A 2ND CLASS ANGEL"

"GUNSHOTS AT DAWN," HUH?

IT'S MY NEW BOOK.

TITLE: *GUNSHOTS AT DAWN*

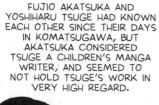

FUJIO AKATSUKA AND YOSHIHARU TSUGE HAD KNOWN EACH OTHER SINCE THEIR DAYS IN KOMATSUGAWA, BUT AKATSUKA CONSIDERED TSUGE A CHILDREN'S MANGA WRITER, AND SEEMED TO NOT HOLD TSUGE'S WORK IN VERY HIGH REGARD.

YAWN

FLIP

THUD
THUD

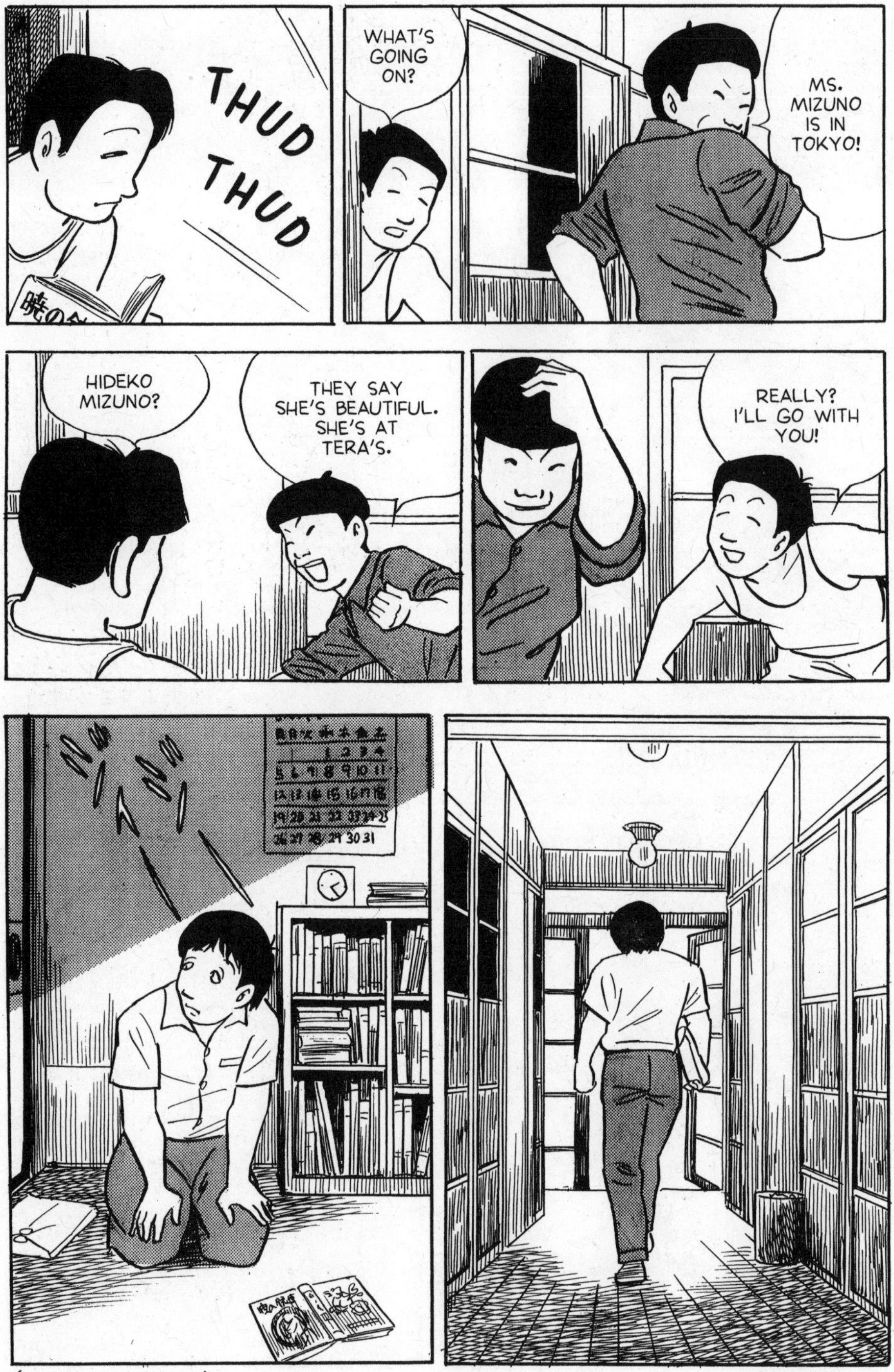
THUD
THUD
WHAT'S GOING ON?
MS. MIZUNO IS IN TOKYO!
HIDEKO MIZUNO?
THEY SAY SHE'S BEAUTIFUL. SHE'S AT TERA'S.
REALLY? I'LL GO WITH YOU!

<SOUND OF CICADAS>

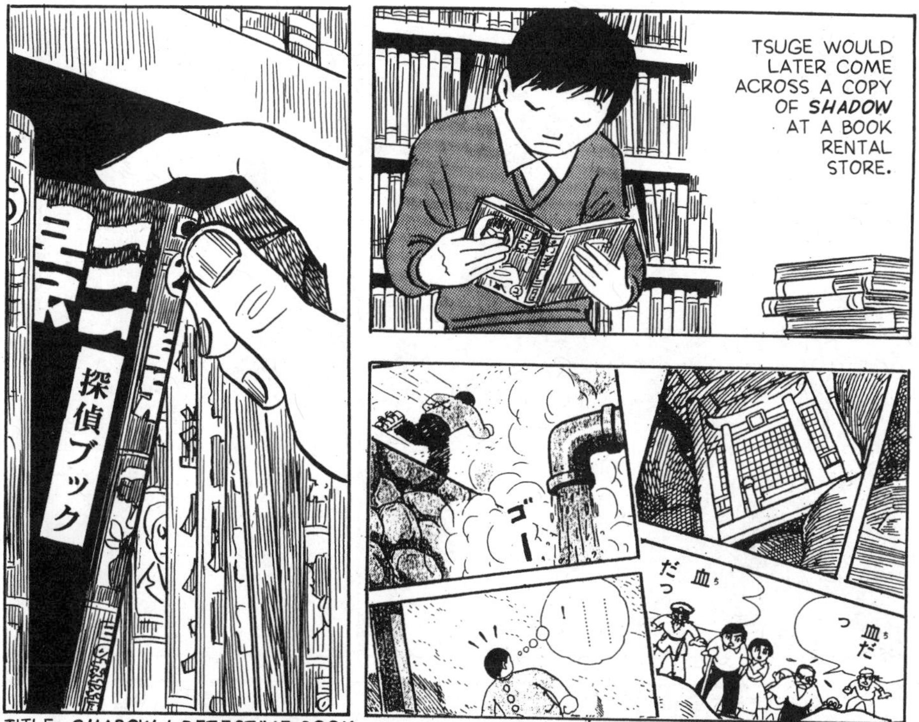
探偵ブック
TSUGE WOULD LATER COME ACROSS A COPY OF SHADOW AT A BOOK RENTAL STORE.
ゴー
!
血だっ
血だっ
TITLE: ***SHADOW I DETECTIVE BOOK***

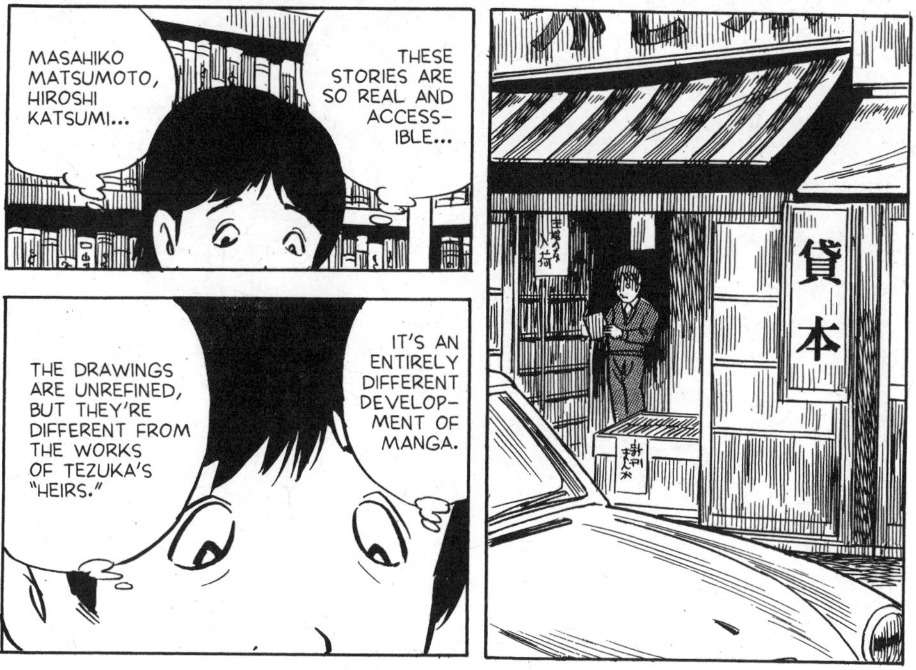
MASAHIKO MATSUMOTO, HIROSHI KATSUMI...
THESE STORIES ARE SO REAL AND ACCESSIBLE...
THE DRAWINGS ARE UNREFINED, BUT THEY'RE DIFFERENT FROM THE WORKS OF TEZUKA'S "HEIRS."
IT'S AN ENTIRELY DIFFERENT DEVELOPMENT OF MANGA.
貸本

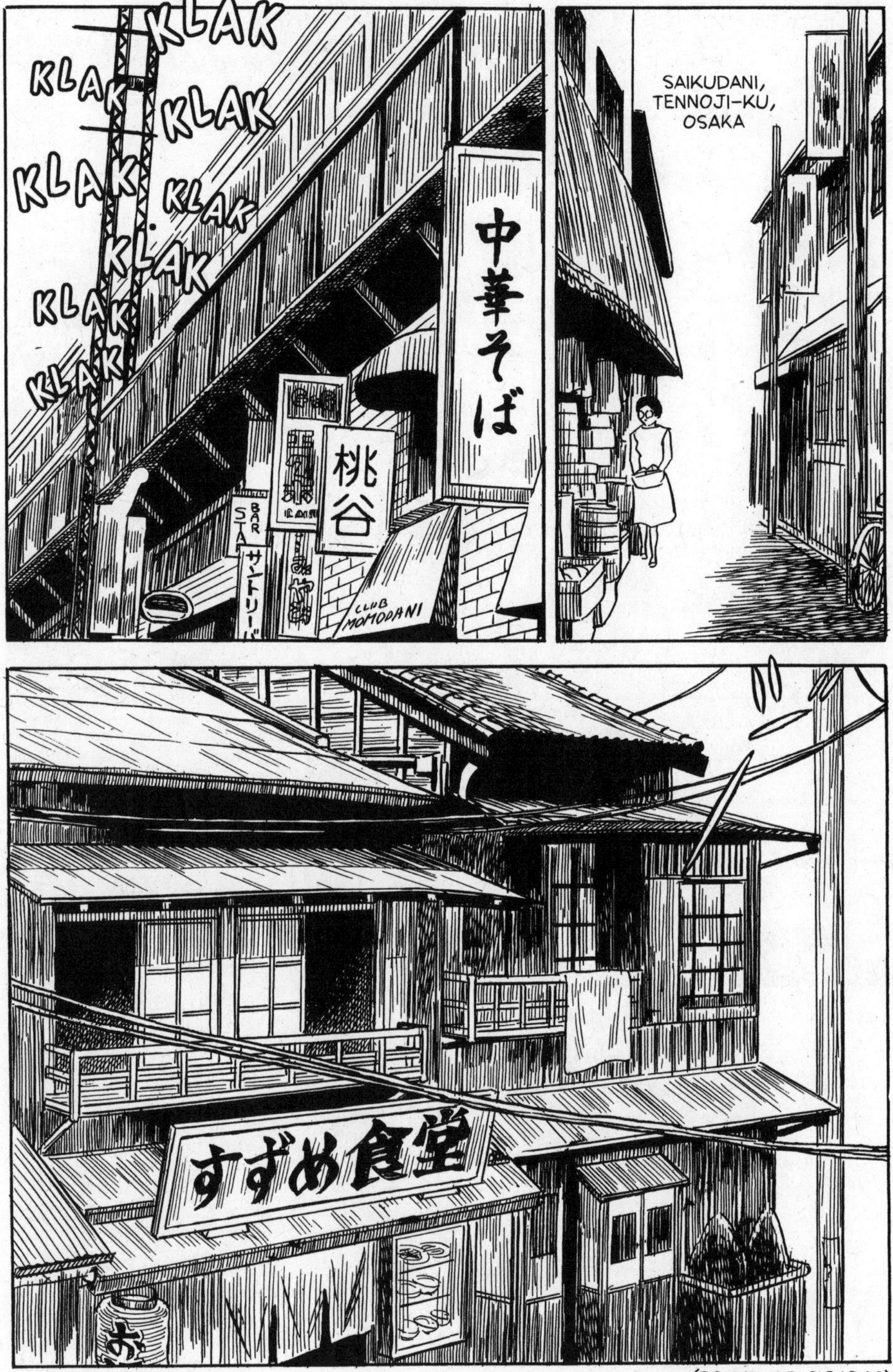
KLAK
KLAK
KLAK
KLAK
KLAK
KLAK
KLAK
KLAK
中華そば
桃谷
CLUB MOMODANI
SAIKUDANI, TENNOJI-KU, OSAKA
すずめ食堂

SIGN: SUZUME DINER

〈SOUND OF CICADAS〉

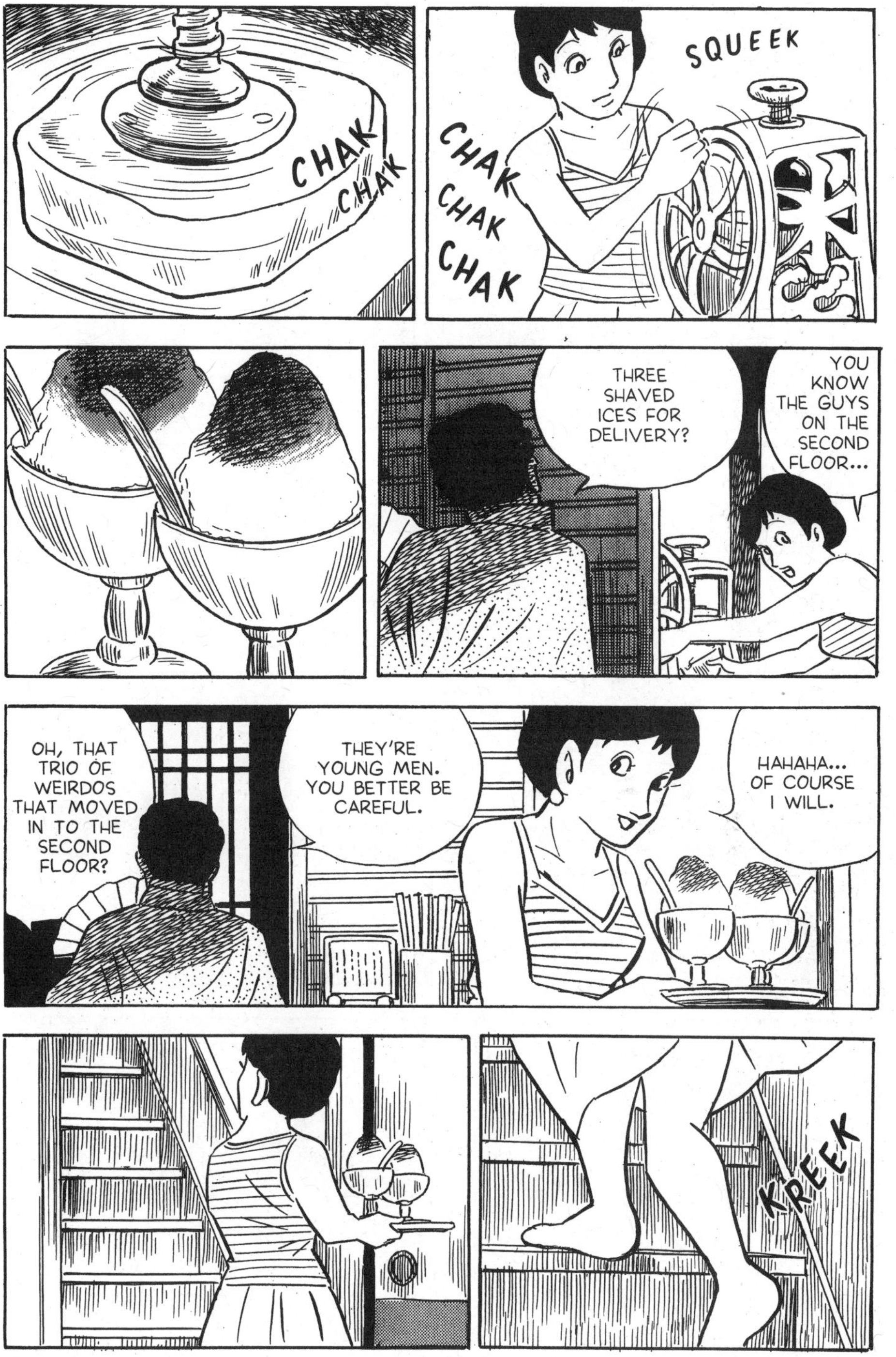

CHAK
CHAK
SQUEEK
CHAK
CHAK
CHAK
THREE SHAVED ICES FOR DELIVERY?
YOU KNOW THE GUYS ON THE SECOND FLOOR...
OH, THAT TRIO OF WEIRDOS THAT MOVED IN TO THE SECOND FLOOR?
THEY'RE YOUNG MEN. YOU BETTER BE CAREFUL.
HAHAHA... OF COURSE I WILL.
KREEK

⟨SOUND OF CICADAS⟩

IT'S SO HOT.

FLAP FLAP

HERE YOU ARE.

OH, I'VE BEEN LOOKING FORWARD TO THESE!

MM-MM...

NOTHING LIKE SHAVED ICE IN THE SUMMER.

OWW!

I ATE IT TOO FAST. MY HEAD IS KILLING ME!

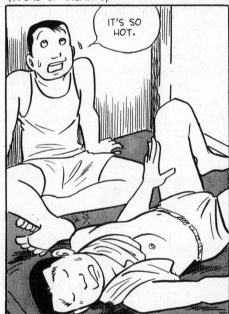

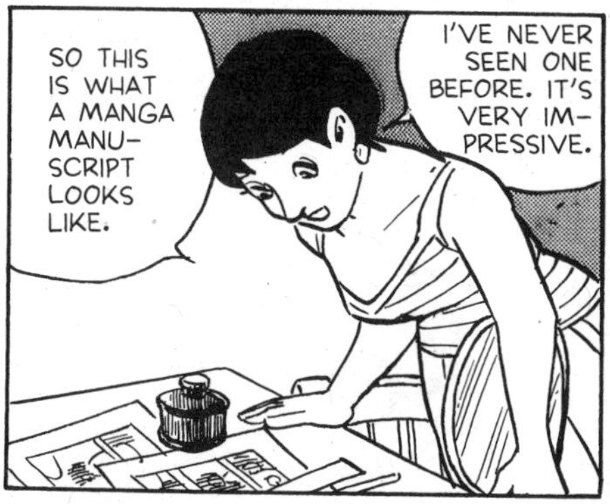
SO THIS IS WHAT A MANGA MANU-SCRIPT LOOKS LIKE.
I'VE NEVER SEEN ONE BEFORE. IT'S VERY IM-PRESSIVE.
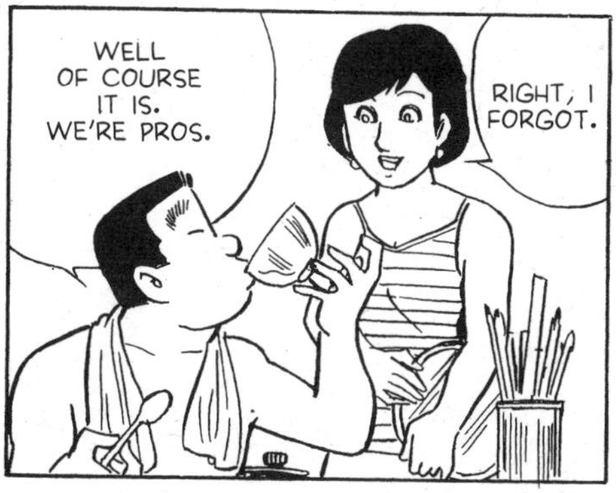
WELL OF COURSE IT IS. WE'RE PROS.
RIGHT, I FORGOT.
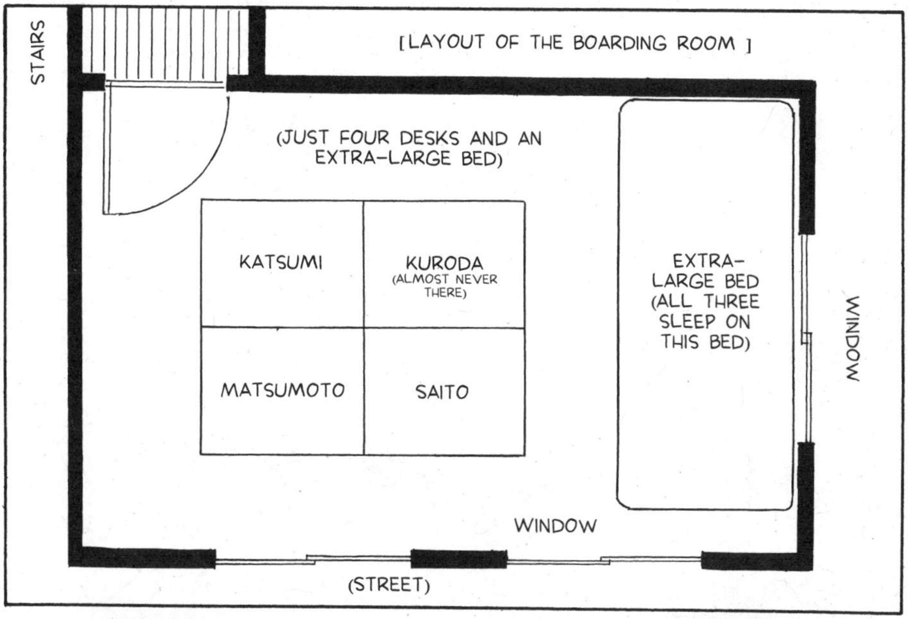
[LAYOUT OF THE BOARDING ROOM]
STAIRS
(JUST FOUR DESKS AND AN EXTRA-LARGE BED)
KATSUMI
KURODA (ALMOST NEVER THERE)
MATSUMOTO
SAITO
EXTRA-LARGE BED (ALL THREE SLEEP ON THIS BED)
WINDOW
WINDOW
(STREET)
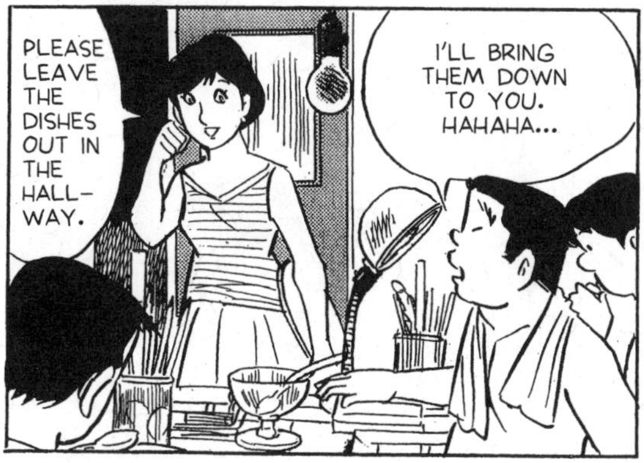
PLEASE LEAVE THE DISHES OUT IN THE HALL-WAY.
I'LL BRING THEM DOWN TO YOU. HAHAHA...
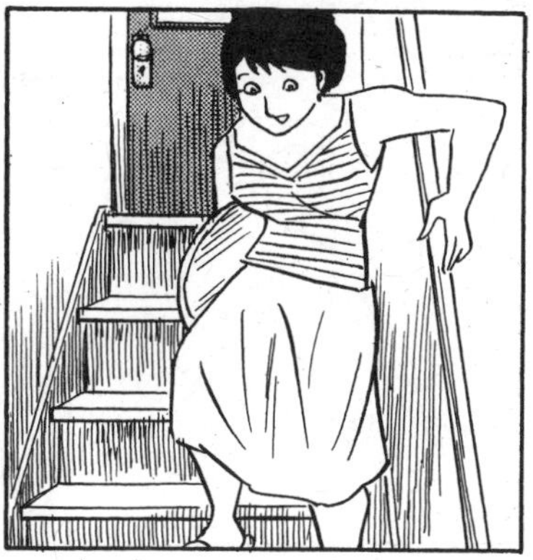

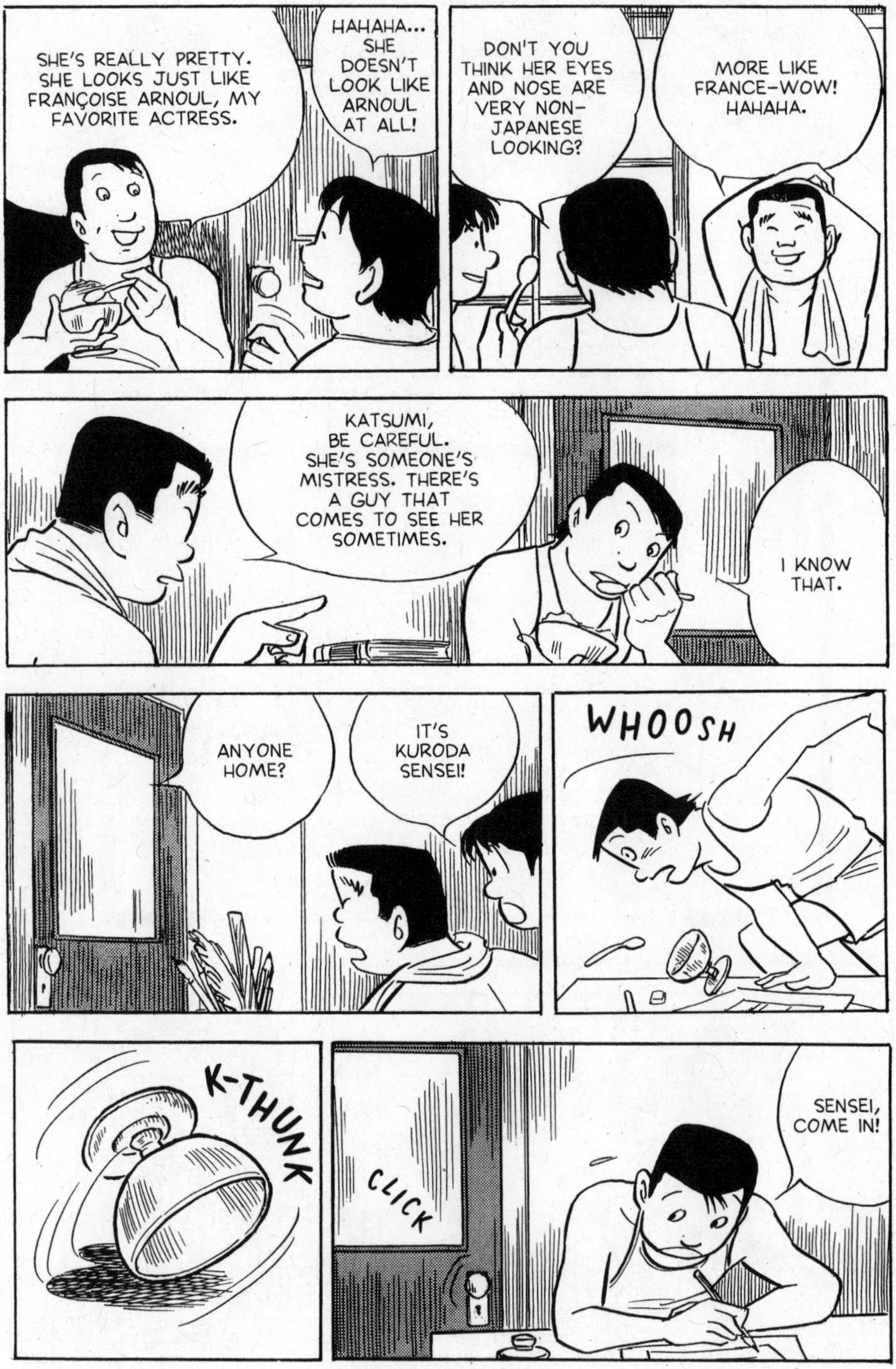
SHE'S REALLY PRETTY. SHE LOOKS JUST LIKE FRANÇOISE ARNOUL, MY FAVORITE ACTRESS.
HAHAHA... SHE DOESN'T LOOK LIKE ARNOUL AT ALL!
DON'T YOU THINK HER EYES AND NOSE ARE VERY NON-JAPANESE LOOKING?
MORE LIKE FRANCE-WOW! HAHAHA.
KATSUMI, BE CAREFUL. SHE'S SOMEONE'S MISTRESS. THERE'S A GUY THAT COMES TO SEE HER SOMETIMES.
I KNOW THAT.
ANYONE HOME?
IT'S KURODA SENSEI!
WHOOSH
K-THUNK
CLICK
SENSEI, COME IN!

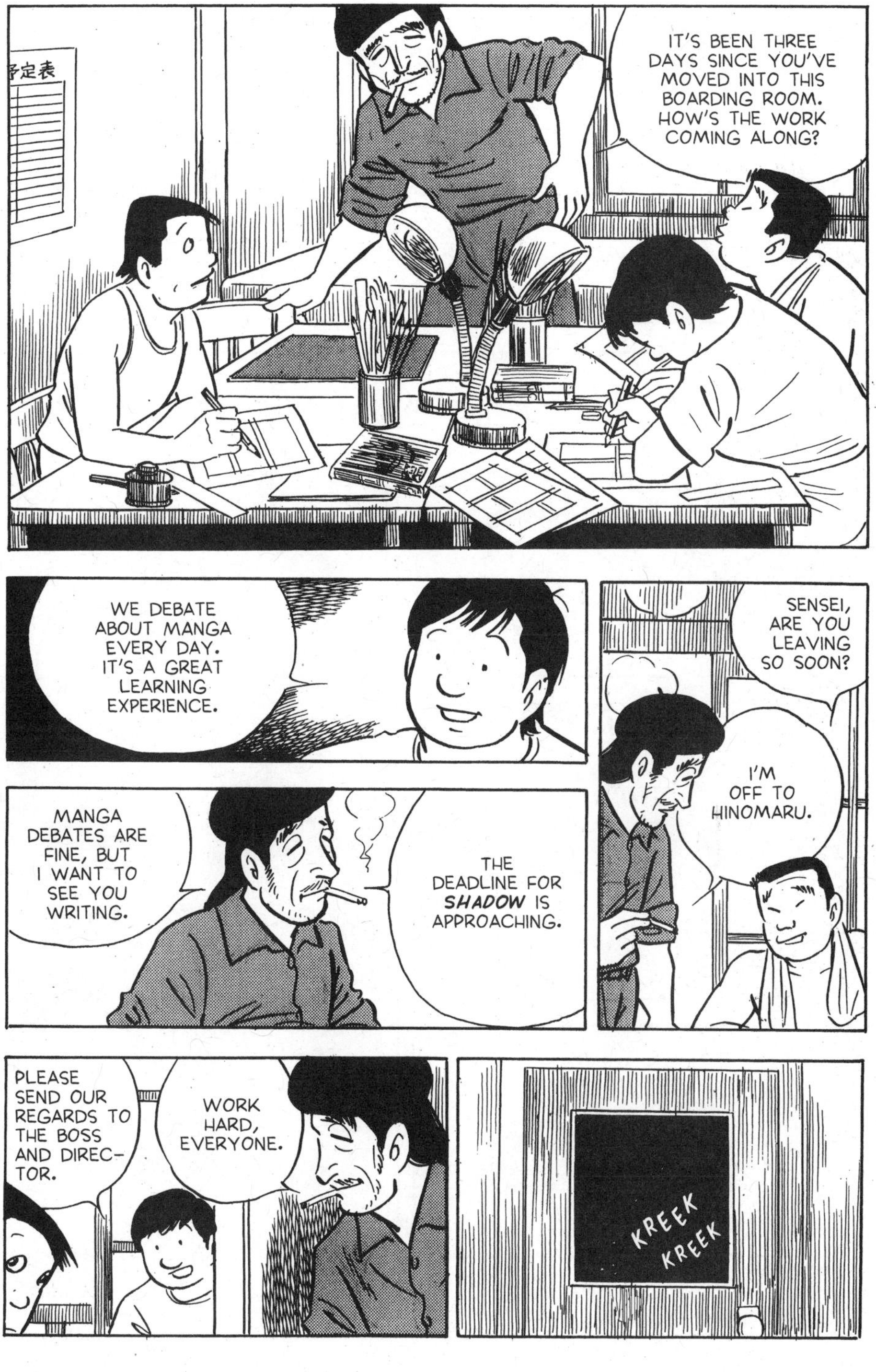
予定表
IT'S BEEN THREE DAYS SINCE YOU'VE MOVED INTO THIS BOARDING ROOM. HOW'S THE WORK COMING ALONG?
WE DEBATE ABOUT MANGA EVERY DAY. IT'S A GREAT LEARNING EXPERIENCE.
MANGA DEBATES ARE FINE, BUT I WANT TO SEE YOU WRITING.
THE DEADLINE FOR SHADOW IS APPROACHING.
SENSEI, ARE YOU LEAVING SO SOON?
I'M OFF TO HINOMARU.
PLEASE SEND OUR REGARDS TO THE BOSS AND DIRECTOR.
WORK HARD, EVERYONE.
KREEK KREEK

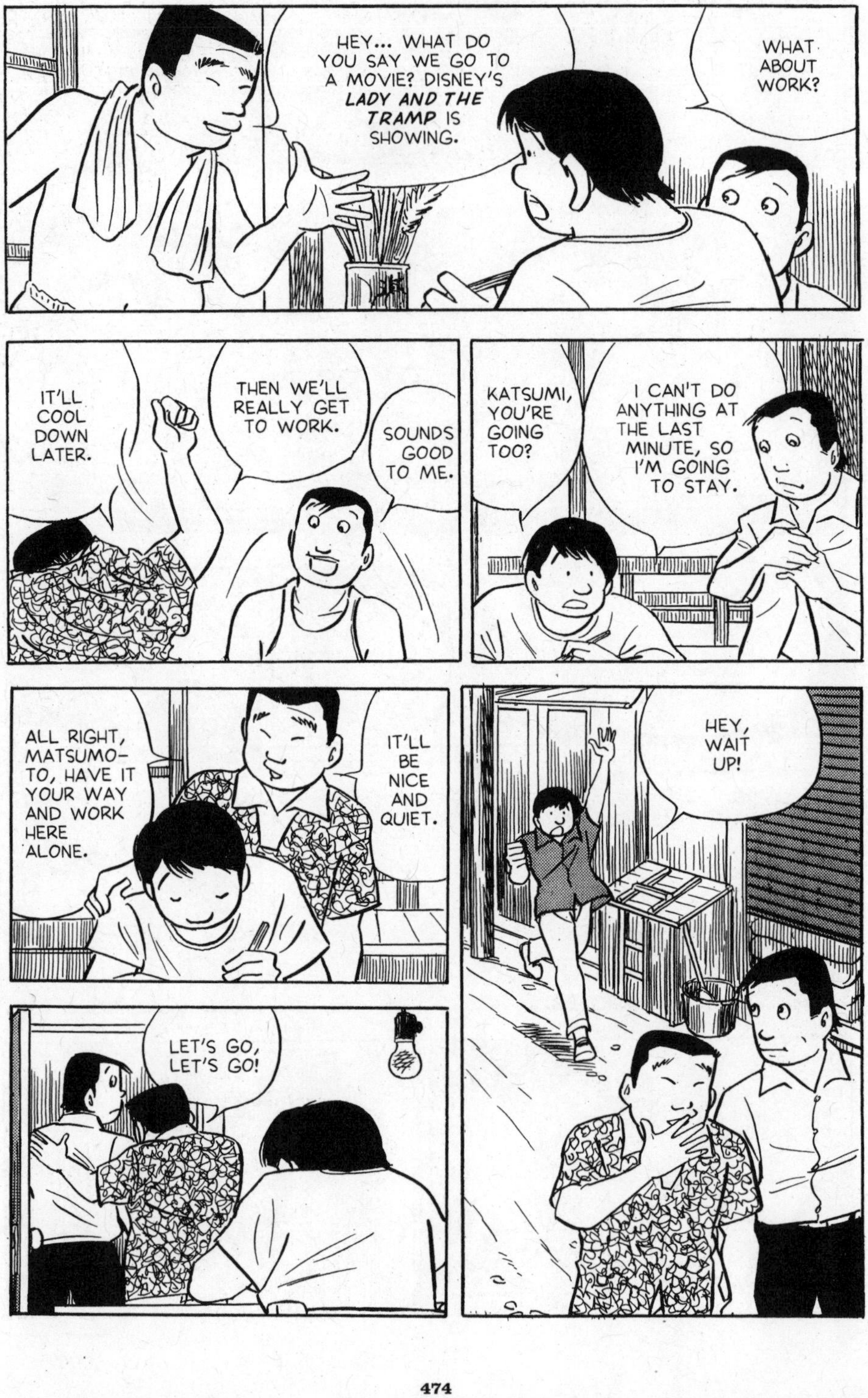
HEY... WHAT DO YOU SAY WE GO TO A MOVIE? DISNEY'S ***LADY AND THE TRAMP*** IS SHOWING.
WHAT ABOUT WORK?
IT'LL COOL DOWN LATER.
THEN WE'LL REALLY GET TO WORK.
SOUNDS GOOD TO ME.
KATSUMI, YOU'RE GOING TOO?
I CAN'T DO ANYTHING AT THE LAST MINUTE, SO I'M GOING TO STAY.
ALL RIGHT, MATSUMOTO, HAVE IT YOUR WAY AND WORK HERE ALONE.
IT'LL BE NICE AND QUIET.
HEY, WAIT UP!
LET'S GO, LET'S GO!

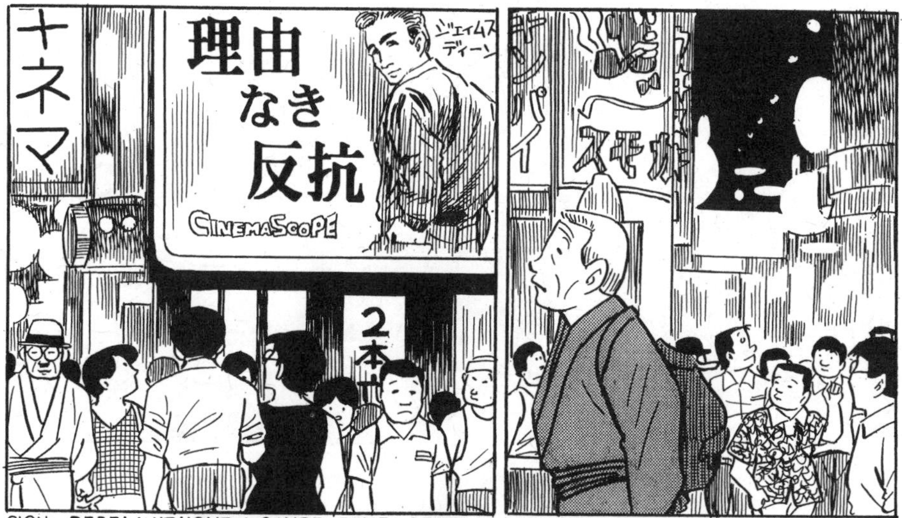
理由なき反抗
ジェイムス
ディーン
CinemaScope
2本

SIGN: *REBEL WITHOUT A CAUSE*, JAMES DEAN

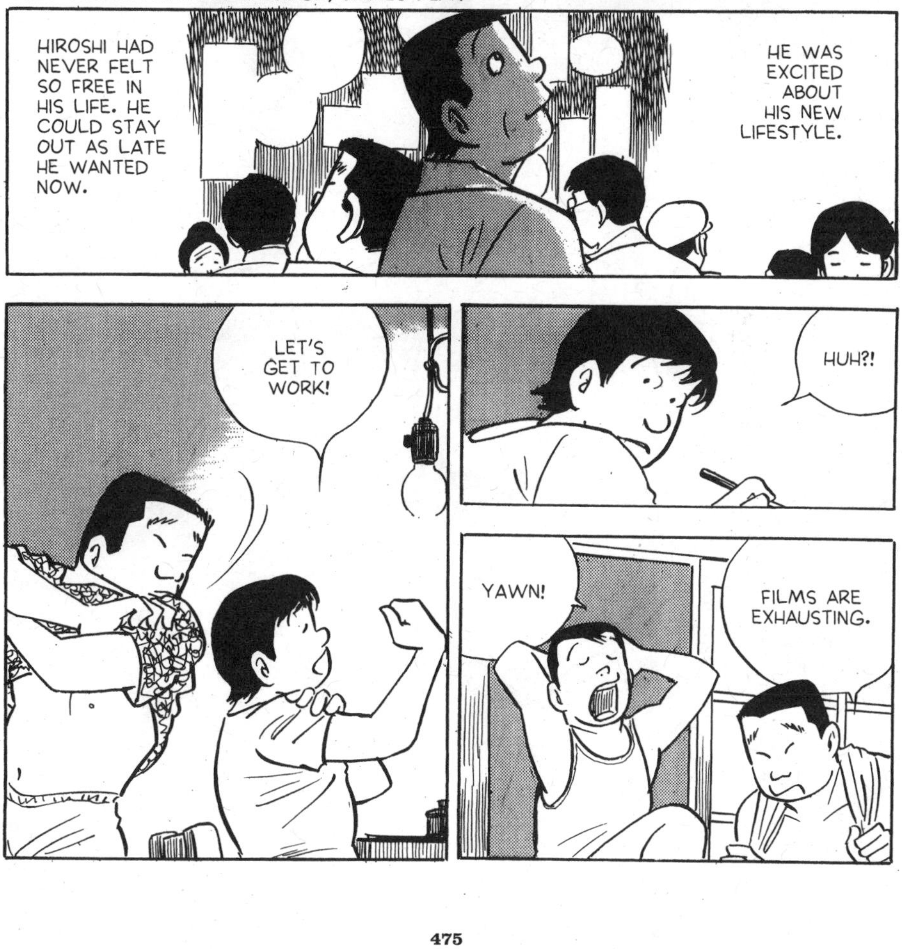
HIROSHI HAD NEVER FELT SO FREE IN HIS LIFE. HE COULD STAY OUT AS LATE HE WANTED NOW.
HE WAS EXCITED ABOUT HIS NEW LIFESTYLE.
LET'S GET TO WORK!
HUH?!
YAWN!
FILMS ARE EXHAUSTING.

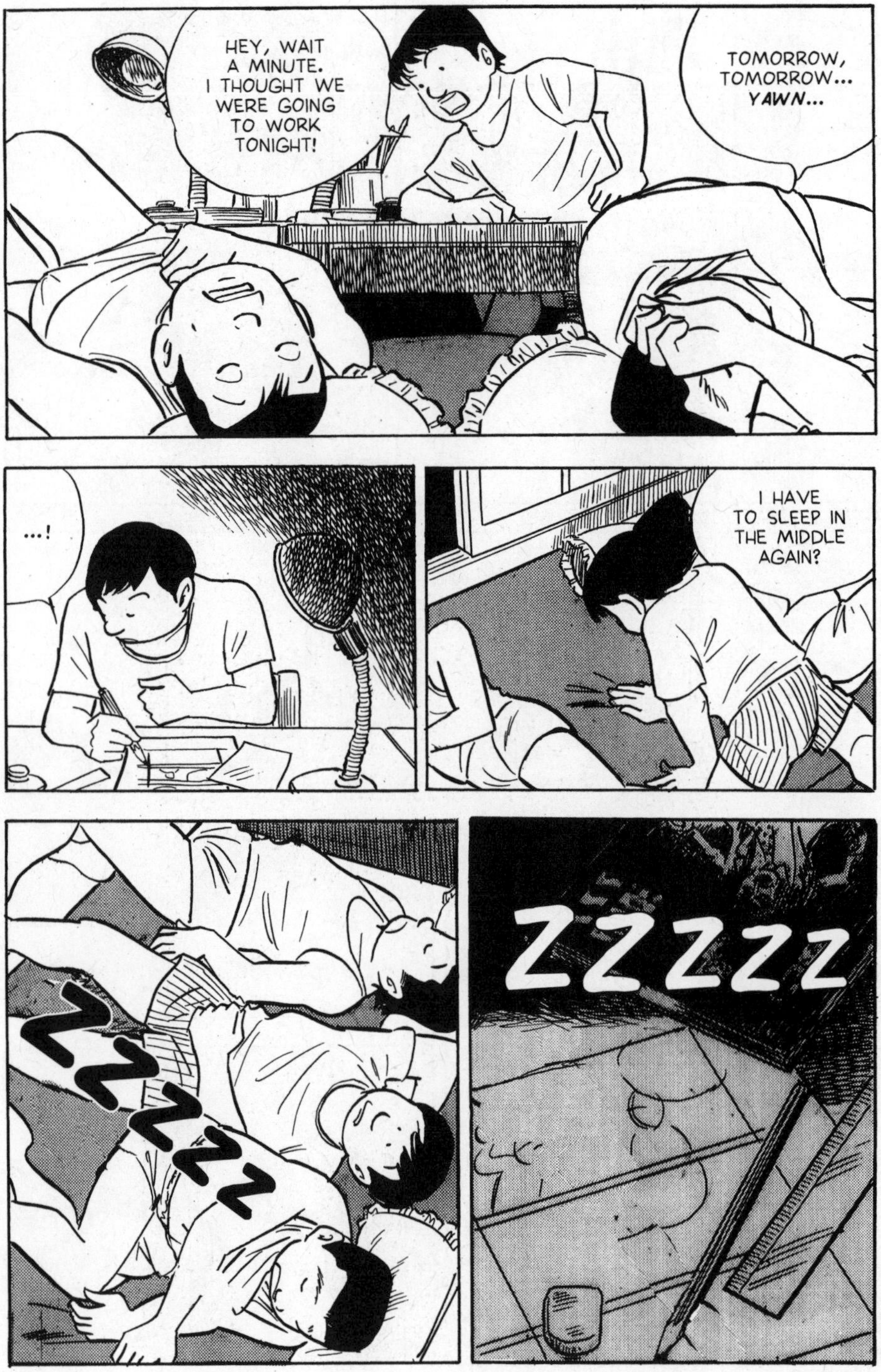
HEY, WAIT A MINUTE. I THOUGHT WE WERE GOING TO WORK TONIGHT!
TOMORROW, TOMORROW... YAWN...
...!
I HAVE TO SLEEP IN THE MIDDLE AGAIN?
ZZZZZ
ZZZZZ

IN THE BALANCE

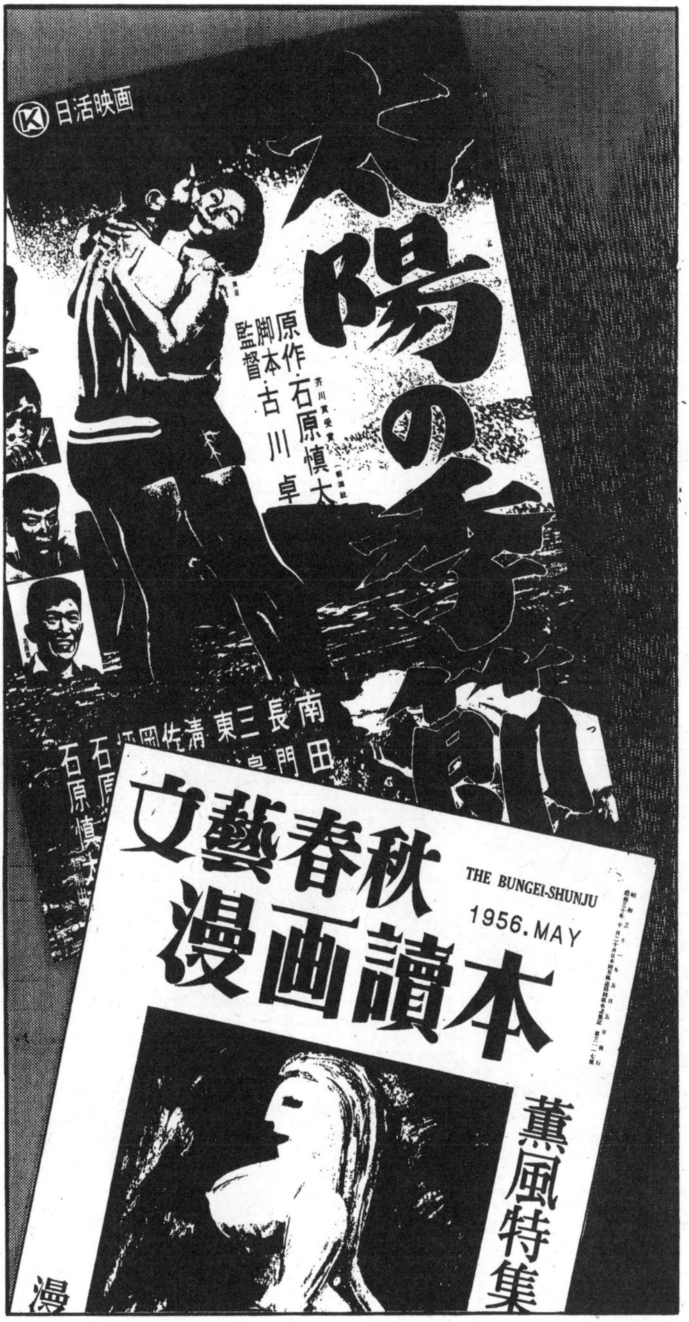
日活映画
原作·石原慎太
脚本
監督·古川卓
文藝春秋
漫画讀本
THE BUNGEI-SHUNJU
1956. MAY
薫風特集

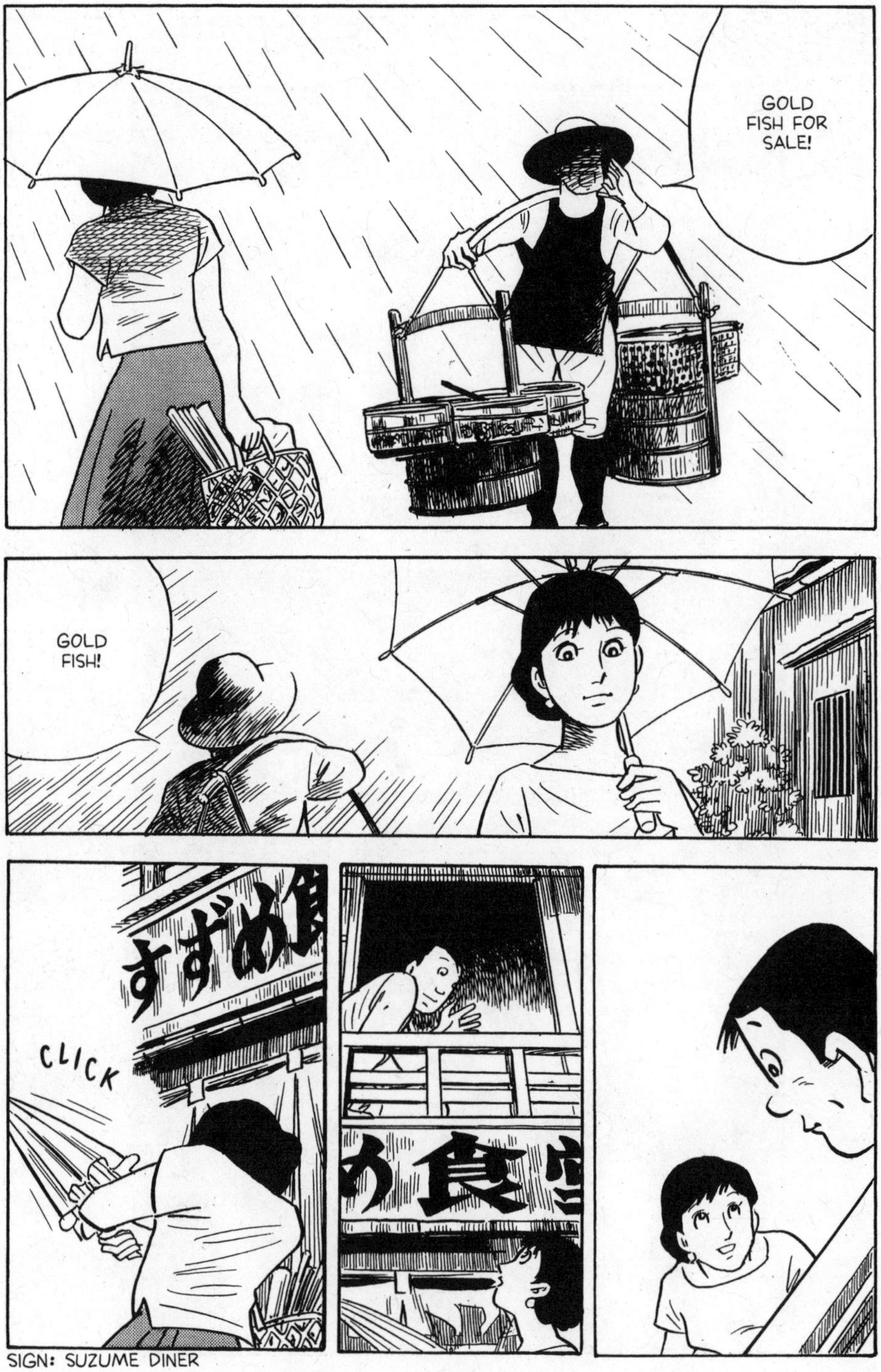
GOLD FISH FOR SALE!
GOLD FISH!
すずめ食
CLICK
め食
SIGN: SUZUME DINER

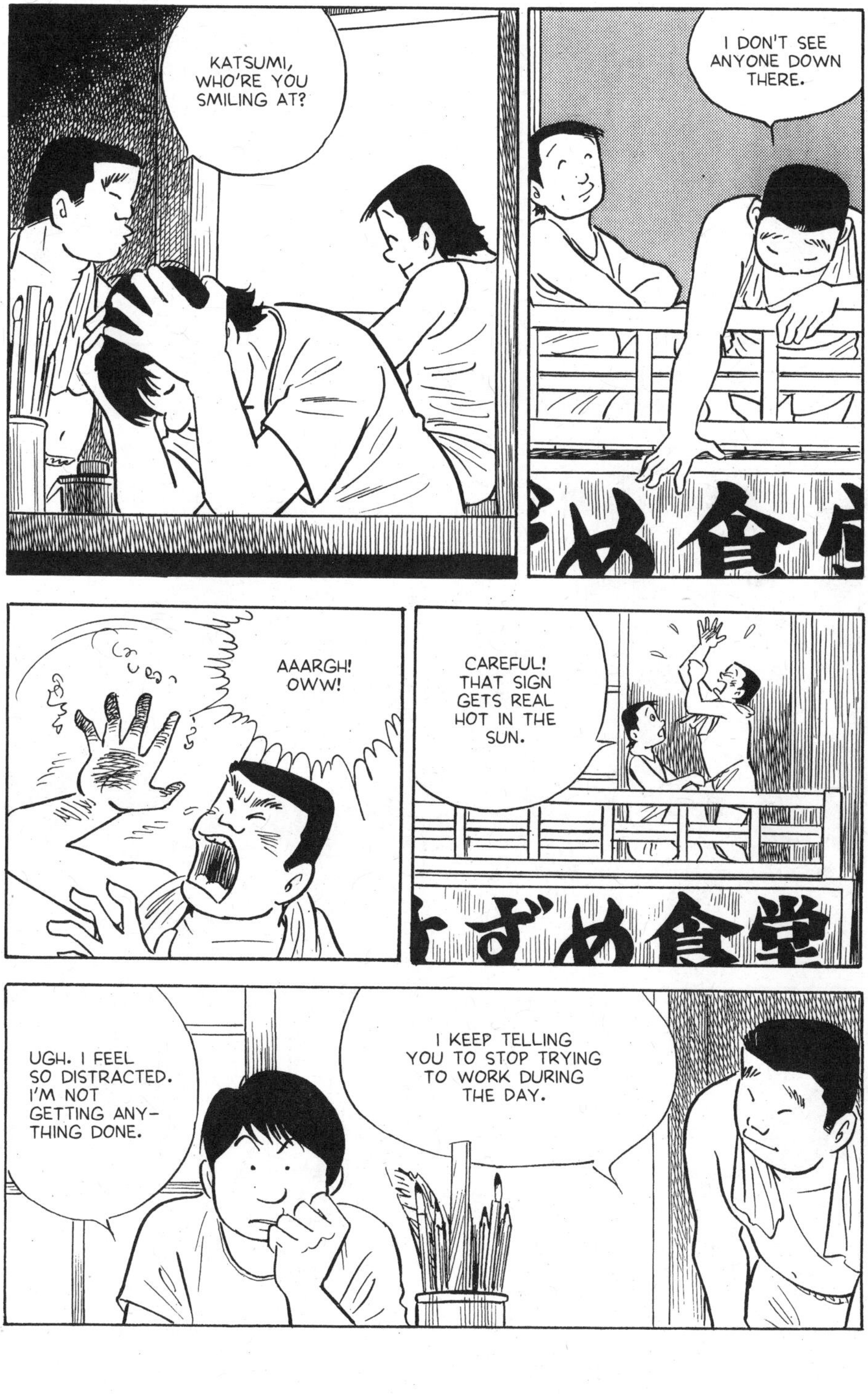
KATSUMI, WHO'RE YOU SMILING AT?
I DON'T SEE ANYONE DOWN THERE.
AAARGH! OWW!
CAREFUL! THAT SIGN GETS REAL HOT IN THE SUN.
ずめ食堂
UGH. I FEEL SO DISTRACTED. I'M NOT GETTING ANY-THING DONE.
I KEEP TELLING YOU TO STOP TRYING TO WORK DURING THE DAY.

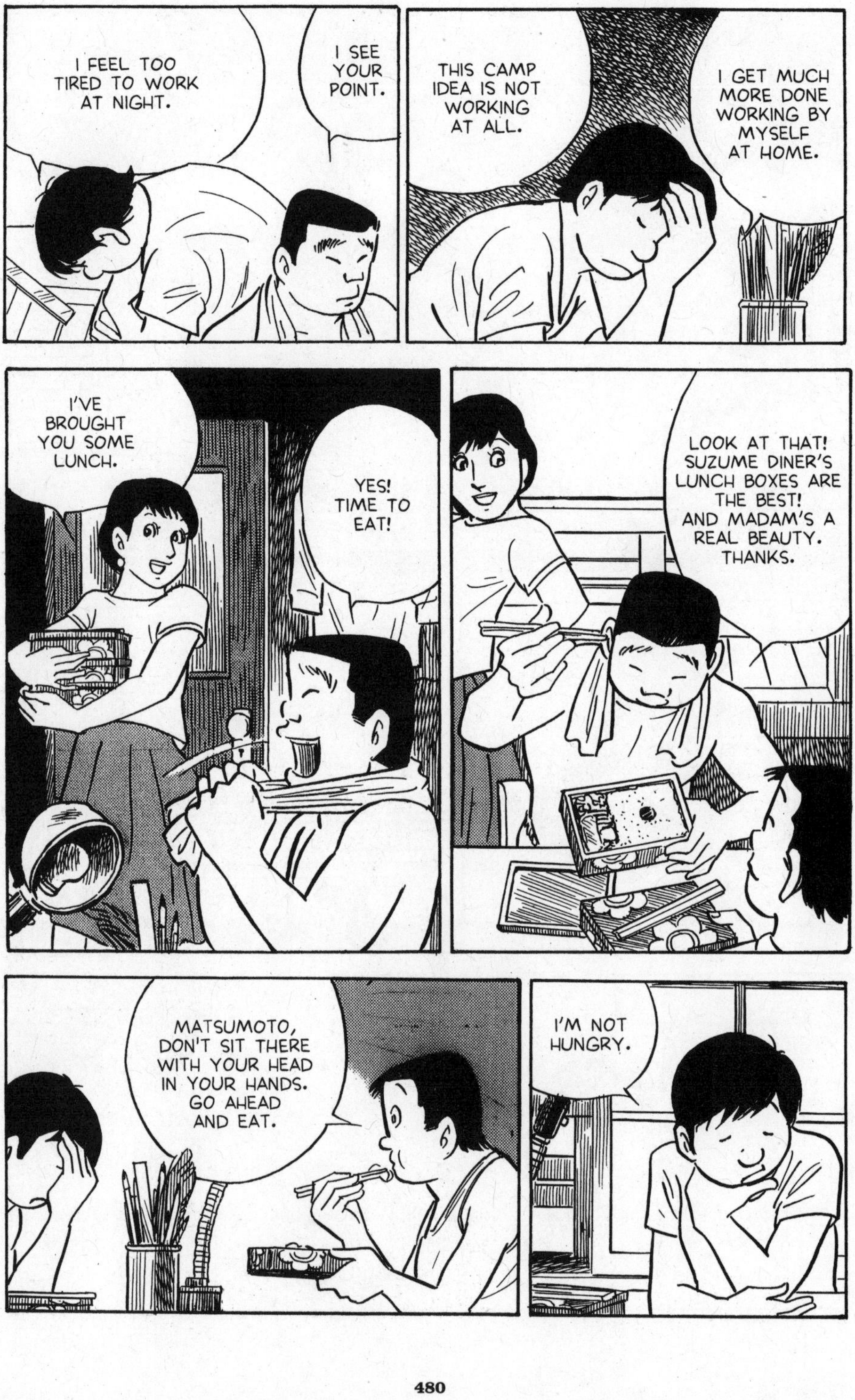
I FEEL TOO TIRED TO WORK AT NIGHT.
I SEE YOUR POINT.
THIS CAMP IDEA IS NOT WORKING AT ALL.
I GET MUCH MORE DONE WORKING BY MYSELF AT HOME.
I'VE BROUGHT YOU SOME LUNCH.
YES! TIME TO EAT!
LOOK AT THAT! SUZUME DINER'S LUNCH BOXES ARE THE BEST! AND MADAM'S A REAL BEAUTY. THANKS.
MATSUMOTO, DON'T SIT THERE WITH YOUR HEAD IN YOUR HANDS. GO AHEAD AND EAT.
I'M NOT HUNGRY.

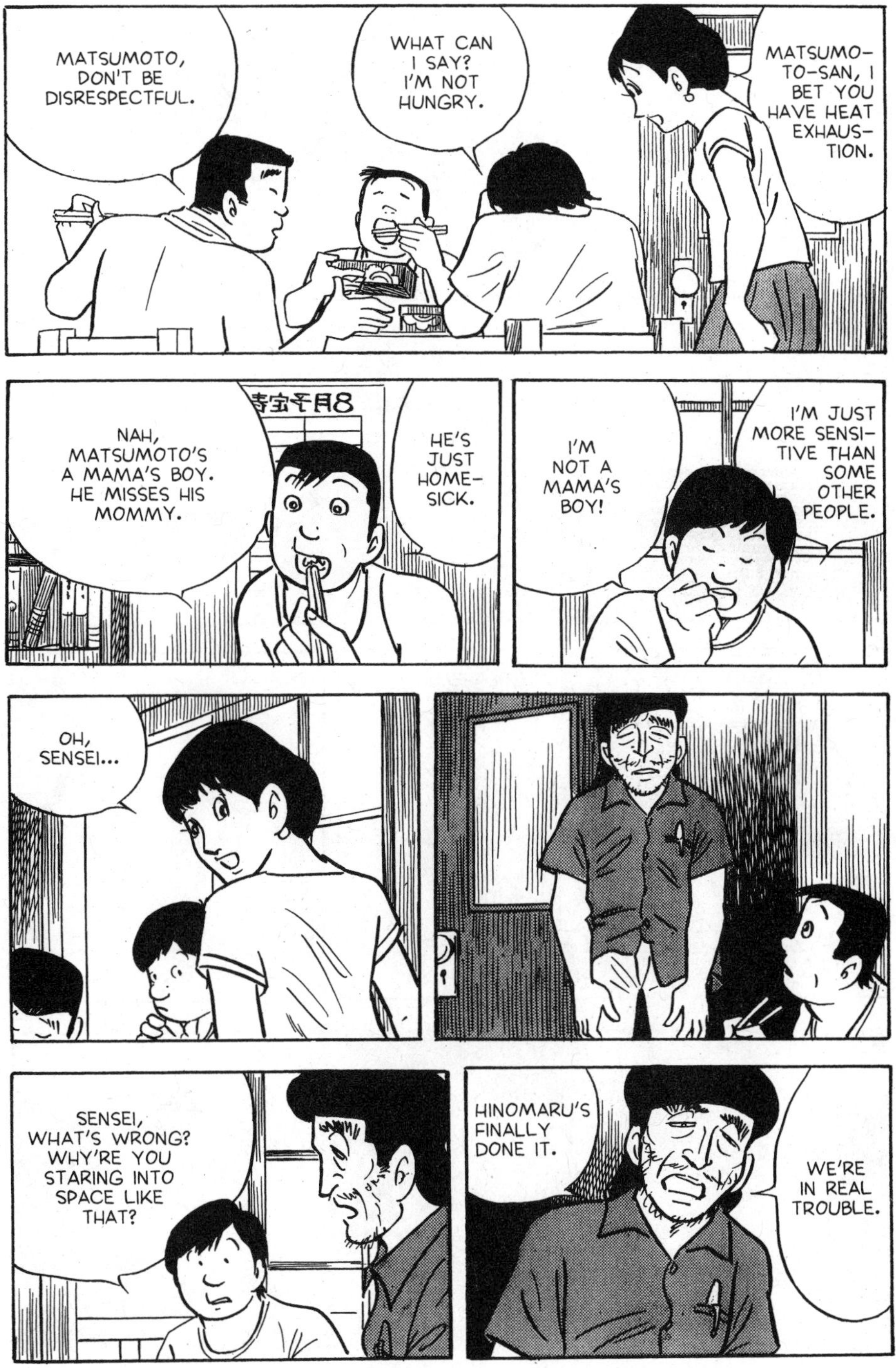
MATSUMOTO, DON'T BE DISRESPECTFUL.
WHAT CAN I SAY? I'M NOT HUNGRY.
MATSUMOTO-SAN, I BET YOU HAVE HEAT EXHAUSTION.
NAH, MATSUMOTO'S A MAMA'S BOY. HE MISSES HIS MOMMY.
HE'S JUST HOMESICK.
I'M NOT A MAMA'S BOY!
I'M JUST MORE SENSITIVE THAN SOME OTHER PEOPLE.
OH, SENSEI...
SENSEI, WHAT'S WRONG? WHY'RE YOU STARING INTO SPACE LIKE THAT?
HINOMARU'S FINALLY DONE IT.
WE'RE IN REAL TROUBLE.

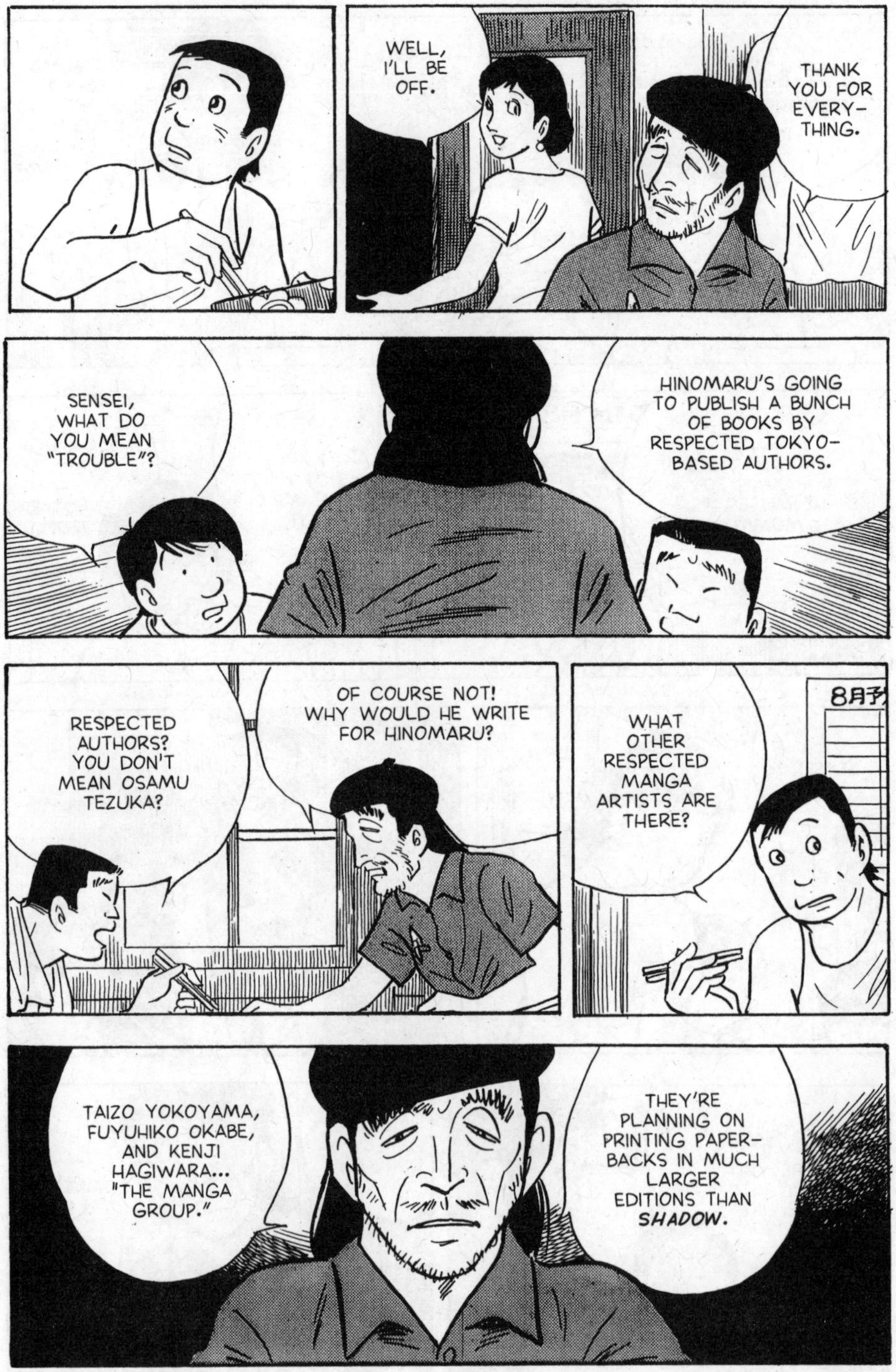

WELL, I'LL BE OFF.
THANK YOU FOR EVERY-THING.
SENSEI, WHAT DO YOU MEAN "TROUBLE"?
HINOMARU'S GOING TO PUBLISH A BUNCH OF BOOKS BY RESPECTED TOKYO-BASED AUTHORS.
RESPECTED AUTHORS? YOU DON'T MEAN OSAMU TEZUKA?
OF COURSE NOT! WHY WOULD HE WRITE FOR HINOMARU?
WHAT OTHER RESPECTED MANGA ARTISTS ARE THERE?
TAIZO YOKOYAMA, FUYUHIKO OKABE, AND KENJI HAGIWARA... "THE MANGA GROUP."
THEY'RE PLANNING ON PRINTING PAPER-BACKS IN MUCH LARGER EDITIONS THAN **SHADOW**.

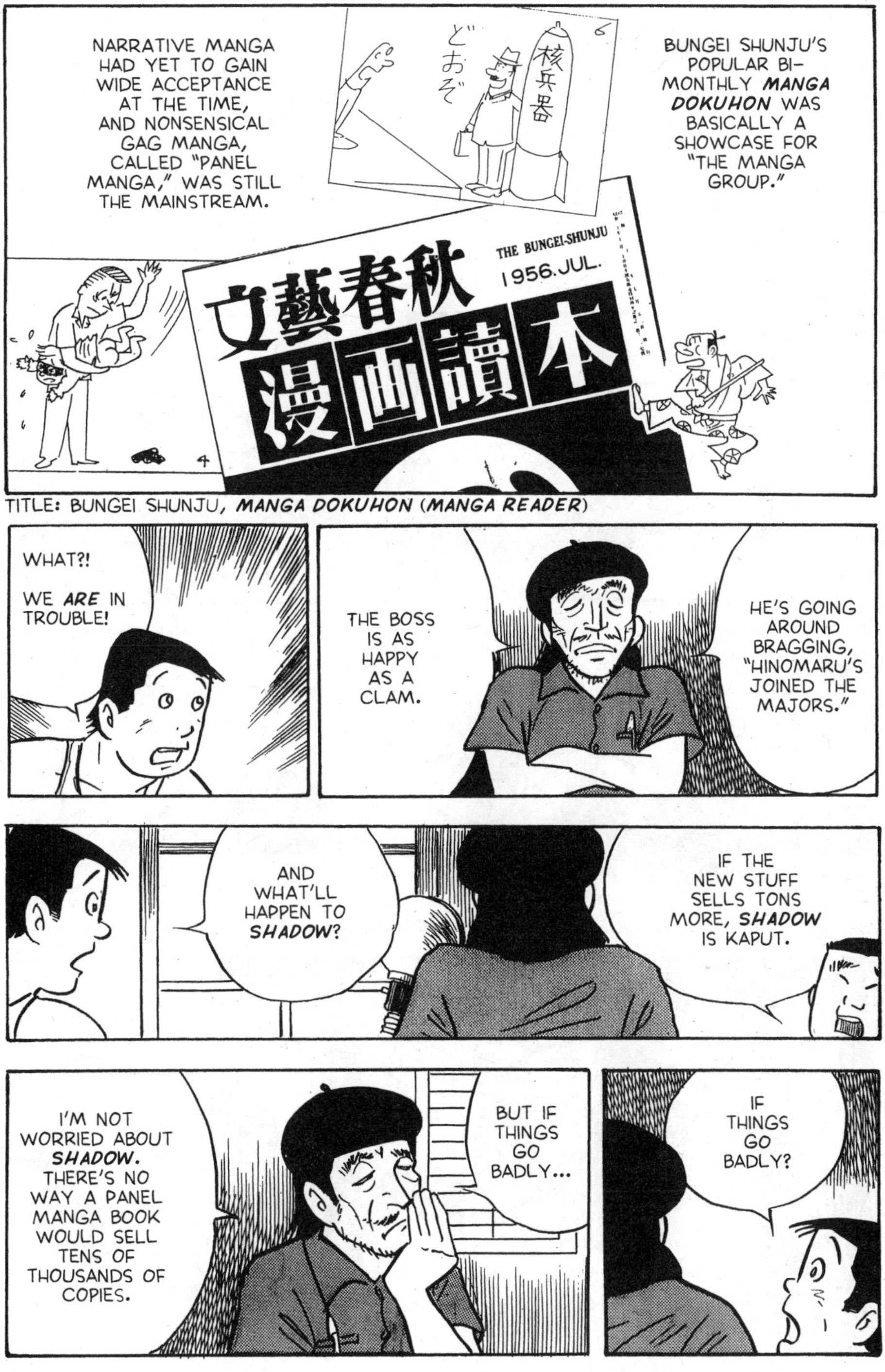

NARRATIVE MANGA HAD YET TO GAIN WIDE ACCEPTANCE AT THE TIME, AND NONSENSICAL GAG MANGA, CALLED "PANEL MANGA," WAS STILL THE MAINSTREAM.
どおぞ
核兵器
BUNGEI SHUNJU'S POPULAR BI-MONTHLY ***MANGA DOKUHON*** WAS BASICALLY A SHOWCASE FOR "THE MANGA GROUP."
THE BUNGEI-SHUNJU
1956.JUL.
文藝春秋
漫画讀本
TITLE: BUNGEI SHUNJU, ***MANGA DOKUHON*** (***MANGA READER***)
WHAT?!
WE ***ARE*** IN TROUBLE!
THE BOSS IS AS HAPPY AS A CLAM.
HE'S GOING AROUND BRAGGING, "HINOMARU'S JOINED THE MAJORS."
AND WHAT'LL HAPPEN TO ***SHADOW***?
IF THE NEW STUFF SELLS TONS MORE, ***SHADOW*** IS KAPUT.
I'M NOT WORRIED ABOUT ***SHADOW***. THERE'S NO WAY A PANEL MANGA BOOK WOULD SELL TENS OF THOUSANDS OF COPIES.
BUT IF THINGS GO BADLY...
IF THINGS GO BADLY?

HINOMARU ITSELF COULD BE AT RISK.

GASP!

WE'LL GO TO HINOMARU RIGHT NOW AND STOP THEM FROM PRINTING PANEL MANGA!

IT'S TOO LATE.

IT'S ALREADY AT THE PRINTERS.

OH, GOD. ONE HEADACHE AFTER ANOTHER.

探偵ブック

影

SHADOW ...

I WAS PREPARED TO DIE WITH YOU, AND THE TIME HAS COME TO MAKE GOOD ON MY PROMISE.

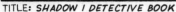

TITLE: *SHADOW / DETECTIVE BOOK*

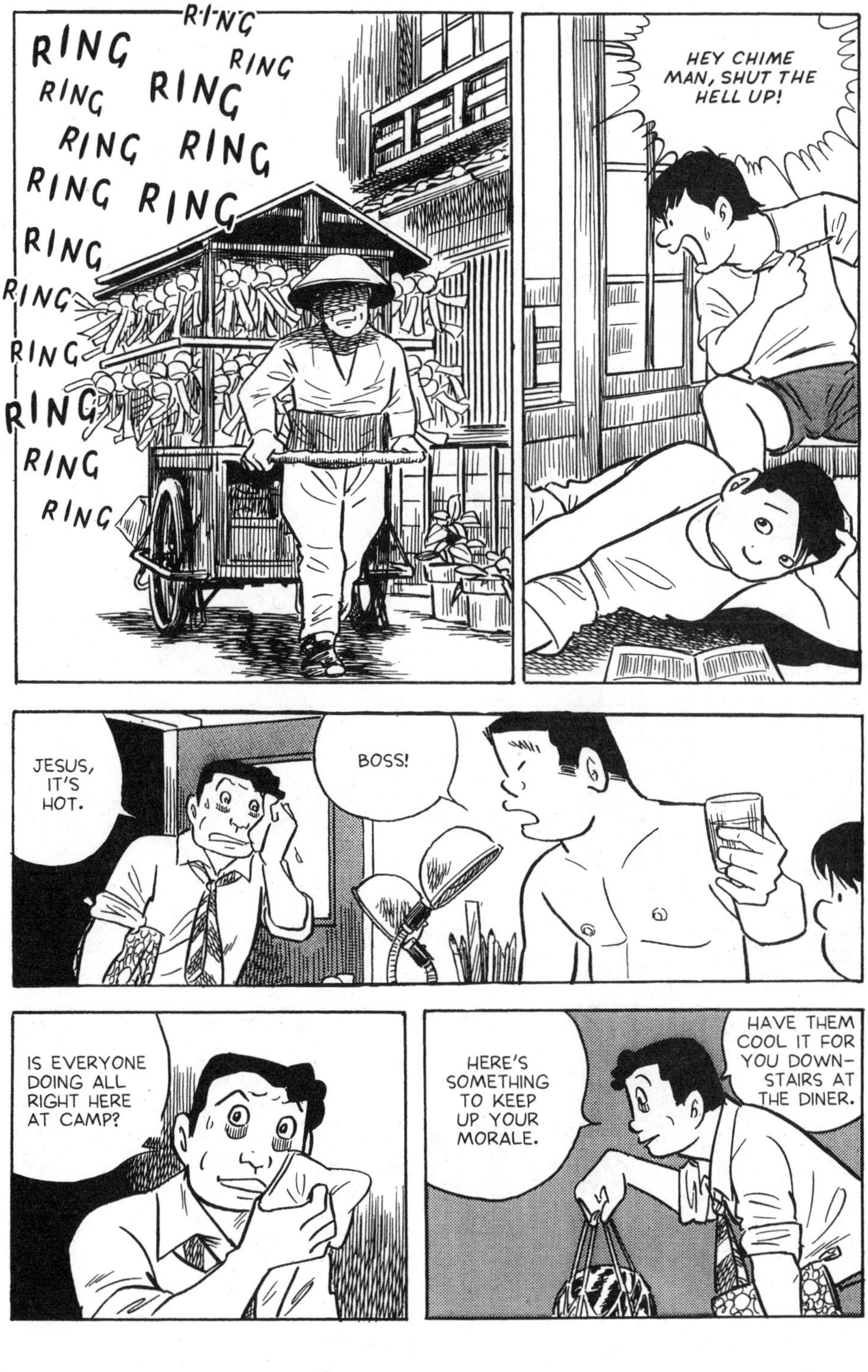
RING
RING
RING
RING
RING
RING
RING
RING
RING
RING
RING
RING
RING
RING
HEY CHIME MAN, SHUT THE HELL UP!
JESUS, IT'S HOT.
BOSS!
IS EVERYONE DOING ALL RIGHT HERE AT CAMP?
HERE'S SOMETHING TO KEEP UP YOUR MORALE.
HAVE THEM COOL IT FOR YOU DOWN-STAIRS AT THE DINER.

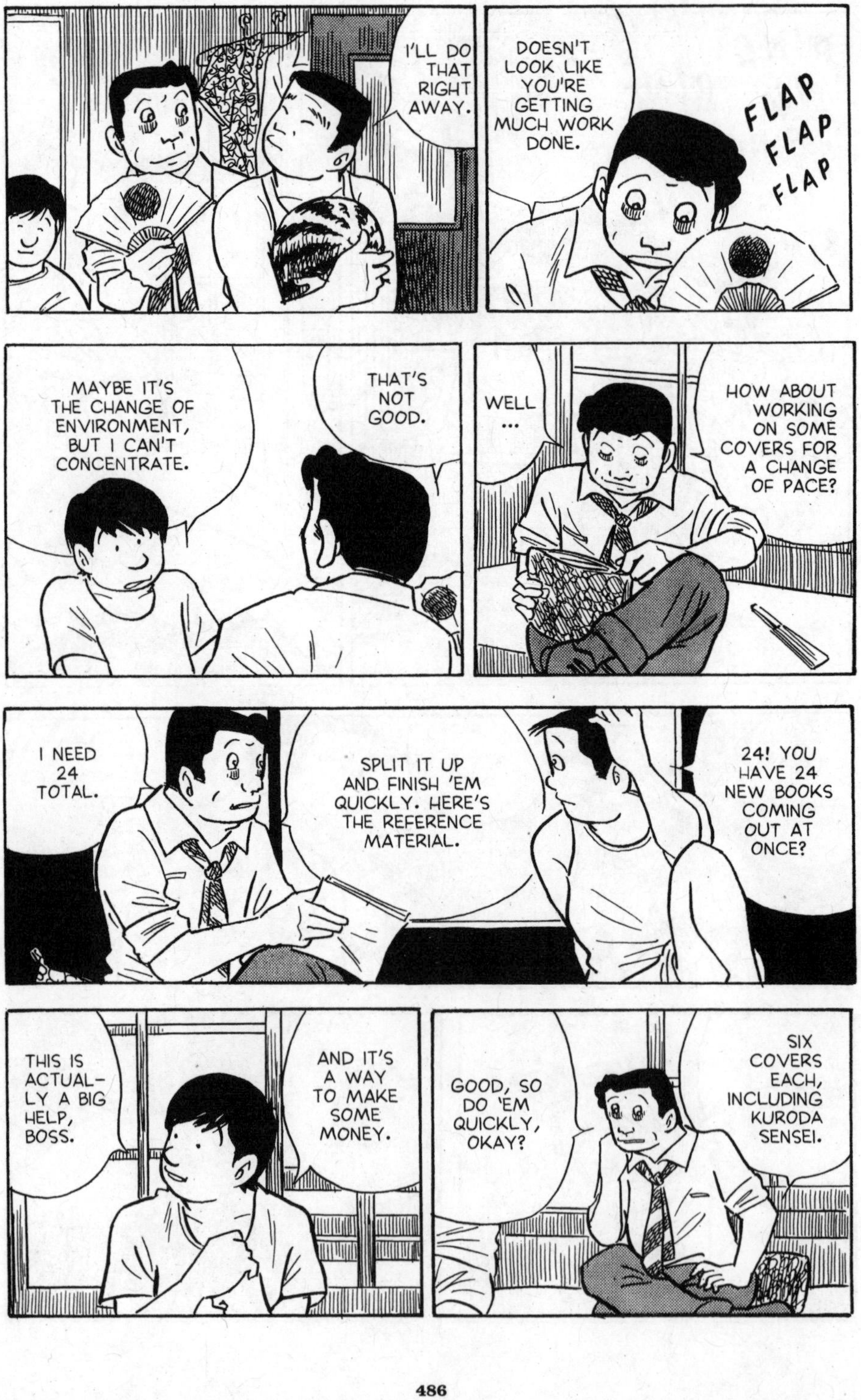
I'LL DO THAT RIGHT AWAY.
DOESN'T LOOK LIKE YOU'RE GETTING MUCH WORK DONE.
FLAP FLAP FLAP
MAYBE IT'S THE CHANGE OF ENVIRONMENT, BUT I CAN'T CONCENTRATE.
THAT'S NOT GOOD.
WELL ...
HOW ABOUT WORKING ON SOME COVERS FOR A CHANGE OF PACE?
I NEED 24 TOTAL.
SPLIT IT UP AND FINISH 'EM QUICKLY. HERE'S THE REFERENCE MATERIAL.
24! YOU HAVE 24 NEW BOOKS COMING OUT AT ONCE?
THIS IS ACTUAL-LY A BIG HELP, BOSS.
AND IT'S A WAY TO MAKE SOME MONEY.
GOOD, SO DO 'EM QUICKLY, OKAY?
SIX COVERS EACH, INCLUDING KURODA SENSEI.

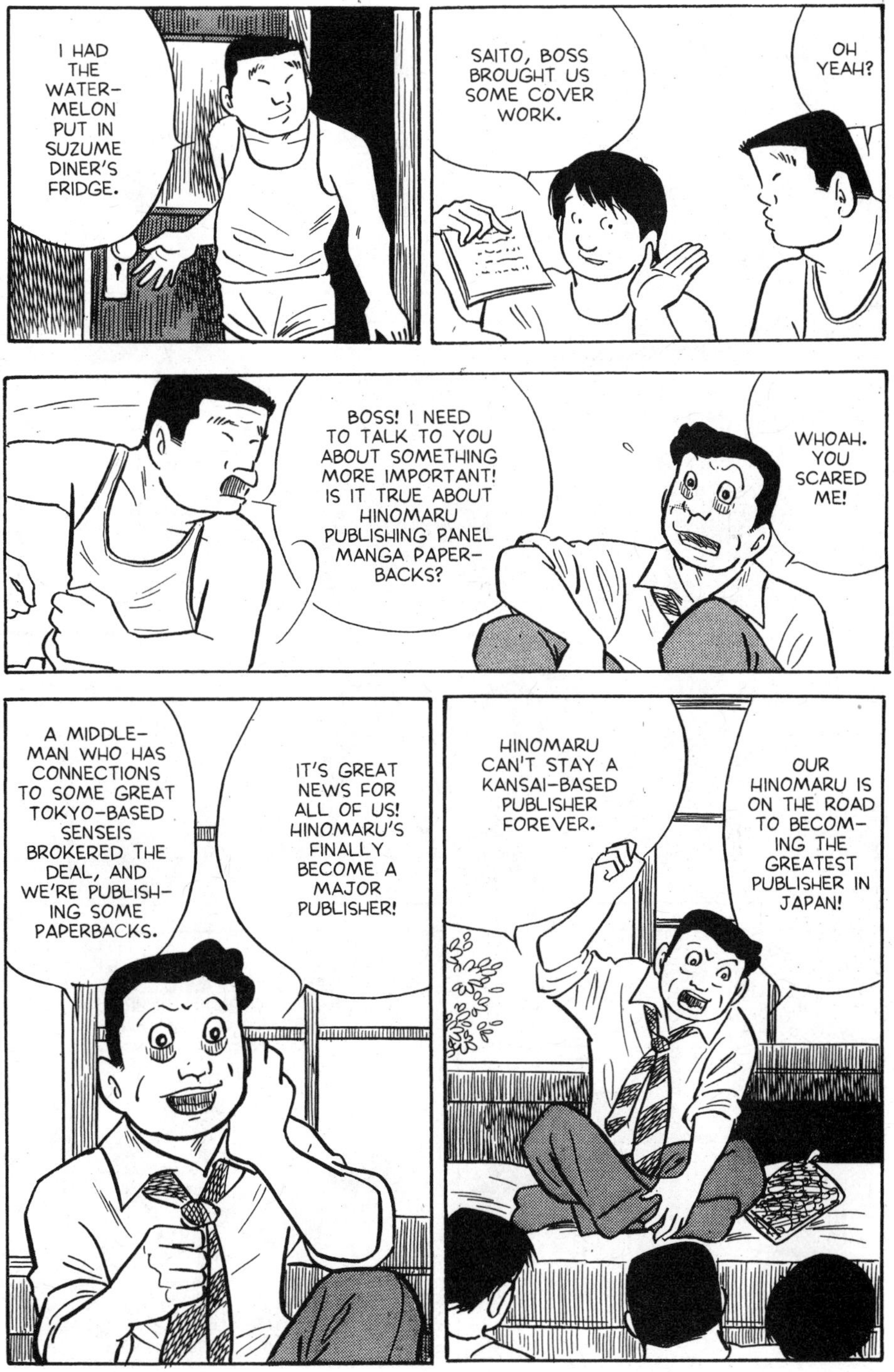
I HAD THE WATER-MELON PUT IN SUZUME DINER'S FRIDGE.
SAITO, BOSS BROUGHT US SOME COVER WORK.
OH YEAH?
BOSS! I NEED TO TALK TO YOU ABOUT SOMETHING MORE IMPORTANT! IS IT TRUE ABOUT HINOMARU PUBLISHING PANEL MANGA PAPER-BACKS?
WHOAH. YOU SCARED ME!
A MIDDLE-MAN WHO HAS CONNECTIONS TO SOME GREAT TOKYO-BASED SENSEIS BROKERED THE DEAL, AND WE'RE PUBLISH-ING SOME PAPERBACKS.
IT'S GREAT NEWS FOR ALL OF US! HINOMARU'S FINALLY BECOME A MAJOR PUBLISHER!
HINOMARU CAN'T STAY A KANSAI-BASED PUBLISHER FOREVER.
OUR HINOMARU IS ON THE ROAD TO BECOM-ING THE GREATEST PUBLISHER IN JAPAN!

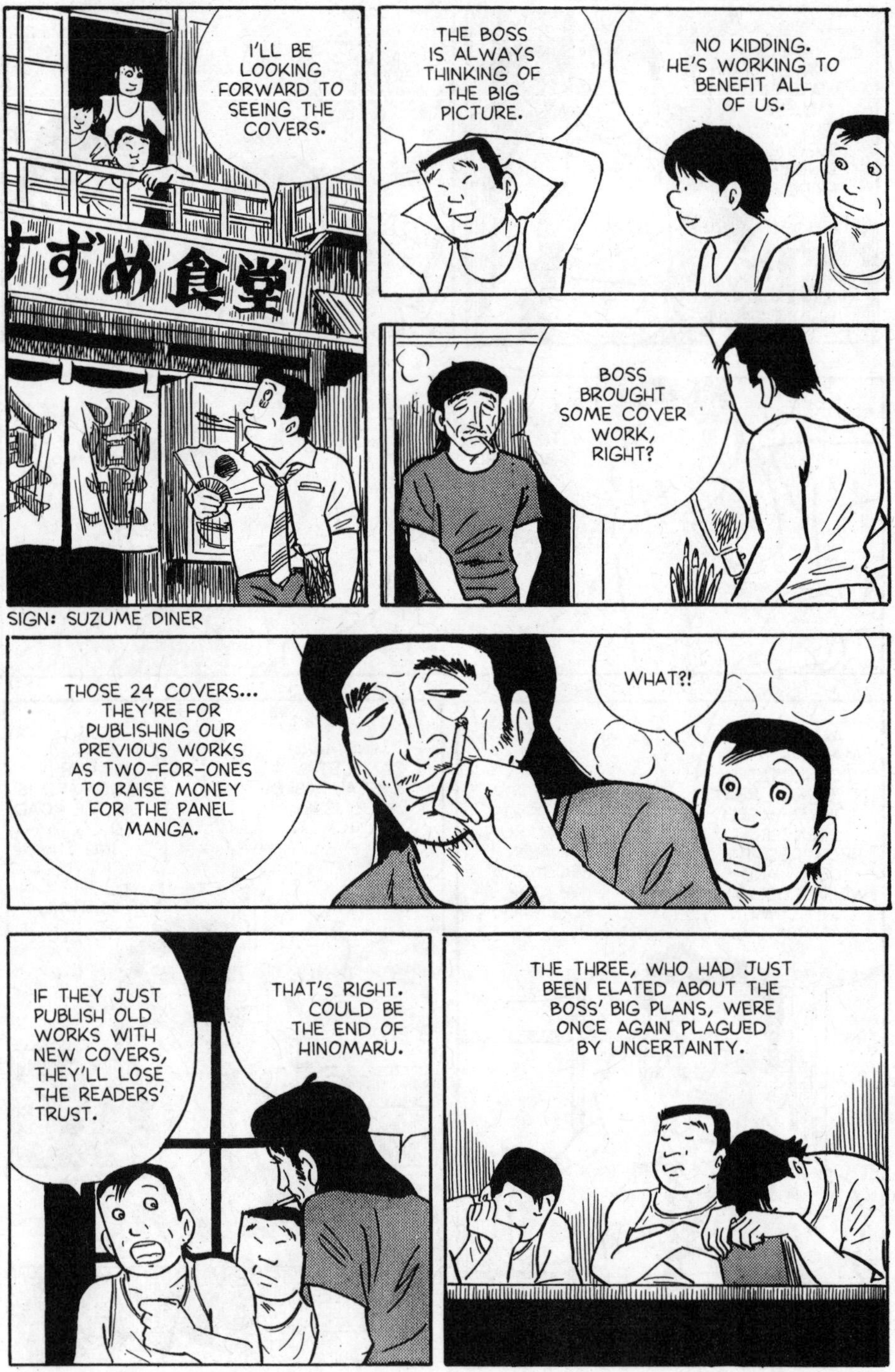

I'LL BE LOOKING FORWARD TO SEEING THE COVERS.
すずめ食堂
SIGN: SUZUME DINER
THE BOSS IS ALWAYS THINKING OF THE BIG PICTURE.
NO KIDDING. HE'S WORKING TO BENEFIT ALL OF US.
BOSS BROUGHT SOME COVER WORK, RIGHT?
THOSE 24 COVERS... THEY'RE FOR PUBLISHING OUR PREVIOUS WORKS AS TWO-FOR-ONES TO RAISE MONEY FOR THE PANEL MANGA.
WHAT?!
IF THEY JUST PUBLISH OLD WORKS WITH NEW COVERS, THEY'LL LOSE THE READERS' TRUST.
THAT'S RIGHT. COULD BE THE END OF HINOMARU.
THE THREE, WHO HAD JUST BEEN ELATED ABOUT THE BOSS' BIG PLANS, WERE ONCE AGAIN PLAGUED BY UNCERTAINTY.

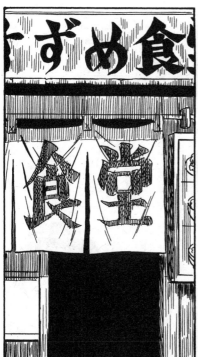

HI.

I'M HERE FOR DINNER.

I'M SUR- PRISED TO SEE YOU HERE ALONE.

SAITO'S ON A DATE, AND MATSUMOTO WENT HOME FOR A VISIT.

A DATE? HOW EXCITING!

HOW ABOUT BARBECUE?

SOUNDS GREAT!

SIZZLE

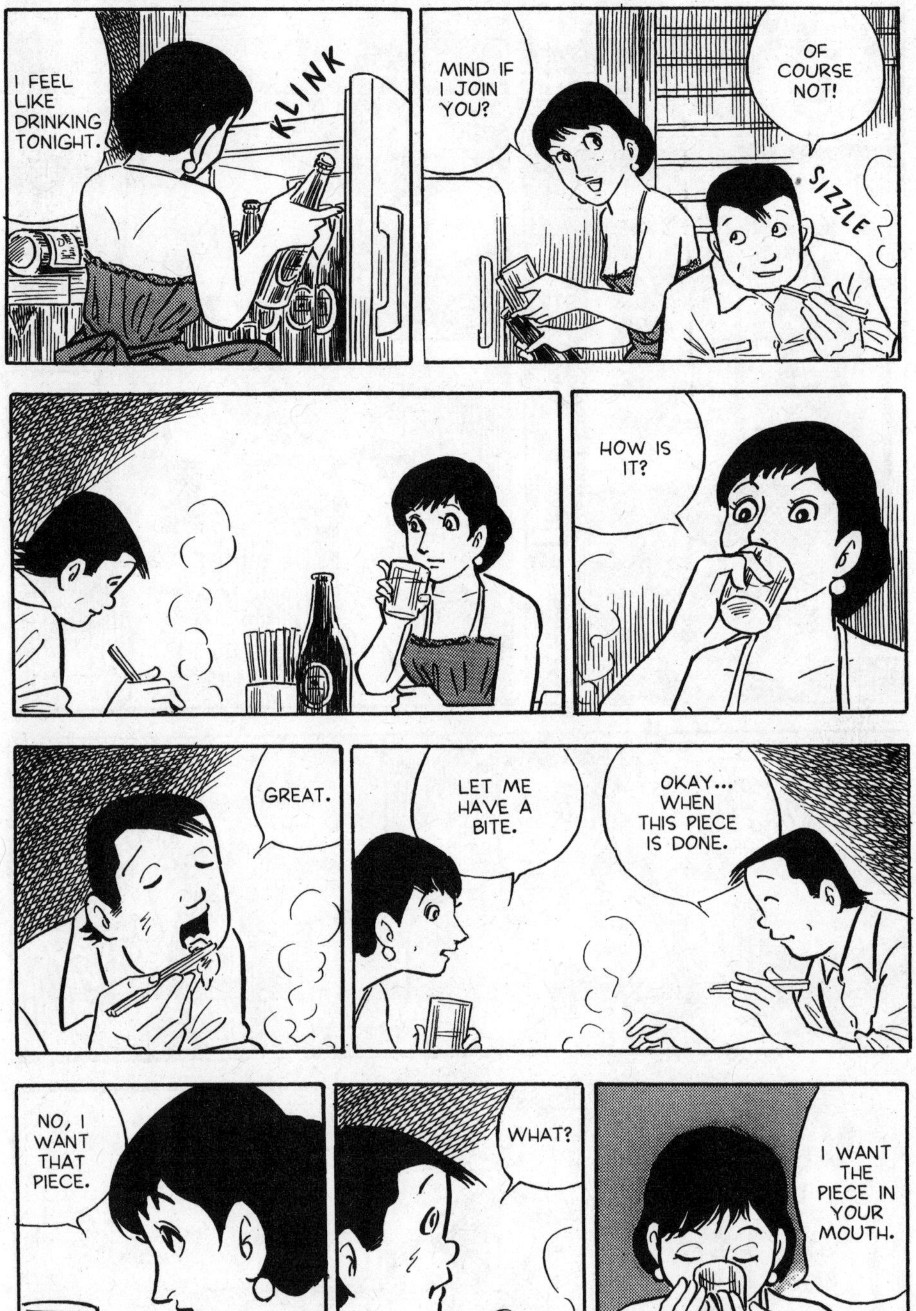
I FEEL LIKE DRINKING TONIGHT.
KLINK
MIND IF I JOIN YOU?
OF COURSE NOT!
SIZZLE
HOW IS IT?
GREAT.
LET ME HAVE A BITE.
OKAY... WHEN THIS PIECE IS DONE.
NO, I WANT THAT PIECE.
WHAT?
I WANT THE PIECE IN YOUR MOUTH.

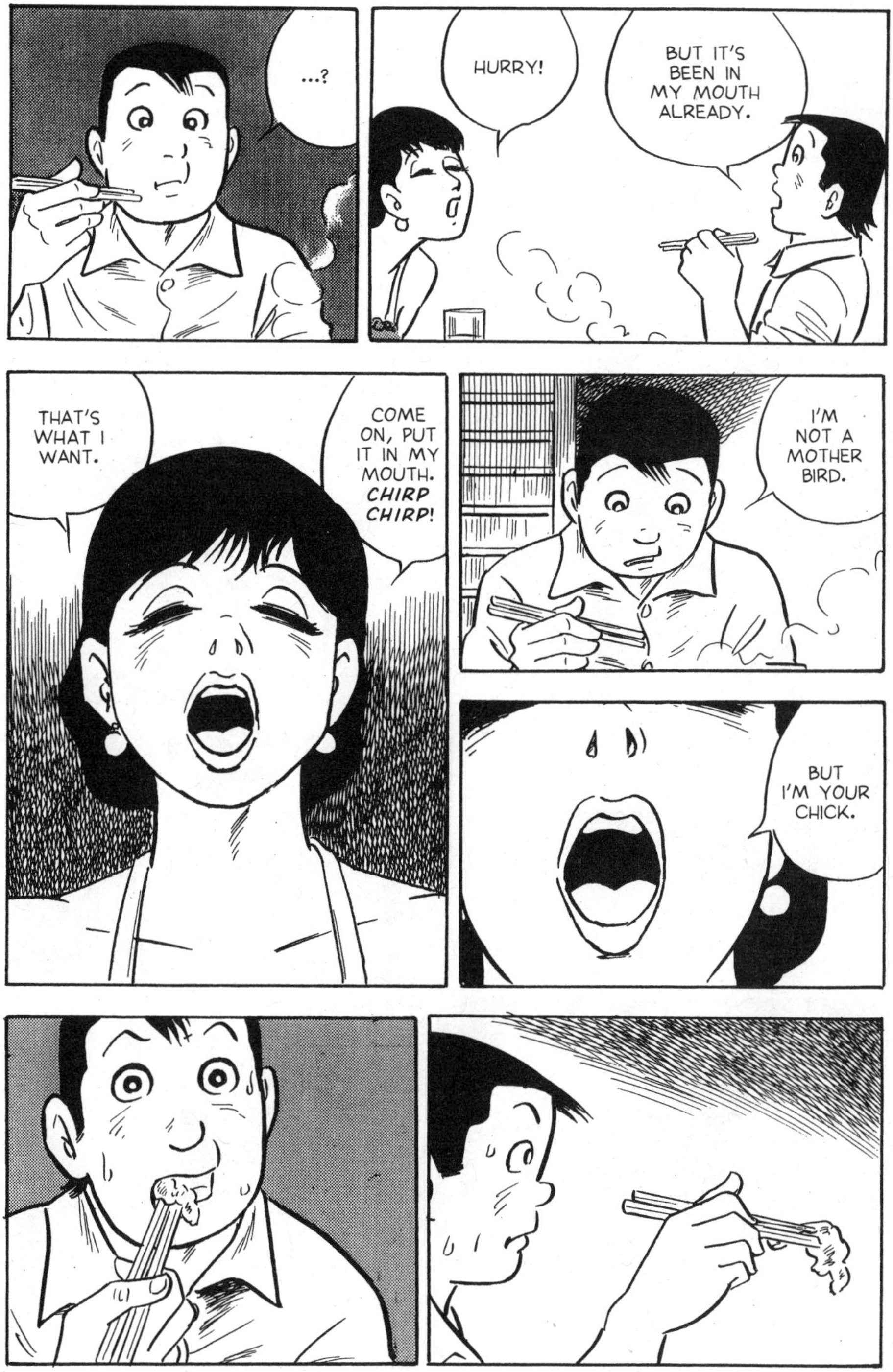
...?
HURRY!
BUT IT'S BEEN IN MY MOUTH ALREADY.
THAT'S WHAT I WANT.
COME ON, PUT IT IN MY MOUTH. CHIRP CHIRP!
I'M NOT A MOTHER BIRD.
BUT I'M YOUR CHICK.

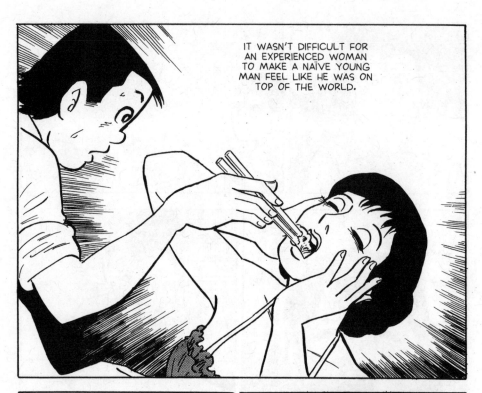

IT WASN'T DIFFICULT FOR AN EXPERIENCED WOMAN TO MAKE A NAÏVE YOUNG MAN FEEL LIKE HE WAS ON TOP OF THE WORLD.

ALREADY ENAMORED OF HER, HIROSHI FELL INTO HER SWEET, LASCIVIOUS TRAP.

DELI-CIOUS!

ESCAPE FROM CAMP

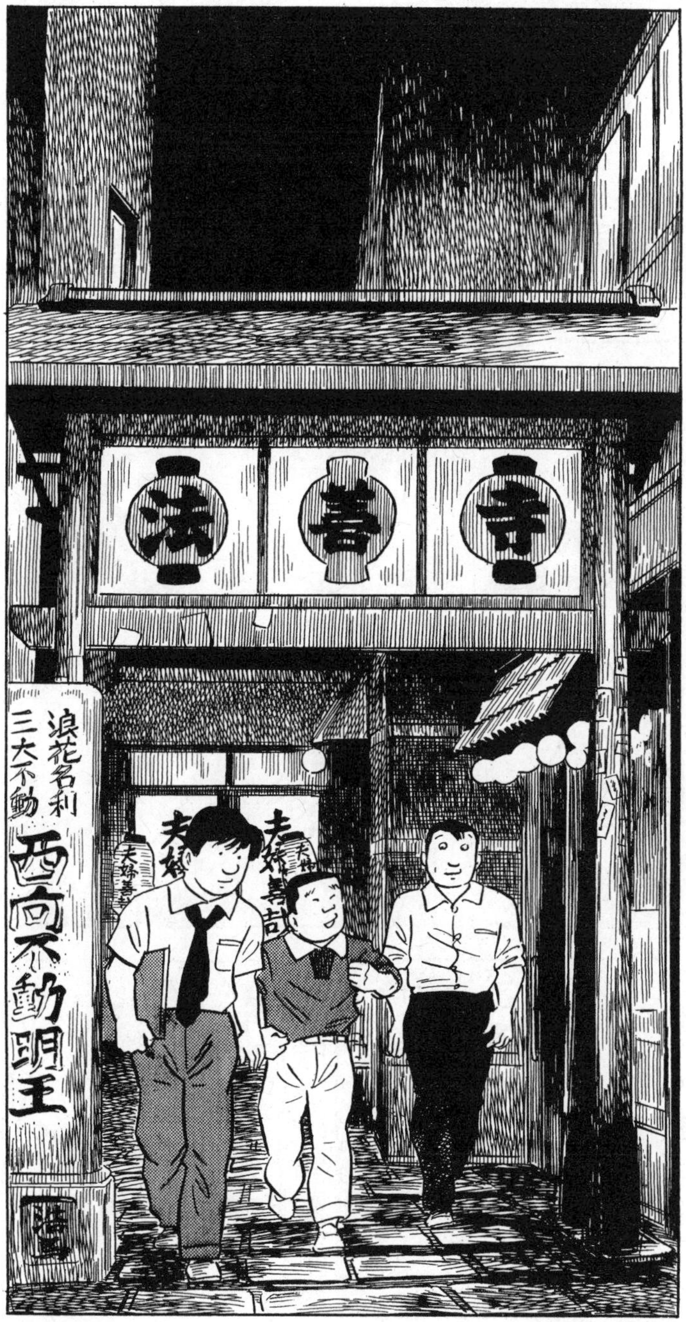

法善寺
浪花名刹
三大不動
西向不動明王

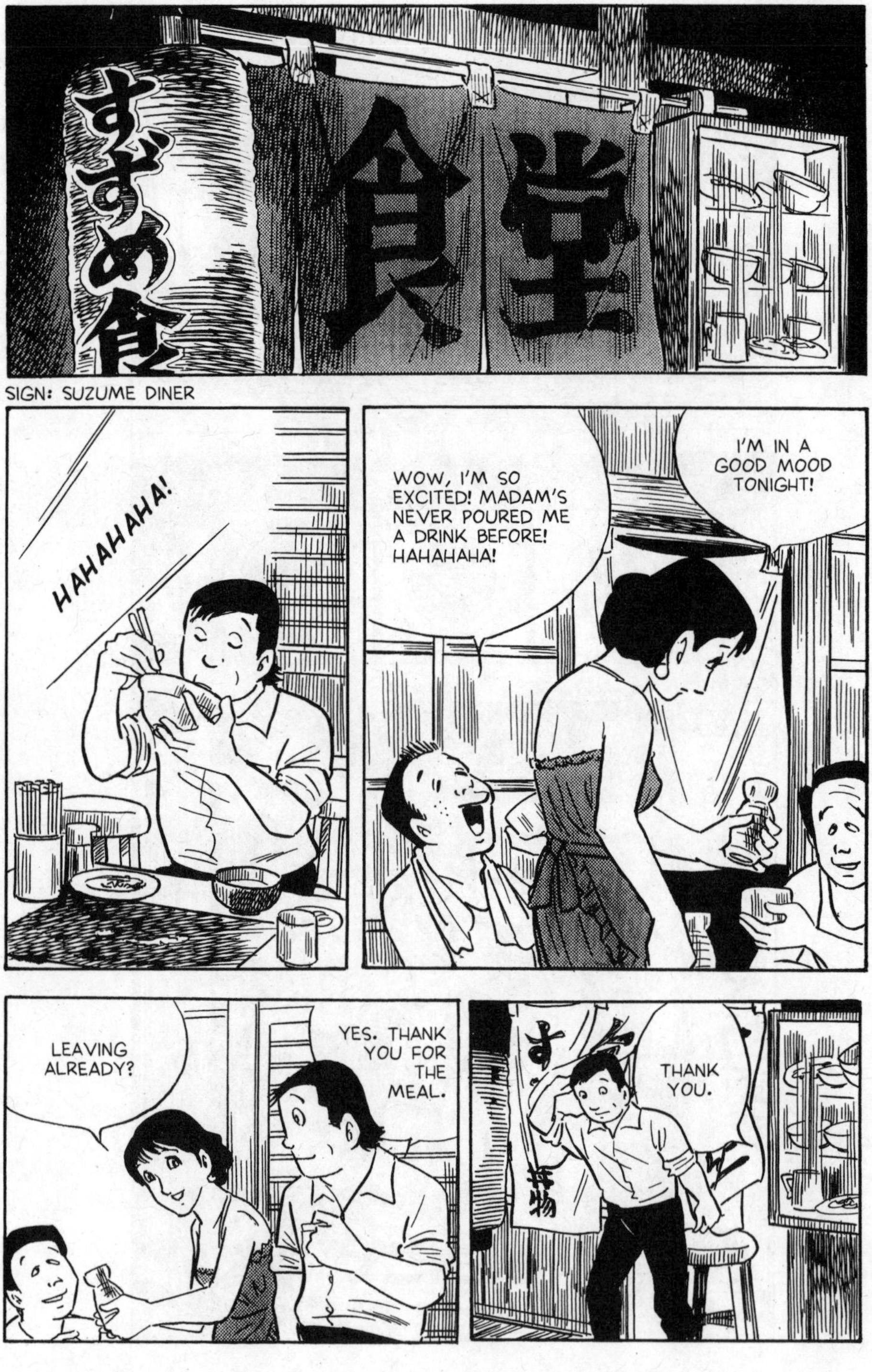
すずめ食
食堂
SIGN: SUZUME DINER
HAHAHAHA!
WOW, I'M SO EXCITED! MADAM'S NEVER POURED ME A DRINK BEFORE! HAHAHAHA!
I'M IN A GOOD MOOD TONIGHT!
LEAVING ALREADY?
YES. THANK YOU FOR THE MEAL.
THANK YOU.

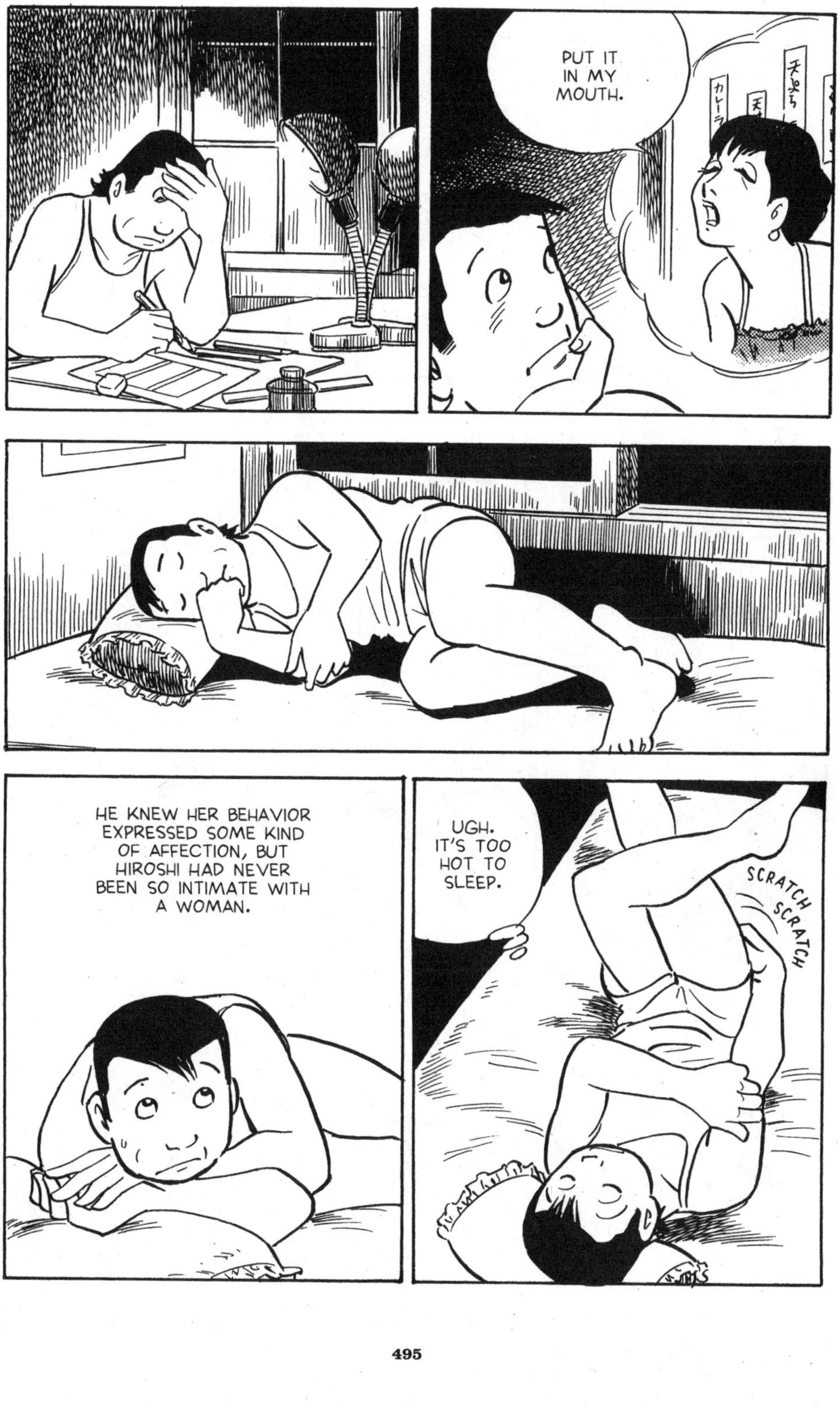
PUT IT IN MY MOUTH.
HE KNEW HER BEHAVIOR EXPRESSED SOME KIND OF AFFECTION, BUT HIROSHI HAD NEVER BEEN SO INTIMATE WITH A WOMAN.
UGH. IT'S TOO HOT TO SLEEP.
SCRATCH SCRATCH

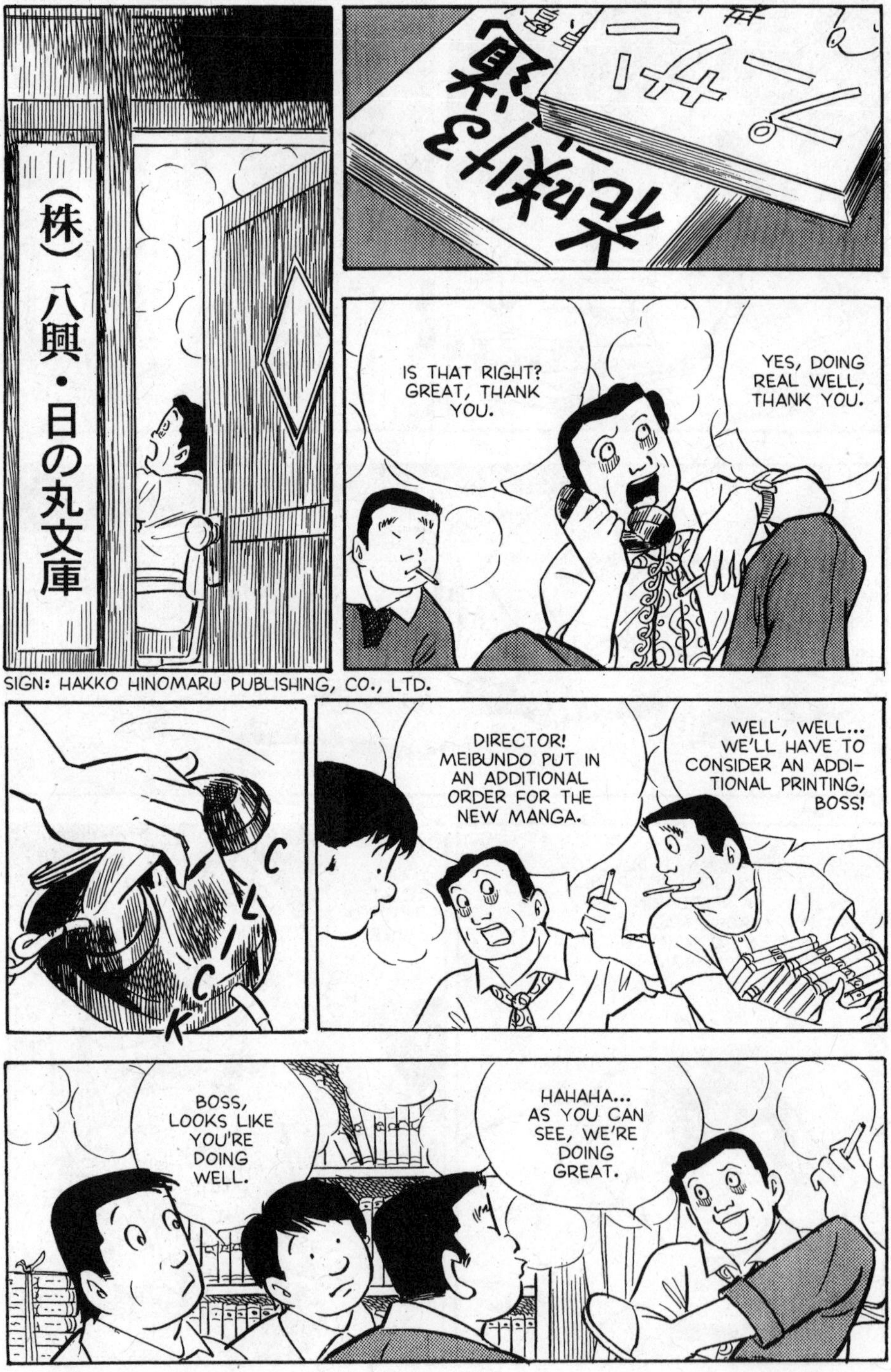

(株)八興・日の丸文庫
IS THAT RIGHT? GREAT, THANK YOU.
YES, DOING REAL WELL, THANK YOU.
SIGN: HAKKO HINOMARU PUBLISHING, CO., LTD.
CLICK
DIRECTOR! MEIBUNDO PUT IN AN ADDITIONAL ORDER FOR THE NEW MANGA.
WELL, WELL... WE'LL HAVE TO CONSIDER AN ADDITIONAL PRINTING, BOSS!
BOSS, LOOKS LIKE YOU'RE DOING WELL.
HAHAHA... AS YOU CAN SEE, WE'RE DOING GREAT.

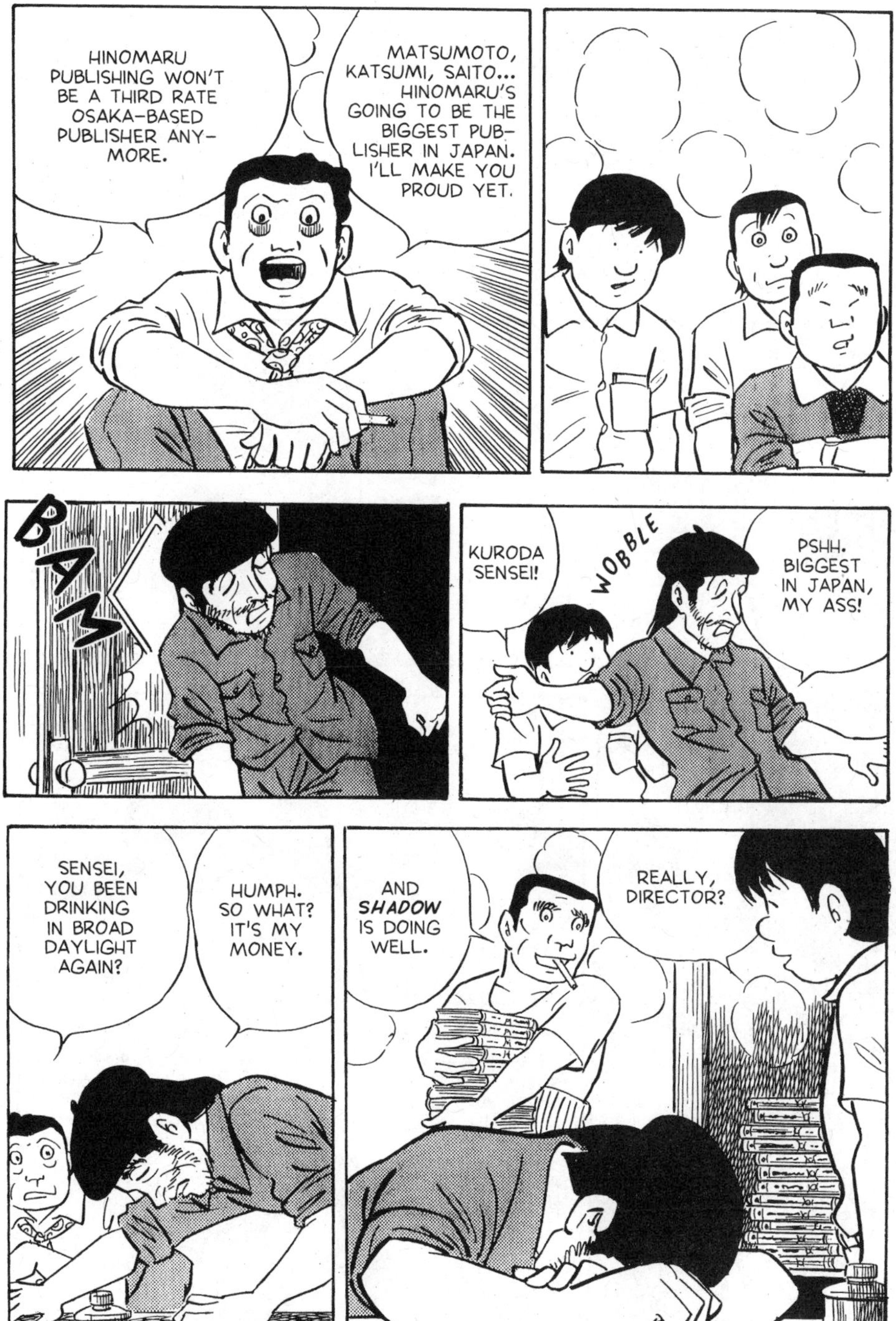
HINOMARU PUBLISHING WON'T BE A THIRD RATE OSAKA-BASED PUBLISHER ANY-MORE.
MATSUMOTO, KATSUMI, SAITO... HINOMARU'S GOING TO BE THE BIGGEST PUB-LISHER IN JAPAN. I'LL MAKE YOU PROUD YET.
BAM
KURODA SENSEI!
WOBBLE
PSHH. BIGGEST IN JAPAN, MY ASS!
SENSEI, YOU BEEN DRINKING IN BROAD DAYLIGHT AGAIN?
HUMPH. SO WHAT? IT'S MY MONEY.
AND *SHADOW* IS DOING WELL.
REALLY, DIRECTOR?

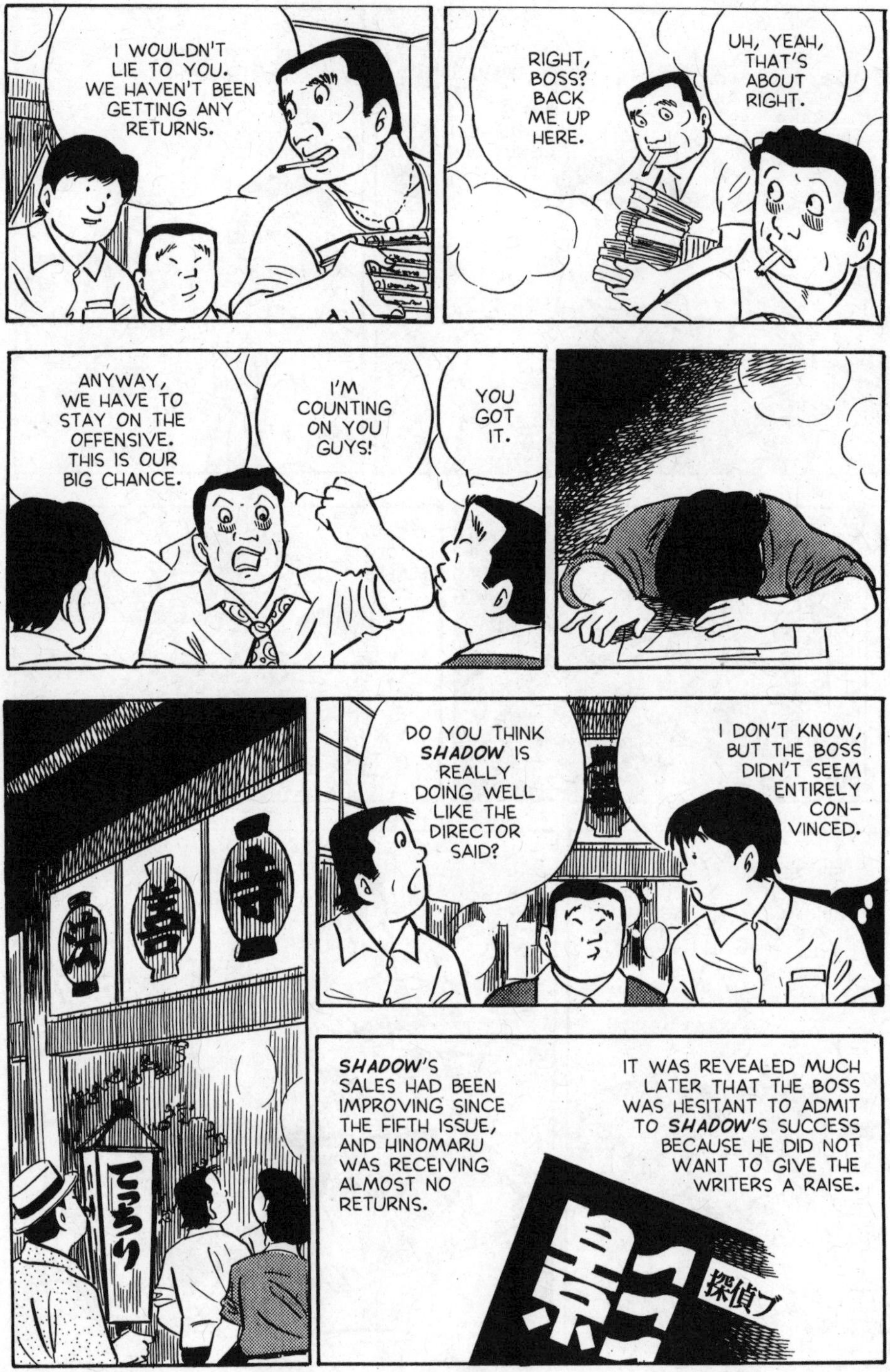
I WOULDN'T LIE TO YOU. WE HAVEN'T BEEN GETTING ANY RETURNS.
RIGHT, BOSS? BACK ME UP HERE.
UH, YEAH, THAT'S ABOUT RIGHT.
ANYWAY, WE HAVE TO STAY ON THE OFFENSIVE. THIS IS OUR BIG CHANCE.
I'M COUNTING ON YOU GUYS!
YOU GOT IT.
法
善
寺
てっちり
DO YOU THINK *SHADOW* IS REALLY DOING WELL LIKE THE DIRECTOR SAID?
I DON'T KNOW, BUT THE BOSS DIDN'T SEEM ENTIRELY CON-VINCED.
SHADOW'S SALES HAD BEEN IMPROVING SINCE THE FIFTH ISSUE, AND HINOMARU WAS RECEIVING ALMOST NO RETURNS.
IT WAS REVEALED MUCH LATER THAT THE BOSS WAS HESITANT TO ADMIT TO *SHADOW*'S SUCCESS BECAUSE HE DID NOT WANT TO GIVE THE WRITERS A RAISE.
探偵ブ

SIGN: HOZENJI

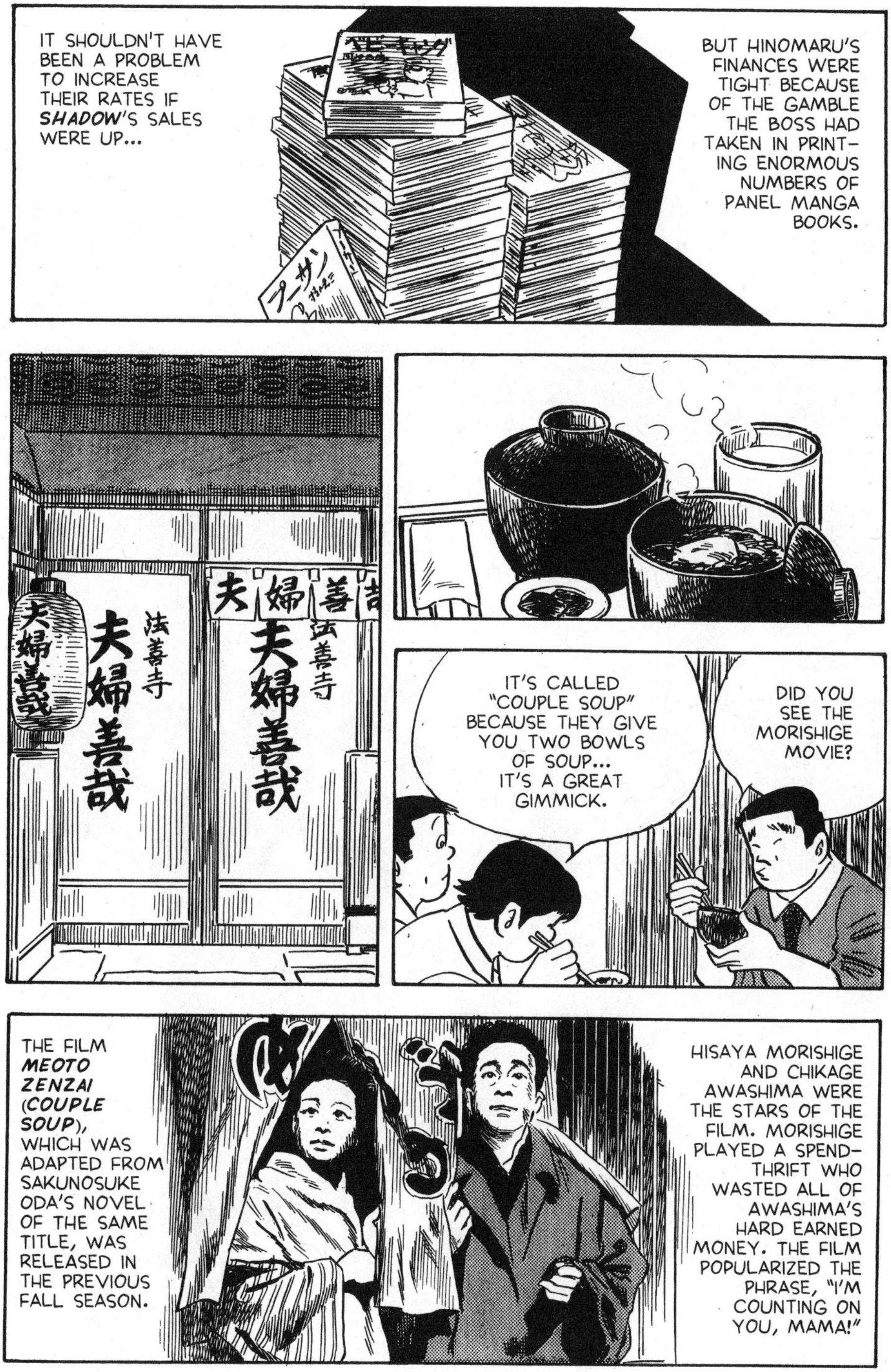
IT SHOULDN'T HAVE BEEN A PROBLEM TO INCREASE THEIR RATES IF ***SHADOW***'S SALES WERE UP...
BUT HINOMARU'S FINANCES WERE TIGHT BECAUSE OF THE GAMBLE THE BOSS HAD TAKEN IN PRINTING ENORMOUS NUMBERS OF PANEL MANGA BOOKS.
夫婦善哉
法善寺
夫婦善哉
夫婦善哉
法善寺
夫婦善哉
IT'S CALLED "COUPLE SOUP" BECAUSE THEY GIVE YOU TWO BOWLS OF SOUP... IT'S A GREAT GIMMICK.
DID YOU SEE THE MORISHIGE MOVIE?
THE FILM ***MEOTO ZENZAI*** (***COUPLE SOUP***), WHICH WAS ADAPTED FROM SAKUNOSUKE ODA'S NOVEL OF THE SAME TITLE, WAS RELEASED IN THE PREVIOUS FALL SEASON.
HISAYA MORISHIGE AND CHIKAGE AWASHIMA WERE THE STARS OF THE FILM. MORISHIGE PLAYED A SPENDTHRIFT WHO WASTED ALL OF AWASHIMA'S HARD EARNED MONEY. THE FILM POPULARIZED THE PHRASE, "I'M COUNTING ON YOU, MAMA!"

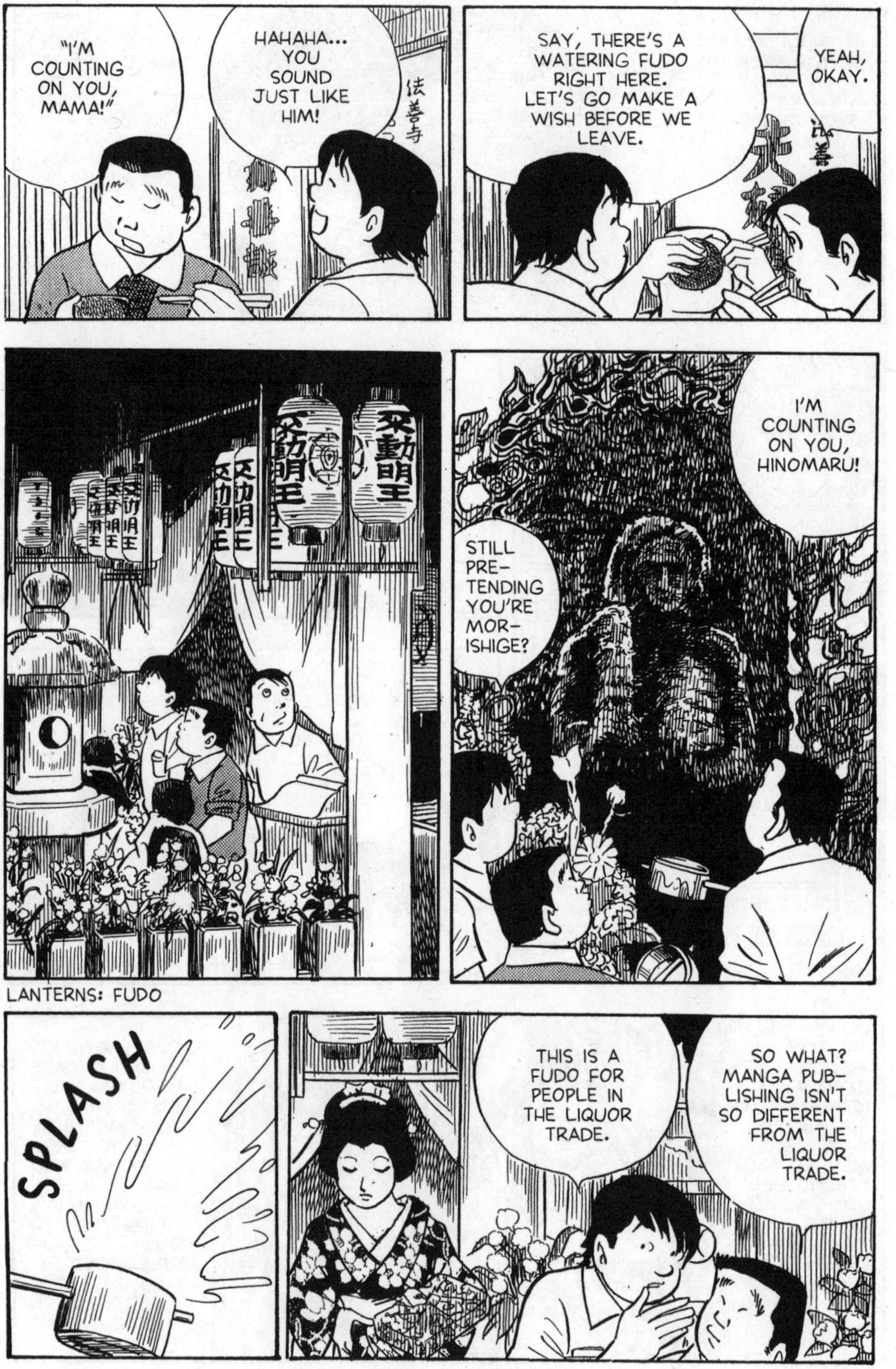

"I'M COUNTING ON YOU, MAMA!"
HAHAHA... YOU SOUND JUST LIKE HIM!
法善寺
SAY, THERE'S A WATERING FUDO RIGHT HERE. LET'S GO MAKE A WISH BEFORE WE LEAVE.
YEAH, OKAY.
不動明王
I'M COUNTING ON YOU, HINOMARU!
STILL PRETENDING YOU'RE MORISHIGE?
LANTERNS: FUDO
SPLASH
THIS IS A FUDO FOR PEOPLE IN THE LIQUOR TRADE.
SO WHAT? MANGA PUBLISHING ISN'T SO DIFFERENT FROM THE LIQUOR TRADE.

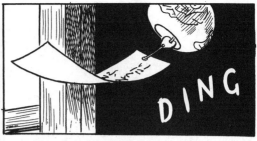

ずめ食
SIGN: SUZUME DINER
DING
ARGH... THIS IS HELL. I'M NOT GETTING ANY WORK DONE AND THAT WIND CHIME IS DRIVING ME NUTS!
HEY, DON'T BLAME THE TRANQUIL WIND CHIME.
WELL, I'M GOING HOME FOR A NIGHT.
I NEED TO DO LAUNDRY ANYWAY.
I WANT TO GO HOME TO KOBE AND WORK THERE, TOO.
BE POSITIVE. WORK HARD, OKAY? BYE-BYE!
HIROSHI FELT A PANG OF LONELINESS AT THE THOUGHT OF GOING A DAY WITHOUT SEEING MADAM.

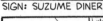

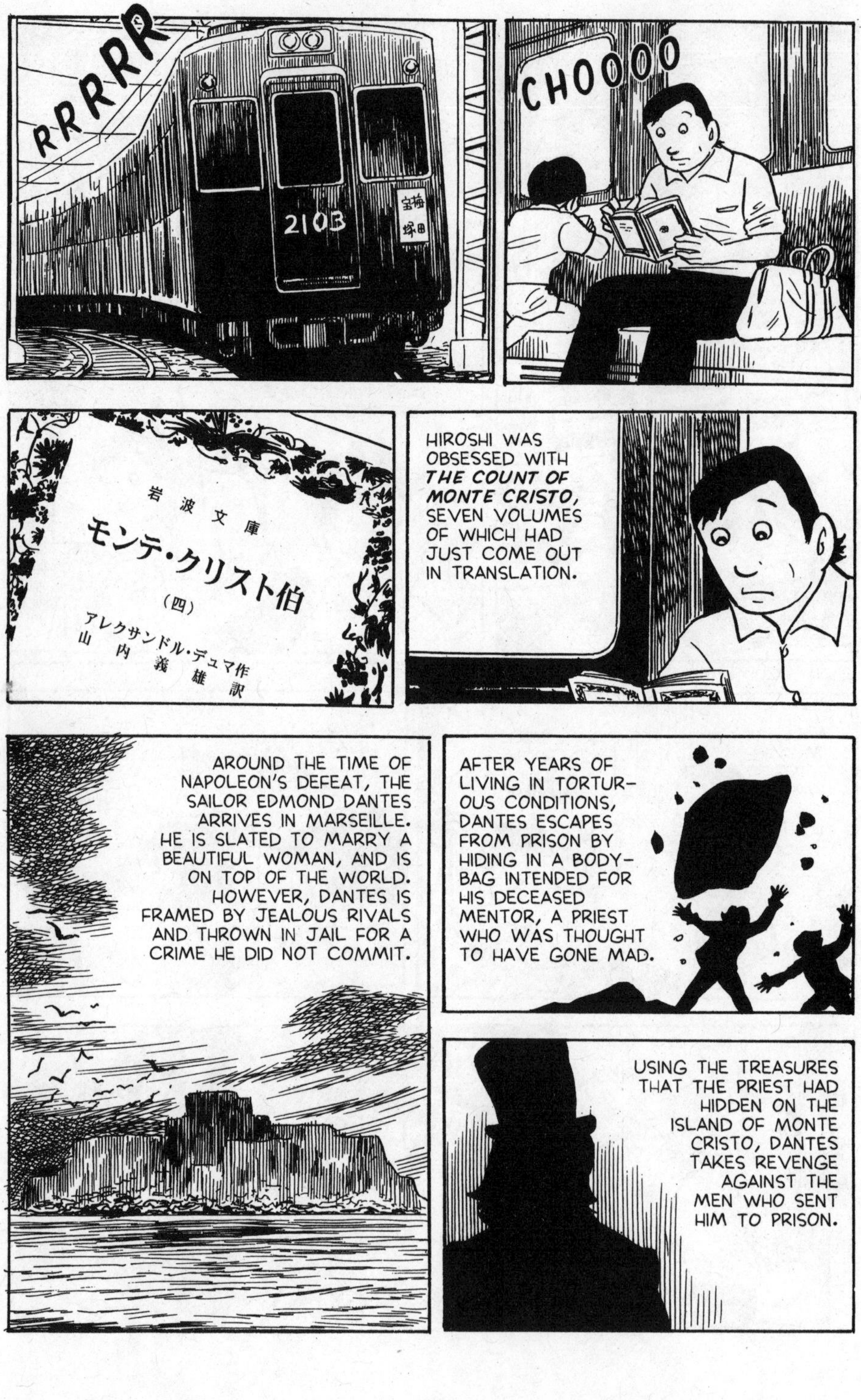
RRRRR
2103
梅田
宝塚
CHOOOO
岩波文庫
モンテ・クリスト伯
（四）
アレクサンドル・デュマ作
山内義雄訳
HIROSHI WAS OBSESSED WITH ***THE COUNT OF MONTE CRISTO,*** SEVEN VOLUMES OF WHICH HAD JUST COME OUT IN TRANSLATION.
AROUND THE TIME OF NAPOLEON'S DEFEAT, THE SAILOR EDMOND DANTES ARRIVES IN MARSEILLE. HE IS SLATED TO MARRY A BEAUTIFUL WOMAN, AND IS ON TOP OF THE WORLD. HOWEVER, DANTES IS FRAMED BY JEALOUS RIVALS AND THROWN IN JAIL FOR A CRIME HE DID NOT COMMIT.
AFTER YEARS OF LIVING IN TORTUR-OUS CONDITIONS, DANTES ESCAPES FROM PRISON BY HIDING IN A BODY-BAG INTENDED FOR HIS DECEASED MENTOR, A PRIEST WHO WAS THOUGHT TO HAVE GONE MAD.
USING THE TREASURES THAT THE PRIEST HAD HIDDEN ON THE ISLAND OF MONTE CRISTO, DANTES TAKES REVENGE AGAINST THE MEN WHO SENT HIM TO PRISON.

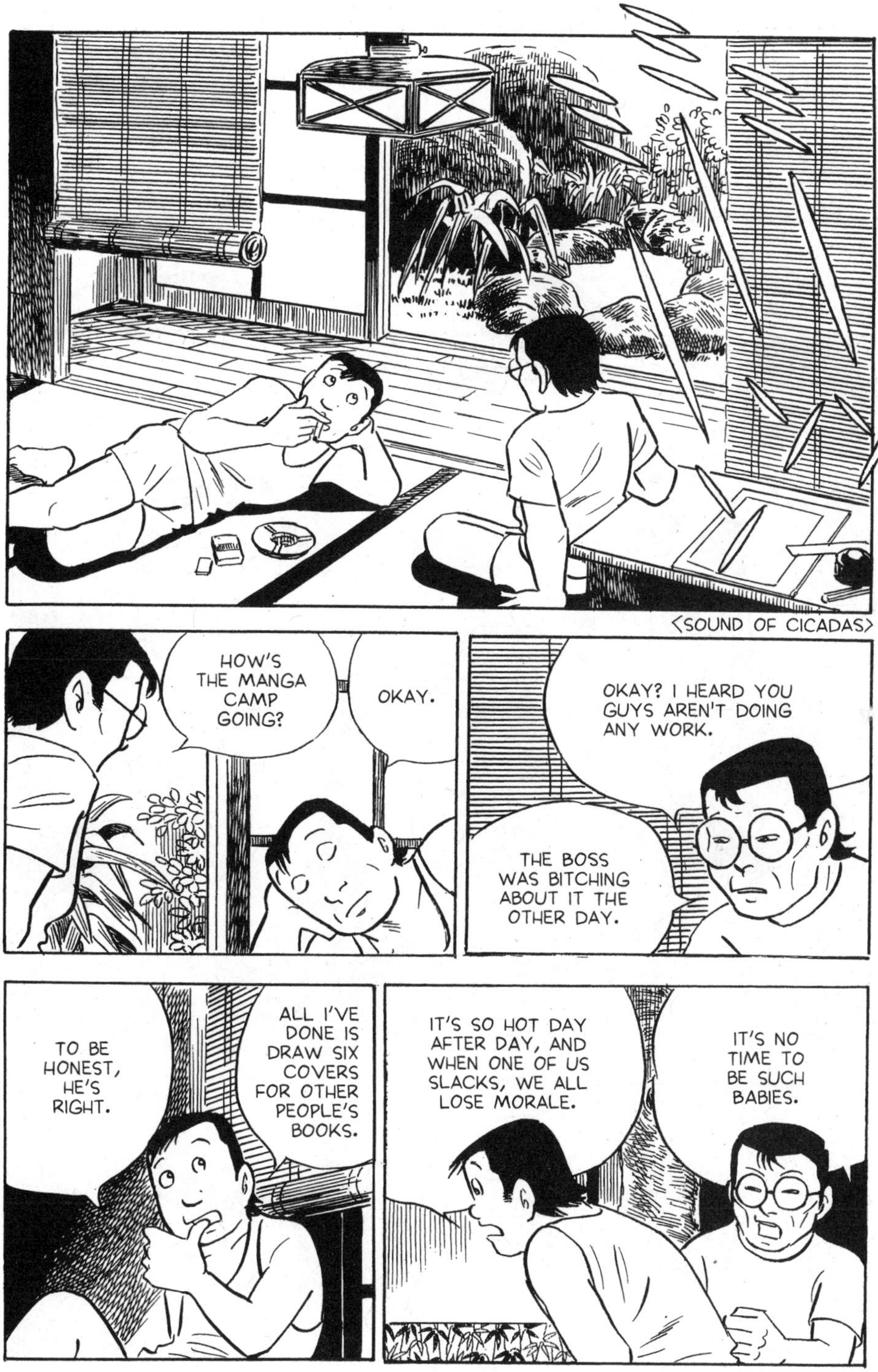

<SOUND OF CICADAS>
HOW'S THE MANGA CAMP GOING?
OKAY.
OKAY? I HEARD YOU GUYS AREN'T DOING ANY WORK.
THE BOSS WAS BITCHING ABOUT IT THE OTHER DAY.
TO BE HONEST, HE'S RIGHT.
ALL I'VE DONE IS DRAW SIX COVERS FOR OTHER PEOPLE'S BOOKS.
IT'S SO HOT DAY AFTER DAY, AND WHEN ONE OF US SLACKS, WE ALL LOSE MORALE.
IT'S NO TIME TO BE SUCH BABIES.

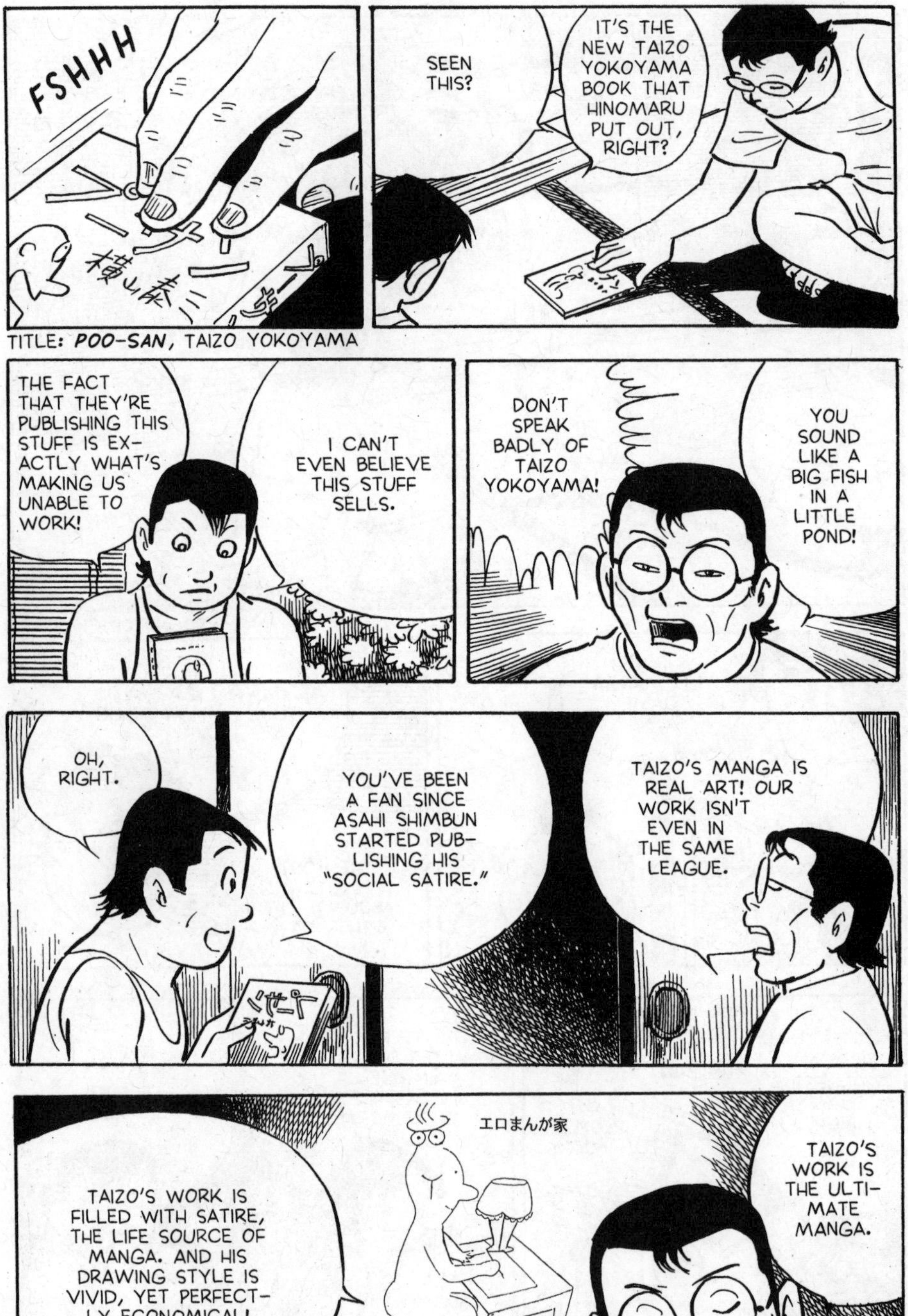
FSHHH
SEEN THIS?
IT'S THE NEW TAIZO YOKOYAMA BOOK THAT HINOMARU PUT OUT, RIGHT?
TITLE: POO-SAN, TAIZO YOKOYAMA
THE FACT THAT THEY'RE PUBLISHING THIS STUFF IS EX-ACTLY WHAT'S MAKING US UNABLE TO WORK!
I CAN'T EVEN BELIEVE THIS STUFF SELLS.
DON'T SPEAK BADLY OF TAIZO YOKOYAMA!
YOU SOUND LIKE A BIG FISH IN A LITTLE POND!
OH, RIGHT.
YOU'VE BEEN A FAN SINCE ASAHI SHIMBUN STARTED PUB-LISHING HIS "SOCIAL SATIRE."
TAIZO'S MANGA IS REAL ART! OUR WORK ISN'T EVEN IN THE SAME LEAGUE.
TAIZO'S WORK IS FILLED WITH SATIRE, THE LIFE SOURCE OF MANGA. AND HIS DRAWING STYLE IS VIVID, YET PERFECT-LY ECONOMICAL!
エロまんが家
TAIZO'S WORK IS THE ULTI-MATE MANGA.

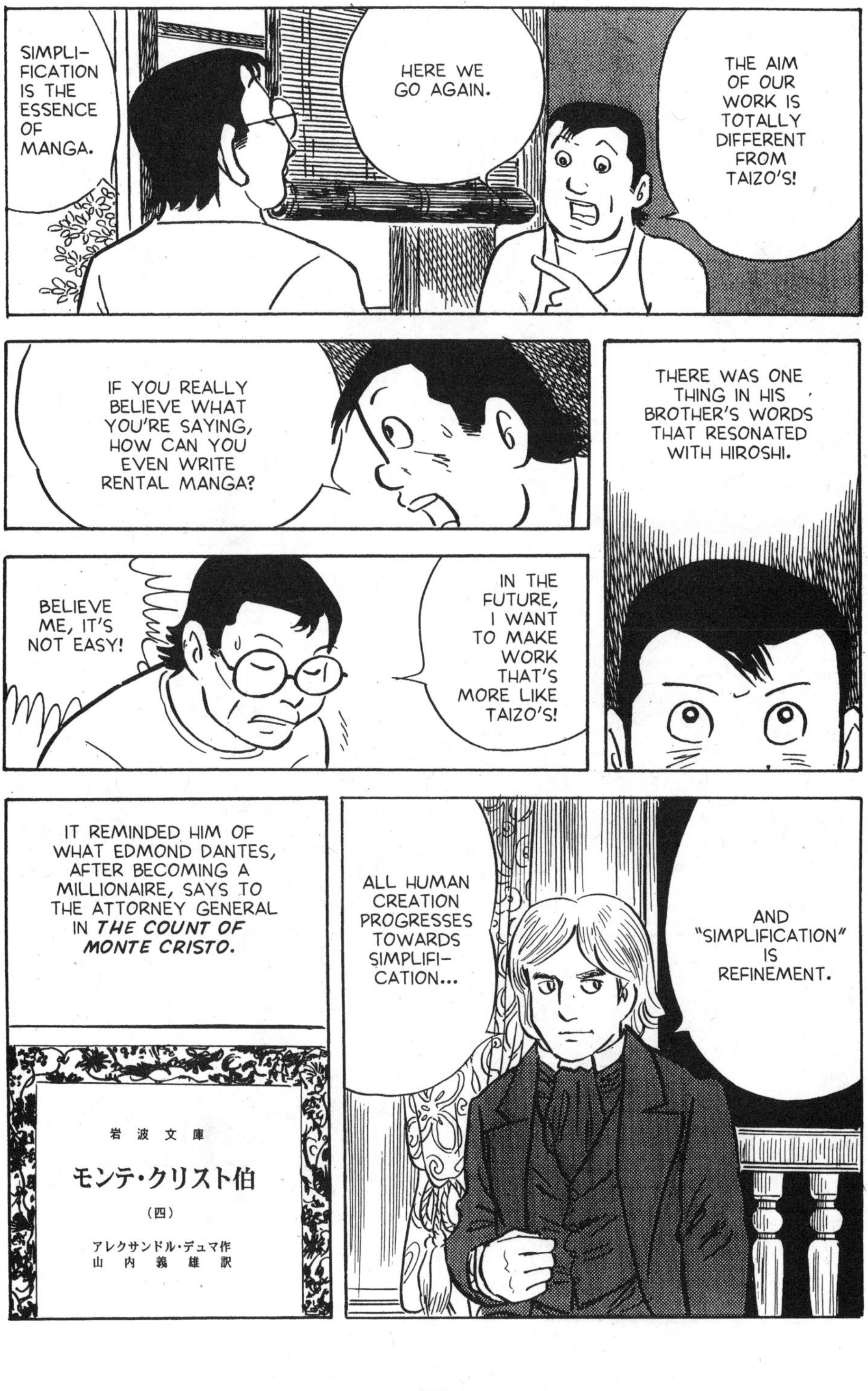
SIMPLIFICATION IS THE ESSENCE OF MANGA.
HERE WE GO AGAIN.
THE AIM OF OUR WORK IS TOTALLY DIFFERENT FROM TAIZO'S!
IF YOU REALLY BELIEVE WHAT YOU'RE SAYING, HOW CAN YOU EVEN WRITE RENTAL MANGA?
BELIEVE ME, IT'S NOT EASY!
IN THE FUTURE, I WANT TO MAKE WORK THAT'S MORE LIKE TAIZO'S!
THERE WAS ONE THING IN HIS BROTHER'S WORDS THAT RESONATED WITH HIROSHI.
IT REMINDED HIM OF WHAT EDMOND DANTES, AFTER BECOMING A MILLIONAIRE, SAYS TO THE ATTORNEY GENERAL IN *THE COUNT OF MONTE CRISTO.*
岩波文庫
モンテ・クリスト伯
（四）
アレクサンドル・デュマ作
山内義雄訳
ALL HUMAN CREATION PROGRESSES TOWARDS SIMPLIFICATION...
AND "SIMPLIFICATION" IS REFINEMENT.

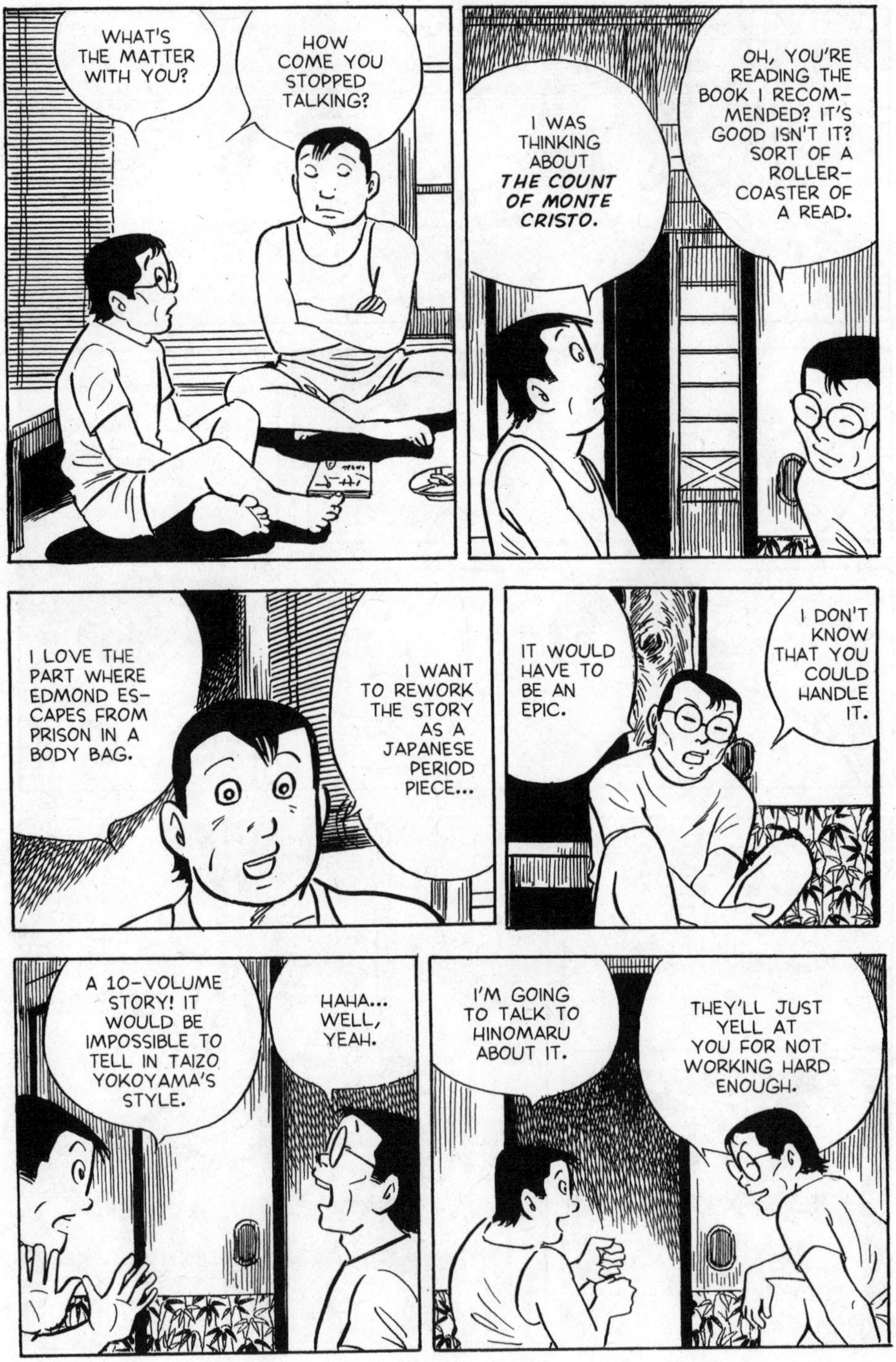
WHAT'S THE MATTER WITH YOU?
HOW COME YOU STOPPED TALKING?
I WAS THINKING ABOUT ***THE COUNT OF MONTE CRISTO.***
OH, YOU'RE READING THE BOOK I RECOM-MENDED? IT'S GOOD ISN'T IT? SORT OF A ROLLER-COASTER OF A READ.
I LOVE THE PART WHERE EDMOND ES-CAPES FROM PRISON IN A BODY BAG.
I WANT TO REWORK THE STORY AS A JAPANESE PERIOD PIECE...
IT WOULD HAVE TO BE AN EPIC.
I DON'T KNOW THAT YOU COULD HANDLE IT.
A 10-VOLUME STORY! IT WOULD BE IMPOSSIBLE TO TELL IN TAIZO YOKOYAMA'S STYLE.
HAHA... WELL, YEAH.
I'M GOING TO TALK TO HINOMARU ABOUT IT.
THEY'LL JUST YELL AT YOU FOR NOT WORKING HARD ENOUGH.

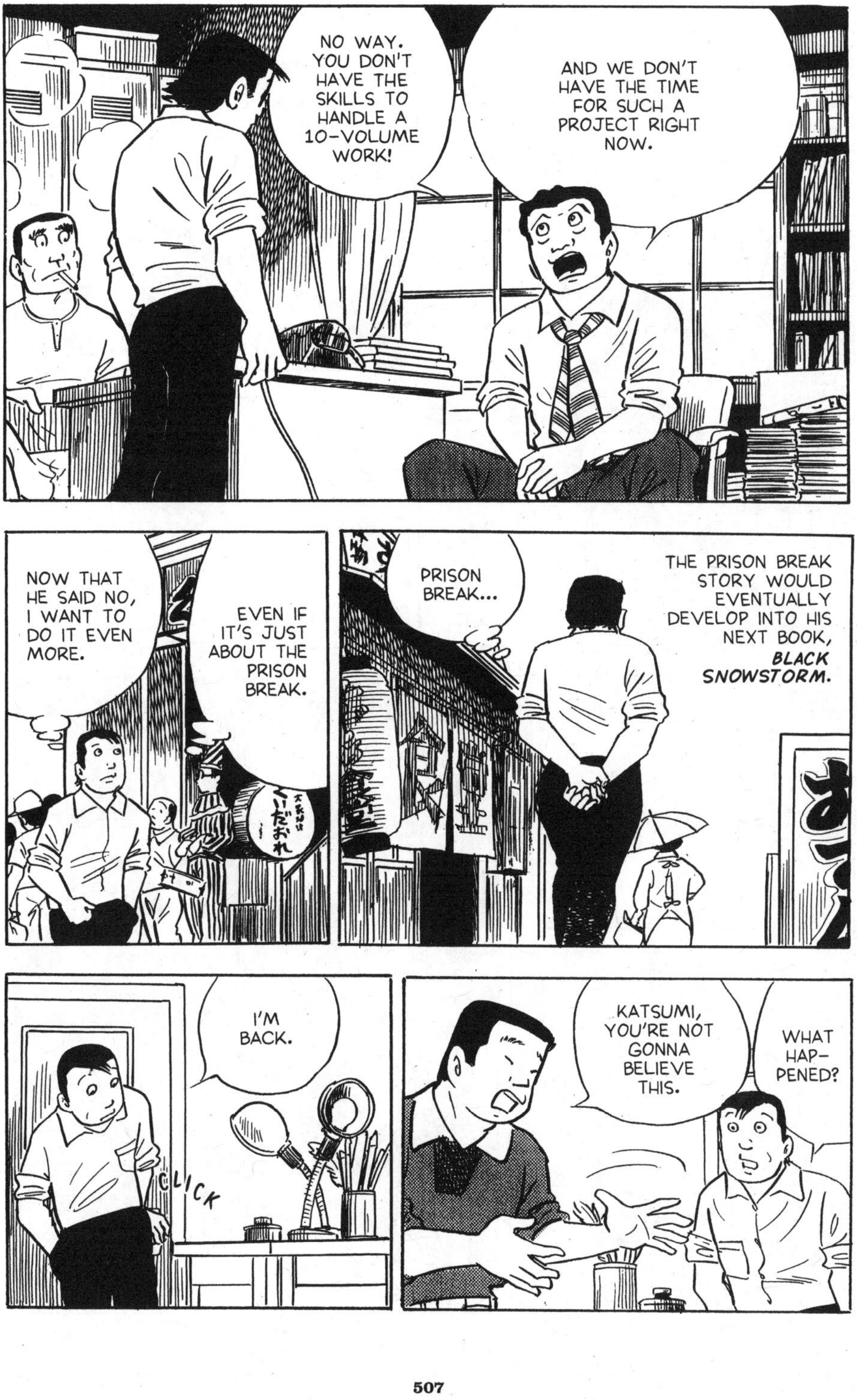
NO WAY. YOU DON'T HAVE THE SKILLS TO HANDLE A 10-VOLUME WORK!
AND WE DON'T HAVE THE TIME FOR SUCH A PROJECT RIGHT NOW.
NOW THAT HE SAID NO, I WANT TO DO IT EVEN MORE.
EVEN IF IT'S JUST ABOUT THE PRISON BREAK.
くいだおれ
PRISON BREAK...
THE PRISON BREAK STORY WOULD EVENTUALLY DEVELOP INTO HIS NEXT BOOK, ***BLACK SNOWSTORM.***
I'M BACK.
CLICK
KATSUMI, YOU'RE NOT GONNA BELIEVE THIS.
WHAT HAP-PENED?

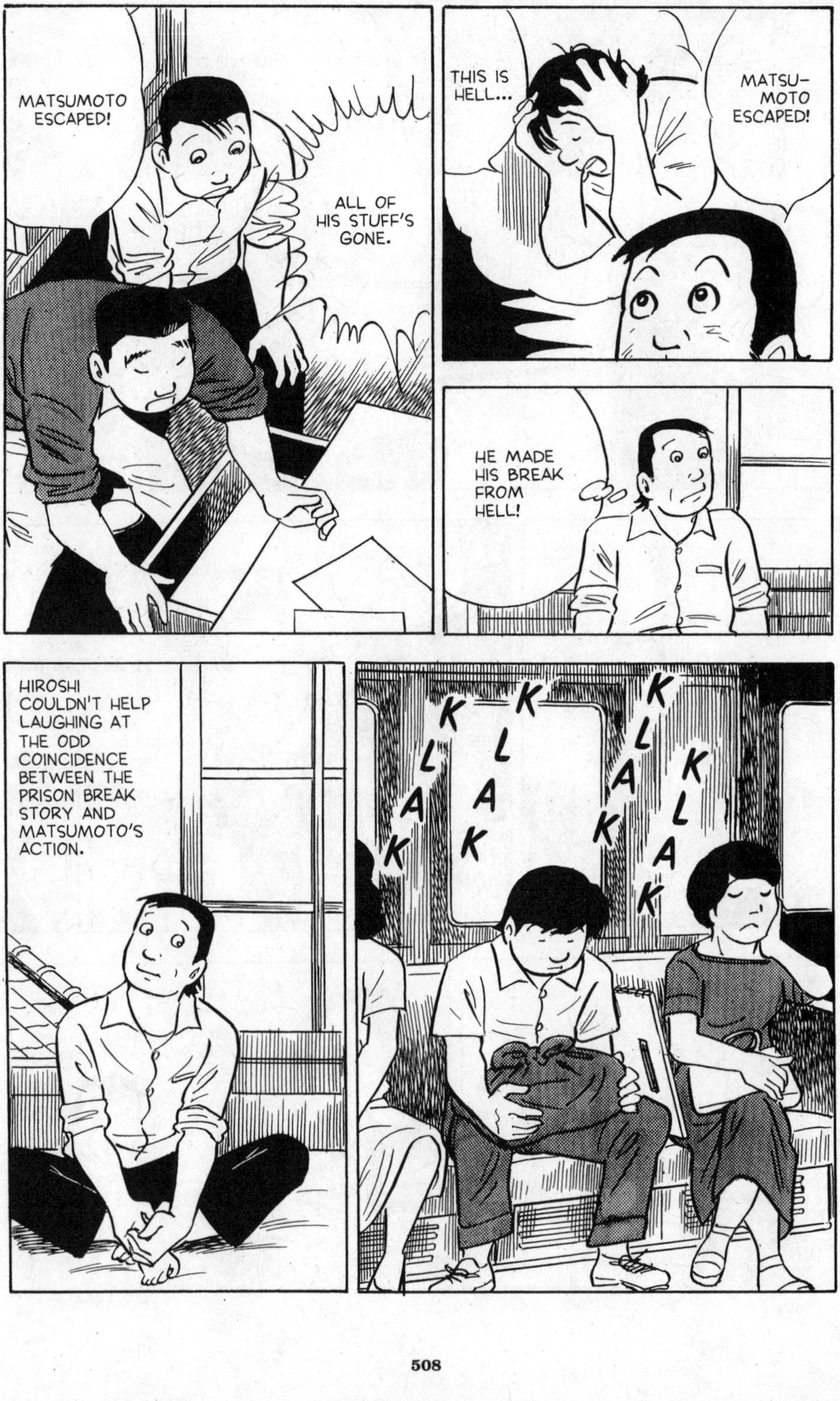
MATSUMOTO ESCAPED!
ALL OF HIS STUFF'S GONE.
THIS IS HELL...
MATSU-MOTO ESCAPED!
HE MADE HIS BREAK FROM HELL!
HIROSHI COULDN'T HELP LAUGHING AT THE ODD COINCIDENCE BETWEEN THE PRISON BREAK STORY AND MATSUMOTO'S ACTION.
KLAK
KLAK
KLAK
KLAK

PASSION AND SEDUCTION

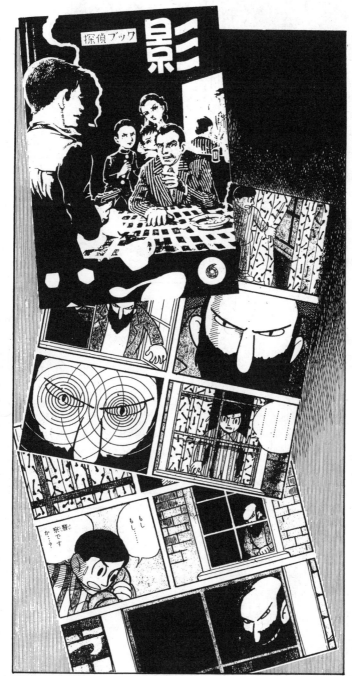

TITLE: *SHADOW DETECTIVE BOOK*

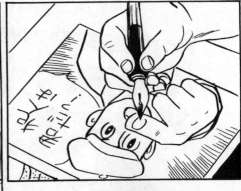

KLAK

AT THIS POINT, IT TOOK HIROSHI AN ENTIRE MONTH TO WRITE A STORY FOR *SHADOW*.

THERE AREN'T ENOUGH PAGES IN *SHADOW* FOR AN EXPERIMENTAL WORK.

I WANT TO WRITE A REALLY LONG STORY USING ENTIRELY NEW NARRATIVE TECHNIQUES.

AN UNFAMILIAR, INDESCRIBABLE FEELING LOOMED OVER HIM AND HE FELT INCREASINGLY FRUSTRATED AS THE DAYS PASSED.

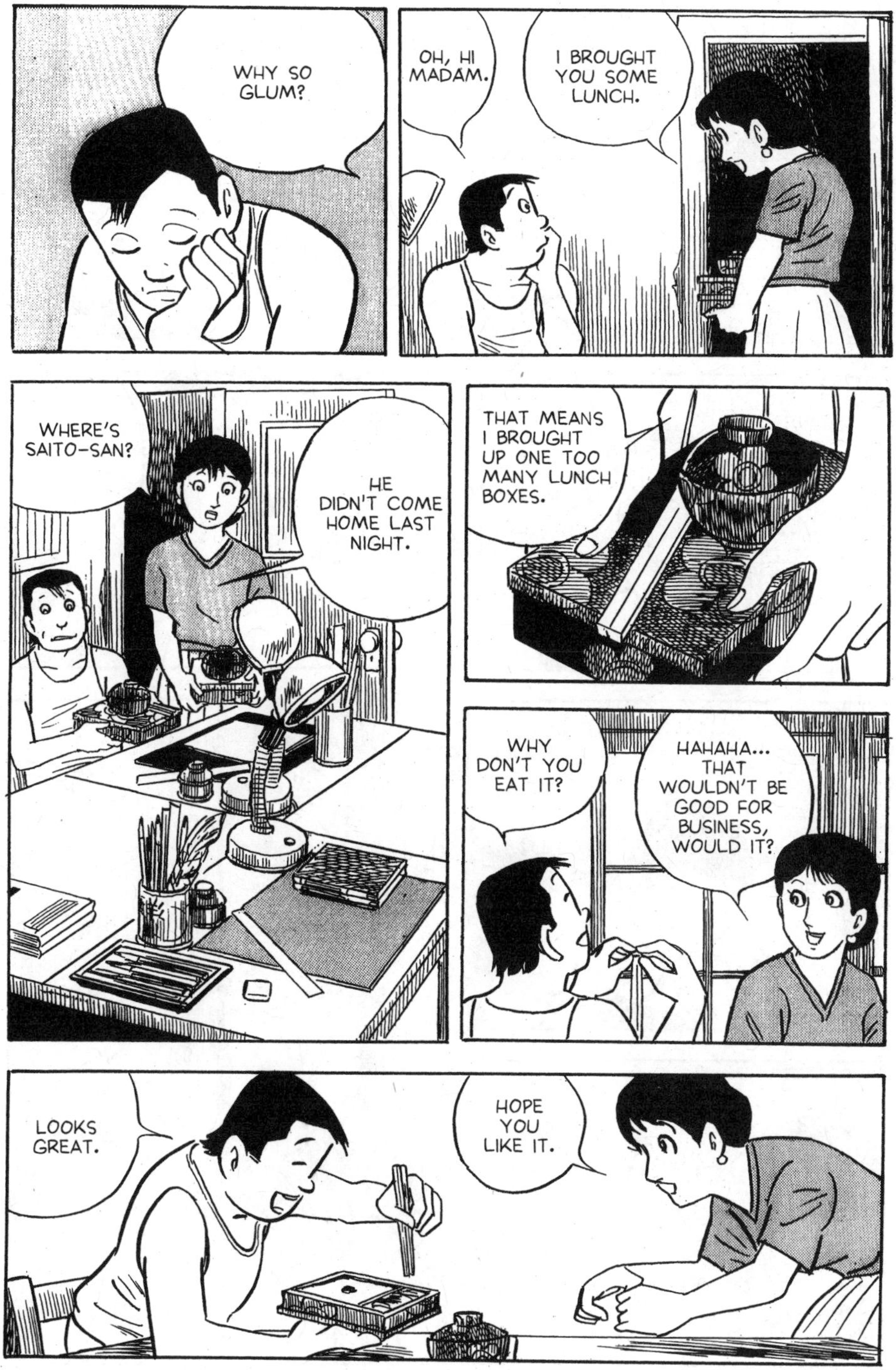
WHY SO GLUM?
OH, HI MADAM.
I BROUGHT YOU SOME LUNCH.
WHERE'S SAITO-SAN?
HE DIDN'T COME HOME LAST NIGHT.
THAT MEANS I BROUGHT UP ONE TOO MANY LUNCH BOXES.
WHY DON'T YOU EAT IT?
HAHAHA... THAT WOULDN'T BE GOOD FOR BUSINESS, WOULD IT?
LOOKS GREAT.
HOPE YOU LIKE IT.

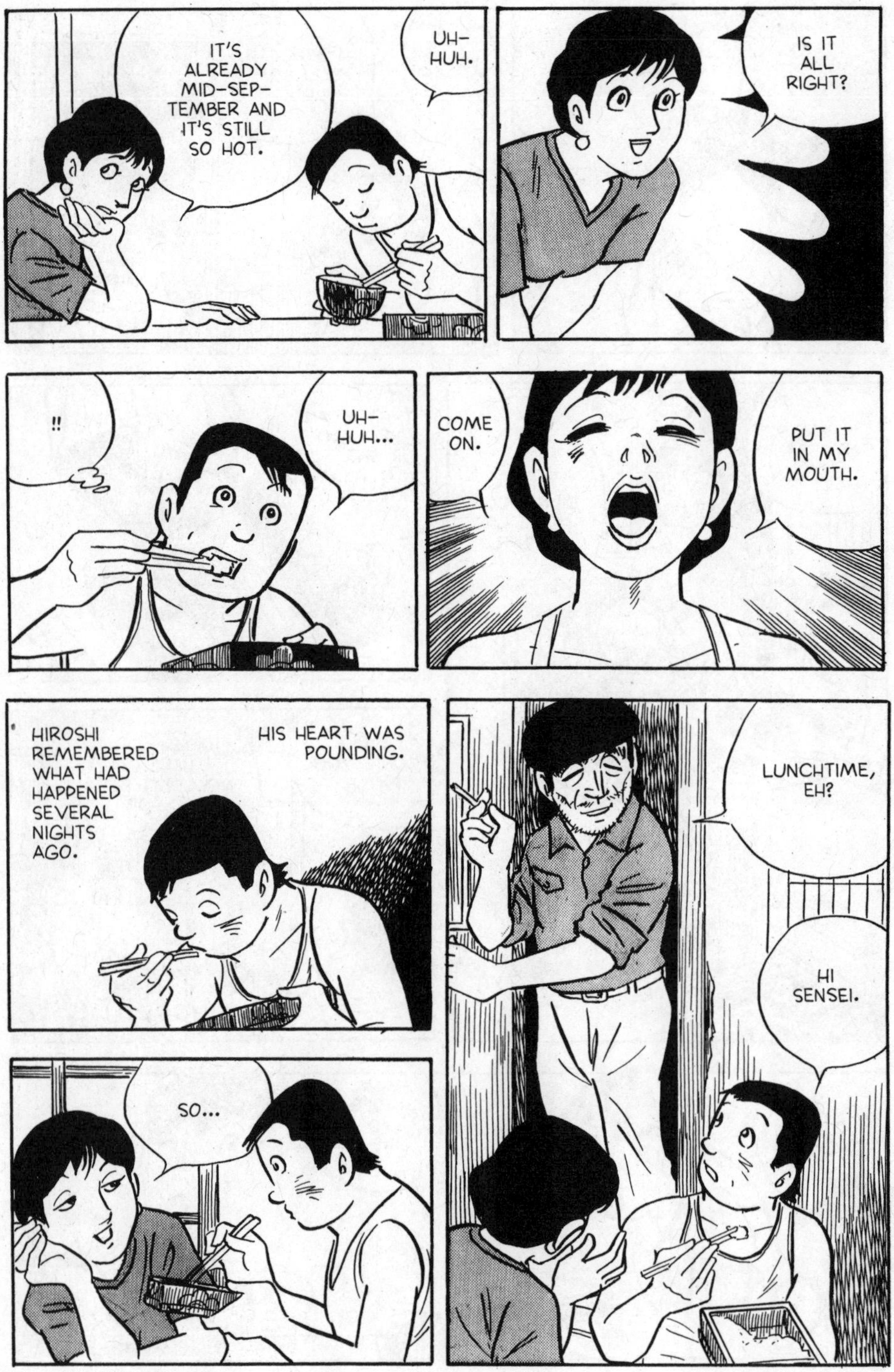
IT'S ALREADY MID-SEP-TEMBER AND IT'S STILL SO HOT.
UH-HUH.
IS IT ALL RIGHT?
!!
UH-HUH...
COME ON.
PUT IT IN MY MOUTH.
HIROSHI REMEMBERED WHAT HAD HAPPENED SEVERAL NIGHTS AGO.
HIS HEART WAS POUNDING.
LUNCHTIME, EH?
HI SENSEI.
SO...

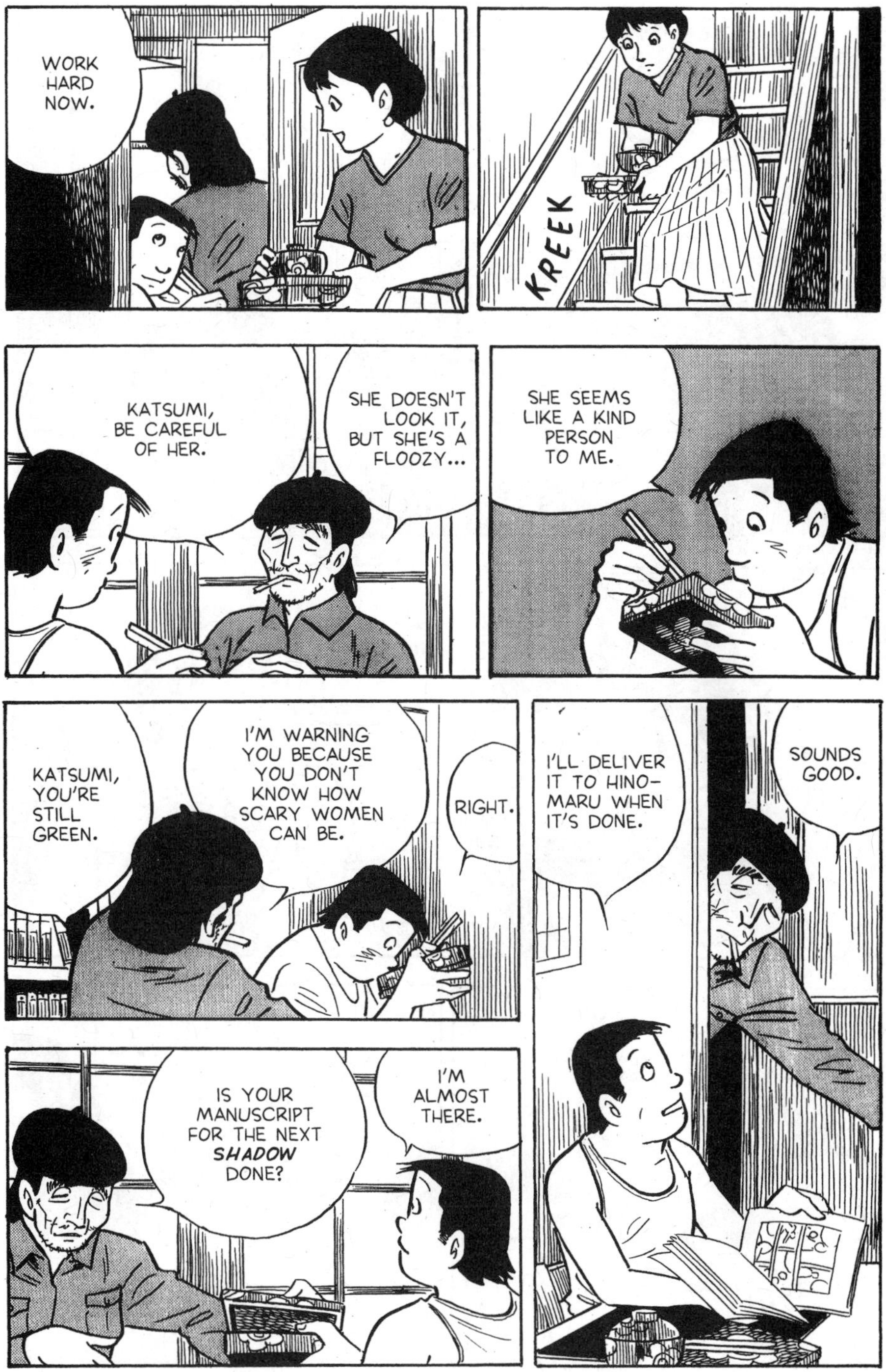
WORK HARD NOW.
KREEK
KATSUMI, BE CAREFUL OF HER.
SHE DOESN'T LOOK IT, BUT SHE'S A FLOOZY...
SHE SEEMS LIKE A KIND PERSON TO ME.
KATSUMI, YOU'RE STILL GREEN.
I'M WARNING YOU BECAUSE YOU DON'T KNOW HOW SCARY WOMEN CAN BE.
RIGHT.
IS YOUR MANUSCRIPT FOR THE NEXT SHADOW DONE?
I'M ALMOST THERE.
I'LL DELIVER IT TO HINO-MARU WHEN IT'S DONE.
SOUNDS GOOD.

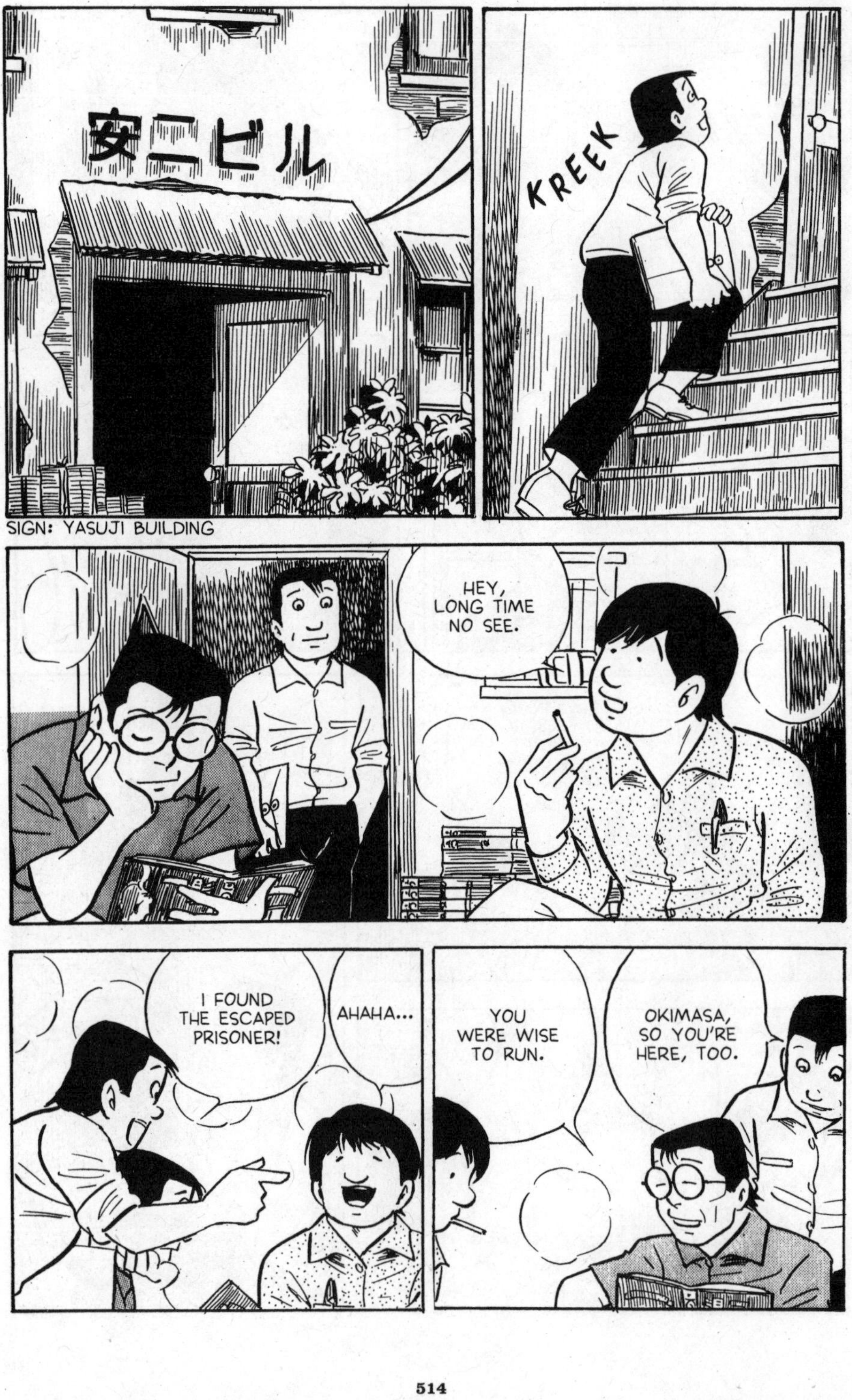
安二ビル
SIGN: YASUJI BUILDING
KREEK
HEY, LONG TIME NO SEE.
I FOUND THE ESCAPED PRISONER!
AHAHA...
YOU WERE WISE TO RUN.
OKIMASA, SO YOU'RE HERE, TOO.

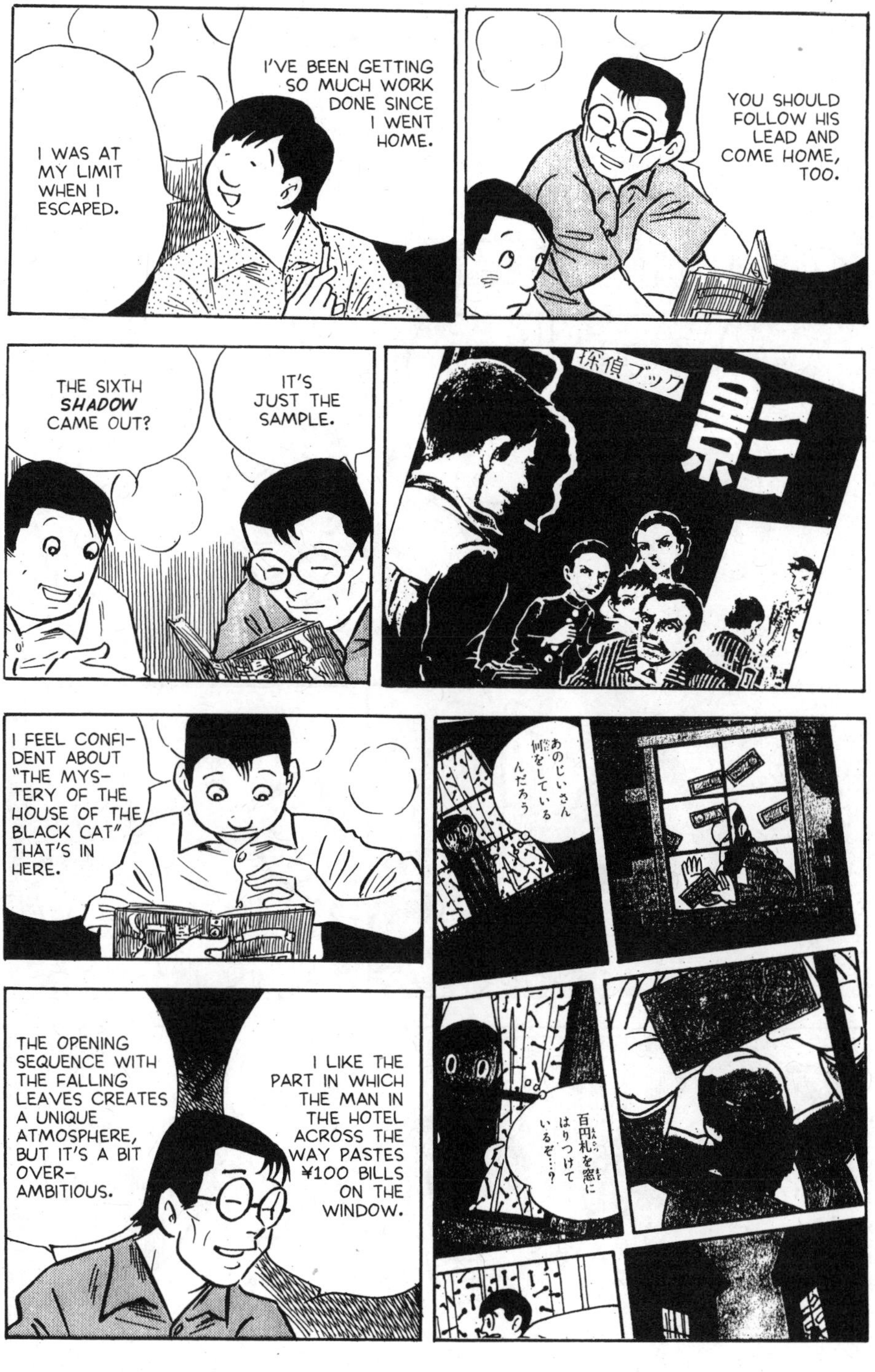
I WAS AT MY LIMIT WHEN I ESCAPED.
I'VE BEEN GETTING SO MUCH WORK DONE SINCE I WENT HOME.
YOU SHOULD FOLLOW HIS LEAD AND COME HOME, TOO.
THE SIXTH *SHADOW* CAME OUT?
IT'S JUST THE SAMPLE.
探偵ブック
I FEEL CONFIDENT ABOUT "THE MYSTERY OF THE HOUSE OF THE BLACK CAT" THAT'S IN HERE.
あのじいさん何をしているんだろう
THE OPENING SEQUENCE WITH THE FALLING LEAVES CREATES A UNIQUE ATMOSPHERE, BUT IT'S A BIT OVER-AMBITIOUS.
I LIKE THE PART IN WHICH THE MAN IN THE HOTEL ACROSS THE WAY PASTES ¥100 BILLS ON THE WINDOW.
百円札を窓にはりつけているぞ…?

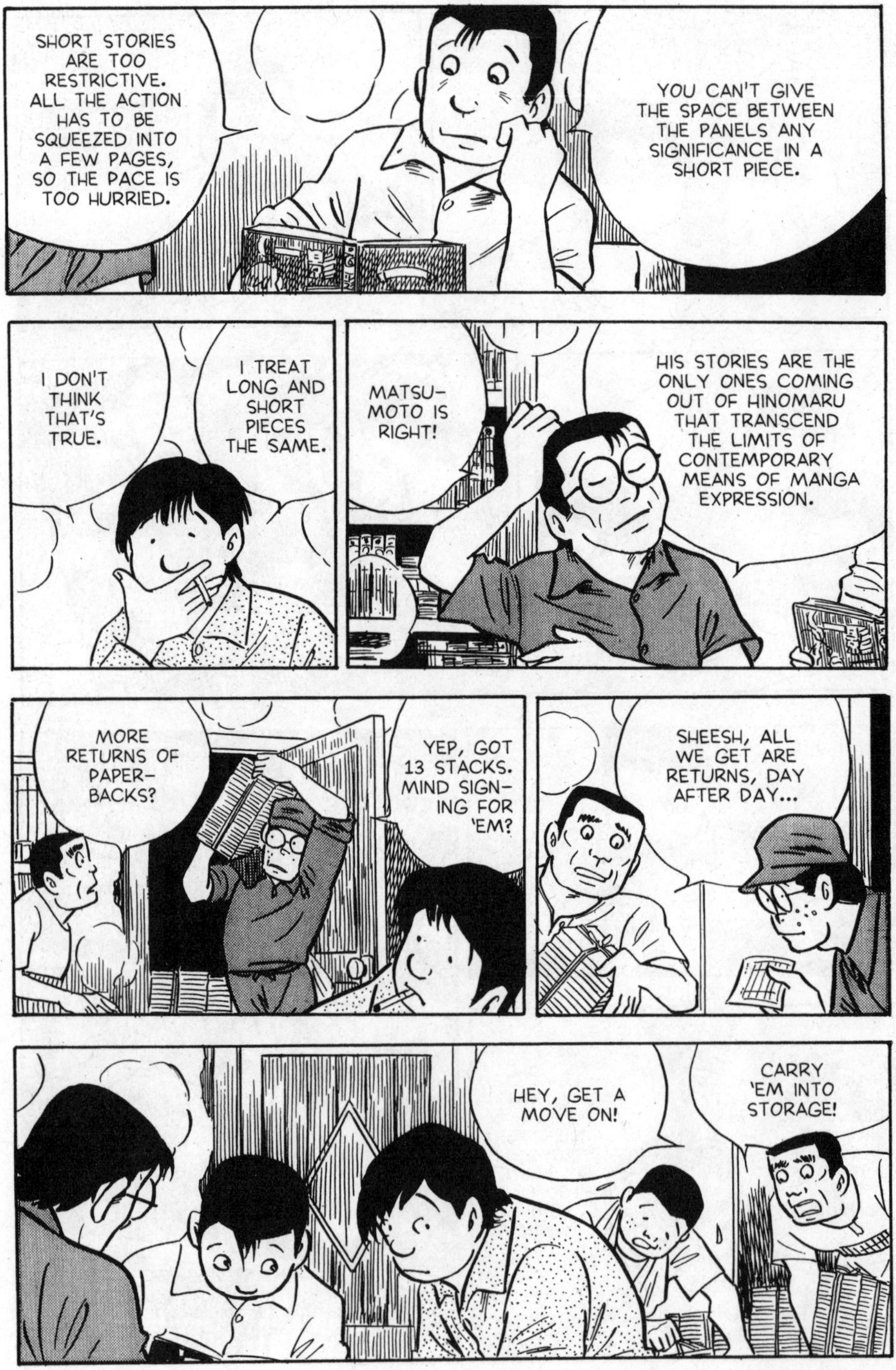
SHORT STORIES ARE TOO RESTRICTIVE. ALL THE ACTION HAS TO BE SQUEEZED INTO A FEW PAGES, SO THE PACE IS TOO HURRIED.
YOU CAN'T GIVE THE SPACE BETWEEN THE PANELS ANY SIGNIFICANCE IN A SHORT PIECE.
I DON'T THINK THAT'S TRUE.
I TREAT LONG AND SHORT PIECES THE SAME.
MATSU-MOTO IS RIGHT!
HIS STORIES ARE THE ONLY ONES COMING OUT OF HINOMARU THAT TRANSCEND THE LIMITS OF CONTEMPORARY MEANS OF MANGA EXPRESSION.
MORE RETURNS OF PAPER-BACKS?
YEP, GOT 13 STACKS. MIND SIGNING FOR 'EM?
SHEESH, ALL WE GET ARE RETURNS, DAY AFTER DAY...
HEY, GET A MOVE ON!
CARRY 'EM INTO STORAGE!

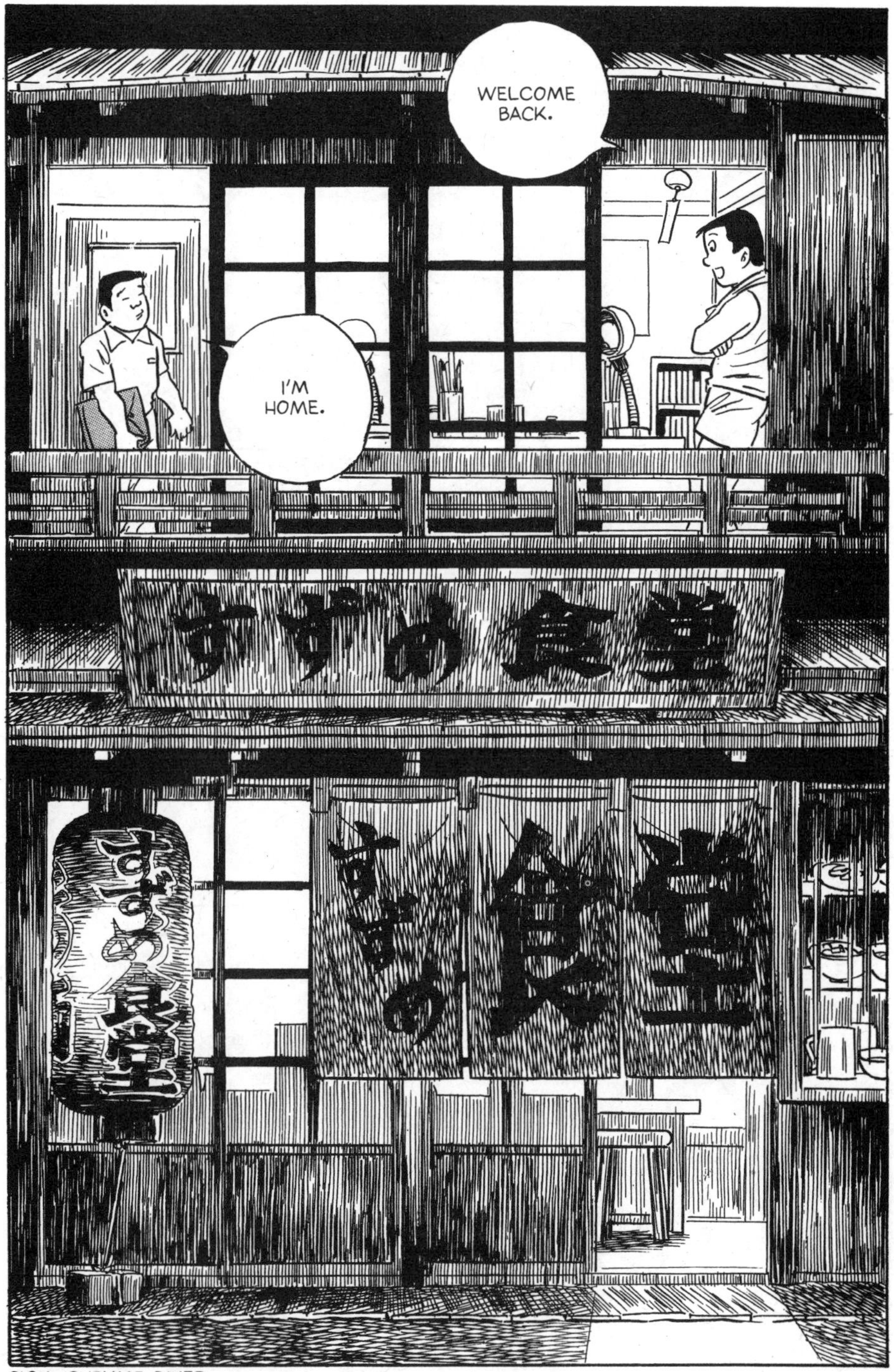
WELCOME BACK.
I'M HOME.
すずめ食堂
すずめ食堂
すずめ食堂

SIGN: SUZUME DINER

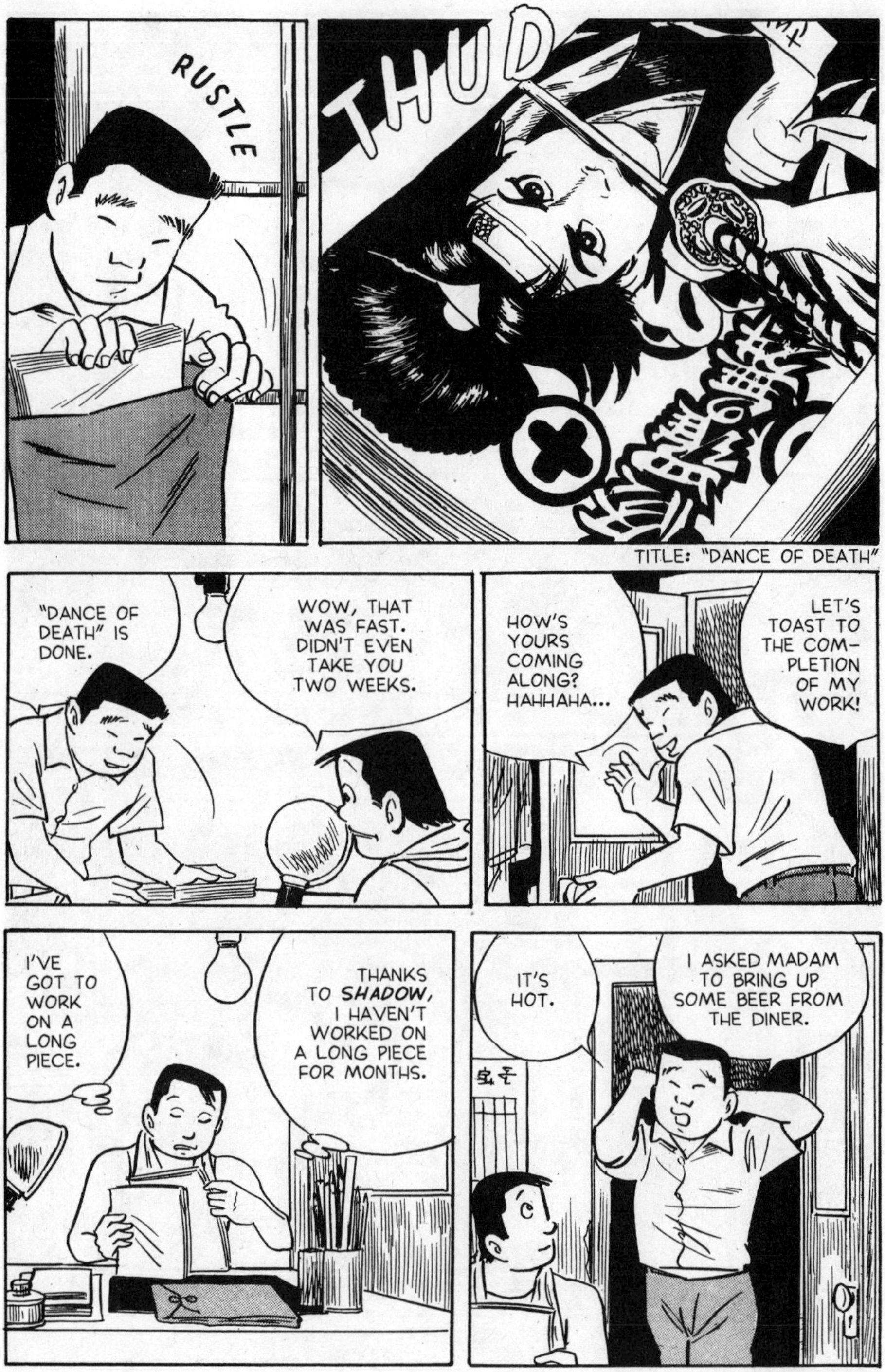
RUSTLE
THUD
TITLE: "DANCE OF DEATH"
"DANCE OF DEATH" IS DONE.
WOW, THAT WAS FAST. DIDN'T EVEN TAKE YOU TWO WEEKS.
HOW'S YOURS COMING ALONG? HAHHAHA...
LET'S TOAST TO THE COMPLETION OF MY WORK!
I'VE GOT TO WORK ON A LONG PIECE.
THANKS TO *SHADOW*, I HAVEN'T WORKED ON A LONG PIECE FOR MONTHS.
IT'S HOT.
I ASKED MADAM TO BRING UP SOME BEER FROM THE DINER.

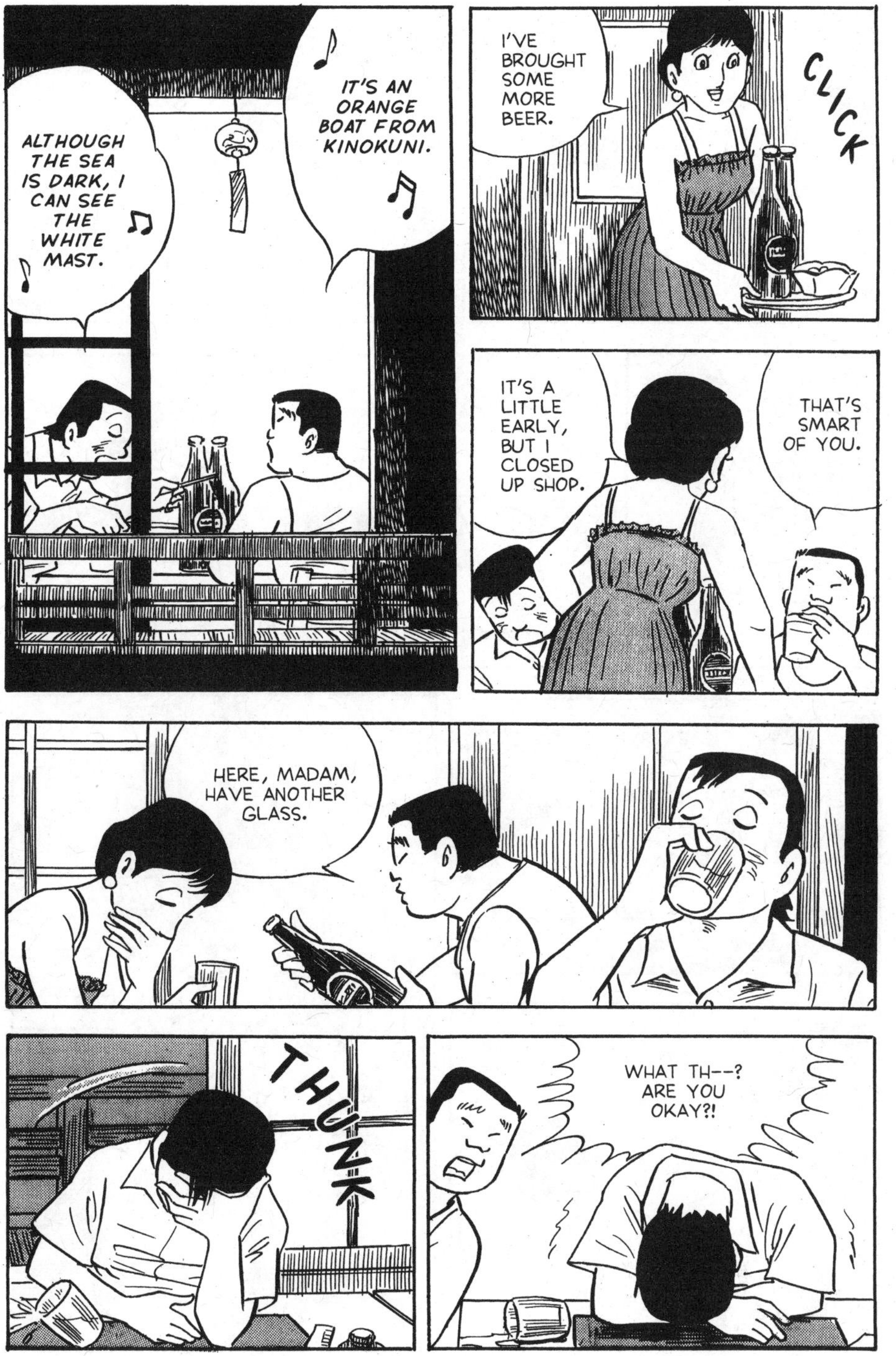
♪ ALTHOUGH THE SEA IS DARK, I CAN SEE THE WHITE MAST. ♫
♪ IT'S AN ORANGE BOAT FROM KINOKUNI. ♫
I'VE BROUGHT SOME MORE BEER.
CLICK
IT'S A LITTLE EARLY, BUT I CLOSED UP SHOP.
THAT'S SMART OF YOU.
HERE, MADAM, HAVE ANOTHER GLASS.
THUNK
WHAT TH--? ARE YOU OKAY?!

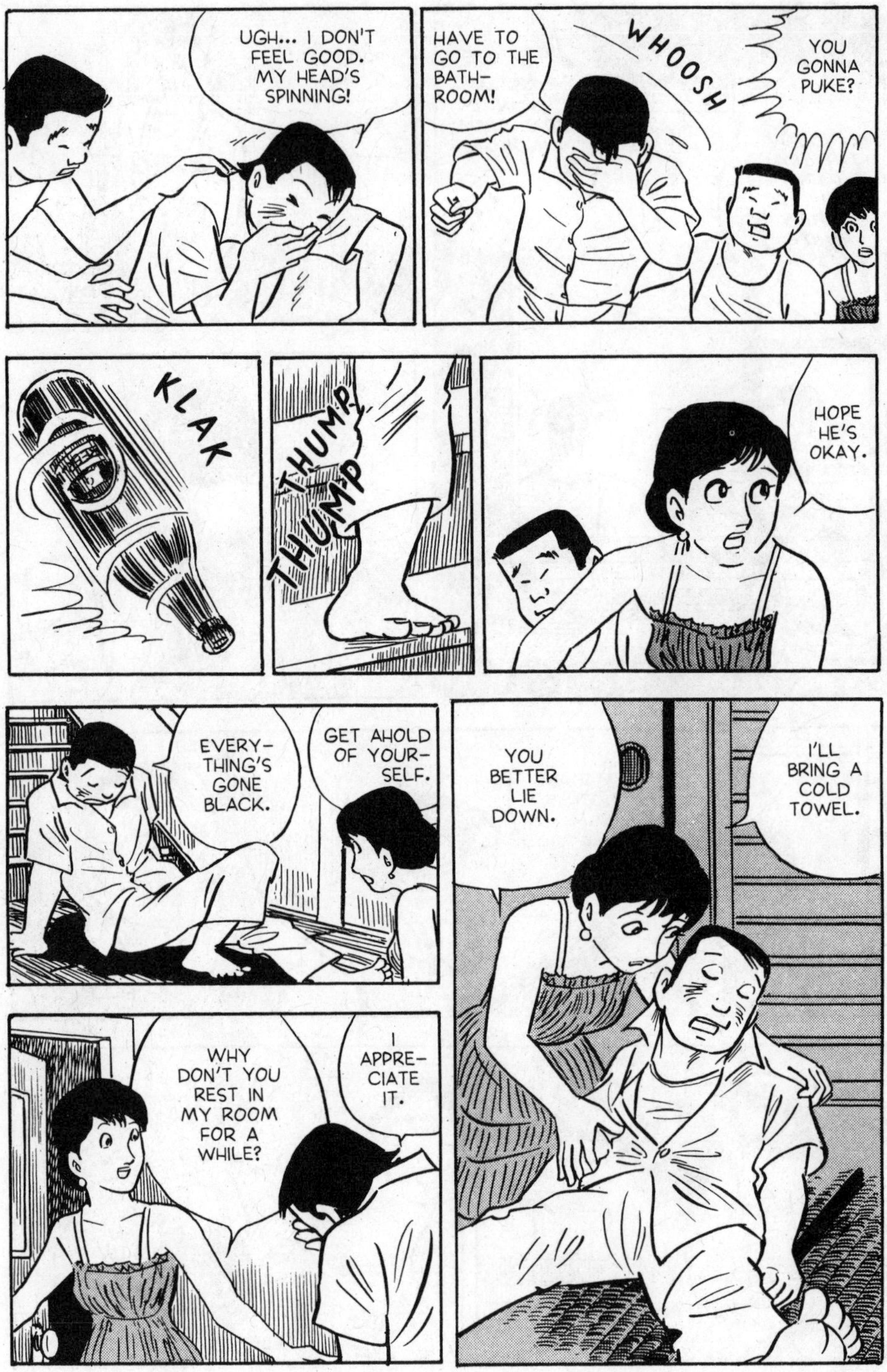
UGH... I DON'T FEEL GOOD. MY HEAD'S SPINNING!
HAVE TO GO TO THE BATH-ROOM!
WHOOSH
YOU GONNA PUKE?
KLAK
THUMP
THUMP
HOPE HE'S OKAY.
EVERY-THING'S GONE BLACK.
GET AHOLD OF YOUR-SELF.
YOU BETTER LIE DOWN.
I'LL BRING A COLD TOWEL.
WHY DON'T YOU REST IN MY ROOM FOR A WHILE?
I APPRECI-ATE IT.

YOU SHOULDN'T HAVE DRANK SO MUCH.

SORRY TO BOTHER YOU.

I BETTER BRING YOU A PILLOW.

I FEEL MUCH BETTER NOW...

THANKS.

HERE, LET ME BRING YOU A NEW COLD TOWEL.

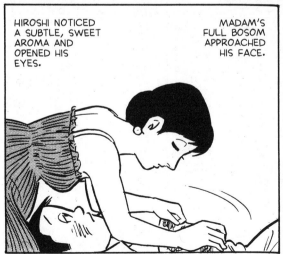

HIROSHI NOTICED A SUBTLE, SWEET AROMA AND OPENED HIS EYES.

MADAM'S FULL BOSOM APPROACHED HIS FACE.

MADAM!

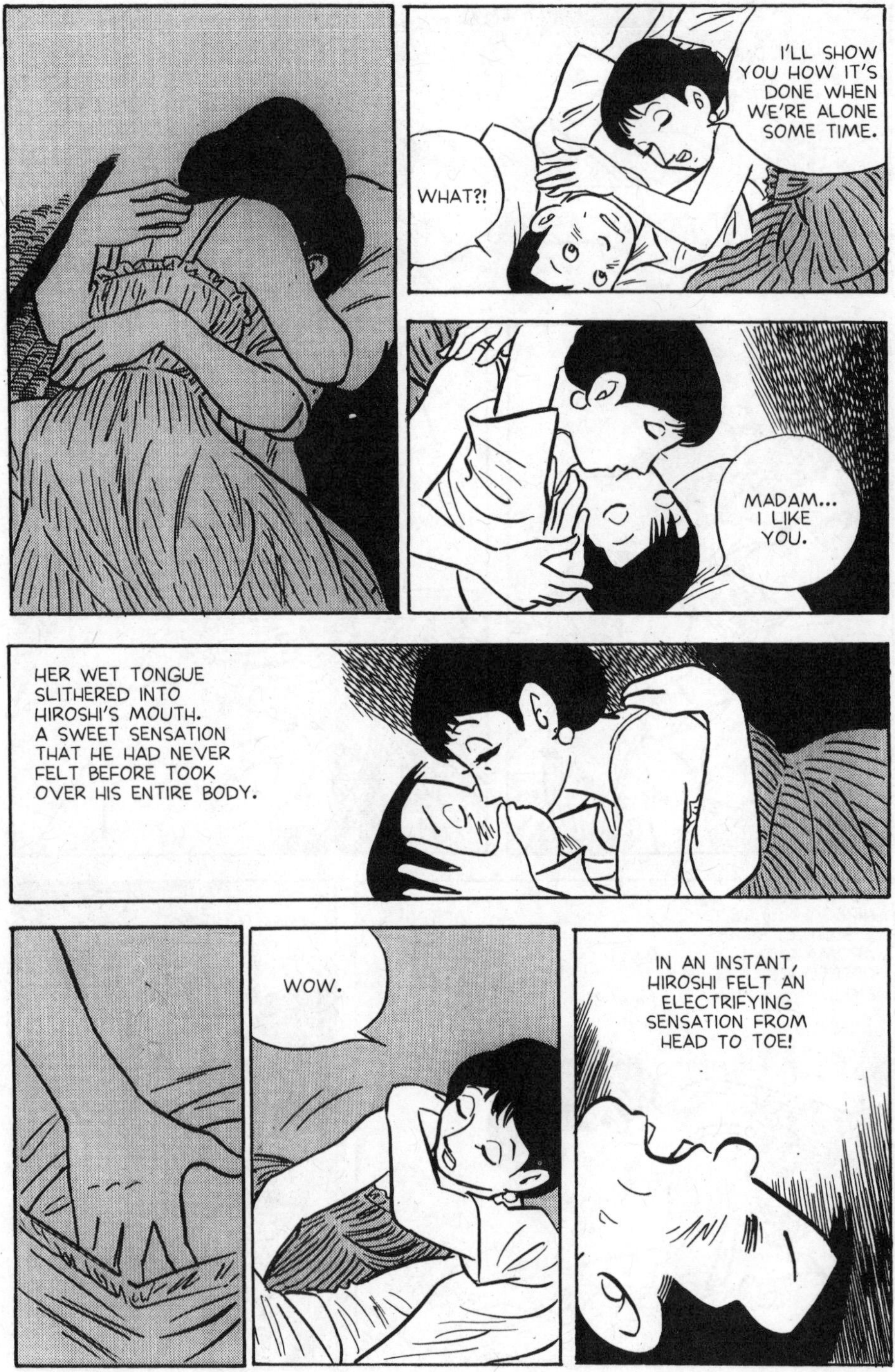
I'LL SHOW YOU HOW IT'S DONE WHEN WE'RE ALONE SOME TIME.
WHAT?!
MADAM... I LIKE YOU.
HER WET TONGUE SLITHERED INTO HIROSHI'S MOUTH. A SWEET SENSATION THAT HE HAD NEVER FELT BEFORE TOOK OVER HIS ENTIRE BODY.
WOW.
IN AN INSTANT, HIROSHI FELT AN ELECTRIFYING SENSATION FROM HEAD TO TOE!

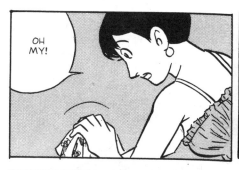

OH MY!

MADAM... I'M SORRY. I'VE WET MY PANTS.

TEE HEE...

HAHA- HAHA

AHA- HAHA- HAHA...

HIROSHI ROLLED ON THE FLOOR, JOINING THE LAUGHTER IN HOPES OF MASKING HIS SELF-HATRED.

KATSUMI, ARE YOU ALL RIGHT?

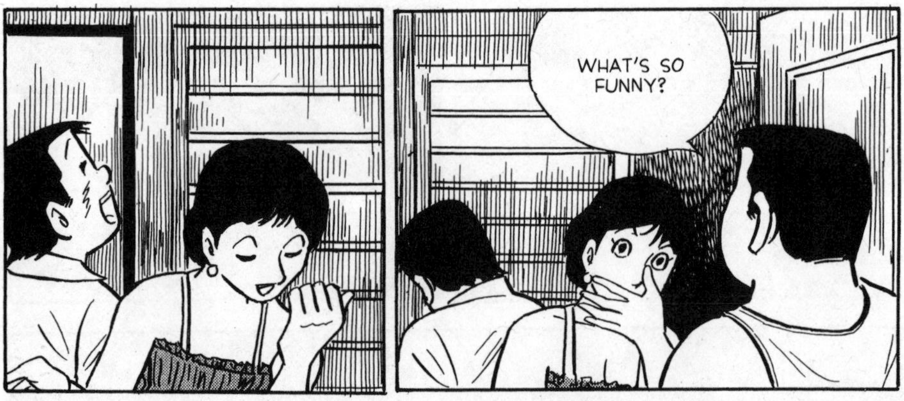
WHAT'S SO FUNNY?

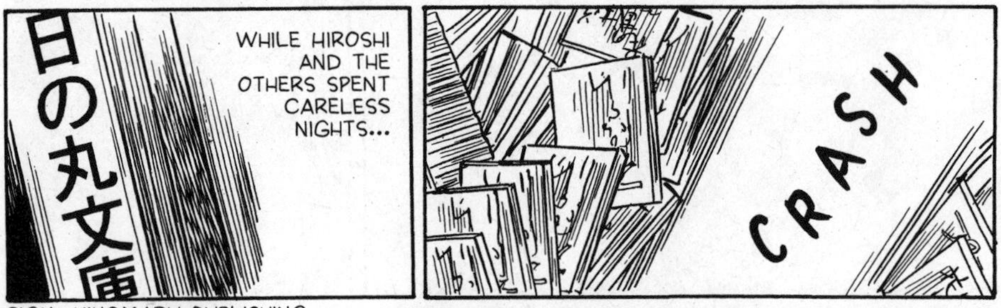
日の丸文庫
WHILE HIROSHI AND THE OTHERS SPENT CARELESS NIGHTS...
CRASH

SIGN: HINOMARU PUBLISHING

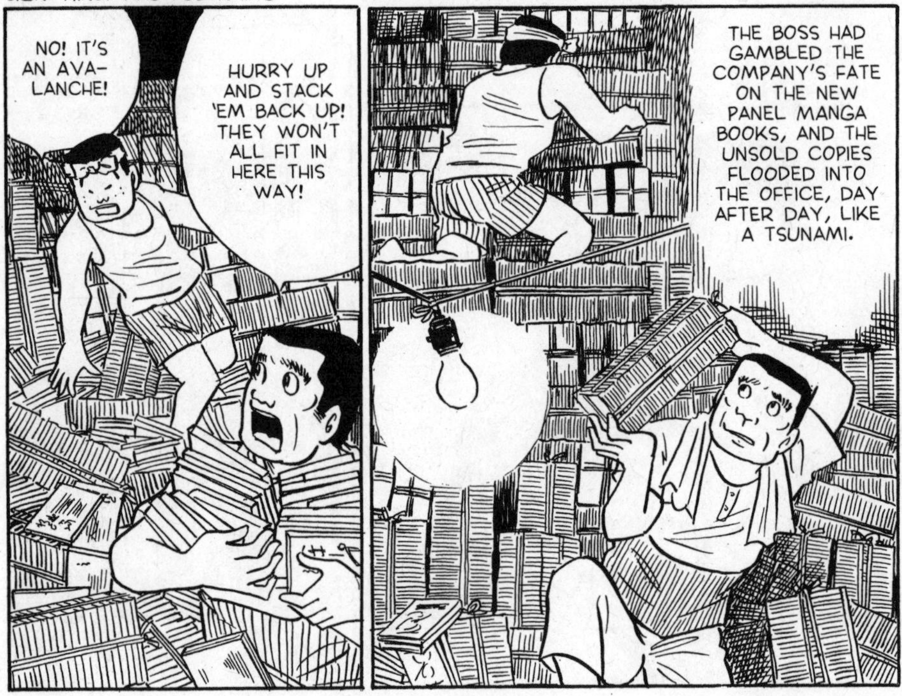
NO! IT'S AN AVA-LANCHE!
HURRY UP AND STACK 'EM BACK UP! THEY WON'T ALL FIT IN HERE THIS WAY!
THE BOSS HAD GAMBLED THE COMPANY'S FATE ON THE NEW PANEL MANGA BOOKS, AND THE UNSOLD COPIES FLOODED INTO THE OFFICE, DAY AFTER DAY, LIKE A TSUNAMI.

A TIME FOR GOOD-BYE

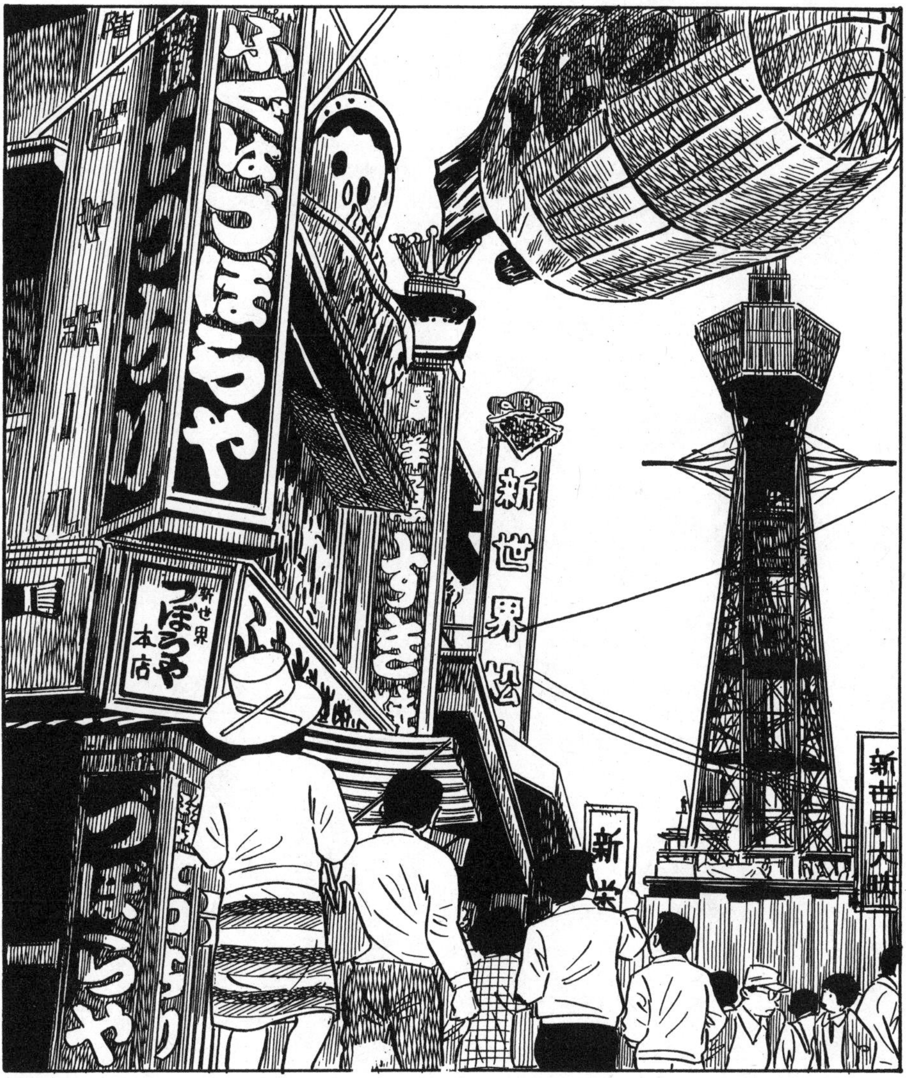
ふぐ つぼらや
新世界 つぼらや 本店

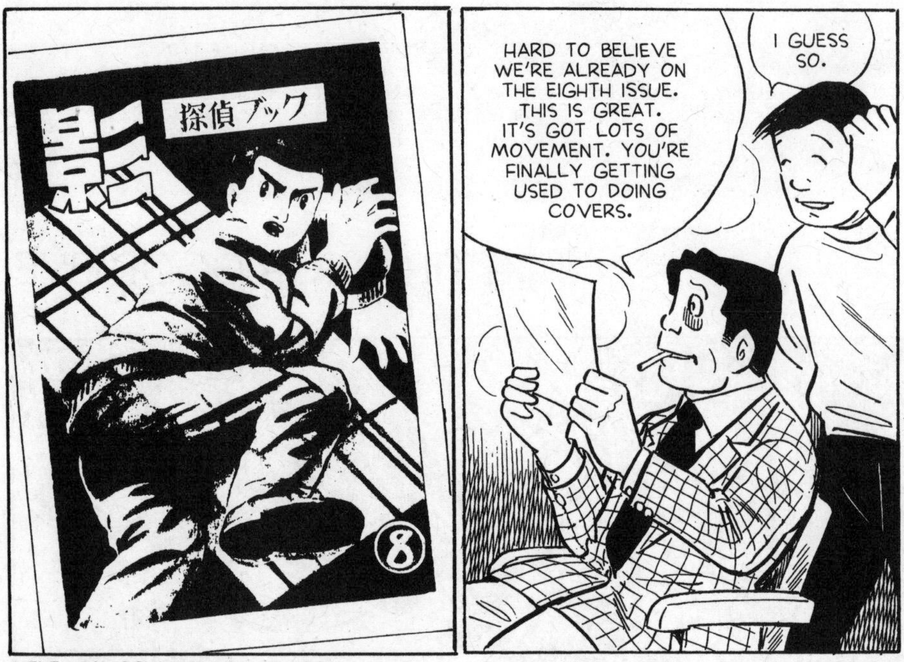
探偵ブック
8
HARD TO BELIEVE WE'RE ALREADY ON THE EIGHTH ISSUE. THIS IS GREAT. IT'S GOT LOTS OF MOVEMENT. YOU'RE FINALLY GETTING USED TO DOING COVERS.
I GUESS SO.

TITLE: *SHADOW DETECTIVE BOOK*

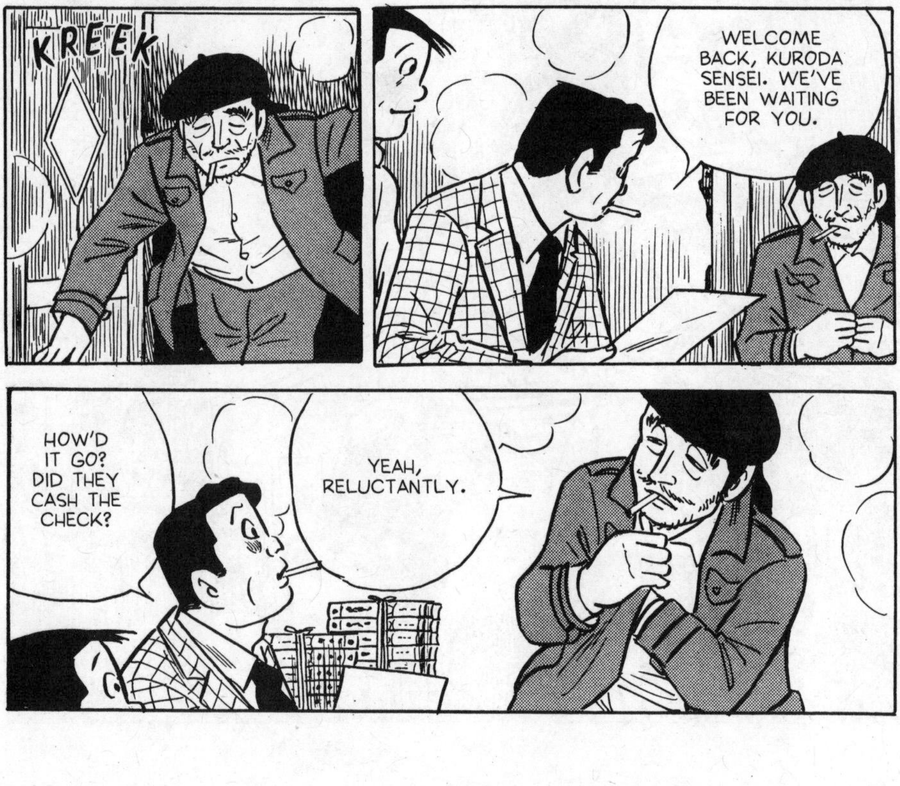
KREEK
WELCOME BACK, KURODA SENSEI. WE'VE BEEN WAITING FOR YOU.
HOW'D IT GO? DID THEY CASH THE CHECK?
YEAH, RELUCTANTLY.

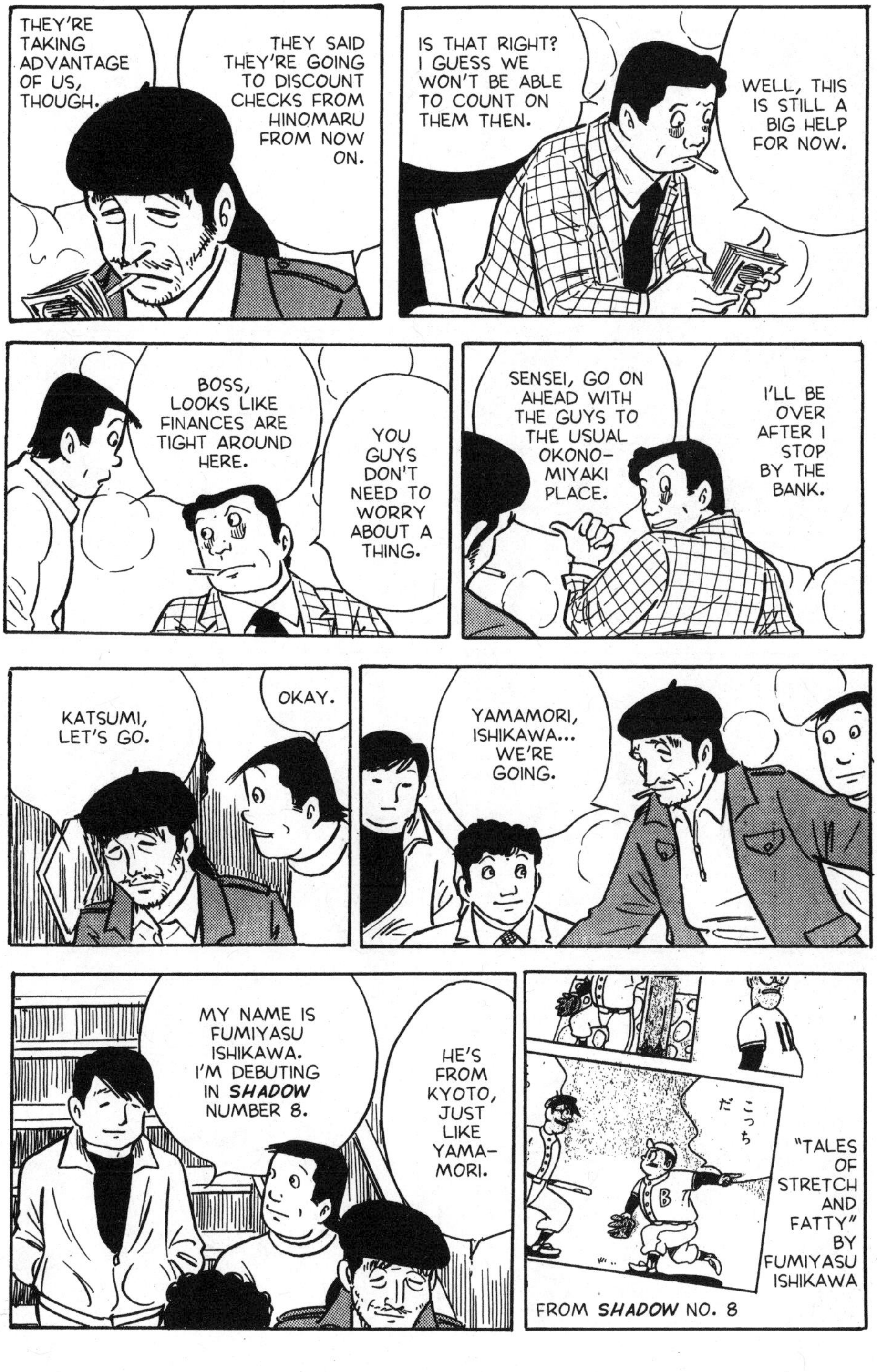
THEY'RE TAKING ADVANTAGE OF US, THOUGH.
THEY SAID THEY'RE GOING TO DISCOUNT CHECKS FROM HINOMARU FROM NOW ON.
IS THAT RIGHT? I GUESS WE WON'T BE ABLE TO COUNT ON THEM THEN.
WELL, THIS IS STILL A BIG HELP FOR NOW.
BOSS, LOOKS LIKE FINANCES ARE TIGHT AROUND HERE.
YOU GUYS DON'T NEED TO WORRY ABOUT A THING.
SENSEI, GO ON AHEAD WITH THE GUYS TO THE USUAL OKONOMIYAKI PLACE.
I'LL BE OVER AFTER I STOP BY THE BANK.
KATSUMI, LET'S GO.
OKAY.
YAMAMORI, ISHIKAWA... WE'RE GOING.
MY NAME IS FUMIYASU ISHIKAWA. I'M DEBUTING IN *SHADOW* NUMBER 8.
HE'S FROM KYOTO, JUST LIKE YAMAMORI.
こっちだ
"TALES OF STRETCH AND FATTY" BY FUMIYASU ISHIKAWA
FROM *SHADOW* NO. 8

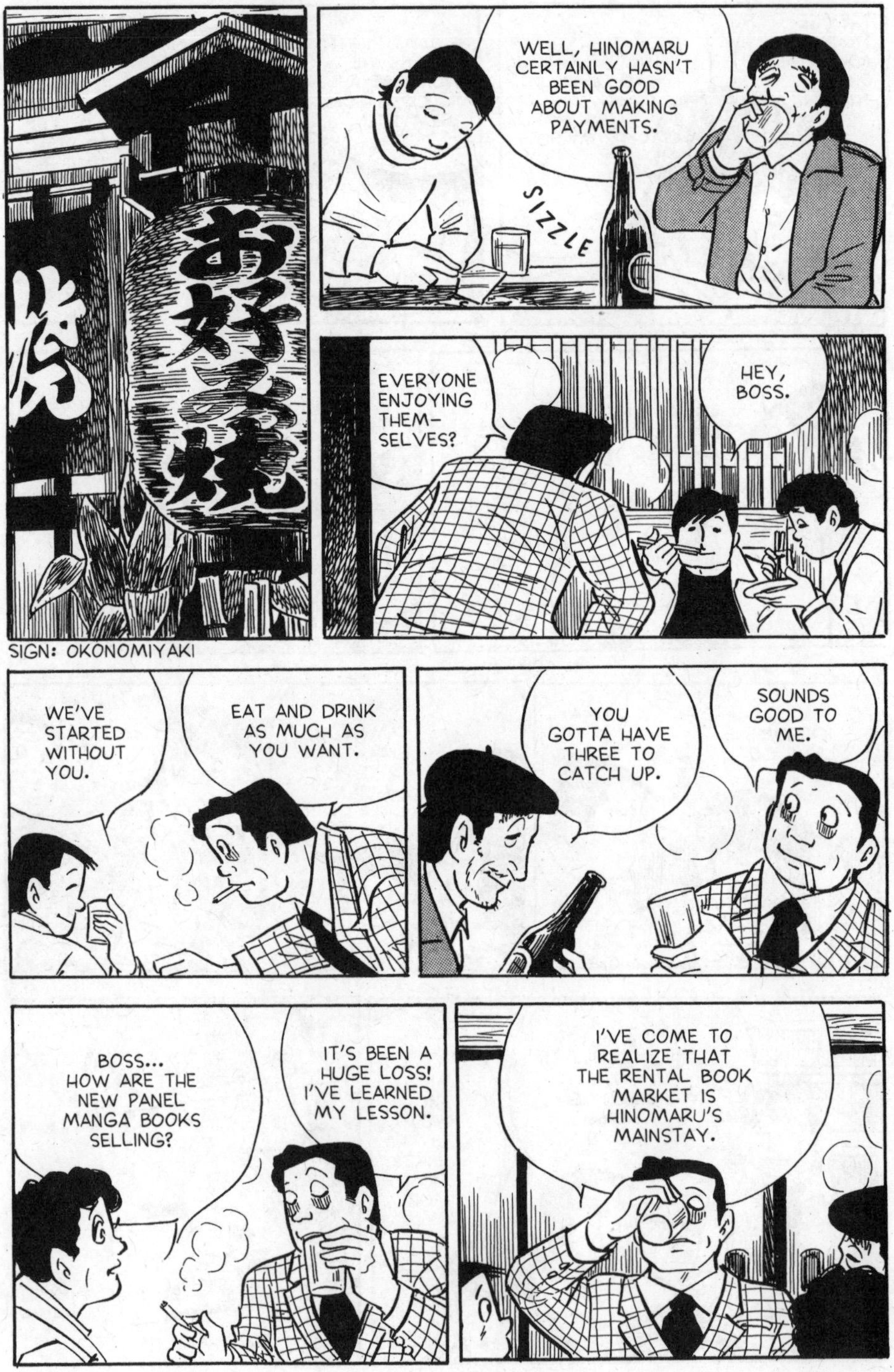
お好み焼
SIGN: OKONOMIYAKI
WELL, HINOMARU CERTAINLY HASN'T BEEN GOOD ABOUT MAKING PAYMENTS.
SIZZLE
EVERYONE ENJOYING THEM-SELVES?
HEY, BOSS.
WE'VE STARTED WITHOUT YOU.
EAT AND DRINK AS MUCH AS YOU WANT.
YOU GOTTA HAVE THREE TO CATCH UP.
SOUNDS GOOD TO ME.
BOSS... HOW ARE THE NEW PANEL MANGA BOOKS SELLING?
IT'S BEEN A HUGE LOSS! I'VE LEARNED MY LESSON.
I'VE COME TO REALIZE THAT THE RENTAL BOOK MARKET IS HINOMARU'S MAINSTAY.

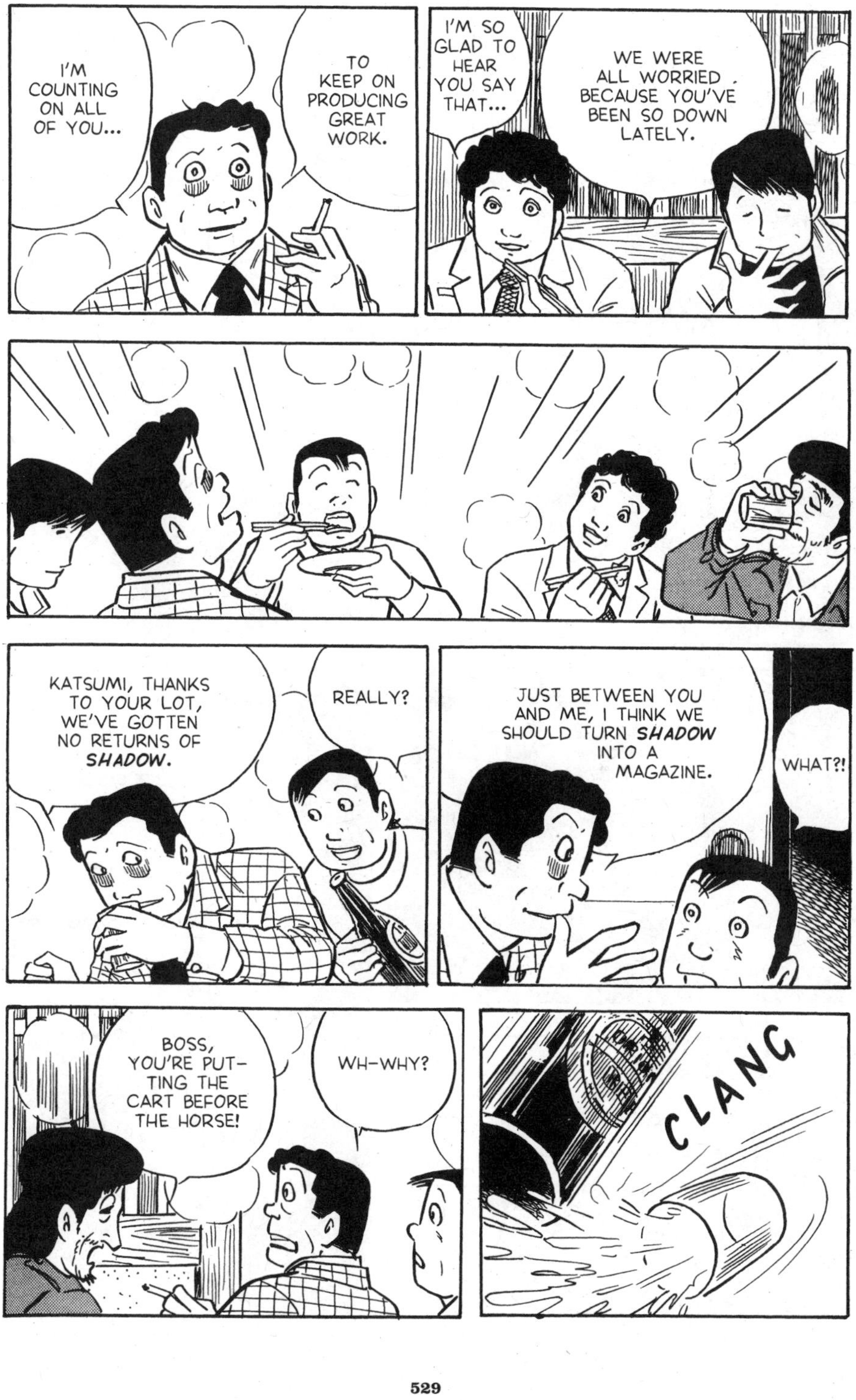
I'M COUNTING ON ALL OF YOU...
TO KEEP ON PRODUCING GREAT WORK.
I'M SO GLAD TO HEAR YOU SAY THAT...
WE WERE ALL WORRIED BECAUSE YOU'VE BEEN SO DOWN LATELY.
KATSUMI, THANKS TO YOUR LOT, WE'VE GOTTEN NO RETURNS OF SHADOW.
REALLY?
JUST BETWEEN YOU AND ME, I THINK WE SHOULD TURN SHADOW INTO A MAGAZINE.
WHAT?!
BOSS, YOU'RE PUT-TING THE CART BEFORE THE HORSE!
WH-WHY?
CLANG

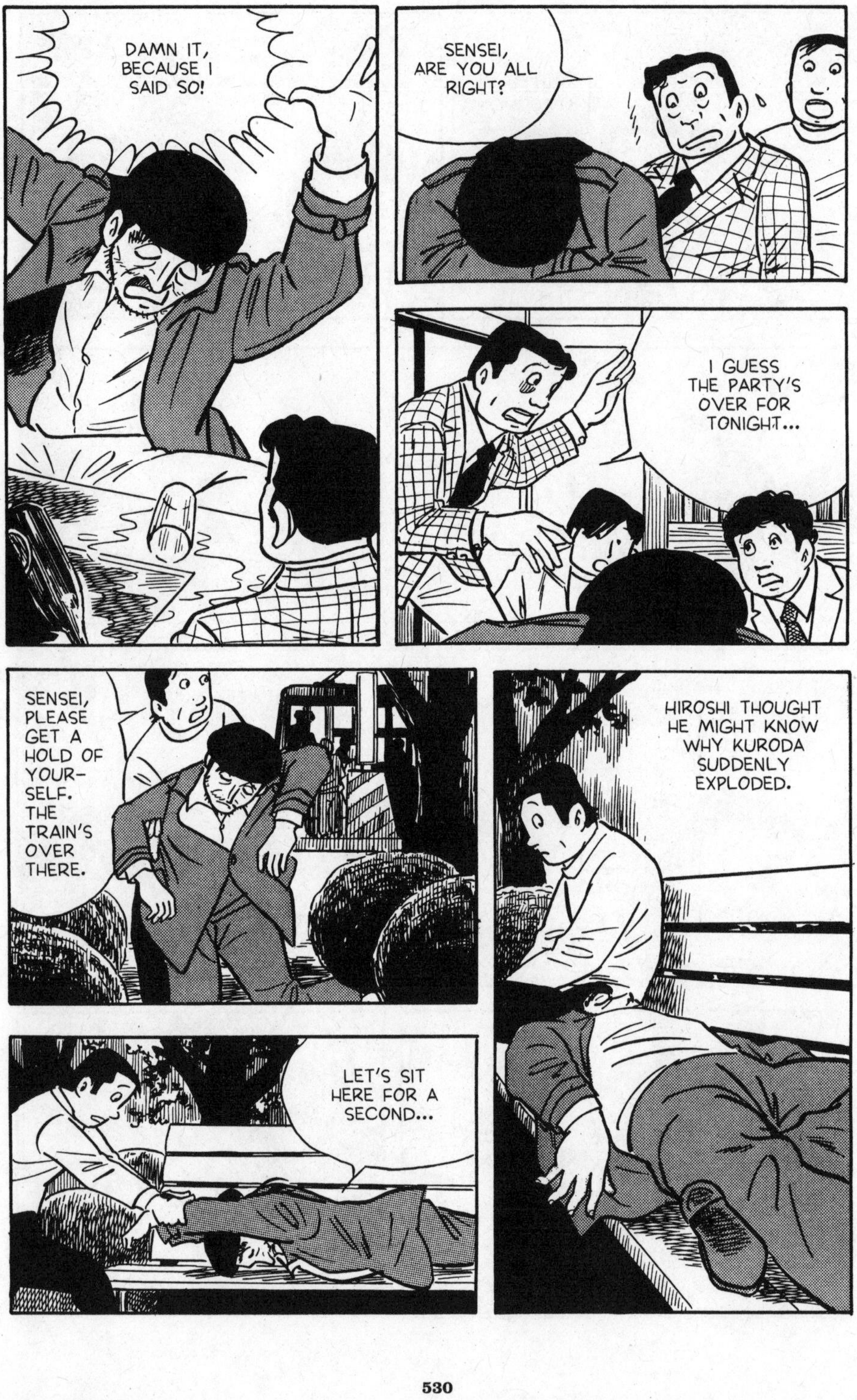
DAMN IT, BECAUSE I SAID SO!
SENSEI, ARE YOU ALL RIGHT?
I GUESS THE PARTY'S OVER FOR TONIGHT...
SENSEI, PLEASE GET A HOLD OF YOURSELF. THE TRAIN'S OVER THERE.
HIROSHI THOUGHT HE MIGHT KNOW WHY KURODA SUDDENLY EXPLODED.
LET'S SIT HERE FOR A SECOND...

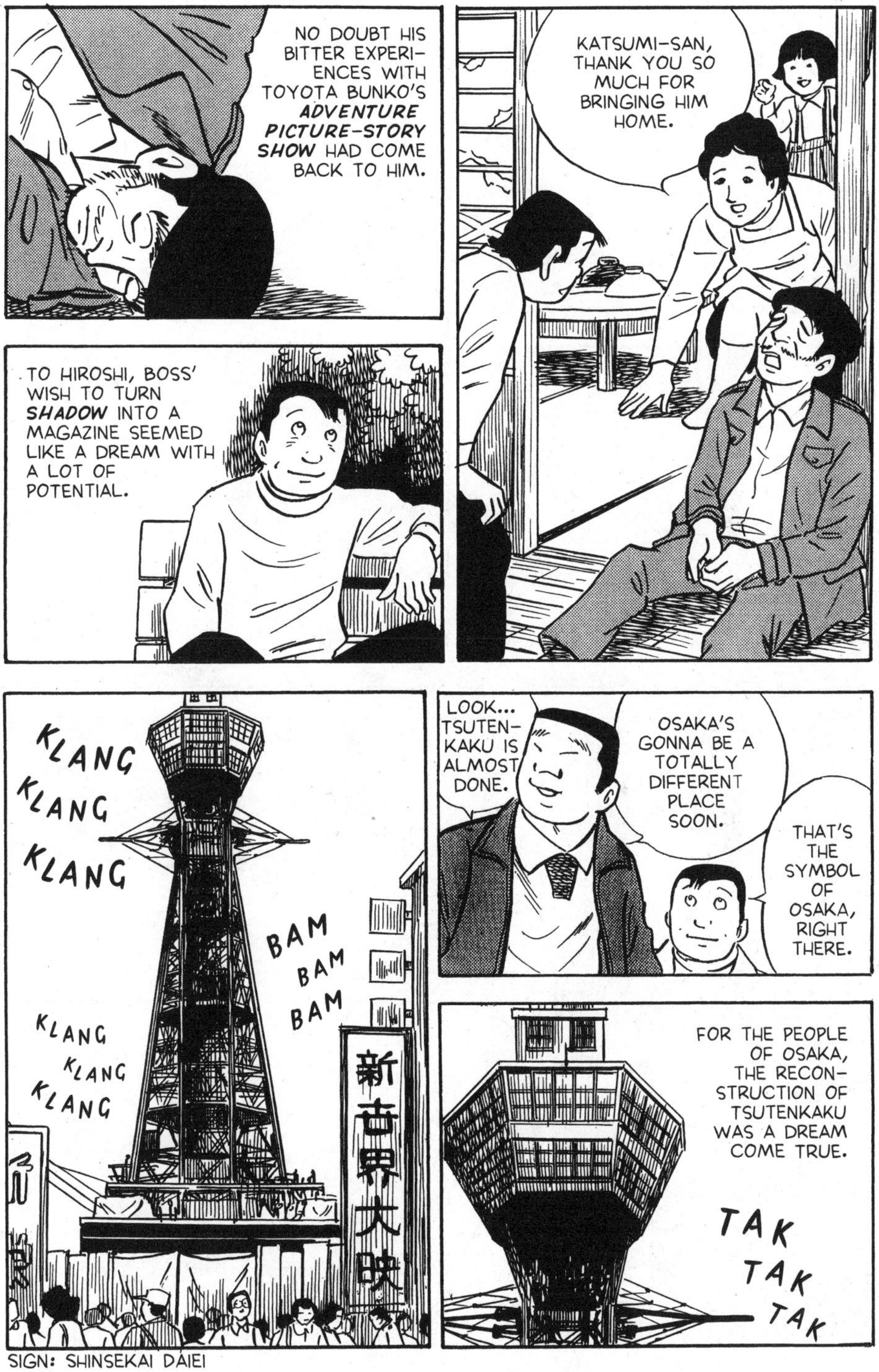
NO DOUBT HIS BITTER EXPERIENCES WITH TOYOTA BUNKO'S ***ADVENTURE PICTURE-STORY SHOW*** HAD COME BACK TO HIM.
TO HIROSHI, BOSS' WISH TO TURN ***SHADOW*** INTO A MAGAZINE SEEMED LIKE A DREAM WITH A LOT OF POTENTIAL.
KATSUMI-SAN, THANK YOU SO MUCH FOR BRINGING HIM HOME.
KLANG KLANG KLANG
BAM BAM BAM
KLANG KLANG KLANG
新世界大映
LOOK... TSUTENKAKU IS ALMOST DONE.
OSAKA'S GONNA BE A TOTALLY DIFFERENT PLACE SOON.
THAT'S THE SYMBOL OF OSAKA, RIGHT THERE.
FOR THE PEOPLE OF OSAKA, THE RECONSTRUCTION OF TSUTENKAKU WAS A DREAM COME TRUE.
TAK TAK TAK
SIGN: SHINSEKAI DAIEI

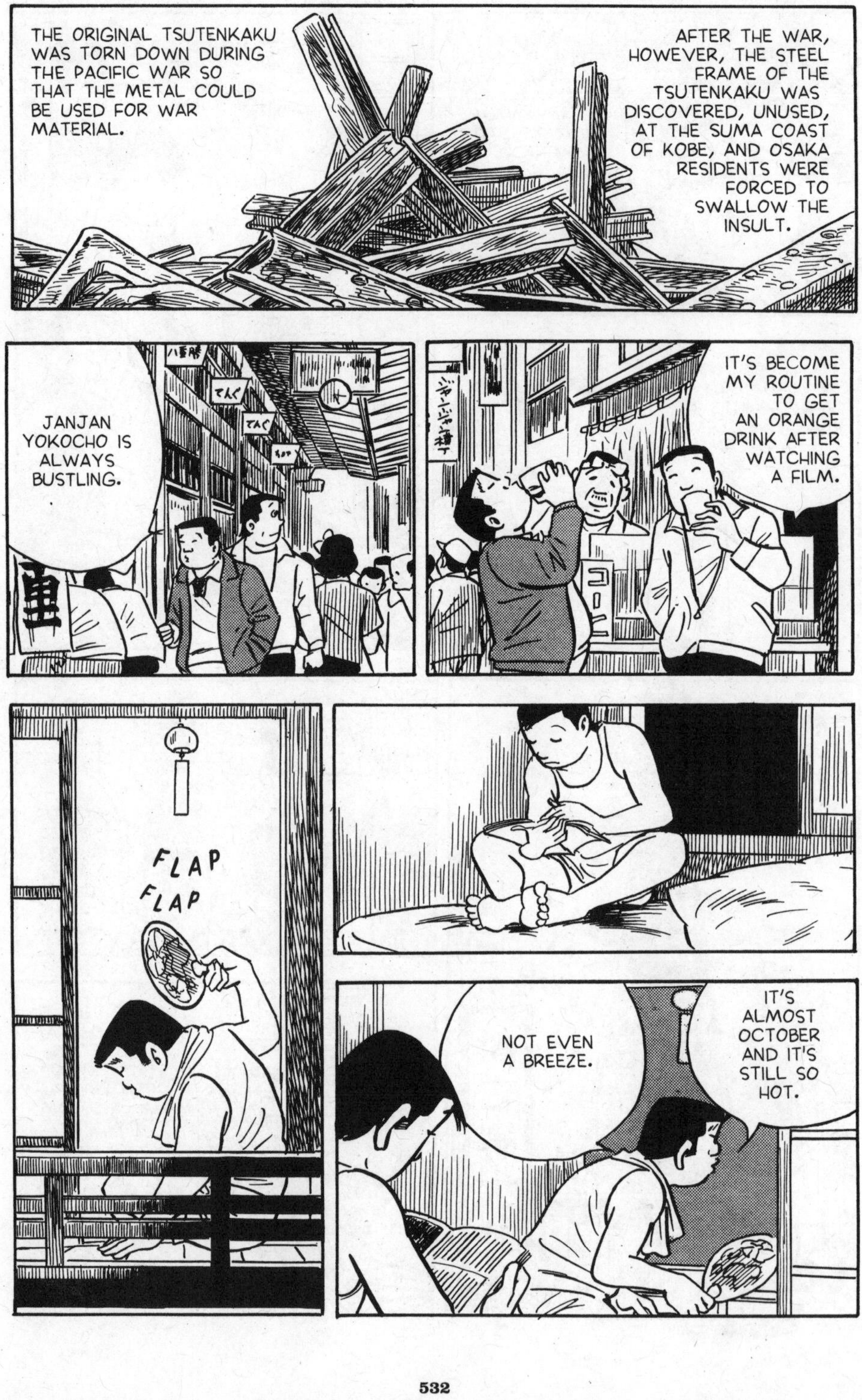
THE ORIGINAL TSUTENKAKU WAS TORN DOWN DURING THE PACIFIC WAR SO THAT THE METAL COULD BE USED FOR WAR MATERIAL.
AFTER THE WAR, HOWEVER, THE STEEL FRAME OF THE TSUTENKAKU WAS DISCOVERED, UNUSED, AT THE SUMA COAST OF KOBE, AND OSAKA RESIDENTS WERE FORCED TO SWALLOW THE INSULT.
JANJAN YOKOCHO IS ALWAYS BUSTLING.
IT'S BECOME MY ROUTINE TO GET AN ORANGE DRINK AFTER WATCHING A FILM.
FLAP
FLAP
NOT EVEN A BREEZE.
IT'S ALMOST OCTOBER AND IT'S STILL SO HOT.

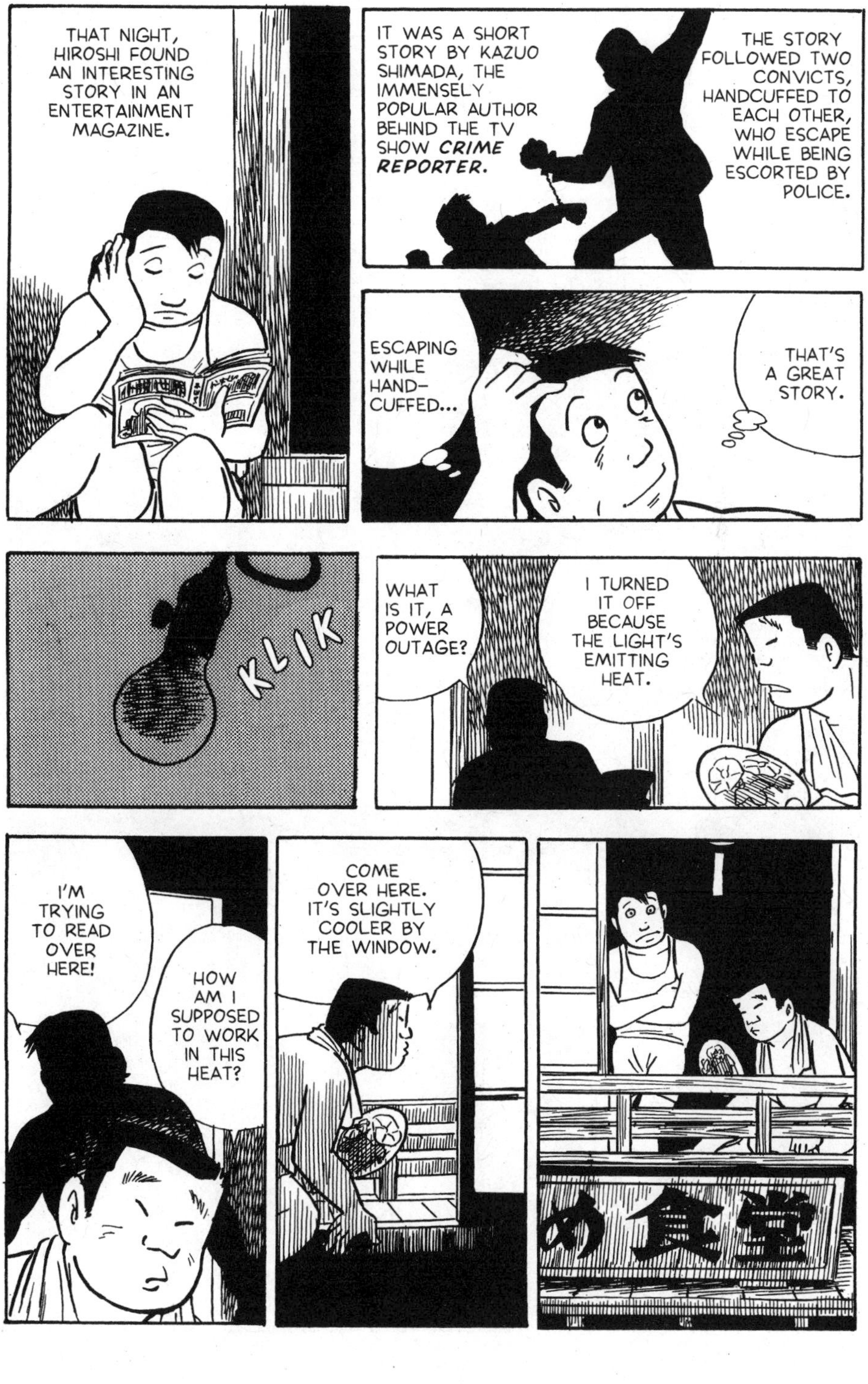
THAT NIGHT, HIROSHI FOUND AN INTERESTING STORY IN AN ENTERTAINMENT MAGAZINE.
IT WAS A SHORT STORY BY KAZUO SHIMADA, THE IMMENSELY POPULAR AUTHOR BEHIND THE TV SHOW CRIME REPORTER.
THE STORY FOLLOWED TWO CONVICTS, HANDCUFFED TO EACH OTHER, WHO ESCAPE WHILE BEING ESCORTED BY POLICE.
ESCAPING WHILE HAND-CUFFED...
THAT'S A GREAT STORY.
KLIK
WHAT IS IT, A POWER OUTAGE?
I TURNED IT OFF BECAUSE THE LIGHT'S EMITTING HEAT.
I'M TRYING TO READ OVER HERE!
HOW AM I SUPPOSED TO WORK IN THIS HEAT?
COME OVER HERE. IT'S SLIGHTLY COOLER BY THE WINDOW.
め食堂

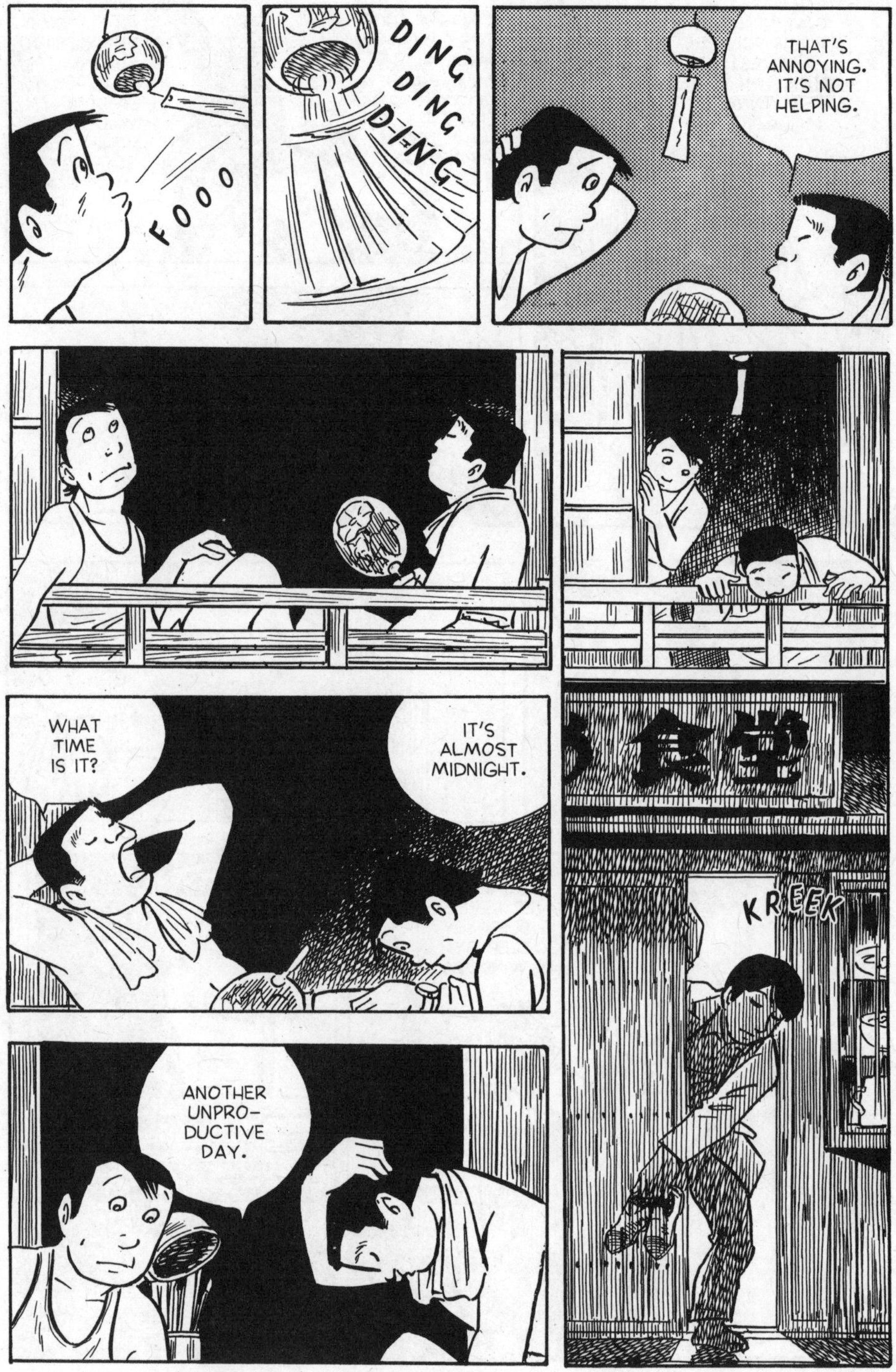
FOOO
DING DING D-I-N-G
THAT'S ANNOYING. IT'S NOT HELPING.
WHAT TIME IS IT?
IT'S ALMOST MIDNIGHT.
食堂
KREEK
ANOTHER UNPRO-DUCTIVE DAY.

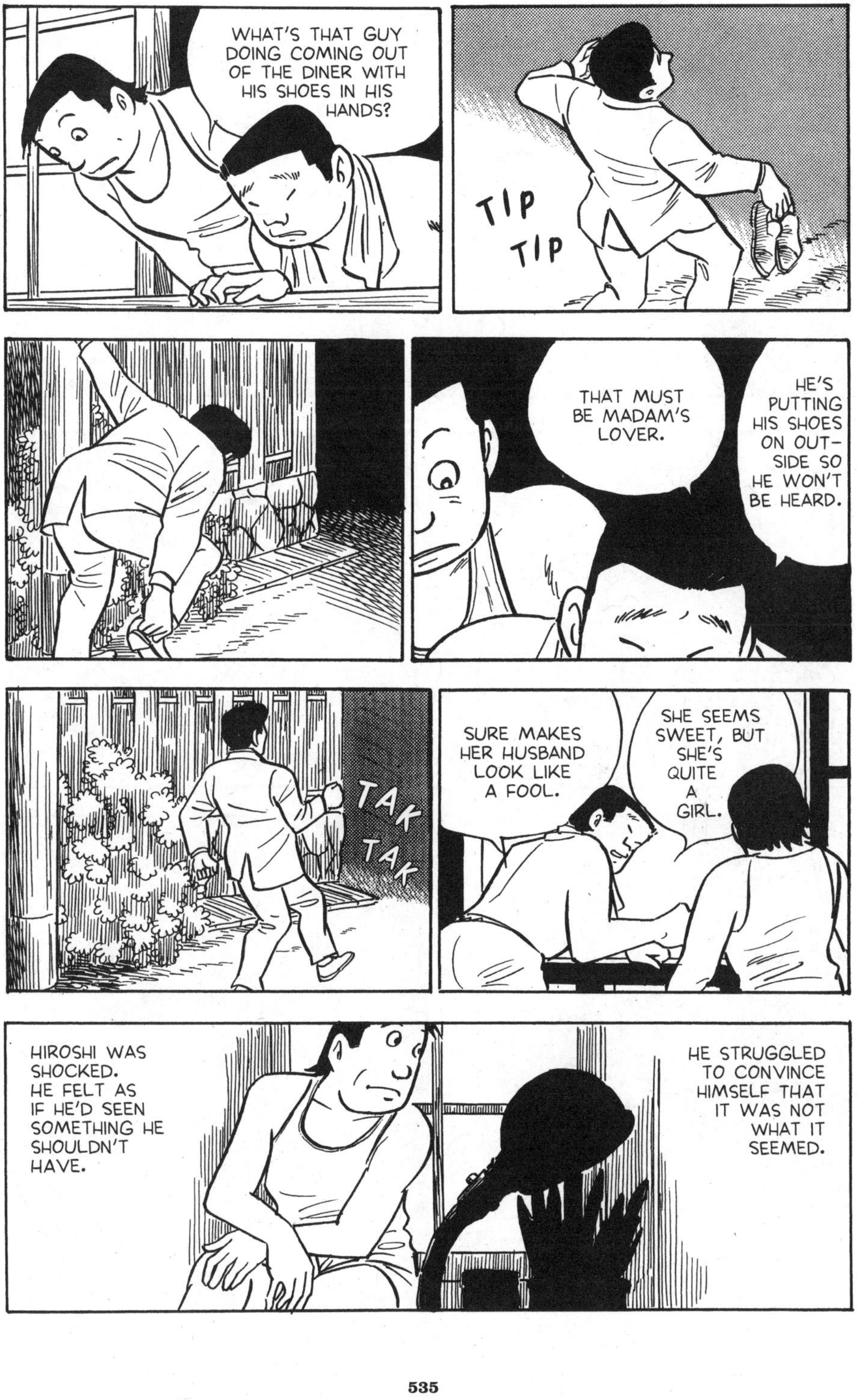
WHAT'S THAT GUY DOING COMING OUT OF THE DINER WITH HIS SHOES IN HIS HANDS?
TIP TIP
THAT MUST BE MADAM'S LOVER.
HE'S PUTTING HIS SHOES ON OUT-SIDE SO HE WON'T BE HEARD.
TAK TAK
SURE MAKES HER HUSBAND LOOK LIKE A FOOL.
SHE SEEMS SWEET, BUT SHE'S QUITE A GIRL.
HIROSHI WAS SHOCKED. HE FELT AS IF HE'D SEEN SOMETHING HE SHOULDN'T HAVE.
HE STRUGGLED TO CONVINCE HIMSELF THAT IT WAS NOT WHAT IT SEEMED.

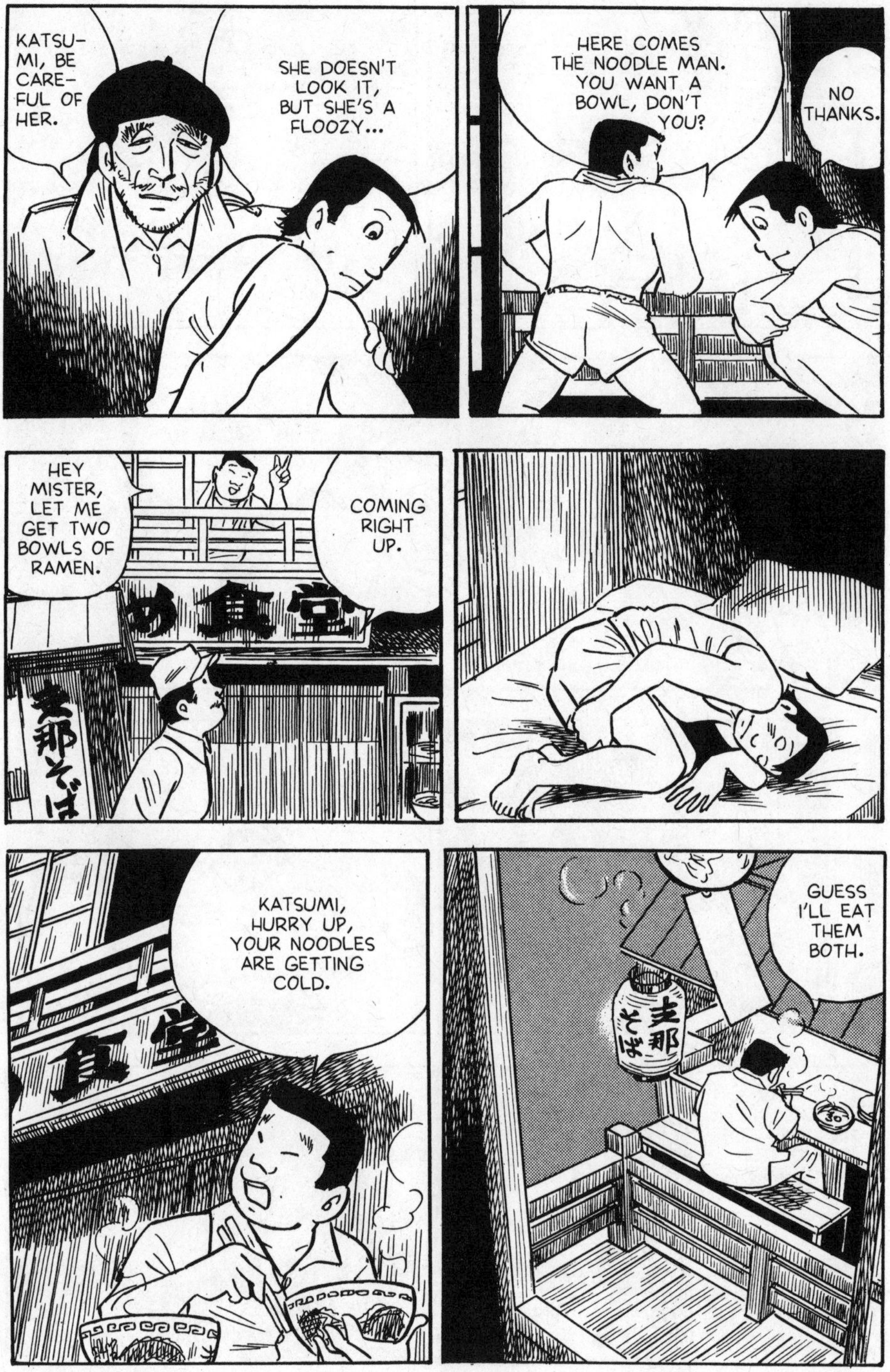
KATSUMI, BE CAREFUL OF HER.
SHE DOESN'T LOOK IT, BUT SHE'S A FLOOZY...
HERE COMES THE NOODLE MAN. YOU WANT A BOWL, DON'T YOU?
NO THANKS.
HEY MISTER, LET ME GET TWO BOWLS OF RAMEN.
COMING RIGHT UP.
食堂
支那そば
KATSUMI, HURRY UP, YOUR NOODLES ARE GETTING COLD.
食堂
GUESS I'LL EAT THEM BOTH.
支那そば

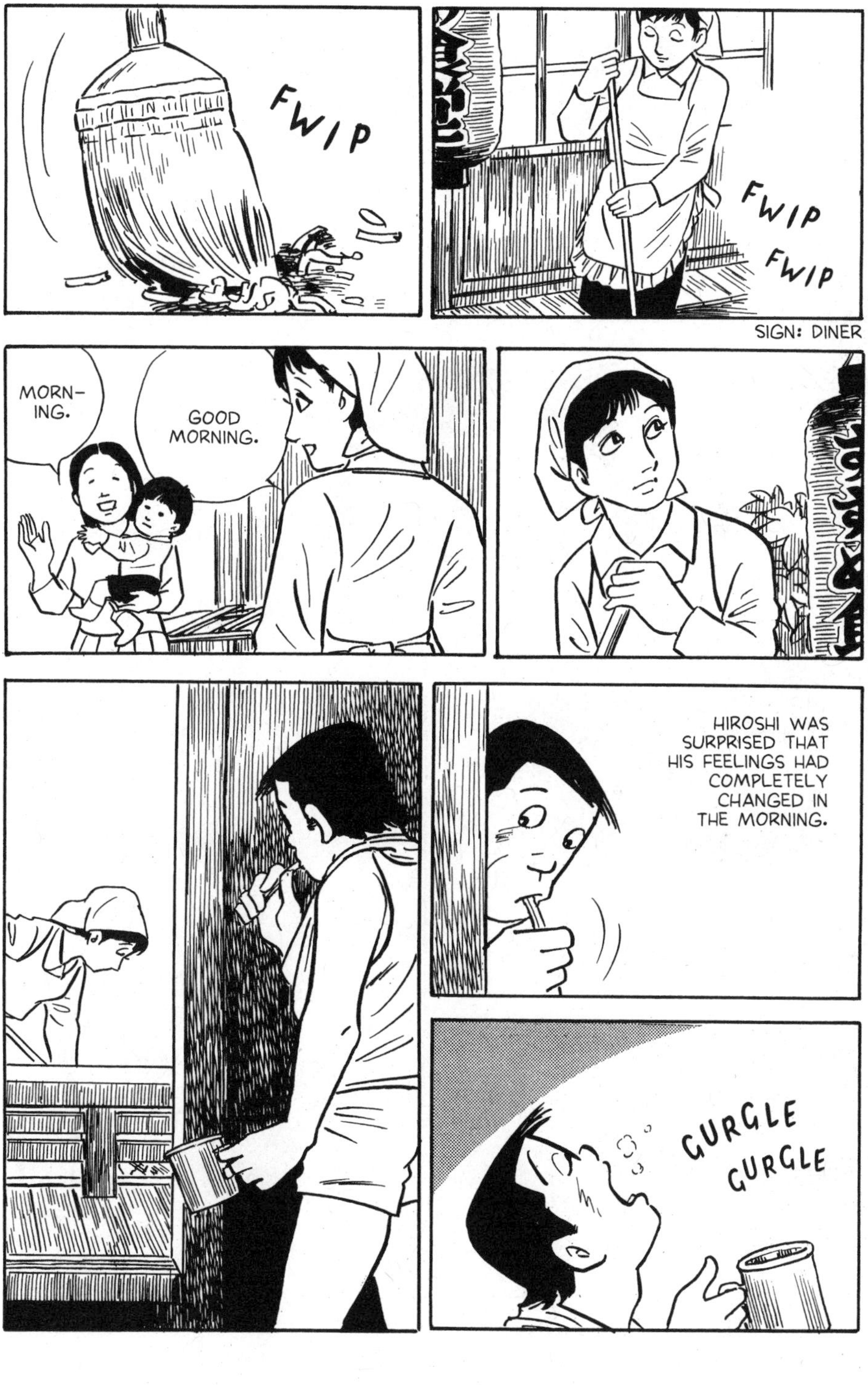
FWIP
FWIP
FWIP
SIGN: DINER
MORN-ING.
GOOD MORNING.
HIROSHI WAS SURPRISED THAT HIS FEELINGS HAD COMPLETELY CHANGED IN THE MORNING.
GURGLE GURGLE

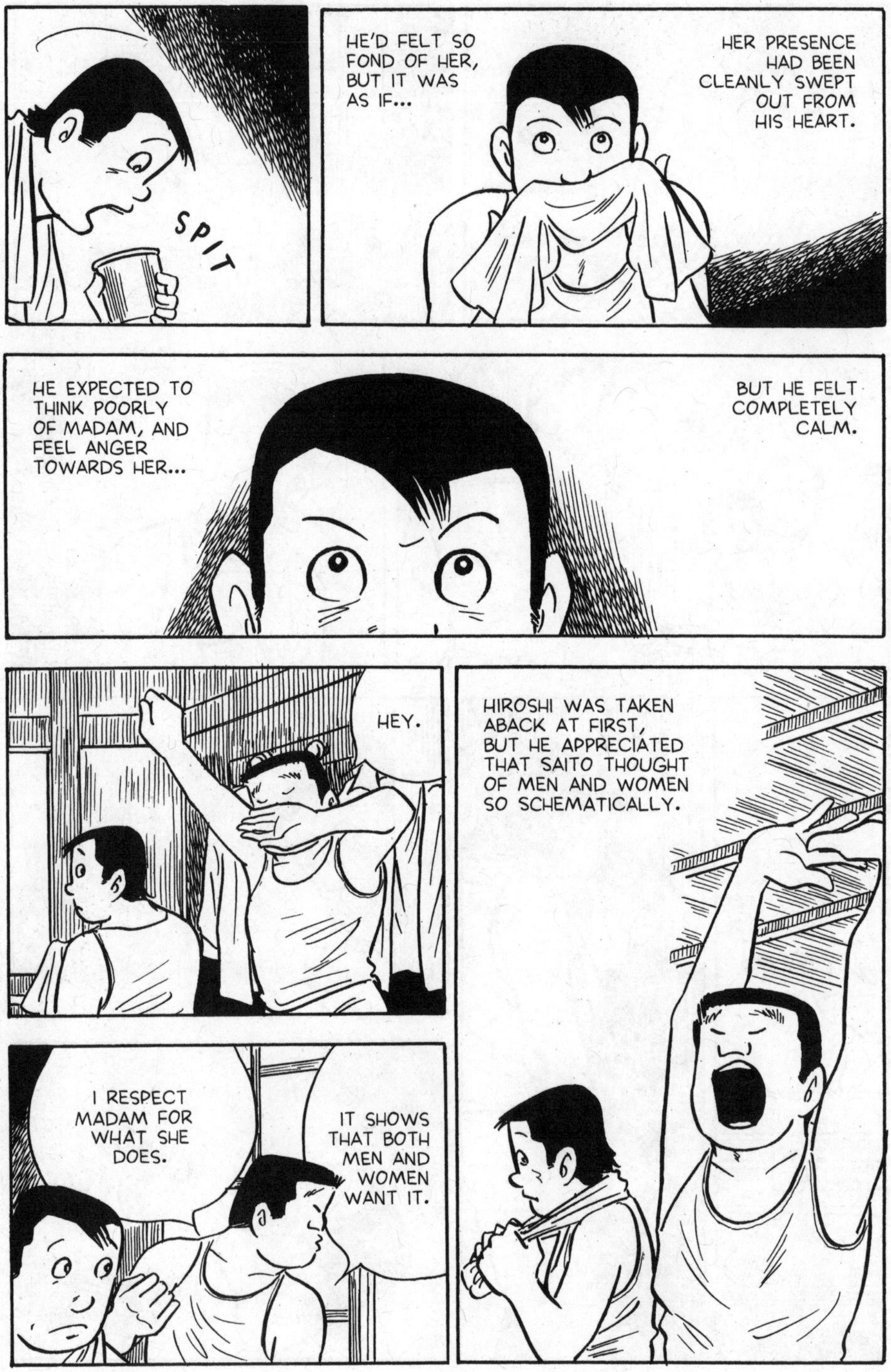
SPIT
HE'D FELT SO FOND OF HER, BUT IT WAS AS IF...
HER PRESENCE HAD BEEN CLEANLY SWEPT OUT FROM HIS HEART.
HE EXPECTED TO THINK POORLY OF MADAM, AND FEEL ANGER TOWARDS HER...
BUT HE FELT COMPLETELY CALM.
HEY.
I RESPECT MADAM FOR WHAT SHE DOES.
IT SHOWS THAT BOTH MEN AND WOMEN WANT IT.
HIROSHI WAS TAKEN ABACK AT FIRST, BUT HE APPRECIATED THAT SAITO THOUGHT OF MEN AND WOMEN SO SCHEMATICALLY.

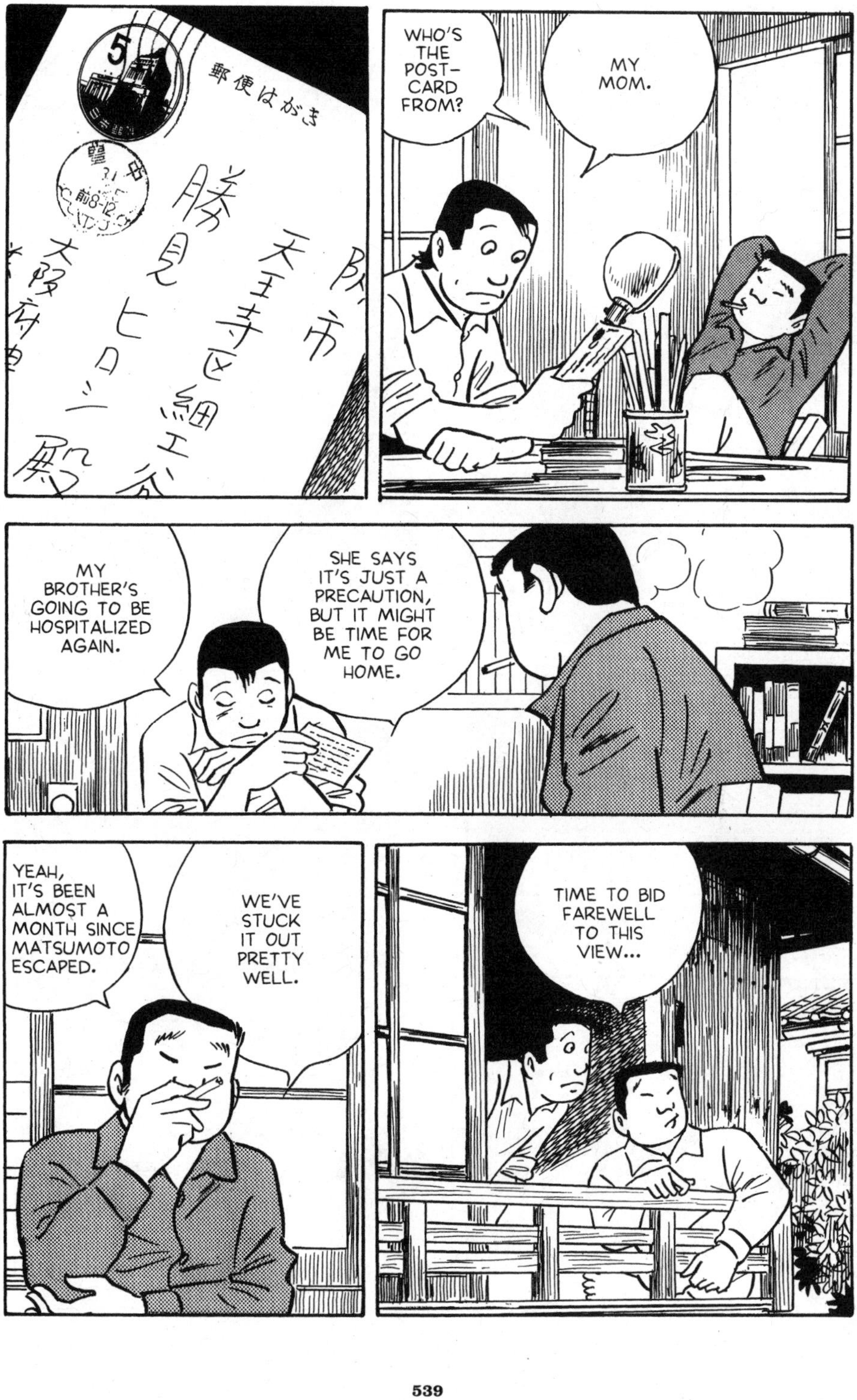
郵便はがき
天王寺区細工谷
勝見ヒロシ殿
WHO'S THE POST-CARD FROM?
MY MOM.
MY BROTHER'S GOING TO BE HOSPITALIZED AGAIN.
SHE SAYS IT'S JUST A PRECAUTION, BUT IT MIGHT BE TIME FOR ME TO GO HOME.
YEAH, IT'S BEEN ALMOST A MONTH SINCE MATSUMOTO ESCAPED.
WE'VE STUCK IT OUT PRETTY WELL.
TIME TO BID FAREWELL TO THIS VIEW...

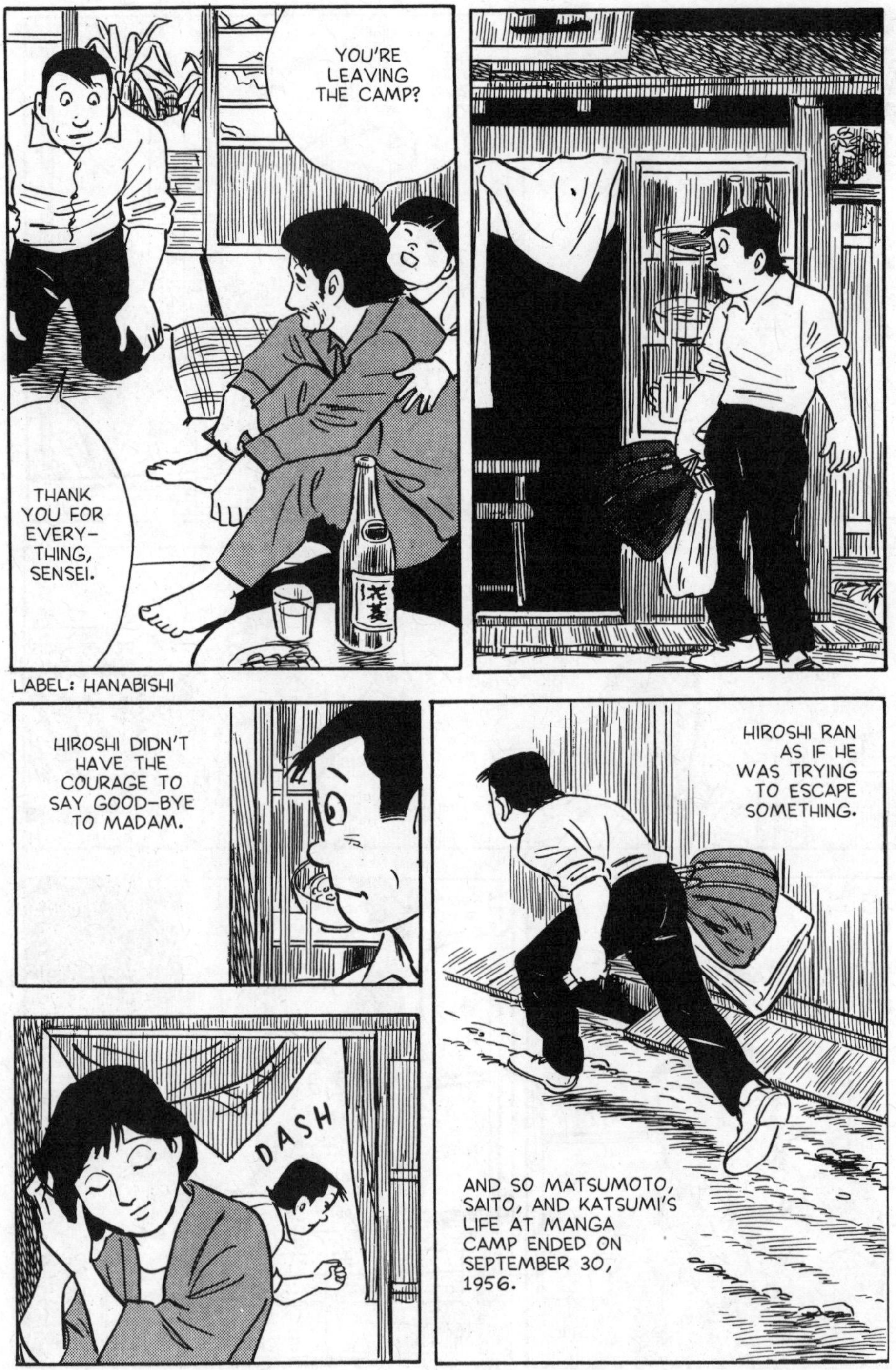

YOU'RE LEAVING THE CAMP?
THANK YOU FOR EVERY-THING, SENSEI.
LABEL: HANABISHI
HIROSHI DIDN'T HAVE THE COURAGE TO SAY GOOD-BYE TO MADAM.
DASH
HIROSHI RAN AS IF HE WAS TRYING TO ESCAPE SOMETHING.
AND SO MATSUMOTO, SAITO, AND KATSUMI'S LIFE AT MANGA CAMP ENDED ON SEPTEMBER 30, 1956.

THE JOY OF CREATION

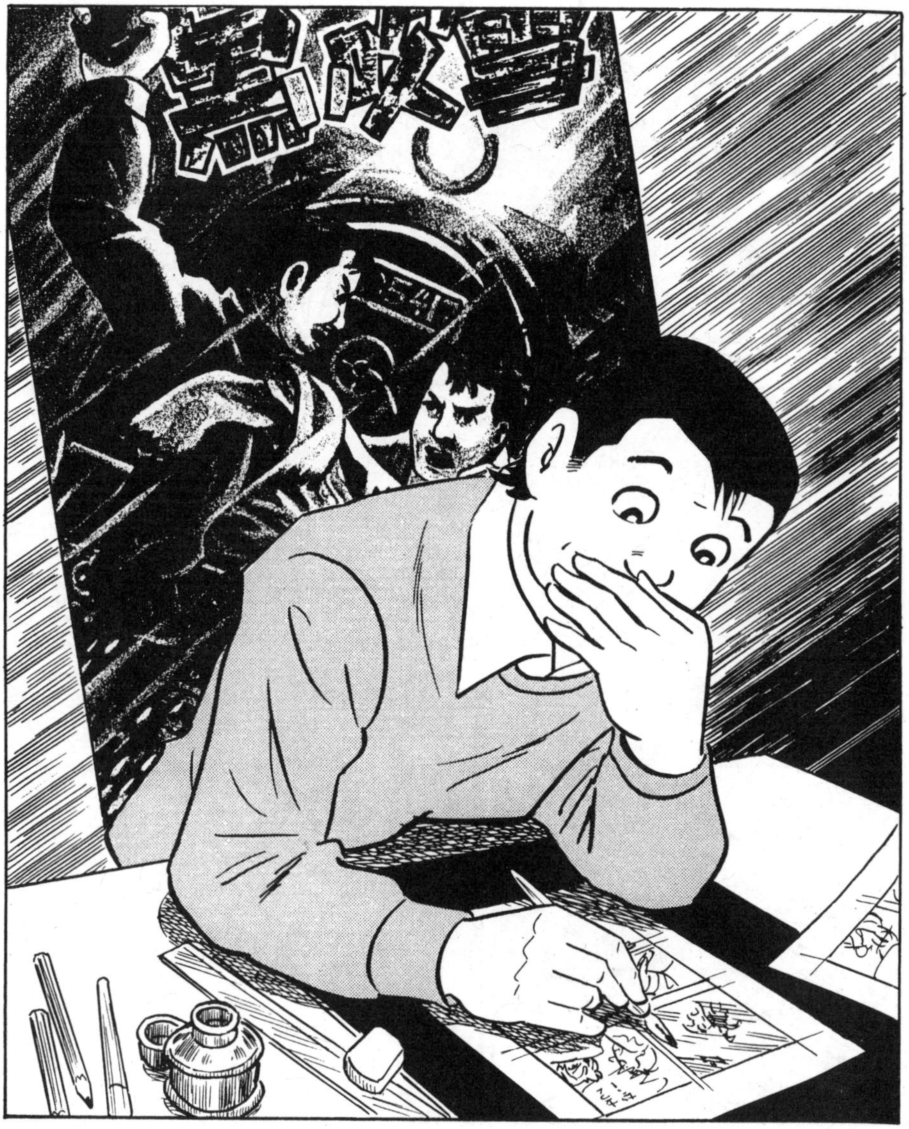

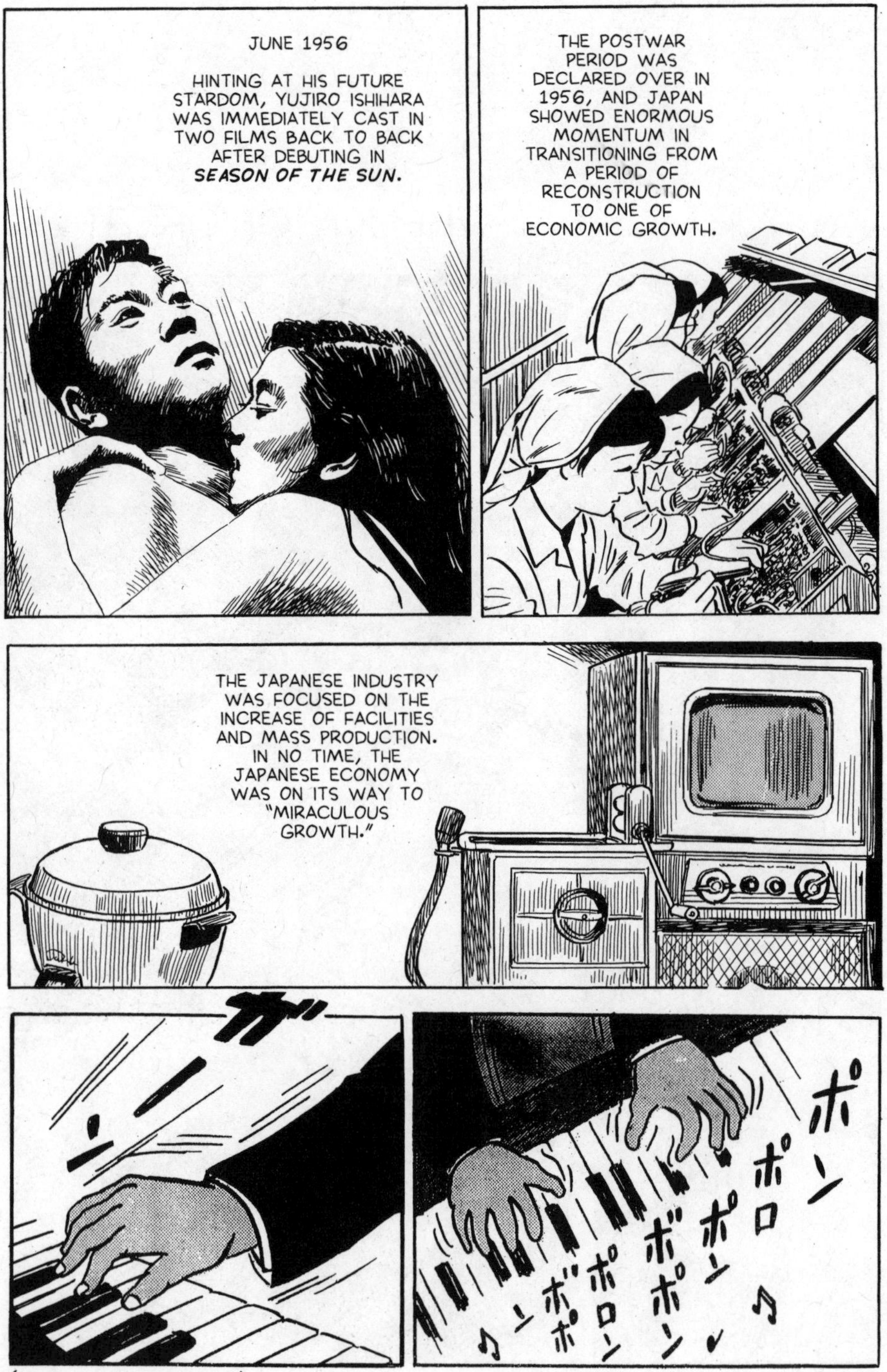
JUNE 1956
HINTING AT HIS FUTURE STARDOM, YUJIRO ISHIHARA WAS IMMEDIATELY CAST IN TWO FILMS BACK TO BACK AFTER DEBUTING IN ***SEASON OF THE SUN.***
THE POSTWAR PERIOD WAS DECLARED OVER IN 1956, AND JAPAN SHOWED ENORMOUS MOMENTUM IN TRANSITIONING FROM A PERIOD OF RECONSTRUCTION TO ONE OF ECONOMIC GROWTH.
THE JAPANESE INDUSTRY WAS FOCUSED ON THE INCREASE OF FACILITIES AND MASS PRODUCTION. IN NO TIME, THE JAPANESE ECONOMY WAS ON ITS WAY TO "MIRACULOUS GROWTH."
ポーン
〈SOUND OF PIANO PLAYING〉

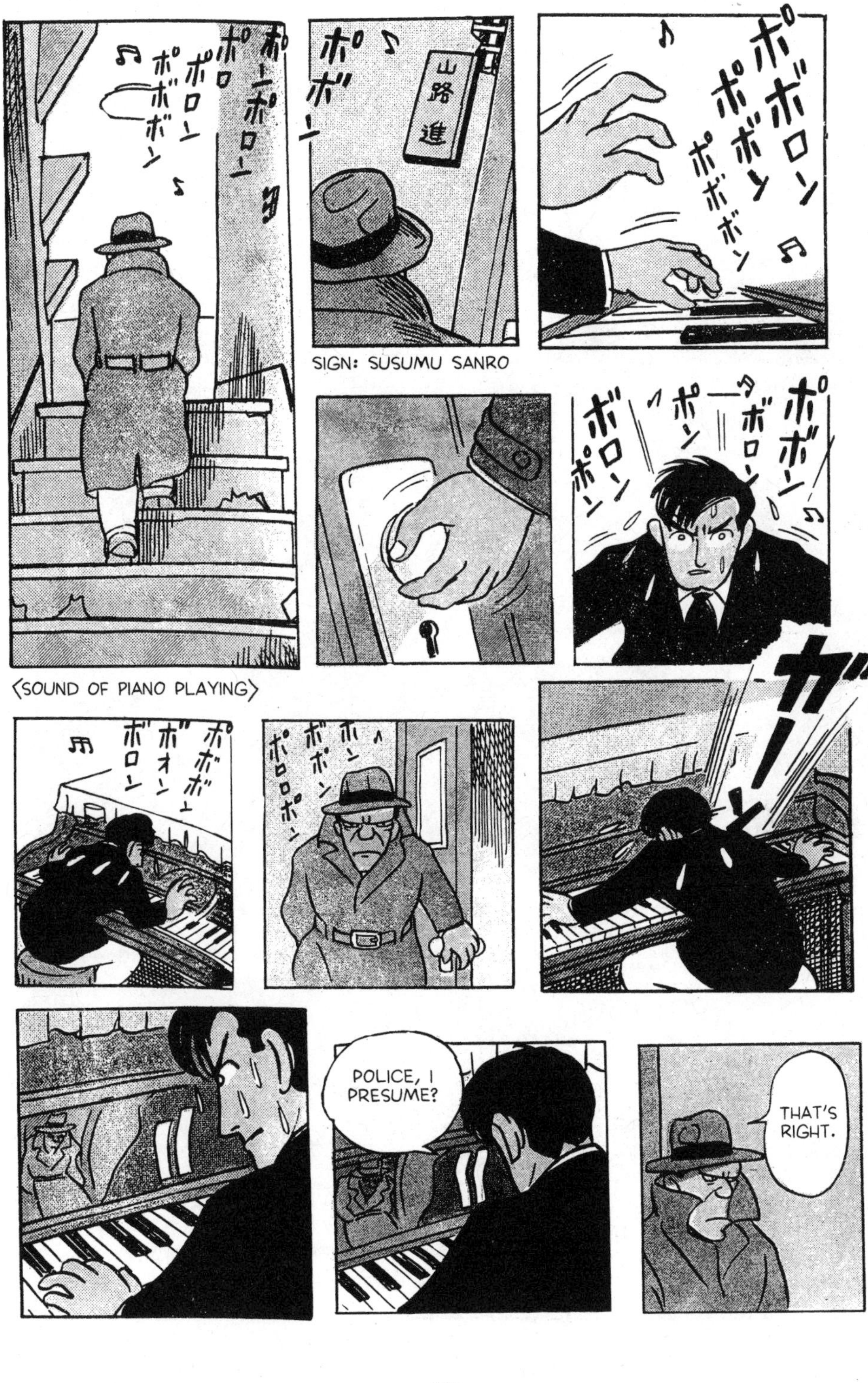
山路進
SIGN: SUSUMU SANRO
⟨SOUND OF PIANO PLAYING⟩
POLICE, I PRESUME?
THAT'S RIGHT.

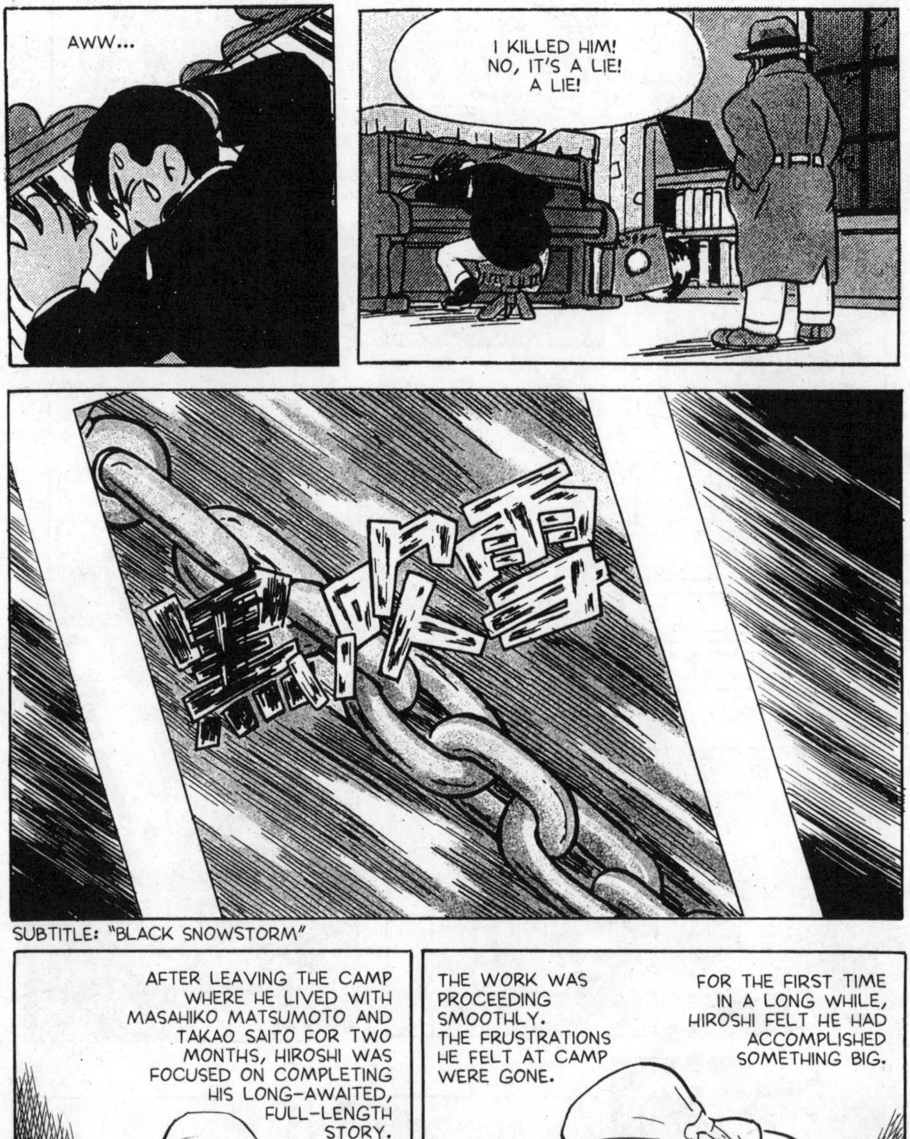
AWW...
I KILLED HIM! NO, IT'S A LIE! A LIE!

SUBTITLE: "BLACK SNOWSTORM"

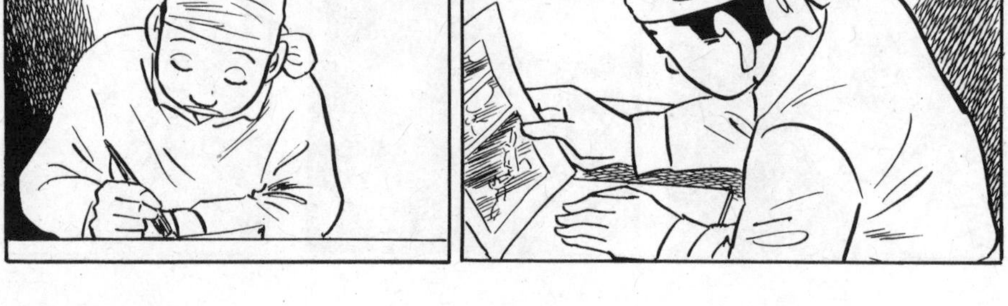
AFTER LEAVING THE CAMP WHERE HE LIVED WITH MASAHIKO MATSUMOTO AND TAKAO SAITO FOR TWO MONTHS, HIROSHI WAS FOCUSED ON COMPLETING HIS LONG-AWAITED, FULL-LENGTH STORY.
THE WORK WAS PROCEEDING SMOOTHLY. THE FRUSTRATIONS HE FELT AT CAMP WERE GONE.
FOR THE FIRST TIME IN A LONG WHILE, HIROSHI FELT HE HAD ACCOMPLISHED SOMETHING BIG.

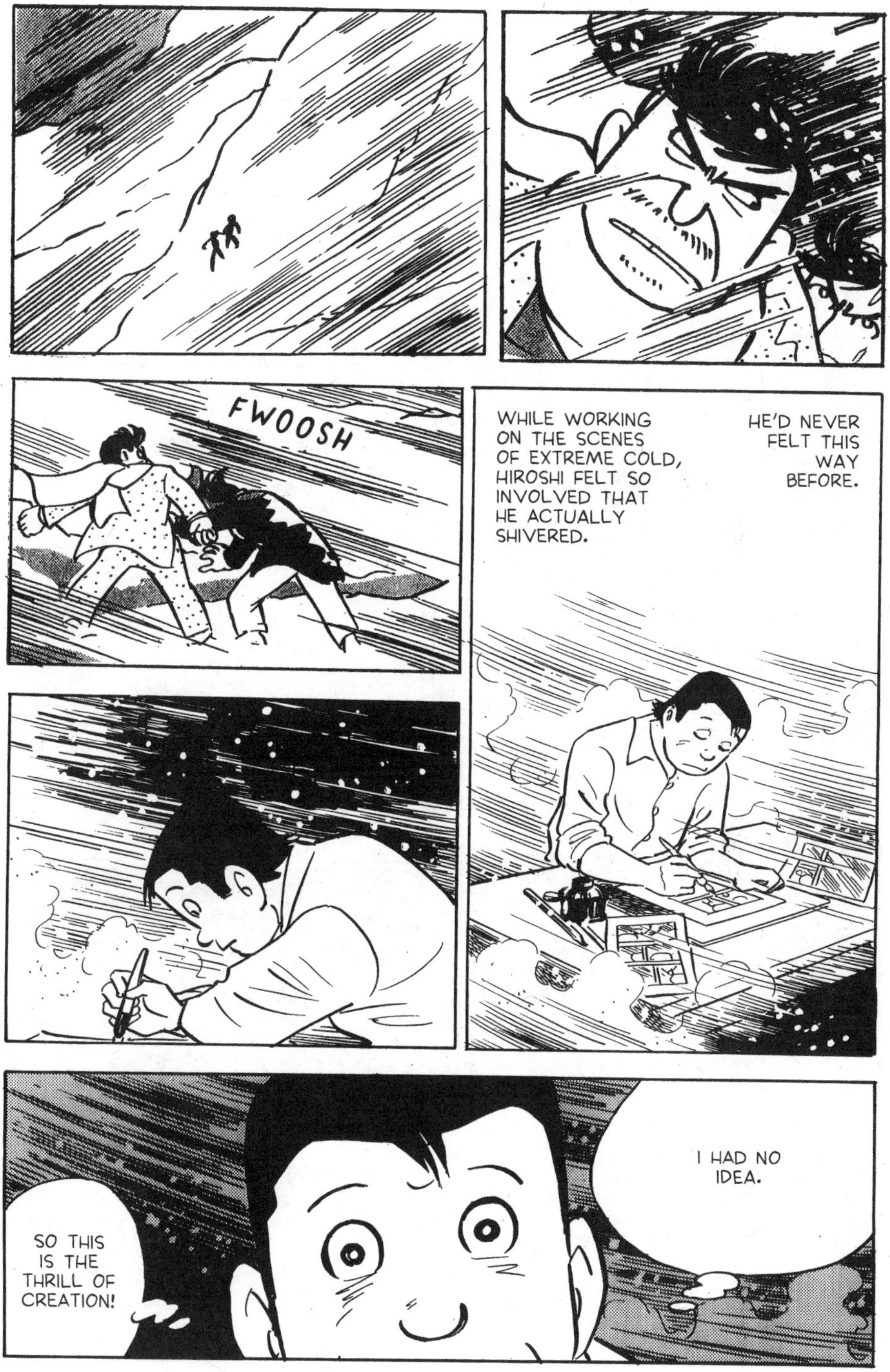
FWOOSH
WHILE WORKING ON THE SCENES OF EXTREME COLD, HIROSHI FELT SO INVOLVED THAT HE ACTUALLY SHIVERED.
HE'D NEVER FELT THIS WAY BEFORE.
SO THIS IS THE THRILL OF CREATION!
I HAD NO IDEA.

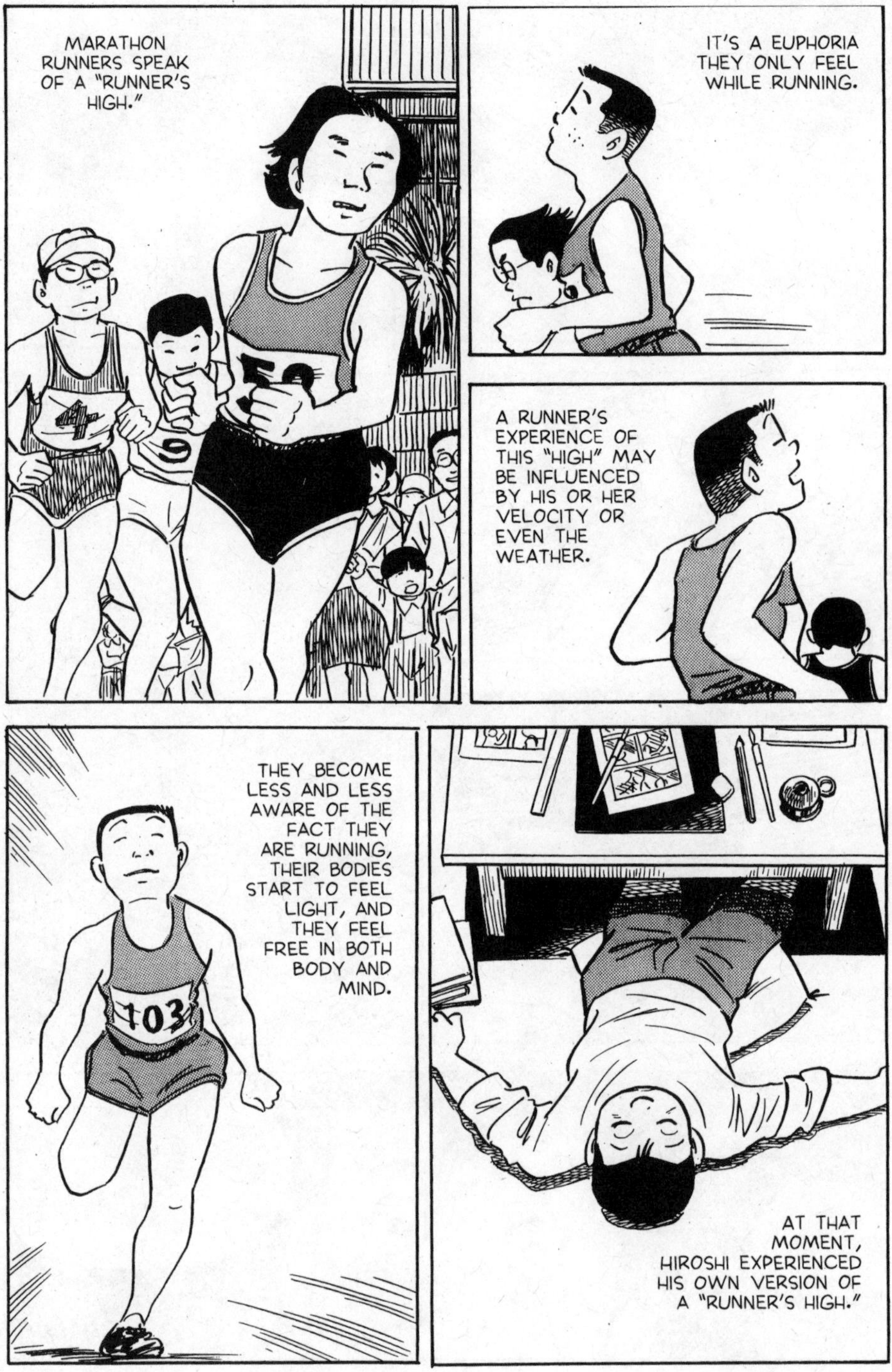
MARATHON RUNNERS SPEAK OF A "RUNNER'S HIGH."
IT'S A EUPHORIA THEY ONLY FEEL WHILE RUNNING.
A RUNNER'S EXPERIENCE OF THIS "HIGH" MAY BE INFLUENCED BY HIS OR HER VELOCITY OR EVEN THE WEATHER.
THEY BECOME LESS AND LESS AWARE OF THE FACT THEY ARE RUNNING, THEIR BODIES START TO FEEL LIGHT, AND THEY FEEL FREE IN BOTH BODY AND MIND.
AT THAT MOMENT, HIROSHI EXPERIENCED HIS OWN VERSION OF A "RUNNER'S HIGH."

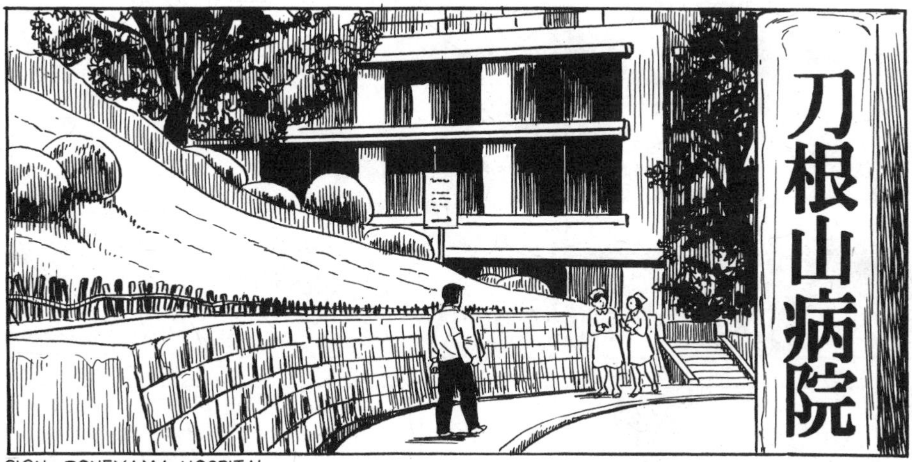
刀根山病院
SIGN: TONEYAMA HOSPITAL

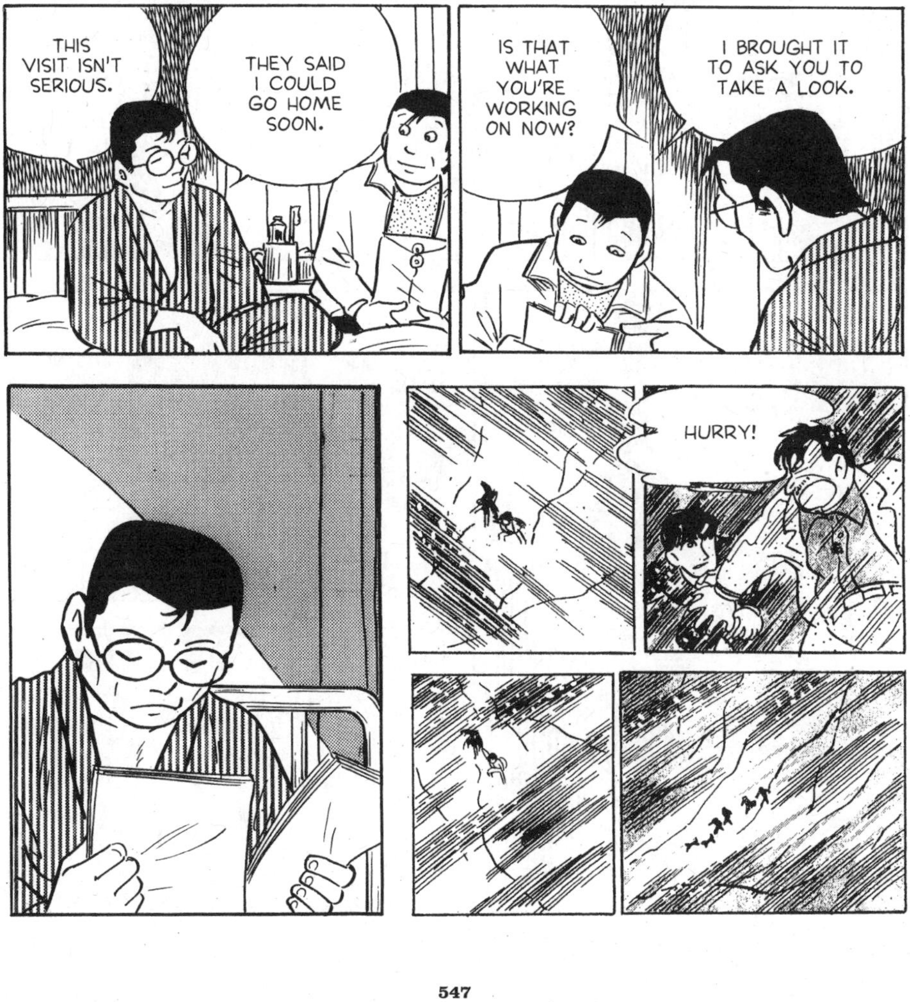
THIS VISIT ISN'T SERIOUS.
THEY SAID I COULD GO HOME SOON.
IS THAT WHAT YOU'RE WORKING ON NOW?
I BROUGHT IT TO ASK YOU TO TAKE A LOOK.
HURRY!

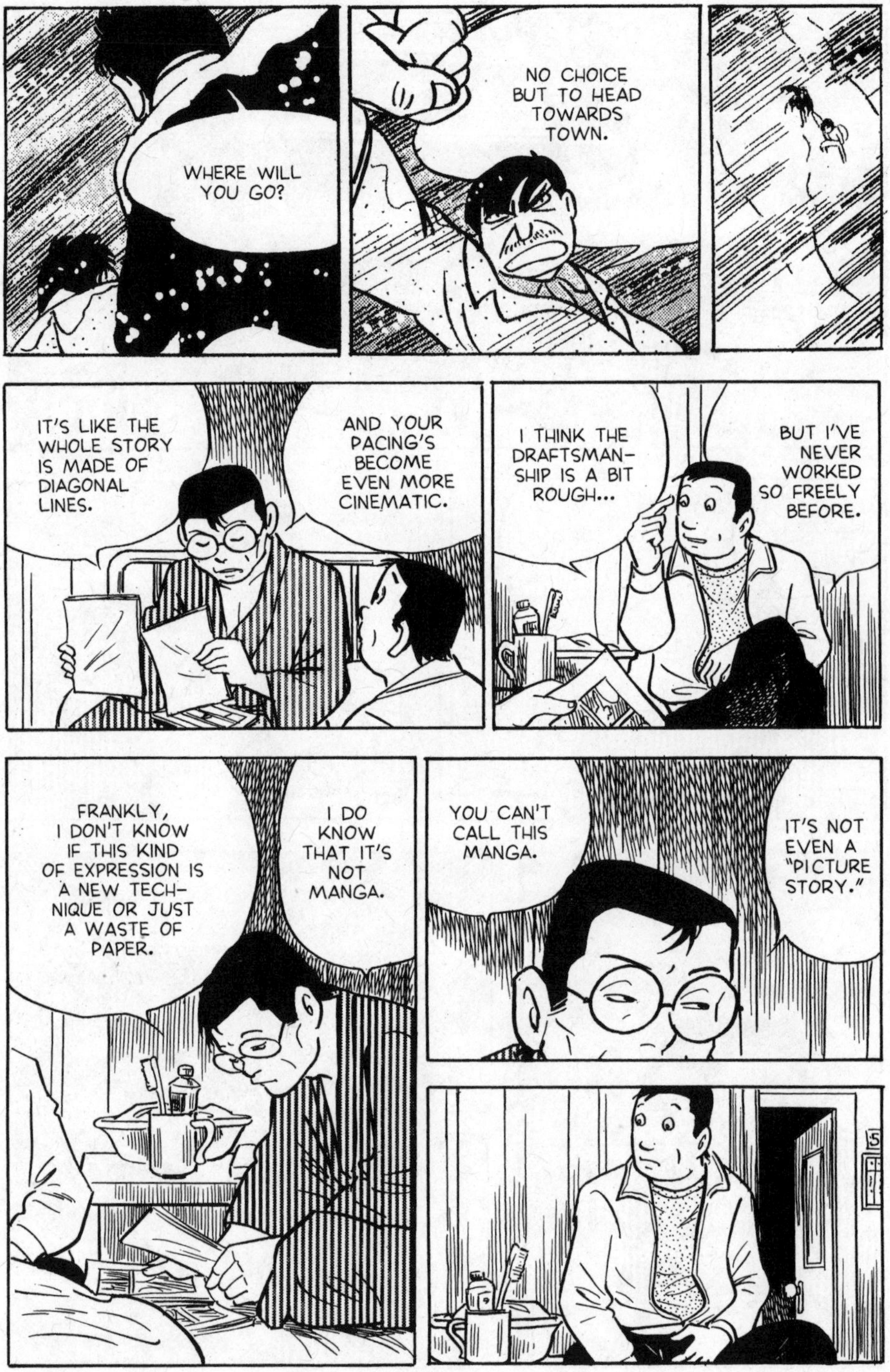
WHERE WILL YOU GO?
NO CHOICE BUT TO HEAD TOWARDS TOWN.
IT'S LIKE THE WHOLE STORY IS MADE OF DIAGONAL LINES.
AND YOUR PACING'S BECOME EVEN MORE CINEMATIC.
I THINK THE DRAFTSMANSHIP IS A BIT ROUGH...
BUT I'VE NEVER WORKED SO FREELY BEFORE.
FRANKLY, I DON'T KNOW IF THIS KIND OF EXPRESSION IS A NEW TECHNIQUE OR JUST A WASTE OF PAPER.
I DO KNOW THAT IT'S NOT MANGA.
YOU CAN'T CALL THIS MANGA.
IT'S NOT EVEN A "PICTURE STORY."

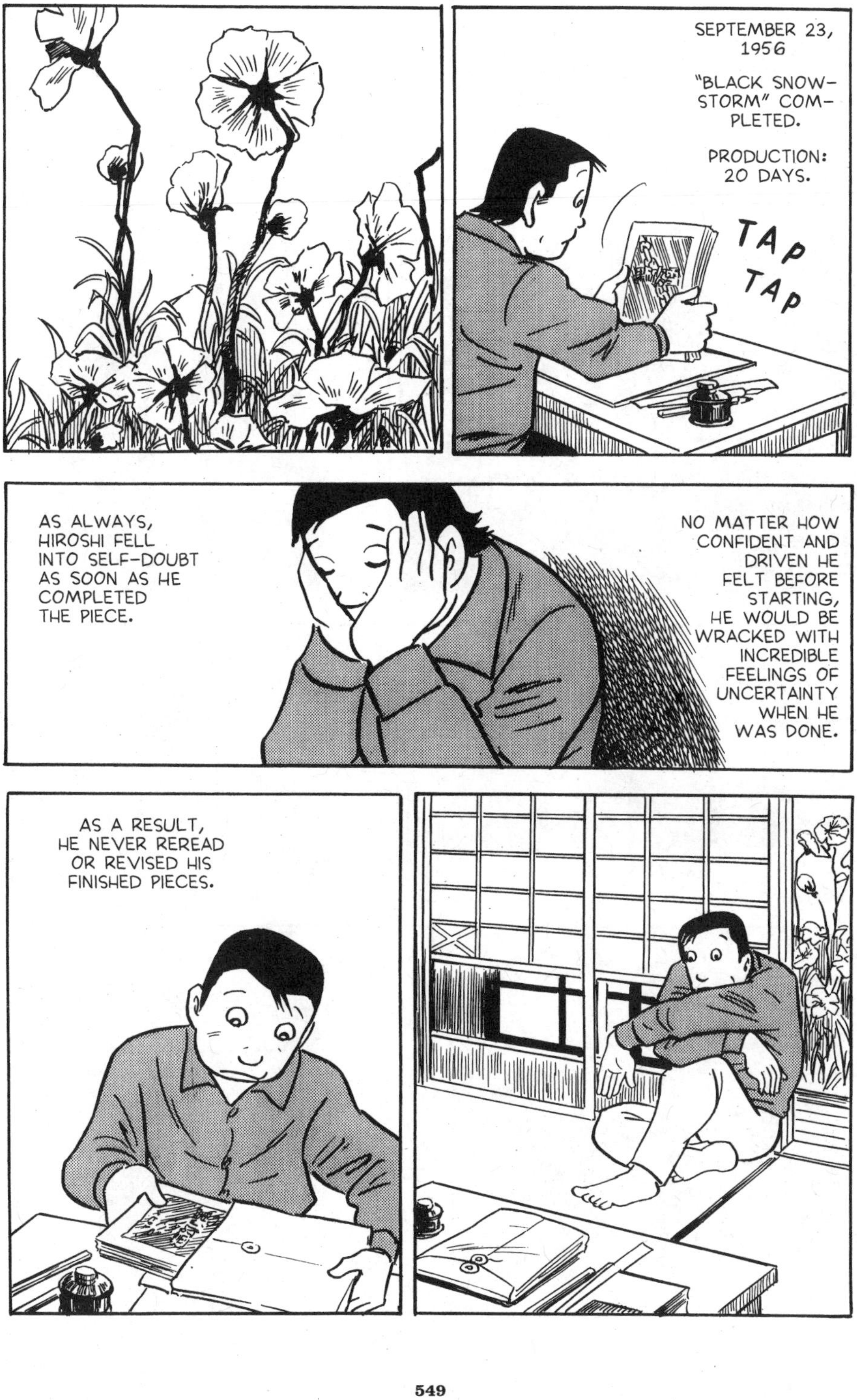
SEPTEMBER 23, 1956
"BLACK SNOW-STORM" COM-PLETED.
PRODUCTION: 20 DAYS.
TAP TAP
AS ALWAYS, HIROSHI FELL INTO SELF-DOUBT AS SOON AS HE COMPLETED THE PIECE.
NO MATTER HOW CONFIDENT AND DRIVEN HE FELT BEFORE STARTING, HE WOULD BE WRACKED WITH INCREDIBLE FEELINGS OF UNCERTAINTY WHEN HE WAS DONE.
AS A RESULT, HE NEVER REREAD OR REVISED HIS FINISHED PIECES.

"BLACK SNOWSTORM" TELLS THE STORY OF A PIANIST WHO HAS BEEN WRONGLY SENTENCED TO PRISON FOR MURDER. WHILE IN TRANSIT THROUGH THE MOUNTAINS, THE PIANIST FINDS HIMSELF HANDCUFFED TO A VIOLENT CRIMINAL, AND TOGETHER THEY HATCH A PLAN TO ESCAPE INTO THE TERRIBLE SNOWSTORM.

THE AMERICAN FILM *THE DEFIANT ONES* WOULD NOT BE RELEASED IN JAPAN UNTIL TWO YEARS LATER, IN 1958.

STAR-RING TONY CURTIS AND SIDNEY POITIER

I'M OFF TO HINOMARU.

OKAY, BE SAFE.

SIGN: YASUJI BUILDING

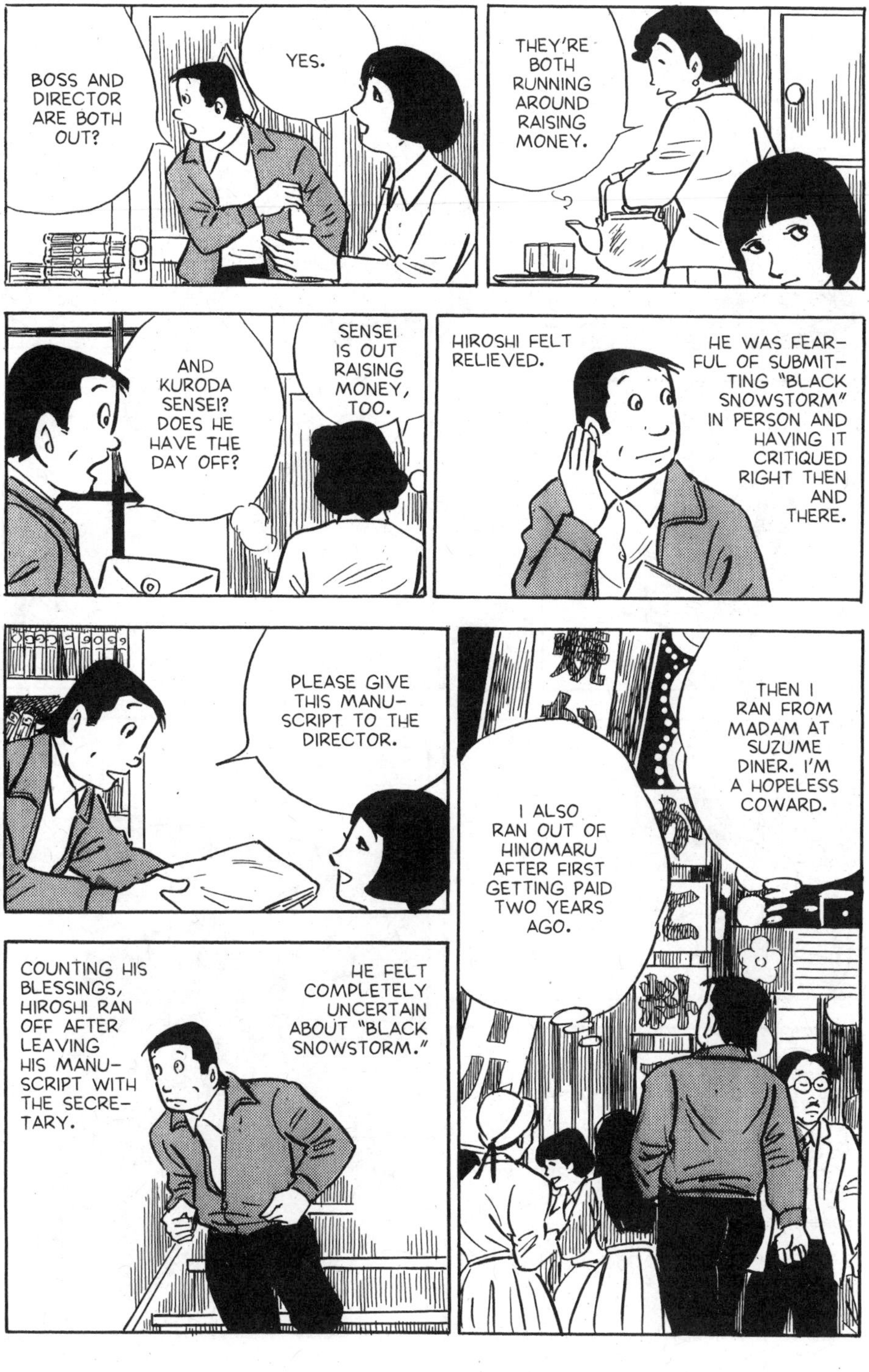
BOSS AND DIRECTOR ARE BOTH OUT?
YES.
THEY'RE BOTH RUNNING AROUND RAISING MONEY.
AND KURODA SENSEI? DOES HE HAVE THE DAY OFF?
SENSEI IS OUT RAISING MONEY, TOO.
HIROSHI FELT RELIEVED.
HE WAS FEARFUL OF SUBMITTING "BLACK SNOWSTORM" IN PERSON AND HAVING IT CRITIQUED RIGHT THEN AND THERE.
PLEASE GIVE THIS MANUSCRIPT TO THE DIRECTOR.
COUNTING HIS BLESSINGS, HIROSHI RAN OFF AFTER LEAVING HIS MANUSCRIPT WITH THE SECRETARY.
HE FELT COMPLETELY UNCERTAIN ABOUT "BLACK SNOWSTORM."
I ALSO RAN OUT OF HINOMARU AFTER FIRST GETTING PAID TWO YEARS AGO.
THEN I RAN FROM MADAM AT SUZUME DINER. I'M A HOPELESS COWARD.

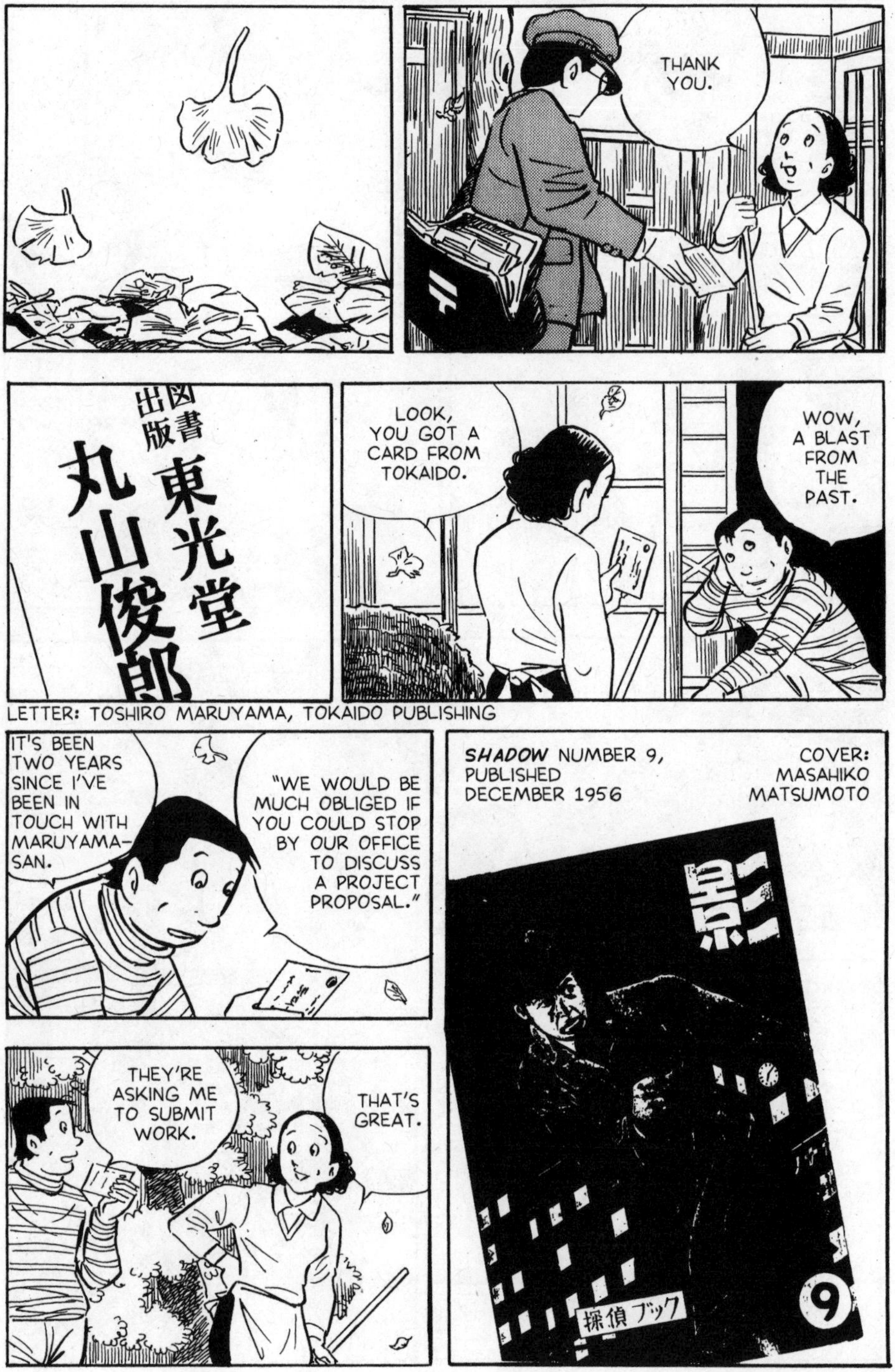
THANK YOU.
図書出版
東光堂
丸山俊郎
LETTER: TOSHIRO MARUYAMA, TOKAIDO PUBLISHING
LOOK, YOU GOT A CARD FROM TOKAIDO.
WOW, A BLAST FROM THE PAST.
IT'S BEEN TWO YEARS SINCE I'VE BEEN IN TOUCH WITH MARUYAMA-SAN.
"WE WOULD BE MUCH OBLIGED IF YOU COULD STOP BY OUR OFFICE TO DISCUSS A PROJECT PROPOSAL."
THEY'RE ASKING ME TO SUBMIT WORK.
THAT'S GREAT.
SHADOW NUMBER 9, PUBLISHED DECEMBER 1956
COVER: MASAHIKO MATSUMOTO
影
9
探偵ブック

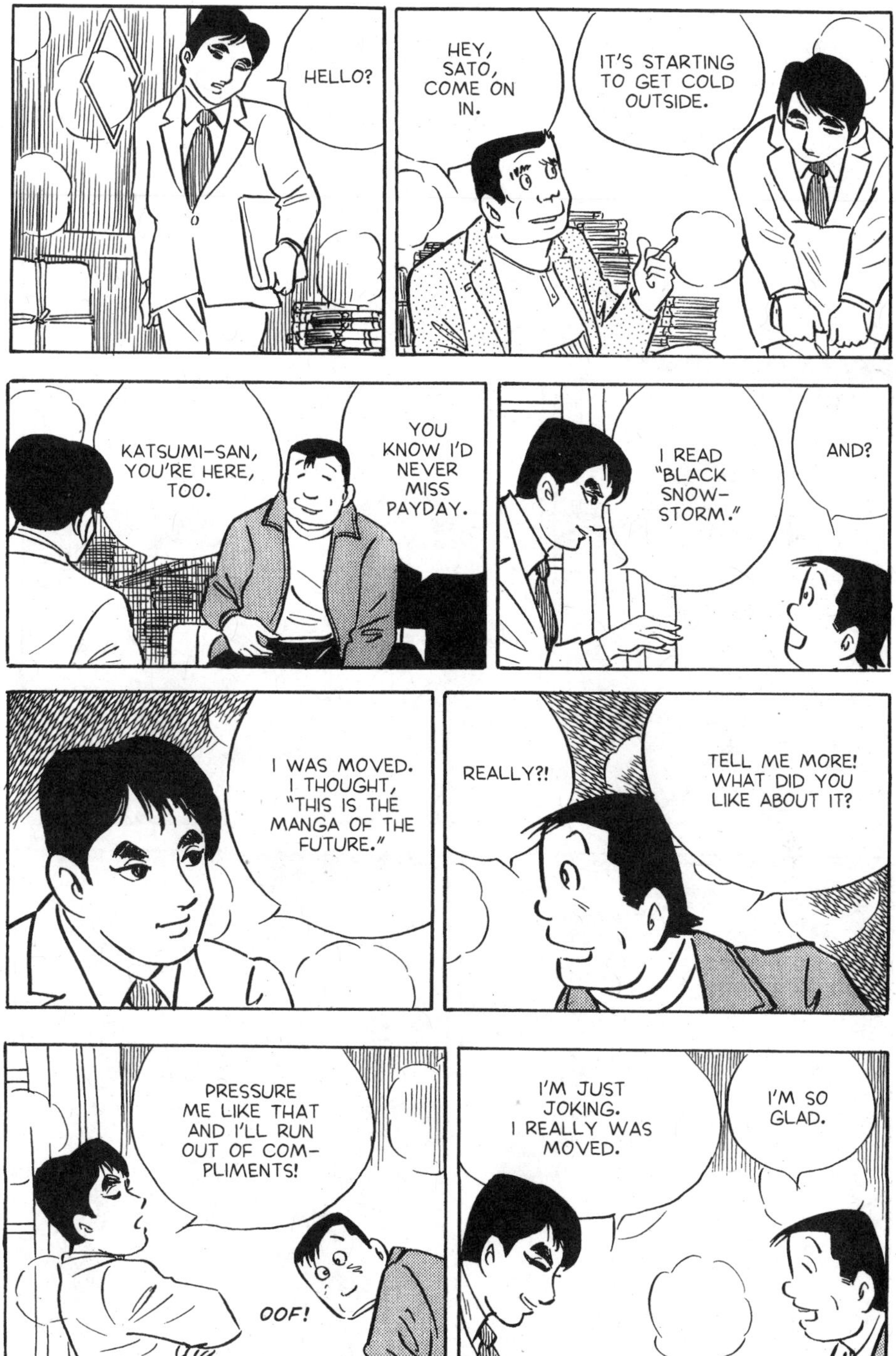
HELLO?
HEY, SATO, COME ON IN.
IT'S STARTING TO GET COLD OUTSIDE.
KATSUMI-SAN, YOU'RE HERE, TOO.
YOU KNOW I'D NEVER MISS PAYDAY.
I READ "BLACK SNOW-STORM."
AND?
I WAS MOVED. I THOUGHT, "THIS IS THE MANGA OF THE FUTURE."
REALLY?!
TELL ME MORE! WHAT DID YOU LIKE ABOUT IT?
PRESSURE ME LIKE THAT AND I'LL RUN OUT OF COM-PLIMENTS!
OOF!
I'M JUST JOKING. I REALLY WAS MOVED.
I'M SO GLAD.

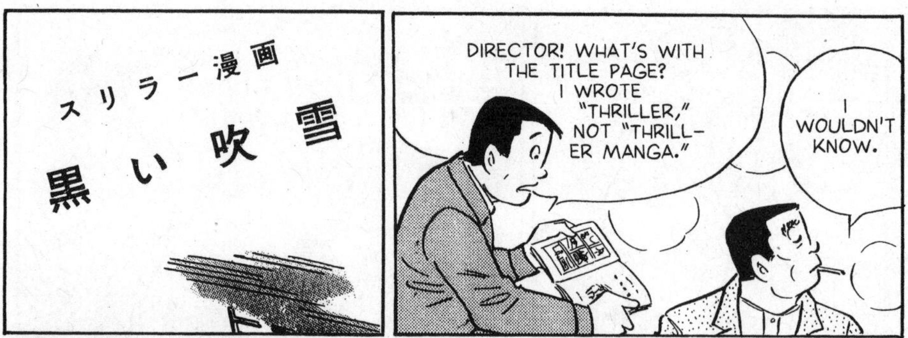
スリラー漫画
黒い吹雪
DIRECTOR! WHAT'S WITH THE TITLE PAGE? I WROTE "THRILLER," NOT "THRILL-ER MANGA."
I WOULDN'T KNOW.
TITLE: THRILLER MANGA "BLACK SNOWSTORM"

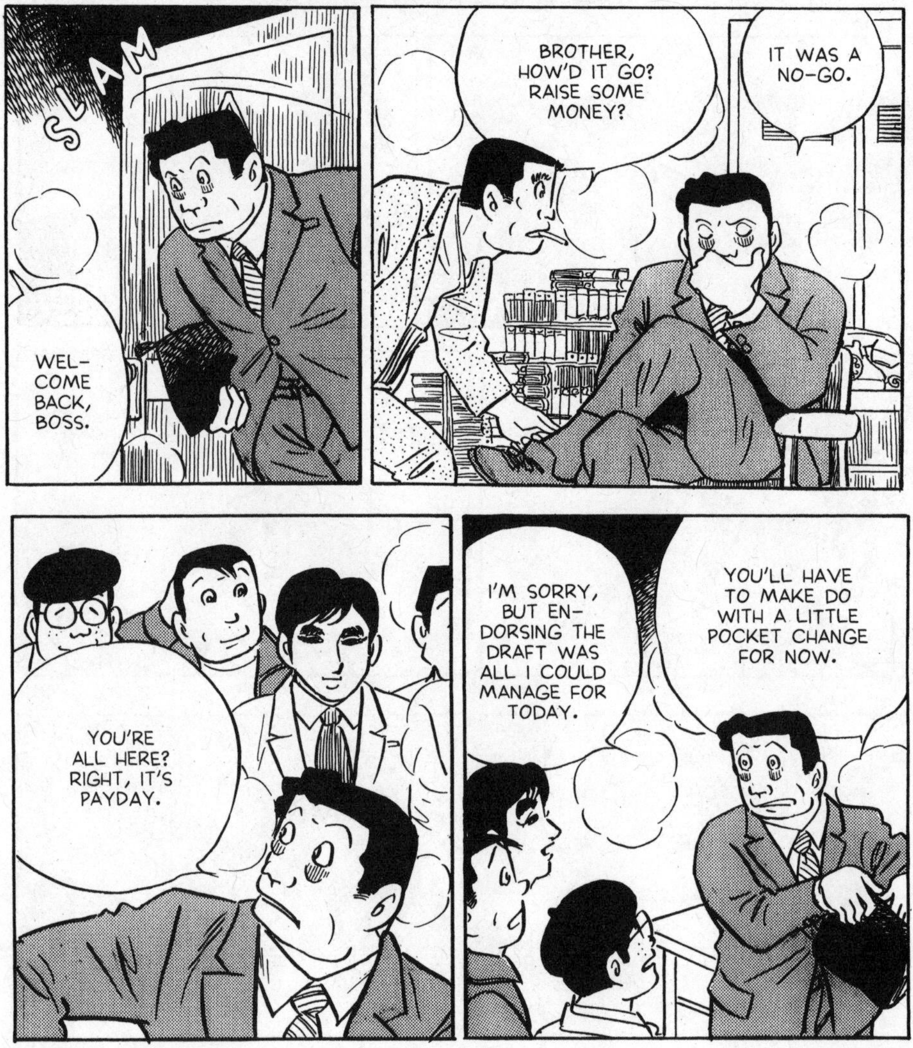
SLAM
WEL-COME BACK, BOSS.
BROTHER, HOW'D IT GO? RAISE SOME MONEY?
IT WAS A NO-GO.
YOU'RE ALL HERE? RIGHT, IT'S PAYDAY.
I'M SORRY, BUT EN-DORSING THE DRAFT WAS ALL I COULD MANAGE FOR TODAY.
YOU'LL HAVE TO MAKE DO WITH A LITTLE POCKET CHANGE FOR NOW.

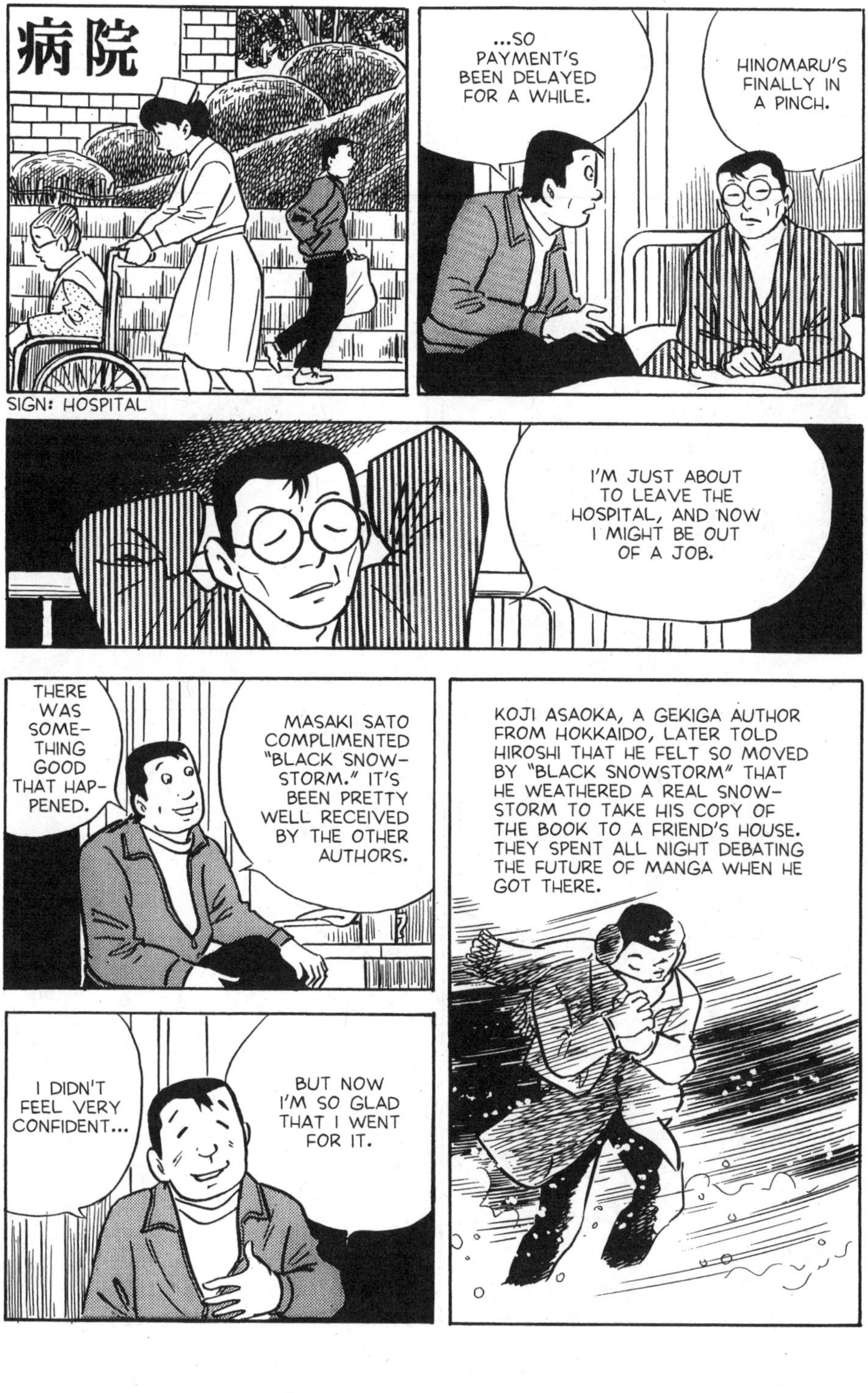
病院
SIGN: HOSPITAL
...SO PAYMENT'S BEEN DELAYED FOR A WHILE.
HINOMARU'S FINALLY IN A PINCH.
I'M JUST ABOUT TO LEAVE THE HOSPITAL, AND NOW I MIGHT BE OUT OF A JOB.
THERE WAS SOME-THING GOOD THAT HAP-PENED.
MASAKI SATO COMPLIMENTED "BLACK SNOW-STORM." IT'S BEEN PRETTY WELL RECEIVED BY THE OTHER AUTHORS.
I DIDN'T FEEL VERY CONFIDENT...
BUT NOW I'M SO GLAD THAT I WENT FOR IT.
KOJI ASAOKA, A GEKIGA AUTHOR FROM HOKKAIDO, LATER TOLD HIROSHI THAT HE FELT SO MOVED BY "BLACK SNOWSTORM" THAT HE WEATHERED A REAL SNOW-STORM TO TAKE HIS COPY OF THE BOOK TO A FRIEND'S HOUSE. THEY SPENT ALL NIGHT DEBATING THE FUTURE OF MANGA WHEN HE GOT THERE.

FEBRUARY 1957

HINOMARU FOUND ITSELF INVOLVED IN AN UNEXPECTED INCIDENT SOON AFTER THE PUBLICATION OF *SHADOW* NUMBER 10.

SIGN: HAKKO HINOMARU PUBLISHING

IS MR. YAMADA IN?

SURE. AND WHO'RE YOU?

POLICE.

I'M HERE TO TAKE MR. YAMADA DOWNTOWN FOR THE COUNTERFEITING OF SECURITIES.

WH-WHAT?!

THE FALL OF HINOMARU BUNKO

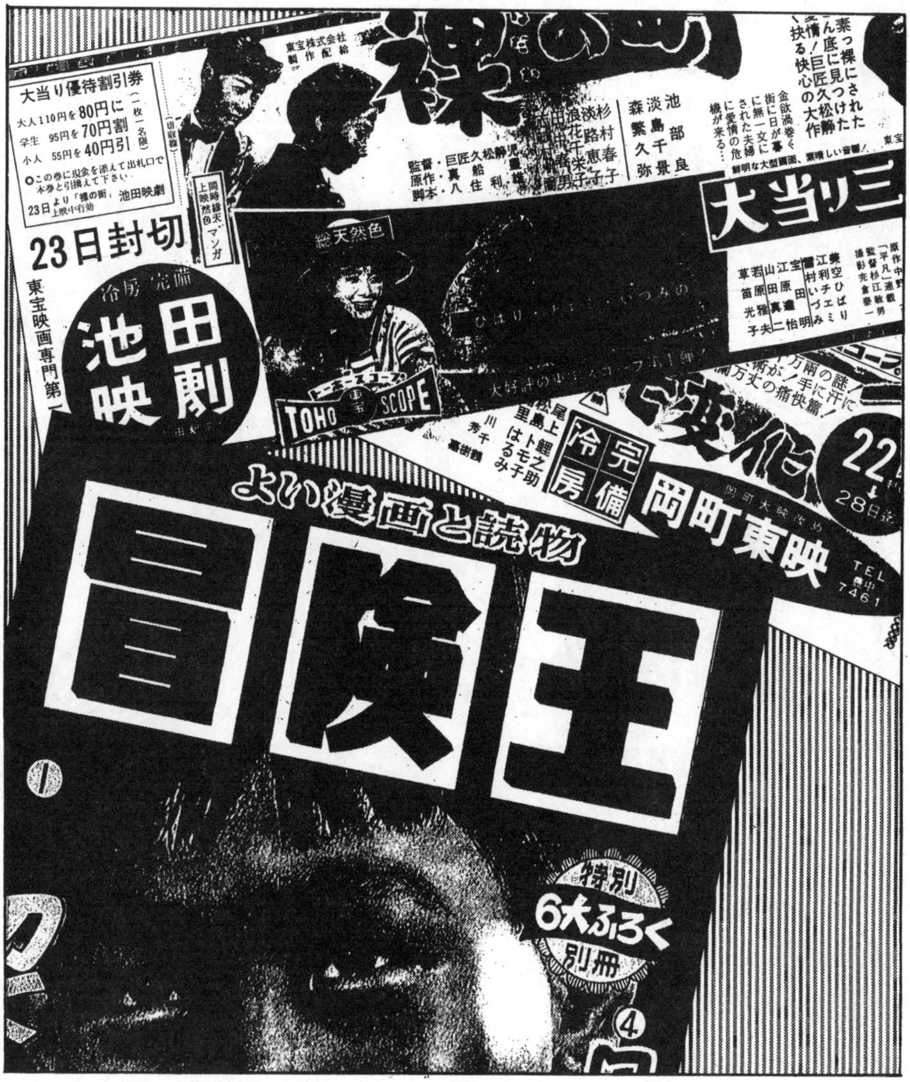
東宝株式会社
製作配給
大当り優待割引券
大人110円を80円に
学生 95円を70円割
小人 55円を40円引
23日封切
東宝映画専門第一
冷房完備
池田映劇
同時上映 総天然色 漫天マンガ
総天然色
TOHO SCOPE
大当り三
冷房完備
岡町東映
22
28日
TEL 7461
よい漫画と読物
冒険王
特別
6大ふろく
別冊

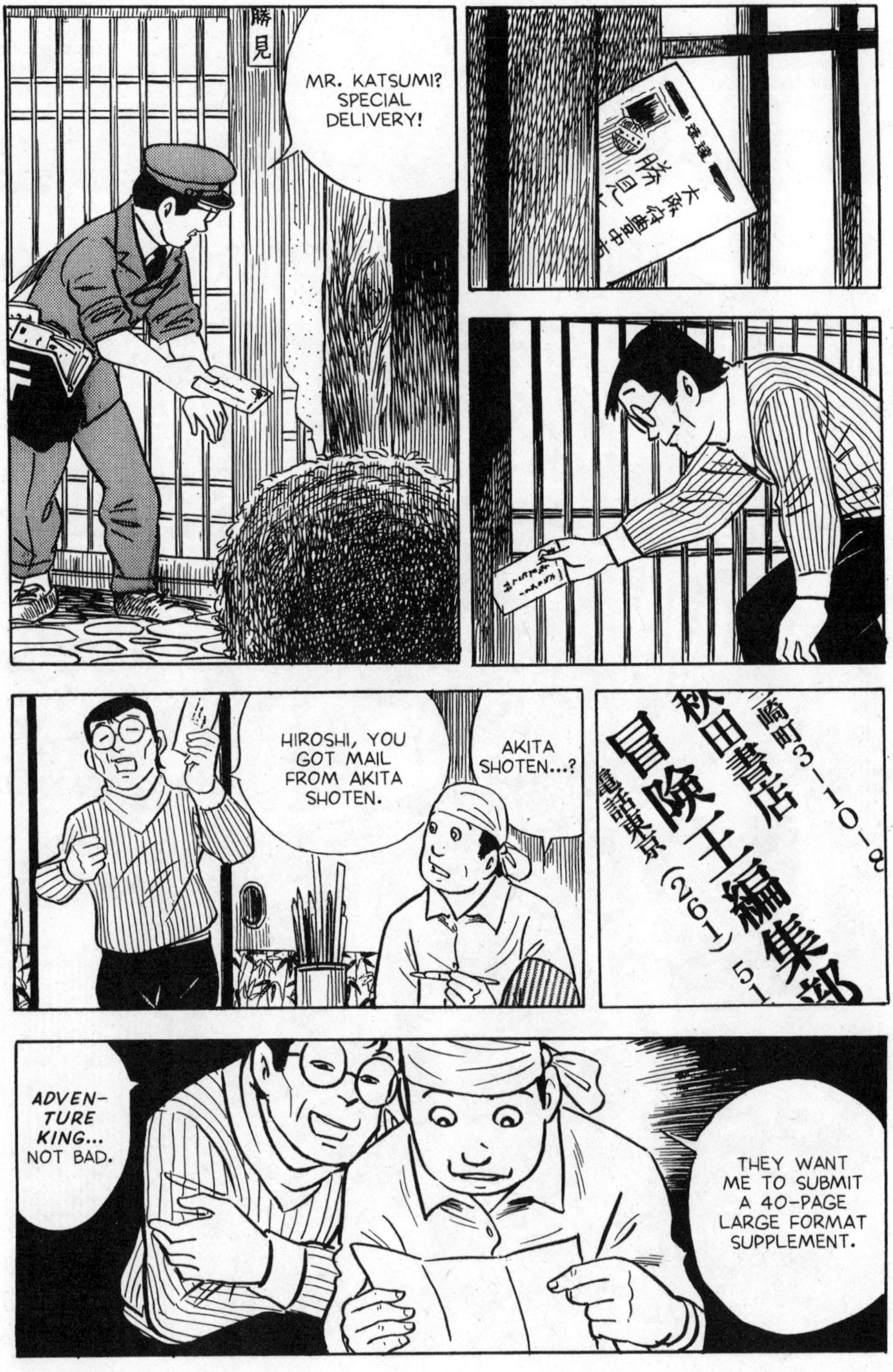
勝見
MR. KATSUMI? SPECIAL DELIVERY!
HIROSHI, YOU GOT MAIL FROM AKITA SHOTEN.
AKITA SHOTEN...?
崎町3-10-8
秋田書店
冒険王編集部
電話東京(261)51
ADVENTURE-KING... NOT BAD.
THEY WANT ME TO SUBMIT A 40-PAGE LARGE FORMAT SUPPLEMENT.

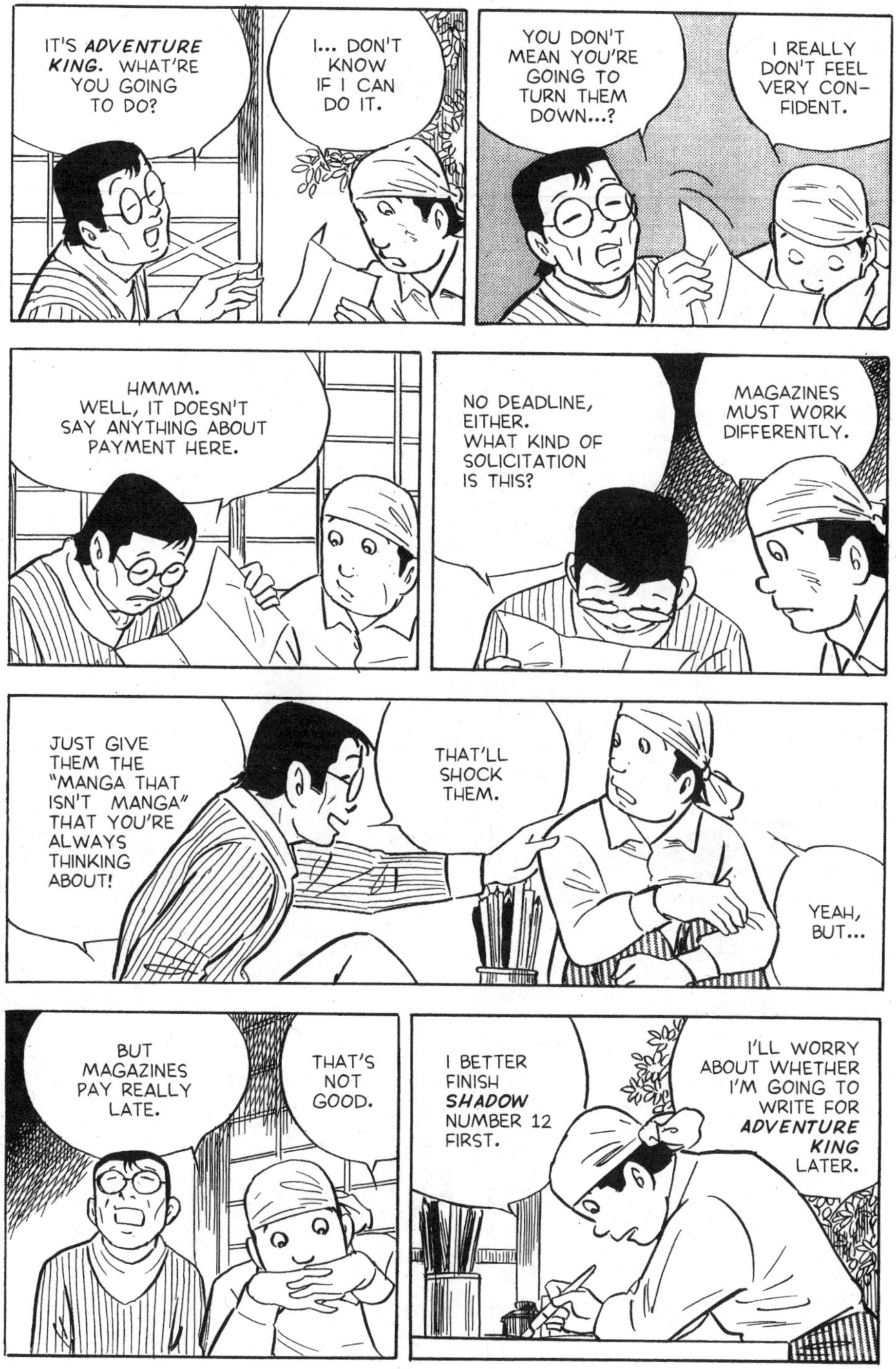
IT'S *ADVENTURE KING*. WHAT'RE YOU GOING TO DO?
I... DON'T KNOW IF I CAN DO IT.
YOU DON'T MEAN YOU'RE GOING TO TURN THEM DOWN...?
I REALLY DON'T FEEL VERY CON-FIDENT.
HMMM. WELL, IT DOESN'T SAY ANYTHING ABOUT PAYMENT HERE.
NO DEADLINE, EITHER. WHAT KIND OF SOLICITATION IS THIS?
MAGAZINES MUST WORK DIFFERENTLY.
JUST GIVE THEM THE "MANGA THAT ISN'T MANGA" THAT YOU'RE ALWAYS THINKING ABOUT!
THAT'LL SHOCK THEM.
YEAH, BUT...
BUT MAGAZINES PAY REALLY LATE.
THAT'S NOT GOOD.
I BETTER FINISH *SHADOW* NUMBER 12 FIRST.
I'LL WORRY ABOUT WHETHER I'M GOING TO WRITE FOR *ADVENTURE KING* LATER.

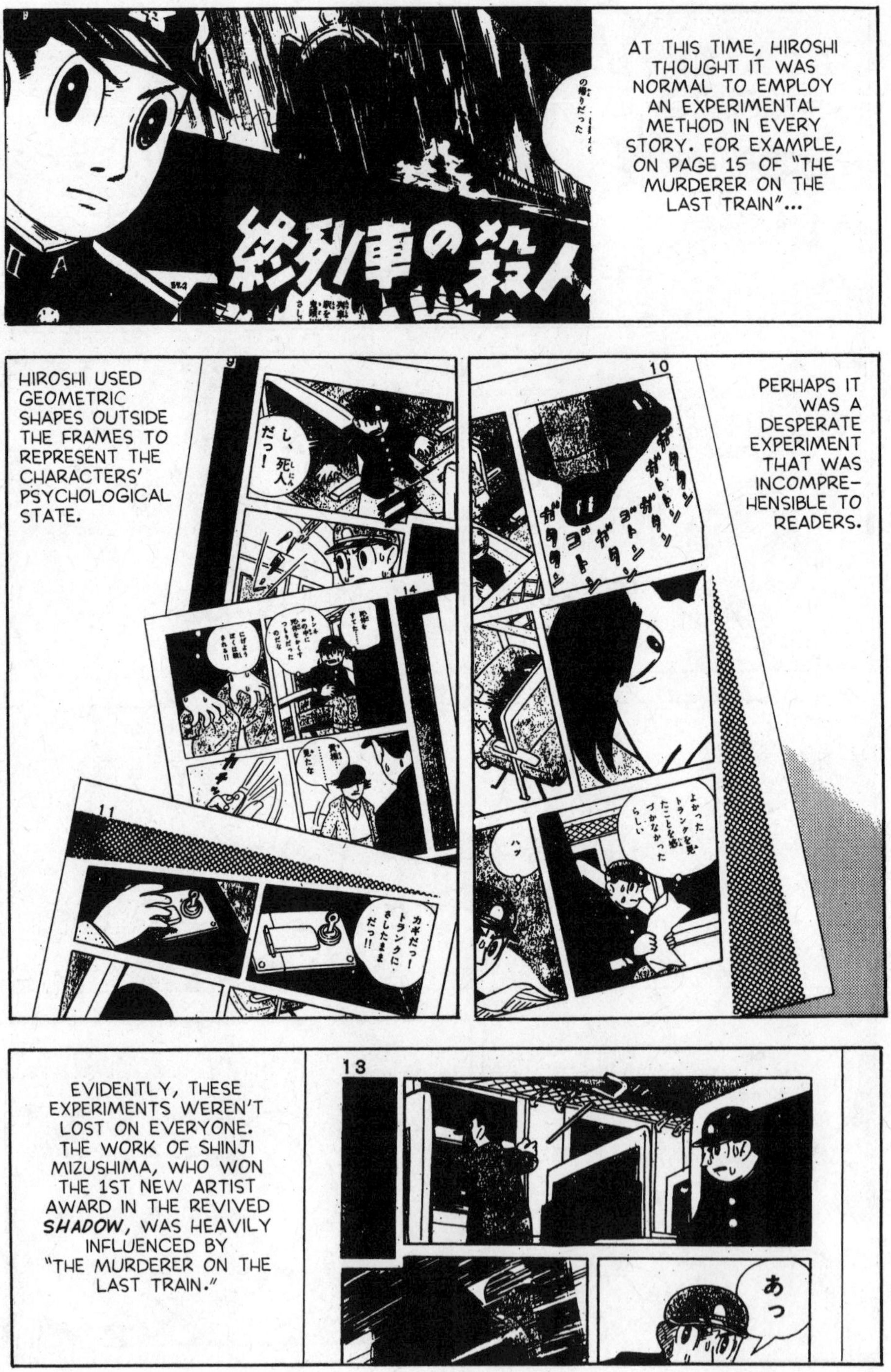
AT THIS TIME, HIROSHI THOUGHT IT WAS NORMAL TO EMPLOY AN EXPERIMENTAL METHOD IN EVERY STORY. FOR EXAMPLE, ON PAGE 15 OF "THE MURDERER ON THE LAST TRAIN"...
終列車の殺人
HIROSHI USED GEOMETRIC SHAPES OUTSIDE THE FRAMES TO REPRESENT THE CHARACTERS' PSYCHOLOGICAL STATE.
し、死人だっ！
カギだっ！トランクにさしたままだっ!!
ハッ
PERHAPS IT WAS A DESPERATE EXPERIMENT THAT WAS INCOMPREHENSIBLE TO READERS.
EVIDENTLY, THESE EXPERIMENTS WEREN'T LOST ON EVERYONE. THE WORK OF SHINJI MIZUSHIMA, WHO WON THE 1ST NEW ARTIST AWARD IN THE REVIVED *SHADOW*, WAS HEAVILY INFLUENCED BY "THE MURDERER ON THE LAST TRAIN."
あっ

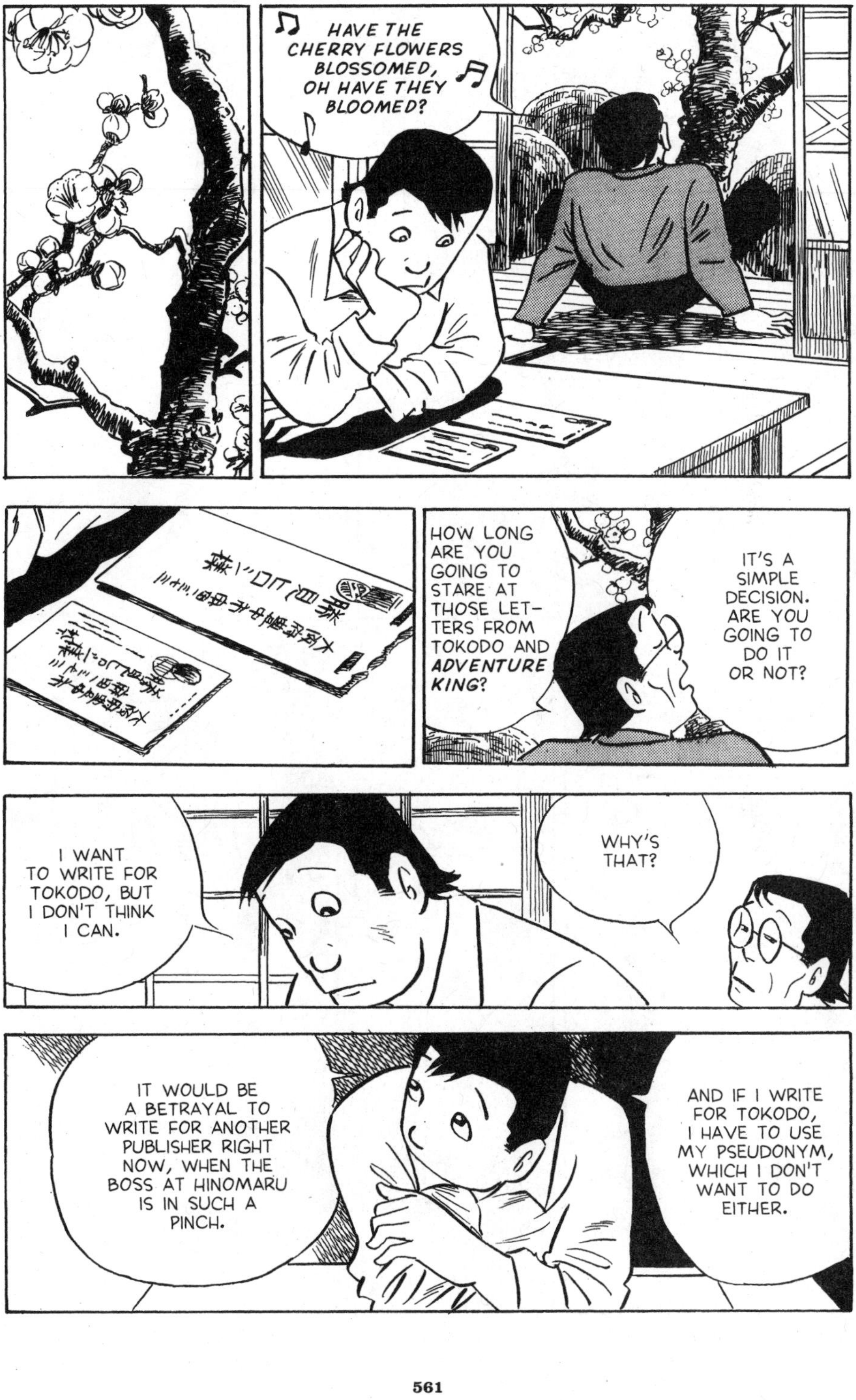
HAVE THE CHERRY FLOWERS BLOSSOMED, OH HAVE THEY BLOOMED?
HOW LONG ARE YOU GOING TO STARE AT THOSE LETTERS FROM TOKODO AND ***ADVENTURE KING***?
IT'S A SIMPLE DECISION. ARE YOU GOING TO DO IT OR NOT?
I WANT TO WRITE FOR TOKODO, BUT I DON'T THINK I CAN.
WHY'S THAT?
IT WOULD BE A BETRAYAL TO WRITE FOR ANOTHER PUBLISHER RIGHT NOW, WHEN THE BOSS AT HINOMARU IS IN SUCH A PINCH.
AND IF I WRITE FOR TOKODO, I HAVE TO USE MY PSEUDONYM, WHICH I DON'T WANT TO DO EITHER.

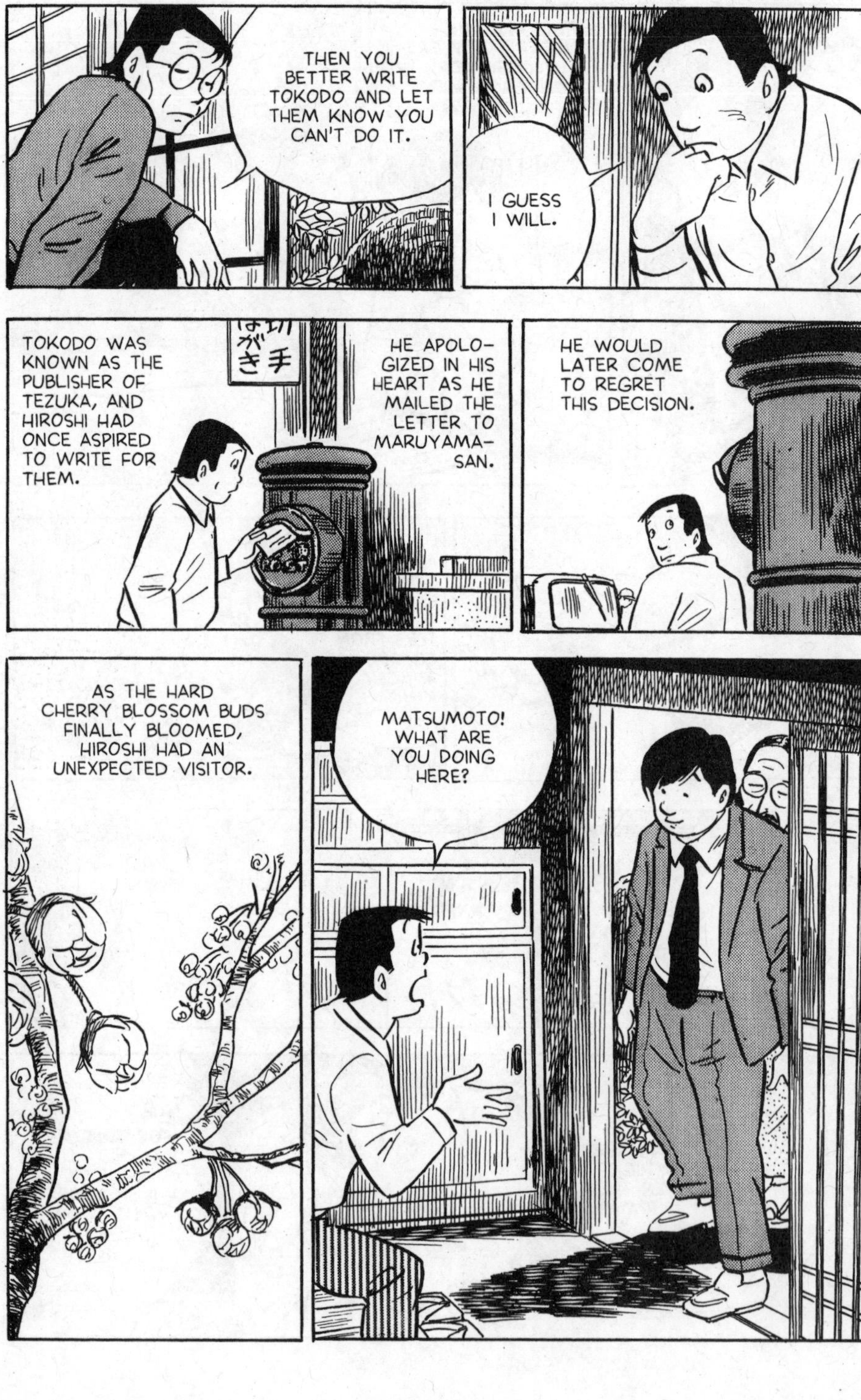
THEN YOU BETTER WRITE TOKODO AND LET THEM KNOW YOU CAN'T DO IT.
I GUESS I WILL.
TOKODO WAS KNOWN AS THE PUBLISHER OF TEZUKA, AND HIROSHI HAD ONCE ASPIRED TO WRITE FOR THEM.
切手
はがき
HE APOLOGIZED IN HIS HEART AS HE MAILED THE LETTER TO MARUYAMA-SAN.
HE WOULD LATER COME TO REGRET THIS DECISION.
AS THE HARD CHERRY BLOSSOM BUDS FINALLY BLOOMED, HIROSHI HAD AN UNEXPECTED VISITOR.
MATSUMOTO! WHAT ARE YOU DOING HERE?

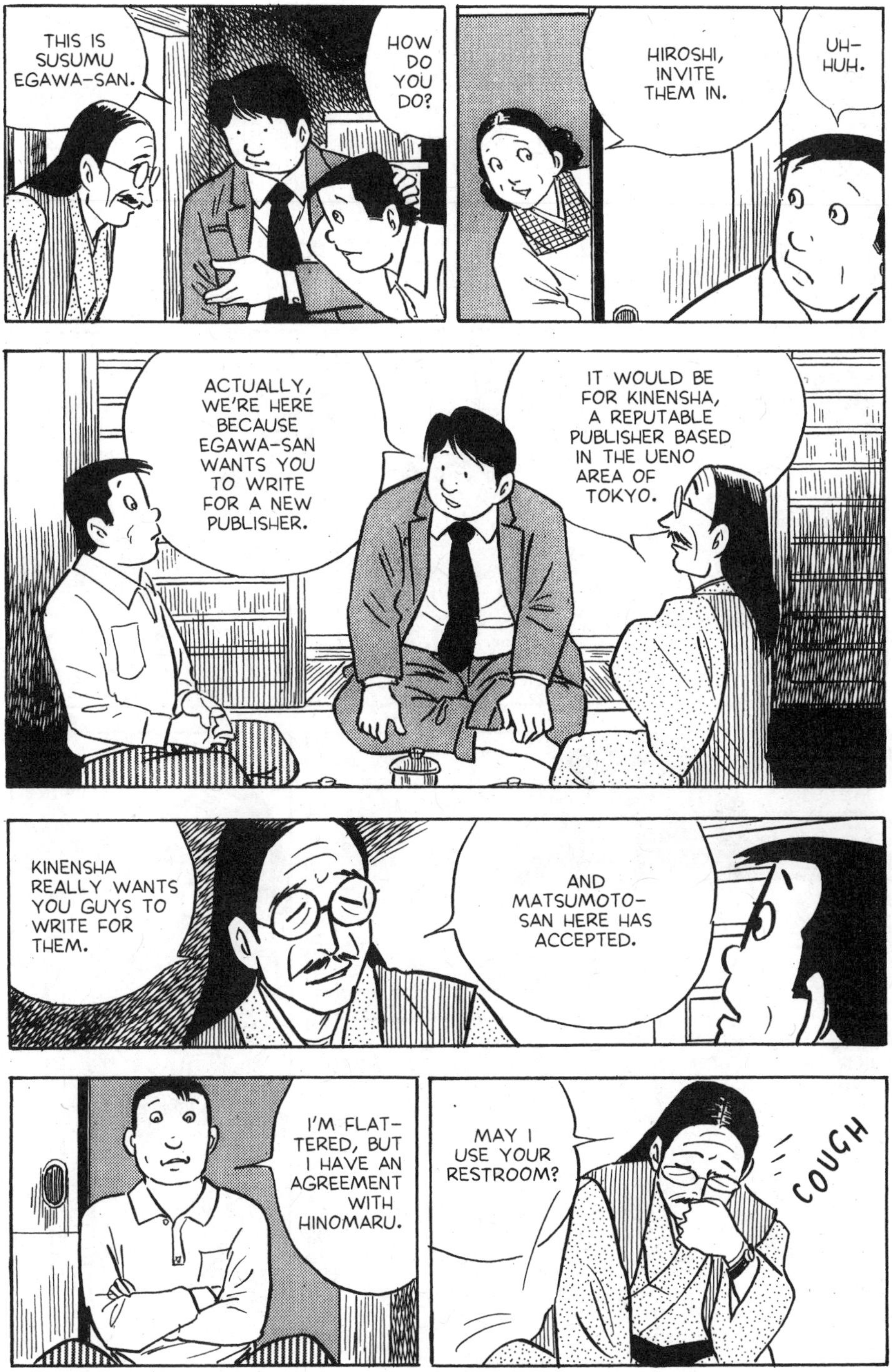
THIS IS SUSUMU EGAWA-SAN.
HOW DO YOU DO?
HIROSHI, INVITE THEM IN.
UH-HUH.
ACTUALLY, WE'RE HERE BECAUSE EGAWA-SAN WANTS YOU TO WRITE FOR A NEW PUBLISHER.
IT WOULD BE FOR KINENSHA, A REPUTABLE PUBLISHER BASED IN THE UENO AREA OF TOKYO.
KINENSHA REALLY WANTS YOU GUYS TO WRITE FOR THEM.
AND MATSUMOTO-SAN HERE HAS ACCEPTED.
I'M FLATTERED, BUT I HAVE AN AGREEMENT WITH HINOMARU.
MAY I USE YOUR RESTROOM?
COUGH

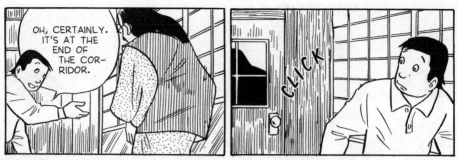

OH, CERTAINLY. IT'S AT THE END OF THE COR-RIDOR.
CLICK
MATSUMOTO, ARE YOU REALLY GOING TO WORK WITH EGAWA-SAN?
HINO-MARU'S GONE BANK-RUPT.
WH-WHAT DID YOU SAY?
I SAID HINOMARU HAS GONE BANKRUPT.
BOSS FINALLY WROTE A BAD DRAFT.
I'M SURE THERE'S CHECKS THAT YOU'RE STILL WAITING FOR.
HIROSHI TURNED PALE.
THE REVELA-TION WAS A BOLT FROM THE BLUE.
SO WHAT DO YOU SAY, KATSUMI-SAN?

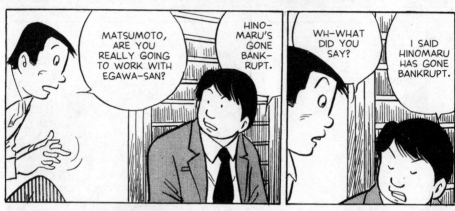

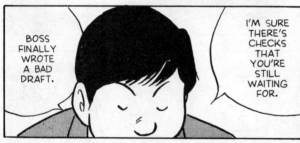

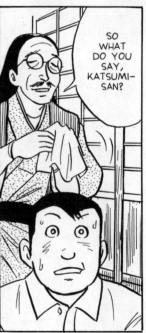

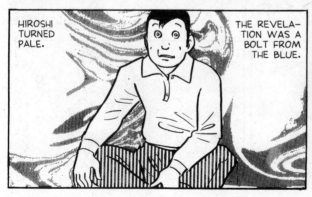

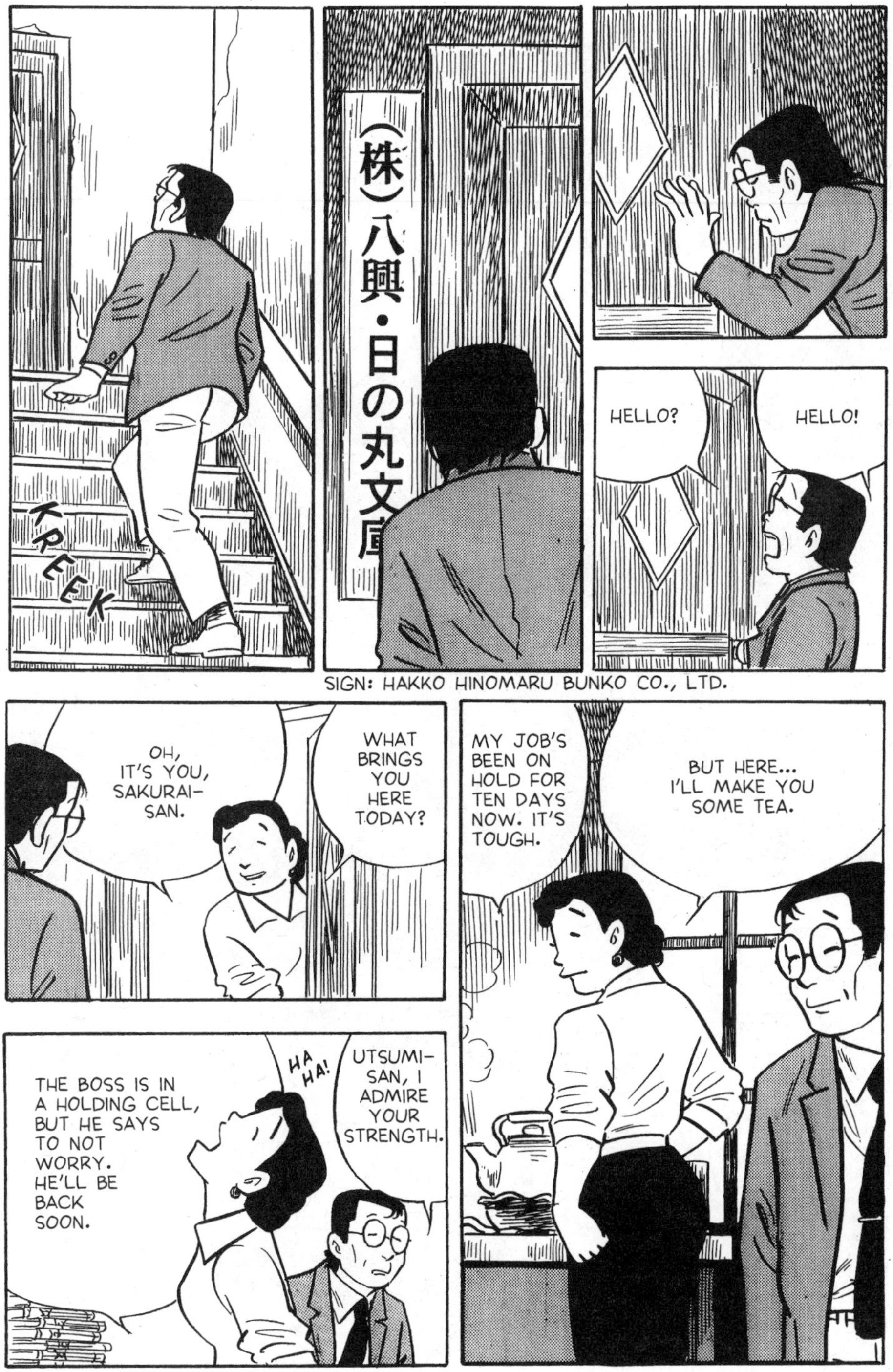
KREEK
（株）八興・日の丸文
HELLO?
HELLO!
SIGN: HAKKO HINOMARU BUNKO CO., LTD.
OH, IT'S YOU, SAKURAI-SAN.
WHAT BRINGS YOU HERE TODAY?
THE BOSS IS IN A HOLDING CELL, BUT HE SAYS TO NOT WORRY. HE'LL BE BACK SOON.
HA HA!
UTSUMI-SAN, I ADMIRE YOUR STRENGTH.
MY JOB'S BEEN ON HOLD FOR TEN DAYS NOW. IT'S TOUGH.
BUT HERE... I'LL MAKE YOU SOME TEA.

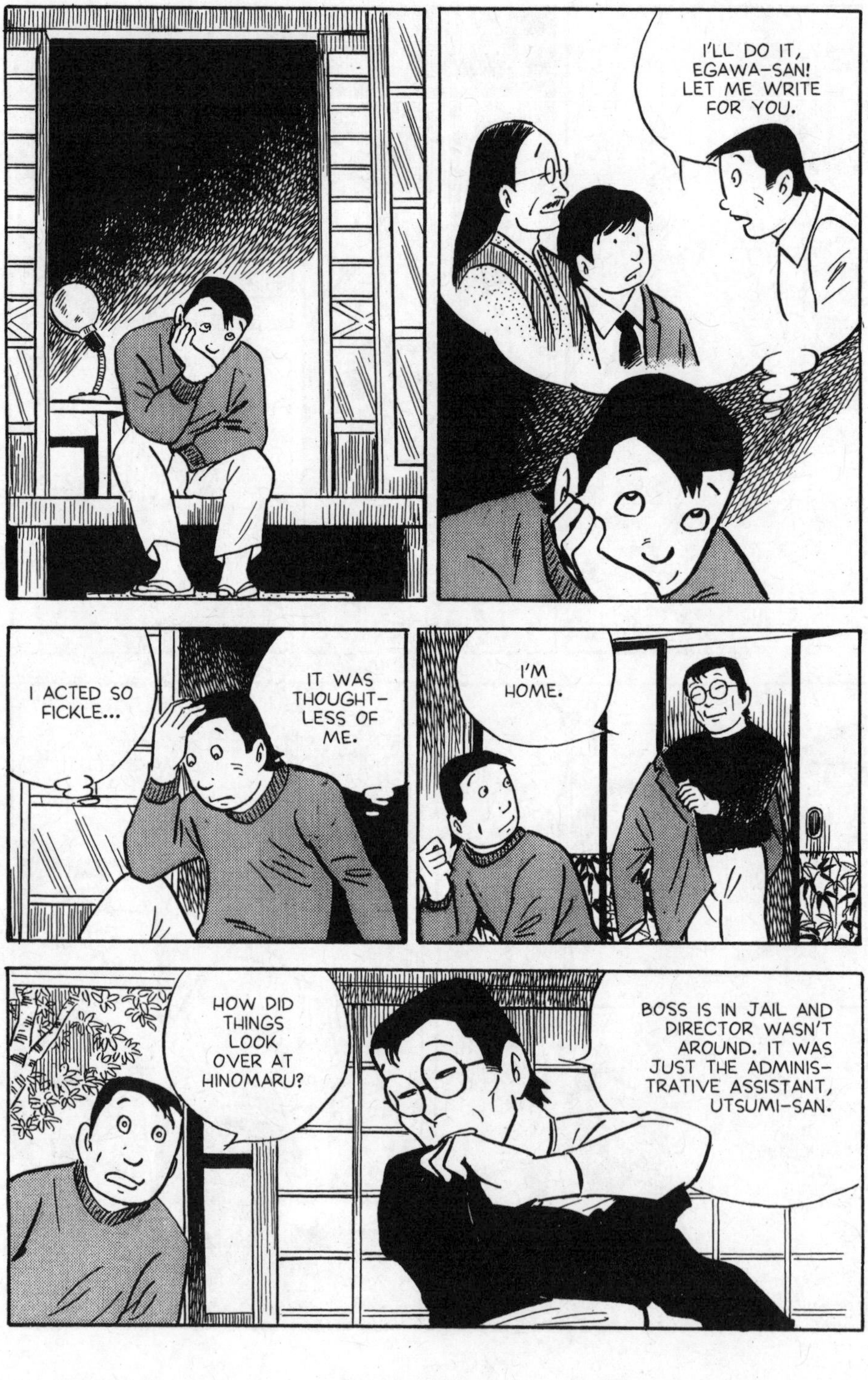
I'LL DO IT, EGAWA-SAN! LET ME WRITE FOR YOU.
I ACTED SO FICKLE...
IT WAS THOUGHT-LESS OF ME.
I'M HOME.
HOW DID THINGS LOOK OVER AT HINOMARU?
BOSS IS IN JAIL AND DIRECTOR WASN'T AROUND. IT WAS JUST THE ADMINIS-TRATIVE ASSISTANT, UTSUMI-SAN.

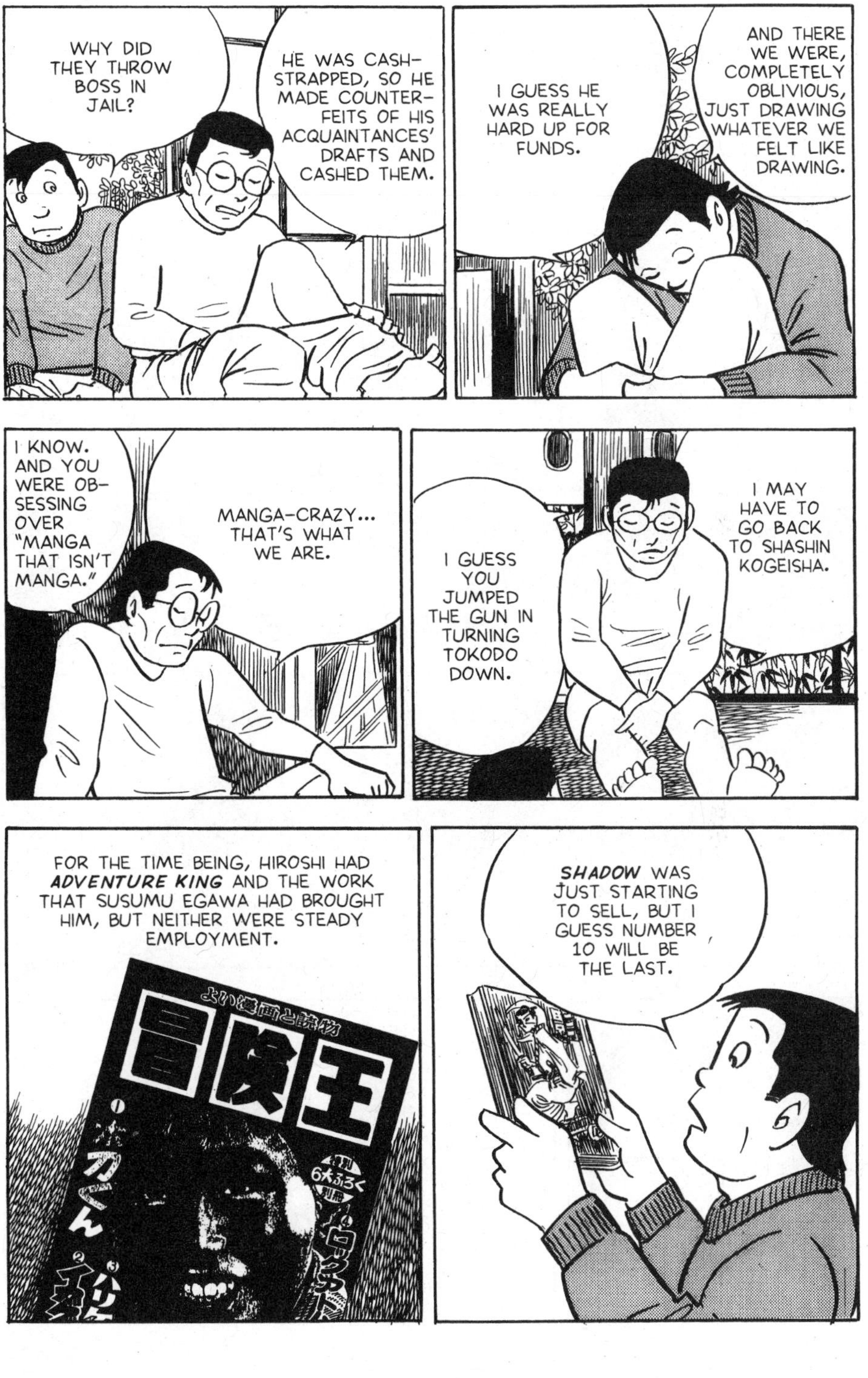
WHY DID THEY THROW BOSS IN JAIL?
HE WAS CASH-STRAPPED, SO HE MADE COUNTER-FEITS OF HIS ACQUAINTANCES' DRAFTS AND CASHED THEM.
I GUESS HE WAS REALLY HARD UP FOR FUNDS.
AND THERE WE WERE, COMPLETELY OBLIVIOUS, JUST DRAWING WHATEVER WE FELT LIKE DRAWING.
I KNOW. AND YOU WERE OB-SESSING OVER "MANGA THAT ISN'T MANGA."
MANGA-CRAZY... THAT'S WHAT WE ARE.
I GUESS YOU JUMPED THE GUN IN TURNING TOKODO DOWN.
I MAY HAVE TO GO BACK TO SHASHIN KOGEISHA.
FOR THE TIME BEING, HIROSHI HAD ADVENTURE KING AND THE WORK THAT SUSUMU EGAWA HAD BROUGHT HIM, BUT NEITHER WERE STEADY EMPLOYMENT.
よい漫画と読物
冒険王
6大ふろく
SHADOW WAS JUST STARTING TO SELL, BUT I GUESS NUMBER 10 WILL BE THE LAST.

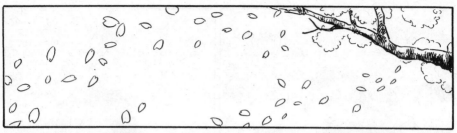

HOW SAD. THE CHERRY BLOSSOMS ARE FALL- ING.

I WAS THINKING... EVERYONE ACTED SO HASTILY ONCE HINOMARU WENT BANKRUPT.

WHAT DO YOU MEAN?

EGAWA-SAN AND MATSUMOTO QUICKLY FOUND WORK AT KINENSHA...

KURODA SENSEI FLEW OFF TO NAGOYA TO FIND HIS NEXT JOB...

NAGO- YA...? WHAT'S THAT ABOUT?

I JUST GOT A LETTER FROM KURODA SENSEI.

IT SAYS HE MADE A DEAL WITH A WHOLESALER IN NAGOYA CALLED "TOKAI TOSHO."

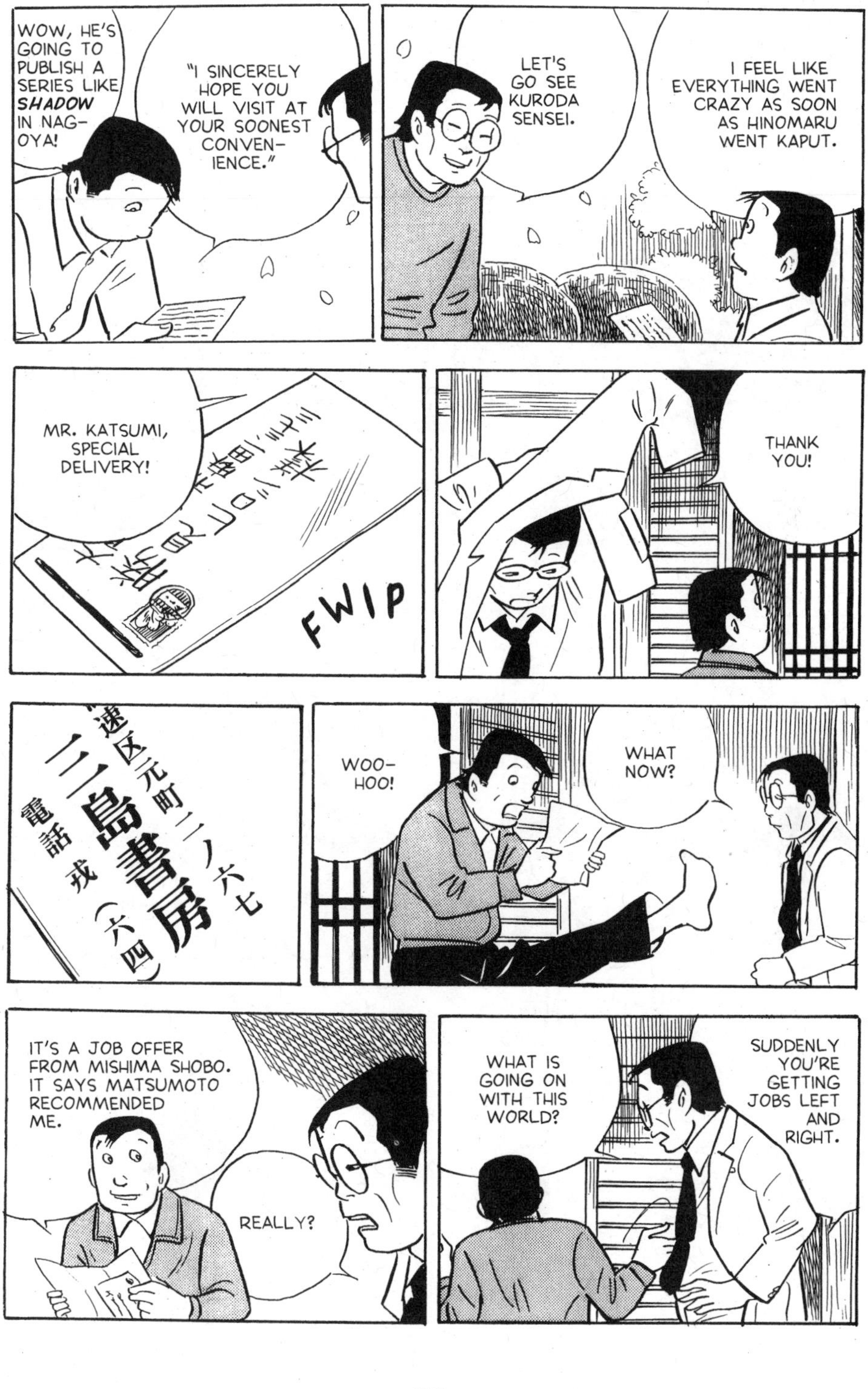
WOW, HE'S GOING TO PUBLISH A SERIES LIKE ***SHADOW*** IN NAG-OYA!
"I SINCERELY HOPE YOU WILL VISIT AT YOUR SOONEST CONVEN-IENCE."
LET'S GO SEE KURODA SENSEI.
I FEEL LIKE EVERYTHING WENT CRAZY AS SOON AS HINOMARU WENT KAPUT.
MR. KATSUMI, SPECIAL DELIVERY!
FWIP
THANK YOU!
速区元町二ノ六七
三島書房
電話 戎 (六四)
WOO-HOO!
WHAT NOW?
IT'S A JOB OFFER FROM MISHIMA SHOBO. IT SAYS MATSUMOTO RECOMMENDED ME.
REALLY?
WHAT IS GOING ON WITH THIS WORLD?
SUDDENLY YOU'RE GETTING JOBS LEFT AND RIGHT.

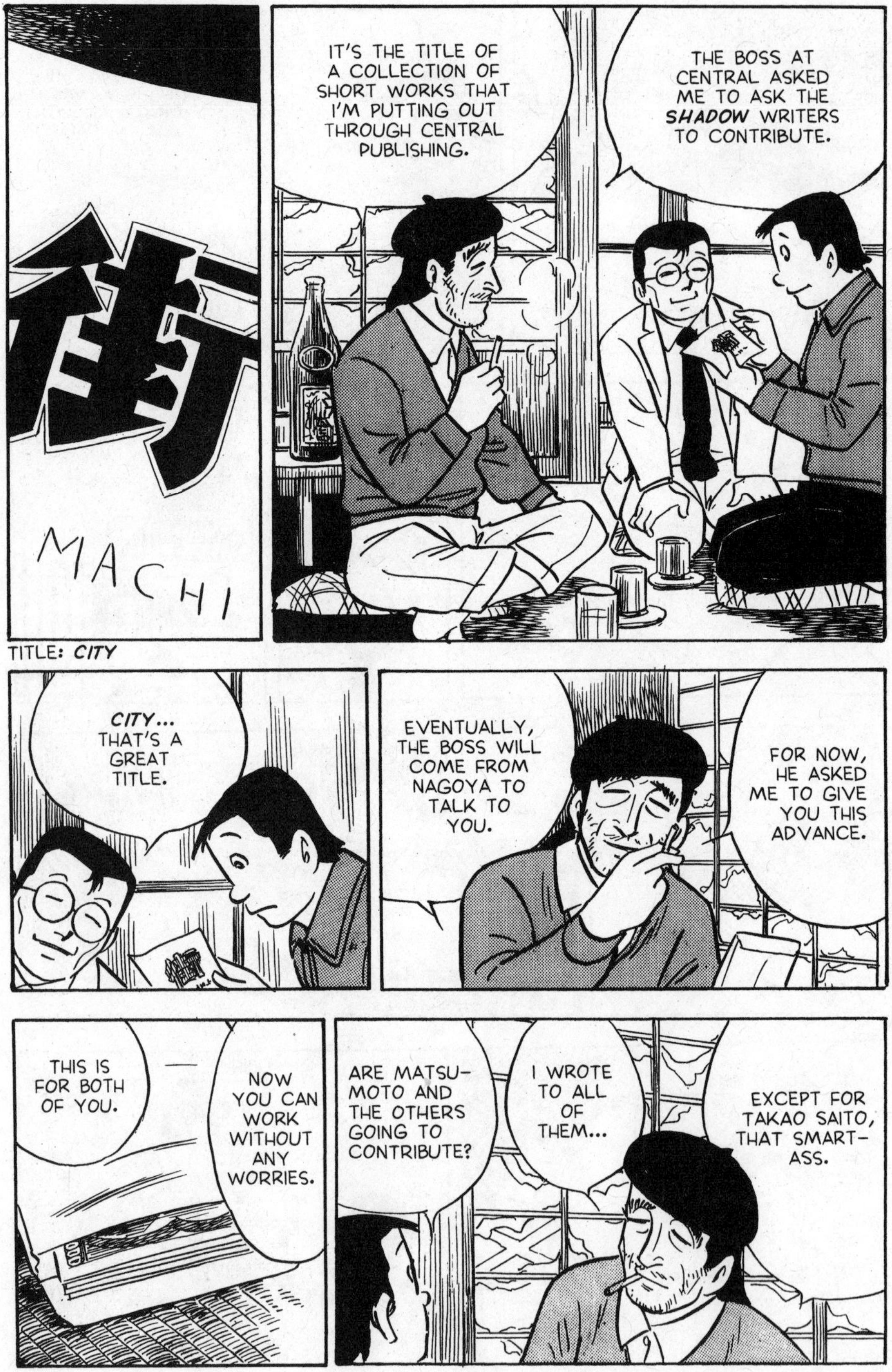
街
MACHI
IT'S THE TITLE OF A COLLECTION OF SHORT WORKS THAT I'M PUTTING OUT THROUGH CENTRAL PUBLISHING.
THE BOSS AT CENTRAL ASKED ME TO ASK THE ***SHADOW*** WRITERS TO CONTRIBUTE.
TITLE: *CITY*
CITY... THAT'S A GREAT TITLE.
EVENTUALLY, THE BOSS WILL COME FROM NAGOYA TO TALK TO YOU.
FOR NOW, HE ASKED ME TO GIVE YOU THIS ADVANCE.
THIS IS FOR BOTH OF YOU.
NOW YOU CAN WORK WITHOUT ANY WORRIES.
ARE MATSU-MOTO AND THE OTHERS GOING TO CONTRIBUTE?
I WROTE TO ALL OF THEM...
EXCEPT FOR TAKAO SAITO, THAT SMART-ASS.

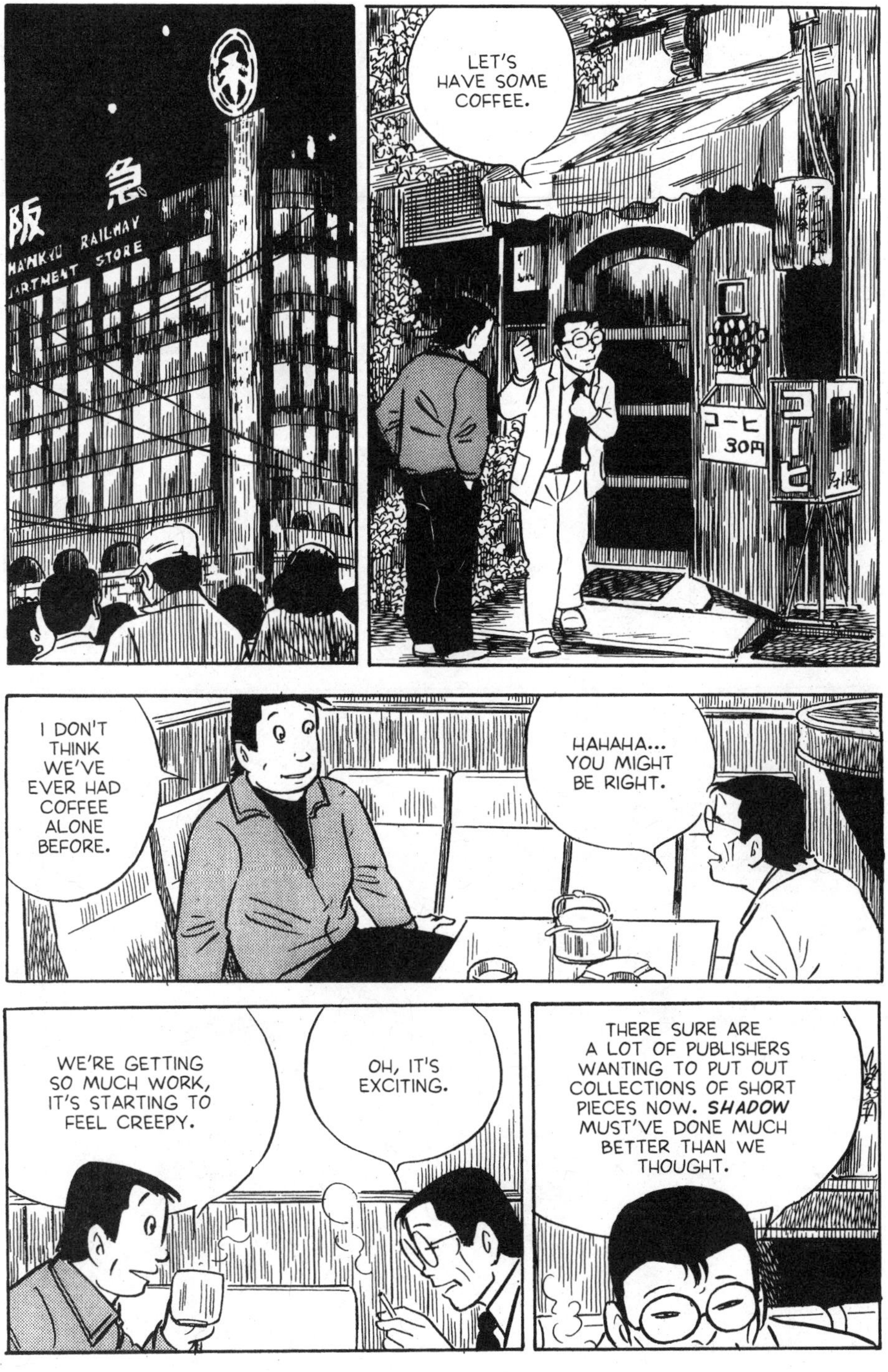

阪 急
HANKYU RAILWAY
ARTMENT STORE
LET'S HAVE SOME COFFEE.
コーヒ 30円
コーヒ
I DON'T THINK WE'VE EVER HAD COFFEE ALONE BEFORE.
HAHAHA... YOU MIGHT BE RIGHT.
WE'RE GETTING SO MUCH WORK, IT'S STARTING TO FEEL CREEPY.
OH, IT'S EXCITING.
THERE SURE ARE A LOT OF PUBLISHERS WANTING TO PUT OUT COLLECTIONS OF SHORT PIECES NOW. ***SHADOW*** MUST'VE DONE MUCH BETTER THAN WE THOUGHT.

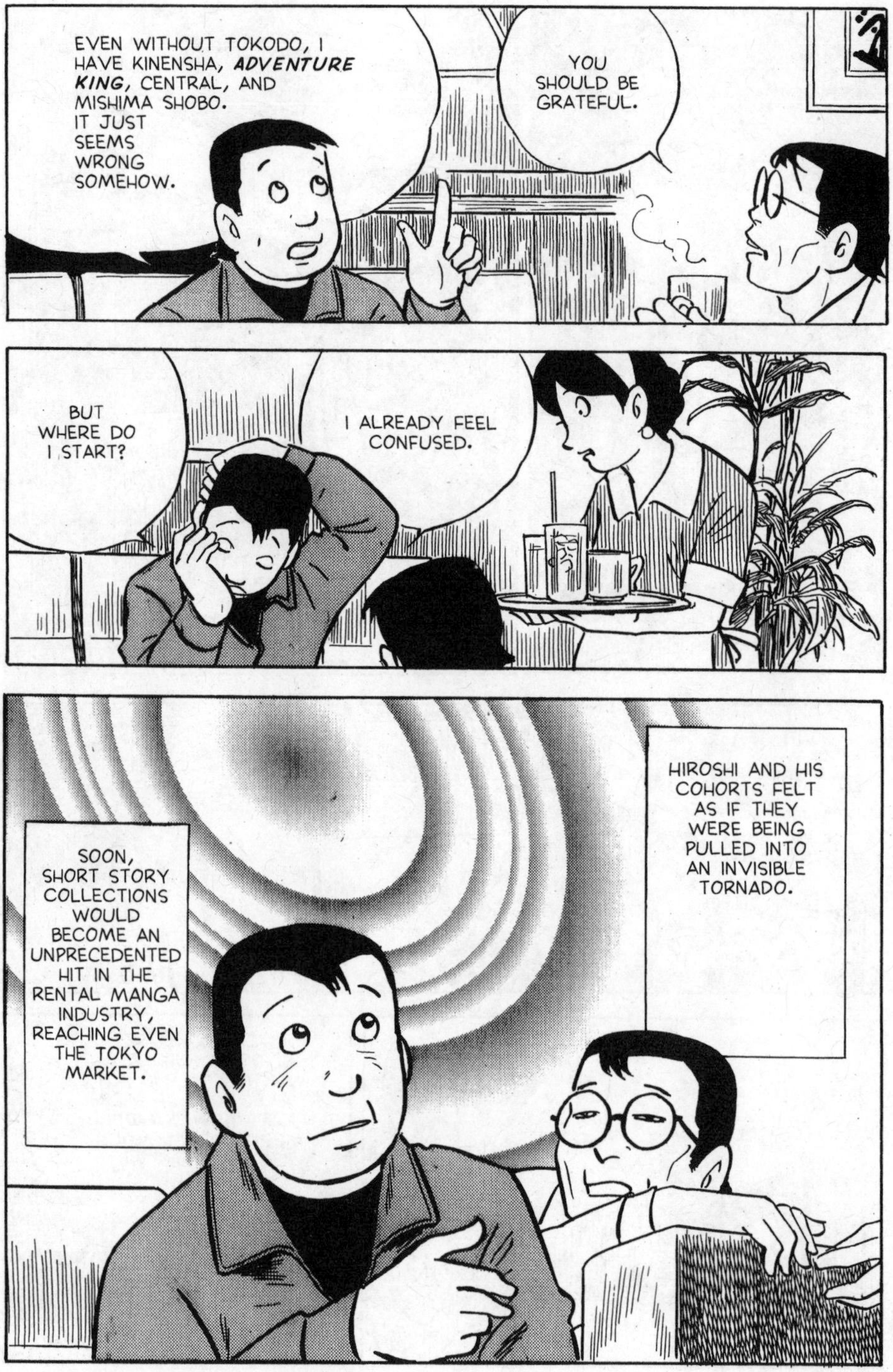
EVEN WITHOUT TOKODO, I HAVE KINENSHA, ***ADVENTURE KING***, CENTRAL, AND MISHIMA SHOBO. IT JUST SEEMS WRONG SOMEHOW.
YOU SHOULD BE GRATEFUL.
BUT WHERE DO I START?
I ALREADY FEEL CONFUSED.
SOON, SHORT STORY COLLECTIONS WOULD BECOME AN UNPRECEDENTED HIT IN THE RENTAL MANGA INDUSTRY, REACHING EVEN THE TOKYO MARKET.
HIROSHI AND HIS COHORTS FELT AS IF THEY WERE BEING PULLED INTO AN INVISIBLE TORNADO.

MANAGING EDITOR

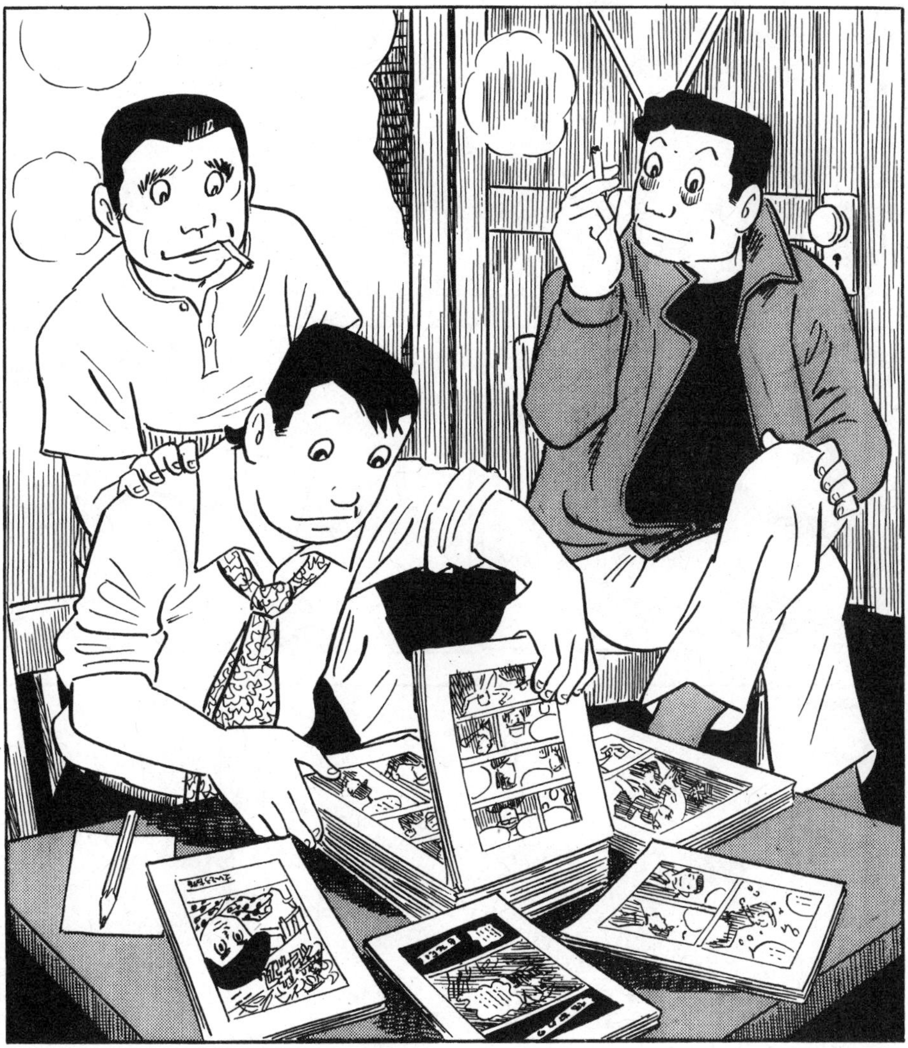

MARCH 1957

HIROSHI WAS SIMULTANEOUSLY WORKING ON THREE STORIES.

"THE MAN WHO LIVED," A 40-PAGE SUPPLEMENT TO *ADVENTURE KING*...

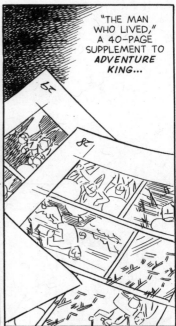

"MURDER AT UGUISUSO," A 21-PAGE STORY FOR CENTRAL BUNKO'S *CITY*...

AND FINALLY, THE 128-PAGE BOOK *BEAT THE BOSS*.

DON'T YOU GET THE STORYLINES CONFUSED WORKING LIKE THAT?

NO, IT ACTUALLY HELPS BECAUSE WHEN I GET BORED WITH ONE, I CAN WORK ON ANOTHER.

I THINK IT'S GOING TO MAKE ME MORE PRODUCTIVE.

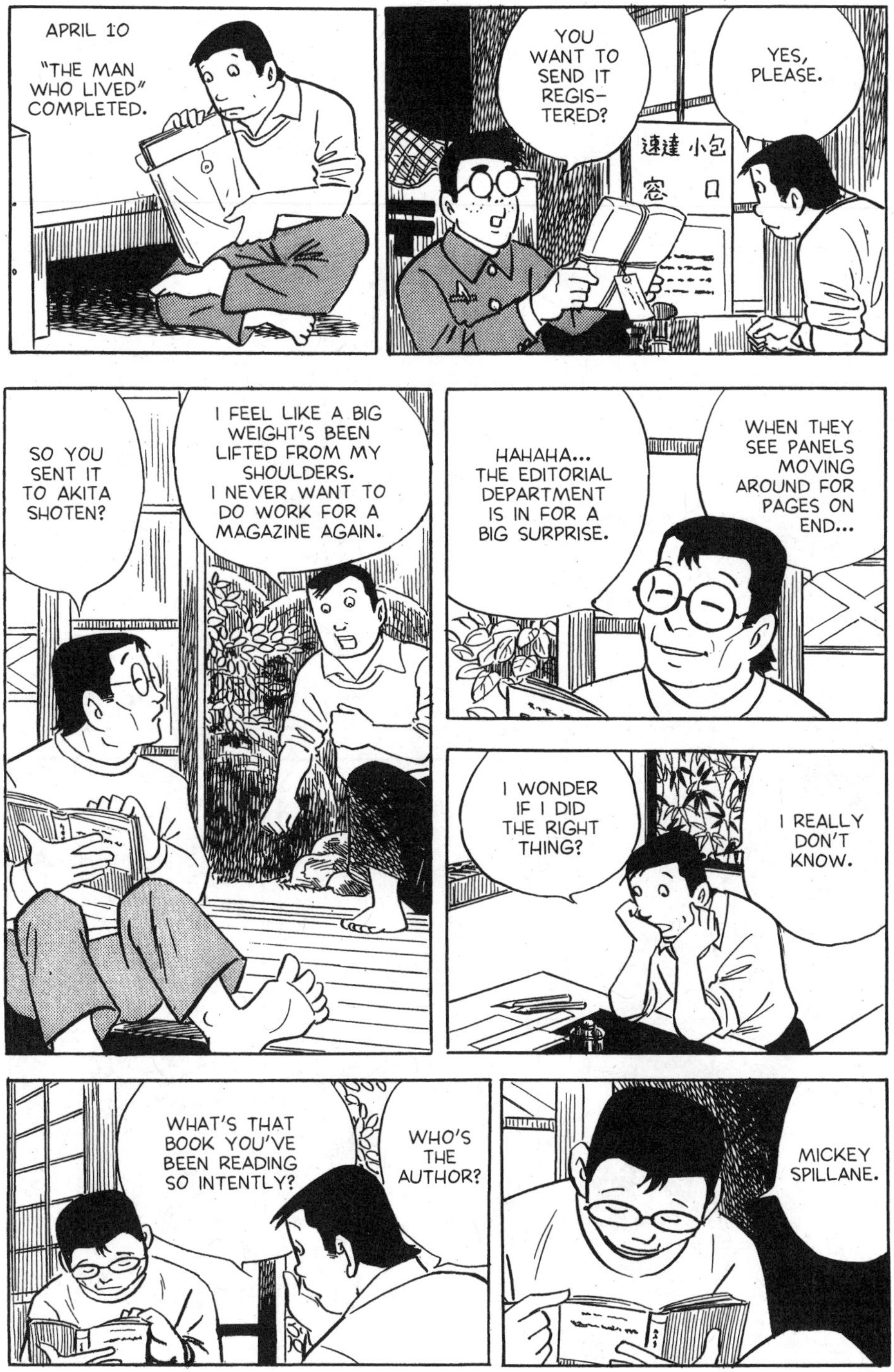
APRIL 10
"THE MAN WHO LIVED" COMPLETED.
YOU WANT TO SEND IT REGIS-TERED?
速達 小包
窓 口
YES, PLEASE.
SO YOU SENT IT TO AKITA SHOTEN?
I FEEL LIKE A BIG WEIGHT'S BEEN LIFTED FROM MY SHOULDERS. I NEVER WANT TO DO WORK FOR A MAGAZINE AGAIN.
HAHAHA... THE EDITORIAL DEPARTMENT IS IN FOR A BIG SURPRISE.
WHEN THEY SEE PANELS MOVING AROUND FOR PAGES ON END...
I WONDER IF I DID THE RIGHT THING?
I REALLY DON'T KNOW.
WHAT'S THAT BOOK YOU'VE BEEN READING SO INTENTLY?
WHO'S THE AUTHOR?
MICKEY SPILLANE.

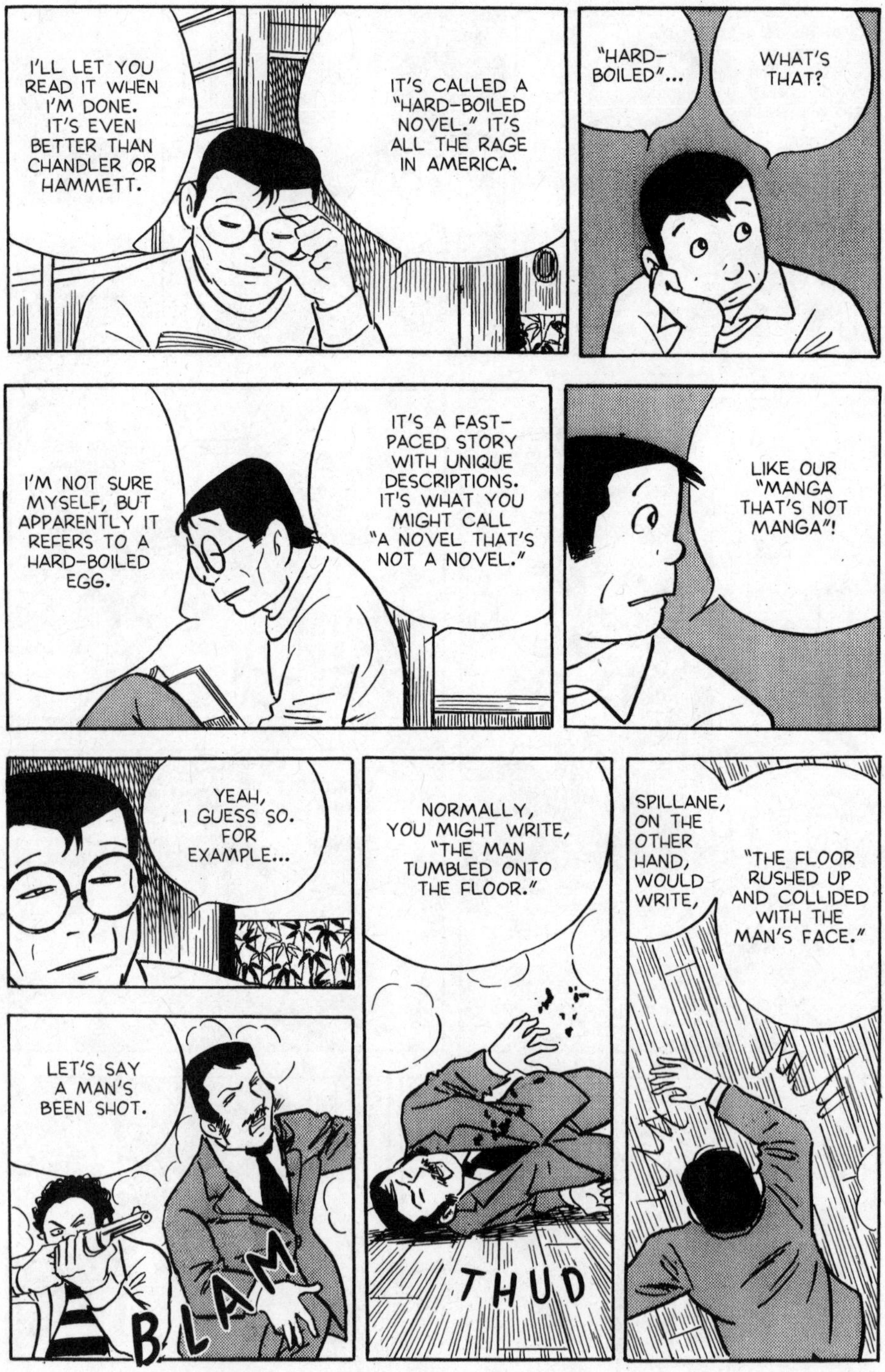
I'LL LET YOU READ IT WHEN I'M DONE. IT'S EVEN BETTER THAN CHANDLER OR HAMMETT.
IT'S CALLED A "HARD-BOILED NOVEL." IT'S ALL THE RAGE IN AMERICA.
"HARD-BOILED"...
WHAT'S THAT?
I'M NOT SURE MYSELF, BUT APPARENTLY IT REFERS TO A HARD-BOILED EGG.
IT'S A FAST-PACED STORY WITH UNIQUE DESCRIPTIONS. IT'S WHAT YOU MIGHT CALL "A NOVEL THAT'S NOT A NOVEL."
LIKE OUR "MANGA THAT'S NOT MANGA"!
YEAH, I GUESS SO. FOR EXAMPLE...
LET'S SAY A MAN'S BEEN SHOT.
BLAM
NORMALLY, YOU MIGHT WRITE, "THE MAN TUMBLED ONTO THE FLOOR."
THUD
SPILLANE, ON THE OTHER HAND, WOULD WRITE,
"THE FLOOR RUSHED UP AND COLLIDED WITH THE MAN'S FACE."

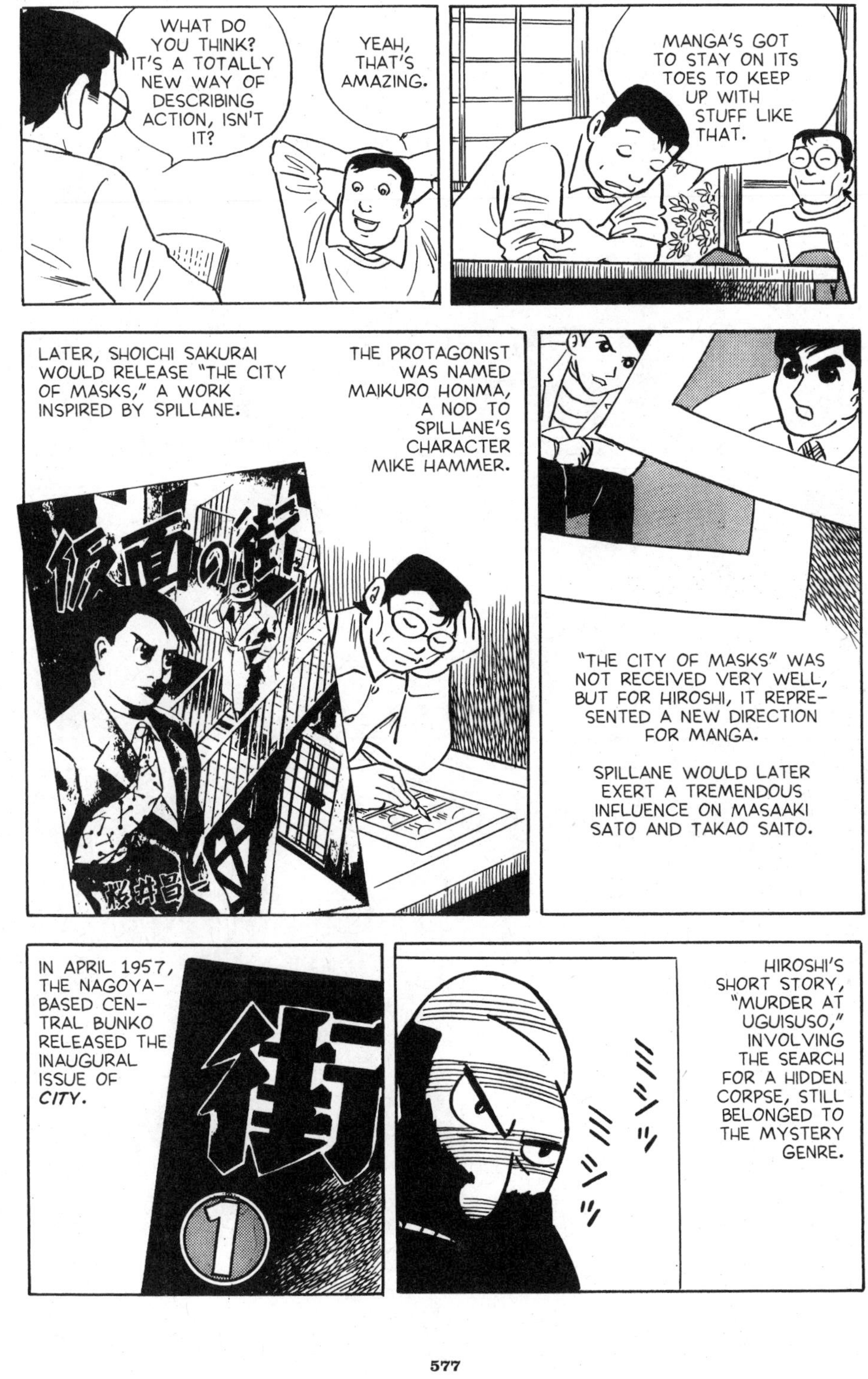
WHAT DO YOU THINK? IT'S A TOTALLY NEW WAY OF DESCRIBING ACTION, ISN'T IT?
YEAH, THAT'S AMAZING.
MANGA'S GOT TO STAY ON ITS TOES TO KEEP UP WITH STUFF LIKE THAT.
LATER, SHOICHI SAKURAI WOULD RELEASE "THE CITY OF MASKS," A WORK INSPIRED BY SPILLANE.
THE PROTAGONIST WAS NAMED MAIKURO HONMA, A NOD TO SPILLANE'S CHARACTER MIKE HAMMER.
仮面の街
"THE CITY OF MASKS" WAS NOT RECEIVED VERY WELL, BUT FOR HIROSHI, IT REPRESENTED A NEW DIRECTION FOR MANGA.
SPILLANE WOULD LATER EXERT A TREMENDOUS INFLUENCE ON MASAAKI SATO AND TAKAO SAITO.
IN APRIL 1957, THE NAGOYA-BASED CENTRAL BUNKO RELEASED THE INAUGURAL ISSUE OF *CITY*.
街
1
HIROSHI'S SHORT STORY, "MURDER AT UGUISUSO," INVOLVING THE SEARCH FOR A HIDDEN CORPSE, STILL BELONGED TO THE MYSTERY GENRE.

HEY, YOU GOT A POSTCARD FROM HINOMARU!

IT SAYS BOSS IS BACK...

AND THAT HINOMARU IS ABOUT TO OPEN FOR BUSINESS AGAIN.

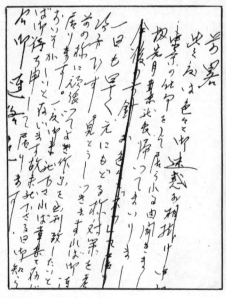

THAT'S GOOD NEWS.

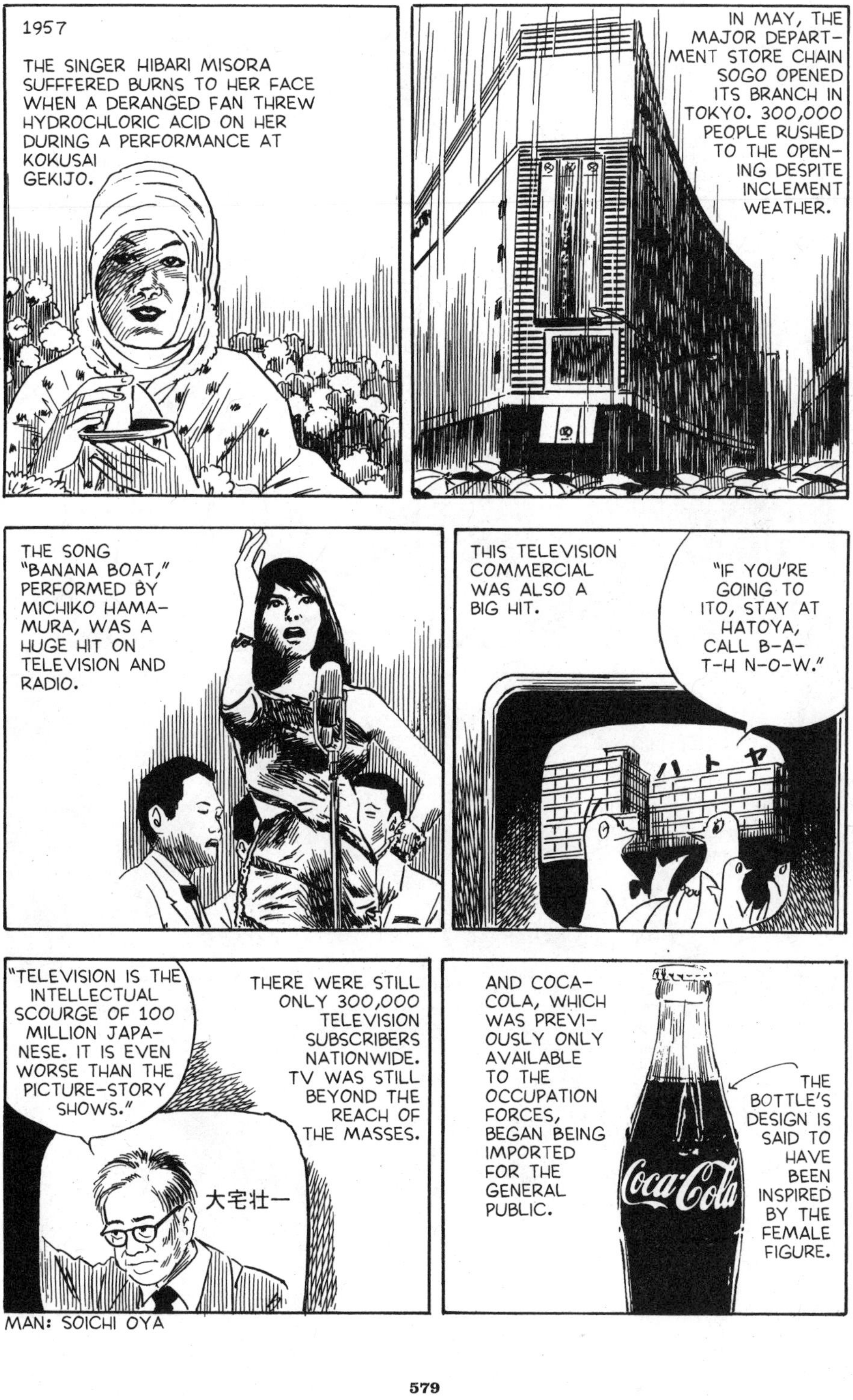
1957
THE SINGER HIBARI MISORA SUFFFERED BURNS TO HER FACE WHEN A DERANGED FAN THREW HYDROCHLORIC ACID ON HER DURING A PERFORMANCE AT KOKUSAI GEKIJO.
IN MAY, THE MAJOR DEPARTMENT STORE CHAIN SOGO OPENED ITS BRANCH IN TOKYO. 300,000 PEOPLE RUSHED TO THE OPENING DESPITE INCLEMENT WEATHER.
THE SONG "BANANA BOAT," PERFORMED BY MICHIKO HAMAMURA, WAS A HUGE HIT ON TELEVISION AND RADIO.
THIS TELEVISION COMMERCIAL WAS ALSO A BIG HIT.
"IF YOU'RE GOING TO ITO, STAY AT HATOYA, CALL B-A-T-H N-O-W."
ハトヤ
"TELEVISION IS THE INTELLECTUAL SCOURGE OF 100 MILLION JAPANESE. IT IS EVEN WORSE THAN THE PICTURE-STORY SHOWS."
大宅壮一
THERE WERE STILL ONLY 300,000 TELEVISION SUBSCRIBERS NATIONWIDE. TV WAS STILL BEYOND THE REACH OF THE MASSES.
AND COCA-COLA, WHICH WAS PREVIOUSLY ONLY AVAILABLE TO THE OCCUPATION FORCES, BEGAN BEING IMPORTED FOR THE GENERAL PUBLIC.
Coca-Cola
THE BOTTLE'S DESIGN IS SAID TO HAVE BEEN INSPIRED BY THE FEMALE FIGURE.

MAN: SOICHI OYA

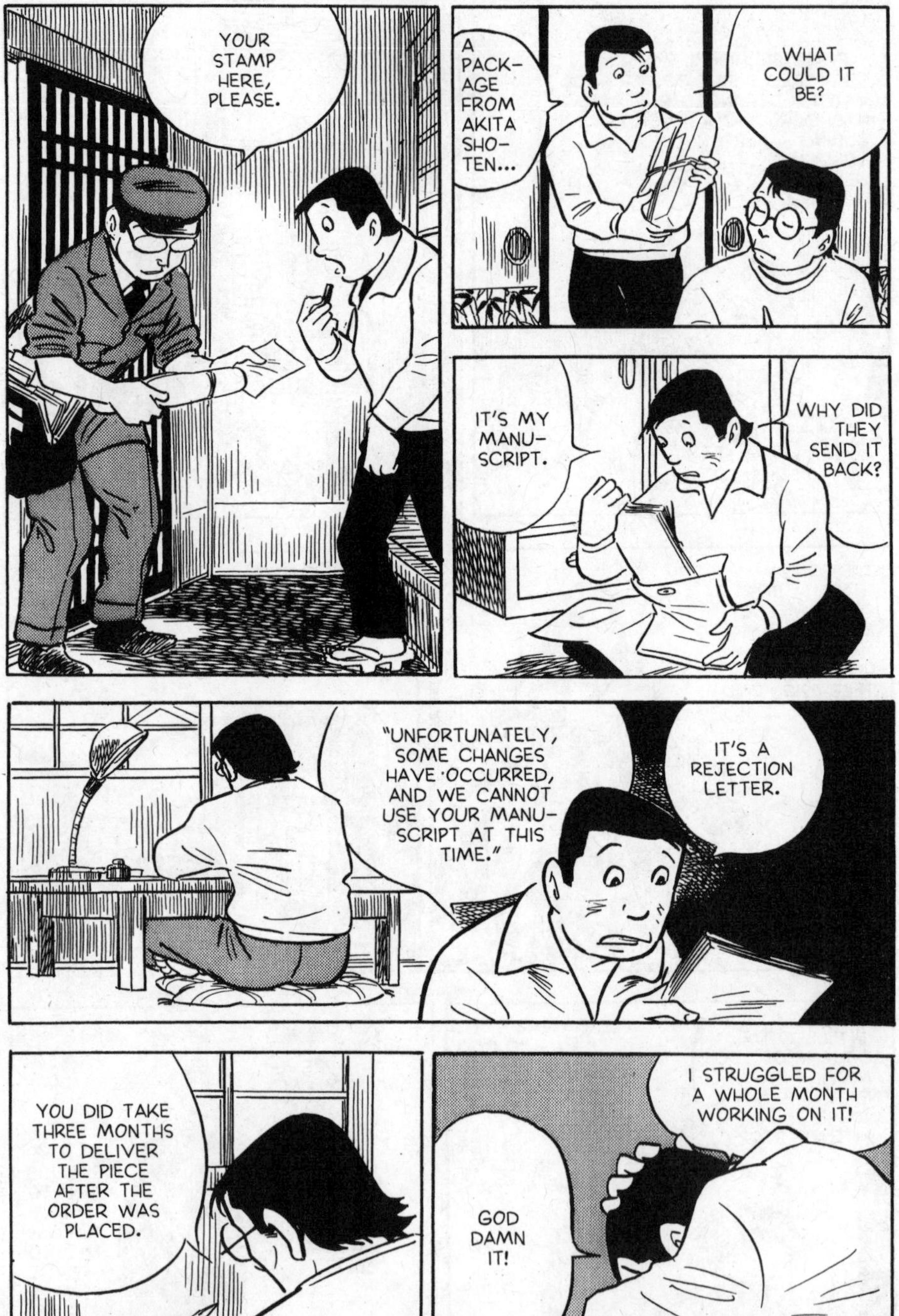
YOUR STAMP HERE, PLEASE.
A PACK-AGE FROM AKITA SHO-TEN...
WHAT COULD IT BE?
IT'S MY MANU-SCRIPT.
WHY DID THEY SEND IT BACK?
"UNFORTUNATELY, SOME CHANGES HAVE OCCURRED, AND WE CANNOT USE YOUR MANU-SCRIPT AT THIS TIME."
IT'S A REJECTION LETTER.
YOU DID TAKE THREE MONTHS TO DELIVER THE PIECE AFTER THE ORDER WAS PLACED.
I STRUGGLED FOR A WHOLE MONTH WORKING ON IT!
GOD DAMN IT!

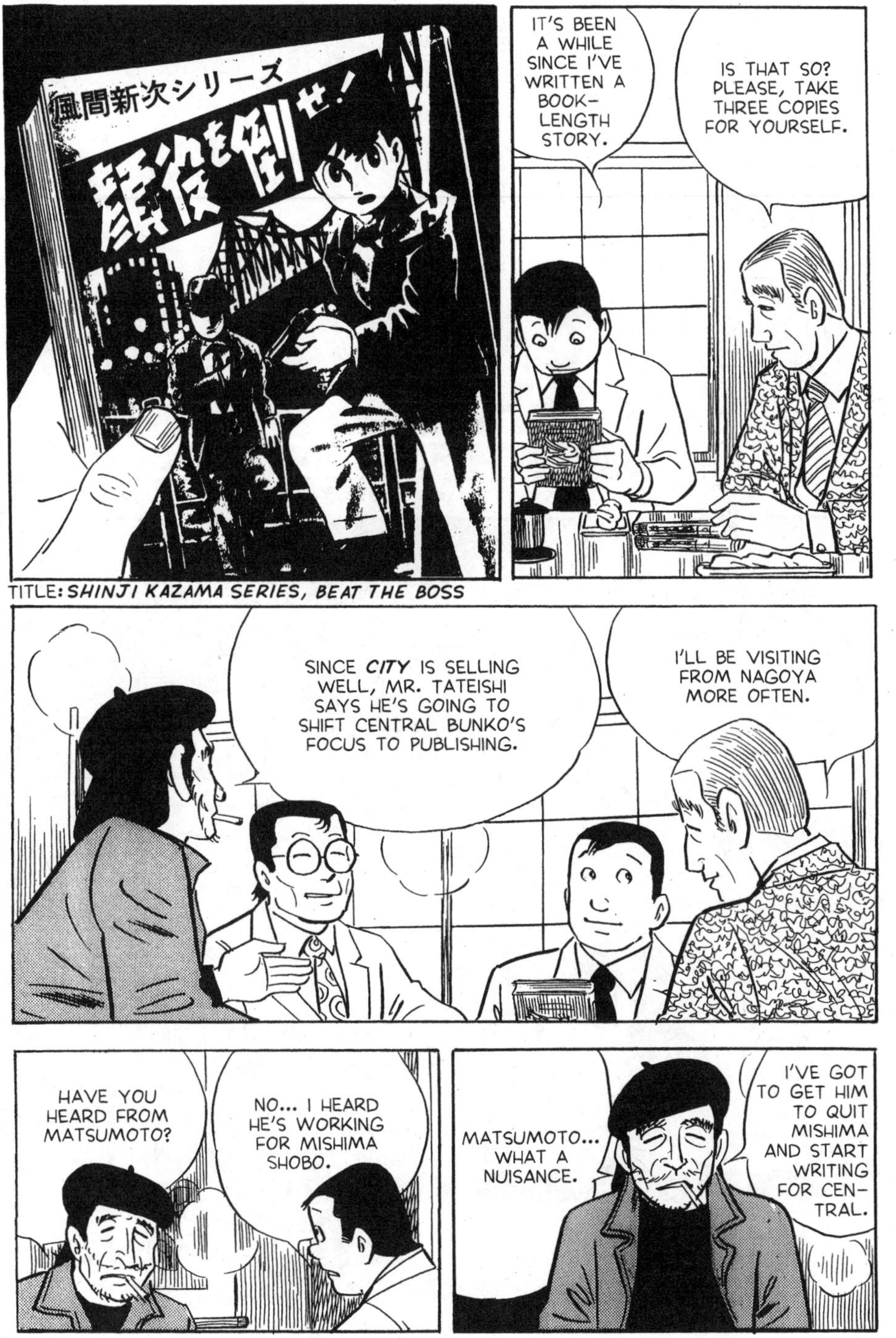
風間新次シリーズ
顔役を倒せ!
TITLE: SHINJI KAZAMA SERIES, BEAT THE BOSS
IT'S BEEN A WHILE SINCE I'VE WRITTEN A BOOK-LENGTH STORY.
IS THAT SO? PLEASE, TAKE THREE COPIES FOR YOURSELF.
SINCE CITY IS SELLING WELL, MR. TATEISHI SAYS HE'S GOING TO SHIFT CENTRAL BUNKO'S FOCUS TO PUBLISHING.
I'LL BE VISITING FROM NAGOYA MORE OFTEN.
HAVE YOU HEARD FROM MATSUMOTO?
NO... I HEARD HE'S WORKING FOR MISHIMA SHOBO.
MATSUMOTO... WHAT A NUISANCE.
I'VE GOT TO GET HIM TO QUIT MISHIMA AND START WRITING FOR CEN-TRAL.

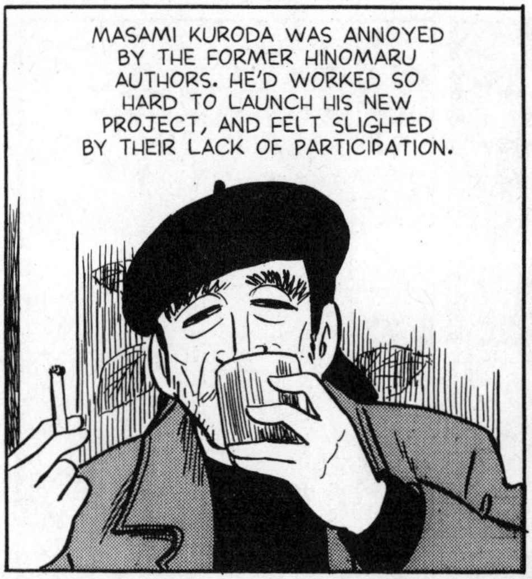
MASAMI KURODA WAS ANNOYED BY THE FORMER HINOMARU AUTHORS. HE'D WORKED SO HARD TO LAUNCH HIS NEW PROJECT, AND FELT SLIGHTED BY THEIR LACK OF PARTICIPATION.

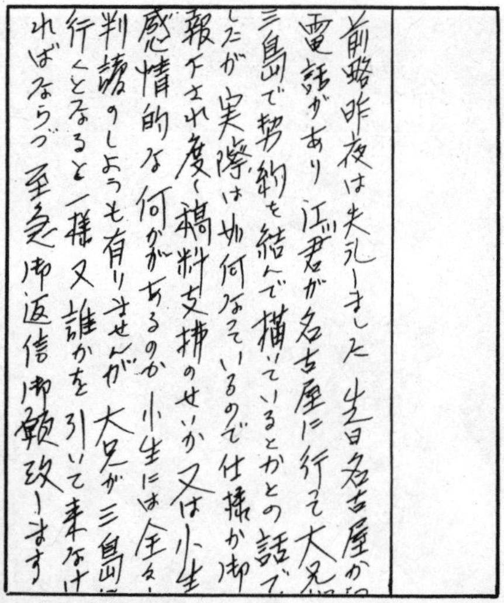
前略昨夜は失礼しました 先日名古屋か
電話があり 江口君が名古屋に行って大兄
三島で契約を結んで描いているとかとの話で
したが実際は如何なっているので仕掛か御
報下され度く稿料支払のせいか又は小生
感情的な何かがあるのか 小生には全く
判読のしようも有りませんが大兄が三島に
行くとなると一様又誰かを引いて来なけ
ればならず 至急御返信御願致します

POSTCARD ADDRESSED TO MASAHIKO MATSUMOTO FROM MASAMI KURODA

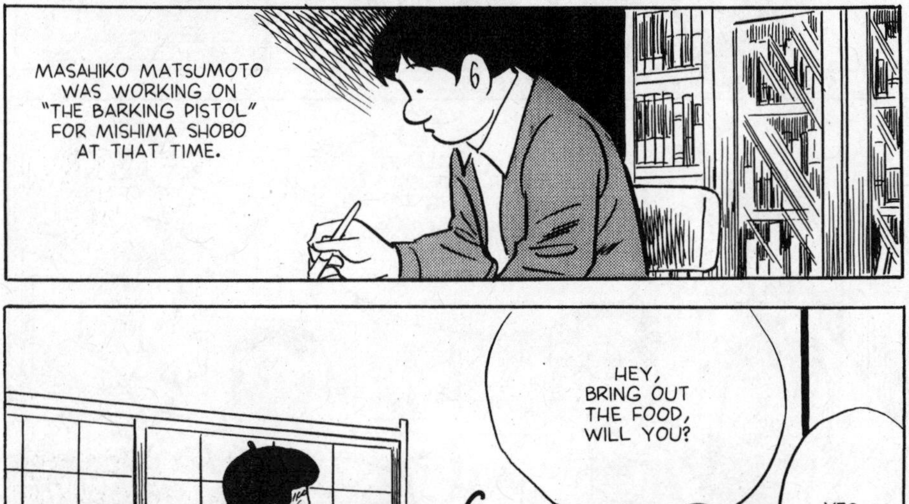
MASAHIKO MATSUMOTO WAS WORKING ON "THE BARKING PISTOL" FOR MISHIMA SHOBO AT THAT TIME.

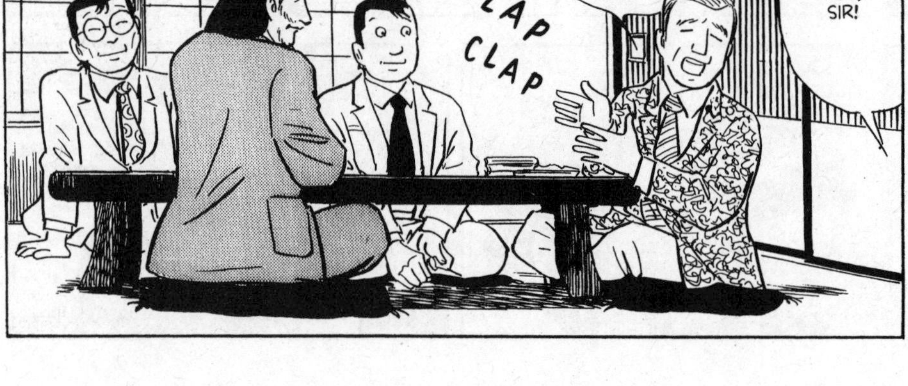
HEY, BRING OUT THE FOOD, WILL YOU?
CLAP CLAP
YES, SIR!

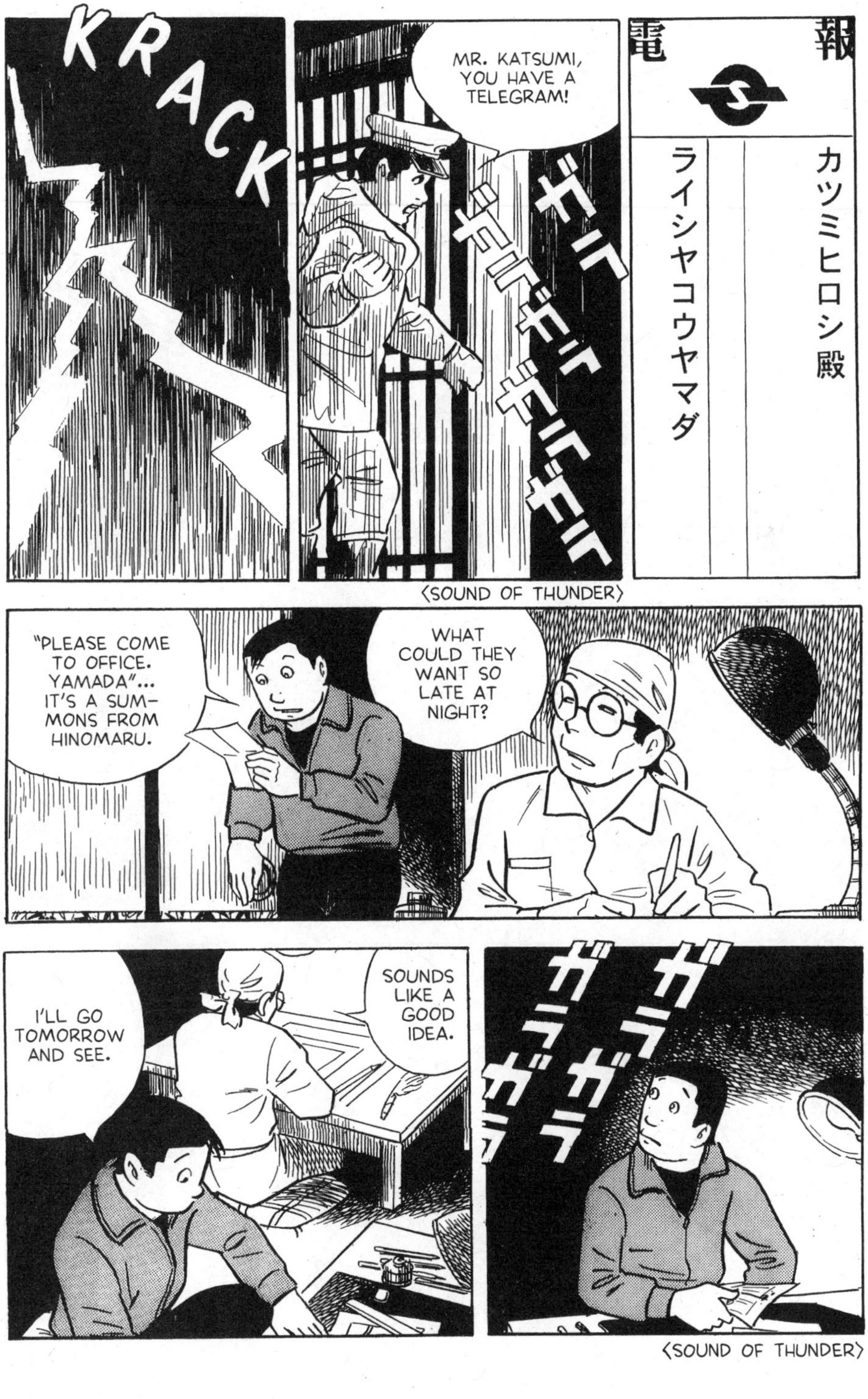
KRACK
MR. KATSUMI, YOU HAVE A TELEGRAM!
電報
カツミヒロシ殿
ライシャコウヤマダ
〈SOUND OF THUNDER〉
"PLEASE COME TO OFFICE. YAMADA"... IT'S A SUMMONS FROM HINOMARU.
WHAT COULD THEY WANT SO LATE AT NIGHT?
I'LL GO TOMORROW AND SEE.
SOUNDS LIKE A GOOD IDEA.
ガラガラ
ガラガラ
〈SOUND OF THUNDER〉

IT'S BEEN SIX MONTHS SINCE MY LAST VISIT TO HINOMARU.

IT LOOKS EXACTLY THE SAME.

KREEK

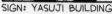

KATSUMI, YOU'VE COME!

BOSS!

I GOT YOUR TELEGRAM, SO I RUSHED OVER HERE.

YOU LOOK WELL. I'M RELIEVED.

HAHAHA... AS YOU CAN SEE, I'M IN GREAT SHAPE.

LISTEN, I'M REAL SORRY ABOUT WHAT HAPPENED. IT MUST'VE BEEN A NUISANCE FOR YOU.

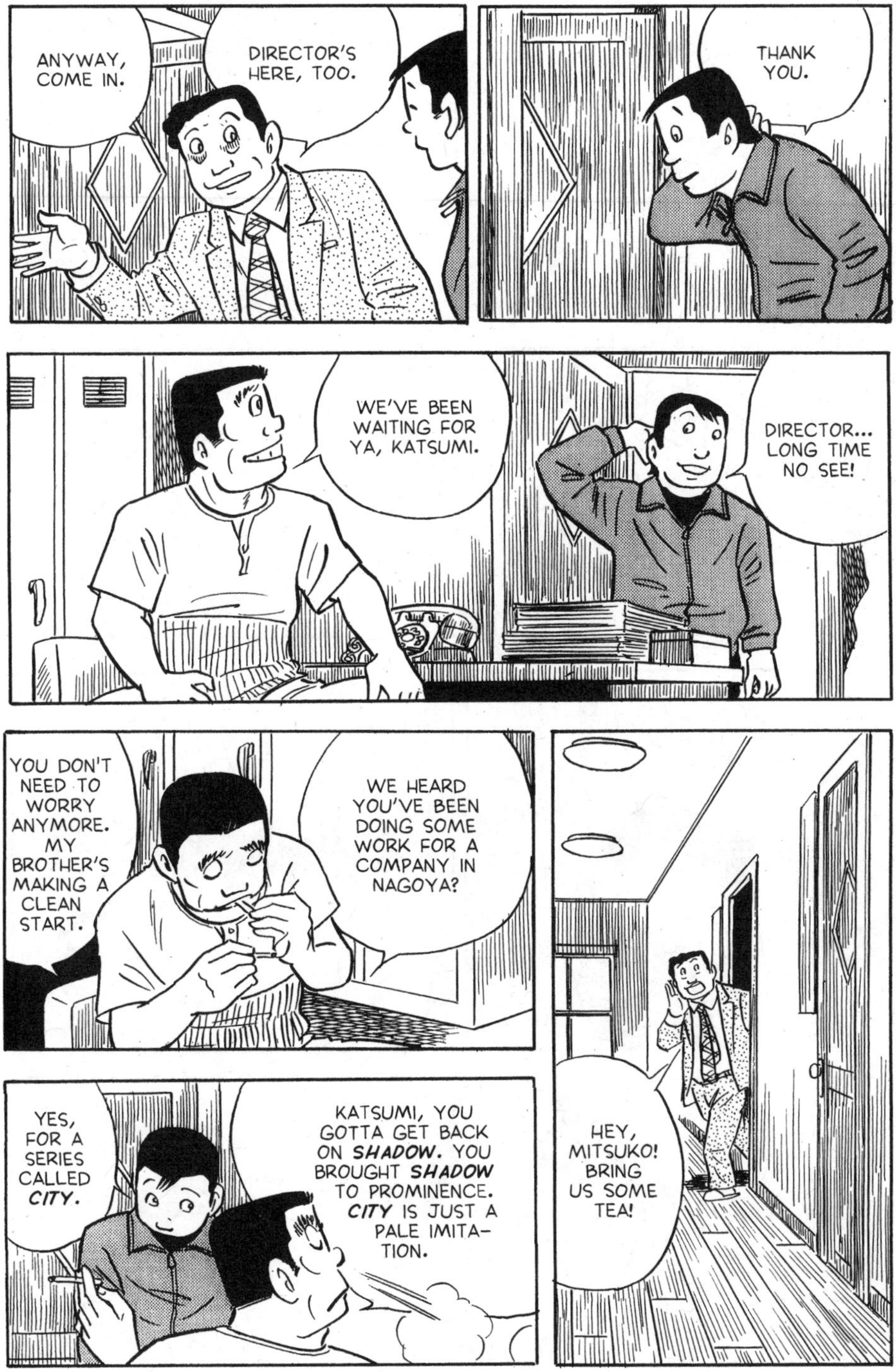
ANYWAY, COME IN.
DIRECTOR'S HERE, TOO.
THANK YOU.
WE'VE BEEN WAITING FOR YA, KATSUMI.
DIRECTOR... LONG TIME NO SEE!
YOU DON'T NEED TO WORRY ANYMORE. MY BROTHER'S MAKING A CLEAN START.
WE HEARD YOU'VE BEEN DOING SOME WORK FOR A COMPANY IN NAGOYA?
YES, FOR A SERIES CALLED *CITY*.
KATSUMI, YOU GOTTA GET BACK ON *SHADOW*. YOU BROUGHT *SHADOW* TO PROMINENCE. *CITY* IS JUST A PALE IMITA-TION.
HEY, MITSUKO! BRING US SOME TEA!

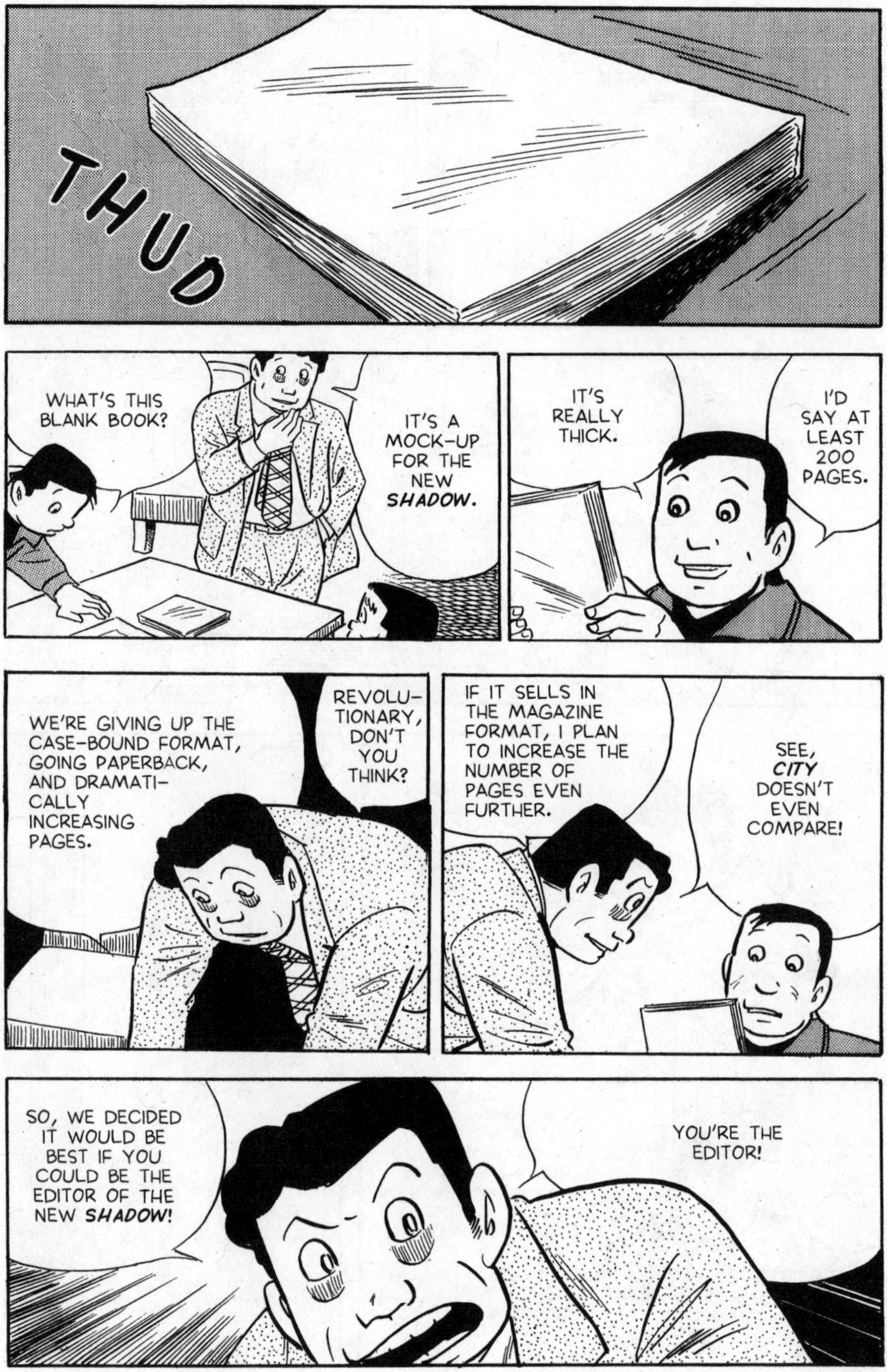
THUD
WHAT'S THIS BLANK BOOK?
IT'S A MOCK-UP FOR THE NEW SHADOW.
IT'S REALLY THICK.
I'D SAY AT LEAST 200 PAGES.
WE'RE GIVING UP THE CASE-BOUND FORMAT, GOING PAPERBACK, AND DRAMATICALLY INCREASING PAGES.
REVOLUTIONARY, DON'T YOU THINK?
IF IT SELLS IN THE MAGAZINE FORMAT, I PLAN TO INCREASE THE NUMBER OF PAGES EVEN FURTHER.
SEE, CITY DOESN'T EVEN COMPARE!
SO, WE DECIDED IT WOULD BE BEST IF YOU COULD BE THE EDITOR OF THE NEW SHADOW!
YOU'RE THE EDITOR!

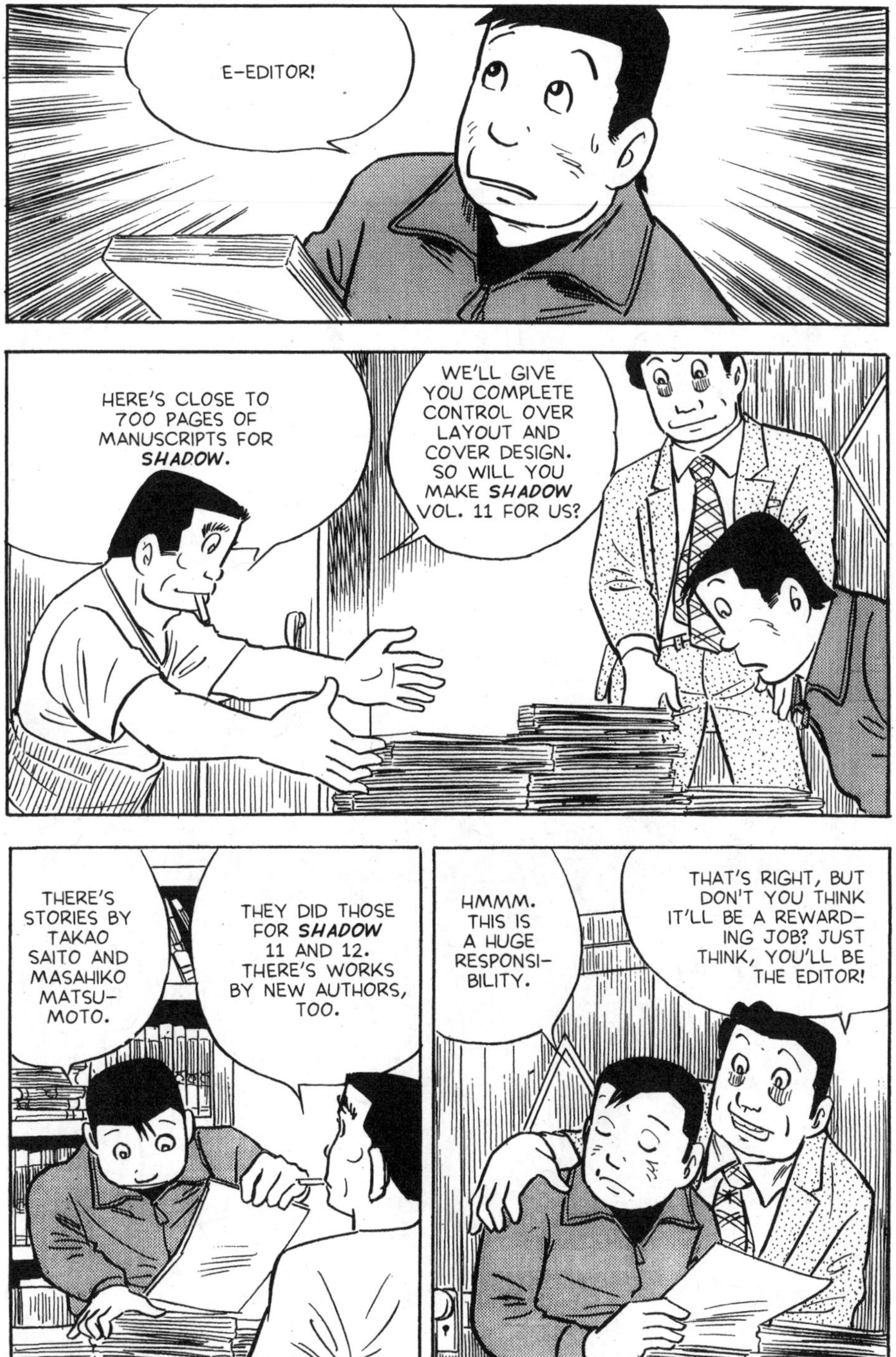
E-EDITOR!
HERE'S CLOSE TO 700 PAGES OF MANUSCRIPTS FOR SHADOW.
WE'LL GIVE YOU COMPLETE CONTROL OVER LAYOUT AND COVER DESIGN. SO WILL YOU MAKE SHADOW VOL. 11 FOR US?
THERE'S STORIES BY TAKAO SAITO AND MASAHIKO MATSU-MOTO.
THEY DID THOSE FOR SHADOW 11 AND 12. THERE'S WORKS BY NEW AUTHORS, TOO.
HMMM. THIS IS A HUGE RESPONSI-BILITY.
THAT'S RIGHT, BUT DON'T YOU THINK IT'LL BE A REWARD-ING JOB? JUST THINK, YOU'LL BE THE EDITOR!

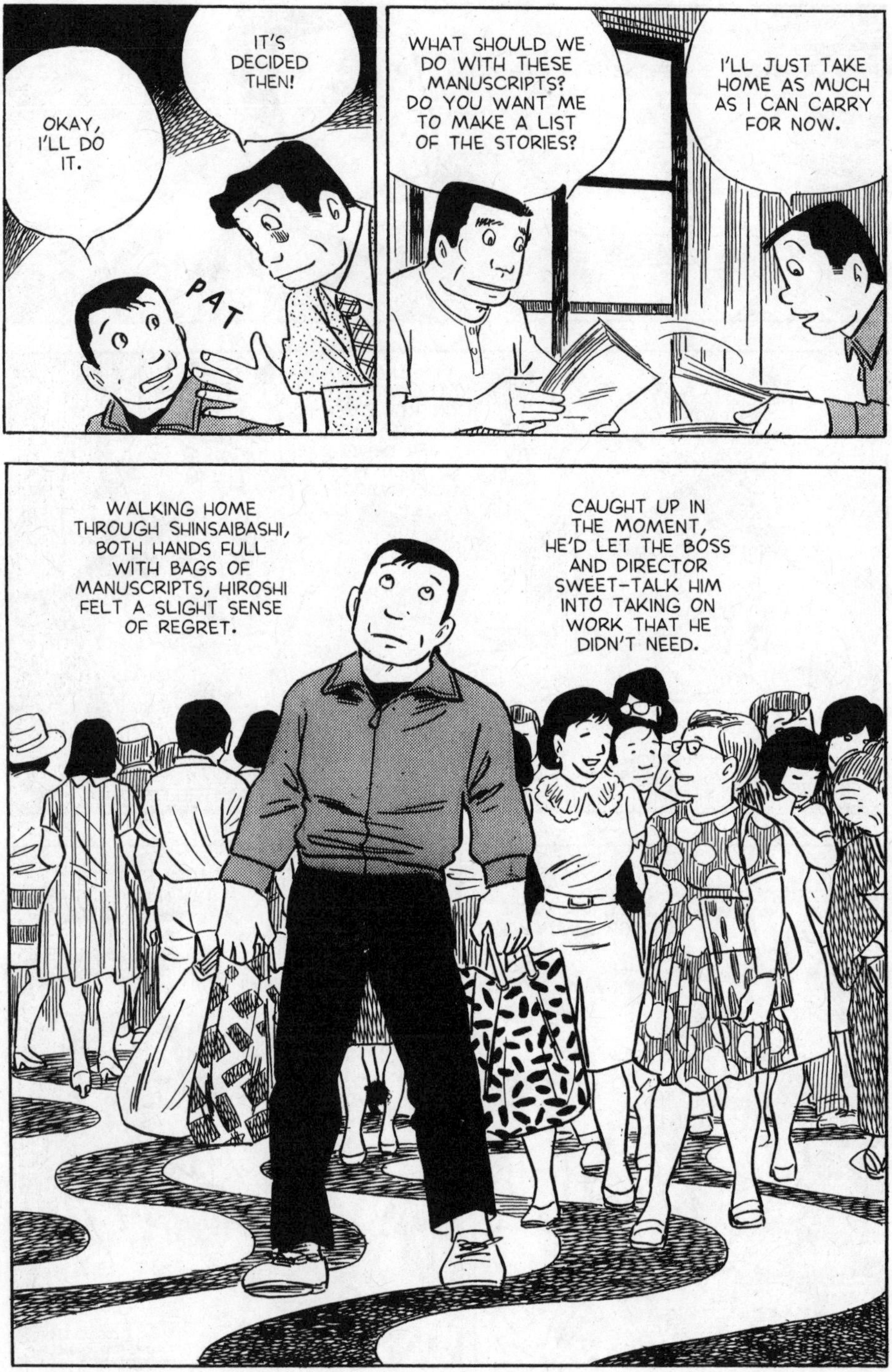
IT'S DECIDED THEN!
OKAY, I'LL DO IT.
PAT
WHAT SHOULD WE DO WITH THESE MANUSCRIPTS? DO YOU WANT ME TO MAKE A LIST OF THE STORIES?
I'LL JUST TAKE HOME AS MUCH AS I CAN CARRY FOR NOW.
WALKING HOME THROUGH SHINSAIBASHI, BOTH HANDS FULL WITH BAGS OF MANUSCRIPTS, HIROSHI FELT A SLIGHT SENSE OF REGRET.
CAUGHT UP IN THE MOMENT, HE'D LET THE BOSS AND DIRECTOR SWEET-TALK HIM INTO TAKING ON WORK THAT HE DIDN'T NEED.

THE SHORT STORY BOOM

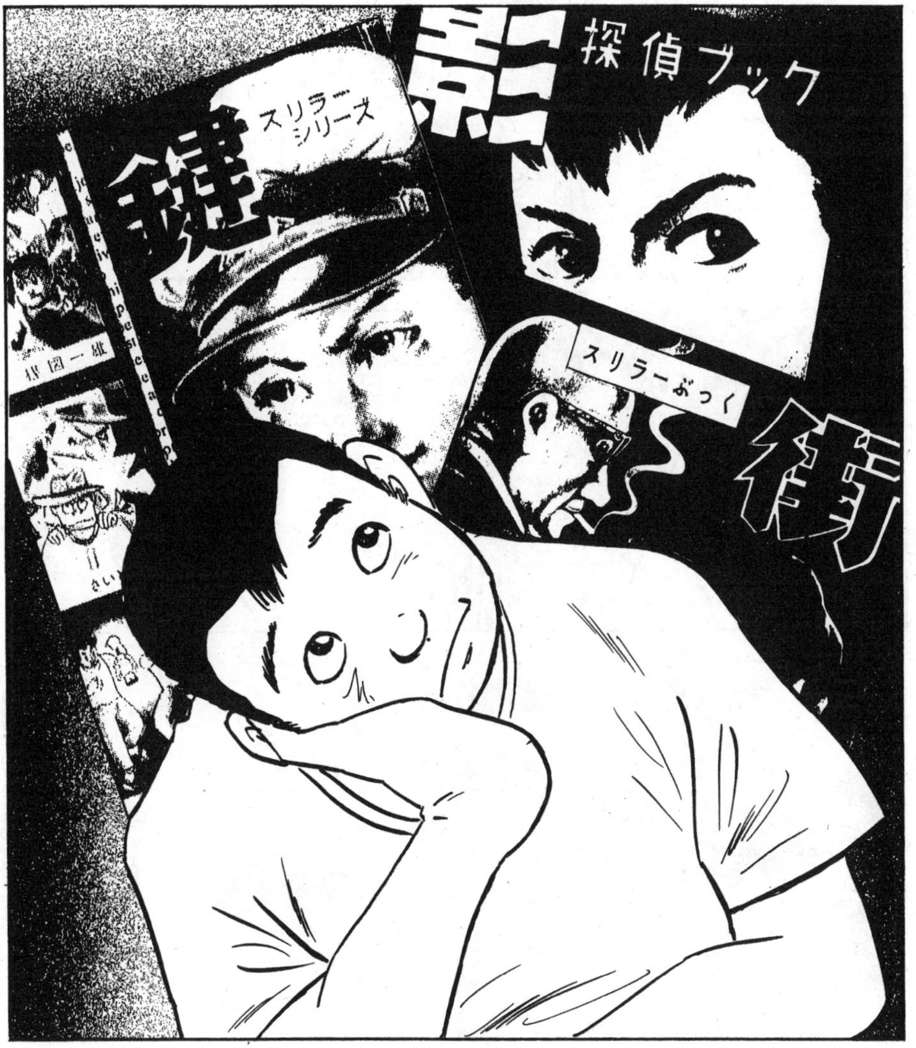
スリラーシリーズ
鍵
影
探偵ブック
スリラーぶっく
街

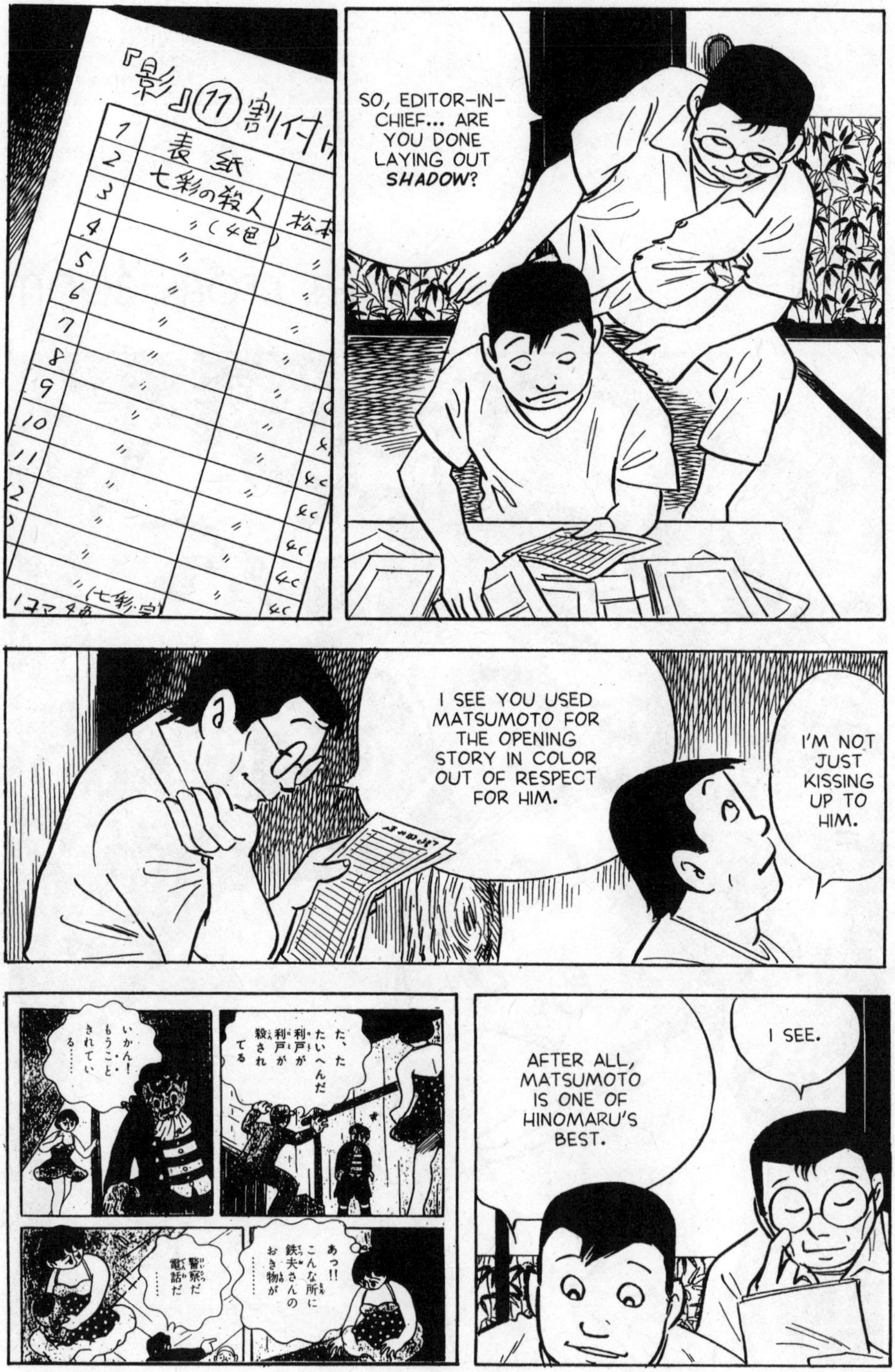
『影』⑪割付
表紙
七彩の殺人
松本
〃（4色）
SO, EDITOR-IN-CHIEF... ARE YOU DONE LAYING OUT *SHADOW*?
I SEE YOU USED MATSUMOTO FOR THE OPENING STORY IN COLOR OUT OF RESPECT FOR HIM.
I'M NOT JUST KISSING UP TO HIM.
いかん！もうことぎれている……
た、たいへんだ利戸が殺されてる
警察だ電話だ……
あっ!!こんな所に鉄夫さんのおき物が……
AFTER ALL, MATSUMOTO IS ONE OF HINOMARU'S BEST.
I SEE.

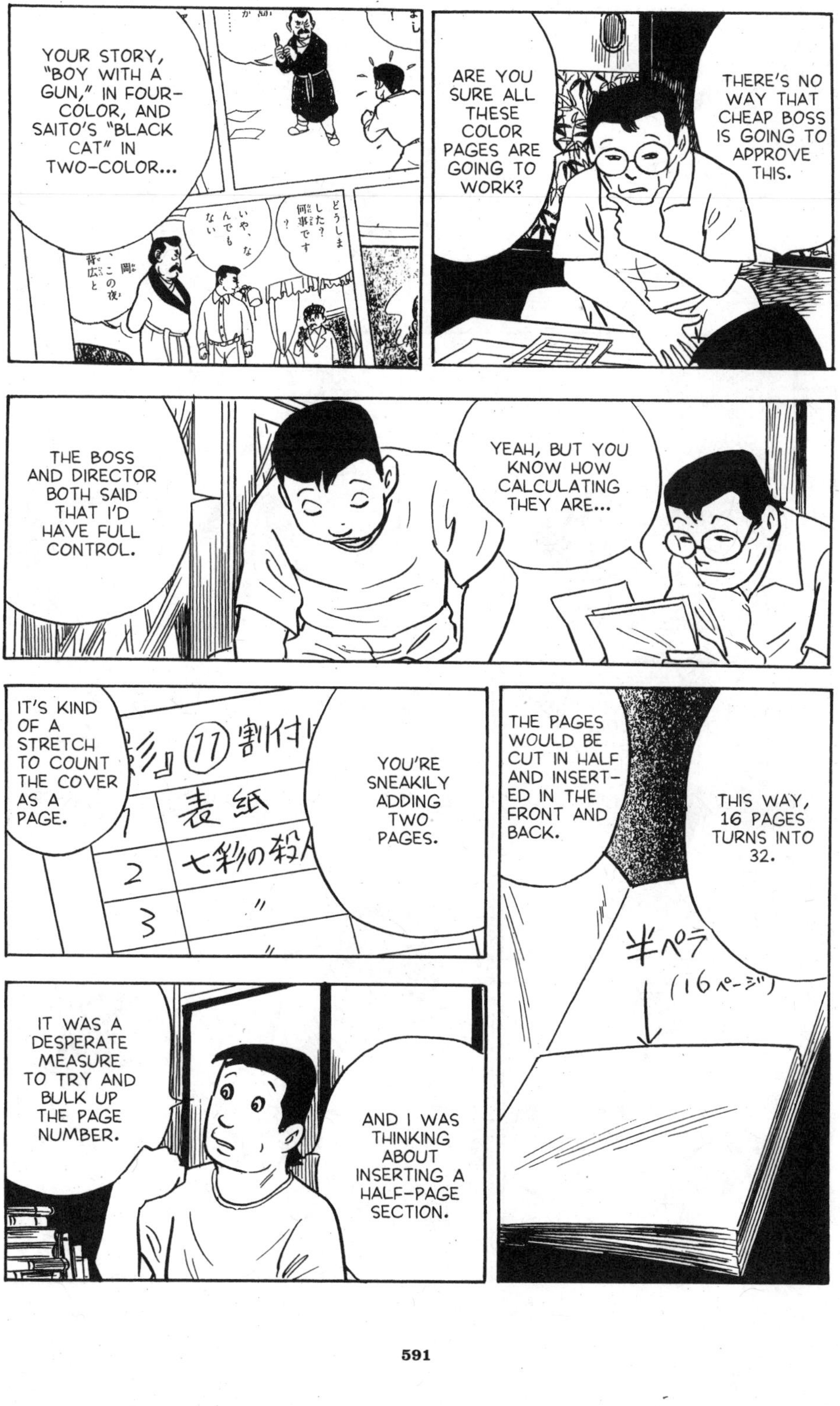
YOUR STORY, "BOY WITH A GUN," IN FOUR-COLOR, AND SAITO'S "BLACK CAT" IN TWO-COLOR...
どうしました？何事です？
いや、なんでもない
ARE YOU SURE ALL THESE COLOR PAGES ARE GOING TO WORK?
THERE'S NO WAY THAT CHEAP BOSS IS GOING TO APPROVE THIS.
THE BOSS AND DIRECTOR BOTH SAID THAT I'D HAVE FULL CONTROL.
YEAH, BUT YOU KNOW HOW CALCULATING THEY ARE...
IT'S KIND OF A STRETCH TO COUNT THE COVER AS A PAGE.
表紙
YOU'RE SNEAKILY ADDING TWO PAGES.
IT WAS A DESPERATE MEASURE TO TRY AND BULK UP THE PAGE NUMBER.
AND I WAS THINKING ABOUT INSERTING A HALF-PAGE SECTION.
THE PAGES WOULD BE CUT IN HALF AND INSERTED IN THE FRONT AND BACK.
THIS WAY, 16 PAGES TURNS INTO 32.
半ペラ
(16ページ)

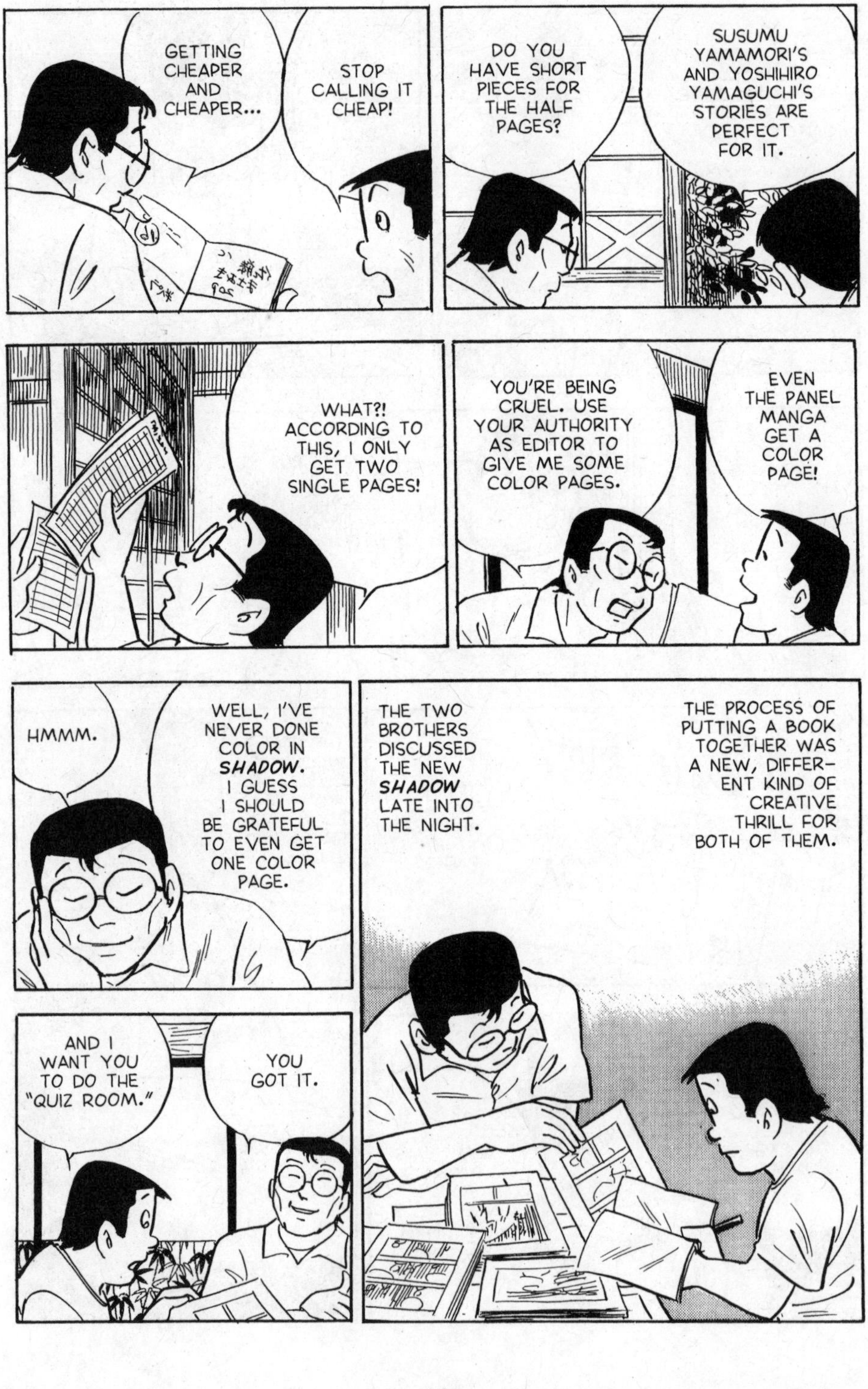
GETTING CHEAPER AND CHEAPER...
STOP CALLING IT CHEAP!
DO YOU HAVE SHORT PIECES FOR THE HALF PAGES?
SUSUMU YAMAMORI'S AND YOSHIHIRO YAMAGUCHI'S STORIES ARE PERFECT FOR IT.
WHAT?! ACCORDING TO THIS, I ONLY GET TWO SINGLE PAGES!
YOU'RE BEING CRUEL. USE YOUR AUTHORITY AS EDITOR TO GIVE ME SOME COLOR PAGES.
EVEN THE PANEL MANGA GET A COLOR PAGE!
HMMM.
WELL, I'VE NEVER DONE COLOR IN SHADOW. I GUESS I SHOULD BE GRATEFUL TO EVEN GET ONE COLOR PAGE.
AND I WANT YOU TO DO THE "QUIZ ROOM."
YOU GOT IT.
THE TWO BROTHERS DISCUSSED THE NEW SHADOW LATE INTO THE NIGHT.
THE PROCESS OF PUTTING A BOOK TOGETHER WAS A NEW, DIFFERENT KIND OF CREATIVE THRILL FOR BOTH OF THEM.

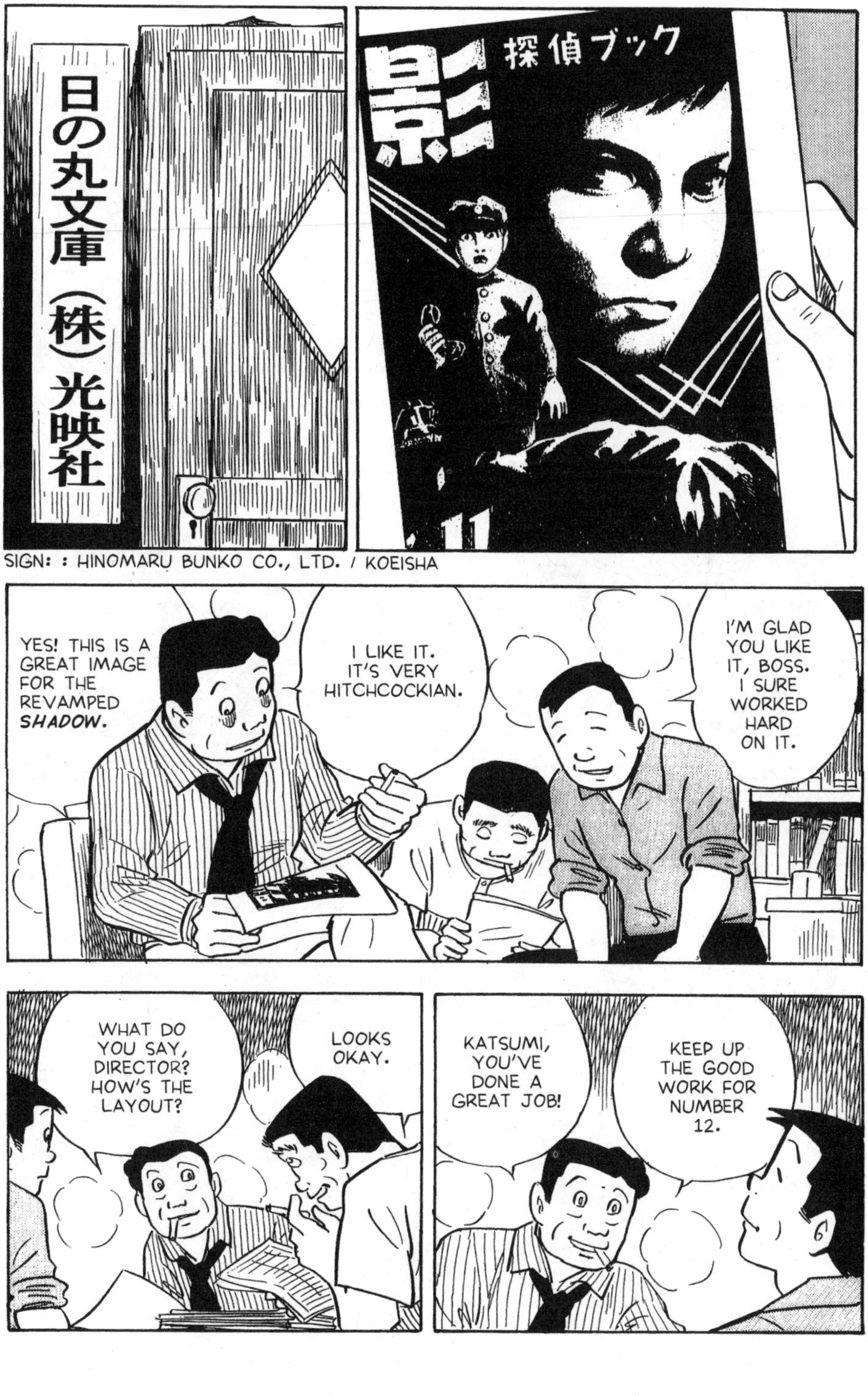
日の丸文庫（株）光映社
探偵ブック
影
11
SIGN: : HINOMARU BUNKO CO., LTD. / KOEISHA
YES! THIS IS A GREAT IMAGE FOR THE REVAMPED *SHADOW*.
I LIKE IT. IT'S VERY HITCHCOCKIAN.
I'M GLAD YOU LIKE IT, BOSS. I SURE WORKED HARD ON IT.
WHAT DO YOU SAY, DIRECTOR? HOW'S THE LAYOUT?
LOOKS OKAY.
KATSUMI, YOU'VE DONE A GREAT JOB!
KEEP UP THE GOOD WORK FOR NUMBER 12.

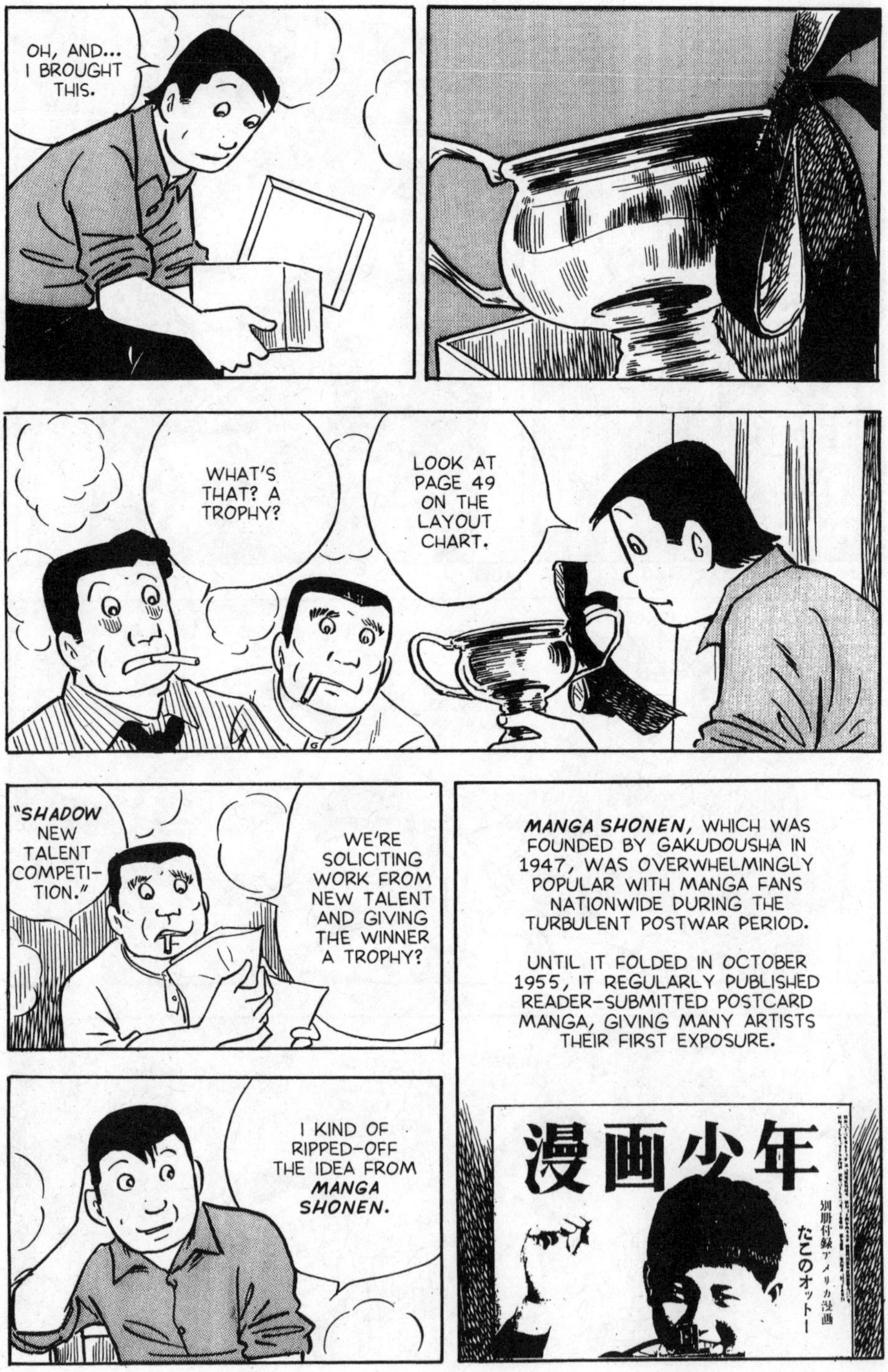
OH, AND... I BROUGHT THIS.
WHAT'S THAT? A TROPHY?
LOOK AT PAGE 49 ON THE LAYOUT CHART.
"SHADOW NEW TALENT COMPETITION."
WE'RE SOLICITING WORK FROM NEW TALENT AND GIVING THE WINNER A TROPHY?
I KIND OF RIPPED-OFF THE IDEA FROM MANGA SHONEN.
MANGA SHONEN, WHICH WAS FOUNDED BY GAKUDOUSHA IN 1947, WAS OVERWHELMINGLY POPULAR WITH MANGA FANS NATIONWIDE DURING THE TURBULENT POSTWAR PERIOD.
UNTIL IT FOLDED IN OCTOBER 1955, IT REGULARLY PUBLISHED READER-SUBMITTED POSTCARD MANGA, GIVING MANY ARTISTS THEIR FIRST EXPOSURE.
漫画少年
別冊付録アメリカ漫画
たこのオットー

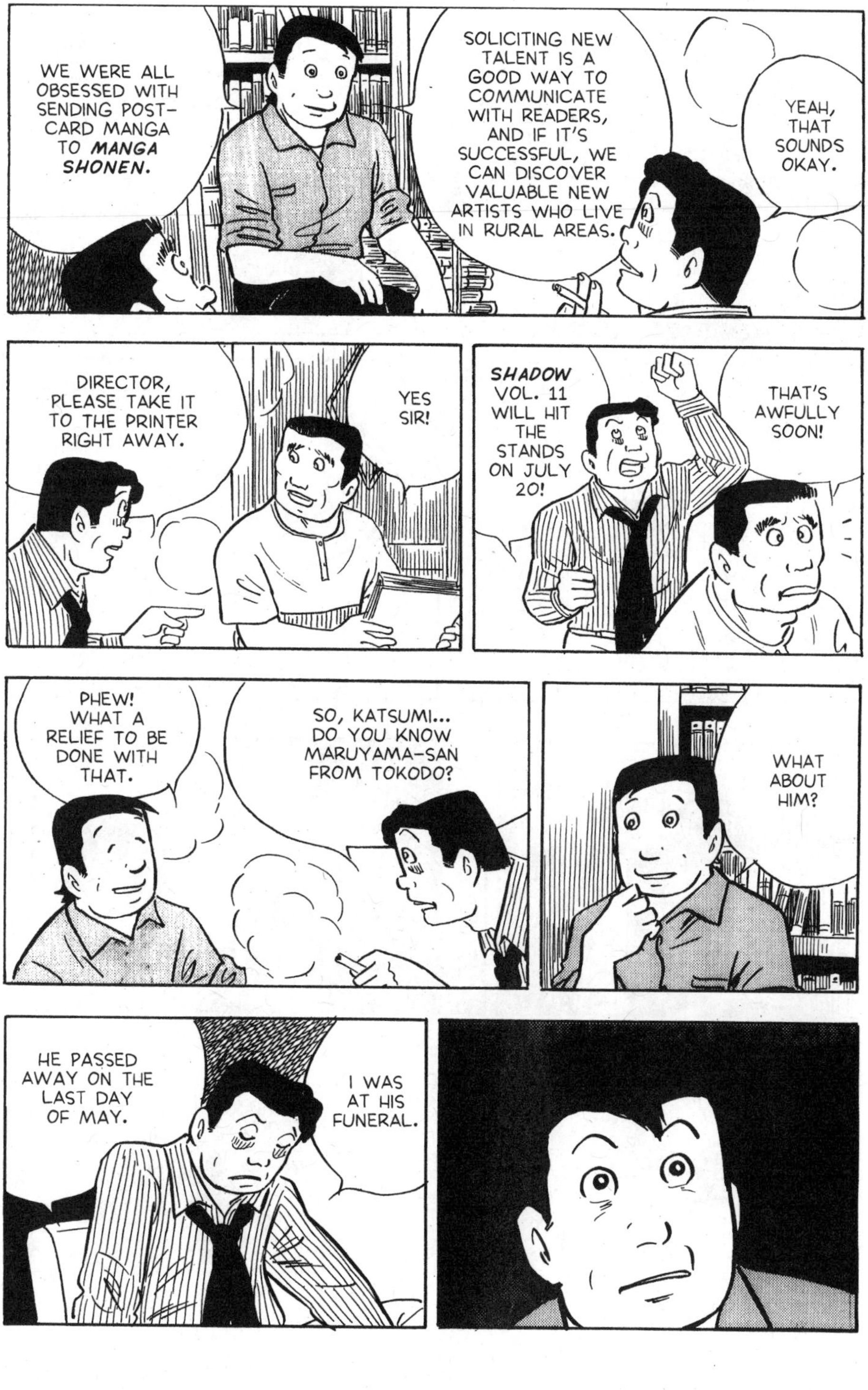
WE WERE ALL OBSESSED WITH SENDING POST-CARD MANGA TO MANGA SHONEN.
SOLICITING NEW TALENT IS A GOOD WAY TO COMMUNICATE WITH READERS, AND IF IT'S SUCCESSFUL, WE CAN DISCOVER VALUABLE NEW ARTISTS WHO LIVE IN RURAL AREAS.
YEAH, THAT SOUNDS OKAY.
DIRECTOR, PLEASE TAKE IT TO THE PRINTER RIGHT AWAY.
YES SIR!
SHADOW VOL. 11 WILL HIT THE STANDS ON JULY 20!
THAT'S AWFULLY SOON!
PHEW! WHAT A RELIEF TO BE DONE WITH THAT.
SO, KATSUMI... DO YOU KNOW MARUYAMA-SAN FROM TOKODO?
WHAT ABOUT HIM?
HE PASSED AWAY ON THE LAST DAY OF MAY.
I WAS AT HIS FUNERAL.

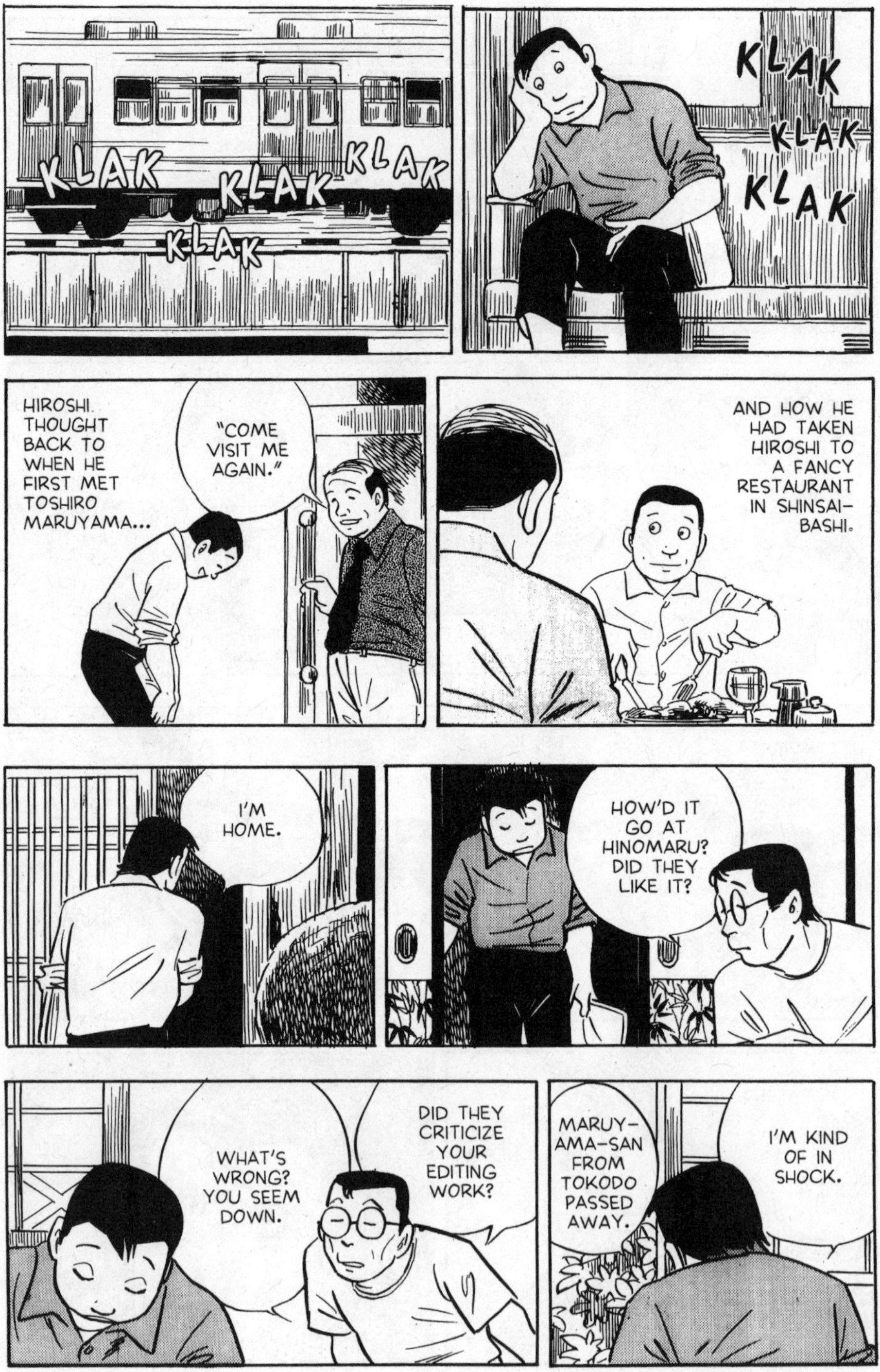
KLAK
KLAK
KLAK
KLAK
KLAK
KLAK
KLAK
HIROSHI THOUGHT BACK TO WHEN HE FIRST MET TOSHIRO MARUYAMA...
"COME VISIT ME AGAIN."
AND HOW HE HAD TAKEN HIROSHI TO A FANCY RESTAURANT IN SHINSAI-BASHI.
I'M HOME.
HOW'D IT GO AT HINOMARU? DID THEY LIKE IT?
WHAT'S WRONG? YOU SEEM DOWN.
DID THEY CRITICIZE YOUR EDITING WORK?
MARUY-AMA-SAN FROM TOKODO PASSED AWAY.
I'M KIND OF IN SHOCK.

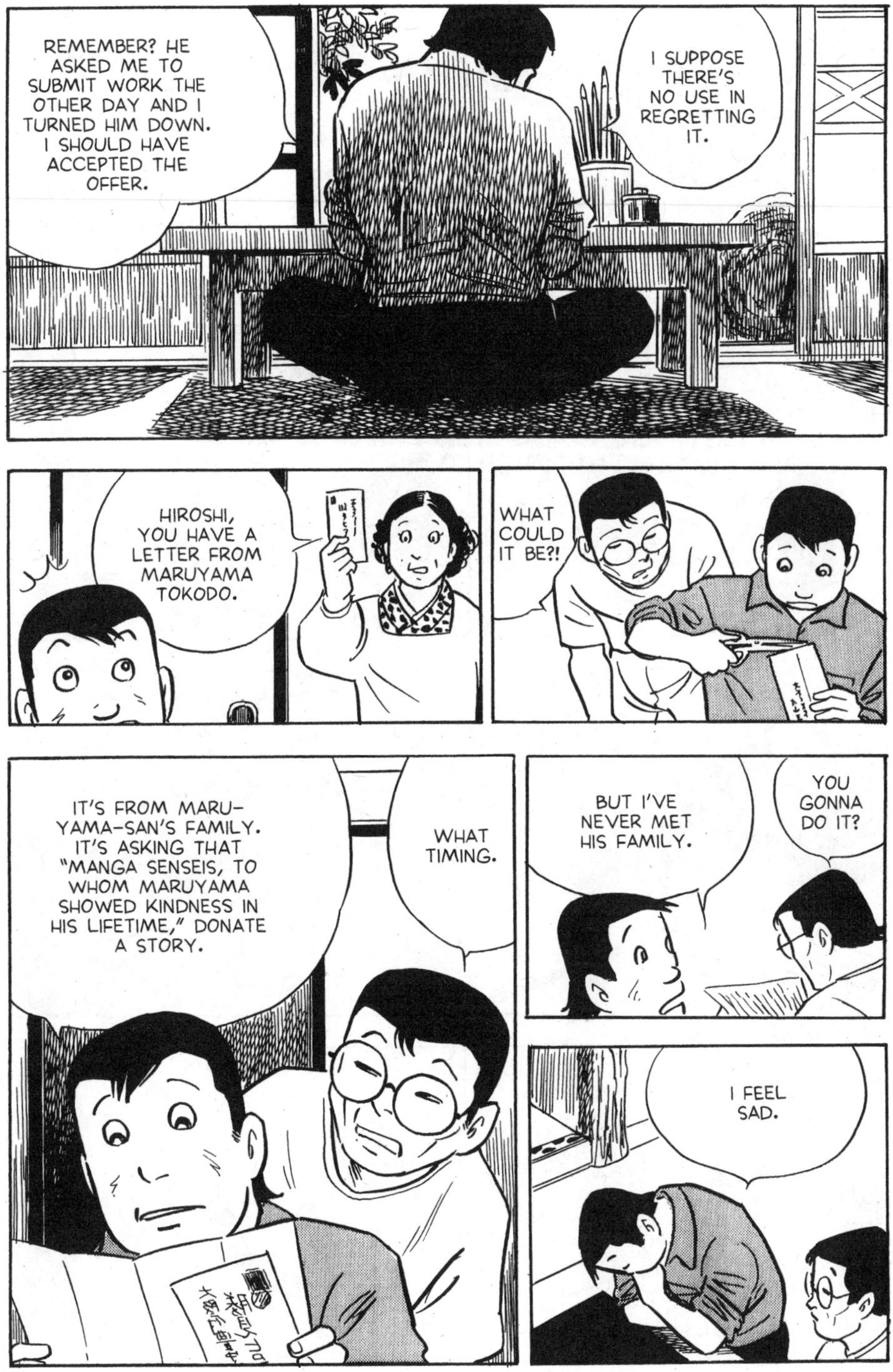
REMEMBER? HE ASKED ME TO SUBMIT WORK THE OTHER DAY AND I TURNED HIM DOWN. I SHOULD HAVE ACCEPTED THE OFFER.
I SUPPOSE THERE'S NO USE IN REGRETTING IT.
HIROSHI, YOU HAVE A LETTER FROM MARUYAMA TOKODO.
WHAT COULD IT BE?!
IT'S FROM MARU-YAMA-SAN'S FAMILY. IT'S ASKING THAT "MANGA SENSEIS, TO WHOM MARUYAMA SHOWED KINDNESS IN HIS LIFETIME," DONATE A STORY.
WHAT TIMING.
BUT I'VE NEVER MET HIS FAMILY.
YOU GONNA DO IT?
I FEEL SAD.

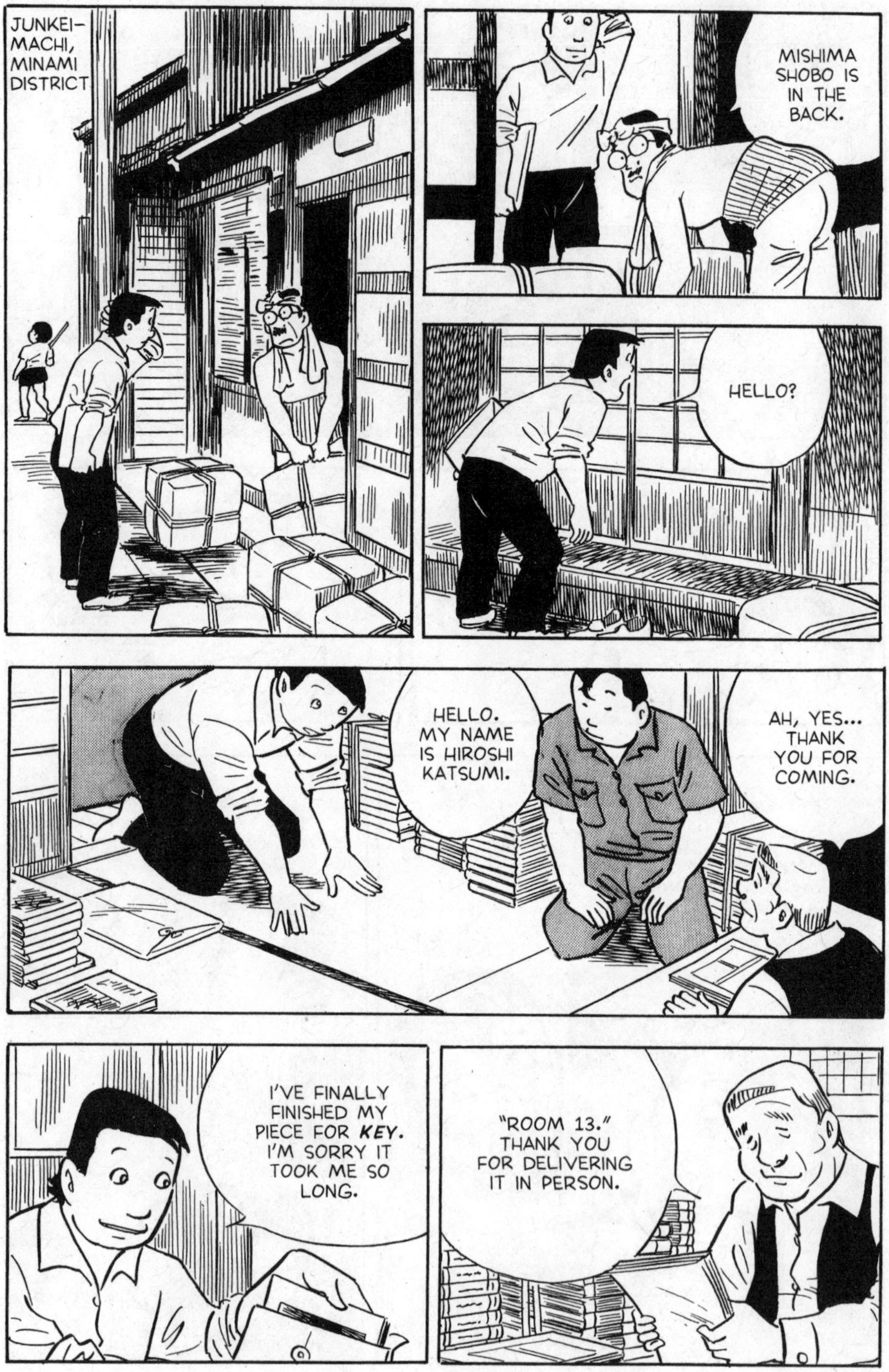
JUNKEI-MACHI, MINAMI DISTRICT
MISHIMA SHOBO IS IN THE BACK.
HELLO?
HELLO. MY NAME IS HIROSHI KATSUMI.
AH, YES... THANK YOU FOR COMING.
I'VE FINALLY FINISHED MY PIECE FOR KEY. I'M SORRY IT TOOK ME SO LONG.
"ROOM 13." THANK YOU FOR DELIVERING IT IN PERSON.

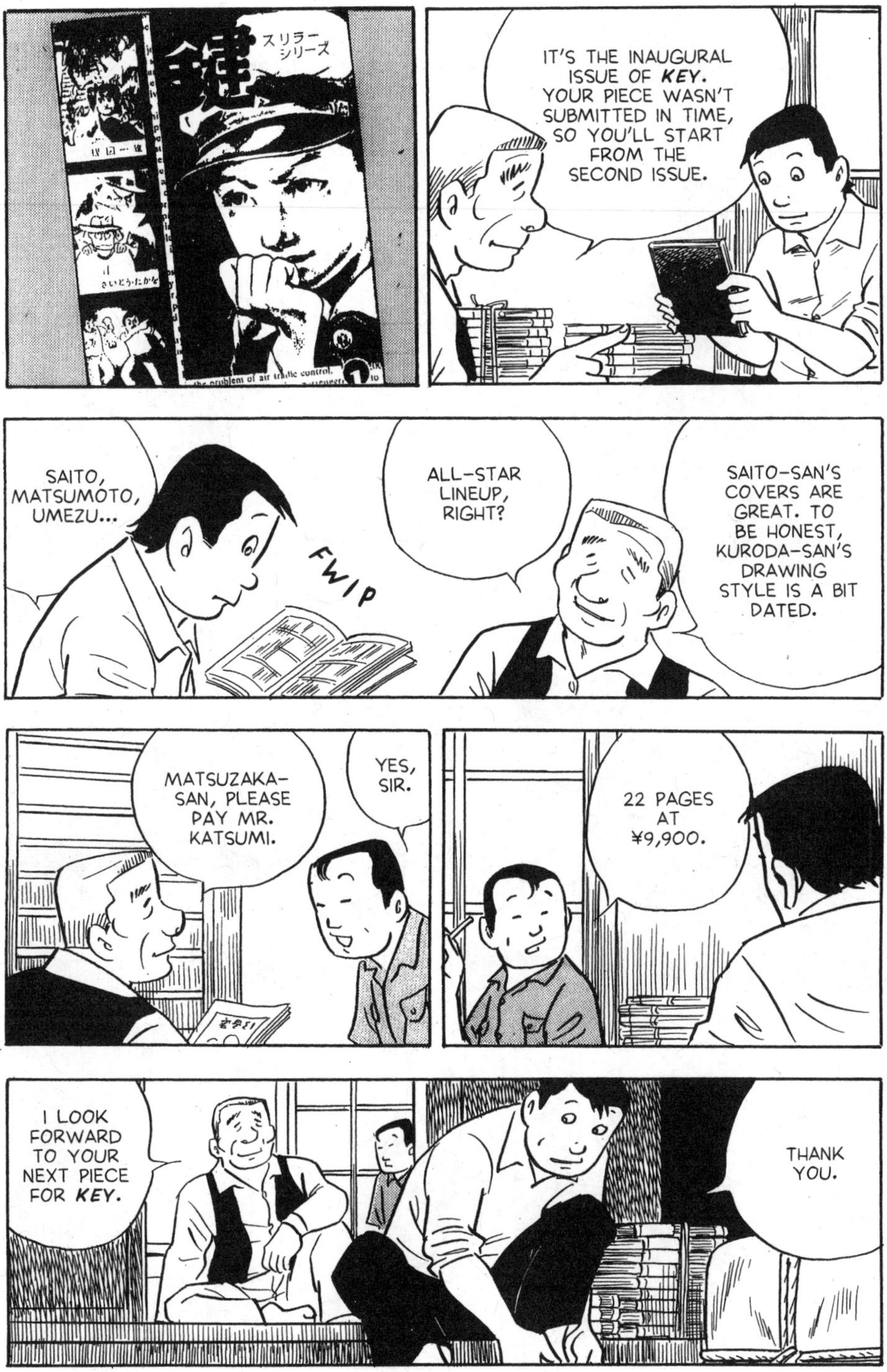
鍵
スリラー
シリーズ
IT'S THE INAUGURAL ISSUE OF **KEY.** YOUR PIECE WASN'T SUBMITTED IN TIME, SO YOU'LL START FROM THE SECOND ISSUE.
SAITO, MATSUMOTO, UMEZU...
FWIP
ALL-STAR LINEUP, RIGHT?
SAITO-SAN'S COVERS ARE GREAT. TO BE HONEST, KURODA-SAN'S DRAWING STYLE IS A BIT DATED.
MATSUZAKA-SAN, PLEASE PAY MR. KATSUMI.
YES, SIR.
22 PAGES AT ¥9,900.
I LOOK FORWARD TO YOUR NEXT PIECE FOR **KEY.**
THANK YOU.

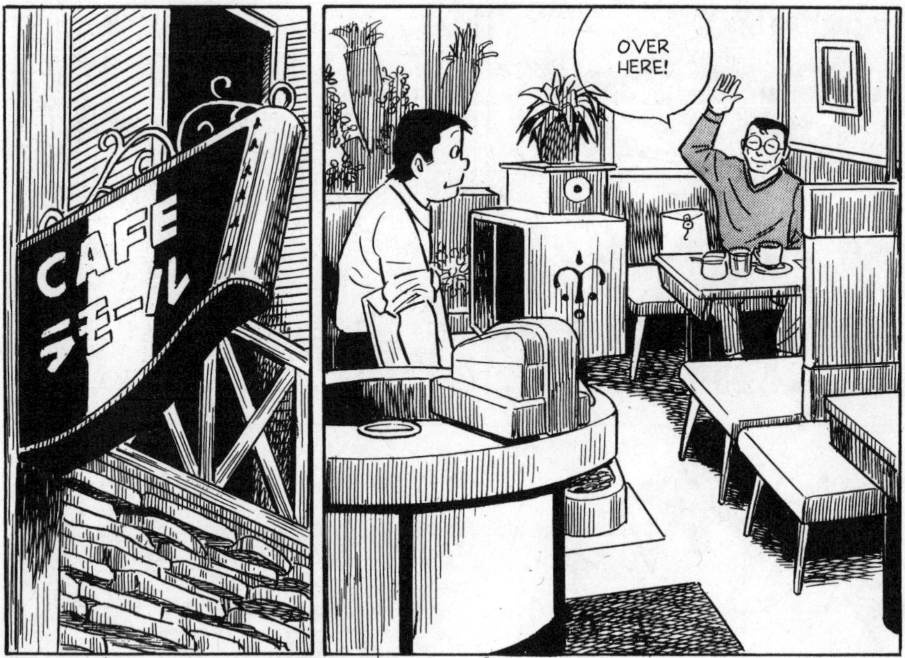
CAFE
ラモール
OVER HERE!

SIGN: CAFÉ L'AMOUR

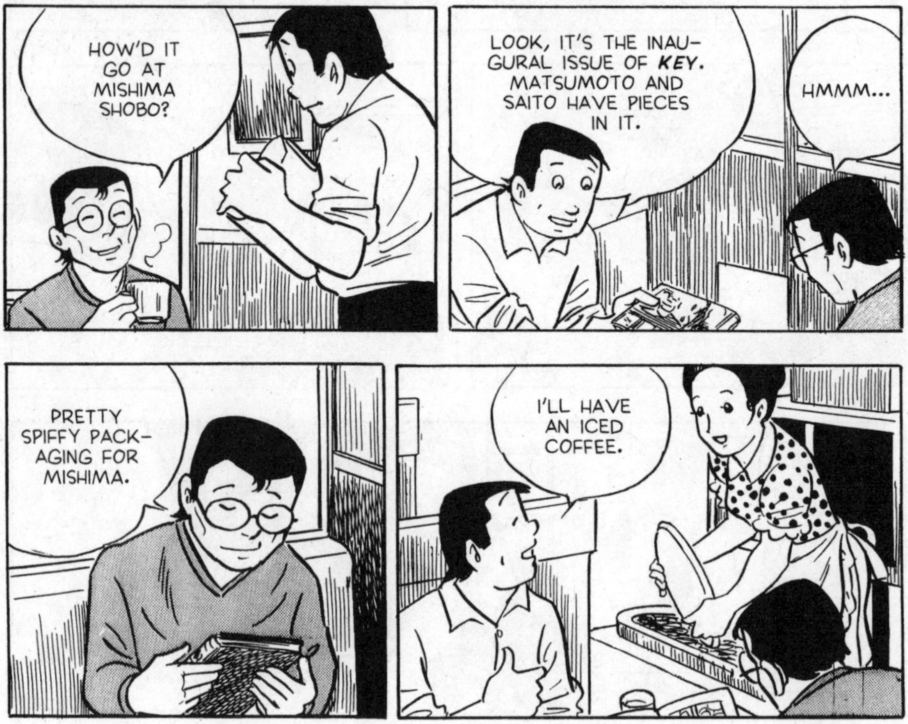
HOW'D IT GO AT MISHIMA SHOBO?
LOOK, IT'S THE INAUGURAL ISSUE OF KEY. MATSUMOTO AND SAITO HAVE PIECES IN IT.
HMMM...
PRETTY SPIFFY PACKAGING FOR MISHIMA.
I'LL HAVE AN ICED COFFEE.

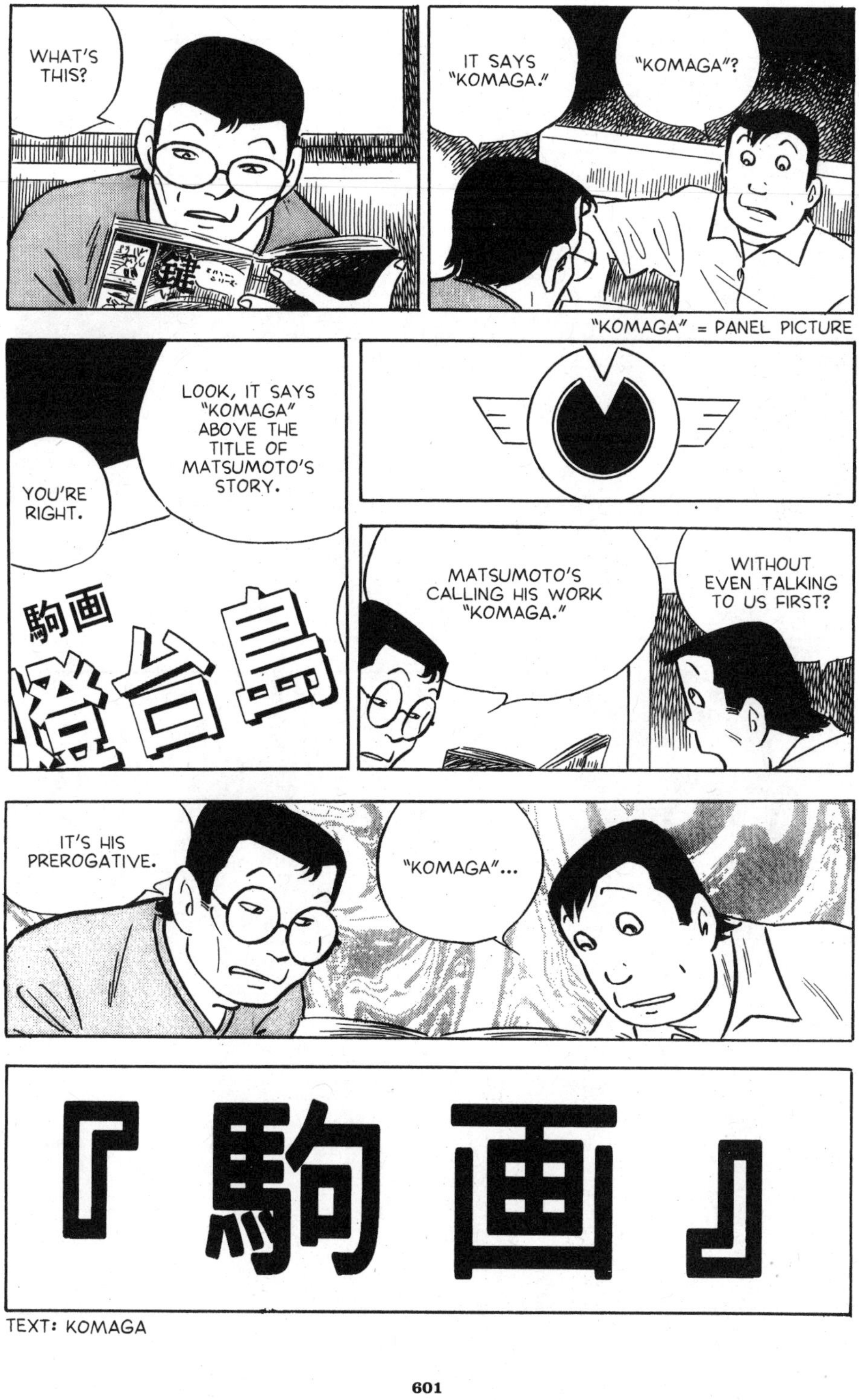
WHAT'S THIS?
IT SAYS "KOMAGA."
"KOMAGA"?
"KOMAGA" = PANEL PICTURE
LOOK, IT SAYS "KOMAGA" ABOVE THE TITLE OF MATSUMOTO'S STORY.
YOU'RE RIGHT.
駒画
燈台島
MATSUMOTO'S CALLING HIS WORK "KOMAGA."
WITHOUT EVEN TALKING TO US FIRST?
IT'S HIS PREROGATIVE.
"KOMAGA"...
『駒画』
TEXT: KOMAGA

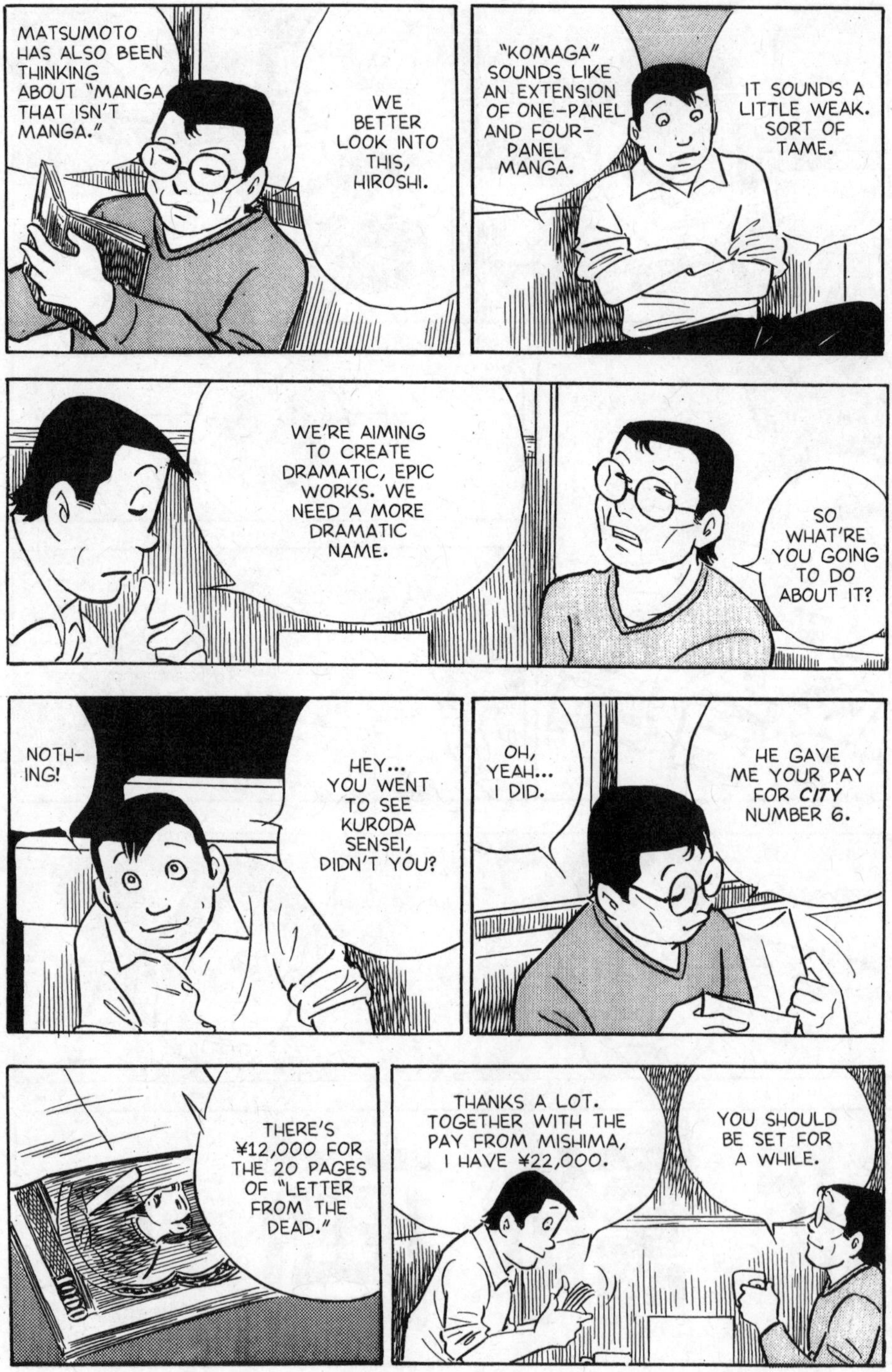
MATSUMOTO HAS ALSO BEEN THINKING ABOUT "MANGA THAT ISN'T MANGA."
WE BETTER LOOK INTO THIS, HIROSHI.
"KOMAGA" SOUNDS LIKE AN EXTENSION OF ONE-PANEL AND FOUR-PANEL MANGA.
IT SOUNDS A LITTLE WEAK. SORT OF TAME.
WE'RE AIMING TO CREATE DRAMATIC, EPIC WORKS. WE NEED A MORE DRAMATIC NAME.
SO WHAT'RE YOU GOING TO DO ABOUT IT?
NOTH-ING!
HEY... YOU WENT TO SEE KURODA SENSEI, DIDN'T YOU?
OH, YEAH... I DID.
HE GAVE ME YOUR PAY FOR *CITY* NUMBER 6.
THERE'S ¥12,000 FOR THE 20 PAGES OF "LETTER FROM THE DEAD."
THANKS A LOT. TOGETHER WITH THE PAY FROM MISHIMA, I HAVE ¥22,000.
YOU SHOULD BE SET FOR A WHILE.

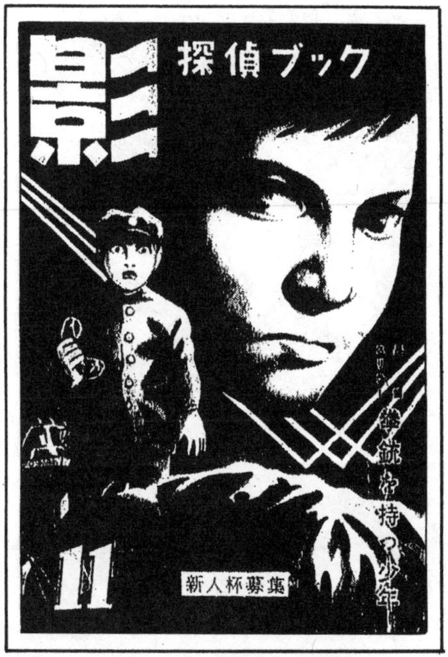
探偵ブック
11
新人杯募集

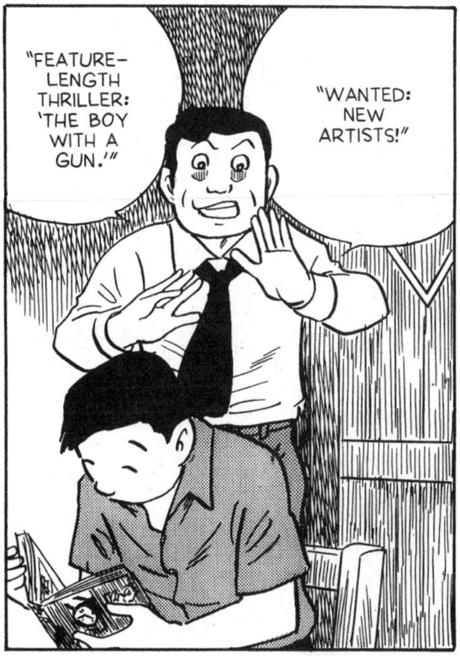
"FEATURE-LENGTH THRILLER: 'THE BOY WITH A GUN.'"
"WANTED: NEW ARTISTS!"

TITLE: *SHADOW I DETECTIVE BOOK*

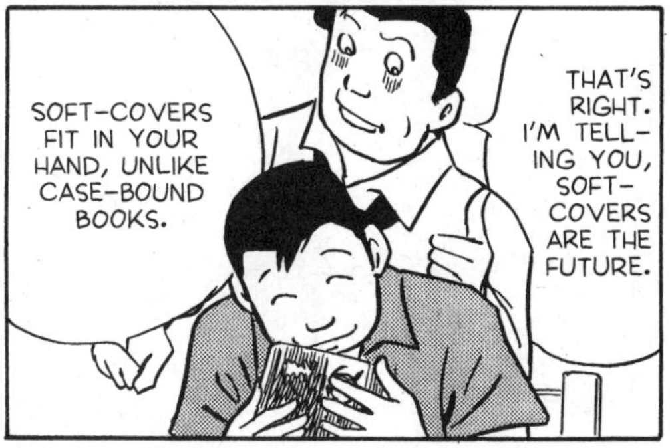
SOFT-COVERS FIT IN YOUR HAND, UNLIKE CASE-BOUND BOOKS.
THAT'S RIGHT. I'M TELL-ING YOU, SOFT-COVERS ARE THE FUTURE.

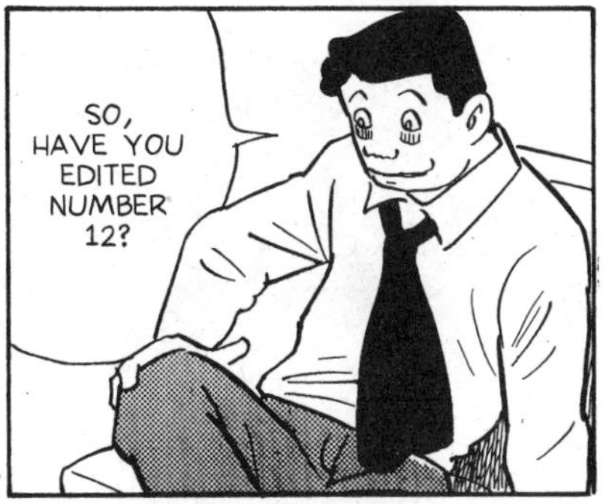
SO, HAVE YOU EDITED NUMBER 12?

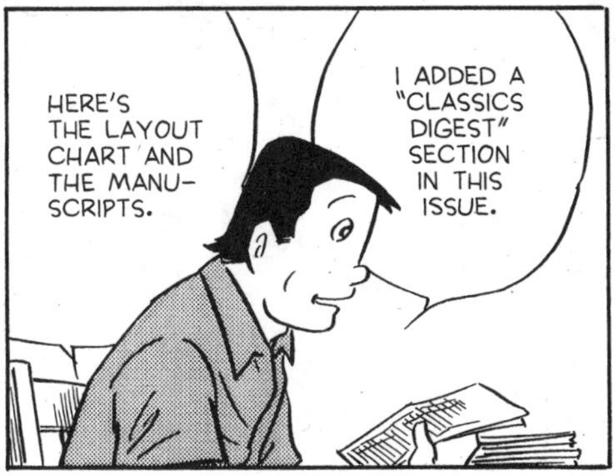
HERE'S THE LAYOUT CHART AND THE MANU-SCRIPTS.
I ADDED A "CLASSICS DIGEST" SECTION IN THIS ISSUE.

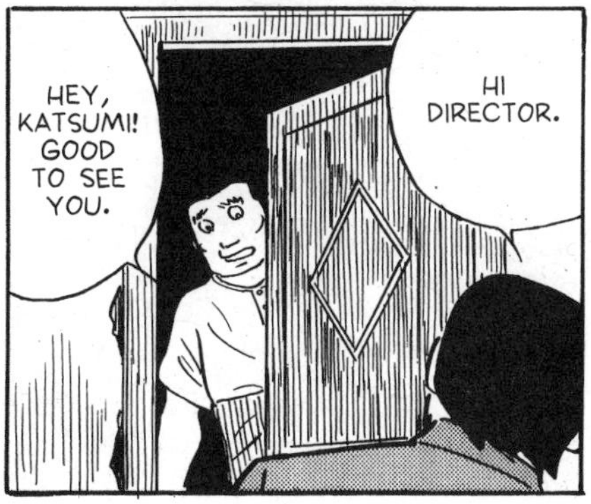
HEY, KATSUMI! GOOD TO SEE YOU.
HI DIRECTOR.

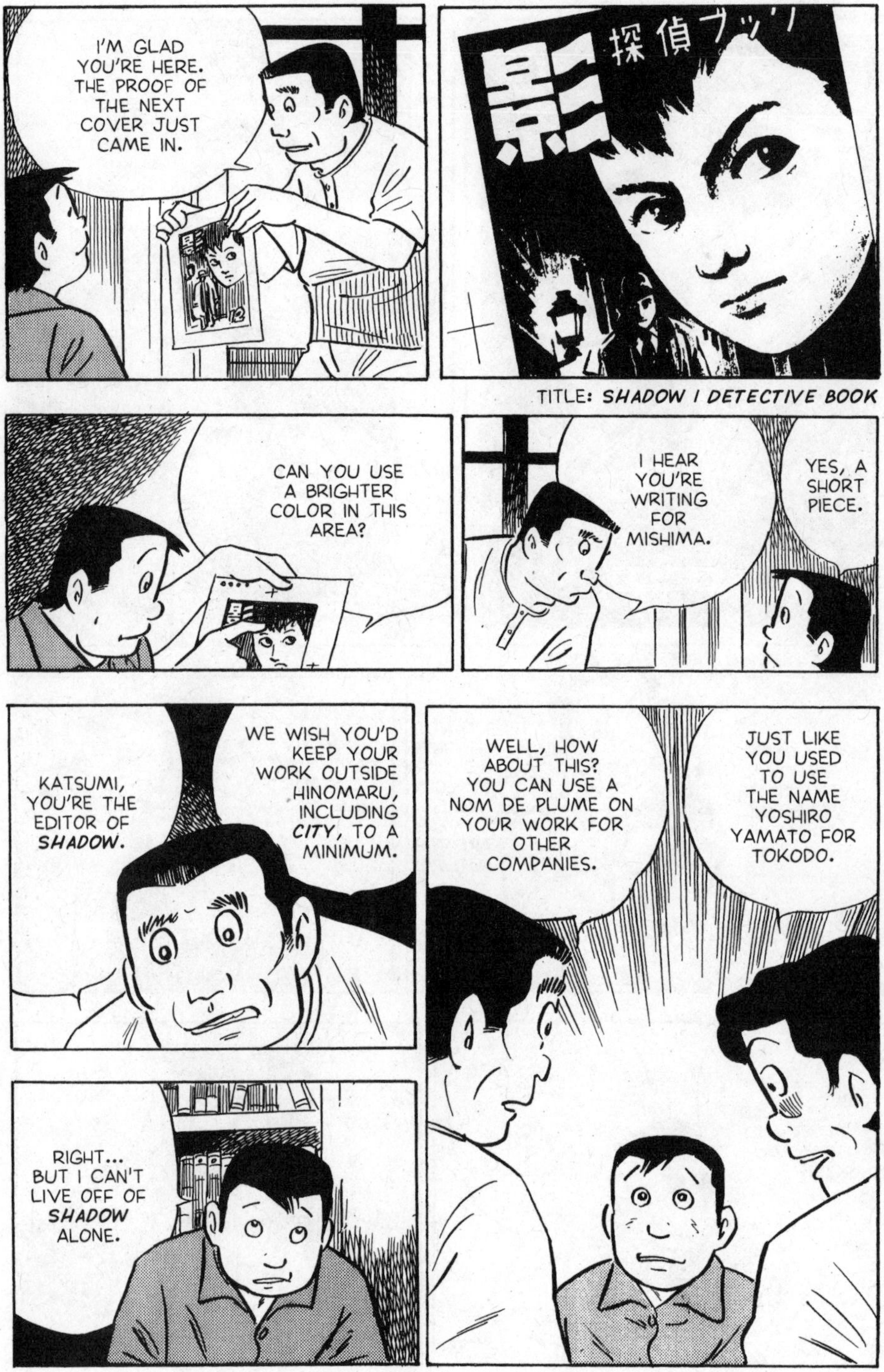
I'M GLAD YOU'RE HERE. THE PROOF OF THE NEXT COVER JUST CAME IN.
TITLE: *SHADOW* | *DETECTIVE BOOK*
CAN YOU USE A BRIGHTER COLOR IN THIS AREA?
I HEAR YOU'RE WRITING FOR MISHIMA.
YES, A SHORT PIECE.
KATSUMI, YOU'RE THE EDITOR OF *SHADOW*.
WE WISH YOU'D KEEP YOUR WORK OUTSIDE HINOMARU, INCLUDING *CITY*, TO A MINIMUM.
RIGHT... BUT I CAN'T LIVE OFF OF *SHADOW* ALONE.
WELL, HOW ABOUT THIS? YOU CAN USE A NOM DE PLUME ON YOUR WORK FOR OTHER COMPANIES.
JUST LIKE YOU USED TO USE THE NAME YOSHIRO YAMATO FOR TOKODO.

DRUNK WITH POWER

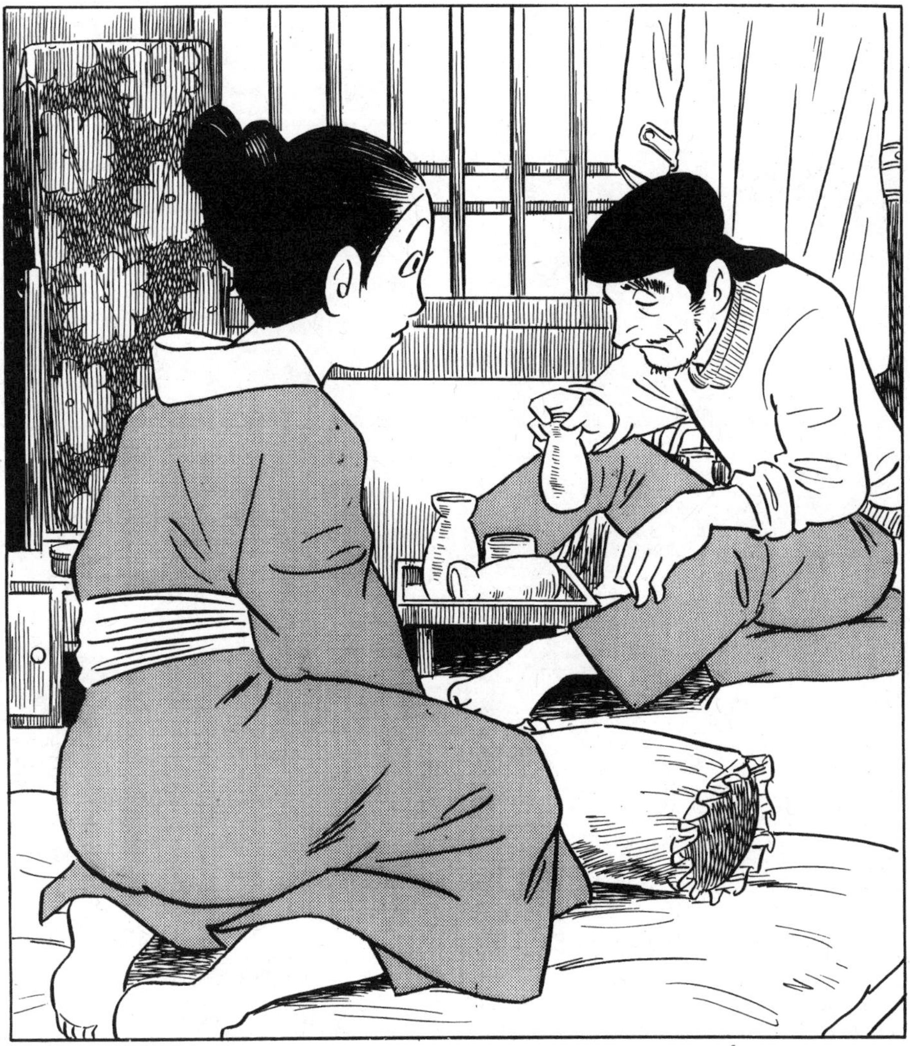

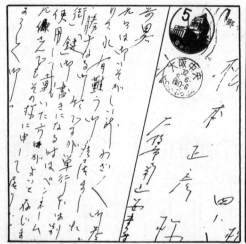

"... WE WOULD LIKE TO SUGGEST THAT YOU USE A DIFFERENT NAME WHEN WRITING FOR *CITY* AND *KEY*."

HOW SELFISH CAN HINOMARU BE?

I WANTED TO KEEP WRITING FOR HINO-MARU...

THEY'RE THE ONES WHO MADE THAT IMPOSSIBLE.

DIRECTOR! WRITE TO ALL *SHADOW* CONTRIBUTORS. AND BE VERY STERN!

GOT IT!

SHORT STORY MAGAZINES WERE POPPING UP ONE AFTER ANOTHER, AND THE YAMADA BROTHERS WORRIED THAT THE ARTISTS THEY'D REARED MIGHT JUMP SHIP.

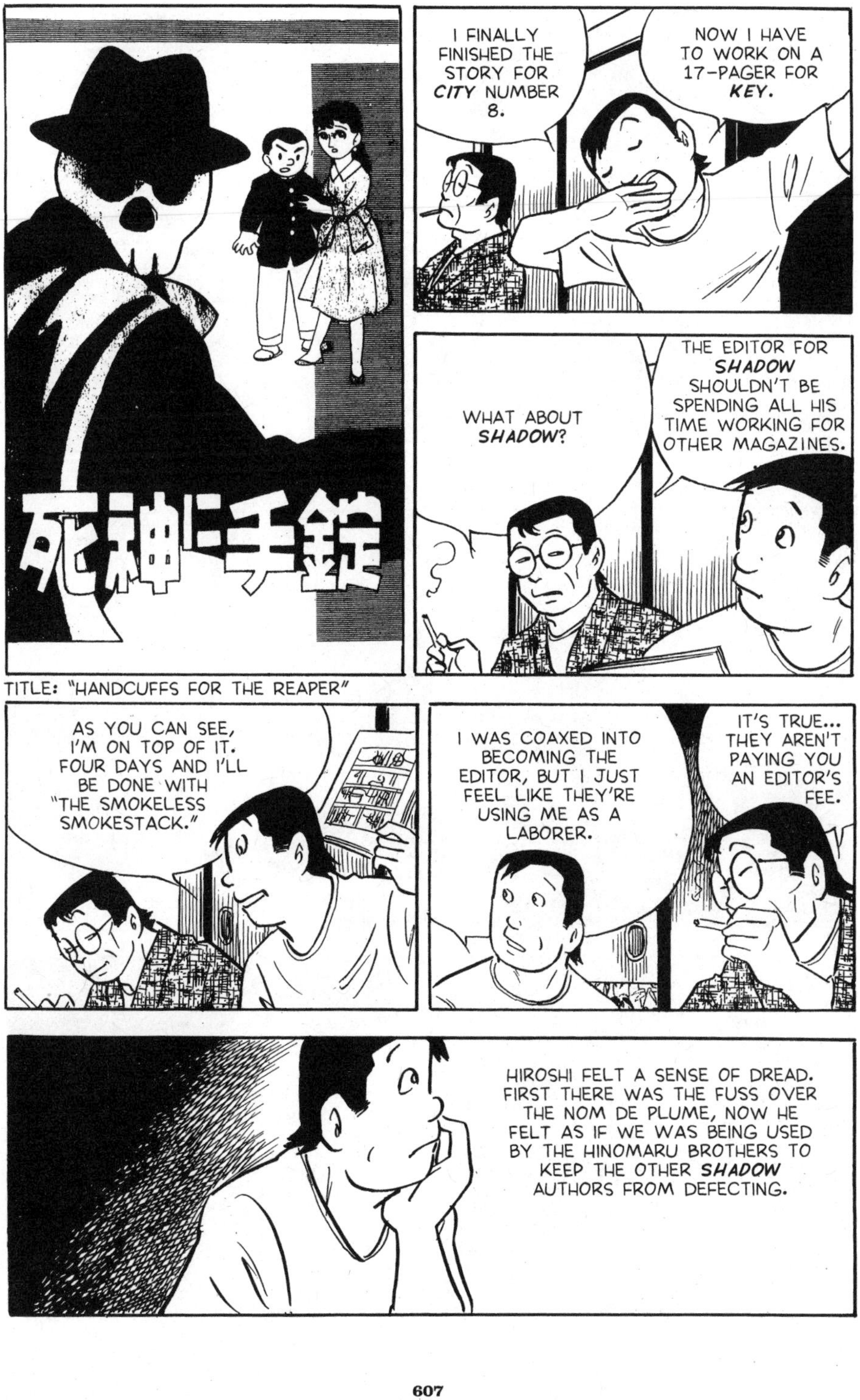
死神に手錠
I FINALLY FINISHED THE STORY FOR CITY NUMBER 8.
NOW I HAVE TO WORK ON A 17-PAGER FOR KEY.
WHAT ABOUT SHADOW?
THE EDITOR FOR SHADOW SHOULDN'T BE SPENDING ALL HIS TIME WORKING FOR OTHER MAGAZINES.
TITLE: "HANDCUFFS FOR THE REAPER"
AS YOU CAN SEE, I'M ON TOP OF IT. FOUR DAYS AND I'LL BE DONE WITH "THE SMOKELESS SMOKESTACK."
I WAS COAXED INTO BECOMING THE EDITOR, BUT I JUST FEEL LIKE THEY'RE USING ME AS A LABORER.
IT'S TRUE... THEY AREN'T PAYING YOU AN EDITOR'S FEE.
HIROSHI FELT A SENSE OF DREAD. FIRST THERE WAS THE FUSS OVER THE NOM DE PLUME, NOW HE FELT AS IF WE WAS BEING USED BY THE HINOMARU BROTHERS TO KEEP THE OTHER SHADOW AUTHORS FROM DEFECTING.

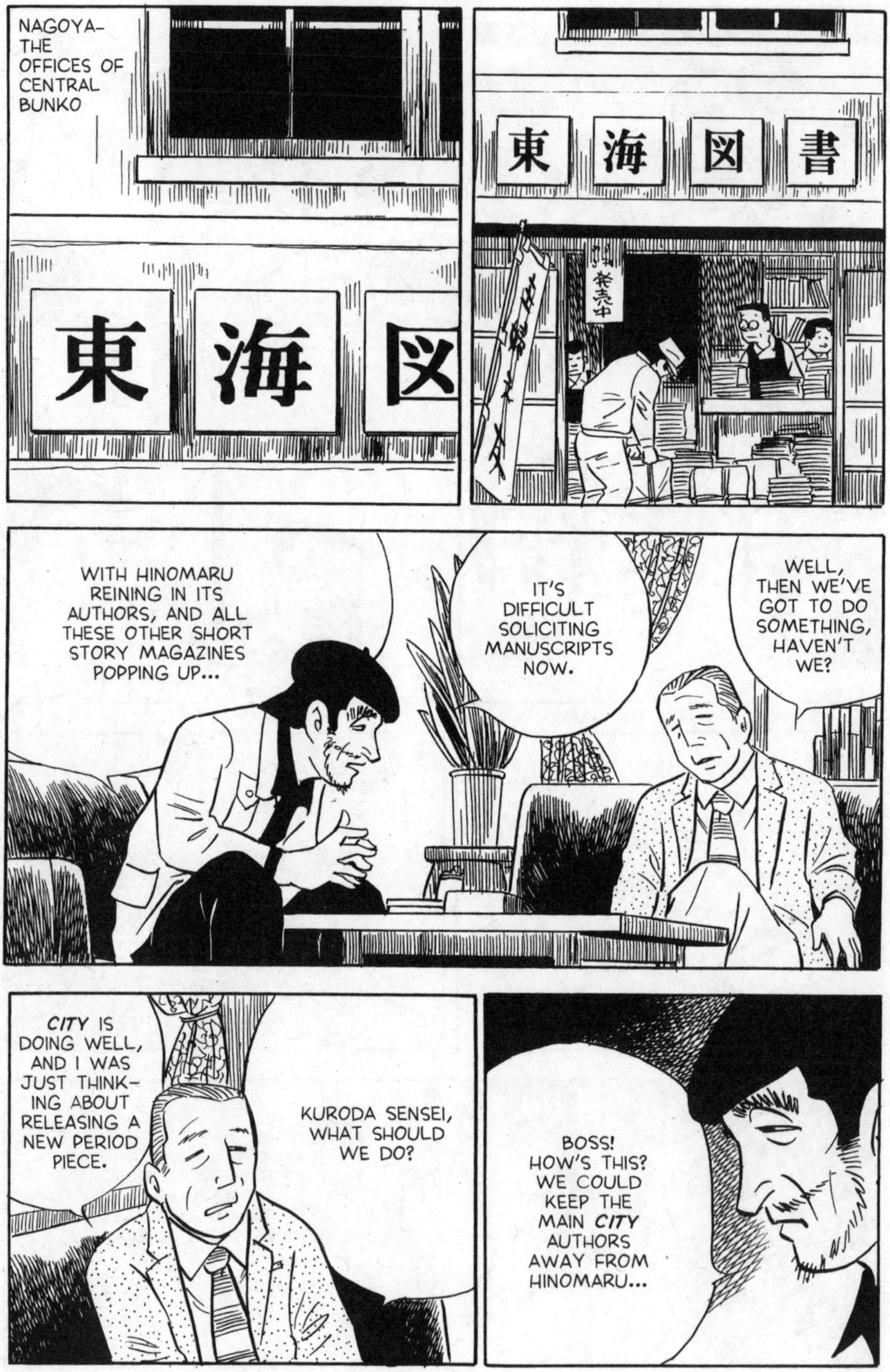
NAGOYA–
THE OFFICES OF CENTRAL BUNKO
東海図
東海図書
WITH HINOMARU REINING IN ITS AUTHORS, AND ALL THESE OTHER SHORT STORY MAGAZINES POPPING UP...
IT'S DIFFICULT SOLICITING MANUSCRIPTS NOW.
WELL, THEN WE'VE GOT TO DO SOMETHING, HAVEN'T WE?
CITY IS DOING WELL, AND I WAS JUST THINK-ING ABOUT RELEASING A NEW PERIOD PIECE.
KURODA SENSEI, WHAT SHOULD WE DO?
BOSS! HOW'S THIS? WE COULD KEEP THE MAIN *CITY* AUTHORS AWAY FROM HINOMARU...

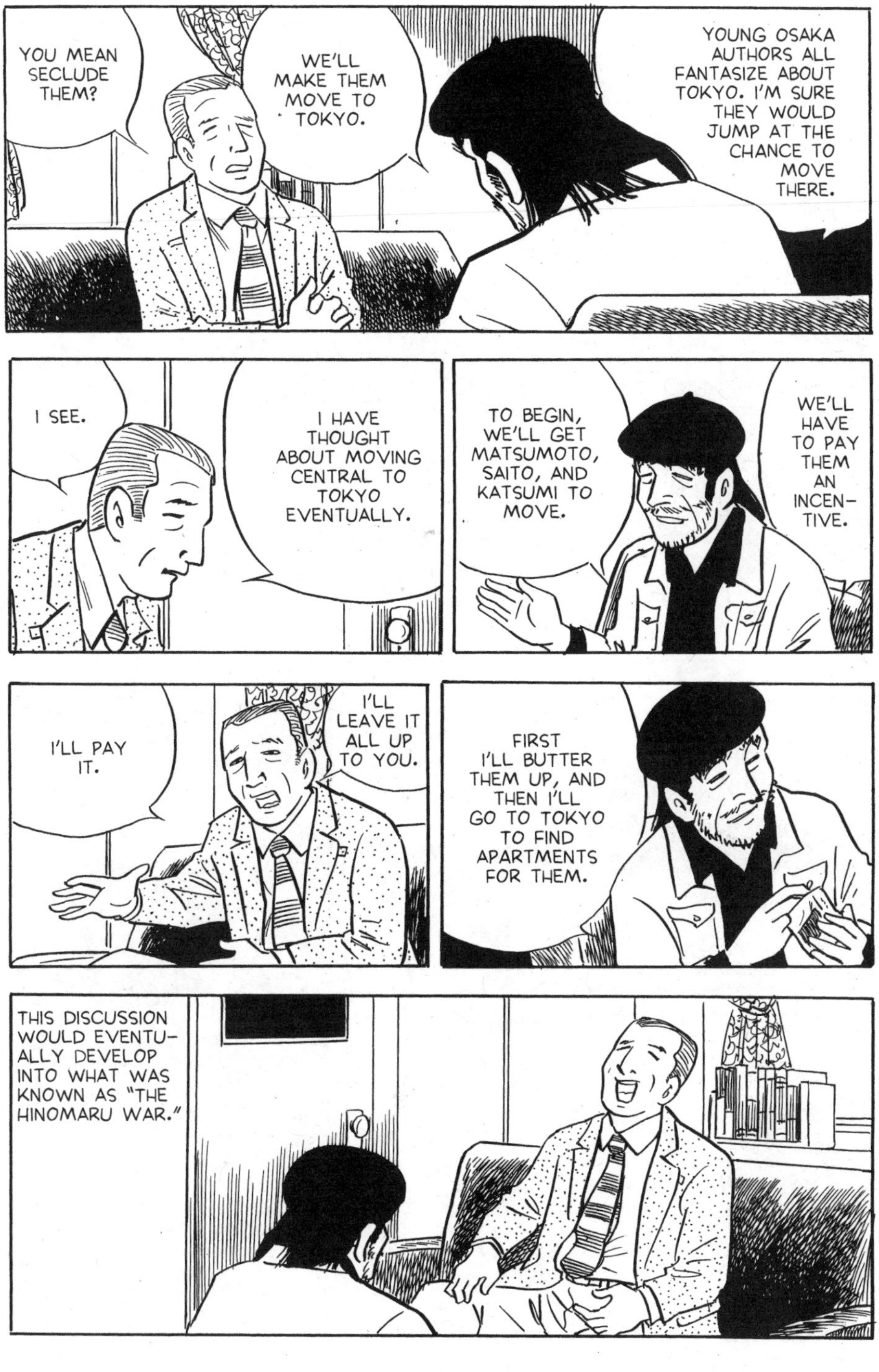
YOU MEAN SECLUDE THEM?
WE'LL MAKE THEM MOVE TO TOKYO.
YOUNG OSAKA AUTHORS ALL FANTASIZE ABOUT TOKYO. I'M SURE THEY WOULD JUMP AT THE CHANCE TO MOVE THERE.
I SEE.
I HAVE THOUGHT ABOUT MOVING CENTRAL TO TOKYO EVENTUALLY.
TO BEGIN, WE'LL GET MATSUMOTO, SAITO, AND KATSUMI TO MOVE.
WE'LL HAVE TO PAY THEM AN INCENTIVE.
I'LL PAY IT.
I'LL LEAVE IT ALL UP TO YOU.
FIRST I'LL BUTTER THEM UP, AND THEN I'LL GO TO TOKYO TO FIND APARTMENTS FOR THEM.
THIS DISCUSSION WOULD EVENTUALLY DEVELOP INTO WHAT WAS KNOWN AS "THE HINOMARU WAR."

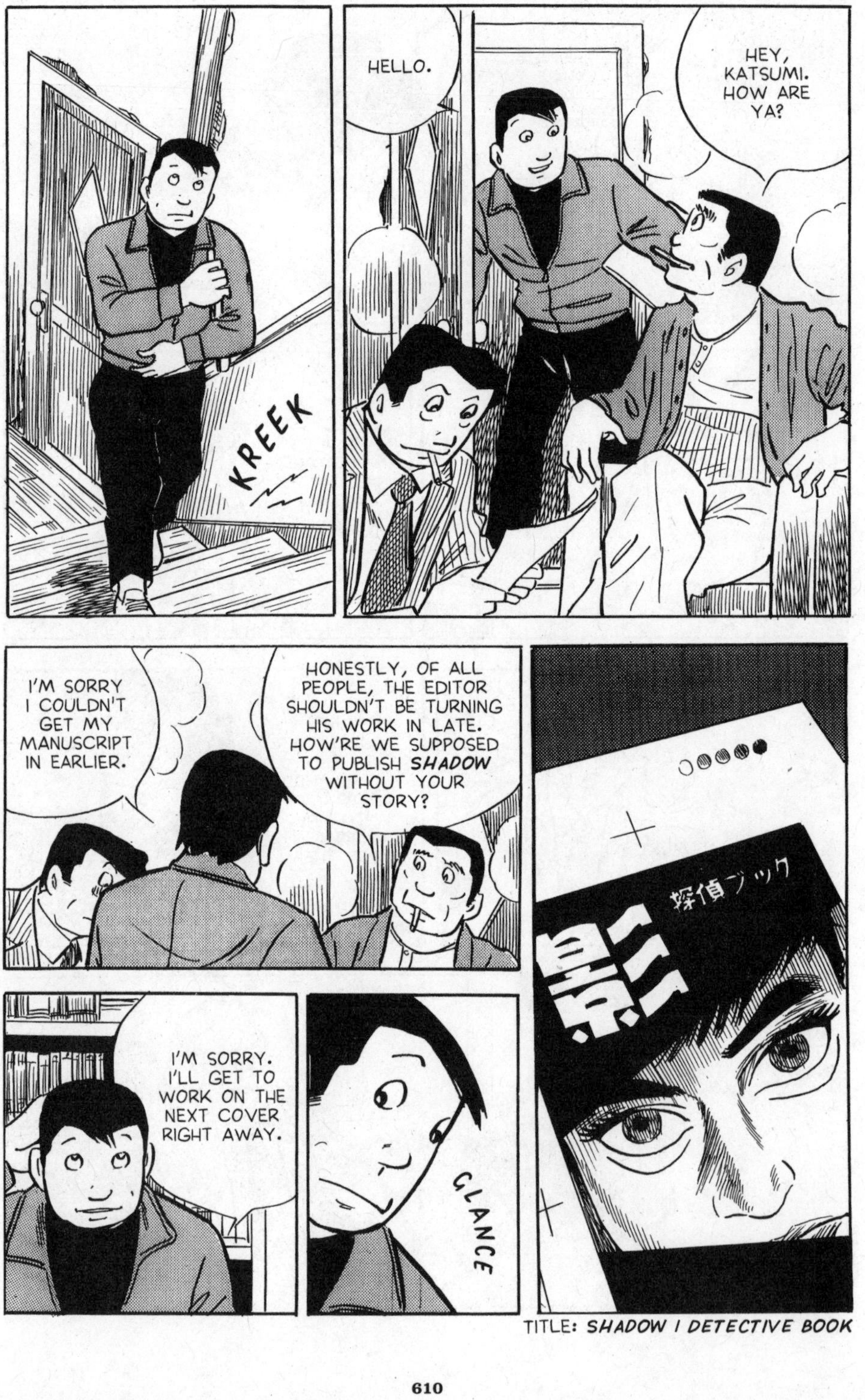
KREEK
HELLO.
HEY, KATSUMI. HOW ARE YA?
I'M SORRY I COULDN'T GET MY MANUSCRIPT IN EARLIER.
HONESTLY, OF ALL PEOPLE, THE EDITOR SHOULDN'T BE TURNING HIS WORK IN LATE. HOW'RE WE SUPPOSED TO PUBLISH *SHADOW* WITHOUT YOUR STORY?
I'M SORRY. I'LL GET TO WORK ON THE NEXT COVER RIGHT AWAY.
GLANCE
探偵ブック

TITLE: ***SHADOW I DETECTIVE BOOK***

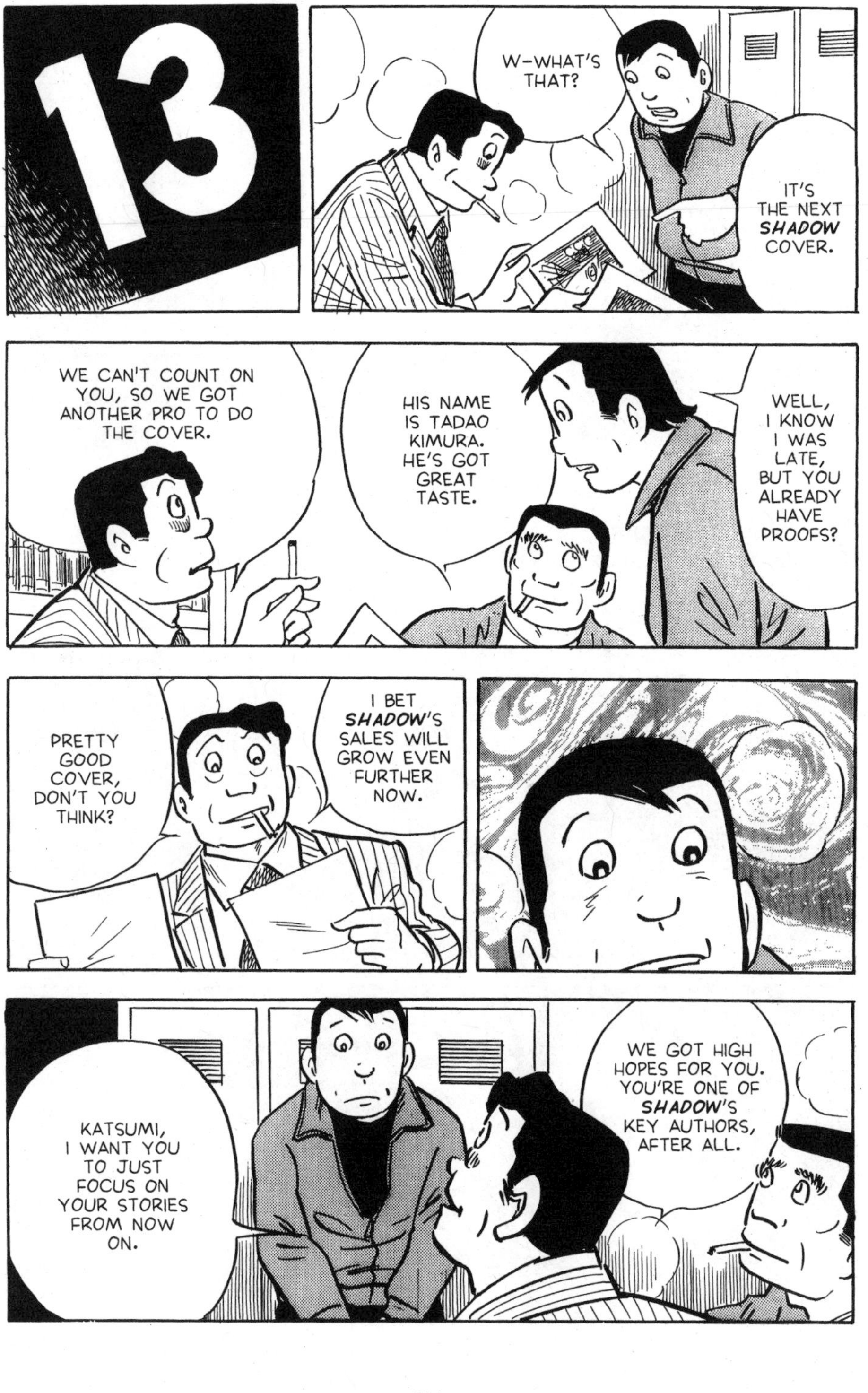
13
W-WHAT'S THAT?
IT'S THE NEXT SHADOW COVER.
WE CAN'T COUNT ON YOU, SO WE GOT ANOTHER PRO TO DO THE COVER.
HIS NAME IS TADAO KIMURA. HE'S GOT GREAT TASTE.
WELL, I KNOW I WAS LATE, BUT YOU ALREADY HAVE PROOFS?
PRETTY GOOD COVER, DON'T YOU THINK?
I BET SHADOW'S SALES WILL GROW EVEN FURTHER NOW.
KATSUMI, I WANT YOU TO JUST FOCUS ON YOUR STORIES FROM NOW ON.
WE GOT HIGH HOPES FOR YOU. YOU'RE ONE OF SHADOW'S KEY AUTHORS, AFTER ALL.

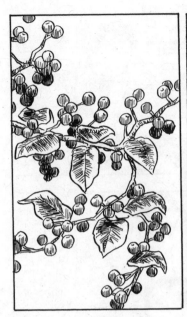

HAHAHA... SO YOU'VE BEEN DEMOTED FROM EDITOR ALREADY!

IT'S NOT FUNNY!

YOU WERE A NON-PAID EDITOR-IN-CHIEF ANYWAY. NOW YOU HAVE LESS ANNOYING WORK TO DO.

I GUESS YOU'RE RIGHT.

I WAS ATTACHED TO *SHADOW*, BUT NOW I CAN WORK FOR OTHER PUBLISHERS WITHOUT APOLOGIZING TO HINOMARU.

AND I CAN FORGET ABOUT THE WHOLE NOM DE PLUME THING.

I PUT MY ALL INTO *SHADOW* NUMBER 11 AND 12. I HAVE NO REGRETS.

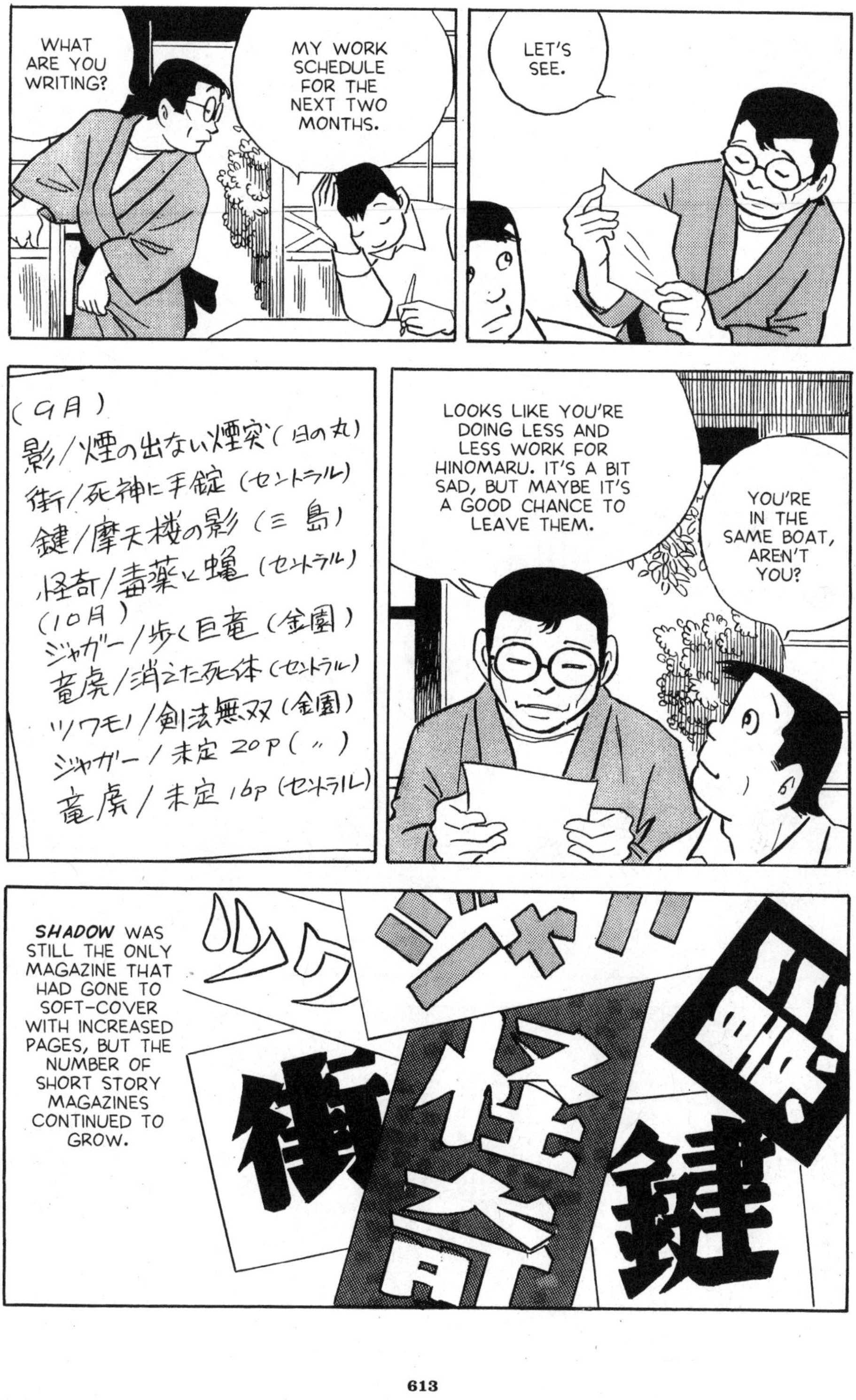
WHAT ARE YOU WRITING?
MY WORK SCHEDULE FOR THE NEXT TWO MONTHS.
LET'S SEE.
（9月）
影／煙の出ない煙突（日の丸）
街／死神に手錠（セントラル）
鍵／摩天楼の影（三島）
怪奇／毒薬と蝿（セントラル）
（10月）
ジャガー／歩く巨竜（金園）
竜虎／消えた死体（セントラル）
ツワモノ／剣法無双（金園）
ジャガー／未定 20P（〃）
竜虎／未定 16P（セントラル）
LOOKS LIKE YOU'RE DOING LESS AND LESS WORK FOR HINOMARU. IT'S A BIT SAD, BUT MAYBE IT'S A GOOD CHANCE TO LEAVE THEM.
YOU'RE IN THE SAME BOAT, AREN'T YOU?
SHADOW WAS STILL THE ONLY MAGAZINE THAT HAD GONE TO SOFT-COVER WITH INCREASED PAGES, BUT THE NUMBER OF SHORT STORY MAGAZINES CONTINUED TO GROW.
街
怪奇
鍵

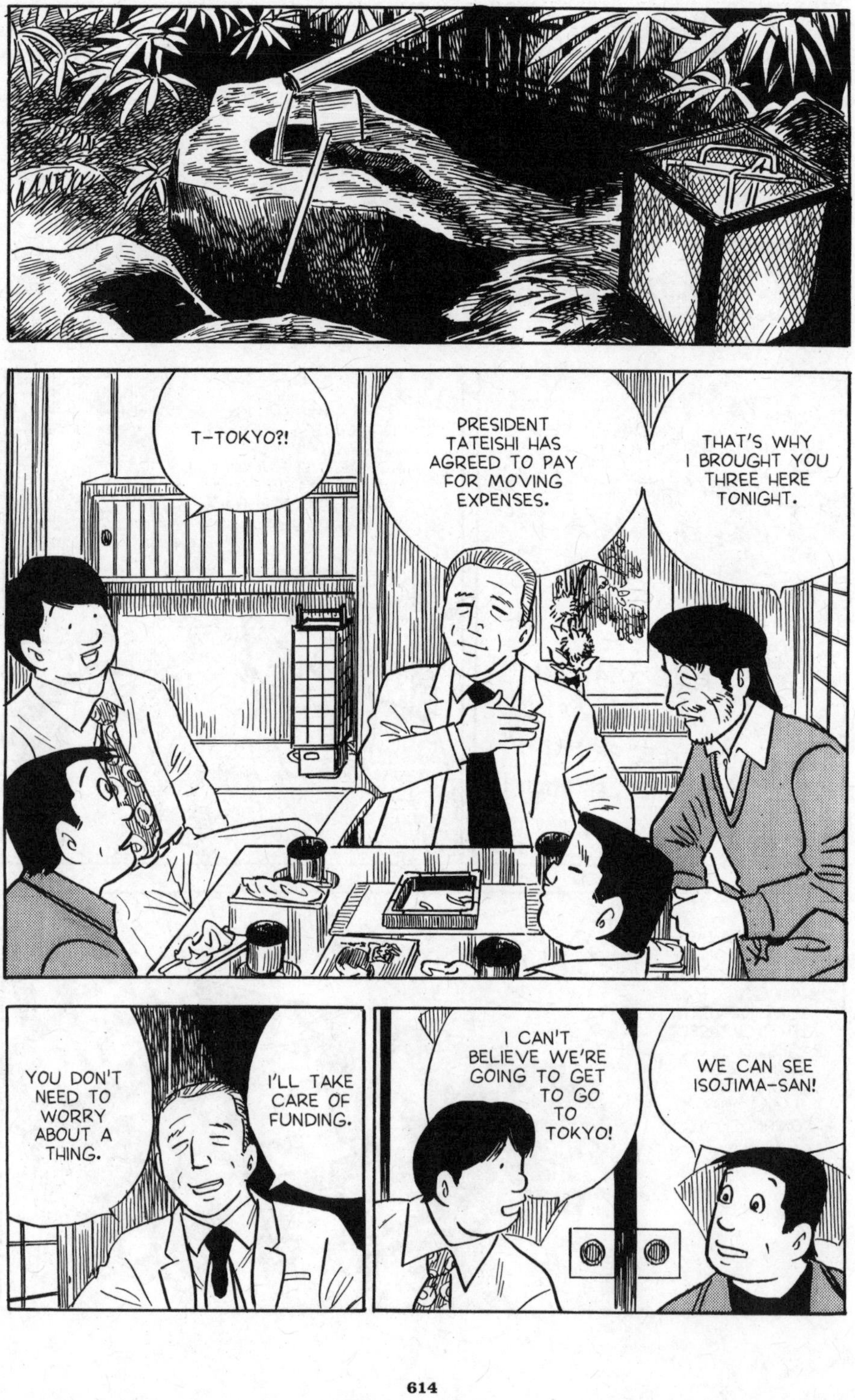
T-TOKYO?!
PRESIDENT TATEISHI HAS AGREED TO PAY FOR MOVING EXPENSES.
THAT'S WHY I BROUGHT YOU THREE HERE TONIGHT.
YOU DON'T NEED TO WORRY ABOUT A THING.
I'LL TAKE CARE OF FUNDING.
I CAN'T BELIEVE WE'RE GOING TO GET TO GO TO TOKYO!
WE CAN SEE ISOJIMA-SAN!

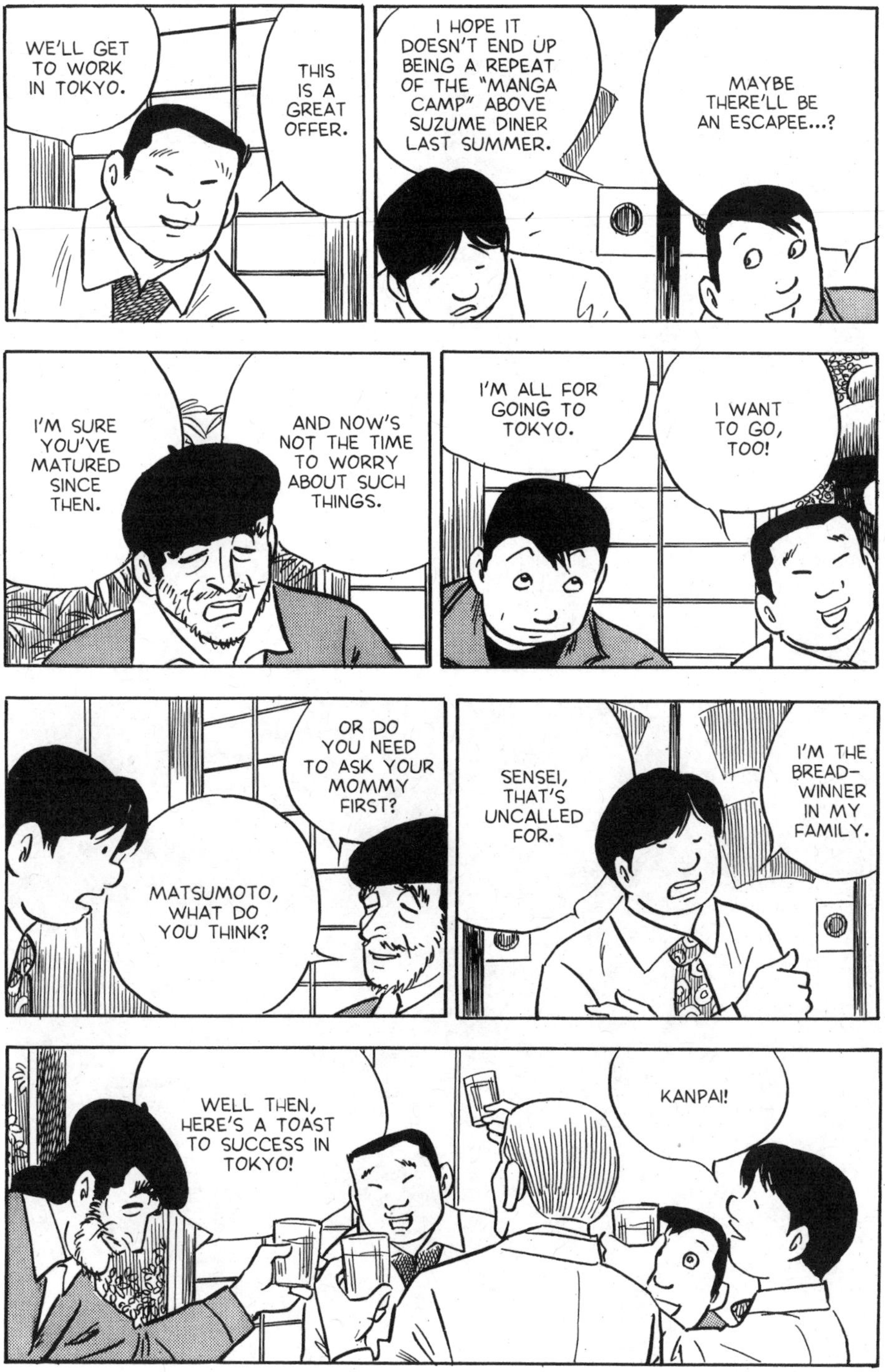
WE'LL GET TO WORK IN TOKYO.
THIS IS A GREAT OFFER.
I HOPE IT DOESN'T END UP BEING A REPEAT OF THE "MANGA CAMP" ABOVE SUZUME DINER LAST SUMMER.
MAYBE THERE'LL BE AN ESCAPEE...?
I'M SURE YOU'VE MATURED SINCE THEN.
AND NOW'S NOT THE TIME TO WORRY ABOUT SUCH THINGS.
I'M ALL FOR GOING TO TOKYO.
I WANT TO GO, TOO!
MATSUMOTO, WHAT DO YOU THINK?
OR DO YOU NEED TO ASK YOUR MOMMY FIRST?
SENSEI, THAT'S UNCALLED FOR.
I'M THE BREAD-WINNER IN MY FAMILY.
WELL THEN, HERE'S A TOAST TO SUCCESS IN TOKYO!
KANPAI!

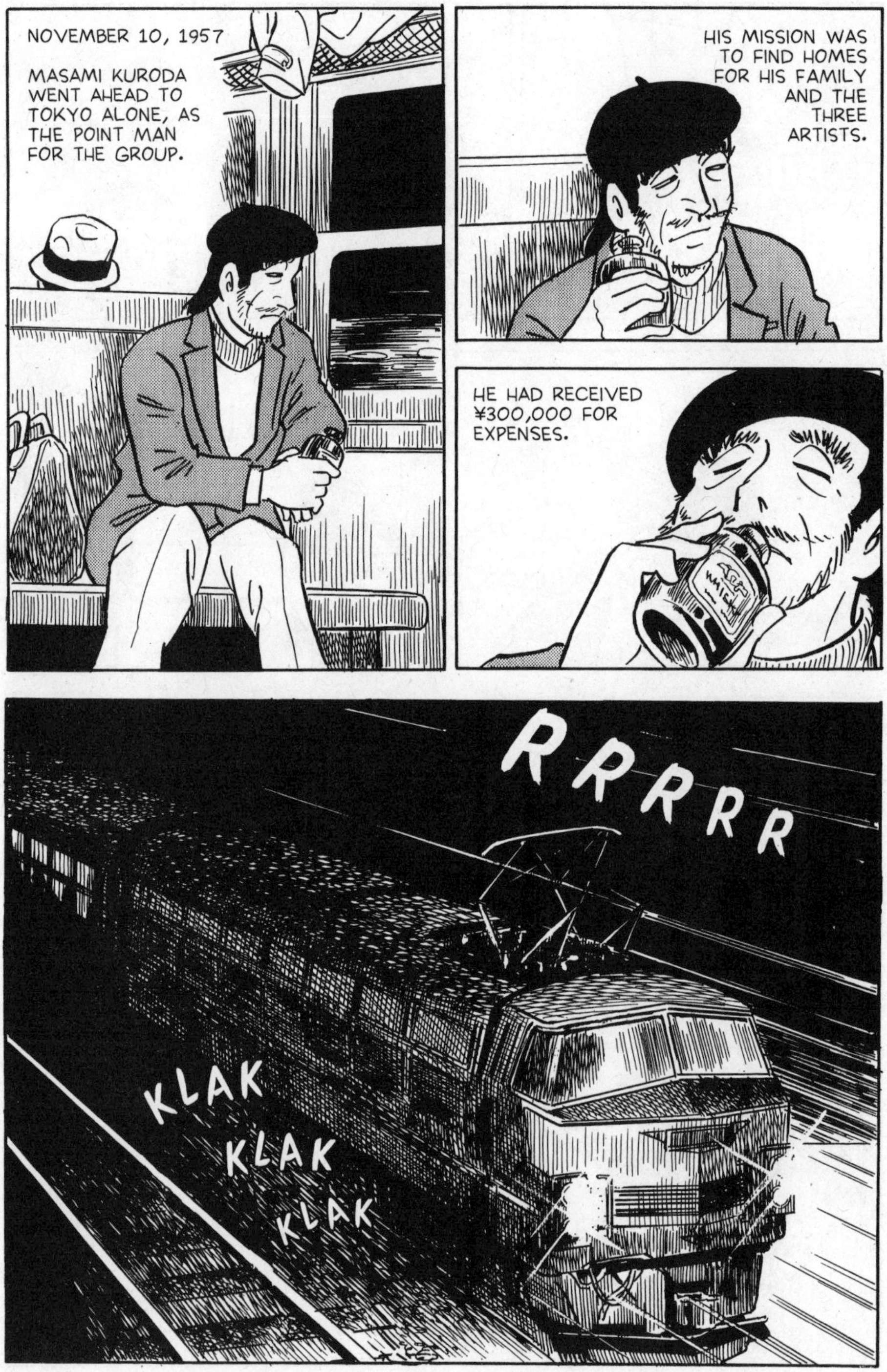
NOVEMBER 10, 1957
MASAMI KURODA WENT AHEAD TO TOKYO ALONE, AS THE POINT MAN FOR THE GROUP.
HIS MISSION WAS TO FIND HOMES FOR HIS FAMILY AND THE THREE ARTISTS.
HE HAD RECEIVED ¥300,000 FOR EXPENSES.
RRRRRR
KLAK
KLAK
KLAK

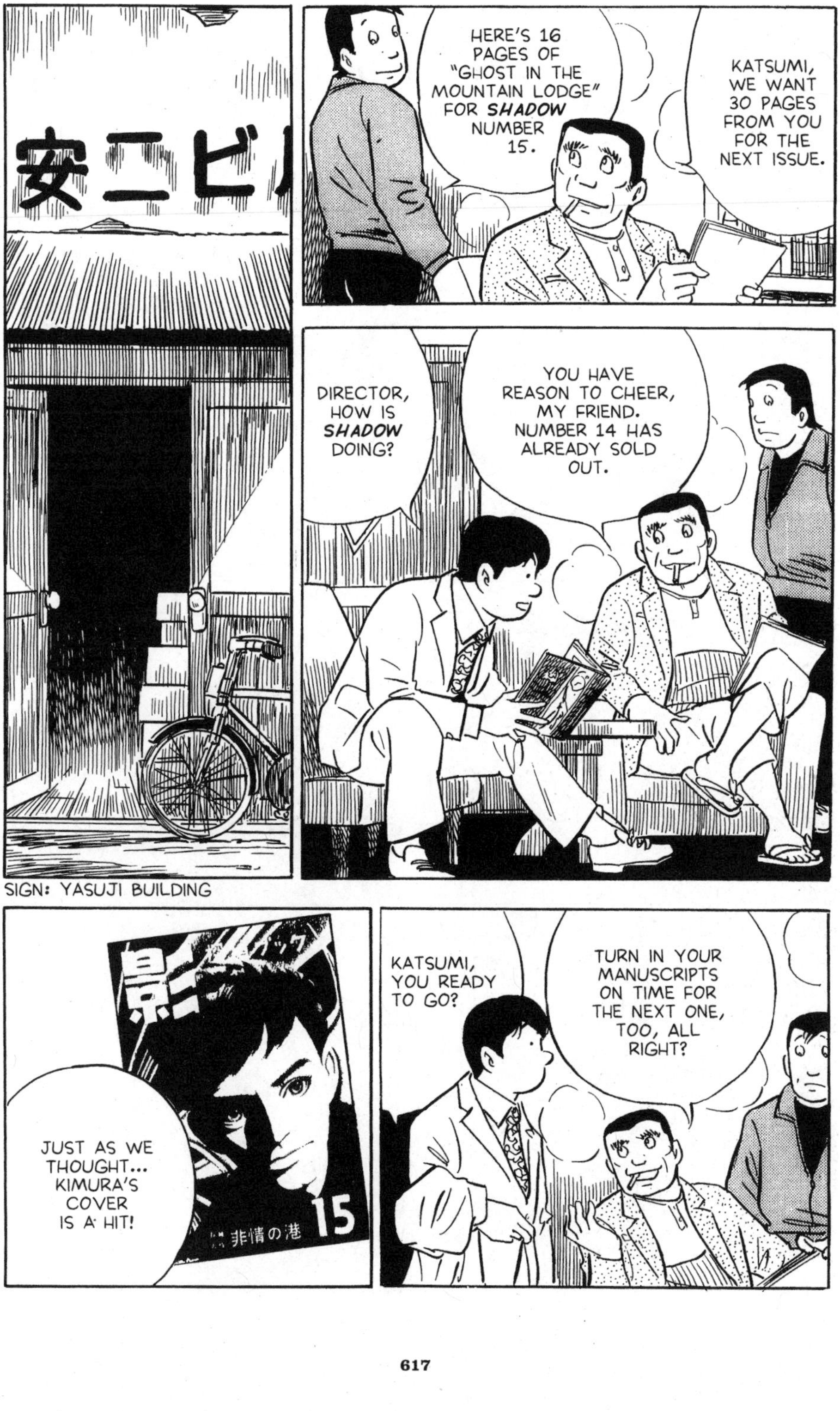
安二ビル
SIGN: YASUJI BUILDING
HERE'S 16 PAGES OF "GHOST IN THE MOUNTAIN LODGE" FOR *SHADOW* NUMBER 15.
KATSUMI, WE WANT 30 PAGES FROM YOU FOR THE NEXT ISSUE.
DIRECTOR, HOW IS *SHADOW* DOING?
YOU HAVE REASON TO CHEER, MY FRIEND. NUMBER 14 HAS ALREADY SOLD OUT.
影
15
非情の港
JUST AS WE THOUGHT... KIMURA'S COVER IS A HIT!
KATSUMI, YOU READY TO GO?
TURN IN YOUR MANUSCRIPTS ON TIME FOR THE NEXT ONE, TOO, ALL RIGHT?

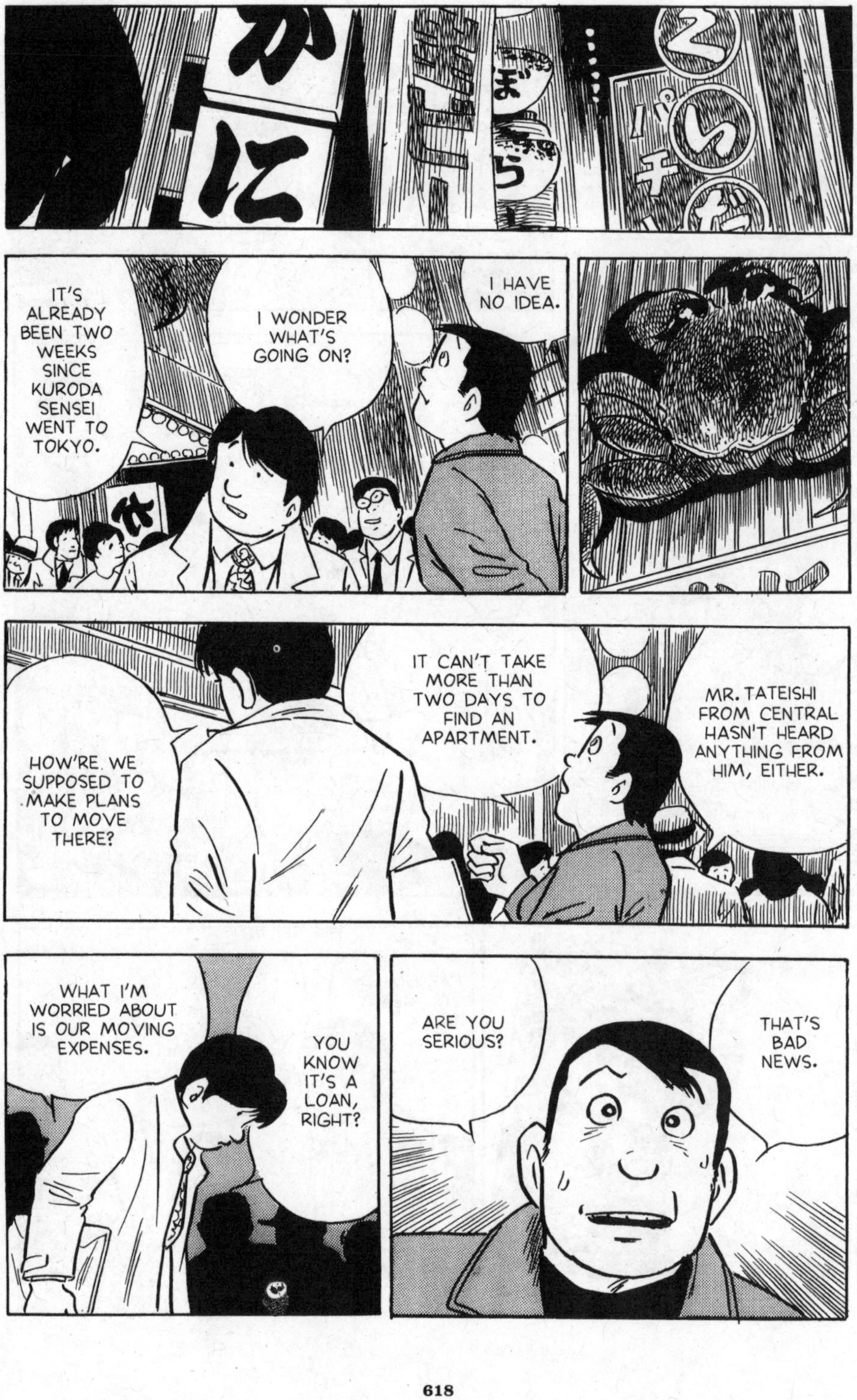
かに
IT'S ALREADY BEEN TWO WEEKS SINCE KURODA SENSEI WENT TO TOKYO.
I WONDER WHAT'S GOING ON?
I HAVE NO IDEA.
HOW'RE WE SUPPOSED TO MAKE PLANS TO MOVE THERE?
IT CAN'T TAKE MORE THAN TWO DAYS TO FIND AN APARTMENT.
MR. TATEISHI FROM CENTRAL HASN'T HEARD ANYTHING FROM HIM, EITHER.
WHAT I'M WORRIED ABOUT IS OUR MOVING EXPENSES.
YOU KNOW IT'S A LOAN, RIGHT?
ARE YOU SERIOUS?
THAT'S BAD NEWS.

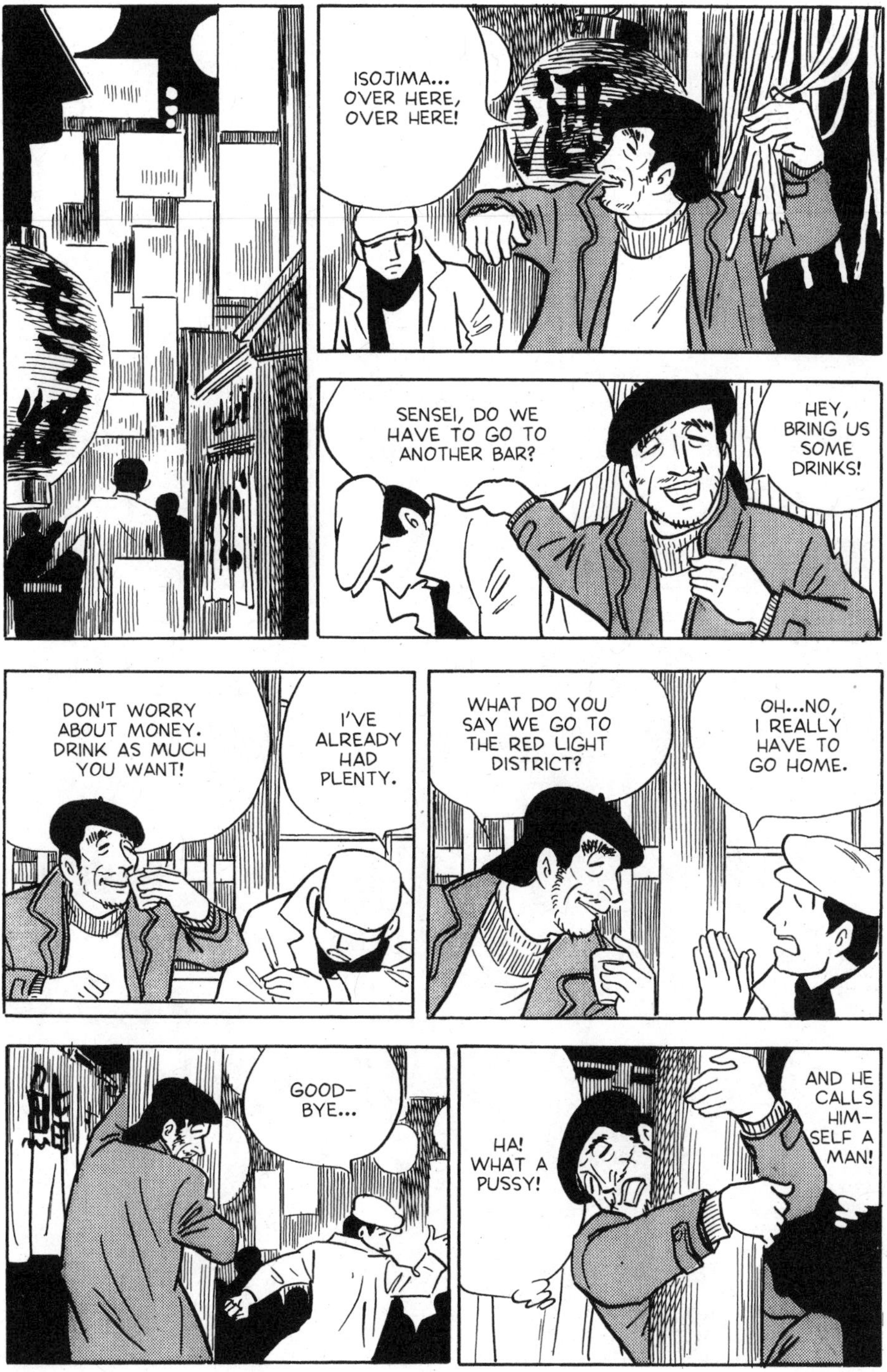
ISOJIMA... OVER HERE, OVER HERE!
SENSEI, DO WE HAVE TO GO TO ANOTHER BAR?
HEY, BRING US SOME DRINKS!
DON'T WORRY ABOUT MONEY. DRINK AS MUCH YOU WANT!
I'VE ALREADY HAD PLENTY.
WHAT DO YOU SAY WE GO TO THE RED LIGHT DISTRICT?
OH...NO, I REALLY HAVE TO GO HOME.
GOOD-BYE...
HA! WHAT A PUSSY!
AND HE CALLS HIM-SELF A MAN!

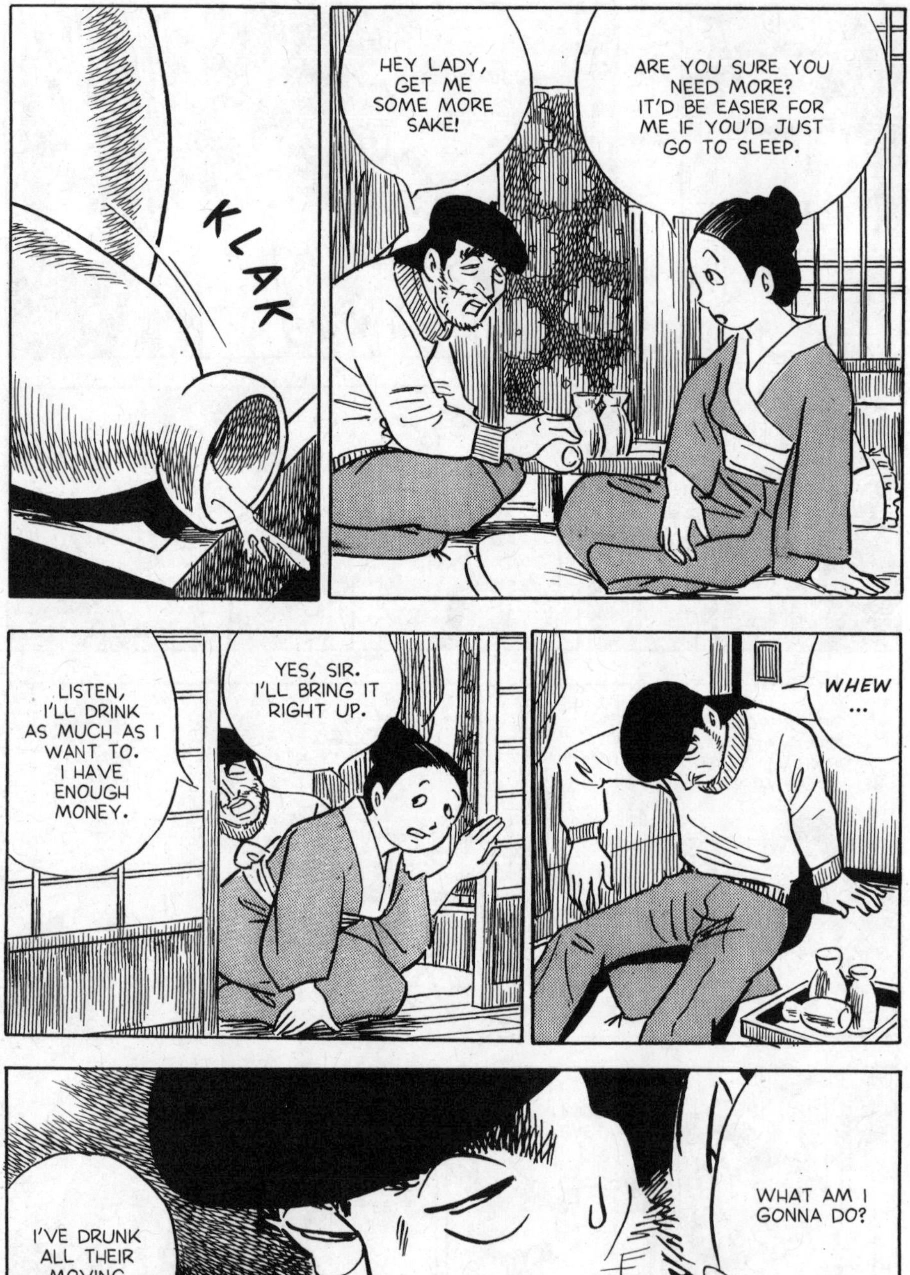
KLAK
HEY LADY, GET ME SOME MORE SAKE!
ARE YOU SURE YOU NEED MORE? IT'D BE EASIER FOR ME IF YOU'D JUST GO TO SLEEP.
LISTEN, I'LL DRINK AS MUCH AS I WANT TO. I HAVE ENOUGH MONEY.
YES, SIR. I'LL BRING IT RIGHT UP.
WHEW ...
I'VE DRUNK ALL THEIR MOVING EXPENSES...
WHAT AM I GONNA DO?

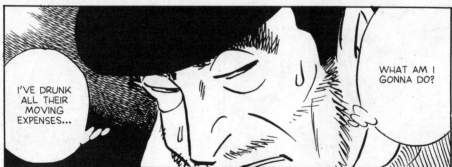

TO TOKYO, AND "GEKIGA"

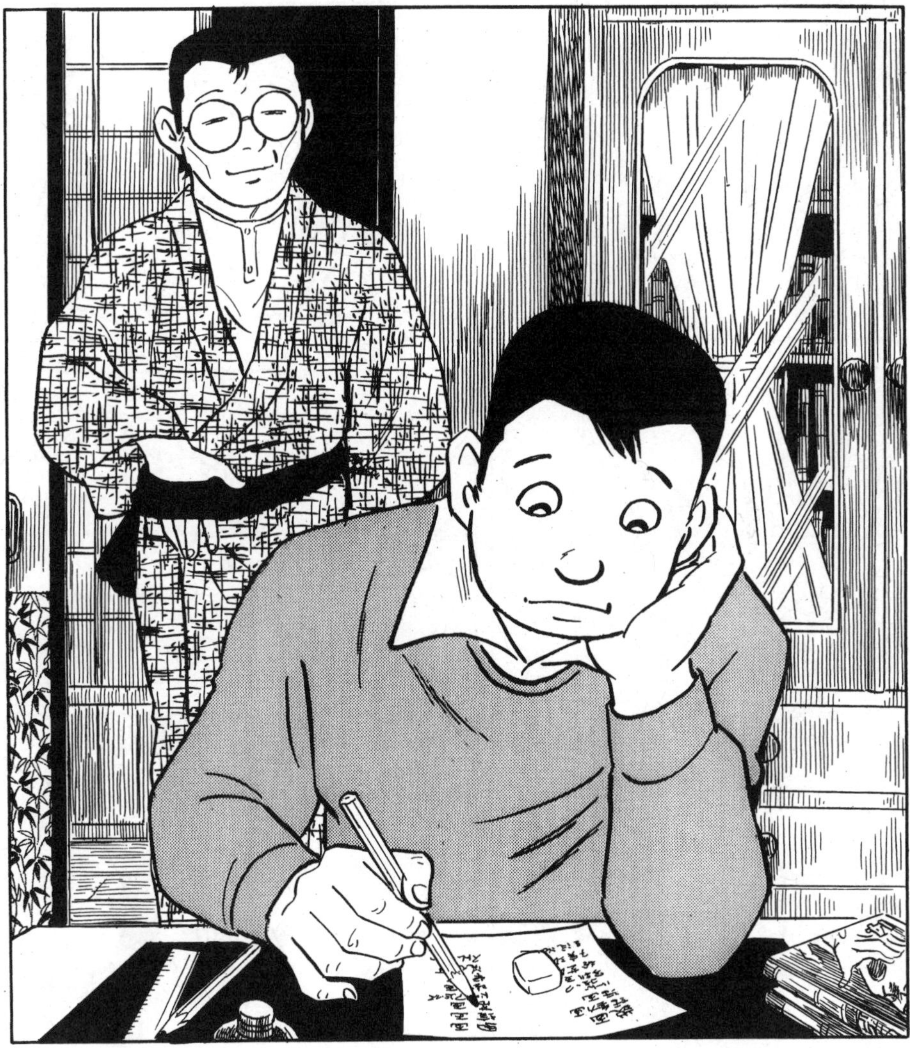

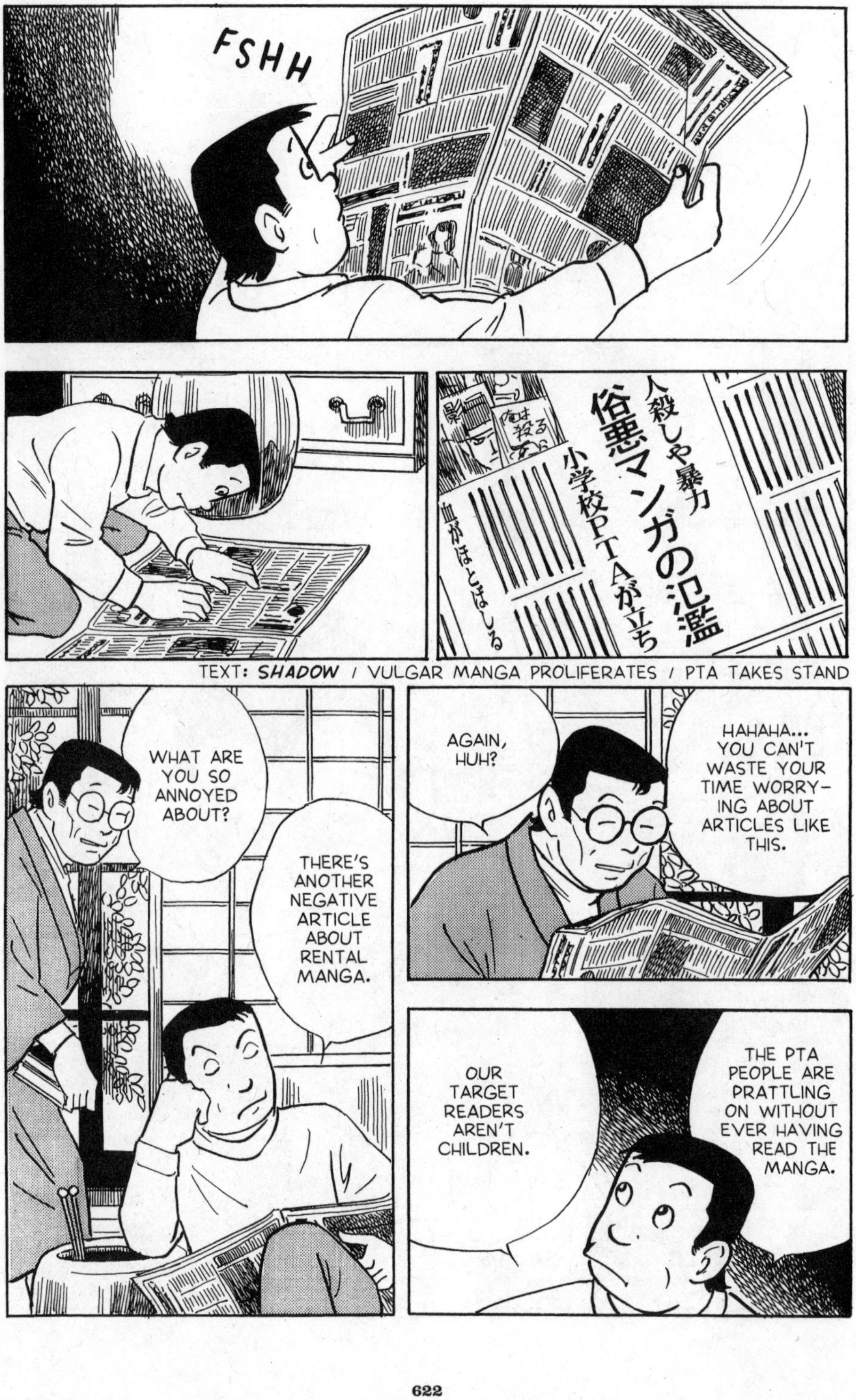
FSHH
人殺しや暴力
俗悪マンガの氾濫
小学校PTAが立ち
血がほとばしる
TEXT: SHADOW / VULGAR MANGA PROLIFERATES / PTA TAKES STAND
WHAT ARE YOU SO ANNOYED ABOUT?
THERE'S ANOTHER NEGATIVE ARTICLE ABOUT RENTAL MANGA.
AGAIN, HUH?
HAHAHA... YOU CAN'T WASTE YOUR TIME WORRYING ABOUT ARTICLES LIKE THIS.
OUR TARGET READERS AREN'T CHILDREN.
THE PTA PEOPLE ARE PRATTLING ON WITHOUT EVER HAVING READ THE MANGA.

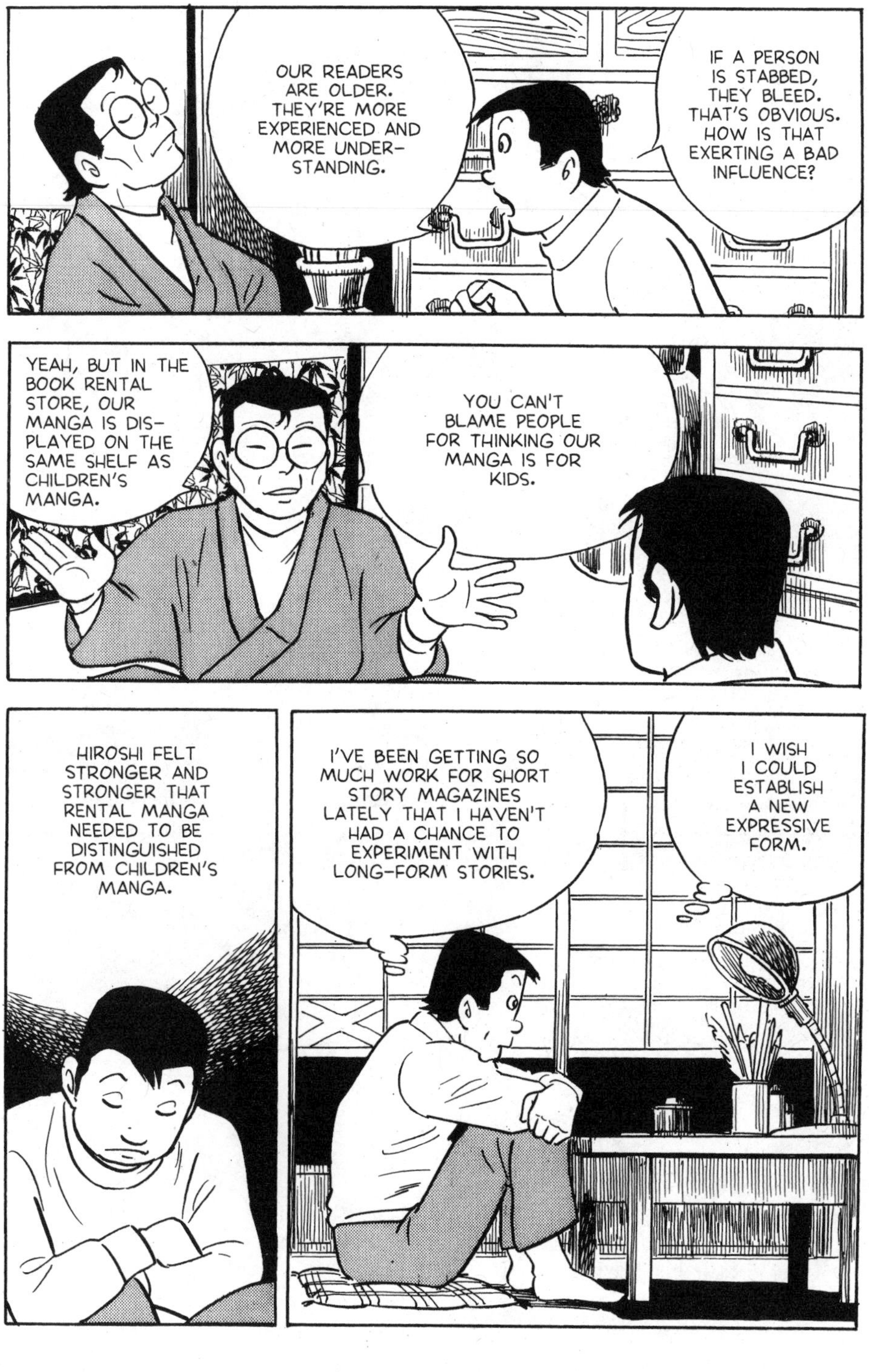
OUR READERS ARE OLDER. THEY'RE MORE EXPERIENCED AND MORE UNDER-STANDING.
IF A PERSON IS STABBED, THEY BLEED. THAT'S OBVIOUS. HOW IS THAT EXERTING A BAD INFLUENCE?
YEAH, BUT IN THE BOOK RENTAL STORE, OUR MANGA IS DIS-PLAYED ON THE SAME SHELF AS CHILDREN'S MANGA.
YOU CAN'T BLAME PEOPLE FOR THINKING OUR MANGA IS FOR KIDS.
HIROSHI FELT STRONGER AND STRONGER THAT RENTAL MANGA NEEDED TO BE DISTINGUISHED FROM CHILDREN'S MANGA.
I'VE BEEN GETTING SO MUCH WORK FOR SHORT STORY MAGAZINES LATELY THAT I HAVEN'T HAD A CHANCE TO EXPERIMENT WITH LONG-FORM STORIES.
I WISH I COULD ESTABLISH A NEW EXPRESSIVE FORM.

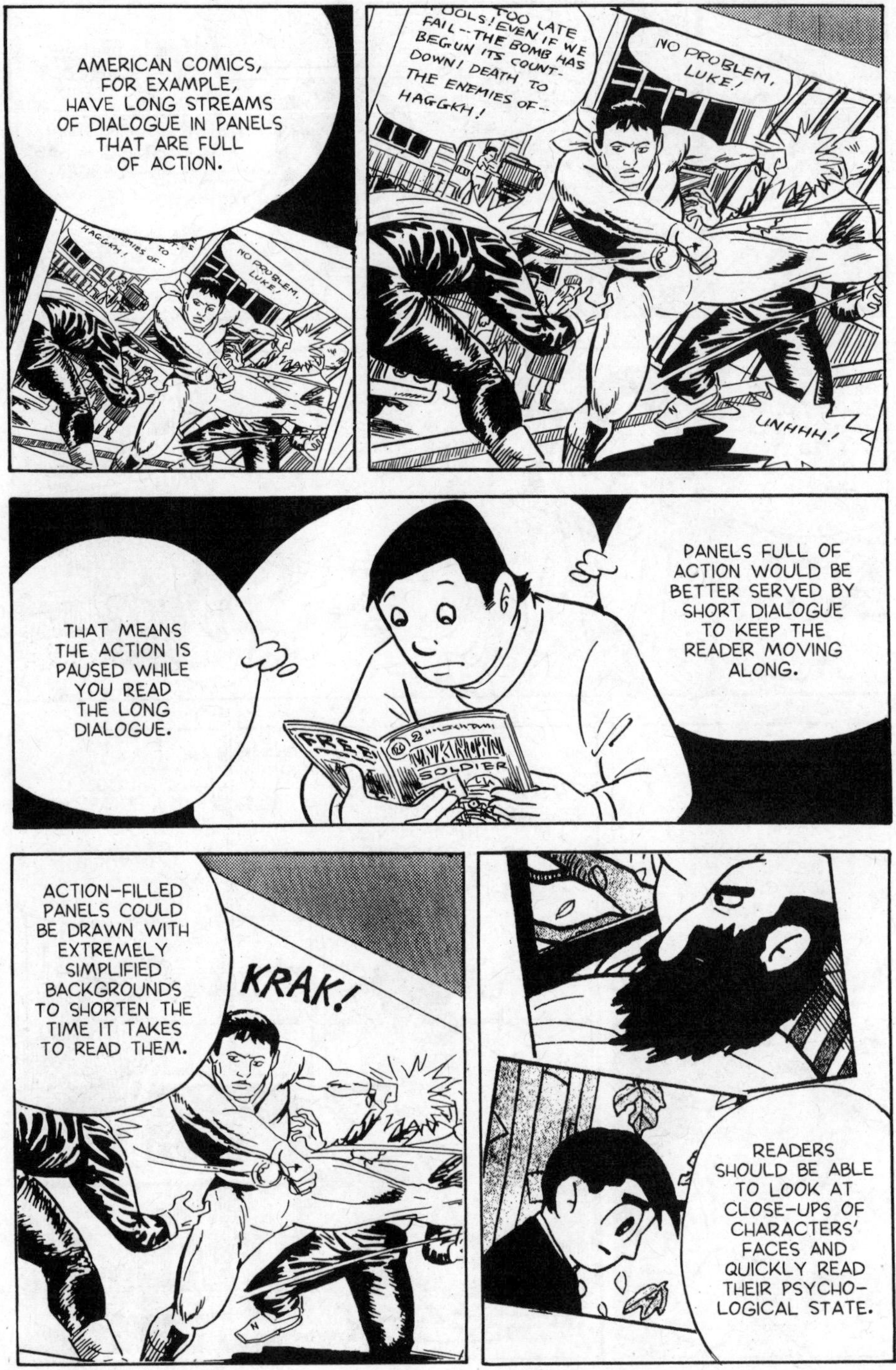
AMERICAN COMICS, FOR EXAMPLE, HAVE LONG STREAMS OF DIALOGUE IN PANELS THAT ARE FULL OF ACTION.
NO PROBLEM, LUKE!
FOOLS! TOO LATE EVEN IF WE FAIL--THE BOMB HAS BEGUN ITS COUNT-DOWN! DEATH TO THE ENEMIES OF-- HAGGKH!
NO PROBLEM, LUKE!
UNHHH!
THAT MEANS THE ACTION IS PAUSED WHILE YOU READ THE LONG DIALOGUE.
SOLDIER
PANELS FULL OF ACTION WOULD BE BETTER SERVED BY SHORT DIALOGUE TO KEEP THE READER MOVING ALONG.
ACTION-FILLED PANELS COULD BE DRAWN WITH EXTREMELY SIMPLIFIED BACKGROUNDS TO SHORTEN THE TIME IT TAKES TO READ THEM.
KRAK!
READERS SHOULD BE ABLE TO LOOK AT CLOSE-UPS OF CHARACTERS' FACES AND QUICKLY READ THEIR PSYCHO-LOGICAL STATE.

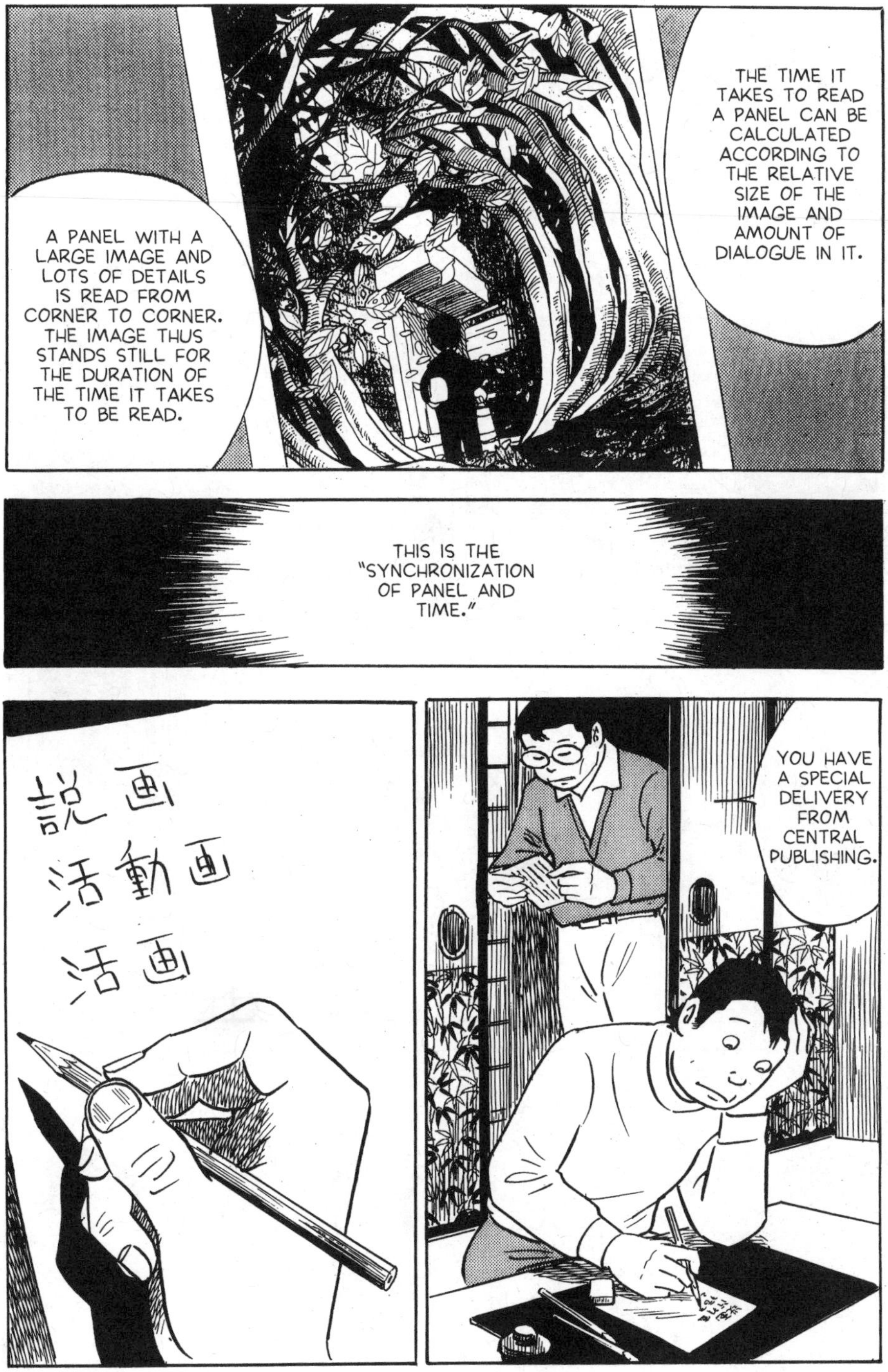
A PANEL WITH A LARGE IMAGE AND LOTS OF DETAILS IS READ FROM CORNER TO CORNER. THE IMAGE THUS STANDS STILL FOR THE DURATION OF THE TIME IT TAKES TO BE READ.
THE TIME IT TAKES TO READ A PANEL CAN BE CALCULATED ACCORDING TO THE RELATIVE SIZE OF THE IMAGE AND AMOUNT OF DIALOGUE IN IT.
THIS IS THE "SYNCHRONIZATION OF PANEL AND TIME."
説画
活動画
活画
YOU HAVE A SPECIAL DELIVERY FROM CENTRAL PUBLISHING.

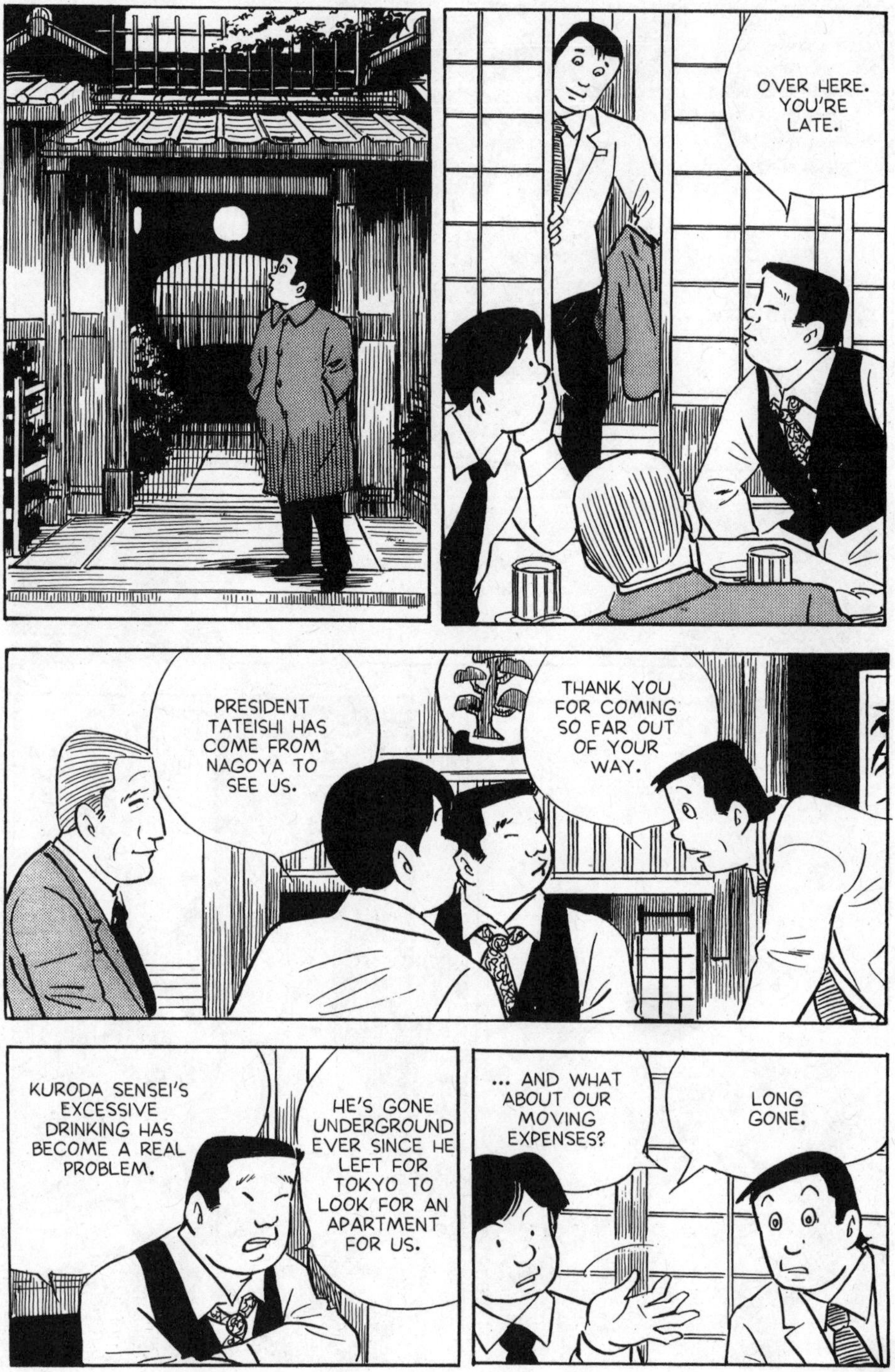

OVER HERE. YOU'RE LATE.
PRESIDENT TATEISHI HAS COME FROM NAGOYA TO SEE US.
THANK YOU FOR COMING SO FAR OUT OF YOUR WAY.
KURODA SENSEI'S EXCESSIVE DRINKING HAS BECOME A REAL PROBLEM.
HE'S GONE UNDERGROUND EVER SINCE HE LEFT FOR TOKYO TO LOOK FOR AN APARTMENT FOR US.
... AND WHAT ABOUT OUR MOVING EXPENSES?
LONG GONE.

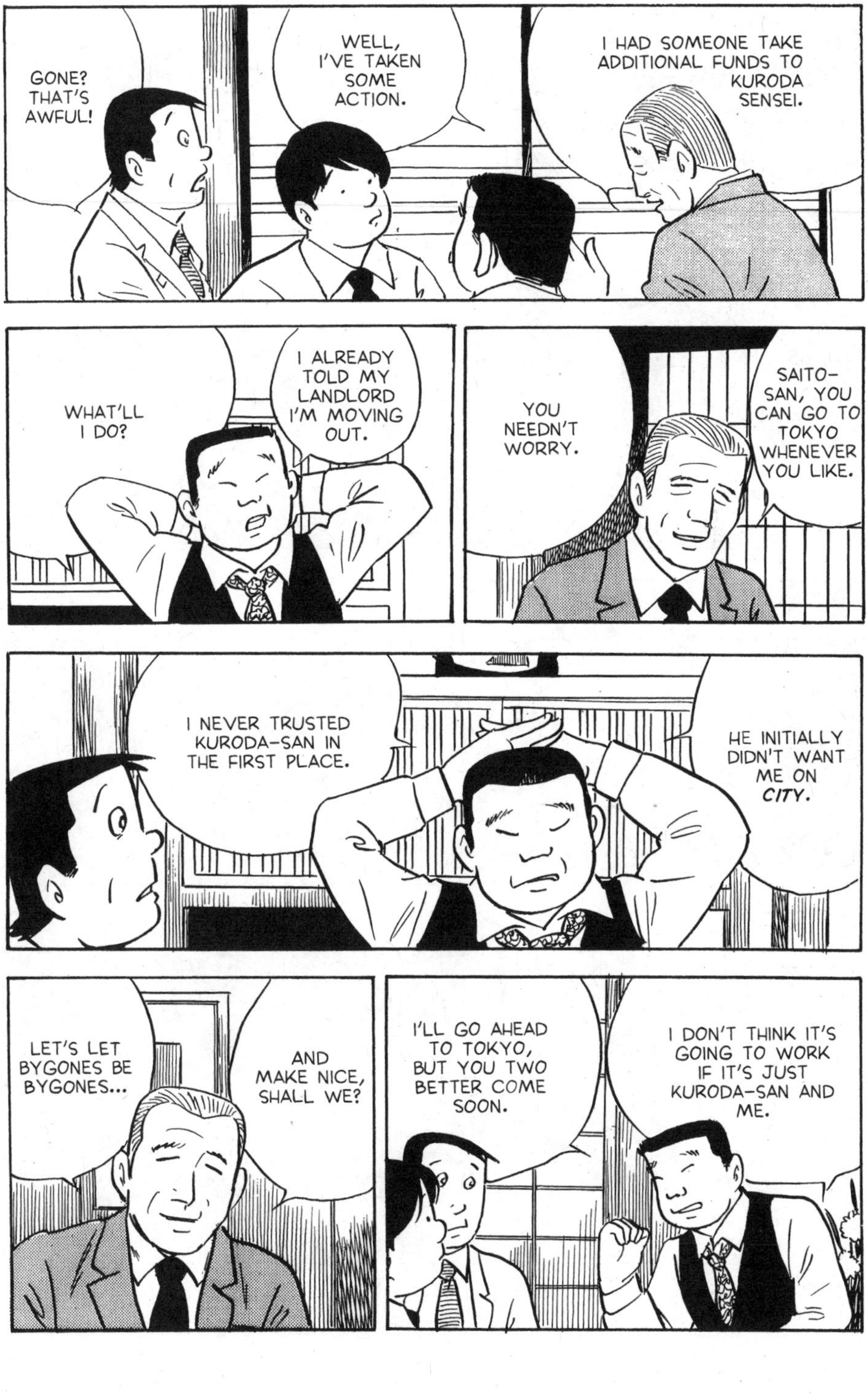
GONE? THAT'S AWFUL!
WELL, I'VE TAKEN SOME ACTION.
I HAD SOMEONE TAKE ADDITIONAL FUNDS TO KURODA SENSEI.
WHAT'LL I DO?
I ALREADY TOLD MY LANDLORD I'M MOVING OUT.
YOU NEEDN'T WORRY.
SAITO-SAN, YOU CAN GO TO TOKYO WHENEVER YOU LIKE.
I NEVER TRUSTED KURODA-SAN IN THE FIRST PLACE.
HE INITIALLY DIDN'T WANT ME ON *CITY*.
LET'S LET BYGONES BE BYGONES...
AND MAKE NICE, SHALL WE?
I'LL GO AHEAD TO TOKYO, BUT YOU TWO BETTER COME SOON.
I DON'T THINK IT'S GOING TO WORK IF IT'S JUST KURODA-SAN AND ME.

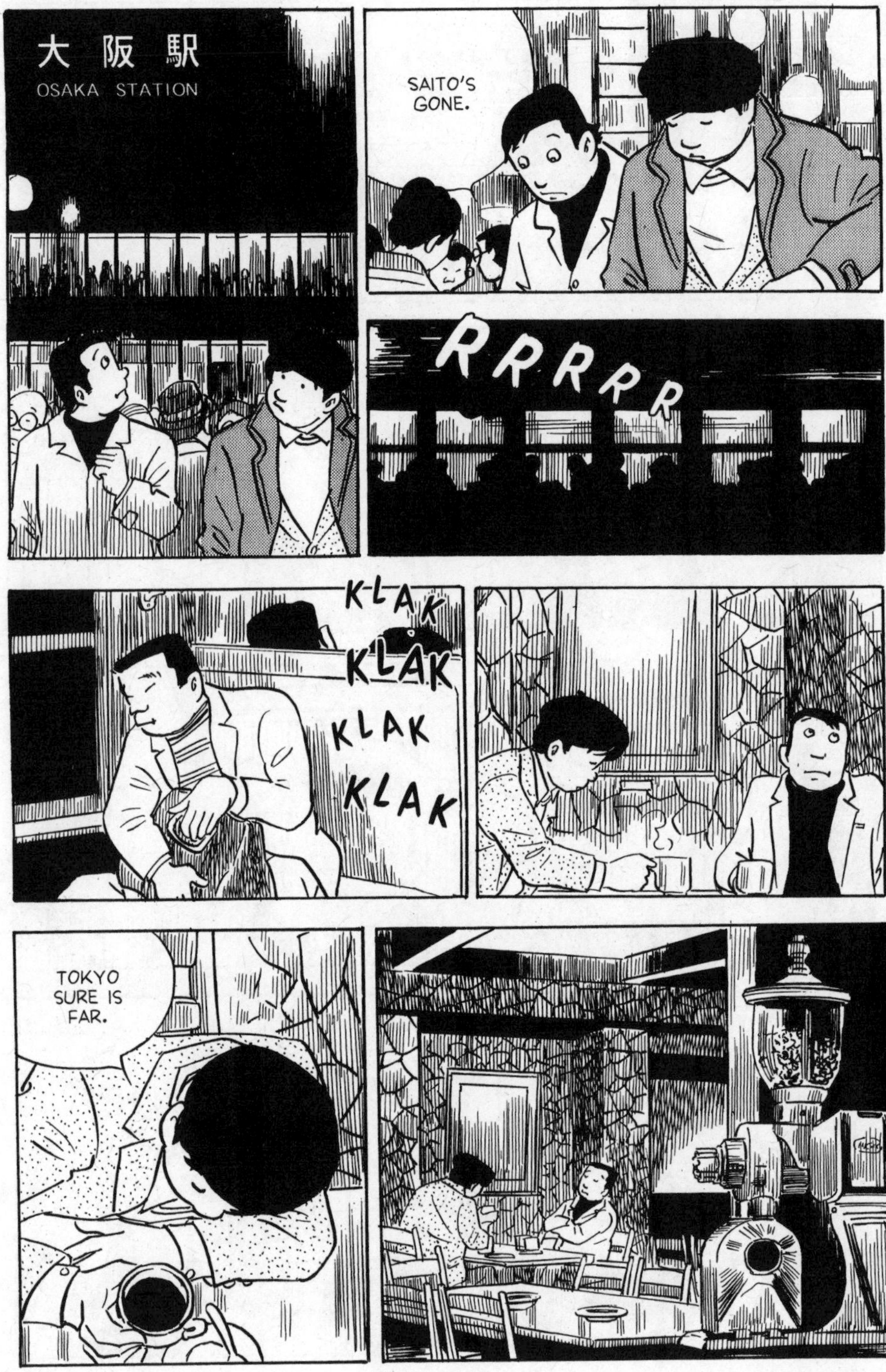
大阪駅
OSAKA STATION
SAITO'S GONE.
RRRRRR
KLAK
KLAK
KLAK
KLAK
TOKYO SURE IS FAR.

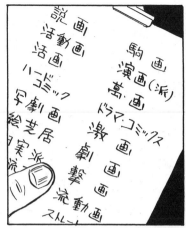

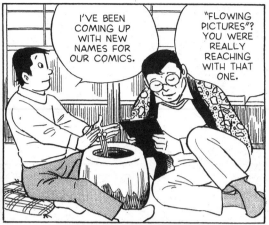

駒画
演画(派)
ドラマ・コミックス
激画
劇画
撃画
流動画
説画
活動画
活画
ハードコミック
写劇画
絵芝居
I'VE BEEN COMING UP WITH NEW NAMES FOR OUR COMICS.
"FLOWING PICTURES"? YOU WERE REALLY REACHING WITH THAT ONE.
YOU'VE INCLUDED MATSUMOTO'S "KOMAGA."
IT'S AN OPTION.
I WANT YOU TO CHOOSE ONE BY PROCESS OF ELIMINATION.
WHY DOES MATSUMOTO LIKE "KOMAGA"?
YOU GUYS TALK ABOUT METHODOLOGY AND STUFF A LOT, DON'T YOU?
NO, NOT AT ALL.
ACTUALLY ALL WE'VE BEEN DOING LATELY IS BITCHING ABOUT HINOMARU.
"SESTUGA" IS INTERESTING...
OKAY, I'M ELIMINATING.
説画
活動画
活画

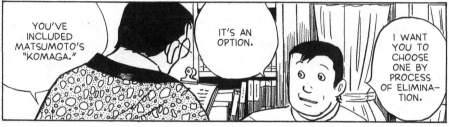

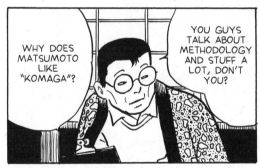

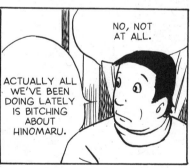

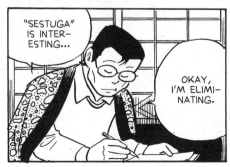

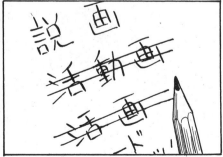

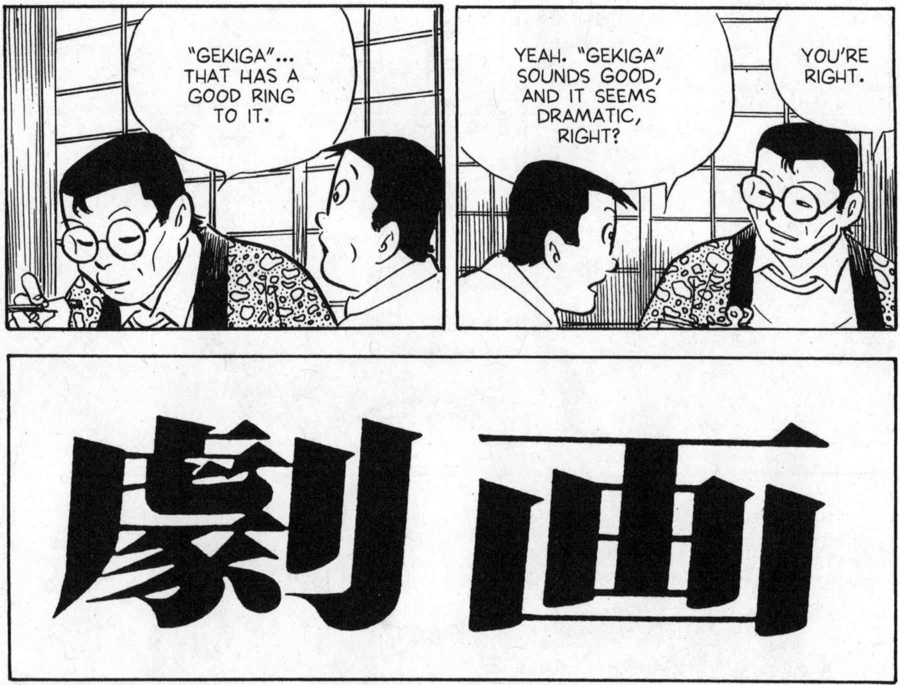
"GEKIGA"... THAT HAS A GOOD RING TO IT.
YEAH. "GEKIGA" SOUNDS GOOD, AND IT SEEMS DRAMATIC, RIGHT?
YOU'RE RIGHT.
劇画
TEXT: GEKIGA

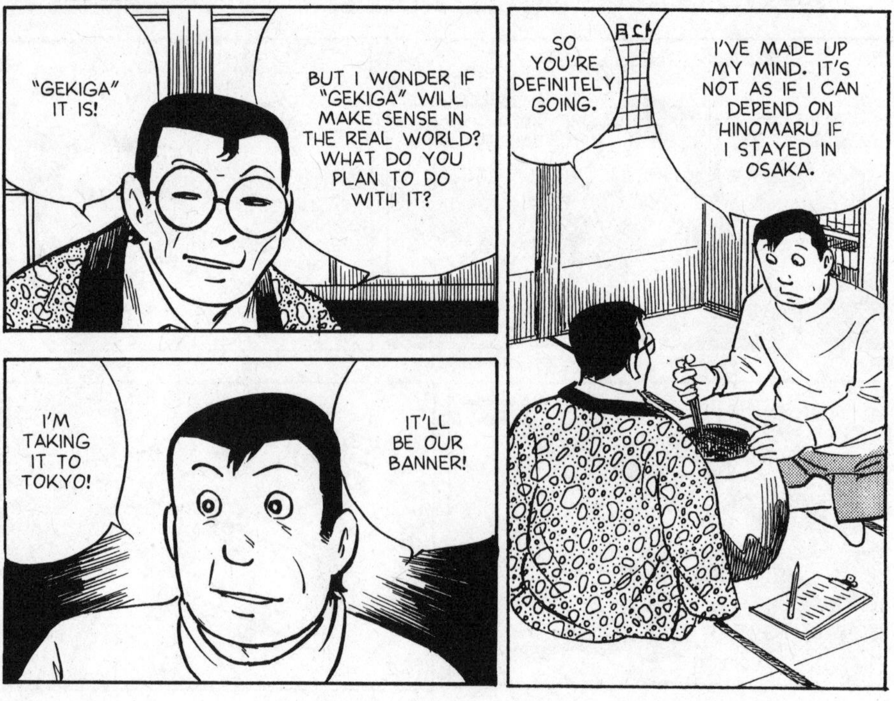
"GEKIGA" IT IS!
BUT I WONDER IF "GEKIGA" WILL MAKE SENSE IN THE REAL WORLD? WHAT DO YOU PLAN TO DO WITH IT?
I'M TAKING IT TO TOKYO!
IT'LL BE OUR BANNER!
SO YOU'RE DEFINITELY GOING.
I'VE MADE UP MY MIND. IT'S NOT AS IF I CAN DEPEND ON HINOMARU IF I STAYED IN OSAKA.

SIGN: HINOMARU BUNKO CO., LTD. / KOEISHA

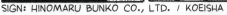

FWIP
FWIP

OUCH!

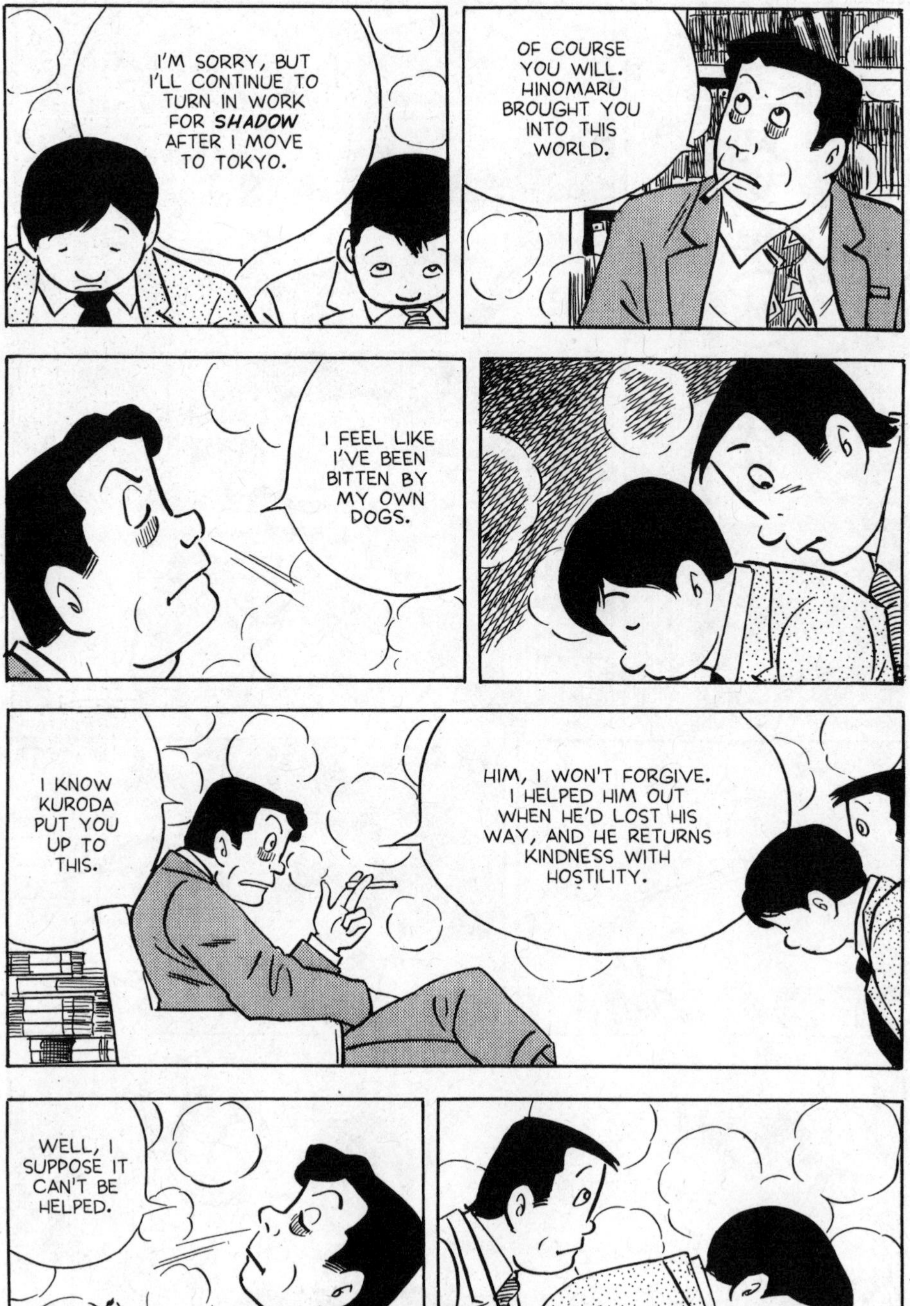
I'M SORRY, BUT I'LL CONTINUE TO TURN IN WORK FOR *SHADOW* AFTER I MOVE TO TOKYO.
OF COURSE YOU WILL. HINOMARU BROUGHT YOU INTO THIS WORLD.
I FEEL LIKE I'VE BEEN BITTEN BY MY OWN DOGS.
I KNOW KURODA PUT YOU UP TO THIS.
HIM, I WON'T FORGIVE. I HELPED HIM OUT WHEN HE'D LOST HIS WAY, AND HE RETURNS KINDNESS WITH HOSTILITY.
WELL, I SUPPOSE IT CAN'T BE HELPED.

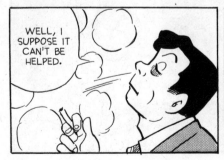

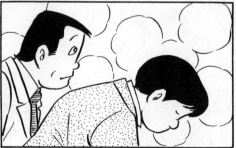

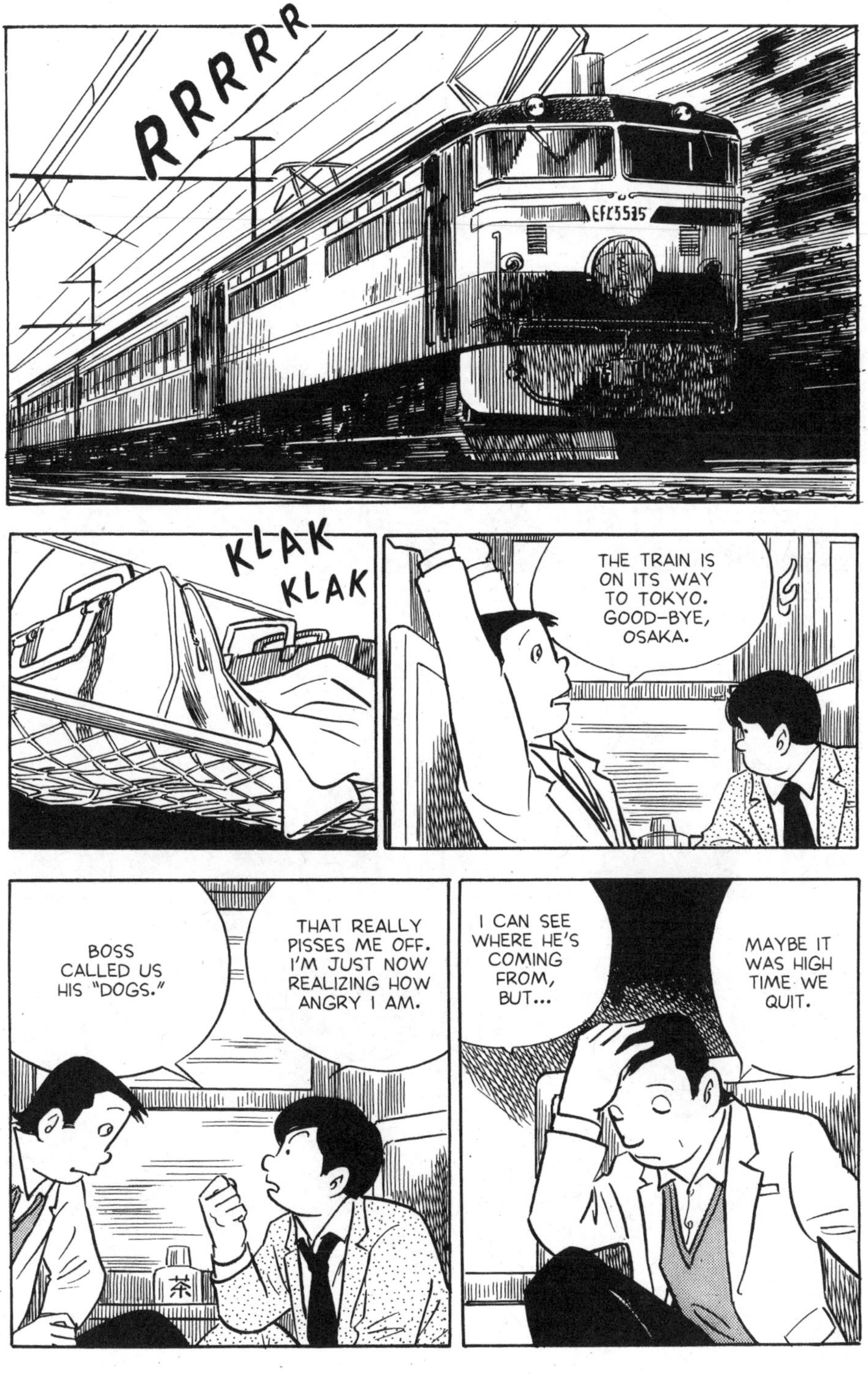
RRRRR
KLAK KLAK
THE TRAIN IS ON ITS WAY TO TOKYO. GOOD-BYE, OSAKA.
BOSS CALLED US HIS "DOGS."
THAT REALLY PISSES ME OFF. I'M JUST NOW REALIZING HOW ANGRY I AM.
茶
I CAN SEE WHERE HE'S COMING FROM, BUT...
MAYBE IT WAS HIGH TIME WE QUIT.

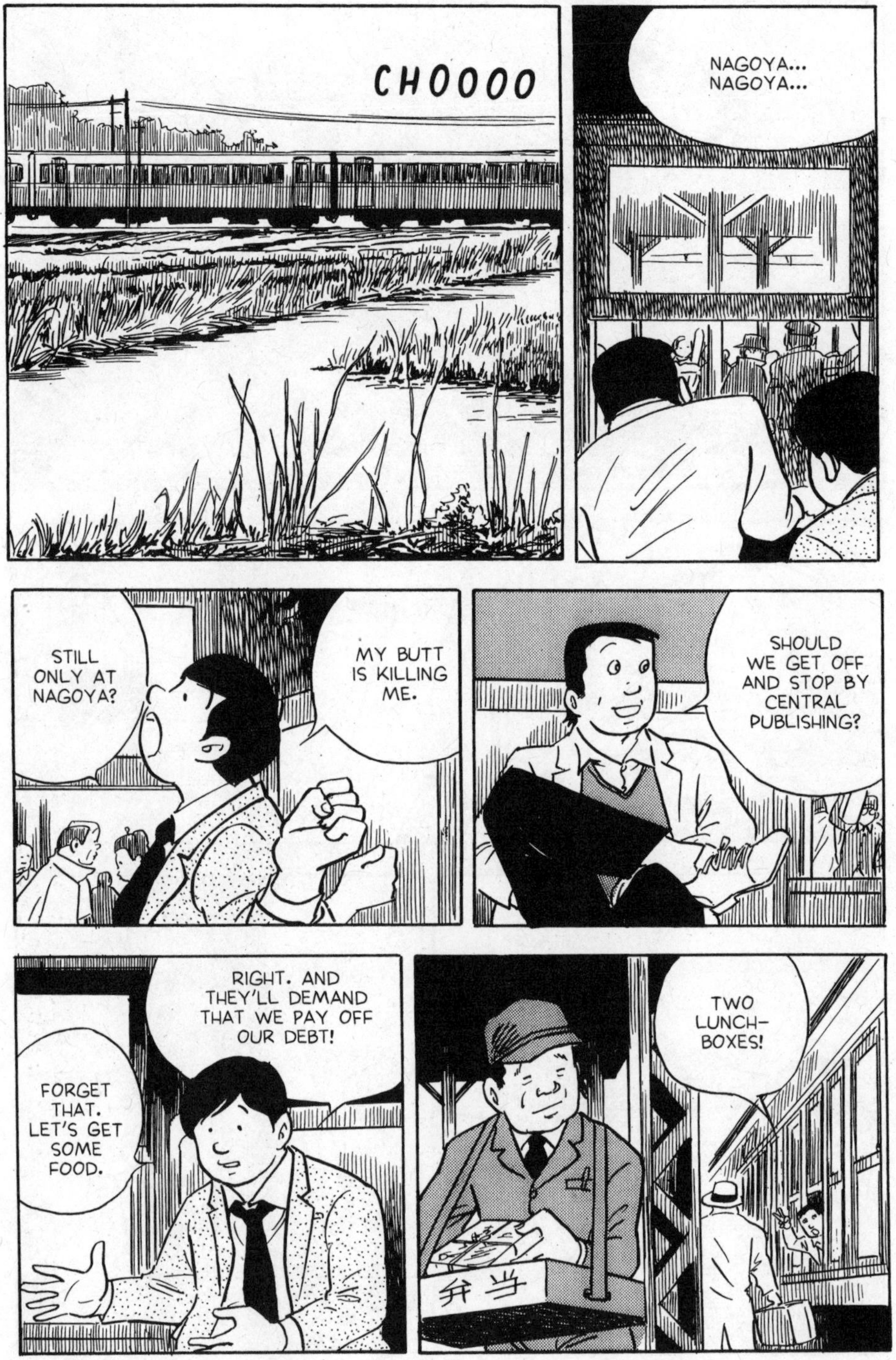
CHOOOO
NAGOYA... NAGOYA...
STILL ONLY AT NAGOYA?
MY BUTT IS KILLING ME.
SHOULD WE GET OFF AND STOP BY CENTRAL PUBLISHING?
RIGHT. AND THEY'LL DEMAND THAT WE PAY OFF OUR DEBT!
FORGET THAT. LET'S GET SOME FOOD.
TWO LUNCH-BOXES!
弁当

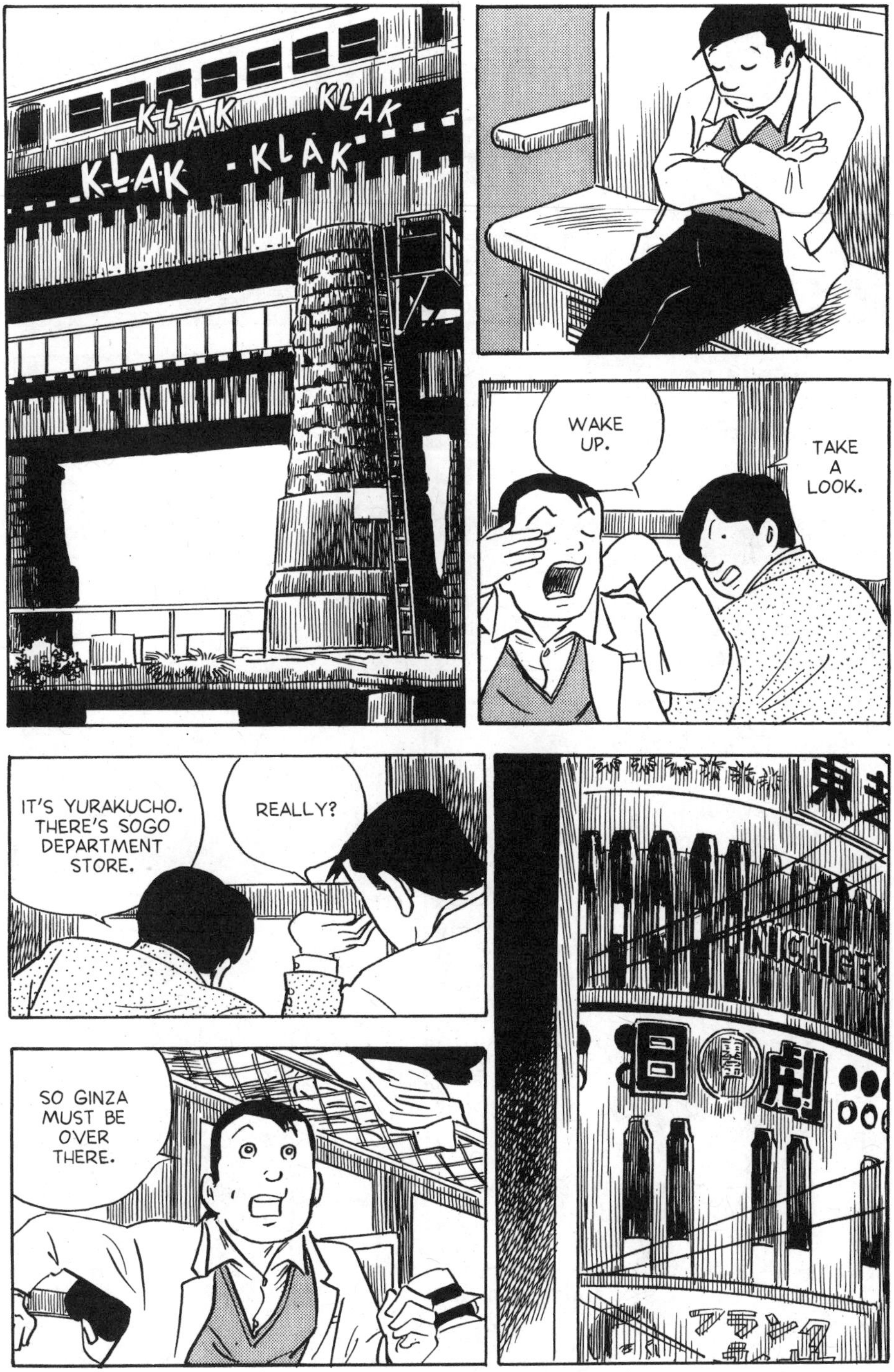
KLAK KLAK
KLAK KLAK
WAKE UP.
TAKE A LOOK.
IT'S YURAKUCHO. THERE'S SOGO DEPARTMENT STORE.
REALLY?
SO GINZA MUST BE OVER THERE.

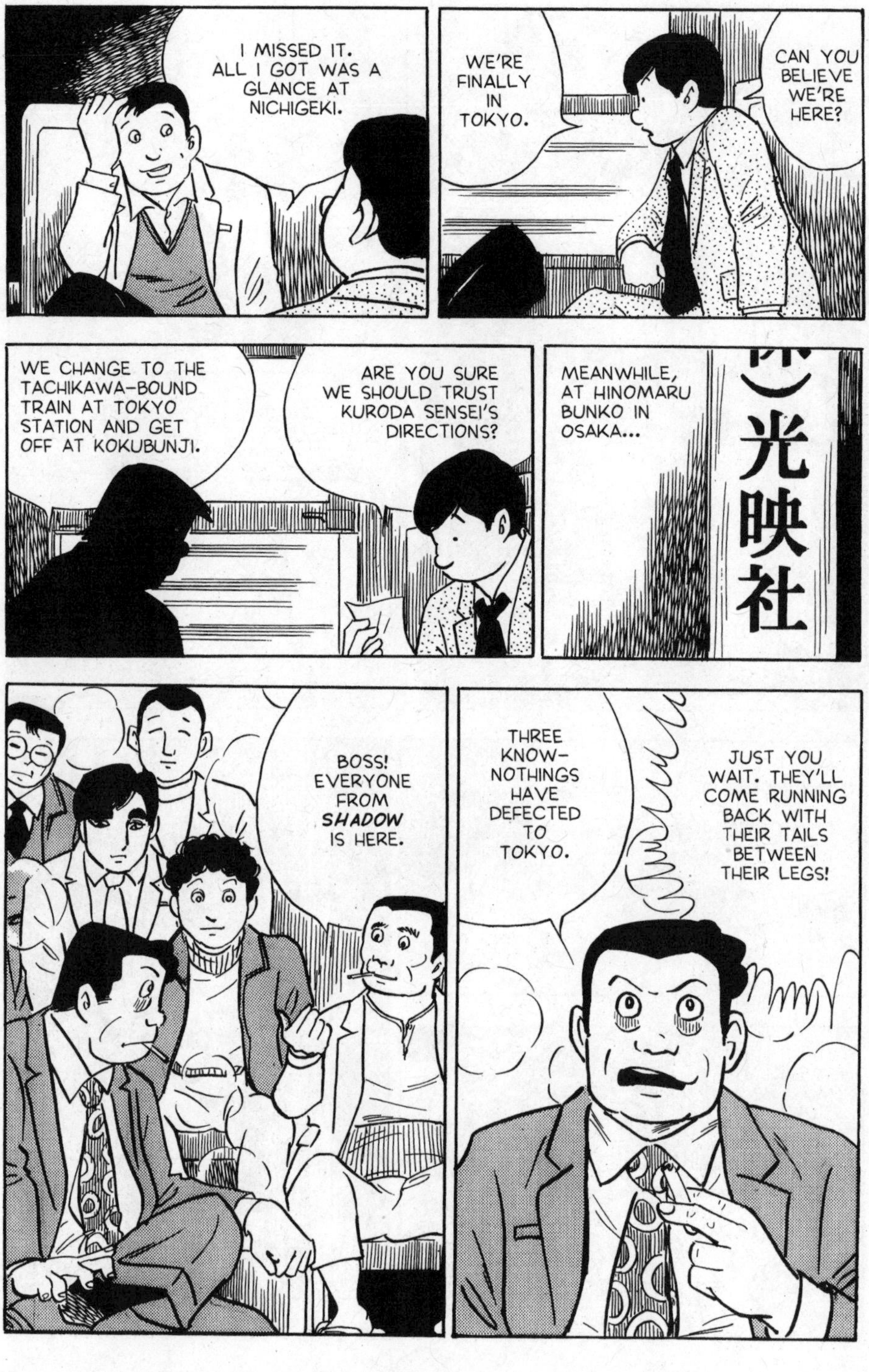
I MISSED IT. ALL I GOT WAS A GLANCE AT NICHIGEKI.
WE'RE FINALLY IN TOKYO.
CAN YOU BELIEVE WE'RE HERE?
WE CHANGE TO THE TACHIKAWA-BOUND TRAIN AT TOKYO STATION AND GET OFF AT KOKUBUNJI.
ARE YOU SURE WE SHOULD TRUST KURODA SENSEI'S DIRECTIONS?
MEANWHILE, AT HINOMARU BUNKO IN OSAKA...
光映社
BOSS! EVERYONE FROM *SHADOW* IS HERE.
THREE KNOW-NOTHINGS HAVE DEFECTED TO TOKYO.
JUST YOU WAIT. THEY'LL COME RUNNING BACK WITH THEIR TAILS BETWEEN THEIR LEGS!

KOTOBUKISO DAYS

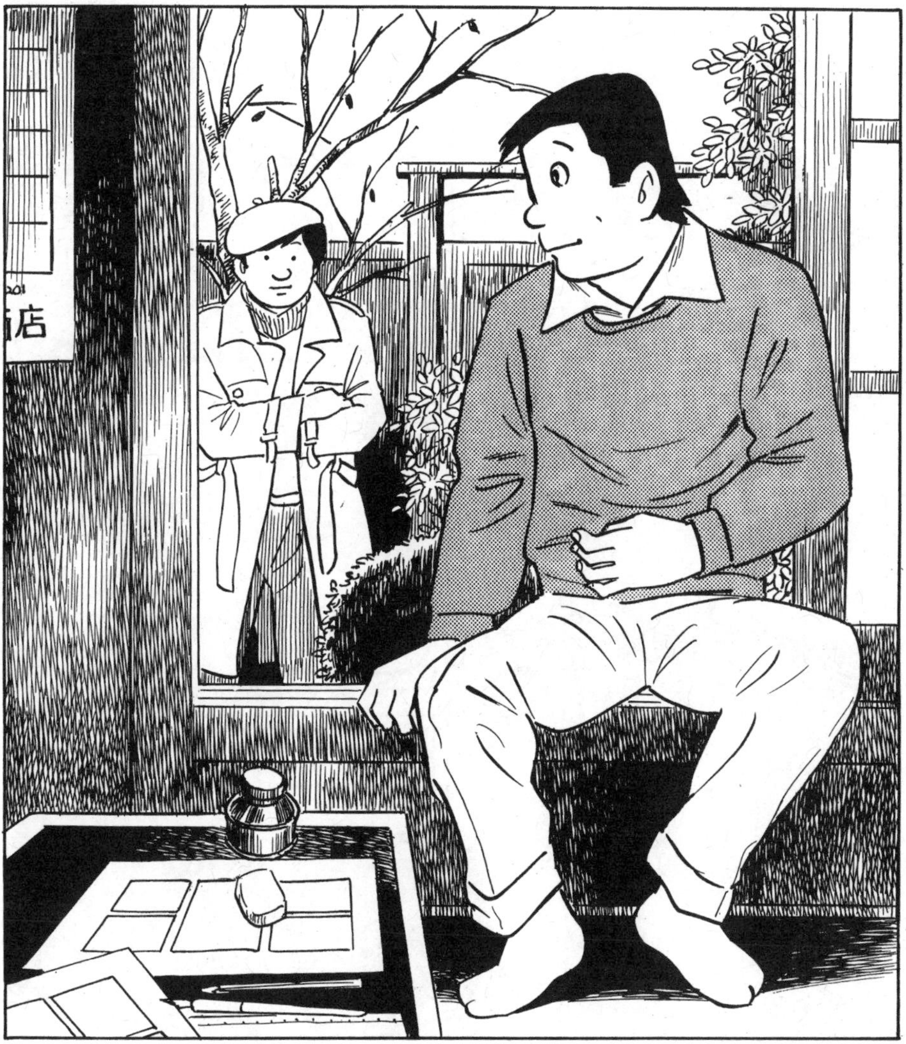

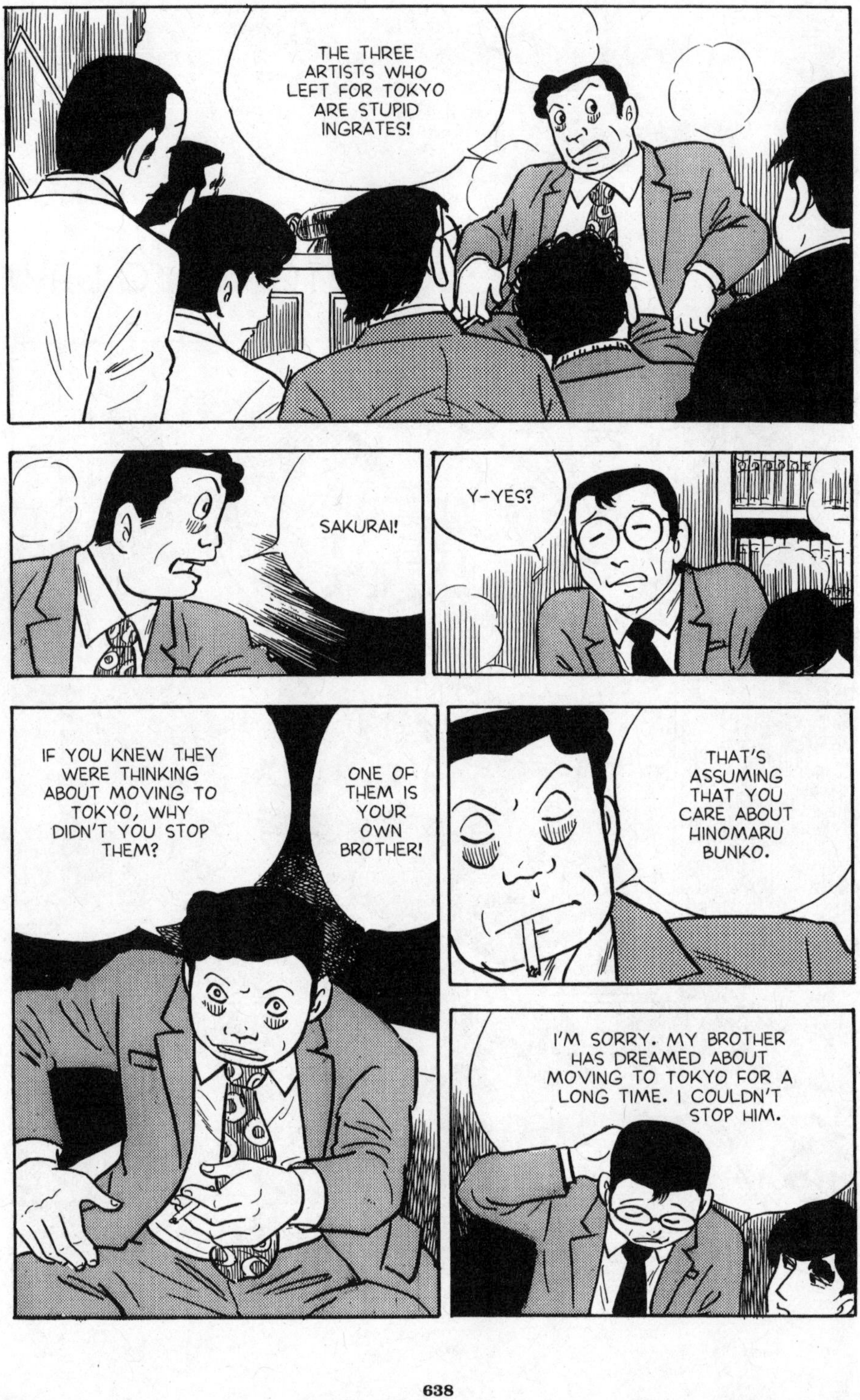
THE THREE ARTISTS WHO LEFT FOR TOKYO ARE STUPID INGRATES!
SAKURAI!
Y-YES?
IF YOU KNEW THEY WERE THINKING ABOUT MOVING TO TOKYO, WHY DIDN'T YOU STOP THEM?
ONE OF THEM IS YOUR OWN BROTHER!
THAT'S ASSUMING THAT YOU CARE ABOUT HINOMARU BUNKO.
I'M SORRY. MY BROTHER HAS DREAMED ABOUT MOVING TO TOKYO FOR A LONG TIME. I COULDN'T STOP HIM.

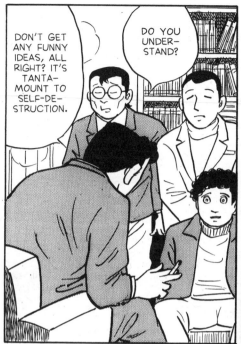

DON'T GET ANY FUNNY IDEAS, ALL RIGHT? IT'S TANTA-MOUNT TO SELF-DE-STRUCTION.
DO YOU UNDER-STAND?
FRANKLY, NOW THAT THOSE THREE HAVE LEFT, IT'S UP TO YOU TO KEEP ***SHADOW*** EXCITING.
I'VE CALLED YOU ALL HERE TODAY TO ASK YOU TO DO JUST THAT.
PHEW...
SO DON'T YOU EVEN ***THINK*** ABOUT GOING TO TOKYO.
AND KEEP YOUR FEET FIRMLY ON THE GROUND.
THANKS TO YOU GUYS, ***SHADOW***'S BEEN SELLING OUT EVERY MONTH AND CIRCULATION IS GROWING.

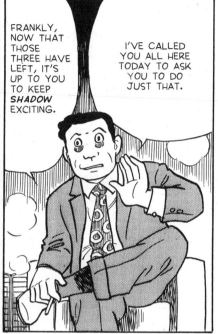

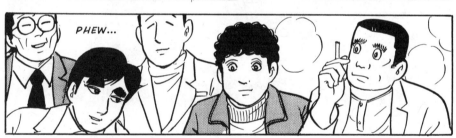

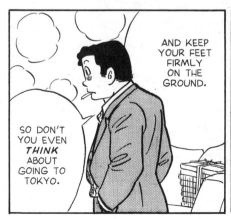

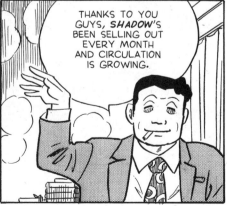

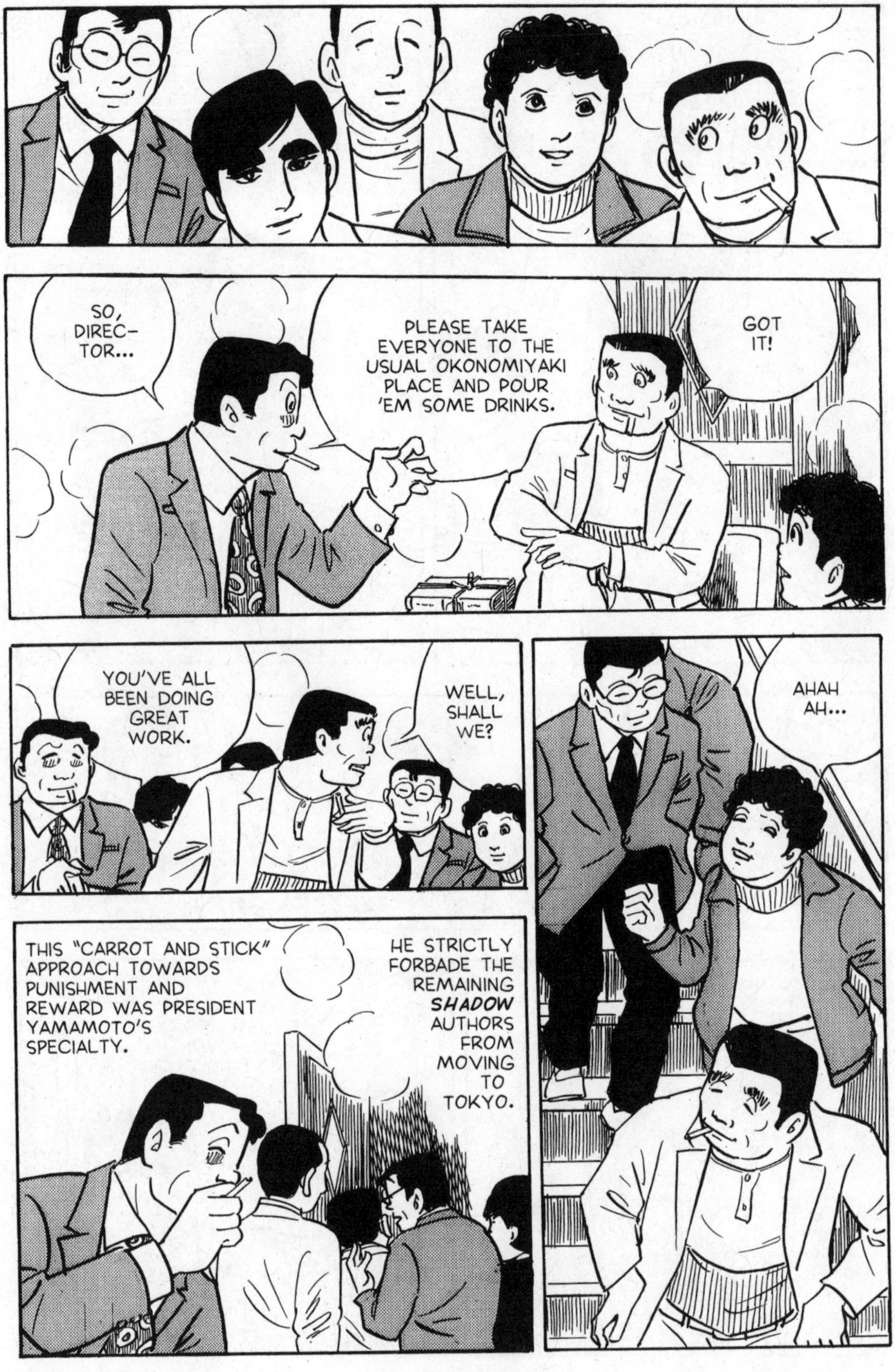
SO, DIREC- TOR...
PLEASE TAKE EVERYONE TO THE USUAL OKONOMIYAKI PLACE AND POUR 'EM SOME DRINKS.
GOT IT!
YOU'VE ALL BEEN DOING GREAT WORK.
WELL, SHALL WE?
THIS "CARROT AND STICK" APPROACH TOWARDS PUNISHMENT AND REWARD WAS PRESIDENT YAMAMOTO'S SPECIALTY.
HE STRICTLY FORBADE THE REMAINING *SHADOW* AUTHORS FROM MOVING TO TOKYO.
AHAH AH...

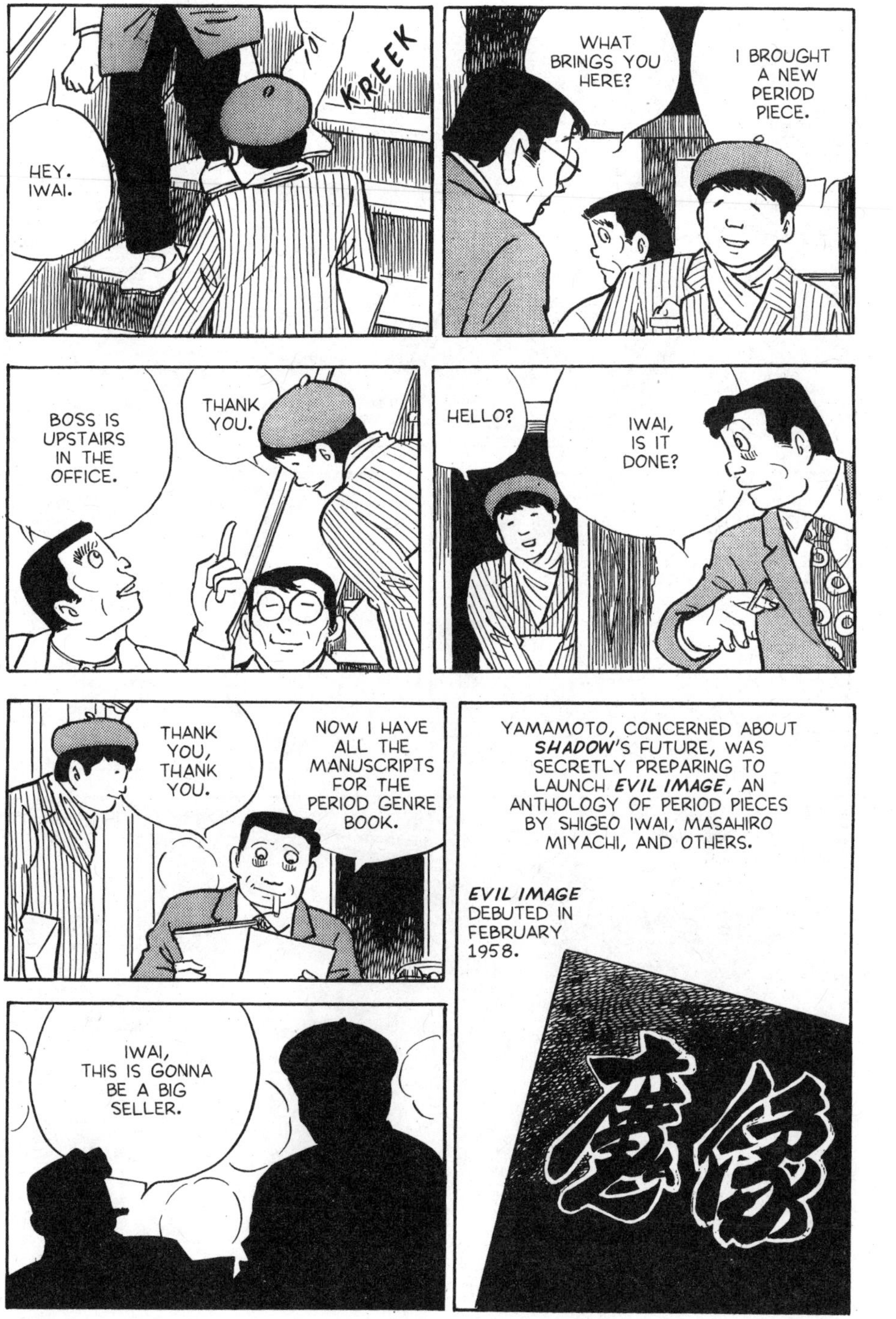
HEY. IWAI.
KREEK
WHAT BRINGS YOU HERE?
I BROUGHT A NEW PERIOD PIECE.
BOSS IS UPSTAIRS IN THE OFFICE.
THANK YOU.
HELLO?
IWAI, IS IT DONE?
THANK YOU, THANK YOU.
NOW I HAVE ALL THE MANUSCRIPTS FOR THE PERIOD GENRE BOOK.
IWAI, THIS IS GONNA BE A BIG SELLER.
YAMAMOTO, CONCERNED ABOUT ***SHADOW***'S FUTURE, WAS SECRETLY PREPARING TO LAUNCH ***EVIL IMAGE***, AN ANTHOLOGY OF PERIOD PIECES BY SHIGEO IWAI, MASAHIRO MIYACHI, AND OTHERS.
EVIL IMAGE DEBUTED IN FEBRUARY 1958.
魔像

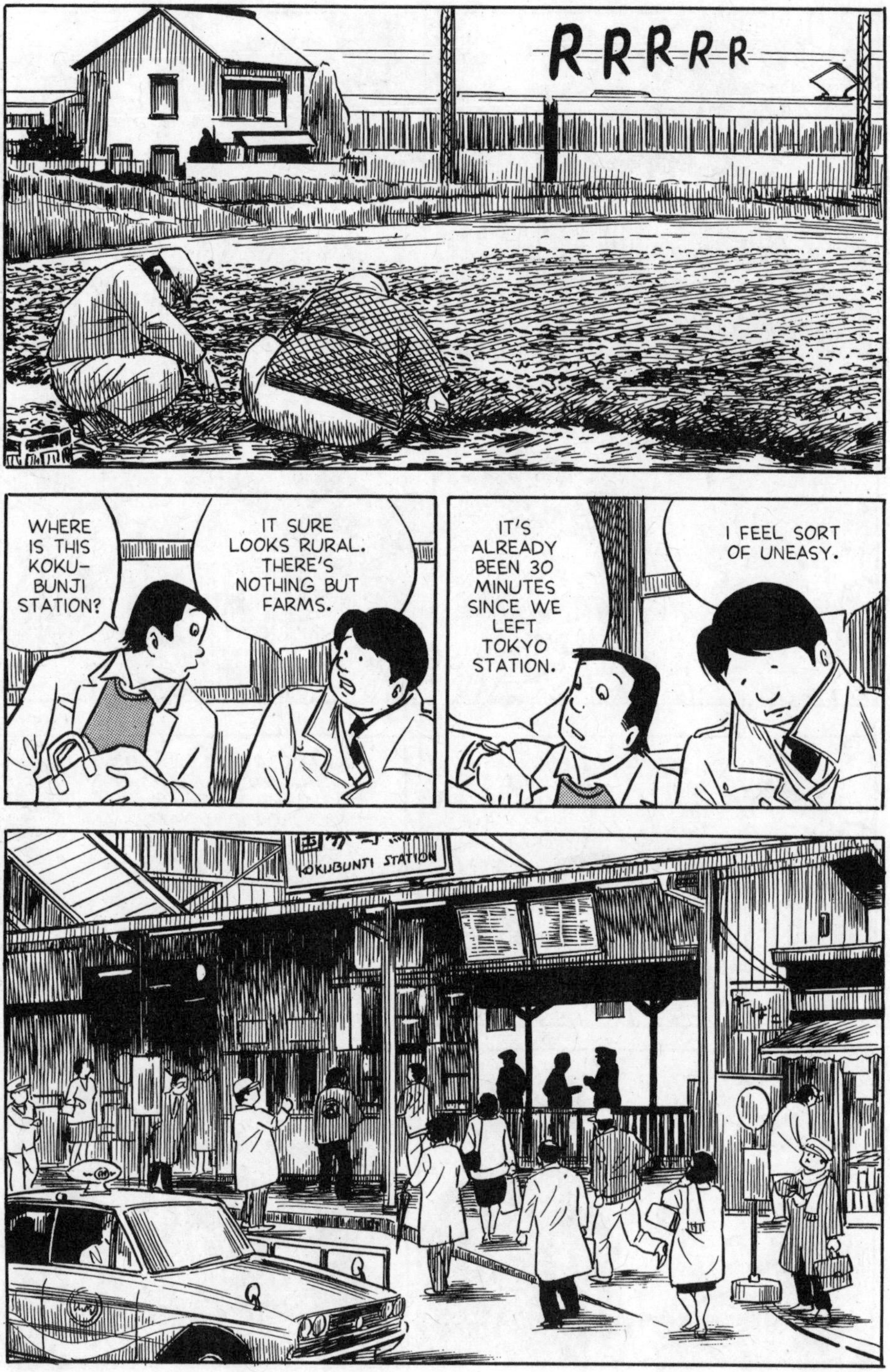
RRRRR
WHERE IS THIS KOKU-BUNJI STATION?
IT SURE LOOKS RURAL. THERE'S NOTHING BUT FARMS.
IT'S ALREADY BEEN 30 MINUTES SINCE WE LEFT TOKYO STATION.
I FEEL SORT OF UNEASY.
KOKUBUNJI STATION

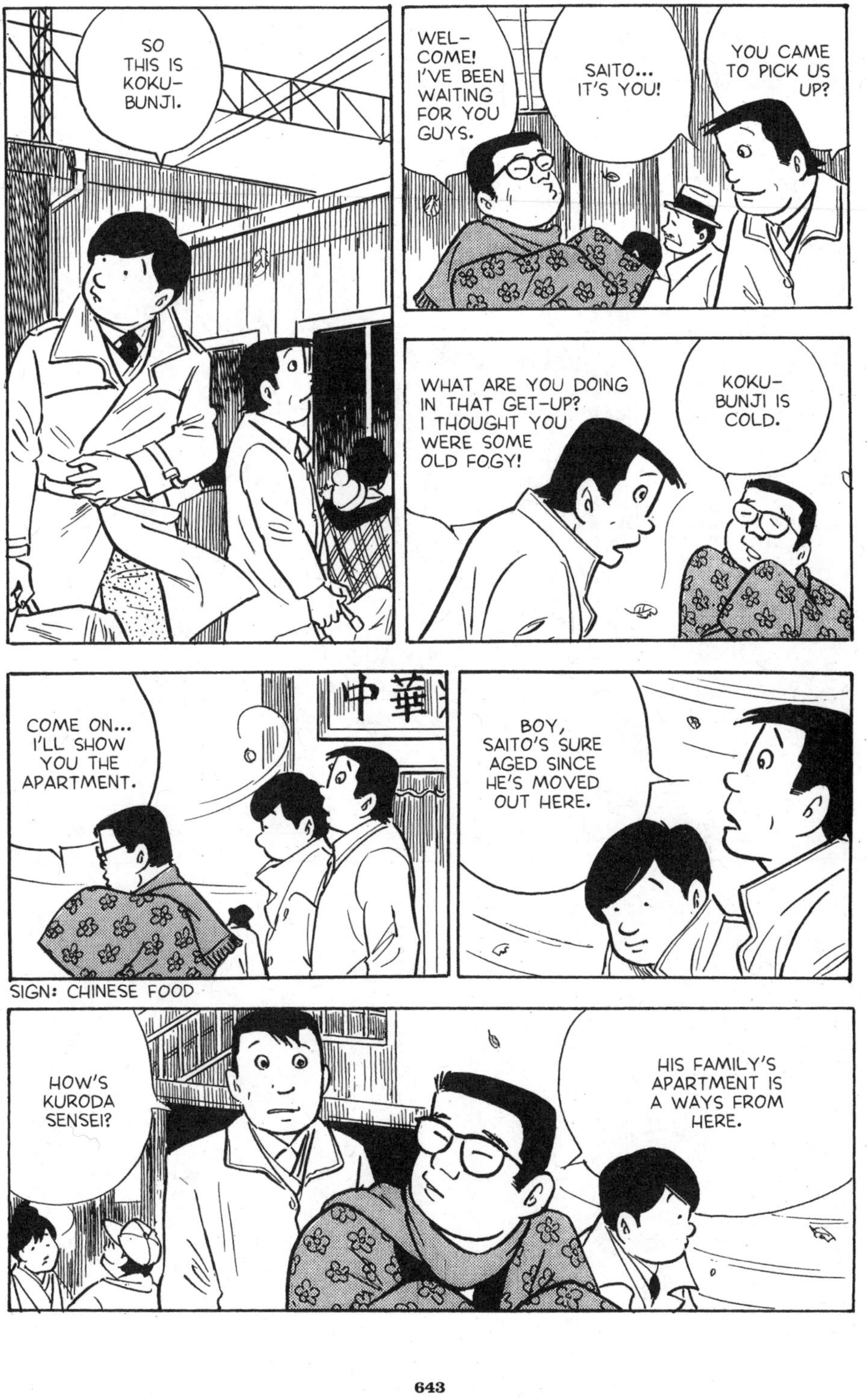
SO THIS IS KOKU-BUNJI.
WEL-COME! I'VE BEEN WAITING FOR YOU GUYS.
SAITO... IT'S YOU!
YOU CAME TO PICK US UP?
WHAT ARE YOU DOING IN THAT GET-UP? I THOUGHT YOU WERE SOME OLD FOGY!
KOKU-BUNJI IS COLD.
COME ON... I'LL SHOW YOU THE APARTMENT.
BOY, SAITO'S SURE AGED SINCE HE'S MOVED OUT HERE.
SIGN: CHINESE FOOD
HOW'S KURODA SENSEI?
HIS FAMILY'S APARTMENT IS A WAYS FROM HERE.

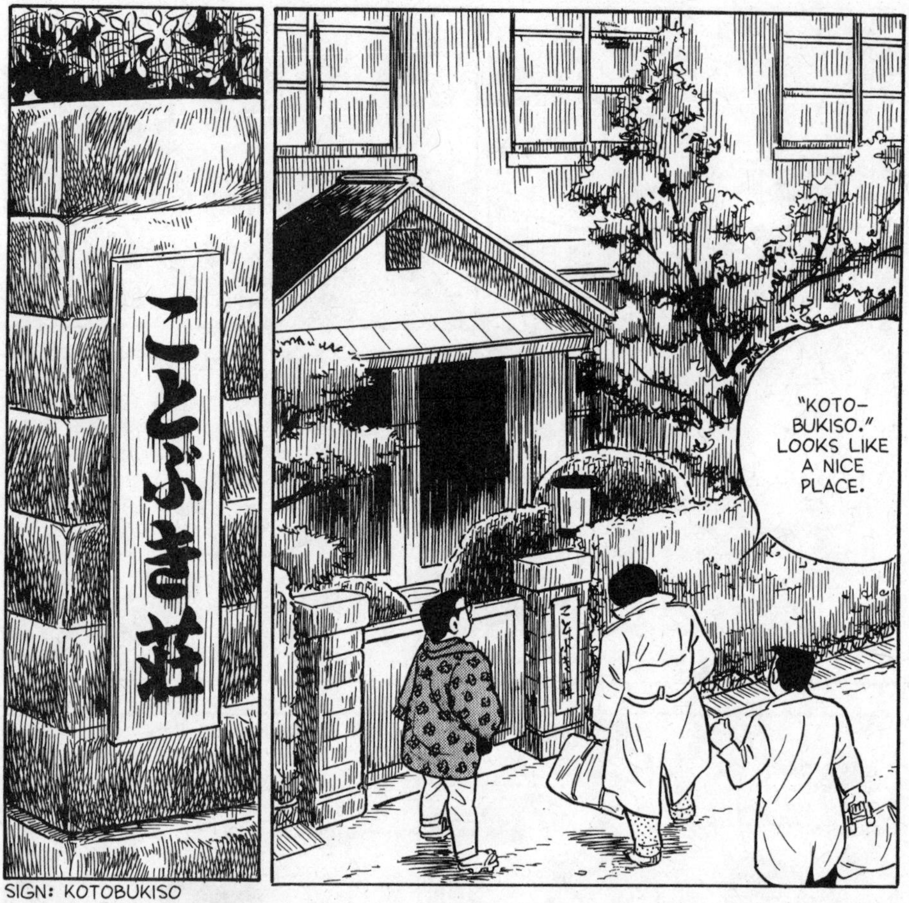
ことぶき荘
"KOTO-BUKISO." LOOKS LIKE A NICE PLACE.
SIGN: KOTOBUKISO

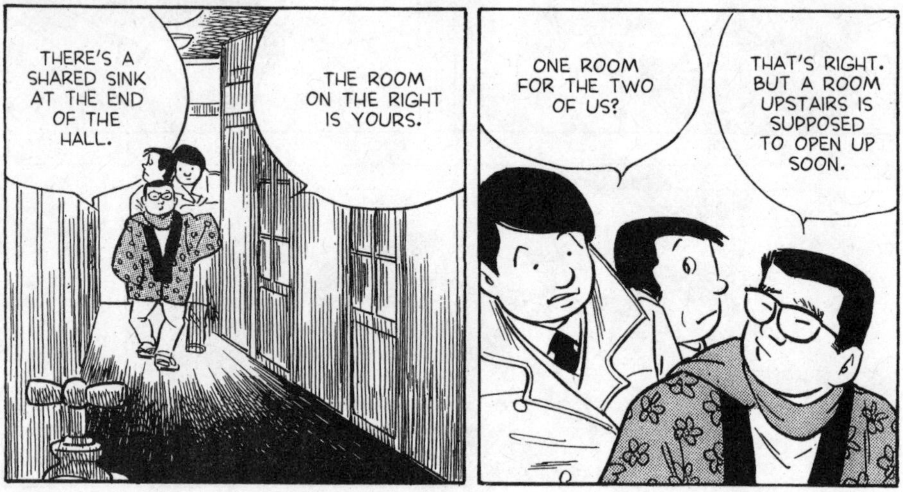
THERE'S A SHARED SINK AT THE END OF THE HALL.
THE ROOM ON THE RIGHT IS YOURS.
ONE ROOM FOR THE TWO OF US?
THAT'S RIGHT. BUT A ROOM UPSTAIRS IS SUPPOSED TO OPEN UP SOON.

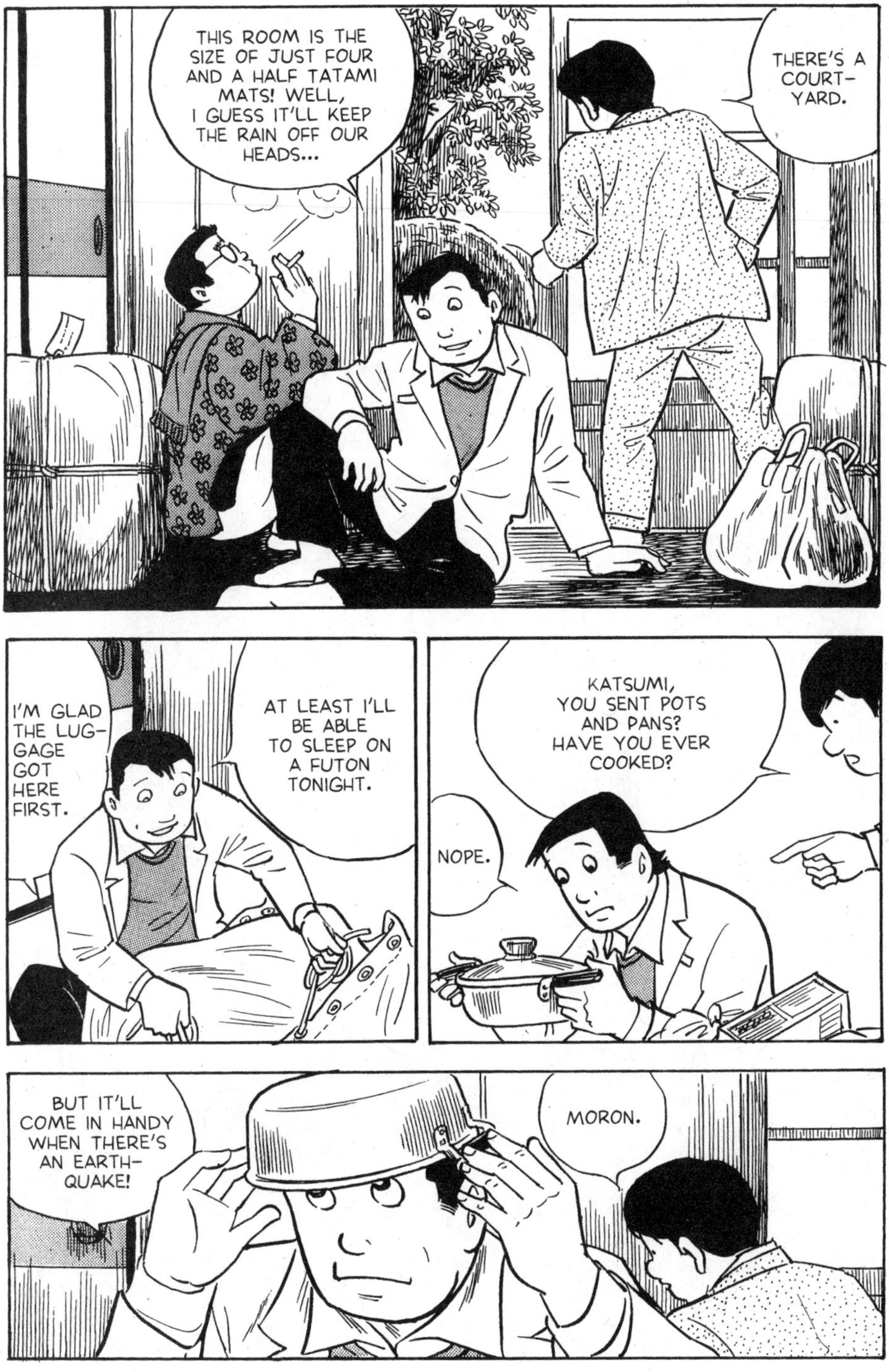
THIS ROOM IS THE SIZE OF JUST FOUR AND A HALF TATAMI MATS! WELL, I GUESS IT'LL KEEP THE RAIN OFF OUR HEADS...
THERE'S A COURT-YARD.
I'M GLAD THE LUG-GAGE GOT HERE FIRST.
AT LEAST I'LL BE ABLE TO SLEEP ON A FUTON TONIGHT.
KATSUMI, YOU SENT POTS AND PANS? HAVE YOU EVER COOKED?
NOPE.
BUT IT'LL COME IN HANDY WHEN THERE'S AN EARTH-QUAKE!
MORON.

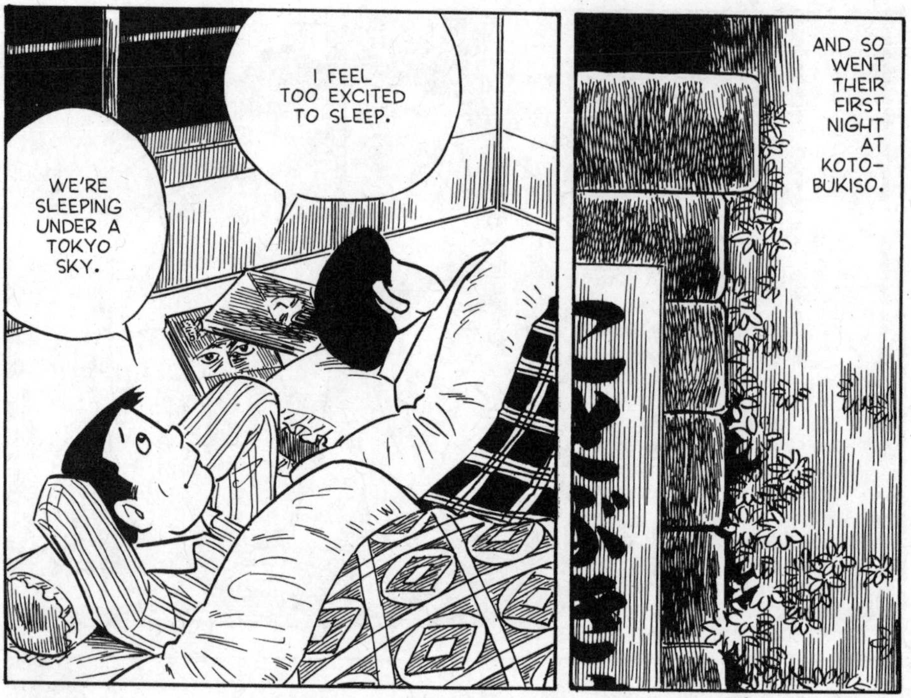
WE'RE SLEEPING UNDER A TOKYO SKY.
I FEEL TOO EXCITED TO SLEEP.
AND SO WENT THEIR FIRST NIGHT AT KOTO-BUKISO.

SIGN: KOTOBUKISO

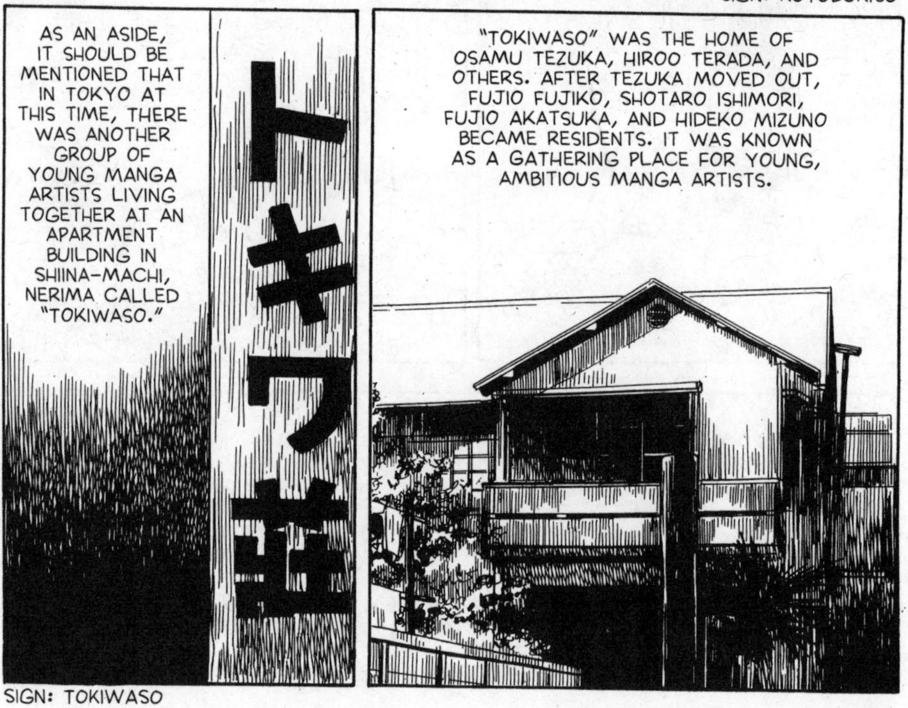
AS AN ASIDE, IT SHOULD BE MENTIONED THAT IN TOKYO AT THIS TIME, THERE WAS ANOTHER GROUP OF YOUNG MANGA ARTISTS LIVING TOGETHER AT AN APARTMENT BUILDING IN SHIINA-MACHI, NERIMA CALLED "TOKIWASO."
トキワ荘
"TOKIWASO" WAS THE HOME OF OSAMU TEZUKA, HIROO TERADA, AND OTHERS. AFTER TEZUKA MOVED OUT, FUJIO FUJIKO, SHOTARO ISHIMORI, FUJIO AKATSUKA, AND HIDEKO MIZUNO BECAME RESIDENTS. IT WAS KNOWN AS A GATHERING PLACE FOR YOUNG, AMBITIOUS MANGA ARTISTS.

SIGN: TOKIWASO

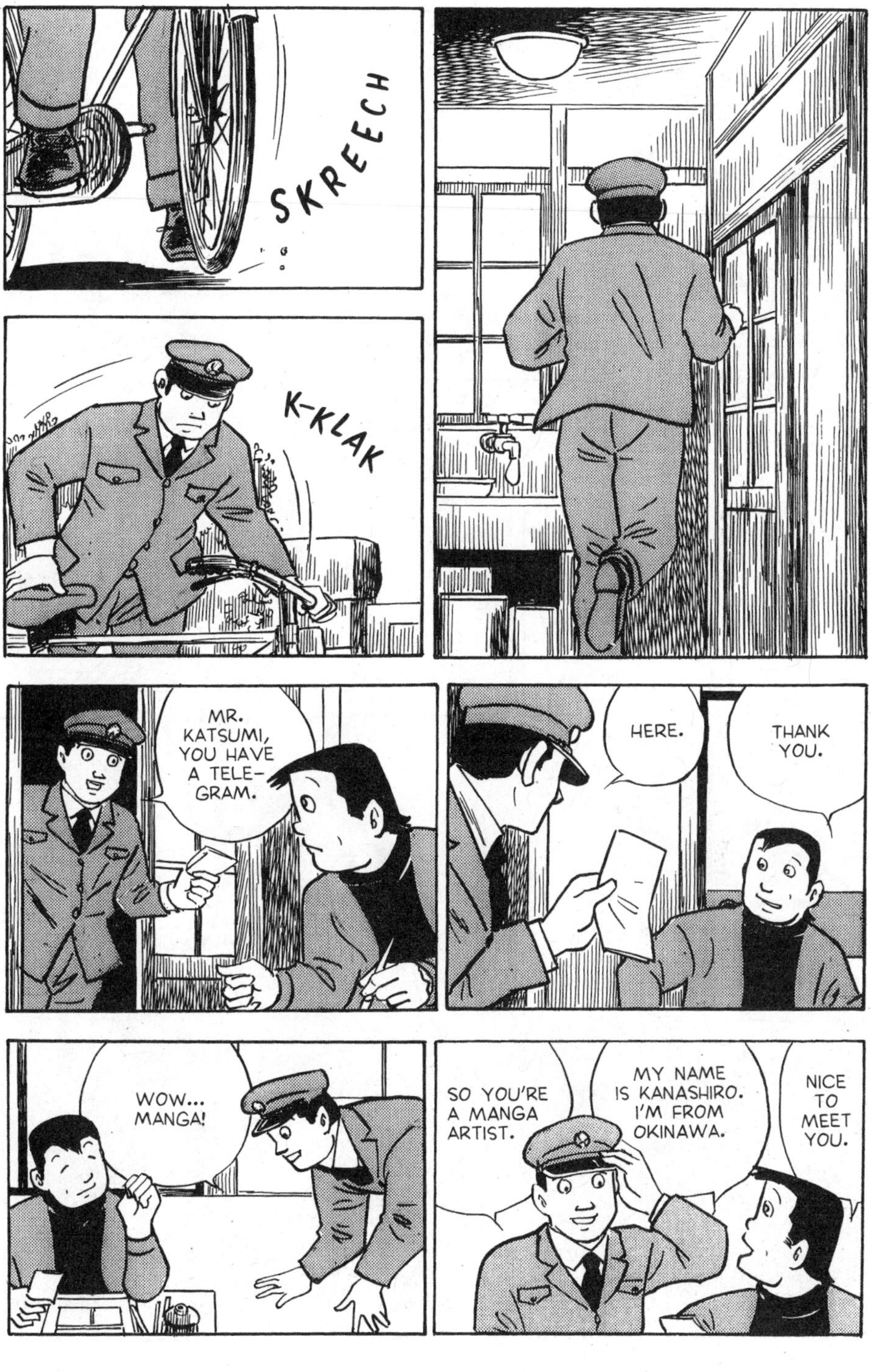
SKREECH
K-KLAK
MR. KATSUMI, YOU HAVE A TELE-GRAM.
HERE.
THANK YOU.
WOW... MANGA!
SO YOU'RE A MANGA ARTIST.
MY NAME IS KANASHIRO. I'M FROM OKINAWA.
NICE TO MEET YOU.

GOOD-BYE.

STRANGE TELEGRAM DELIVERER, HUH?

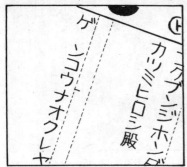

FROM HINOMARU, RIGHT?

"SEND MANUSCRIPT -- YAMADA." EXACTLY TWENTY LETTERS.

BAM BAM

COMING...

KURODA SENSEI.

I KNOW YOU'RE IN A NEW, UNFAMILIAR PLACE. HAVE YOU MADE YOURSELVES COMFORTABLE?

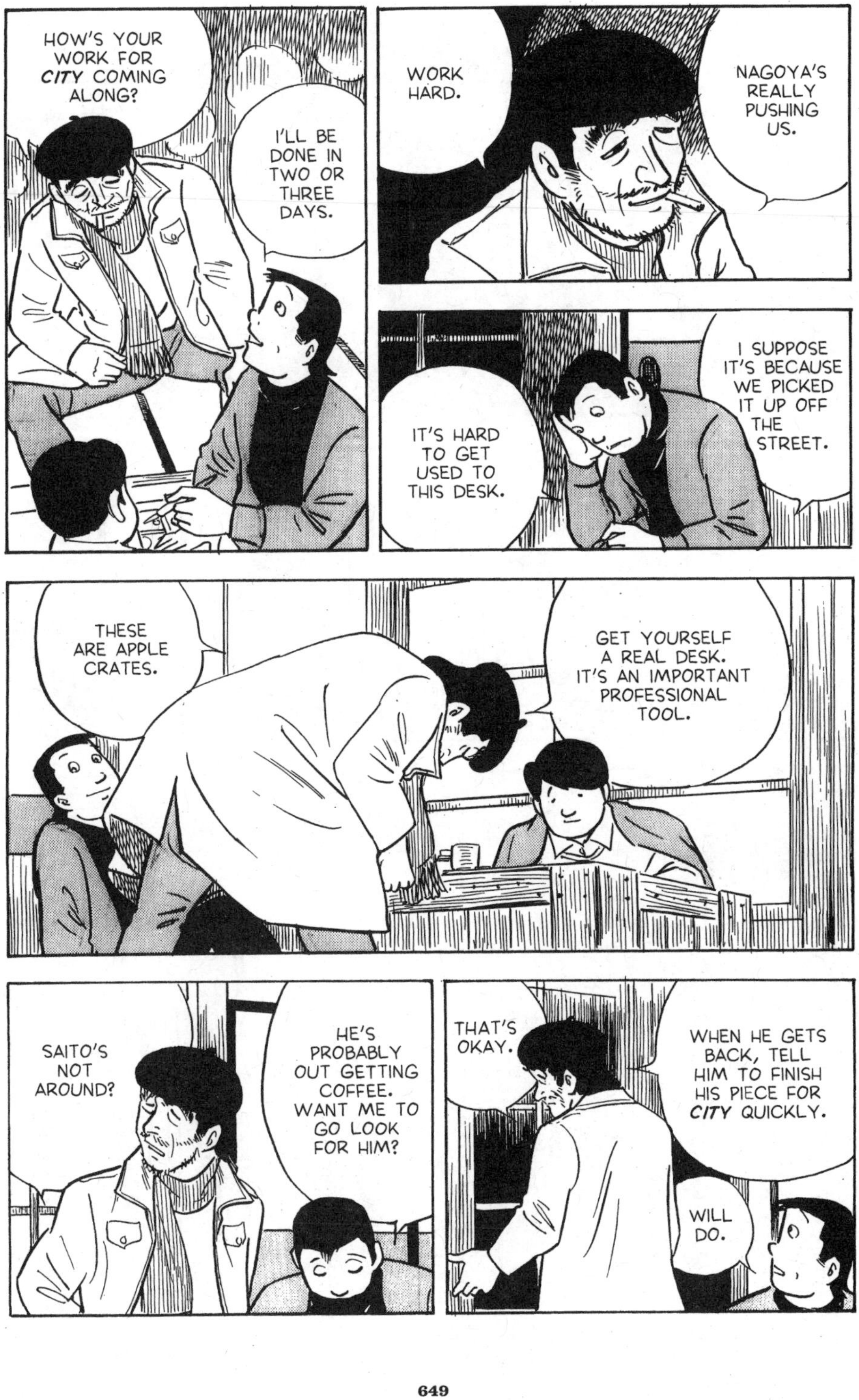
HOW'S YOUR WORK FOR CITY COMING ALONG?
I'LL BE DONE IN TWO OR THREE DAYS.
WORK HARD.
NAGOYA'S REALLY PUSHING US.
IT'S HARD TO GET USED TO THIS DESK.
I SUPPOSE IT'S BECAUSE WE PICKED IT UP OFF THE STREET.
THESE ARE APPLE CRATES.
GET YOURSELF A REAL DESK. IT'S AN IMPORTANT PROFESSIONAL TOOL.
SAITO'S NOT AROUND?
HE'S PROBABLY OUT GETTING COFFEE. WANT ME TO GO LOOK FOR HIM?
THAT'S OKAY.
WHEN HE GETS BACK, TELL HIM TO FINISH HIS PIECE FOR CITY QUICKLY.
WILL DO.

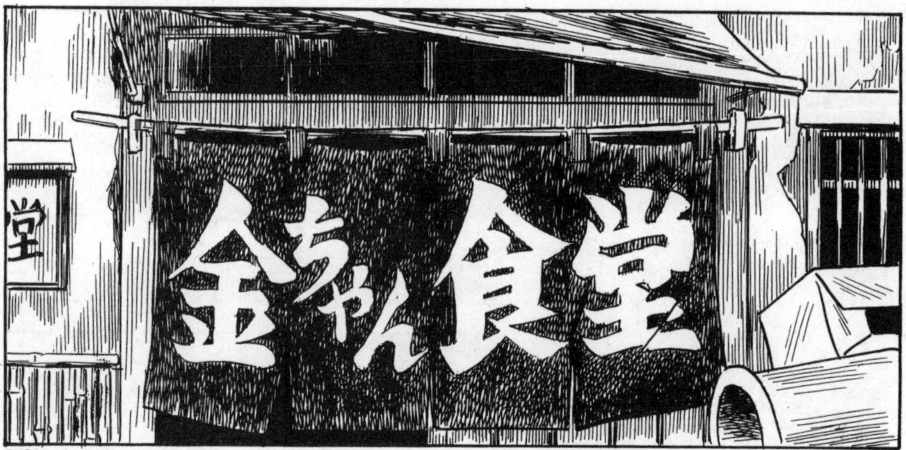
金ちゃん食堂

SIGN: KIN-CHAN DINER

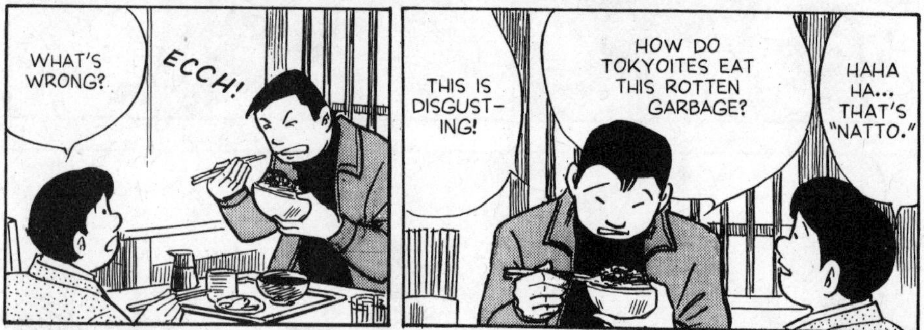
WHAT'S WRONG?
ECCH!
THIS IS DISGUST-ING!
HOW DO TOKYOITES EAT THIS ROTTEN GARBAGE?
HAHA HA... THAT'S "NATTO."

"NATTO" = FERMENTED SOYBEANS

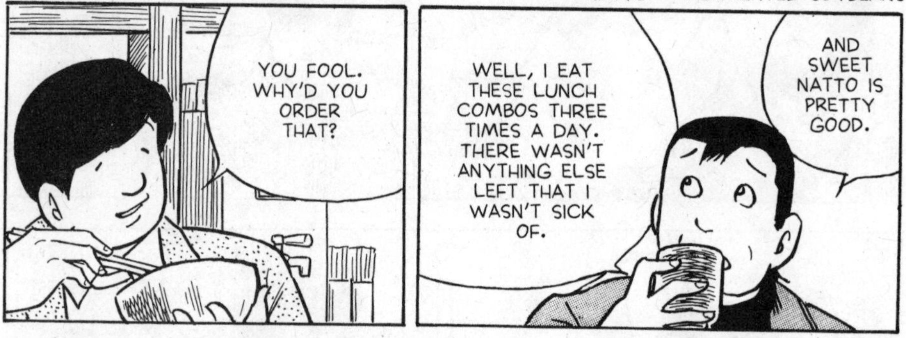
YOU FOOL. WHY'D YOU ORDER THAT?
WELL, I EAT THESE LUNCH COMBOS THREE TIMES A DAY. THERE WASN'T ANYTHING ELSE LEFT THAT I WASN'T SICK OF.
AND SWEET NATTO IS PRETTY GOOD.

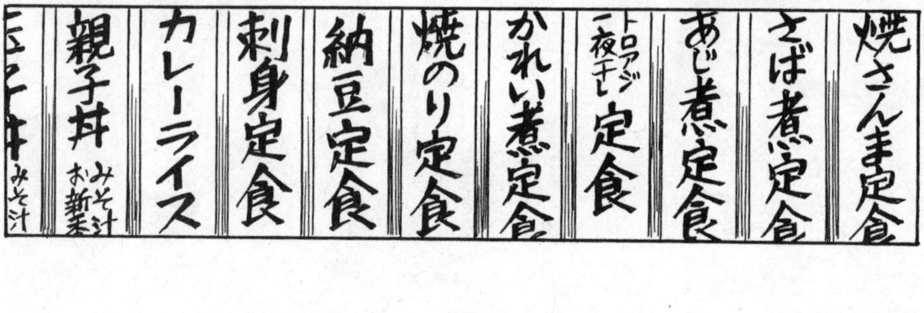
焼さんま定食
さば煮定食
あじ煮定食
トロアジ一夜干し定食
かれい煮定食
焼のり定食
納豆定食
刺身定食
カレーライス
親子丼 みそ汁 お新香

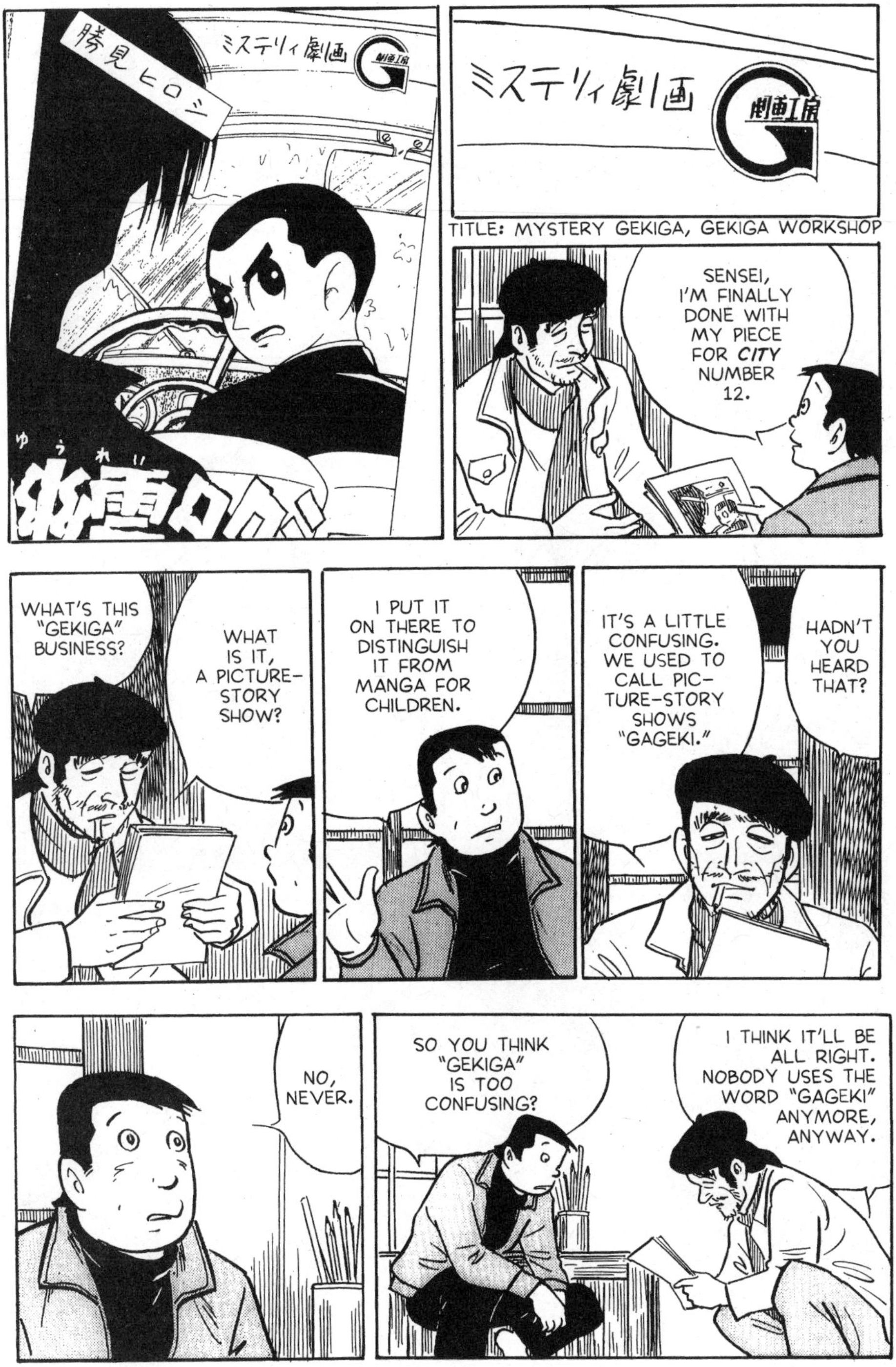
勝見ヒロシ
ミステリィ劇画
劇画工房
ミステリィ劇画
劇画工房
TITLE: MYSTERY GEKIGA, GEKIGA WORKSHOP
SENSEI, I'M FINALLY DONE WITH MY PIECE FOR *CITY* NUMBER 12.
WHAT'S THIS "GEKIGA" BUSINESS?
WHAT IS IT, A PICTURE-STORY SHOW?
I PUT IT ON THERE TO DISTINGUISH IT FROM MANGA FOR CHILDREN.
IT'S A LITTLE CONFUSING. WE USED TO CALL PICTURE-STORY SHOWS "GAGEKI."
HADN'T YOU HEARD THAT?
NO, NEVER.
SO YOU THINK "GEKIGA" IS TOO CONFUSING?
I THINK IT'LL BE ALL RIGHT. NOBODY USES THE WORD "GAGEKI" ANYMORE, ANYWAY.

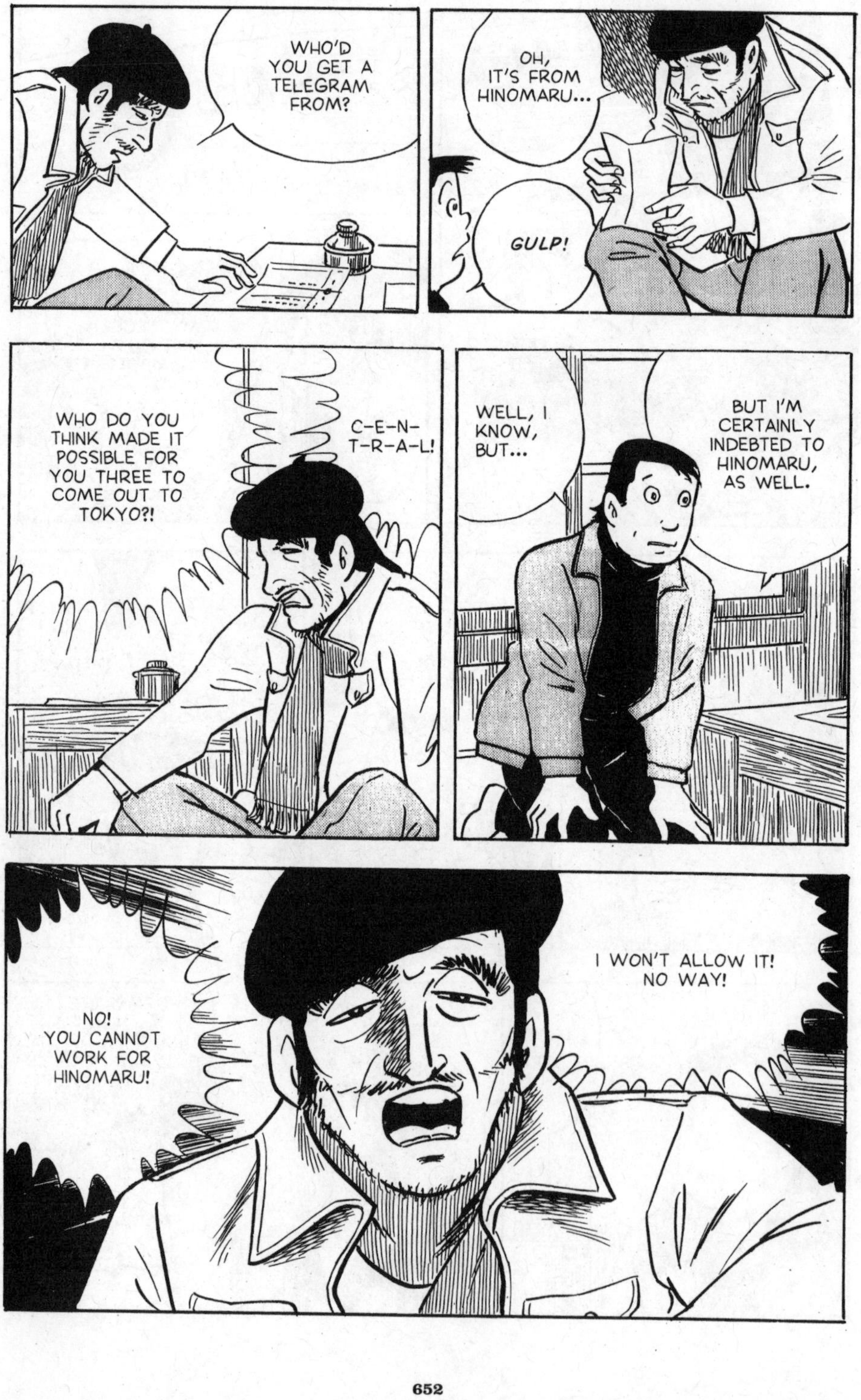
WHO'D YOU GET A TELEGRAM FROM?
OH, IT'S FROM HINOMARU...
GULP!
WHO DO YOU THINK MADE IT POSSIBLE FOR YOU THREE TO COME OUT TO TOKYO?!
C-E-N-T-R-A-L!
WELL, I KNOW, BUT...
BUT I'M CERTAINLY INDEBTED TO HINOMARU, AS WELL.
NO! YOU CANNOT WORK FOR HINOMARU!
I WON'T ALLOW IT! NO WAY!

THE BOOM CONTINUES

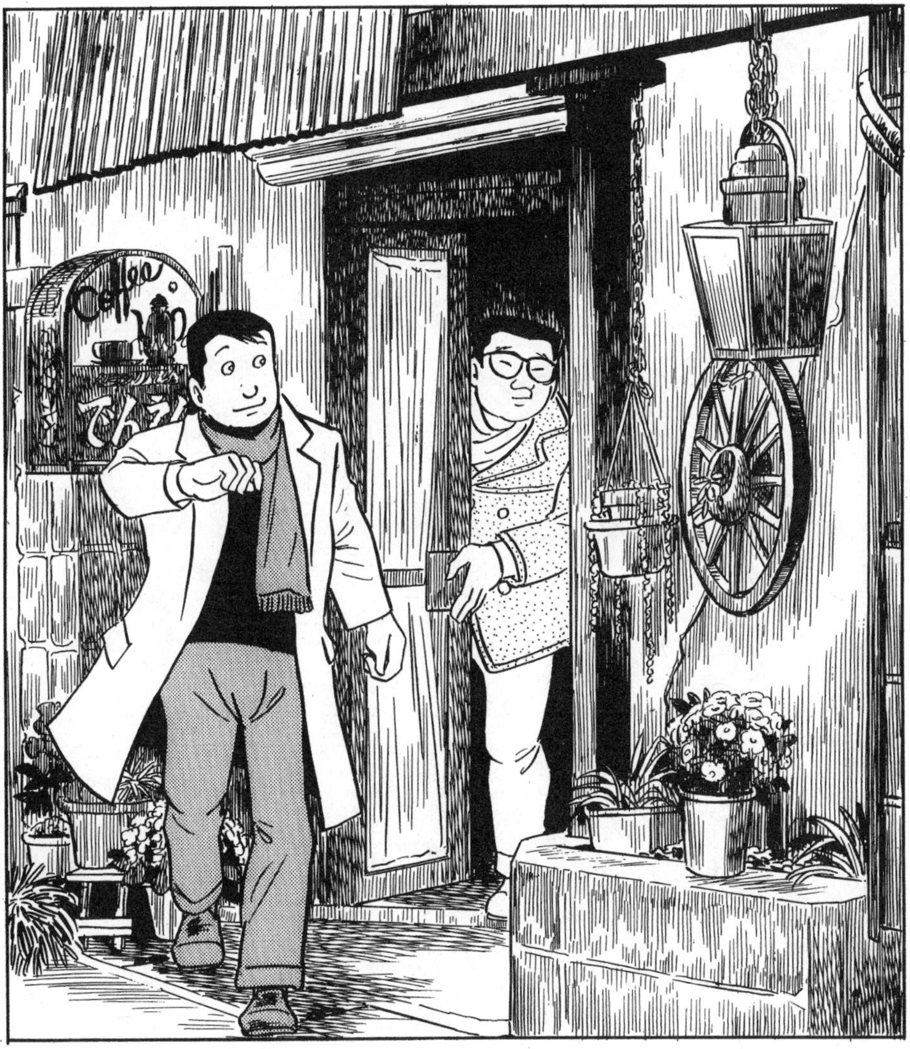
Coffee

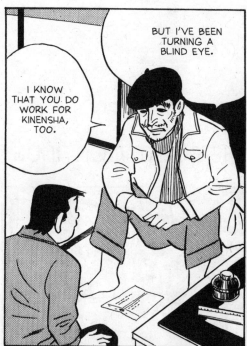

I KNOW THAT YOU DO WORK FOR KINENSHA, TOO.

BUT I'VE BEEN TURNING A BLIND EYE.

I WILL NOT LET YOU WORK FOR HINOMARU!

DO YOU UNDER-STAND?

YES...

MR. TATEISHI IS COMING TO TOKYO SOON.

HE SAYS CENTRAL IS GOING TO DROP ITS BOOK BUSINESS AND BECOME STRICT-LY A COMICS PUBLISHER.

THEY'RE GOING TO STOP ITS WHOLESALE BUSINESS?!

YOU'RE GOING TO HAVE A LOT MORE WORK FOR CENTRAL FROM NOW ON.

YOU WON'T HAVE TIME TO WORK FOR ANYBODY ELSE.

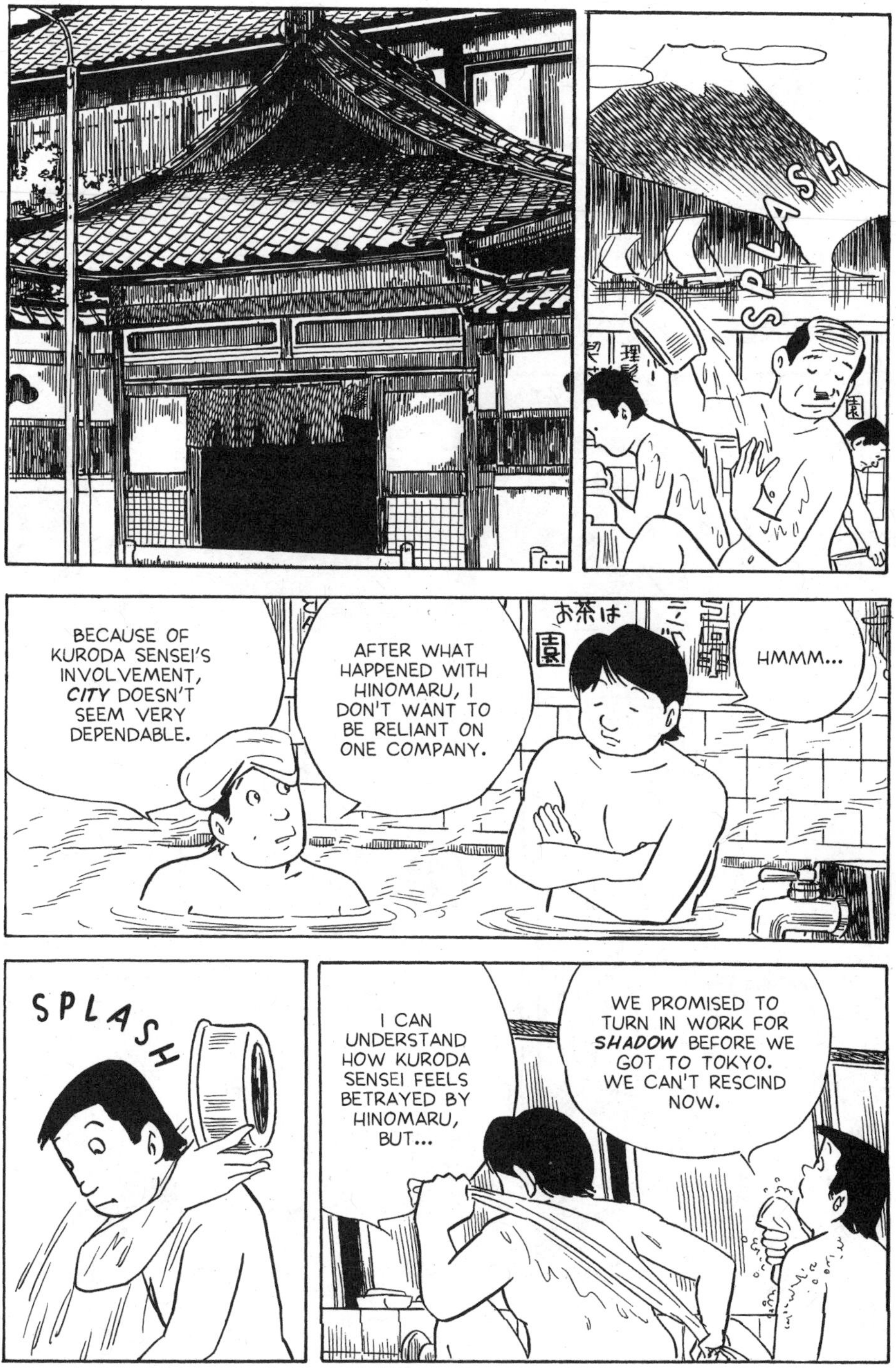
SPLASH
BECAUSE OF KURODA SENSEI'S INVOLVEMENT, CITY DOESN'T SEEM VERY DEPENDABLE.
AFTER WHAT HAPPENED WITH HINOMARU, I DON'T WANT TO BE RELIANT ON ONE COMPANY.
お茶は
園
HMMM...
SPLASH
I CAN UNDERSTAND HOW KURODA SENSEI FEELS BETRAYED BY HINOMARU, BUT...
WE PROMISED TO TURN IN WORK FOR SHADOW BEFORE WE GOT TO TOKYO. WE CAN'T RESCIND NOW.

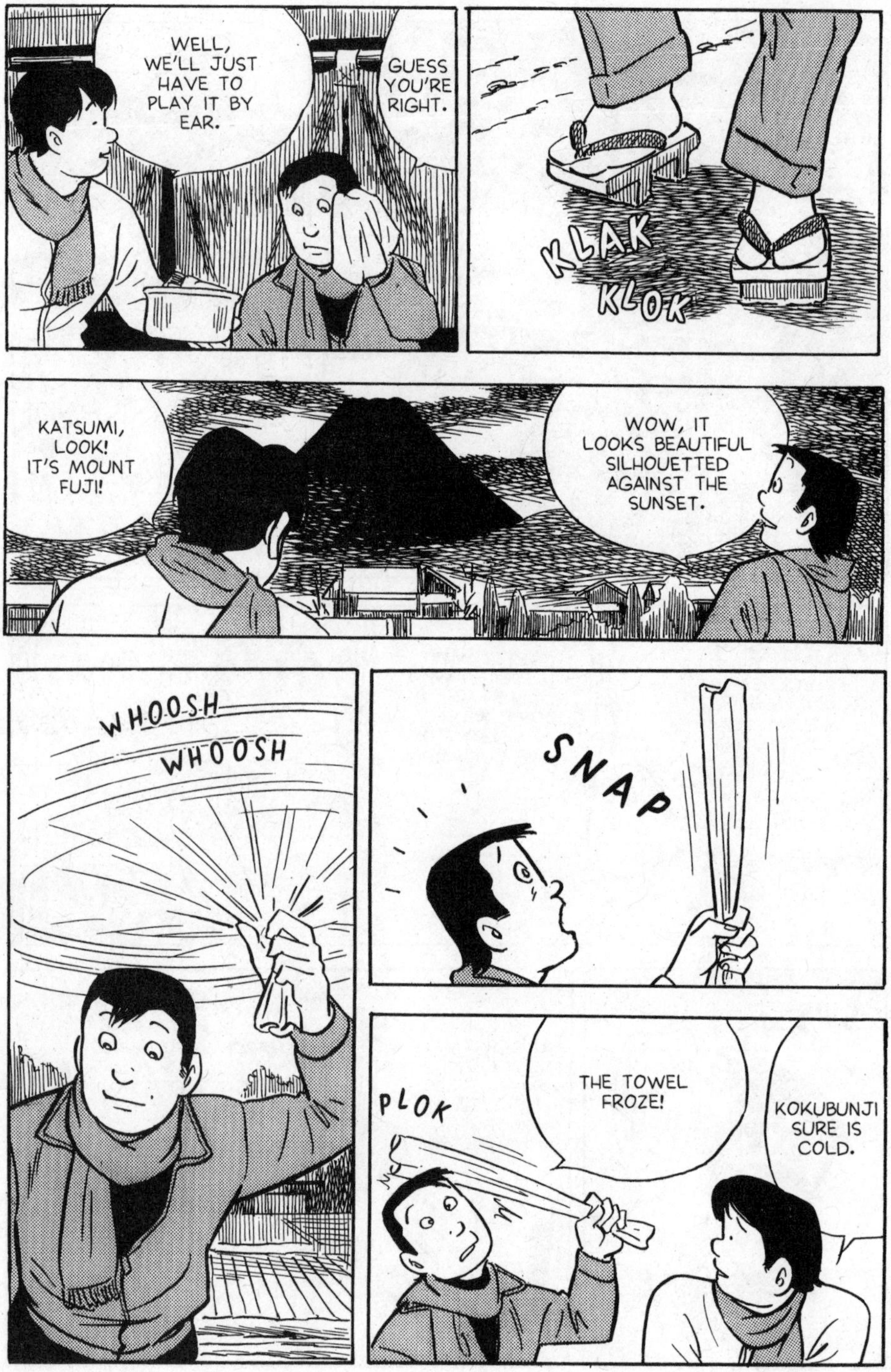
WELL, WE'LL JUST HAVE TO PLAY IT BY EAR.
GUESS YOU'RE RIGHT.
KLAK
KLOK
KATSUMI, LOOK! IT'S MOUNT FUJI!
WOW, IT LOOKS BEAUTIFUL SILHOUETTED AGAINST THE SUNSET.
WHOOSH
WHOOSH
SNAP
PLOK
THE TOWEL FROZE!
KOKUBUNJI SURE IS COLD.

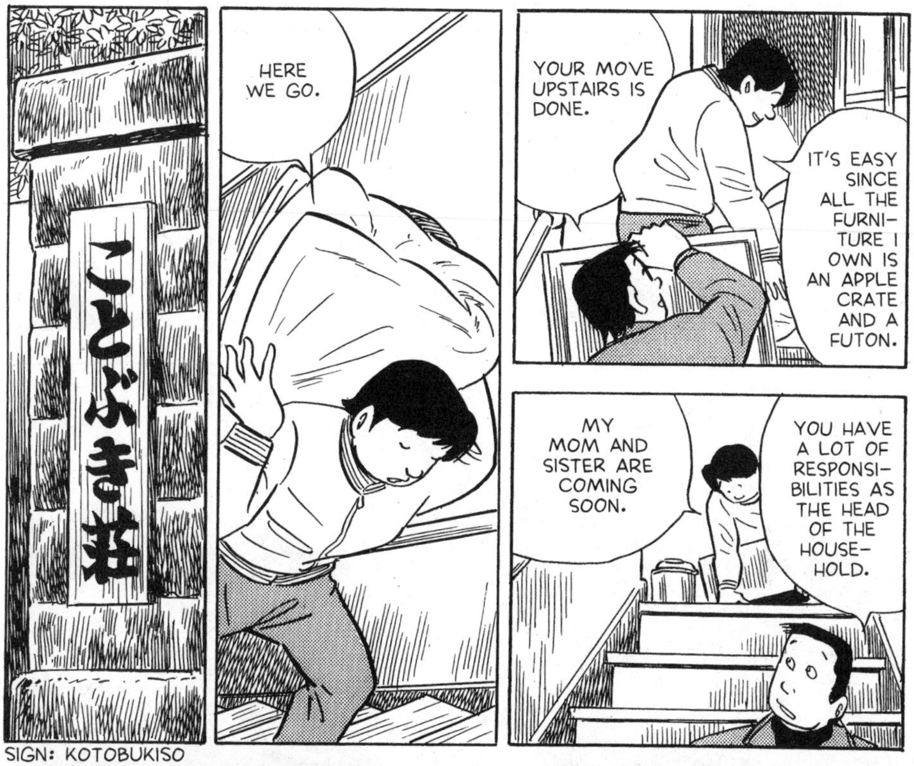
ことぶき荘
HERE WE GO.
YOUR MOVE UPSTAIRS IS DONE.
IT'S EASY SINCE ALL THE FURNI-TURE I OWN IS AN APPLE CRATE AND A FUTON.
MY MOM AND SISTER ARE COMING SOON.
YOU HAVE A LOT OF RESPONSI-BILITIES AS THE HEAD OF THE HOUSE-HOLD.
SIGN: KOTOBUKISO

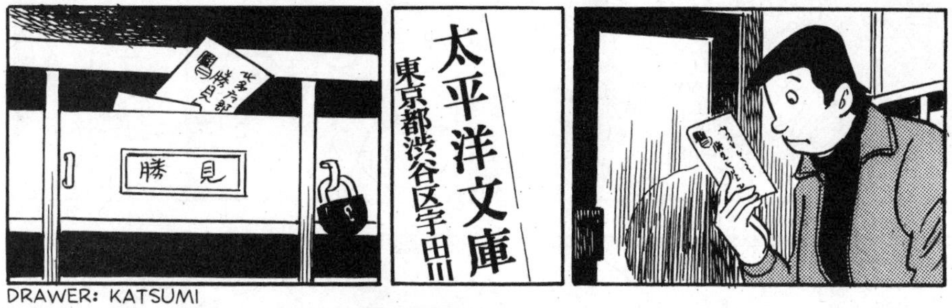
勝見
太平洋文庫
東京都渋谷区宇田川
DRAWER: KATSUMI

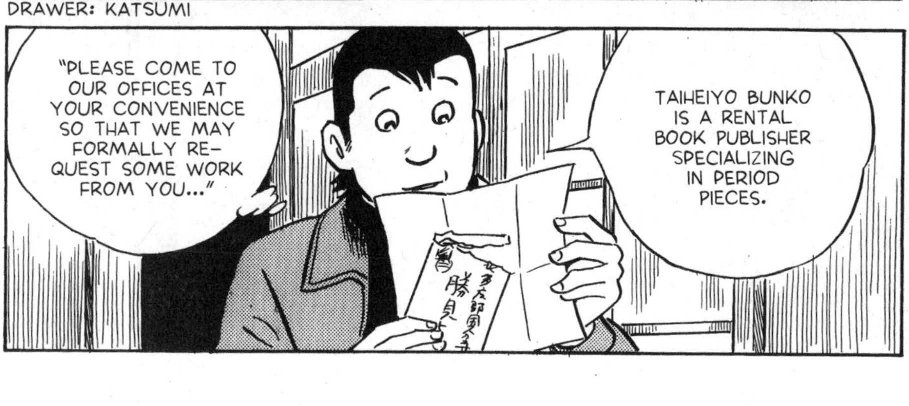
"PLEASE COME TO OUR OFFICES AT YOUR CONVENIENCE SO THAT WE MAY FORMALLY RE-QUEST SOME WORK FROM YOU..."
TAIHEIYO BUNKO IS A RENTAL BOOK PUBLISHER SPECIALIZING IN PERIOD PIECES.

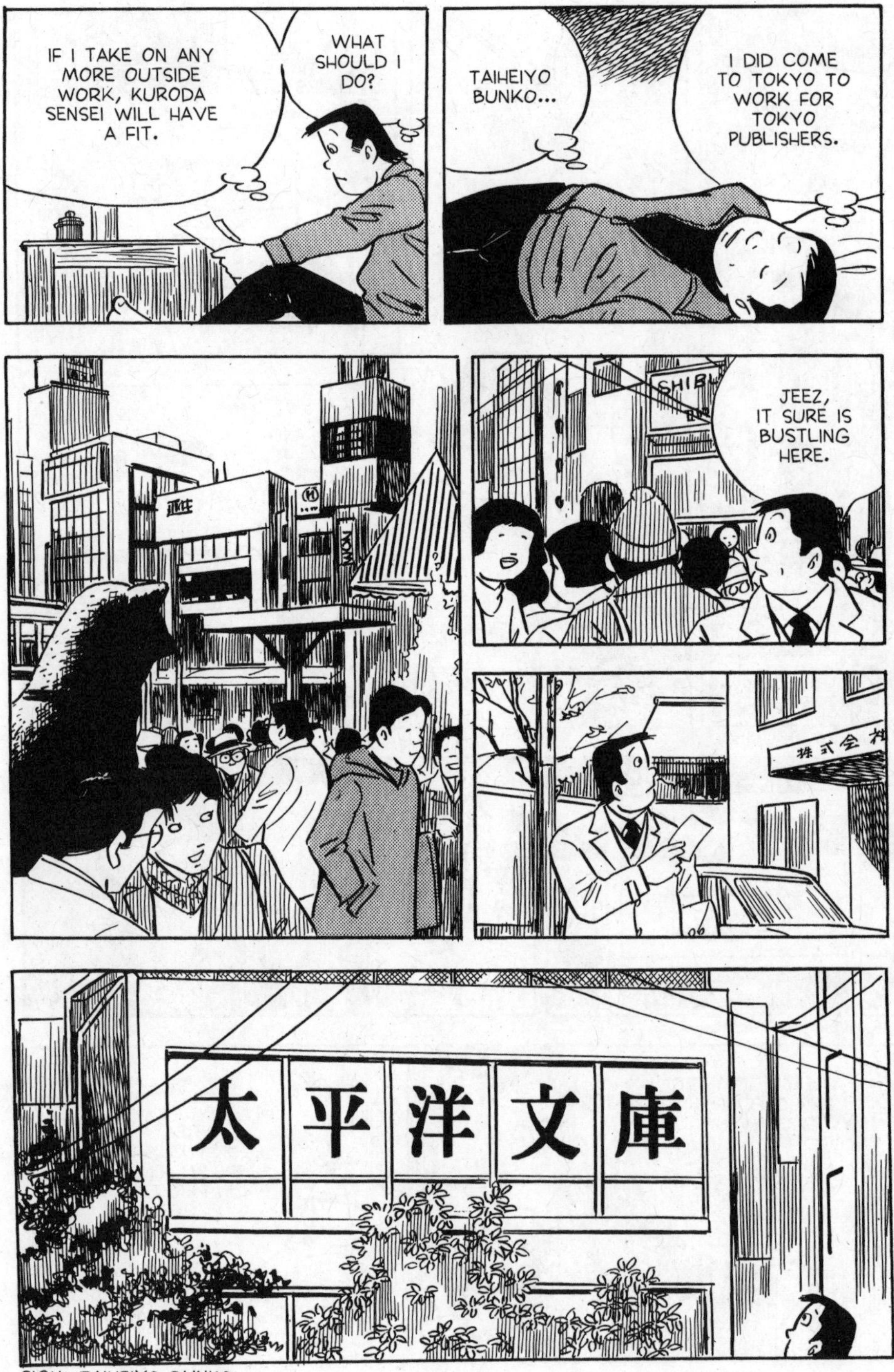
IF I TAKE ON ANY MORE OUTSIDE WORK, KURODA SENSEI WILL HAVE A FIT.
WHAT SHOULD I DO?
TAIHEIYO BUNKO...
I DID COME TO TOKYO TO WORK FOR TOKYO PUBLISHERS.
JEEZ, IT SURE IS BUSTLING HERE.
太平洋文庫
SIGN: TAIHEIYO BUNKO

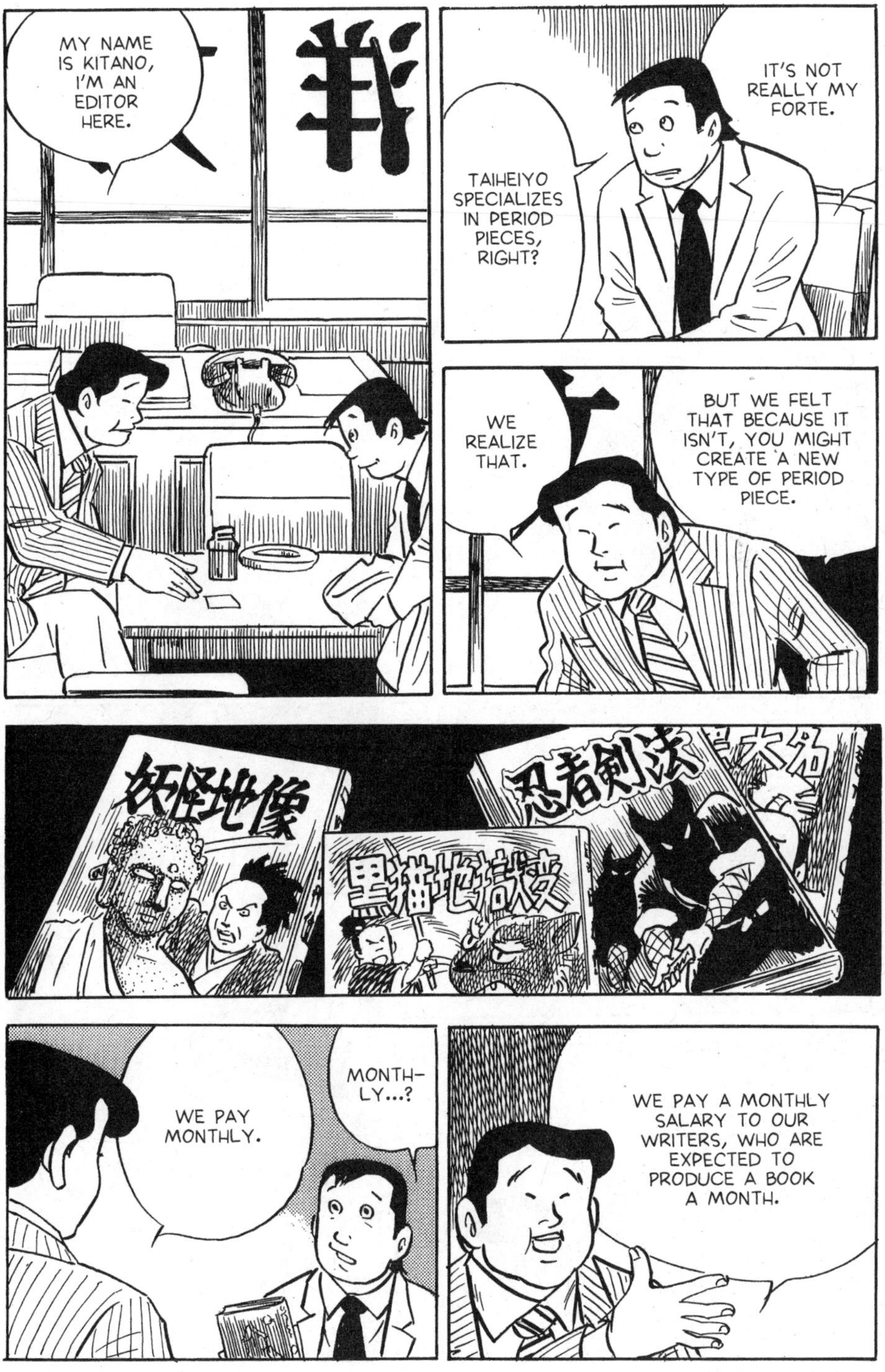
MY NAME IS KITANO, I'M AN EDITOR HERE.
TAIHEIYO SPECIALIZES IN PERIOD PIECES, RIGHT?
IT'S NOT REALLY MY FORTE.
WE REALIZE THAT.
BUT WE FELT THAT BECAUSE IT ISN'T, YOU MIGHT CREATE A NEW TYPE OF PERIOD PIECE.
WE PAY MONTHLY.
MONTH-LY...?
WE PAY A MONTHLY SALARY TO OUR WRITERS, WHO ARE EXPECTED TO PRODUCE A BOOK A MONTH.

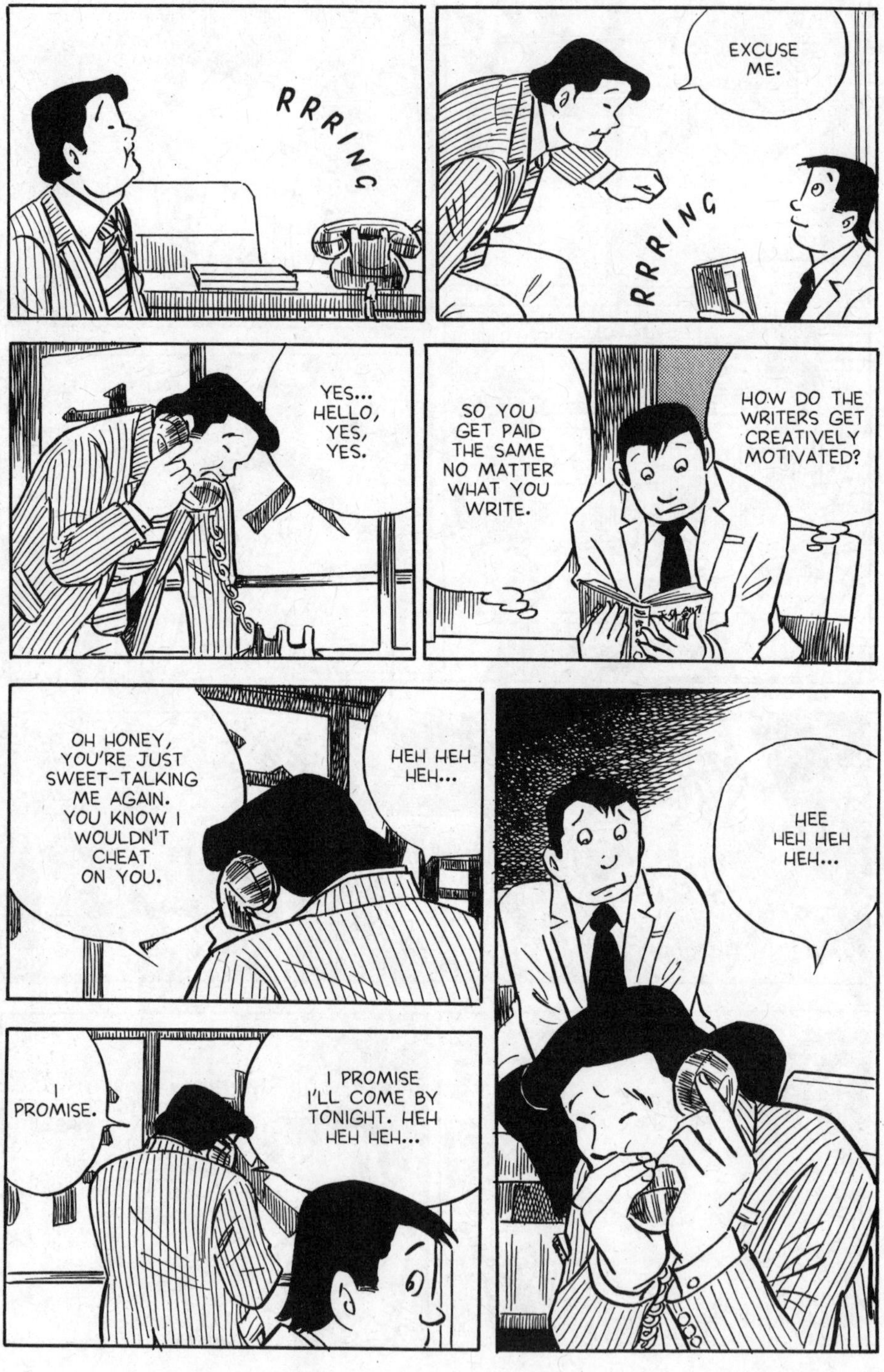
RRRING
EXCUSE ME.
RRRING
YES... HELLO, YES, YES.
SO YOU GET PAID THE SAME NO MATTER WHAT YOU WRITE.
HOW DO THE WRITERS GET CREATIVELY MOTIVATED?
OH HONEY, YOU'RE JUST SWEET-TALKING ME AGAIN. YOU KNOW I WOULDN'T CHEAT ON YOU.
HEH HEH HEH...
I PROMISE.
I PROMISE I'LL COME BY TONIGHT. HEH HEH HEH...
HEE HEH HEH HEH...

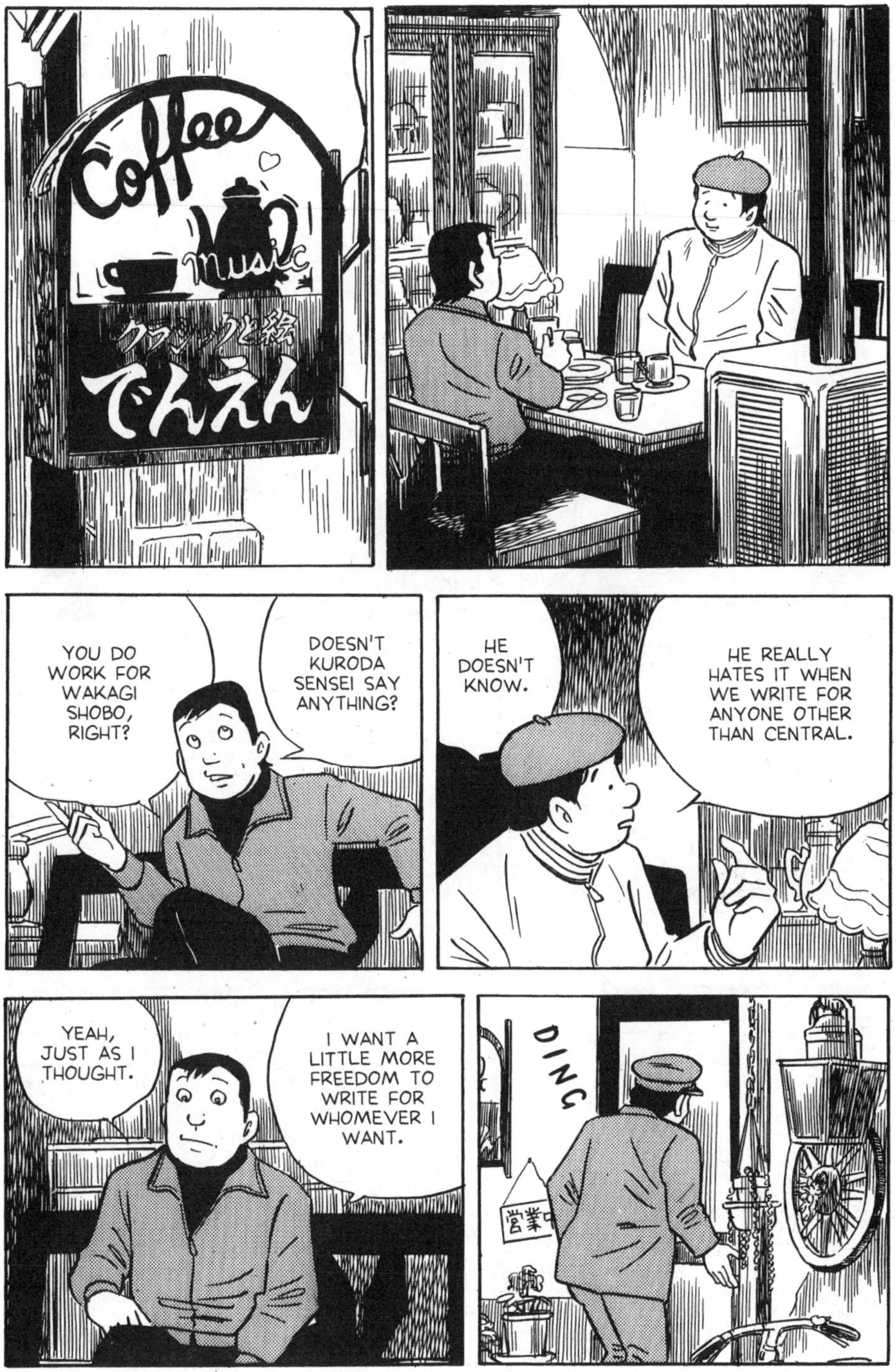
Coffee
music
でんえん
YOU DO WORK FOR WAKAGI SHOBO, RIGHT?
DOESN'T KURODA SENSEI SAY ANYTHING?
HE DOESN'T KNOW.
HE REALLY HATES IT WHEN WE WRITE FOR ANYONE OTHER THAN CENTRAL.
YEAH, JUST AS I THOUGHT.
I WANT A LITTLE MORE FREEDOM TO WRITE FOR WHOMEVER I WANT.
DING

HEY, YOU'RE THE TELEGRAM MAN.

OH, I'M GLAD I FINALLY FOUND YOU.

MR. KATSUMI, YOU HAVE A TELEGRAM FROM NAGOYA.

THANK YOU! BUT HOW'D YOU KNOW I'D BE HERE?

I ASKED AROUND, AND NOW I PRETTY MUCH KNOW YOUR FIELD OF ACTION.

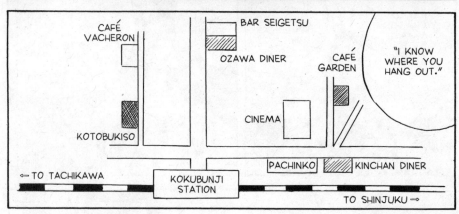

CAFÉ VACHERON

KOTOBUKISO

BAR SEIGETSU

OZAWA DINER

CINEMA

CAFÉ GARDEN

"I KNOW WHERE YOU HANG OUT."

PACHINKO KINCHAN DINER

⇐ TO TACHIKAWA

KOKUBUNJI STATION

TO SHINJUKU ⇒

YOU'RE REALLY JUST A TELEGRAM MAN?

OR ARE YOU A DETECTIVE AS WELL?

WANNA JOIN ME FOR COFFEE?

NO, THANK YOU. I'M ON THE CLOCK.

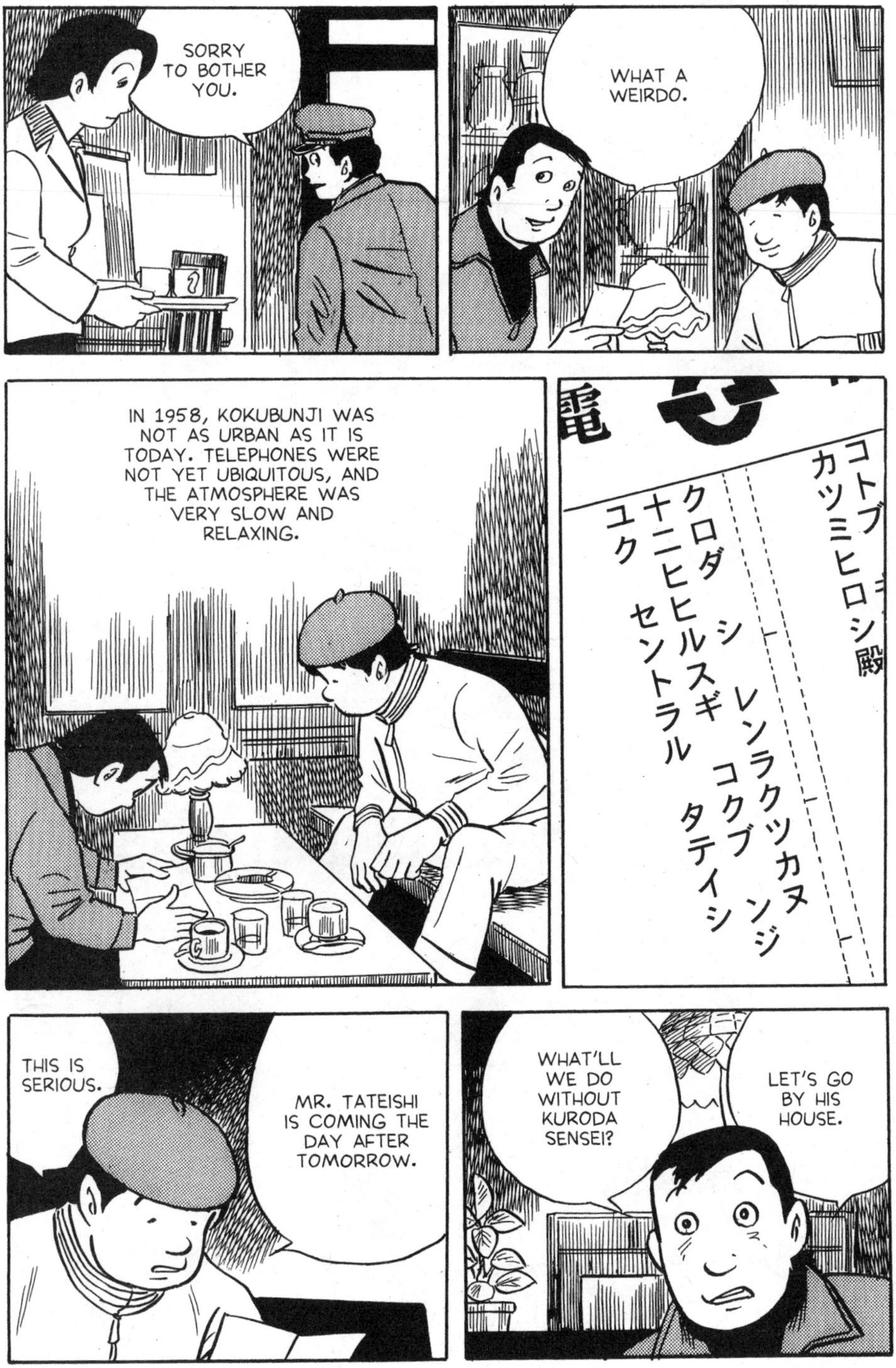
SORRY TO BOTHER YOU.
WHAT A WEIRDO.
IN 1958, KOKUBUNJI WAS NOT AS URBAN AS IT IS TODAY. TELEPHONES WERE NOT YET UBIQUITOUS, AND THE ATMOSPHERE WAS VERY SLOW AND RELAXING.
電
コトブ
カツミヒロシ殿
クロダ シ レンラクツカヌ
十二ヒヒルスギ コクブンジ
ユク セントラル タテイシ
THIS IS SERIOUS.
MR. TATEISHI IS COMING THE DAY AFTER TOMORROW.
WHAT'LL WE DO WITHOUT KURODA SENSEI?
LET'S GO BY HIS HOUSE.

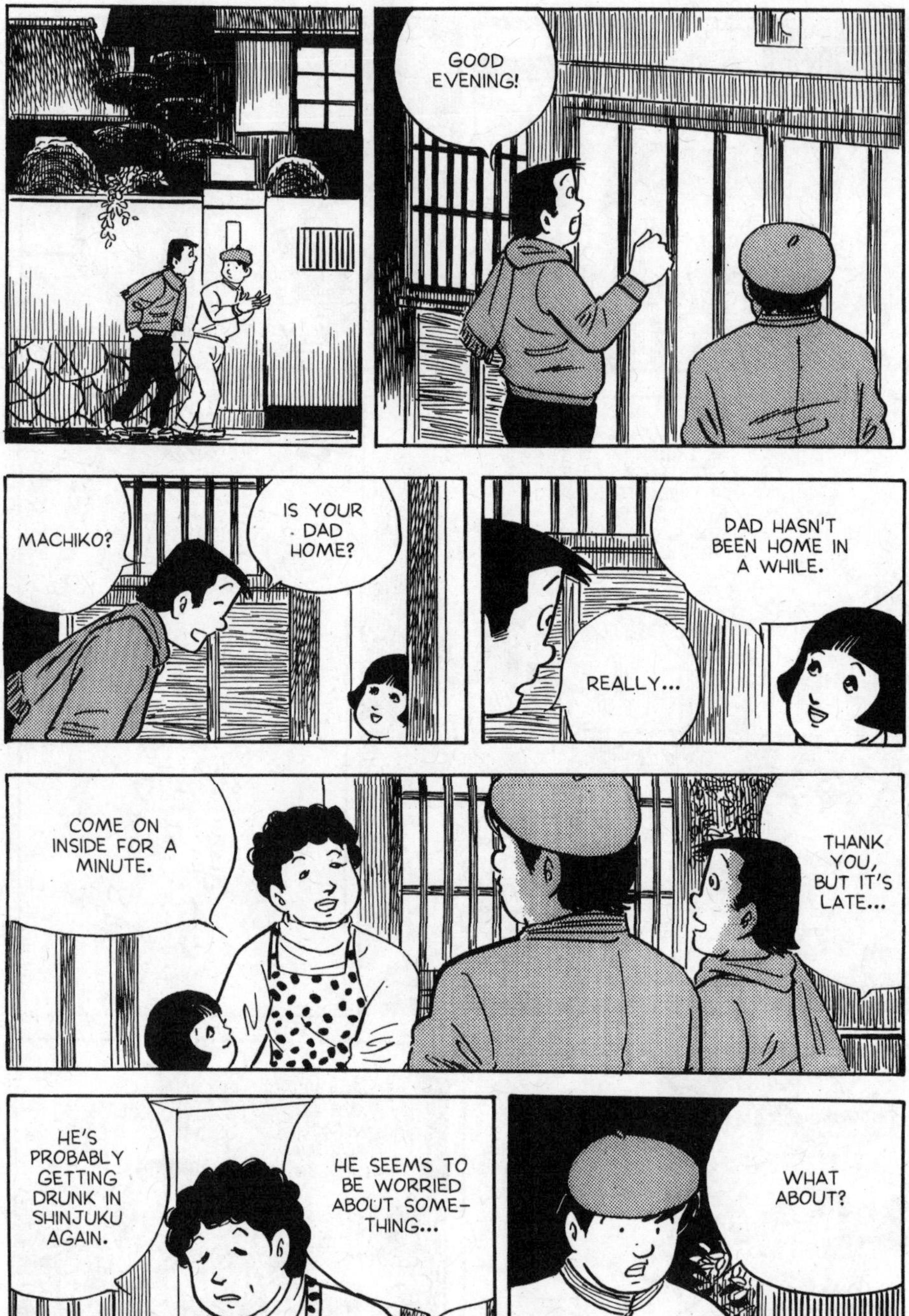
GOOD EVENING!
MACHIKO?
IS YOUR DAD HOME?
DAD HASN'T BEEN HOME IN A WHILE.
REALLY...
COME ON INSIDE FOR A MINUTE.
THANK YOU, BUT IT'S LATE...
HE'S PROBABLY GETTING DRUNK IN SHINJUKU AGAIN.
HE SEEMS TO BE WORRIED ABOUT SOMETHING...
WHAT ABOUT?

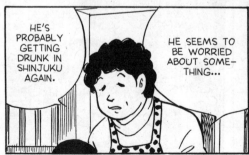

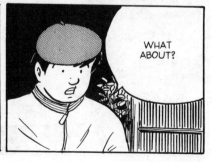

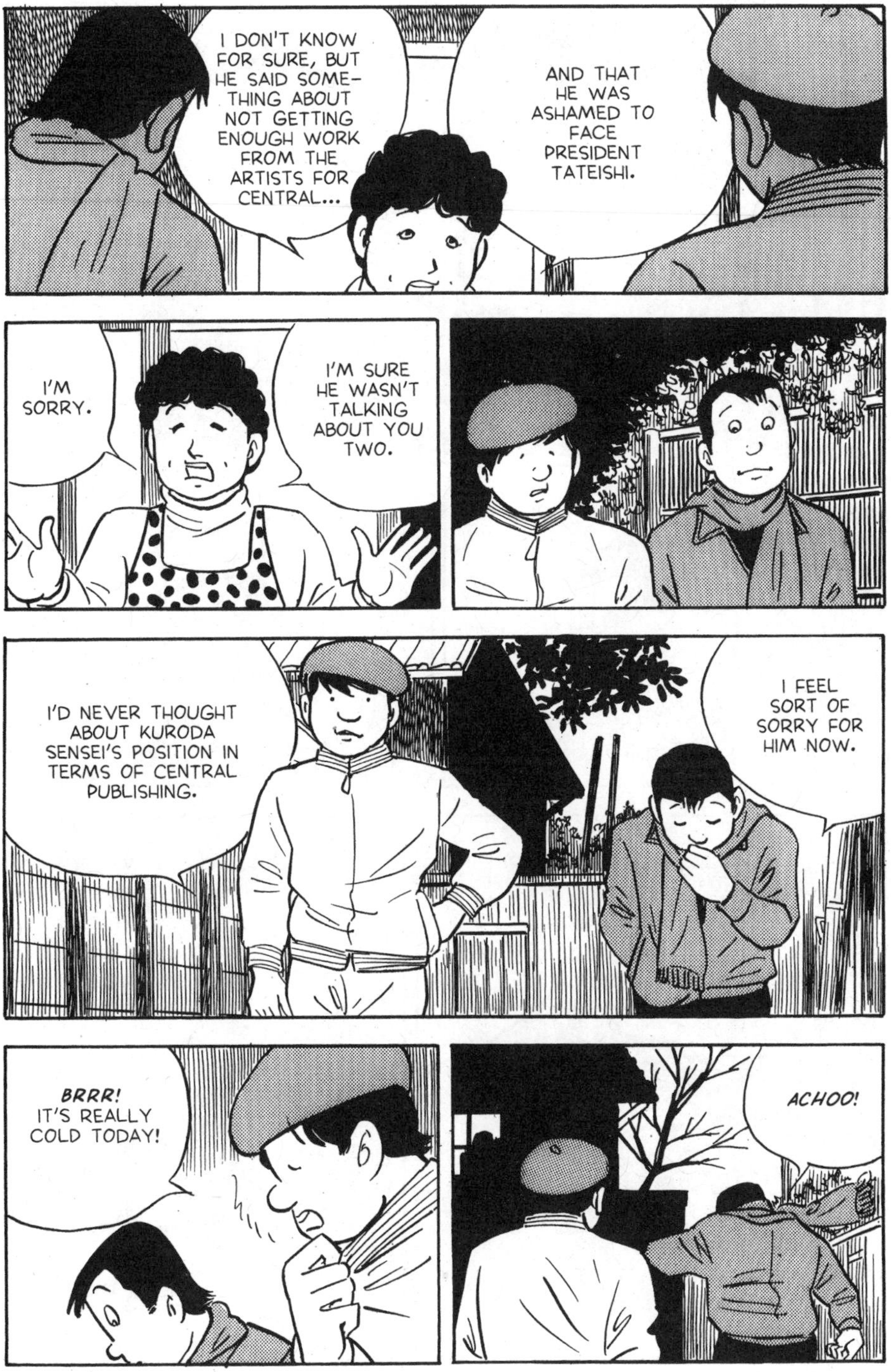
I DON'T KNOW FOR SURE, BUT HE SAID SOME-THING ABOUT NOT GETTING ENOUGH WORK FROM THE ARTISTS FOR CENTRAL...
AND THAT HE WAS ASHAMED TO FACE PRESIDENT TATEISHI.
I'M SORRY.
I'M SURE HE WASN'T TALKING ABOUT YOU TWO.
I'D NEVER THOUGHT ABOUT KURODA SENSEI'S POSITION IN TERMS OF CENTRAL PUBLISHING.
I FEEL SORT OF SORRY FOR HIM NOW.
BRRR! IT'S REALLY COLD TODAY!
ACHOO!

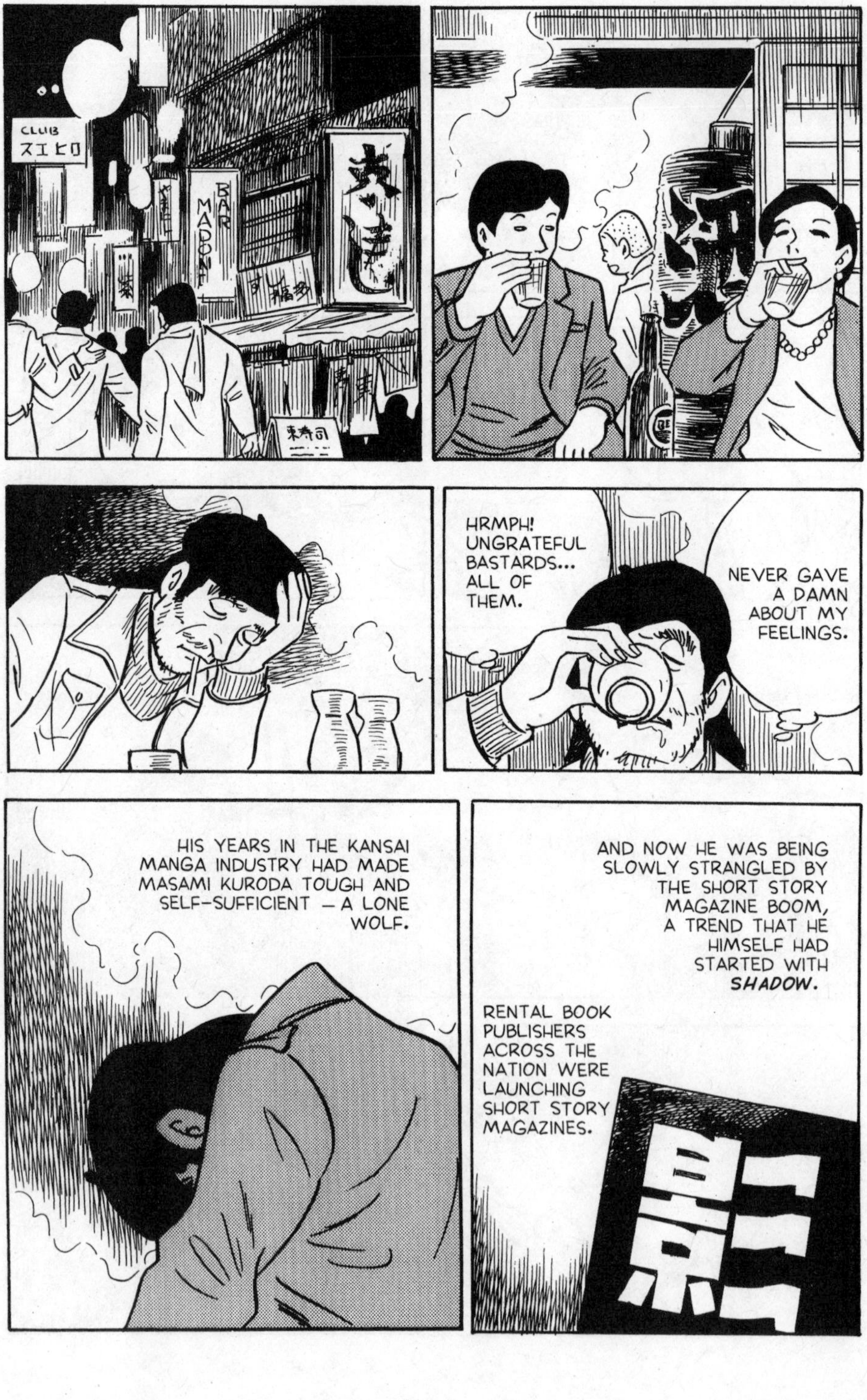
CLUB
スエヒロ
BAR
HRMPH! UNGRATEFUL BASTARDS... ALL OF THEM.
NEVER GAVE A DAMN ABOUT MY FEELINGS.
HIS YEARS IN THE KANSAI MANGA INDUSTRY HAD MADE MASAMI KURODA TOUGH AND SELF-SUFFICIENT – A LONE WOLF.
AND NOW HE WAS BEING SLOWLY STRANGLED BY THE SHORT STORY MAGAZINE BOOM, A TREND THAT HE HIMSELF HAD STARTED WITH *SHADOW*.
RENTAL BOOK PUBLISHERS ACROSS THE NATION WERE LAUNCHING SHORT STORY MAGAZINES.

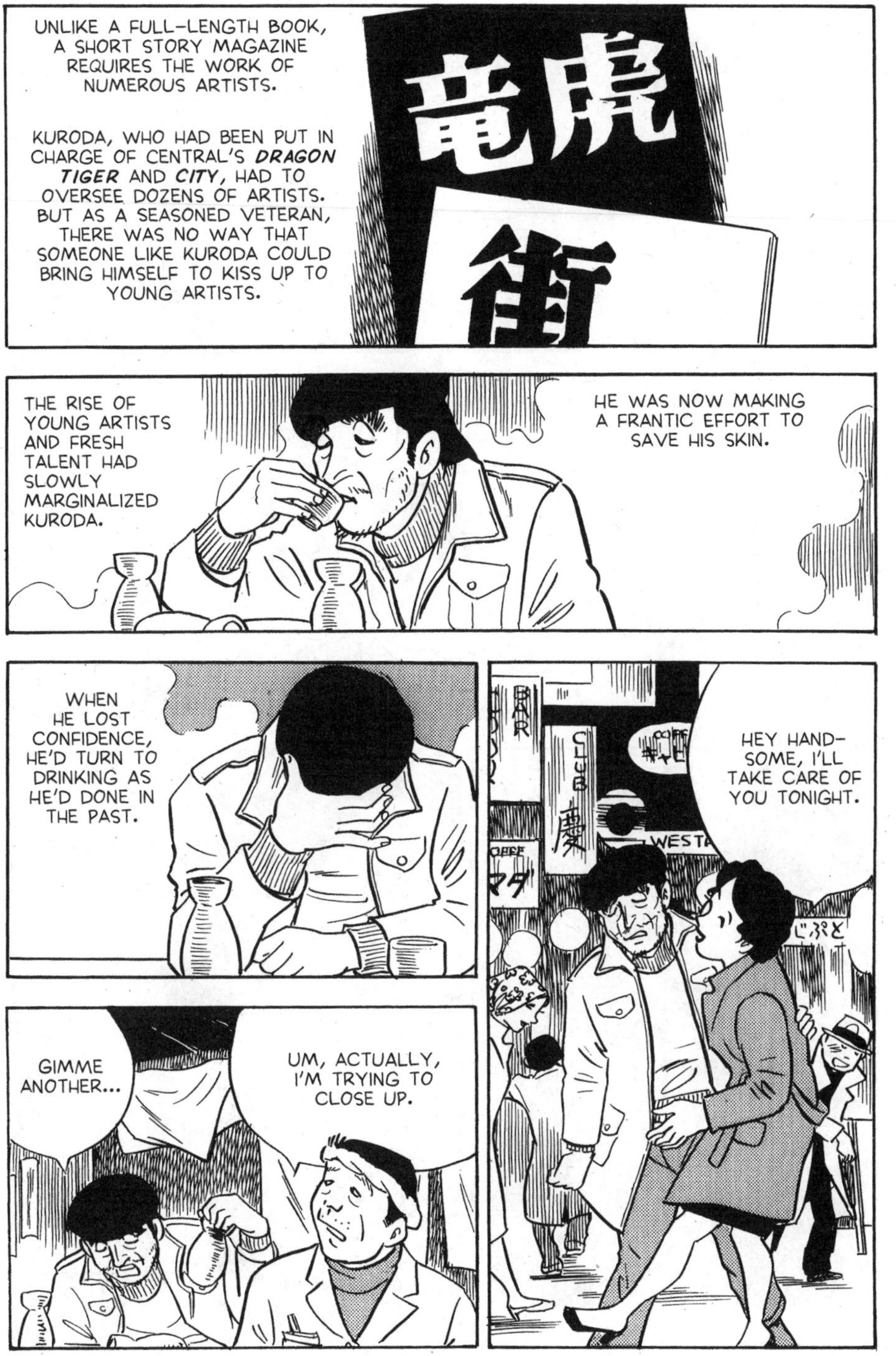
UNLIKE A FULL-LENGTH BOOK, A SHORT STORY MAGAZINE REQUIRES THE WORK OF NUMEROUS ARTISTS.
KURODA, WHO HAD BEEN PUT IN CHARGE OF CENTRAL'S ***DRAGON TIGER*** AND ***CITY***, HAD TO OVERSEE DOZENS OF ARTISTS. BUT AS A SEASONED VETERAN, THERE WAS NO WAY THAT SOMEONE LIKE KURODA COULD BRING HIMSELF TO KISS UP TO YOUNG ARTISTS.
竜虎
街
THE RISE OF YOUNG ARTISTS AND FRESH TALENT HAD SLOWLY MARGINALIZED KURODA.
HE WAS NOW MAKING A FRANTIC EFFORT TO SAVE HIS SKIN.
WHEN HE LOST CONFIDENCE, HE'D TURN TO DRINKING AS HE'D DONE IN THE PAST.
GIMME ANOTHER...
UM, ACTUALLY, I'M TRYING TO CLOSE UP.
BAR
CLUB
HEY HAND-SOME, I'LL TAKE CARE OF YOU TONIGHT.

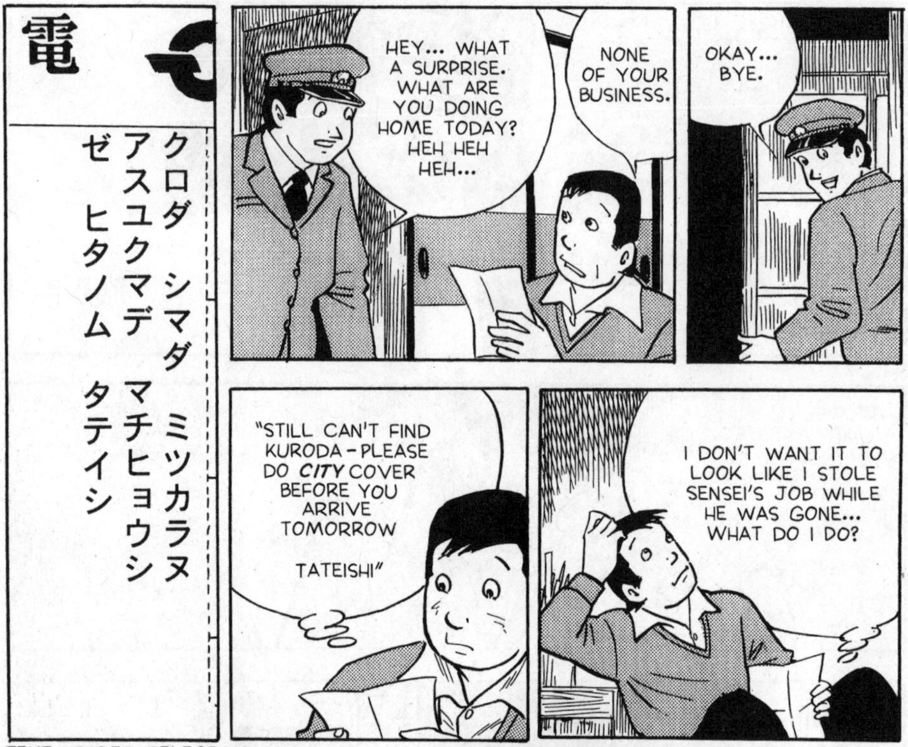
電
クロダ シマダ ミツカラヌ
アスユクマデ マチヒョウシ
ゼ ヒタノム タテイシ
HEY... WHAT A SURPRISE. WHAT ARE YOU DOING HOME TODAY? HEH HEH HEH...
NONE OF YOUR BUSINESS.
OKAY... BYE.
"STILL CAN'T FIND KURODA - PLEASE DO CITY COVER BEFORE YOU ARRIVE TOMORROW TATEISHI"
I DON'T WANT IT TO LOOK LIKE I STOLE SENSEI'S JOB WHILE HE WAS GONE... WHAT DO I DO?

TEXT HEADER: TELEGRAM

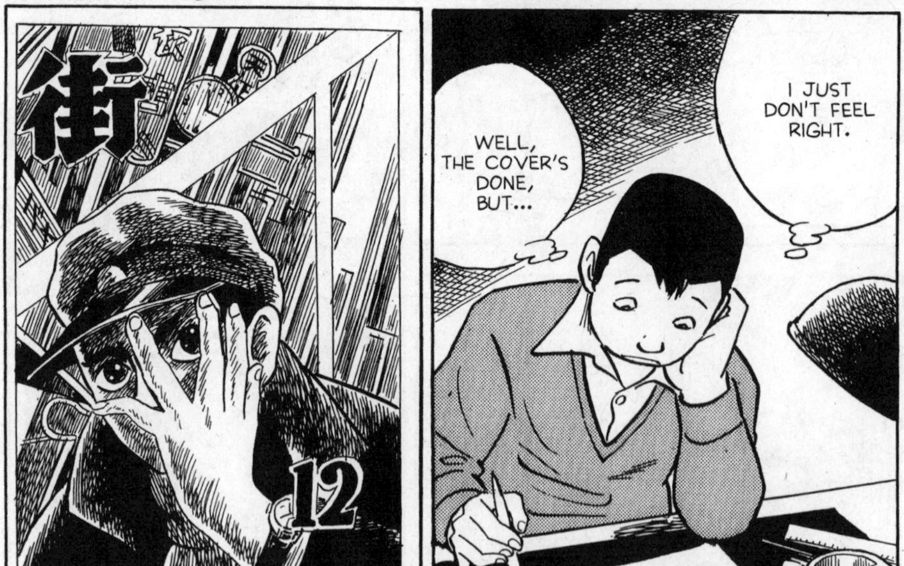
街
12
WELL, THE COVER'S DONE, BUT...
I JUST DON'T FEEL RIGHT.

RENTAL MANGA WARS

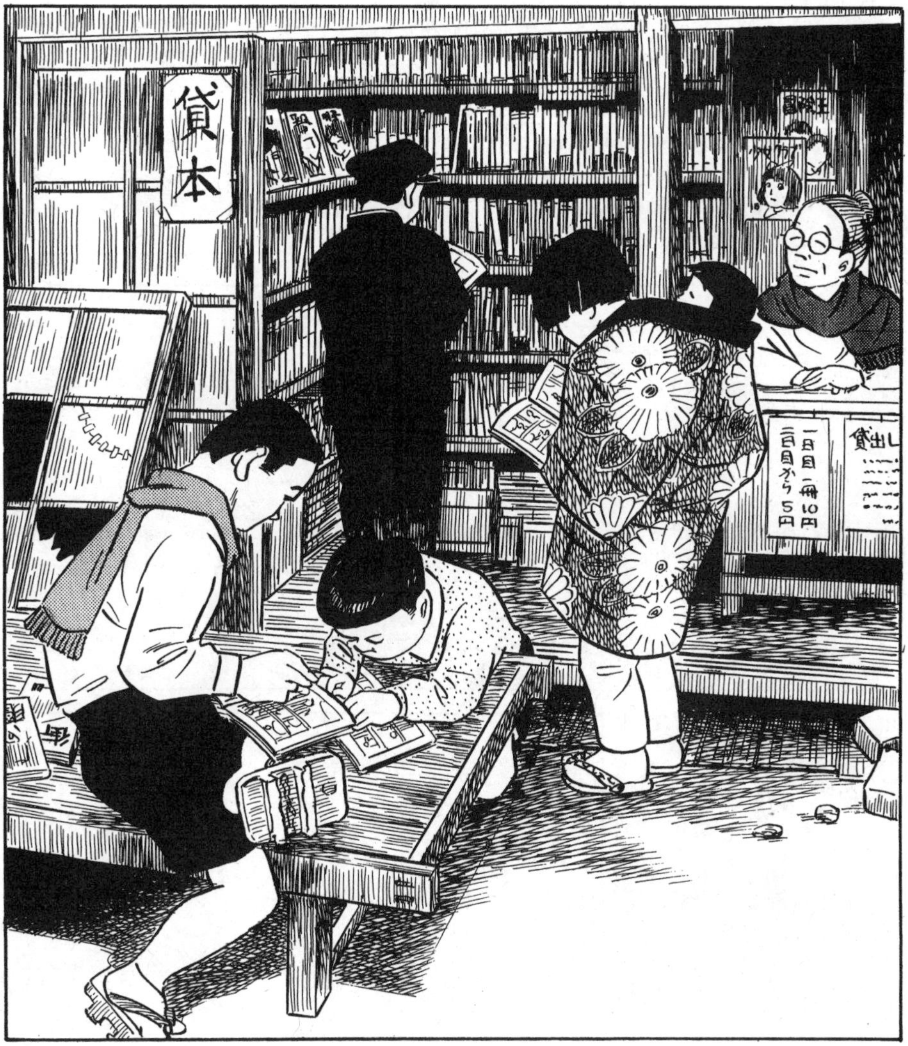

貸本
一日目二冊10円
二日目から5円
貸出し

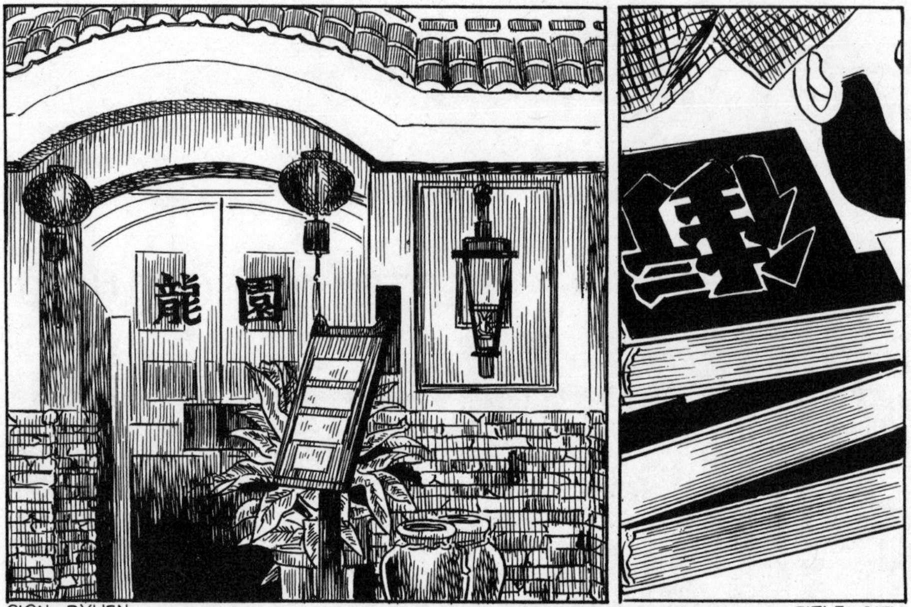
龍園
SIGN: RYUEN

TITLE: *CITY*

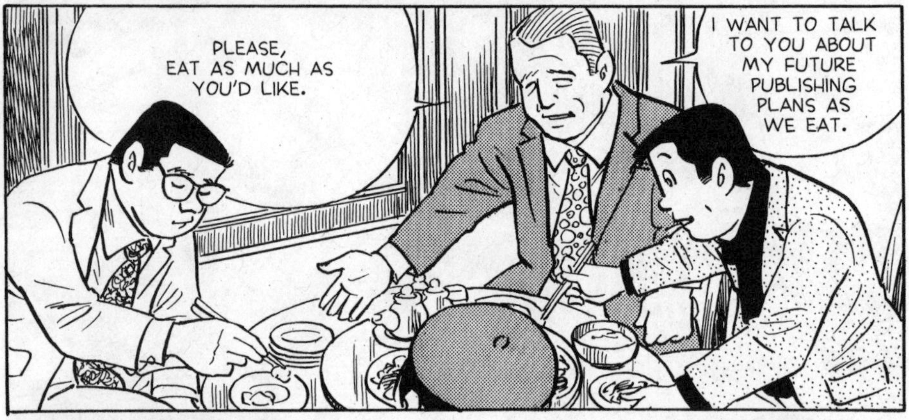
PLEASE, EAT AS MUCH AS YOU'D LIKE.
I WANT TO TALK TO YOU ABOUT MY FUTURE PUBLISHING PLANS AS WE EAT.

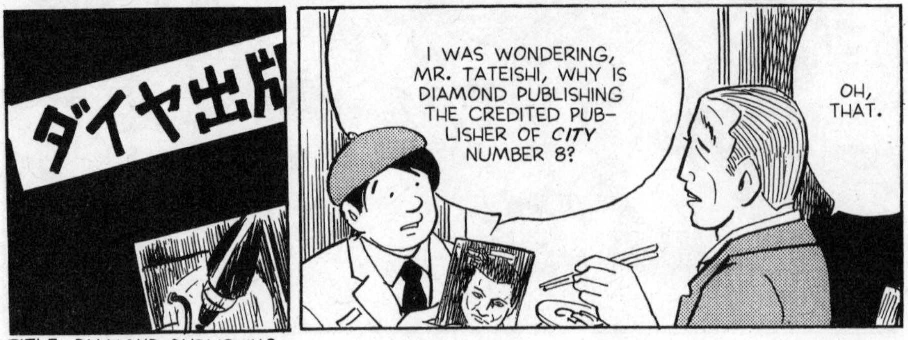
ダイヤ出
I WAS WONDERING, MR. TATEISHI, WHY IS DIAMOND PUBLISHING THE CREDITED PUBLISHER OF *CITY* NUMBER 8?
OH, THAT.
TITLE: DIAMOND PUBLISHING

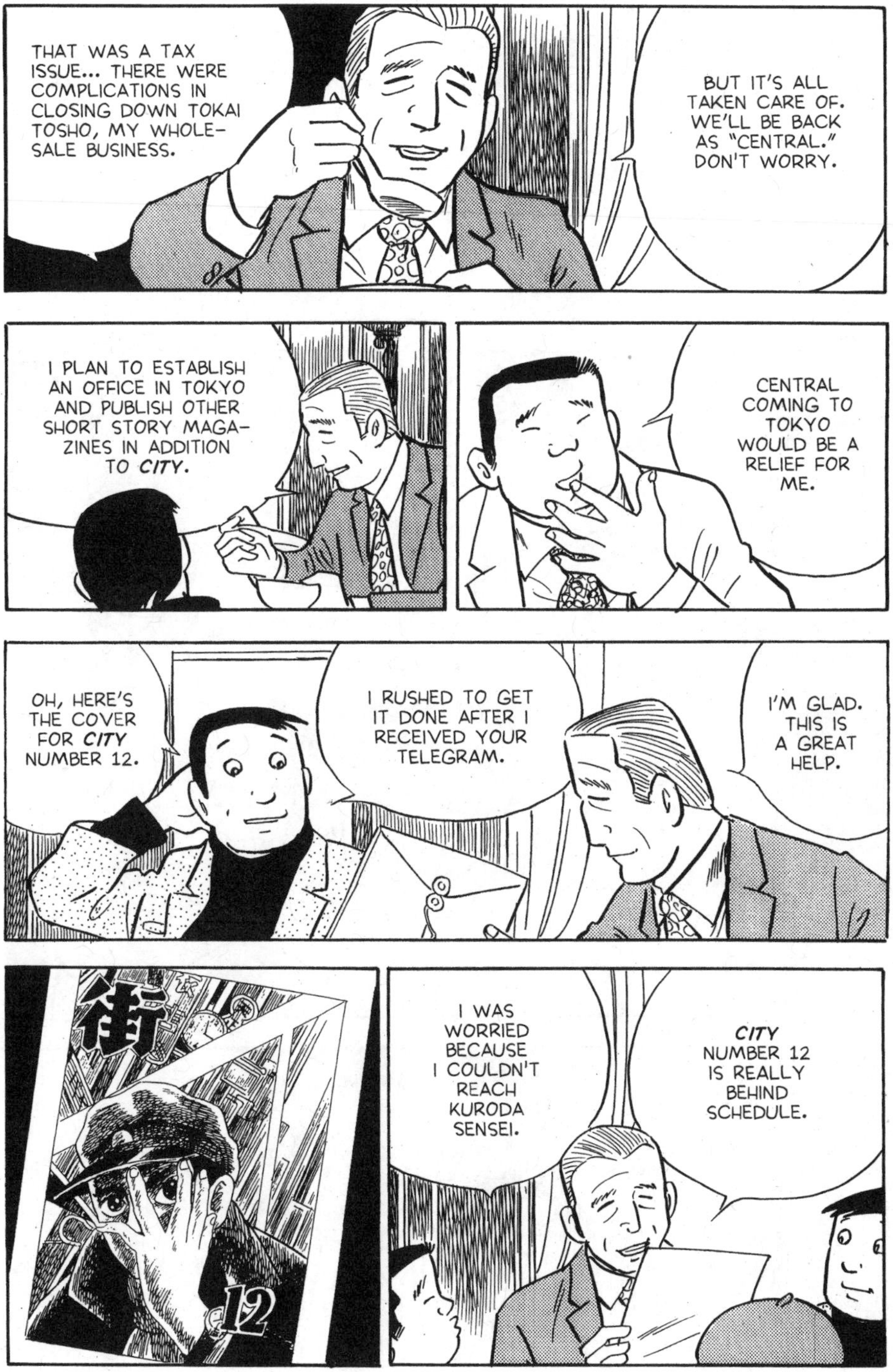
THAT WAS A TAX ISSUE... THERE WERE COMPLICATIONS IN CLOSING DOWN TOKAI TOSHO, MY WHOLE-SALE BUSINESS.
BUT IT'S ALL TAKEN CARE OF. WE'LL BE BACK AS "CENTRAL." DON'T WORRY.
I PLAN TO ESTABLISH AN OFFICE IN TOKYO AND PUBLISH OTHER SHORT STORY MAGA-ZINES IN ADDITION TO *CITY*.
CENTRAL COMING TO TOKYO WOULD BE A RELIEF FOR ME.
OH, HERE'S THE COVER FOR *CITY* NUMBER 12.
I RUSHED TO GET IT DONE AFTER I RECEIVED YOUR TELEGRAM.
I'M GLAD. THIS IS A GREAT HELP.
街
12
I WAS WORRIED BECAUSE I COULDN'T REACH KURODA SENSEI.
CITY NUMBER 12 IS REALLY BEHIND SCHEDULE.

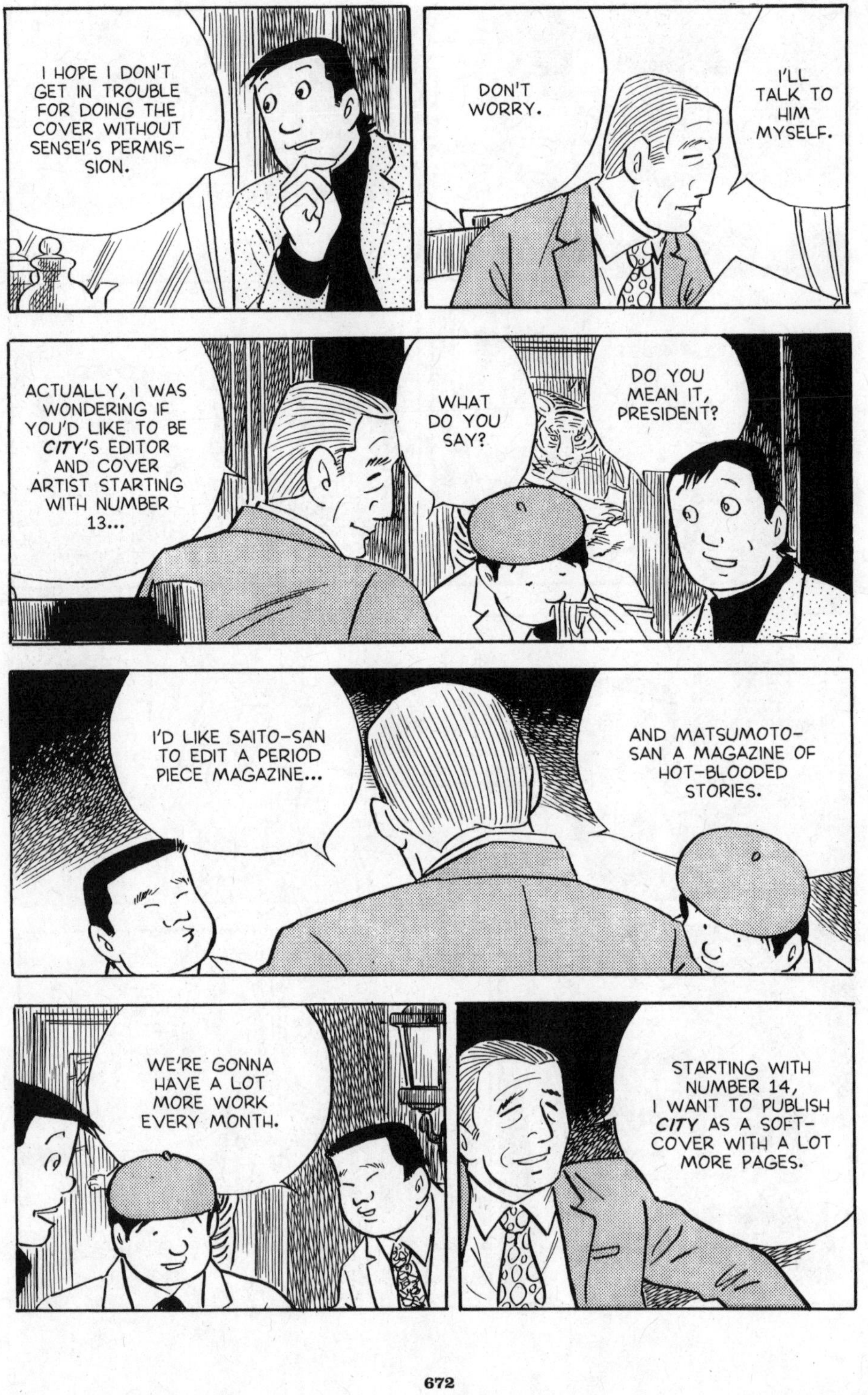
I HOPE I DON'T GET IN TROUBLE FOR DOING THE COVER WITHOUT SENSEI'S PERMIS-SION.
DON'T WORRY.
I'LL TALK TO HIM MYSELF.
ACTUALLY, I WAS WONDERING IF YOU'D LIKE TO BE *CITY*'S EDITOR AND COVER ARTIST STARTING WITH NUMBER 13...
WHAT DO YOU SAY?
DO YOU MEAN IT, PRESIDENT?
I'D LIKE SAITO-SAN TO EDIT A PERIOD PIECE MAGAZINE...
AND MATSUMOTO-SAN A MAGAZINE OF HOT-BLOODED STORIES.
WE'RE GONNA HAVE A LOT MORE WORK EVERY MONTH.
STARTING WITH NUMBER 14, I WANT TO PUBLISH *CITY* AS A SOFT-COVER WITH A LOT MORE PAGES.

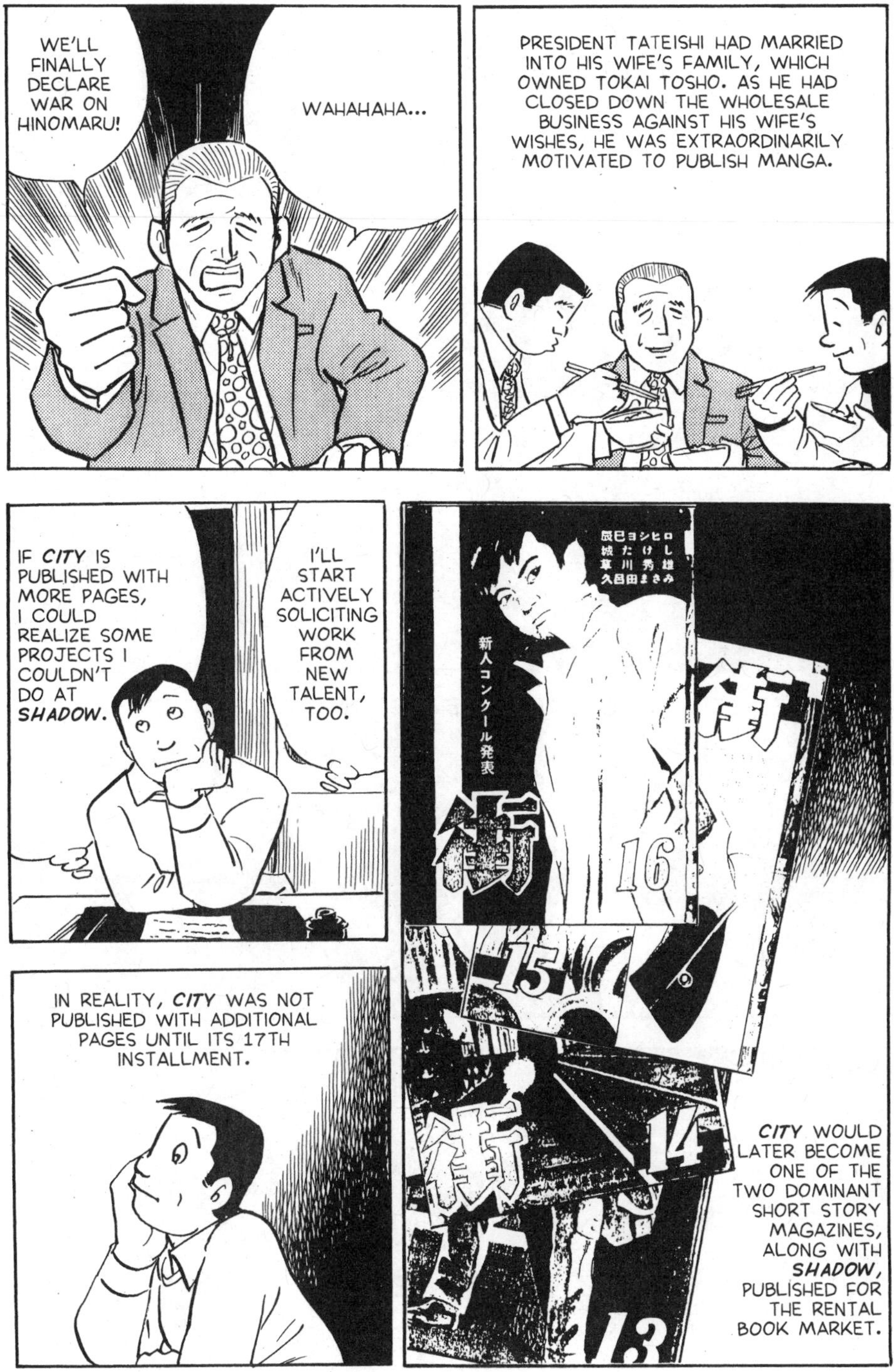
WE'LL FINALLY DECLARE WAR ON HINOMARU!
WAHAHAHA...
PRESIDENT TATEISHI HAD MARRIED INTO HIS WIFE'S FAMILY, WHICH OWNED TOKAI TOSHO. AS HE HAD CLOSED DOWN THE WHOLESALE BUSINESS AGAINST HIS WIFE'S WISHES, HE WAS EXTRAORDINARILY MOTIVATED TO PUBLISH MANGA.
IF ***CITY*** IS PUBLISHED WITH MORE PAGES, I COULD REALIZE SOME PROJECTS I COULDN'T DO AT ***SHADOW***.
I'LL START ACTIVELY SOLICITING WORK FROM NEW TALENT, TOO.
IN REALITY, ***CITY*** WAS NOT PUBLISHED WITH ADDITIONAL PAGES UNTIL ITS 17TH INSTALLMENT.
辰巳ヨシヒロ
城たけし
草川秀雄
久呂田まさみ
新人コンクール発表
街
16
街
15
街
14
13
CITY WOULD LATER BECOME ONE OF THE TWO DOMINANT SHORT STORY MAGAZINES, ALONG WITH ***SHADOW***, PUBLISHED FOR THE RENTAL BOOK MARKET.

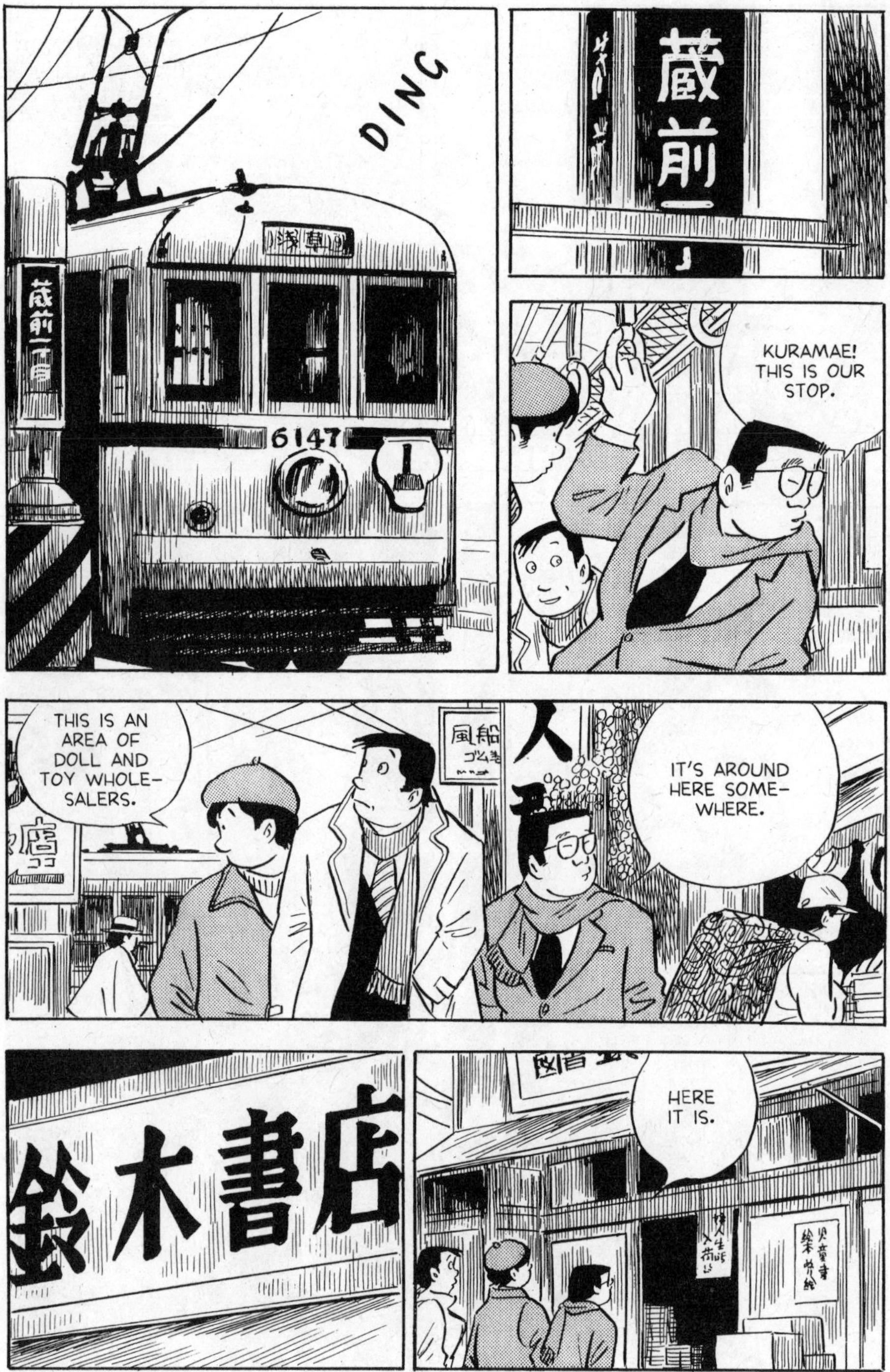
DING
蔵前
KURAMAE! THIS IS OUR STOP.
THIS IS AN AREA OF DOLL AND TOY WHOLE-SALERS.
風船
IT'S AROUND HERE SOME-WHERE.
鈴木書店
HERE IT IS.
SIGN: SUZUKI SHOTEN

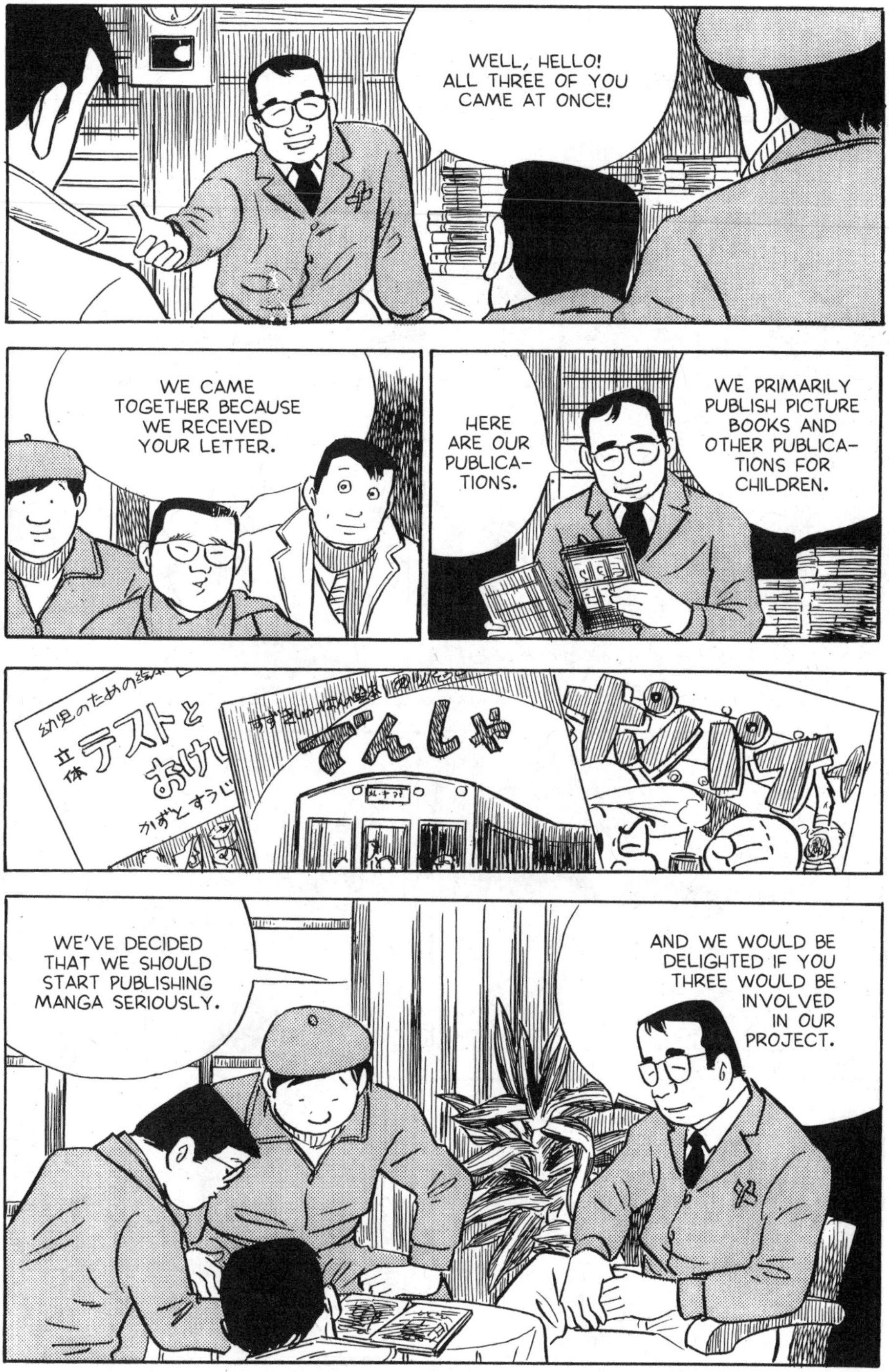
WELL, HELLO! ALL THREE OF YOU CAME AT ONCE!
WE CAME TOGETHER BECAUSE WE RECEIVED YOUR LETTER.
HERE ARE OUR PUBLICATIONS.
WE PRIMARILY PUBLISH PICTURE BOOKS AND OTHER PUBLICATIONS FOR CHILDREN.
かずとすうじ
でんしゃ
ポパイ
WE'VE DECIDED THAT WE SHOULD START PUBLISHING MANGA SERIOUSLY.
AND WE WOULD BE DELIGHTED IF YOU THREE WOULD BE INVOLVED IN OUR PROJECT.

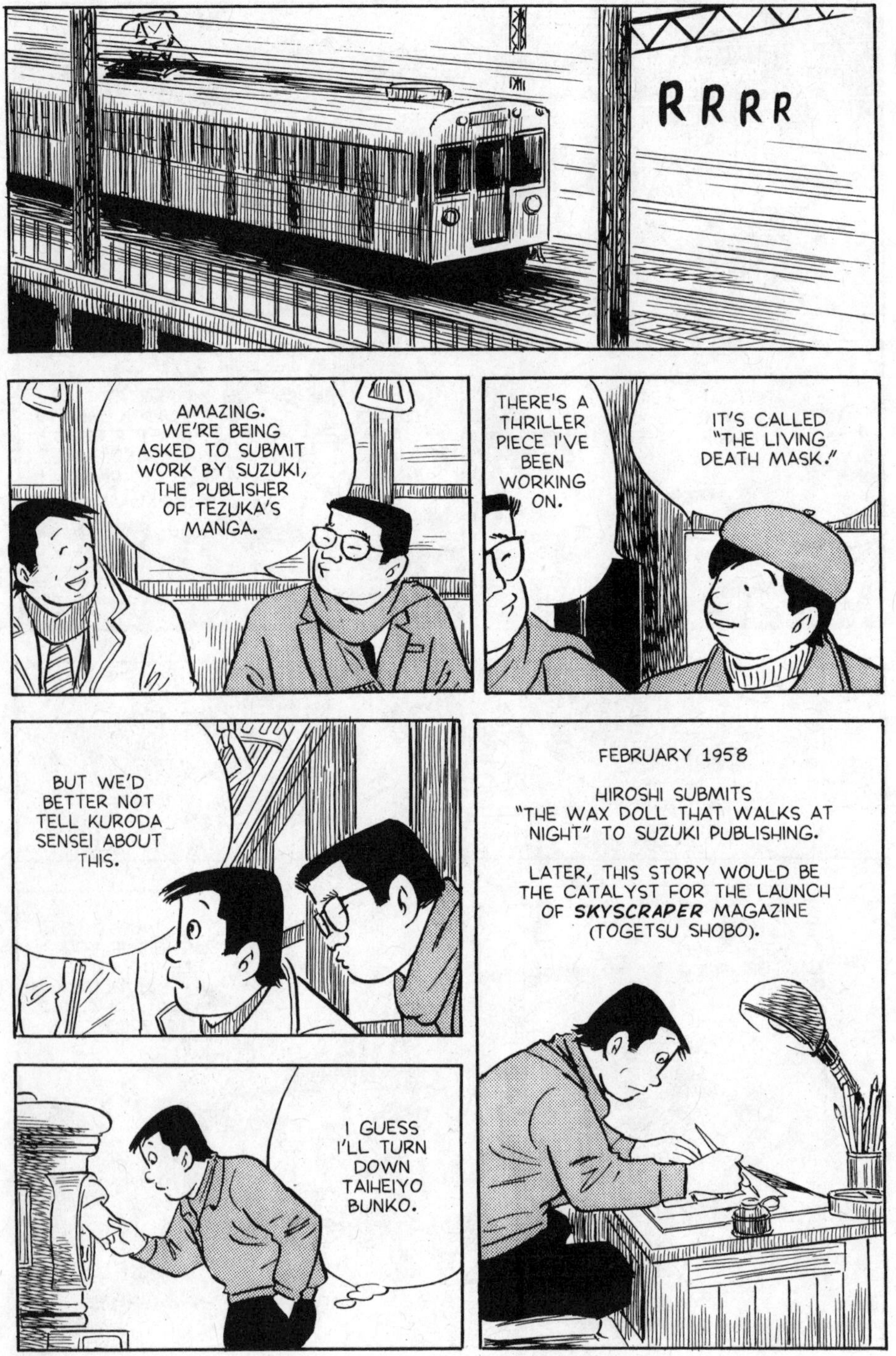
RRRR
AMAZING. WE'RE BEING ASKED TO SUBMIT WORK BY SUZUKI, THE PUBLISHER OF TEZUKA'S MANGA.
THERE'S A THRILLER PIECE I'VE BEEN WORKING ON.
IT'S CALLED "THE LIVING DEATH MASK."
BUT WE'D BETTER NOT TELL KURODA SENSEI ABOUT THIS.
FEBRUARY 1958
HIROSHI SUBMITS "THE WAX DOLL THAT WALKS AT NIGHT" TO SUZUKI PUBLISHING.
LATER, THIS STORY WOULD BE THE CATALYST FOR THE LAUNCH OF ***SKYSCRAPER*** MAGAZINE (TOGETSU SHOBO).
I GUESS I'LL TURN DOWN TAIHEIYO BUNKO.

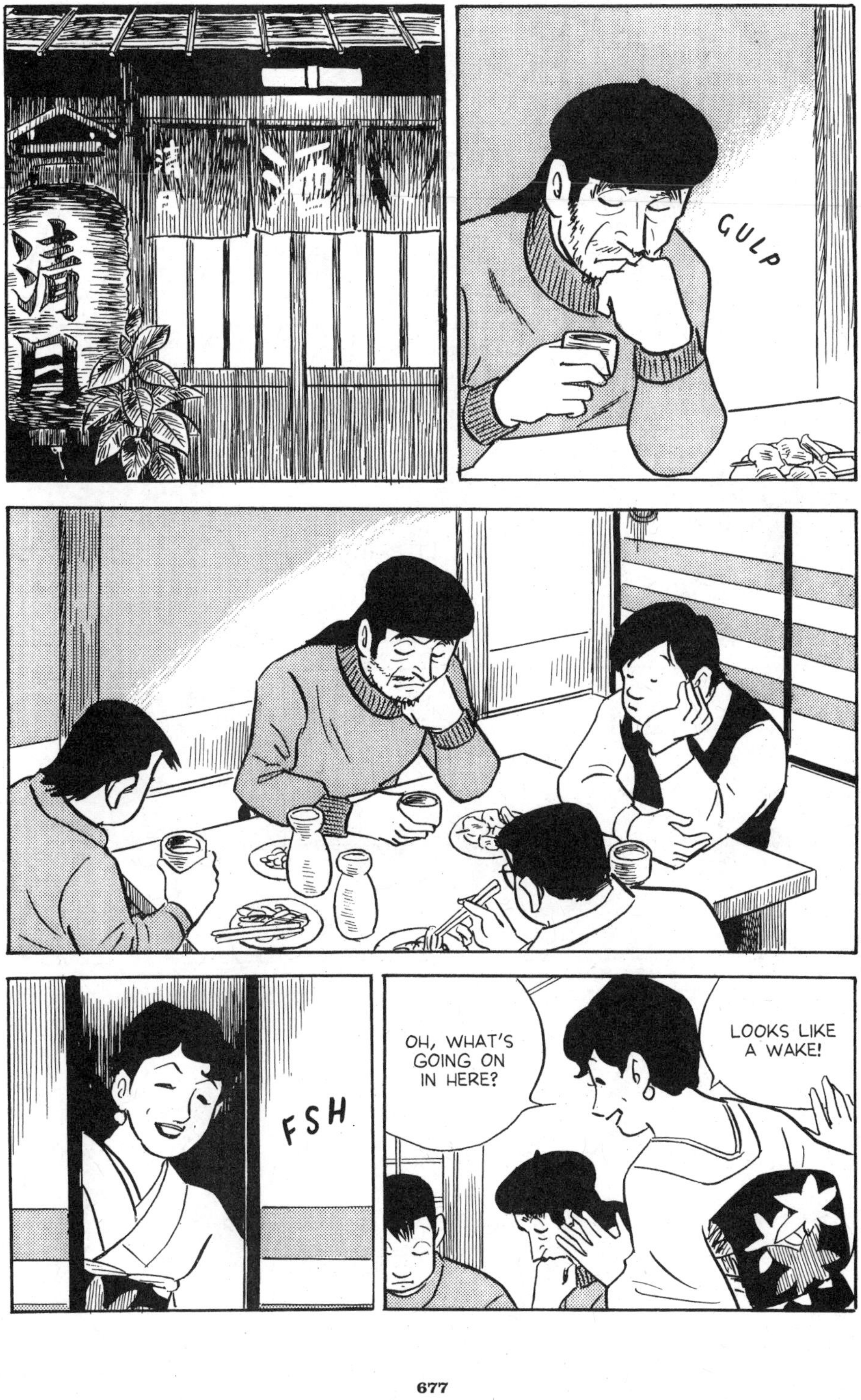
清月
酒
GULP
FSH
OH, WHAT'S GOING ON IN HERE?
LOOKS LIKE A WAKE!

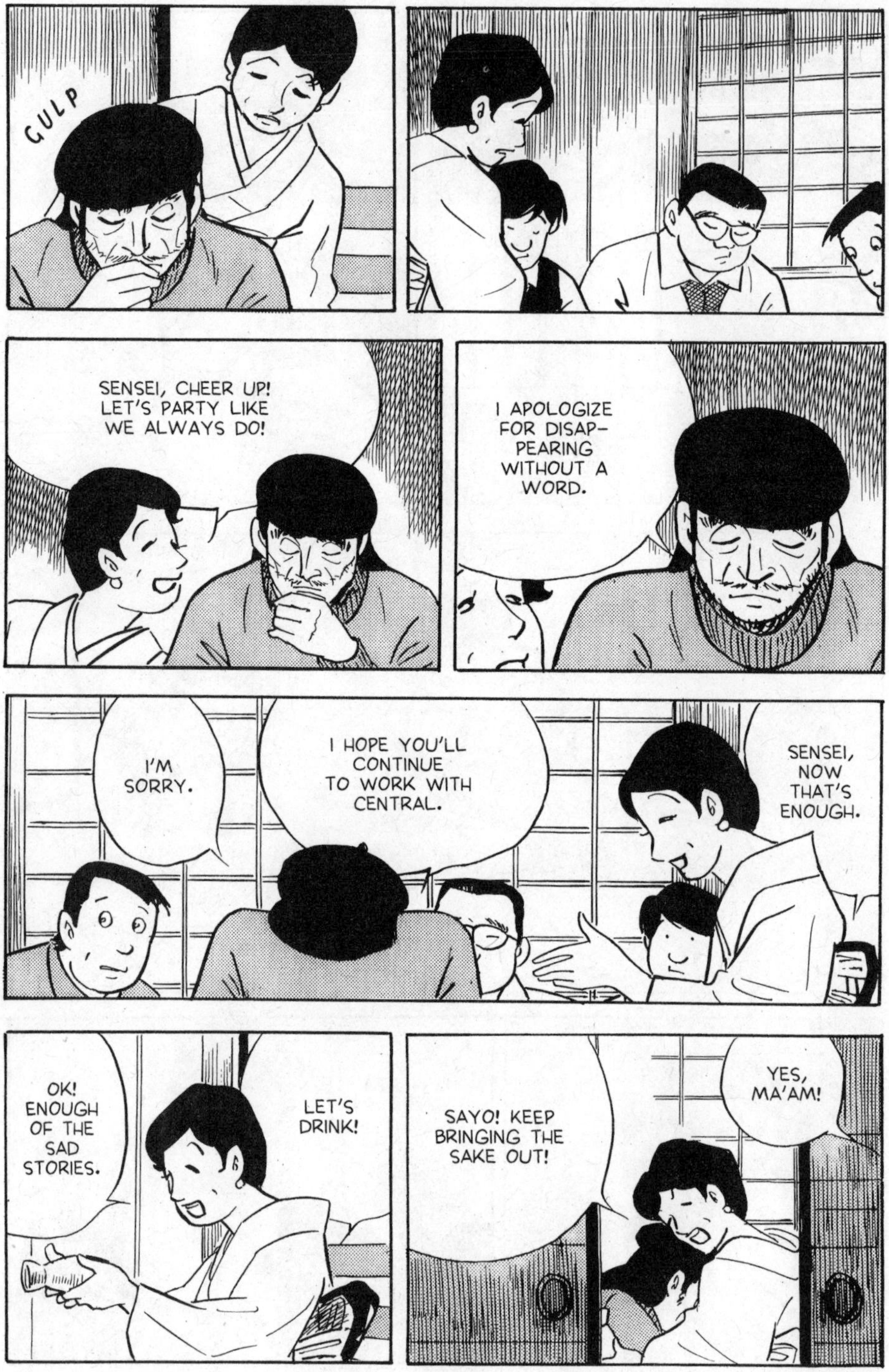
GULP
SENSEI, CHEER UP! LET'S PARTY LIKE WE ALWAYS DO!
I APOLOGIZE FOR DISAP-PEARING WITHOUT A WORD.
I'M SORRY.
I HOPE YOU'LL CONTINUE TO WORK WITH CENTRAL.
SENSEI, NOW THAT'S ENOUGH.
OK! ENOUGH OF THE SAD STORIES.
LET'S DRINK!
SAYO! KEEP BRINGING THE SAKE OUT!
YES, MA'AM!

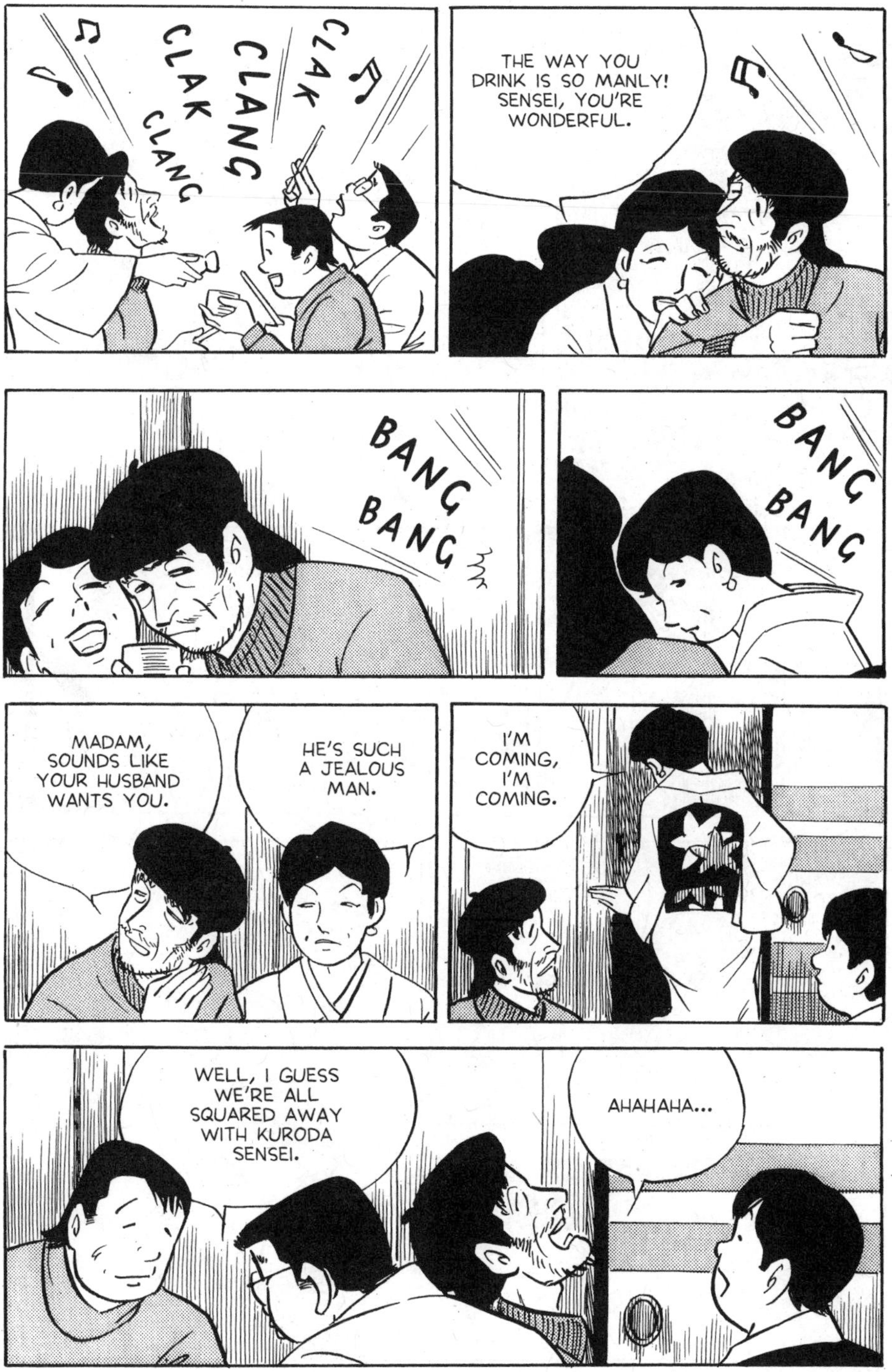
CLAK CLAK CLAK
CLANG CLANG
THE WAY YOU DRINK IS SO MANLY! SENSEI, YOU'RE WONDERFUL.
BANG BANG
BANG BANG
MADAM, SOUNDS LIKE YOUR HUSBAND WANTS YOU.
HE'S SUCH A JEALOUS MAN.
I'M COMING, I'M COMING.
WELL, I GUESS WE'RE ALL SQUARED AWAY WITH KURODA SENSEI.
AHAHAHA...

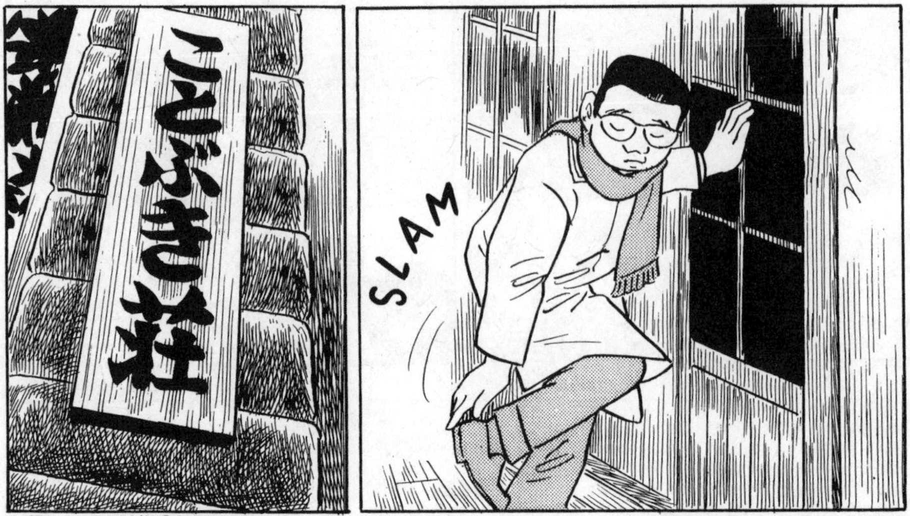
ことぶき荘
SLAM

SIGN: KOTOBUKISO

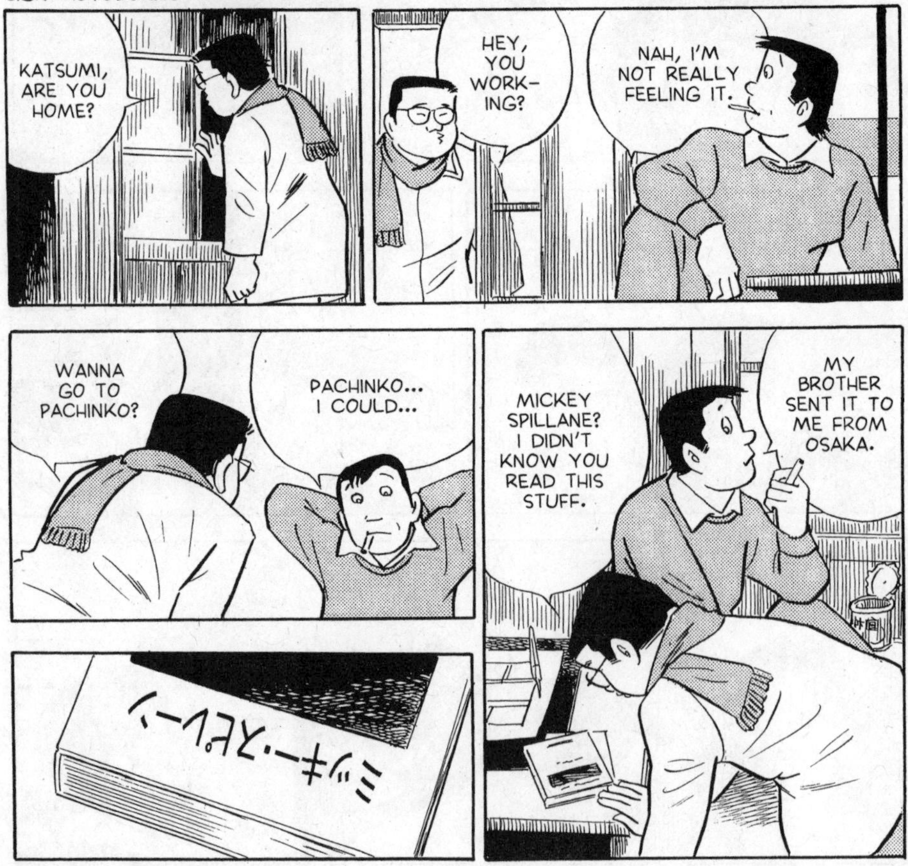
KATSUMI, ARE YOU HOME?
HEY, YOU WORK-ING?
NAH, I'M NOT REALLY FEELING IT.
WANNA GO TO PACHINKO?
PACHINKO... I COULD...
ミッキー・スピレーン
MICKEY SPILLANE? I DIDN'T KNOW YOU READ THIS STUFF.
MY BROTHER SENT IT TO ME FROM OSAKA.

AUTHOR: MICKEY SPILLANE

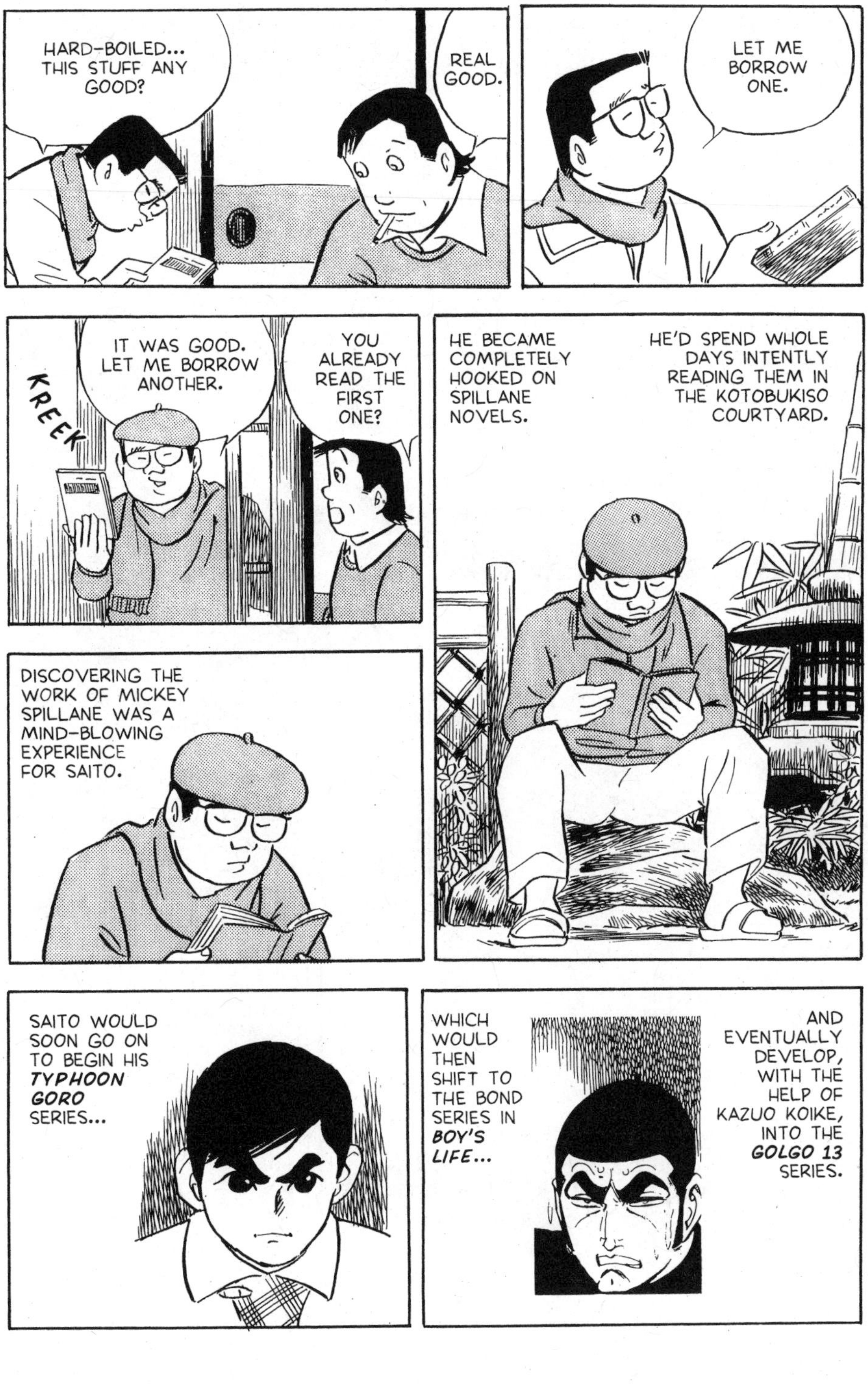
HARD-BOILED... THIS STUFF ANY GOOD?
REAL GOOD.
LET ME BORROW ONE.
KREEK
IT WAS GOOD. LET ME BORROW ANOTHER.
YOU ALREADY READ THE FIRST ONE?
DISCOVERING THE WORK OF MICKEY SPILLANE WAS A MIND-BLOWING EXPERIENCE FOR SAITO.
HE BECAME COMPLETELY HOOKED ON SPILLANE NOVELS.
HE'D SPEND WHOLE DAYS INTENTLY READING THEM IN THE KOTOBUKISO COURTYARD.
SAITO WOULD SOON GO ON TO BEGIN HIS ***TYPHOON GORO*** SERIES...
WHICH WOULD THEN SHIFT TO THE BOND SERIES IN ***BOY'S LIFE...***
AND EVENTUALLY DEVELOP, WITH THE HELP OF KAZUO KOIKE, INTO THE ***GOLGO 13*** SERIES.

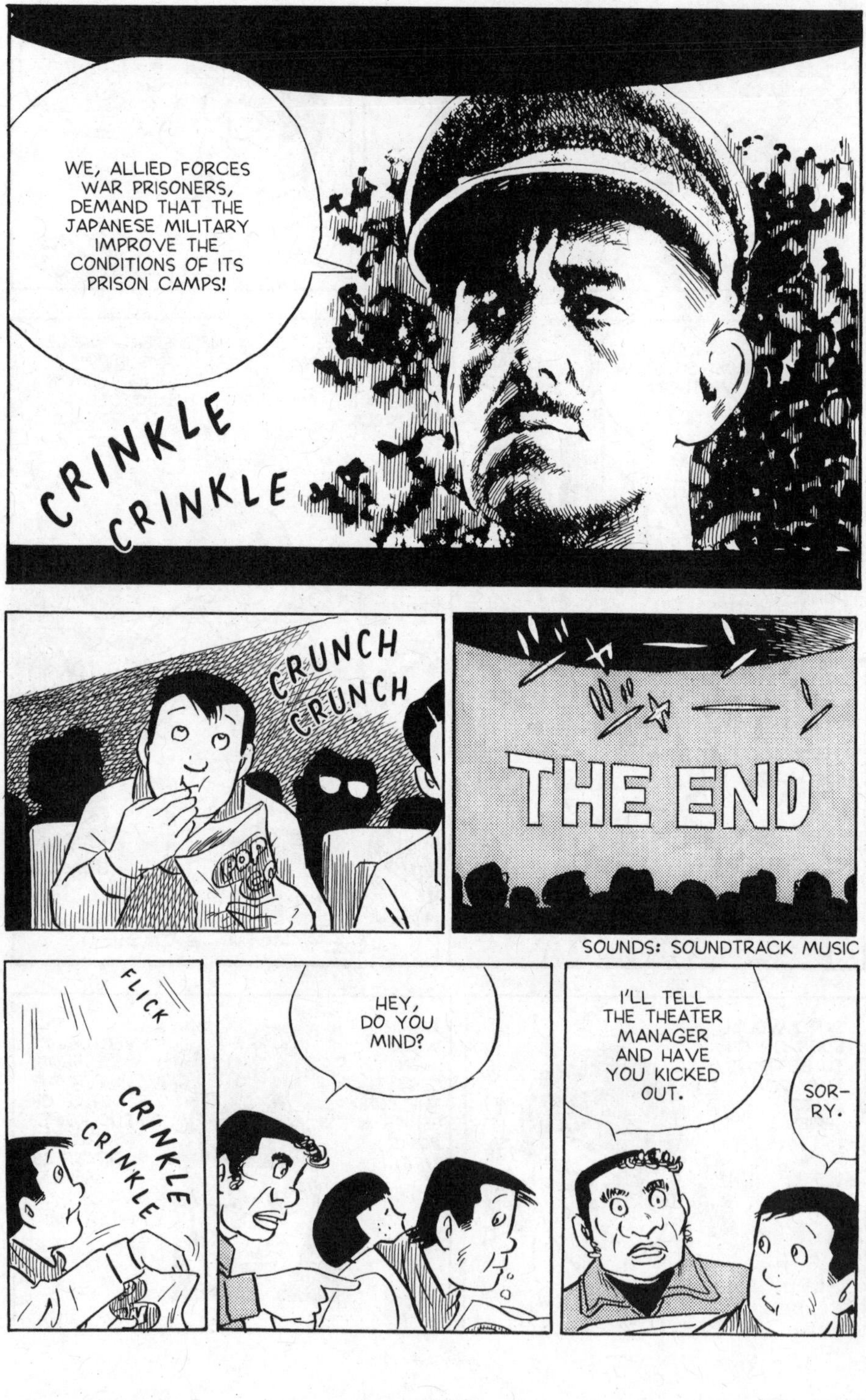
WE, ALLIED FORCES WAR PRISONERS, DEMAND THAT THE JAPANESE MILITARY IMPROVE THE CONDITIONS OF ITS PRISON CAMPS!
CRINKLE CRINKLE
CRUNCH CRUNCH
THE END
SOUNDS: SOUNDTRACK MUSIC
FLICK
CRINKLE CRINKLE
HEY, DO YOU MIND?
I'LL TELL THE THEATER MANAGER AND HAVE YOU KICKED OUT.
SOR-RY.

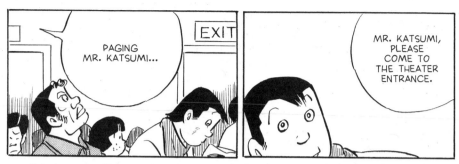

EXIT
PAGING MR. KATSUMI...
MR. KATSUMI, PLEASE COME TO THE THEATER ENTRANCE.
EXIT
GUESS YOU ALREADY TOLD THE MANAGER.
総天然色
ウィリアム ホールデン
アレック・ギネス
2本立
同時上映 人工衛星X号
OH... TELEGRAM MAN. IT'S YOU.
SORRY TO DISTURB YOU. I THOUGHT YOU'D BE HERE.

SIGN: CINEMA

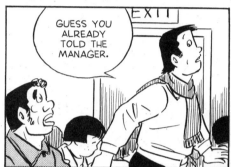

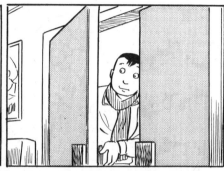

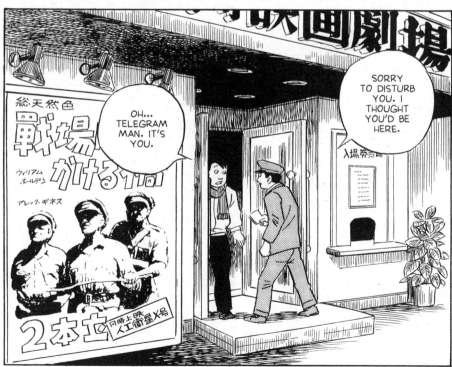

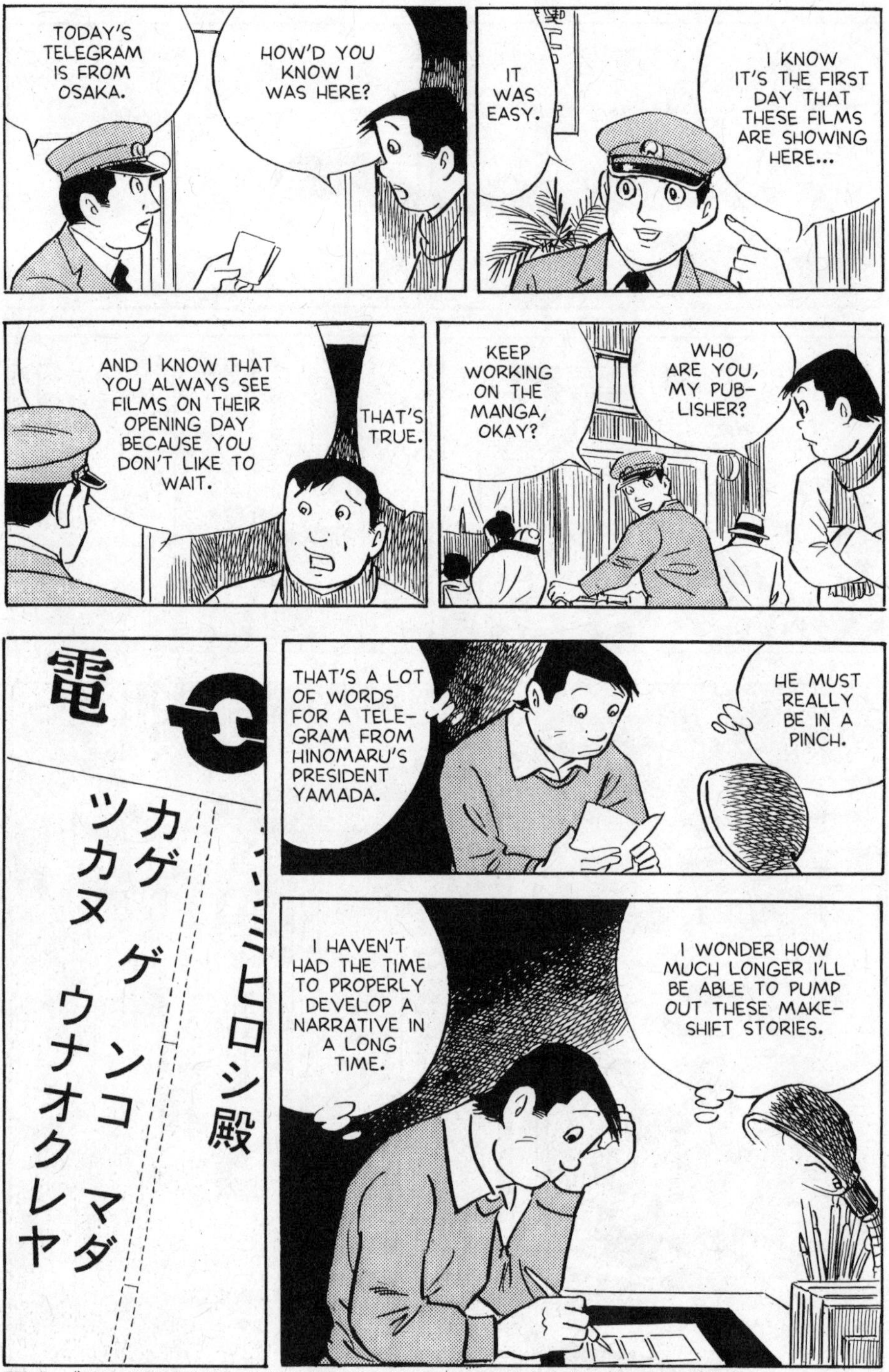
TODAY'S TELEGRAM IS FROM OSAKA.
HOW'D YOU KNOW I WAS HERE?
IT WAS EASY.
I KNOW IT'S THE FIRST DAY THAT THESE FILMS ARE SHOWING HERE...
AND I KNOW THAT YOU ALWAYS SEE FILMS ON THEIR OPENING DAY BECAUSE YOU DON'T LIKE TO WAIT.
THAT'S TRUE.
KEEP WORKING ON THE MANGA, OKAY?
WHO ARE YOU, MY PUBLISHER?
電
ミヒロシ殿
カゲ　ゲンコ　マダ
ツカヌ　ウナオクレヤ
THAT'S A LOT OF WORDS FOR A TELEGRAM FROM HINOMARU'S PRESIDENT YAMADA.
HE MUST REALLY BE IN A PINCH.
I HAVEN'T HAD THE TIME TO PROPERLY DEVELOP A NARRATIVE IN A LONG TIME.
I WONDER HOW MUCH LONGER I'LL BE ABLE TO PUMP OUT THESE MAKE-SHIFT STORIES.

TEXT: "MR. HIROSHI KATSUMI / HAVE NOT RECEIVED ***SHADOW*** SCRIPT YET / SEND SOON"

DRAWING FROM TURMOIL

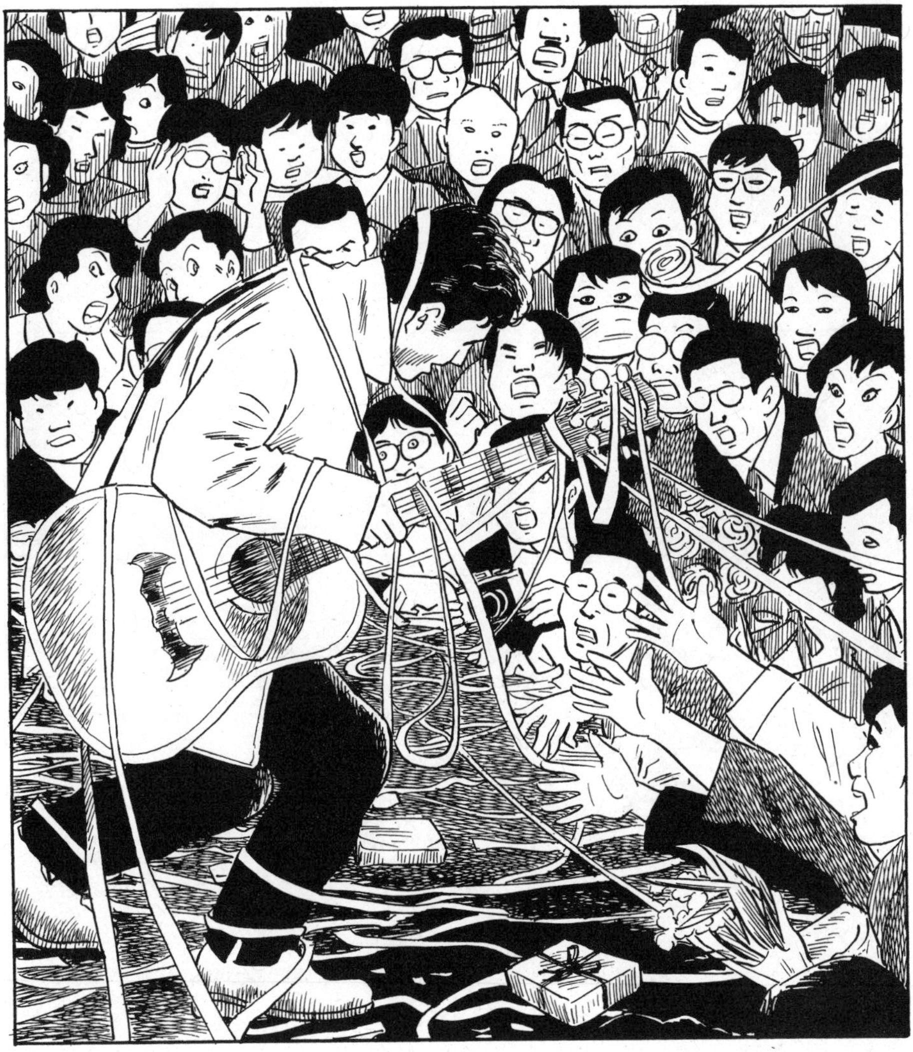

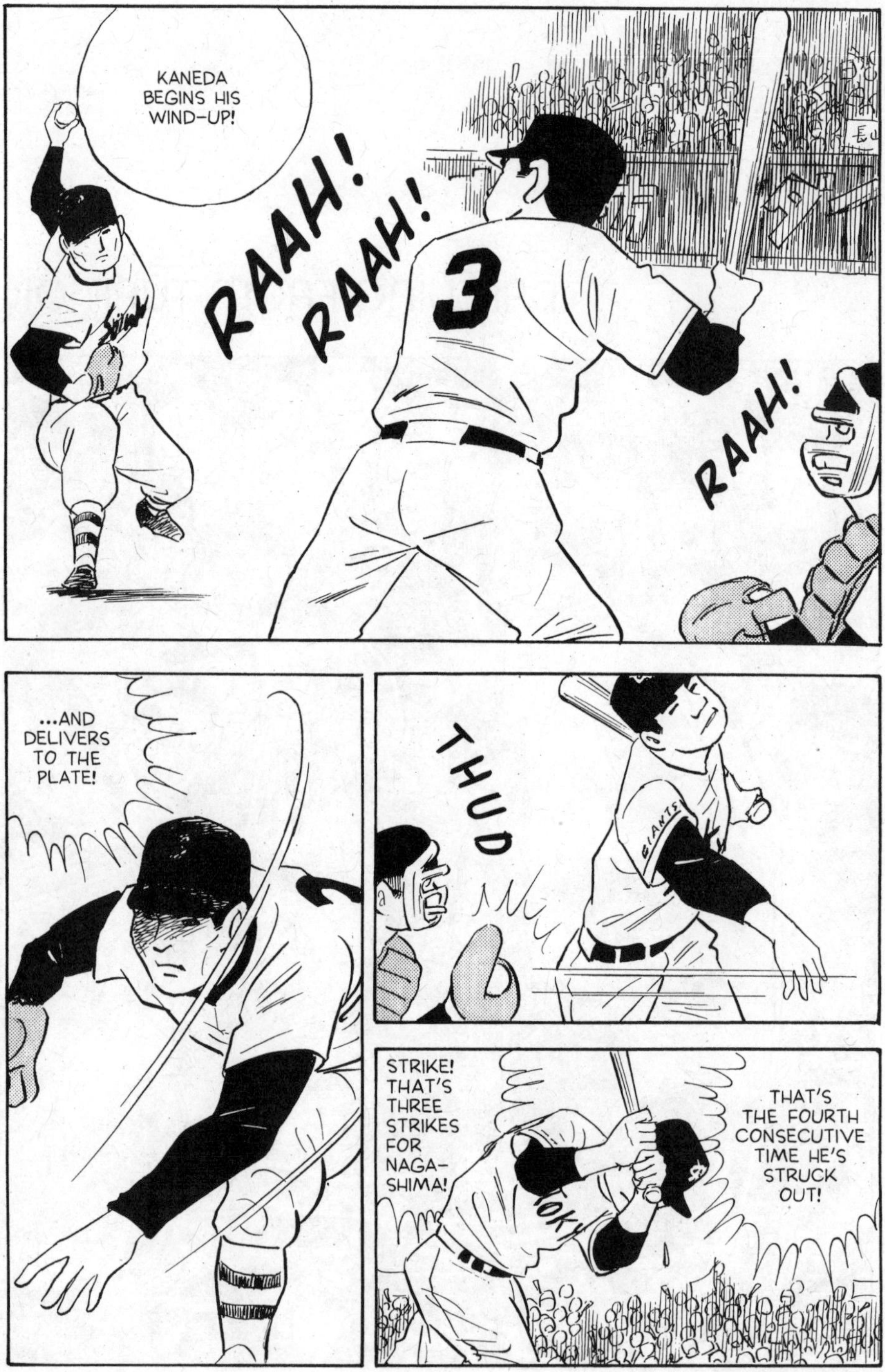
KANEDA BEGINS HIS WIND-UP!
RAAH!
RAAH!
RAAH!
...AND DELIVERS TO THE PLATE!
THUD
GIANTS
STRIKE! THAT'S THREE STRIKES FOR NAGA-SHIMA!
THAT'S THE FOURTH CONSECUTIVE TIME HE'S STRUCK OUT!

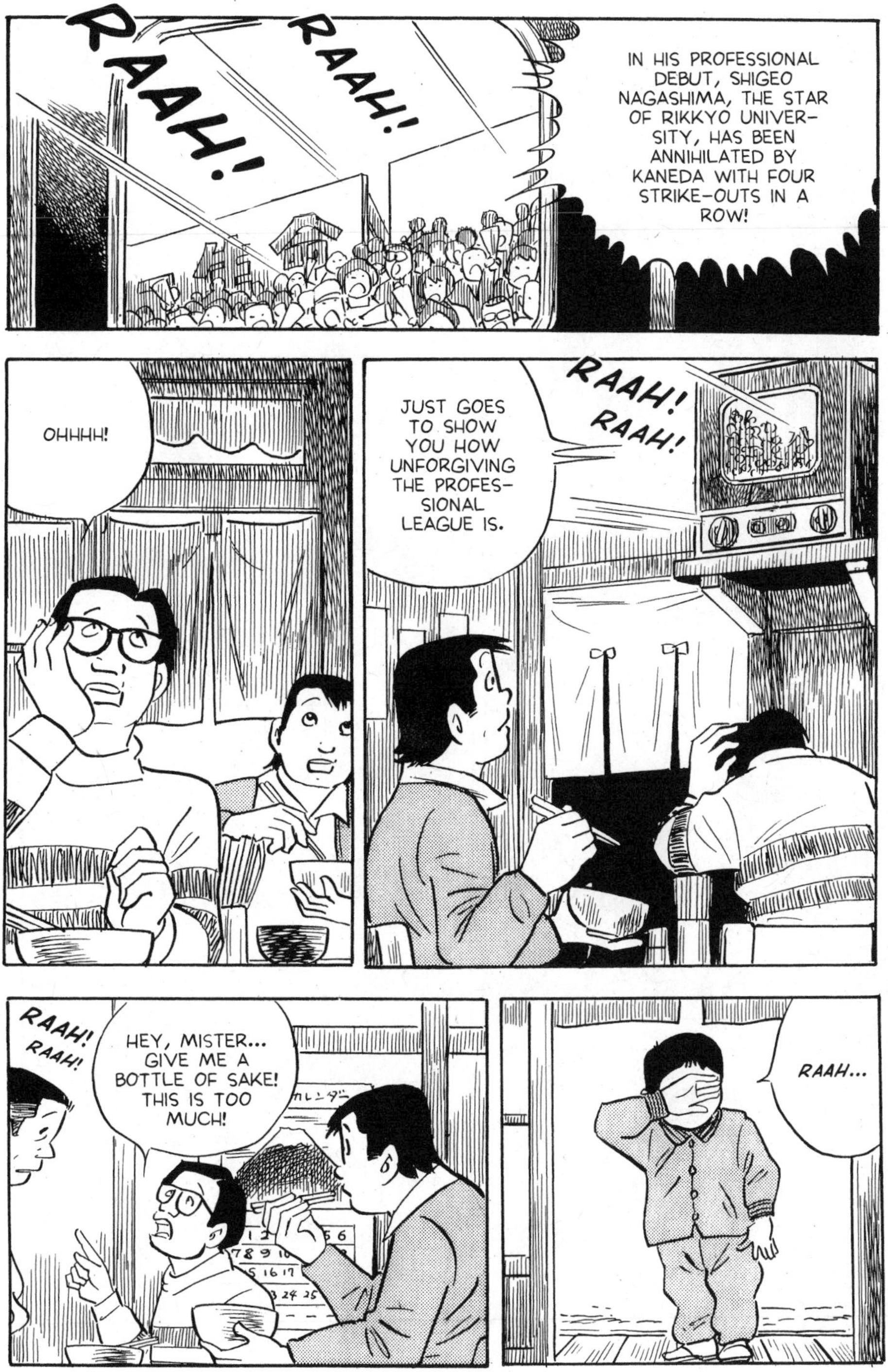
RAAH!
RAAH!
IN HIS PROFESSIONAL DEBUT, SHIGEO NAGASHIMA, THE STAR OF RIKKYO UNIVERSITY, HAS BEEN ANNIHILATED BY KANEDA WITH FOUR STRIKE-OUTS IN A ROW!
OHHHH!
JUST GOES TO SHOW YOU HOW UNFORGIVING THE PROFESSIONAL LEAGUE IS.
RAAH!
RAAH!
RAAH!
RAAH!
HEY, MISTER... GIVE ME A BOTTLE OF SAKE! THIS IS TOO MUCH!
カレンダー
RAAH...

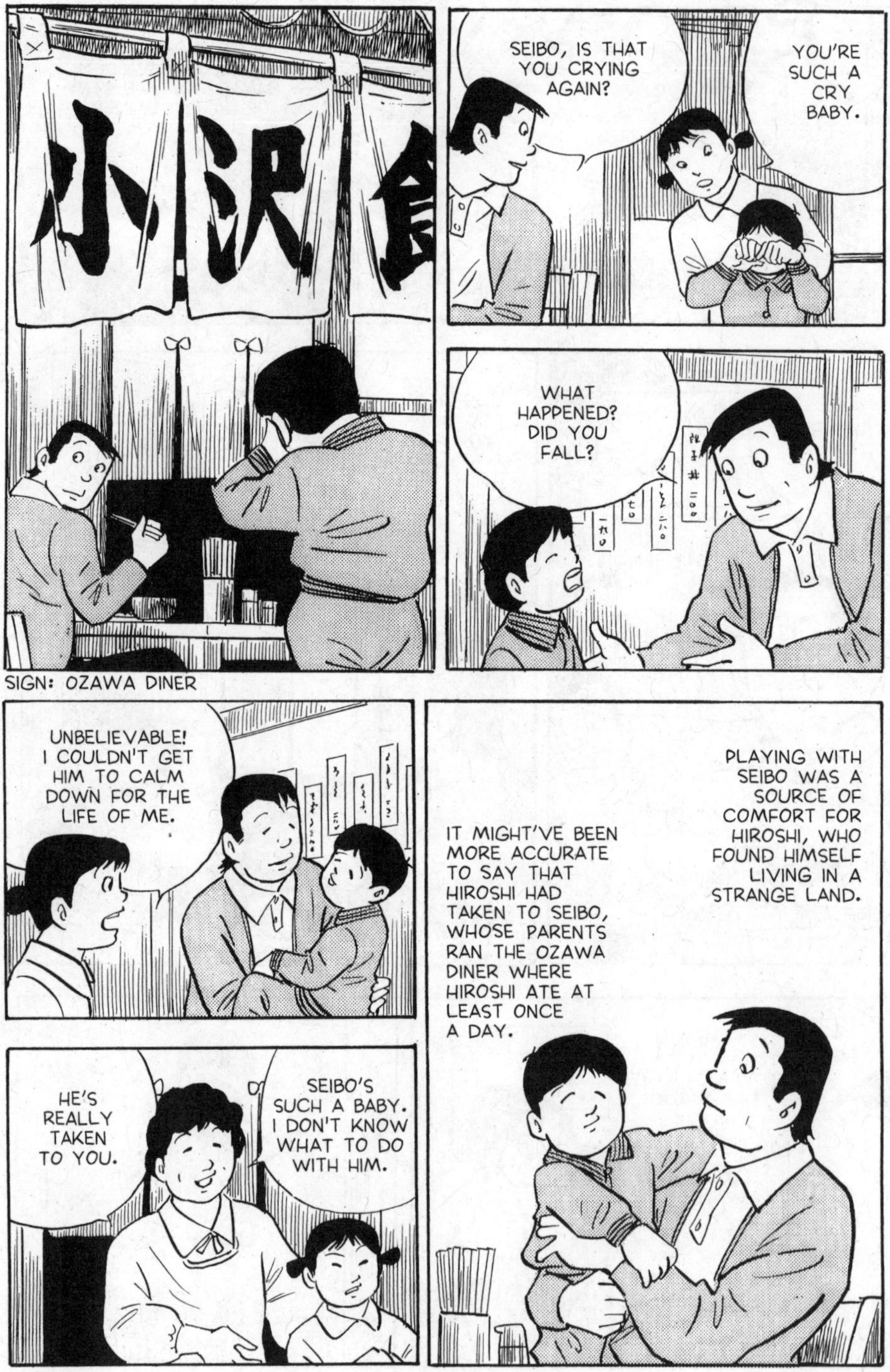

小沢食
SIGN: OZAWA DINER
SEIBO, IS THAT YOU CRYING AGAIN?
YOU'RE SUCH A CRY BABY.
WHAT HAPPENED? DID YOU FALL?
UNBELIEVABLE! I COULDN'T GET HIM TO CALM DOWN FOR THE LIFE OF ME.
HE'S REALLY TAKEN TO YOU.
SEIBO'S SUCH A BABY. I DON'T KNOW WHAT TO DO WITH HIM.
PLAYING WITH SEIBO WAS A SOURCE OF COMFORT FOR HIROSHI, WHO FOUND HIMSELF LIVING IN A STRANGE LAND.
IT MIGHT'VE BEEN MORE ACCURATE TO SAY THAT HIROSHI HAD TAKEN TO SEIBO, WHOSE PARENTS RAN THE OZAWA DINER WHERE HIROSHI ATE AT LEAST ONCE A DAY.

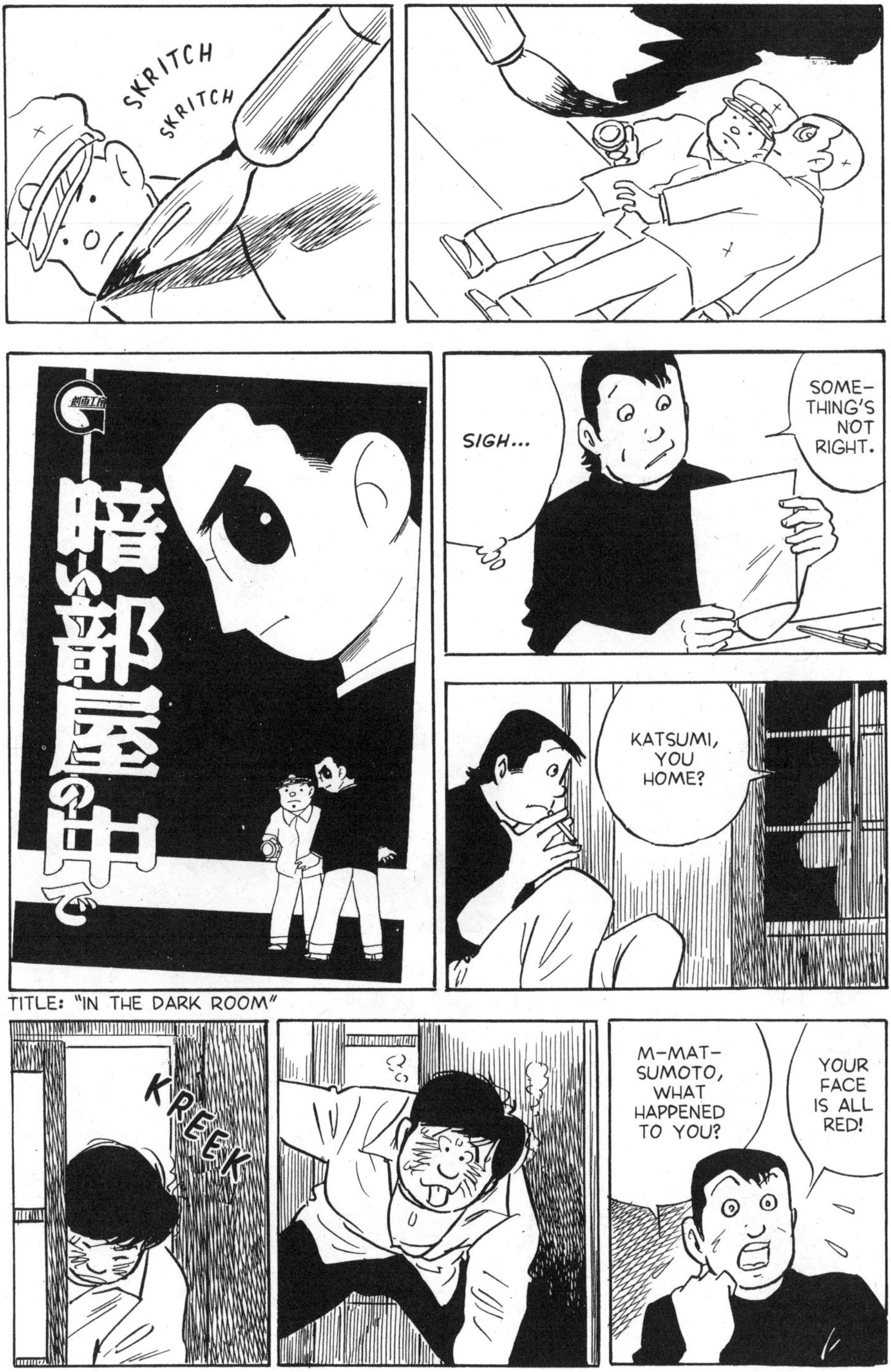
SKRITCH
SKRITCH
暗い部屋の中で
SIGH...
SOME-THING'S NOT RIGHT.
KATSUMI, YOU HOME?
TITLE: "IN THE DARK ROOM"
KREEK
M-MAT-SUMOTO, WHAT HAPPENED TO YOU?
YOUR FACE IS ALL RED!

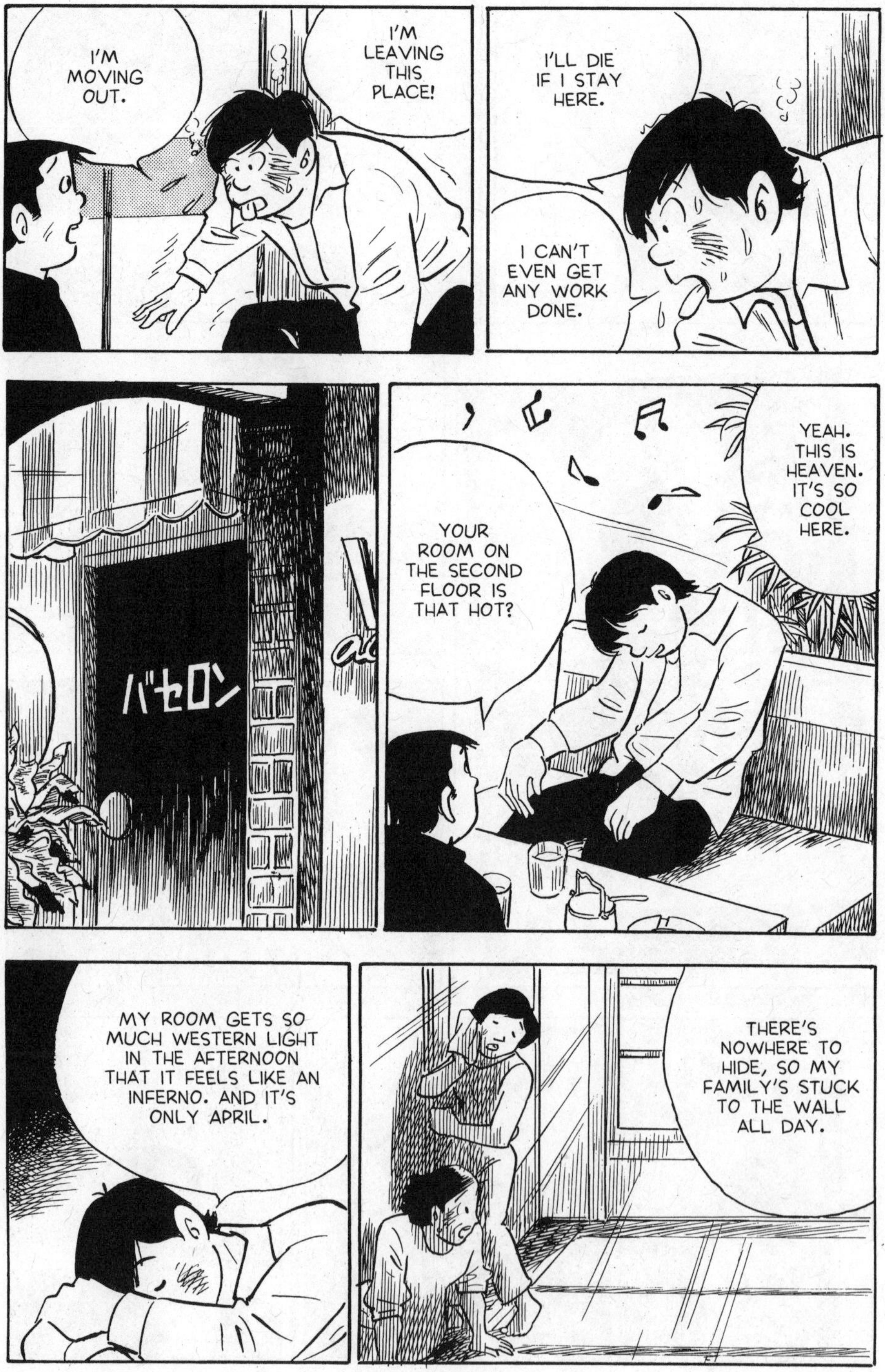
I'M MOVING OUT.
I'M LEAVING THIS PLACE!
I'LL DIE IF I STAY HERE.
I CAN'T EVEN GET ANY WORK DONE.
バセロン
YEAH. THIS IS HEAVEN. IT'S SO COOL HERE.
YOUR ROOM ON THE SECOND FLOOR IS THAT HOT?
MY ROOM GETS SO MUCH WESTERN LIGHT IN THE AFTERNOON THAT IT FEELS LIKE AN INFERNO. AND IT'S ONLY APRIL.
THERE'S NOWHERE TO HIDE, SO MY FAMILY'S STUCK TO THE WALL ALL DAY.

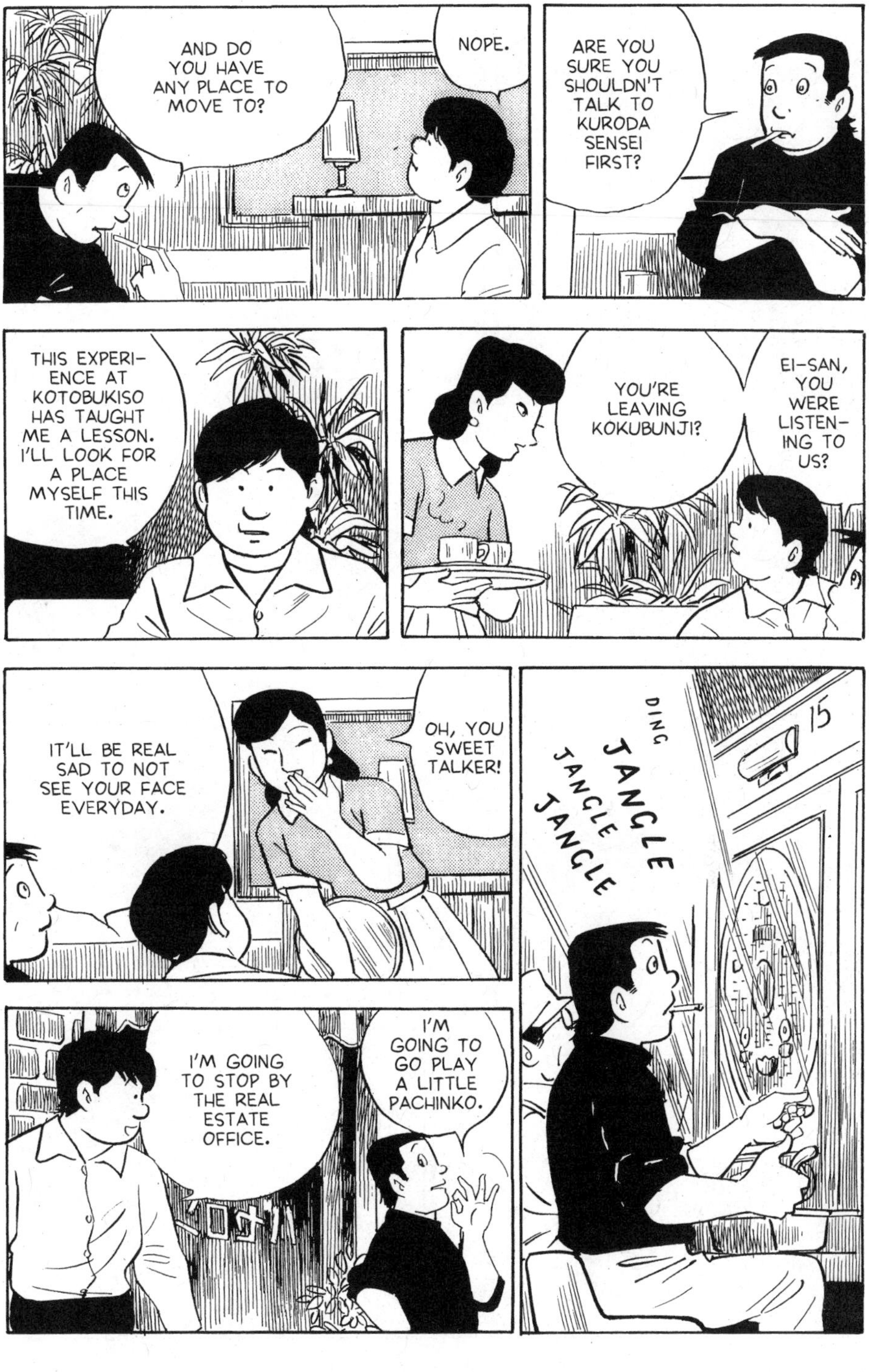
AND DO YOU HAVE ANY PLACE TO MOVE TO?
NOPE.
ARE YOU SURE YOU SHOULDN'T TALK TO KURODA SENSEI FIRST?
THIS EXPERIENCE AT KOTOBUKISO HAS TAUGHT ME A LESSON. I'LL LOOK FOR A PLACE MYSELF THIS TIME.
YOU'RE LEAVING KOKUBUNJI?
EI-SAN, YOU WERE LISTENING TO US?
IT'LL BE REAL SAD TO NOT SEE YOUR FACE EVERYDAY.
OH, YOU SWEET TALKER!
DING
JANGLE
JANGLE
JANGLE
15
I'M GOING TO STOP BY THE REAL ESTATE OFFICE.
I'M GOING TO GO PLAY A LITTLE PACHINKO.

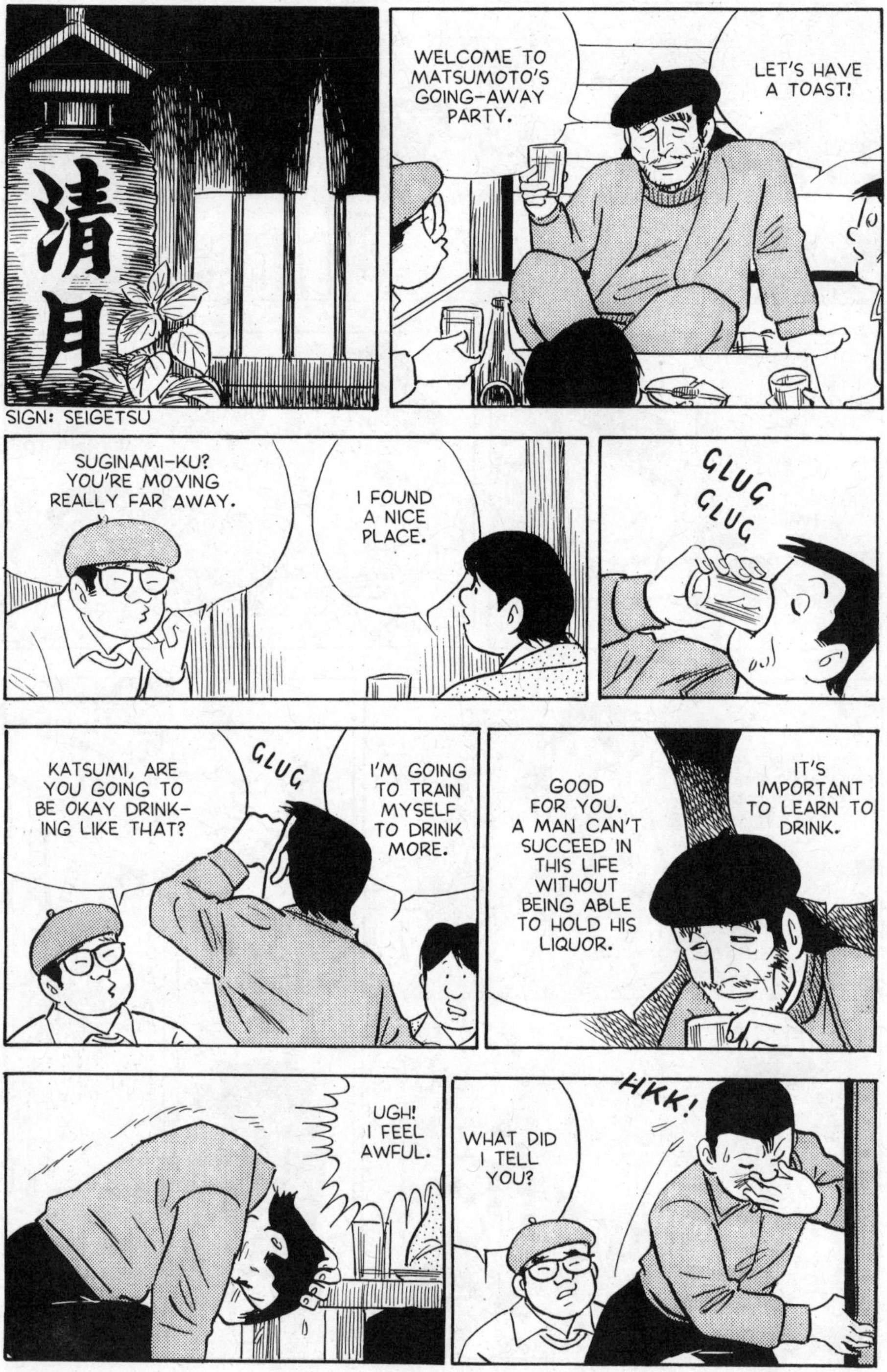
清月
SIGN: SEIGETSU
WELCOME TO MATSUMOTO'S GOING-AWAY PARTY.
LET'S HAVE A TOAST!
SUGINAMI-KU? YOU'RE MOVING REALLY FAR AWAY.
I FOUND A NICE PLACE.
GLUG GLUG
KATSUMI, ARE YOU GOING TO BE OKAY DRINK-ING LIKE THAT?
GLUG
I'M GOING TO TRAIN MYSELF TO DRINK MORE.
GOOD FOR YOU. A MAN CAN'T SUCCEED IN THIS LIFE WITHOUT BEING ABLE TO HOLD HIS LIQUOR.
IT'S IMPORTANT TO LEARN TO DRINK.
UGH! I FEEL AWFUL.
HKK!
WHAT DID I TELL YOU?

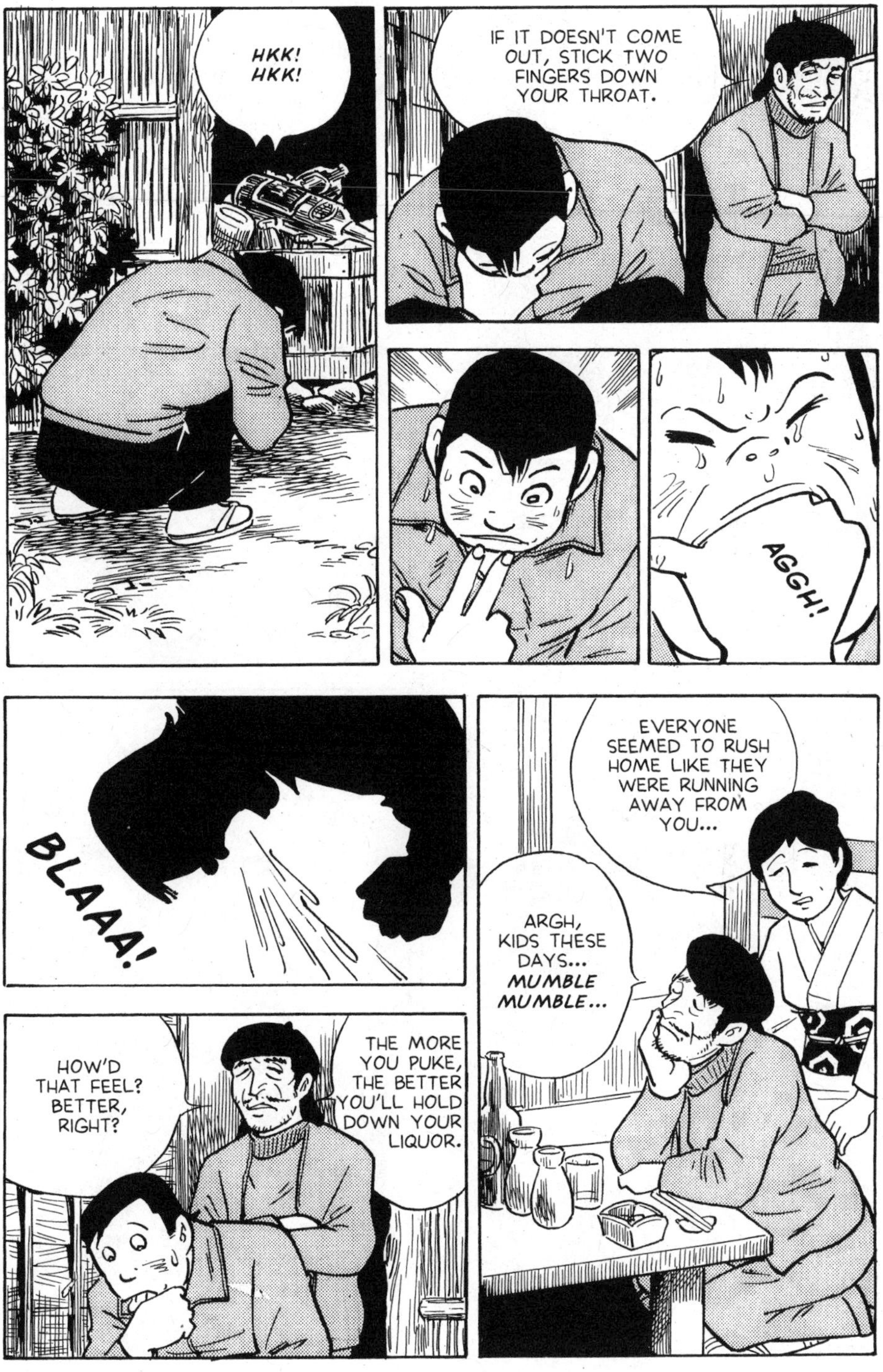
HKK! HKK!
IF IT DOESN'T COME OUT, STICK TWO FINGERS DOWN YOUR THROAT.
AGGH!
BLAAA!
EVERYONE SEEMED TO RUSH HOME LIKE THEY WERE RUNNING AWAY FROM YOU...
ARGH, KIDS THESE DAYS... MUMBLE MUMBLE...
HOW'D THAT FEEL? BETTER, RIGHT?
THE MORE YOU PUKE, THE BETTER YOU'LL HOLD DOWN YOUR LIQUOR.

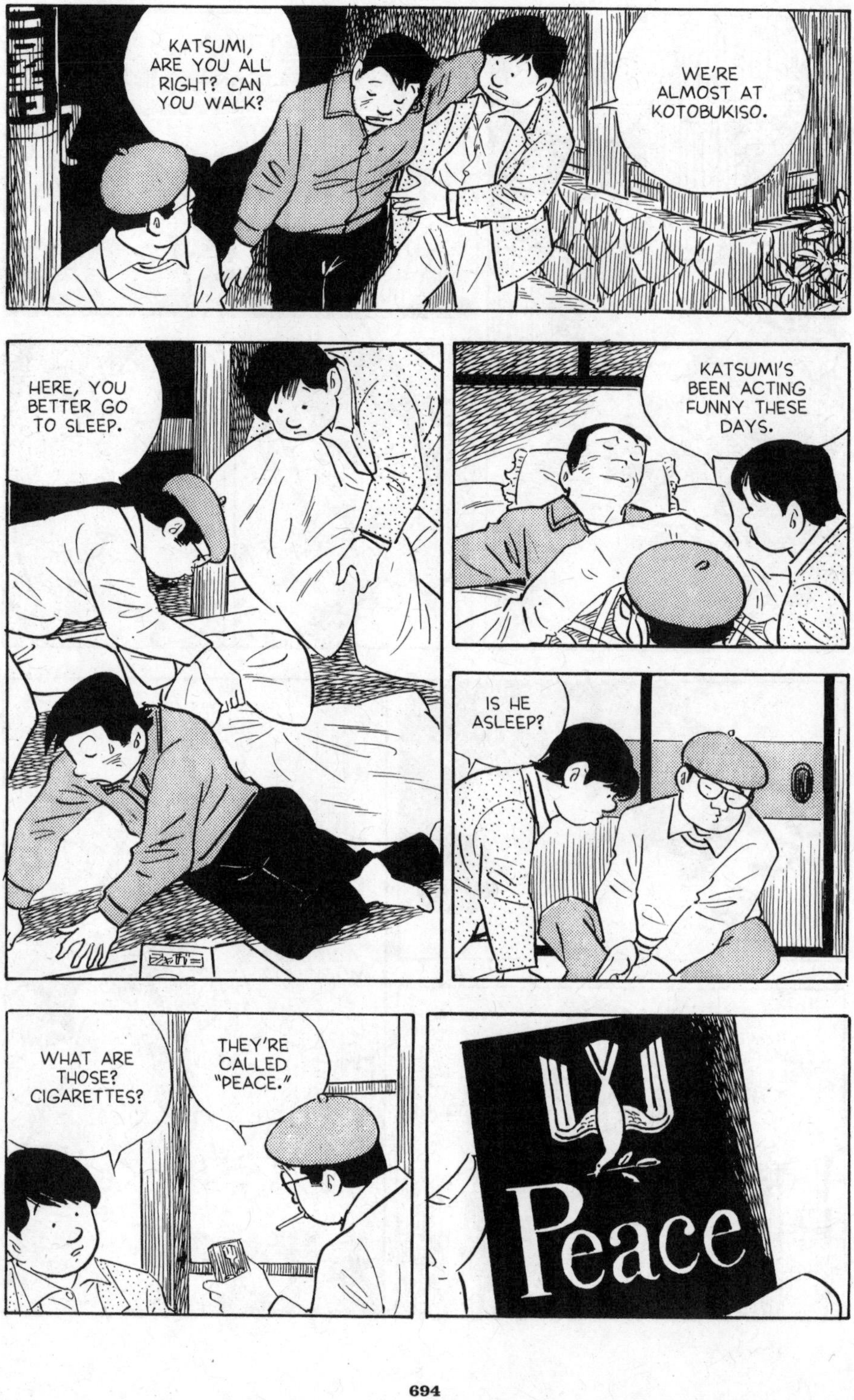
KATSUMI, ARE YOU ALL RIGHT? CAN YOU WALK?
WE'RE ALMOST AT KOTOBUKISO.
HERE, YOU BETTER GO TO SLEEP.
KATSUMI'S BEEN ACTING FUNNY THESE DAYS.
IS HE ASLEEP?
WHAT ARE THOSE? CIGARETTES?
THEY'RE CALLED "PEACE."
Peace

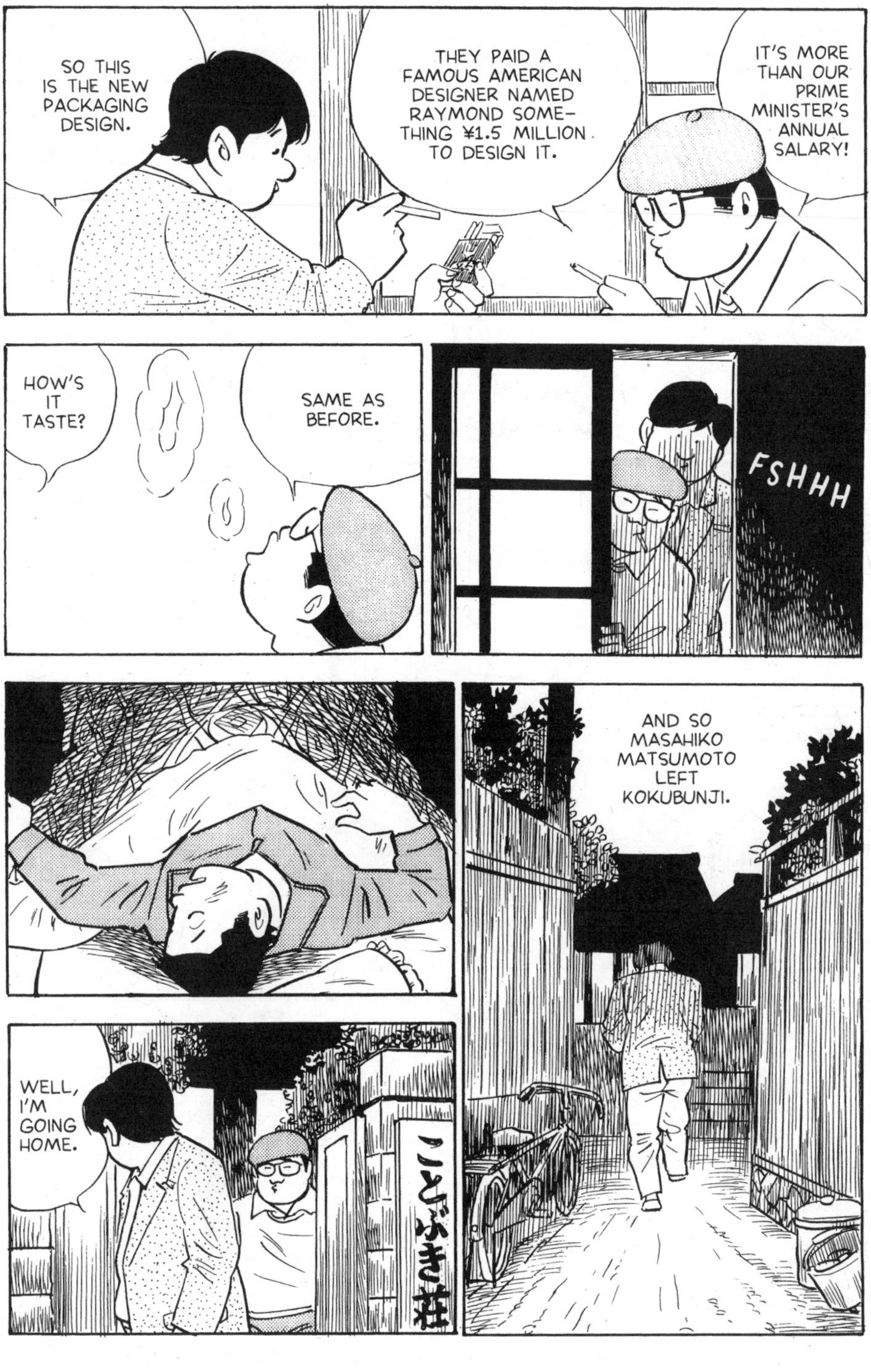
SO THIS IS THE NEW PACKAGING DESIGN.
THEY PAID A FAMOUS AMERICAN DESIGNER NAMED RAYMOND SOME-THING ¥1.5 MILLION TO DESIGN IT.
IT'S MORE THAN OUR PRIME MINISTER'S ANNUAL SALARY!
HOW'S IT TASTE?
SAME AS BEFORE.
FSHHH
WELL, I'M GOING HOME.
ことぶき荘
AND SO MASAHIKO MATSUMOTO LEFT KOKUBUNJI.

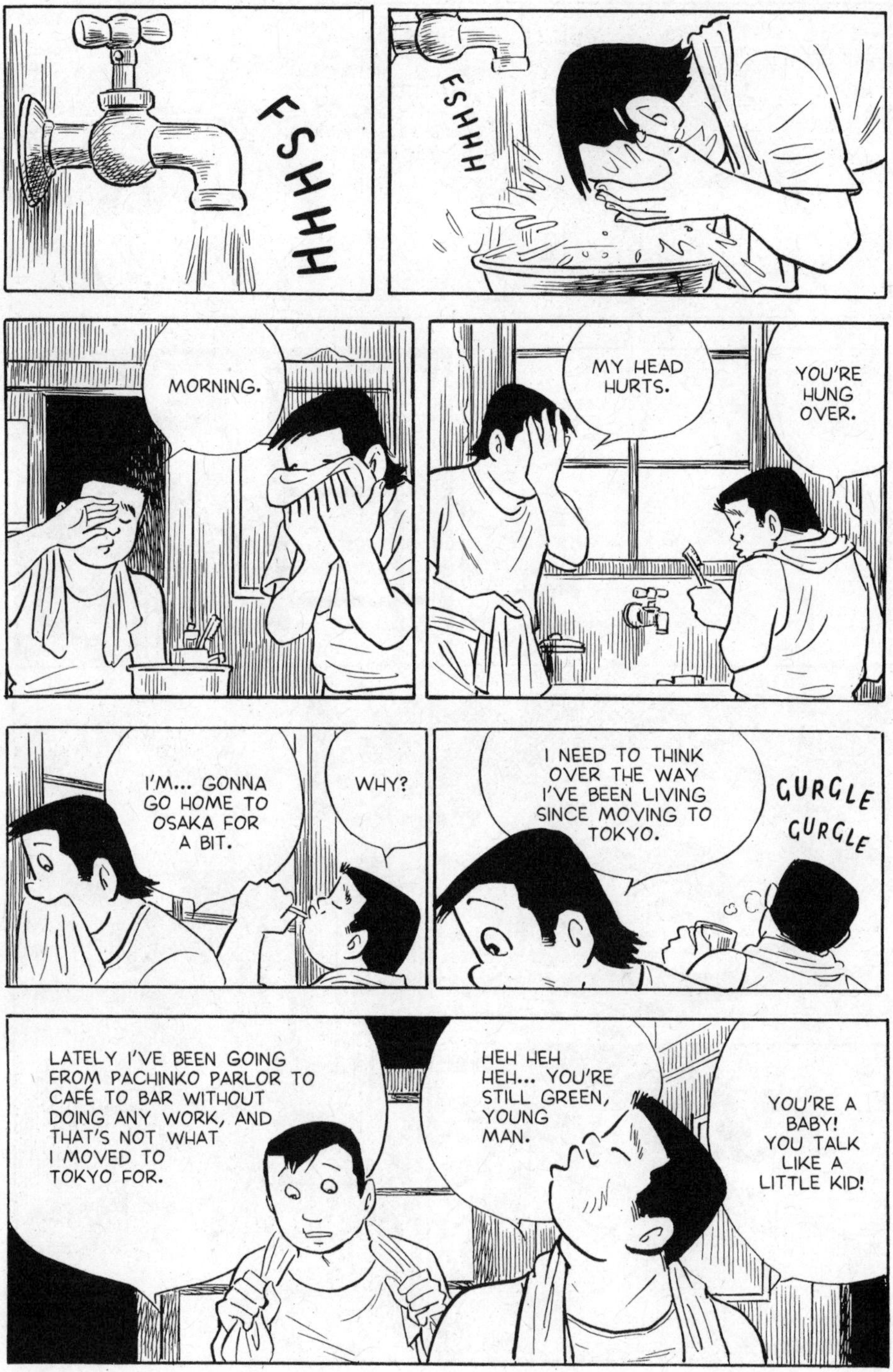
FSHHH
FSHHH
MORNING.
MY HEAD HURTS.
YOU'RE HUNG OVER.
I'M... GONNA GO HOME TO OSAKA FOR A BIT.
WHY?
I NEED TO THINK OVER THE WAY I'VE BEEN LIVING SINCE MOVING TO TOKYO.
GURGLE
GURGLE
LATELY I'VE BEEN GOING FROM PACHINKO PARLOR TO CAFÉ TO BAR WITHOUT DOING ANY WORK, AND THAT'S NOT WHAT I MOVED TO TOKYO FOR.
HEH HEH HEH... YOU'RE STILL GREEN, YOUNG MAN.
YOU'RE A BABY! YOU TALK LIKE A LITTLE KID!

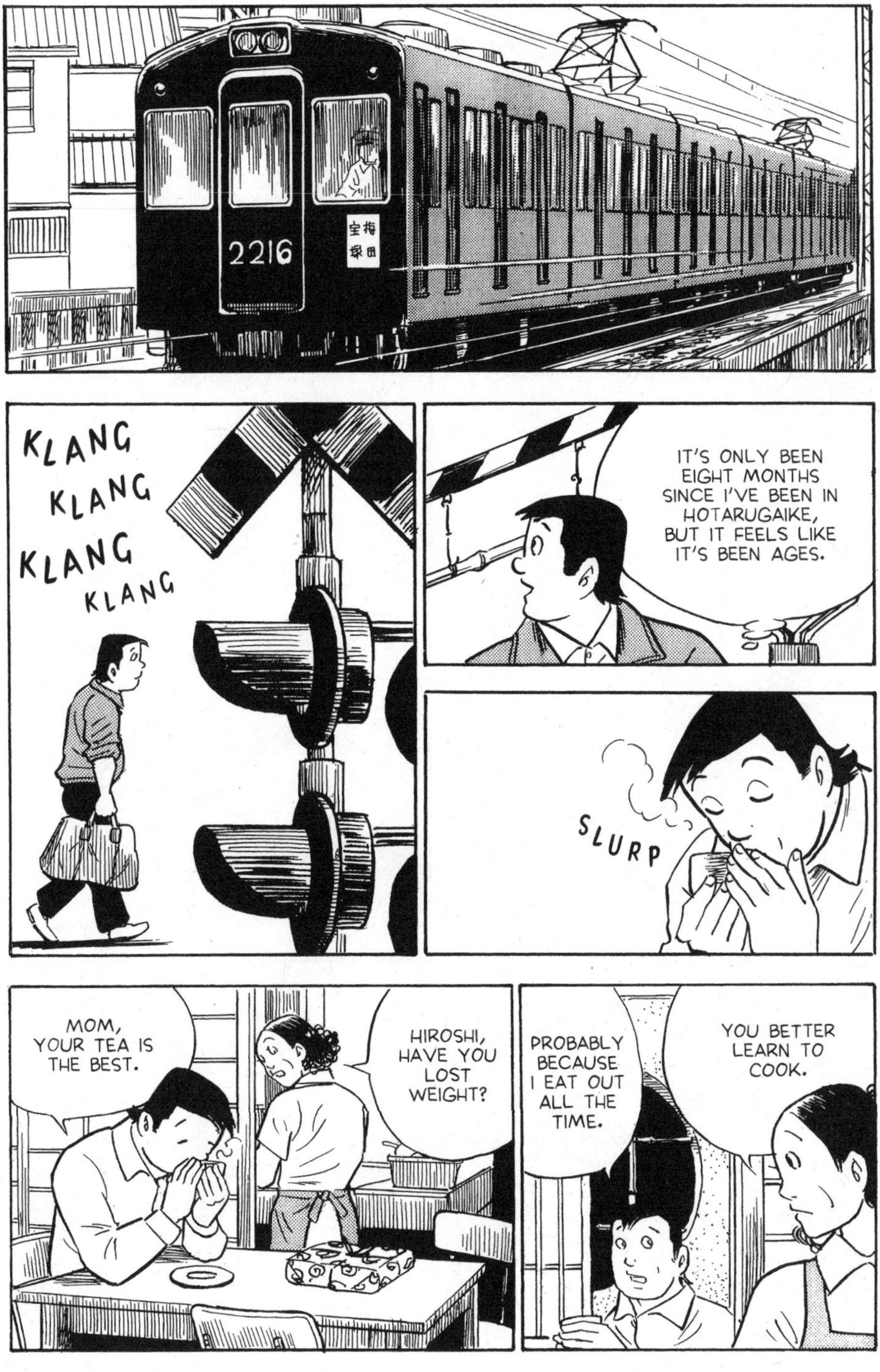

宝塚
梅田
2216
KLANG
KLANG
KLANG
KLANG
IT'S ONLY BEEN EIGHT MONTHS SINCE I'VE BEEN IN HOTARUGAIKE, BUT IT FEELS LIKE IT'S BEEN AGES.
SLURP
MOM, YOUR TEA IS THE BEST.
HIROSHI, HAVE YOU LOST WEIGHT?
PROBABLY BECAUSE I EAT OUT ALL THE TIME.
YOU BETTER LEARN TO COOK.

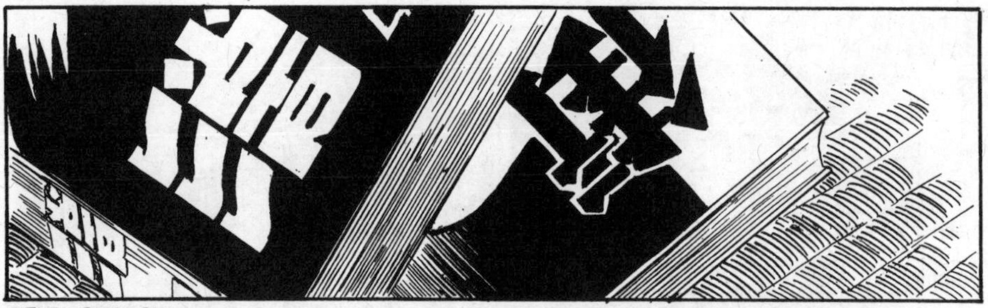

TITLE: *SHADOW*

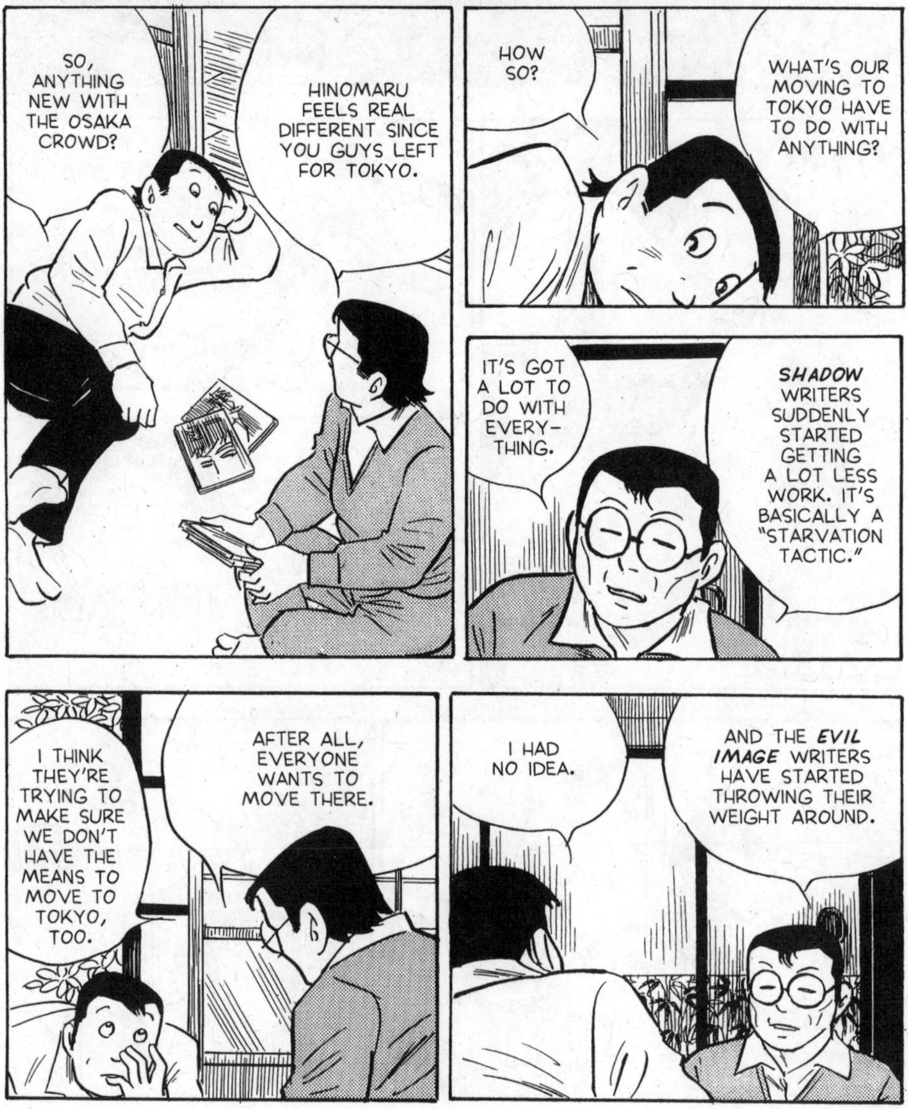

SO, ANYTHING NEW WITH THE OSAKA CROWD?
HINOMARU FEELS REAL DIFFERENT SINCE YOU GUYS LEFT FOR TOKYO.
HOW SO?
WHAT'S *OUR* MOVING TO TOKYO HAVE TO DO WITH ANYTHING?
IT'S GOT A LOT TO DO WITH EVERY-THING.
SHADOW WRITERS SUDDENLY STARTED GETTING A LOT LESS WORK. IT'S BASICALLY A "STARVATION TACTIC."
I THINK THEY'RE TRYING TO MAKE SURE WE DON'T HAVE THE MEANS TO MOVE TO TOKYO, TOO.
AFTER ALL, EVERYONE WANTS TO MOVE THERE.
I HAD NO IDEA.
AND THE *EVIL IMAGE* WRITERS HAVE STARTED THROWING THEIR WEIGHT AROUND.

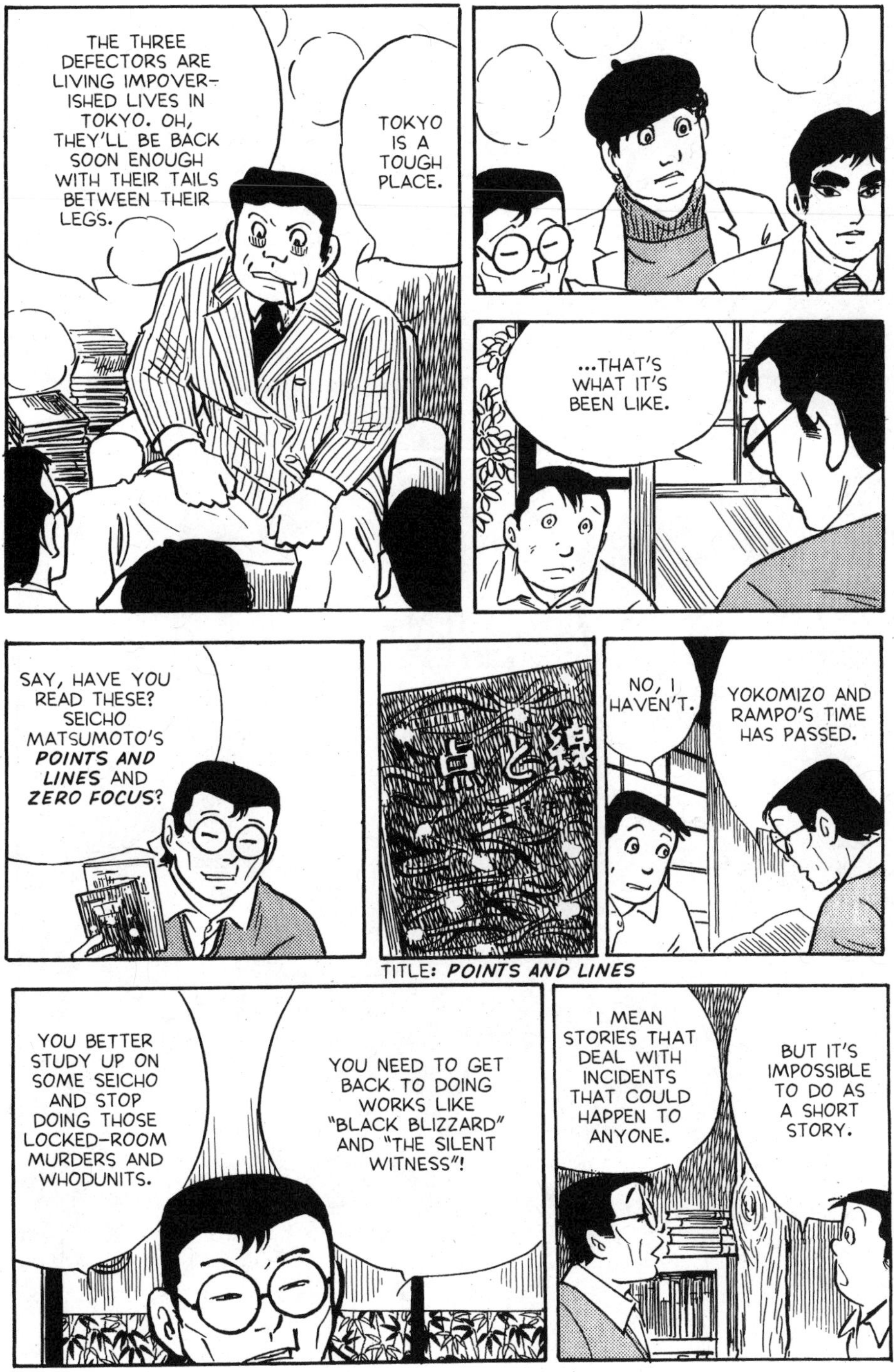
THE THREE DEFECTORS ARE LIVING IMPOVER-ISHED LIVES IN TOKYO. OH, THEY'LL BE BACK SOON ENOUGH WITH THEIR TAILS BETWEEN THEIR LEGS.
TOKYO IS A TOUGH PLACE.
...THAT'S WHAT IT'S BEEN LIKE.
SAY, HAVE YOU READ THESE? SEICHO MATSUMOTO'S ***POINTS AND LINES*** AND ***ZERO FOCUS***?
点と線
NO, I HAVEN'T.
YOKOMIZO AND RAMPO'S TIME HAS PASSED.
TITLE: ***POINTS AND LINES***
YOU BETTER STUDY UP ON SOME SEICHO AND STOP DOING THOSE LOCKED-ROOM MURDERS AND WHODUNITS.
YOU NEED TO GET BACK TO DOING WORKS LIKE "BLACK BLIZZARD" AND "THE SILENT WITNESS"!
I MEAN STORIES THAT DEAL WITH INCIDENTS THAT COULD HAPPEN TO ANYONE.
BUT IT'S IMPOSSIBLE TO DO AS A SHORT STORY.

WHAT'S HAPPENED TO YOUR IDEA OF "GEKIGA"?!

YOUR RECENT WORKS AREN'T "GEKIGA" AT ALL!

BUT...

THE WORK YOU'VE BEEN MAKING IN TOKYO IS CRAP.

YOU'RE LIVING RECKLESSLY AND IT SHOWS IN YOUR WORK!

...

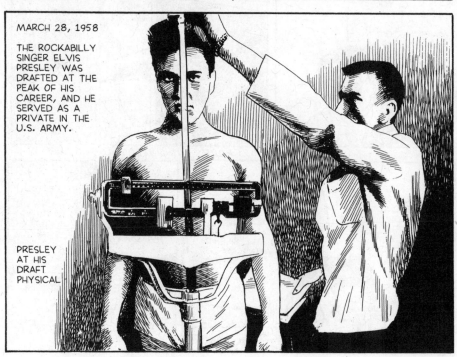

MARCH 28, 1958

THE ROCKABILLY SINGER ELVIS PRESLEY WAS DRAFTED AT THE PEAK OF HIS CAREER, AND HE SERVED AS A PRIVATE IN THE U.S. ARMY.

PRESLEY AT HIS DRAFT PHYSICAL

REACHING TOWARDS GEKIGA

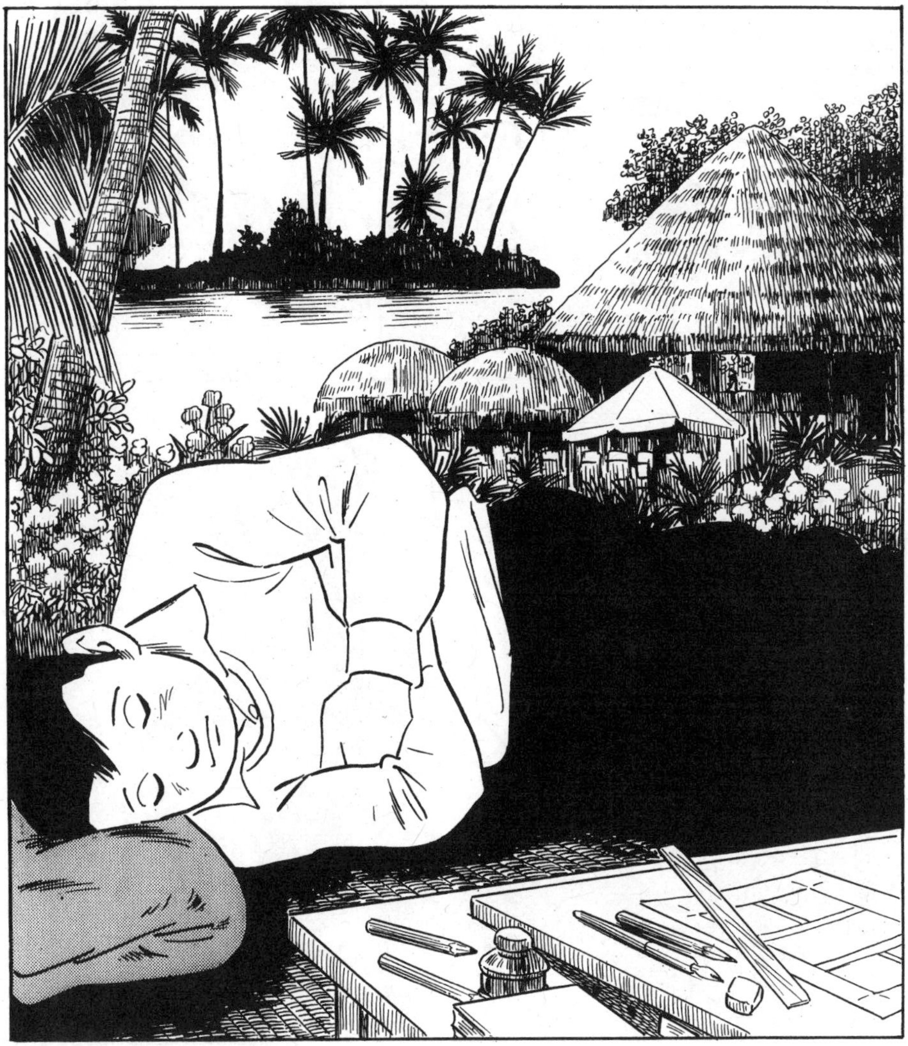

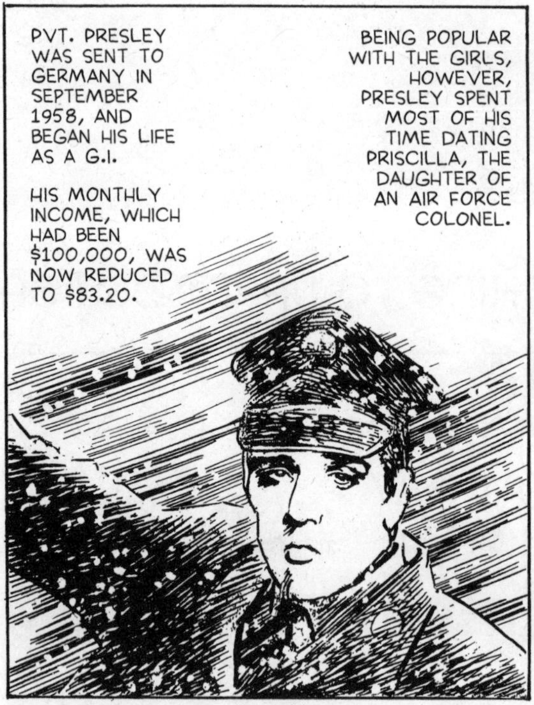
PVT. PRESLEY WAS SENT TO GERMANY IN SEPTEMBER 1958, AND BEGAN HIS LIFE AS A G.I.
HIS MONTHLY INCOME, WHICH HAD BEEN $100,000, WAS NOW REDUCED TO $83.20.
BEING POPULAR WITH THE GIRLS, HOWEVER, PRESLEY SPENT MOST OF HIS TIME DATING PRISCILLA, THE DAUGHTER OF AN AIR FORCE COLONEL.
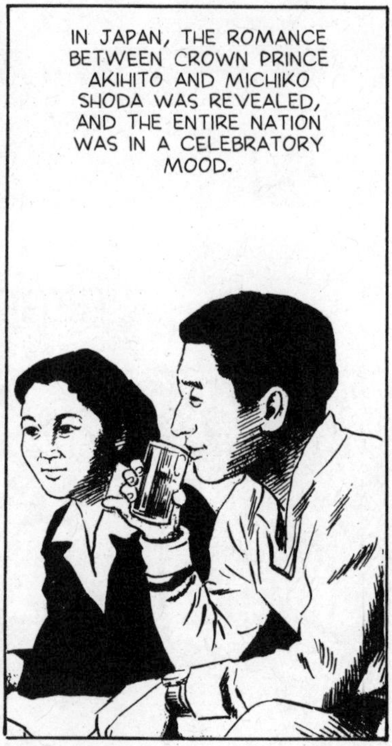
IN JAPAN, THE ROMANCE BETWEEN CROWN PRINCE AKIHITO AND MICHIKO SHODA WAS REVEALED, AND THE ENTIRE NATION WAS IN A CELEBRATORY MOOD.
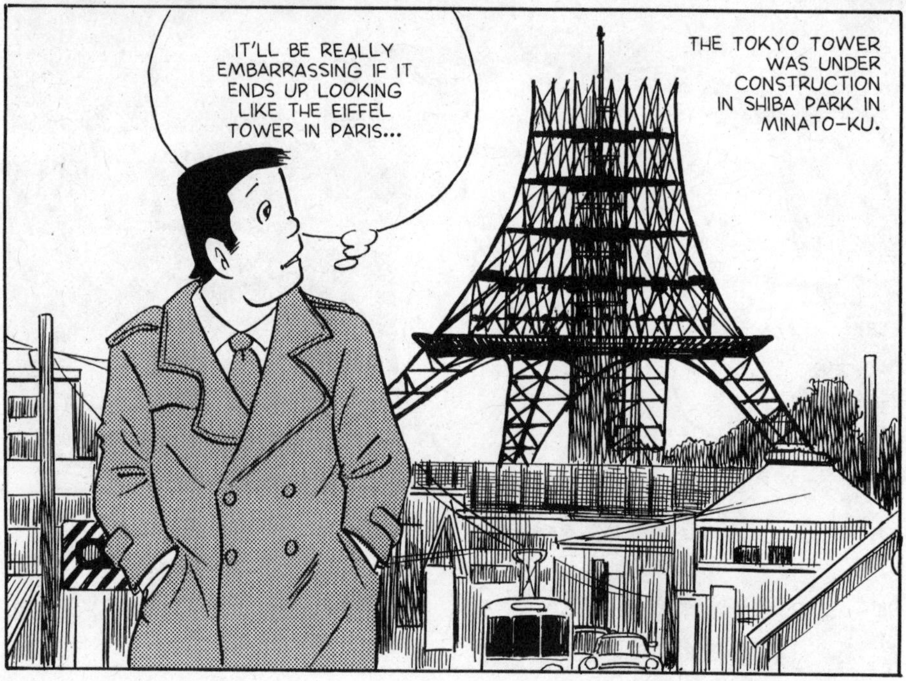
IT'LL BE REALLY EMBARRASSING IF IT ENDS UP LOOKING LIKE THE EIFFEL TOWER IN PARIS...
THE TOKYO TOWER WAS UNDER CONSTRUCTION IN SHIBA PARK IN MINATO-KU.

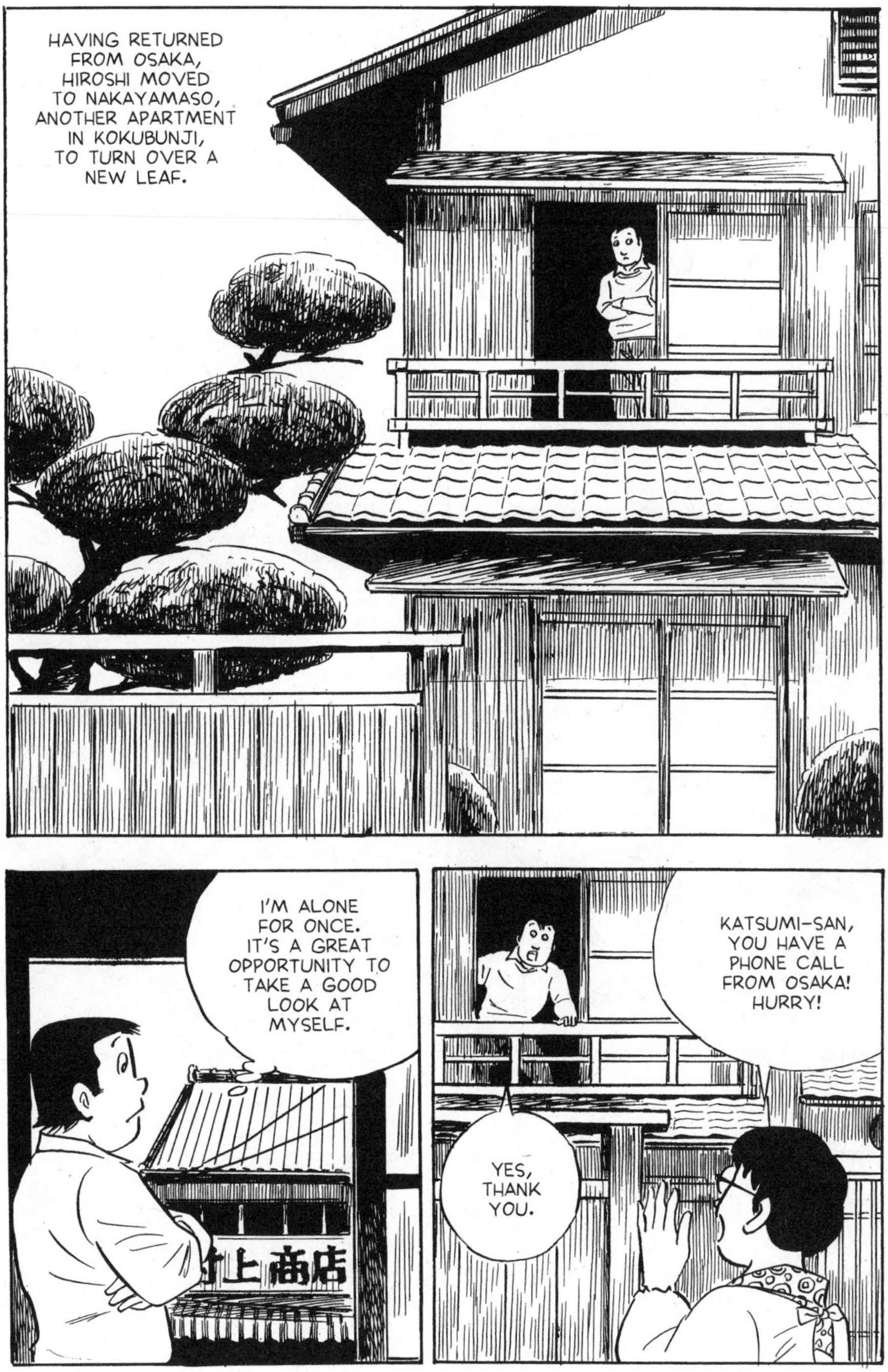
HAVING RETURNED FROM OSAKA, HIROSHI MOVED TO NAKAYAMASO, ANOTHER APARTMENT IN KOKUBUNJI, TO TURN OVER A NEW LEAF.
I'M ALONE FOR ONCE. IT'S A GREAT OPPORTUNITY TO TAKE A GOOD LOOK AT MYSELF.
KATSUMI-SAN, YOU HAVE A PHONE CALL FROM OSAKA! HURRY!
YES, THANK YOU.

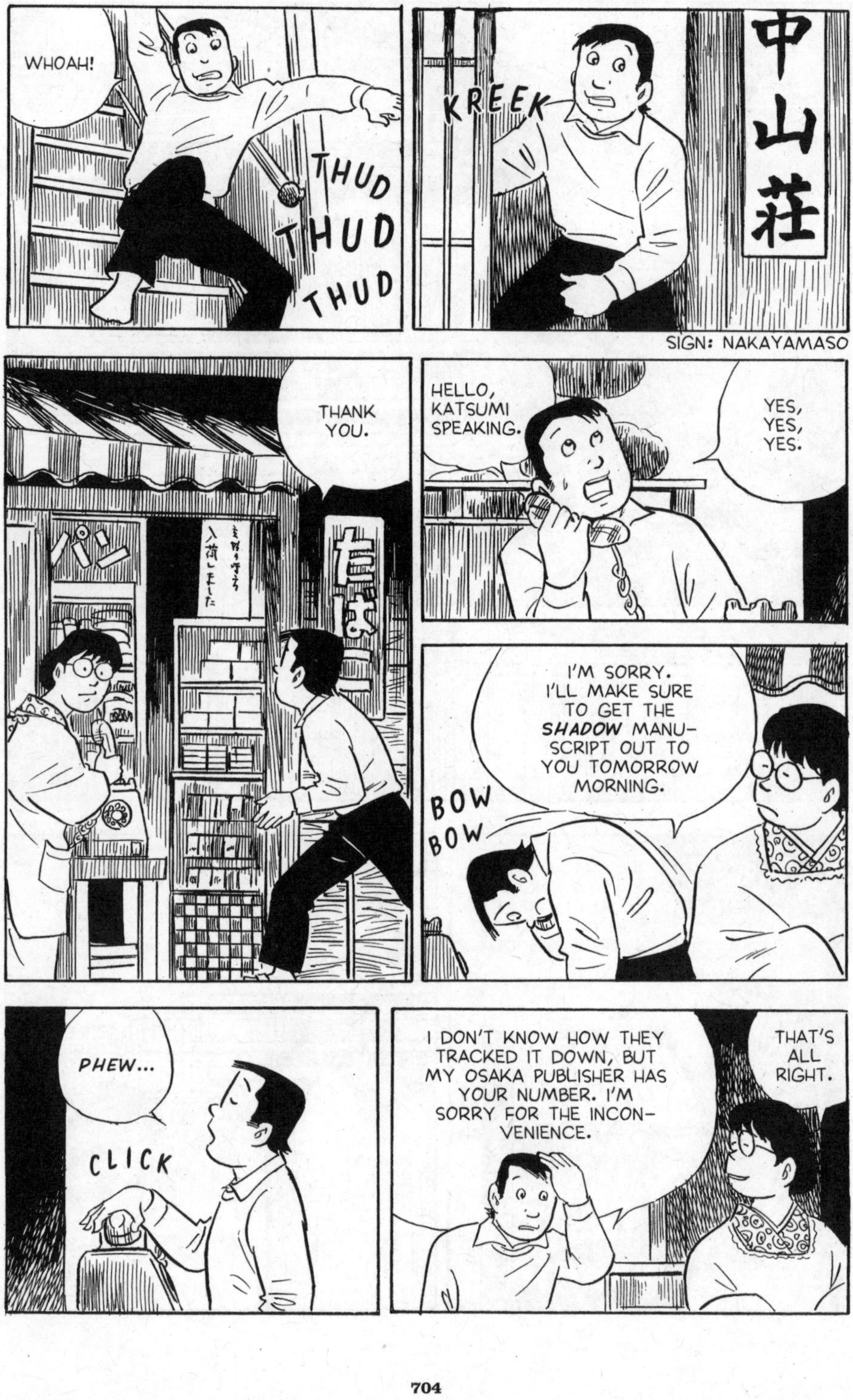

WHOAH!
THUD
THUD
THUD
KREEK
中山荘
SIGN: NAKAYAMASO
THANK YOU.
パン
HELLO, KATSUMI SPEAKING.
YES, YES, YES.
I'M SORRY. I'LL MAKE SURE TO GET THE ***SHADOW*** MANU-SCRIPT OUT TO YOU TOMORROW MORNING.
BOW
BOW
PHEW...
CLICK
I DON'T KNOW HOW THEY TRACKED IT DOWN, BUT MY OSAKA PUBLISHER HAS YOUR NUMBER. I'M SORRY FOR THE INCON-VENIENCE.
THAT'S ALL RIGHT.

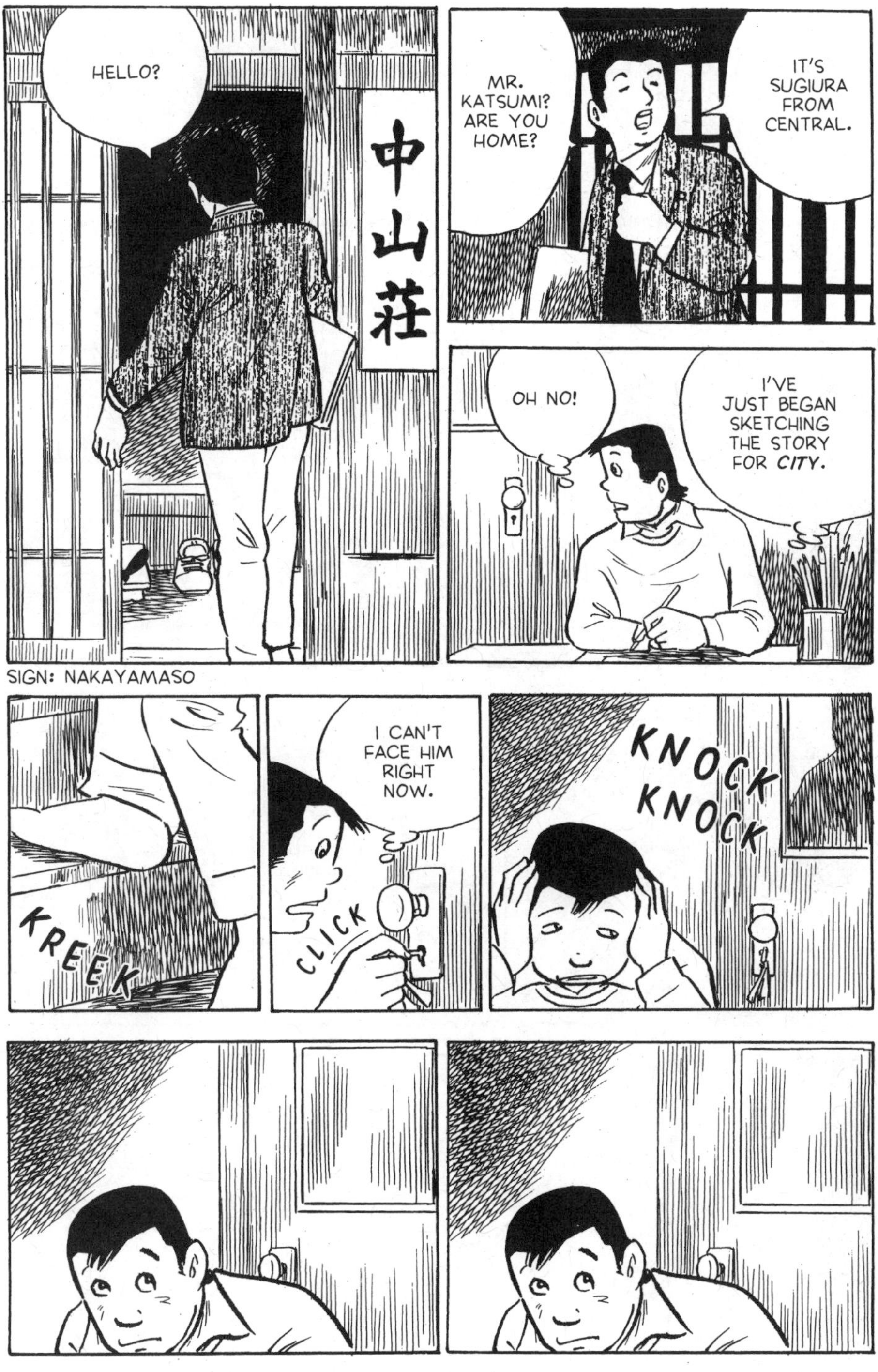
HELLO?
中山荘
SIGN: NAKAYAMASO
MR. KATSUMI? ARE YOU HOME?
IT'S SUGIURA FROM CENTRAL.
OH NO!
I'VE JUST BEGAN SKETCHING THE STORY FOR *CITY*.
KREEK
I CAN'T FACE HIM RIGHT NOW.
CLICK
KNOCK KNOCK

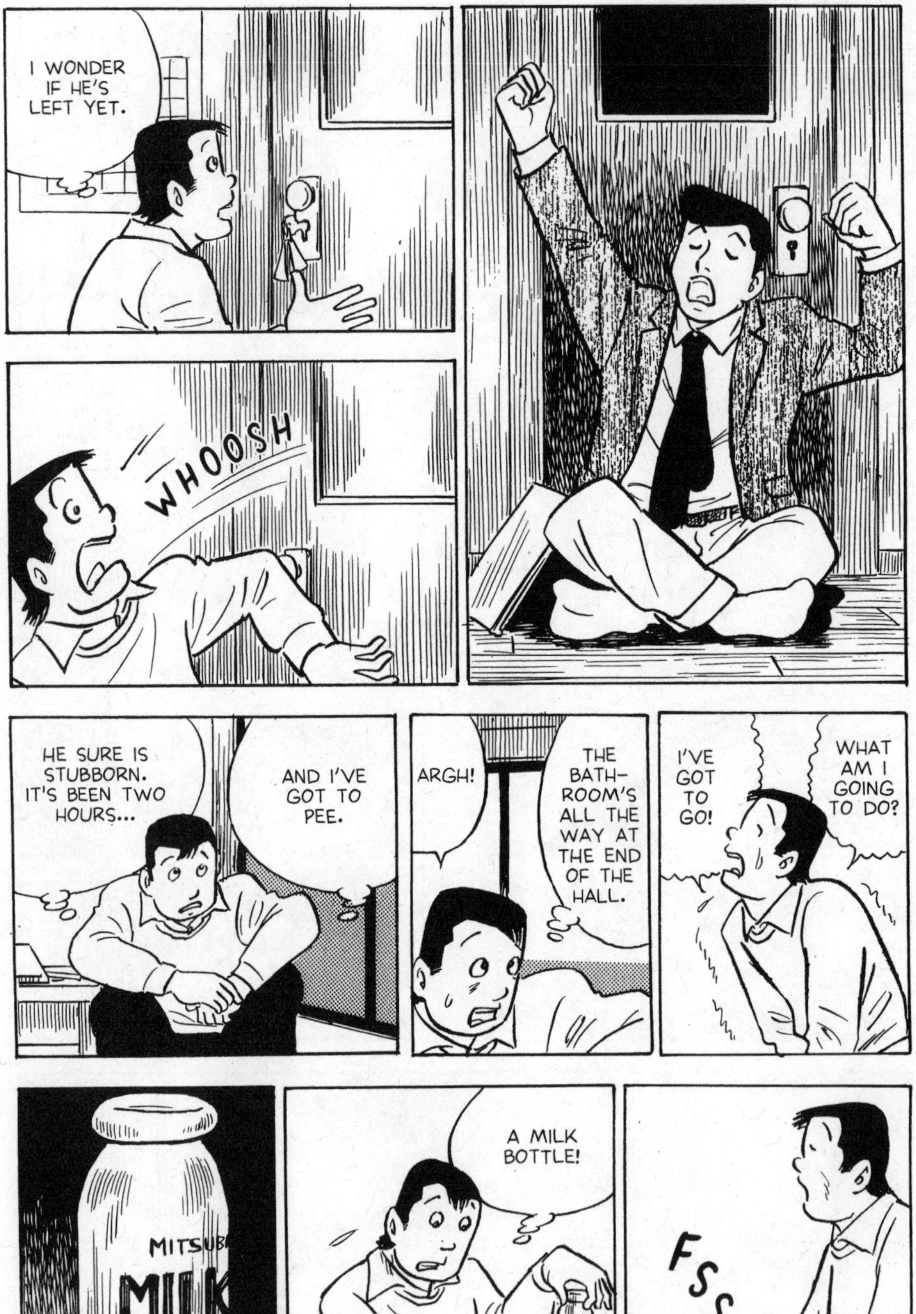
I WONDER IF HE'S LEFT YET.
WHOOSH
HE SURE IS STUBBORN. IT'S BEEN TWO HOURS...
AND I'VE GOT TO PEE.
ARGH!
THE BATH-ROOM'S ALL THE WAY AT THE END OF THE HALL.
I'VE GOT TO GO!
WHAT AM I GOING TO DO?
MILK
A MILK BOTTLE!
FSSSS

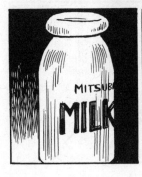

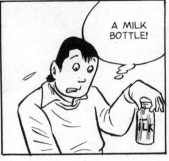

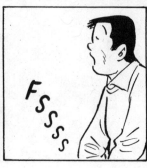

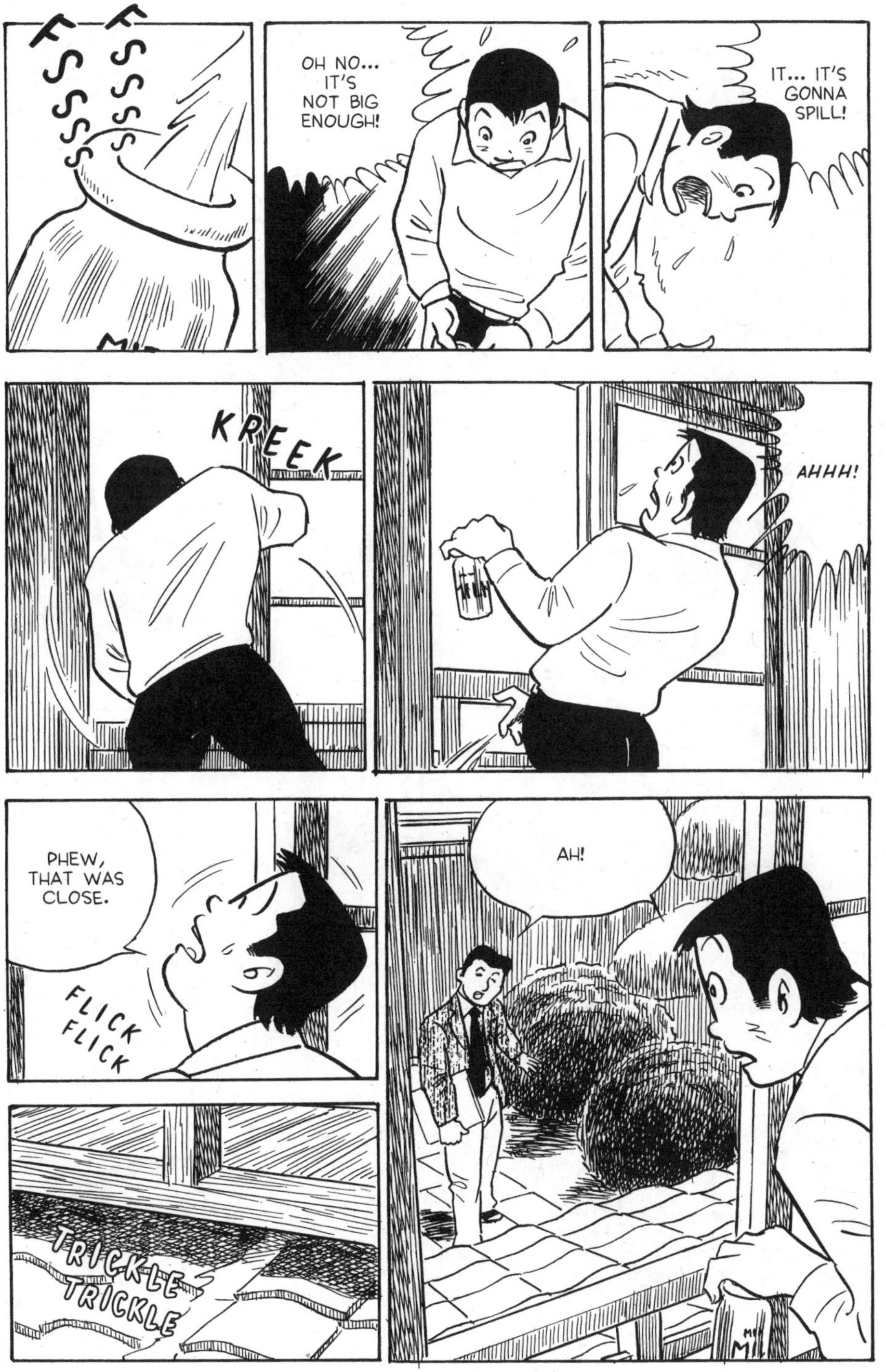
FSSSS
FSSSS
OH NO... IT'S NOT BIG ENOUGH!
IT... IT'S GONNA SPILL!
KREEK
AHHH!
PHEW, THAT WAS CLOSE.
FLICK FLICK
TRICKLE TRICKLE
AH!

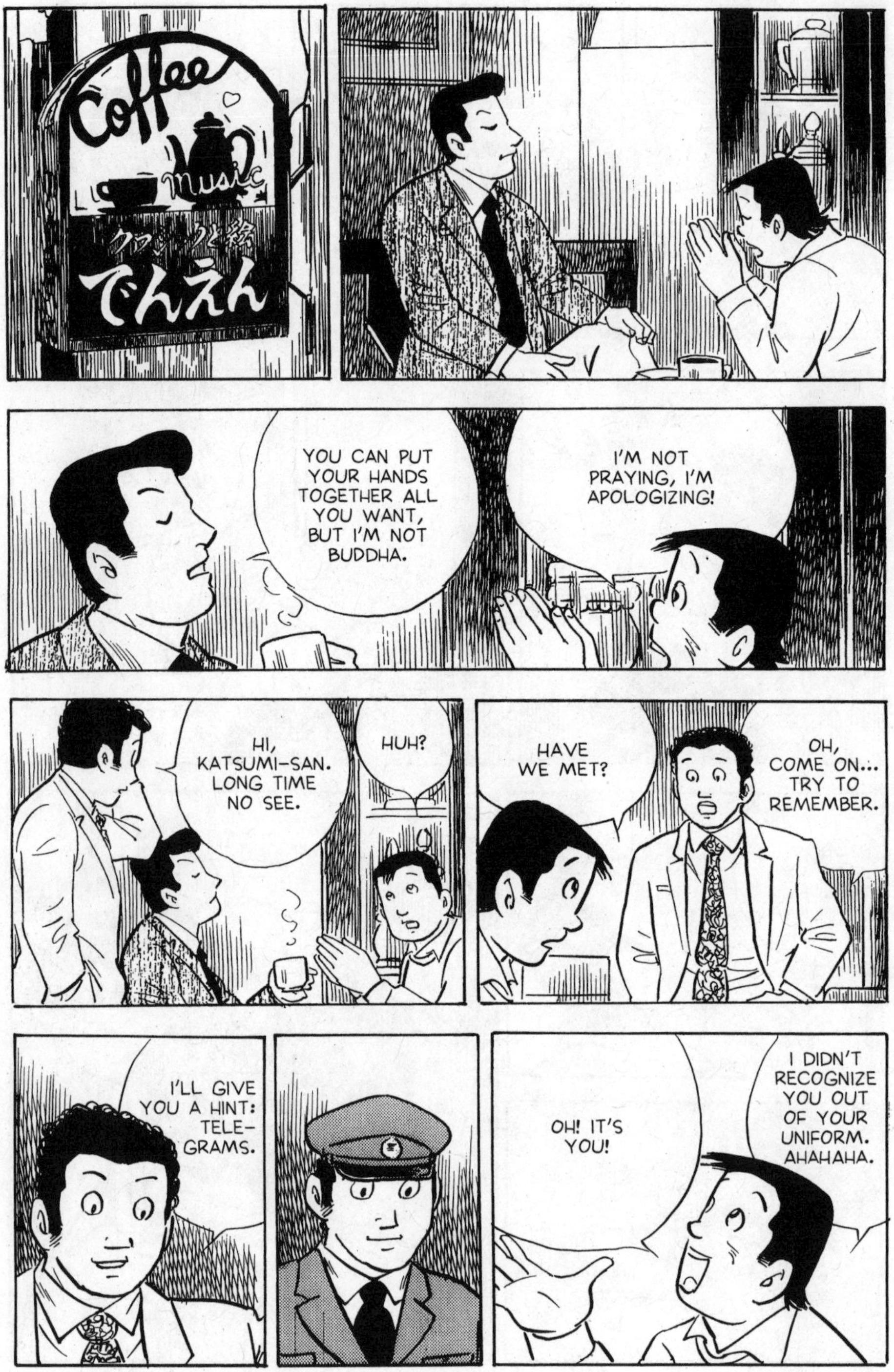
Coffee
music
でんえん
YOU CAN PUT YOUR HANDS TOGETHER ALL YOU WANT, BUT I'M NOT BUDDHA.
I'M NOT PRAYING, I'M APOLOGIZING!
HI, KATSUMI-SAN. LONG TIME NO SEE.
HUH?
HAVE WE MET?
OH, COME ON... TRY TO REMEMBER.
I'LL GIVE YOU A HINT: TELE-GRAMS.
OH! IT'S YOU!
I DIDN'T RECOGNIZE YOU OUT OF YOUR UNIFORM. AHAHAHA.

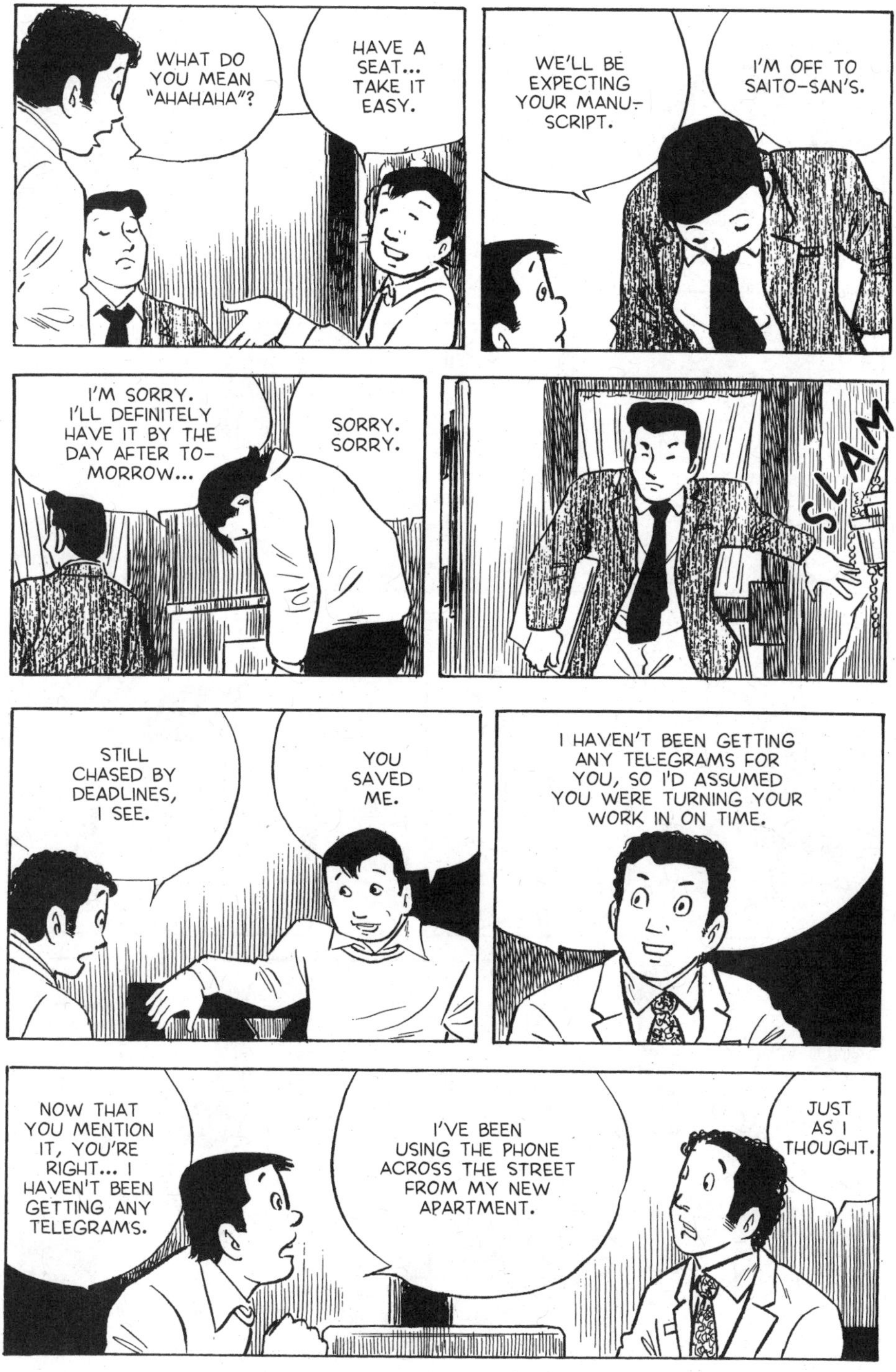
WHAT DO YOU MEAN "AHAHAHA"?
HAVE A SEAT... TAKE IT EASY.
WE'LL BE EXPECTING YOUR MANU-SCRIPT.
I'M OFF TO SAITO-SAN'S.
I'M SORRY. I'LL DEFINITELY HAVE IT BY THE DAY AFTER TO-MORROW...
SORRY. SORRY.
SLAM
STILL CHASED BY DEADLINES, I SEE.
YOU SAVED ME.
I HAVEN'T BEEN GETTING ANY TELEGRAMS FOR YOU, SO I'D ASSUMED YOU WERE TURNING YOUR WORK IN ON TIME.
NOW THAT YOU MENTION IT, YOU'RE RIGHT... I HAVEN'T BEEN GETTING ANY TELEGRAMS.
I'VE BEEN USING THE PHONE ACROSS THE STREET FROM MY NEW APARTMENT.
JUST AS I THOUGHT.

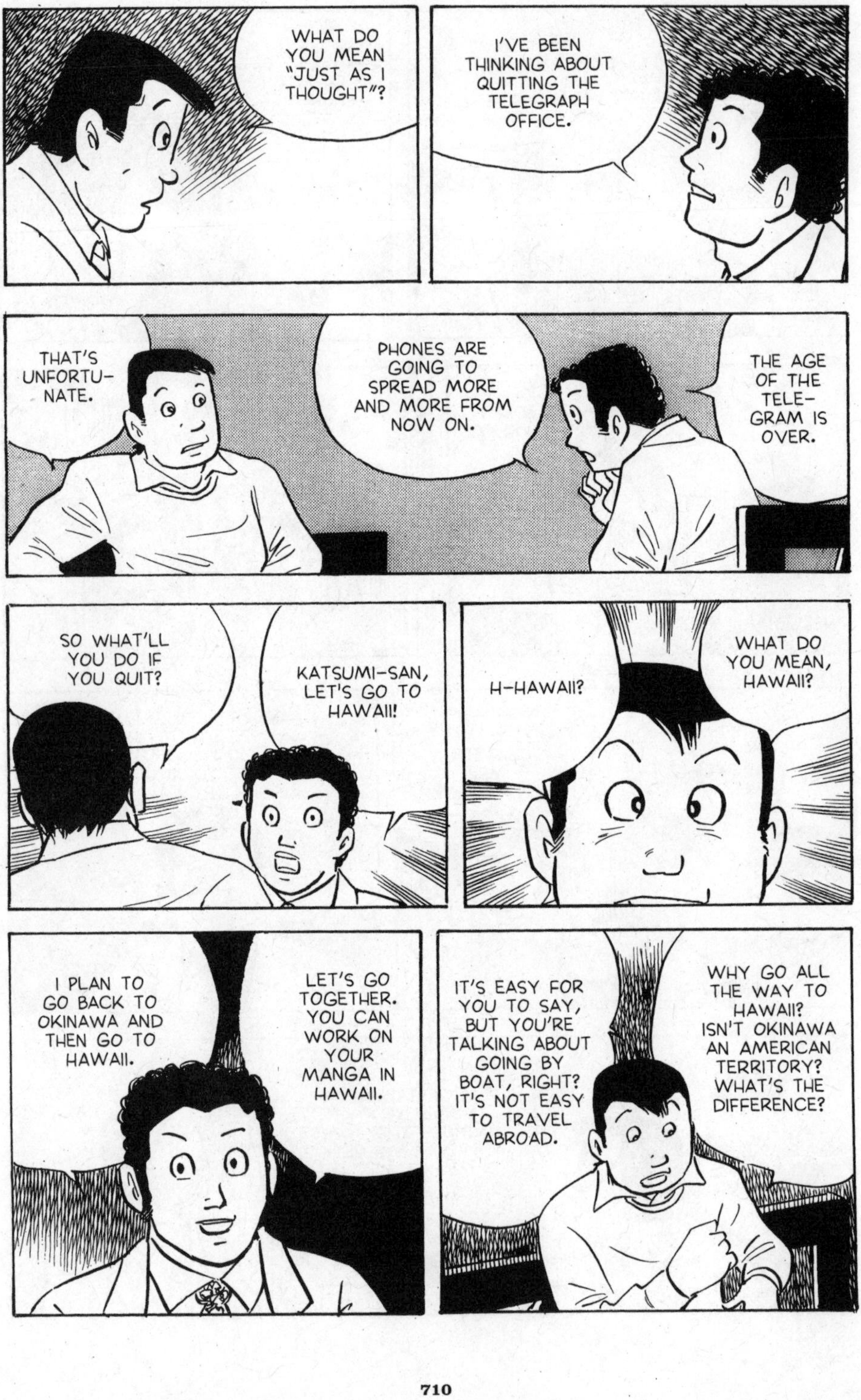
WHAT DO YOU MEAN "JUST AS I THOUGHT"?
I'VE BEEN THINKING ABOUT QUITTING THE TELEGRAPH OFFICE.
THAT'S UNFORTU-NATE.
PHONES ARE GOING TO SPREAD MORE AND MORE FROM NOW ON.
THE AGE OF THE TELE-GRAM IS OVER.
SO WHAT'LL YOU DO IF YOU QUIT?
KATSUMI-SAN, LET'S GO TO HAWAII!
H-HAWAII?
WHAT DO YOU MEAN, HAWAII?
I PLAN TO GO BACK TO OKINAWA AND THEN GO TO HAWAII.
LET'S GO TOGETHER. YOU CAN WORK ON YOUR MANGA IN HAWAII.
IT'S EASY FOR YOU TO SAY, BUT YOU'RE TALKING ABOUT GOING BY BOAT, RIGHT? IT'S NOT EASY TO TRAVEL ABROAD.
WHY GO ALL THE WAY TO HAWAII? ISN'T OKINAWA AN AMERICAN TERRITORY? WHAT'S THE DIFFERENCE?

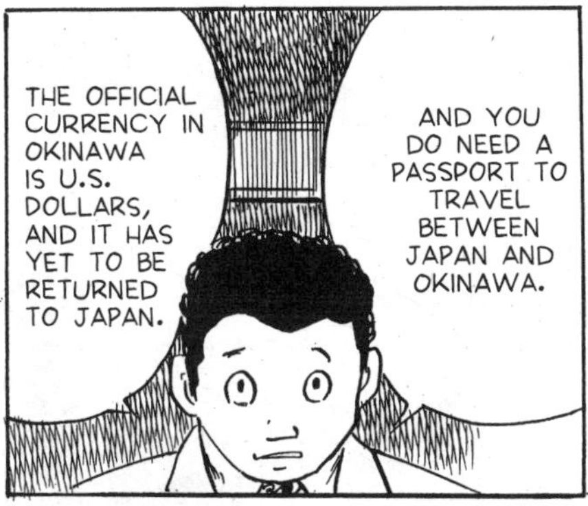
THE OFFICIAL CURRENCY IN OKINAWA IS U.S. DOLLARS, AND IT HAS YET TO BE RETURNED TO JAPAN.
AND YOU DO NEED A PASSPORT TO TRAVEL BETWEEN JAPAN AND OKINAWA.

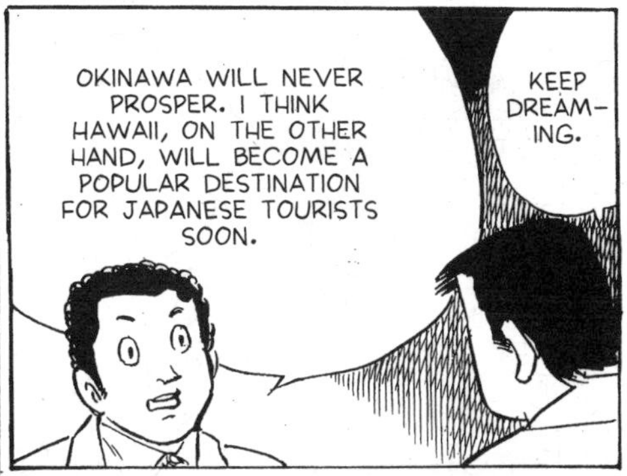
OKINAWA WILL NEVER PROSPER. I THINK HAWAII, ON THE OTHER HAND, WILL BECOME A POPULAR DESTINATION FOR JAPANESE TOURISTS SOON.
KEEP DREAMING.

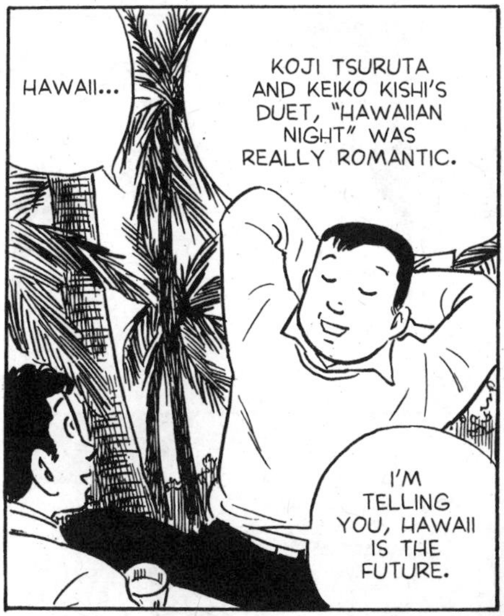
HAWAII...
KOJI TSURUTA AND KEIKO KISHI'S DUET, "HAWAIIAN NIGHT" WAS REALLY ROMANTIC.
I'M TELLING YOU, HAWAII IS THE FUTURE.

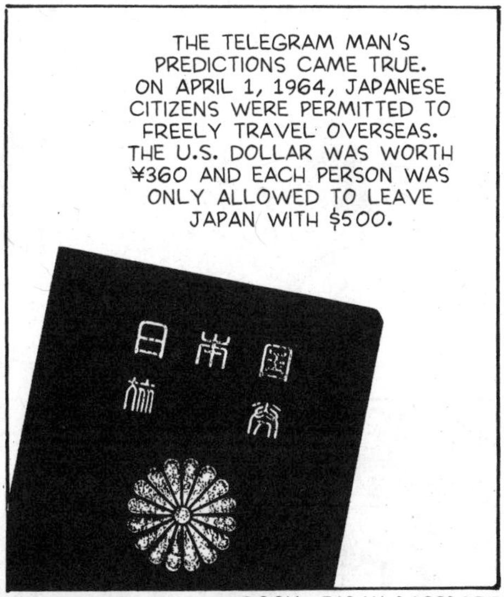
THE TELEGRAM MAN'S PREDICTIONS CAME TRUE. ON APRIL 1, 1964, JAPANESE CITIZENS WERE PERMITTED TO FREELY TRAVEL OVERSEAS. THE U.S. DOLLAR WAS WORTH ¥360 AND EACH PERSON WAS ONLY ALLOWED TO LEAVE JAPAN WITH $500.

BOOK: JAPAN PASSPORT

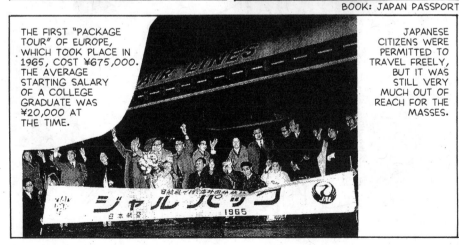

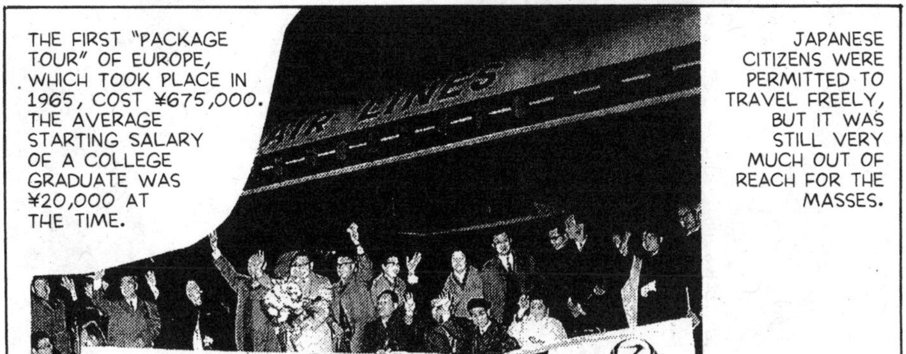
THE FIRST "PACKAGE TOUR" OF EUROPE, WHICH TOOK PLACE IN 1965, COST ¥675,000. THE AVERAGE STARTING SALARY OF A COLLEGE GRADUATE WAS ¥20,000 AT THE TIME.
JAPANESE CITIZENS WERE PERMITTED TO TRAVEL FREELY, BUT IT WAS STILL VERY MUCH OUT OF REACH FOR THE MASSES.
ジャルパック
1965

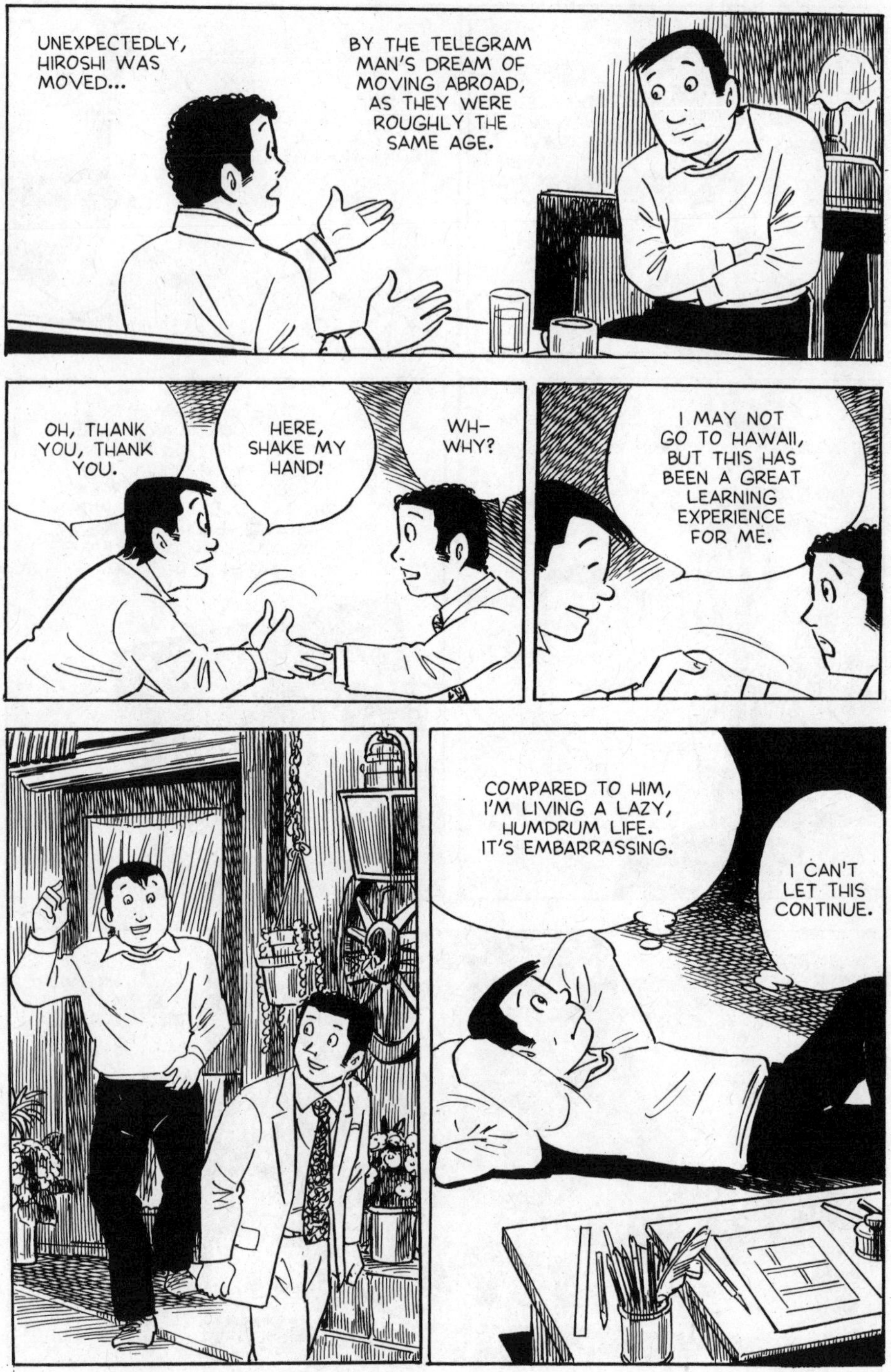
UNEXPECTEDLY, HIROSHI WAS MOVED...
BY THE TELEGRAM MAN'S DREAM OF MOVING ABROAD, AS THEY WERE ROUGHLY THE SAME AGE.
OH, THANK YOU, THANK YOU.
HERE, SHAKE MY HAND!
WH- WHY?
I MAY NOT GO TO HAWAII, BUT THIS HAS BEEN A GREAT LEARNING EXPERIENCE FOR ME.
COMPARED TO HIM, I'M LIVING A LAZY, HUMDRUM LIFE. IT'S EMBARRASSING.
I CAN'T LET THIS CONTINUE.

I'VE GOT TO CREATE "GEKIGA"!

IT'S "GEKIGA" OR NOTHING!

THERE'S NO FUTURE IN ONLY DOING THESE HALF-ASSED SHORT PIECES THAT THE PUBLISHERS ASSIGN ME.

NO MORE SHORT STORIES!

AS SOON AS I'M DONE WITH THE SHORT STORIES I'M WORKING ON NOW, I'M FOCUSING ALL MY ENERGY ON A BOOK-LENGTH "GEKIGA" PIECE.

HIROSHI'S DESIRE TO WRITE LONGER WORKS WAS QUICKLY THWARTED BY THE RAGING SHORT STORY MAGAZINE BOOM THAT HIT THE RENTAL BOOK INDUSTRY.

TAP TAP

KATSUMI SENSEI?

MY NAME IS AOYAMA. I'M FROM TOGETSU SHOBO.

TITLE: *FOG | DETECTIVE THRILLER SERIES*

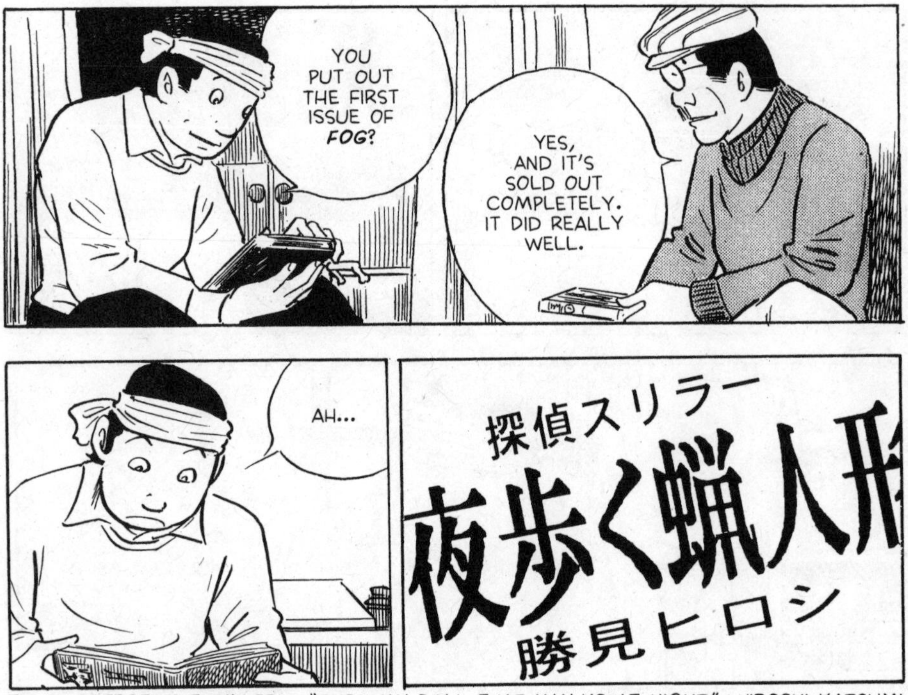
YOU PUT OUT THE FIRST ISSUE OF *FOG*?
YES, AND IT'S SOLD OUT COMPLETELY. IT DID REALLY WELL.
AH...
探偵スリラー
夜歩く蝋人形
勝見ヒロシ

TITLE: DETECTIVE THRILLER / "THE WAX DOLL THAT WALKS AT NIGHT" / HIROSHI KATSUMI

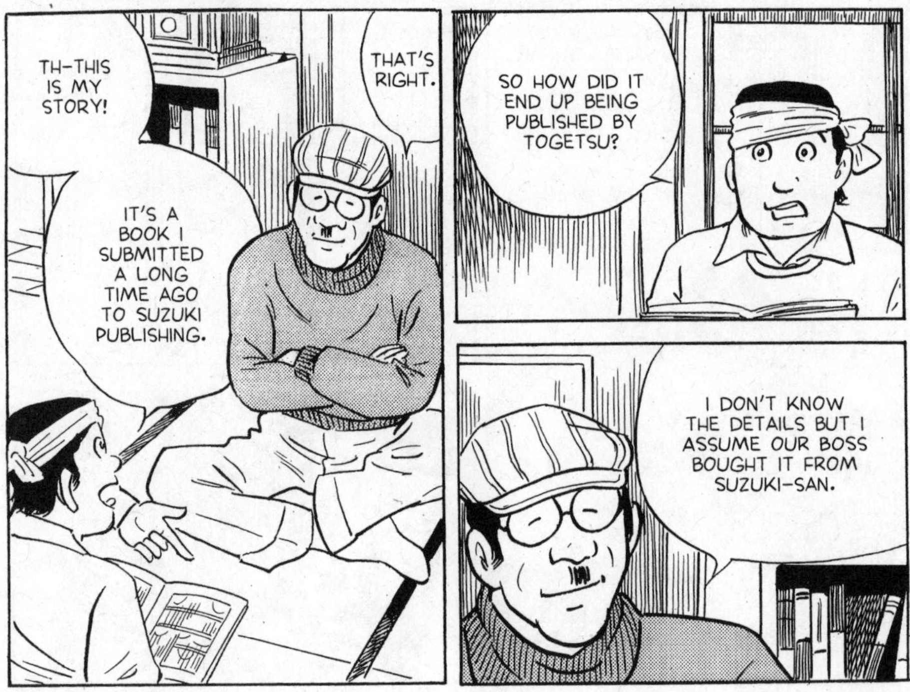
TH-THIS IS MY STORY!
THAT'S RIGHT.
IT'S A BOOK I SUBMITTED A LONG TIME AGO TO SUZUKI PUBLISHING.
SO HOW DID IT END UP BEING PUBLISHED BY TOGETSU?
I DON'T KNOW THE DETAILS BUT I ASSUME OUR BOSS BOUGHT IT FROM SUZUKI-SAN.

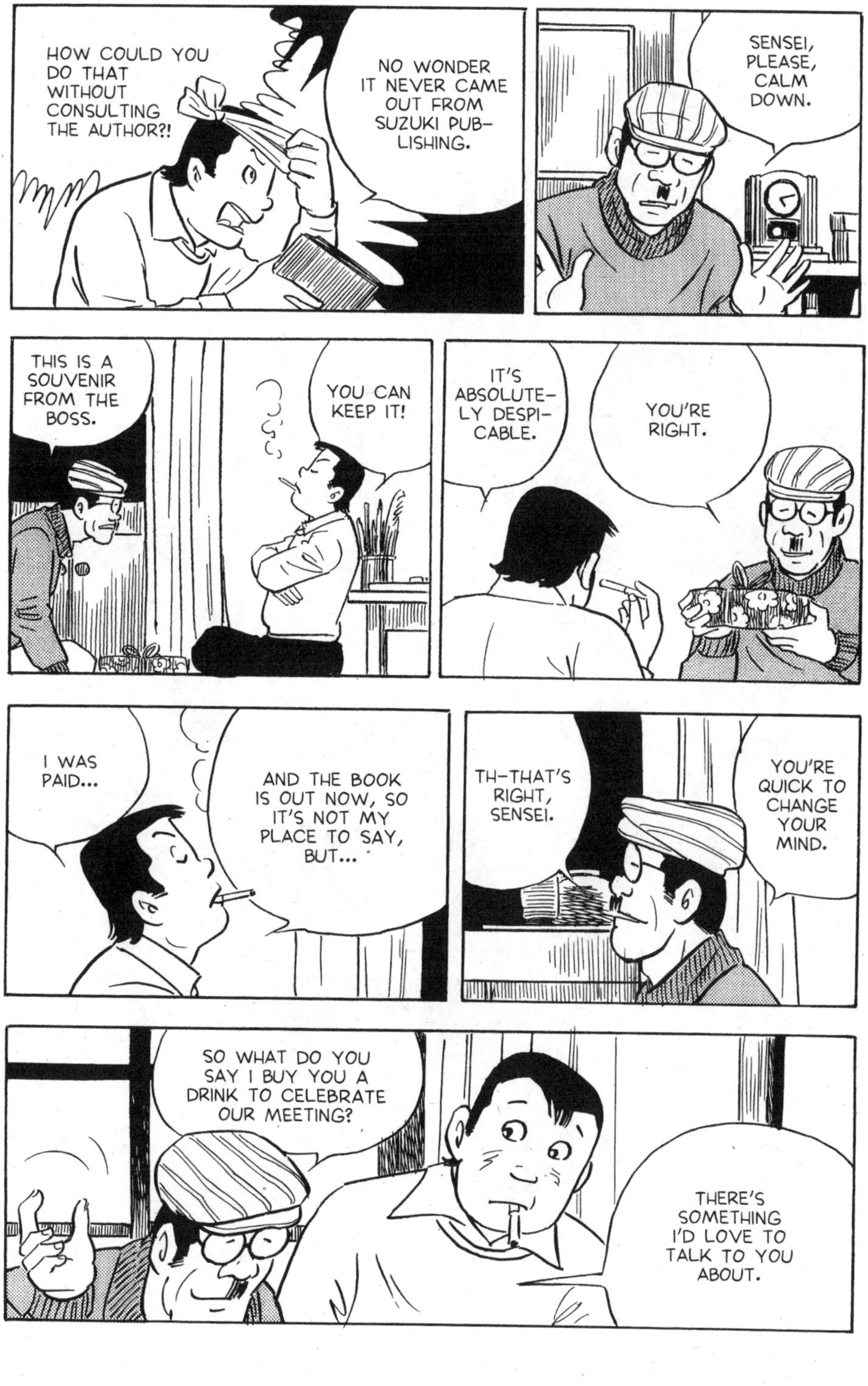

HOW COULD YOU DO THAT WITHOUT CONSULTING THE AUTHOR?!
NO WONDER IT NEVER CAME OUT FROM SUZUKI PUB-LISHING.
SENSEI, PLEASE, CALM DOWN.
THIS IS A SOUVENIR FROM THE BOSS.
YOU CAN KEEP IT!
IT'S ABSOLUTE-LY DESPI-CABLE.
YOU'RE RIGHT.
I WAS PAID...
AND THE BOOK IS OUT NOW, SO IT'S NOT MY PLACE TO SAY, BUT...
TH-THAT'S RIGHT, SENSEI.
YOU'RE QUICK TO CHANGE YOUR MIND.
SO WHAT DO YOU SAY I BUY YOU A DRINK TO CELEBRATE OUR MEETING?
THERE'S SOMETHING I'D LOVE TO TALK TO YOU ABOUT.

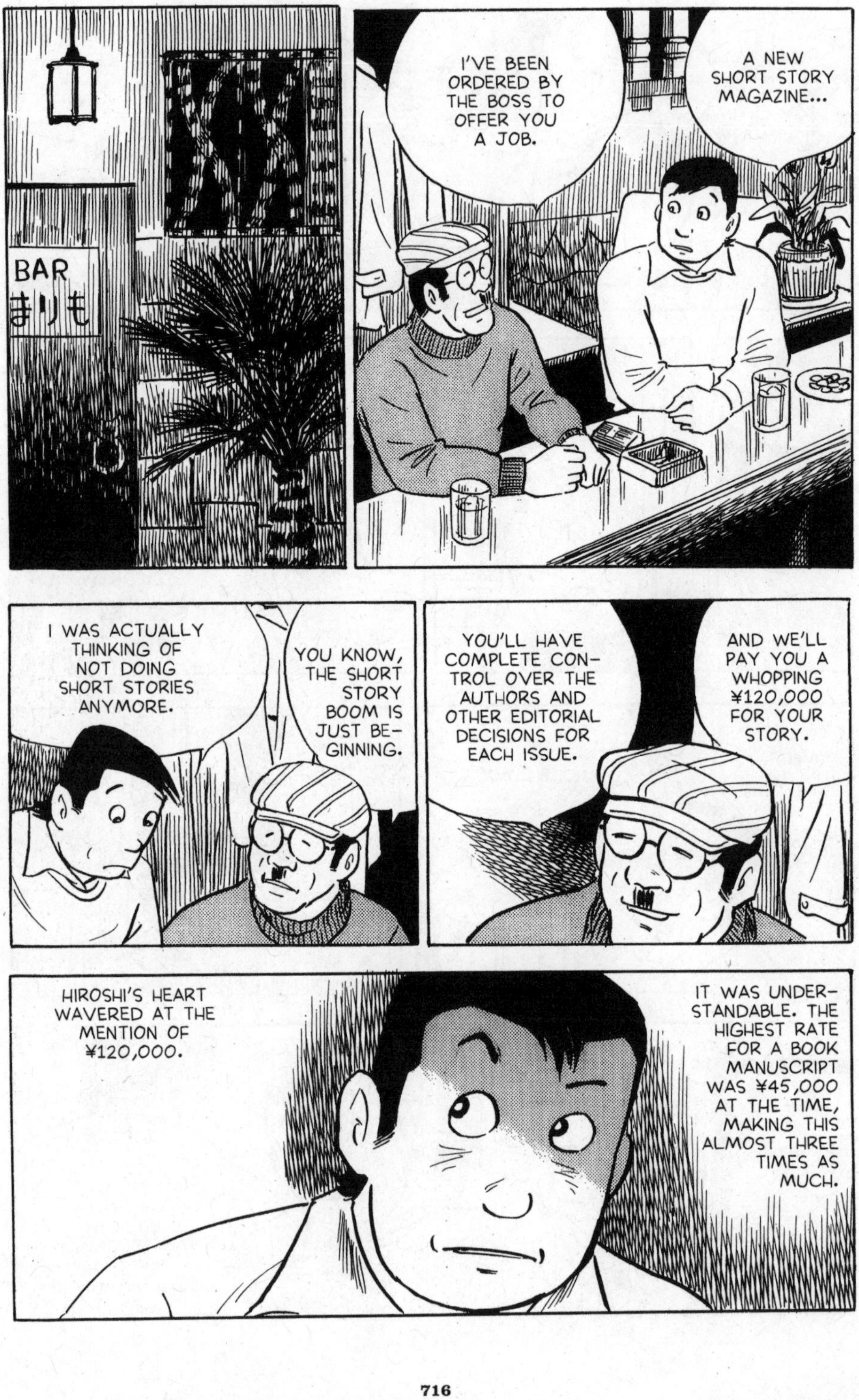
BAR
まりも
I'VE BEEN ORDERED BY THE BOSS TO OFFER YOU A JOB.
A NEW SHORT STORY MAGAZINE...
I WAS ACTUALLY THINKING OF NOT DOING SHORT STORIES ANYMORE.
YOU KNOW, THE SHORT STORY BOOM IS JUST BE-GINNING.
YOU'LL HAVE COMPLETE CON-TROL OVER THE AUTHORS AND OTHER EDITORIAL DECISIONS FOR EACH ISSUE.
AND WE'LL PAY YOU A WHOPPING ¥120,000 FOR YOUR STORY.
HIROSHI'S HEART WAVERED AT THE MENTION OF ¥120,000.
IT WAS UNDER-STANDABLE. THE HIGHEST RATE FOR A BOOK MANUSCRIPT WAS ¥45,000 AT THE TIME, MAKING THIS ALMOST THREE TIMES AS MUCH.

THE BIRTH OF THE GEKIGA WORKSHOP

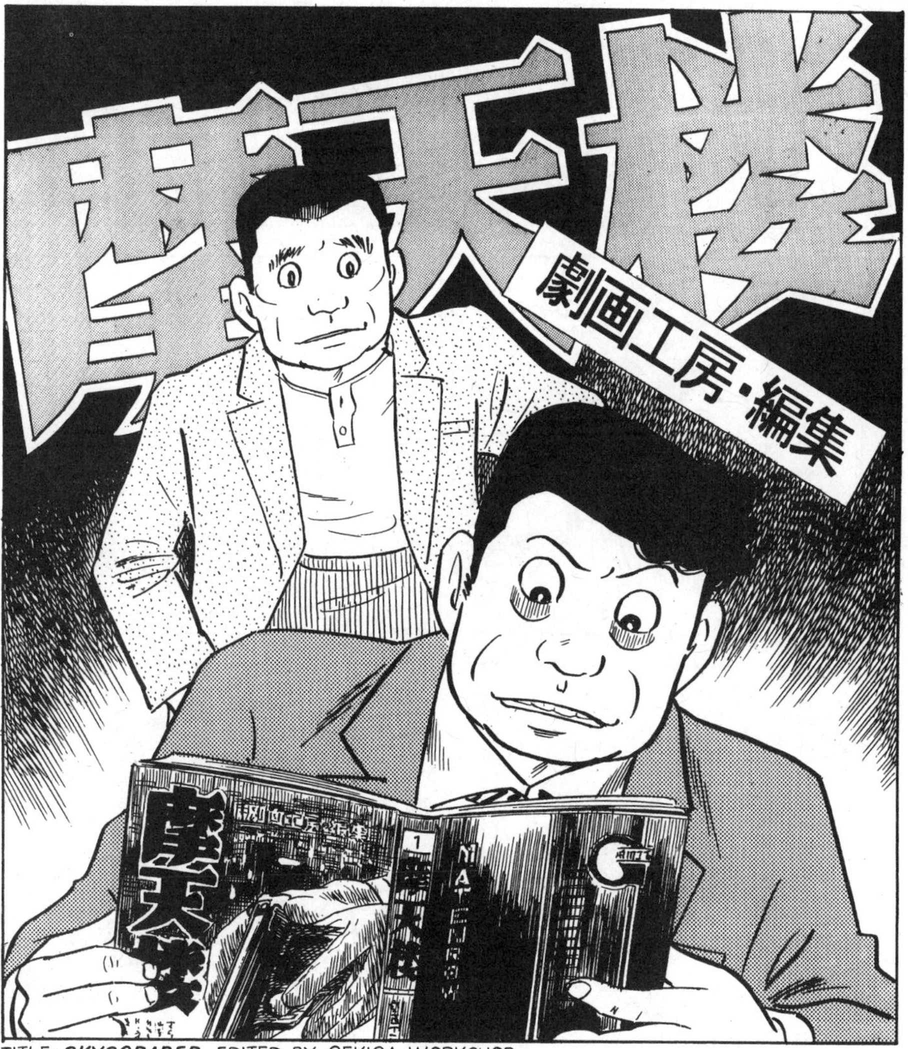

摩天楼
劇画工房・編集

TITLE: *SKYSCRAPER,* EDITED BY GEKIGA WORKSHOP

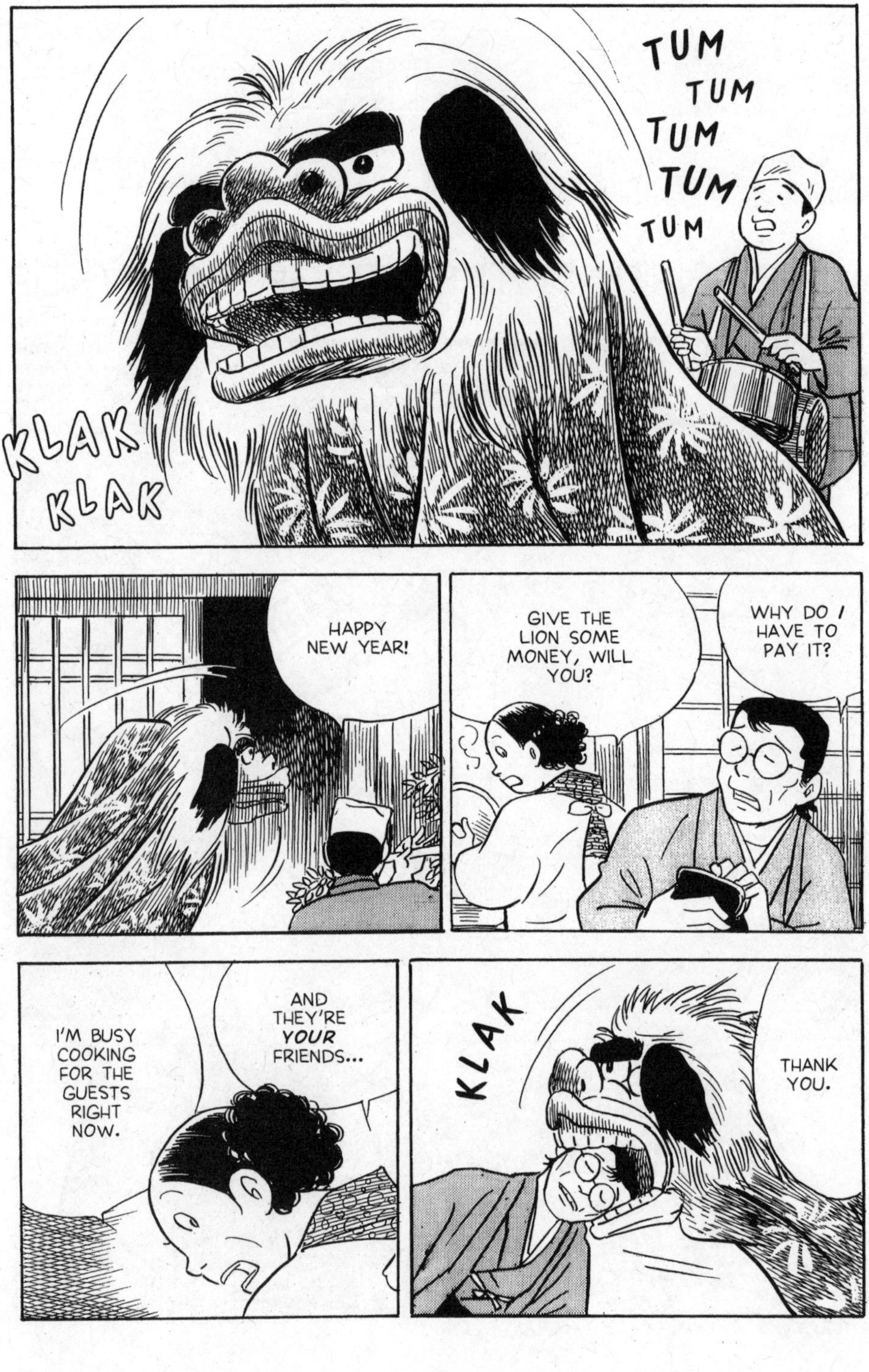
TUM
TUM
TUM
TUM
TUM
KLAK
KLAK
HAPPY NEW YEAR!
GIVE THE LION SOME MONEY, WILL YOU?
WHY DO *I* HAVE TO PAY IT?
I'M BUSY COOKING FOR THE GUESTS RIGHT NOW.
AND THEY'RE ***YOUR*** FRIENDS...
KLAK
THANK YOU.

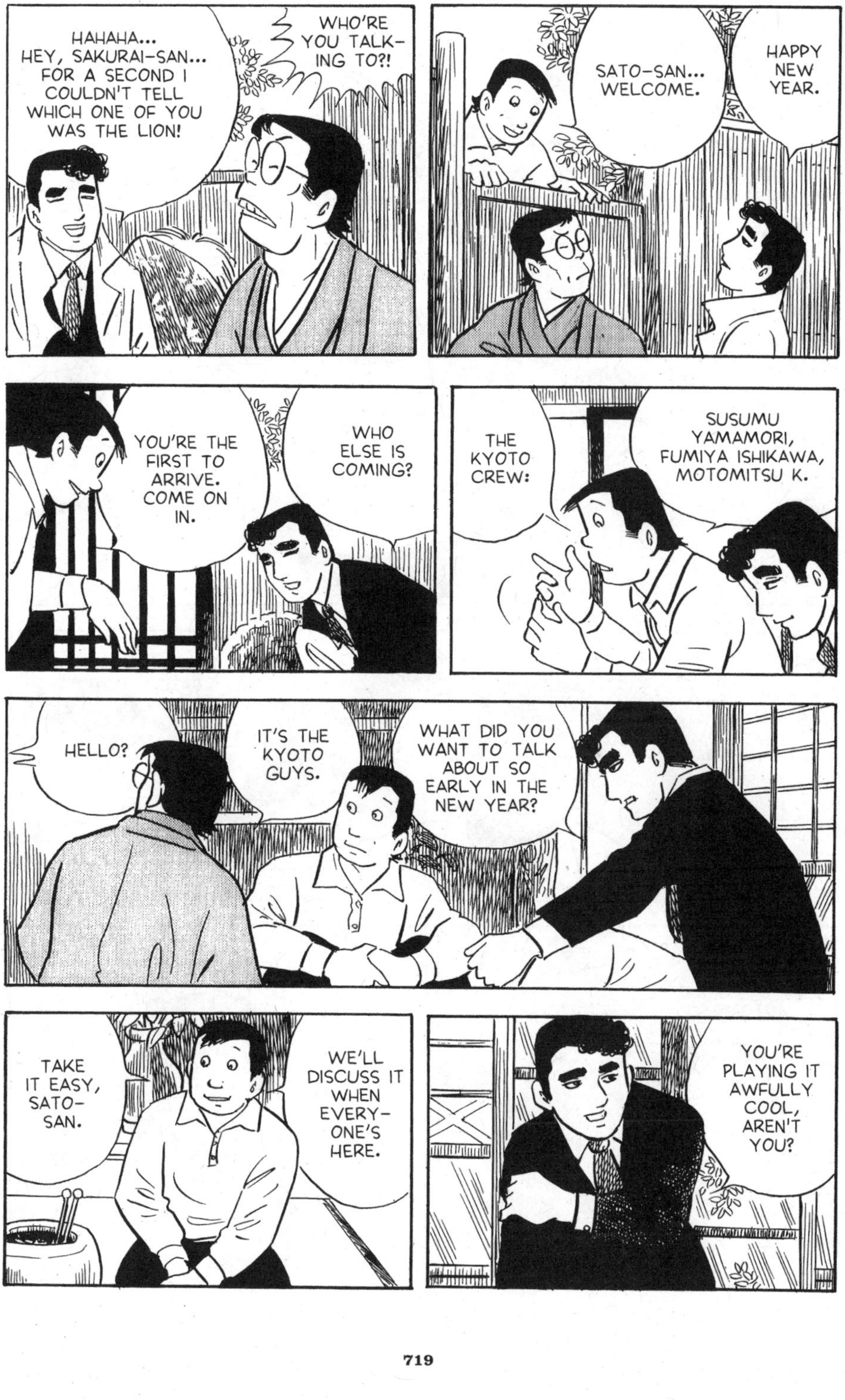
HAHAHA... HEY, SAKURAI-SAN... FOR A SECOND I COULDN'T TELL WHICH ONE OF YOU WAS THE LION!
WHO'RE YOU TALKING TO?!
SATO-SAN... WELCOME.
HAPPY NEW YEAR.
YOU'RE THE FIRST TO ARRIVE. COME ON IN.
WHO ELSE IS COMING?
THE KYOTO CREW:
SUSUMU YAMAMORI, FUMIYA ISHIKAWA, MOTOMITSU K.
HELLO?
IT'S THE KYOTO GUYS.
WHAT DID YOU WANT TO TALK ABOUT SO EARLY IN THE NEW YEAR?
TAKE IT EASY, SATO-SAN.
WE'LL DISCUSS IT WHEN EVERYONE'S HERE.
YOU'RE PLAYING IT AWFULLY COOL, AREN'T YOU?

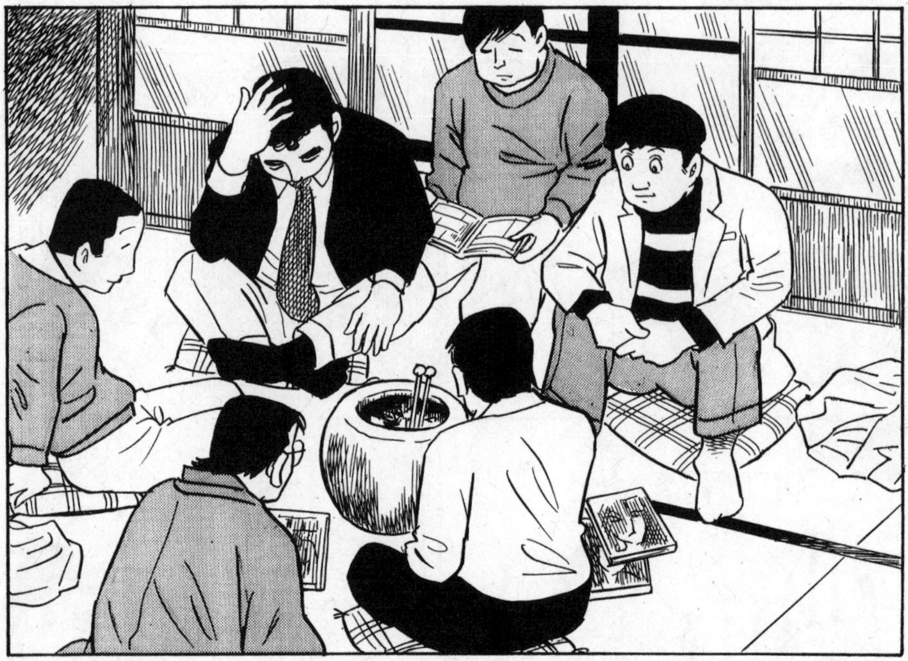

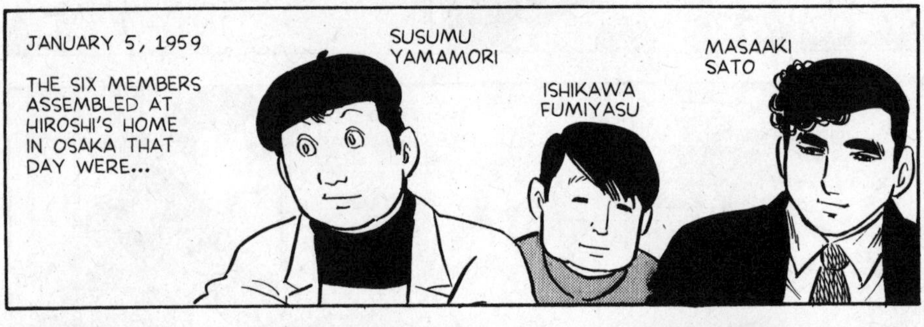
JANUARY 5, 1959
THE SIX MEMBERS ASSEMBLED AT HIROSHI'S HOME IN OSAKA THAT DAY WERE...
SUSUMU YAMAMORI
ISHIKAWA FUMIYASU
MASAAKI SATO

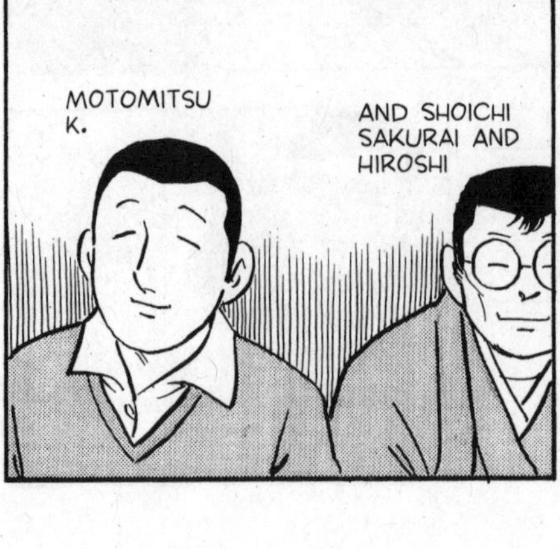
MOTOMITSU K.
AND SHOICHI SAKURAI AND HIROSHI

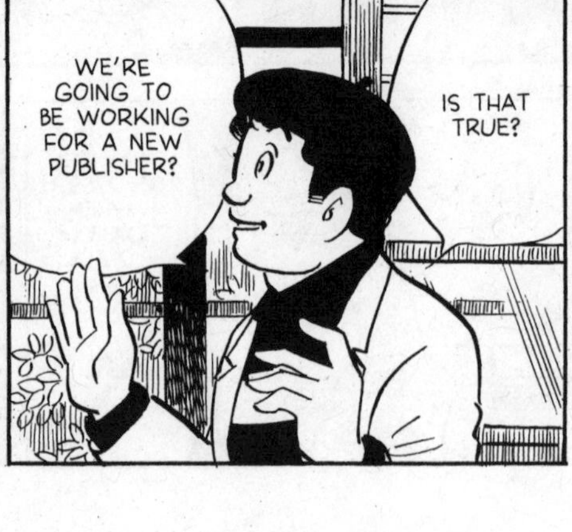
WE'RE GOING TO BE WORKING FOR A NEW PUBLISHER?
IS THAT TRUE?

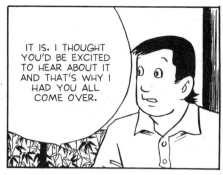

IT IS. I THOUGHT YOU'D BE EXCITED TO HEAR ABOUT IT AND THAT'S WHY I HAD YOU ALL COME OVER.
THAT'S GREAT NEWS.
THERE'S BEEN LESS AND LESS WORK FROM HINOMARU, SO IT'S REALLY A GODSEND.
SO YOU'LL PARTICI-PATE THEN?
ISHIKAWA, HOW ABOUT YOU?
IF EVERYONE ELSE IS GOING TO DO IT, I WILL, TOO.
TOGESTU SHOBO WANTS TO PUBLISH SOMETHING LIKE ***SHADOW*** OR ***CITY***, RIGHT?
I PROMISE TO PAY ALL MEMBERS EQUALLY FOR THEIR MANU-SCRIPTS.
AND THE PAY WILL DEFINITELY BE COMPA-RABLE OR BETTER THAN ***SHADOW*** OR ***CITY***.
AND WHO WILL BE THE MEMBERS OF THIS NEW MAGAZINE?
THE SIX OF US HERE NOW...
AND I'D LIKE TO GET MASAHIKO MATSUMOTO AND TAKAO SAITO INVOLVED.

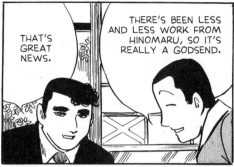

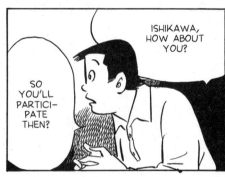

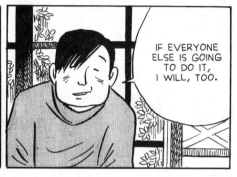

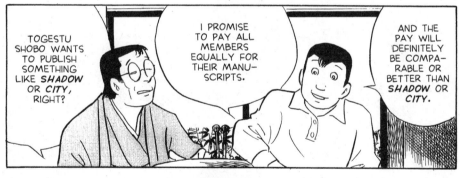

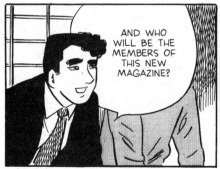

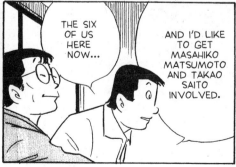

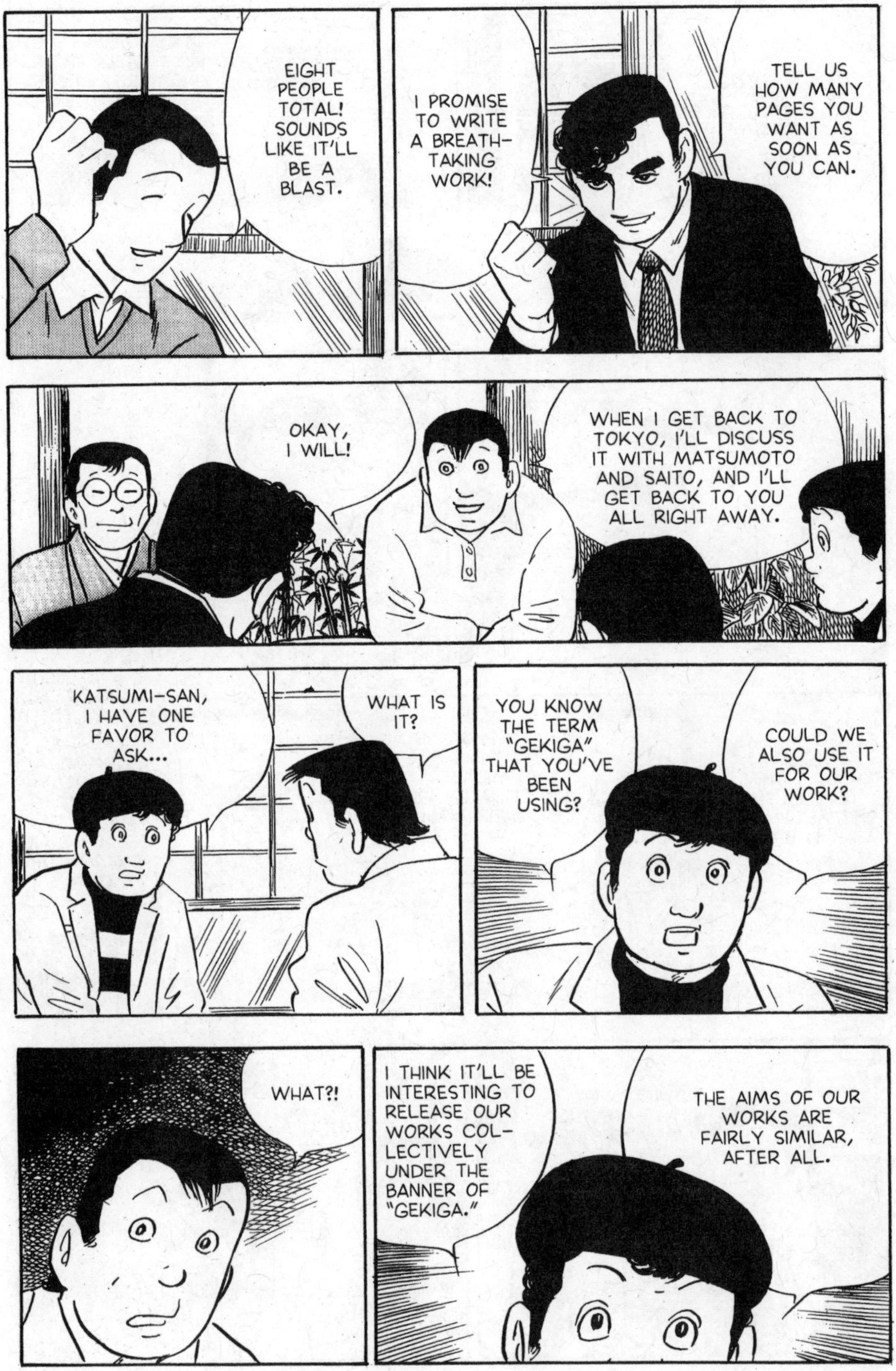
EIGHT PEOPLE TOTAL! SOUNDS LIKE IT'LL BE A BLAST.
I PROMISE TO WRITE A BREATH-TAKING WORK!
TELL US HOW MANY PAGES YOU WANT AS SOON AS YOU CAN.
OKAY, I WILL!
WHEN I GET BACK TO TOKYO, I'LL DISCUSS IT WITH MATSUMOTO AND SAITO, AND I'LL GET BACK TO YOU ALL RIGHT AWAY.
KATSUMI-SAN, I HAVE ONE FAVOR TO ASK...
WHAT IS IT?
YOU KNOW THE TERM "GEKIGA" THAT YOU'VE BEEN USING?
COULD WE ALSO USE IT FOR OUR WORK?
WHAT?!
I THINK IT'LL BE INTERESTING TO RELEASE OUR WORKS COL-LECTIVELY UNDER THE BANNER OF "GEKIGA."
THE AIMS OF OUR WORKS ARE FAIRLY SIMILAR, AFTER ALL.

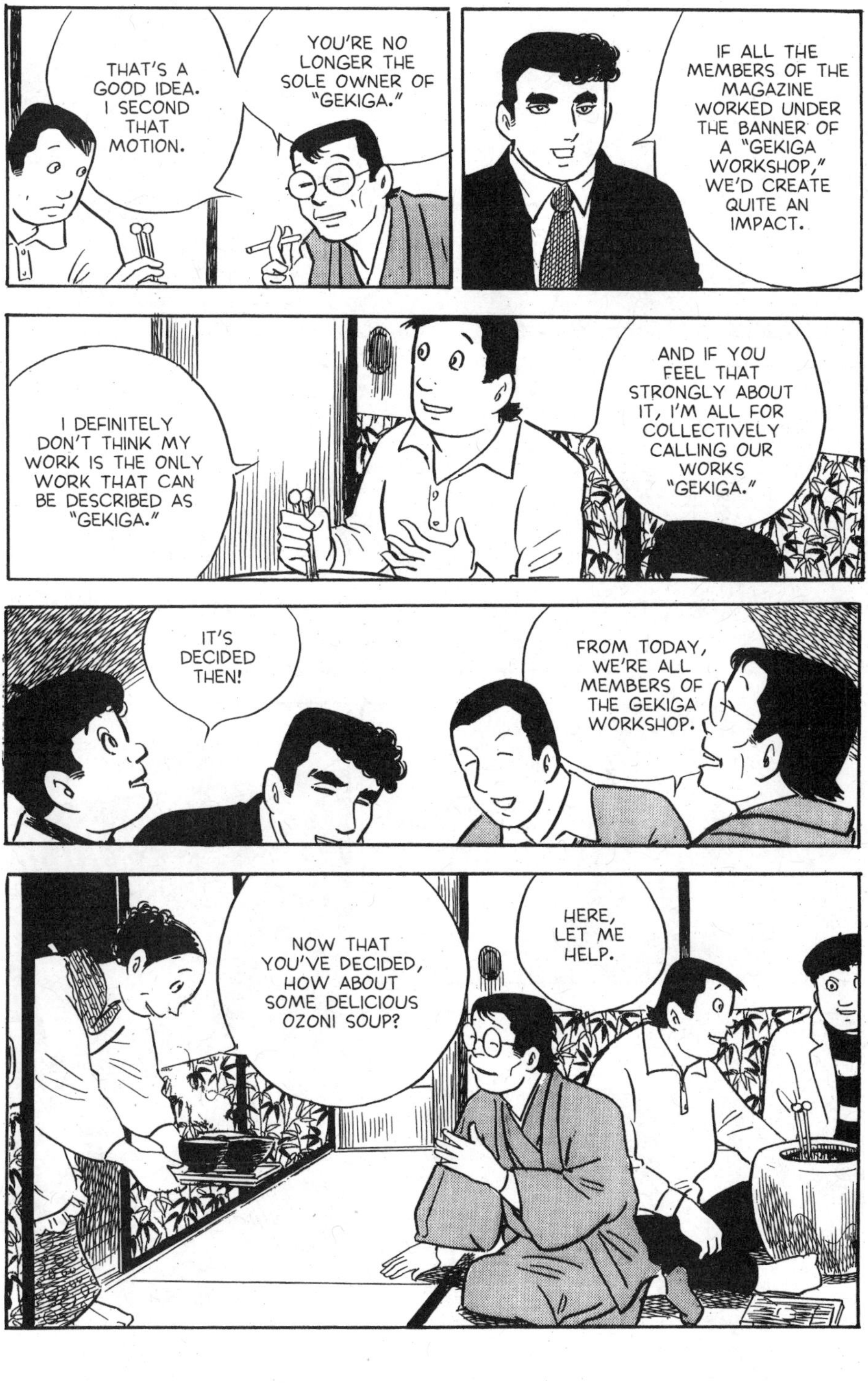
THAT'S A GOOD IDEA. I SECOND THAT MOTION.
YOU'RE NO LONGER THE SOLE OWNER OF "GEKIGA."
IF ALL THE MEMBERS OF THE MAGAZINE WORKED UNDER THE BANNER OF A "GEKIGA WORKSHOP," WE'D CREATE QUITE AN IMPACT.
I DEFINITELY DON'T THINK MY WORK IS THE ONLY WORK THAT CAN BE DESCRIBED AS "GEKIGA."
AND IF YOU FEEL THAT STRONGLY ABOUT IT, I'M ALL FOR COLLECTIVELY CALLING OUR WORKS "GEKIGA."
IT'S DECIDED THEN!
FROM TODAY, WE'RE ALL MEMBERS OF THE GEKIGA WORKSHOP.
NOW THAT YOU'VE DECIDED, HOW ABOUT SOME DELICIOUS OZONI SOUP?
HERE, LET ME HELP.

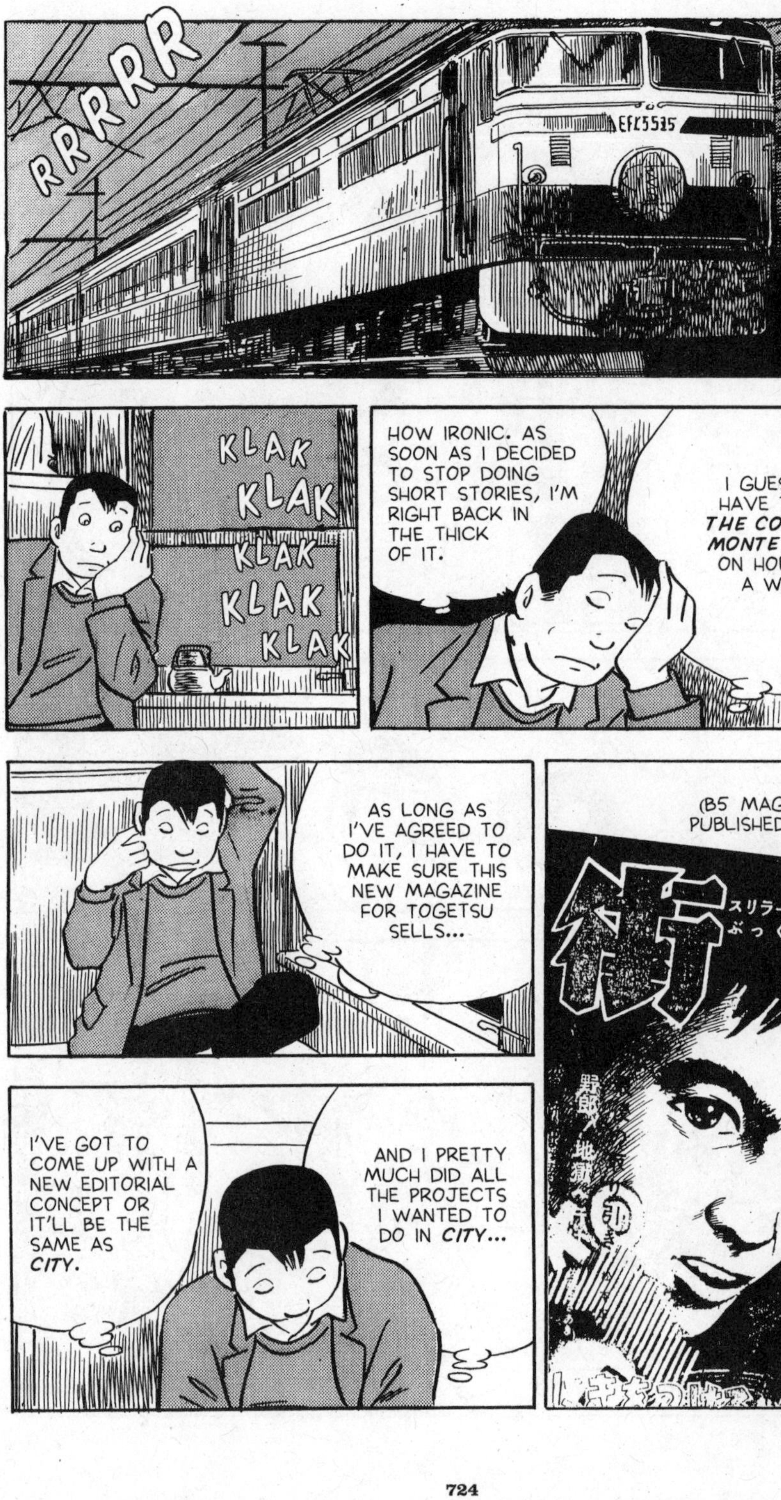
RRRRRR
KLAK KLAK KLAK KLAK KLAK
HOW IRONIC. AS SOON AS I DECIDED TO STOP DOING SHORT STORIES, I'M RIGHT BACK IN THE THICK OF IT.
I GUESS I'LL HAVE TO PUT ***THE COUNT OF MONTE CRISTO*** ON HOLD FOR A WHILE.
AS LONG AS I'VE AGREED TO DO IT, I HAVE TO MAKE SURE THIS NEW MAGAZINE FOR TOGETSU SELLS...
I'VE GOT TO COME UP WITH A NEW EDITORIAL CONCEPT OR IT'LL BE THE SAME AS ***CITY***.
AND I PRETTY MUCH DID ALL THE PROJECTS I WANTED TO DO IN ***CITY***...
CITY (B5 MAGAZINE SIZE, PUBLISHED JANUARY, 1959)
街
スリラー ぶっく
別冊
アクション特集

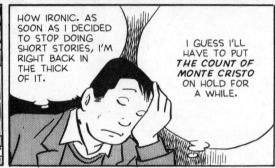

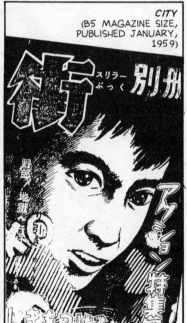

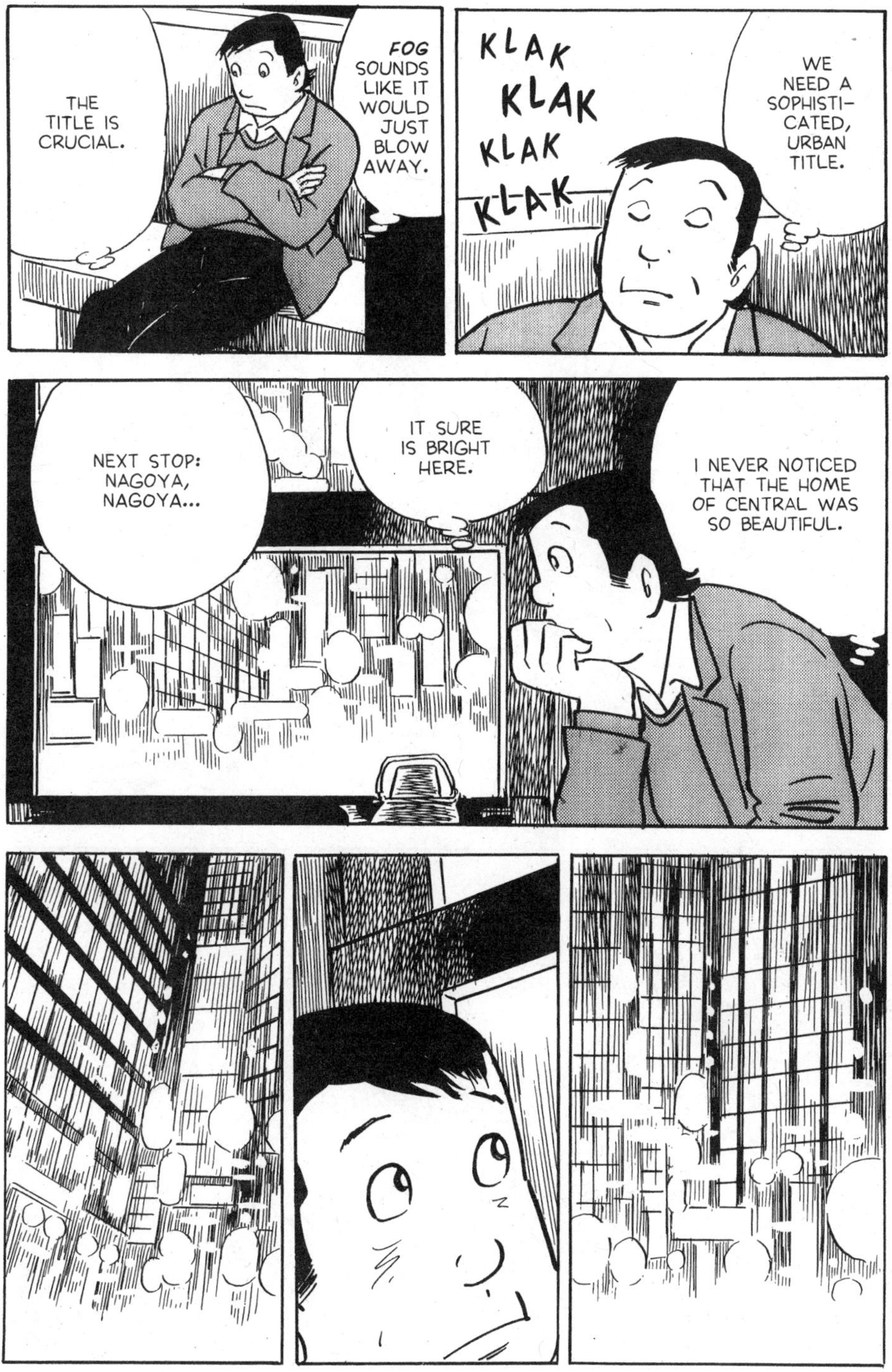

THE TITLE IS CRUCIAL.
FOG SOUNDS LIKE IT WOULD JUST BLOW AWAY.
KLAK KLAK KLAK KLAK
WE NEED A SOPHISTI-CATED, URBAN TITLE.
NEXT STOP: NAGOYA, NAGOYA...
IT SURE IS BRIGHT HERE.
I NEVER NOTICED THAT THE HOME OF CENTRAL WAS SO BEAUTIFUL.

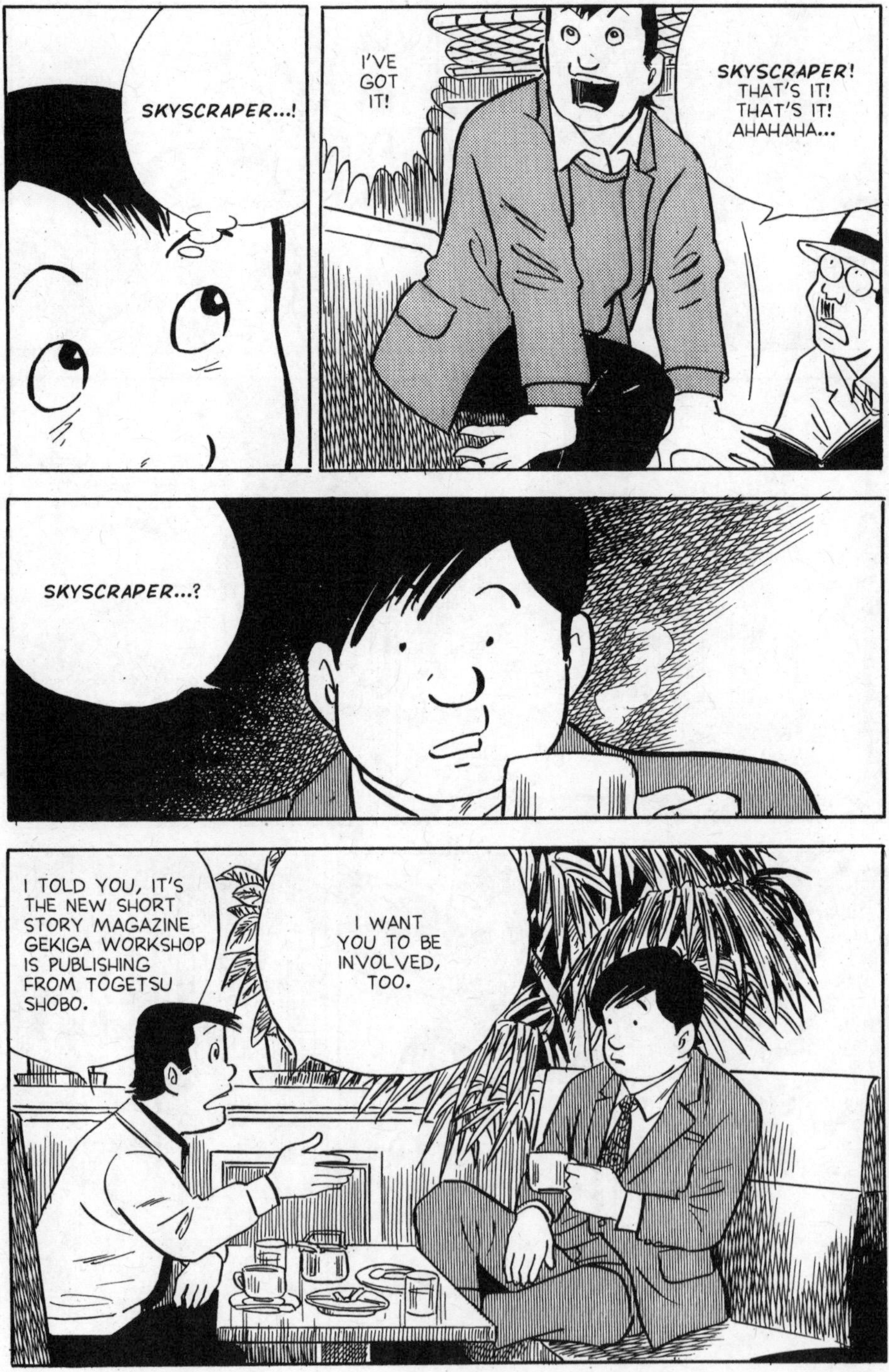
SKYSCRAPER...!
I'VE GOT IT!
SKYSCRAPER! THAT'S IT! THAT'S IT! AHAHAHA...
SKYSCRAPER...?
I TOLD YOU, IT'S THE NEW SHORT STORY MAGAZINE GEKIGA WORKSHOP IS PUBLISHING FROM TOGETSU SHOBO.
I WANT YOU TO BE INVOLVED, TOO.

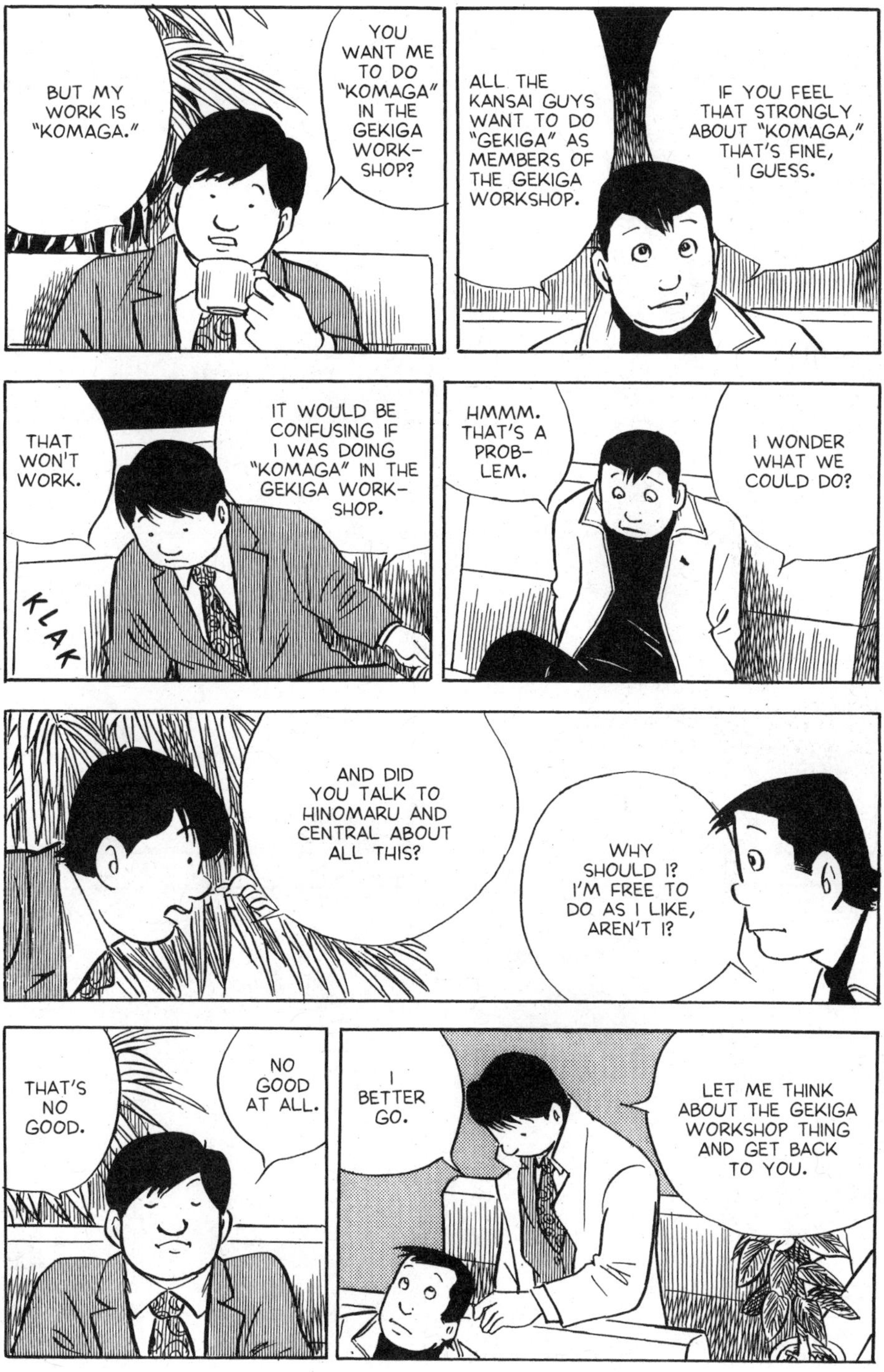
BUT MY WORK IS "KOMAGA."
YOU WANT ME TO DO "KOMAGA" IN THE GEKIGA WORK-SHOP?
ALL THE KANSAI GUYS WANT TO DO "GEKIGA" AS MEMBERS OF THE GEKIGA WORKSHOP.
IF YOU FEEL THAT STRONGLY ABOUT "KOMAGA," THAT'S FINE, I GUESS.
THAT WON'T WORK.
KLAK
IT WOULD BE CONFUSING IF I WAS DOING "KOMAGA" IN THE GEKIGA WORK-SHOP.
HMMM. THAT'S A PROB-LEM.
I WONDER WHAT WE COULD DO?
AND DID YOU TALK TO HINOMARU AND CENTRAL ABOUT ALL THIS?
WHY SHOULD I? I'M FREE TO DO AS I LIKE, AREN'T I?
THAT'S NO GOOD.
NO GOOD AT ALL.
I BETTER GO.
LET ME THINK ABOUT THE GEKIGA WORKSHOP THING AND GET BACK TO YOU.

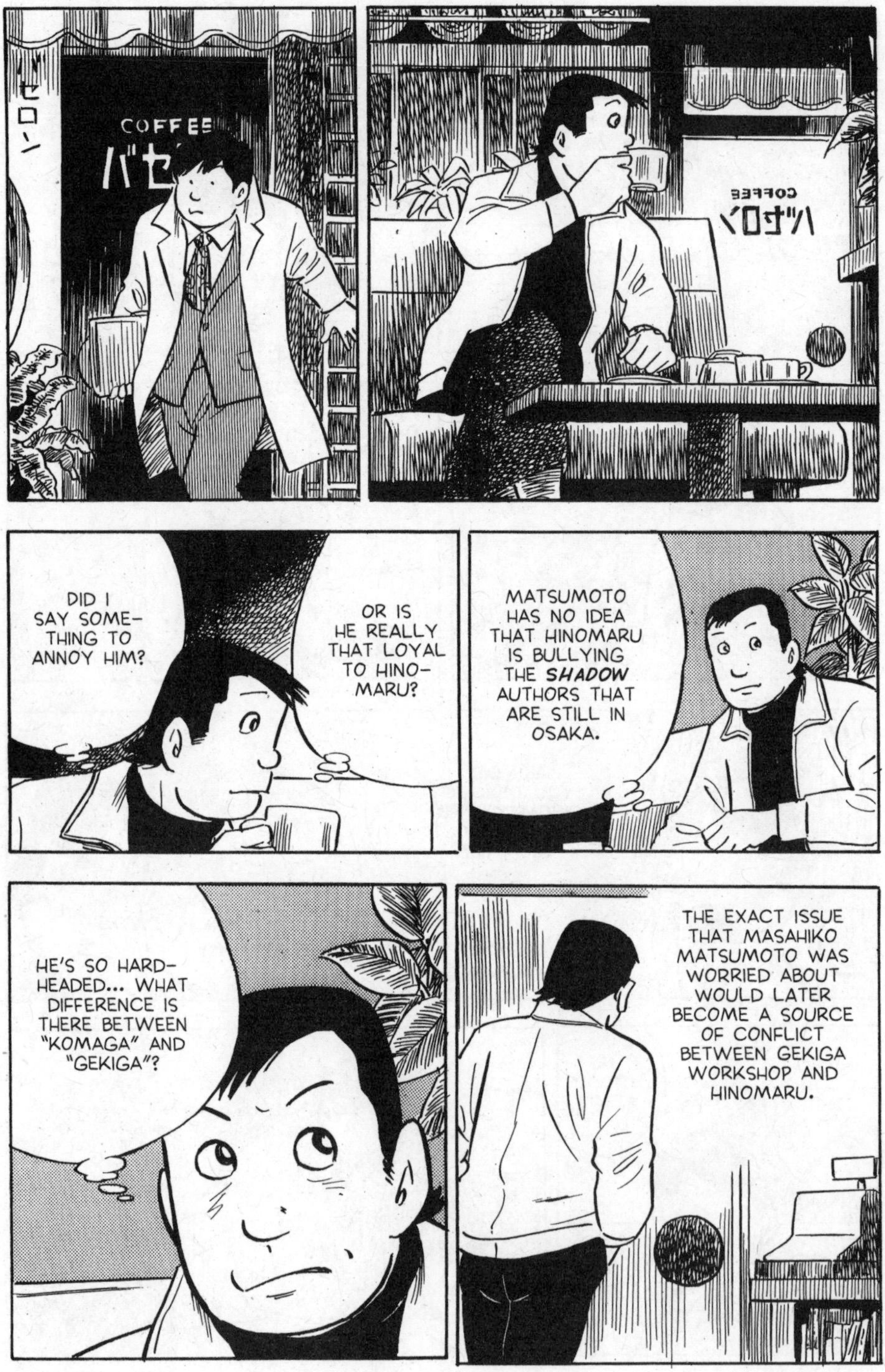

DID I SAY SOME-THING TO ANNOY HIM?
OR IS HE REALLY THAT LOYAL TO HINO-MARU?
MATSUMOTO HAS NO IDEA THAT HINOMARU IS BULLYING THE ***SHADOW*** AUTHORS THAT ARE STILL IN OSAKA.
HE'S SO HARD-HEADED... WHAT DIFFERENCE IS THERE BETWEEN "KOMAGA" AND "GEKIGA"?
THE EXACT ISSUE THAT MASAHIKO MATSUMOTO WAS WORRIED ABOUT WOULD LATER BECOME A SOURCE OF CONFLICT BETWEEN GEKIGA WORKSHOP AND HINOMARU.

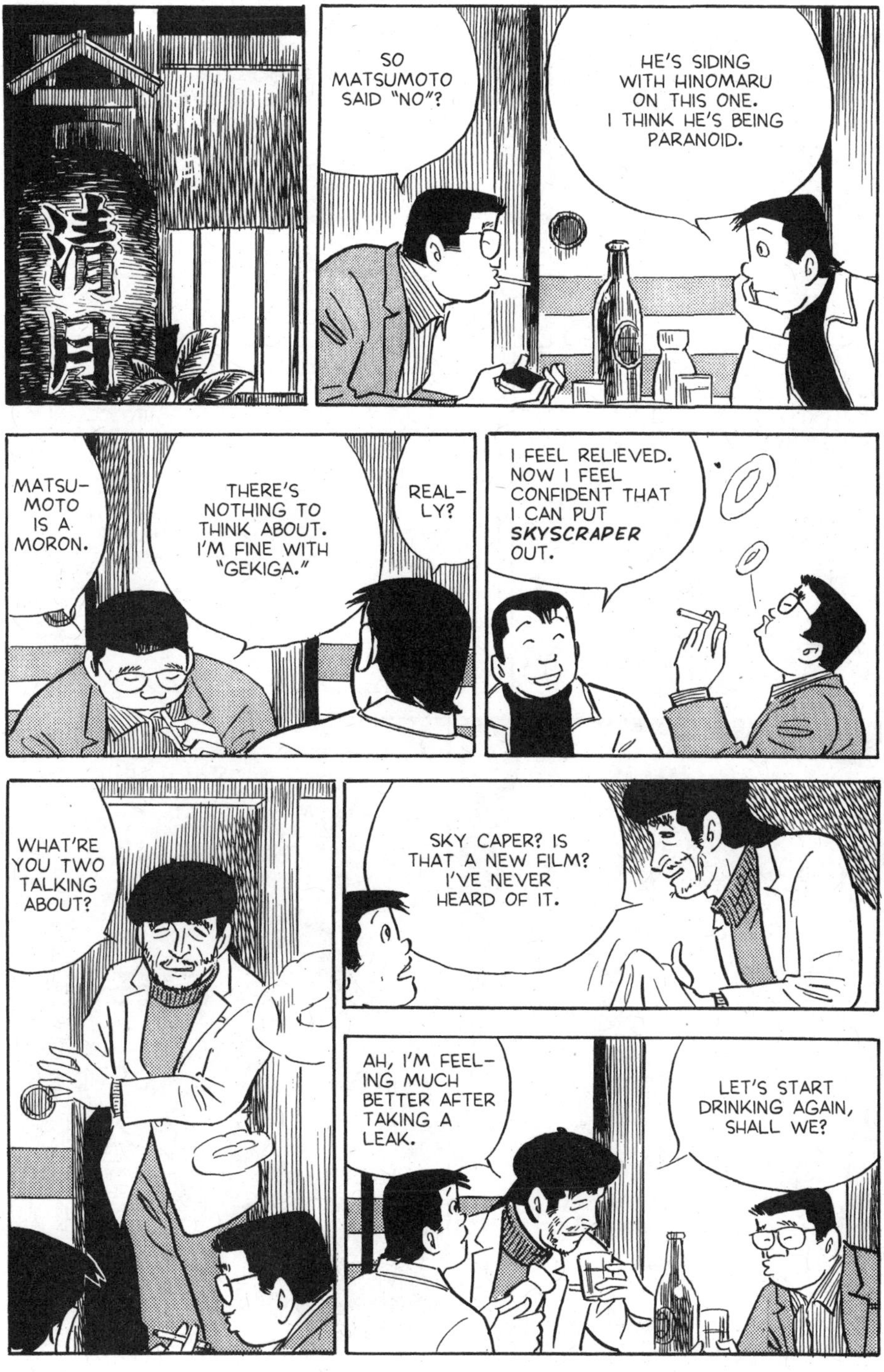
清月
SO MATSUMOTO SAID "NO"?
HE'S SIDING WITH HINOMARU ON THIS ONE. I THINK HE'S BEING PARANOID.
MATSU-MOTO IS A MORON.
THERE'S NOTHING TO THINK ABOUT. I'M FINE WITH "GEKIGA."
REAL-LY?
I FEEL RELIEVED. NOW I FEEL CONFIDENT THAT I CAN PUT **SKYSCRAPER** OUT.
WHAT'RE YOU TWO TALKING ABOUT?
SKY CAPER? IS THAT A NEW FILM? I'VE NEVER HEARD OF IT.
AH, I'M FEEL-ING MUCH BETTER AFTER TAKING A LEAK.
LET'S START DRINKING AGAIN, SHALL WE?

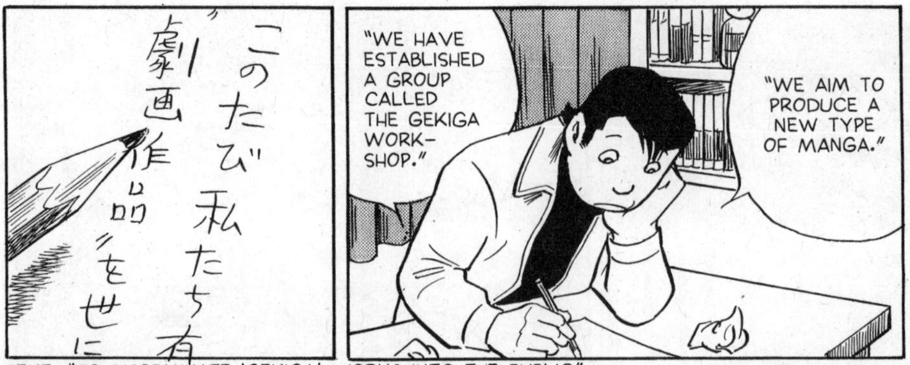
このたび私たち有
〝劇画作品〟を世に
"WE HAVE ESTABLISHED A GROUP CALLED THE GEKIGA WORKSHOP."
"WE AIM TO PRODUCE A NEW TYPE OF MANGA."

TEXT: "TO DISSEMINATE 'GEKIGA' WORKS INTO THE PUBLIC"

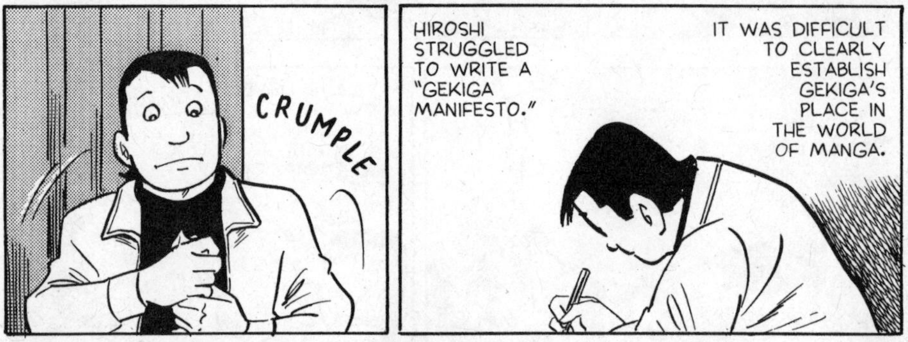
CRUMPLE
HIROSHI STRUGGLED TO WRITE A "GEKIGA MANIFESTO."
IT WAS DIFFICULT TO CLEARLY ESTABLISH GEKIGA'S PLACE IN THE WORLD OF MANGA.

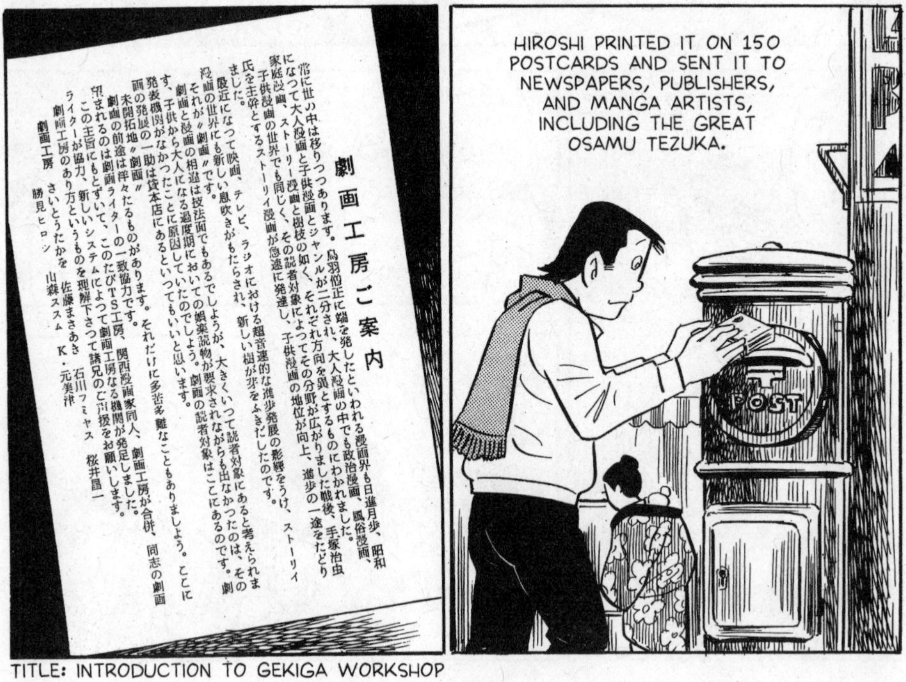
劇画工房ご案内
常に世の中は移りつつあります。鳥羽僧正に端を発したといわれる漫画界も日進月歩、昭和
になつて大人漫画と子供漫画とジャンルが二分され、大人漫画の中でも政治漫画、風俗漫画、
家庭漫画、ストーリー漫画と樹枝の如く、それぞれ方向を異とするものにわかれました。
子供漫画の世界でも同じく、その読者対象によつてその分野が広がりました戦後、手塚治虫
氏を主幹とするストーリイ漫画が急速に発達し、子供漫画の地位が向上、進歩の一途をたどり
ました。
最近になつて映画、テレビ、ラジオにおける超音速的な進歩発展の影響をうけ、ストーリイ
漫画の世界にも新しい息吹きがもたらされ、新しい樹が芽をふきだしたのです。
それが〝劇画〟です。
劇画と漫画の相違は技法面でもあるでしょうが、大きくいつて読者対象にあると考えられま
す、子供から大人になる過度期においての娯楽読物が要求されながらも出なかつたのは、その
発表機関がなかつたことに原因していたのでしょう。劇画の読者対象はここにあるのです。劇
画の発展の一助は貸本店にあるといつてもいいと思います。
未開拓地〝劇画〟
劇画の前途は洋々たるものがあります。それだけに多苦多難なこともありましょう。ここに
望まれるのは劇画ライターの一致協力です。
この主旨にもとずいて、このたびTS工房、関西漫画家同人、劇画工房が合併、同志の劇画
ライターが協力、新しいシステムによつて劇画工房なる機関が発足しました。
劇画工房のあり方というものを理解下さつて諸兄のご声援をお願いします。
劇画工房
さいとうたかを 佐藤まさあき 石川フミヤス 桜井昌一
勝見ヒロシ 山森ススム K・元美津
HIROSHI PRINTED IT ON 150 POSTCARDS AND SENT IT TO NEWSPAPERS, PUBLISHERS, AND MANGA ARTISTS, INCLUDING THE GREAT OSAMU TEZUKA.
POST

TITLE: INTRODUCTION TO GEKIGA WORKSHOP

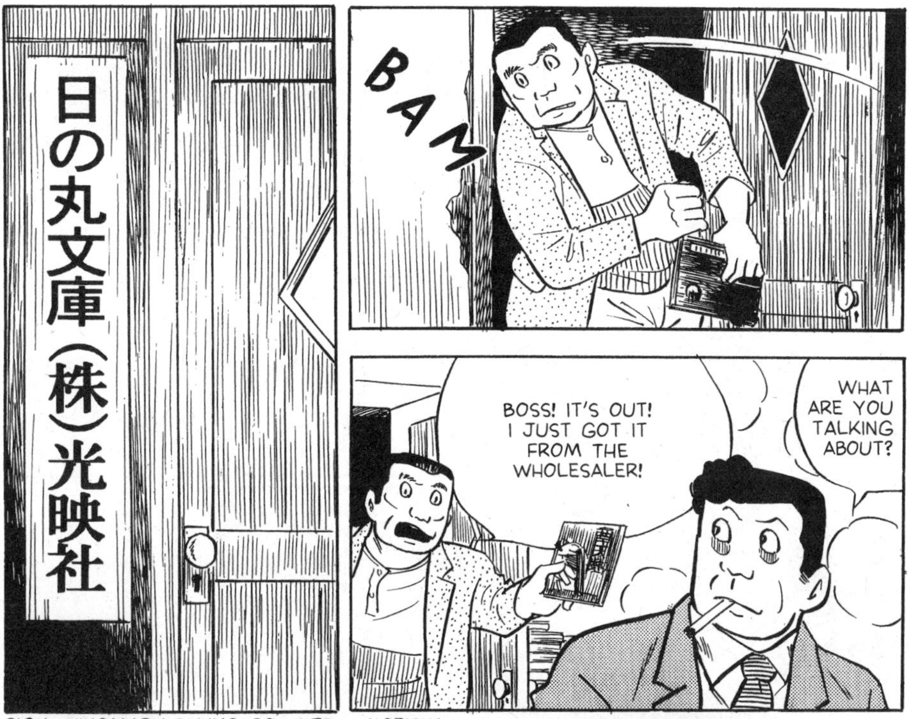
日の丸文庫（株）光映社
BAM
BOSS! IT'S OUT! I JUST GOT IT FROM THE WHOLESALER!
WHAT ARE YOU TALKING ABOUT?
SIGN: HINOMARU BUNKO CO., LTD. / KOEISHA

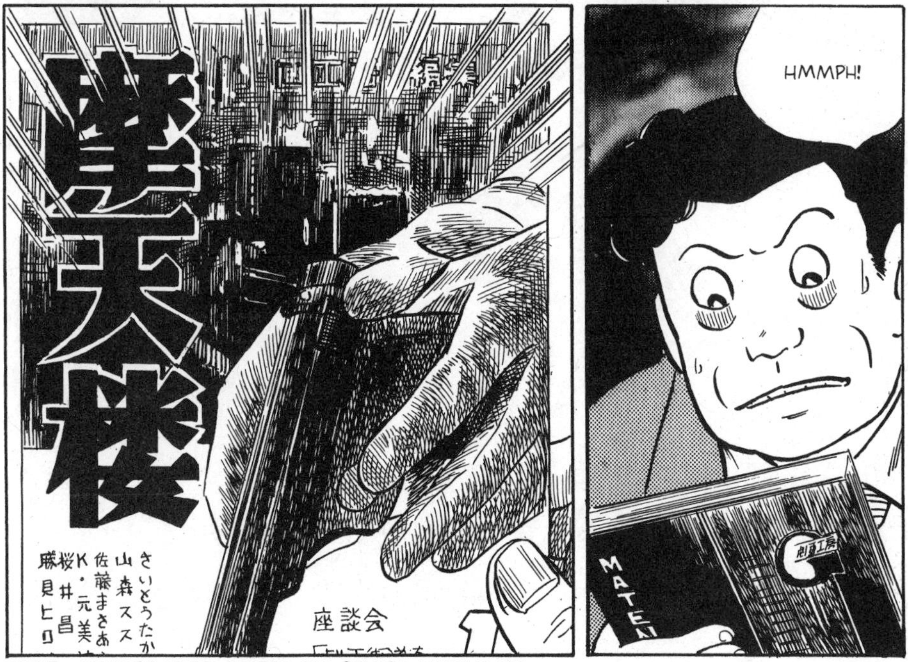
摩天楼
座談会
HMMPH!
MATEN
TITLE: *SKYSCRAPER*, EDITED BY GEKIGA WORKSHOP

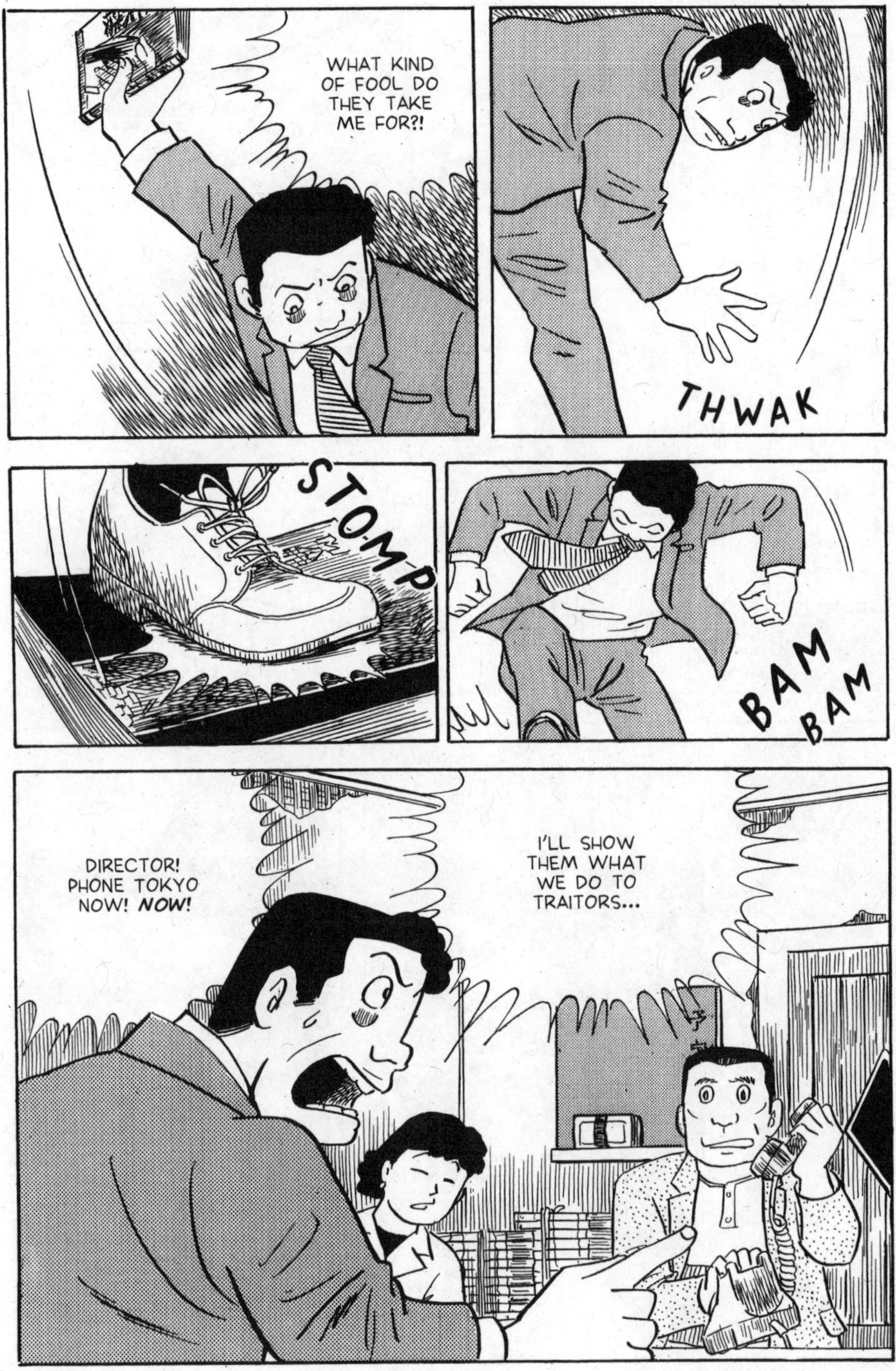
WHAT KIND OF FOOL DO THEY TAKE ME FOR?!
THWAK
STOMP
BAM
BAM
DIRECTOR! PHONE TOKYO NOW! ***NOW!***
I'LL SHOW THEM WHAT WE DO TO TRAITORS...

PROS AND CONS

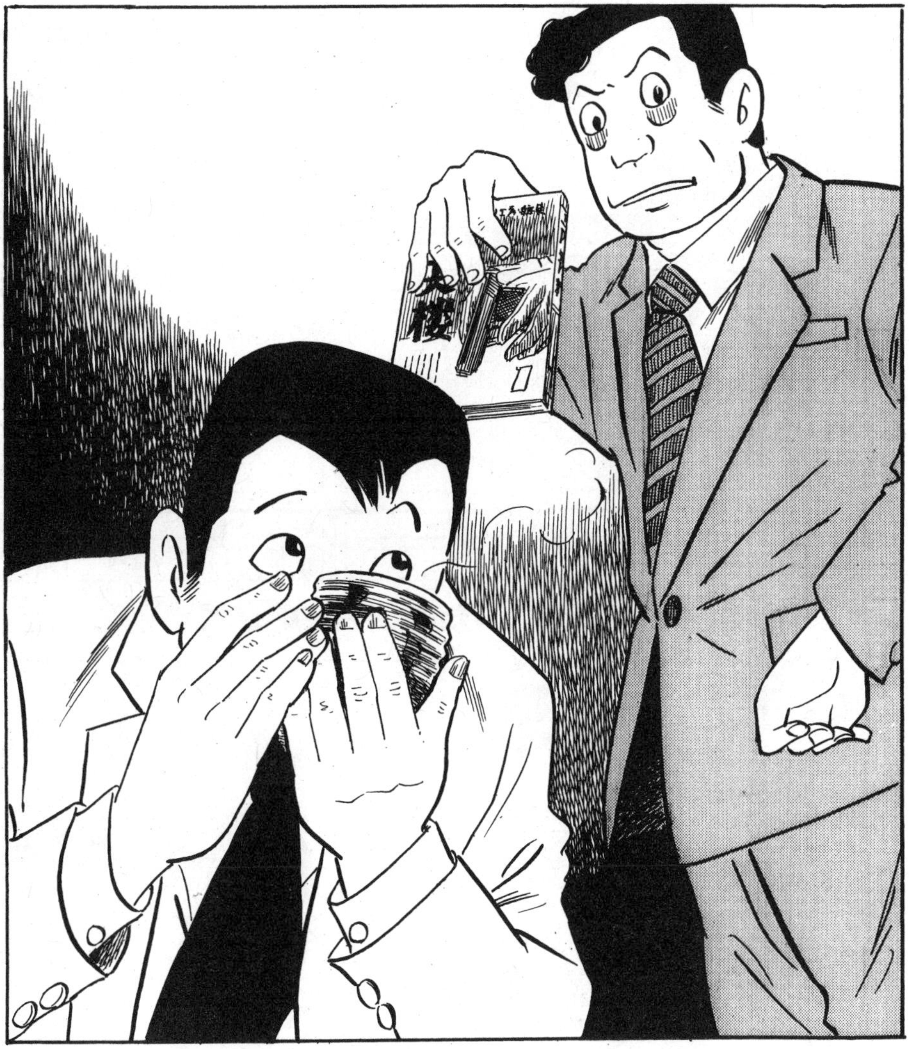

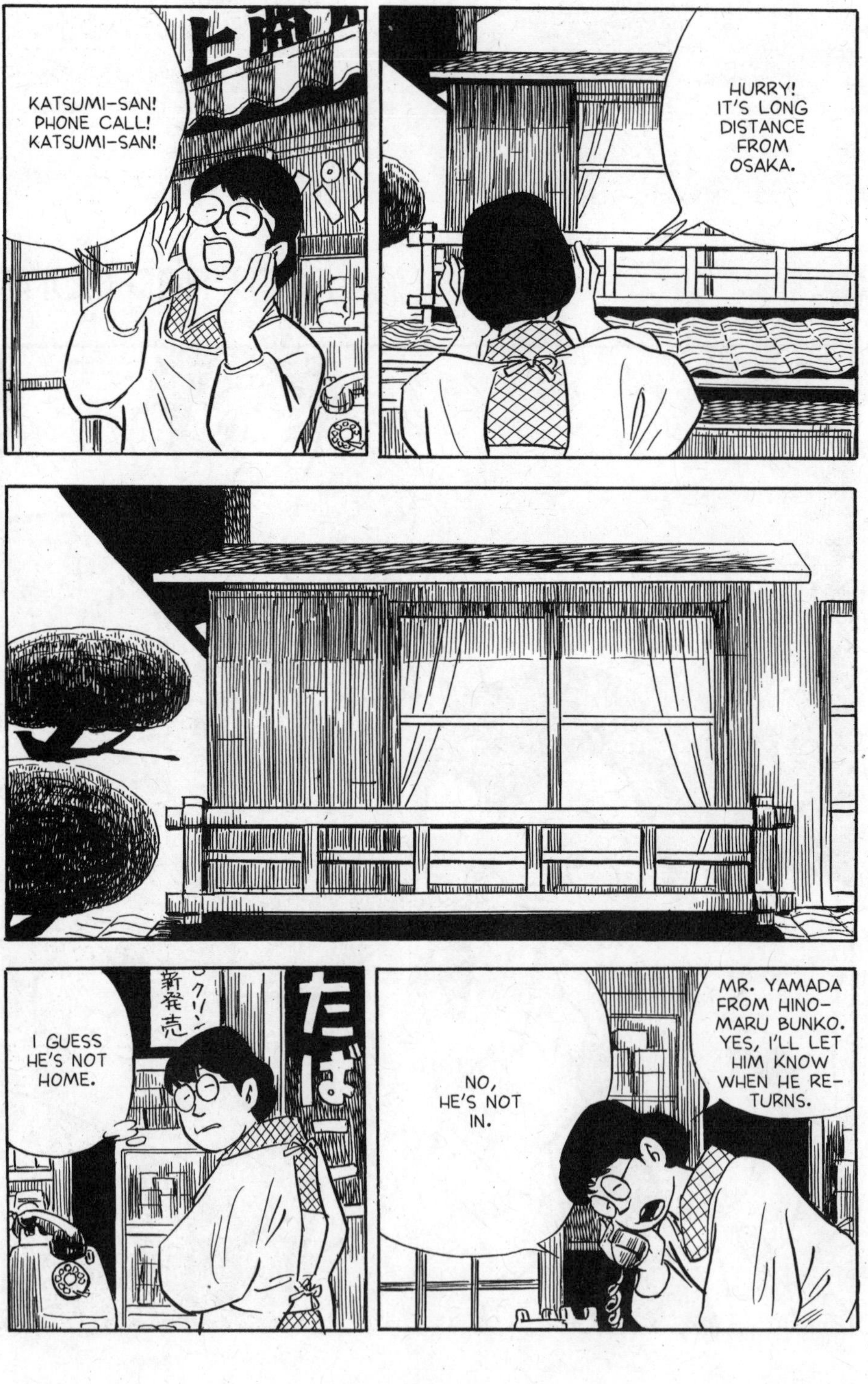
KATSUMI-SAN! PHONE CALL! KATSUMI-SAN!
HURRY! IT'S LONG DISTANCE FROM OSAKA.
I GUESS HE'S NOT HOME.
新発売
NO, HE'S NOT IN.
MR. YAMADA FROM HINO-MARU BUNKO. YES, I'LL LET HIM KNOW WHEN HE RE-TURNS.

I WONDER WHERE HE'S PROWLING ABOUT AT THIS TIME OF DAY.

HE SHOULD BE HOME WORKING!

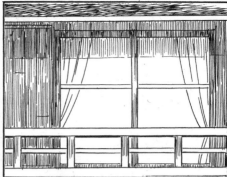

FORGIVE ME, TOBACCO SHOP LADY...

FOR PRETENDING TO NOT BE HOME.

WHAT SHOULD I DO?

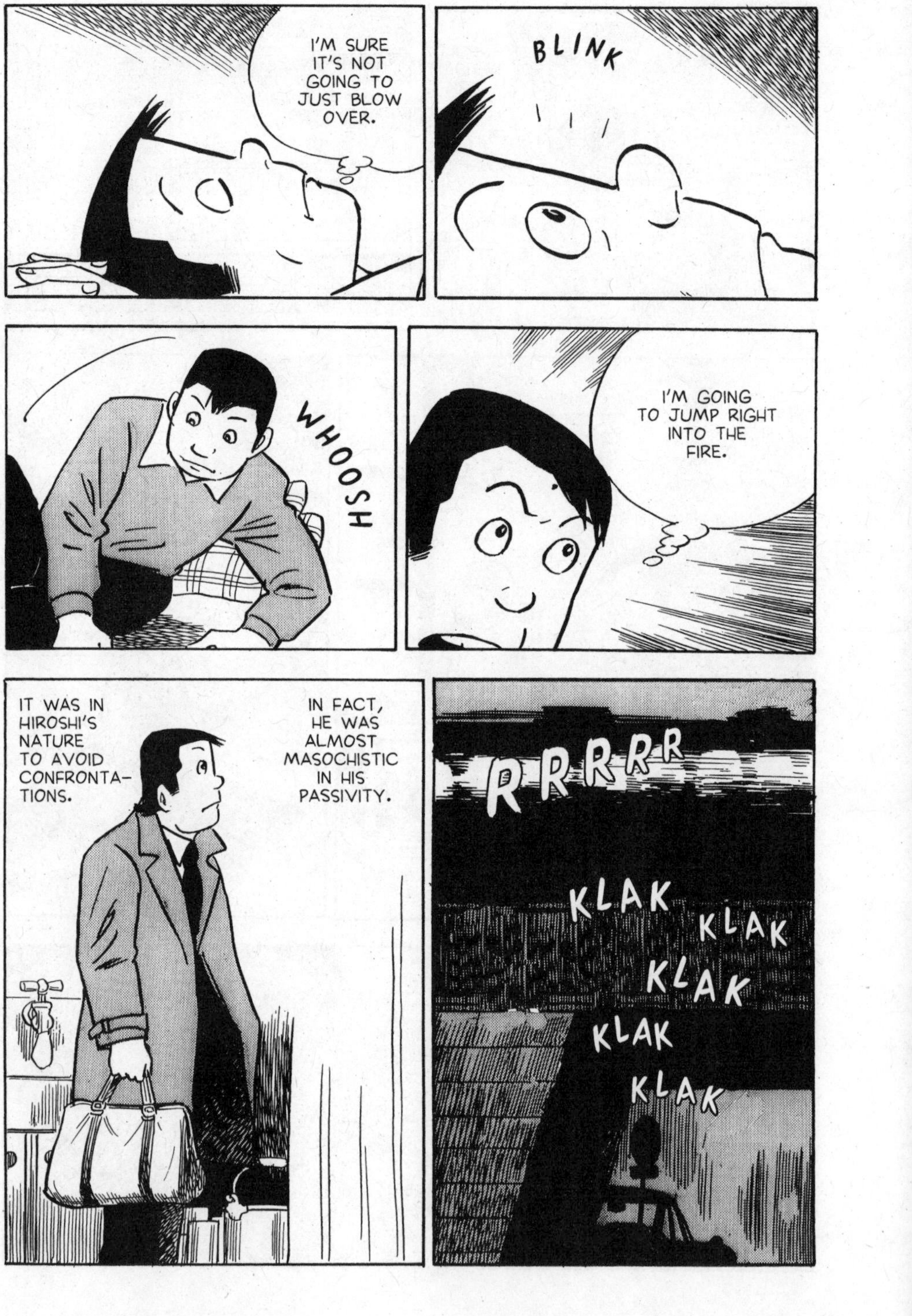
I'M SURE IT'S NOT GOING TO JUST BLOW OVER.
BLINK
WHOOSH
I'M GOING TO JUMP RIGHT INTO THE FIRE.
IT WAS IN HIROSHI'S NATURE TO AVOID CONFRONTATIONS.
IN FACT, HE WAS ALMOST MASOCHISTIC IN HIS PASSIVITY.
RRRRR
KLAK
KLAK
KLAK
KLAK
KLAK

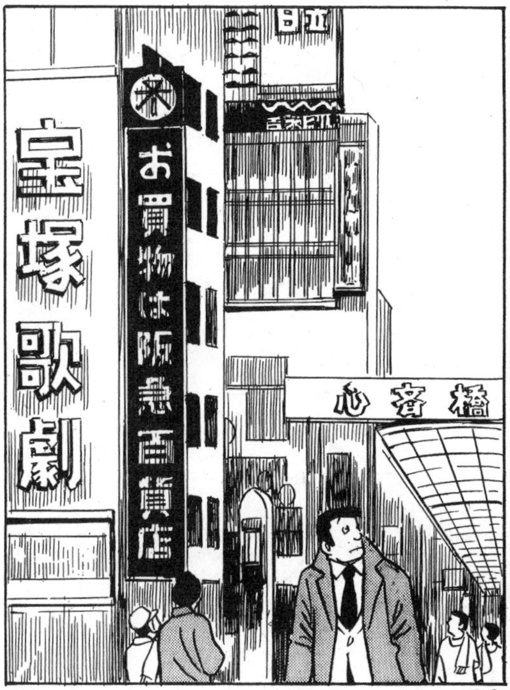
宝塚歌劇
お買物は阪急百貨店
心斎橋

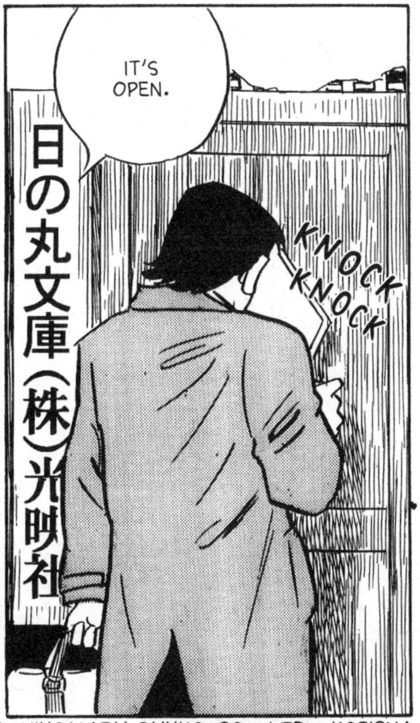
IT'S OPEN.
日の丸文庫(株)光映社
KNOCK KNOCK

SIGN: HINOMARU BUNKO CO., LTD., KOEISHA

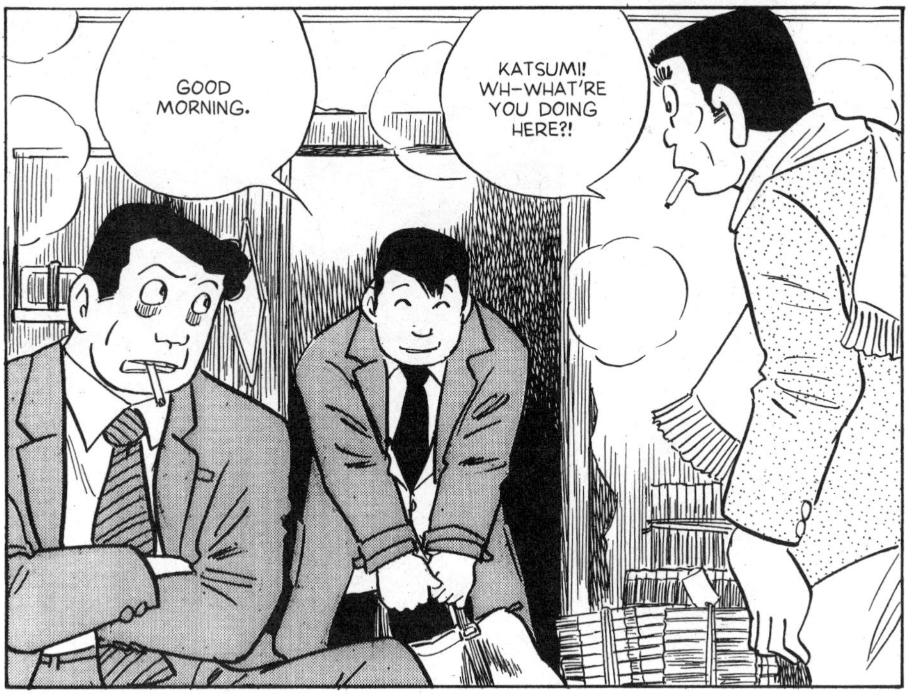
GOOD MORNING.
KATSUMI! WH-WHAT'RE YOU DOING HERE?!

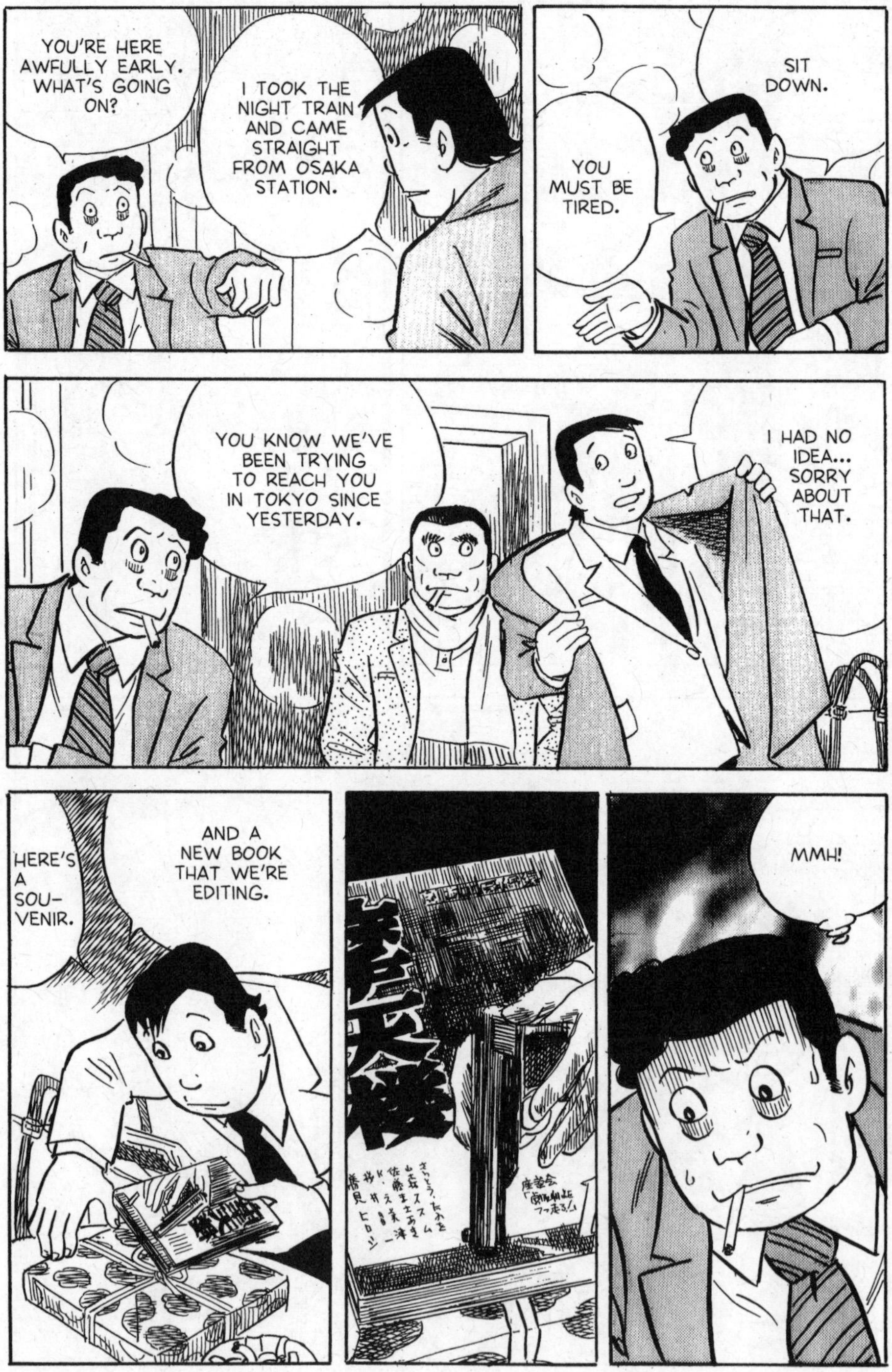
YOU'RE HERE AWFULLY EARLY. WHAT'S GOING ON?
I TOOK THE NIGHT TRAIN AND CAME STRAIGHT FROM OSAKA STATION.
YOU MUST BE TIRED.
SIT DOWN.
YOU KNOW WE'VE BEEN TRYING TO REACH YOU IN TOKYO SINCE YESTERDAY.
I HAD NO IDEA... SORRY ABOUT THAT.
HERE'S A SOU-VENIR.
AND A NEW BOOK THAT WE'RE EDITING.
MMH!

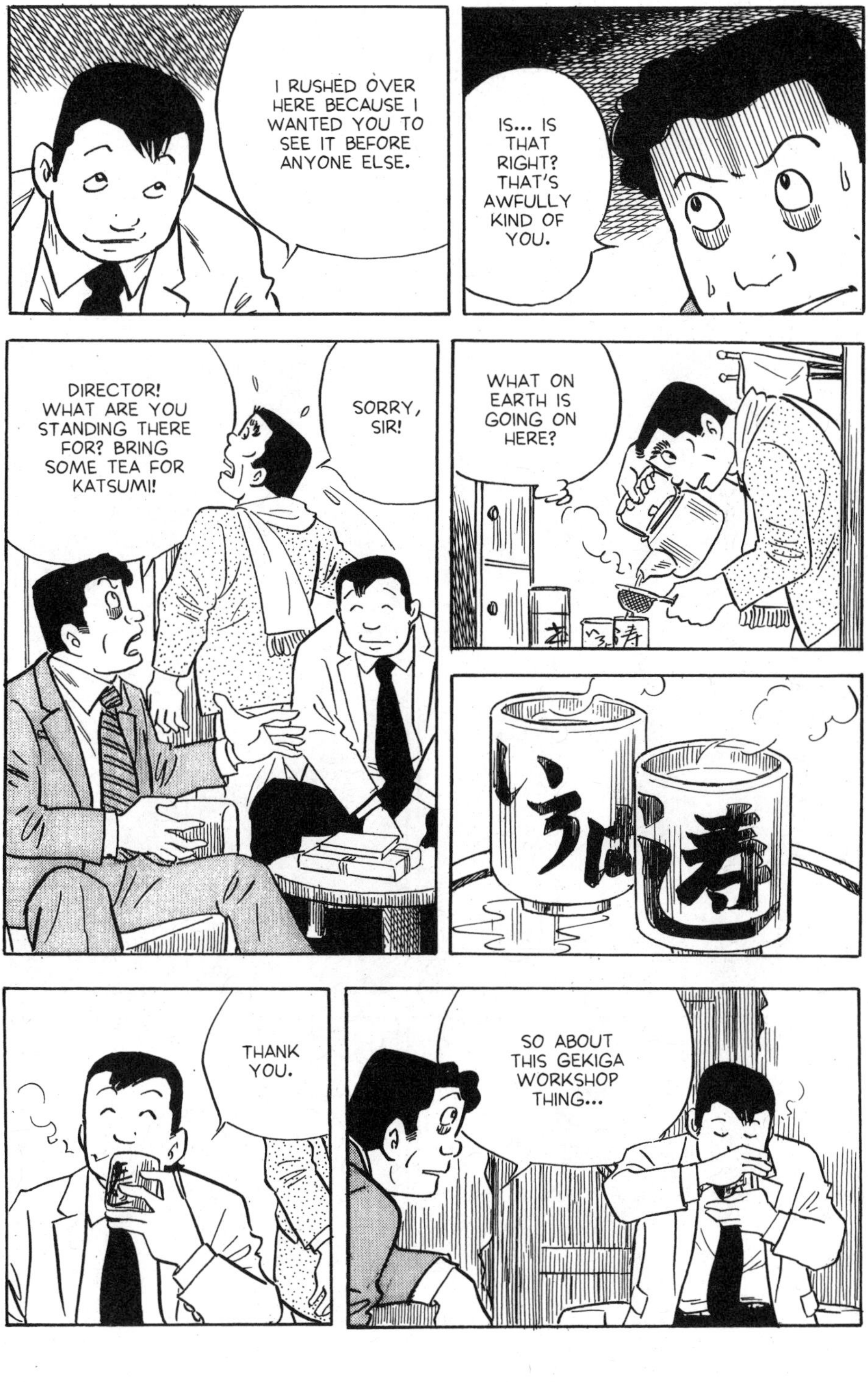
I RUSHED OVER HERE BECAUSE I WANTED YOU TO SEE IT BEFORE ANYONE ELSE.
IS... IS THAT RIGHT? THAT'S AWFULLY KIND OF YOU.
DIRECTOR! WHAT ARE YOU STANDING THERE FOR? BRING SOME TEA FOR KATSUMI!
SORRY, SIR!
WHAT ON EARTH IS GOING ON HERE?
THANK YOU.
SO ABOUT THIS GEKIGA WORKSHOP THING...

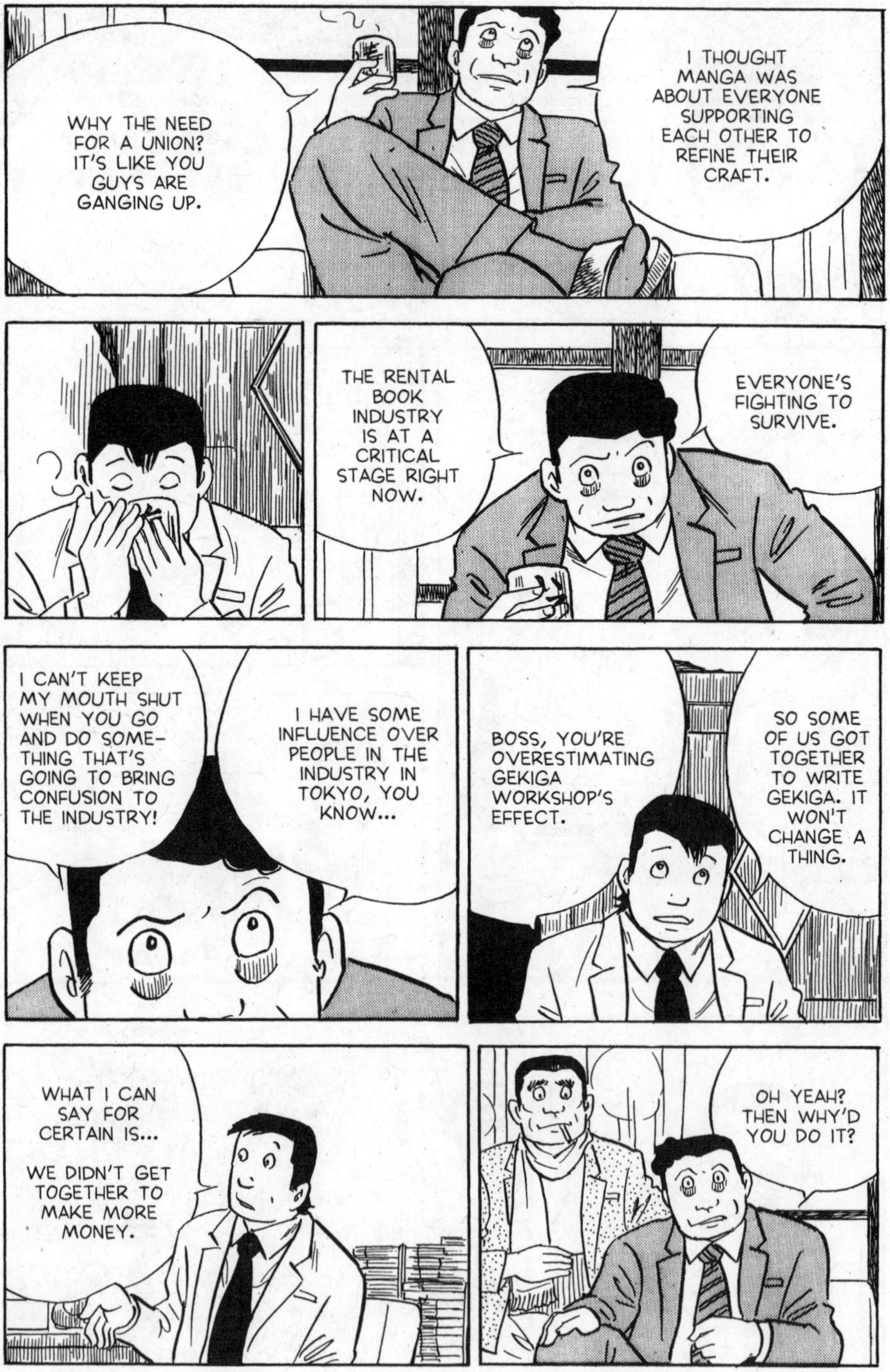
WHY THE NEED FOR A UNION? IT'S LIKE YOU GUYS ARE GANGING UP.
I THOUGHT MANGA WAS ABOUT EVERYONE SUPPORTING EACH OTHER TO REFINE THEIR CRAFT.
THE RENTAL BOOK INDUSTRY IS AT A CRITICAL STAGE RIGHT NOW.
EVERYONE'S FIGHTING TO SURVIVE.
I CAN'T KEEP MY MOUTH SHUT WHEN YOU GO AND DO SOME-THING THAT'S GOING TO BRING CONFUSION TO THE INDUSTRY!
I HAVE SOME INFLUENCE OVER PEOPLE IN THE INDUSTRY IN TOKYO, YOU KNOW...
BOSS, YOU'RE OVERESTIMATING GEKIGA WORKSHOP'S EFFECT.
SO SOME OF US GOT TOGETHER TO WRITE GEKIGA. IT WON'T CHANGE A THING.
WHAT I CAN SAY FOR CERTAIN IS...
WE DIDN'T GET TOGETHER TO MAKE MORE MONEY.
OH YEAH? THEN WHY'D YOU DO IT?

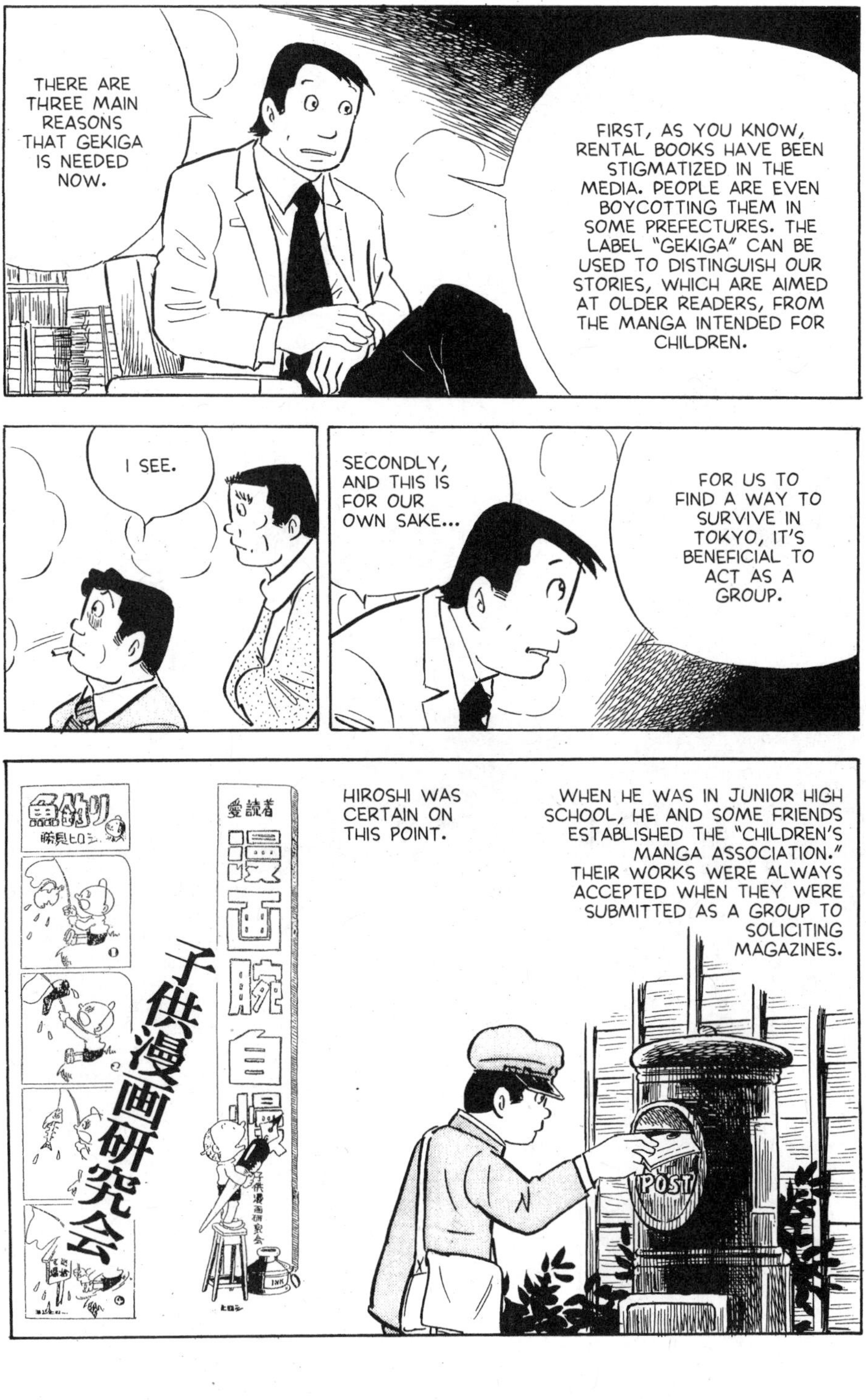
THERE ARE THREE MAIN REASONS THAT GEKIGA IS NEEDED NOW.
FIRST, AS YOU KNOW, RENTAL BOOKS HAVE BEEN STIGMATIZED IN THE MEDIA. PEOPLE ARE EVEN BOYCOTTING THEM IN SOME PREFECTURES. THE LABEL "GEKIGA" CAN BE USED TO DISTINGUISH OUR STORIES, WHICH ARE AIMED AT OLDER READERS, FROM THE MANGA INTENDED FOR CHILDREN.
I SEE.
SECONDLY, AND THIS IS FOR OUR OWN SAKE...
FOR US TO FIND A WAY TO SURVIVE IN TOKYO, IT'S BENEFICIAL TO ACT AS A GROUP.
HIROSHI WAS CERTAIN ON THIS POINT.
WHEN HE WAS IN JUNIOR HIGH SCHOOL, HE AND SOME FRIENDS ESTABLISHED THE "CHILDREN'S MANGA ASSOCIATION." THEIR WORKS WERE ALWAYS ACCEPTED WHEN THEY WERE SUBMITTED AS A GROUP TO SOLICITING MAGAZINES.
魚釣り
愛読者
漫画腕自慢
子供漫画研究会
INK
POST

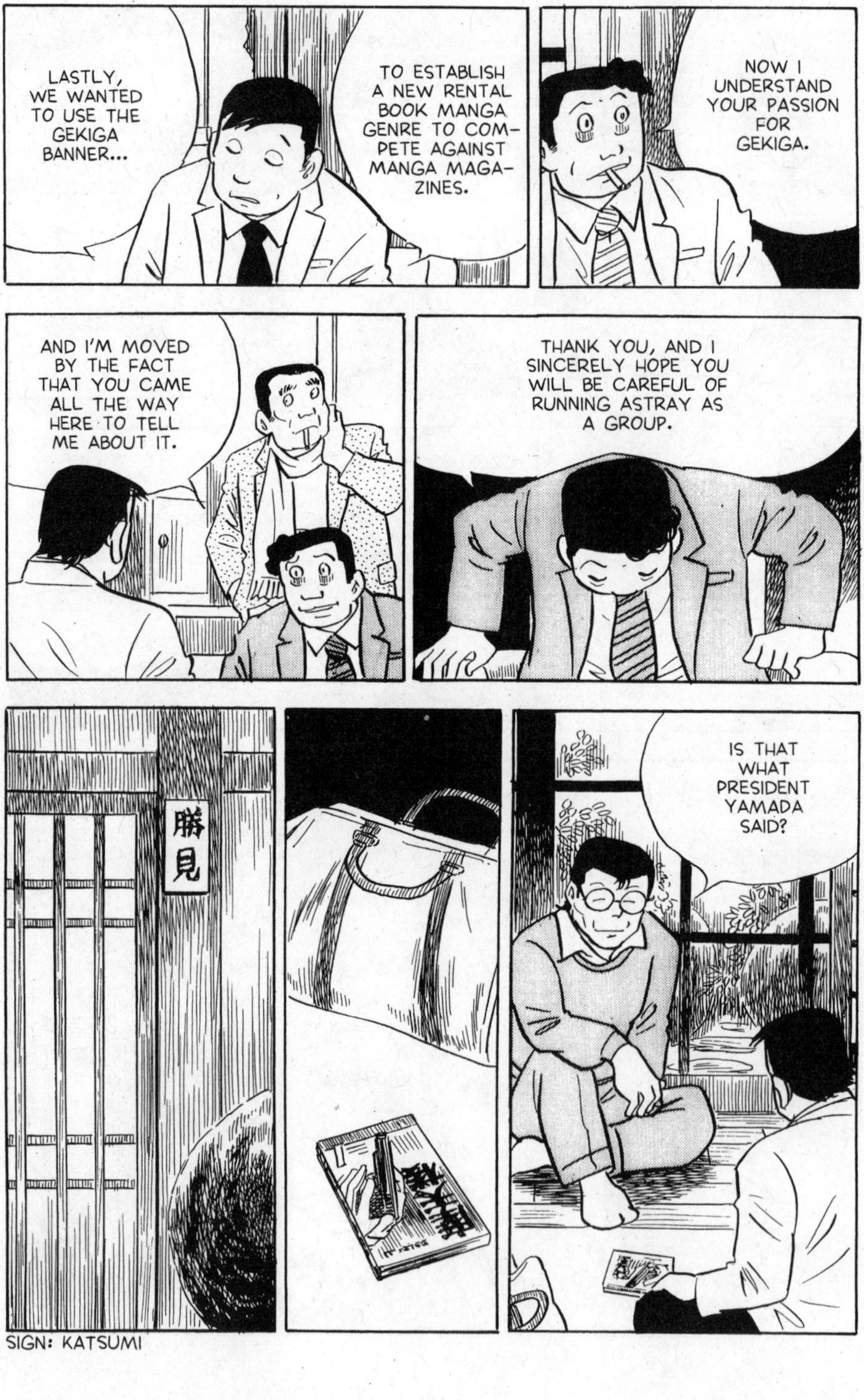
LASTLY, WE WANTED TO USE THE GEKIGA BANNER...
TO ESTABLISH A NEW RENTAL BOOK MANGA GENRE TO COMPETE AGAINST MANGA MAGAZINES.
NOW I UNDERSTAND YOUR PASSION FOR GEKIGA.
AND I'M MOVED BY THE FACT THAT YOU CAME ALL THE WAY HERE TO TELL ME ABOUT IT.
THANK YOU, AND I SINCERELY HOPE YOU WILL BE CAREFUL OF RUNNING ASTRAY AS A GROUP.
勝見
IS THAT WHAT PRESIDENT YAMADA SAID?

SIGN: KATSUMI

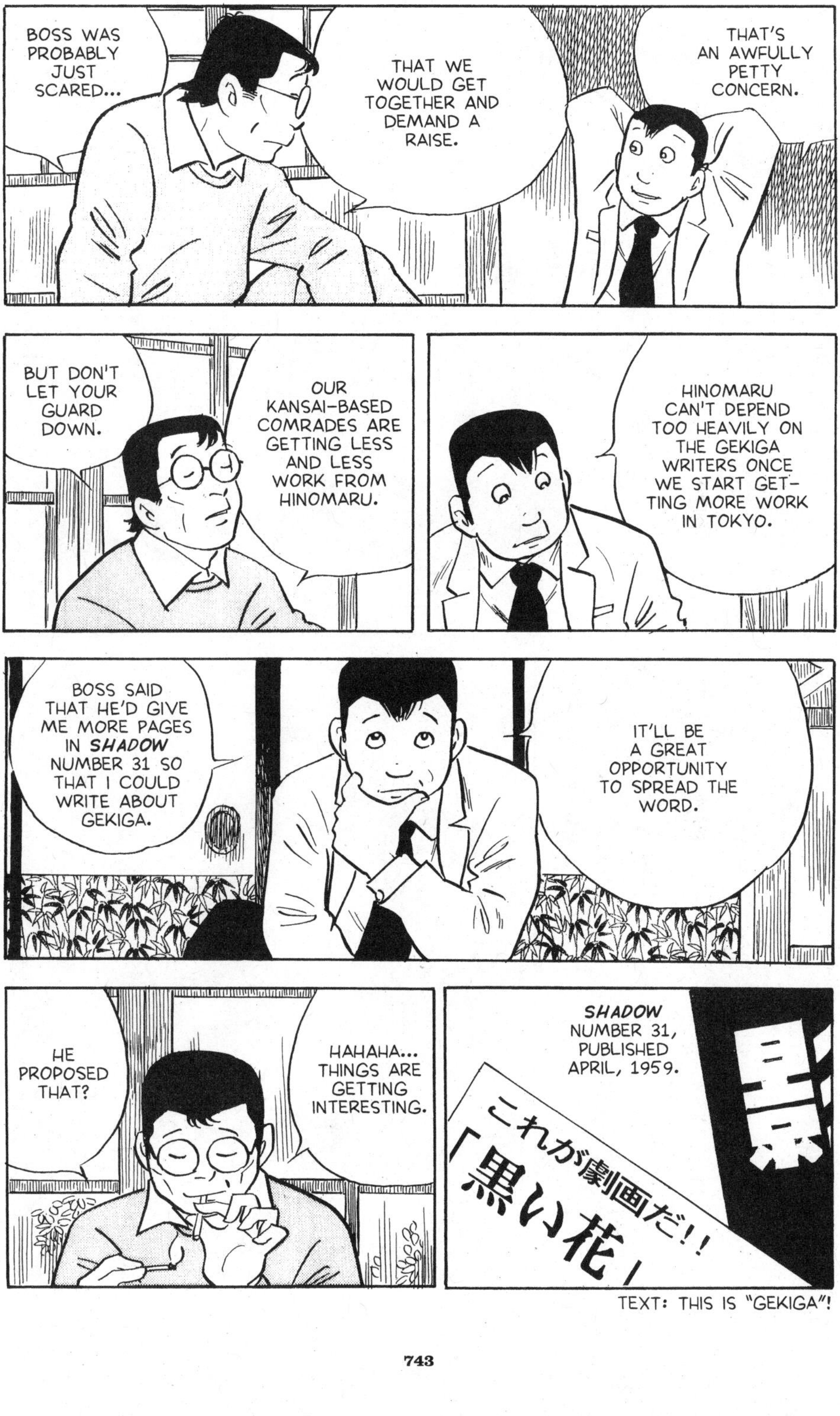
BOSS WAS PROBABLY JUST SCARED...
THAT WE WOULD GET TOGETHER AND DEMAND A RAISE.
THAT'S AN AWFULLY PETTY CONCERN.
BUT DON'T LET YOUR GUARD DOWN.
OUR KANSAI-BASED COMRADES ARE GETTING LESS AND LESS WORK FROM HINOMARU.
HINOMARU CAN'T DEPEND TOO HEAVILY ON THE GEKIGA WRITERS ONCE WE START GETTING MORE WORK IN TOKYO.
BOSS SAID THAT HE'D GIVE ME MORE PAGES IN *SHADOW* NUMBER 31 SO THAT I COULD WRITE ABOUT GEKIGA.
IT'LL BE A GREAT OPPORTUNITY TO SPREAD THE WORD.
HE PROPOSED THAT?
HAHAHA... THINGS ARE GETTING INTERESTING.
SHADOW NUMBER 31, PUBLISHED APRIL, 1959.
これが劇画だ!!
「黒い花」
TEXT: THIS IS "GEKIGA"!

I GUESS IT PAYS TO MAKE THE FIRST MOVE. WELL, LOOKS LIKE YOU WRAPPED THINGS UP PRETTY WELL WITH HINOMARU.

I HAVE WORK TO DO, SO I'LL BE GOING BACK TO TOKYO ON THE KODAMA TRAIN THIS AFTERNOON.

BUT THINGS WERE NOT SO EASILY RESOLVED.

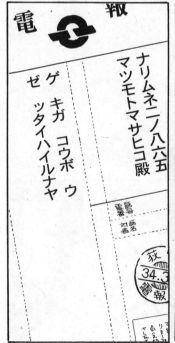

電報

ナリムネノ八六五
マツモトマサヒコ殿

ゼゲ
ッキガ
タコ
イウ
ハボ
イウ
ルナ
ヤ

荻
34.3

MASAHIKO, YOU RECEIVED ANOTHER TELEGRAM?

A TELEGRAM FROM PRESIDENT YAMADA, IMPLORING ME TO NOT JOIN THE GEKIGA WORKSHOP. WHAT A PEST.

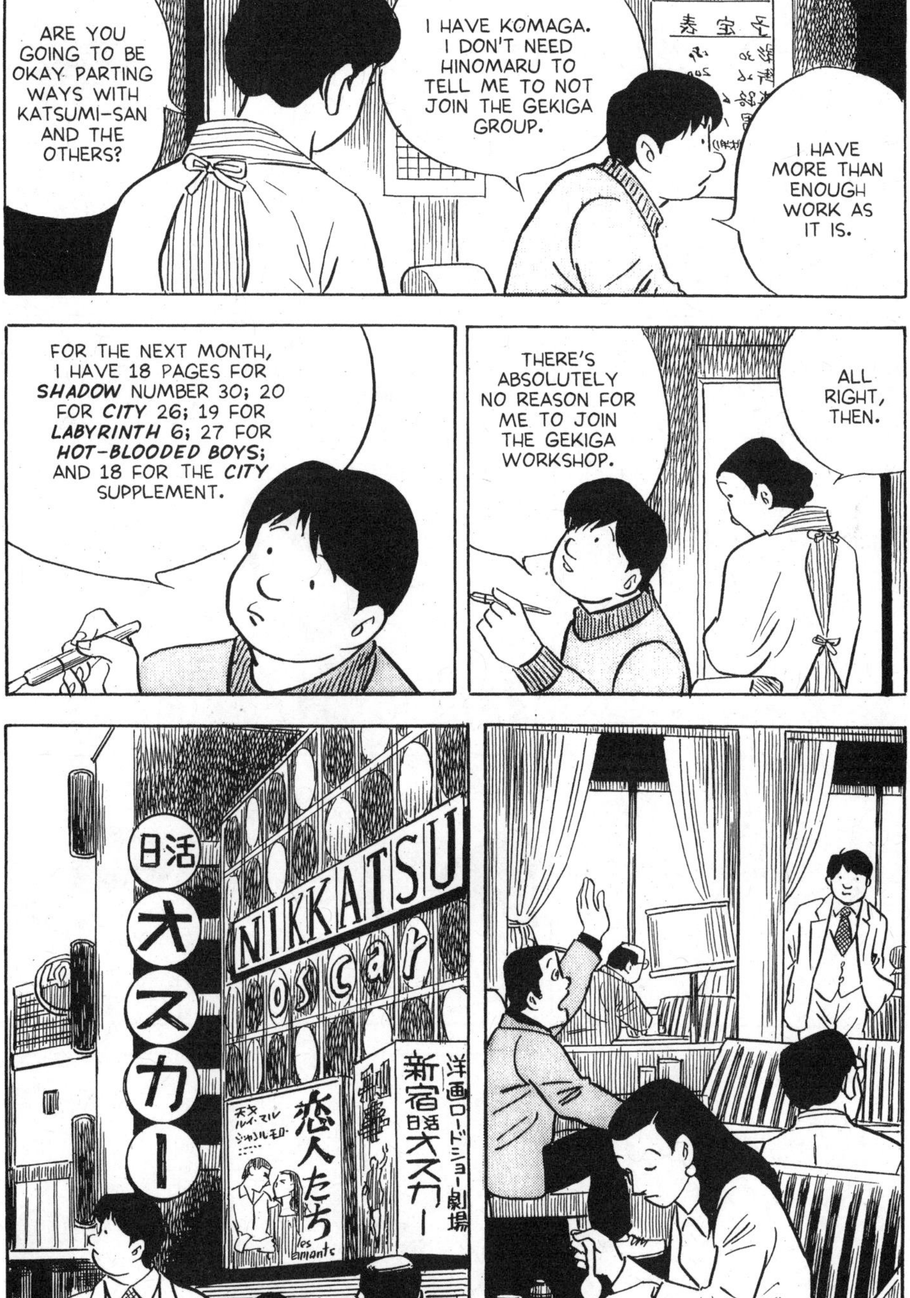

ARE YOU GOING TO BE OKAY PARTING WAYS WITH KATSUMI-SAN AND THE OTHERS?
I HAVE KOMAGA. I DON'T NEED HINOMARU TO TELL ME TO NOT JOIN THE GEKIGA GROUP.
I HAVE MORE THAN ENOUGH WORK AS IT IS.
FOR THE NEXT MONTH, I HAVE 18 PAGES FOR SHADOW NUMBER 30; 20 FOR CITY 26; 19 FOR LABYRINTH 6; 27 FOR HOT-BLOODED BOYS; AND 18 FOR THE CITY SUPPLEMENT.
THERE'S ABSOLUTELY NO REASON FOR ME TO JOIN THE GEKIGA WORKSHOP.
ALL RIGHT, THEN.
日活
オスカー
NIKKATSU
oscar
恋人たち
les amants
洋画ロードショー劇場
新宿日活オスカー

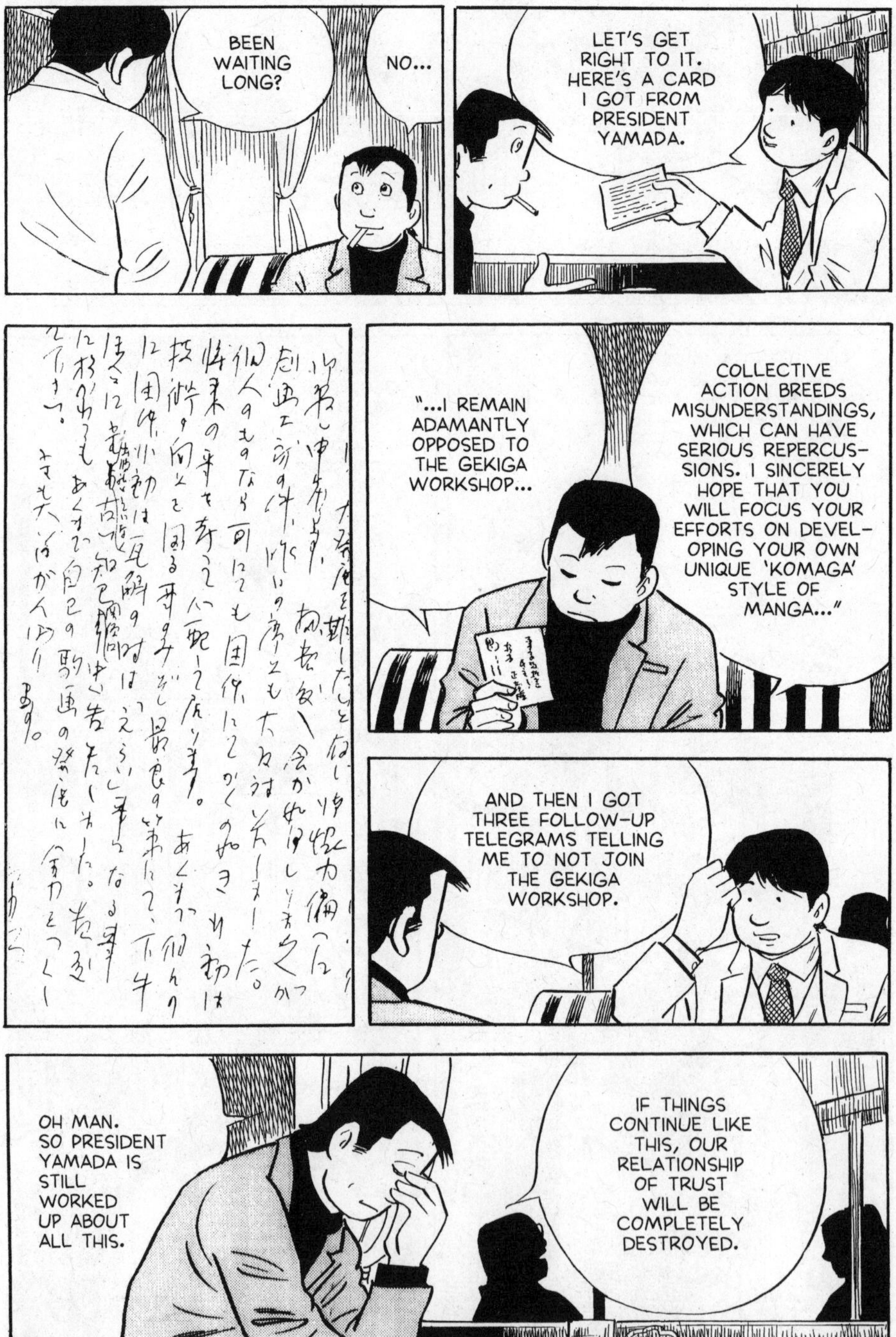
BEEN WAITING LONG?
NO...
LET'S GET RIGHT TO IT. HERE'S A CARD I GOT FROM PRESIDENT YAMADA.
"...I REMAIN ADAMANTLY OPPOSED TO THE GEKIGA WORKSHOP...
COLLECTIVE ACTION BREEDS MISUNDERSTANDINGS, WHICH CAN HAVE SERIOUS REPERCUSSIONS. I SINCERELY HOPE THAT YOU WILL FOCUS YOUR EFFORTS ON DEVELOPING YOUR OWN UNIQUE 'KOMAGA' STYLE OF MANGA..."
AND THEN I GOT THREE FOLLOW-UP TELEGRAMS TELLING ME TO NOT JOIN THE GEKIGA WORKSHOP.
OH MAN. SO PRESIDENT YAMADA IS STILL WORKED UP ABOUT ALL THIS.
IF THINGS CONTINUE LIKE THIS, OUR RELATIONSHIP OF TRUST WILL BE COMPLETELY DESTROYED.

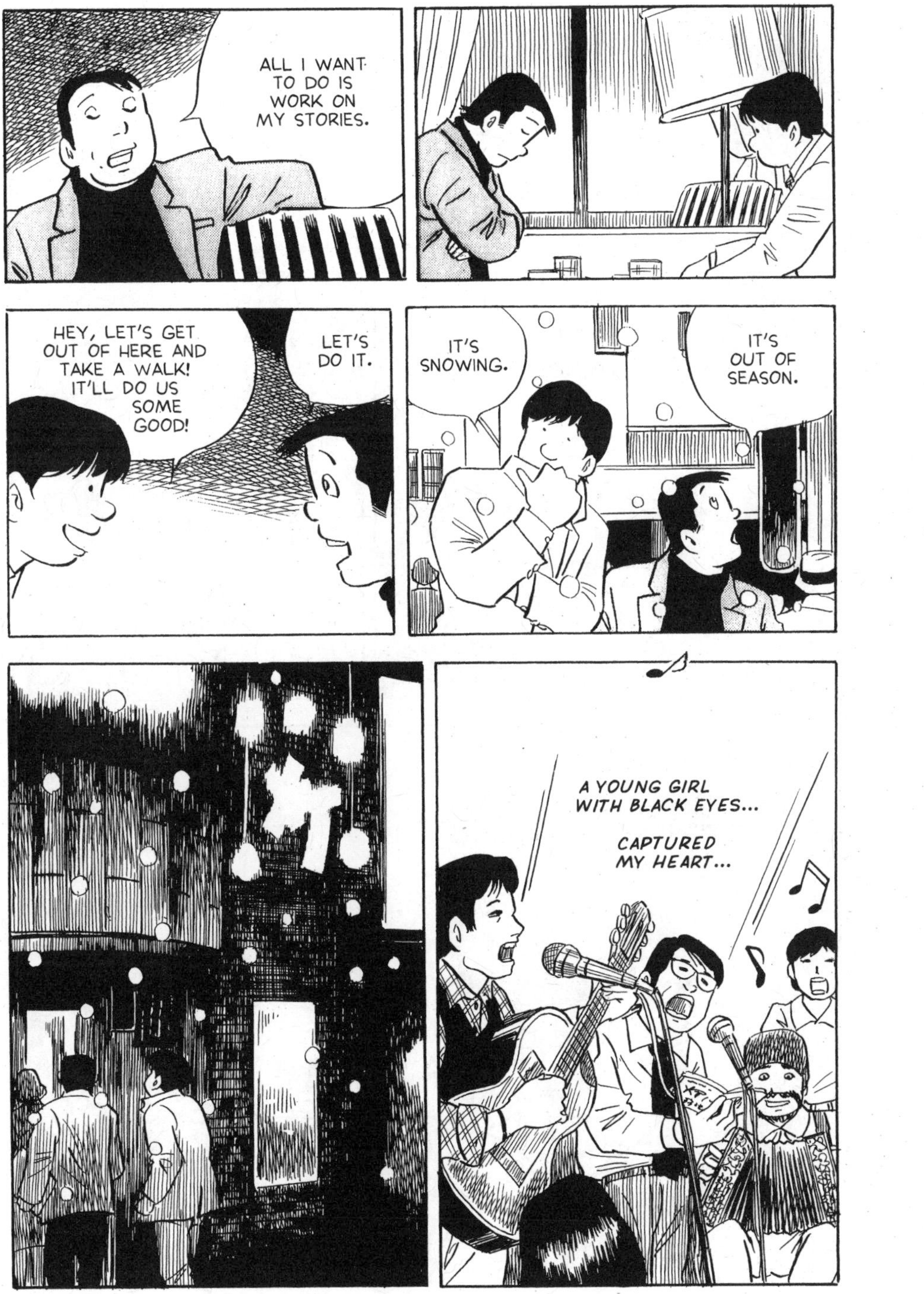
ALL I WANT TO DO IS WORK ON MY STORIES.
HEY, LET'S GET OUT OF HERE AND TAKE A WALK! IT'LL DO US SOME GOOD!
LET'S DO IT.
IT'S SNOWING.
IT'S OUT OF SEASON.
A YOUNG GIRL WITH BLACK EYES...
CAPTURED MY HEART...

うたごえ喫茶
灯（ともしび）
歌唱集⑧
"SINGING CAFES" WERE POPULAR AMONG YOUNG PEOPLE AT THE TIME.
THERE WOULD BE AN M.C., AND THE CUSTOMERS WOULD SING RUSSIAN FOLK SONGS ACCOMPANIED BY A LIVE BAND. IT WAS THE "KARAOKE" OF THE PERIOD.
SOME OF THE WAITRESSES WERE RUSSIAN. THESE VENUES WERE ALWAYS BUSTLING.
FOR KATSUMI AND MASAHIKO, A SIMPLE CHILDHOOD HOBBY HAD EVOLVED INTO A WEB OF COMPLEX INTERPERSONAL RELATIONS AND POLITICS.
THE MELAN-CHOLIC SONGS ASSUAGED THE BITTERSWEET PAIN, AND THE TWO MEN SANG AS STRONGLY AS THEY COULD.
UTA GOE
うたごえ喫茶
灯（ともしび）
UTA GOE

THE VAMPIRE KILLER BECOMES A VAMPIRE

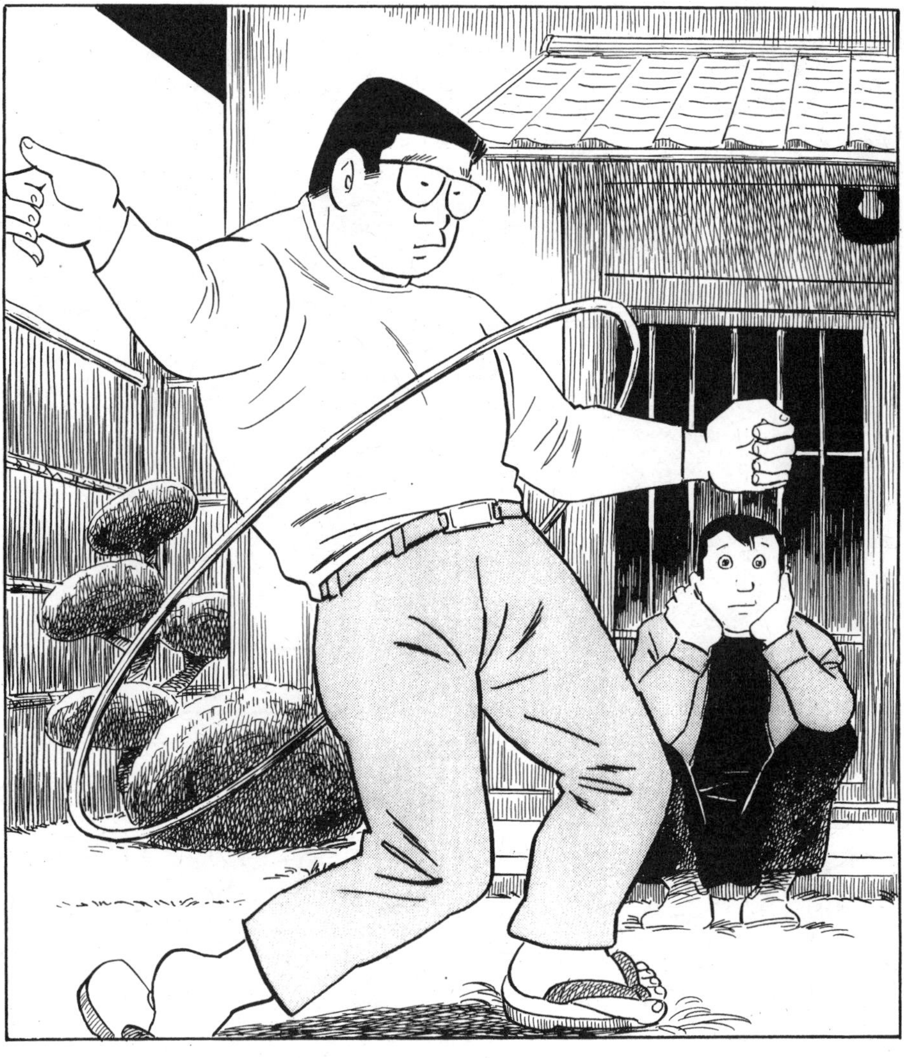

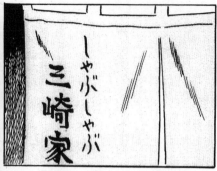

HALF OF THE BEEF THEY SERVE HERE IS FROM KOBE, AND THE OTHER HALF IS FROM MATSUZAKA. THEY SPECIFY WHAT THE CATTLE EATS SO THAT THEY GET PERFECTLY MARBLED CUTS OF BEEF.

LET'S EAT!

THANKS TO YOU ALL, *SKYSCRAPER* IS A BIG SUCCESS.

THE GEKIGA WORKSHOP IS TOGETSU SHOTEN'S SAVIOR.

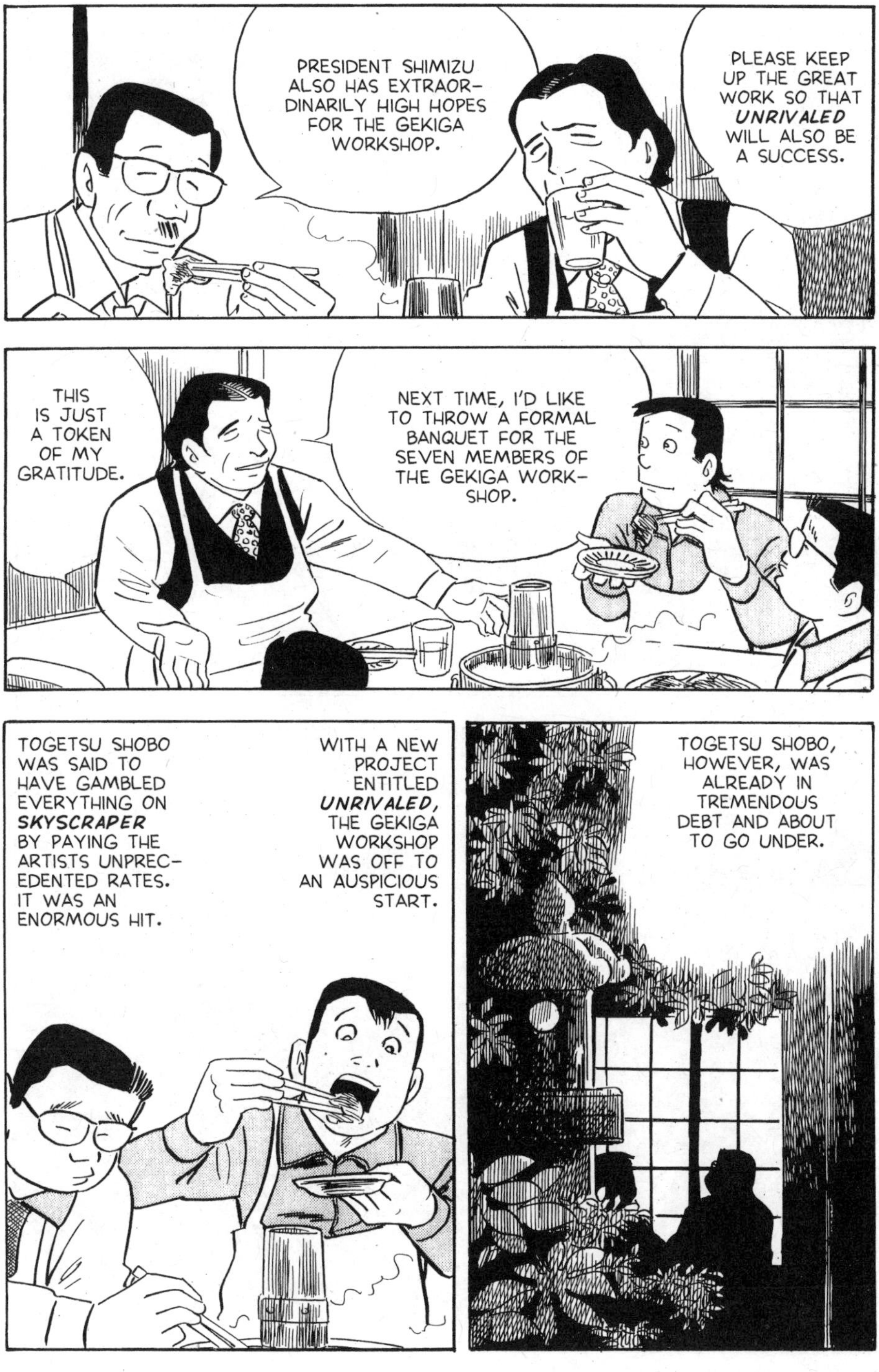
PRESIDENT SHIMIZU ALSO HAS EXTRAOR-DINARILY HIGH HOPES FOR THE GEKIGA WORKSHOP.
PLEASE KEEP UP THE GREAT WORK SO THAT *UNRIVALED* WILL ALSO BE A SUCCESS.
THIS IS JUST A TOKEN OF MY GRATITUDE.
NEXT TIME, I'D LIKE TO THROW A FORMAL BANQUET FOR THE SEVEN MEMBERS OF THE GEKIGA WORK-SHOP.
TOGETSU SHOBO WAS SAID TO HAVE GAMBLED EVERYTHING ON *SKYSCRAPER* BY PAYING THE ARTISTS UNPREC-EDENTED RATES. IT WAS AN ENORMOUS HIT.
WITH A NEW PROJECT ENTITLED *UNRIVALED*, THE GEKIGA WORKSHOP WAS OFF TO AN AUSPICIOUS START.
TOGETSU SHOBO, HOWEVER, WAS ALREADY IN TREMENDOUS DEBT AND ABOUT TO GO UNDER.

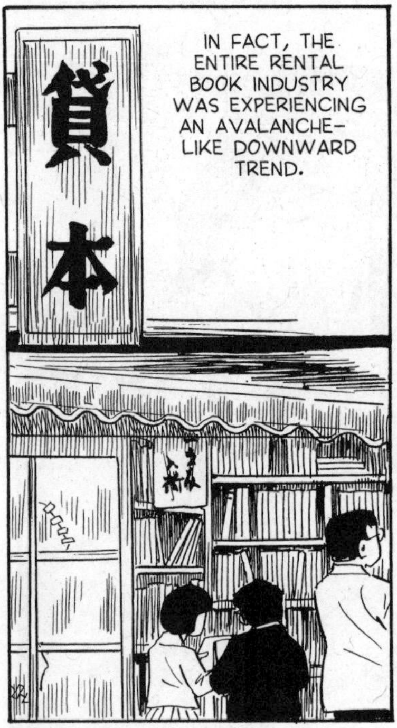
IN FACT, THE ENTIRE RENTAL BOOK INDUSTRY WAS EXPERIENCING AN AVALANCHE-LIKE DOWNWARD TREND.
貸本

SIGN: BOOK RENTAL

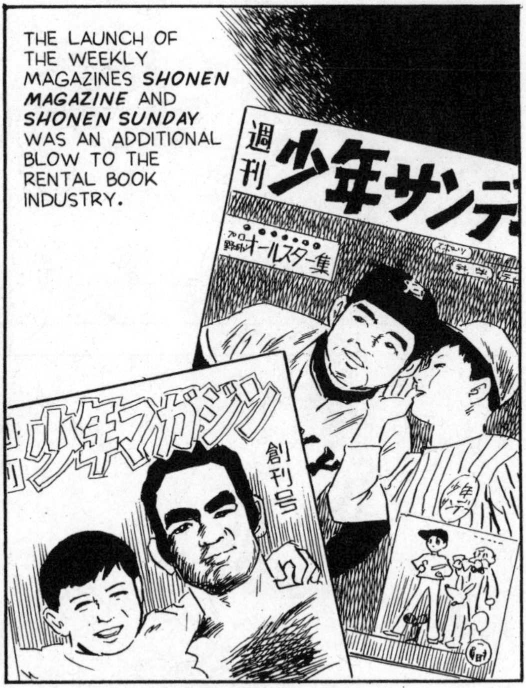
THE LAUNCH OF THE WEEKLY MAGAZINES ***SHONEN MAGAZINE*** AND ***SHONEN SUNDAY*** WAS AN ADDITIONAL BLOW TO THE RENTAL BOOK INDUSTRY.
週刊
少年マガジン
創刊号

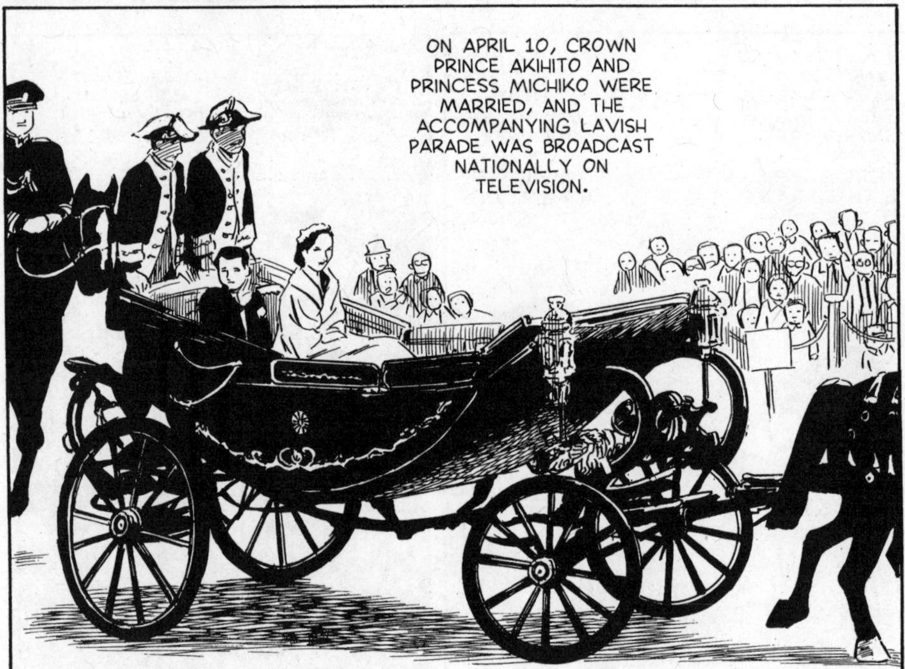
ON APRIL 10, CROWN PRINCE AKIHITO AND PRINCESS MICHIKO WERE MARRIED, AND THE ACCOMPANYING LAVISH PARADE WAS BROADCAST NATIONALLY ON TELEVISION.

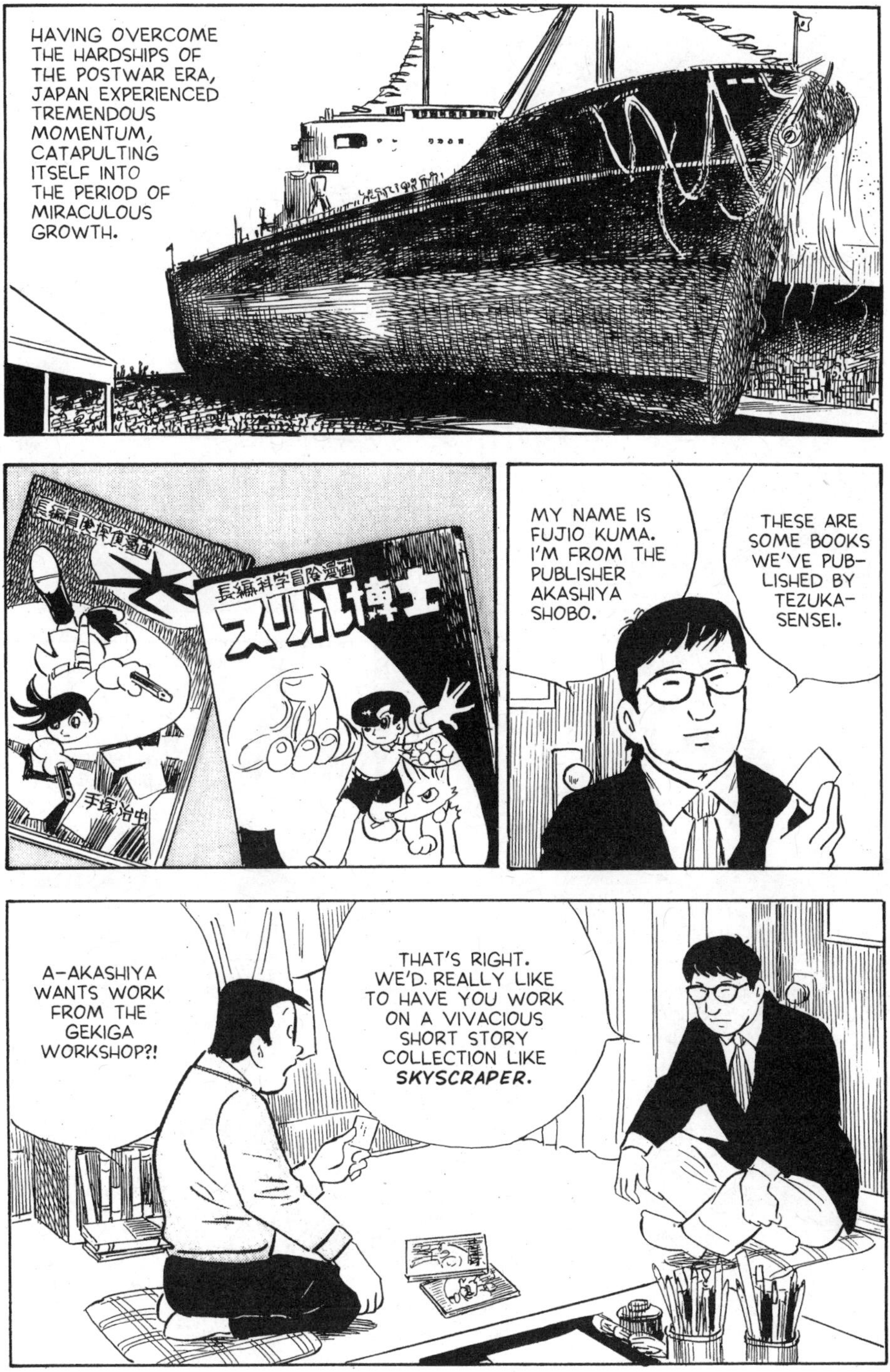
HAVING OVERCOME THE HARDSHIPS OF THE POSTWAR ERA, JAPAN EXPERIENCED TREMENDOUS MOMENTUM, CATAPULTING ITSELF INTO THE PERIOD OF MIRACULOUS GROWTH.
長編科学冒険漫画
スリル博士
MY NAME IS FUJIO KUMA. I'M FROM THE PUBLISHER AKASHIYA SHOBO.
THESE ARE SOME BOOKS WE'VE PUB-LISHED BY TEZUKA-SENSEI.
A-AKASHIYA WANTS WORK FROM THE GEKIGA WORKSHOP?!
THAT'S RIGHT. WE'D REALLY LIKE TO HAVE YOU WORK ON A VIVACIOUS SHORT STORY COLLECTION LIKE **SKYSCRAPER**.

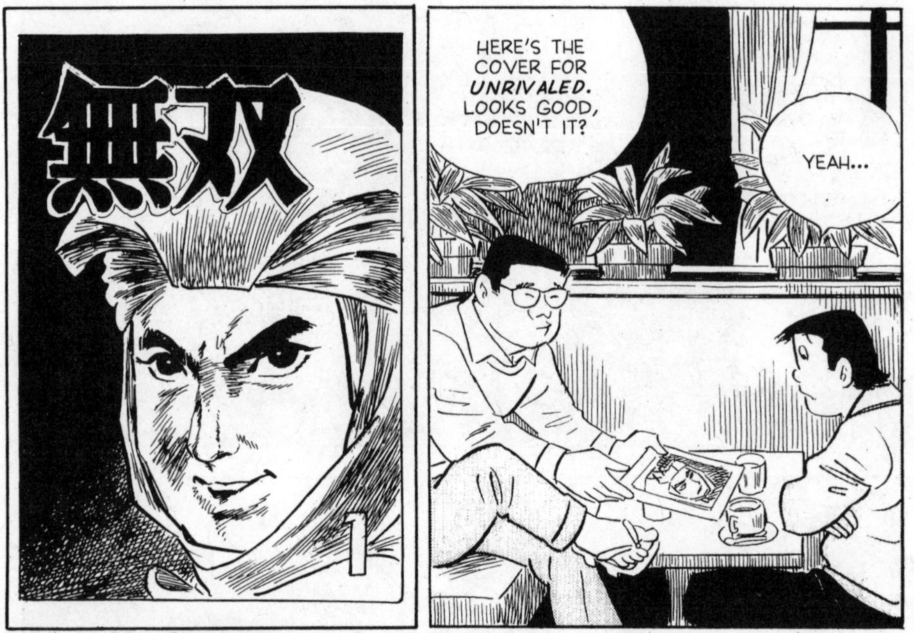
無双
1
HERE'S THE COVER FOR *UNRIVALED.* LOOKS GOOD, DOESN'T IT?
YEAH...
TITLE: *UNRIVALED*

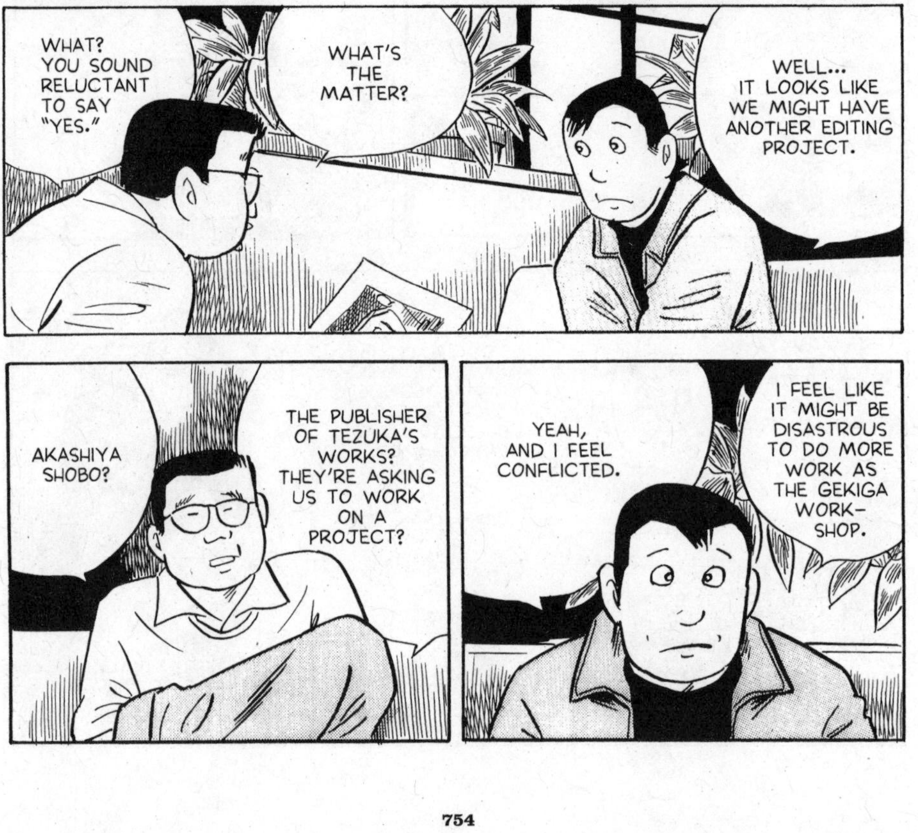
WHAT? YOU SOUND RELUCTANT TO SAY "YES."
WHAT'S THE MATTER?
WELL... IT LOOKS LIKE WE MIGHT HAVE ANOTHER EDITING PROJECT.
AKASHIYA SHOBO?
THE PUBLISHER OF TEZUKA'S WORKS? THEY'RE ASKING US TO WORK ON A PROJECT?
YEAH, AND I FEEL CONFLICTED.
I FEEL LIKE IT MIGHT BE DISASTROUS TO DO MORE WORK AS THE GEKIGA WORK-SHOP.

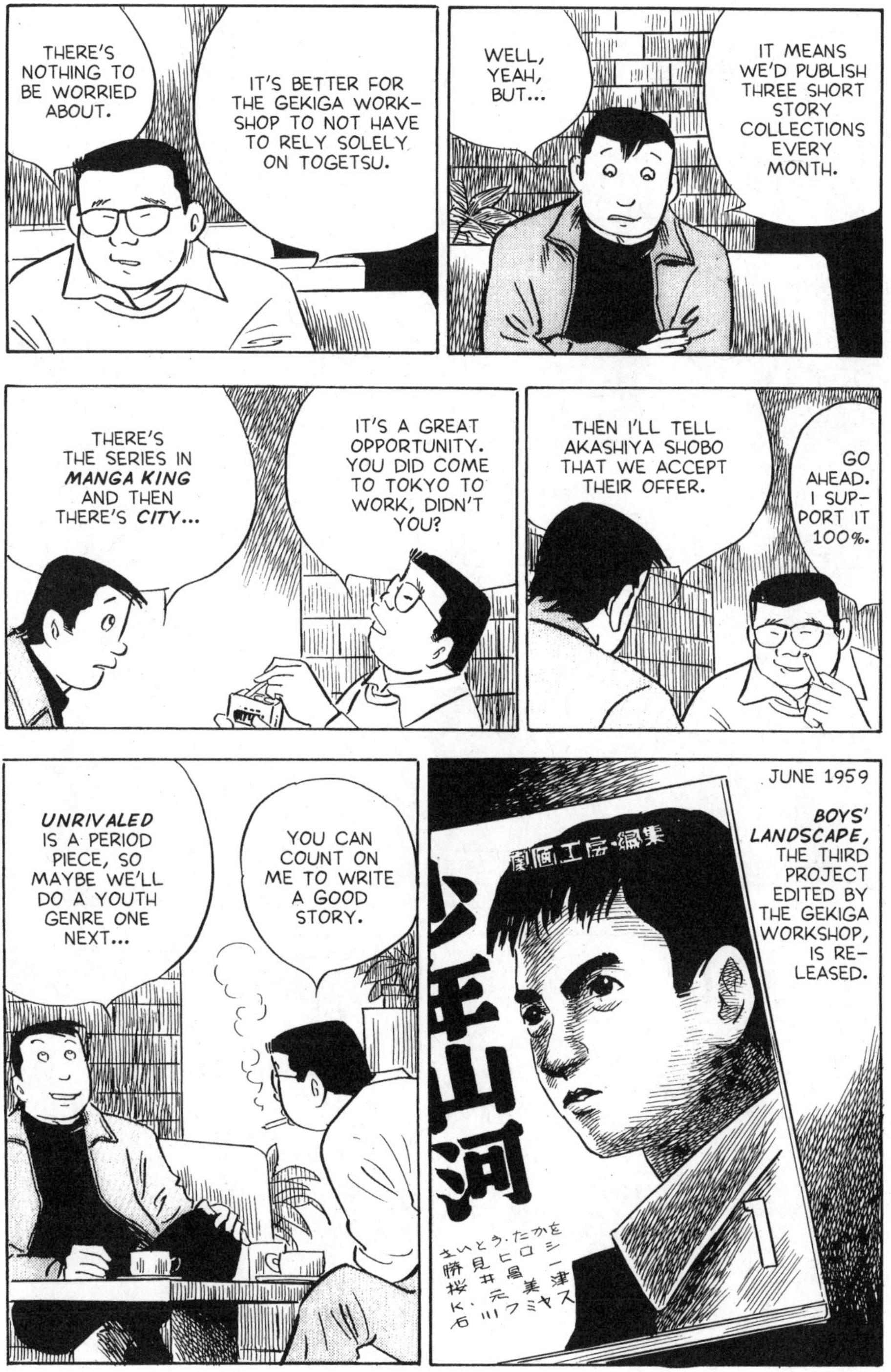

THERE'S NOTHING TO BE WORRIED ABOUT.
IT'S BETTER FOR THE GEKIGA WORK-SHOP TO NOT HAVE TO RELY SOLELY ON TOGETSU.
WELL, YEAH, BUT...
IT MEANS WE'D PUBLISH THREE SHORT STORY COLLECTIONS EVERY MONTH.
THERE'S THE SERIES IN *MANGA KING* AND THEN THERE'S *CITY*...
IT'S A GREAT OPPORTUNITY. YOU DID COME TO TOKYO TO WORK, DIDN'T YOU?
THEN I'LL TELL AKASHIYA SHOBO THAT WE ACCEPT THEIR OFFER.
GO AHEAD. I SUP-PORT IT 100%.
UNRIVALED IS A PERIOD PIECE, SO MAYBE WE'LL DO A YOUTH GENRE ONE NEXT...
YOU CAN COUNT ON ME TO WRITE A GOOD STORY.
JUNE 1959
BOYS' LANDSCAPE, THE THIRD PROJECT EDITED BY THE GEKIGA WORKSHOP, IS RE-LEASED.
劇画工房・編集
さいとう・たかを
勝見ヒロシ
桜井昌一
K・元美津
石川フミヤス

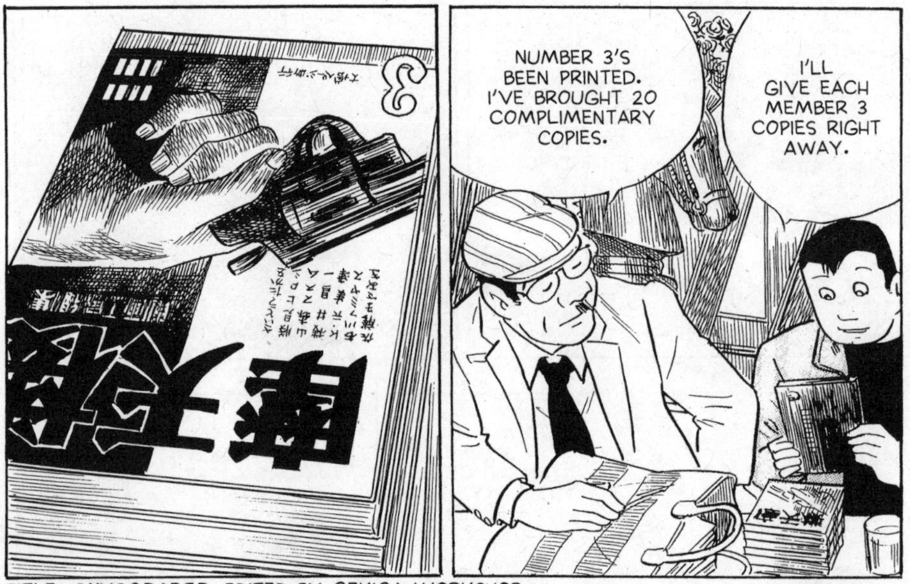
NUMBER 3'S BEEN PRINTED. I'VE BROUGHT 20 COMPLIMENTARY COPIES.
I'LL GIVE EACH MEMBER 3 COPIES RIGHT AWAY.

TITLE: ***SKYSCRAPER,*** EDITED BY GEKIGA WORKSHOP

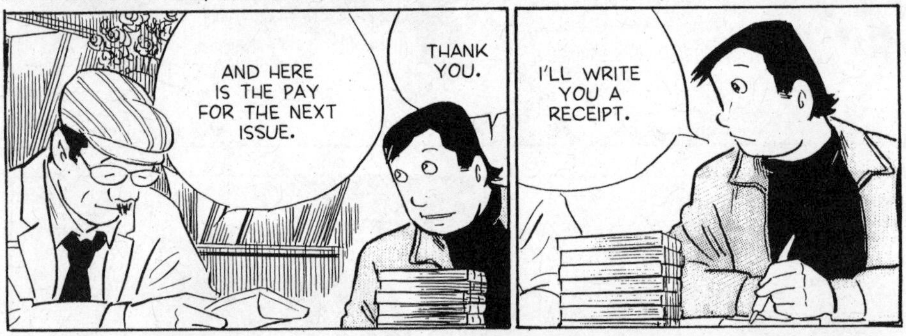
AND HERE IS THE PAY FOR THE NEXT ISSUE.
THANK YOU.
I'LL WRITE YOU A RECEIPT.

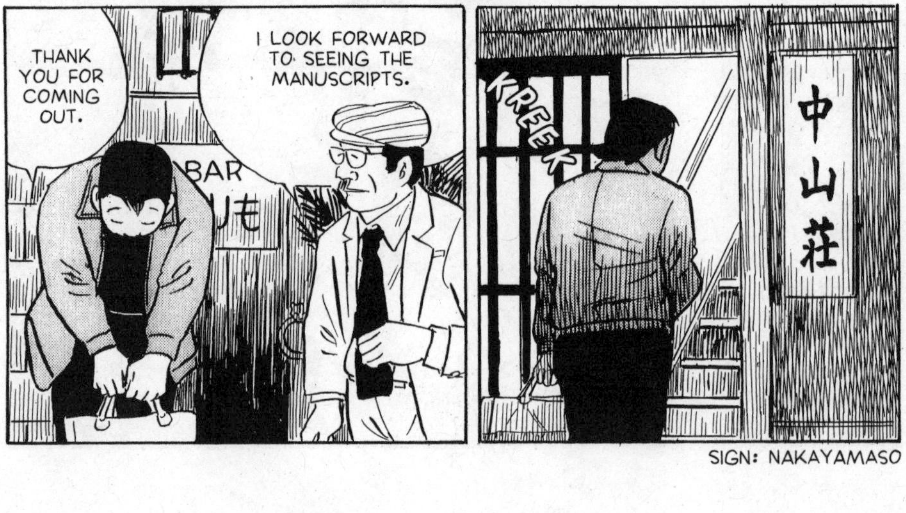
THANK YOU FOR COMING OUT.
I LOOK FORWARD TO SEEING THE MANUSCRIPTS.
BAR
KREEK
中山荘

SIGN: NAKAYAMASO

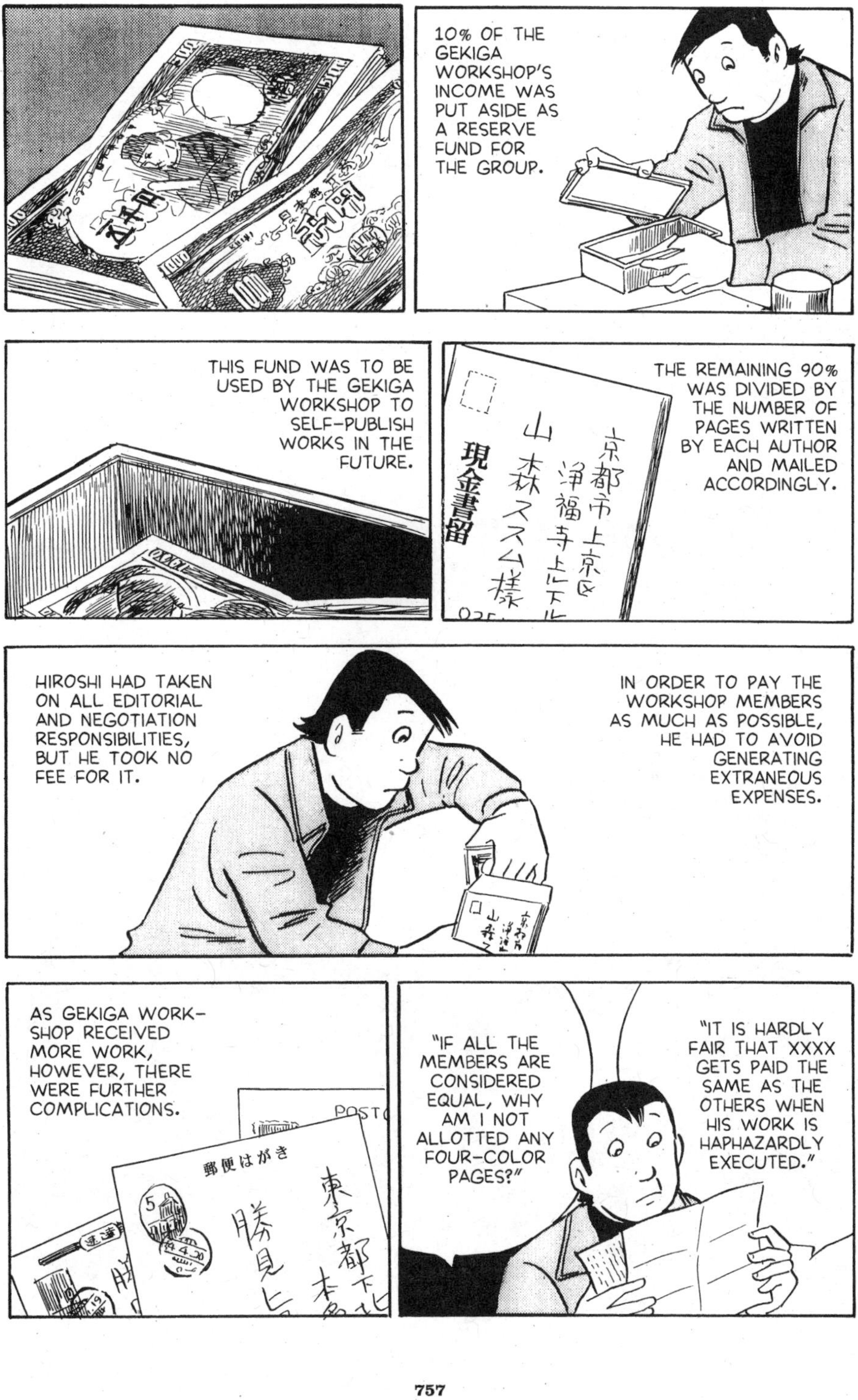
10% OF THE GEKIGA WORKSHOP'S INCOME WAS PUT ASIDE AS A RESERVE FUND FOR THE GROUP.
THIS FUND WAS TO BE USED BY THE GEKIGA WORKSHOP TO SELF-PUBLISH WORKS IN THE FUTURE.
現金書留
山森ススム様
THE REMAINING 90% WAS DIVIDED BY THE NUMBER OF PAGES WRITTEN BY EACH AUTHOR AND MAILED ACCORDINGLY.
HIROSHI HAD TAKEN ON ALL EDITORIAL AND NEGOTIATION RESPONSIBILITIES, BUT HE TOOK NO FEE FOR IT.
IN ORDER TO PAY THE WORKSHOP MEMBERS AS MUCH AS POSSIBLE, HE HAD TO AVOID GENERATING EXTRANEOUS EXPENSES.
AS GEKIGA WORK-SHOP RECEIVED MORE WORK, HOWEVER, THERE WERE FURTHER COMPLICATIONS.
郵便はがき
"IF ALL THE MEMBERS ARE CONSIDERED EQUAL, WHY AM I NOT ALLOTTED ANY FOUR-COLOR PAGES?"
"IT IS HARDLY FAIR THAT XXXX GETS PAID THE SAME AS THE OTHERS WHEN HIS WORK IS HAPHAZARDLY EXECUTED."

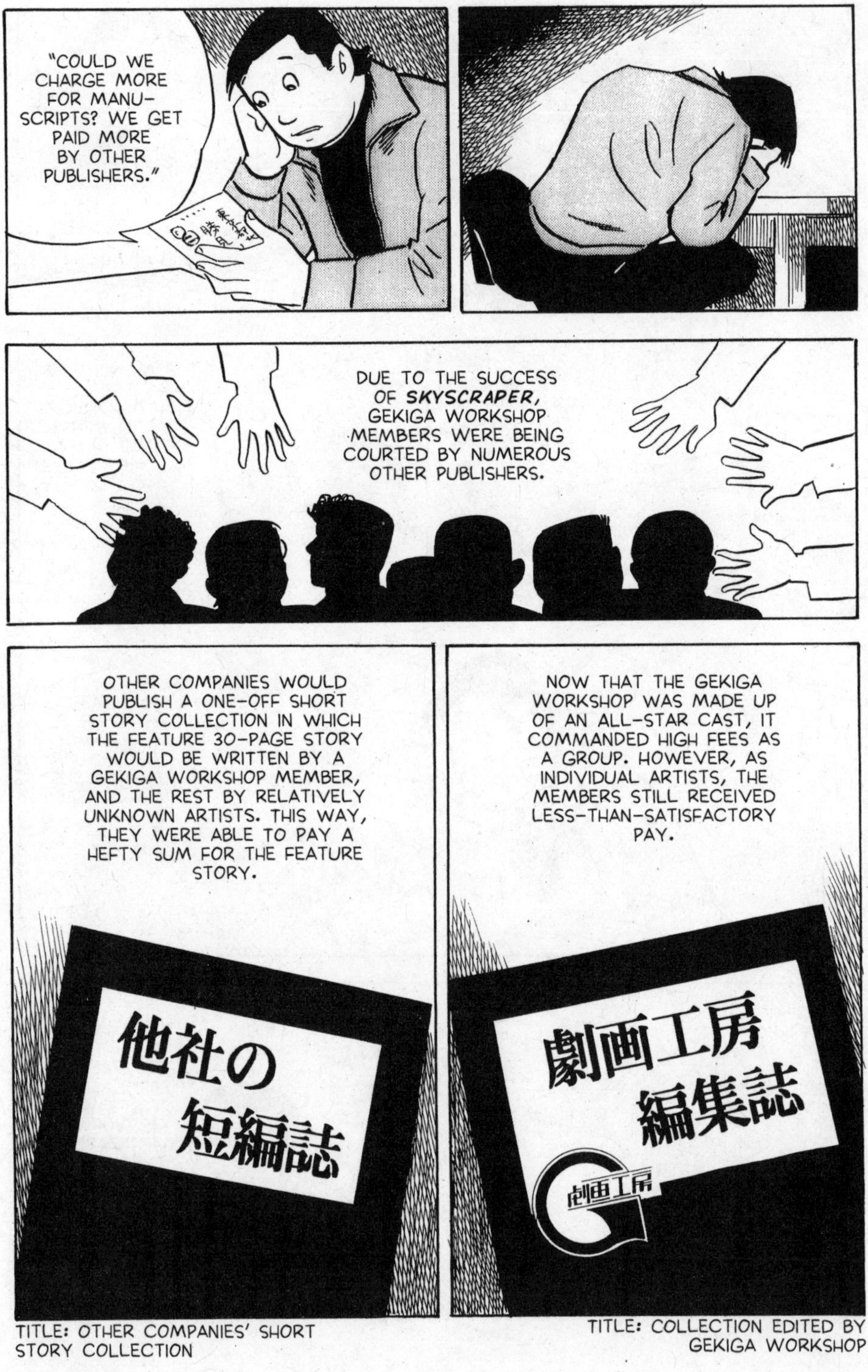
"COULD WE CHARGE MORE FOR MANU-SCRIPTS? WE GET PAID MORE BY OTHER PUBLISHERS."
DUE TO THE SUCCESS OF **SKYSCRAPER**, GEKIGA WORKSHOP MEMBERS WERE BEING COURTED BY NUMEROUS OTHER PUBLISHERS.
OTHER COMPANIES WOULD PUBLISH A ONE-OFF SHORT STORY COLLECTION IN WHICH THE FEATURE 30-PAGE STORY WOULD BE WRITTEN BY A GEKIGA WORKSHOP MEMBER, AND THE REST BY RELATIVELY UNKNOWN ARTISTS. THIS WAY, THEY WERE ABLE TO PAY A HEFTY SUM FOR THE FEATURE STORY.
他社の短編誌
NOW THAT THE GEKIGA WORKSHOP WAS MADE UP OF AN ALL-STAR CAST, IT COMMANDED HIGH FEES AS A GROUP. HOWEVER, AS INDIVIDUAL ARTISTS, THE MEMBERS STILL RECEIVED LESS-THAN-SATISFACTORY PAY.
劇画工房編集誌
劇画工房

TITLE: OTHER COMPANIES' SHORT STORY COLLECTION

TITLE: COLLECTION EDITED BY GEKIGA WORKSHOP

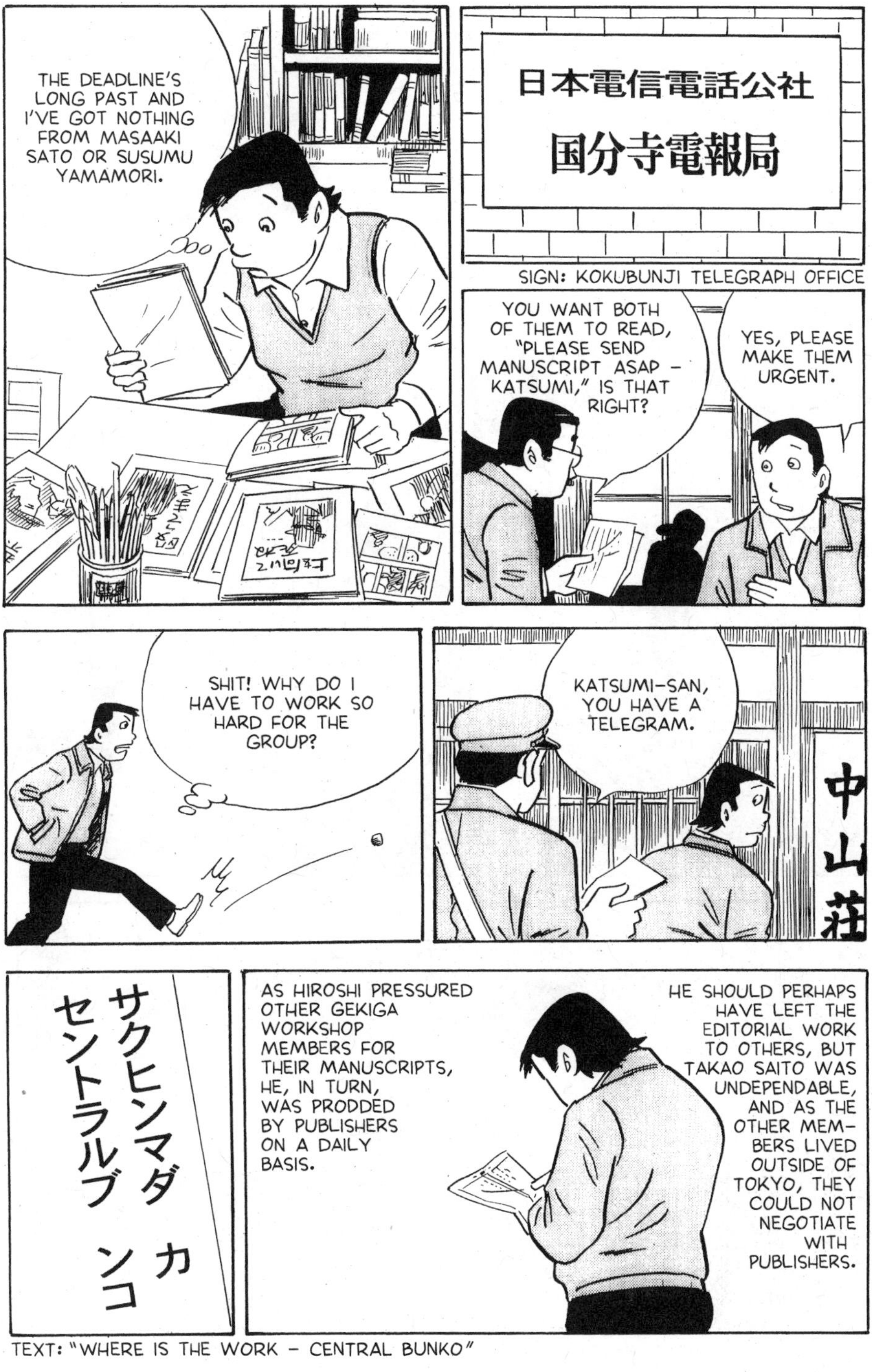
THE DEADLINE'S LONG PAST AND I'VE GOT NOTHING FROM MASAAKI SATO OR SUSUMU YAMAMORI.
日本電信電話公社
国分寺電報局
SIGN: KOKUBUNJI TELEGRAPH OFFICE
YOU WANT BOTH OF THEM TO READ, "PLEASE SEND MANUSCRIPT ASAP – KATSUMI," IS THAT RIGHT?
YES, PLEASE MAKE THEM URGENT.
SHIT! WHY DO I HAVE TO WORK SO HARD FOR THE GROUP?
KATSUMI-SAN, YOU HAVE A TELEGRAM.
中山荘
サクヒンマダカ
セントラルブンコ
TEXT: "WHERE IS THE WORK – CENTRAL BUNKO"
AS HIROSHI PRESSURED OTHER GEKIGA WORKSHOP MEMBERS FOR THEIR MANUSCRIPTS, HE, IN TURN, WAS PRODDED BY PUBLISHERS ON A DAILY BASIS.
HE SHOULD PERHAPS HAVE LEFT THE EDITORIAL WORK TO OTHERS, BUT TAKAO SAITO WAS UNDEPENDABLE, AND AS THE OTHER MEM-BERS LIVED OUTSIDE OF TOKYO, THEY COULD NOT NEGOTIATE WITH PUBLISHERS.

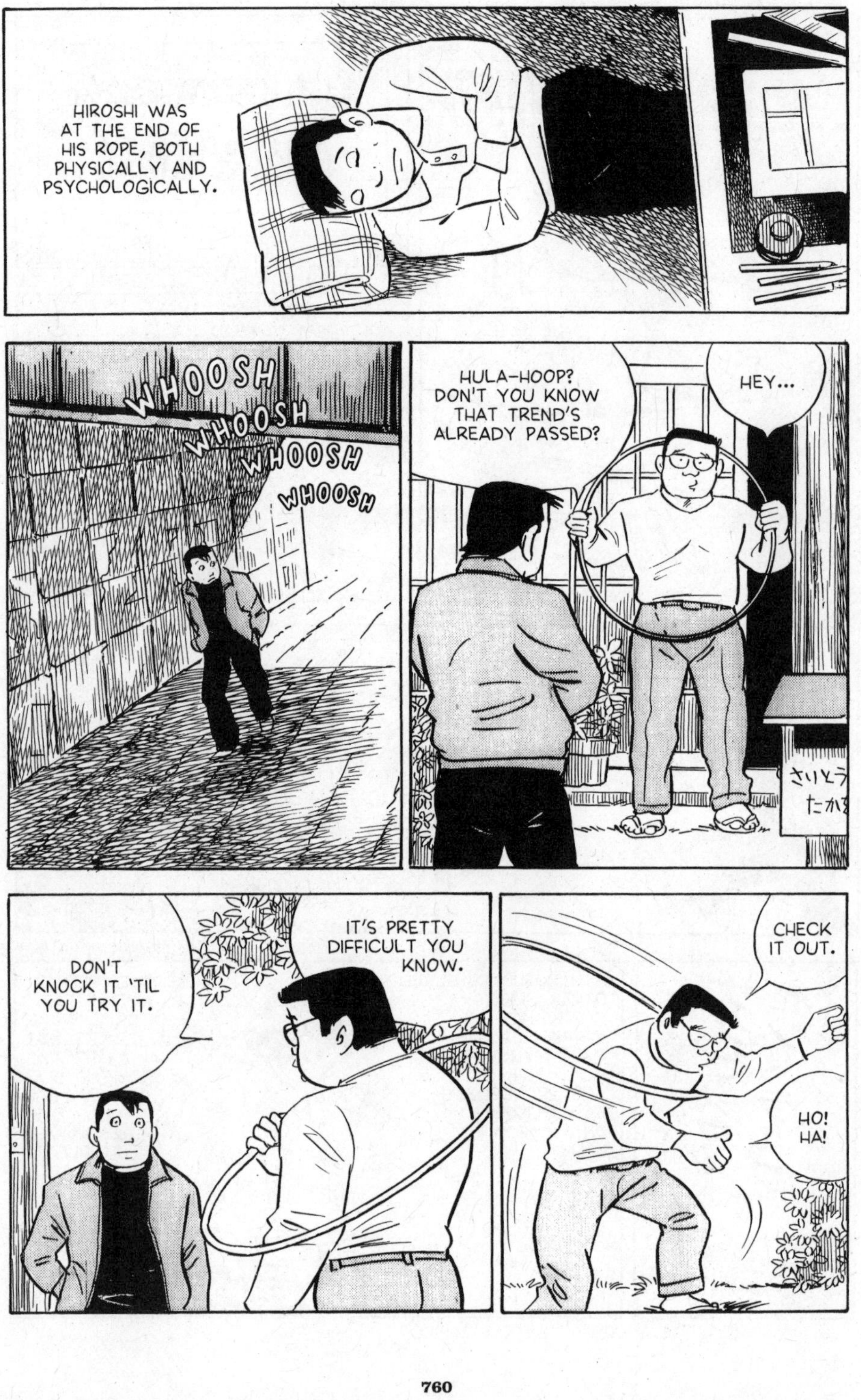
HIROSHI WAS AT THE END OF HIS ROPE, BOTH PHYSICALLY AND PSYCHOLOGICALLY.
WHOOSH
WHOOSH
WHOOSH
WHOOSH
HEY...
HULA-HOOP? DON'T YOU KNOW THAT TREND'S ALREADY PASSED?
DON'T KNOCK IT 'TIL YOU TRY IT.
IT'S PRETTY DIFFICULT YOU KNOW.
CHECK IT OUT.
HO! HA!

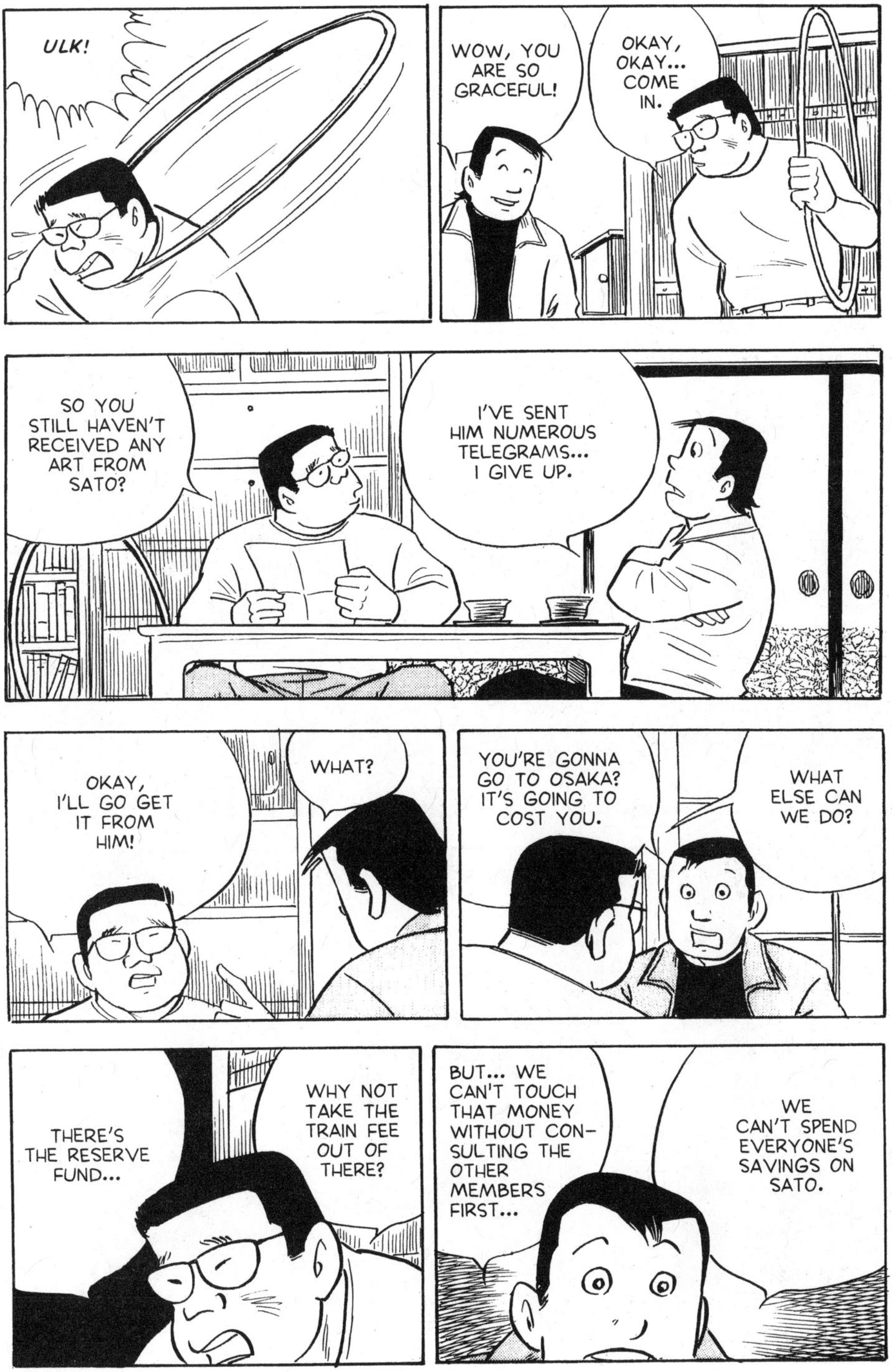
ULK!
WOW, YOU ARE SO GRACEFUL!
OKAY, OKAY... COME IN.
SO YOU STILL HAVEN'T RECEIVED ANY ART FROM SATO?
I'VE SENT HIM NUMEROUS TELEGRAMS... I GIVE UP.
OKAY, I'LL GO GET IT FROM HIM!
WHAT?
YOU'RE GONNA GO TO OSAKA? IT'S GOING TO COST YOU.
WHAT ELSE CAN WE DO?
THERE'S THE RESERVE FUND...
WHY NOT TAKE THE TRAIN FEE OUT OF THERE?
BUT... WE CAN'T TOUCH THAT MONEY WITHOUT CON-SULTING THE OTHER MEMBERS FIRST...
WE CAN'T SPEND EVERYONE'S SAVINGS ON SATO.

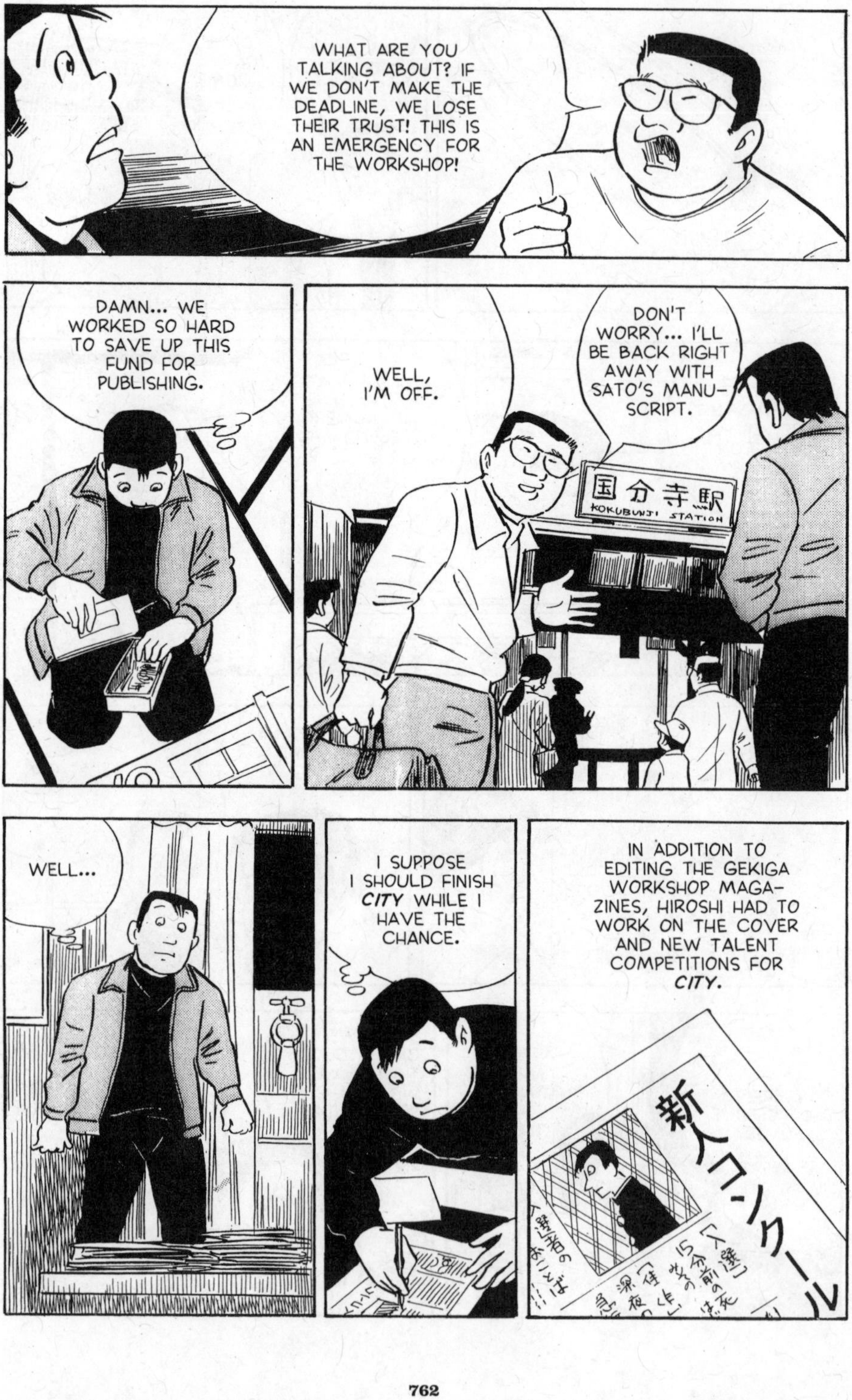
WHAT ARE YOU TALKING ABOUT? IF WE DON'T MAKE THE DEADLINE, WE LOSE THEIR TRUST! THIS IS AN EMERGENCY FOR THE WORKSHOP!
DAMN... WE WORKED SO HARD TO SAVE UP THIS FUND FOR PUBLISHING.
WELL, I'M OFF.
DON'T WORRY... I'LL BE BACK RIGHT AWAY WITH SATO'S MANU-SCRIPT.
国分寺駅
KOKUBUNJI STATION
WELL...
I SUPPOSE I SHOULD FINISH *CITY* WHILE I HAVE THE CHANCE.
IN ADDITION TO EDITING THE GEKIGA WORKSHOP MAGA-ZINES, HIROSHI HAD TO WORK ON THE COVER AND NEW TALENT COMPETITIONS FOR *CITY*.
新人コンクール

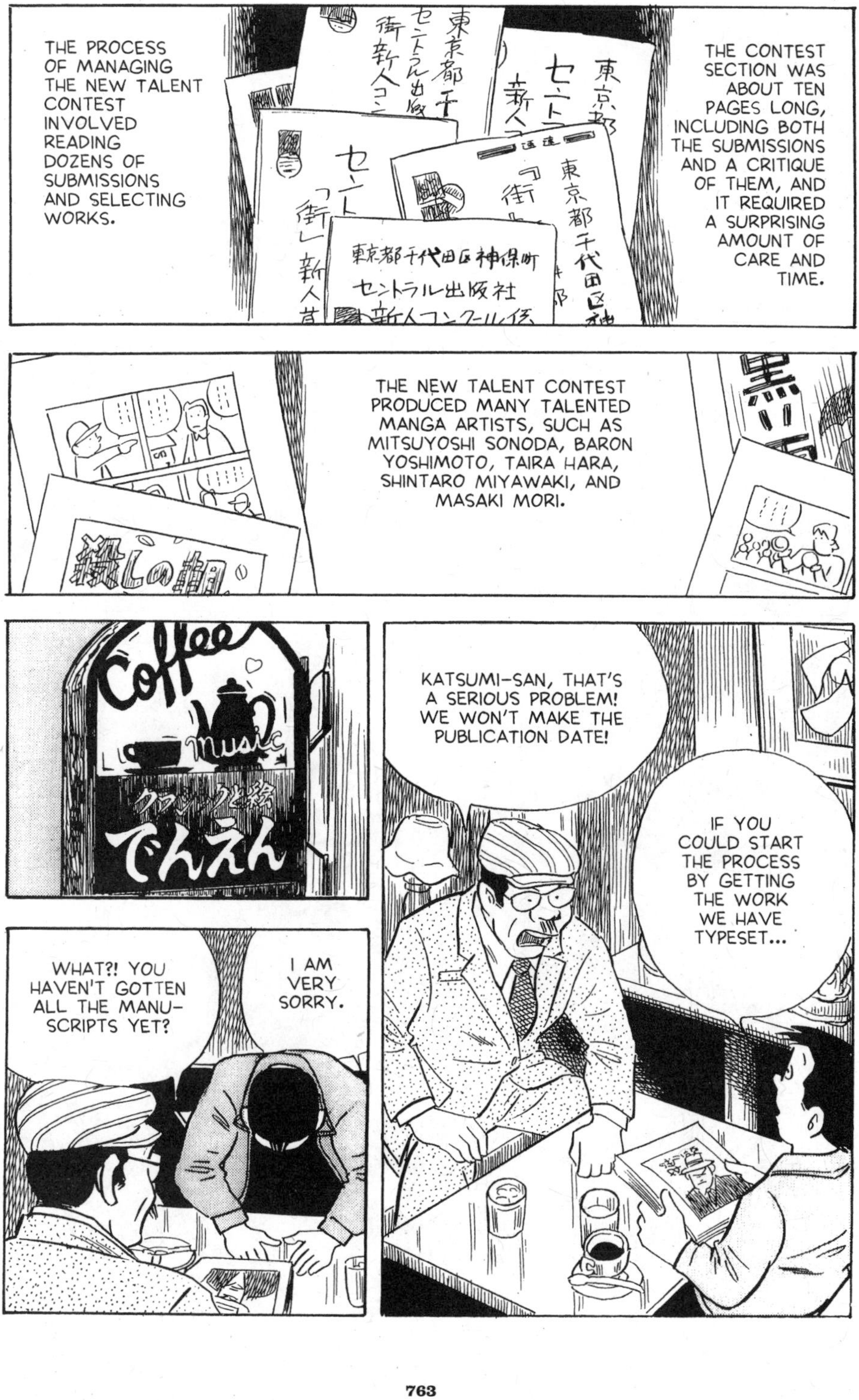
THE PROCESS OF MANAGING THE NEW TALENT CONTEST INVOLVED READING DOZENS OF SUBMISSIONS AND SELECTING WORKS.
東京都千代田区神保町
セントラル出版社
THE CONTEST SECTION WAS ABOUT TEN PAGES LONG, INCLUDING BOTH THE SUBMISSIONS AND A CRITIQUE OF THEM, AND IT REQUIRED A SURPRISING AMOUNT OF CARE AND TIME.
THE NEW TALENT CONTEST PRODUCED MANY TALENTED MANGA ARTISTS, SUCH AS MITSUYOSHI SONODA, BARON YOSHIMOTO, TAIRA HARA, SHINTARO MIYAWAKI, AND MASAKI MORI.
Coffee
music
でんえん
WHAT?! YOU HAVEN'T GOTTEN ALL THE MANU-SCRIPTS YET?
I AM VERY SORRY.
KATSUMI-SAN, THAT'S A SERIOUS PROBLEM! WE WON'T MAKE THE PUBLICATION DATE!
IF YOU COULD START THE PROCESS BY GETTING THE WORK WE HAVE TYPESET...

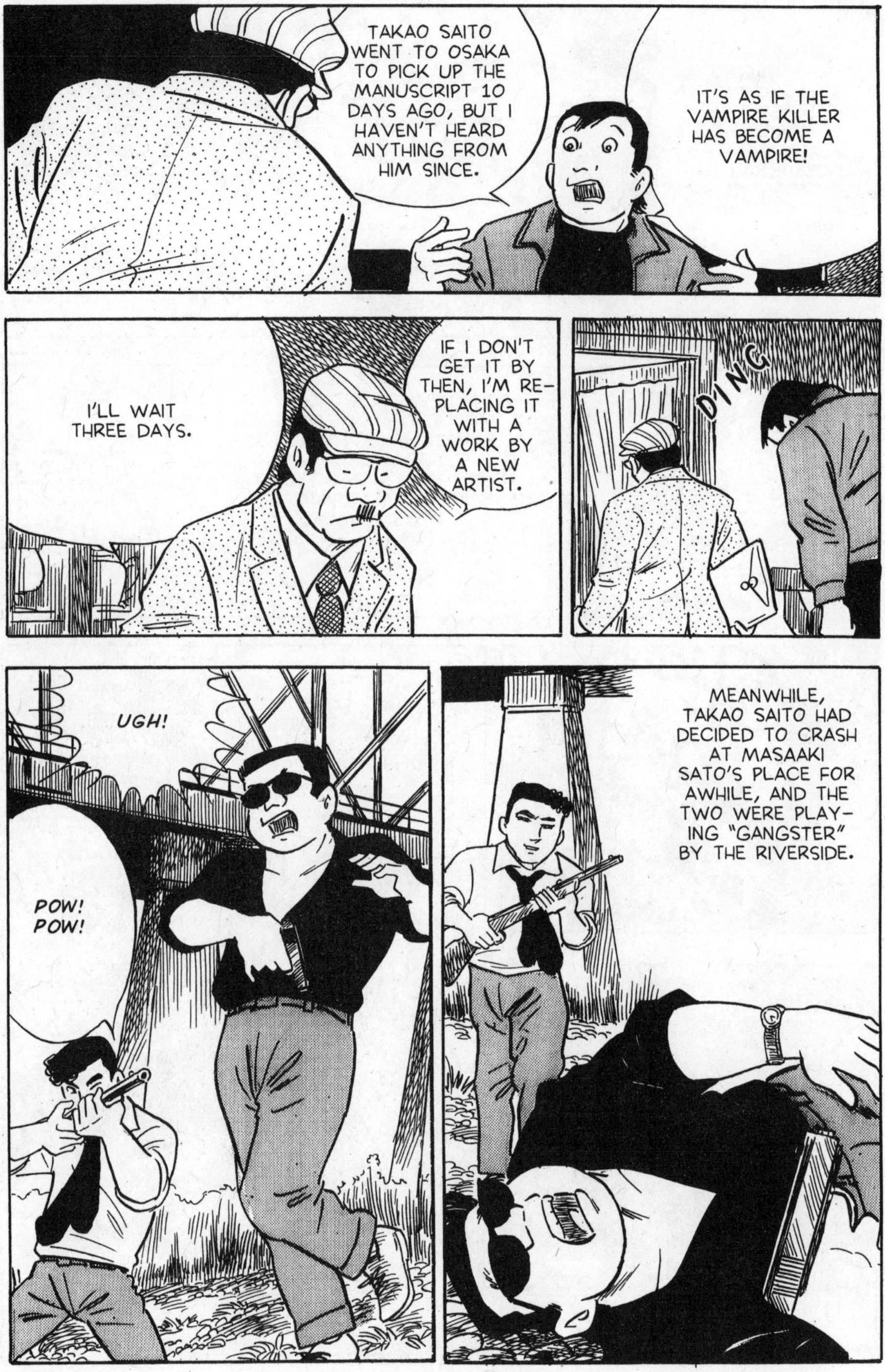
TAKAO SAITO WENT TO OSAKA TO PICK UP THE MANUSCRIPT 10 DAYS AGO, BUT I HAVEN'T HEARD ANYTHING FROM HIM SINCE.
IT'S AS IF THE VAMPIRE KILLER HAS BECOME A VAMPIRE!
I'LL WAIT THREE DAYS.
IF I DON'T GET IT BY THEN, I'M RE-PLACING IT WITH A WORK BY A NEW ARTIST.
DING
UGH!
POW! POW!
MEANWHILE, TAKAO SAITO HAD DECIDED TO CRASH AT MASAAKI SATO'S PLACE FOR AWHILE, AND THE TWO WERE PLAY-ING "GANGSTER" BY THE RIVERSIDE.

PASSION FOR GEKIGA DWINDLES

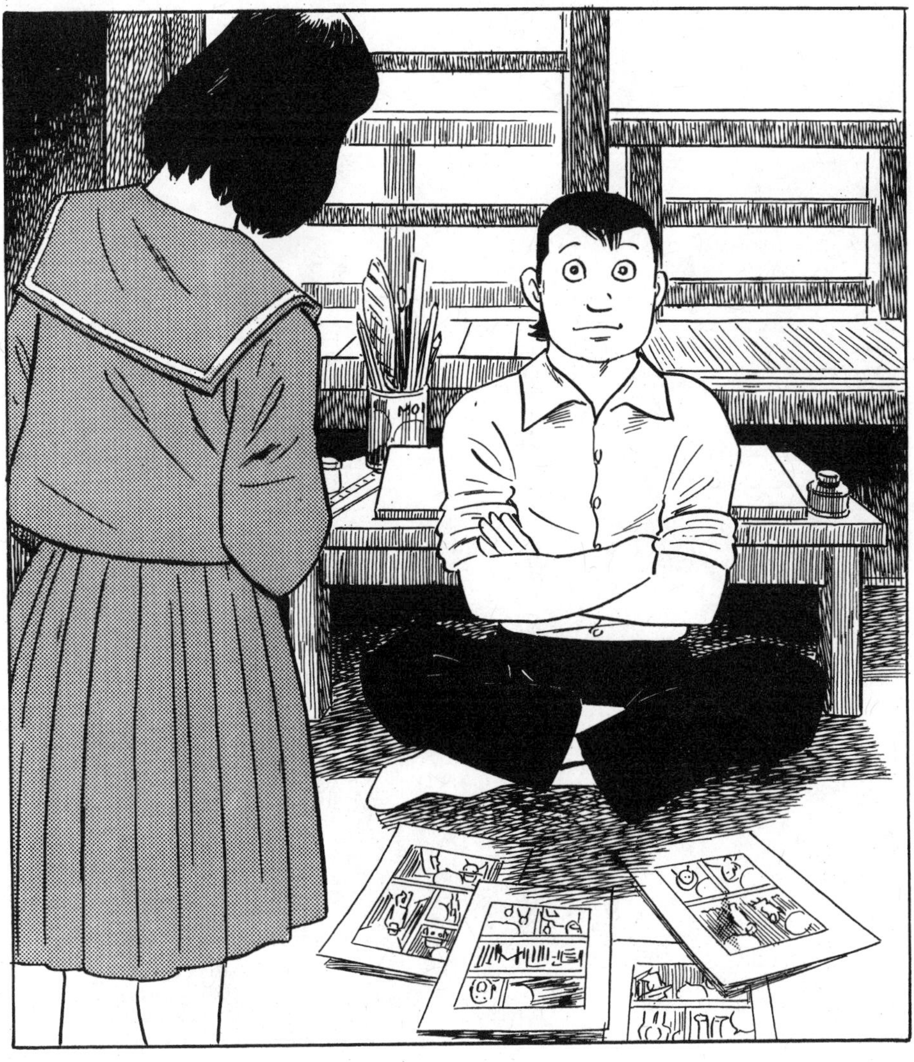

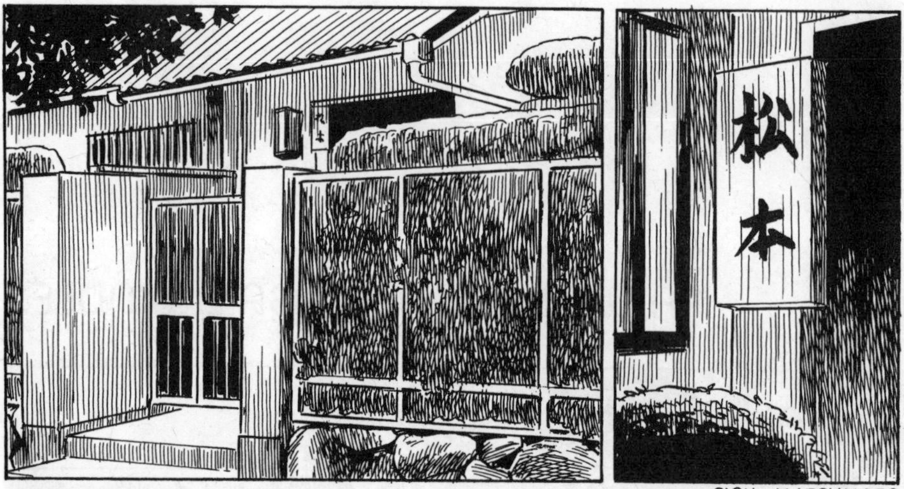
松本

SIGN: MATSUMOTO

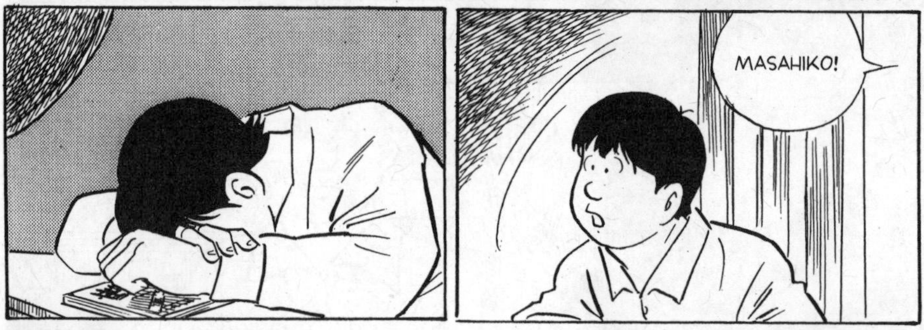
MASAHIKO!

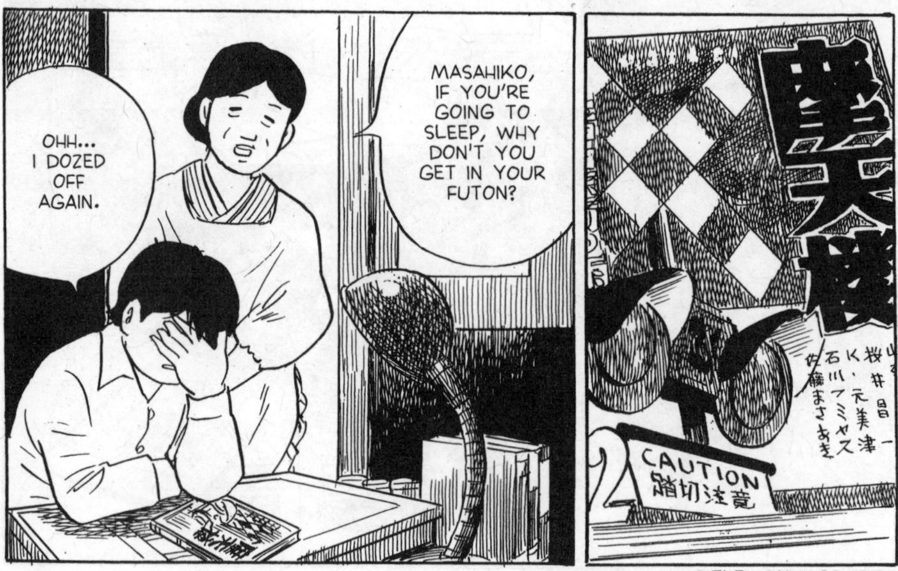
OHH... I DOZED OFF AGAIN.
MASAHIKO, IF YOU'RE GOING TO SLEEP, WHY DON'T YOU GET IN YOUR FUTON?
CAUTION

TITLE: ***SKYSCRAPER***

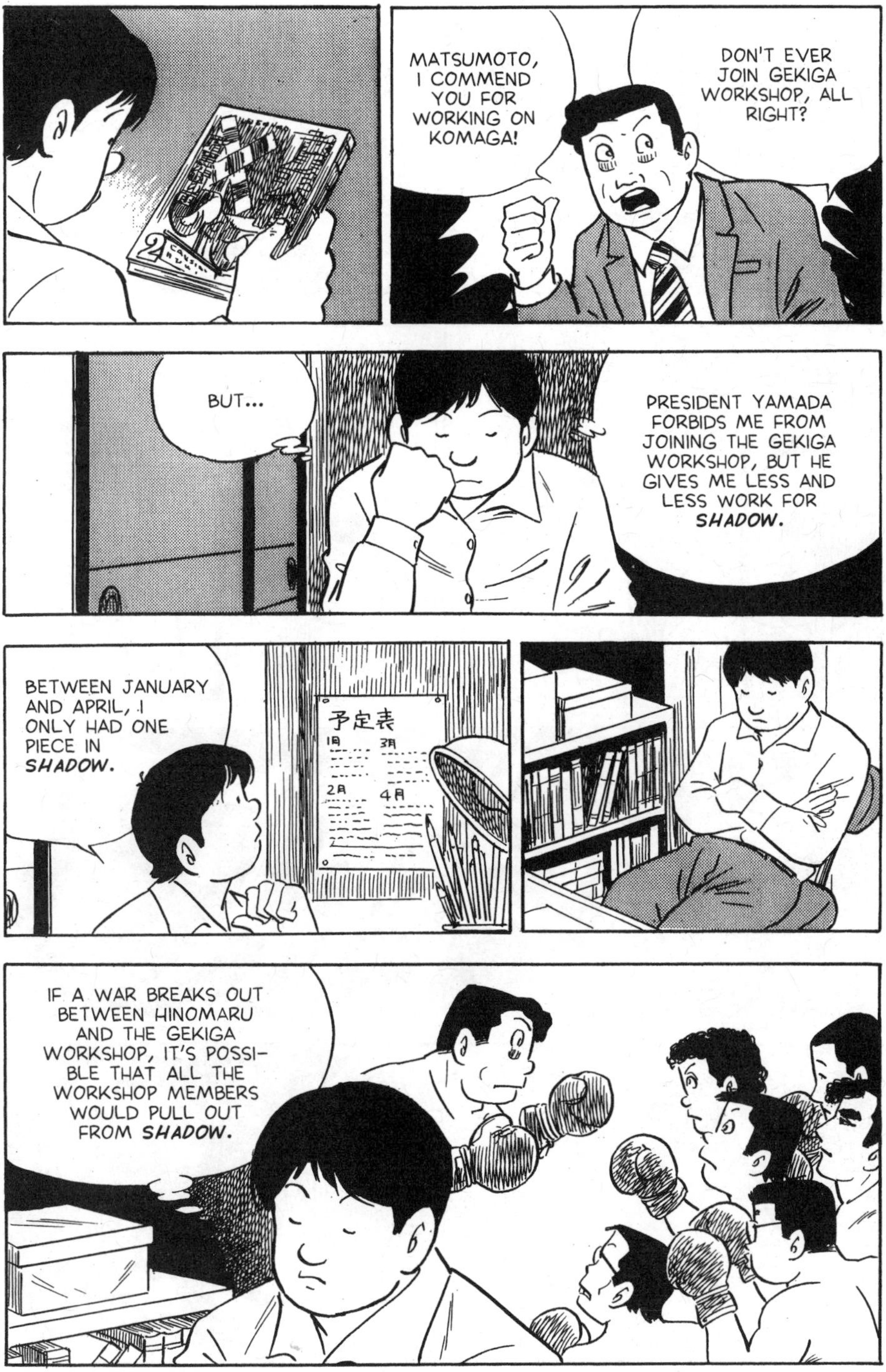
MATSUMOTO, I COMMEND YOU FOR WORKING ON KOMAGA!
DON'T EVER JOIN GEKIGA WORKSHOP, ALL RIGHT?
BUT...
PRESIDENT YAMADA FORBIDS ME FROM JOINING THE GEKIGA WORKSHOP, BUT HE GIVES ME LESS AND LESS WORK FOR SHADOW.
BETWEEN JANUARY AND APRIL, I ONLY HAD ONE PIECE IN SHADOW.
予定表
1月 3月
2月 4月
IF A WAR BREAKS OUT BETWEEN HINOMARU AND THE GEKIGA WORKSHOP, IT'S POSSIBLE THAT ALL THE WORKSHOP MEMBERS WOULD PULL OUT FROM SHADOW.

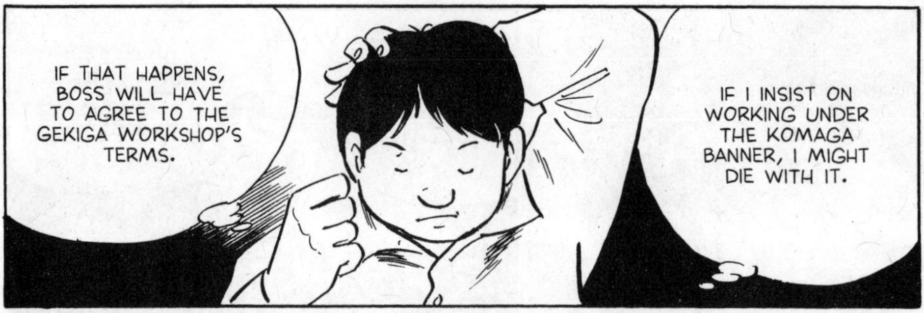
IF THAT HAPPENS, BOSS WILL HAVE TO AGREE TO THE GEKIGA WORKSHOP'S TERMS.
IF I INSIST ON WORKING UNDER THE KOMAGA BANNER, I MIGHT DIE WITH IT.

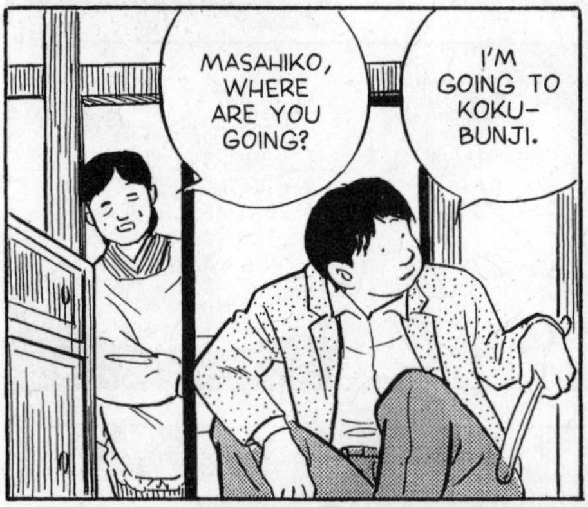
MASAHIKO, WHERE ARE YOU GOING?
I'M GOING TO KOKU-BUNJI.

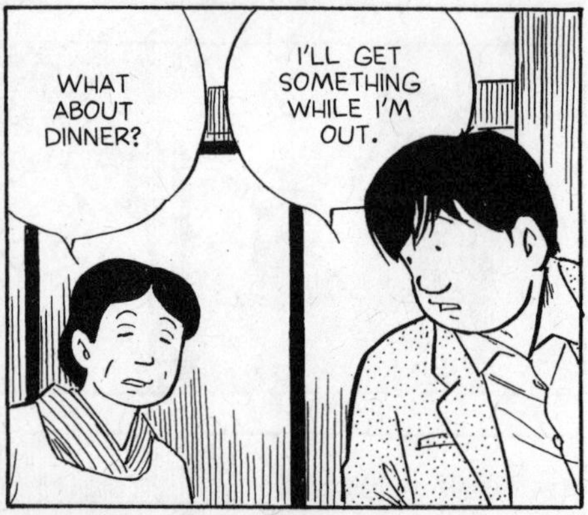
WHAT ABOUT DINNER?
I'LL GET SOMETHING WHILE I'M OUT.

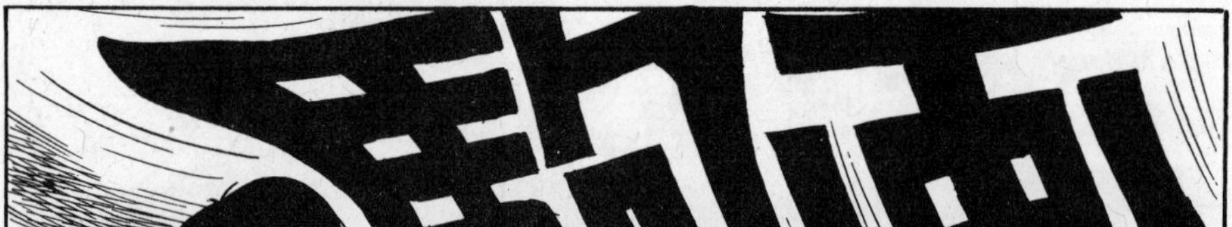
駒画

TEXT: : KOMAGA

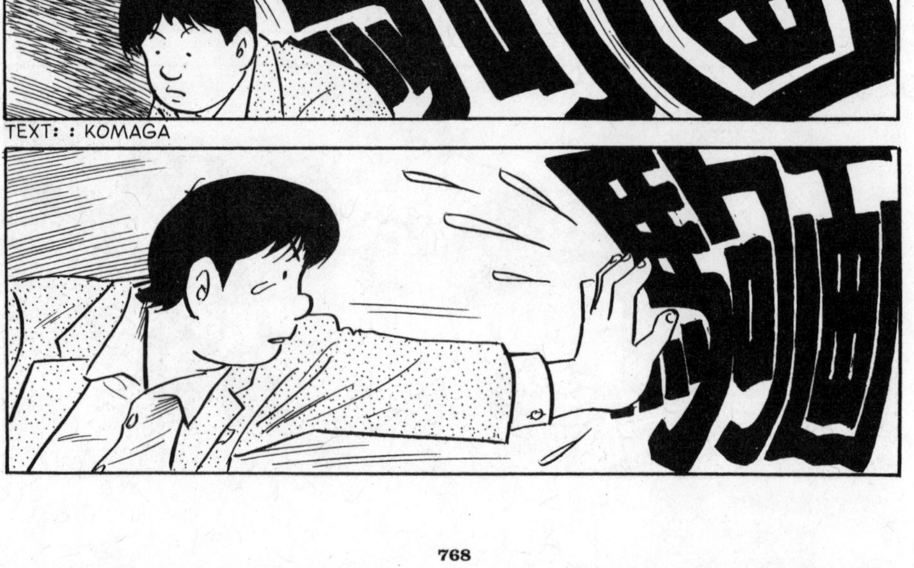
駒画

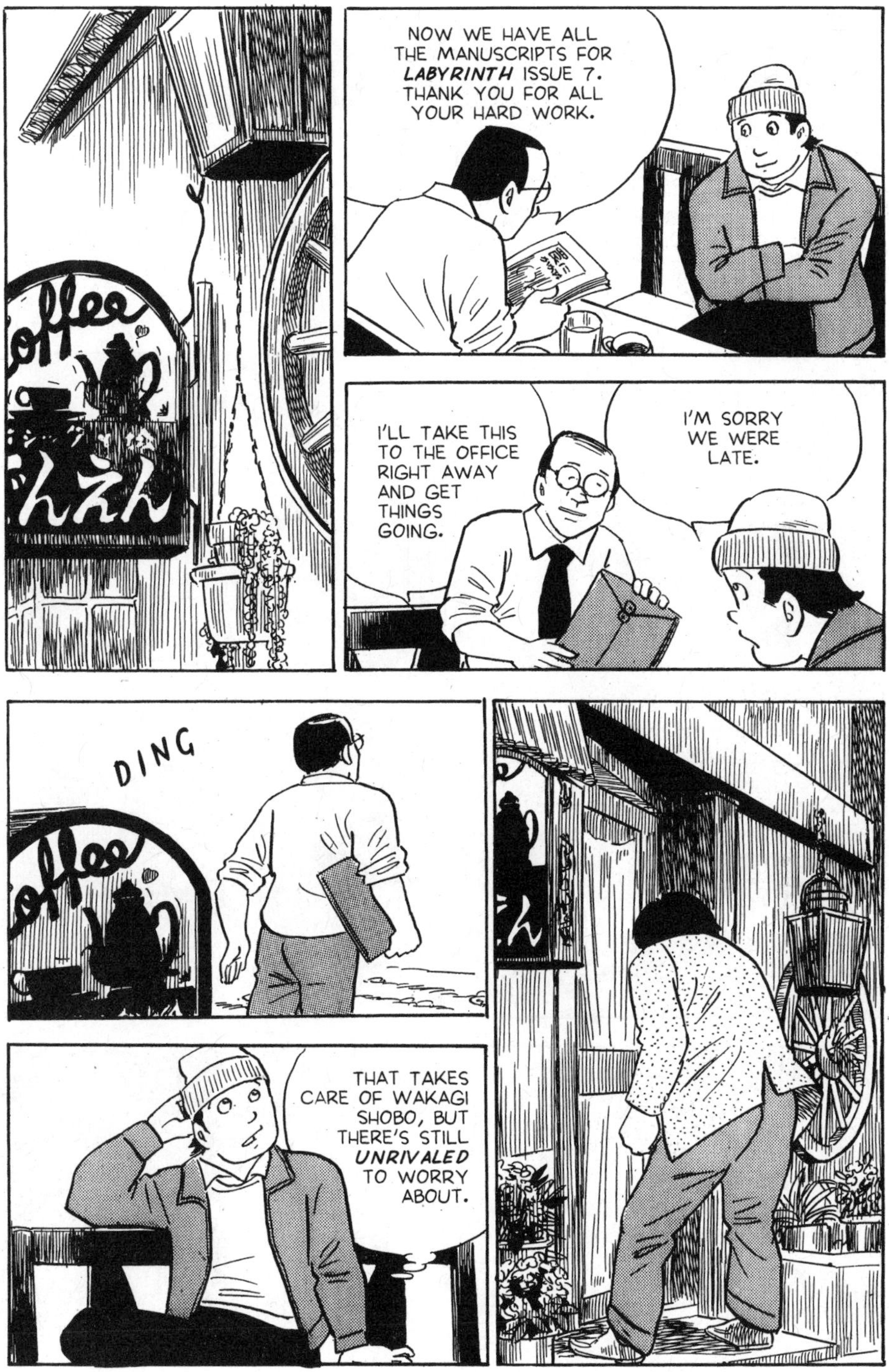
NOW WE HAVE ALL THE MANUSCRIPTS FOR *LABYRINTH* ISSUE 7. THANK YOU FOR ALL YOUR HARD WORK.
I'LL TAKE THIS TO THE OFFICE RIGHT AWAY AND GET THINGS GOING.
I'M SORRY WE WERE LATE.
DING
THAT TAKES CARE OF WAKAGI SHOBO, BUT THERE'S STILL *UNRIVALED* TO WORRY ABOUT.

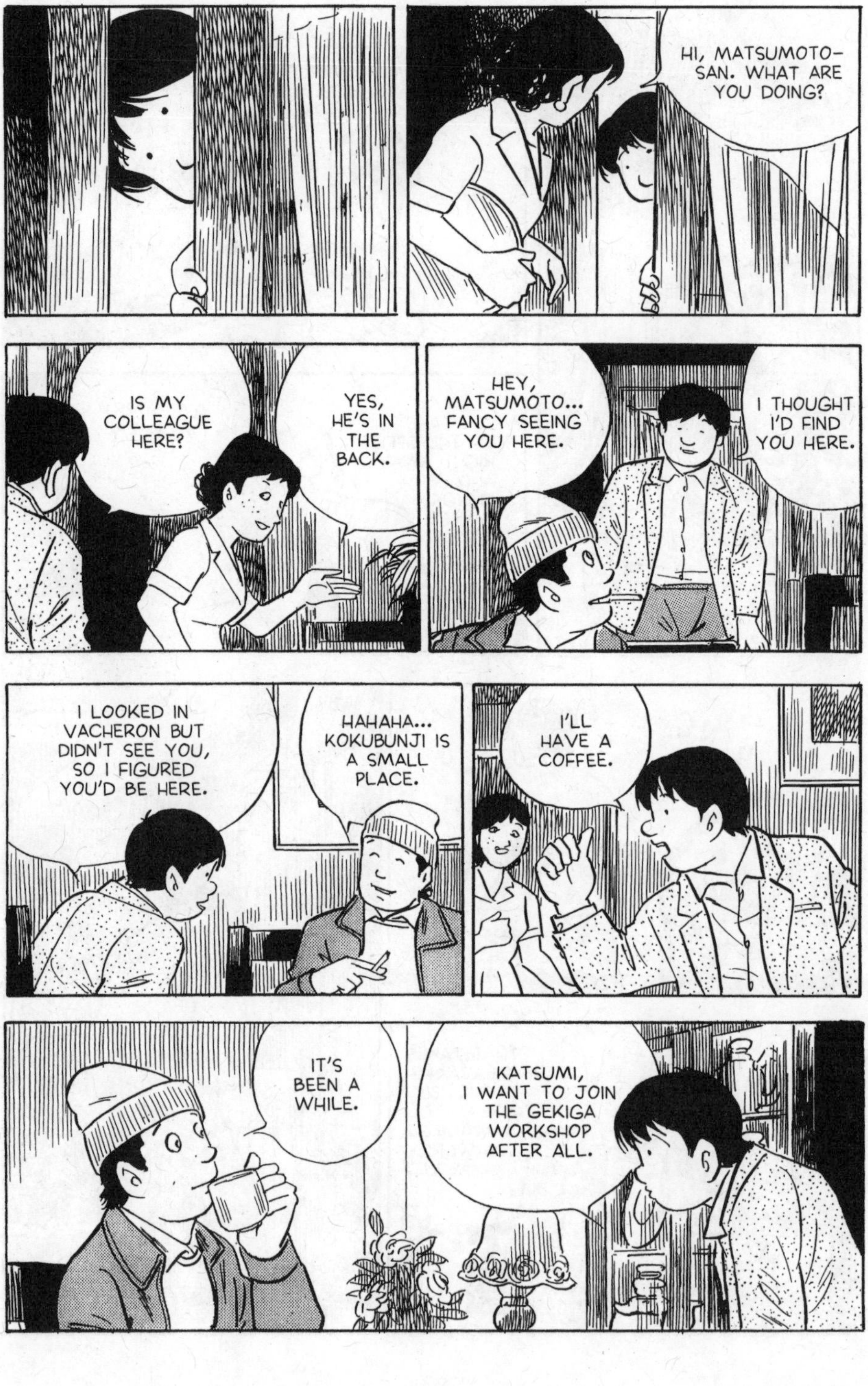
HI, MATSUMOTO-SAN. WHAT ARE YOU DOING?
IS MY COLLEAGUE HERE?
YES, HE'S IN THE BACK.
HEY, MATSUMOTO... FANCY SEEING YOU HERE.
I THOUGHT I'D FIND YOU HERE.
I LOOKED IN VACHERON BUT DIDN'T SEE YOU, SO I FIGURED YOU'D BE HERE.
HAHAHA... KOKUBUNJI IS A SMALL PLACE.
I'LL HAVE A COFFEE.
IT'S BEEN A WHILE.
KATSUMI, I WANT TO JOIN THE GEKIGA WORKSHOP AFTER ALL.

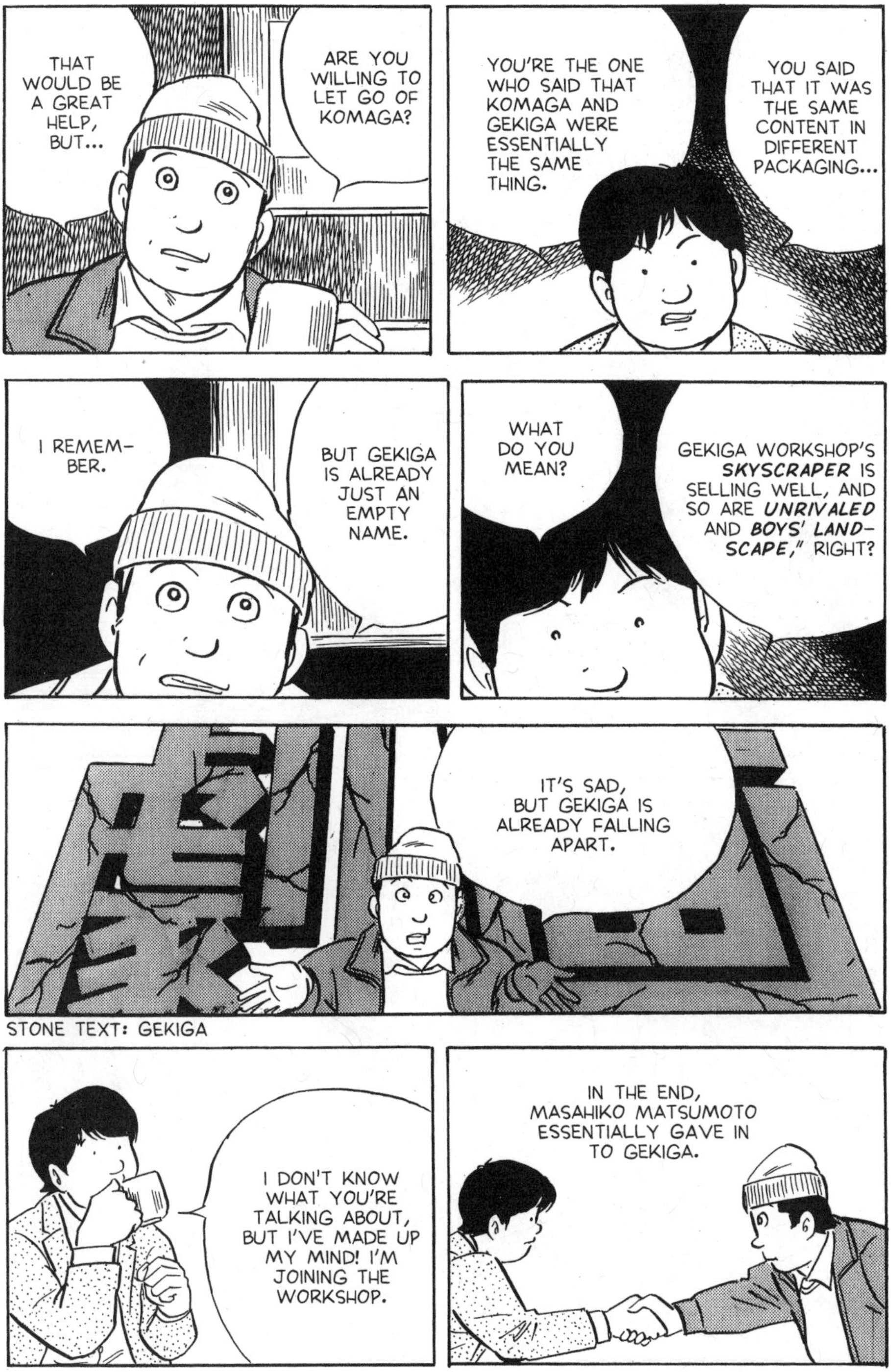
THAT WOULD BE A GREAT HELP, BUT...
ARE YOU WILLING TO LET GO OF KOMAGA?
YOU'RE THE ONE WHO SAID THAT KOMAGA AND GEKIGA WERE ESSENTIALLY THE SAME THING.
YOU SAID THAT IT WAS THE SAME CONTENT IN DIFFERENT PACKAGING...
I REMEM-BER.
BUT GEKIGA IS ALREADY JUST AN EMPTY NAME.
WHAT DO YOU MEAN?
GEKIGA WORKSHOP'S ***SKYSCRAPER*** IS SELLING WELL, AND SO ARE ***UNRIVALED*** AND ***BOYS' LAND-SCAPE***," RIGHT?
IT'S SAD, BUT GEKIGA IS ALREADY FALLING APART.
STONE TEXT: GEKIGA
I DON'T KNOW WHAT YOU'RE TALKING ABOUT, BUT I'VE MADE UP MY MIND! I'M JOINING THE WORKSHOP.
IN THE END, MASAHIKO MATSUMOTO ESSENTIALLY GAVE IN TO GEKIGA.

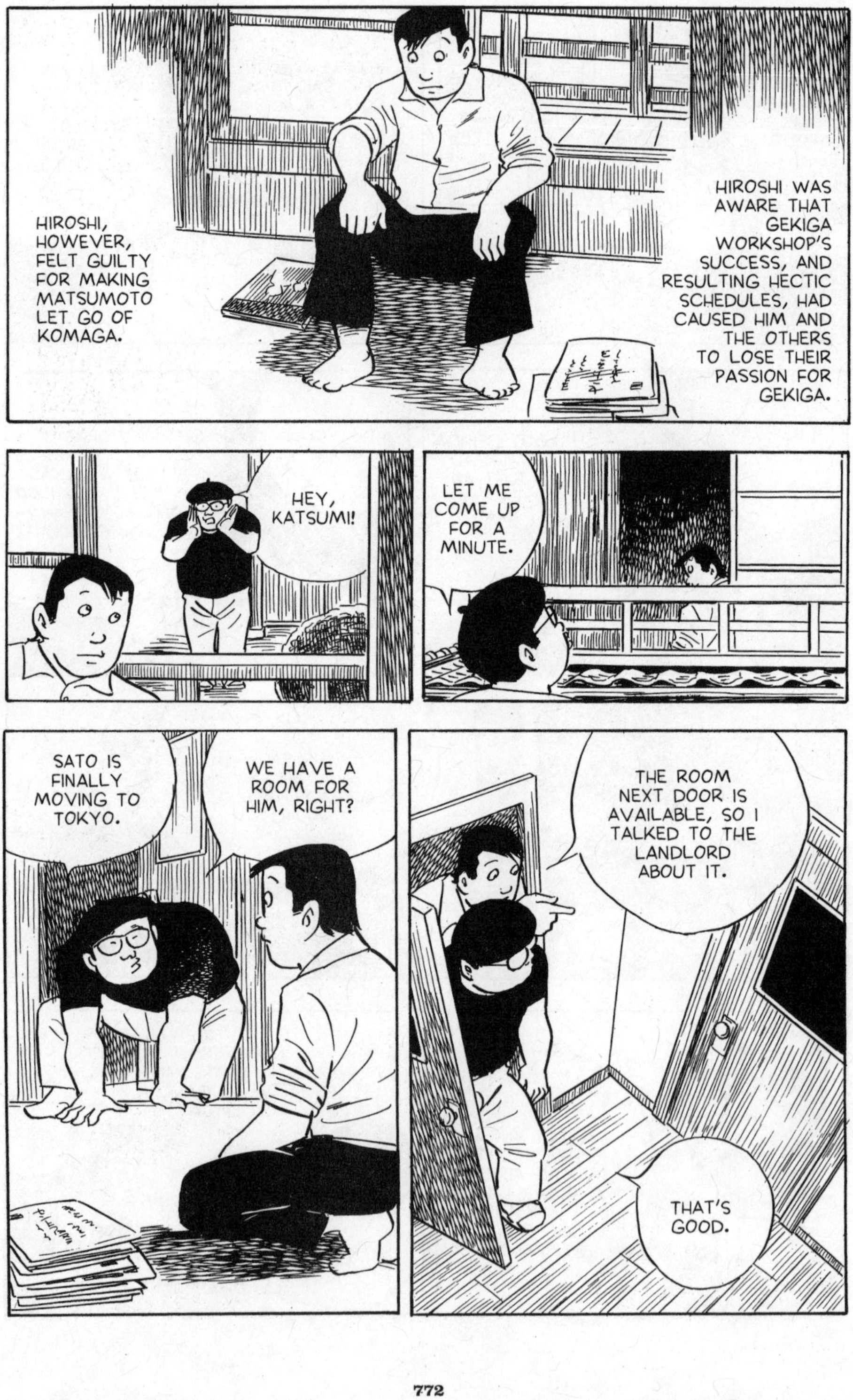
HIROSHI, HOWEVER, FELT GUILTY FOR MAKING MATSUMOTO LET GO OF KOMAGA.
HIROSHI WAS AWARE THAT GEKIGA WORKSHOP'S SUCCESS, AND RESULTING HECTIC SCHEDULES, HAD CAUSED HIM AND THE OTHERS TO LOSE THEIR PASSION FOR GEKIGA.
HEY, KATSUMI!
LET ME COME UP FOR A MINUTE.
SATO IS FINALLY MOVING TO TOKYO.
WE HAVE A ROOM FOR HIM, RIGHT?
THE ROOM NEXT DOOR IS AVAILABLE, SO I TALKED TO THE LANDLORD ABOUT IT.
THAT'S GOOD.

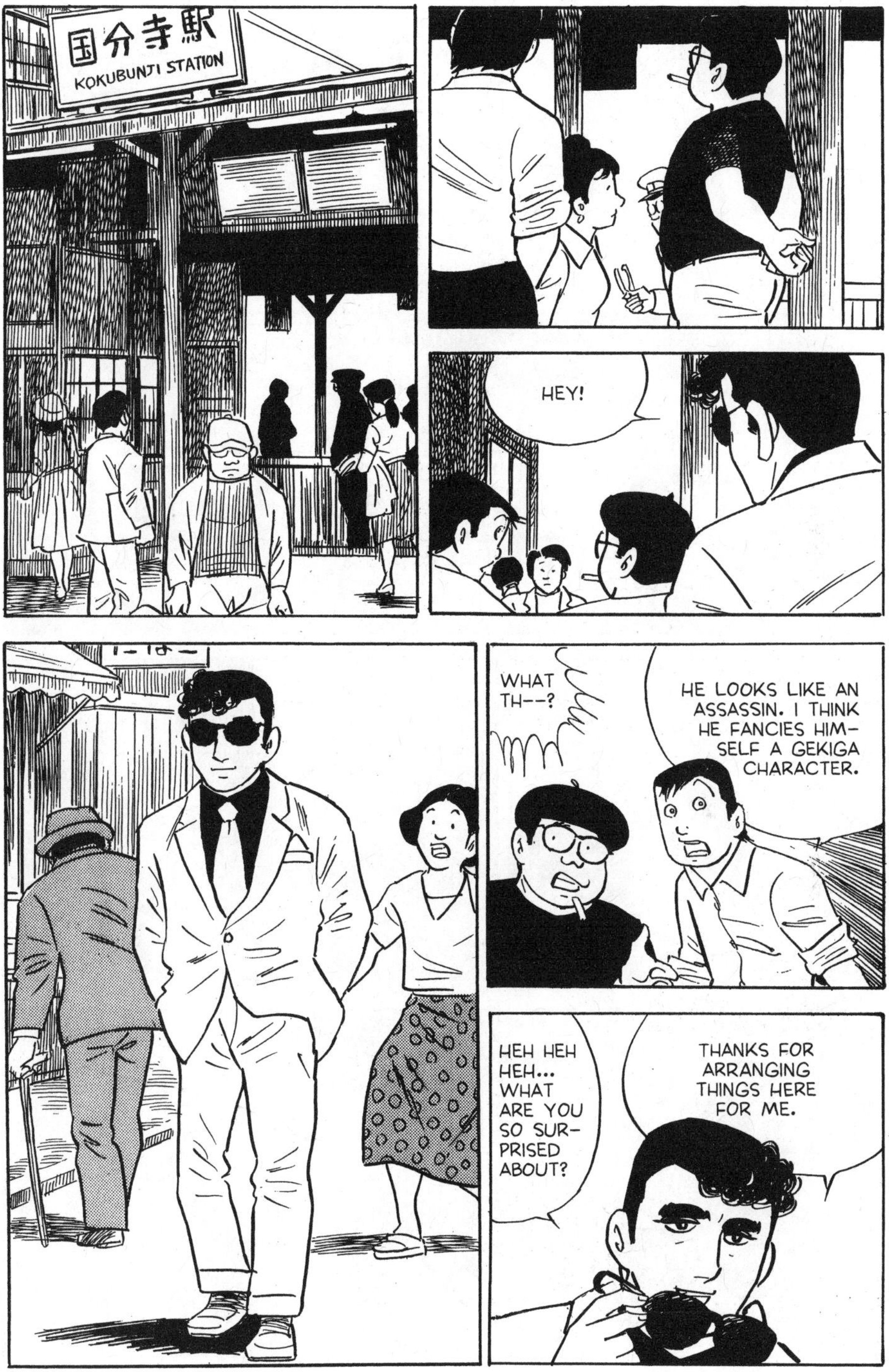
国分寺駅
KOKUBUNJI STATION
HEY!
WHAT TH--?
HE LOOKS LIKE AN ASSASSIN. I THINK HE FANCIES HIMSELF A GEKIGA CHARACTER.
HEH HEH HEH... WHAT ARE YOU SO SURPRISED ABOUT?
THANKS FOR ARRANGING THINGS HERE FOR ME.

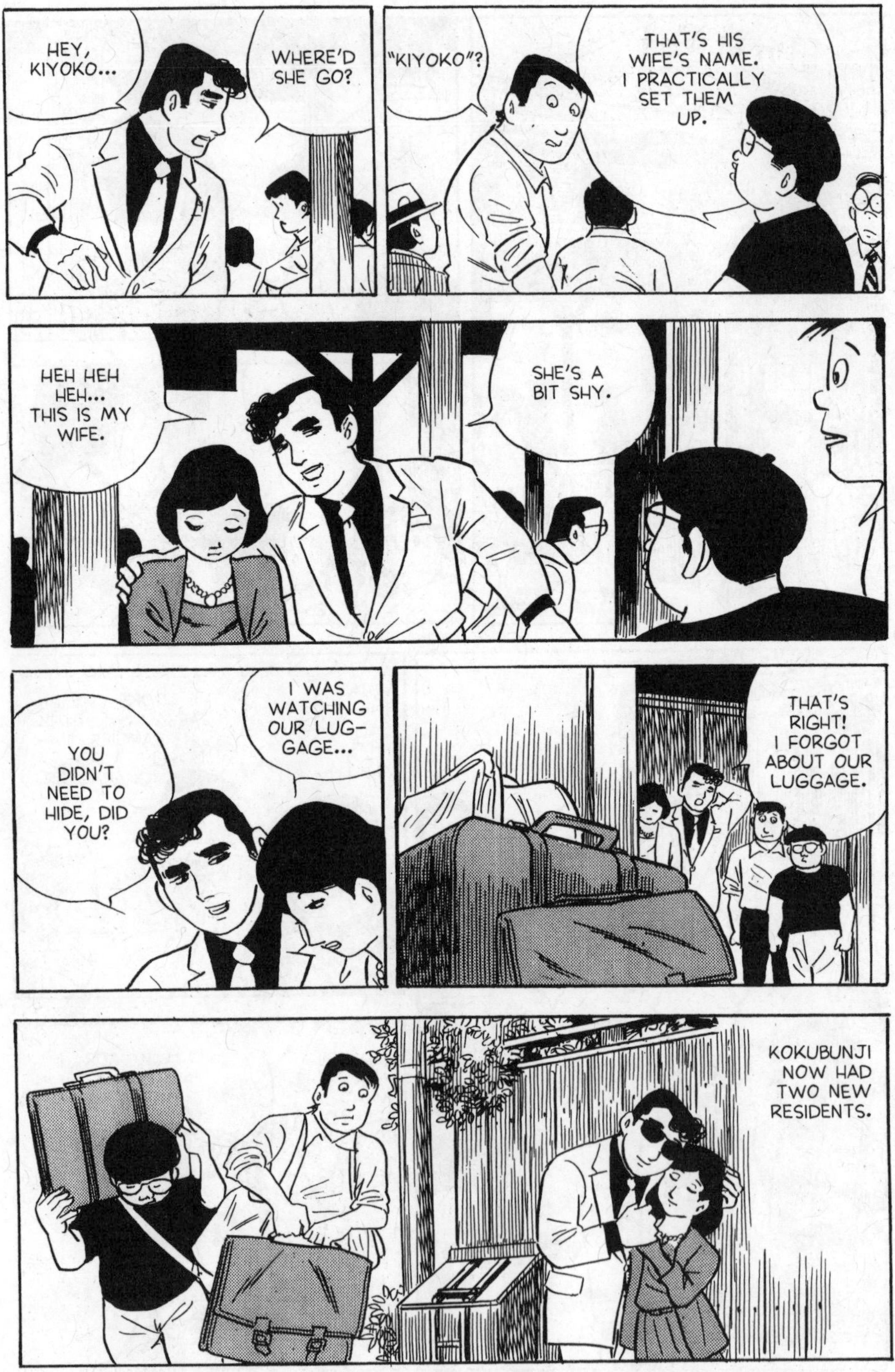
HEY, KIYOKO...
WHERE'D SHE GO?
"KIYOKO"?
THAT'S HIS WIFE'S NAME. I PRACTICALLY SET THEM UP.
HEH HEH HEH... THIS IS MY WIFE.
SHE'S A BIT SHY.
YOU DIDN'T NEED TO HIDE, DID YOU?
I WAS WATCHING OUR LUG-GAGE...
THAT'S RIGHT! I FORGOT ABOUT OUR LUGGAGE.
KOKUBUNJI NOW HAD TWO NEW RESIDENTS.

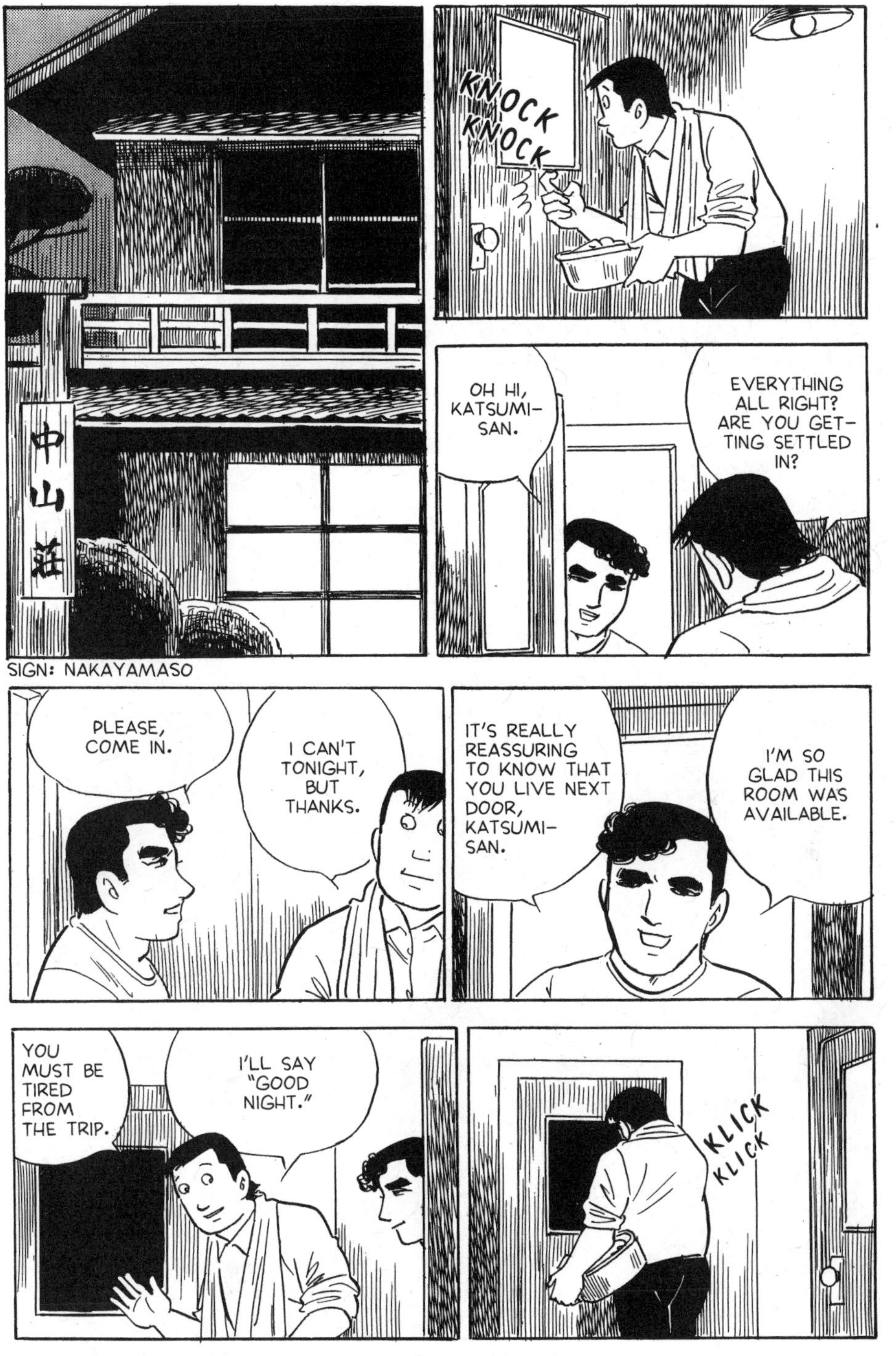

中山荘
SIGN: NAKAYAMASO
KNOCK KNOCK
OH HI, KATSUMI-SAN.
EVERYTHING ALL RIGHT? ARE YOU GETTING SETTLED IN?
PLEASE, COME IN.
I CAN'T TONIGHT, BUT THANKS.
IT'S REALLY REASSURING TO KNOW THAT YOU LIVE NEXT DOOR, KATSUMI-SAN.
I'M SO GLAD THIS ROOM WAS AVAILABLE.
YOU MUST BE TIRED FROM THE TRIP.
I'LL SAY "GOOD NIGHT."
KLICK KLICK

HIROSHI HAD WANTED TO TURN IN HIS BEST WORK FOR ***SKYSCRAPER,*** WHICH WAS RECEIVING QUITE A BIT OF ATTENTION...
BUT BEING SO BUSY, HE SETTLED FOR A VERY UN-GEKIGA-LIKE GAG STRIP FOR NUMBERS FOUR THROUGH SIX.
TITLE: "SKYSCRAPPER"
IT WAS A COMPROMISE – A CONTINGENCY PLAN IN CASE ONE OF THE OTHER MEMBERS FAILED TO MEET THE DEADLINE.
HE HAD TO SAVE ENOUGH ENERGY TO BE ABLE TO WRITE A LAST-MINUTE REPLACEMENT STORY IF NEEDED.
KATSUMI'S WORRIES SEEMED TO BE FOR NAUGHT, AND AFTER HIS CONTRIBUTORS HAD MET THEIR DEADLINES FOR THREE CONSECUTIVE ISSUES, HE WAS ABLE TO DISCONTINUE HIS GAG STRIP.
BUT HE ALSO RECEIVED SEVERE CRITICISM FROM HIS COLLEAGUES REGARDING THIS UNCHARACTERISTIC OUTPUT.
THEY DON'T KNOW MY TROUBLES...
AH... AH...
YES!

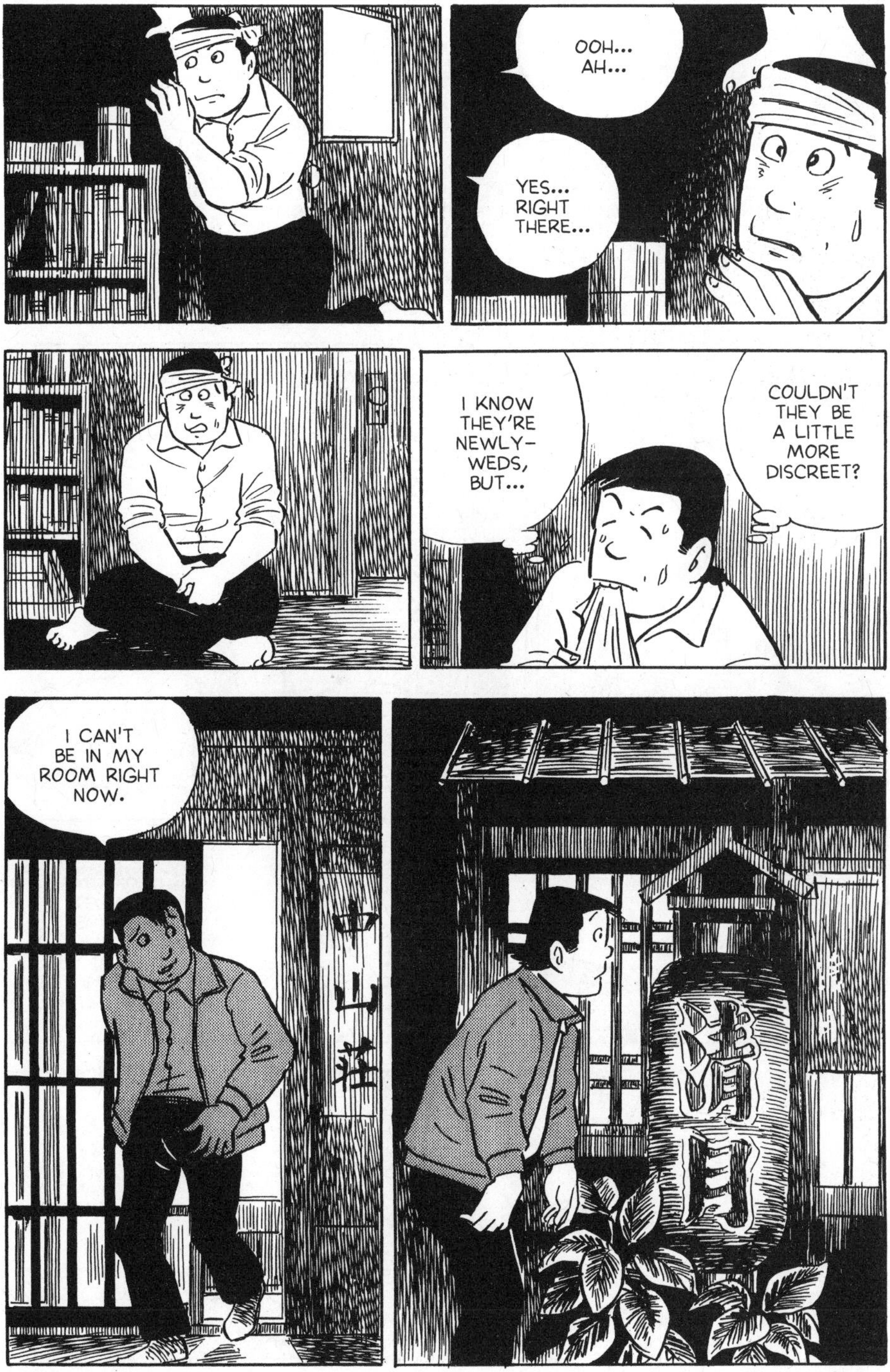
OOH... AH...
YES... RIGHT THERE...
I KNOW THEY'RE NEWLY-WEDS, BUT...
COULDN'T THEY BE A LITTLE MORE DISCREET?
I CAN'T BE IN MY ROOM RIGHT NOW.
SIGN: NAKAYAMASO

TEXT: SEIGETSU

IT'S NOT LIKE YOU TO SHOW UP BY YOUR-SELF.

WHAT'S GOTTEN INTO YOU?

AS HIROSHI FORCED THE DRINKS DOWN HIS THROAT, HE WAS OVERCOME BY A FEELING OF EMPTI-NESS.

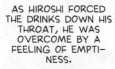

IT HAD BEEN A YEAR AND A HALF SINCE HE HAD MOVED TO TOKYO. IN THAT TIME, HE HAD DASHED OFF PAGES OF INCONSEQUENTIAL WORK JUST TO MEET DEAD-LINES...

BUT HE HADN'T CHALLENGED HIMSELF, AND HE HADN'T PRODUCED A THING OF SUBSTANCE.

THE GEKIGA WORKSHOP'S SHORT STORY COLLECTIONS WERE OFF TO A GOOD START...

BUT HIROSHI REALIZED THAT HE HAD LOST SIGHT OF HIMSELF AMIDST THE UNEXPECTED DELUGE OF WORK THEY HAD BEEN RECEIVING.

WHERE DID MY PASSION FOR GEKIGA GO?!

WHAT DOES GEKIGA WORK-SHOP EVEN STAND FOR NOW?

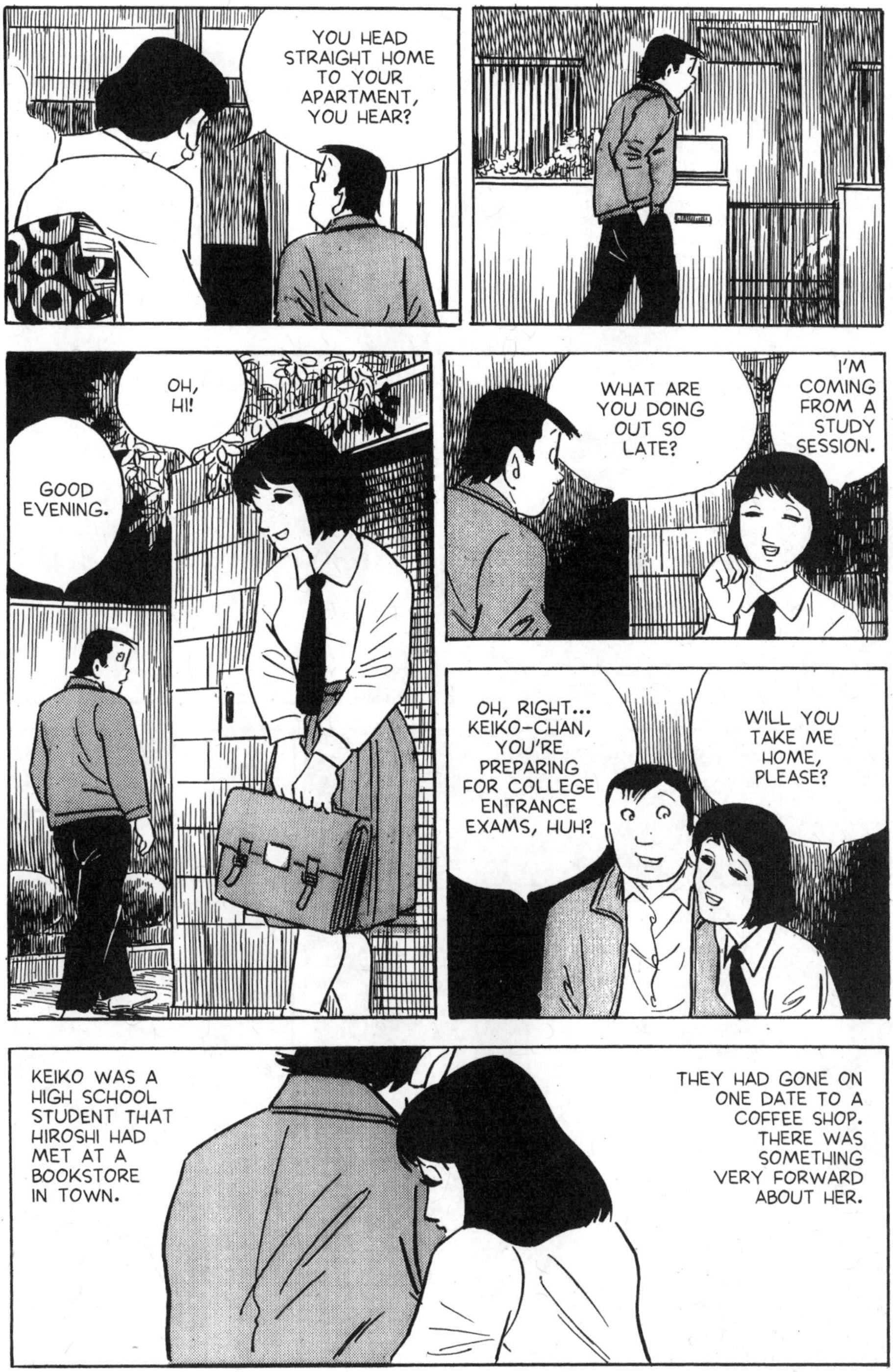
YOU HEAD STRAIGHT HOME TO YOUR APARTMENT, YOU HEAR?
GOOD EVENING.
OH, HI!
WHAT ARE YOU DOING OUT SO LATE?
I'M COMING FROM A STUDY SESSION.
OH, RIGHT... KEIKO-CHAN, YOU'RE PREPARING FOR COLLEGE ENTRANCE EXAMS, HUH?
WILL YOU TAKE ME HOME, PLEASE?
KEIKO WAS A HIGH SCHOOL STUDENT THAT HIROSHI HAD MET AT A BOOKSTORE IN TOWN.
THEY HAD GONE ON ONE DATE TO A COFFEE SHOP. THERE WAS SOMETHING VERY FORWARD ABOUT HER.

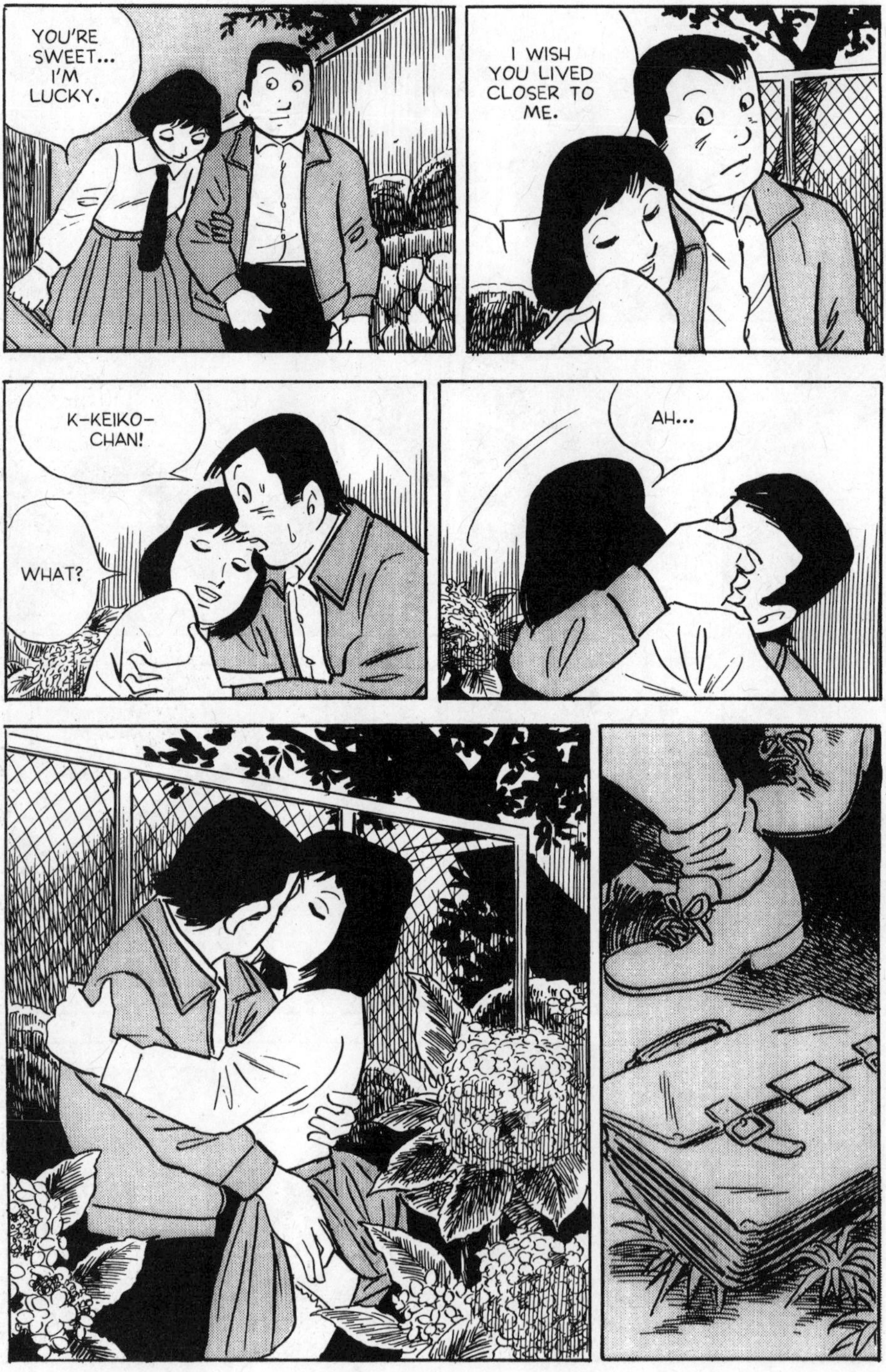
YOU'RE SWEET... I'M LUCKY.
I WISH YOU LIVED CLOSER TO ME.
K-KEIKO-CHAN!
WHAT?
AH...

JEALOUSY AND FRUSTRATION

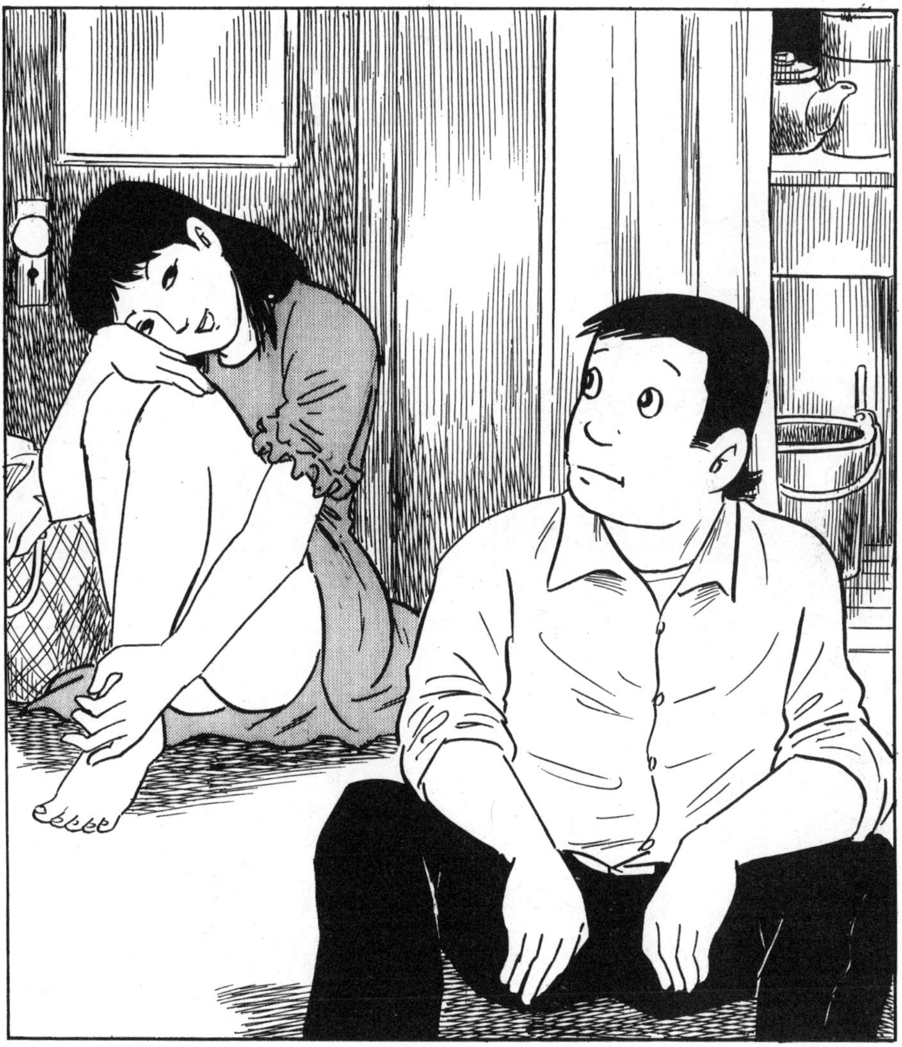

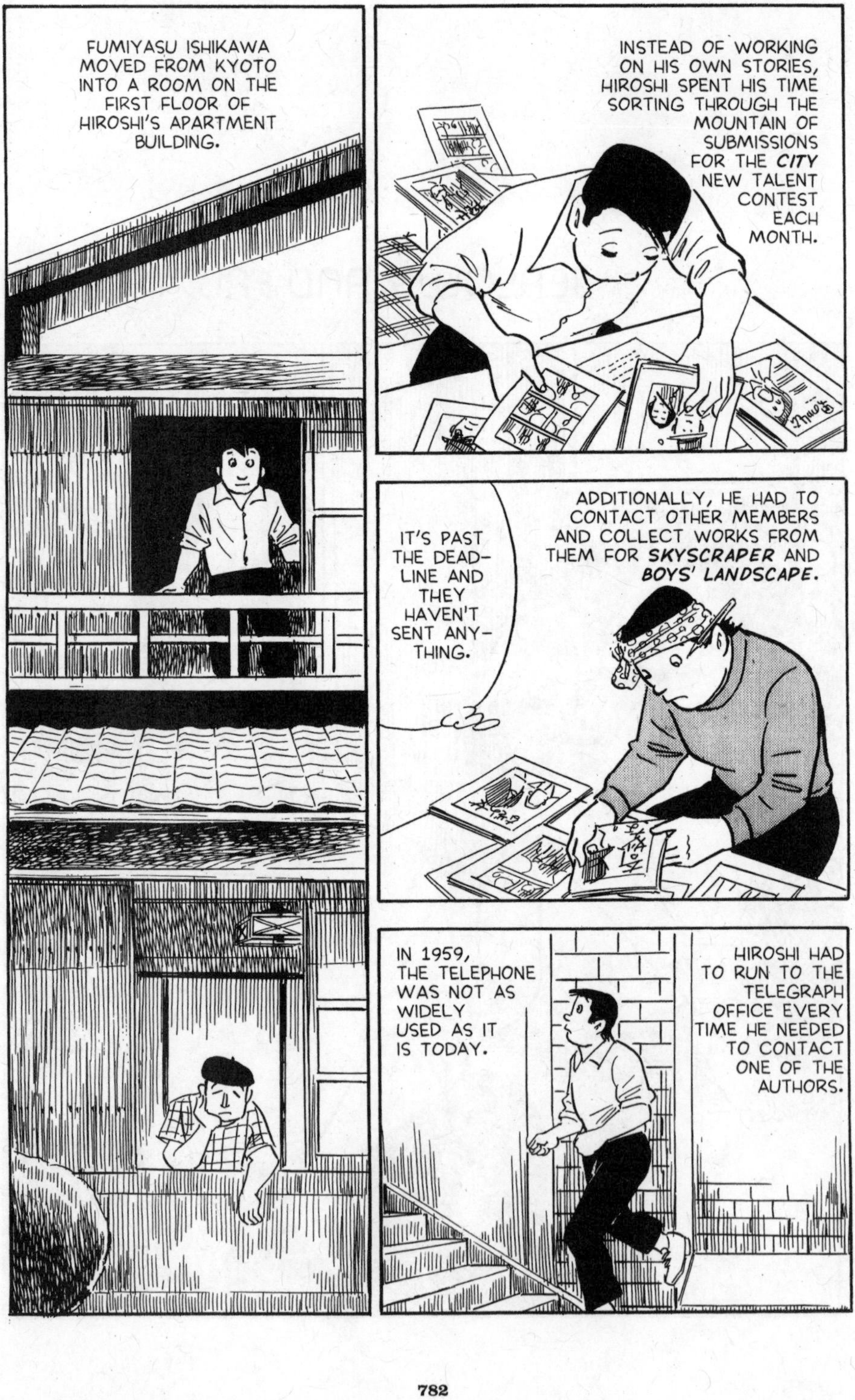
FUMIYASU ISHIKAWA MOVED FROM KYOTO INTO A ROOM ON THE FIRST FLOOR OF HIROSHI'S APARTMENT BUILDING.
INSTEAD OF WORKING ON HIS OWN STORIES, HIROSHI SPENT HIS TIME SORTING THROUGH THE MOUNTAIN OF SUBMISSIONS FOR THE CITY NEW TALENT CONTEST EACH MONTH.
ADDITIONALLY, HE HAD TO CONTACT OTHER MEMBERS AND COLLECT WORKS FROM THEM FOR SKYSCRAPER AND BOYS' LANDSCAPE.
IT'S PAST THE DEAD-LINE AND THEY HAVEN'T SENT ANY-THING.
IN 1959, THE TELEPHONE WAS NOT AS WIDELY USED AS IT IS TODAY.
HIROSHI HAD TO RUN TO THE TELEGRAPH OFFICE EVERY TIME HE NEEDED TO CONTACT ONE OF THE AUTHORS.

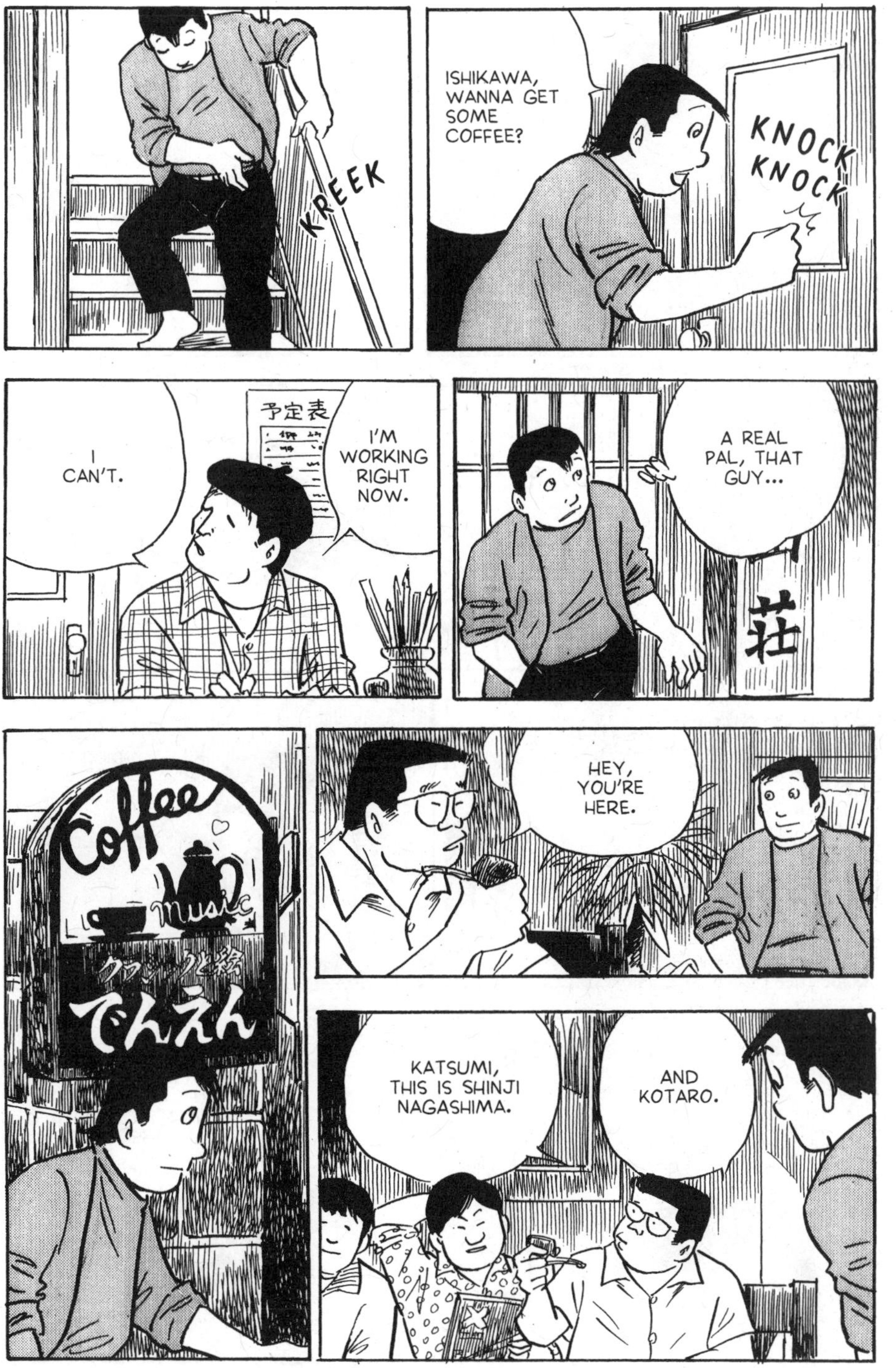
KREEK
ISHIKAWA, WANNA GET SOME COFFEE?
KNOCK KNOCK
I CAN'T.
予定表
I'M WORKING RIGHT NOW.
A REAL PAL, THAT GUY...
荘
Coffee
music
クラシックと絵
でんえん
HEY, YOU'RE HERE.
KATSUMI, THIS IS SHINJI NAGASHIMA.
AND KOTARO.

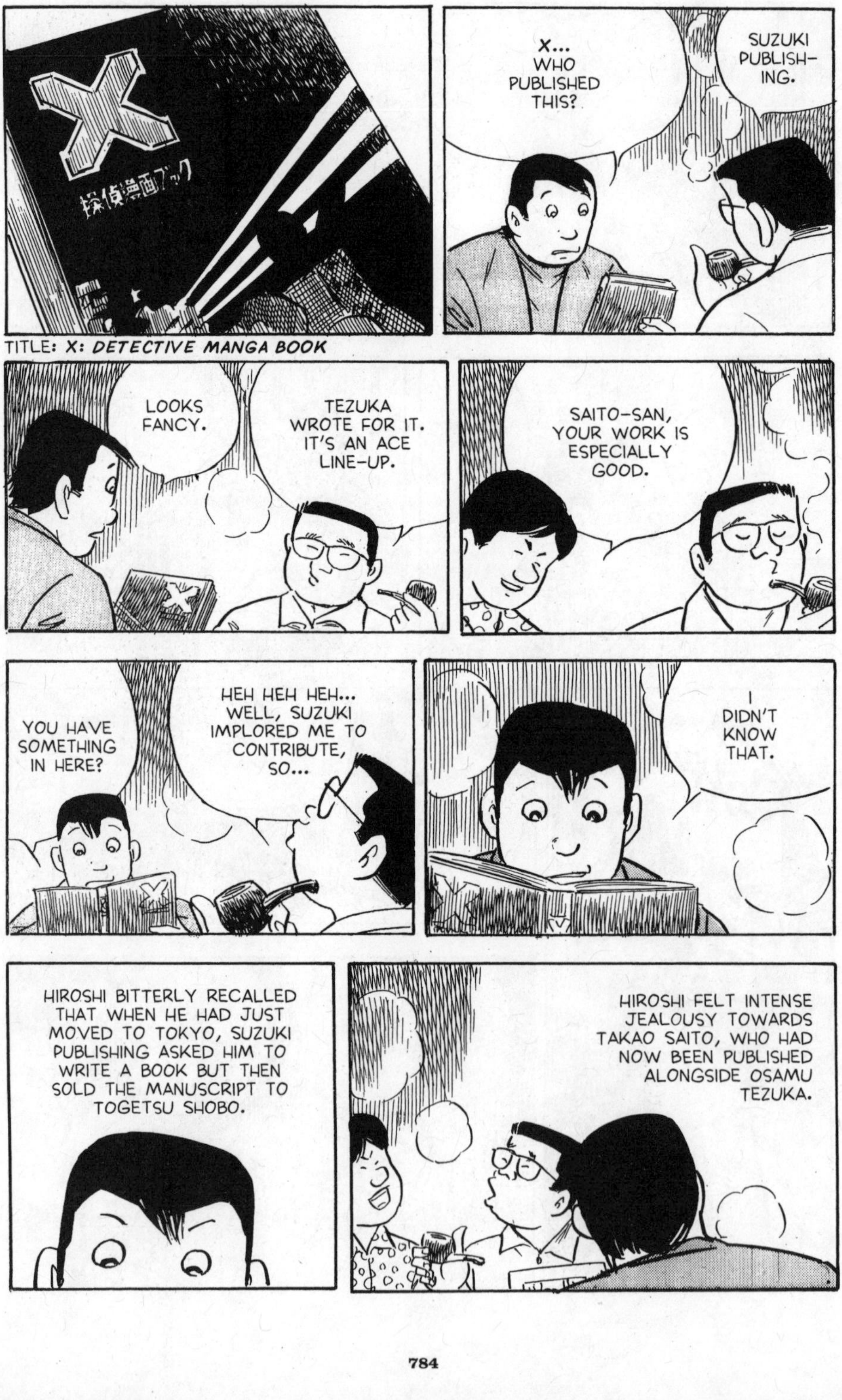
探偵漫画ブック
TITLE: X: DETECTIVE MANGA BOOK
X... WHO PUBLISHED THIS?
SUZUKI PUBLISHING.
LOOKS FANCY.
TEZUKA WROTE FOR IT. IT'S AN ACE LINE-UP.
SAITO-SAN, YOUR WORK IS ESPECIALLY GOOD.
YOU HAVE SOMETHING IN HERE?
HEH HEH HEH... WELL, SUZUKI IMPLORED ME TO CONTRIBUTE, SO...
I DIDN'T KNOW THAT.
HIROSHI BITTERLY RECALLED THAT WHEN HE HAD JUST MOVED TO TOKYO, SUZUKI PUBLISHING ASKED HIM TO WRITE A BOOK BUT THEN SOLD THE MANUSCRIPT TO TOGETSU SHOBO.
HIROSHI FELT INTENSE JEALOUSY TOWARDS TAKAO SAITO, WHO HAD NOW BEEN PUBLISHED ALONGSIDE OSAMU TEZUKA.

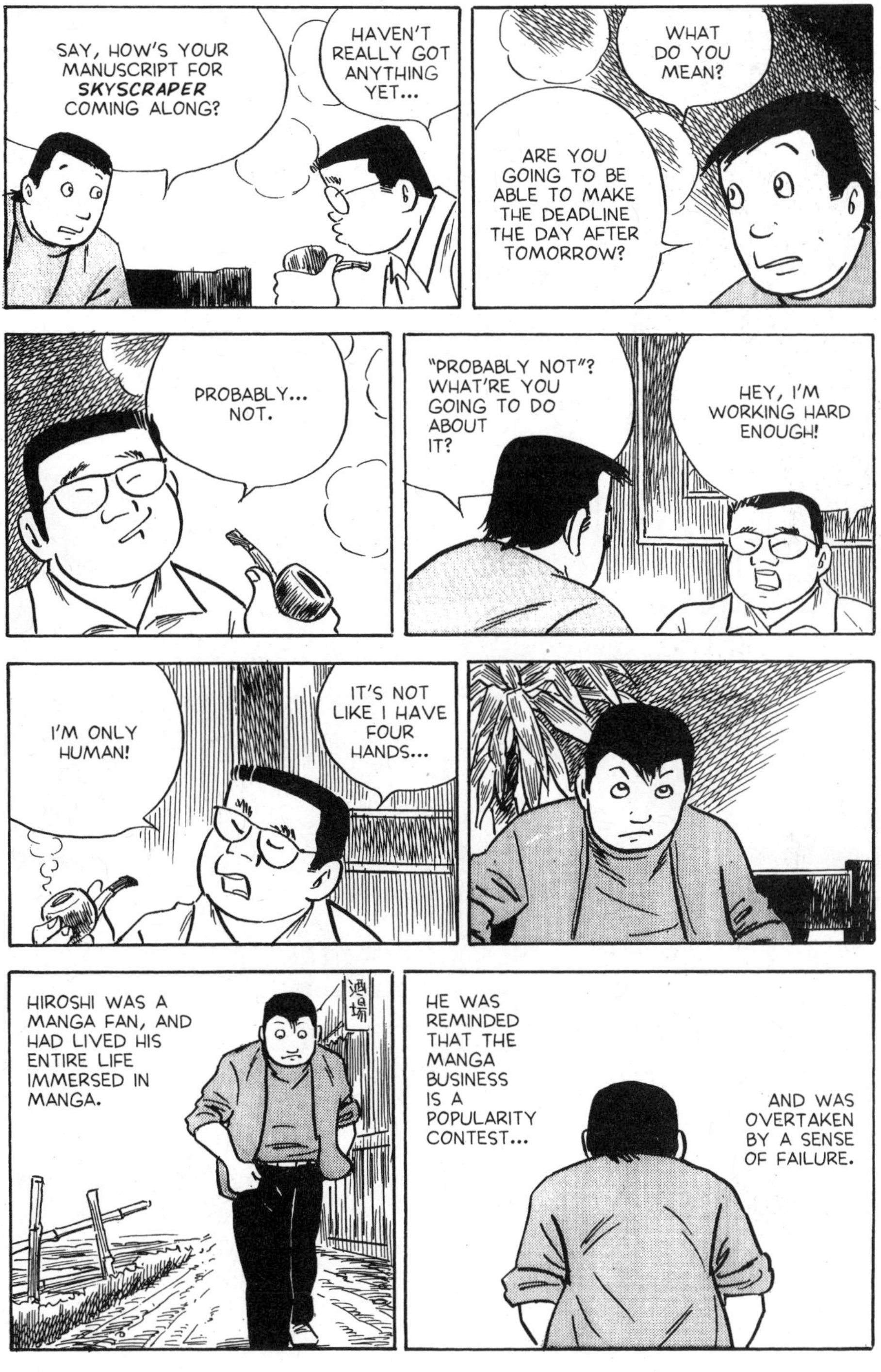
SAY, HOW'S YOUR MANUSCRIPT FOR ***SKYSCRAPER*** COMING ALONG?
HAVEN'T REALLY GOT ANYTHING YET...
WHAT DO YOU MEAN?
ARE YOU GOING TO BE ABLE TO MAKE THE DEADLINE THE DAY AFTER TOMORROW?
PROBABLY... NOT.
"PROBABLY NOT"? WHAT'RE YOU GOING TO DO ABOUT IT?
HEY, I'M WORKING HARD ENOUGH!
I'M ONLY HUMAN!
IT'S NOT LIKE I HAVE FOUR HANDS...
HIROSHI WAS A MANGA FAN, AND HAD LIVED HIS ENTIRE LIFE IMMERSED IN MANGA.
HE WAS REMINDED THAT THE MANGA BUSINESS IS A POPULARITY CONTEST...
AND WAS OVERTAKEN BY A SENSE OF FAILURE.

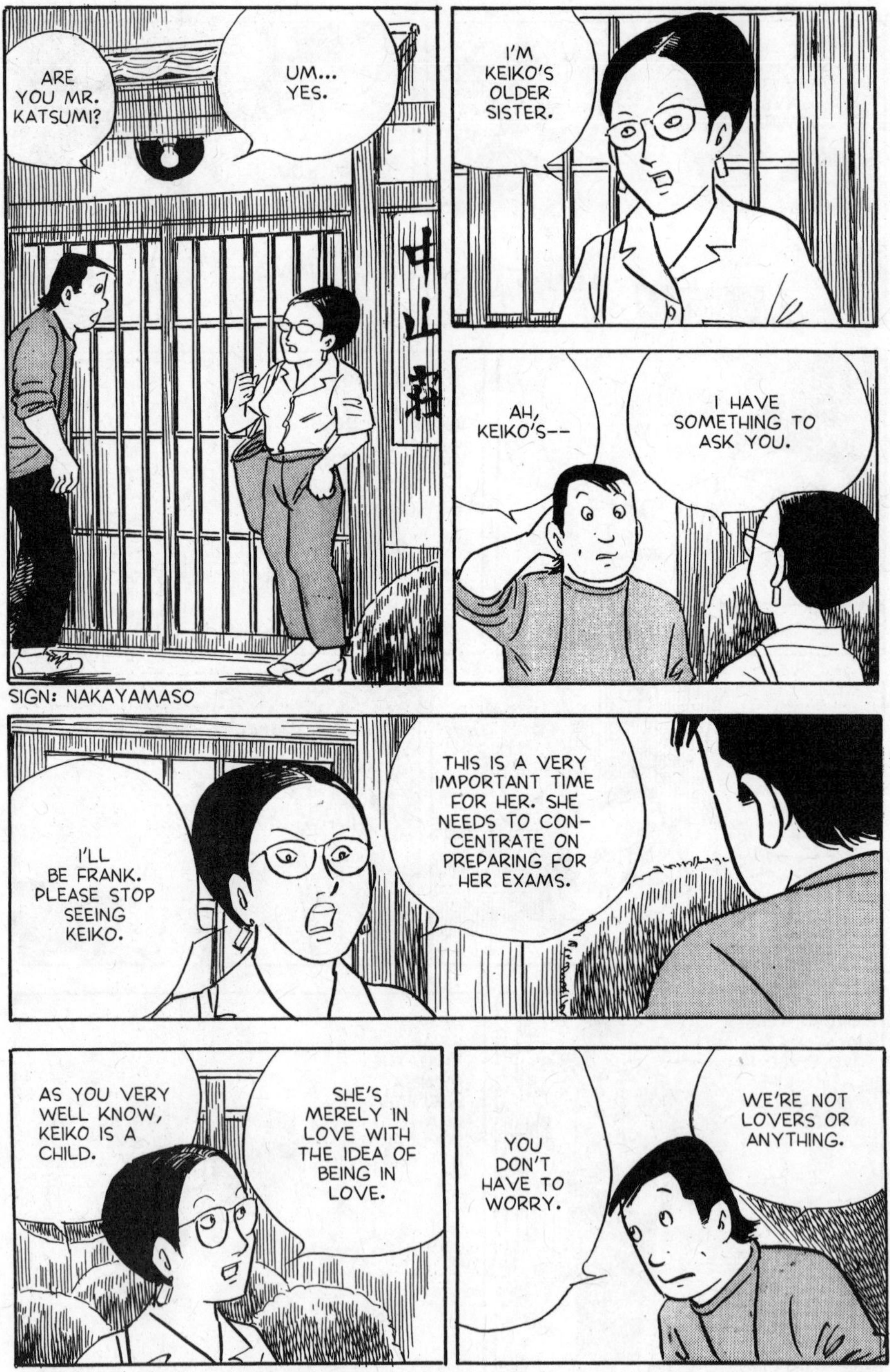
ARE YOU MR. KATSUMI?
UM... YES.
中山荘
SIGN: NAKAYAMASO
I'M KEIKO'S OLDER SISTER.
AH, KEIKO'S--
I HAVE SOMETHING TO ASK YOU.
I'LL BE FRANK. PLEASE STOP SEEING KEIKO.
THIS IS A VERY IMPORTANT TIME FOR HER. SHE NEEDS TO CON-CENTRATE ON PREPARING FOR HER EXAMS.
AS YOU VERY WELL KNOW, KEIKO IS A CHILD.
SHE'S MERELY IN LOVE WITH THE IDEA OF BEING IN LOVE.
YOU DON'T HAVE TO WORRY.
WE'RE NOT LOVERS OR ANYTHING.

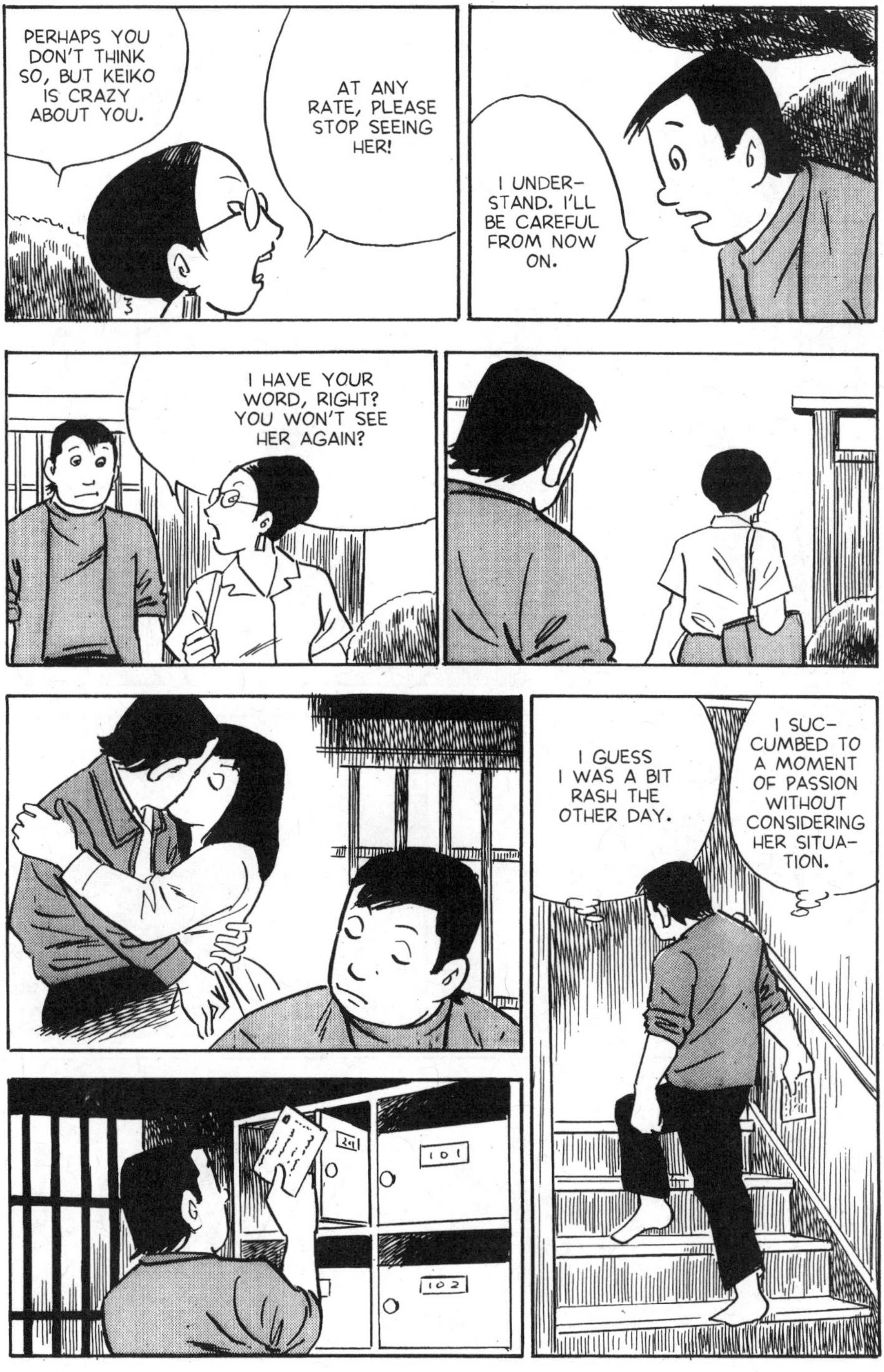
PERHAPS YOU DON'T THINK SO, BUT KEIKO IS CRAZY ABOUT YOU.
AT ANY RATE, PLEASE STOP SEEING HER!
I UNDER-STAND. I'LL BE CAREFUL FROM NOW ON.
I HAVE YOUR WORD, RIGHT? YOU WON'T SEE HER AGAIN?
I GUESS I WAS A BIT RASH THE OTHER DAY.
I SUC-CUMBED TO A MOMENT OF PASSION WITHOUT CONSIDERING HER SITUA-TION.
101
102

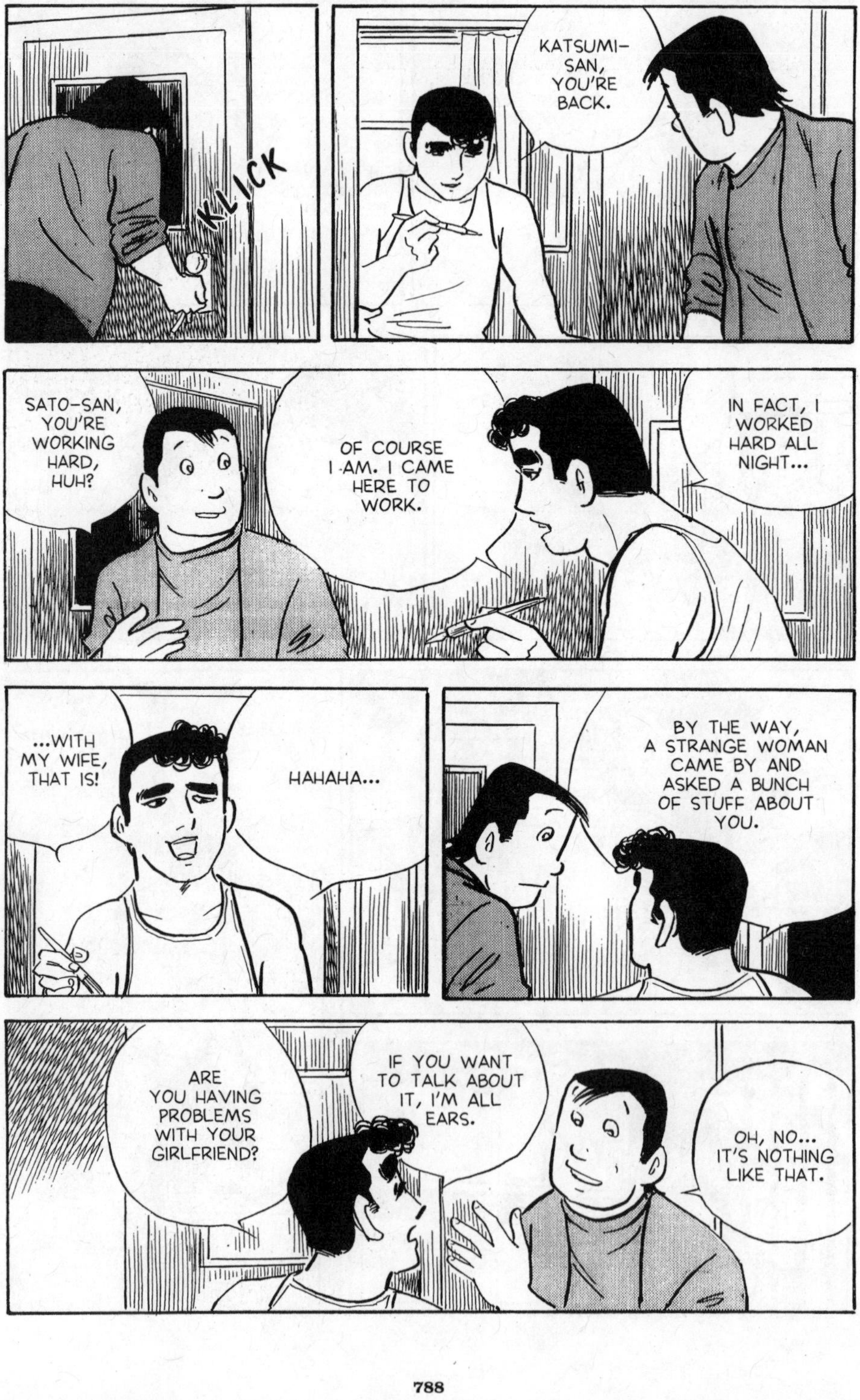
KLICK
KATSUMI-SAN, YOU'RE BACK.
SATO-SAN, YOU'RE WORKING HARD, HUH?
OF COURSE I AM. I CAME HERE TO WORK.
IN FACT, I WORKED HARD ALL NIGHT...
...WITH MY WIFE, THAT IS!
HAHAHA...
BY THE WAY, A STRANGE WOMAN CAME BY AND ASKED A BUNCH OF STUFF ABOUT YOU.
ARE YOU HAVING PROBLEMS WITH YOUR GIRLFRIEND?
IF YOU WANT TO TALK ABOUT IT, I'M ALL EARS.
OH, NO... IT'S NOTHING LIKE THAT.

LETTER: "YOU SHOULD BE CAREFUL AS YOUR RECENT WORK HAS BEEN VERY ROUGH AND POORLY EXECUTED. PRESIDENT YAMADA AT HINOMARU HAS BEEN SAYING THAT THERE IS INFIGHTING WITHIN THE GEKIGA WORKSHOP. I HOPE EVERYTHING IS OKAY. I WILL BE MOVING TO TOKYO MYSELF SOON. PLEASE WATCH YOURSELF AND YOUR WORK. -SHOICHI SARKURAI"

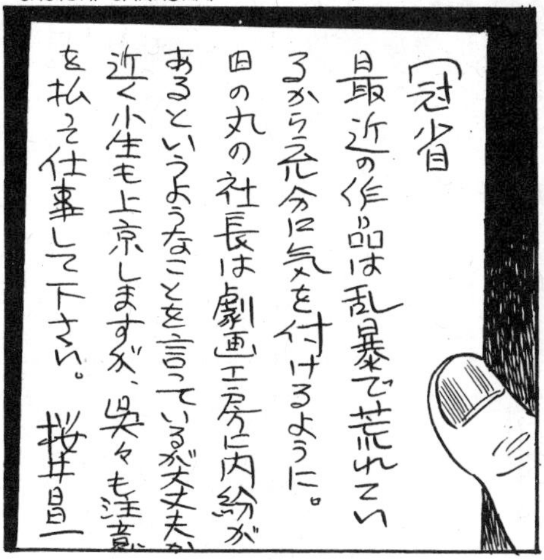
冠省
最近の作品は乱暴で荒れてい
るから充分に気を付けるように。
日の丸の社長は劇画工房に内紛が
あるというようなことを言っているが大丈夫か
近く小生も上京しますが、呉々も注意
を払って仕事して下さい。
桜井昌一

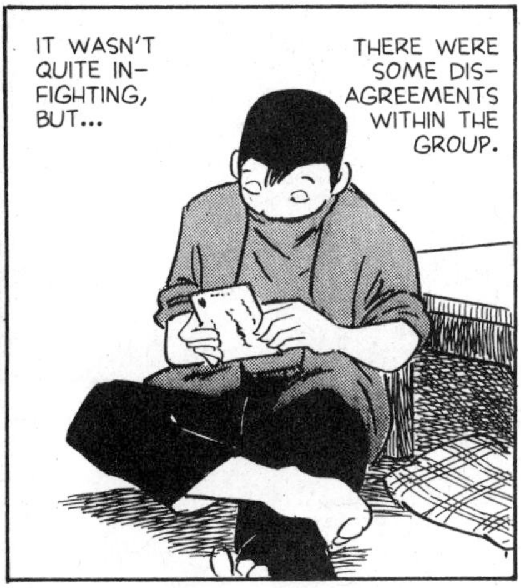
IT WASN'T QUITE IN-FIGHTING, BUT...
THERE WERE SOME DIS-AGREEMENTS WITHIN THE GROUP.

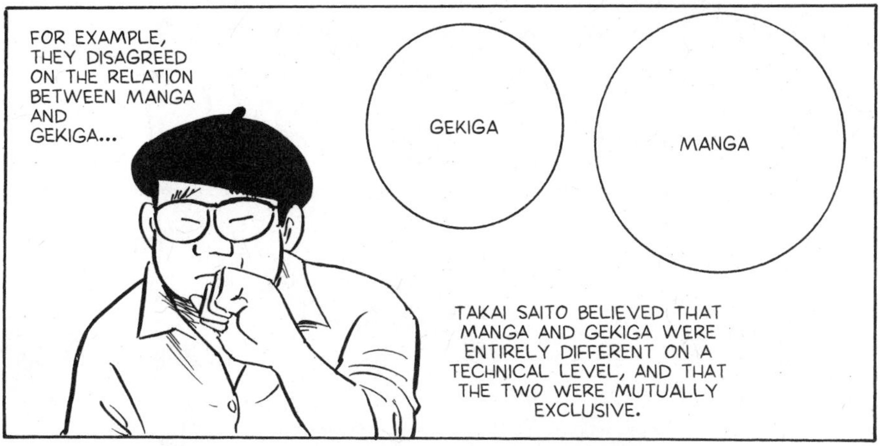
FOR EXAMPLE, THEY DISAGREED ON THE RELATION BETWEEN MANGA AND GEKIGA...
GEKIGA
MANGA
TAKAI SAITO BELIEVED THAT MANGA AND GEKIGA WERE ENTIRELY DIFFERENT ON A TECHNICAL LEVEL, AND THAT THE TWO WERE MUTUALLY EXCLUSIVE.

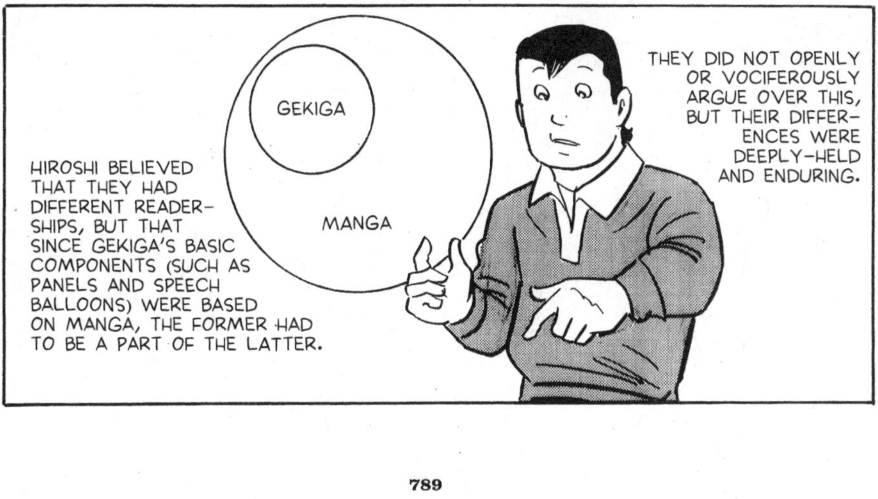
GEKIGA
MANGA
HIROSHI BELIEVED THAT THEY HAD DIFFERENT READER-SHIPS, BUT THAT SINCE GEKIGA'S BASIC COMPONENTS (SUCH AS PANELS AND SPEECH BALLOONS) WERE BASED ON MANGA, THE FORMER HAD TO BE A PART OF THE LATTER.
THEY DID NOT OPENLY OR VOCIFEROUSLY ARGUE OVER THIS, BUT THEIR DIFFER-ENCES WERE DEEPLY-HELD AND ENDURING.

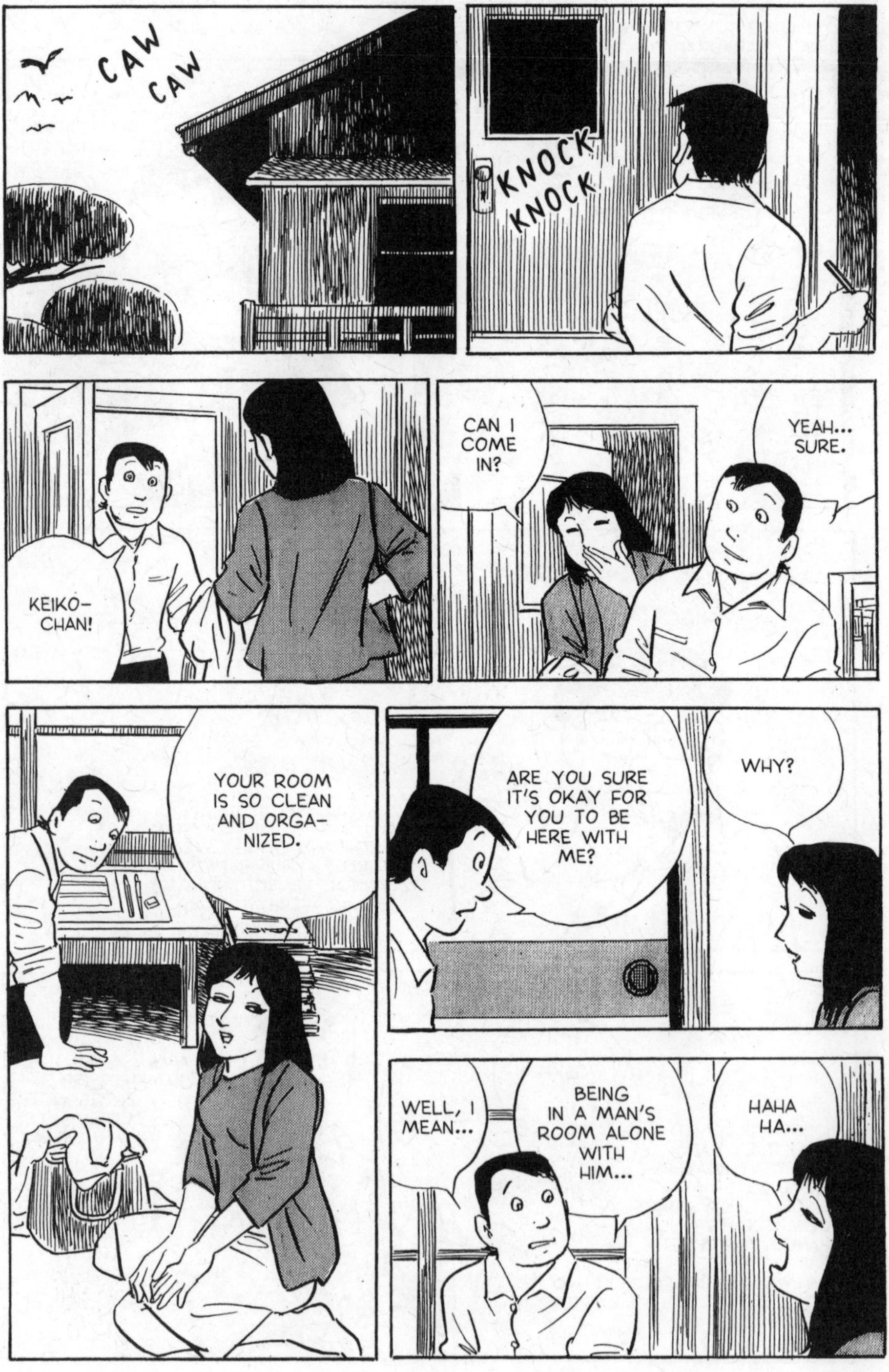
CAW CAW
KNOCK KNOCK
KEIKO-CHAN!
CAN I COME IN?
YEAH... SURE.
YOUR ROOM IS SO CLEAN AND ORGA-NIZED.
ARE YOU SURE IT'S OKAY FOR YOU TO BE HERE WITH ME?
WHY?
WELL, I MEAN...
BEING IN A MAN'S ROOM ALONE WITH HIM...
HAHA HA...

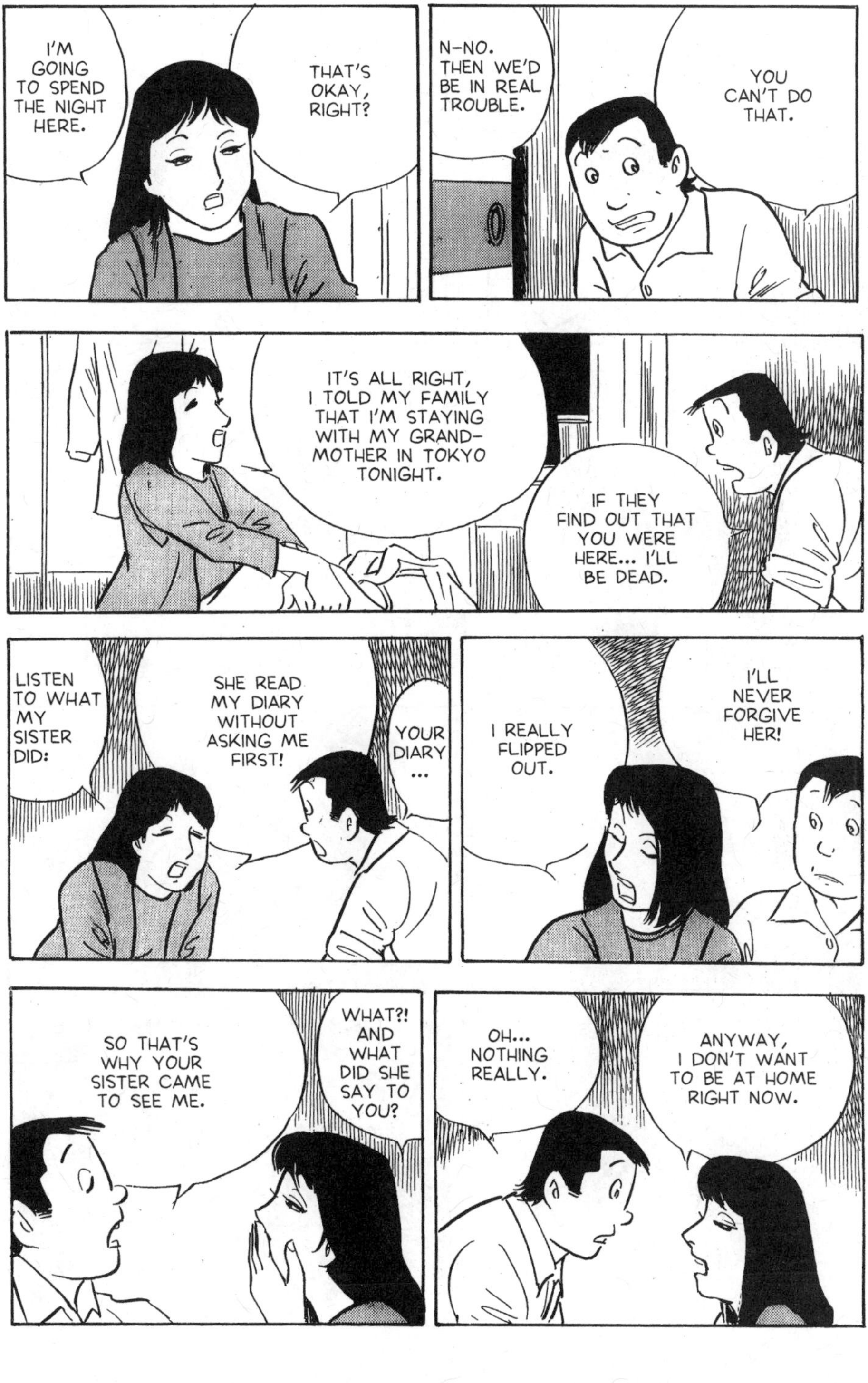
I'M GOING TO SPEND THE NIGHT HERE.
THAT'S OKAY, RIGHT?
N-NO. THEN WE'D BE IN REAL TROUBLE.
YOU CAN'T DO THAT.
IT'S ALL RIGHT, I TOLD MY FAMILY THAT I'M STAYING WITH MY GRAND-MOTHER IN TOKYO TONIGHT.
IF THEY FIND OUT THAT YOU WERE HERE... I'LL BE DEAD.
LISTEN TO WHAT MY SISTER DID:
SHE READ MY DIARY WITHOUT ASKING ME FIRST!
YOUR DIARY...
I REALLY FLIPPED OUT.
I'LL NEVER FORGIVE HER!
SO THAT'S WHY YOUR SISTER CAME TO SEE ME.
WHAT?! AND WHAT DID SHE SAY TO YOU?
OH... NOTHING REALLY.
ANYWAY, I DON'T WANT TO BE AT HOME RIGHT NOW.

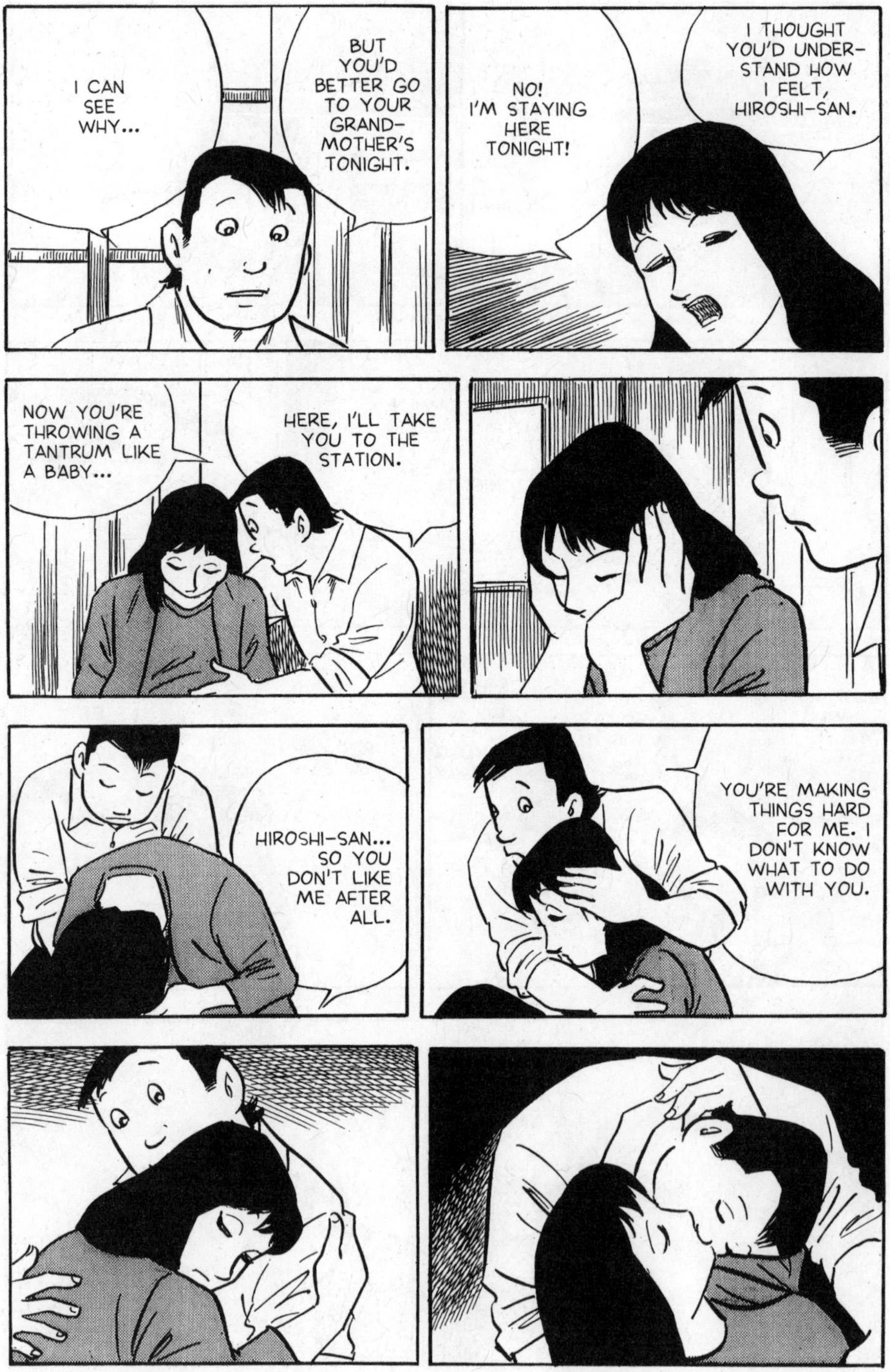
I CAN SEE WHY...
BUT YOU'D BETTER GO TO YOUR GRAND-MOTHER'S TONIGHT.
NO! I'M STAYING HERE TONIGHT!
I THOUGHT YOU'D UNDER-STAND HOW I FELT, HIROSHI-SAN.
NOW YOU'RE THROWING A TANTRUM LIKE A BABY...
HERE, I'LL TAKE YOU TO THE STATION.
HIROSHI-SAN... SO YOU DON'T LIKE ME AFTER ALL.
YOU'RE MAKING THINGS HARD FOR ME. I DON'T KNOW WHAT TO DO WITH YOU.

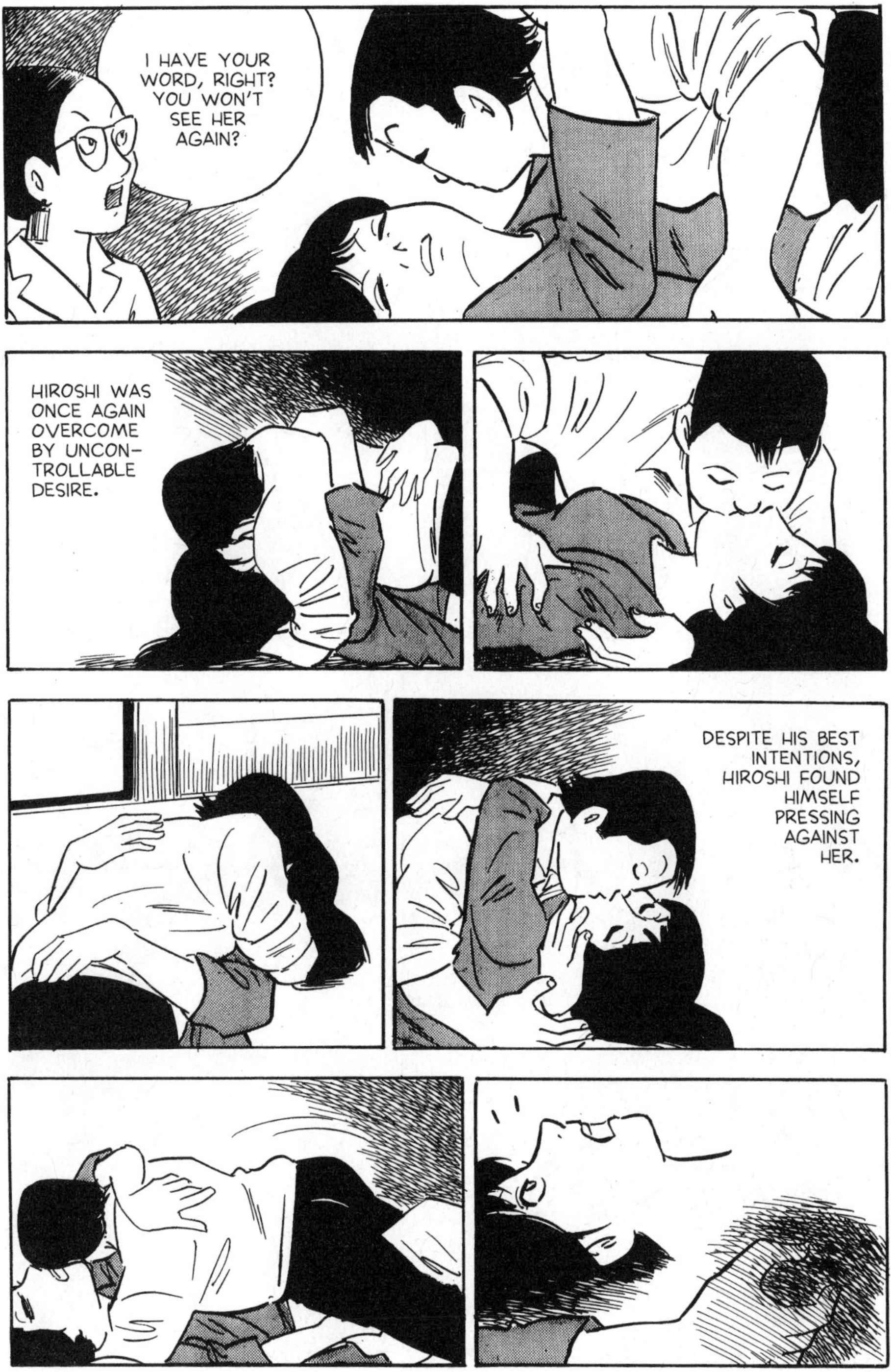
I HAVE YOUR WORD, RIGHT? YOU WON'T SEE HER AGAIN?
HIROSHI WAS ONCE AGAIN OVERCOME BY UNCON-TROLLABLE DESIRE.
DESPITE HIS BEST INTENTIONS, HIROSHI FOUND HIMSELF PRESSING AGAINST HER.

AH!

HEY, WHAT'S THIS HARD THING IN YOUR POCKET?

UH...

IT'S... IT'S A PIPE...

I'VE STARTED SMOKING ONE RECENTLY...

HE DIDN'T KNOW IF KEIKO KNEW THAT HE WAS LYING...

BUT SHE DIDN'T SAY ANYTHING EITHER WAY.

HIROSHI ALREADY FELT DISCOURAGED.

SO YOU'LL GO TO YOUR GRAND-MOTHER'S, THEN?

YES... I WILL.

国分寺駅
KOKUBUNJI STATION

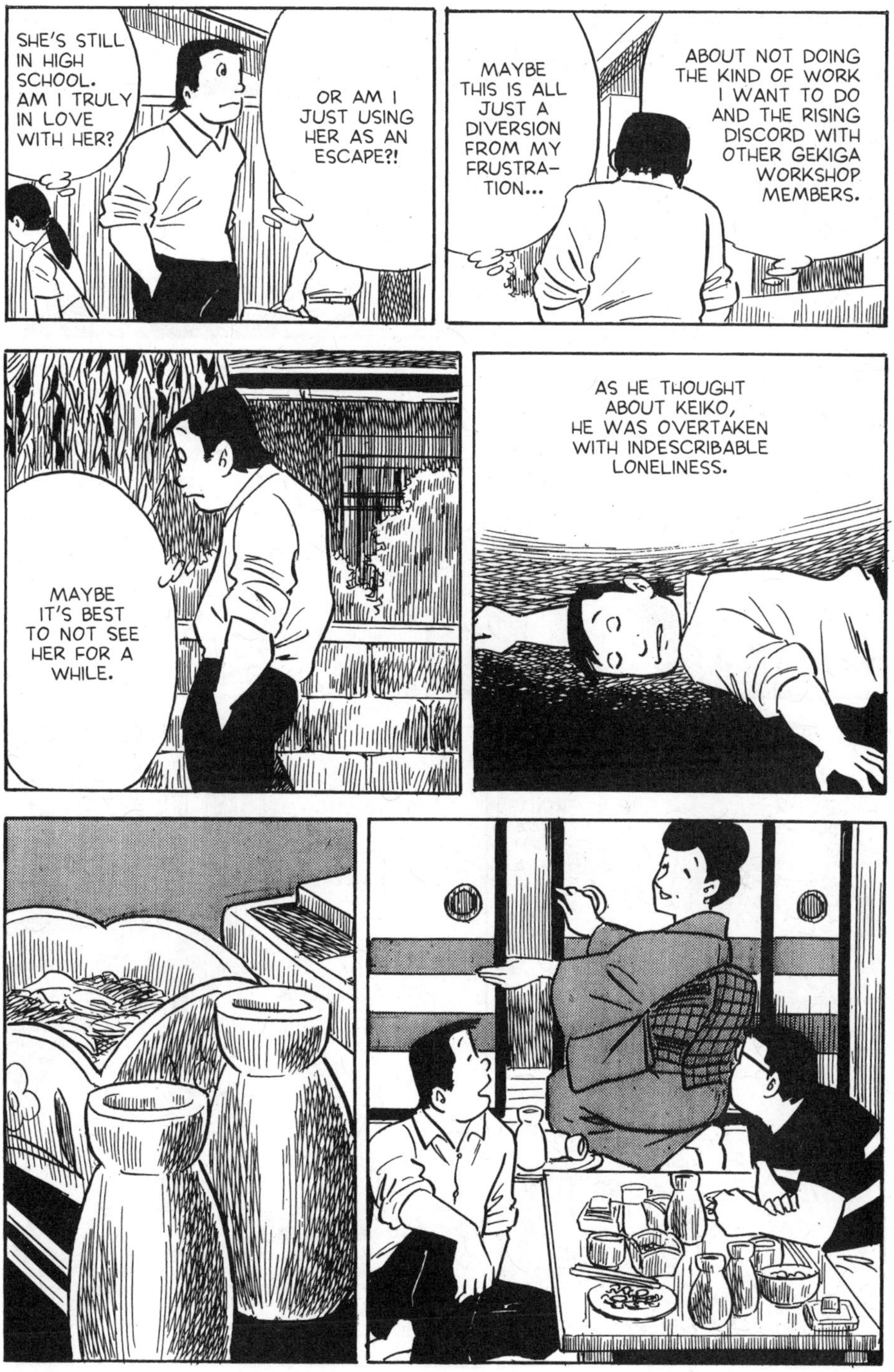
SHE'S STILL IN HIGH SCHOOL. AM I TRULY IN LOVE WITH HER?
OR AM I JUST USING HER AS AN ESCAPE?!
MAYBE THIS IS ALL JUST A DIVERSION FROM MY FRUSTRATION...
ABOUT NOT DOING THE KIND OF WORK I WANT TO DO AND THE RISING DISCORD WITH OTHER GEKIGA WORKSHOP MEMBERS.
MAYBE IT'S BEST TO NOT SEE HER FOR A WHILE.
AS HE THOUGHT ABOUT KEIKO, HE WAS OVERTAKEN WITH INDESCRIBABLE LONELINESS.

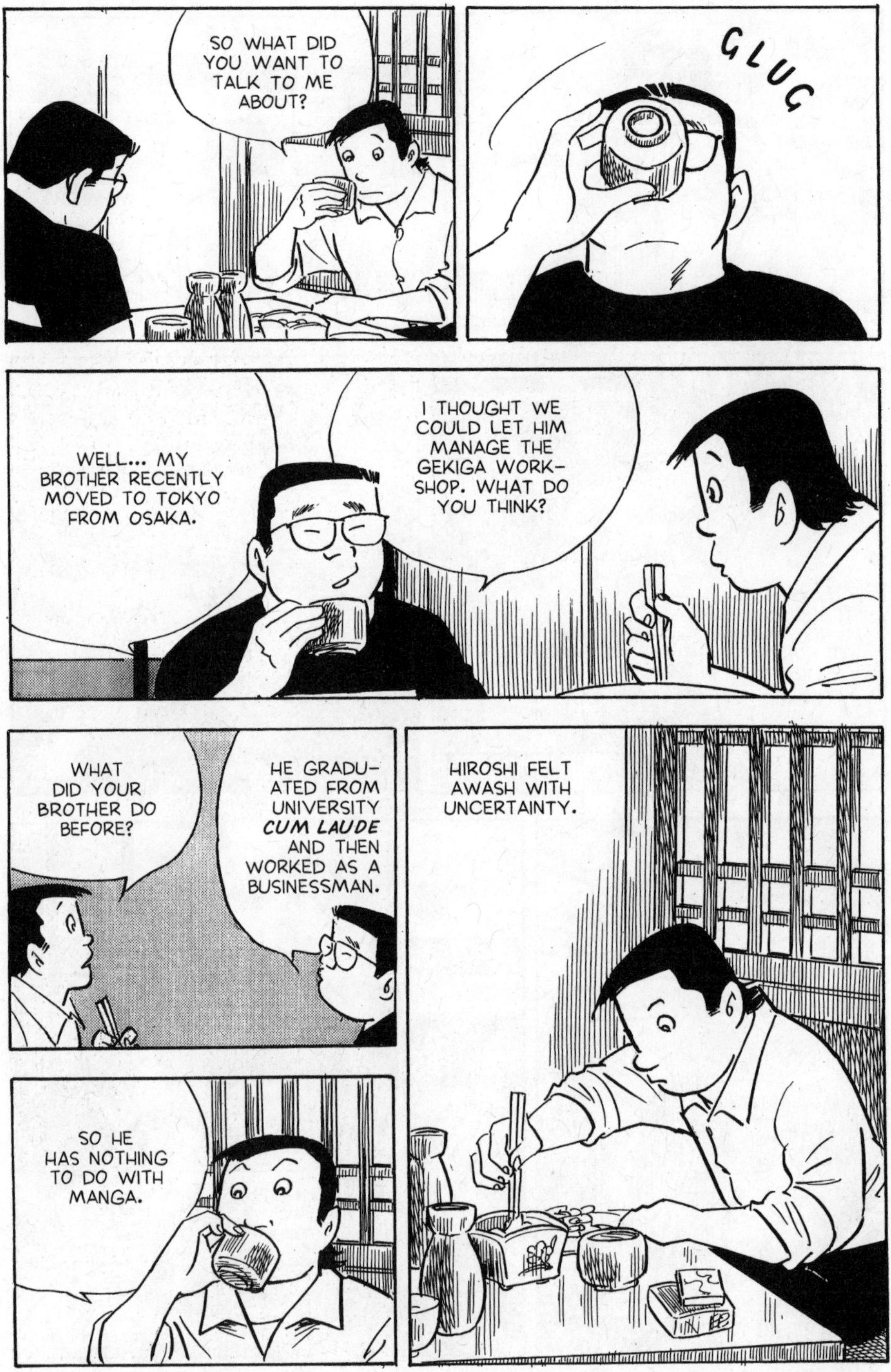
SO WHAT DID YOU WANT TO TALK TO ME ABOUT?
GLUG
WELL... MY BROTHER RECENTLY MOVED TO TOKYO FROM OSAKA.
I THOUGHT WE COULD LET HIM MANAGE THE GEKIGA WORK-SHOP. WHAT DO YOU THINK?
WHAT DID YOUR BROTHER DO BEFORE?
HE GRADU-ATED FROM UNIVERSITY *CUM LAUDE* AND THEN WORKED AS A BUSINESSMAN.
SO HE HAS NOTHING TO DO WITH MANGA.
HIROSHI FELT AWASH WITH UNCERTAINTY.

THE QUICK DISSOLUTION OF THE GEKIGA WORKSHOP

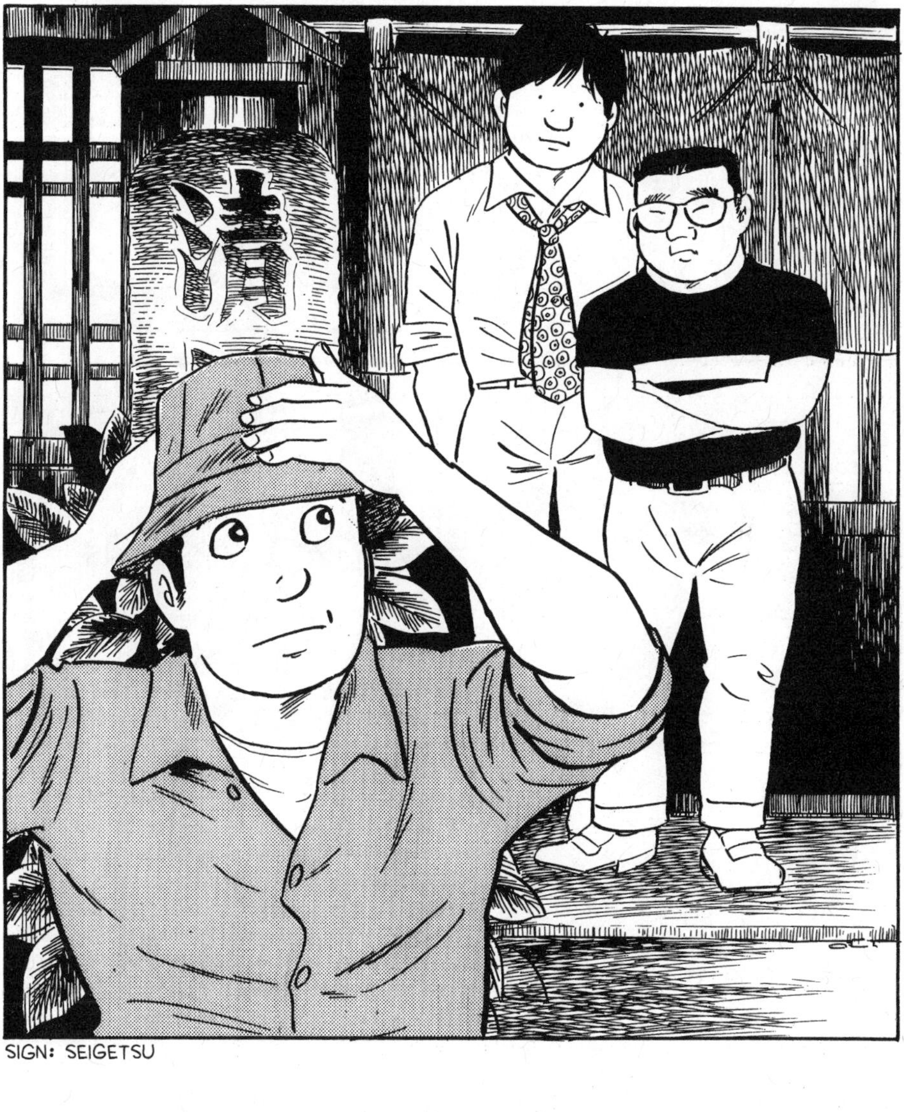

SIGN: SEIGETSU

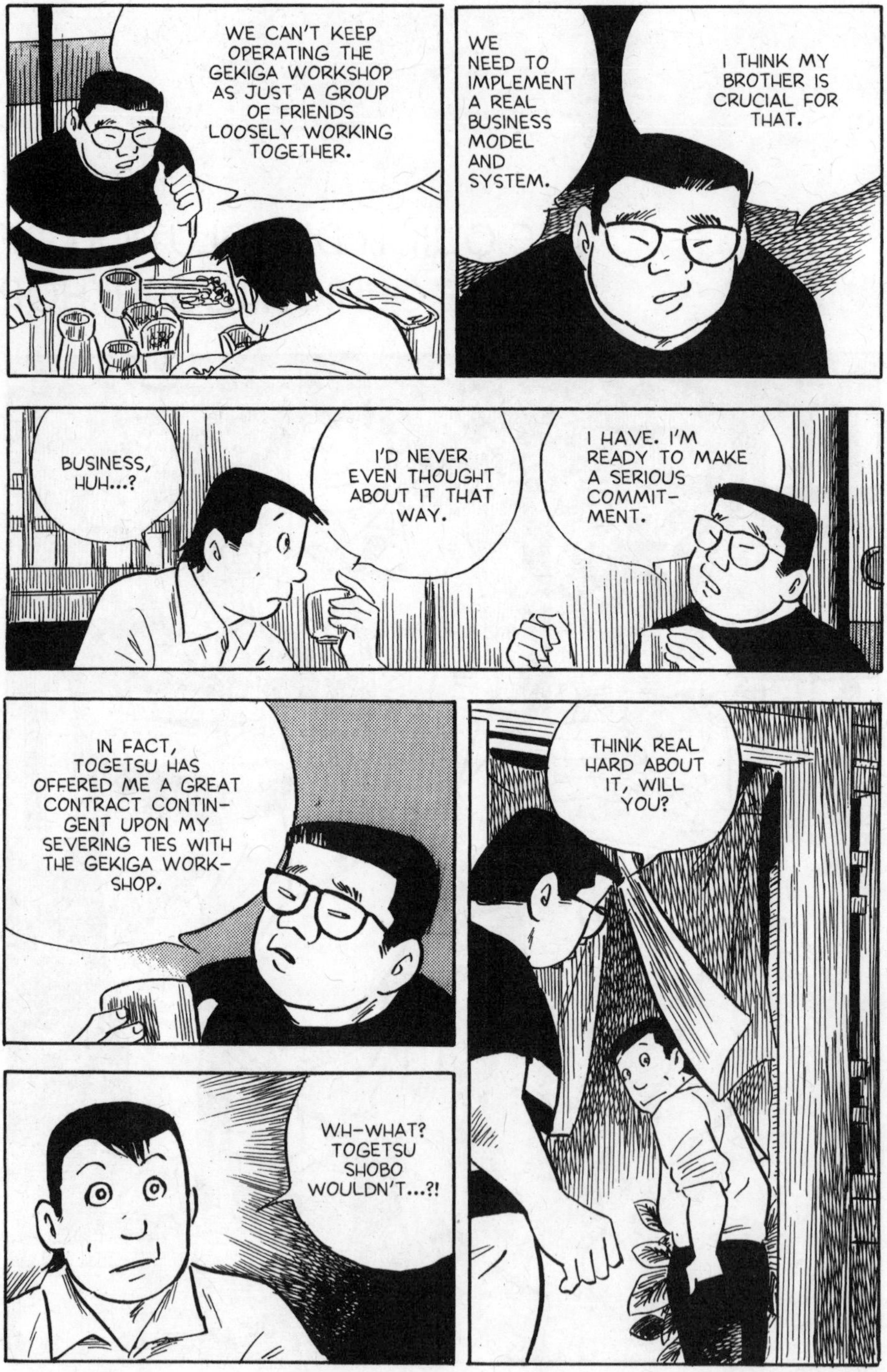
WE CAN'T KEEP OPERATING THE GEKIGA WORKSHOP AS JUST A GROUP OF FRIENDS LOOSELY WORKING TOGETHER.
WE NEED TO IMPLEMENT A REAL BUSINESS MODEL AND SYSTEM.
I THINK MY BROTHER IS CRUCIAL FOR THAT.
BUSINESS, HUH...?
I'D NEVER EVEN THOUGHT ABOUT IT THAT WAY.
I HAVE. I'M READY TO MAKE A SERIOUS COMMIT-MENT.
IN FACT, TOGETSU HAS OFFERED ME A GREAT CONTRACT CONTIN-GENT UPON MY SEVERING TIES WITH THE GEKIGA WORK-SHOP.
WH-WHAT? TOGETSU SHOBO WOULDN'T...?!
THINK REAL HARD ABOUT IT, WILL YOU?

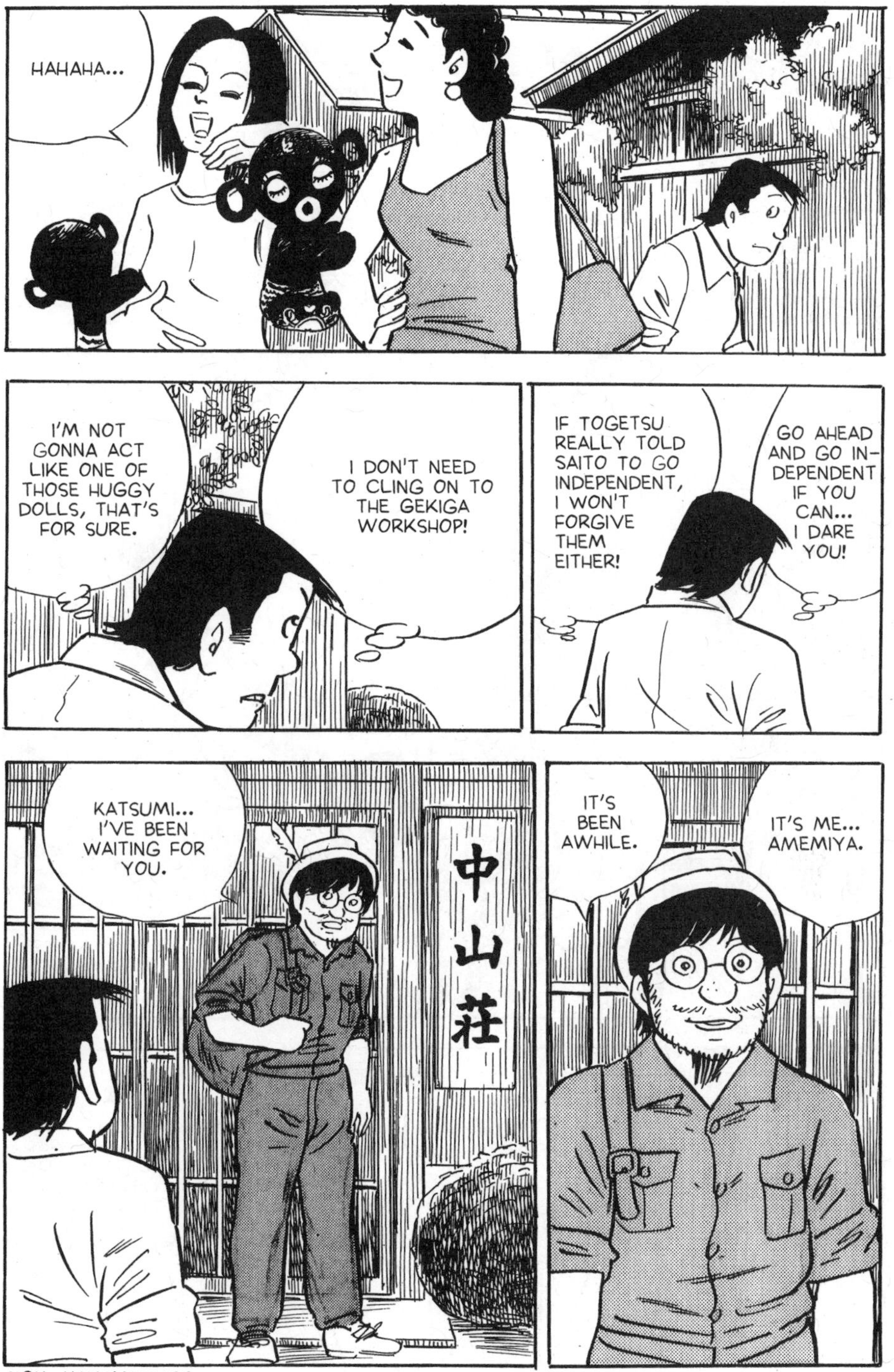
HAHAHA...
I'M NOT GONNA ACT LIKE ONE OF THOSE HUGGY DOLLS, THAT'S FOR SURE.
I DON'T NEED TO CLING ON TO THE GEKIGA WORKSHOP!
IF TOGETSU REALLY TOLD SAITO TO GO INDEPENDENT, I WON'T FORGIVE THEM EITHER!
GO AHEAD AND GO INDEPENDENT IF YOU CAN... I DARE YOU!
KATSUMI... I'VE BEEN WAITING FOR YOU.
中山荘
IT'S BEEN AWHILE.
IT'S ME... AMEMIYA.
SIGN: NAKAYAMASO

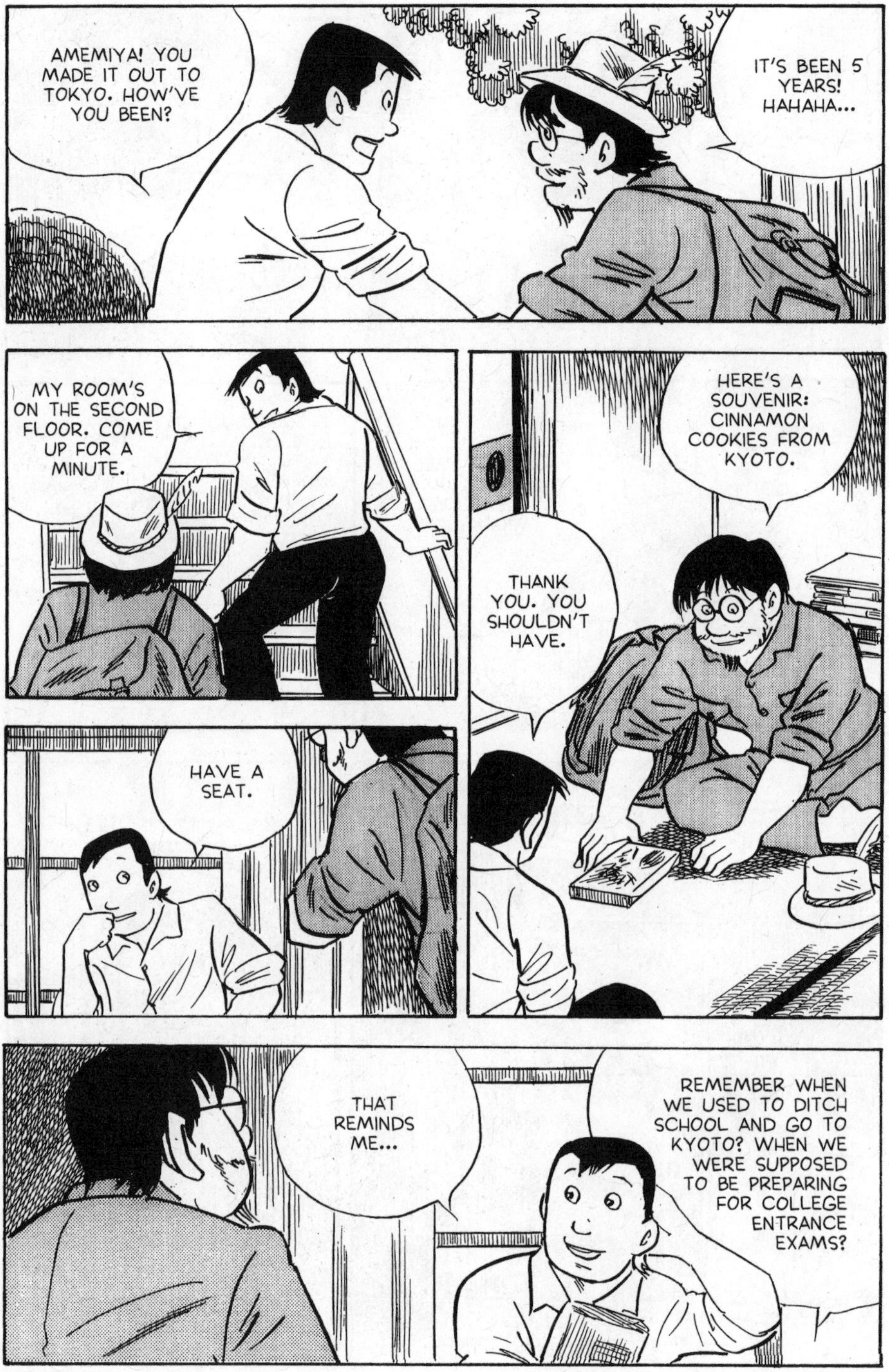
AMEMIYA! YOU MADE IT OUT TO TOKYO. HOW'VE YOU BEEN?
IT'S BEEN 5 YEARS! HAHAHA...
MY ROOM'S ON THE SECOND FLOOR. COME UP FOR A MINUTE.
HERE'S A SOUVENIR: CINNAMON COOKIES FROM KYOTO.
THANK YOU. YOU SHOULDN'T HAVE.
HAVE A SEAT.
THAT REMINDS ME...
REMEMBER WHEN WE USED TO DITCH SCHOOL AND GO TO KYOTO? WHEN WE WERE SUPPOSED TO BE PREPARING FOR COLLEGE ENTRANCE EXAMS?

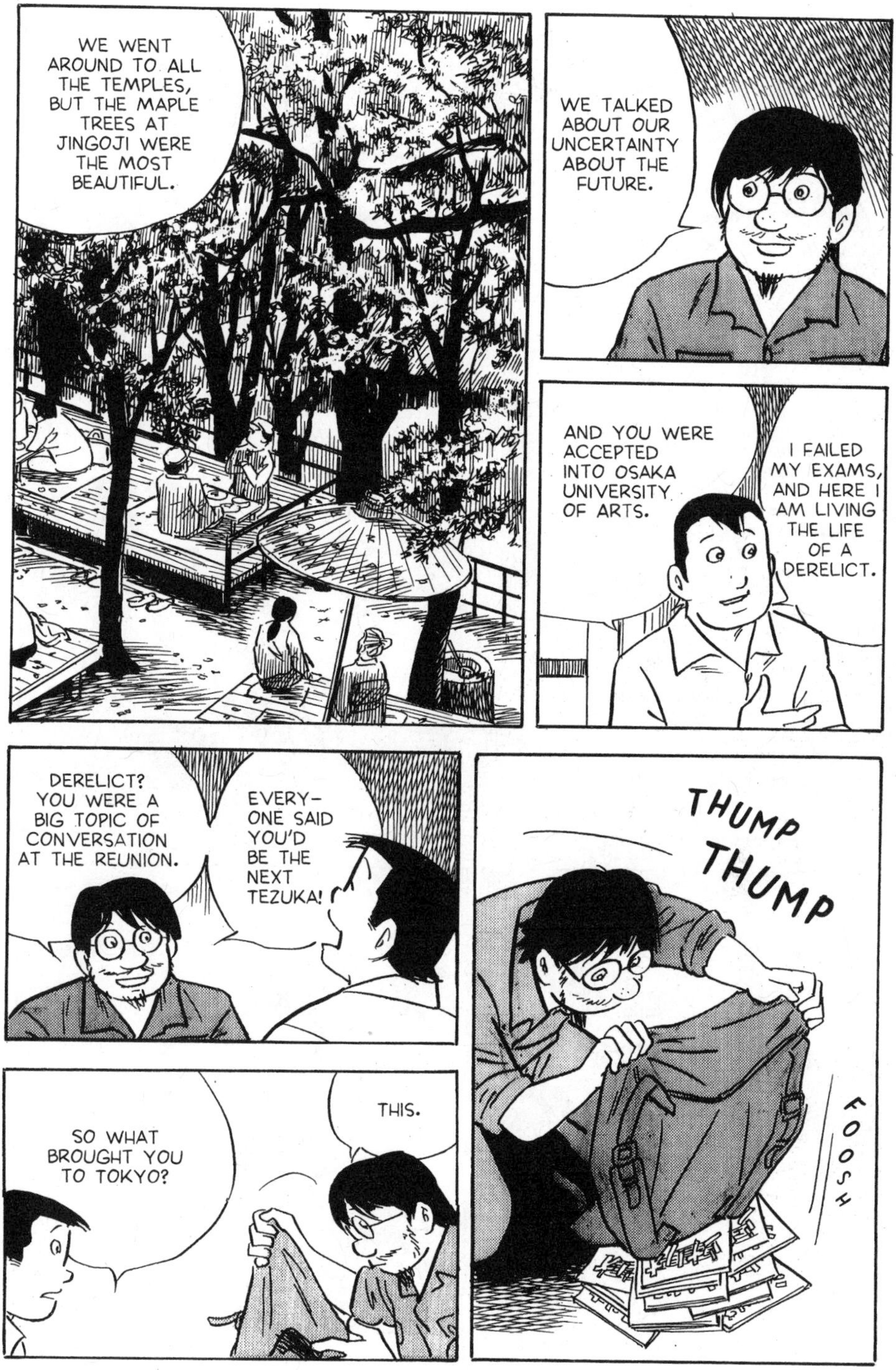
WE WENT AROUND TO ALL THE TEMPLES, BUT THE MAPLE TREES AT JINGOJI WERE THE MOST BEAUTIFUL.
WE TALKED ABOUT OUR UNCERTAINTY ABOUT THE FUTURE.
AND YOU WERE ACCEPTED INTO OSAKA UNIVERSITY OF ARTS.
I FAILED MY EXAMS, AND HERE I AM LIVING THE LIFE OF A DERELICT.
DERELICT? YOU WERE A BIG TOPIC OF CONVERSATION AT THE REUNION.
EVERY-ONE SAID YOU'D BE THE NEXT TEZUKA!
SO WHAT BROUGHT YOU TO TOKYO?
THIS.
THUMP
THUMP
FOOSH

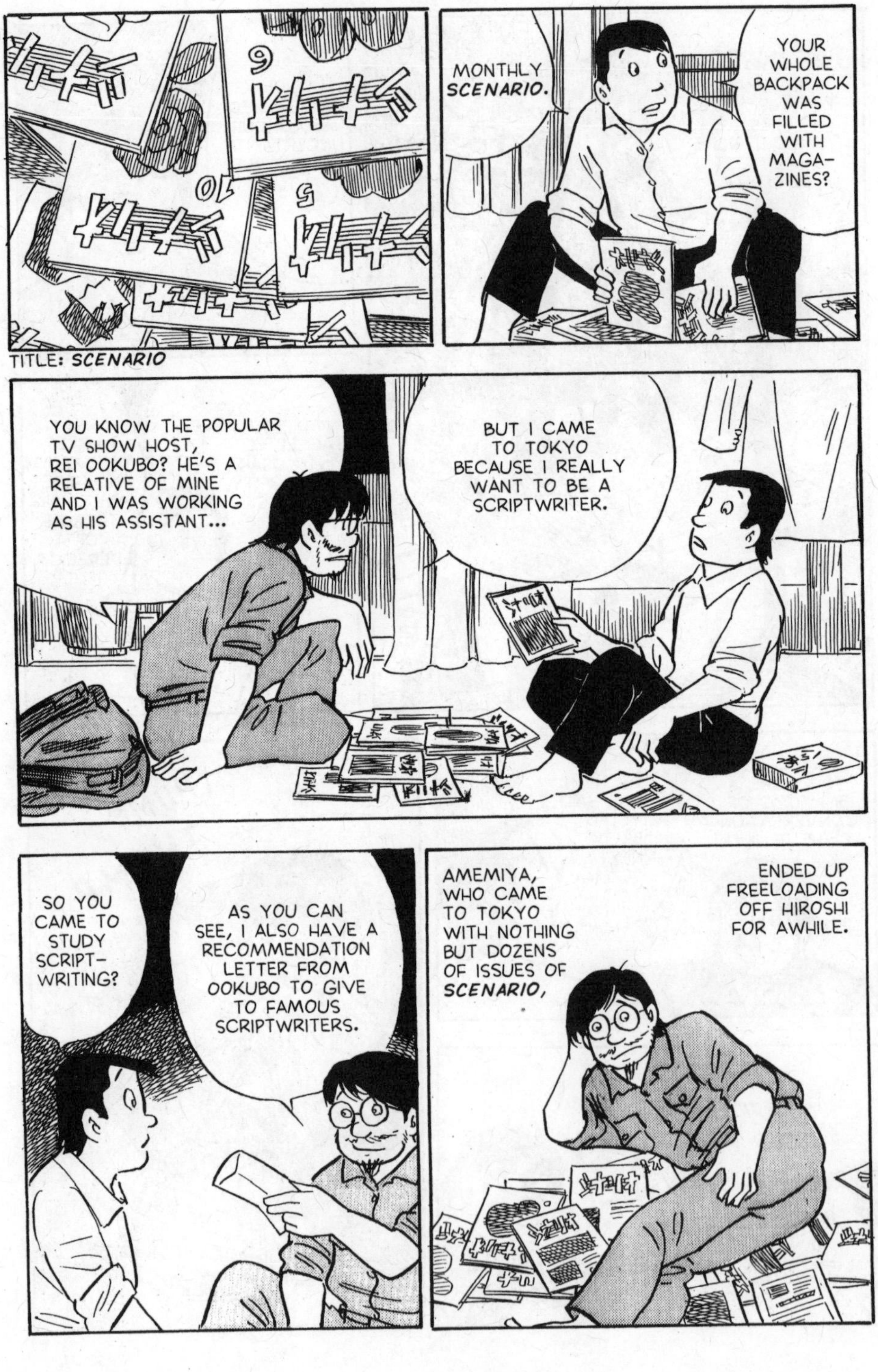

MONTHLY SCENARIO.
YOUR WHOLE BACKPACK WAS FILLED WITH MAGA-ZINES?
TITLE: SCENARIO
YOU KNOW THE POPULAR TV SHOW HOST, REI OOKUBO? HE'S A RELATIVE OF MINE AND I WAS WORKING AS HIS ASSISTANT...
BUT I CAME TO TOKYO BECAUSE I REALLY WANT TO BE A SCRIPTWRITER.
SO YOU CAME TO STUDY SCRIPT-WRITING?
AS YOU CAN SEE, I ALSO HAVE A RECOMMENDATION LETTER FROM OOKUBO TO GIVE TO FAMOUS SCRIPTWRITERS.
AMEMIYA, WHO CAME TO TOKYO WITH NOTHING BUT DOZENS OF ISSUES OF SCENARIO,
ENDED UP FREELOADING OFF HIROSHI FOR AWHILE.

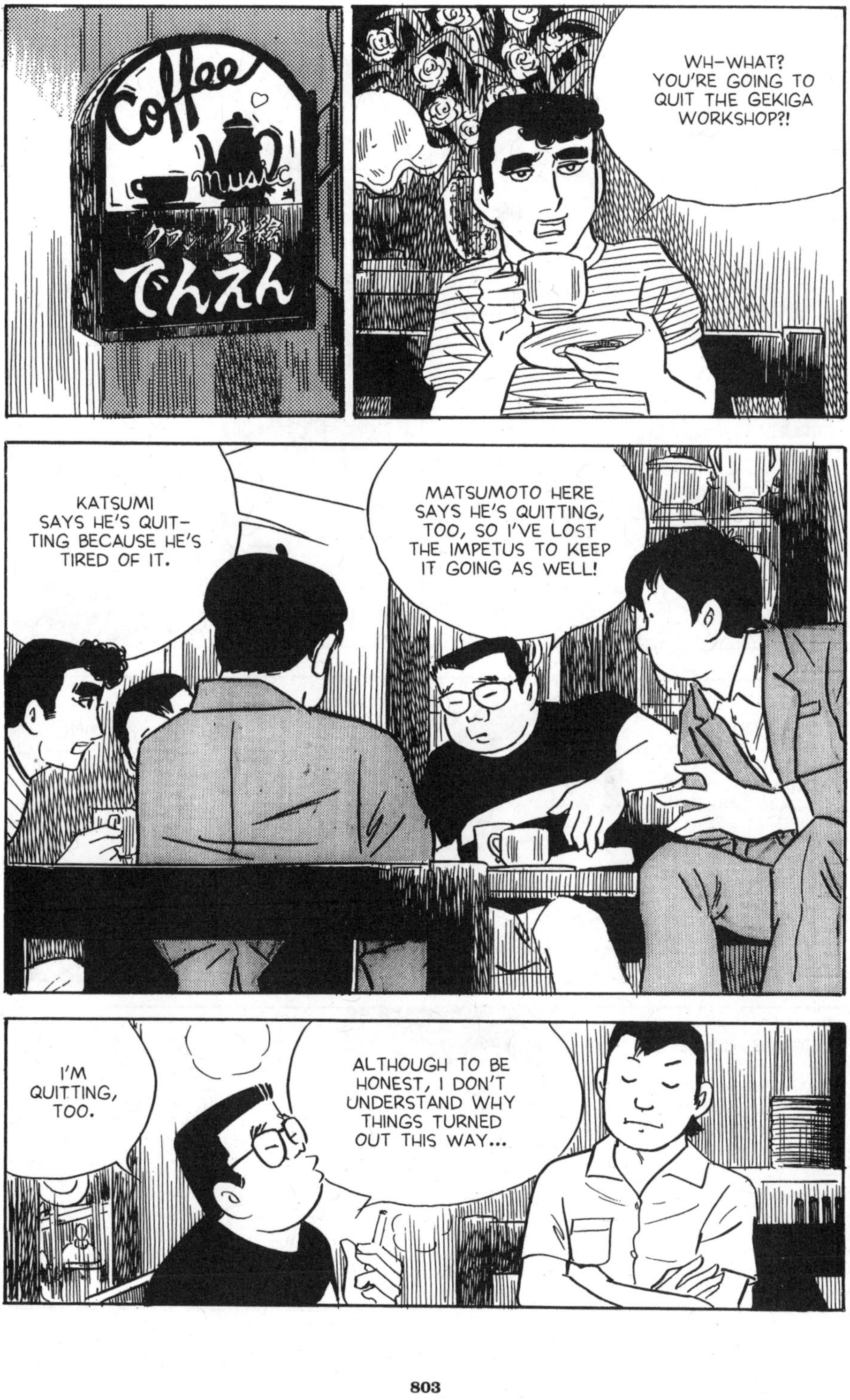
Coffee
music
でんえん
WH-WHAT? YOU'RE GOING TO QUIT THE GEKIGA WORKSHOP?!
KATSUMI SAYS HE'S QUIT-TING BECAUSE HE'S TIRED OF IT.
MATSUMOTO HERE SAYS HE'S QUITTING, TOO, SO I'VE LOST THE IMPETUS TO KEEP IT GOING AS WELL!
I'M QUITTING, TOO.
ALTHOUGH TO BE HONEST, I DON'T UNDERSTAND WHY THINGS TURNED OUT THIS WAY...

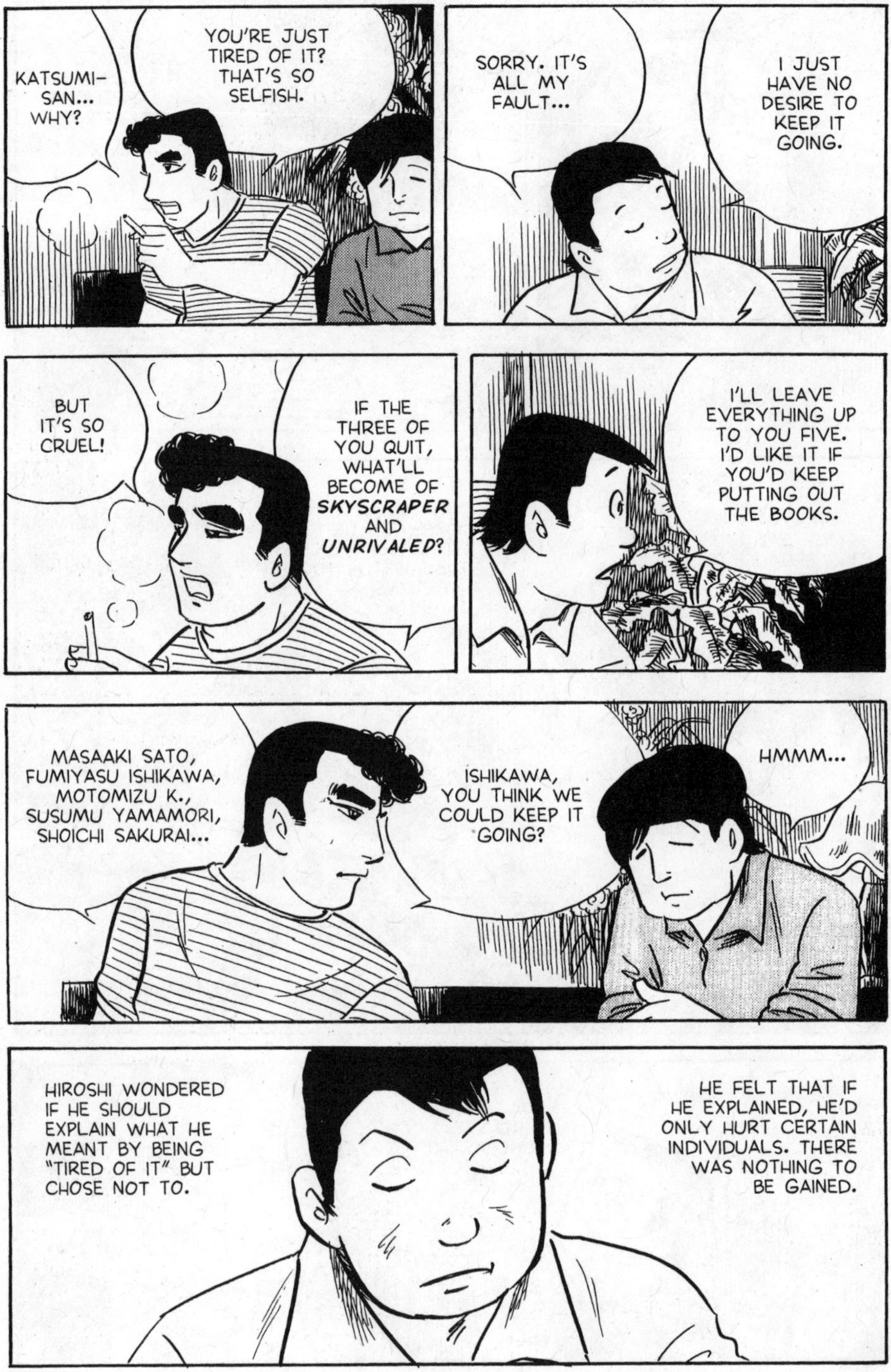
KATSUMI-SAN... WHY?
YOU'RE JUST TIRED OF IT? THAT'S SO SELFISH.
SORRY. IT'S ALL MY FAULT...
I JUST HAVE NO DESIRE TO KEEP IT GOING.
BUT IT'S SO CRUEL!
IF THE THREE OF YOU QUIT, WHAT'LL BECOME OF SKYSCRAPER AND UNRIVALED?
I'LL LEAVE EVERYTHING UP TO YOU FIVE. I'D LIKE IT IF YOU'D KEEP PUTTING OUT THE BOOKS.
MASAAKI SATO, FUMIYASU ISHIKAWA, MOTOMIZU K., SUSUMU YAMAMORI, SHOICHI SAKURAI...
ISHIKAWA, YOU THINK WE COULD KEEP IT GOING?
HMMM...
HIROSHI WONDERED IF HE SHOULD EXPLAIN WHAT HE MEANT BY BEING "TIRED OF IT" BUT CHOSE NOT TO.
HE FELT THAT IF HE EXPLAINED, HE'D ONLY HURT CERTAIN INDIVIDUALS. THERE WAS NOTHING TO BE GAINED.

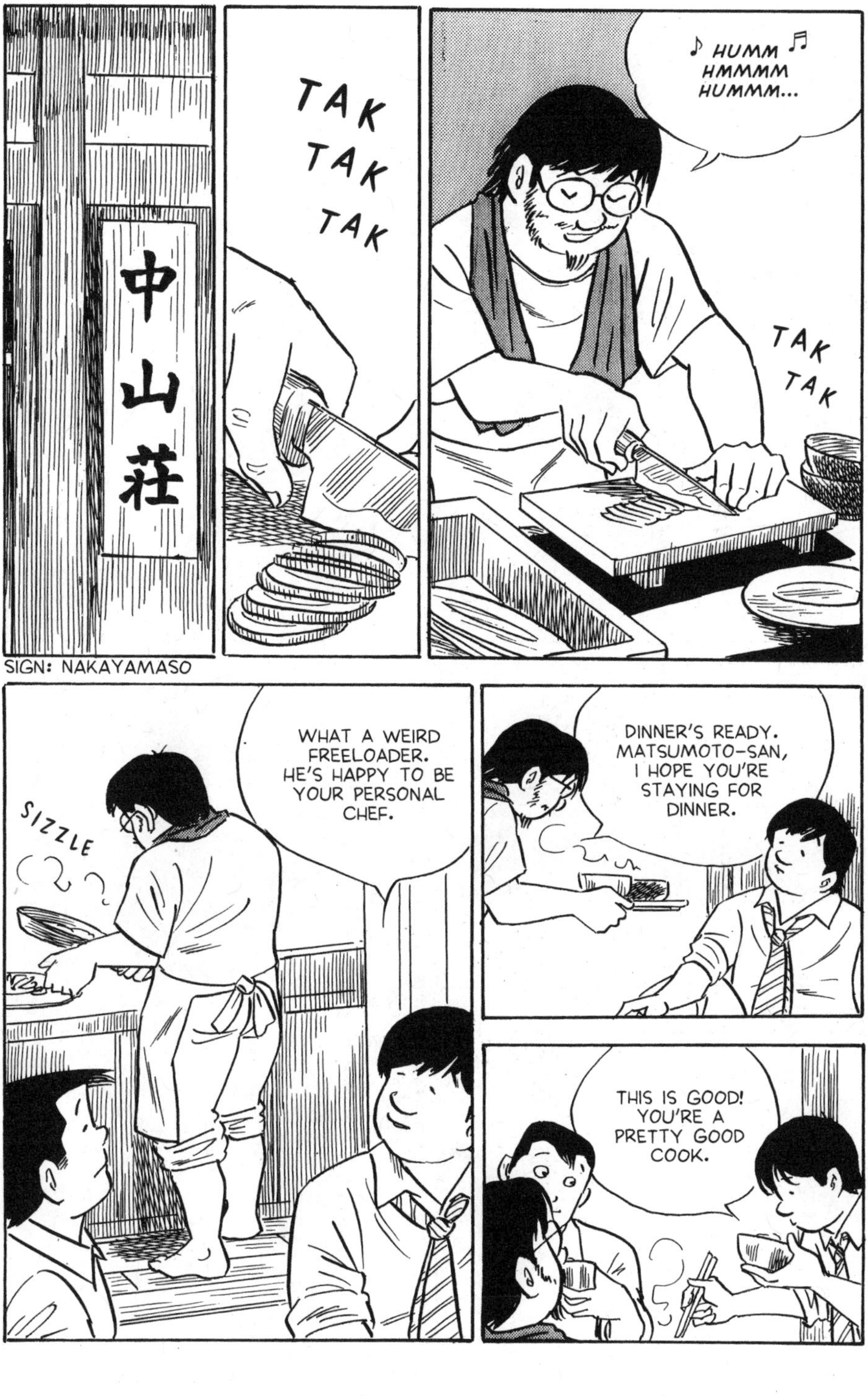
中山荘
SIGN: NAKAYAMASO
TAK TAK TAK
♪ HUMM ♫ HMMMM HUMMM...
TAK TAK
SIZZLE
WHAT A WEIRD FREELOADER. HE'S HAPPY TO BE YOUR PERSONAL CHEF.
DINNER'S READY. MATSUMOTO-SAN, I HOPE YOU'RE STAYING FOR DINNER.
THIS IS GOOD! YOU'RE A PRETTY GOOD COOK.

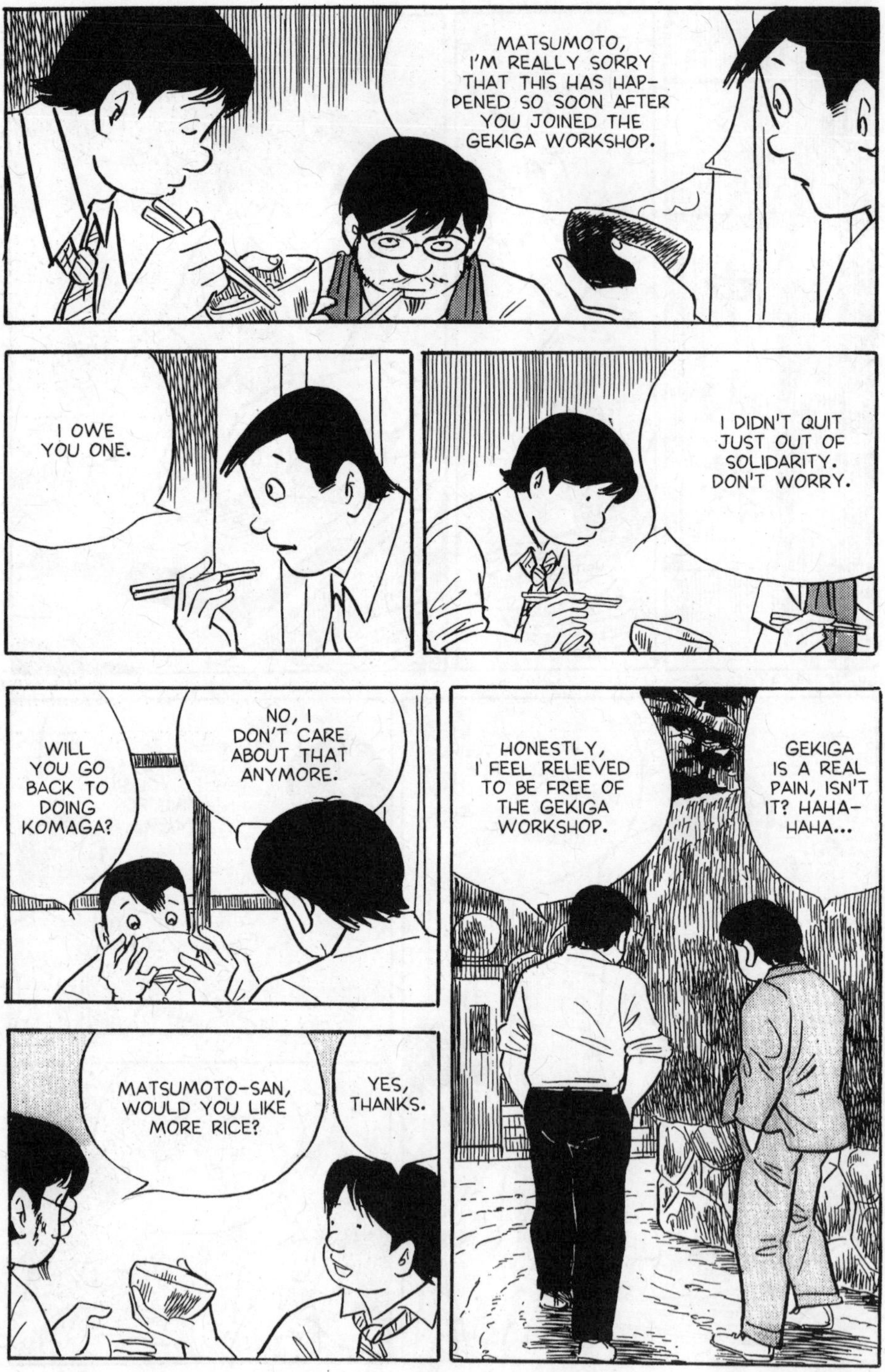
MATSUMOTO, I'M REALLY SORRY THAT THIS HAS HAP-PENED SO SOON AFTER YOU JOINED THE GEKIGA WORKSHOP.
I OWE YOU ONE.
I DIDN'T QUIT JUST OUT OF SOLIDARITY. DON'T WORRY.
WILL YOU GO BACK TO DOING KOMAGA?
NO, I DON'T CARE ABOUT THAT ANYMORE.
MATSUMOTO-SAN, WOULD YOU LIKE MORE RICE?
YES, THANKS.
HONESTLY, I FEEL RELIEVED TO BE FREE OF THE GEKIGA WORKSHOP.
GEKIGA IS A REAL PAIN, ISN'T IT? HAHA-HAHA...

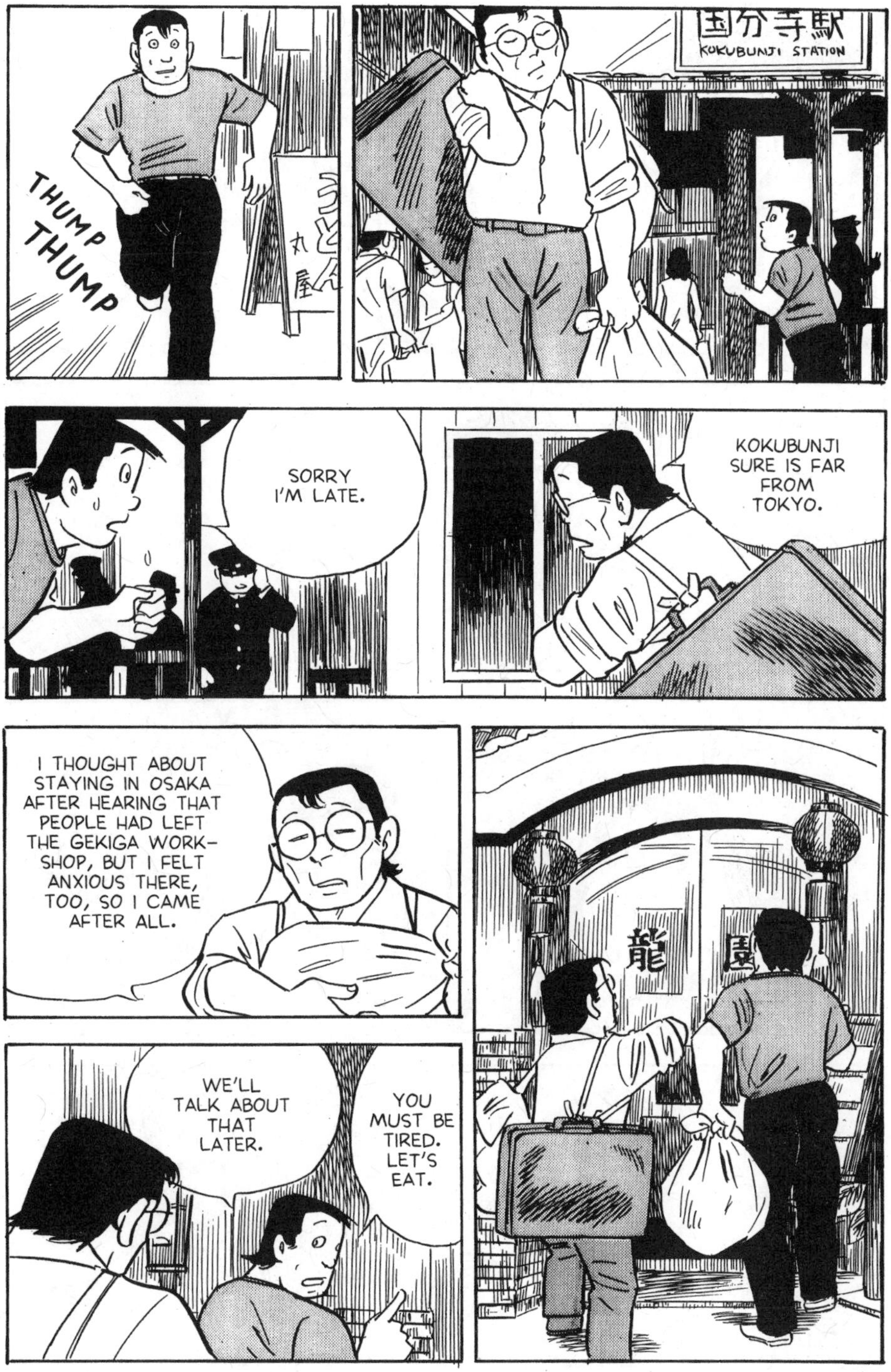
THUMP THUMP
うどん 丸屋
国分寺駅
KOKUBUNJI STATION
SORRY I'M LATE.
KOKUBUNJI SURE IS FAR FROM TOKYO.
I THOUGHT ABOUT STAYING IN OSAKA AFTER HEARING THAT PEOPLE HAD LEFT THE GEKIGA WORK-SHOP, BUT I FELT ANXIOUS THERE, TOO, SO I CAME AFTER ALL.
龍 園
WE'LL TALK ABOUT THAT LATER.
YOU MUST BE TIRED. LET'S EAT.

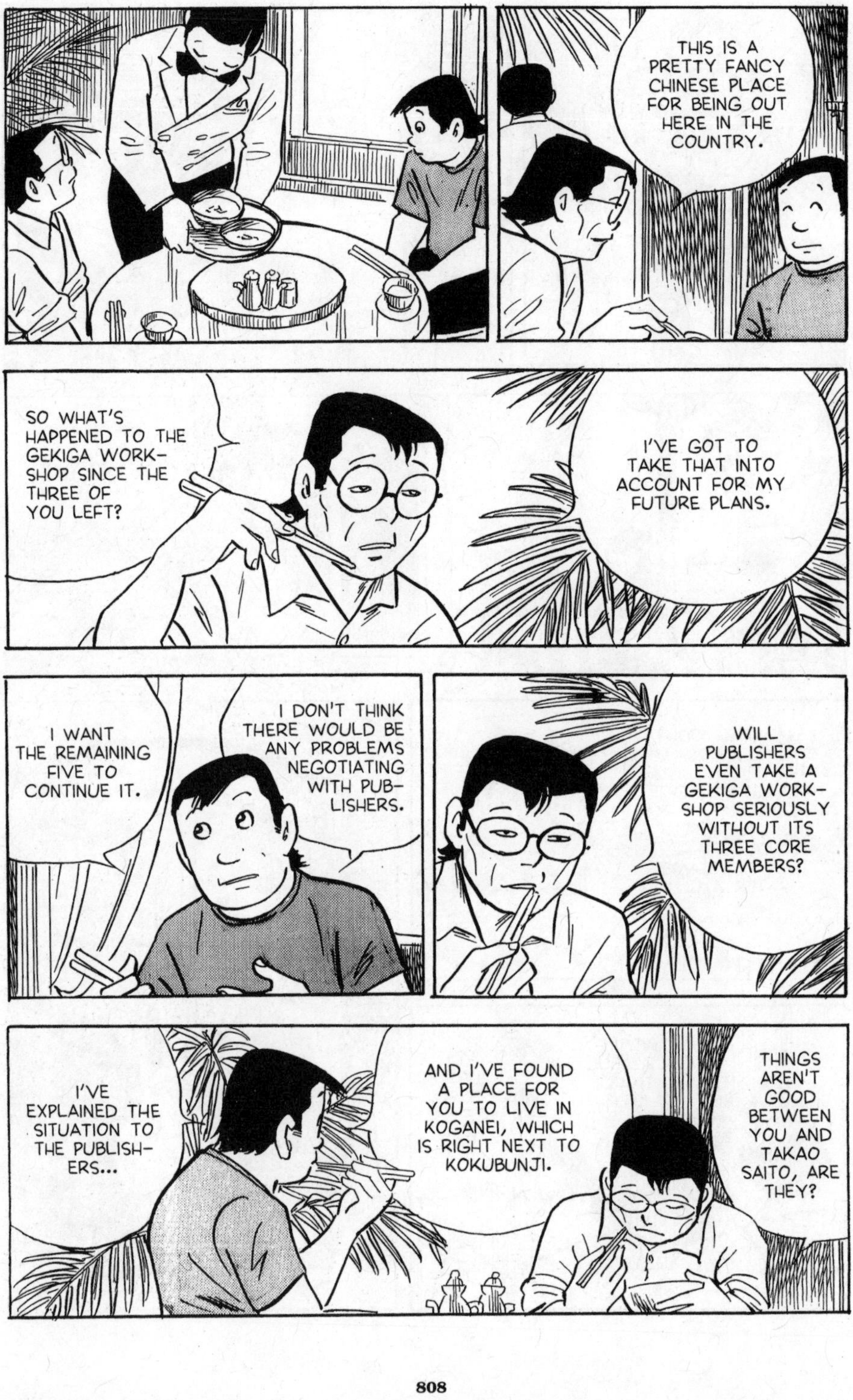
THIS IS A PRETTY FANCY CHINESE PLACE FOR BEING OUT HERE IN THE COUNTRY.
SO WHAT'S HAPPENED TO THE GEKIGA WORK-SHOP SINCE THE THREE OF YOU LEFT?
I'VE GOT TO TAKE THAT INTO ACCOUNT FOR MY FUTURE PLANS.
I WANT THE REMAINING FIVE TO CONTINUE IT.
I DON'T THINK THERE WOULD BE ANY PROBLEMS NEGOTIATING WITH PUB-LISHERS.
WILL PUBLISHERS EVEN TAKE A GEKIGA WORK-SHOP SERIOUSLY WITHOUT ITS THREE CORE MEMBERS?
I'VE EXPLAINED THE SITUATION TO THE PUBLISH-ERS...
AND I'VE FOUND A PLACE FOR YOU TO LIVE IN KOGANEI, WHICH IS RIGHT NEXT TO KOKUBUNJI.
THINGS AREN'T GOOD BETWEEN YOU AND TAKAO SAITO, ARE THEY?

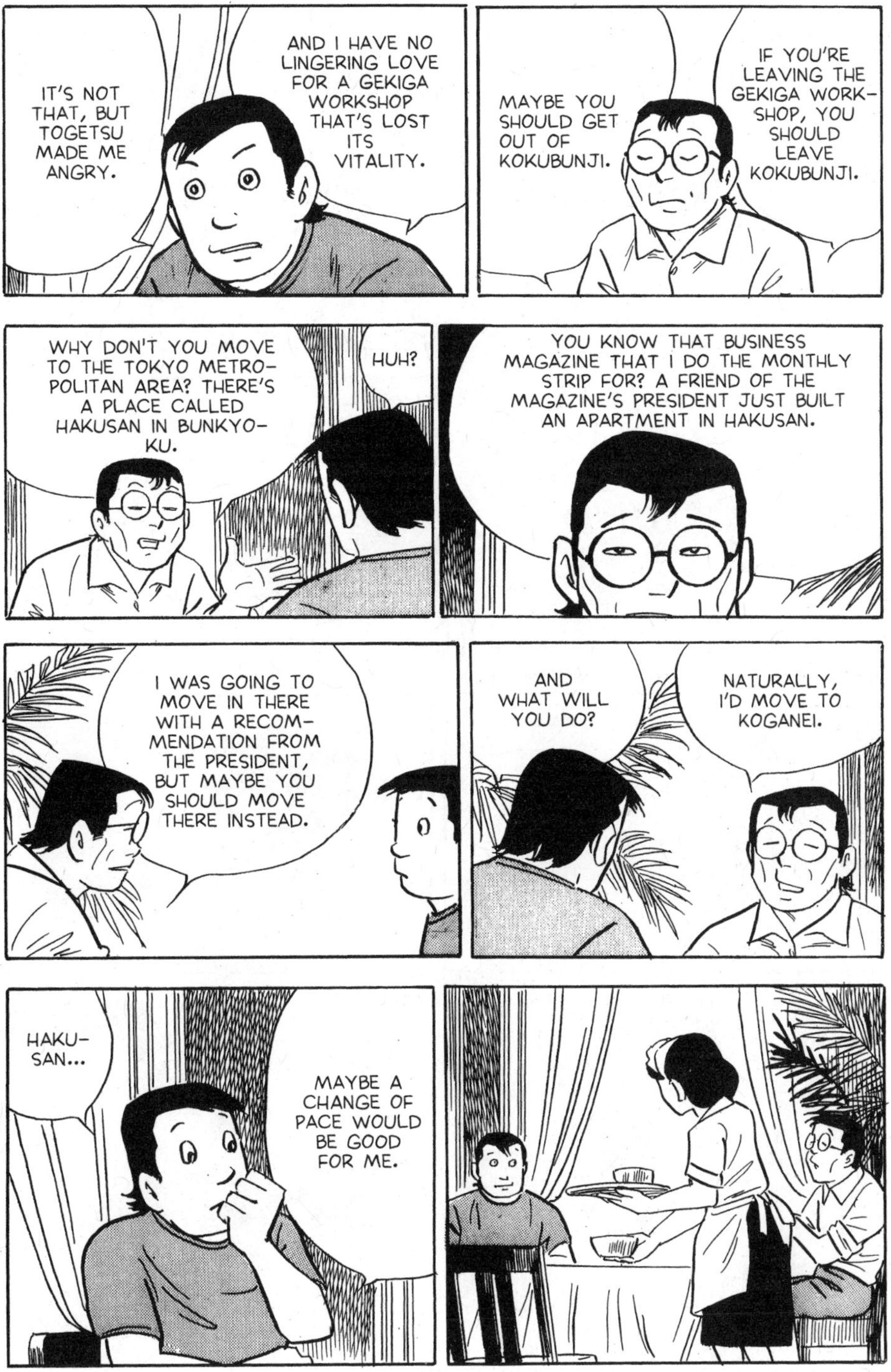

IT'S NOT THAT, BUT TOGETSU MADE ME ANGRY.
AND I HAVE NO LINGERING LOVE FOR A GEKIGA WORKSHOP THAT'S LOST ITS VITALITY.
MAYBE YOU SHOULD GET OUT OF KOKUBUNJI.
IF YOU'RE LEAVING THE GEKIGA WORK-SHOP, YOU SHOULD LEAVE KOKUBUNJI.
WHY DON'T YOU MOVE TO THE TOKYO METRO-POLITAN AREA? THERE'S A PLACE CALLED HAKUSAN IN BUNKYO-KU.
HUH?
YOU KNOW THAT BUSINESS MAGAZINE THAT I DO THE MONTHLY STRIP FOR? A FRIEND OF THE MAGAZINE'S PRESIDENT JUST BUILT AN APARTMENT IN HAKUSAN.
I WAS GOING TO MOVE IN THERE WITH A RECOM-MENDATION FROM THE PRESIDENT, BUT MAYBE YOU SHOULD MOVE THERE INSTEAD.
AND WHAT WILL YOU DO?
NATURALLY, I'D MOVE TO KOGANEI.
HAKU-SAN...
MAYBE A CHANGE OF PACE WOULD BE GOOD FOR ME.

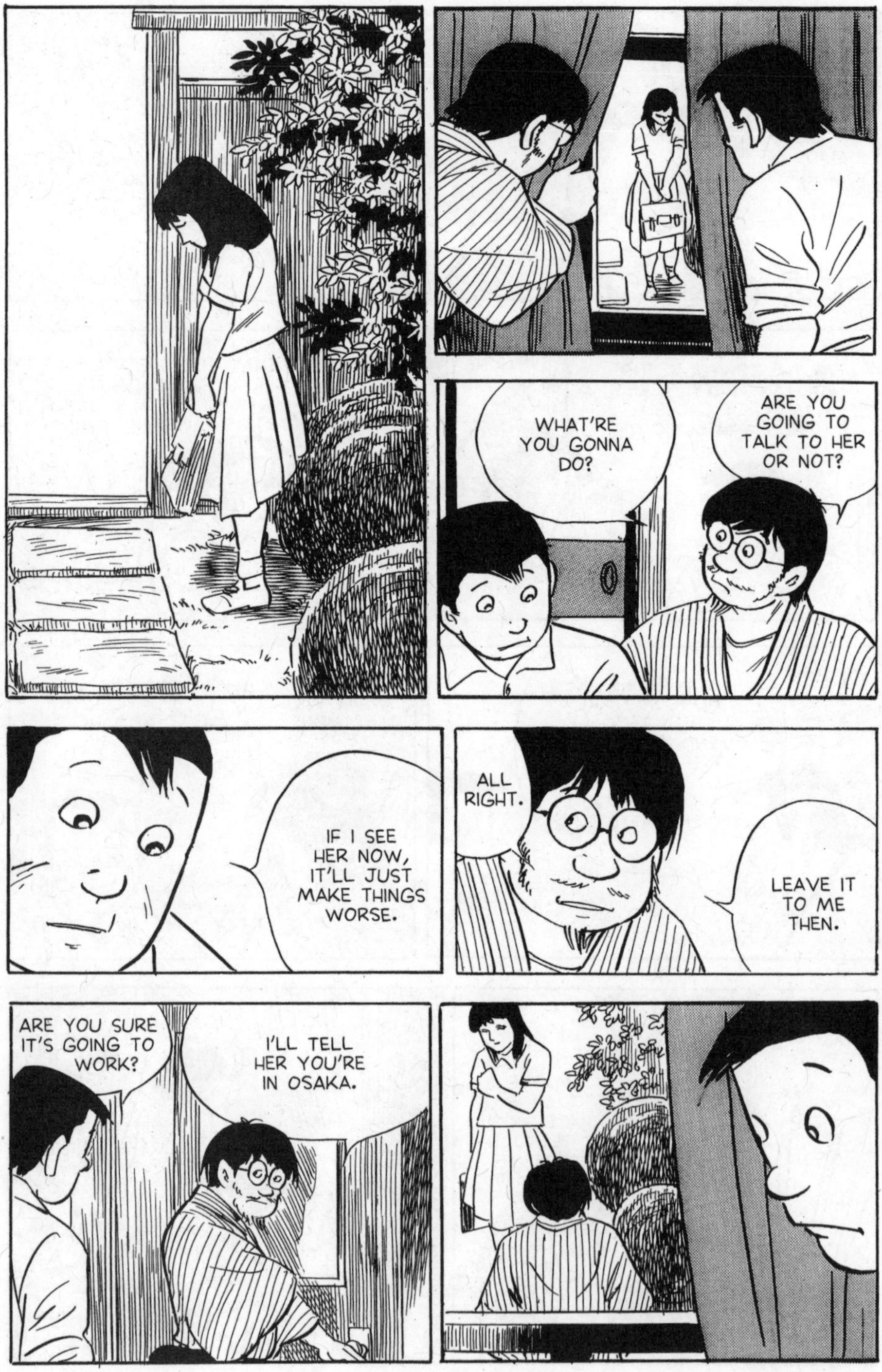
WHAT'RE YOU GONNA DO?
ARE YOU GOING TO TALK TO HER OR NOT?
IF I SEE HER NOW, IT'LL JUST MAKE THINGS WORSE.
ALL RIGHT.
LEAVE IT TO ME THEN.
ARE YOU SURE IT'S GOING TO WORK?
I'LL TELL HER YOU'RE IN OSAKA.

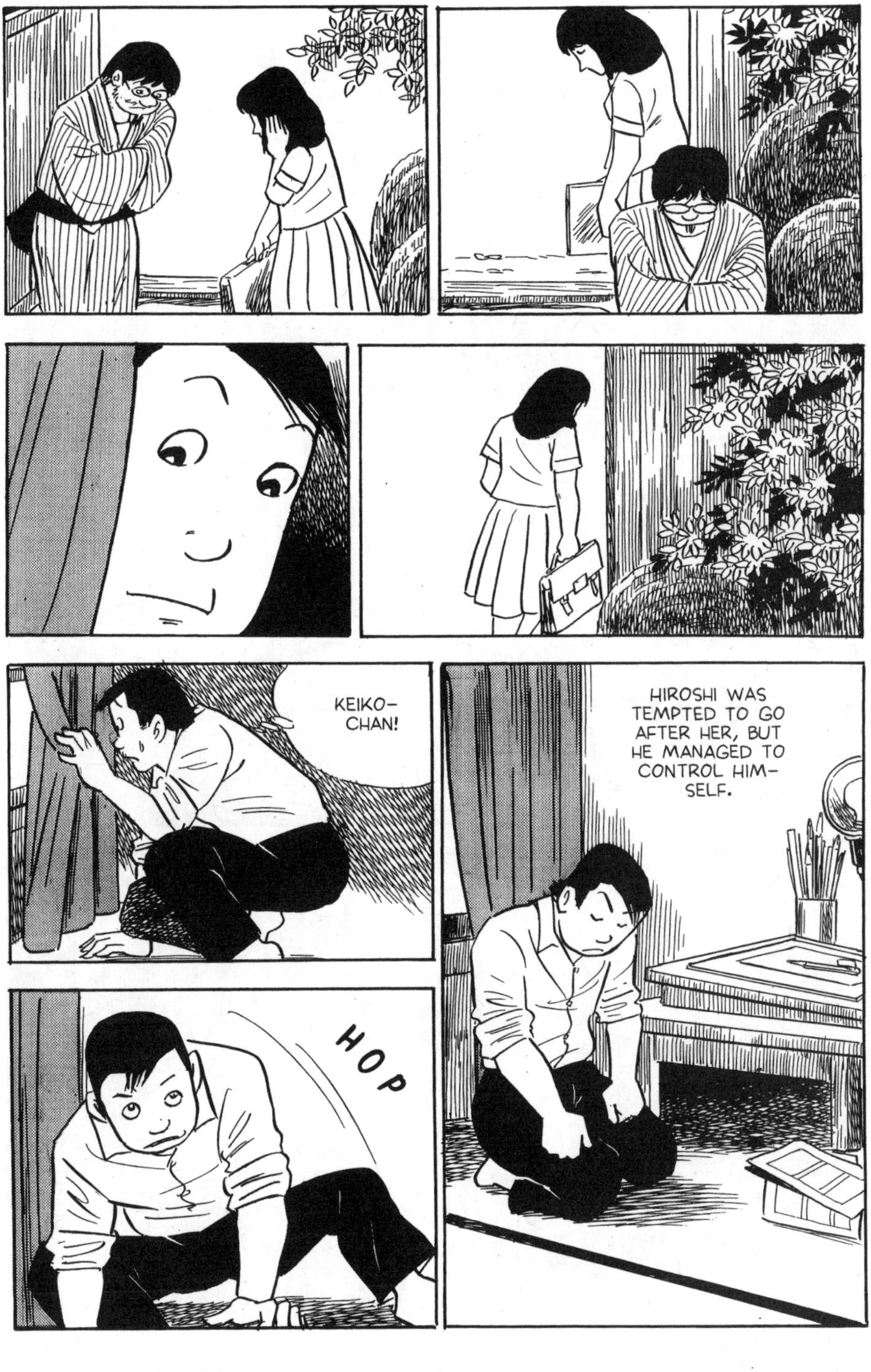
KEIKO-CHAN!
HIROSHI WAS TEMPTED TO GO AFTER HER, BUT HE MANAGED TO CONTROL HIM-SELF.
HOP

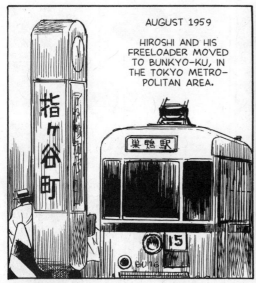

AUGUST 1959

HIROSHI AND HIS FREELOADER MOVED TO BUNKYO-KU, IN THE TOKYO METRO-POLITAN AREA.

HIROSHI HAD BECOME OBSESSED WITH AMEMIYA'S *SCENARIO* MAGAZINES.

WITHIN THEIR PAGES WAS A WORLD OF FILM THAT HIROSHI HAD PREVIOUSLY KNOWN NOTHING ABOUT.

DINNER'S READY!

COME EAT BEFORE IT GETS COLD.

FUELED BY ANGER

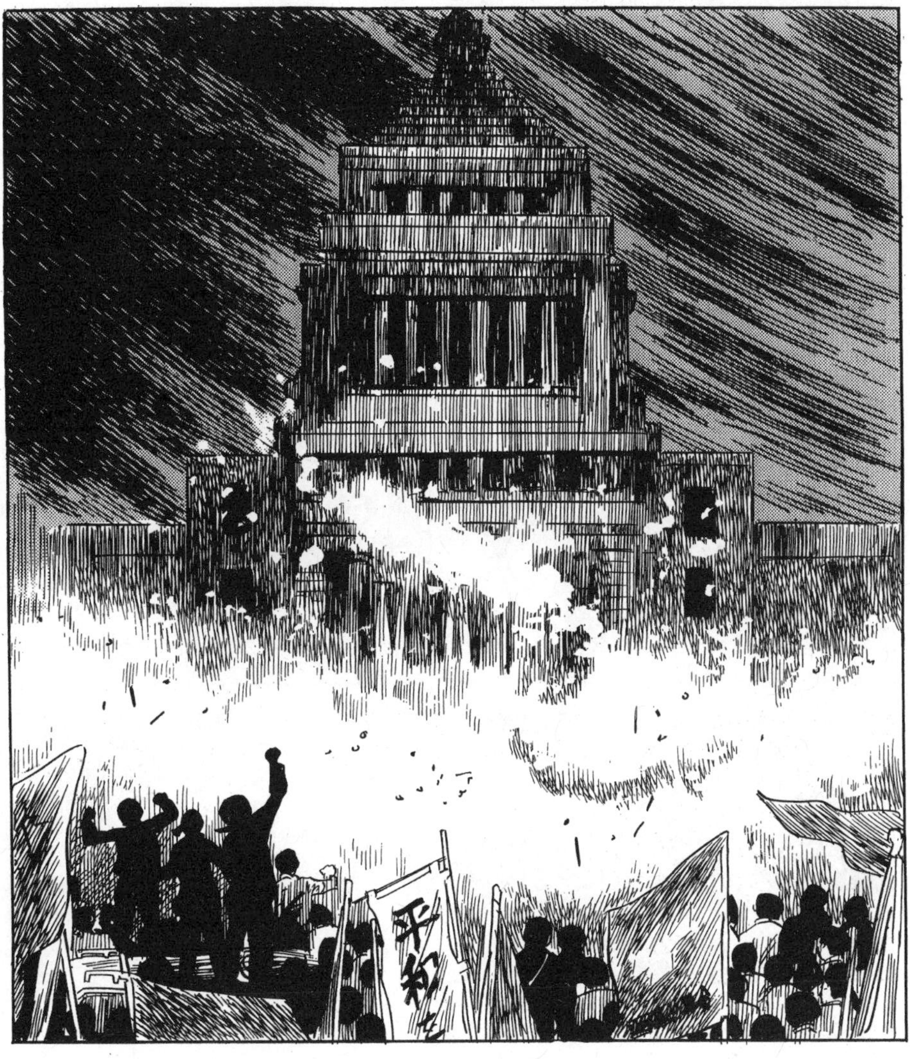
平和

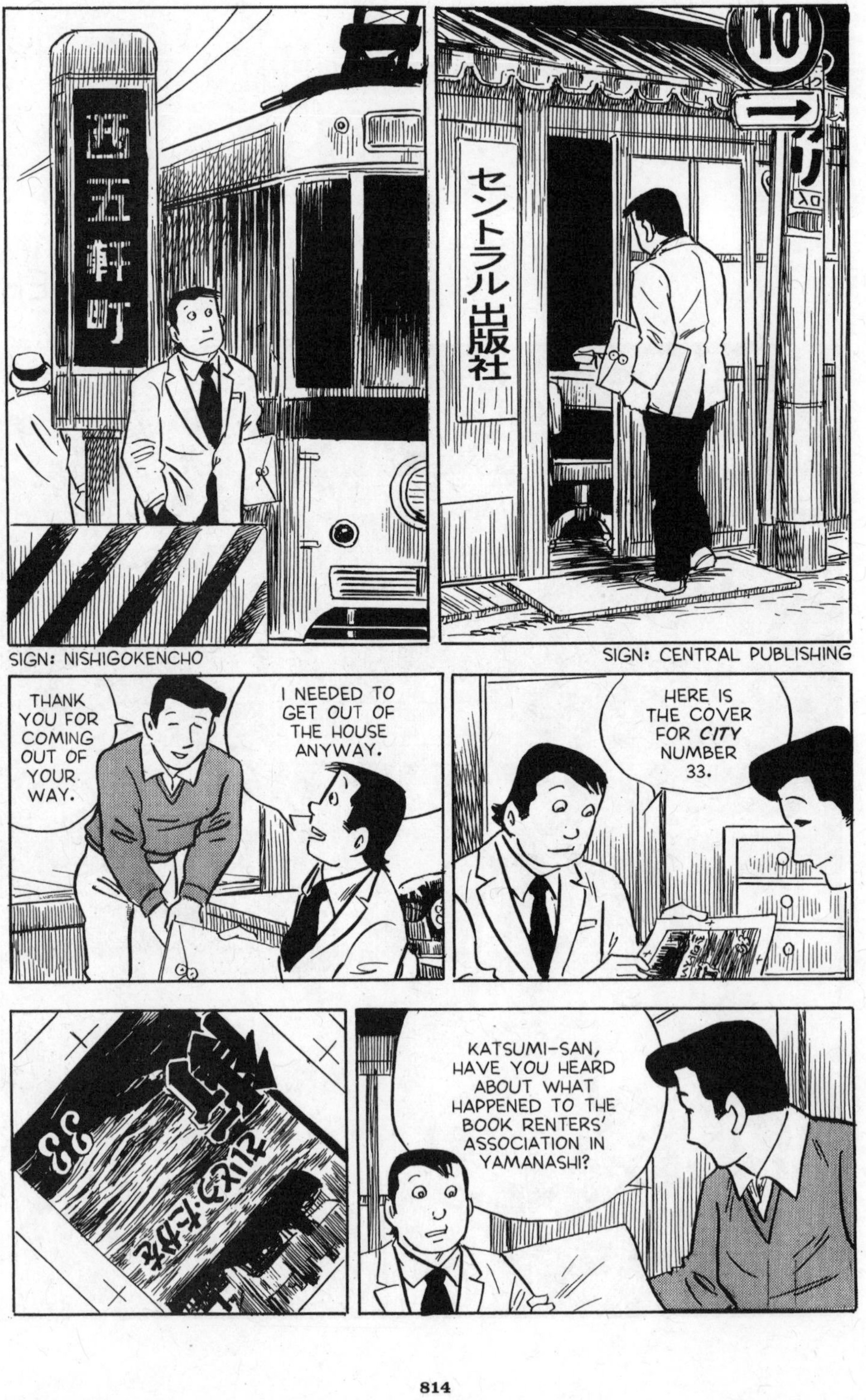
西五軒町
SIGN: NISHIGOKENCHO
セントラル出版社
SIGN: CENTRAL PUBLISHING
THANK YOU FOR COMING OUT OF YOUR WAY.
I NEEDED TO GET OUT OF THE HOUSE ANYWAY.
HERE IS THE COVER FOR *CITY* NUMBER 33.
33
KATSUMI-SAN, HAVE YOU HEARD ABOUT WHAT HAPPENED TO THE BOOK RENTERS' ASSOCIATION IN YAMANASHI?

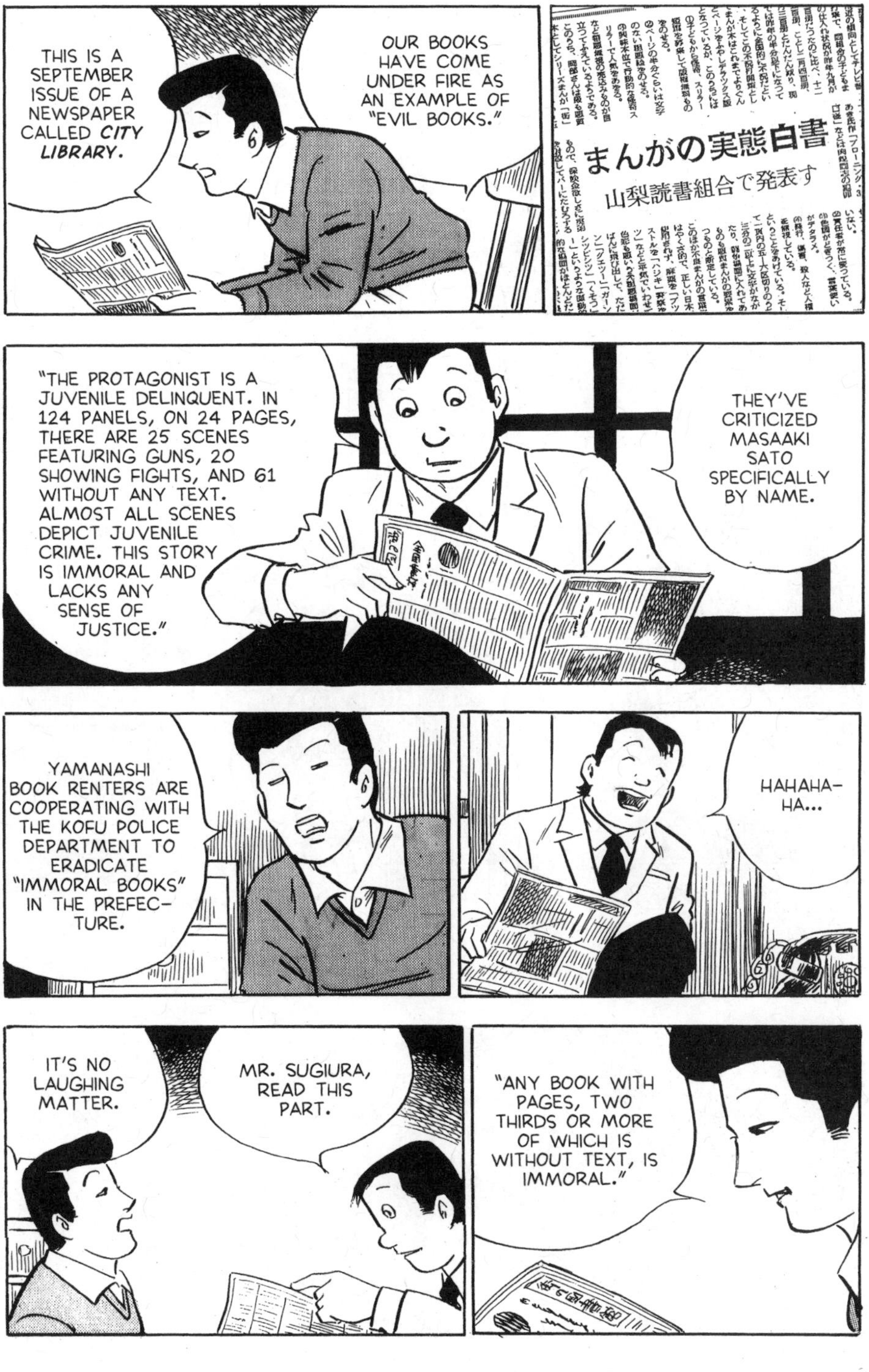
THIS IS A SEPTEMBER ISSUE OF A NEWSPAPER CALLED *CITY LIBRARY*.
OUR BOOKS HAVE COME UNDER FIRE AS AN EXAMPLE OF "EVIL BOOKS."
まんがの実態白書
山梨読書組合で発表す
"THE PROTAGONIST IS A JUVENILE DELINQUENT. IN 124 PANELS, ON 24 PAGES, THERE ARE 25 SCENES FEATURING GUNS, 20 SHOWING FIGHTS, AND 61 WITHOUT ANY TEXT. ALMOST ALL SCENES DEPICT JUVENILE CRIME. THIS STORY IS IMMORAL AND LACKS ANY SENSE OF JUSTICE."
THEY'VE CRITICIZED MASAAKI SATO SPECIFICALLY BY NAME.
YAMANASHI BOOK RENTERS ARE COOPERATING WITH THE KOFU POLICE DEPARTMENT TO ERADICATE "IMMORAL BOOKS" IN THE PREFEC-TURE.
HAHAHA-HA...
IT'S NO LAUGHING MATTER.
MR. SUGIURA, READ THIS PART.
"ANY BOOK WITH PAGES, TWO THIRDS OR MORE OF WHICH IS WITHOUT TEXT, IS IMMORAL."

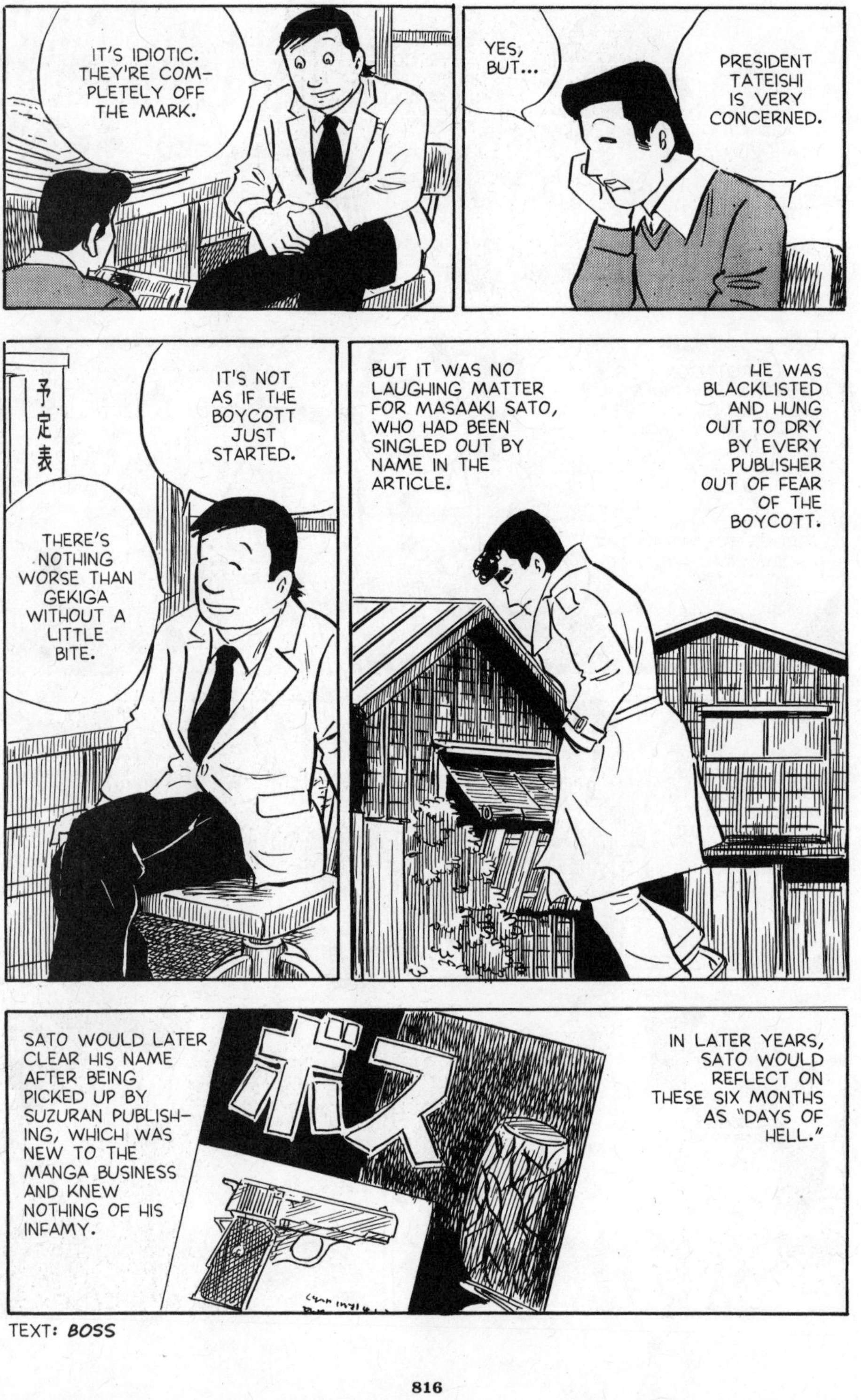
IT'S IDIOTIC. THEY'RE COMPLETELY OFF THE MARK.
YES, BUT...
PRESIDENT TATEISHI IS VERY CONCERNED.
予定表
IT'S NOT AS IF THE BOYCOTT JUST STARTED.
THERE'S NOTHING WORSE THAN GEKIGA WITHOUT A LITTLE BITE.
BUT IT WAS NO LAUGHING MATTER FOR MASAAKI SATO, WHO HAD BEEN SINGLED OUT BY NAME IN THE ARTICLE.
HE WAS BLACKLISTED AND HUNG OUT TO DRY BY EVERY PUBLISHER OUT OF FEAR OF THE BOYCOTT.
SATO WOULD LATER CLEAR HIS NAME AFTER BEING PICKED UP BY SUZURAN PUBLISHING, WHICH WAS NEW TO THE MANGA BUSINESS AND KNEW NOTHING OF HIS INFAMY.
ボス
IN LATER YEARS, SATO WOULD REFLECT ON THESE SIX MONTHS AS "DAYS OF HELL."

TEXT: ***BOSS***

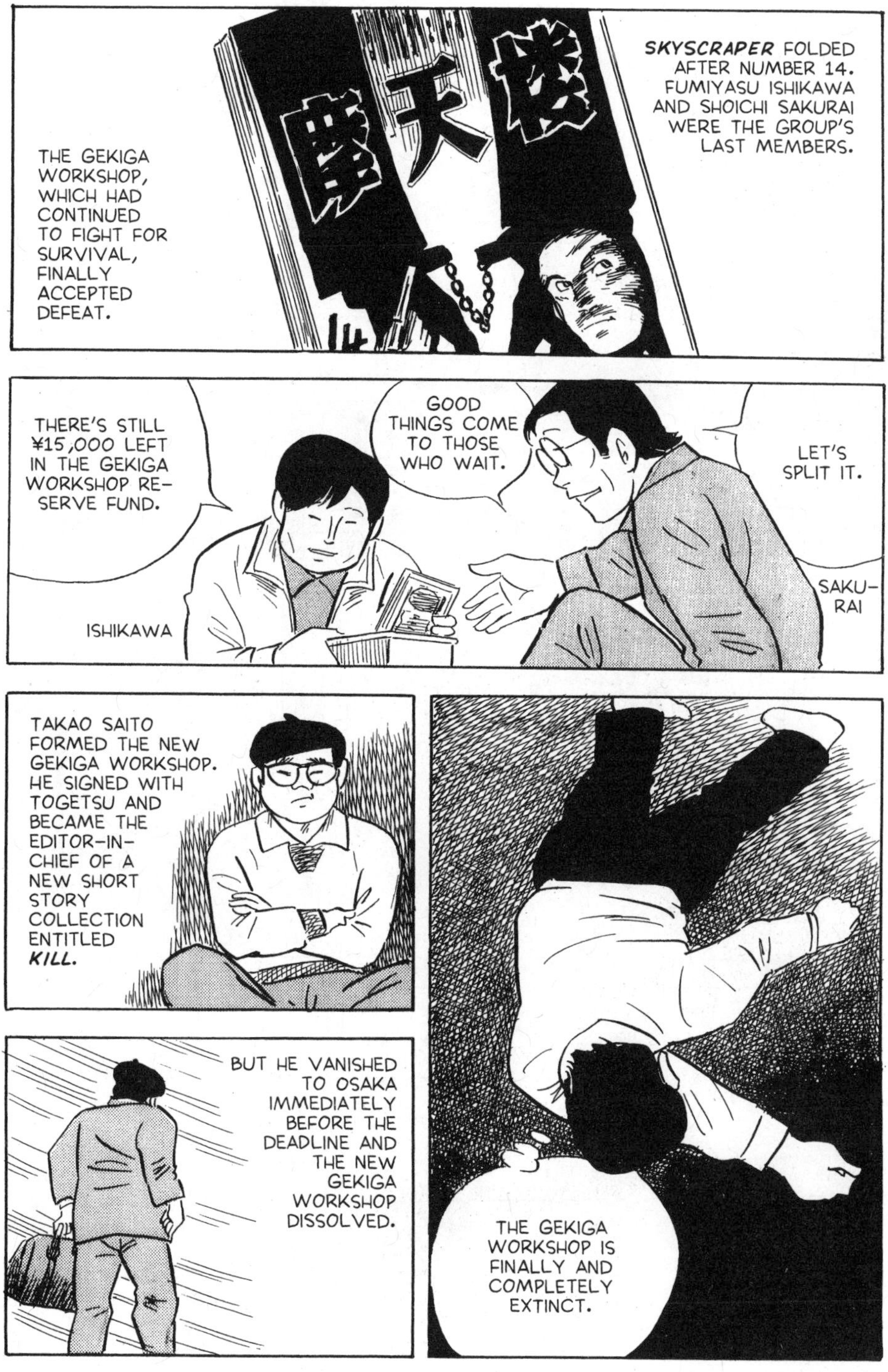
THE GEKIGA WORKSHOP, WHICH HAD CONTINUED TO FIGHT FOR SURVIVAL, FINALLY ACCEPTED DEFEAT.
摩天楼
SKYSCRAPER FOLDED AFTER NUMBER 14. FUMIYASU ISHIKAWA AND SHOICHI SAKURAI WERE THE GROUP'S LAST MEMBERS.
THERE'S STILL ¥15,000 LEFT IN THE GEKIGA WORKSHOP RE-SERVE FUND.
ISHIKAWA
GOOD THINGS COME TO THOSE WHO WAIT.
LET'S SPLIT IT.
SAKU-RAI
TAKAO SAITO FORMED THE NEW GEKIGA WORKSHOP. HE SIGNED WITH TOGETSU AND BECAME THE EDITOR-IN-CHIEF OF A NEW SHORT STORY COLLECTION ENTITLED ***KILL***.
BUT HE VANISHED TO OSAKA IMMEDIATELY BEFORE THE DEADLINE AND THE NEW GEKIGA WORKSHOP DISSOLVED.
THE GEKIGA WORKSHOP IS FINALLY AND COMPLETELY EXTINCT.

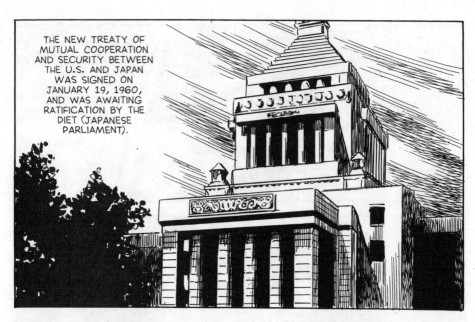

THE NEW TREATY OF MUTUAL COOPERATION AND SECURITY BETWEEN THE U.S. AND JAPAN WAS SIGNED ON JANUARY 19, 1960, AND WAS AWAITING RATIFICATION BY THE DIET (JAPANESE PARLIAMENT).

THE NEW SECURITY TREATY MAY HAVE BEEN RATIFIED, BUT JAPAN IS STILL DEPENDENT ON THE U.S.

HOW COME?

APPARENTLY, THE U.S. CAN CONTINUE TO FREELY MAINTAIN MILITARY BASES ON JAPANESE SOIL UNDER THE NEW TREATY.

SOUNDS MORE LIKE AN INSECURITY TREATY.

AS LONG AS WE HAVE AMERICAN BASES IN JAPAN, WE'RE GOING TO BE DRAGGED INTO ALL U.S. WARS.

TITLE: *SCENARIO*, OCTOBER ISSUE

"KANETO SHINDO, THE YOUNG SCRIPT-WRITER, HAS SHOWN HIS PASSION FOR CINEMA BY CRAFTING A SCRIPT WHICH ADDRESSES A VERY UNLIKELY SUBJECT MATTER: HANSEN'S DISEASE."

HIROSHI READ THE *SCENARIO* MAGAZINES, THE ONLY POSSESSIONS AMEMIYA BROUGHT WITH HIM, FROM COVER TO COVER.

HIROSHI LEARNED A LOT FROM *SCENARIO*.

ONE LESSON WAS THAT "VISUALS SHOULD BE THE PRIMARY METHOD OF EXPRESSION", AND THAT "DIALOGUE SHOULD BE AS ABBREVIATED AS POSSIBLE."

THERE ARE STILL EXPRESSIVE METHODS LEFT FOR GEKIGA TO EXPLORE.

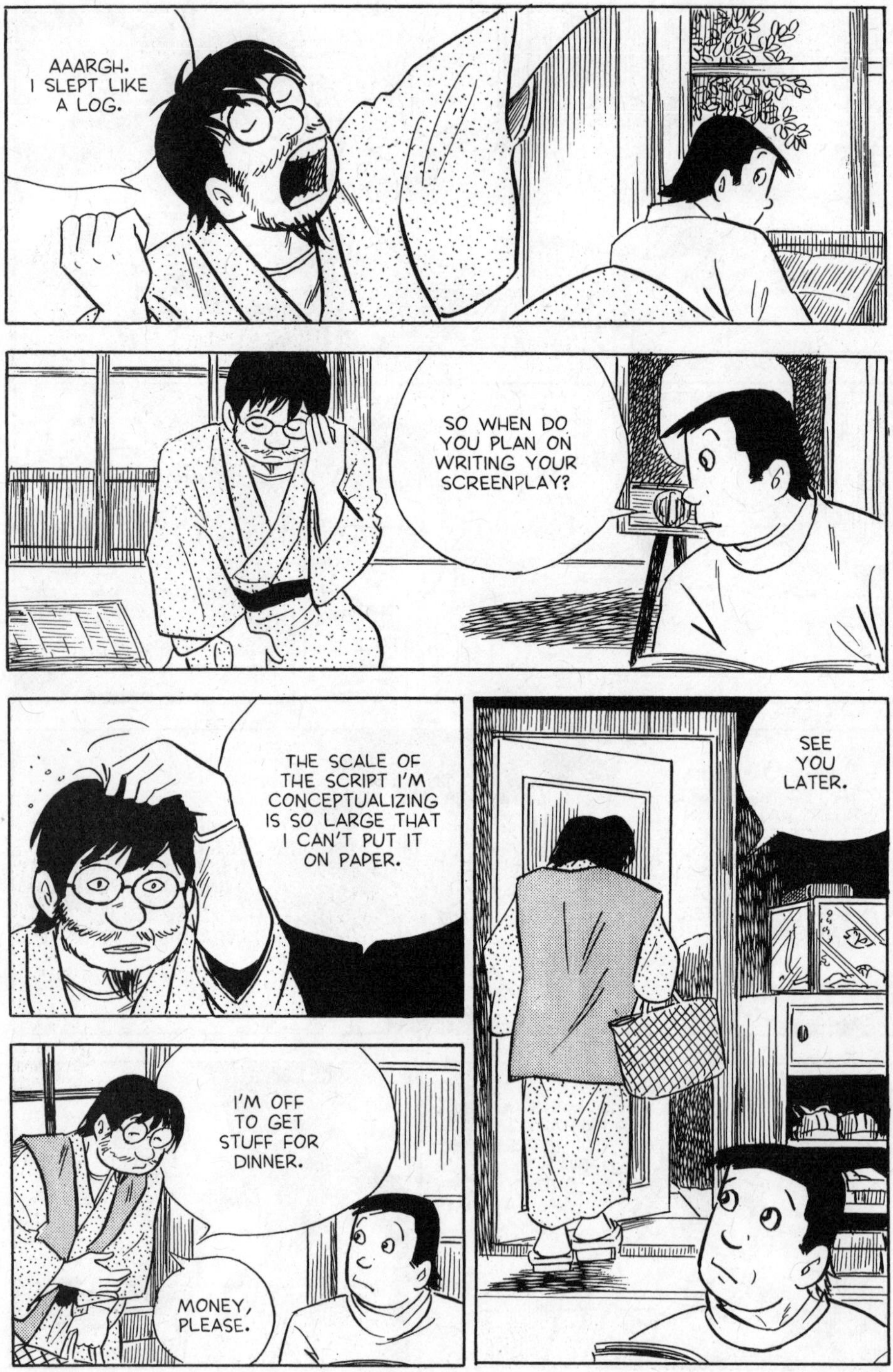
AAARGH. I SLEPT LIKE A LOG.
SO WHEN DO YOU PLAN ON WRITING YOUR SCREENPLAY?
THE SCALE OF THE SCRIPT I'M CONCEPTUALIZING IS SO LARGE THAT I CAN'T PUT IT ON PAPER.
I'M OFF TO GET STUFF FOR DINNER.
MONEY, PLEASE.
SEE YOU LATER.

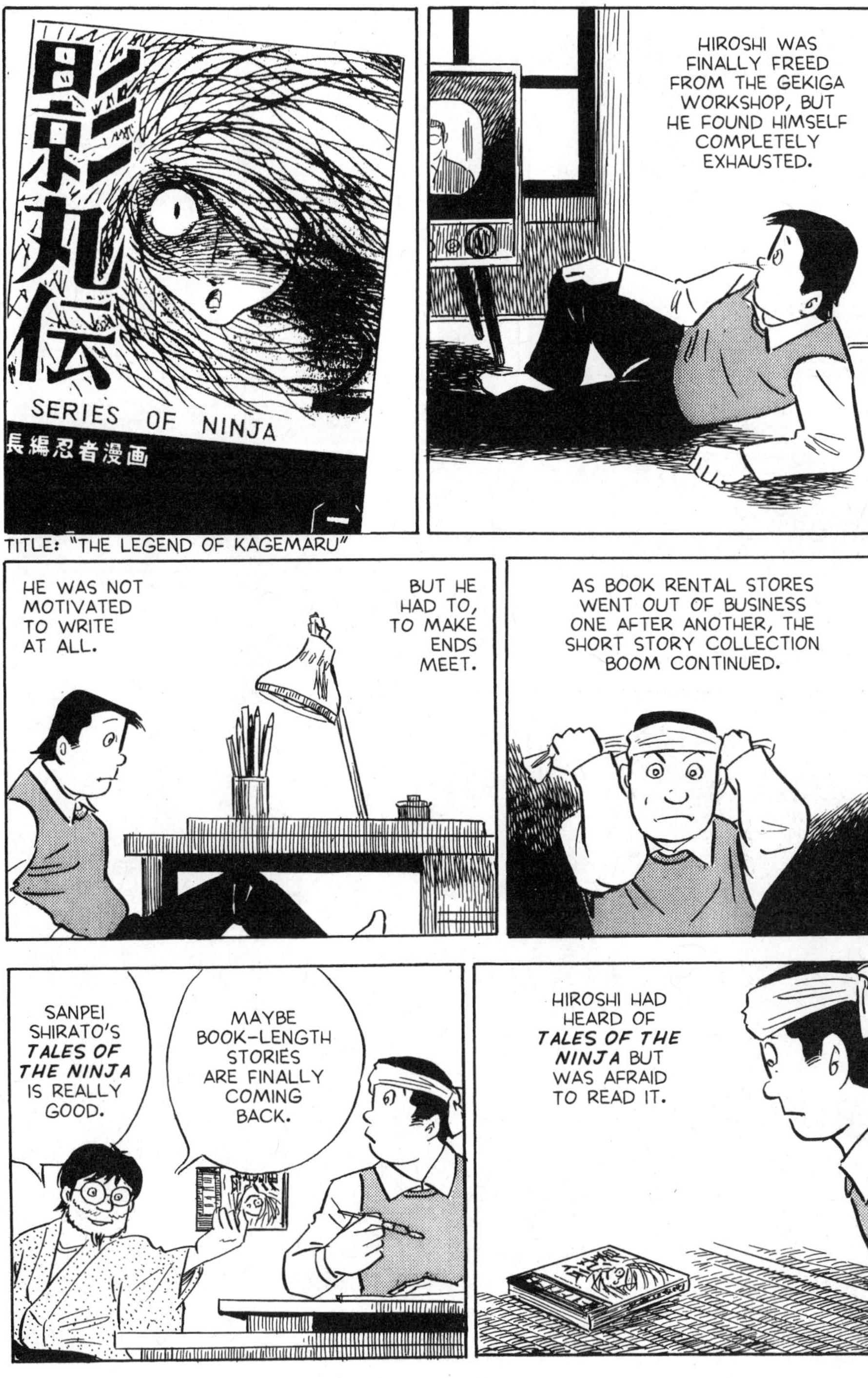
影丸伝
SERIES OF NINJA
長編忍者漫画
TITLE: "THE LEGEND OF KAGEMARU"
HIROSHI WAS FINALLY FREED FROM THE GEKIGA WORKSHOP, BUT HE FOUND HIMSELF COMPLETELY EXHAUSTED.
HE WAS NOT MOTIVATED TO WRITE AT ALL.
BUT HE HAD TO, TO MAKE ENDS MEET.
AS BOOK RENTAL STORES WENT OUT OF BUSINESS ONE AFTER ANOTHER, THE SHORT STORY COLLECTION BOOM CONTINUED.
SANPEI SHIRATO'S TALES OF THE NINJA IS REALLY GOOD.
MAYBE BOOK-LENGTH STORIES ARE FINALLY COMING BACK.
HIROSHI HAD HEARD OF TALES OF THE NINJA BUT WAS AFRAID TO READ IT.

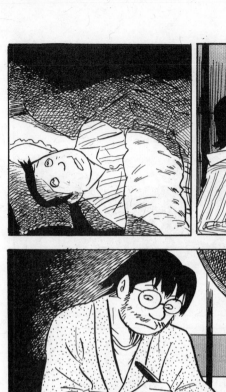

IT'S THE THIRD NIGHT IN A ROW HE HASN'T SLEPT.

WHY DON'T YOU SLEEP A LITTLE?

YOU DON'T WANT TO OVEREXERT YOURSELF AND GET SICK.

I USED TO WORK LIKE THAT...

OH, THE DAYS OF WORKING ON B6-SIZED RENTAL BOOKS...

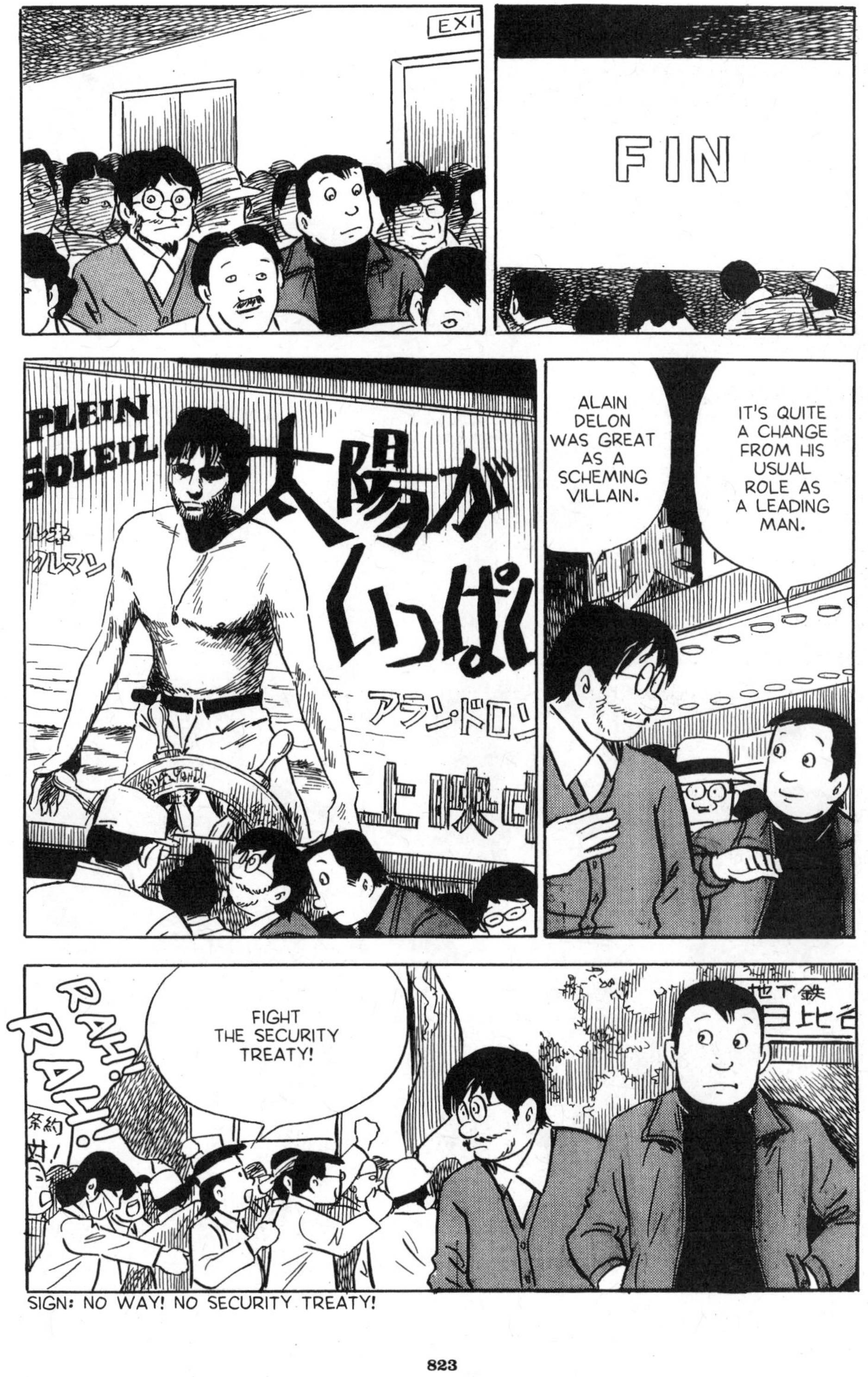
FIN
PLEIN SOLEIL
太陽がいっぱい
アラン・ドロン
ALAIN DELON WAS GREAT AS A SCHEMING VILLAIN.
IT'S QUITE A CHANGE FROM HIS USUAL ROLE AS A LEADING MAN.
RAH! RAH!
FIGHT THE SECURITY TREATY!
地下鉄
日比谷

SIGN: NO WAY! NO SECURITY TREATY!

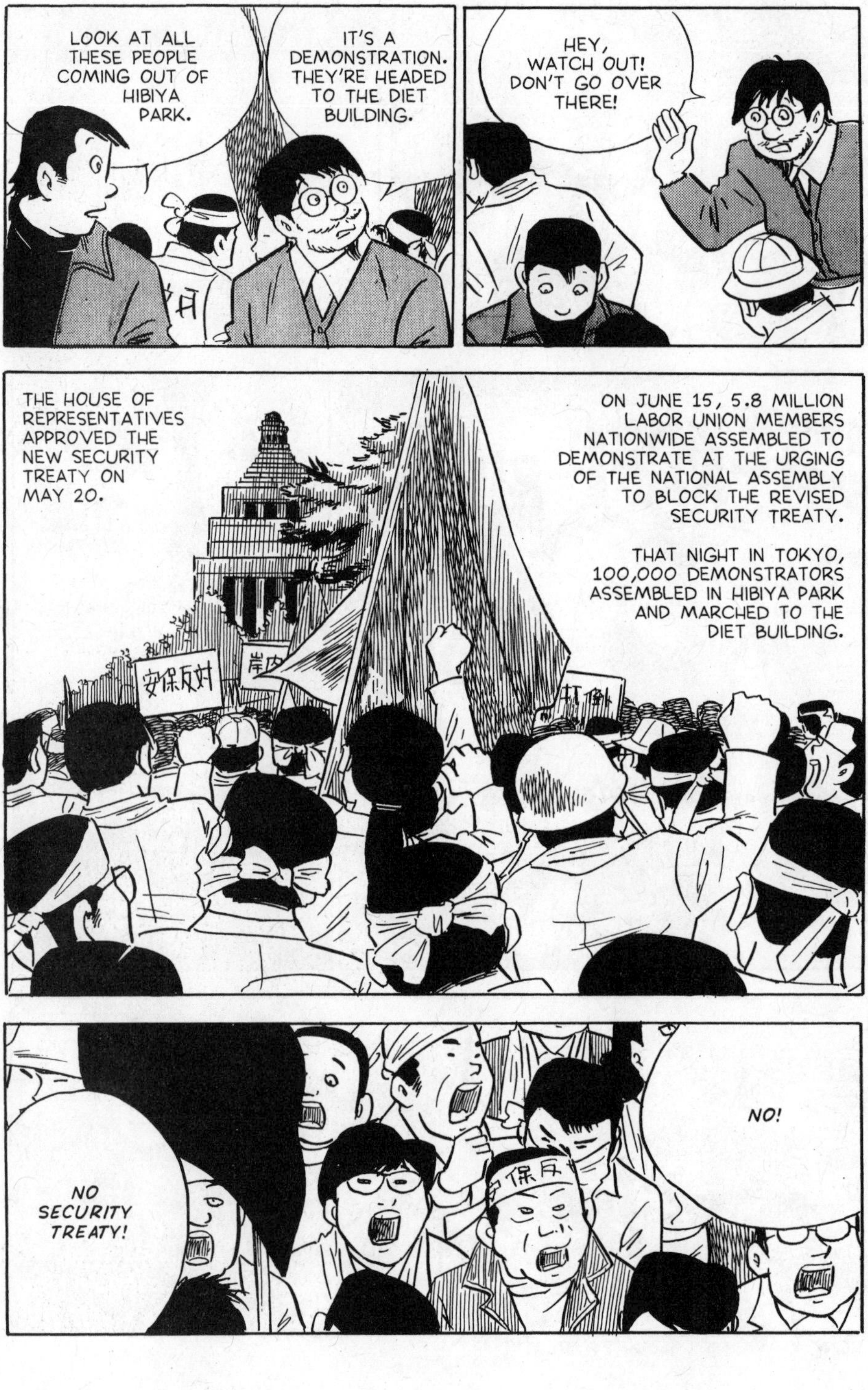
LOOK AT ALL THESE PEOPLE COMING OUT OF HIBIYA PARK.
IT'S A DEMONSTRATION. THEY'RE HEADED TO THE DIET BUILDING.
HEY, WATCH OUT! DON'T GO OVER THERE!
THE HOUSE OF REPRESENTATIVES APPROVED THE NEW SECURITY TREATY ON MAY 20.
ON JUNE 15, 5.8 MILLION LABOR UNION MEMBERS NATIONWIDE ASSEMBLED TO DEMONSTRATE AT THE URGING OF THE NATIONAL ASSEMBLY TO BLOCK THE REVISED SECURITY TREATY.
THAT NIGHT IN TOKYO, 100,000 DEMONSTRATORS ASSEMBLED IN HIBIYA PARK AND MARCHED TO THE DIET BUILDING.
安保反対
NO SECURITY TREATY!
NO!

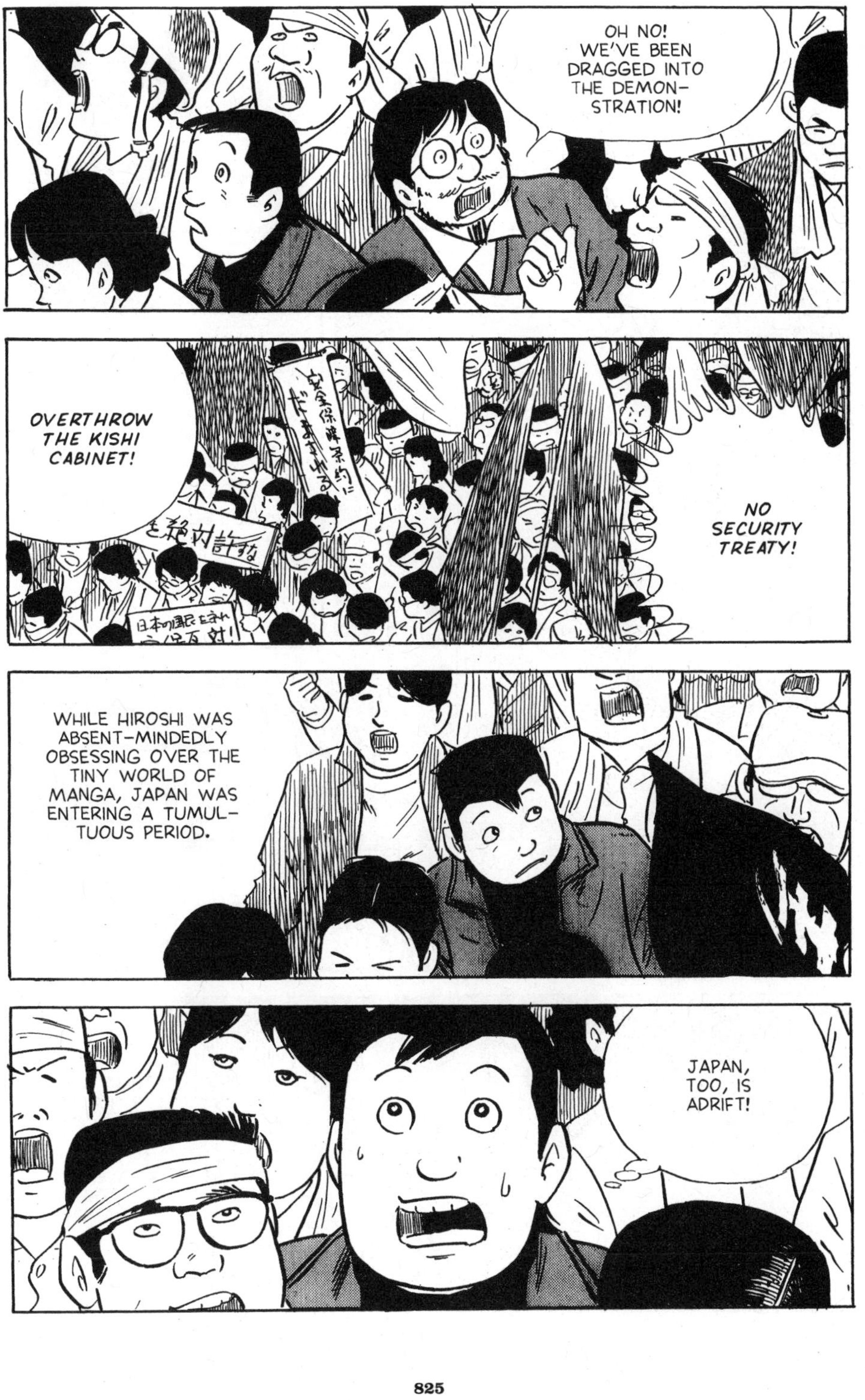
OH NO! WE'VE BEEN DRAGGED INTO THE DEMON-STRATION!
OVERTHROW THE KISHI CABINET!
NO SECURITY TREATY!
WHILE HIROSHI WAS ABSENT-MINDEDLY OBSESSING OVER THE TINY WORLD OF MANGA, JAPAN WAS ENTERING A TUMUL-TUOUS PERIOD.
JAPAN, TOO, IS ADRIFT!

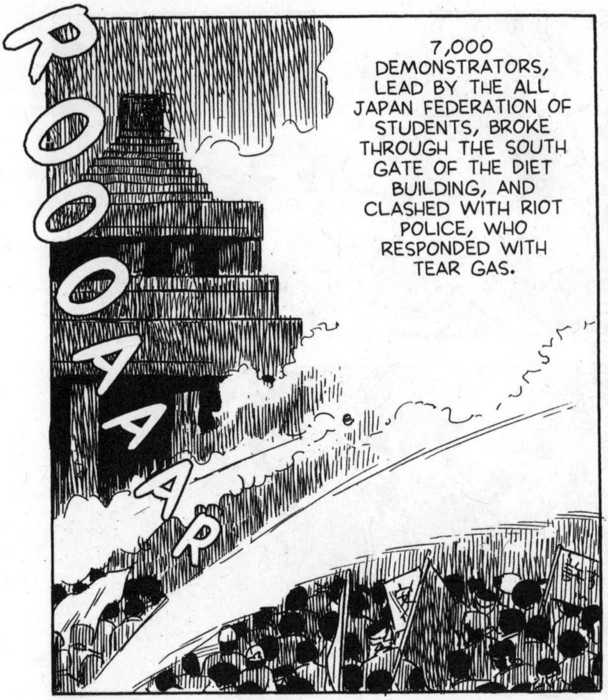
ROOOOAAAAR
7,000 DEMONSTRATORS, LEAD BY THE ALL JAPAN FEDERATION OF STUDENTS, BROKE THROUGH THE SOUTH GATE OF THE DIET BUILDING, AND CLASHED WITH RIOT POLICE, WHO RESPONDED WITH TEAR GAS.

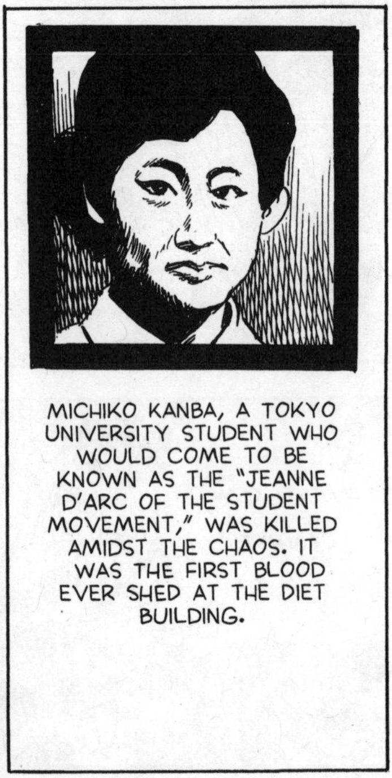
MICHIKO KANBA, A TOKYO UNIVERSITY STUDENT WHO WOULD COME TO BE KNOWN AS THE "JEANNE D'ARC OF THE STUDENT MOVEMENT," WAS KILLED AMIDST THE CHAOS. IT WAS THE FIRST BLOOD EVER SHED AT THE DIET BUILDING.

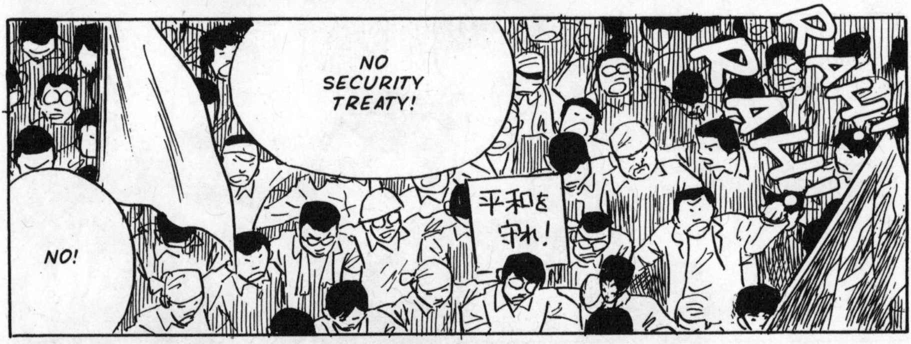
NO SECURITY TREATY!
NO!
平和を守れ!
RAH! RAH!

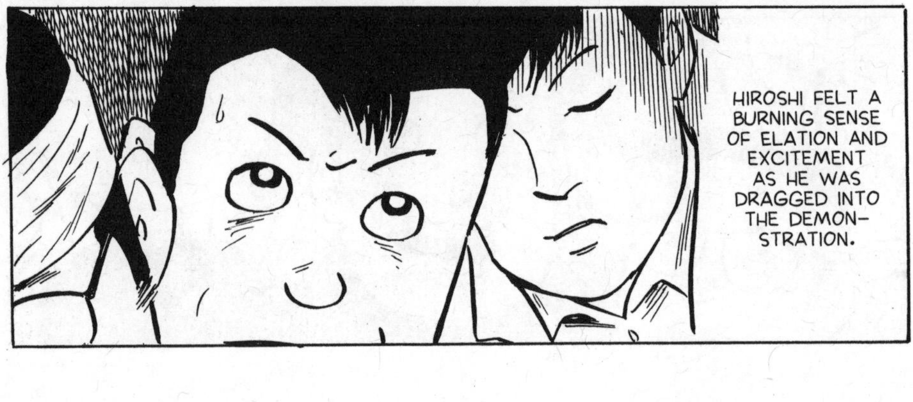
HIROSHI FELT A BURNING SENSE OF ELATION AND EXCITEMENT AS HE WAS DRAGGED INTO THE DEMON-STRATION.

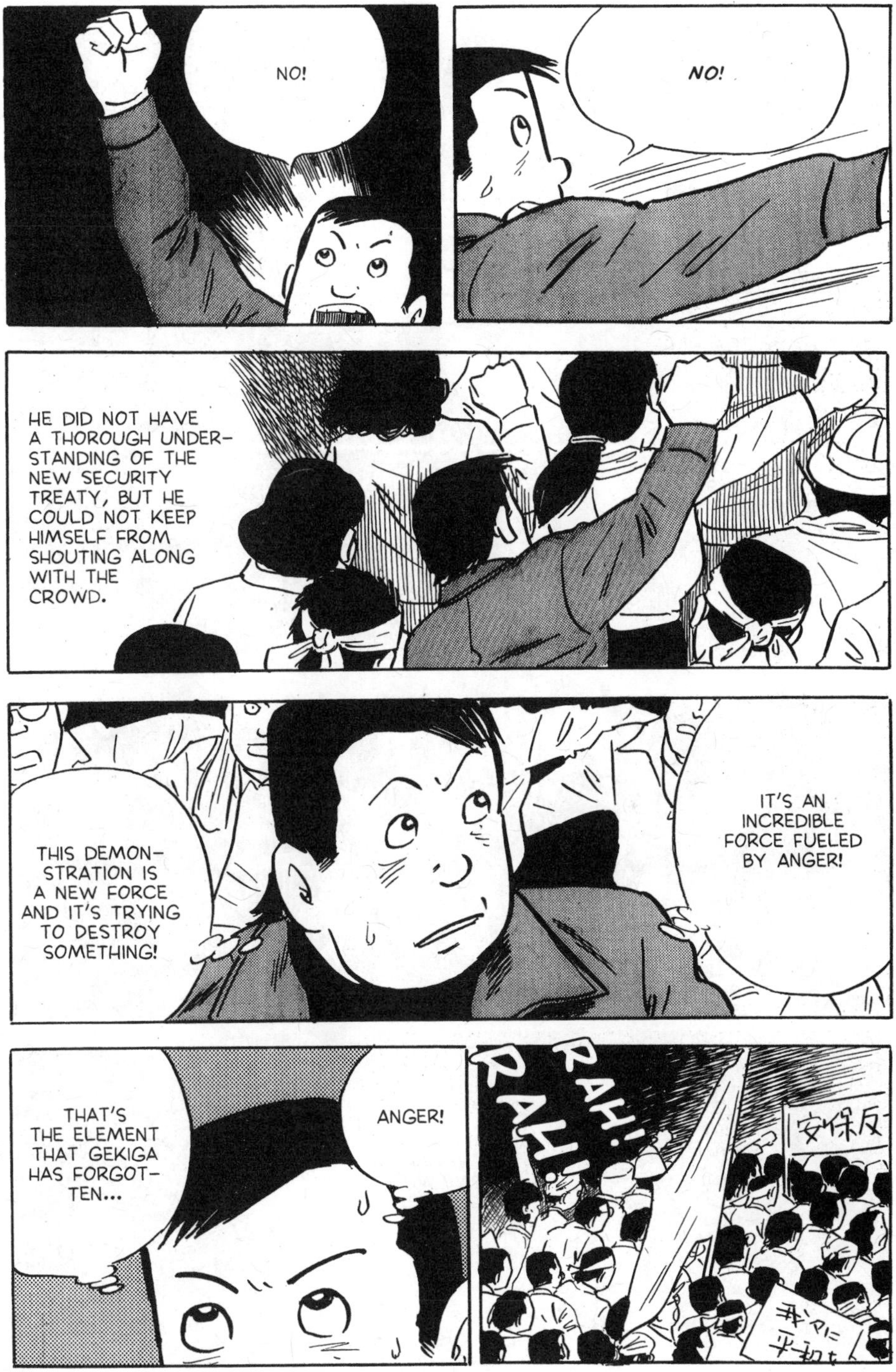
NO!
NO!
HE DID NOT HAVE A THOROUGH UNDERSTANDING OF THE NEW SECURITY TREATY, BUT HE COULD NOT KEEP HIMSELF FROM SHOUTING ALONG WITH THE CROWD.
THIS DEMONSTRATION IS A NEW FORCE AND IT'S TRYING TO DESTROY SOMETHING!
IT'S AN INCREDIBLE FORCE FUELED BY ANGER!
THAT'S THE ELEMENT THAT GEKIGA HAS FORGOTTEN...
ANGER!
RAH! RAH!
安保反

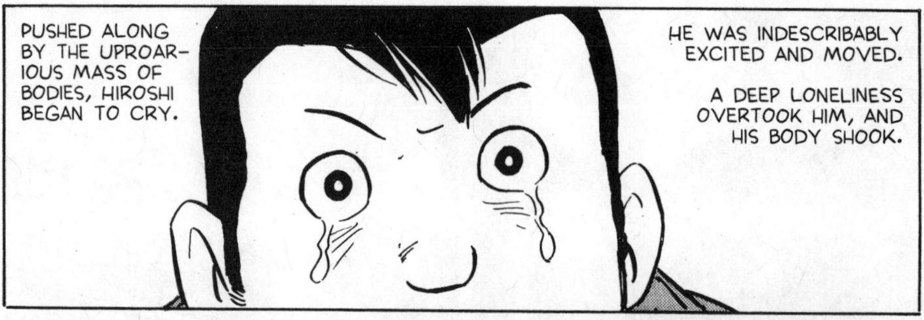
PUSHED ALONG BY THE UPROAR-IOUS MASS OF BODIES, HIROSHI BEGAN TO CRY.
HE WAS INDESCRIBABLY EXCITED AND MOVED.
A DEEP LONELINESS OVERTOOK HIM, AND HIS BODY SHOOK.
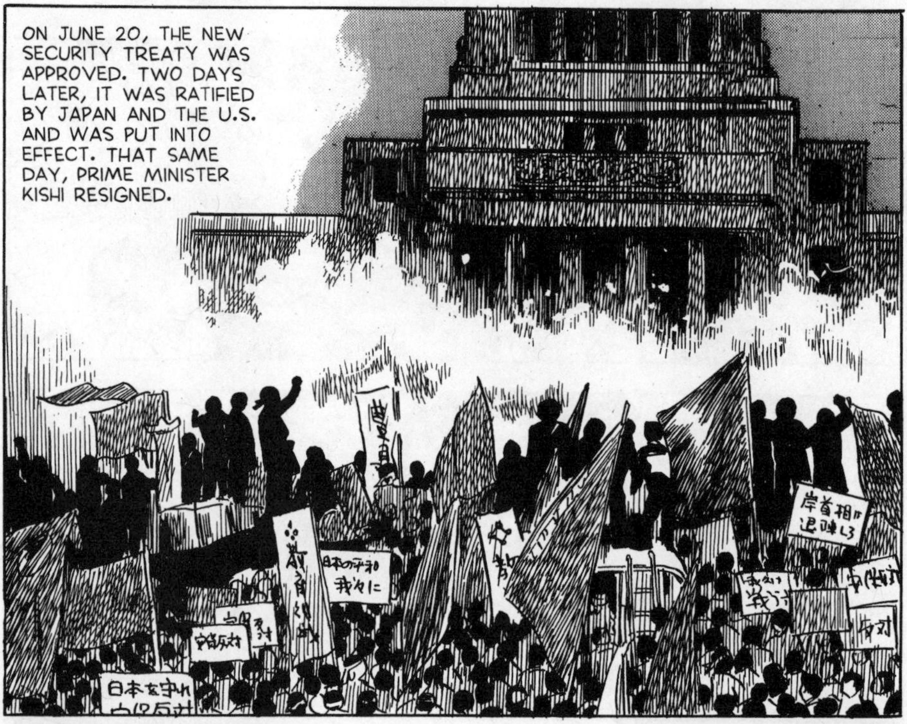
ON JUNE 20, THE NEW SECURITY TREATY WAS APPROVED. TWO DAYS LATER, IT WAS RATIFIED BY JAPAN AND THE U.S. AND WAS PUT INTO EFFECT. THAT SAME DAY, PRIME MINISTER KISHI RESIGNED.
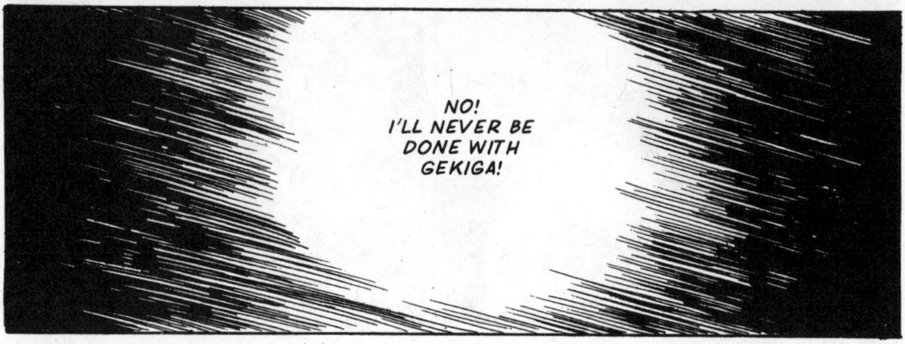
NO! I'LL NEVER BE DONE WITH GEKIGA!

EPILOGUE

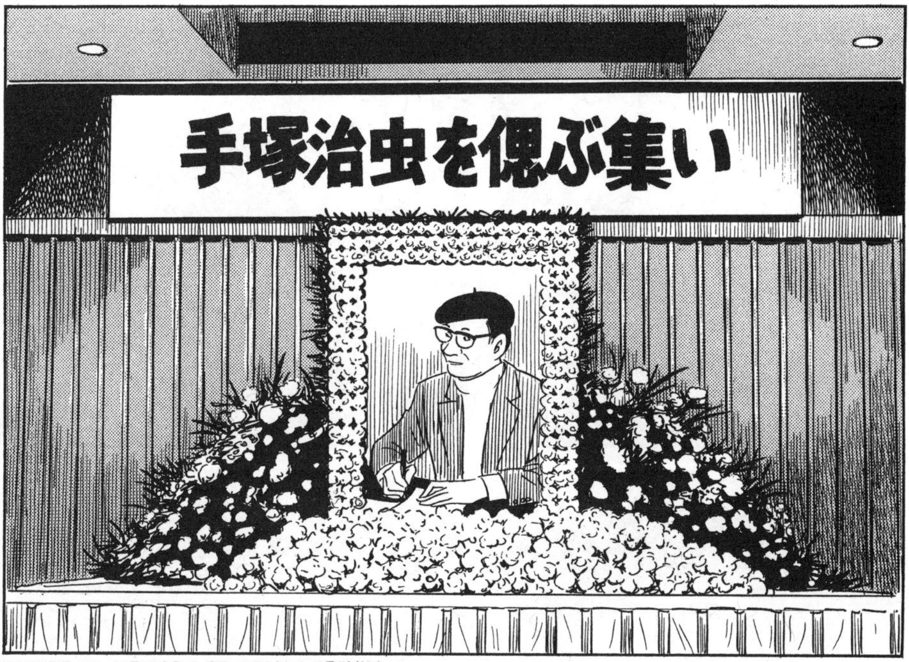
手塚治虫を偲ぶ集い

BANNER: IN MEMORY OF OSAMU TEZUKA

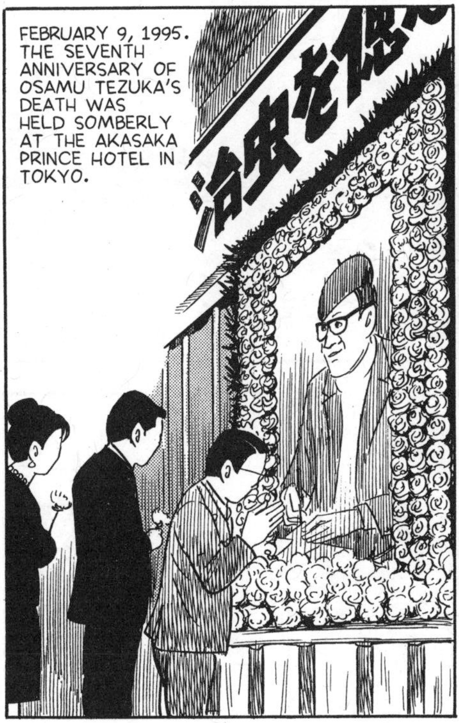
FEBRUARY 9, 1995. THE SEVENTH ANNIVERSARY OF OSAMU TEZUKA'S DEATH WAS HELD SOMBERLY AT THE AKASAKA PRINCE HOTEL IN TOKYO.

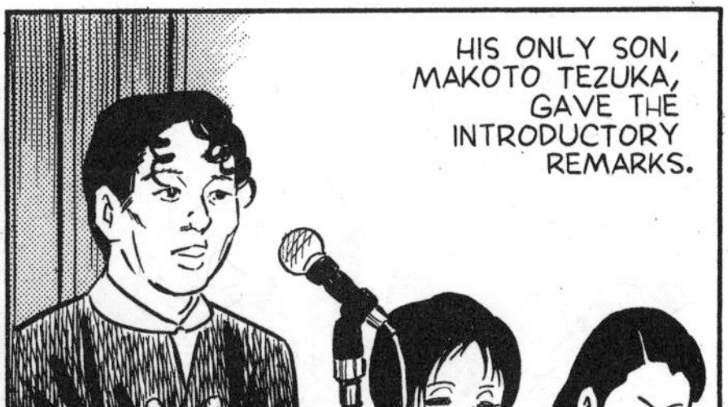
HIS ONLY SON, MAKOTO TEZUKA, GAVE THE INTRODUCTORY REMARKS.

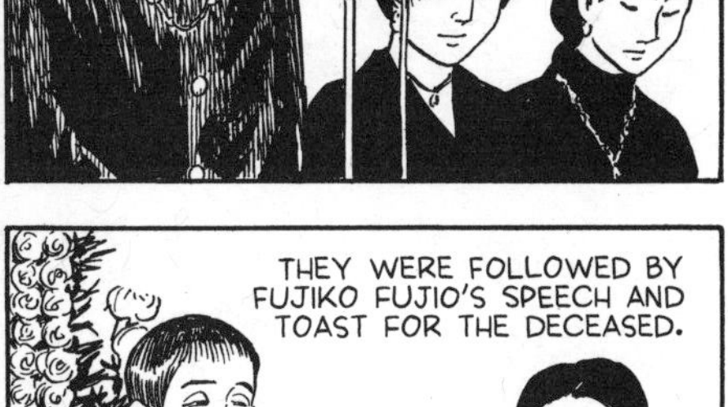
THEY WERE FOLLOWED BY FUJIKO FUJIO'S SPEECH AND TOAST FOR THE DECEASED.

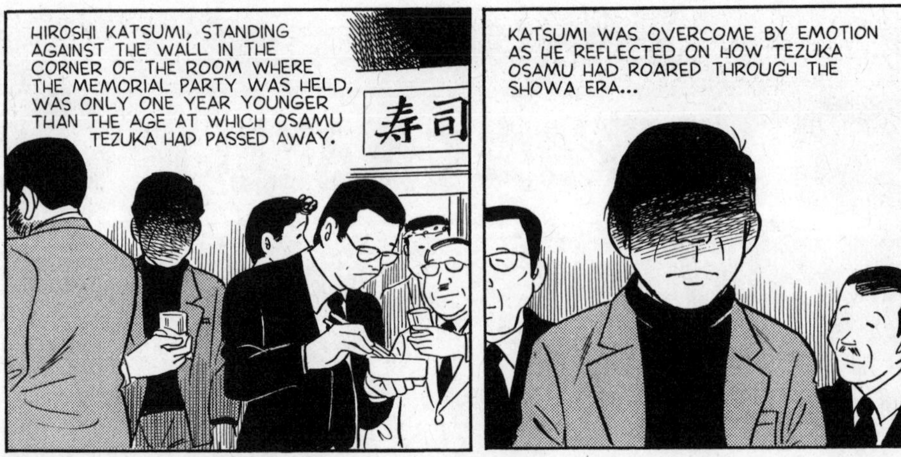
HIROSHI KATSUMI, STANDING AGAINST THE WALL IN THE CORNER OF THE ROOM WHERE THE MEMORIAL PARTY WAS HELD, WAS ONLY ONE YEAR YOUNGER THAN THE AGE AT WHICH OSAMU TEZUKA HAD PASSED AWAY.
寿司
KATSUMI WAS OVERCOME BY EMOTION AS HE REFLECTED ON HOW TEZUKA OSAMU HAD ROARED THROUGH THE SHOWA ERA...

SIGN: SUSHI

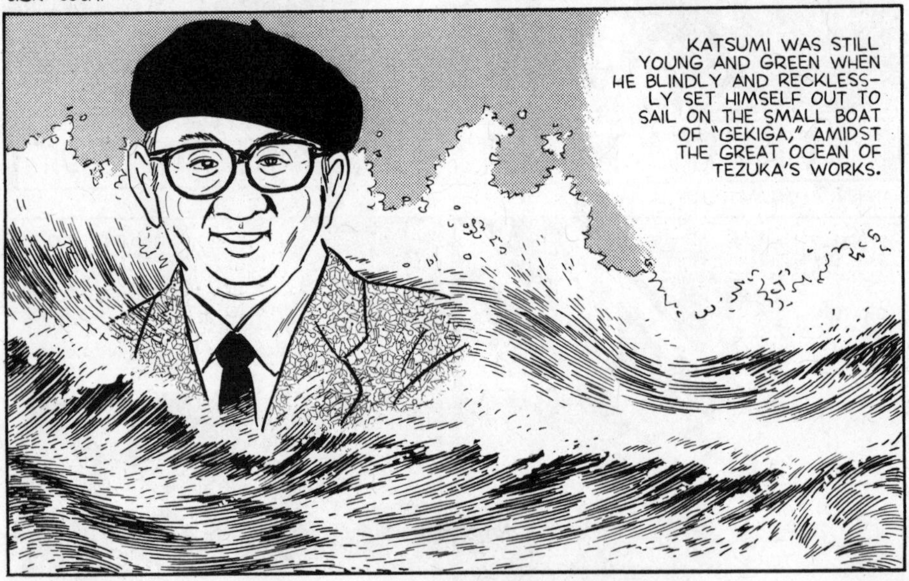
KATSUMI WAS STILL YOUNG AND GREEN WHEN HE BLINDLY AND RECKLESS-LY SET HIMSELF OUT TO SAIL ON THE SMALL BOAT OF "GEKIGA," AMIDST THE GREAT OCEAN OF TEZUKA'S WORKS.

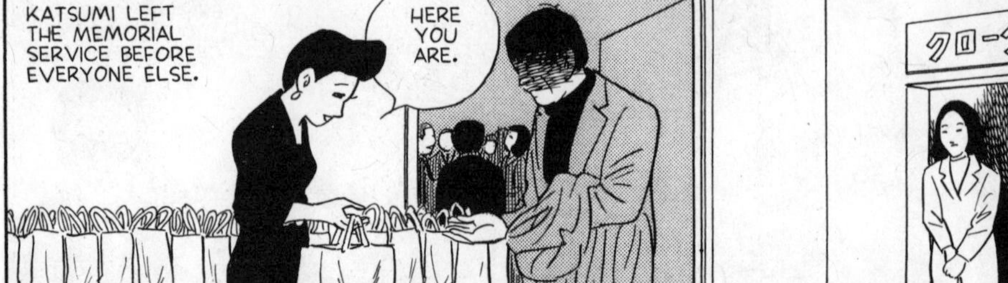
KATSUMI LEFT THE MEMORIAL SERVICE BEFORE EVERYONE ELSE.
HERE YOU ARE.

SIGNS: COAT CHECK / CHECK YOUR BAGS HERE

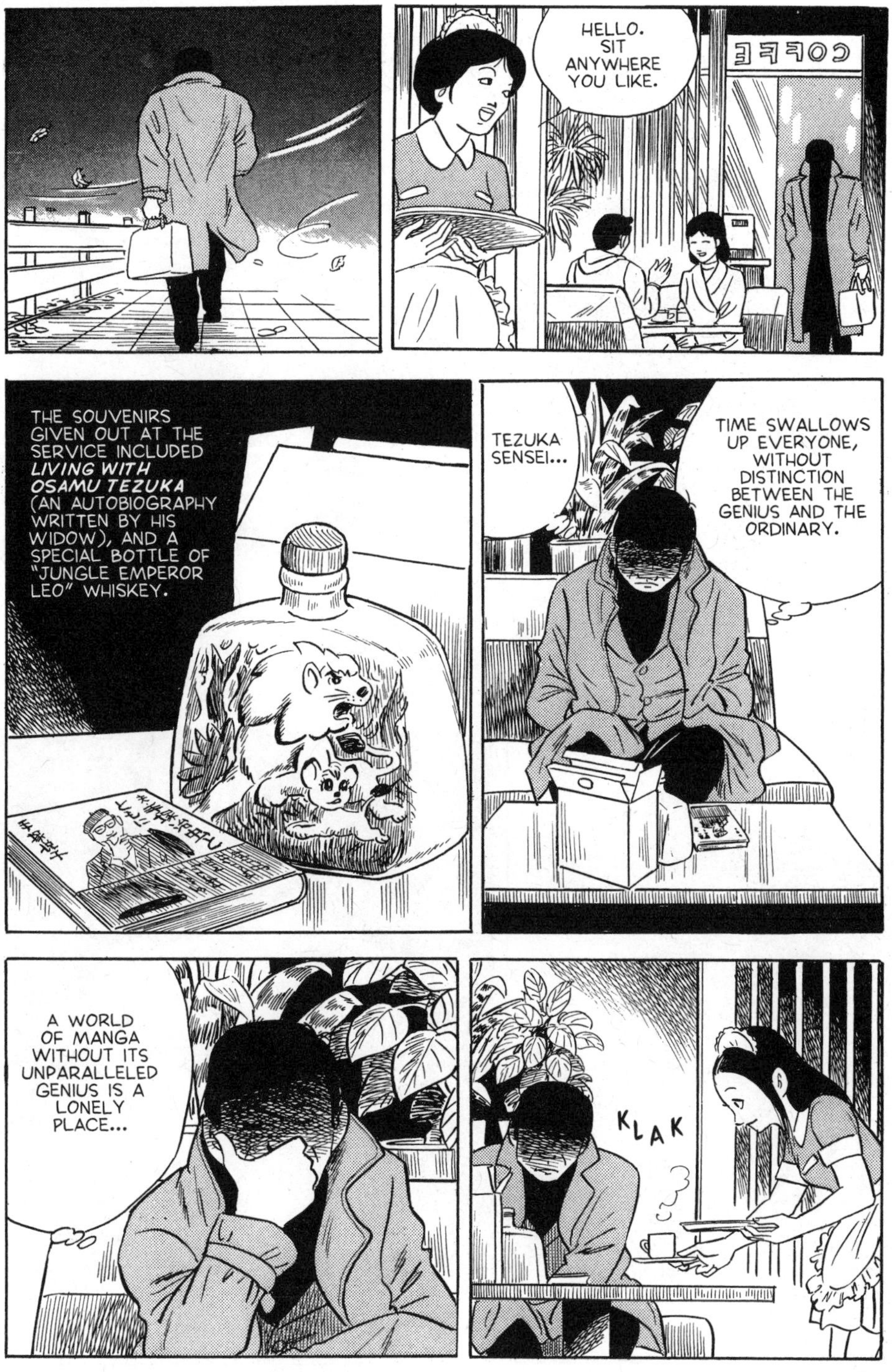

HELLO. SIT ANYWHERE YOU LIKE.
THE SOUVENIRS GIVEN OUT AT THE SERVICE INCLUDED *LIVING WITH OSAMU TEZUKA* (AN AUTOBIOGRAPHY WRITTEN BY HIS WIDOW), AND A SPECIAL BOTTLE OF "JUNGLE EMPEROR LEO" WHISKEY.
TEZUKA SENSEI...
TIME SWALLOWS UP EVERYONE, WITHOUT DISTINCTION BETWEEN THE GENIUS AND THE ORDINARY.
A WORLD OF MANGA WITHOUT ITS UNPARALLELED GENIUS IS A LONELY PLACE...
KLAK

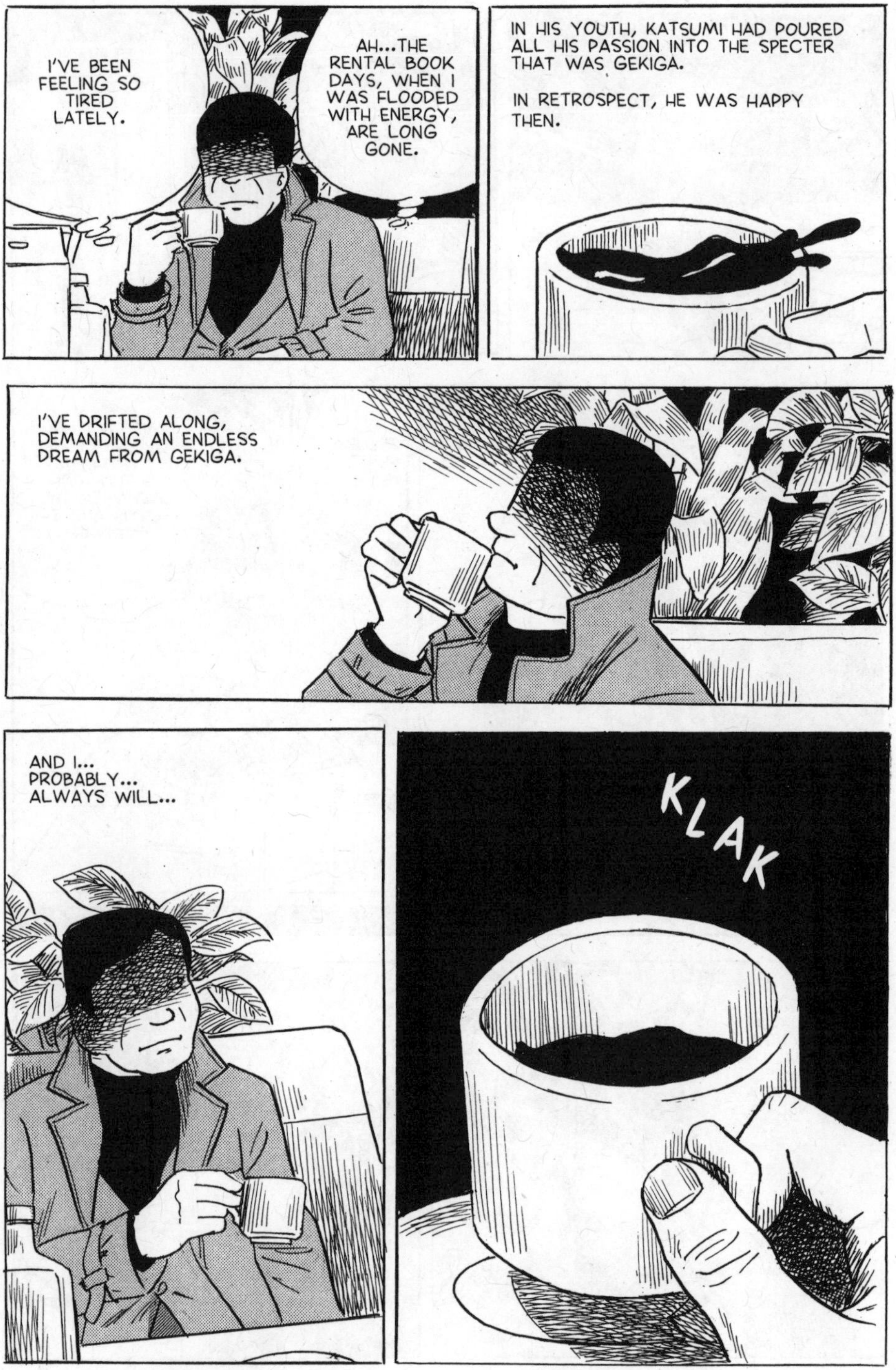
I'VE BEEN FEELING SO TIRED LATELY.
AH...THE RENTAL BOOK DAYS, WHEN I WAS FLOODED WITH ENERGY, ARE LONG GONE.
IN HIS YOUTH, KATSUMI HAD POURED ALL HIS PASSION INTO THE SPECTER THAT WAS GEKIGA.
IN RETROSPECT, HE WAS HAPPY THEN.
I'VE DRIFTED ALONG, DEMANDING AN ENDLESS DREAM FROM GEKIGA.
AND I... PROBABLY... ALWAYS WILL...
KLAK

APPENDIX

PAGE 15, PANEL 1
Published December, 1948 by Fuji Shobo.
¥80.

PAGE 16, PANEL 2
Text within comic:
– "AARGH"
– "POW"

PAGE 27, PANEL 5
Sign within bookstore:
Just Arrived—*Women's Friend*

PAGE 31, PANEL 1
Text within comic:
– "Doh!"

PAGE 33, PANEL 6
Source: Mainichi Shimbun, *Ichiokunin no Showa-shi
(The History of 100 Million People in Showa)*

PAGE 34, PANEL 1
Source: Mainichi Shimbun, *Shinnhion no Genten no
Kiroku (A Document of the Origin of the New Japan)*

PAGE 34, PANEL 4
Source: Nihon Bunka-sha Nihon Rekishi Series,
Gendai (Contemporary Times)

PAGE 35, PANEL 1
Source: Mainichi Shimbun, *Shinnhion no Genten no
Kiroku (A Document of the Origin of the New Japan)*

PAGE 38, PANEL 1
"Deko" was the nickname of the actress
Hideko Takamine.

PAGE 39, PANEL 1
Signs and book titles:
– New magazine
– Just In!
– *Literary World*
– *Mainichi Graph*
– *Takarazuka Graph*
– *Asahi Graph*
– Baseball
– Airplane
– *Shonen Club* on sale

PAGE 39, PANEL 2
Text within comic:
– *Manga to Yomimono (Manga and Literature)*
– A reader-submitted manga printed in the April
1949 issue of *Manga to Yomimono*
– The pitcher makes his first throw
– And it's a hit
– The pitcher catches the ball
– And throws to first
– Thought it was out, but it was a piece of the bat

PAGE 41, PANEL 4
Text on envelope:
– Hiroshi Katsumi
– Asada Toyonaka-shi Osaka

PAGE 48, PANEL 5
Text within comic:
– *Sho-chan*
– I'm going to get the packages
– Oh wow, there sure is a lot of them

PAGE 52, PANEL 1
Text:
3. If the left side of the equation is resolved, we get
4. If the left side of the equation is factored, we get
(2) Answer the following questions
1. In the quadratic equation P=x..., x is...
Compared to its value, the minimum value of P is
2. In the quadratic equation x..., x is $-ab$
In the inequation, x has to be $-d$
In the quadratic function y=x2, P
Draw a parallel line with X as its axis
The rectangle PQQ'P is = e.
In triangle ABC, two points are placed above BC
So that F fulfills the following
AB, CF=FD
Where BC=18cm, resolve the following

PAGE 63, PANEL 5
Source: *Shin Takara Jima (New Treasure Island)*, *Ryusenkei Jiken (Streamlined Case)*, *Faust*, and *Fushigi Ryokouki (The Wonderful Journey)*

PAGE 71, PANEL 1
Full text:
– Katsumi Family Tree (as of 1950)
– Mother: Miyako
– Father: Yoshio
– Eldest son: Nobuyoshi (preparing for university entrance exam, which he failed previously)
– Second son: Okimasa (under medical treatment)
– Third son: Hiroshi (9th grade)
– Eldest daughter: Michiko (5th grade)

PAGE 72, PANEL 4
Text:
The social significance of manga has surprising breadth and depth. Manga tickles its readers with wit and puts the world at ease. Manga has become a trend in the postwar period, and it is our job to keep the manga of the future wholesome. We invited three manga artists currently in middle school for a roundtable discussion with the astonishingly popular Osamu Tezuka.

PAGE 72, PANEL 5
Text:
Hiroshi Katsumi: 9th grade, Toyonaka No. 2 Middle School (Toyonaka–shi, Osaka)
Began drawing manga about two years ago. His work has been accepted into over 50 boys' magazines. His address is Asada, Toyonaka–shi, Osaka.
Masuda Hiroshi:
Began drawing under Mr. Tezuka's tutelage in fourth grade. He draws about 10 pages a day on average. He says that on some nights he stays up until midnight or 1:00 AM working on manga. His address is Minoh City, Toyono–gun, Osaka.

PAGE 72, PANEL 6
Text:
– Share and critique each other's works.

– What does the group do?
– We show each other our works and critique them.
– What format do you use most often?
– Okanishi: I use the four–panel format.
– Katsumi: Me too.
– Sudden ideas while walking or in bed.
– Masuda: I am working on longer pieces.
– Tezuka: each panel of a four–panel comic must articulate an introduction, development, climax, and conclusion, respectively.

PAGE 73, PANEL 4
Text within comic:
– Shotaro Nanbu, *Yaneura 3–chan* Shogakkan.
– I brought some salt and bran paste.
– Thanks!
– Making pickles?
– HAHAHA

PAGE 79, PANEL 2
– *Manga Shonen*, October 1950
– Reader Manga Dojo
– Children's Manga Association
– *Fishing*

PAGE 83, PANEL 7
– *Devil of Science* by Tanaka Masa
– *Adventures of a Cub* by...
– *Ghost Doctor* by Kikuo Tagawa
– *Joyous Whale Hunting Boat* by Noboru Ooshiro
– *Adventures of Tarzan* by Fukujiro Yokoi
– *Comic Doctor's Botched Expeditions* by Noboru Ooshiro
– *Don Quixote* by Bontaro Shaka

PAGE 87, PANEL 5
– *Golden Bat*
– *The Mysterious Underground Man*
– *The Magic House*
– *Monster Detective Group*
– *The Jungle Kingdom*
– *Mars Exploration Corps*
– *Q–chan's Detective Story*
– *Four Swordsmen of the Forest*
– *The Masked Child Adventurer*

- *Sky Devil*
- *The World 1,000 Years After*
- *Streamlined Case*
- *Tuberculoses*
- *Tarzan's Cave*
- *Lost World (Terrestrial)*
- *Lost World (Extra Terrestrial)*
- *Angel Gunfighter*
- *The Miracle Forest*

PAGE 92, PANEL 7
Text within comic:
- CATCH
- PACHINKO

PAGE 93, PANEL 4
Text within comic:
- Are you sure you can do it alone?
- No, I'm not
- Your plans have gone awry again
- I feel so angry!
- Junko, I hate you!
- WAAA
  - From *Song of Chocolate,* by Satoo Tomoe

PAGE 114, PANEL 3
Full text on envelope:
- To: Mr. Okimasa Katsumi
- From: Nakamura Bookstore
2–8 Asakusabashi, Taito–ku, Tokyo
TEL: Hamamachi 851–1932
Acct#: Tokyo 11616

PAGE 118, PANEL 3
Image source: Mainichi Shimbun, *Ichiokunin no Showa–shi (The History of 100 Million People in Showa)*

PAGE 119, PANEL 1
Image source: Mainichi Shimbun, *Ichiokunin no Showa–shi (The History of 100 Million People in Showa)*

PAGE 129, PANEL 2
Text within comic:
- I'm thirsty

- SODA
- Asada, Toyonaka–shi
- Red Party
- Red Feather Party
- by Sanpei Inoue

PAGE 159, PANEL 3
Sign:
- NO TRESPASSING
- ENTRY WITHOUT PERMISSION IS FORBIDDEN AND VIOLATORS WILL BE PUNISHED BY LAW

PAGE 166, PANEL 3
Text within comic:
- They call me Komekichi the cop
- Cut! Let's try that again

PAGE 166, PANEL 5
Text within comic:
- Mr. Anahist (the preparation)
- by Sanpei Inoue
- "New Year's Civil Aviation"
- Departure
- Arrival
- "Cough"
- Where did I put the Asmaret?
- COUGH COUGH

PAGE 175, PANEL 1
Headlines and text:
- *Asahi Graph*
- Pictures of A–bomb victims made available for the first time.
- Hiroshima: the first victim of the atomic bomb.

PAGE 175, PANEL 3
Film posters:
- *Rashomon*
- *To Live*
- *The Third Man*

PAGE 197, PANEL 2
Text within comic:

– *Sazae–san*
– Machiko Hasegawa
– Sis, I'll go

PAGE 200, PANEL 1
Text within comic:
– *The Cautious Hen–pecked Husband*
– But I ordered a long–handled broom…"
– Michiko Katsumi

PAGE 236, PANEL 2
Text within comic:
– "Children's Island"
– Hiroshi Katsumi

PAGE 236, PANEL 3
Text within comic:
– Team of Five Friends
– An underwater palace?
– A rabbit! A rabbit was in it
– That's the culprit
– Let's get him
– He went over here
– The strong rainstorm continued all night
– Morning
– The yacht's been washed away…

PAGE 236, PANEL 4
Text within comic:
– *Friends' Theatre*
– What are you doing with the extension cord?
– Hahaha, you'll see
– Go over there until we're finished
– Published March 15, 1954
– ¥100
– Author: Hiroshi Katsumi
– Publisher: Tsurayuki Tanaka
– Printer: Hironobu Suzuki
– Printed by: Asahi Printing Co., Ltd.
– Published by: Tsuru Shobo Co., Ltd. 1–8
Fujimi–cho, Chiyoda–ku, Tokyo, TEL: (33) 4707

PAGE 238, PANEL 2
Repeat of last six lines above.

PAGE 251, PANELS 5 AND 6
Text in letter:
Dear Mr. Katsumi,
Thank you for your hard work. We hope that your
exam preparations are going well. We have had an
editorial meeting and wish to inform you of a change
in policy…<Fragmented in original> We will be proceeding with the new project as described … Submission will… <Fragmented in original>

PAGE 255, PANEL 2
Full text on signs:
– Kyoto City University of the Arts
– Entrance exam
– Western painting
– Japanese painting
– Visual design
– Dyeing

PAGE 256, PANEL 1
Image on lunchbox: Pickled plum in white rice
symbolizing Japanese flag and victory.

PAGE 278, PANEL 3
Text within comic:
– Ready? I'm letting the panther loose!
– SOB
– SOB
– SOB
– SOB

PAGE 282, PANEL 1
Text within comics:
– *Pinocchio*
– *Rock Home*
– *Manga University*
– *Tokodo*

PAGE 291, PANEL 2
Text within comic:
– New Manga Series
– *Akado Suzunosuke*
– By Eiichi Fukui
– RYAAA

– one game match!
– (2) Do! (body)
– (3) Game! Suzunosuke Kinno wins with a do! (body)
– Good job, Suzunosuke. We'll attach an origami to it starting today
– so... it will... right? (fragmented in original)
– Suzunosuke... hurry... (fragmented in original)

PAGE 292, PANEL I
Text within comic:
– KRAAK

PAGE 293, PANEL 4
Text within comic:
– Boy detective appears
– BWOOO
– BWOOO
– ZAZAAN
– ZAAA
– ZAAA

PAGE 303, PANEL 3
Signs:
– TOYS
– CABARET
– WHISKEY BAR
– KARAOKE
– SALE
– SIGNS

PAGE 306, PANEL I
Signs:
– Wholesale Books Enomoto
– Enomoto Shoten
– Enomoto Horeikan (repeated three times)

PAGE 309, PANEL 6
Signs:
– Menswear
– Marukin Co., Ltd
– Daimon Clothing
– Maruya
– Dock

PAGE 311, PANEL 2
Text on directory:
– Yasuji Building
– Nekoya Co., Ltd.
– Hakko Hinomaru Bunko Co.
– Asahiya Co., Ltd.
– Marumaru Industries

PAGE 316, PANEL 5
Text within comic:
– That man...
– He went into the jungle...

PAGE 344, PANEL 5
– "Humor University"
– Bocchan Sensei
– Sensei
– by Masahiko Matsumoto

PAGE 346, PANEL 4
Signs:
– KOBE LINE
– TAKRAZUKA THEATER

PAGE 350, PANEL I
1. *Sun Boy,* Osamu Iwatani
2. *Boy Momotaro,* Masami Kuroda
3. *Toraohmaru,* Mizuo Higashiura
4. *Humor School,* Masahiko Matsumoto
5. *Samurai Nippon,* Masami Kuroda
6. *Detective Bocchan,* Masahiko Matsumoto
7. *Three Samurai,* Masami Kuroda
8. *Saboten-kun,* Masahiko Matsumoto
9. *A Song for Mother,* Shigeji Isojima
10. *Seven Faces,* Hiroshi Katsumi
11. *Saboten-kun Moves to Tokyo*
12. *Crescent Moon Samurai,* Ichiro Kudo
13. *King of Wrestling,* Satoshi Imabashi
14. *13 Eyes,* Hiroshi Katsumi
15. *Ukkari-kun and Chakkari-kun,* Shigeji Isojima
16. *Go For It, Santa!,* Masahiko Matsumoto
17. *The Naked Magistrate,* Ichiro Kudo
18. *The Awesome Karate Chop,* Masami Kuroda
19. *Pika Don Sensei,* Hiroshi Katsumi

20. *Aozora Wakasama,* Shigeo Iwai
21. *A Lady Jumps Out,* Shigeji Isojima
22. *The Acorn Child,* Masami Okada
23. *Tiger of the University,* Masahiko Matsumoto

PAGE 352, PANEL 3
Text in index:
– *Transformation,* Ichiro Kudo
– *King of Wrestling,* Satoshi Imabashi
– *21 Fingerprints,* Hiroshi Katsumi
– *The Man Who Disappeared Yesterday,* Ichiro Kudo
– *The Komori Family,* Shigeo Iwai
– *Balloon Samurai,* Masami Okada
– *A Star is Born,* Shigeji Isoji
– *The Purple Devil,* Masahiko Matsumoto
– *The Absent–Minded Cop,* Susumu Egawa
– *The Burning Buddha Statue,* Mitsuo Shiozawa
– *Gates of Hell,* Masami Okada
– *Mountain Brothers,* Shinmin Yamaguchi
– *Two Tengus,* Ichiro Kudo
– *Wooden Sword Sensei,* Hiroshi Katsumi

PAGE 353, PANEL 5
Text within comic:
– Anyone who learns the way of the sword will progress up to a certain point.
– But a real swordsman must go beyond that point.
– Only I don't know how to get there.
– What do I do?
– Psh, it's just a kid. Maybe he has some cash.

PAGE 362, PANEL 3
Text within comic:
– PON PON PON

PAGE 367, PANEL 5
Image source:
Godzilla film poster (1954)

PAGE 369, PANEL 1
Text within comic:
– The acclaimed number
– *Detective Manga*
– Hinomaru Bunko

– Volume size: B6 128 pages
– ¥130 available now
– *Seven Faces*
– Hiroshi Katsumi
– Despite protection provided by over 100 cops, a major painting disappears from a windowless room! The scandal causes even more scandals!
– *13 Eyes*
– Hiroshi Katsumi
– A mysterious doctor disappears from a luxury liner during a terrible storm!
– A blue cape drawn by a mouse! One mysterious incident unfolds after another! The *13 Eyes* glimmer!
– *21 Fingerprints*
– Hiroshi Katsumi
– What is the "Bizarre Club"?
– The mysterious case of the elusive "neck man"

PAGE 373, PANEL 1
Image source:
Poster for *The Beast From 20,000 Fathoms* (1953)

PAGE 373, PANEL 2
Image source:
Poster for *Them* (1954)

PAGE 378, PANEL 6
Text within comic:
– THUMP
– WAAAR

PAGE 380, PANEL 1
"A5" refers to the paper size 5.8 x 8.3 inches and is a term used in Europe and Japan.

PAGE 387, PANEL 4
Signs:
– Appliances
– Rice cookers available

PAGE 397
Titles of comics:
– *Todoroki Sensei*
– *Igaguri–kun*

– *Sazae–san*

PAGE 398, PANEL 1
Text within newspaper:
– A dream comes true for manga artist.
– Work recognized and published as "hardcover."
– Takao, who works at a barber, will soon release his second book.
– A 30–year–old woman who can't remarry.

PAGE 398, PANEL 2
Text within newspaper:
– Local Edition
– To report a newsworthy event, call:
– A dream comes true for manga artist.
– Work recognized and published as "hardcover."
– Takao, who works at a barber, will soon release his second book.
– A 30–year–old woman who can't remarry.
– Matriculated students defer.
– Public high school tuition increases.
– Takechi Police.

PAGE 403, PANEL 4
Text within comic:
– Poisoner
– Why won't you fight?
– Kong, don't you get it?

PAGE 404, PANEL 2
Text on magazine cover:
– The city of Kazusa
– Is a line of freight trains
– Where the sea is level with the watchtower
– Sanpei Mejiro's *Abscondence*

PAGE 411, PANEL 5
Text on note:
– Detective Manga Book
– Subtitle
– Black Cat
– Shadow
– Action (Manga) Books
– Mystery (or Mysterious Room)

– Darkness

PAGE 413
Table of contents:
– *The Menacing Detective,* Takao Saito
– *The Man Next Door,* Masahiko Matsumoto
– *The Cursed Jewel,* Shoichi Sakurai
– *The Mottled Rope,* Makoto Takahashi
– *Parrot,* Masami Kuroda
– *I Saw It,* Hiroshi Katsumi
Frontispiece:
– Masahiko Matsumoto
– Makoto Takahashi
– Hiroshi Katsumi
Cover, inside cover, and content:
– Masami Kuroda

PAGE 414
Text within comic:
– Okay, stop.
– Going to kill them?
– The train should drown out the shots.
– HONKKK
– Don't move!
– CHOOO
– CHOOO
– CHOOO
– CHOOO
– CHOOO
– CHOOO
– CHOOO
– CHOOO
– CHOOO

PAGE 415, LEFT ROW
Text within comic:
– Now that you've seen my face, I have no choice but to kill you!
– CHOOO
– BAM BAM
– CHOOO
– CHOOO
– CHOOO
– THUMP

PAGE 423, PANEL 3
Text on movie posters:
(Right)
– *Floating Clouds*
– Now playing:
– *Summer Time*
– In Technicolor
(Left)
– *A Kid for Two Farthings*
– Akira Kurosawa's *To Live*

PAGE 423, PANEL 5
Text on movie poster:
– *The Wages of Fear*
– Now playing

PAGE 427, PANEL 5
Text within comic:
– And he takes a nap right there every day. He's like a machine, going through the same motions day after day... (Image provided by Masahiko Matsumoto)

PAGE 428, PANEL 4
Text within comic:
– I've got it!
– ZZZZZ

PAGE 429
Text within comic:
– *The Cursed Jewel*
– *Hahahahaha*
– *Hahahahaha*
– Mottled... mottled rope...
– Mottled rope...?
– Suspense Manga
– *Parrot*
– By Masami Kuroda
– Works from inaugural issue (April 1956) of *Shadow:* Takao Saito, Shoichi Sakurai, Masahiko Matsumoto, Makoto Takahashi, Masami Kuroda.

PAGE 430, PANEL 1
Text within comic:
– Meow

– Damn that pestering cat
– Take that!
(Image provided by Masahiko Matsumoto)

PAGE 454, PANEL 2
Sign:
– Special Sake: ¥90

PAGE 460, PANEL 7
Sign:
– Hitachi
– Shinsekai

PAGE 465, PANEL 1
Title at right:
Manga Shonen, October, 1955

PAGE 467, PANEL 3
Text within comic:
– Blood!
– It's blood!
– GOOO

PAGE 467, PANEL 6
Signs:
– Book Rental
– We now have *Shufu no Tomo*
– New comics are in

PAGE 468, PANEL 1
Signs:
– Chinese Noodles
– Momodani
– Ekubo
– Miyabi
– Suntory Bar

PAGE 477
Poster for the Nikkatsu film *Season of the Sun,* which opened on May 17, 1956.

PAGE 483, PANEL 1
Text written on bomb in middle comic strip:
– Nuclear bomb

PAGE 496, PANEL 2
Titles on books:
– *Poo-san*
– *Blooming Way of the Samurai*

PAGE 498, PANEL 5
Second sign:
– Blowfish Stew

PAGE 499, PANEL 2
Signs:
– Couple Soup
– Hozenji

PAGE 500, PANEL 2
A "watering fudo" is a statue of a Shinto deity
that one pours water on.

PAGE 500, PANEL 6
Note:
"liquor trade" has negative connotations in Japan and
refers to much more than just liquor. In this context
it refers to businesses who hire women to keep customers company as they drink, etc.

PAGE 502, PANEL 3
Text on book:
– Iwanami Bunko
– *The Count of Monte Cristo*
– Alexandre Dumas
– Translated by Yoshio Yamauchi

PAGE 504, PANEL 6
Text next to cartoon drawing:
– Porn manga author
Credit:
Taizo Yokoyama (from *Bunshun Manga Dokuhon*,
January 1956)

PAGE 507, PANEL 2
Sign:
– Osaka's Famous Restaurant

PAGE 509

Text within comic:
– Hello? Hello?
– Is this the police?

PAGE 510, PANEL 2
Text within comic:
– You're the perpetrator!

PAGE 515, PANEL 4
Text within comic:
– *Detective Book Shadow*
– Published September 1956 (cover by
Makoto Takahashi)

PAGE 515, PANEL 7
Text within comic:
– What is that old man doing?
– ¥100
– Why is he pasting ¥100 bills on the window?

PAGE 525
Signs:
(Left to right, top to bottom)
– Upstairs BEER HALL
– BLOW FISH STEW
– TRY ZUBORAYA FOR BLOWFISH
– Shionsekai Zuboraya Original Store
– ZUBORAYA
– BLOWFISH STEW
– BLOWFISH
– SUKIYAKI
– Shinsekai Shochiku
– ZUBORAYA (on balloon)
– Shinei
– Shinsekai Daiei

PAGE 527, PANEL 8
Text within comic:
– Over here.

PAGE 531, PANEL 4
The original Tsutenkaku Tower was torn down in
1943 when the Japanese government dismantled it
over fears that it could have been a target for bomb-

ing raids over Osaka. The new tower shown here was constructed in 1956 and has appeared in several stories by Tatsumi.

PAGE 532, PANEL 1
"Pacific War" refers to World War II.

PAGE 532, PANEL 2
Janjan Yokocho is a popular shopping area centered around Tsutenkaku Tower.

PAGE 539, PANEL 1
Text on postcard:
- Mr. Hiroshi Katsumi
- Saikudani, Tennoji-ku, Osaka
- Osaka

PAGE 556, PANEL 1
Text on cover:
- *Shadow*
- *Detective Book*
- Special Feature

PAGE 558, PANEL 5
Text on card:
- Akita Shoten
- Adventure King Editorial Department
- 3-10-8 Misakicho
- TEL: Tokyo (261) 51

PAGE 560, PANEL 2
Text within comic:
- It was on the way home from...
- *The Murderer on the Last Train*
- The train left the station.
- It, it's a corpse!
- SLAM
- He got rid of the body...
- He was planning to hide the body in the tunnel.
- I better run before I'm killed.
- You saw me do it, didn't you?
- FLICK
- A key left in the trunk!

PAGE 561, PANEL 3
Text on both envelope and postcard:
Mr. Hiroshi Katsumi
1-37-3 Asada Toyonaka-shi
Osaka

PAGE 567, PANEL 5
Text on cover:
- Good Manga and Other Reading
- *Adventure King*
- With 6 special supplements
- *Rock Atom*
- Mr. Wooden Sword
- Igaguri
- Harike

PAGE 569, PANEL 5
Text on paper:
Mishima Shobo
2-67 Motomachi Naniwa-ku
TEL: 1 (64)

PAGE 571, PANEL 2
Signs:
- Café Forest
- Coffee ¥30

PAGE 578, PANEL 4
Text in letter:
Please accept our sincere apologies for the many troubles we have caused with the unfortunate recent incident at our office. The president returned safely last month and we are currently taking every possible measure to get back on our feet as soon as possible. We will let you know as soon as we have a better idea of when we might start operations again. When our operations are back in order, we would be very grateful to publish your work once again.
We look forward to hearing from you.
Yours sincerely,
Yamamoto
Director, Hinomaru Bunko
(Source: Masahiko Matsumoto)

PAGE 582, PANEL 2

Postcard addressed to Masahiko Matsumoto from Masami Kuroda (May 8, 1957):

Excuse me for the other night. I received a call from Nagoya the other day, and heard that you had signed a contract with Mishima. I do not know if your decision is based on pay or emotional matters, but please do let me know directly of your decision, as I will need to find a replacement for you should you have decided to not work for me.

(Source: Masahiko Matsumoto)

PAGE 583, PANEL 3

Text on telegram:

– TELEGRAM
– Mr. Hiroshi Katsumi
– Please come to office
– Yamada

PAGE 589

Text within comic (background):

– *Key*
– *Thriller Series*
– *Shadow*
– *Detective Book*
– *Thriller Book*
– *City*

PAGE 590, PANEL 1

Text on paper:

Shadow (11) Layout
1. Cover
2. *Murder in Seven Colors,* Matsumoto
(4–color)
(*Seven Colors* ends)
1 panel 4 colors

PAGE 590, PANEL 4

Text within comic:

– Oh...oh my god! R–Rito's been murdered!
– No! He's already gone...
– Ah! It's Tetsuo–san's figurine...
– The police! Call the police!!

PAGE 591, PANEL 1

Text within comic:

– What's happened? Anything wrong?
– No, nothing.
– ...night suit... <fragmented in original>

PAGE 594, PANEL 5

Text on cover:

– *Manga Shonen*
– Supplementary volume of American comics
– *Otto the Octopus*

PAGE 599, PANEL 1

Text on cover:

– *Key*
– Thriller Series
– Kazuo Umezu
– Takao Saito

PAGE 606, PANEL 1

Text in letter:

Mr. Masahiko Matsumoto

Thank you for writing to us despite your busy schedule. We apologize in advance for any inconvenience, but we would like to suggest that you use a different name when writing for *City* and *Key*. We have decided to recommend this system to all of our writers. Thank you for your consideration.

PAGE 608, PANEL 2

Sign:

– To kai To sho
Banner:
– *Shufunotomo*
– On sale

PAGE 613, PANEL 3

Text in letter:

– (September)
– *Shadow:* "The Smokeless Smokestack" (Hinomaru)
– *City:* "Handcuffs for the Reaper" (Central)
– *Key:* "In the Shadow of the Skyscraper" (Mishima)
– *Bizarre:* "The Poison and the ??" (Kinen)
– (October)

– *Jaguar:* "The Giant Walking Dragon" (Kinen)
– *Dragon and Tiger:* "The Missing Corpse" (Central)
– *The Strong:* "The Unrivaled Swordsman" (Kinen)
– *Jaguar:* TBA 20 pages (same)
– *Dragon and Tiger:* TBA 16 pages (Central)

PAGE 617, PANEL 4
Text on cover:
– *Shadow*
– *Detective Book*
– *The Heartless Harbor*

PAGE 618, PANEL 1
Signs:
(left to right)
– CRAB
– DRAFT BEER
– ZUBORAYA
– PACHINKO
– KUIDAORE

PAGE 622, PANEL 3
Newspaper headlines:
– Vulgar Manga Proliferates
– Elementary PTA Takes Stand

PAGE 625, PANEL 3
Handwritten text:
– Setsuga (Story Pictures)
– Katsudouga (Active Pictures)
– Katsuga (Action Pictures)

PAGE 629, PANEL 1
Text in letter:
– Setsuga (Story Pictures)
– Katsudouga (Active Pictures)
– Katsuga (Action Pictures)
– Hard Comics
– Shagekiga (Realistic Drama Pictures)
– Eshibai (Picture Play)
– Genjitsuha (Realist)
– Komaga (Panel Picture)
– Enga(ha) (Theatrical Picture)
– Manga (Omnipicture)

– Drama Comics
– Gekiga (Intense Picture)
– Gekiga (Dramatic Picture)
– Gekiga (Hard–hitting Picture)
– Ryudouga (Flowing Picture)
– Straight Comics

PAGE 629, PANEL 7
Handwritten text:
– Setsuga
– Katsudouga
– Katsuga

PAGE 635, PANEL 6
Signs:
– TOSHIBA
– NICHIGEKI
– FRANK SINATRA

PAGE 648, PANEL 3
Text on telegram:
– MR. HIROSHI KATSUMI
– KOKUBUNJI HONDA
– SEND MANUSCRIPT

PAGE 650, PANEL 6
Menu:
– Egg Bowl w/pickles and miso soup
– Family Bowl w/pickles and miso soup
– Curry with Rice
– Sashimi Lunch
– Natto Lunch
– Roasted Seaweed Lunch
– Sole Stew Lunch
– Horse Mackerel Lunch
– Horse Mackerel Stew Lunch
– Mackerel Stew Lunch
– Grilled Mackerel Pike Horse Mackerel Stew Lunch
– Mackerel Stew Lunch
– Grilled Mackerel Pike

PAGE 651, PANEL 1
Text on cover:
– Mystery Gekiga

– Gekiga Workshop
– Hiroshi Katsumi
– *Ghost Taxi*

PAGE 657, PANEL 6
Text on letter:
– Taiheiyo Bunko
– Utagwa, Shibuya–ku
– Tokyo

PAGE 659, PANEL 4
Text on covers:
– *Ghost Buddha Statue*
– *Black Cat from Hell*
– *Ninja Swordsman*
– *Feudal Lord*

PAGE 661, PANEL 1
Sign:
– Classical Music and Paintings
– Garden

PAGE 663, PANEL 4
Text on telegram:
– MR. HIROSHI KATSUMI
– KOTOBUKISO
– CANNOT REACH KURODA
– COMING TO KOKUBUNJI ON 12TH AFTER-NOON
– TATEISHI
– CENTRAL

PAGE 666, PANEL 1
Signs:
(left to right)
– SuehiroTEA
– Yamamnishi
– Sushi Fukuda
– Higashi Sushi

PAGE 668, PANEL 1
Text on telegram:
– STILL CAN'T REACH KURODA
– PLEASE DO CITY COVER

– BEFORE YOU ARRIVE TOMORROW

PAGE 669
Signs:
– Book Rental
– ¥10 per book per day for the first day
– ¥5 from the second day on

PAGE 673, PANEL 5
Text on covers:
– *City*
– New Talent Contest Results Announced
– Yoshihiro Tatsumi
– Takeshi Kizuki
– Hidetake Kusakawa
– Masami Kuroda

PAGE 674, PANEL 1
Sign on post:
– KURAMAE ICCHOME

PAGE 674, PANEL 2
Sign on post:
– KURAMAE ICCHOME

PAGE 674, PANEL 5
Signs:
– DOLLS
– BALLOONS
– RUBBER

PAGE 674, PANEL 6
Signs:
– BOOKS
– JUST ARRIVED: *FUJIN SEIKATSU (Women's Life)*
– CHILDREN'S BOOKS
– PICTURE BOOKS
– COLORING BOOKS

PAGE 675, PANEL 4
Text on covers:
– Picture books for children
– 3D Lessons and Tests

– Numbers and Numerals
– A Suzuki Picture Book
– *Trains*
– *Popeye*

PAGE 677, PANEL 1
Signs:
– SEIGETSU
– SAKE

PAGE 683, PANEL 5
Signs:
– TECHNICOLOR
– *The Bridge on the River Kwai*
– William Holden
– Alec Guinness
– Double Feature: *Satellite in the Sky*
– Tickets

PAGE 688, PANEL 3
Menu items:
– ¥190
– FAMILY BOWL
– ¥200
– ¥280

PAGE 697, PANEL 1
Sign on train:
– TAKARAZUKA UMEDA

PAGE 704, PANEL 3
Signs:
– BREAD
– TOBACCO

PAGE 708, PANEL 1
Sign:
– Classical Music and Paintings
– GARDEN

PAGE 724, PANEL 6
Text on cover:
– *City*
– Thriller Book Supplement
– Action Special

PAGE 730, PANEL 5
Text on paper:

The world is changing constantly. The world of manga, created by Sojo Toba in the 12th century, is no exception. Manga is a fast-evolving field, and in the Showa period, it has been bifurcated into manga for adults, and manga for children. Today, manga for adults alone comprises various genres such as political manga, realist manga, family manga, and story manga.

Children's manga has also become diversified and it now includes different genres for different readerships. In the postwar period, the story manga rapidly rose to prominence, principally due to Osamu Tezuka's efforts. With this new prominence, children's manga also improved its social status and continued to develop steadily.

More recently, the story manga has been vitalized through the influence exerted by the supersonic development of other media such as film, television, and radio. This vitalization has given birth to a new genre, which we have named "gekiga."

Manga and "gekiga" differ in methodology, but perhaps more importantly, in their readerships. The demand for manga, written for adolescents, i.e. those readers between childhood and adulthood, has never been answered, because there has never been a forum for such works. This hitherto neglected reader segment is "gekiga's" intended target. It was, in fact, the rental book market that contributed significantly to the development of "gekiga."

"GEKIGA": THE NEW FRONTIER

Gekiga has a great future. It will also, doubtless, face some difficulties. Success will require unanimous cooperation from all gekiga writers.

In light of the above, the former TS Workshop and Kansai Manga Artists Group have been consolidated into Gekiga Workshop. Gekiga writers have united to establish a new system under the banner of "Gekiga Workshop."

It is our sincere hope to have your support and understanding for the future endeavors of the Gekiga

Workshop.
Gekiga Workshop
Takao Saito
Masaaki Sato
Fumiyasu Ishikawa
Shoichi Sakurai
Hiroshi Katsumi
Susumu Yamamori
Motomizu K.

PAGE 731, PANEL 4
Names and text on magazine cover:
- Hiroshi Katsumi
- Shoichi Sakurai
- Motomizu K.
- Masaki Sato
- Susumu Yamamori
- Takao Saito
- ROUNDTABLE

PAGE 734, PANEL 4
Signs:
- NEW Cleaner
- TOBACCO

PAGE 737, PANEL 1
Signs:
- TAKARAZUKA REVUE
- SHOP AT HANKYU DEPARTMENT STORE
- HITACHI
- SHINSAIBASHI

PAGE 738, PANEL 5
Text on cover:
- *Skyscraper*
- Edited by Gekiga Workshop
- Hiroshi Katsumi
- Shoichi Sakurai
- Motomizu K.
- Masaki Sato
- Susumu Yamamori
- Takao Saito
- ROUNDTABLE
- "Going full throttle with 'gekiga'"

PAGE 741, PANEL 4
Text within comic:
- READER SUBMISSION
- Manga Dojo
- Children's Manga Association
- *Fishing*
- Hiroshi Katsumi

PAGE 744, PANEL 3
Text on telegram:
- MR. MASAHIKO MATSUMOTO
- 2–865 NARIMUNE
- DO NOT JOIN GEKIGA WORKSHOP EVER

PAGE 745, PANEL 1
Text on bulletin board:
- SCHEDULE
- *Shadow* # 30: 18 pages
- *City* # 26: 20 pages
- *Labyrinth* # 6
- *Hot–Blooded Boys*
- *City* Supplement (large format)

PAGE 745, PANEL 4
Signs:
- NIKKATSU OSCAR
- From the Genius of Louis Malle
- Starring Jeanne Moreau
- *Les Amants*
- DETECTIVE
- CINEMA
- SHINJUKU NIKKATSU OSCAR

PAGE 746, PANEL 3
Text in letter:
I ask you for your cooperation in this matter. As I mentioned during our last meeting, I remain adamantly opposed to the Gekiga Workshop. Out of concern for the future, I am extremely worried about group actions like this one. Individual action is the best way to improve one's skills. Collective action breeds misunderstandings, which can have serious repercussions. I sincerely hope that you will focus

your efforts on developing your own unique "ko-maga" style of manga. We too will work diligently in our endeavors.

(Source: Masahiko Matsumoto)

PAGE 748, PANEL 1

Text:

- Singing Café
- LAMP
- Songbook

PAGE 750, PANEL 1

Text:

- Shabu Shabu
- MISAKIYA

PAGE 752, PANEL 2

Text on covers:

- Weekly
- *Shonen Sunday*
- All-star baseball issue
- *Shonen* magazine
- Inaugural Issue

PAGE 753, PANEL 2

Text on covers:

- Full-length Science Adventure Manga
- *Dr. Thrill*
- Full-length Adventure Detective Manga
- *Hikari*

PAGE 755, PANEL 6

Text on cover:

- Edited by Gekiga Workshop
- *Boys' Landscape*
- Takao Saito
- Hiroshi Katsumi
- Shoichi Sakurai
- Motomizu K.
- Fumiyasu Ishikawa

PAGE 756, PANEL 1

Text on cover:

- Takao Saito

- Hiroshi Katsumi
- Susumu Yamamori
- Shoichi Sakurai
- Motomizu K.
- Fumiyasu Ishikawa
- Masaaki Sato
- Now with more pages!

PAGE 757, PANEL 4

Text on envelope:

- REGISTERED CASH ENVELOPE
- Mr. Susumu Yamamori
- Upper Jofukuji
- Kamigyoku, Kyoto

PAGE 757, PANEL 6

Text postcard:

- Mr. Hiroshi Katsumi
- Honda
- Shimokita
- Tokyo
- EXPRESS
- Mr. Hiroshi

PAGE 759, PANEL 1

Text on comics pages:

- *Die Looking Up*
- *Hit 'em*

PAGE 759, PANEL 2

Sign:

- NIPPON TELEGRAPH AND TELEPHONE PUBLIC CORPORATION
- KOKUBUNJI TELEGRAPH OFFICE

PAGE 762, PANEL 6

Text:

- New Talent Competition
- Selected
- *A Death 15 from Minutes Ago*
- Hajime Misono
- Honorable Mention
- *Midnight*

PAGE 763, PANEL 1

Text:

– Central Publishing

– *City* New Talent Contest Committee

– Jinbo–cho, Chiyoda–ku

– Tokyo

– EXPRESS

– Central Publishing

– *City* New Talent Contest Committee

– Jinbo–cho, Chiyoda–ku

– Tokyo

PAGE 763, PANEL 2

Text on comics pages:

– *Black Rain*

– *Morning of The Murder*

PAGE 766, PANEL 6

Text:

– Masaaki Sato

– Fumiyasu Ishikawa

– Motomizu K.

– Shoichi Sakurai

– CAUTION

– RAILROAD CROSSING

PAGE 812, PANEL 1

Text on sign:

– SASUGAYA

– SUGAMO

PAGE 814, PANEL 5

Text on cover:

– Takao Saito

– *City*

PAGE 815, PANEL 2

Text:

– A report on current manga

– by Yamanashi Reader's Group

PAGE 819, PANEL 2

Text on cover:

– Film Scenario School of Japan

PAGE 823, PANEL 3

Sign:

– Now showing:

– *Plein Soleil*

– Directed by René Clément

– Alain Delon

PAGE 823, PANEL 5

Sign:

– SUBWAY HIBIYA

PAGE 824, PANEL 3

Protest signs:

– NO SECURITY TREATY

– OVERTHROW PRIME MINISTER KISHI

PAGE 826, PANEL 3

Protest signs:

– MAINTAIN PEACE

PAGE 827, PANEL 6

Protest signs:

– No Security Treaty

– Give Us Peace

PAGE 828, PANEL 2

Protest signs:

– PROTECT JAPAN

– NO SECURITY TREATY

– EDUCATIONAL ASSOCIATION

– PEACE IN JAPAN

– IMPEACH KISHI

– NO TREATY

– NO WAR

Yoshihiro Tatsumi was born in Osaka 1935.
He lives and works in Tokyo.